Countries, Peoples & Cultures

Western & Central Africa

First Edition

Volume 7

Editor

Michael Shally-Jensen, PhD

SALEM PRESS
A Division of EBSCO Information Services, Inc.
Ipswich, Massachusetts

Grey House
Publishing

Publisher's Cataloging-In-Publication Data
(Prepared by The Donohue Group, Inc.)

Western & Central Africa / editor, Michael Shally-Jensen, PhD. – First edition.

   pages : illustrations ; cm. – (Countries, peoples & cultures ; v. 7)

   Includes bibliographical references and index.
   ISBN: 978-1-61925-784-9 (v. 7)
   ISBN: 978-1-61925-800-6 (set)

   1. Africa, West – History. 2. Africa, Central – History. 3. Africa, West – Economic conditions. 4. Africa, Central – Economic conditions. 5. Africa, West – Social life and customs. 6. Africa, Central – Social life and customs. 7. Religions. 8. Comparative government. I. Shally-Jensen, Michael. II. Title: Western and Central Africa III. Series: Countries, peoples & cultures ; v. 7.

DT471 .W47 2015
966

First Printing
PRINTED IN CANADA

Contents

Publisher's Note

Countries, Peoples & Cultures: Western & Central Africa is the seventh volume of a new 9-volume series from Salem Press. *Countries, Peoples & Cultures* offers valuable insight into the social, cultural, economic, historical and religious practices and beliefs of nearly every country around the globe.

Following the extensive introduction that summarizes this politically and physically complex part of the world, this volume provides 20-page profiles of the 25 countries that make up this region of the world. Each includes colorful maps—one highlighting the country's location in the world, and one with its major cities and natural landmarks—and a country flag, plus 10 categories of information: General Information; Environment & Geography; Customs & Courtesies; Lifestyle; Cultural History; Culture; Society; Social Development; Government; and Economy.

Each profile also includes full color photographs, valuable tables of information including fun "Do You Know?" facts, and a comprehensive Bibliography. Each country profile combines must-have statistics, such as population, language, size, climate, and currency, with the flavor and feel of the land. You'll read about favorite foods, arts & entertainment, youth culture, women's rights, health care, and tourism, for a comprehensive picture of the country, its people, and their culture.

Appendix One: World Governments, focuses on 21 types of governments found around the world today, from Commonwealth and Communism to Treaty System and Failed State. Each government profile includes its Guiding Premise, Structure, Citizen's Role, and modern day examples.

Appendix Two: World Religions, focuses on 10 of the world's major religions from African religious traditions to Sikhism. Each religion profile includes a number of adherents, basic tenets, major figures and holy sites, and major rites and celebrations. The nine volumes of *Countries, Peoples & Cultures* are: *Central & South America; Central, South & Southeast Asia; Western Europe; Eastern Europe; Middle East & North Africa; Eastern & Southern Africa; Western & Central Africa; North America & the Caribbean;* and *East Asia & the Pacific.*

Introduction

The continent of Africa is traditionally divided into five, or sometimes six, major regions. The five-region model consists of Northern (or North) Africa, Western (or West) Africa, Central Africa, Eastern (or East) Africa, and Southern Africa. Under the six-region model, Eastern Africa is further divided into East Africa (with Lake Victoria at its center) and the Horn and Middle Nile region (encompassing the Horn of Africa and inland areas). In the present series, we keep it simple and follow the five-region scheme. North Africa is, for cultural and historical reasons, included in a volume entitled *The Middle East and North Africa*. Eastern and Southern Africa are likewise dealt with in a separate volume. In the present volume we focus on Western and Central Africa.

The first of these two regions, the western part, is made up of the following 16 countries: Benin, Burkina Faso, Cape Verde, Cote d'Ivoire (Ivory Coast), The Gambia, Ghana, Guinea, Guinea-Bissau, Liberia, Mali, Mauritania, Niger, Nigeria, Senegal, Sierra Leone, and Togo. The second region, Central Africa, consists of the following 9 countries: Angola, Cameroon, Central African Republic, Chad, Democratic Republic of the Congo, Republic of the Congo, Equatorial Guinea, Gabon, São Tomé & Príncipe. All told, then, 25 nations are examined in this volume.

Geography and Environment

One feature of the African continent as a whole is the vast plateau that makes up most of it. The continent is essentially a single plateau covered with flat terrain and gently rolling hills, along with a few high peaks and rift valleys. The plateau is lower in the north and west than in the east and south, and it falls more sharply to the coast in the latter area, forming a rock face known as the Great Escarpment. The northern and western portion of the plateau has elevations of 500 to 2,000 feet, whereas the southern and eastern half generally stands above 3,000 feet. Few areas rise above 7,500 feet, however. Mount Kilimanjaro, the highest peak, reaches over 19,000 feet. Other high peaks, most of them associated with volcanic activity (as is Kilimanjaro), include mounts Meru, Kenya, and Elgon.

Although the tropical rainforest is one prominent feature of Africa's makeup, it is by no means the only or even the most prominent feature. Much of Eastern and Southern Africa, for example, consists of tropical and temperate grassland, and most of the Horn region is characterized by a steppe and desert environment. The rainforest areas are limited largely to the equatorial zone and a long coastal strip on the east extending from southern Kenya to southern Mozambique. Eastern Madagascar, too, features such a tropical strip. Inland from the coast, in the case of both Madagascar and mainland Africa, one encounters savanna grasslands and what is called tropical thorn forest, an area of mixed vegetation falling between rainforest and savanna conditions. Desert and steppes are again encountered in the Kalahari region of the south, which shades into a more temperate zone along the southern coast of South Africa. The western and central regions dealt with in the present volume are predominantly tropical, although the northern portions of Mali, Mauritania, Niger, and Chad belong to the Sahara Desert.

Much of the area in Africa is unfavorable to agriculture. Moreover, because of population growth, drought, environmental degradation, and political corruption, food shortages and outright famine have occurred frequently. The worst famines in recent times, however, have been associated not simply with drought or any one of these other conditions, but rather with wars in addition to one or more of these other conditions. Civil unrest has created millions of refugees over the decades and has disrupted the lives of millions more, exacerbating existing environmental problems—which include the depletion of animal and plant resources, the destruction of forests, the denuding and spoliation of the land, and the spreading of pollutants—and putting a strain on economies. Government neglect, and policies that actually discourage agricultural production, add further to the problem. The oil industry in and around Nigeria has contributed its share to regional socioeconomic and environmental problems.

The obstacles to overcoming Africa's food production and environmental problems are considerable, but some leaders have begun linking economic difficulties with environmental abuse and civil conflict. Such linkage is an important first step toward improved management of agricultural commodities and other resources including the region's flora, fauna, oil, and minerals.

People

There are no fewer than 1,000 different and mutually unintelligible languages spoken in Africa, perhaps as many as half of them spoken in the eastern and southern regions with which we are concerned here. This situation has, to a degree, hindered communication between the various African peoples, since people living relatively close to one another may speak entirely separate languages. Before French, English, and, to a lesser extent, Portuguese came to be spoken as second languages by colonized African populations, certain African languages gained usage outside their native areas, thus serving as "lingua francas." One such language was Swahili, centered in the Great Lakes region (lakes Victoria and Tanganyika) of East Africa. Over time, Swahili acquired a large number of loan words from Arabic, brought by Arab traders. Even today, one or another dialect of Swahili is current as a lingua franca in many parts of East Africa. In Western and Central Africa, on the other hand, the picture is more complicated and no one language has achieved the status that Swahili has in the east.

Traditional Africa is composed primarily of rural dwellers situated in small villages or dispersed hamlets and of semi-nomadic peoples.

This picture has begun to change in recent years, however, as urbanization has become an increasingly dominant trend. Interestingly, two parts of West Africa—a region along the Niger River and an area of the Guinea Coast—have histories of urban settlements that predate the arrival of the Europeans.

The Guinea Coast, lying above the Gulf of Guinea at the "crotch" of Africa, consists of a forested belt that has long sustained a large human population. The people of this area are supported by agriculture, trade, and, especially in Nigeria, oil. In the central part of the region such peoples as the Ashanti, Dahomeans, Bini, and Yoruba developed complex and relatively wealthy states in medieval times and after—as late as the 19th century. They established efficient market and trading systems, marked by the use of controlled currencies, and evolved comparatively elaborate trade and labor specializations. Politically, authority was centralized under chiefs and elders but also allowed for input from quasi-democratic organizations, or societies, made up of commoners. In the area of religion, people here developed a rich, largely ritual-based set practices accompanied by a fairly detailed theology. In later years, however, Christianity took hold, even as traditional spiritualism continued to be practiced. Finally, the region's sculpture, music, and dance have become legion, and have left a profound mark on Western art itself.

To the north and west of the Guinea Coast, below the Sahara and reaching into the western "bulge" of Africa, is another large area characterized by cultural diversity. This region too is noted for its well-developed trading networks, its labor specialization, its political sophistication, and its selected pockets of dense population, along with its artistic production. But the people here traditionally have been more dependent on cattle raising than the people of the forest zone. Styles of clothing and housing, naturally, differ from those of the south. More important, Islam is the dominant religion of the region, particularly among the ruling classes and in the cities. In its early history, before the 18th century, the region gave rise to a string of notable empires, including

Ghana (not to be confused with the modern country of the same name), Mali, Songhai, Kanem-Bornu, and the Fulani-Hausa empire. Islam was, in most cases, part of that history. The succession of these native states ended only with the start of heavy European colonization in the 19th century. Today, there continues to be significant tension, and occasional violence, between northern and southern—Islamic and Christian—sections of West Africa.

In Central Africa, except for Chad in the north and parts of Angola in the south, much of the area is tropical rainforest. The Congo Basin, lying at the center, is home to numerous ethnic groups but is popularly known as the land of various pygmy peoples. The pygmies' classic hunting-and-gathering lifestyle contrasts with those of the other peoples of the area, even as they often trade among themselves. Congo peoples rely extensively on agriculture and, in the modern era, the mining of natural resources. Trade involving the use of barter systems and, since the 19th century, money is widespread. A number of peoples, including the Kongo, Kuba, and Lunda, created sizeable, complex states via conquest and confederation. Most peoples of the area, however, traditionally lived in smaller, less complex societies centered politically on the village or village cluster. Here too, craft specializations in weaving, woodcarving, and iron working are notable, their products long collected outside of Africa. The early influence of Portuguese Catholicism later gave way to other forms of Christianity as well as a continuance of African traditional religion. In Chad and parts of the Central African Republic, Islam is present.

History

Prior to the 19th century, most of the Europeans conducting business in sub-Saharan Africa were content to operate on the coasts and have slaves, gold, and ivory brought to them from the interior for shipment abroad. In the early 1800s, however, a more systematic exploration of the continent by European interests got underway. The so-called "scramble for Africa" was a massive effort by British, French, German, Belgian, Portuguese,

and other powers to expand their control of selected areas and exploit whatever resources were present there. The colonial history of the continent is too complex to summarize here. Suffice it to say that colonialism brought repression and exploitation along with the introduction of Christianity, literacy, and Western education, the beginning of modern cities, a shift toward market economies, the introduction of Western medicine and public health, and the emergence of transportation and communication networks. It also brought, especially in later decades, a desire for independence along with a new class of African politicians who sought to share in or seize the perquisites of power. Thus, even as traditional ways remained strong in the countryside, with its village-based or semi-nomadic lifestyle, its social life based on the family, the lineage, and the clan, major changes were introduced as a result of European hegemony.

After World War I the colonial era began to draw to a close, or at least to change. The British emphasized a strategy of "indirect rule," which promoted chosen local chiefs at the expense of others. The chiefs in office typically exploited their status and created rifts in traditional society. France, in contrast, pursued a policy of assimilation by the populace and direct rule by French colonial leaders. Most Africans, however, were not prepared to assume a French way of life or bow forever to French ministers. They eventually revolted. Portuguese and Belgian systems of colonial rule likewise underwent dramatic change, while German and Italian interests largely disappeared from the region between the first and second world wars. Indeed, World War II served to accelerate the rise of African nationalism. By the early 1950s, the political transformation of Africa was complete. The postwar era brought into existence some 50 new nations, with nearly as many distinct forms of government and unique, albeit often controversial, heads of state.

After a promising start, however, the years since the 1960s have been characterized by economic stasis or decline, and political instability. Many African leaders have eliminated or weakened parliamentary structures and oppositional groups in order to maintain authoritarian rule. Democratic institutions such as political parties, trade unions, and the press have suffered as a result. Since independence, most African states have experienced at least one coup d'état, and many of them more than one. Ethnic and religious conflicts have also arisen, reaching, in some cases, genocidal proportions. Yet, there is room for optimism, as African and international leaders begin to deal more realistically with the region's socioeconomic and political problems. It is notable in this regard that a Ghanaian, Kofi Annan, headed the United Nations recently, and Annan and a number of other contemporary Africans, including Wangari Maathai of Kenya, Albert Luthuli and Nelson Mandela of South Africa, and Ellen Johnson Sirleaf and Leymah Gbowee of Liberia, have won the Nobel Peace Prize.

Michael Shally-Jensen, PhD

Bibliography

Akyeampong, Emmanuel Kwaku. *Themes in West African History*. Athens, OH: Ohio University Press, 2006.

Gordon, April A. and Donald L. Gordon, eds. *Understanding Contemporary Africa*. Boulder, CO, Lynne Rienner, 2012.

Grinker, Roy Richard, et al., eds. *Perspectives on Africa: A Reader in Culture, History and Representation*. Malden, MA: Wiley-Blackwell, 2010.

Pakenham, Thomas. *The Scramble for Africa: White Man's Conquest of the Dark Continent from 1876 to 1912*. New York: Random House, 1991.

Van Reybrouck, David. *Congo: The Epic History of a People*. New York: Ecco, 2014.

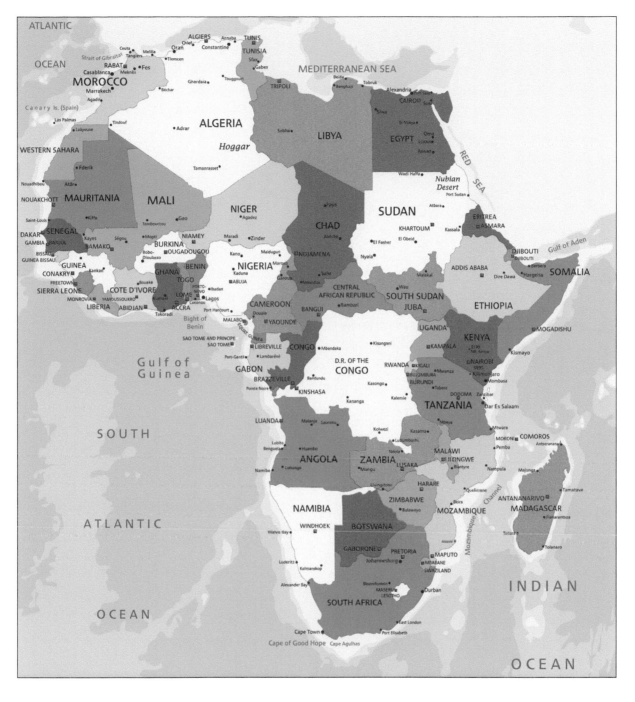

WESTERN & CENTRAL
AFRICA

Map of the African continent from 1914.

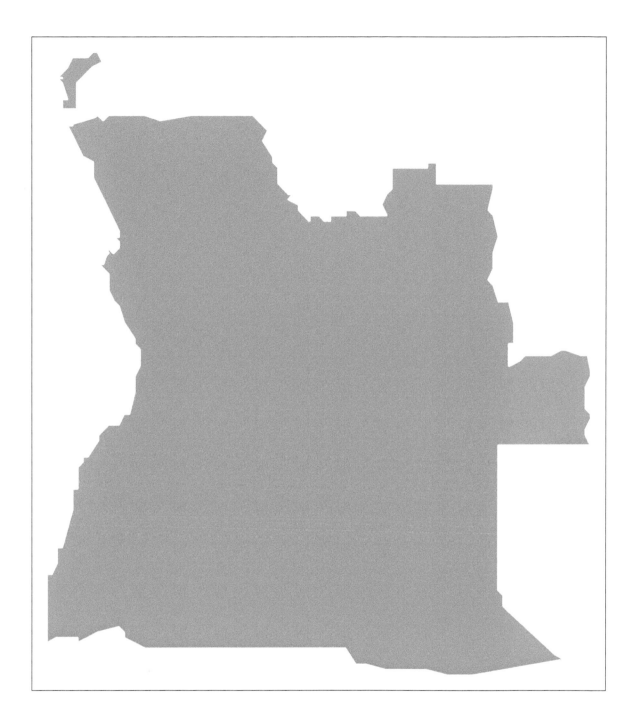

ANGOLA

Introduction

The West African nation of Angola lies on the southwest coast of Africa. It is bordered on the north by the Republic of the Congo and the Democratic Republic of the Congo, on the east by Zambia, on the south by Namibia, and on the west by the Atlantic Ocean.

The Portuguese used Angola as a base for the slave trade in the 16th century. By the 20th century, the Southern African country was the main source of slaves for the Americas. Later, Angola became an overseas province of Portugal. After independence was won in 1975, some of the groups engaged in near-continuous civil war, which formally ended in 2002. A constitution was ratified in 2010, and the first national elections were held in 2012.

Government corruption and lack of economic development has kept a significant portion of Angola's population below the poverty line. However, the economy is growing, primarily because of the discovery and development of oil deposits. Diamond production is also an important source of revenue in Angola.

Angolan traditional arts are closely tied to cultural rituals such as birth, death, and adulthood, and to seasonal activities such as hunting and harvesting. Because of the slave trade, much of Angola's traditional musical styles and instruments were exported to Latin America and the Caribbean.

GENERAL INFORMATION

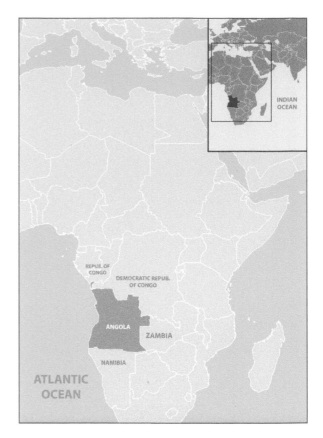

Official Language: Portuguese
Population: 24,300,00 (2014 estimate)
Currency: Angolan kwanza
Coins: Coins are available in denominations of 1, 2, and 5 kwanzas.
Land Area: 1,246,700 square kilometers (481,354 square miles)
National Motto: "Virtus Unita Fortior" (Latin, "Unity Provides Strength")
National Anthem: "Angola Avante" ("Forward Angola")
Capital: Luanda
Time Zone: GMT +1
Flag Description: The flag of Angola features two horizontal bands of color, one red and one black. The red represents the blood shed during the country's fight for independence while the black represents Africa. The flag also features a yellow cog wheel, machete, and star. This centered imagery, which represents the communist ideals of workers and industry, was included during the years Angola was administered by a single-party socialist government.

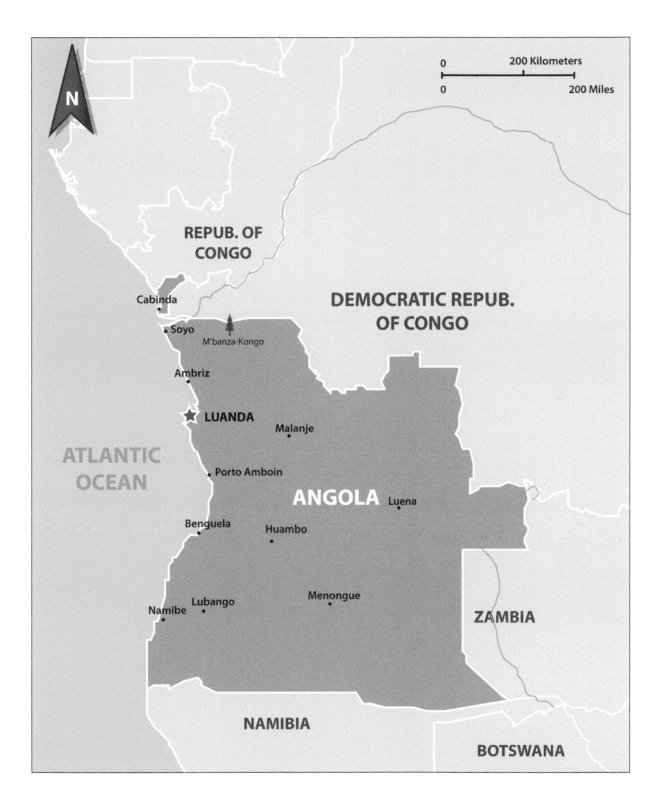

Principal Cities by Population (2009-10, unless otherwise specified):

- Luanda (5,506,000) (2015)
- Huambo (1,269,000) (2015)
- Lobito (805,000)
- Cabinda (377,931)
- Lubango (256,713)
- Kuito (185,302)
- Malanje (156,829)
- Benguela (131,281)
- Uíge (119,815)
- Namibe (86,366) (2008)

Population

The majority (60 percent) of Angola's population lives in rural areas. The country is urbanizing at a rate of almost five percent per year. Before independence, more than 400,000 Europeans and mestiços (of mixed black African and European descent) lived in Angola. Many fled during the wars; most of those who remain live in the country's cities.

Most Angolans are descended from one of several primary African ethnic groups. The Ovimbundu, who constitute 37 percent of the population, speak the Umbundu language and live mostly in central and southern Angola. The Mbundu (Kimbundu) account for 25 percent of the population. They are speakers of Kimbundu, and they live in the capital and in the central and southern areas. Straddling Angola's borders with the Republic of the Congo and the Democratic Republic of the Congo is the homeland of the Bakongo, who speak Kikongo dialects. The Bakongo comprise 13 percent of the population.

Other ethnic groups in Angola include the Kongo, Lwena, Chokwe, Kwanyama, Nyaneka, Luchazi, Ambo, Mbwela, and Nyemba peoples. These account for the remaining 25 percent of the population.

Languages

The official language of Angola is Portuguese and it is spoken by more than 90 percent of the population. French is also spoken to a lesser extent. In addition, more than 60 regional languages belonging to the Bantu group are also spoken. Some of the major languages include Umbundu, Kimbundu, Kikongo, Tchokwe, Ofambo, Bakongo, and Kwanyama.

Native People & Ethnic Groups

Angola has been inhabited since prehistoric times. Approximately 2,000 years ago, Bantu-speaking people settled in the area. When the Portuguese arrived in 1482, the area was dominated by the Kingdom of Ndongo. Through wars and treaties, the Portuguese gained control and turned the country into a major base for the slave trade. Angola was often referred to as "Portuguese West Africa."

After slavery was abolished, Angola became a Portuguese colony and then an overseas province. In the 1950s, Portuguese people were encouraged to move to Angola and start businesses. The resulting economic advances did little for the black Angolans, most of who lived in a state of virtual forced labor. This disparity led to increased racial tensions. Today most black Angolans are subsistence farmers and herders who live below the poverty line.

Religions

Angola's constitution states that the country is a secular state that respects all religions. Within its region of Southwest Africa, Angola has been looked to as a standard for religious freedom. About half of all Angolans follow indigenous beliefs. The other half is Christian; the majority of this half is Roman Catholic.

Climate

The northern part of Angola, nearer the equator, has a tropical climate. The southern area is subtropical. Temperate conditions prevail, however, at altitudes above 1,500 meters (5,000 feet), where frost sometimes occurs.

Average temperatures on the coastal plain range from 21° Celsius (70° Fahrenheit) in January (sub-equatorial summer) to 16° Celsius (60° Fahrenheit) in June. The coast is cooler than most tropical areas at the same latitude because of sea breezes from the Benguela Current. The interior experiences temperatures close to 19° Celsius (66° Fahrenheit). The rainy seasons lasts from October to March, while the dry season is from November to April.

The northern coast and most of the interior experience between 1,000 and 1,500 millimeters (40 and 60 inches) of annual rainfall, whereas the desert area receives only about 50 millimeters (two inches) of rain each year. Local heavy rains on the plateau often cause floods.

ENVIRONMENT & GEOGRAPHY

Topography

Almost twice the size of the American state of Texas, Angola lies on the southwest coast of Africa. It is bordered by the Republic of the Congo and the Democratic Republic of the Congo (formerly Zaire), Zambia, and Namibia, and on the west by the Atlantic Ocean. The province of Cabinda, in the northwest, is separated from the rest of the country by the estuary of the Congo River.

Angola is part of southern Africa's inland plateau. A dry coastal plain rises to a wet agricultural plateau in the interior. The land then slopes gradually to the savannah (grasslands) of the east. The southwestern part of the county is rocky semi-desert, and borders the Kalahari Desert of Namibia. The northern part (including Cabinda) is rainforest.

Luanda, a major African seaport, is situated on the Angolan coast, which stretches approximately 1,610 kilometers (1,000 miles) along the Atlantic Ocean. The city is located along a narrow and relatively dry coastal zone, known colloquially as the "flat land." A small peninsula, known as the Ilha de Luanda (Island of Luanda), extends off the coast of Luanda and features numerous beaches, recreational facilities, and small fisheries. Other seaports include Ambriz, Cabinda, Lobito, Malongo, Namibe, Porto Amboim, and Soyo.

Angola is traversed by 1,400 kilometers (more than 900 miles) of navigable rivers. Primary watercourses into the interior include the Cunene (1,207 kilometers/750 miles), the Cuango (1,127 kilometers/700 miles), and the Kwanza (966 kilometers/600 miles). The Zambezi, Africa's fourth-largest river, rises in Angola and flows south into Zambia. The lower Congo River forms part of the border between Angola and the Democratic Republic of the Congo.

Plants & Animals

Other than palm trees there is little vegetation along Angola's dry coastal plain. The northern tropical forests are home to such tree species as African sandalwood, ebony, rosewood, tola, and mahogany. Aloe grows in the highlands. Grasses and shrubs grow abundantly in the savannah. The south and east are characterized by grasslands. Sparse desert vegetation grows in the southwest.

War and deforestation have caused Angola to lose much of its biodiversity, especially large animals. However, the country is still home to Angolan giant sables (a mountain goat-antelope), gorillas, elephants, crocodiles, hippopotamuses, elands, reedbucks, oribis, black sables, impalas, antelope, lions, white rhinoceroses, zebras, bushpigs, duikers, buffalo, leopards, baboons, giraffes, and cheetahs. Smaller animals include porcupines, pangolins, aardwolves, genets (a type of cat), adders, and mound-building termites.

About 360 bird species have been identified in the highlands alone, including cave-chats, francolins, swifts, togins, thrushes, and the slaty flycatcher. Mackerel, tuna, and sardines flourish in Angola's coastal waters.

CUSTOMS & COURTESIES

Greetings

The basic greeting in Angola involves a handshake, while close acquaintances and family may embrace. Women often kiss on the cheek and younger children are expected to respectfully bow or curtsy when greeting elders. Most Angolans will greet in Portuguese, their tribal language, or both. Portuguese is prominent in urban areas, but may be followed by indigenous greetings if two individuals share the same ethnicity. Commonly heard phrases include "Bomdia" ("Good morning"), "Boa tarde" ("Good afternoon"), and "Boa noite" ("Good evening"); the Portuguese "Ola" ("Hello") is common in informal greetings. Additionally, greetings in Angola may also customarily involve inquiring about one's well-being and family, and refraining from carrying out this lengthy enquiry may cause offense or disrespect.

Gestures & Etiquette
Generally, Angolans are a very friendly people. Common gestures include handshaking, patting on the back, kissing another's cheek, and sucking teeth in disapproval. Most identify with their larger cultural groups and adhere strictly to societal codes of conduct. Each ethnicity has its own strict rule of etiquette, but all ethnic and tribal groups share in common the deference shown to elders. This includes bowing for males and curtsying for females, and the serving of elders first at family meals.

The Ovimbundu have developed the social tradition of passing a communal pipe. Both men and women smoke pipes, but never in the same circles. Men often enjoy a communal pipe among friends after dinner, while women will usually do the same in the evening, once all of their household duties have been completed. It is said among the Ovimbundu that if a man asks a woman for her pipe, he is essentially asking for her hand in marriage.

Eating/Meals
Traditionally, Angolans eat three meals per day, with most meals generally eaten at home, depending on available resources. Food shortages in the late 20th and early 21st centuries has impacted eating customs, and eating one or two meals per day has also become commonplace. In fact, in 2004, following the end to the drawn-out civil war, the United Nations World Food Programme (WFP) was feeding an estimated 1.9 million Angolans. Despite a severe food shortage and debilitated infrastructure for bringing in food supplies, Angolans are slowly regaining their ability to make traditional meals.

Before civil conflict, Angolans shared a relatively universal eating style. Per tradition, meals were cooked by women, though men often grilled the meat. Breakfast is generally taken at home, and may consist of leftovers or porridge. Dinner is traditionally eaten as a family, with all members sitting around communal dishes, either on a mat on the floor or at a table. The dishes include sauces and porridges, and are eaten with spoons. Drinks may be served after dinner.

Visiting
Visiting in Angola is a common and often daily practice. Generally, visiting does not include eating, as guests traditionally visit after dinner has been served. Women, however, may visit during meal preparations, while men typically gather in the evening. Women may also generally visit each other during the day when their husbands are away at work, and will commonly bring over their children to socialize.

LIFESTYLE

Family
Traditional Angolan family structure resembles that of other African societies. The extended family unit in Angola includes a husband, his wife (or wives), their children, and other relatives or extended family also living in their compound. All members of an extended family household must share in daily domestic responsibilities, including child rearing and financial contributions. Even the eldest children are expected to help raise their younger siblings. In traditional polygamous households, in which the practice of plural wives is observed, the husband lives among all of his wives. However, in urban areas, husbands have taken up the practice of living with one wife and supporting the other wives, who may live with their parents or in individual apartments with their children. Nonetheless, the husband is required by law to support them.

In addition to these traditional family units, more modern family structures, such as the nuclear family unit (a husband, a wife, and their children) are finding their way into Angolan society as a direct result of overcrowding and Western influence. Another factor that has changed the traditional Angolan family structure was the decades-long civil war that displaced thousands. Countless Angolans were forced from their homes, disrupting the kinship relationships of many communities that had been established for centuries. According to many conflict studies experts, such a disruption can cause an irreversible transition from focusing on the community to a heightened sense of individualism. One immediate result is that Angolan women are now charging a fee to babysit other children because they have no other means of making a living.

Housing

Housing differs greatly between urban and rural Angola. This is largely due to lifestyle, space, and availability of materials. In rural Angola, where most Angolans live, the housing is generally uniform from region to region and among all ethnic groups. Most homes are constructed from wattle and daub techniques, and consist of mud walls and thatched roofs, commonly called raffia. Families, depending on income and number, will construct several of these living units on their property to form a compound. Homes that are more modern are constructed from mud bricks with corrugated tin roofs.

Housing also varies in urban Angola, particularly Luanda. The wealthy or upper middle class Angolans and foreigners living in Luanda usually inhabit concrete bungalows or high-rise apartments. The bungalows and larger homes typically feature wraparound porches or single verandas, and may be surrounded by concrete walls. Barrios, or overcrowded neighborhoods, are common and have characteristic architecture, including housing units called musseque. Built from mud, scrap metal, cardboard, plastic bags or any other extraneous material, these single-room living units typically share walls with the surrounding homes. These informal settlements are commonly without running water, sanitation, or paved roads.

Food

The staples of the Angolan diet are a healthy mix of grains, greens, and protein. The national cuisine has long been influenced by outside forces that date back to the original Bantu peoples, who introduced starches into the diet. The Portuguese then introduced olive oil and other Mediterranean staples. The main items used in contemporary Angolan cooking include tilapia or other whitefish, and meats such as chicken, goat, or beef. Beans, dendem (palm oil), sweet potato and sweet potato leaves, tomato, onions, okra, yucca and manioc flour, and corn flour are other common ingredients. These are used to make a variety of traditional porridges and stews that are eaten at family meals.

Perhaps the most likely dish one would encounter when visiting Angola is funge, a thick, smooth porridge made from corn flour. This staple is traditionally served alongside stews that feature meat, greens, garlic, onion, and spices. The other main starch is a rendition of funge made from yucca or manioc flour. The manioc flour dish is also commonly known as bombo. Occasionally piripiri, or pilli-pilli, a spicy mix of fresh peppers and olive oil, is served with these dishes. Perhaps the most famous dish is calulu, which is a stew made from a mix of dried and fresh fish, okra and greens, and served either with funge or beans cooked in dendem.

Drinks are numerous and shared on all sorts of occasions. Families often have soft drinks after dinner or may even have beer or wine. Maluvu is a popular palm wine and kissangua is a corn-flour beer commonly consumed. Mongozo is a world-famous brew made by the Chokwe people.

Life's Milestones

Birth is celebrated as both a major milestone heralding the life of a new child, and as a major achievement of the new parents. Marriage is generally considered unsuccessful if a couple is unable to conceive. Thus, when a woman becomes pregnant she will customarily rest throughout the duration of her pregnancy and be cared for by elder female relatives. In some more contemporary families in urban Angola, women may work through their third trimester.

Youth celebrate initiation into adulthood when they come of a certain age: 15 for boys, and the age at which they can conceive for girls. For boys, this initiation involves entering the wilderness to prove their manhood. Traditionally, the boys will spend anywhere from one to a few weeks in the wilderness, at first accompanied by older, male villagers. During that last few days, they are isolated and forced to fend for themselves. When they return to their villages, they are considered men. A ceremony generally follows and includes the newly appointed young men donning masks and dancing. Girls are said to come of age when once they are able to have children. Their ceremony involves ceremonial bathing and being dressed up in beads and make-up. They execute elaborate dances that emphasize their subservience to men.

Marriage is considered very important in Angolan society. In most traditional households, marriage is arranged by family members and the match is typically based on politics. Brides are expected to be far younger than their matches to reinforce the dominant role of the male in the relationship. When a member of a community or family dies, it is believed by nearly all Angolans that his spirit passes on into another life. Therefore, it is of the utmost importance to Angolans that the deceased receive the proper funerary rites. This involves cleaning and dressing the body. Significant artifacts used by the deceased are also collected and placed with the body to accompany it to the afterlife.

CULTURAL HISTORY

Art

The earliest known inhabitants of Angola were the Khoisan- and Khoe-speaking tribes and Saan Bushmen. These groups were not noted for their artistic expression and were skilled cattle farmers or hunter-gatherers. Two significant migrations of Bantu tribes occurred—2500–2000 BCE and 1500–500 BCE—into Western Africa,

displacing the Khoisan- and Khoe-speaking tribes. The Bantu brought with them their knowledge of metallurgy and ceramics (while also adopting the cattle farming trade). The next significant cultural influx arrived in the 15th century with the arrival of Portuguese colonists. After the Portuguese arrival, the cultural make-up of Angola underwent significant change. Colonialism brought about organized education, and Portuguese was taught in urban areas. However, traditional arts suffered, as they were deemed as inferior and forbidden.

Some ethnic groups continued to hold fast to their traditional arts. The Chokwe, for example, still practice their famed basket weaving and ceramic crafting. The ceramic and terra cotta pots are often intricately designed with dark, geometric patterns and sometimes hung with strings of handmade beads. They are functional in nature, and used to store grains, onions and garlic, and textiles. *The Thinker*, a bronze sculpture of Chokwe origin, is one of the oldest and best-known pieces of traditional Angolan art.

Textiles are important to many of the ethnic groups and tribes. Primarily created by women, textiles are woven from handmade and hand-dyed thread. The patches of weaving are then sewn together and embroidered with elaborate patterns on top of the bold, colorful designs.

Each culture in Angola produces a distinctive style of mask.

Masks of bronze, ivory, malachite, ceramics, and wood are distinct for each culture. Lubunda-Chokwe masks, for instance, represent mythological figures and are used with music and storytelling.

Architecture

Angola's diverse architecture includes Portuguese colonial architecture and modern architecture that took root in the 1970s, following independence. The colonial imprint of Portugal is still extant, and the buildings are reminiscent of Spanish architecture. Distinct elements include domes, white pillars, and repetitive archways. One prominent example is the National Bank Building, built in Luanda in the mid-1900s. True to its colonial roots, the two-story building boasts a centerpiece gold dome and a rose-colored façade adorned with white pillars and archways. Older examples of Portuguese architecture are the numerous baroque churches that still remain. The Igrejada Nossa Senhora do Cabo, originally built in 1575 and rebuilt in 1669, still stands in Luanda, along with churches from the same era in Benguela. However, the Angolan Civil War (1975–2002) wreaked terrible havoc on buildings in many rural cities. In Huambo, in particular, most of the Portuguese architecture was destroyed.

Drama

From the 1970s through the late 1990s, international filmmakers mostly dominated Angolan film. Since the end of the civil war, Angola's film industry has made significant headway. In 2004, numerous feature length films were released, *O Herói* (*The Hero,* 2004), by writer and director Zézé Gamboa (1955–), follows the lives of three people following the Angolan Civil War. The film won the Sundance Film Festival's World Cinema Grand Jury Prize and the Best Feature Film Award at the Pan African Film Festival in Los Angeles, both in 2005. Gamboa followed up *O Herói* with *O Grande Kilapy* (*The Great Kilapy,* 2012). *Na Cidade Vazia* (*Hollow City,* 2004), directed by Maria João Ganga (1964–), is the first Angolan film produced by a woman.

Music

Music and dance both play a crucial role in Angolan society, dating back to the region's first inhabitants. The Bantu tribes that settled in the region during the great migration brought with them or developed elaborate musical traditions. Among these groups, music functioned not only as the backdrop of all celebrations and ceremonies, but also as a necessary element. For example, songs were composed for naming ceremonies, marriage, initiation, death, harvesting, royal ceremonies, and battle. The Ovimbundu are famous for their large drums and flutes, used particularly during royal ceremonies.

When the Portuguese arrived, they systematically suppressed indigenous Angolan art forms, including music. However, by the 1940s, Angolan musicians reemerged with the founding of Ngola Ritmos, a group of nine musicians. Led by musical groundbreaker Carlos "Liceu" Vieira Dias (c. 1933–2008), considered the father of contemporary Angolan popular music, it was one of the first Angolan groups to incorporate electric guitar and Cuban and Brazilian sounds into traditional music. The lyrics were critical of the Portuguese government, and the group remained influential during Angola's fight for independence. Jose Adelino Barceló de Carvalho (1943–), known as Bonga, was the next largely popular musician to emerge from Angola. Carvalho grew up in Luanda and wrote politically and socio-economically charged lyrics. He also helped popularize semba, a traditional Angolan music, believed to have inspired samba in Brazil.

During the country's civil war, musicians were often persecuted and exiled by the government. However, in spite of limited resources and freedoms, hip-hop emerged as one of the most popular musical styles in the country. Kuduru is Angolan hip-hop and is a blend of traditional Angolan music mixed with contemporary European and American beats. Kuduru also refers to the dance that accompanies the music.

Literature

Angolan literature can trace its roots to the region's oral traditions, long practiced by indigenous ethnic groups, and the written literary traditions of the Portuguese. Before the arrival of the Portuguese, there existed a thriving storytelling tradition, in the form of myths, folklore, and proverbs, among all indigenous ethnic groups. The memorization and verbal dissemination of these cultural treasures was sacred to each tribe as a means of transmitting history and values from one generation to the next. Many stories were creation myths, while others traced lineage back to the first tribal members. Legends usually involve an individual achieving superhuman feats, in the same fashion as American tall tales. Folktales, the equivalent of moralistic fables, typically involve a trickster animal who demonstrates crafty human characteristics. Proverbs are traditionally short (one or two sentences) sayings that hide a valuable moral lesson.

When the Portuguese arrived, they brought their written language and educational system. The first authors in Angola were Portuguese who wrote tales glorifying European culture while degrading "savage" African culture. However, a few Europeans lauded African lifestyles while admonishing the rough practices of the Portuguese. Fernando Monteiro de castor Soromenho (1910–1968) is considered the "father of the Angolan novel" for his works decrying the acts of his compatriots. His 1949 novel, *Terra Morta*, recounts the region-wide destruction Portugal was causing. Literary achievement by both the mestiços and black Angolans followed.

By the 1950s, with increased nationalism and focus on the rights of indigenous Angolans, Angolan literature began to fully develop a distinct identity. Authors such as playwright José Mena Abrantes (1945–) and fiction writer Artur Carlos Maurício Pestana dos Santos (1941–), who writes under the pseudonym Pepetela, helped develop the Angolan literary voice. Before the civil war, António Agostinho Neto (1922–1979) was a well-known poet before he became Angola's first president. Today most Angolan literature is rife with traditional motifs and political, economic, and social commentary. Literature remains a crucial aspect of Angolan culture and, following the cultural destruction

during the civil war, the Ministry of Culture created a commission of fourteen experts to write the history of Angolan literature in 2005.

CULTURE

Arts & Entertainment
The contemporary arts in Angola are characterized by a strong desire to transcend the cultural destruction incurred by both Portuguese colonialism and the decades-long civil conflict that began in the 1970s. In 2002, as part of a new effort to support the arts, the government pledged to create the Medium and Higher Institutes of the Arts and the Museum of Contemporary Arts.

Outside of the traditional world of art, the contemporary art scene is strong, though patronage and government support is often lacking. Several national arts organizations and endeavors have been instituted since the civil war, the most important of which is perhaps the Uniao Nacional Artisticos Plasticos, or National Union for Plastic Artists, founded in 1977. Today, it boasts as members some of Angola's most famed artists, and has helped boost the careers of upstart artists through exhibitions and publicity. This organization was partially responsible for the rise of notable Angolan artists during the civil war era, including Vitor Teixeira (1940–1993), or Viteix, and António Ole (1951–).

Viteix created work in many media including oils, sculpture, and photography. Ole is a prolific artist who also uses many mediums including photography, oils, scrap collages, and sculpture. His work often decries the socio-economic tragedies of Angola. A notable exhibit was composed of discarded tin doors from one of the numerous musseque neighborhoods surrounding Luanda. The doors are accompanied by destroyed street signs, painted bright colors, and situated to recreate these barrios. His goal was to highlight, literally with the vibrant colors, the dire circumstances of life in these shantytowns (informal settlements).

Most contemporary Angolan artists have not been formally trained. They learn from trial and error or through apprenticeship, common among craftsmen and women. For those who have the opportunity to train formally, there are a surprising number of options. Escola Nacional de Artes Plásticos, or the Luanda National School of Plastic Arts, and the School of Arts, Media and Painting have turned out Angola's most famous contemporary artists. Manuel José Ventura (1981–) is among them, and his works depict traditional Angolan scenes in abstract forms. Other famous artists educated in country are Aurelio Fernandes Cabenda (1974–) and painter Francisco Domingos Van-Dúnem (1959–).

The national sports of Angola, football (soccer) and basketball, are major recreational activities in Luanda. Angola's national football team, the Palancas Negros ("Black Antelopes"), competes internationally. They were runners-up in the 2011 African Nations Championship.

Cultural Sites & Landmarks

The city of M'banza-Kongo is home to some of the most prized historical sites in Angola. At the height of the Kongo Kingdom (1400–1914), which extended from Central Africa to the southern tip of Africa's western coast, M'banza functioned as the capital for its centralized and elevated location. The city is situated atop the flattened peak of a mountain, and remnants of the kingdom remain, including the residences and tombs of the Kongo kings. The Jalankuwo, or judgment tree, used by the king to determine the fate of criminals, also still stands in the center of the city. Also near the center lie the famous ruins of a cathedral built by the Portuguese in the 16th century. The United Nations Educational, Scientific, and Cultural Organization (UNESCO) list the city as a tentative World Heritage Site.

While Angola remains a bastion of natural beauty and diverse flora and fauna, poachers have long devastated the region. The Iona National Park, the nation's largest geographic protected area, has suffered such devastation at the hands of game hunters. Despite the diminished mammalian population, the park still boasts a recorded 114 species of birds; scientists claim that many more are yet to be discovered. The

Quiçama (or Kissama) National Park in northwest Angola is the nation's only fully functioning national park. It was founded in 1938 as a game reserve, but was transformed into a national park in 1957. Also suffering from wildlife decimation, the park spearheaded Operation Noah's Ark in September 2000. As part of this initiative, 30 elephants and other large mammals were transported from the overpopulated natural reserves in South Africa and Botswana.

Founded by the Portuguese in the 16th century, Luanda was once referred to as the "Paris of Africa" due to its European-influenced architecture and heritage. It is home to many cultural landmarks, including Estádio da Cidadela, Angola's main stadium; the colonial architecture of the National Bank of Angola building; Museo Nacional de Antropologia (National Anthropology Museum); and Fort San Miguel, a 17th-century white Portuguese fort.

Luanda also has a number of Roman Catholic churches that have become tourist attractions for their architectural and historical significance. The Church of Jesus, located in the center of downtown Luanda, was constructed in 1636 and restored after 2002. The Cathedral of Luanda, a modern worship site, is also a popular location for tourists drawn to the gardens that surround the site. On Ilha de Cabo (Island of the End) off the coast of Luanda, is the city's oldest church, which was founded by Portuguese missionaries in 1575 and still holds services for residents and visiting Catholics.

Libraries & Museums

Museums and cultural centers in Luanda include the National Museum of Natural History, which contains a preserved animal collection documenting the flora and fauna of Angola, and the National Museum of Anthropology, which has collections of art, clothing, and tools representing Angola's tribal history. The Central Museum of the Forces Assembled is a military museum containing information on the history of Angola and Luanda from a military perspective.

The National Library of Angola, founded in 1969, is located in Luanda. In 2010, the Angolan government announced plans to build six multi-media libraries in six provinces, an investment of $48 million (USD).

Holidays

Official holidays observed in Angola include Martyrs' Day (January 4), Peace and National Reconciliation Day (April 4), Africa Day (May 25), and Independence Day (November 11). Liberation Day (February 4) marks the anniversary of the outbreak of armed resistance against the Portuguese. National Heroes' Day (September 17) is also the birthday of António Agostinho Neto (1922–1979), the country's first president.

Youth Culture

Respecting one's elders is an important part of youth culture in Angolan society, regardless of ethnic affiliation. This is most often demonstrated through an ingrained series of actions that includes bowing or curtsying when greeting, allowing elders to sit and eat first, and the seeking out of advice from family or tribal elders in all life matters. Girls and boys are also acculturated into their traditional societal roles by their corresponding parent. For example, girls are taught domestic responsibilities from an early age, including child rearing and cooking, while boys may be taken to work with their fathers or simply allowed to extend their schooling. Generally, among most ethnicities, male children are the most likely to achieve an extended education.

The Angolan Civil War, which spanned three decades, had a devastating effect on Angolan youth. Not only were their traditional roles disrupted, but they were often forced to participate in the conflict. UNITA, in particular, recruited and forced orphaned youth to join the conflict, often doing so after having executed the parents; other children were forced into prostitution. It is estimated that roughly 100,000 children lost their families and homes due to the civil war. An estimated two million suffered from malnutrition or starvation as recently as 2005, three years after the conflict officially ended. In addition, because

of social stigma, young men and women who were shamed by the violent or sexual acts committed against them have been reluctant to rejoin society.

SOCIETY

Transportation

As of 2015, Angola has one of the lowest rates of car ownership in the world. Buses and minibuses are the most common form of public transportation. National bus services connect all major cities (though practices are often unregulated). Schedules may be infrequent and overcrowding is common. Traffic moves on the right-hand side of the road in Angola.

Transportation Infrastructure

The transportation infrastructure in Angola, including the Luanda Railway, was damaged during the country's years of civil war. Conditions are improving in the early 21st century due to international aid, particularly from China. Still, most rural roads in Angola remain impassable during rainy seasons.

The train system is the most important mode of moving goods from inland Angola to the coast for international trade. However, some river systems—Angola is traversed by 1,400 kilometers (more than 900 miles) of navigable rivers—are also useful for transporting. Small ships are able to make trips up and down the Cuanza River in the north, and large ocean liners are able to travel up the lower Congo River.

Media & Communications

Angola's media has nearly always been dominated by the state and criticism of the government has been frowned upon. After independence, in 1975, the government nationalized all forms of media and communications. Private journalists were often persecuted, tortured, exiled, incarcerated or even exiled for simply criticizing policies. In 1994, in an effort to improve its international reputation, the Angolan government established the Lusaka Protocol. This agreement between the government and the emerging rebels groups vying for power stated that the media would no longer be inhibited by government control, but would function as a tool for national reconciliation. However, government censorship persists and privatization of the press and television is limited.

The largest newspapers in circulation are government owned and operated, and include the *Jornal de Angola*. There are numerous private papers published weekly, but radio is more readily available nationwide. The government owns and operates the only national radio station, Rádio Nacional de Angola (RNA), as well as Televisao Popular de Angola (TPA). A notable critical radio station is the Rádio Ecclesia run by the Catholic Church, started in 1954.

Access to the Internet is limited in Angola but has been growing rapidly in recent years. Nevertheless, there is still much room for improvement, in 2014, there were an estimated 3.7 million Internet users, representing 19.4 percent of the population. Landline telephones are rare in Angola, used by a mere one percent of the population. However, approximately three quarters of the population uses cell phones according to a 2014 estimate.

SOCIAL DEVELOPMENT

Standard of Living
Angola ranked 149th out of 187 countries on the 2013 United Nations Human Development Index, which measures quality of life and standard of living indicators.

Water Consumption
Clean drinking water is not readily available or abundant in Angola. Most Angolans obtain water from shared wells and springs, which are often polluted. Although clean water is regularly trucked into areas that are without it, the process of delivery and transportation can often result in the water being contaminated. Incidents of waterborne diseases remain common. The Angolan government and the World Bank have pledged hundreds of millions of dollars in funding in the hopes of developing a sustainable water system in the country.

Education
Officially, education is compulsory for children between seven and 15 years. In reality, only roughly half of this age group is enrolled in primary and secondary school. All state education is free.

Primary school begins at age six and lasts for four years. Secondary school begins at age 10 and lasts for up to seven years. Instruction used to be solely in Portuguese, but today it is usually offered in local languages.

Angola has several universities, all in major urban areas. The two largest are in Luanda. The Universidade Agostinho Neto began in 1962 as Estudos Gerais Universitarios de Angola. A Catholic institution, it was part of the Portuguese educational system. After independence, private schools were banned. In 1979, the institution was re-established as Universidade de Angola, a state school. In 1985, the name was changed to Universidade Agostinho Neto, in honor of the first president of the independent republic.

Eventually, the ban on private schools was lifted. The Universidade Catolica de Angola, established in 1977, is the first private university in the country since independence. The literacy rate in Angola is 74 percent overall (82 percent among men and 61 percent among women).

Women's Rights
Due to unequal administration of the law, limited access to education, and the traditional belief that women must occupy a subservient role, Angolan women continue to face challenges in the early 21st century. For centuries, women have been raised to fill a subordinate role in Angolan society. Tradition mandates that Angola women marry at a young age, act as the primary caregivers for their children, and obey the wishes of their husband and other male family members. Often, this means that Angolan girls receive the bare minimum of required education, if any at all, in favor of learning

domestic responsibilities. As such, they are ill-equipped to enter the workforce, and in some cases, lack the understanding or knowledge of their guaranteed rights under the law. It has also resulted in a severely unbalanced literacy rate that favors men.

Angola's constitution provides equal laws for both men and women and protects women from most forms of violent abuse. However, these laws are widely unenforced and domestic abuse and violence against women remains widespread. Spousal abuse, for example, is not explicitly prohibited by law, but can be filed as general assault. Rape, including spousal rape, is constitutionally illegal and punishable by law with up to eight years in prison. However, most cases remain unreported or unprosecuted.

The government formed the Ministry of Women and Family Affairs to oversee protection of women's rights. The ministry is currently working in conjunction with the Angolan Bar Association to inform women of their rights under Angolan and international human rights law. From September through October 2007, the government also sponsored a program to raise awareness of women's rights and spousal abuse through a series of roundtables and ads in the national newspaper.

Health Care

In general, public health in Angola is poor. Life expectancy is only 56 years overall (54 years for men and 57 years for women). Only 3.8 percent of the GDP is spent on health expenditures, which ranks at 172nd out of 191 nations.

With an average of only 1.7 physicians for every 10,000 people, many people do not have the health care access they need. High-risk diseases in Angola include bacterial and protozoal diarrhea, typhoid fever, hepatitis A, sleeping sickness, malaria, meningitis, and schistosomiasis, a disease transmitted by contact with contaminated water.

At 2.4 percent, Angola's incidence of HIV-AIDS is officially much lower than in the rest of Africa. United Nations epidemiologists and Angolan activists, however, believe the incidence

is actually much higher, and blame insufficient testing for the low number. Inexpensive drug treatment is virtually nonexistent.

GOVERNMENT

Structure

An armed rebellion against Portuguese imperialism, begun in 1961, was unsuccessful. Severe repression followed, but violence kept breaking out for more than a decade. Finally, after a 1974 coup d'etat (an event in which the government is overthrown) in Portugal, the new military leaders agreed to grant Angola its independence. The republic was officially established on November 11, 1975. Cultural divisions between the north and south resulted in a long civil war after independence.

Today, Angola is a multiparty democracy. The first national elections were held in 2012. Suffrage, at age 18, is universal.

The president is head of state and head of government. According to the constitution established in 2010, the president is elected directly every five years, and can serve for a total of two terms. The president appoints the prime minister and the Council of Ministers.

The unicameral legislature, the Assembleia Nacional (National Assembly), has 220 members who are elected by proportional representation for five-year terms.

Political Parties

The most widely known political party in Angola is the Popular Movement for the Liberation of Angola (MPLA). The MPLA has been in control of the government of Angola since 1979. During the civil war, some of the country remained under the control of the rebel group UNITA, the National Union for the Total Independence of Angola, and the National Liberation Front of Angola. Since the civil war, these organizations have remained as opposition political parties. Other major political parties in Angola today include Liberal Democratic Party and the Republican Party of Angola.

Local Government

The country is organized into 18 provincias (provinces). Each province is administered by a governor appointed by the president. Angola's provinces are subdivided into 163 municipalities, which are further subdivided into 618 communes. Municipal administrators and traditional tribal authorities operate government at a local level. The country's central government appoints each non-traditional head of municipal government in Angola. Communal administrators are nominated by Ministry of Territorial Affairs. In February 2007, the Angolan government passed the Local Administration Law. The legislation aims to decentralize authority in Angola and increase the efficiency and viability of municipal services.

Judicial System

As a former Portuguese colony, Angola's judicial system is based in Portuguese civil law. During the years of single-party Marxist-Leninist socialist rule, citizens were provided few protections under the law and subjected to abuse of authority on the part of the government. Angola's transition to democracy has not resulted in significant changes in this system of "unified popular justice."

Taxation

Domestic corporations operating in Angola pay a flat income tax rate of 35 percent. Agriculture industries pay a discounted rate of 20 percent. Other taxes on businesses include taxes on interest, royalties, and real estate. Employers also pay eight percent for employee social security. Angolan citizens pay a variable income tax rate of up to 17 percent and a social security tax of three percent. All Angolans file taxes individually as joint filing is not permitted. Taxes are not collected from Angola's informal economy and less than 10 percent of the country's population has bank accounts.

Armed Forces

The Angolan Armed Forces (FAA), formed in 1991, consists of an army, navy, and national air force. Conscription is compulsory and universal,

and lasts twenty-four months. The armed forces have advanced bilateral military relations with China in recent years. In addition, much of the army's weaponry and equipment is Russian-made. The FAA had an estimated 100,000 active personnel in 2012. That same year, military spending accounted for an estimated 3.6 percent of Angola's GDP.

Foreign Policy

Angola's foreign policy since the 1950s has been plagued by conflicting factions supported by external agents vying for influence within Africa. These include the Popular Movement for the Liberation of Angola (MPLA), aligned politically with Russia; the National Front for Liberation of Angola (FNLA), supported by the US and the Democratic Republic of Congo (DRC); and the National Union for the Total Independence of Angola (UNITA), linked to South Africa and the People's Republic of China. During the 1960s, each faction fought the Portuguese government for control, with the MPLA eventually declaring independence in 1975. From the 1970s through the early 1990s, the country was engulfed in widespread civil war, and Angola was aligned with the East and the former Soviet Union. With the fall of communism, however, Angola opened itself up to Western nations.

The fighting continued until 1989, when the U.S. stepped in to broker a peace deal. The Bresse Accord was signed and the first democratic elections took place in the nation's history, yet bloodshed continued. In 1994, the Lusaka Protocol aimed for a similar peace, but failed yet again. Eventually UNITA lost credibility in the international community and the UN implemented sanctions to breakup their hold over the Huambo region. UNITA continued to fight until the death of its leader in 2002. That April, the Luena Memorandum of Understanding (MOU) was signed and returned control of all of Angola's land to the government; there have been two successful elections since.

In the postwar era of the early 21st century, Angola's economy is seeing rapid growth as it develops its oil industry. It enjoys strong economic relations with China, and that country loaned the national government $7 billion (USD) to develop infrastructure. Angola is a member of the UN is slated to serve on the UN Security Council (UNSC) from 2015–2016. Angola's foreign relations, including those with the US and the European Union (EU), are focused on sustainable development and health initiatives. In Africa, its influence over the central region is increasing since the late 1990s. Angola holds membership in the South African Development Community (SADC), the Organization of Petroleum Exporting Countries (OPEC), and the African Union (AU).

Human Rights Profile

International human rights law insists that states respect civil and political rights, and promote an individual's economic, social, and cultural rights. The United Nations (UN) Universal Declaration of Human Rights is recognized as the standard for international human rights. Its authors sought the counsel of the world's great thinkers, philosophers, and religious leaders, and were careful to create a document that reflects the core values shared by every world culture. (To read this document or view the articles relating to cultural human rights, visit http://www.udhr.org/UDHR/default.htm.)

In general, Angola's human rights practices have improved in the years following the drawn-out Angolan Civil War. The government has made headway in lessening police and security brutality and arbitrary arrest and detention. Furthermore, on the African continent, Angola stands out as a strong supporter of religious freedom and the freedom of association. However, many international human rights groups continue to contend that certain human rights and practices still require drastic improvement.

Generally, returning refugees were given mixed treatment. In the case of refugees returning to Angola from other, nearby nations, human rights organizations accused border patrols of extortion, as well as higher than normal taxes charged to impoverished families. Often, these taxed families had to give up the only goods they

had to cross back into Angola. For internally displaced families returning to their destroyed homes, the government pledged to compensate them for their losses and rebuild their homes. However, when presented with contracts for housing, Angola's government allowed families who were squatting in their gutted homes to be removed without compensation. Some families were offered compensation to move far from their original homes, often to other towns. In certain cases, if they did not accept the deal, they lost both their land and offer.

Prison conditions are considered terribly dangerous. Nearly every prison is overcrowded and has no sanitation and health services. As a result, violence, disease, and death are commonplace. The government claims that limited resources prevent them from correcting the situation. The judicial process is similarly under attack from human rights monitoring agencies. Although everyone is constitutionally allowed the right to a free and fair trial, most local courts were demolished during the civil war, and there are not enough judges to serve all localities. Thus, many villages are left to arbitrate their own criminal proceedings.

Lastly, the Angolan government is seen as a corrupt and obtuse institution, by citizens and human rights agencies alike. In general, many human rights groups found that the government needed to improve upon its transparency and address poverty and the use of funds, particularly in the oil revenue department. The government has also been accused of cronyism with awarding contracts to certain business owners.

ECONOMY

Overview of the Economy

The civil war that ended in 2002 left Angola's economy in ruin. It is among Africa's fastest-growing economies, however, thanks to its oil output. Oil exports account for nearly half of the country's gross domestic product (GDP), and Angola is one of the largest oil-producing countries in Africa. Diamonds are also economically important, but other sectors, such as fishing and manufacturing, are growing. In 2014, its estimated per capita GDP was $7,200 (USD). China is the largest trading partner for Angola, followed by the United States and Europe.

Industry

Industry, including mining and manufacturing, employs just over 10 percent of the workforce, and generates roughly 60 percent of the GDP. Industrial products include beer, petroleum, bread, flour, and cement. Angola's major exports, earning $69.46 billion (USD) annually, include crude and refined oil, diamonds, coffee, timber, sisal, fish, cotton, and minerals.

Labor

The vast majority of the population, about 85 percent, makes its living by subsistence farming. The remainder works in the industries listed above.

Energy/Power/Natural Resources

Angola's major natural resources are petroleum, diamonds, and timber. Others important resources include gold, diamonds, iron ore, fish, copper, phosphates, bauxite, feldspar, and uranium.

The country suffers many environmental problems. The pressure of a growing population pressures have led to overgrazing and resultant soil erosion. In turn, soil erosion contributes to water pollution. Deforestation in the tropical rainforest has resulted from the use of wood for fuel, causing a loss of biodiversity. Conservation groups are working to preserve and increase animal and plant populations. Desertification is another problem.

Fishing

Luanda has a number of productive fisheries and fish-processing facilities to make use of the coastal resources, though overfishing has damaged fish stocks in the coastal regions. In particular, the fishing industry has been challenged by illegal and unregulated fishing activities. While tuna and shellfish are developing as commercially viable resources, horse mackerel and sardines are the two primary commercial species.

Forestry

In 2013, an estimated 46.8 percent of Angolan territory was forested, much of it in the country's northern regions. The country's forestry resources are considered undeveloped. Angola exports a limited amount of mahogany and ebony to foreign markets. Part of the reason that Angola's forests are not more developed is due to the presence of the Angolan UNITA rebel movement.

Mining/Metals

A major industry in Angola is diamond mining. Other mineral resources include gold, copper, phosphates, bauxite, and iron ore. Though the nation has a rich mineralogical resource base, diamond and gem mining has been controversial because of the numbers of workers exploited by those that control the industry.

Agriculture

Major agricultural products include coffee, sugar cane, corn, millet, sisal, bananas, manioc, tobacco, cotton, plantains, vegetables, sweet potatoes, oil palm fruit, and tobacco. Timber, fish, and livestock are also important to the agricultural sector.

Before the civil war, Angola was the fourth-largest coffee producer in the world. The International Coffee Organization (ICO) is helping coffee growers to revive production.

Less than four percent of the land in Angola is arable, and subsistence farmers are unable to grow enough food to feed their families. Today, Angola imports much of its food. Drought also contributes to low agricultural productivity.

Animal Husbandry

Cattle and pigs are the primary livestock raised. Livestock products include cows' milk, beef and veal, pork, honey, hides, goat meat, poultry, game, eggs, beeswax, mutton, and lamb.

Tourism

Civil war has caused significant damage to Angola's tourist industry. However, tourism has grown significantly in the past years. Some 530,000 tourists visited the country in 2012, and the annual numbers continue to rise. Popular tourist attractions include white beaches, tropical rainforests, dramatic landscapes in both mountains and plains, waterfalls, unusual rock formations, rivers, and deep gorges. Tourists also enjoy safaris in game parks and national parks. Several years after the end of the war, however, the country remains unstable.

Kristen Pappas, Ellen Bailey, Micah Issitt

DO YOU KNOW?

- Capoeira, a blend of martial arts and dancing that that was developed by Africans and Brazilians during the slave era, is popular in Angola. Luanda has a number of capoeira schools and capoeira competitions are sometimes part of local festivals.

- During the long struggle for independence, Queen Nzinga Mbande (1582–1663) became a symbol of resistance. An expert at guerilla warfare, she continued to personally lead her warriors into battle against the Portuguese until well into her 60s. The Dutch supplanted the Portuguese from 1641 to 1648, partly with Queen Nzinga's aid. However, instead of abolishing the slave trade, they simply took it over.

Bibliography

Bender, Gerald J. "Angola under the Portuguese: The Myth and Reality." Trenton, NJ: *Africa World Press*, January 2004.

Chatelain, Heli. "Folk-Tales of Angola: Fifty Tales with Ki-Mbundu Text, Literal English Translation, Introduction, and Notes." *Kessinger Publishing*, May 2006.

Oyebade, Adebayo O. "Culture and Customs of Angola." Westport, CT: *Greenwood Press*, November 2006.

Pierce, Justin. "Political Identity and Conflict in Angola, 1975–2002." New York: *Cambridge University Press*, 2015.

Soares de Oliveira, Ricardo. "Magnificent and Beggar Land: Angola since the Civil War." New York: *Oxford University Press*, May 2015.

Works Cited

"Angola – Amnesty International Report 2008." *Amnesty International*. http://www.amnesty.org/en/region/angola/report-2008.

"Angola builds studio city to revive film industry." June 2007. *BizCommunity.com*. http://www.bizcommunity.com/Article/7/97/15203.html

"Angola by Bus." February 2003. *BBC Online*. Accessed Online March 10, 2009. http://news.bbc.co.uk/2/hi/programmes/from_our_own_correspondent/2736325.stm

"Angola." *City Population*. Accessed Online September 22, 2015. http://www.citypopulation.de/Angola.html

"Angola." 2009. *Encyclopædia Britannica Online*. http://www.britannica.com/EBchecked/topic/25137/Angola.

"Angola." *CIA World Factbook*. Accessed Online September 23, 2015. https://www.cia.gov/library/publications/the-world-factbook/geos/ao.html.

"Angola." January 2009. U.S. Department of State. Accessed Online September 23, 2015. http://www.state.gov/r/pa/ei/bgn/6619.htm.

"Angola." *The World Cookbook for Students*. Greenwood Press. 2007. http://books.google.com/books?id=LohMBqO3nBYC&printsec=copyright&dq=funge+angola#PPR4,M1

"Angola." *Transparency International Corruption Stats*. Accessed Online on September 18, 2015. http://www.transparency.org/country#AGO.

"Angola." *UN Data*. Accessed Online September 23, 2015. http://data.un.org/CountryProfile.aspx?crName=Angola.

"Angola." *UN Human Development Index*. Accessed Online on September 18, 2015. http://hdr.undp.org/en/countries/profiles/AGO.

"Angola." *World Health Org Stats*. Accessed Online on September 18, 2015. http://www.who.int/gho/countries/ago/country_profiles/en/.

"Angola: Country Reports on Human Rights Practices." March 2007. *U.S. Department of State*. http://www.state.gov/g/drl/rls/hrrpt/2006/78718.htm

"Angolan Cinema Flourishes After the War." *The Power of Culture: Cinema in Africa*. Accessed online. http://www.powerofculture.nl/uk/specials/cinema_in_africa/angola.html

"Artists in Dialogue: Antonio Ole and AimeMpane."
  February 13, 2009. *Going Out Guide: Editorial Review*.
  http://www.washingtonpost.com/gog/exhibits/artists-in-
  dialogue-antonio-ole-and-aime-mpane,1155362.html

"Country profile: Angola." *BBC World News*. Accessed
  Online September 23, 2015. http://news.bbc.co.uk/2/hi/
  africa/country_profiles/1063073.stm#media

"Fernando Monteiro de Castro Soromenho."
  EncyclopædiaBritannica. 2009. http://www.britannica.
  com/EBchecked/topic/554948/Fernando-Monteiro-de-
  Castro-Soromenho.

"Fortress of Kambambe." *UNESCO: World Heritage*.
  http://whc.unesco.org/en/tentativelists/926/

"Huambo." 2009. *EncyclopædiaBritannica*. http://www.
  britannica.com/EBchecked/topic/274269/Huambo.

"Iona National Park." BirdLife IBA Fact Sheet: *Bird Life
  International*. http://www.birdlife.org/datazone/sites/
  index.html?action=SitHTMDetails.asp&sid=6011&m=0

"Jumbos journey to Angola." September 2000. *BBC World
  News*. http://news.bbc.co.uk/2/hi/africa/915226.stm

"Little Fort of Kikombo." 1996. UNESCO: *World
  Heritage*. http://whc.unesco.org/en/tentativelists/929/

"Luanda." 2009. *Encyclopædia Britannica Online*. http://
  www.britannica.com/EBchecked/topic/350301/Luanda

"Mbundu." 2009. *Encyclopædia Britannica Online*.
  http://www.britannica.com/EBchecked/topic/371373/
  Mbundu.

"Operation Noah's Ark, the largest airborne wildlife
  restocking operation ever, has begun, and can be viewed
  on the internet." *PR Newswire Europe Ltd*. http://www.
  prnewswire.co.uk/cgi/news/release?id=72597

"OT Africa Line Angola's Container Painting Competition
  2005 - Comes to Europe!" 2005. *OT Africa Line*. http://
  www.otal.com/Services/paintingcompetition.htm

Barnard, Alan. "Hunters and Herders of Southern Africa."
  Cambridge University Press 1992. http://books.google.
  com/books?id=2nBx83jMc48C&dq=kwadi+history&so
  urce=gbs_summary_s&cad=0

Hambly, Wilfred D. "The Ovimbundu of Angola." 1934.
  Chicago Press. Accessed Online March 10, 2009. http://
  www.archive.org/stream/ovimbunduofangol212hamb/
  ovimbunduofangol212hamb_djvu.txt

Oyebade, Adebayo. "Culture and Customs of Angola."
  2007. *Greenwood Publishing Group*. http://books.
  google.com/books?id=DeVqVy21g9sC&dq=national+in
  stitute+for+artistic+training+angola&source=
  gbs_summary_s&cad=0.

King's drums are an important part of Benin's culture. iStock.com/YovoPhoto.

BENIN

Introduction

Benin is a nation in West Africa. It is bordered by Niger to the north, Nigeria to the east, Burkina Faso to the northwest, Togo to the west, and the Bight of Benin to the south. Despite the discovery of petroleum deposits in the 1990s, Benin has an underdeveloped economy and most of its population is involved in subsistence agriculture.

A former part of French West Africa, Benin was a colony of France from 1904 to 1960. Until 1975, the country was known as Dahomey, and much of Benin's traditional folk art comes from the Dahomey Empire. Examples of this artwork include appliqué tapestries and bronze castings.

Benin is also known for its Vodun (or "Voodoo") religion and culture. One of the central concepts in West African Voodoo is reverence for one's ancestors and for this reason, Beninese culture has traditionally included a number of ceremonies and celebrations meant to venerate the living and deceased members of the family.

GENERAL INFORMATION

Official Language: French
Population: 10,448,647 (2015 estimate)
Currency: West African CFA franc
Coins: Coins are available in denominations of 1, 5, 10, 25, 50, 100, 200, 250, and 500 francs.
Land Area: 110,622 square kilometers (42,700 square miles)
Water Area: 2,000 square kilometers (772 square miles)

National Motto: "Fraternit, Justice, Travail" (French, "Brotherhood, Justice, Labor")
National Anthem: "L'Aube Nouvelle" (French, "The New Dawn")
Capital: Porto Novo
Time Zone: GMT +1
Flag Description: The flag of Benin depicts three solid colors: a vertical band of green extending along the whole of the hoist (left side), and two equal and horizontal bands of yellow (top) and red (bottom). The red represents courage, the green represents hope, and yellow symbolizes wealth. These colors are considered the official colors of the Pan-Africa (African unity) movement.

Population

The population of Benin is comprised of more than 60 different ethnic groups. Over 50 percent of all Beninese belong to two closely-related ethnic groups called the Fon and the Adja. Along with the Yoruba, who make up 10 percent of the population, the Fon and the Adja live primarily in

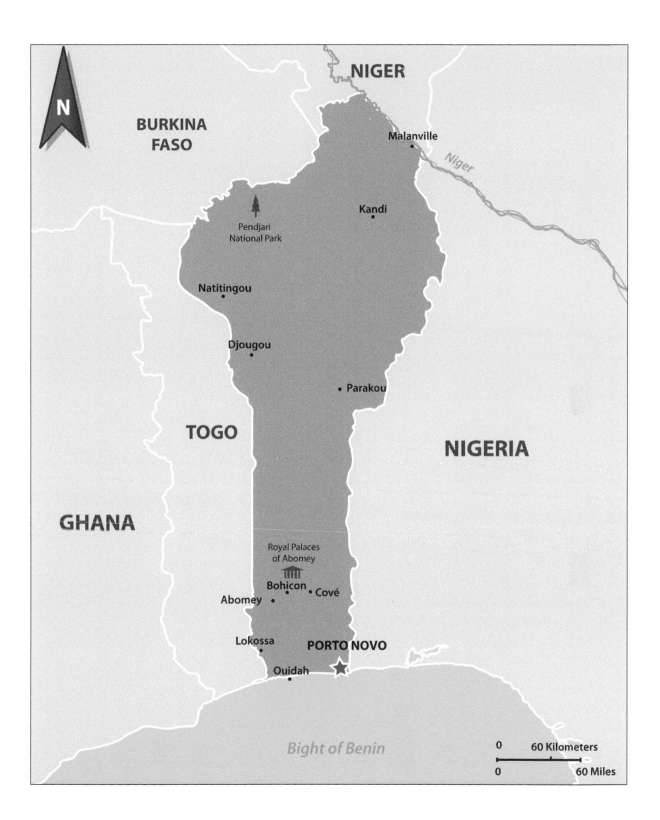

Principal Cities by Population (2012):

- Abomey-Calavi (757,000) (2015)
- Cotonou (682,000) (2015)
- Porto Novo (268,000) (2014)
- Djougou (237,040)
- Parakou (206,667)
- Bohicon (149,271)
- Kandi (128,172)
- Lokossa (106,081)
- Savé (97,309)
- Ouidah (91,688)

the southern parts of Benin. The northern region is dominated by the Bariba people, who account for an additional 10 percent of the population. The Somba people are also prevalent in the northern areas.

Around 1.6 percent of Beninese is European immigrants and descendants. In large cities, like Porto-Novo and Cotonou, European and mixed-European and African ethnicities compose a larger portion of the population than in rural Benin. The majority of the Europeans in Benin are of Portuguese and French descent.

Nearly two-thirds of the population resides in the southern part of the country, where the major cities are located. However, many Beninese are subsistence farmers who live in rural areas. Porto Novo is the national capital, but Cotonou is the largest city and the main commercial port. Over 40 percent of Beninese people live in urban areas. Most of Benin's cultural activity occurs in Cotonou, which is considerably more crowded than Porto Novo; the population of Porto-Novo was estimated in 2014 at 268,000, while as of 2015, Cotonou has a population of 682,000.

Other major cities and villages include Ganvié, which is famous for its houses built on stilts in a lagoon; Ouidah, the center of the Voodoo culture; Grand Popo, a beach resort; Abomey, famous as the capital of the Dahomey Empire; Natitingou, the home of the Somba people; Parakou, a trade center; and Malanville, which lies at the border of Benin, Nigeria, and Niger.

Languages

French is the official language of Benin, though nearly 50 other tribal languages are also spoken. Along the southern coast, Yoruba and Fon are the most widely spoken dialects. Some residents of Porto-Novo also speak Portuguese (imported from Brazil) and Spanish. Names of streets, buildings, and public facilities are generally listed in French, sometimes with African dialect translations.

Native People & Ethnic Groups

Benin was home to two major ethnic groups in the 13th century. The Ewé-speaking people lived in the southern regions, while the Voltaiques inhabited the north. In the 16th century, the Dahomey people established their kingdom in southern Benin and assumed dominance over the other Fon states in the nation.

Dahomians became the most powerful group in Benin because they settled the southern coast, where they established a slave trade with European colonists. By selling other ethnic Africans into slavery, the Dahomians built a powerful empire that existed for centuries. When European slavery was abolished in the 19th century, France overtook the Dahomians and established the colonies of French West Africa.

The largest ethnic groups in the country today include the Yoruba, Dendi, and Bariba. Recent years have seen the arrival of people from other African nations in Benin, including Togolese, Malians, and Nigerians.

Religions

Traditional religion exerts a lasting presence in Benin. Roughly a third of Beninese practice some form of animism, the most common of which is Vodun, or Voodoo. The Vodun religion and culture is highly significant in Benin; Voodoo cultural rituals exert a strong influence over both rural and urban life in Benin and play an important role in the nation's social fabric. The term "gris-gris," which means "curse," is a Voodoo colloquialism that alternately refers to good and bad luck. Roughly 43 percent of

Beninese practice Christianity and 24 percent practice Islam. Most Christians live in the south, and most Muslims live in the north.

Climate

Benin's climate is hot and humid throughout the country. The southern region experiences an equatorial climate, while the northern region's climate is tropical. Benin's average annual temperature ranges from 20° to 34° Celsius (68° to 93° Fahrenheit).

Rainfall is heavier in the equatorial south than in the tropical north. The central region receives the most rainfall, with an annual average of 1,300 millimeters (50 inches). In the south, there are two wet seasons. From April through July and from September through October, the south receives an average rainfall of 510 millimeters (20 inches). The northern region receives nearly 900 millimeters (35 inches) during its wet season, from June to October.

Drought, desertification, tornadoes, and the harmattan desert wind are common natural hazards in Benin.

ENVIRONMENT & GEOGRAPHY

Topography

The Atakora Mountains are the only significant topographical feature of Benin, which is otherwise relatively flat. The coast, which has no natural harbors, is made up of dunes and marshes. The central area of the country, which is mostly lowlands, is known as the terre de barre.

Northern Benin features a high plateau that rises to an elevation of 488 meters (1,600 feet). The highest point in the country is Mount Sokbaro in the Atakora Mountains, which rises to 658 meters (2,158 feet) above sea level.

The Ouémé River is Benin's longest, at 451 kilometers (280 miles) long. Other rivers include the Couffo in the south, the Mono in the southwest, and the Niger, Sota, Mékrou, and Alibori in the north. The country's largest freshwater body is Lake Nokoug.

Plants & Animals

Animals native to Benin include hippopotamuses, elephants, lions, panthers, crocodiles, antelope, buffalo, baboons, and warthogs. Poaching is a significant threat to Beninese wildlife. Despite government bans on illegal hunting and the establishment of national parks, poaching remains an epidemic. The two main national parks are the Parc National de la Pendjari, which is considered one of the best in Africa, and the Parc National du W, which is shared with neighboring Burkina Faso and Niger.

Benin's many species of birds include rose ringed parakeets, yellow-billed kites, African thrushes, tinkerbirds, laughing doves, common bulbuls, and Senegal parrots.

Much of Benin's plant life is threatened by deforestation, desertification, and drought. Trees in Benin's south have been mostly destroyed by deforestation, particularly along the coastal strip, which was once a dense rainforest. Most of the remaining trees are varieties of palms, clustered in the southern part of the country. Woodlands are found in the central region, while the northern area is mostly grassland.

CUSTOMS & COURTESIES

Greetings

The official language of Benin is French. The style of speaking and vocabulary used in Benin is closer to standard French than French dialects in other parts of Africa. The expressions "Bonjour" ("Good day") and "Bonsoir" ("Goodnight") are common greetings. Informally, Beninois may greet each other with the abbreviated expression "Salut" ("Hi").

There are a variety of tribal languages spoken in Benin, with the two most common being Fon and Yoruba. In Yoruba, individuals say "E kaaaro" ("Good morning"), "E kaasan" ("Good afternoon"), and "E kuurole" ("Good evening"). In the Fon language, basic greetings are more familiar. A Fon may greet a new person by saying "A do gangi a?" ("Are you well?").

Alternatively, the Fon may use more formal expressions such as "Kudo zan" ("Good morning") "Kudo hweme" ("Good afternoon"), and "Kudo gbada" ("Goodnight").

Rank and social status are very important in Benin, and it is considered rude to speak informally to someone older or of higher social status. Formal French is therefore used in initial greetings and when speaking to someone older. Greetings should always be initiated by the older person. Visitors should wait for women, authority figures, or older individuals to extend their hands before offering their own.

When greeting, men usually shake right hands, standing roughly at arm's length from one another. (As in Muslim culture, the left hand is considered unsanitary, as it is traditionally the hand used for hygienic activities.) Individuals of the same sex who know each other well may greet with a series of kisses, beginning on the cheeks and ending on the lips. It is considered impolite to make physical contact with strangers, and contact is generally reserved for close acquaintances and kin. Informal forms of address should also be reserved for friends and close acquaintances. Beninois also take care to address elders and authority figures by their family name or title rather than their given name.

Gestures & Etiquette

Eye contact is very important in Beninese culture and direct eye contact is taken as a sign of forthright behavior. As such, it is considered disrespectful to stare directly at individuals of the opposite sex or at older individuals. Such prolonged eye contact can be interpreted as a symbol of desire or a challenge to authority. Similarly, winking one's eyes can be perceived as a signal of deception. It is also considered respectful to bow one's head slightly when greeting older individuals.

The Beninois use a variety of facial expressions and hand gestures while speaking. For example, slapping one's hand against the leg is an expression of frustration that is commonly used. Additionally, as the left hand is considered unsanitary, it is considered impolite to gesture with the left hand.

Eating/Meals

The Beninois eat between two and three meals each day, roughly corresponding to the European traditions of breakfast, lunch, and dinner. In rural environments, it is more common for families to eat twice each day, once in the morning and once in the evening.

The morning meal generally consists of light fare such as tropical fruits and baked goods. Meat is not served with every meal because it is expensive and reserved for special occasions (or served at one of the two to three daily meals). Though some urban families may use utensils, it is common to eat with one's hands. (Again, the right hand is used out of hygienic concerns; the left hand is never used to eat). Beninois meals are served from communal dishes, with individuals reaching into a shared bowl and taking handfuls of food. Customs differ in urban areas, where diners may be given individual plates or bowls. Families usually serve food in two bowls, one for children and one for adults.

As with other aspects of Beninois culture, age and rank are important in traditional dining customs. The eldest male of a household is served first and, if there are male guests present, the men may eat separately from the women. Children and women are traditionally served only when the male members of the family have been given their food.

Visiting

The Beninois generally maintain a relaxed attitude about visiting, and it is not always necessary to arrange a visit in advance. Visitors customarily ask for permission before entering a house and before leaving, and wait for their host to show them to the door. It is also considered polite to reciprocate social invitations, and visitors should take care to extend a return invitation when appropriate. Whether or not visitors arrive in time for a meal, many Beninois hosts will offer water and/or food to their guests. It is considered impolite to refuse any food or drink offered, as families are making a significant gesture by offering some of their often-limited food supply to their guests.

LIFESTYLE

Family

As in many West African cultures, extended kin groups form the basis of Beninois society. Marriages are traditionally arranged between families for strategic reasons, with both families hoping to gain in status and prosperity through the union. In rural areas, marriages are often handled in a traditional manner, with the bridal family's eldest female member accepting the proposal on behalf of the bride. That member is also responsible for organizing the ceremonies. The groom is required to present gifts to the family that symbolize his suitability to provide for the bride's well-being, as well as that of any children who arise from the union.

Young couples generally require the help of extended family to establish their homes and care for children. For this reason, most young couples settle close to parents and other relatives. It is common for families to live in shared housing, with several closely related nuclear families sharing a single plot of land, including crops or livestock. Female family members are generally responsible for a majority of the agricultural work, in addition to child rearing and other forms of domestic maintenance. Men are expected to earn an income and provide food.

Because traditional marriage can be a significant drain on a family's resources, cohabitation has become increasingly common in Benin. Couples may wait months or years before deciding to marry and may have one or more children during this time, despite traditional and religious prohibitions. It has also become more common, particularly in cities such as Cotonou and Porto Novo, for young couples to establish nuclear households, though they may stay in close contact with their extended kin group.

Housing

Most homes in Benin are simple, with wooden walls and thatched roofing surrounding an earthen floor. In cities, some families live in concrete or stone houses with tile roofing. Apartment buildings or complexes are most common in Porto Novo and Cotonou. Apartments are usually small with a single bedroom, which may be shared by a couple and their children.

In rural areas, most Beninois families have no indoor plumbing or electricity. Electricity is only widely available (and reliable) in the cities and the areas immediately surrounding urban centers. The open-air markets are the primary place for recreation and socialization and form an essential component of every Beninese community. Markets consist of simple shacks with thatched roofing held in place by wooden stakes to cover a few tables or other surfaces on which vendors sell their goods.

Food

Most families subsist on a diet heavy in grains and vegetables; millet, couscous, rice, okra, yams, and beans are staples of the Beninese diet. In addition, spicy sauces such as pilipili are part of most Beninese meals. Meat is a delicacy and may be served only once daily or when feeding a group for special occasions.

One of the more popular peasant dishes in Benin is a stew called amiwo, which is usually made from corn flour mixed with vegetables and spices. There are dozens of regional varieties of amiwo, some of which mix in seafood or beef for extra flavor. Amiwo porridge may be eaten for breakfast or lunch, when it is usually served with several side dishes, including various preparations of spinach, cassava, yams or potatoes.

Cassava is one the most important crops grown in Benin. Families may eat cassava flesh boiled, fried, roasted, or mashed, or may make flour from cassava, which is used to bake bread. Peanuts are also widely grown in Benin and have become a common component in both sweet and savory dishes. Peanuts may be crushed into pulp and used to make "butter" or may be added whole to a dish.

Seafood is popular in coastal areas and a variety of fish and shellfish are added to the local diet. Fried fish are often served with peppers used to flavor the fish or to provide a sauce. Similar spicy sauces are used to flavor roasted chicken, beef, and lamb. Dahomey fish stew is a popular dish in the coast that includes a base of tomatoes and onions, combined with any variety of floured fish fried in oil and seasoned with salt and pepper. Though primarily a peasant dish, some Beninese restaurants serve a gourmet version that includes several types of fish mixed with fresh vegetables.

For special occasions, when families slaughter livestock or purchase meat for a meal, lamb with peanut sauce is one of the most popular dishes. The sauce is prepared with crushed peanuts, tomatoes, garlic, and onion and then poured over a stew of lamb with cassava, carrots, and potatoes. Some variations alternately call for spicy peppers to replace the garlic. Peanut sauce is also used with roasted chicken and sometimes with fish or other seafood dishes.

Beer and palm wine are the most common beverages. Tchapallo and the much stronger sodabe are popular varieties of palm wine.

Life's Milestones

Rites of passage in Beninois culture vary depending on the religious and cultural affiliation of the family. In Christian and Catholic families, the traditions of baptism, first communion, and marriage are the primary events marking the stages of life. Baptism is a cause for family celebration and usually accompanied by a feast with family and friends. Some families also mark a child's first communion with a celebration featuring the child's friends and family.

Those who practice Vodun (also spelled as Vodoun or Voodoo), one of the nation's oldest and most popular religious traditions, tend to adhere to standard Christian or Catholic traditions, but with different ceremonial practices. The animistic spiritualism of Vodun has been blended with Christian and Catholic rites through the centuries, creating a creole religion that takes elements from both traditions. The Vodun practice of animal sacrifice, for instance, may accompany baptism, marriage, or other rites of passage in Vodun families.

The traditional Beninois marriage is an elaborate ceremony and celebration that can last for several days. Customarily, family and friends enjoy dancing, singing, and feasting to celebrate the joining of two families. The ceremonies mark not only the transition to adulthood for the couple, but also an important opportunity for both families to advance in social status through the union. The celebration, therefore, is seen as an important time to form and strengthen the bonds between extended family members.

CULTURAL HISTORY

Art

Many examples of native Beninese art and sculpture come from the Fon kingdom of Dahomey. This state flourished in the 17th to the late 19th centuries in the West African region that now encompasses modern-day Benin. Fon artisans used wood and bronze to create detailed sculptures and ritual objects that provide insight into their daily life and culture. Animal imagery featured prominently in Dahomean art; it was a common theme for painting, sculpture, and metalwork. Royal scepters fashioned from bronze, for example, are usually tipped with an animal head, like a dog or serpent, which are seen as symbols of authority.

Many sculptors were also inspired to create wooden or bronze images of the ruling family. King Glele, who presided over the end of the Dahomey Kingdom from 1858 to 1889, is the subject of numerous sculptures produced in the late 19th century. In some sculptures, the body of the king is blended with that of an animal, like a shark or a lion, symbolizing both the king's authority and the perceived powers of animals in their environment.

Architecture

One important element of Benin's architectural heritage were the bas-reliefs (stone wall carvings depicting people and events) created by Dahomey artisans. Made from wood or earth, they serve as the best existing archaeological record of Dahomey culture. While the kingdom maintained no written records, these bas-reliefs depict important military victories, royal celebrations, and the myths and legends that formed part of the culture's basic worldview. The bas-reliefs decorated the walls of Dahomey palaces, which were usually constructed anew for each successive king.

Another early artistic technique that was popularized by the Fon is the creation of appliqué wall hangings made from dyed cloth stitched into pictures or abstract designs. Fon wall hangings sometimes depict landscapes or images of people engaged in daily activities. Many wall hangings feature animals native to the region, such as giraffes, lions, and birds.

Drama

Benin's theater culture has its roots in the country's tribal history, when storytellers played an integral role in everyday life. Today, Benin is home to several celebrated playwrights, including Ousmane Aledji (1970–). Aledji was named chairman of the Association of Beninese Playwrights in 1995. Aledji's 2010 work *Traumatism* examines the cultural, social, and political changes that occurred during the first 50 years of African independence. The International Festival of Theatre of Benin (FITHEB) is held annually and features theatrical works by performers and playwrights from around the world.

Music & Dance

The music of Benin is a blend of influences from Europe, Africa, and South America. The native music of the Fon and Yoruba (a West African ethnicity) includes a variety of rhythmic orchestral styles in which large or small groups gather to play various percussion instruments while singers recount myths, legends, and stories of everyday life. After Benin gained its independence from France, native artists began to blend African and European sounds to create new, innovative genres.

Angelique Kidjo (1960–) ranks as one of the most successful recording artists to emerge from Africa. Kidjo was born in Cotonou, Benin's second largest city, and received her early musical education through the traditional songs of the Fon and Yoruba. Kidjo fuses traditional African sounds with pop and reggae rhythms. She also blends elements from other disparate musical styles, including American gospel and South American samba and salsa. Her music provides an example of the kind of innovation that swept through Benin in the era immediately following independence. Gnonnas Pedro (1943–2004) and Lionel Loueke (1973–) are among other well know musicians born in Benin.

During the reign of the Dahomey kingdom, many Fon and Yoruba were sold to slave owners in Brazil as laborers. The influx of Africans to Brazil played a role in the formation of Brazil's unique musical traditions, in which African rhythms are blended with Spanish and French classical music. After independence, thousands of Beninois returned from Brazil to Benin and clustered together, creating small pockets of Afro-Brazilian culture in Benin. Some Beninese musicians have combined Brazilian styles, like samba and choro, with native African music, creating innovative combinations. In the Bahia region of Brazil, the influence of Fon and Yoruba music is evident in local variations on popular Brazilian songs.

Dance is a significant art form in Benin, and is often spiritual in nature. Voodoo dances are usually performed at celebrations which honor the spirit in all things. Unlike the dances of many African cultures, Beninese dances are typically performed by individuals rather than groups. The celebration of La Gani incorporates many spiritual dances that are rituals of self-affirmation.

Literature

The early history of Beninese literature is heavily influenced by the country's years as a French colony. One of the first works by a native Beninese novelist is *The Slave* by Felix Couchoro, which was published in 1929. Other well known Beninese novelists include Arnold Senou, Edgar Zinsou, and Dominique Titus. Benin's Raouf Mama is the recipient of the 2008 National

Multicultural Children's Book Award and the 2009 Kwabo Trophy of Literary Excellence. He is known for his short story collections *The Barefoot Book of Tropical Tales* and *Pearls of Wisdom*.

CULTURE

Arts & Entertainment

While the Beninois are proud of their artistic traditions and the accomplishments of local artists, the government provides little in the form of support for the arts. Most artistic projects are privately funded, while some artists are fortunate enough to obtain funding from foreign sources. Artists may obtain scholarships to study art, music, or performance in nearby countries or in Europe, and many of the nation's most talented artists trained and lived abroad while developing their work.

Government-funded museums and former official buildings contain collections of tribal and historic art. Artists today usually resort to showing their work in their homes or in makeshift community galleries. In Porto Novo and Cotonou, residents have set up several permanent galleries where artists can show and sell their work. Cotonou's Center de Promotion de l'Artisant, located on Boulevard Saint Michel, is one of the few locations for the sale and exhibition of local art. Visitors to the center can purchase reproductions of tribal art as well as the creations of modern artists.

Contemporary artists from Benin create a variety of works inspired by traditional culture and modern influences. One of the most prominent modern artists is Meschac Gaba (1961–), who uses unusual materials, such as Beninese coins and bills, to create sculptures and other installation pieces. One of Gaba's most unusual projects is a collection of "tresses," which are headpieces that take the shape of buildings or architectural structures. Gaba also creates wigs, using traditional African hair braiding techniques, to recreate architectural shapes in the body of the wig. Modern textile artists have found a market for their work by selling wall hangings to tourists or to overseas art customers through brokers in the cities.

Music and dance performances are an important component of Beninois culture and accompany almost all government and official functions. The government of Benin displays its pride in native traditions by featuring the native singing and dances of the Fon at government celebrations, particularly when the country receives foreign dignitaries.

Cultural Sites & Landmarks

The Royal Palaces of Abomey, located in the center of the territory occupied by the former Dahomey Kingdom, have been designated as a World Heritage Site by the United Nations Educational, Scientific, and Cultural Organization (UNESCO). The palaces still contain preserved examples of the art and architecture of the Fon during the height of their power. Also, as the Dahomey Kingdom came to power through the slave trade, the palaces of the Fon rulers are also considered an important artifact for scholars studying the history of slavery in Africa.

The Royal Palace of King Toffa, whose reign (1874–1908) as one of the last royal leaders of the royal lineage in Porto Novo stood in opposition to the Dahomey, is another prominent cultural site. After the French subdued the Dahomey, they merged the two territories, and the influence of Toffa's regime declined. The former palace houses artifacts and photos from Toffa's reign. The capital of Cotonou, located on the coast and popular for its beaches, also boasts an important collection of historic landmarks and museums. The Notre Dame Cathedral, located in the middle of the city, is a small wooden structure painted with alternating white and red stripes. The cathedral is an important gathering site for the nation's Catholic community and one of the most notable buildings in the city. Cotonou, the seat of the national government, also features the Presidential Palace, a pink building that occupies a prominent location in the center of the city.

Benin's natural environment is preserved and on display in the Pendjari National Park in northwestern Benin. It is the country's largest and most ecologically diverse wildlife reserve. Walking in the park is forbidden, and visitors are required to hire transportation or obtain a rented car before visiting. There are hundreds of species of animals and plants in the park, including many of Africa's most famous large mammals, such as lions, giraffes, hippopotamuses, and buffalo. The park occupies 2,750 square kilometers (1,064 square miles) of bush habitat, including savannah and dry forest.

Though the Adjarra Market is actually located approximately 10 kilometers (6.2 miles) from the city of Porto Novo, most residents frequent the market, which is held every four days, regularly. There are a variety of products offered, from traditional African handicrafts and art, to modern amenities such as video and music recordings. The Adjarra Market also caters to the local Voodoo religion by offering a variety of herbs and charms used in traditional Voodoo ceremonies.

Libraries & Museums

The Alexandre Sènou Adandé Ethnographic Museum in Porto Novo, founded in 1957, is one of the nation's most respected museums. The building housing the museum is designed in the Afro-Brazilian style, with concrete pillars supporting a wooden structure. Within the small museum is an extensive collection of artifacts representing the country's cultural heritage. Among the more prominent collections are the Fon and Yoruba tribal weaponry collection and a collection of items and clothing associated with Beninois royalty. In addition, the museum houses a collection of drums and other musical instruments from the Fon and Yoruba traditions.

The da Silva Museum (Musée da Silva) is in a modern building located in the center of Porto Novo that contains exhibits and a small library with information about the history of Brazilian immigration into Porto-Novo. The museum also has a small, attached hotel and restaurant. The da

Silva museum is the center of an Afro-Brazilian festival held annually in January.

The capital of Porto Novo is also home to the country's National Archives and National Library. The National Library (Bibliothèque nationale du Bénin), Benin's legal depository, was established in 1975.

Holidays

Benin's biggest national holiday is Voodoo Day. Celebrated on January 10, Voodoo Day is a celebration during which people go to the beaches in Ouidah to perform sacrifices and prayers. The celebration, which involves dancing and music, is the most popular annual event in Benin. Muslim holidays are also widely observed throughout the year.

Other public holidays include Martyr's Day (January 16), Liberation Day (February 28), Armed Forces Day (October 26), and Republic Day (December 4).

Youth Culture

Despite widespread poverty, teenagers in Benin enjoy a wide variety of recreational activities, from sports to music. In Cotonou, fashion and pop media imported from France and the United States have become trendy with teenagers. American influence has also spawned the development of a lively Beninois hip-hop scene. Both French and Senegalese hip-hop are among the most popular styles of music imported into the country.

Football (soccer) is the most popular youth sport in the country. Tennis is another popular sport, but is most popular with the affluent sector of Beninois society, as the cost of equipment prohibits most youth participation in the sport. Many Beninois children in rural areas may not have access to recreational equipment or other toys, and therefore play with items collected from the "bush." This includes items and sporting goods made from stone, sticks, or nuts and berries.

Beninois children often entertain themselves by singing and dancing. There are a variety of musical styles native to the country, including tribal rhythmic choruses, Afro-Brazilian pop and samba, and various types of West African stringed music. Young children often learn traditional songs from their parents, which may have been passed down through several generations. Many children's songs are designed to teach moral or cultural lessons, with lyrics relating a problem and the appropriate solution.

SOCIETY

Transportation

Generally, Benin lacks a cohesive public transportation system. Private taxi services and rental car companies are available in Cotonou or Porto Novo. Porto-Novo does have some public transportation options, including busses, taxis, and boats that travel along the coast, taking visitors to nearby towns and other cities. Part of the Trans West African Coastal Highway passes through Benin and links the country to Nigeria, Ghana, and the Ivory Coast. Traffic moves on the right-hand side of the road.

Transportation Infrastructure

There are approximately 16,000 kilometers (9,942 miles) of roads in Benin, of which 1,400 kilometers (870 miles) are paved. Road conditions are poor largely due to a lack of funding for maintenance. While most streets in Cotonou and Porto Novo are paved, damaged sections of road may remain in poor condition for months or years before they are repaired.

Approximately 150 kilometers (93 miles) of the Niger River run through Benin and accommodates local passenger and commercial traffic. Though the waterways are infrequently used by tourists, they are an important component of the transport system for residents living in the area surrounding the river. These waterways are also important for the commercial shipping industry, serving as a route for goods to make their way inland from the coast.

Benin has a single international airport, Cotonou International Airport, which is one of six airports in the country (and only one with

paved runways). Cotonou International offers connecting flights to locations across Africa, as well as routes with access to Europe and the United States. Alternatively, some visitors enter Benin by flying into neighboring Ghana, traveling by car or bus across the border.

Media & Communications

Benin has a variety of domestic and imported print publications, including the government-operated *La Nacion* and the private daily newspapers *Le Matinal* and *Fraternite*. Because of poor literacy rates, newspaper and magazine readership is low and most Beninois receive their news from radio and television broadcasts. In cities such as Cotonou and Porto Novo merchants import dozens of international publications, most in French and English.

The Office of Radio and Television (ORTB) owns most of the nation's radio and television stations, including Radio Nationale, which focuses on news and information and a small number of rural stations providing local news. The government also operates Television Nationale, which provides news and entertainment programming and is broadcast nationally. In addition to government-owned outlets, there are several privately owned stations broadcasting in the cities and some of the larger towns. In Cotonou, residents and visitors can also receive Radio France International and British Broadcasting Corporation (BBC) programs via radio.

While the government owns most of the nation's major news outlets, there are no censorship restrictions and all media outlets are allowed to express views critical of government policy. Some media rights organizations have criticized the government for maintaining severe penalties against libel that, in some cases, restrict the activities of journalists. A media ethics commission is active in Benin and responsible for upholding quality of broadcast and print media. While the commission is not an official government body, it is responsible for prosecuting journalists and media managers whose agencies broadcast or print information that is inaccurate or libelous.

Telecommunications infrastructure in Benin is fair but underdeveloped. Benin was one of the first West African states to receive an Internet connection. In 2014, Internet usage was measured for about four percent of the total population.

SOCIAL DEVELOPMENT

Standard of Living
Benin ranked 165th out of 187 countries on the 2013 United Nations Human Development Index, which measures quality of life and standard of living indicators.

Water Consumption
In 2013, the United Nations Development Programme (UNDP) reported that access to clean drinking water is improving in Benin but at a rate slower than they had hoped.

Although the percentage of the population with access to "an improved drinking water source" rose to 63.6 percent by 2011, the UNDP states "access to drinking water and basic sanitation continues to be a major worry for a large part of the Beninese population."

Education
Education is free and compulsory for Beninese children between ages six and eleven. The literacy rate among all Beninese is 38.4 percent. However, the literacy rate among women remains low (27.3 percent) due to sexism in the government and society.

In 2012, UNICEF estimated that approximately 89.3 percent of eligible Beninese children attended primary school. However, enrollment rates for secondary school and further education remain low. The University of Abomey-Calavi (formerly The National University of Benin and The University of Dahomey) is the nation's largest university. The university was founded in 1970 and offers undergraduate, postgraduate, diploma, and certificate programs. In 2015, enrollment at the university was estimated at over 45,000.

Women's Rights
While the Beninese constitution guarantees equal rights between the sexes, women's rights are a major concern in Benin, largely resulting from cultural norms that allow spousal abuse and domestic violence. While the penal code prohibits rape, domestic violence, and other types of spousal abuse, the legal system is ill equipped to adequately protect women and penalize offenders.

According to the penal code, rape carries penalties of up to five years imprisonment depending on the circumstances of the crime. The penal code has special provisions covering domestic violence, with penalties ranging from six months to three years imprisonment. Cases rarely come before the courts, however, as few women choose to prosecute and police are reportedly reluctant to investigate domestic issues. Societal norms holding that domestic issues should be addressed within the family contribute to the reluctance of women to seek outside aid. Several non-governmental organizations (NGOs) in Benin provide counseling and legal aid for abuse victims and their children.

Female genital mutilation (FGM) is one of the primary human rights concerns facing women in Benin and elsewhere in Africa. According to UNICEF estimates, approximately 12.7 percent of Beninois women have undergone genital mutilation for the purposes of promoting sexual fidelity. Though the penal code prohibits genital mutilation and provides penalties, including fines and prison sentences of up to ten years, the practice remains commonplace, especially in rural areas. Both government-sponsored and NGO-mediated groups are active in Benin providing public education programs and medical care for victims of mutilation. The Ministry of Family sends representatives to Beninois schools to educate children about the dangers of genital mutilation and the legal concerns surrounding the practice.

While women are equal under the law, social norms discourage women from seeking positions in the professional sector. As a result, the number of women working in management and technical positions remains small. Women are more likely to find employment in the educational, health and agricultural sectors, or in retail sales positions. Women are far less likely to be chosen for government jobs and earn, on average, less than male counterparts.

Health Care

Benin has a substandard health care system. Most Beninese do not receive adequate medical attention, as there are few medical centers and a lack of trained professionals and medicines. As a result, Beninese are at high risk for a number of deadly diseases and life expectancy is low. As of 2015, 61 years is the estimated average life expectancy in Benin.

World health experts have denounced the Beninese practice of female circumcision, which is also known as female genital mutilation (FGM). The ritual of circumcision has been performed on a large percentage of Beninese women, despite its enormous health risks.

Benin's lack of potable water and high levels of urban pollution are causes of many health problems. The HIV/AIDS epidemic is widespread in Benin; roughly 77,900 Beninese are living with HIV/AIDS. Other common diseases and infections are bacterial and protozoal diarrhea, hepatitis A, typhoid fever, yellow fever, and meningitis.

GOVERNMENT

Structure

Upon gaining independence, Benin's government was subject to numerous overthrows. In 1960, the Dahomians were the first of several groups to attempt a coup d'état (overthrow of government). Because of threats from many rebel groups, Benin changed governments nine times in its first 12 years as a sovereign state.

Major Mathieu Kreign state.) launched a successful coup in 1972 and took control of Benin. Throughout the 1970s and 1980s, Kérékou's Benin was a communist dictatorship. Kérékou stepped down in 1990, under pressure

from France to establish democracy in Benin following the fall of communism in Europe.

Benin is now a democratic republic, and free elections have been held in Benin since 1991. However, elections in Benin have been characterized by corruption, poor voter turnout, and allegations of vote tampering. Kérékou won elections from 1996 through 2006. In April 2006, Thomas Yayi Boni (1952–) was elected president, and in April 2011, he won re-election.

The president is the chief executive and head of state, and is elected by popular vote to a five-year term. The executive cabinet is the Cabinet of Ministers. An 83-member National Assembly, whose members are elected to four-year terms, is the nation's legislative body. The judicial branch consists of the Constitutional Court, the Supreme Court, and the High Court of Justice. Eighteen is the age of suffrage in Benin.

Political Parties

Benin's multi-party system has given rise to a large number of political organizations that support a range of political philosophies. Major political parties in Benin are the Alliance of Progress Forces (AFP), the African Movement for Democracy and Progress (MADEP), the Benin Renaissance (RB), and the Democratic Renewal Party (PRD). There are more than 20 minor political parties in Benin, which include the Union for Homeland and Labour, the Communist Party of Benin, and the Chameleon Alliance.

Local Government

Benin is organized administratively into 12 departments. The country's departments are further subdivided into communes. There are 77 communes in all. Local government consists of city districts and villages that form arrondissements (a French term meaning "administrative division"). Benin's communes are comprised of arrondisements. This system of municipal government has been in place in Benin since 1999. The country continues to face challenges in its efforts to decentralize the power of the central government and establish a more efficiently functioning nationwide democracy.

Judicial System

Benin's legal system was established when the country was a French colony and is based on French civil law. Courts are overseen by the Ministry of Justice. Judges are appointed to civil courts by the president. Although the Supreme Court of Benin is the highest level of appeal, Benin's Constitutional Court adjudicates changes to the constitution as well as conflicts between the president and National Assembly. Benin's court system faces significant challenges related to corruption and inadequate facilities. The lack of efficiency in the court system makes incidences of mob justice and vigilantism common in Benin.

Taxation

Citizens of Benin pay a variable income tax ranging from 10 to 35 percent. As of 2015, a flat rate of 3.6 percent is collected for Social Security. Businesses pay a standard corporate income tax of 30 percent, but oil companies operating in Benin pay a higher rate. Other corporate taxes include a capital duty, payroll tax, and property tax. Corporations also contribute to employee Social Security and insurance.

Armed Forces

The service branches of Benin's military consist of an army, air force, navy, and national gendarmerie (military police force). Military service is compulsory and lasts eighteen months. The Beninese Armed Forces regularly trains with other armed forces of the ECOWAS (Economic Community of West African States), a regional group of West African states. Since 2010, the ECOWAS Standby Force consists of 6,500 military personnel.

Foreign Policy

The Republic of Benin is a member of the United Nations (UN) and several of its specialized African groups, including the Economic Community of West African States (ECOWAS). Benin has retained strong diplomatic and economic relations with France, the nation's former colonial power, and has strong diplomatic ties with other Francophone (French speaking) coun-

tries in Africa. Though Benin has been involved in the mediating efforts of neighboring conflicts, its continental influence is generally limited.

Benin has a long-standing border dispute with Burkina Faso regarding ownership of a small plot of land on the nation's shared borders. Citizens of Burkina Faso have established three small villages in the contested zone and have alleged that Beninois citizens and security forces occasionally try to expel them from the area. In 2005, members of a small Burkina Faso school in the contested area were expelled by force. While negotiations temporarily stalled the potential for military conflict, the issue became heated again in 2007 when Beninois authorities arrested a Burkina Faso man in the contested zone. In 2008, the Beninois government agreed to a truce in which they would allow the Burkina Faso communities to remain as long as no national flags were erected in the area. Additionally, the Burkina Faso government agreed not to establish military or police in the area.

The U.S. is one of Benin's strongest sources of development aid, particularly through the U.S. Agency for International Development (USAID), which contributes to programs involving education, family planning, and AIDS relief. While the U.S. is deeply involved in Beninois aid, China and India are the nation's strongest economic partners. The Peoples Republic of China accounts for over a quarter of the Beninois export industry, which includes palm, cashews, cotton, and seafood products.

Human Rights Profile

International human rights law insists that states respect civil and political rights, and promote an individual's economic, social, and cultural rights. The United Nations (UN) Universal Declaration of Human Rights (UDHR) is recognized as the standard for international human rights. Its authors sought the counsel of the world's great thinkers, philosophers, and religious leaders, and were careful to create a document that reflects the core values shared by every world culture. (To read this document or view the articles relating to cultural human rights, visit http://www.udhr.org/UDHR/default.htm.)

While the government of Benin generally respects the rights of its citizens and establishes laws in keeping with the principles of UDHR, widespread poverty and discriminatory cultural norms create situations in which violations against basic human rights occasionally occur.

Both the national police force and the presidential guard have been charged with using excessive force to control crowds and detain suspects. Some reports indicate that police and security personnel have occasionally unlawfully killed citizens, while human rights organizations allege that civilian authorities do not have adequate police oversight. In some areas, citizens concerned about crime have formed vigilante gangs to eliminate criminals. Failure of the police to address the rise in mob violence and vigilante killings constitutes a failure to ensure right to life, freedom from abuse, and equal protection under the law. Though vigilante justice is illegal under the penal code, Amnesty International (AI) reports indicate that police have done little to prohibit vigilantism.

The Beninois prison system, which consists of eight prisons and a number of holding and detention facilities, is burdened by overcrowding and insufficient facilities. Many prisoners lack access to basic sanitary and medical facilities, constituting cruel punishment as defined by the UDHR. According to the U.S. Department of State, the nationwide prison population in 2010 was 6,908, in a system with an official capacity of 1,900 prisoners. The overburdened Beninois court system contributes to human rights concerns by forcing detainees to remain in holding for excessive periods while awaiting trial.

Beninois law prohibits discrimination based on race, gender, or disability, and provides special protections for women and children. However, the safety of children remains a serious issue in Benin as child abuse is reportedly common and police coverage is insufficient. Underage marriage has been reported in some rural communities, involving children under the age of 14, and usually arranged by parents and guardians. According to some reports, children born with developmental disabilities are some-times killed because of folk customs. In 2012, a national forum to try to combat infanticide was held in Parakou. Lack of funding and personnel make it difficult for police to appropriately address child welfare, especially in rural areas.

ECONOMY

Overview of the Economy

In 1972, Benin was under the leadership of Major Mathieu Kérékou, who established a Marxist economy. During this era, Benin received foreign aid from the Eastern European communist bloc. In 1988, Benin's socialist economy collapsed, shortly before the Soviet Union disbanded. Benin then shifted to a free-market economy and democracy with help from France.

As one of the poorest nations in the world, Benin is highly dependent on foreign aid. A member of the Economic Community of West African States (ECOWAS), Benin receives economic and development aid from neighboring countries. In 2014, the estimated per capita GDP of Benin was estimated at $1,900 (USD). The largest contributor to the GDP is the services industry, which includes banking and tourism and accounts for more than 50 percent of the nation's annual revenues. Benin's primary trading partners are China, France, India, Algeria, and Nigeria.

Industry

Industrial activity is limited in Benin, as the economy is focused on the agricultural sector. Cotton is Benin's biggest export. In addition to cotton, major exports include palm products, cashews, crude oil, and cacao.

Other than light production of petroleum and limestone, several commercial plants conduct the majority of Benin's industrial activity. Industrial facilities include palm oil refineries, breweries, bakeries, and cotton mills.

Labor

Benin's labor market is separated into two parts, based on the country's formal and informal economy. Agriculture, particularly the production of cotton, remains Benin's largest employment sector. Benin's agricultural sector includes both subsistence farming and formal agro-business. The service industry, including construction, restaurants, and transportation, is the country's second largest employment sector. Unemployment remains high in urban areas, particularly Cotonou and Abomey-Bohicon. Stagnantly low wages, low demand for Beninese exports, and lack of significant economic development initiatives continue to exacerbate widespread poverty in Benin.

Energy/Power/Natural Resources

Benin's most significant natural resource is an oil field off the coast of Cotonou. In addition to oil, the nation has deposits of iron ore, phosphates, chromium, clay, marble, and diamonds. Geological estimates indicate that Benin has deposits of limestone that are currently unexploited.

Benin's trees provide a timber resource that could generate revenues if properly exploited, but the majority of Benin's wood is used as a fuel resource for the nation's people.

Fishing

Development initiatives between Benin, Senegal, and Libya have helped improve the country's fishing industry. Benin's total fish catch averaged approximately 40,000 tons as of 2006. Fisheries make up about two percent of the GDP. Freshwater fishing remains an important part of subsistence agriculture in Benin.

Forestry

In a 2013 estimate, 40 percent of Benin was covered with forests. However, of that percentage, only a small amount is considered commercially viable. Wood continues to be the primary source of domestic fuel in much of Benin.

Mining/Metals

Benin is not a major mineral producer, but does have limited supplies of clay, gold, and sand. In 2014, Benin produced 2.1 million metric tons of cement. U.S.-based oil companies continue to explore the country's land and waters for potential petroleum reserves. Drilling of Benin's offshore Seme oil field was completed in 1998.

Agriculture

Agriculture is Benin's most important economic sector, and the nation is heavily dependent on agricultural activity. Agricultural exports account for almost 31.8 percent of the nation's GDP. Although it is the primary economic sector, revenues from agriculture are limited by the fact that most farming is done at the subsistence level.

Cash crops include beans, cacao, cassava, coffee, corn, cotton, palm oil, palm kernels, peanuts, sorghum, cashews, and yams. Drought is a large threat to agricultural activity, and thus Benin's economy is vulnerable to recessions during dry seasons.

Animal Husbandry

Livestock herding includes cattle, goats, pigs, and sheep. The United States African Development Foundation (USADF) plays a large role in the management of Benin's livestock industry, helping to broker trade arrangements between farmers and buyers. In October 2010, USADF signed three separate grants aimed at improving the infrastructure of the country's livestock industry, including transportation and animal housing facilities.

Tourism

Benin, like most West African countries, benefits greatly from tourism. One of the most popular tourist destinations in Africa is Ganvié, a Beninese village built in a lagoon. The bamboo huts of the village are built on stilts with high walkways. Tourists often take boat rides through the lagoon. Ganvié's nickname is the "Venice of Africa."

Other popular tourist attractions are the Dahomey palaces in Abomey, the beach resort in Ouidah, and the National Museum in Cotonou. The capital of Porto Novo is noted for its colonial architecture.

Micah Issitt, Richard Means

DO YOU KNOW?

- The name "Benin" refers to the "Bight of Benin," on the coast of the Gulf of Guinea. Prior to 1975, the country was known as "Dahomey," a reference to one of the nation's former African kingdoms. The name was changed in an effort to choose a politically neutral title, whereas "Dahomey" refers to a specific ethnic group.

- The royal palace in Abomey was constructed in 1645 by the third king of Dahomey. Every Dahomey king thereafter built his own addition to the compound, and the entire palace now covers 100 acres. Most of the palace was burned by the 10th Dahomey king.

Bibliography

Bartley, Nigel and Kevin Lovelock. "The Art of Benin." London, UK: *British Museum Press*, 2010.

Ben-Amos, Paula. "Art, Innovation, and Politics in Eighteenth-century Benin." Bloomington, IN: *Indiana University Press*, 1999.

Broughton, Simon and Mark Ellingham, eds. "The Rough Guide to World Music Volume 1: Africa, Europe, and the Middle East." 2nd ed., London, UK: *Rough Guides*, 2000.

Butler, Stuart. "Benin: The Bradt Travel Guide." Bucks, UK: *Bradt Travel Guides*, 2006.

Gangbe Guedou, Georges A. *Xó et gbè, langage et culture chez les Fon (Bénin): langage et culture chez les Fon.* Belgium: *Peeters Publishers*, 1985.

Harris, Jessica B. *The Africa Cookbook.* New York: *Simon & Schuster*, 1998.

Nugent, Paul. "Africa Since Independence: A Comparative History." New York: *Palgrave Macmillan*, 2004.

Preston-Blier, Suzanne. "African Vodoun: Art, Psychology, and Power." Chicago: *University of Chicago Press*, 1996.

Rush, Dana. "Vodun in Coastal Benin: Unfinished, Open-Ended, Global." Nashville, TN: *Vanderbilt University Press*, 2013.

Trillo, Richard. "The Rough Guide to West Africa." 5th ed. London, UK: *Rough Guides*, 2008.

Works Cited

"Benin." Bureau of African Affairs. *U.S. Department of State Online.* January 2009. http://www.state.gov/r/pa/ei/bgn/6761.htm

"Benin: Country Reports on Human Rights Practices." *U.S. Department of State Online.* http://www.state.gov/g/drl/rls/hrrpt/2007/100466.htm

"Benin: largest cities and towns and statistics of their population." *World Gazetteer.* http://archive.is/3zGtL#selection-127.0-127.66

"Benin." Country Overview. *Lonely Planet Online.* http://www.lonelyplanet.com/benin

"Benin: News and Publications." *Amnesty International.* http://www.amnesty.org/en/region/benin

"Benin." Central Intelligence Agency. *The World Factbook Online.* https://www.cia.gov/library/publications/the-world-factbook/geos/bn.html

"Benin." *Food and Agriculture Organizations of the United Nations.* http://www.fao.org/countryprofiles/index/en/?iso3=BEN

"Country Profile: Benin." *BBC News Online.* http://news.bbc.co.uk/2/hi/africa/country_profiles/1064527.stm

"Facts About the Republic of Benin: Official Document." African Studies Center. *University of Pennsylvania Online.*

"Middle Africa's cement sector: Explosive Growth." *Ecobank.* July 2014. http://www.ecobank.com/upload/20140724011129637822cPHHGNvnw6.pdf

"La population béninoise en 2006 par arrondissement et celle en âge de voter" *Institut National de la Statistique Benin.* http://www.insae-bj.org/.

"République du Bénin, gouvernement et ministères du Bénin" *Official Government of Benin Online.* http://www.gouv.bj/

"Republic of Benin MDG Acceleration Framework: Access to Safe Drinking Water and Basic Sanitation." *Ministry of Development, Economic Analysis and Forecasting (MDAEP) of the Republic of Benin.* May 2013. http://www.undp.org/content/dam/undp/library/MDG/MDG percent20Acceleration percent20Framework/MAF percent20Reports/RBA/Benin percent20- percent20ENG percent20may percent2014 percent20WEB.pdf

"Statistics: Benin." *UNICEF.* (Accessed September 25, 2014.) http://www.unicef.org/infobycountry/benin_statistics.html

BURKINA FASO

Introduction

Burkina Faso is a completely landlocked African country, bordered by Benin, Côte d'Ivoire, Ghana, Mali, Niger, and Togo. Once known as Upper Volta, Burkina Faso became a parliamentary republic when it gained independence from France in 1960. Burkina Faso is one of the poorest countries in the world and a majority of the population engages in subsistence agriculture.

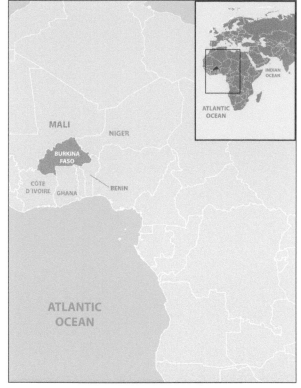

GENERAL INFORMATION

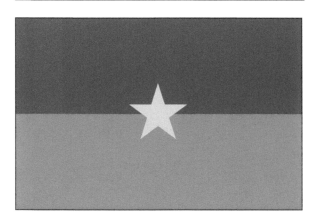

stands for revolution; and the gold star is the guiding star of revolution.

Official Language: French
Population: 18,931,686 (2015 estimate)
Currency: West African CFA franc
Coins: Coins are available in denominations of 1, 5, 10, 25, 50, 100, 200, 250, and 500 francs.
Land Area: 272,967 square kilometers (105,393 square miles)
Water Area: 400 square kilometers (154 square miles)
National Motto: "Unité, Progrès, Justice" (French, "Unity, Progress, Justice")
National Anthem: "Une Seule Nuit" (French, "One Single Night")
Capital: Ouagadougou
Time Zone: GMT +0
Flag Description: The flag of Burkina Faso shares the colors of its African neighbors, featuring two equal horizontal stripes of red (top) and green (bottom) with a central golden star. The green is said to symbolize the country's riches; the red

Population

Although the nearly 18.9 million people in Burkina Faso are known by the generic term "Burkinabe," each falls into one of two significant West African cultural groups: the Voltaic or the Mande.

Accounting for roughly 40 percent of the population, the Voltaic Mossi is the most prominent ethnic group in Burkina Faso. The Mossi speak the indigenous language of Mòoré (Voltaic), and are mostly farmers. The Bobo, Lobi, Grunshi, and Senufo are also part of the Voltaic group. The Mande speak Dioula and are also predominantly farmers. The Fulani, Busani, Marka, Samo, and Dyula are part of the Mande culture.

Compared to most other African countries, Burkina Faso is densely populated, with roughly 60.3 people per square kilometer (156 people per square mile). Most Burkinabe reside in rural areas in the south and central parts of the country.

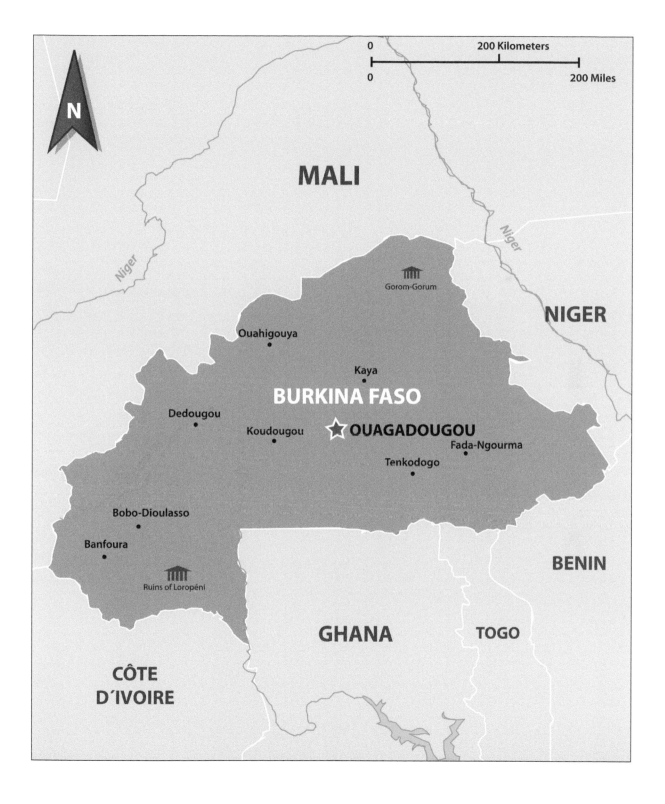

Principal Cities by Population (2012):

- Ouagadougou (2,741,000) (2015)
- Bobo Dioulasso (537,728)
- Banfora (93,750)
- Koudougou (91,981)
- Oahiygouya (86,569)
- Pouytenga (84,156)
- Kaya (66,851)
- Garango(63,527)
- Fada N'gourma (51,421)
- Tenkodogo (48,534)

An estimated 30 percent of the total population is urban (2015).

Languages

The majority of Burkinabe speak French in addition to their culture's native tongue. French is also the administrative and educational language of Ouagadougou, the capital. Mòoré & Dioula (Bambara) are also recognized.

Native People & Ethnic Groups

There are 63 indigenous cultures in Burkina Faso. The most prominent are the Mossi, Mande, Bobo, Lobi, Fulani, Gurunsi, and Senufo.

Since they account for 40 percent of the population of Burkina Faso, the Mossi are the most powerful and influential ethnic group. Before the French settled the country in the late 1800s, the Mossi were the undisputed rulers. Their roots in the country can be traced back to the 10th century. The Bobo, Lobi, and Gurunsi were established in Burkina Faso even before the Mossi arrived.

The Mossi have a complex hierarchy. Their emperor, known as the Moro Naba, resides in the capital of Ouagadougou, along with the republic's president and prime minister. In each region of Mossi territory, a chief (Naba) is chosen from the ruling class (Nakomse). These chiefs tax the citizens in their region and give a portion of that money to their emperor. The ethnic traditions and modern republic manage to coexist peacefully.

Religions

Both Islam and Christianity have left their mark on Burkina Faso, but they are forced to exist alongside traditional beliefs. Although the Mossi rulers first fought against the introduction of Islam, it is now the dominant religion of the country by a long shot; 60.5 percent of the population identifies as Muslim. Christians account for about one-quarter of the population.

Climate

Burkina Faso is a tropical country with distinct dry and rainy seasons. The weather is coolest during the dry months between November and February. In the north, the dry season is brings hot, dry desert winds, known as the harmattan. March through June is the hottest time of year.

From July to September, the rainy season brings cooler temperatures of 29° Celsius (85° Fahrenheit) during the day and 16° Celsius (60° Fahrenheit) at night, although there is also an increase in humidity. Average annual rainfall is between 25 and 100 centimeters (10 and 40 inches).

Because of its elevation and location in the Sahel, Ouagadougou's weather tends to be hot and dry. Temperatures during the dry season can climb as high as 45° Celsius (113° Fahrenheit), while lows hover around 19° Celsius (66.2° Fahrenheit). Ouagadougou is most affected by two climactic phenomena: the harmattan, or dry wind that blows across the Sahel, and the monsoon season, which brings rain.

ENVIRONMENT & GEOGRAPHY

Topography

Burkina Faso is a completely landlocked country. There are three major rivers, the Black, Red, and White Voltas, which run through the center of the country. The largest river is the Black Volta, also known as the Mouhoun. Ouagadougou, the capital, is situated on a central plateau between the Red and White Voltas in the central-south region of Burkina Faso. (Its strategic position in the Sahel—the middle region between the Sahara Desert and the rainforests of West Africa—made Ouagadougou a major nexus of trade and culture during the trans-Saharan trading era, and an ideal location for an administrative and cultural center in the modern era.)

There are several different types of terrain throughout Burkina Faso. The Sahel, between the Sahara Desert and the coastal rainforests, lies in the north of the country. The most fertile farmland is found in wooded savanna to the south, while central Burkina Faso is mostly flat savanna. There are several hills in the west, the highest of which is Mount Tenakourou at 762 meters (2,500 feet), on the border of Mali.

Plants & Animals

Most of Burkina Faso is thinly covered with short grasses, scrub brush, and small trees. There are small forests of fruit trees in the southern and central parts of the country.

There are a number of game preserves, which offer sanctuary for a variety of typical African animals such as elephants, lions, hippos, monkeys, warthogs, African buffalos, and antelope. Crocodiles and caimans are also common.

CUSTOMS & COURTESIES

Greetings

French is Burkina's official language. In the urban areas, people typically greet each other with "Bonjour" ("Hello"). "Salut" is more informal and common among younger people and between friends. For friends or those who know each other's language, greetings will be made in the native language of Dioula (also called Jula). Though not shared among many groups, this language is known to many. In urban areas, men will shake hands with men and sometimes with women (especially if the woman is a foreigner who has some kind of status). Urban women often adhere to the customary French greeting of a light kiss on each cheek. In rural areas, men and women avoid personal contact.

In conversations that extend longer than a brief interaction, it is important to inquire about the health of the other person's family before getting into other topics. It is also considered rude to have even the briefest of conversations without first making a customary greeting. Additionally, acknowledging the status or position of the person with whom one is speaking is important. Thus, the "vous" form is used with strangers, elders, and those in positions of power. Strangers are also customarily addressed with their titles, including "Madame" (for an older or married woman), "Monsieur" (for a man), or "Mademoiselle" (for a young or unmarried woman).

Gestures & Etiquette

In general, showing emotion publicly is frowned upon. People are expected to be reserved, except in ritualized situations such as funerals or weddings. Customarily, respect is based on appearance and attire. Women wear dresses or below-the-knee skirts and tops. Men wear long pants and long-sleeved shirts to work, often with a jacket and tie. The traditional boubou, a long cotton gown, is also common for men. Young people occasionally wear jeans, but it is uncommon for women to wear pants in any situation.

While the younger generation and people in urban areas are starting to modify tradition somewhat, touching is generally limited to those of the same gender. Men may hold hands with male friends and women with female friends, but public displays of affection between romantic couples are frowned upon, even in urban areas. Touching the right forearm with the left hand when greeting an elder or superior is a gesture of respect. Additionally, as in Muslim culture, people refrain from using the left hand as it is associated with the cleansing of the body, and is thus considered impure. In addition, direct eye contact between adults is common, but in some northern cultures it can be interpreted as threatening if it goes on too long. Children tend to only look adults in the eye for a brief period.

Speaking about family is always the safest topic of conversation and can continue for quite some time as family includes grandparents, aunts, uncles, and cousins. Work is considered a secondary topic, and conversations about religion or politics should only be introduced between people who know each other quite well. In addition, the amount of personal space left between people who are in a conversation varies depending on status. Elders or people of high social status should be given more space. People of the same age and social rank often stand closer together than is typical in North American social interactions.

Eating/Meals
Breakfast in Burkina Faso is still strongly influenced by the French colonial period, and might consist of a cup of coffee and a fried egg on a baguette. Lunch is traditionally the biggest meal of the day, and may constitute the only meal in rural areas. In the cities, men who have come in from the countryside for work typically eat lunch at food stalls on the street corners. These stalls sell inexpensive food such as brochette (grilled meat) with sauce gombo (okra sauce), or riz gras (rice with a tomato-based sauce). In rural areas, it is customary to sit on the ground in a circle, sharing a single plate of food. In addition, chapolo (also called dolo), a home-brewed millet beer, is also sold in rural villages. Many Burkinabé follow the French custom of a brief rest period following lunch. Dinner is a smaller meal, and typically consists of a meat or fish for those who can afford it.

Visiting
Burkinabé are very welcoming people, and family and friends are not generally expected to call or make plans before visiting. It is not necessary to bring a gift, although for extended visits it is a good idea to bring some sort of food. If food is offered, the guest should accept or risk appearing rude. Eating even a few bites is better than eating nothing. Visits also tend to be long according to Westerns standards. However, guests should not directly express their desire to leave a host's

home, as that might be perceived as insulting. Instead, the guest will make hints until the host decides that it is time to end the visit.

A typical afternoon visit would involve drinking tea, which is a ritualized process with very specific steps. Sugar is added to the tea and the mixture is poured back and forth between the pot and a small glass cup about a dozen times before it is consumed. Visitors usually go through at least three rounds of tea. Refusing a drink is considered rude. Bissap, a drink made from steeped hibiscus flower petals, is another popular social beverage in Burkina Faso.

LIFESTYLE

Family
In Burkina Faso, several generations of a family typically live together, although this practice is not as common in urban areas. Large families are common—the average Burkinabé woman bears more than six children. Polygamy, which remains legal, is also common within certain groups. Traditionally, there are defined roles for men and women within the various groups in Burkina Faso. Women are responsible for domestic duties and child rearing, and assume agricultural responsibilities in rural areas. Taking care of elders is of the utmost importance, and usually falls to the oldest son. Arranged marriages are still quite common throughout the country, although this is increasingly less common in urban areas.

Many families in Burkina Faso have been separated because of work migration and labor mobility. While this separation may only be temporary during the harvest season, other times the father of the family may live and work abroad for years. This causes hardship for families who must stay behind and work the land while caring for children and elders. There is also a caste system among some peoples of Burkina Faso that is based primarily on the family occupation. Among the Mande-speaking people, for example, griots (storytellers) and blacksmiths traditionally belong to their own castes and live in certain areas of the villages.

Some dwellings in Burkina Faso are painted with decorative patterns.

Housing

Seventy percent of Burkinabé families live in rural areas. A typical arrangement is a compound of separate houses built around a courtyard, which then serves as a type of living room. Residency depends on the culture. Among some groups, male and female members of the family live in separate houses. In polygamist cultures, each wife and her offspring have separate dwellings.

While the style of home depends on the ethnic group, most houses are made of mud-brick construction. Many groups live in round dwellings with thatched, conical roofs, while others favor rectangular homes or flat roofs accessed by ladders. Some homes are painted with decorative patterns on the outside and others are plain. The Tuareg people in the north are nomadic and live in tents made from goatskin. Most people in cities live in single-story houses, often with corrugated metal roofs. There are few apartment buildings, except in Ouagadougou or Bobo Dioulosso.

Food

Traditionally, the cuisine of Burkina Faso is similar to other West African cuisines. Food is sometimes scarce due to drought and poor soil, and Burkinabé rely on dishes made with a few reliable staples such as millet, yams, peanuts, maize, and rice. Local crops such as sorghum, potatoes, beans, and okra also make up the majority of the Burkinabé diet. Sauces are a common part of meals and are often flavored with néré seeds.

A typical meal might consist of tô, which is a sticky paste of millet, sorghum, or maize flour topped with a vegetable or peanut sauce. Another common dish is a type of fried dumpling called soubala or maggi Africain that is made from dried, fermented néré seeds. Meat is expensive, so it is typically eaten only on special occasions in most rural areas. In the larger towns or cities, grilled chicken or fish and skewered beef (called brochettes) are common and can be found at relatively affordable prizes. The nomadic people of the north have a different diet that is relies on goat milk, meat, and cheese.

In Ouagadougou, there are restaurants that serve French, Chinese, and Italian food as well as fast food similar to that found in Western cultures. Lebanese or Senegalese food is also easy to find in larger towns. The French influence is still strong in Burkina Faso, and there are still patisseries and boulangeries in the bigger towns. While over half of the population is Muslim and refrains from alcohol, millet beer called dolo or chopolo is a popular accompaniment to meals. Another popular beverage is zoom koom ("flour water" in the Mooré language), which is a soft drink made from millet flour, ginger, and lemon.

Life's Milestones

Many of the age-old traditions of the various ethnic groups of Burkina Faso are still practiced today. Scarification, which is the intentional creation of scars on the skin for decorative purposes, is still common among some Burkinabé ethnic groups, and typically happens either shortly after a baby is born or at a coming-of-age ritual.

Initiation rituals are still common for boys and girls. Boys in the Lobi group in the southwest undergo a three- to six-month period of difficult tasks designed to prove their manhood. At the same time, the elders of the group teach them the oral history of their people.

Ancestors are important to all of the animist cultures of Burkina Faso. After a person dies, elaborate ceremonies are held to ensure that evil spirits does not take their souls. In addition, community burial grounds are located in sacred groves, which are off-limits except to certain members of the group.

CULTURAL HISTORY

Art
Artistically, the Lobi people have always been known for their sculpture, characterized by wooden human figurines and simple lines. The Mossi are celebrated for their masks, which vary from exaggerated human faces to fantastical animals. Their horned antelope masks are especially highly valued. Blacksmiths hold a special place in Bobo society, and are known for their sacred objects and jewelry.

Architecture
In the 12th century, Burkina Faso was part of the Mossi kingdoms, a trio of independently ruled states that ruled until French colonization. The third kingdom, known as Wagadougou, ruled from the capital of Wagdugu, the precursor to the modern-day capital of Ouagadougou. There, the Mossi built a large city in the Sahelian architecture style. This fired mud on timber construction is best exemplified by the Grand Mosque at Djenné in Senegal, the world's largest mud-brick building. During the over 700-year history of the kingdoms, architectural styles changed very little. People used materials they had on hand, such as millet stalks for thatched roofs, mud-bricks for the walls, and timber when available.

Modern-day Burkinabé use the same materials, but each ethnic group has developed its own style. The Dogons (who live near the border with Mali) are known for their homes built into cliffs and the thatched-roof granary towers that sit next to the dwellings. Wooden doors and windows shutters with elaborate carving also distinguish their homes. While most mud-brick construction homes are simple, the Gourounsi people in the southeast paint the exterior of their unfired mud homes with abstract patterns.

Music & Dance
In the culture of Burkina Faso, music rarely is unaccompanied by dancing and storytelling. Each of the more than sixty ethnic groups in Burkina Faso has distinctive musical, dance, and dramatic traditions. There are many similarities between them, and the different disciplines are closely linked. There are also different categories of performance: those for secular celebrations and those for sacred occasions (such a funerals or rites of passage). Historically, music also served a practical purpose, and many groups have praise songs to kings or chiefs and work songs.

Common instruments used by the various Burkinabé ethnic groups are the balafon and the djembe. The balafon is a kind of wooden xylophone made from gourds. The djembe is a percussive instrument with a wide top that tapers into a narrower base and is held between the legs and played with the hand. Two distinct instruments of the Mossi people are percussive instruments. The dondo is a drum played with a long, cane-like stick, and bendre are drums made from a goatskin-covered calabash (gourd) that are played by hand. The Tuareg people, who live in the far north of the country, have a different musical style that focuses largely on a one-stringed violin. Fulani music also features the tambin (a type of flute), the riti (one-stringed violin), and the hoddu (lute). The "talking" buuba drums imitate the sounds of the Fulani language.

Masks have traditionally been an important part of sacred dance in Burkina Faso. Only certain members of the community could only do masked dances, and in some cultures, the dancer's identity was a closely guarded secret. While dancing, a masked dancer was said to actually become the spirit that his mask represented, whether that spirit was an animal, ancestor, or king. In some of the Dongon masked dances, performers wear masks up to 15 feet in length or use stilts. In secular dance, all members of the community could take part, and men and women typically did separate dances. Tuareg dances are often accompanied only by chanting, singing, clapping, and the clanging of bracelets.

Literature
Most of the ethnic groups of Burkina Faso have never had a written tradition. Instead, storytelling was the most important way to preserve history

and transmit cultural values. (There were some exceptions, however, such as the Tuareg, who used tifinagh, a Berber alphabet common among the desert people of the Sahara and its border region.) Many of the cultures in Burkina Faso had official storytellers, called griots in French or djeli in Mande (which is spoken by several groups in the country). Griots traveled from town to town, sometimes wore costumes, and were accompanied by musicians. Some were praise singers who sang to glorify the king or chief, while others told comical stories.

The French introduced the written tradition to Burkina Faso at the turn of the 20th century. The first book published by a Burkinabé was *Maximes, Pensees, et Devinettes Mossi* (1934), which is the retelling of Mossi oral history in French. The first post-colonial Burkinabé novel was *Crépuscule Des Temps Anciens* (*The Dawn of Ancient Times*, 1962) by Nazi Boni (1909–1969) which explored the country's pre-colonial history. A number of Burkinabé writers have since gone on to gain recognition, especially in francophone Africa. The poet Frédéric Pacéré Titinga (1943–) was awarded the Grand Prix of Black African Literature for *Poèmes pour l'Angola* (1982) and *La Poésie des Griots* (1982), both volumes of poetry. Sarah Bouyain (1968–), a French-Burkinabé novelist and film-maker, is considered one of Burkina's most promising writers of the younger generation. Many Burkinabé writers incorporate legends or traditional storytelling techniques into their work in order to reflect their own cultural identity.

CULTURE

Arts & Entertainment

Burkina Faso's biggest art event is FESPACO (Festival Pan-Africain du Cinema) the pan-African film festival held in February and March in odd-numbered years in Ouagadougou. Over the course of the festival, over 100 films by filmmakers from all over Africa are screened. The festival brings tens of thousands of people to Ouagadougou from all over the world. FESPACO has had a big influence on the cultural life of Ouagadougou, and there is now an Ouagadougou Fashion Show for designers from all over Africa, as well as photography and painting exhibitions and shopping bazaars. In addition, the government has invested money in the film industry. Several Burkinabé filmmakers have also won international acclaim, including Idrissa Ouedraogo (1954–) and Gaston Kaboré (1951–). These filmmakers have gained audiences in French-speaking countries in Africa, and to a lesser extent in Europe and North America.

On even-numbered years when FESPACO is not held, Ouagadougou is home to SIAO (Le Salon International de l'Artisant de Ouagadougou). This international art and craft fair features jewelry, pottery, textiles, sculpture, housewares, and art objects made in countries across Africa. At this event, artisans have a chance to show and sell their work, as well as participate in workshops and seminars that help them expand the market for their work or develop effective business practices. In addition, importers from around the world come to the fair to develop trade relationships with these artisans.

Like many of its neighboring countries, Burkina Faso also has a vibrant musical culture. Afropop, reggae, and Caribbean-influenced music developed there, as in other West African countries, from the 1970s on. More recently, hip-hop and coup-decale from neighboring Côte d'Ivoire have become popular, while traditional music is still respected. Koudougou is home to the music festival Les Nuits Atypiques, which celebrates traditional drumming, dance, and song. Jazz is also popular in Burkina, and Ouagadougou hosts a bi-annual jazz festival.

Traditional theatrical performances continue to be popular in Burkina Faso. Often, these performances use dramatic storytelling to touch upon modern social issues such as HIV/AIDS. This kind of performance, which is based on the belief that theater can contribute to social development, is the focus of the International Theater Festival for Development, which is held every other year in Ouagadougou and Kadiogo. Some of the plays at the festival use participatory techniques such as "collective creation," or open debate between the audience and actors after the performance. Others use traditional griot storytelling techniques or puppets. Playwright and director Jean-Pierre Guingane—one of only two Burkinabé playwrights in the country to have published plays in French—founded the Ouagadougou International Theatre and Marionette Festival to promote modern and traditional use of puppets in storytelling and performance. In 2008, a comedy festival was launched in Ouagadougou, and a storytelling festival in Boussé.

Burkina Faso's National Culture Week, which takes place every other year in Bobo Dioulosso, brings together representatives from all aspects of Burkinabé culture. It highlights visual artists, performing artists (including modern and traditional music and dance), comedians, photographers, fashion designers, writers, competitors in traditional sports such as archery, and chefs. At the end of the event, prizes for distinction in each category are awarded. Laongo, just outside of Ouagadougou, is known for its sculptors who work in granite and the periodic sculpture conventions held there.

One of the most popular festivals in Burkina Faso is the Festival International des Masques et des Arts de Dédougou (FESTIMA). The bi-annual celebration features dancers from over thirty ethnic groups from around West Africa (and sometimes other areas of the world) doing sacred traditional masked dances. The festival, which was designed to preserve cultural traditions in the face of Westernization, has become a major tourist draw.

Cultural Sites & Landmarks

While Ouagadougou is Burkina's capital, Bobo Dioulosso, with its French-style tree-lined boulevards and slow pace of life, is the preferred cultural destination. Among the city's main attractions is the Grand Mosquée, built in 1893. A striking mud-brick construction building, it features numerous cone-shaped towers of varying height and width. Wooden beams stick out from the white-painted surface, giving the mosque a dramatic, unusual appearance. The Grand Marche (central market) caters to local people, but is also popular with tourists. There are numerous workshops in the old quarter of the city where the public can watch artisans make pottery, drums, batik cloth, and other handmade items. Also in the old quarter is the Konsa House, the oldest structure in the city, which dates back to the 15th century.

The Thursday market at Gorom is considered one of the most diverse markets in West Africa. Located in the northern part of the country, the market brings together ethnic groups from the region and features a variety of goods, from vegetables to cattle to homemade soap and textiles. Tuareg men from the far north desert arrive on camels wearing blue or black turbans and often carrying swords. Fulani women—known throughout Burkina Faso for their beauty—wear colorful dresses, lots of jewelry, and elaborate hairstyles. Fulani men—who often arrive at the market on horseback—wear turbans and flowing gowns, except for the herders, who wear woven, cone-shaped hats.

Spectacular in a different way are the ruins of Loropéni. The walls are remnants of a fortress area in the Lobi region, testaments to the age of the trans-Saharan gold trade. Situated near the borders of Côte d'Ivoire, Ghana, and Togo, the ruins have recently been shown to be at least 1,000 years old.

There are several "sacred crocodile lakes" in Burkina Faso. Local legends say the crocodiles and humans share the same spirit, and in the past, people often prayed to the crocodiles asking for success and protection against enemies. It was believed among these people that if a crocodile died, a human in a nearby village would also die. Today, the lakes at Bazoulé and Sabou are tourist attractions where visitors can go to observe crocodiles in their natural habitat.

Libraries & Museums

The National Museum of Burkina Faso is located in the capital. Established in 1962, it houses numerous artifacts from the country's various cultures and ethnicities. Ouagadougou is also home to the two-story National Museum of Music.

Museums showcasing Burkinabé art include the Musee de Manega (Manega Museum), which celebrates Burkina Faso's varied and rich cultural heritage; Musee du Poni art Lobi (or Poni Museum), which celebrates the Lobi culture; and Musee Provinciel du Houet, located in Bobo Dioulasso.

The National Library of Burkina Faso (Bibliothèque nationale du Burkina) was established in 1996, and is the country's legal depository for all Burkinabé publications. The Friends of African Village (FAVL) Libraries, which works to establish and maintain libraries in rural Africa, manages eight libraries in the country.

Holidays

Burkina Faso celebrates a number of Islamic and Christian religious holidays, including Ramadan and Christmas. Independence Day is August 5, celebrating the break from France in 1960. This day is also known as National Day or the Anniversary of the Revolution. The Proclamation of the Republic is commemorated on December 11.

Youth Culture

Football (soccer), basketball, and handball are all popular among the youth of Burkina Faso. Girls are more limited in the sports they typically pursue, but both boys and girls participate in track and field sports. Young people closely follow the national football team, as well as some of the European and African teams that have Burkinabé players. In rural areas, youth typically socialize in the common areas of the village. Groups are usually divided by gender and it is not considered acceptable for teens of the opposite sex to spend time together except in large groups. Because of the poverty in Burkina Faso, many teens and preteens have to work or take care of their younger siblings. In the cities, young people like to go dancing and frequent clubs or bars called maquis.

Education in Burkina Faso consists of primary, secondary, and higher education. However, universal primary education, which is provided for by the government, is not adequately funded. Agriculture remains a primary topic of study, and integrating technology into education remains an underdeveloped aspect of education in Burkina Faso. In addition, many youth also leave school early to participate in the labor market. Burkina Faso is also considered one of the world's least literate countries, with an average literacy rate of 36 percent.

SOCIETY

Transportation

There is bus service between Burkina and its neighboring countries and within major cities. Urban transportation also commonly consists of bicycles, mopeds, or taxis. Informal taxis known as bush taxis, which are often about the size of a large van, are a common mode of transportation in Burkina Faso. Often, these taxis have no fixed route and usually originate from larger cities. In rural areas, donkey carts are still a frequent sight, while in the northerly desert areas, riding camels and horses for transportation are a common practice. Traffic moves on the right-hand side of the road.

Transportation Infrastructure

The major cities of Burkina Faso are connected by a paved road system, though many roads are in poor condition. Secondary and rural roads are not paved. As one of the major cities of West Africa, Ouagadougou is connected by rail to Abidjan, Côte d'Ivoire, and by a highway to Niamey, the capital of Niger. Several roads connect the city to other points in the region. There is also domestic passenger rail service between Ouagadougou and Kaya and Bobo Dioulosso.

There are two international airports in Ouagadougou with flights to other cities in Africa and to France. Air travel is also possible within Burkina Faso from Ouagadougou to some

of the bigger cities. According to a 2013 estimate, the country hosts 23 airports.

Media & Communications

Since almost two-thirds of the population is
illiterate and many people do not have electricity
or access to television, radio is the most popular
medium in Burkina Faso. There are small community radio stations throughout the country,
many of which broadcast in the local language
rather than French (the country's official language). There are four high-wattage private
radio stations and a high-wattage government
radio station that reach wide areas. The big international radio stations—British Broadcasting
Corporation (BBC), Voice of America (VOA),
and Radio France Internationale (RFI)—also
broadcast from Ouagadougou.

Burkina Faso has three televisions stations—
one government-run and two private. It is possible to get international satellite TV at the larger
hotels in Ouagadougou and Bobo Dioulosso.
There are three daily newspapers in Burkina
Faso: one state-run newspaper and several privately run newspapers, all published in French.
There are also several weekly newspapers and a
government news agency.

Telephone service did not reach all areas
of the country until very recently, and only
about one percent of Burkinabé has a telephone
landline. However, cell phone use is more widespread, less expensive, and increasing. More than
two thirds of Burkinabé have a cell phone as of
a 2014 estimate. Internet usage is low, but growing. In a 2014 estimate, 782,400 Burkinabé use
the Internet. Although this number corresponds
to only 4.3 percent of the population, it more than
quadrupled over the previous five year.

SOCIAL DEVELOPMENT

Standard of Living

Burkina Faso ranked 181th out of 187 countries on the 2013 United Nations Human
Development Index, which measures quality of
life and standard of living indicators.

Average life expectancy in Burkina Faso
is 53 years for males and 57 years for females
(2015 estimate).

Water Consumption

According to UNICEF (United Nations
Children's Fund), 82 percent of the population
have access to improved drinking water, with the
urban population at 97 percent improved access
and 76 percent for the rural population. In terms
of improved sanitation, UNICEF reports that
19 percent of the total population has improved
access—with 50 percent of the urban population
having improved access and only seven percent
of the rural population.

Education

By law, children in Burkina Faso are required to
attend school until 16 years old. However, only
26 percent of children advance to the secondary
level. Although there is no tuition, many families
cannot afford to buy school supplies, and choose
to send their children to work instead. The country's average literacy rate is only 36 percent.

The University of Ouagadougou was
Burkina's first university. It opened in 1974. The
other three institutions of higher learning are the
Bobo-Dioulasso Polytechnic University, Institut
Supérieur d'Informatique et de Gestion, and the
Koudougou École Normale Supérieure.

Women's Rights

Burkina Faso ratified the Convention on the
Elimination of All Forms of Discrimination
against Women (CEDAW) and the Optional
Protocol to the Convention on the Elimination
of All Forms of Discrimination against Women
(CEDAWOP). The government has also undertaken campaigns to reverse the traditional societal views that women are inferior, second-class
citizens. However, despite the government's
commitment to women's rights, in reality,
women still have little protection against discrimination and abuse.

Sexual harassment and discrimination is
illegal in Burkina Faso, but it is reportedly common and most women are reluctant to report it.

Although there are some women in relatively high-level positions in the educational, public, health, and legal sectors, most women in Burkina work in the informal agricultural sector. Equal access to education for girls has been a persistent problem in the rural areas of Burkina Faso. Many families do not have enough money to send all their children to school. In those cases, the boys of the family are sent first and the girls are denied education. Since this lack of education limits a women's ability to obtain employment, the government has recently undertaken a large education project with the help of international aid.

By law, women are allowed to own and inherit property; in reality, few women are aware of their rights and follow customary law (the law of the woman's ethnic group). Most groups prohibit a woman from owning property independent of her husband or from inheriting property should her husband die. In some cultures, if a woman's husband dies, she then belongs to his brother. If a woman dies, her sister is given to the dead woman's husband. The government and women's rights groups have undertaken campaigns to increase women's awareness of their rights under the law.

There is no specific law against domestic violence in Burkina Faso and there are no official statistics about its prevalence; it is thought to be a widespread problem. Women generally do not report abuse because of the social stigma associated with it. Rape is illegal, but like domestic violence, it is not always reported and very few cases are actually prosecuted. In cases that are brought to trial, some attackers have been successfully prosecuted.

In 1996, Burkina Faso became one of the first countries to outlaw female genital mutilation (FGM). However, as of a 2010 estimate, three quarters of women aged 15–49 have experienced FGM. The government has undertaken campaigns to stop it and has successfully prosecuted some of those found to be continuing this tradition. However, the practice persists, regardless of the government's efforts to introduce alternative ceremonies that are not harmful.

Polygamy is legal in Burkina Faso and remains a common practice, especially in the northern part of the country. Forced marriage is against the law, but it still exists. Girls have been kidnapped in order to be married, even in urban areas. Women are allowed to seek divorce in Burkina Faso.

Health Care

Access to health care is extremely limited in the rural areas of Burkina Faso, despite the fact that the majority of the population lives there. The infant mortality rate is 75 deaths for every 1,000 births (2015 estimate). The average life expectancy for Burkinabe is 55 years.

Major diseases include food and waterborne diseases, such as bacterial and protozoal diarrhea, hepatitis A, and typhoid fever; respiratory disease, such as meningitis; malaria; and HIV/AIDS. About 110,000 people living in Burkina Faso have HIV/AIDS (2013 estimate).

The country experienced outbreaks of meningitis in 1996, 2001, and 2002. Together, these nearly epidemic occurrences killed thousands of people.

GOVERNMENT

Structure

Since gaining its independence from France in 1960, the government of Burkina Faso has been a parliamentary republic. The executive branch includes a president, who acts as chief of state, and a prime minister, who acts as the head of government. The president determines the members of the cabinet, called the Council of Ministers, with help from the prime minister. The president is voted into office for a term of five years and can only be reelected once.

The legislative branch, like the entire government, is in a state of transition. In 2002, the upper of the two houses was dissolved. Agreements made in 2012 to reinstate it under a new name have not been carried out. That leaves the 127-member National Assembly as a unicameral legislature as of October 2015.

On October 31, 2014, President Blaise Compaore resigned after his efforts to change the constitution to run for an additional term led to violent protests. Various military leaders acted as the head of state before Michel Kafando became interim president on November 18, 2014. A military coup briefly took over the government on September 16, 2015; however, Kafando came back to power after just one week. Elections are set for late 2015.

Political Parties

Of the more than 140 political parties in Burkina Faso, the dominant political party is the Congress for Democracy and Progress, a left-wing socialist party that has dominated the country's presidency since 1992 and has progressively gained more power in the National Assembly. In the 2012 election, the Congress for Democracy and Progress took almost half of the vote, securing 70 seats. Other parties include the African Democratic Rally-Alliance for Democracy and Federation, which won 19 seats in the 2012 vote; the Union for Progress and Reform, which also won 19 seats; as wells as over 100 smaller parties.

Local Government

Local government in Burkina Faso is divided into 13 regions, 45 provinces, and 351 departments. The Congress for Democracy and Progress party holds a majority of positions in local government. Decentralization efforts since 2006 have increased the number of election positions, in the hope that an increase in local participation by women will result.

Judicial System

Communities in Burkina Faso have local (traditional) courts. The judicial system is overwhelmed because of a shortage of courts and an unstable judiciary that has been characterized as corrupt. The Court of Appeal and Supreme Court are the country's highest courts.

Taxation

The government of Burkina Faso levies income, corporate, value-added, real estate, sales, social security, payroll, and other taxes. Tax rates are average, with 30 percent as both the highest corporate tax rate and personal income tax rate.

Armed Forces

The Burkina Faso military consists of five service branches: Army, Air Force, National Gendarmerie (military police), National Police, and People's Militia. There is no conscription. Armed forces personnel numbered approximately 11,200 in 2012.

Foreign Policy

Burkina Faso gained independence from France in 1960, and it has undergone a good deal of political upheaval since then. The government is proactive with its regional relations. Burkina Faso holds membership in the United Nations (UN), the African Union (AU), the Organization of African Unity (OAU), the World Trade Organization (WTO), the International Monetary Fund (IMF), and the World Bank, among other international organizations. In 2008, Burkina Faso was elected to the UN Security Council (UNSC) as a non-permanent member, a position that lasted two years. The country has also ratified many international environmental, human rights, and peace treaties, including the Nuclear Non-Proliferation Treaty and the Kyoto Protocol on global climate change.

However, Burkina Faso has been involved in regional conflicts with neighboring countries. When civil war erupted in Côte d'Ivoire in 2000, Burkinabé who had emigrated because of economic opportunity became the target of Ivorian nationalists. Additionally, the Ivorian government accused Burkina Faso of supporting the rebels who were fighting for control of the country. The relationship between the two countries improved when former Burkina President Blaise Compaoré (1951–) helped to negotiate a peace agreement between the Ivorian rebels and the government in 2007.

The governments of Liberia and Sierra Leone also claimed at one time that Burkina Faso had supported rebel groups in their countries. The UN found evidence that the Burkinabé government was supplying arms to the Liberian rebel forces, which violated an arms sanction against the group. The Liberian arms-dealing situation created a rift between Burkina Faso and many of its allies, but the situation later improved. In 2004, the government of nearby Mauritania accused Burkina Faso of trying to provoke a civil war in that country.

Burkina Faso maintains good relations with the Group of Eight (G8), the major industrialized nations that include the United States, the United Kingdom, Canada, Germany, France, Japan, Italy, and Russia, as well as the European Union (EU). France remains Burkina's major ally and largest trading partner, and has provided the Burkinabé military with training in the years since independence. In addition to aid from the IMF and World Bank, it has received direct financial assistance from the US, the EU, France, Germany, Denmark, the Netherlands, Belgium, Canada, Libya, and Taiwan. Trade between the US and Burkina is limited.

Human Rights Profile
International human rights law insists that states respect civil and political rights, and promote an individual's economic, social, and cultural rights. The United Nations Universal Declaration on Human Rights (UDHR) is recognized as the standard for international human rights. Its authors sought the counsel of the world's great thinkers, philosophers, and religious leaders, and were careful to create a document that reflected the core values shared by every world culture. (To read this document or view the articles relating to cultural human rights, visit http://www.udhr.org/UDHR/default.htm.)

Burkina Faso has ratified the major international human rights conventions, including the International Covenant on Economic, Social, and Cultural Rights (CESCR), the International Covenant on Civil and Political Rights (CCPR), the Convention on the Rights of the Child (CRC), and the International Convention on the Protection of the Rights of All Migrant Workers and Members of Their Families. Despite being home to over 60 ethnic groups, the country also

has a history of harmony among its people, and there is no evidence of official discrimination due to religion or ethnicity. In general, the privacy of individuals and groups is respected in Burkina Faso, and citizens are permitted to assemble freely without government interference. However, there are still a number of concerns.

The 1998 murder of journalist Norbert Zongo (1949–1998), who published an independent newspaper, caused international outcry and political unrest. Zongo was investigating members of the president's family when he and several associates were killed and their car set on fire. No one was ever charged for the murder. Since then, there have been incidents of harassment of journalists. Regardless, there are no reports of government limits on foreign media or the Internet in Burkina Faso.

Elections in Burkina Faso are generally considered free, but some have questioned whether they are entirely fair, as there have been reports of voter fraud. The ruling party has control of both the executive and legislative branches and there are reports that the executive branch has strong influence over the judiciary, calling into question the fairness of trials. Corruption and bribes among government officials are reported to be common. There are also many reports of human rights abuses by police and security forces in Burkina Faso. The police have made arbitrary arrests and have been accused of brutality and torture. Additionally, prisons in Burkina Faso are overcrowded and lack adequate sanitation and food for prisoners.

Human trafficking is an issue in Burkina Faso. Although there is some protection against trafficking for children, it is not specifically against the law to traffic in adults. While some have been arrested for trafficking for children, there have not been many successful prosecutions for the crime. The country has child labor laws, but they are not commonly enforced.

Migration
Migration in Burkina Faso has traditionally followed a cyclical pattern tied to the seasons and

agricultural work, but in the 20th century, that changed, and the migration cycle (usually to Côte d'Ivoire, its neighbor to the south) has extended to several years. According to a 2013 estimate by the United Nations, Burkina Faso loses about 1.5 out of 1,000 people per year in net migration.

ECONOMY

Overview of the Economy

Most Burkinabe live in extreme poverty, with a 2013 United Nations estimate declaring 82 percent of Burkinabe live in multidimensional poverty. In 2013, the country's gross domestic product (GDP) was estimated at $29.31 billion (USD), with a per capita GDP of $1,700 (USD). Burkina Faso relies on other countries for a substantial amount of economic aid. Because of the country's few natural resources, little industry, and reliance on agriculture, natural disasters, such as drought, threaten the livelihood of the people.

Burkina Faso mainly trades with its neighboring nations. However, political instability in many of these countries severely limits Burkina's opportunities for trade. In 2002–2003, for example, the country's border with Côte d'Ivoire was completely closed.

Industry

Burkina Faso's industrial structure is underdeveloped. Industry accounts for almost 22 percent of the GDP. Industrial activities include mining (mostly for gold) as well as the manufacture of cotton lint, beverages, agricultural processing, soap, cigarettes, and textiles.

A significant portion of Ouagadougou's industry is based on craft exports; the city has become a crafts center in Africa and many businesses in the city are oriented towards the production of arts and crafts. Ouagadougou also serves as Burkina Faso's export center and thus handles most of the country's exports of cotton, sorghum, and millet.

Labor

Burkina Faso's labor force numbers 7,468 million people; the unemployment rate in 2013 was measured at 2.3 percent. Ninety percent are employed in the agricultural sector, with 10 percent working in the service and industry sectors.

Energy/Power/Natural Resources

Burkina Faso's limited natural resources include manganese, limestone, marble, and phosphate. The country has rich deposits of gold and silver, but has insufficient resources to exploit them.

Since most Burkinabe are farmers, the greatest threats to the Burkinabe way of life are the frequent droughts, deforestation, and overgrazing, all of which make farming difficult. Because of these environmental problems, many men seek work in neighboring countries, leaving their families behind to attempt to cultivate the land.

Fishing

As a landlocked country, Burkina Faso's fishing industry, comprised of mostly artisanal fishers, is focused in lakes and reservoirs. The fishing industry does not contribute to the country's GDP as most of the fish feeds communities and families, although fees for permits and licenses do contribute to government revenues.

Forestry

About 20 percent of Burkina Faso is forested, and existing forests are threatened by deforestation. Estimates place the contribution of the forestry industry to the GDP between 1.5 and three percent. For 97 percent of the population, firewood and charcoal serve as the country's primary fuel source (90 percent). This heavy dependency has caused a degradation of available resources, especially around urban areas.

Mining/Metals

Burkina Faso lies in the midst of the Birimian Greenstone Belt, one of the highest producing gold areas in the world. According to the government of Burkina Faso, gold production doubled between 2008 and 2009. The government is also interested in promoting manganese mining, as well as exploring the possibilities for further exploitation of oil and uranium. Phosphate is another plentiful resource.

Agriculture

Approximately 90 percent of Burkina Faso's population is engaged in farming, mostly at the subsistence level. Agriculture is the main source of goods for export, accounting for 38 percent of the GDP.

Cotton is the chief crop; rises in the GDP are often directly related to increasing cotton prices. Other crops include millet, sorghum, rice, livestock, peanuts, shea nuts, and maize. These crops are chosen because they need little water to survive, as drought is a continuing problem throughout the country. Agricultural workers from all cultural groups frequently immigrate to the adjoining countries of Côte d'Ivoire and Ghana in order to obtain seasonal work. This is essential to their survival, since it is difficult to find work in Burkina Faso due to its frequent droughts.

The Burkina government is seeking to export cotton and other crops to more nations outside of Africa, including the European Union and Taiwan, in the hopes that a wider market might bring higher prices.

Animal Husbandry

Cattle are a major contributor to the country's agricultural sector (accounting for eight percent of exports) but such exports have been decreasing in the past decade. Mobile herds comb the countryside looking for grazing land, which has become increasingly more challenging in recent years of drought. Sheep and goats are kept in small numbers, as they face the same grazing challenges facing cattle herders.

Tourism

Tourism is not a well-developed industry in Burkina Faso. However, the Burkinabé are known for their hospitality, and there is much to see in the country. The country's most popular attraction is the biennial FESPACO, or the Pan-African Cinema and Television Festival.

Burkina Faso offers plenty of opportunities for hiking and biking, with or without guides. Visitors can go on safari and watch the wildlife in the country's many national parks, including Arly National Park, Park of Pô (Kaboré Tembi National Park), Nazinga Game Reserve, Deux-Balé conservation forest, and Hippopotami Lake.

Encouraged by the United Nations (UN) and non-profit organizations, Ouagadougou has tried to bolster its image as a West African tourist destination. Burkina Faso has been able to establish many internationally renowned cultural events revolving around African arts, music, and culture. In addition, Ouagadougou frequently hosts UN summits and conferences. Eco-tourism in Ouagadougou has also generated revenue and attracted visitors from around the world.

Joanne O'Sullivan, Rebekah Painter,
Pilar Quezzaire

DO YOU KNOW?

- The name "Ouagadougou" is a French conversion of the city's original name, "Wogodogo." Residents call the city "Ouaga."

- The name Burkina Faso means "land of the incorruptible," "land of the honorable men," or "country of integrity," depending on the translation. It is a combination of the Mòoré and Gur languages and was chosen in an attempt to keep peace between ethnic groups.

Bibliography

Banham, Martin, Errol Hill, and George Woodyard, eds. "The Cambridge Guide to African and Caribbean Theater." Cambridge: *Cambridge University Press*, 1994.

Letarte, Martine. "Women and the Patriarchal Society in Burkina Faso." *L'Itinaire* 15 September 2007.

Manson, Katrina. "Burkina Faso (Bradt Travel Guide)." Guilford, CT: *Globe Pequot*, 2012.

Rupley, Lawrence. "Historical Dictionary of Burkina Faso." Lanham, MD: *Scarecrow Press*, 2013.

Trillo, Richard. "The Rough Guide to West Africa," 5th ed. London: *Pearson*, 2008.

Works Cited

"Burkina Faso." *Bureau of African Affairs United States Department of State.* http://www.state.gov

"Burkina Faso: Country Specific Information." *U.S. State Department.* http://travel.state.gov

"Burkina Faso." Foreign and Commonwealth office of the Government of the UK http://www.fco.uk.gov

"Burkina Faso Fact File: International Relations." *Institute for Security Studies* http://www.issafrica.org.

"Burkina Faso: Largest Cities and Towns and Statistics of their Population." *World Gazetteer.* http://archive. is/20130111131816/http://www.world-gazetteer.com/ wg.php. 2 October 2015.

"Burkina Faso Opts for Internet Boom." *Afrol News.* www. afrol.com

"Burkina Faso: Population." *Emporis.* http://www.emporis. com

"Burkina Faso." U.S.-Africa.Org http://www.us-africa. tripodcom

"Burkina Faso." *United Nations.* http://data.un.org/ CountryProfile.aspx?crName=Burkina percent20Faso. 3 October 2015.

"Burkina Faso." *World Health Organization.* http://apps. who.int/gho/data/node.country.country-BFA?lang=en. 3 October 2015.

"Country Insights: Burkina Faso." *Center for Intercultural Learning.* www.intercultures.ca.

"Country Profile: Burkina Faso." *BBC.* http://news.bbc. co.uk.

"Female Genital Mutilation/Cutting: Data and Trends." *Population Reference Bureau.* http://www.prb.org/pdf14/ fgm-wallchart2014.pdf. 2 October 2015.

"HDI: Burkina Faso." *United Nations Development Programme.* http://hdr.undp.org/en/countries/profiles/ BFA. 3 October 2015.

"Ouagadougou Cultural Life Blossoms During FESPACO." 3 March 2005. *Afrol News.*

"Portals of the World: Burkina Faso." *Library of Congress.* http://www.loc.gov.

"The World Factbook: Burkina Faso." *Central Intelligence Agency.* http://www.cia.gov. 2 October 2015.

"Trade Overview: Burkina Faso." *UN Comtrade.* file:///Users/anthonyvivian/Downloads/Burkina percent20Faso2010.pdf. 3 October 2015.

"Young People From Burkina Faso Reveal Their Hopes and Dreams For the Future." *Cool Planet.* Oxfam http:www. Oxfam.uk.org.

Eyre, Banning. "Burkina Faso." *Afropop Worldwide.* www. afropop.org

Roy, Christopher. "The Lobi of Burkina Faso." *University of Iowa*, 2002.

Sollie, Emily. "In Burkina Faso, Literacy Training Helps Women Fight for Rights." *Monday Developments.* 29 August 2005.

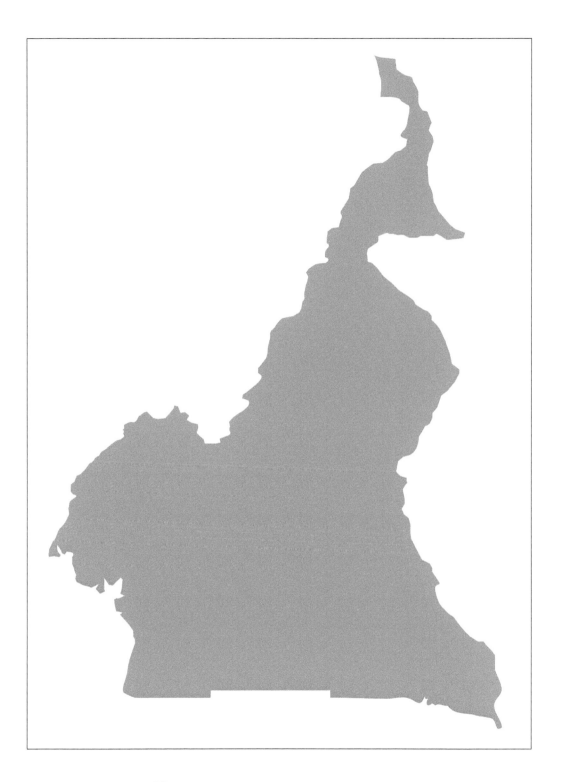

CAMEROON

Introduction

The Republic of Cameroon is a country on the central western shore of the continent of Africa. Because of its location, it is often called the "Hinge of Africa." It is bordered to the east by Chad and the Central African Republic, to the south by Congo, Equatorial Guinea, and Gabon, and to the west by Nigeria and the Bight of Biafra. Relations with neighboring countries are generally good, although some borders are closed periodically. Most of Cameroon's political struggles occur internally. Despite the democratic structure of its government, the nation has been accused of operating as a dictatorship.

Cameroon's culture and people have been greatly affected by the legacy of European colonialism. The founding of the capital, Yaoundé, can even be attributed to the arrival of German traders who settled there to facilitate the ivory trade in 1888. Since that time, the French, British, Dutch, and Germans have all controlled parts of Cameroon at one time or another.

While Cameroon comprises some 250 distinct ethnicities, some of country's most prominent native arts come from the Bamiléké and Bamoun people, and include woodcarving and masks. Dance remains an important and popular tradition in Cameroon, and public celebrations and holidays often involve traditional forms of group dancing. In addition, many traditional African musical instruments such as the thumb piano, a stringed instrument called the mvet, and a xylophone called the balafon are used in both traditional and modern Cameroonian music. Bikutsi music, a traditional Beti musical form that has blended with modern dance-beat music, and makossa, which has developed into a form of modern African jazz, are two of the essential styles of music found in Cameroon.

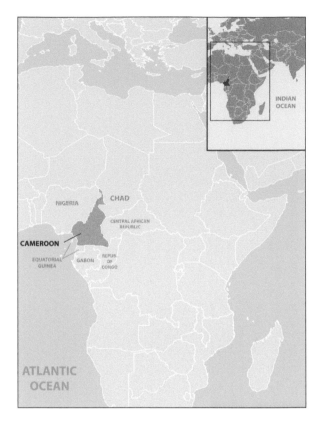

GENERAL INFORMATION

Official Language: French, English
Population: 23,739,218 (2015 estimate)
Currency: Central African franc
Coins: Coins are available in denominations of 1, 2, 5, 10, 25, 50, 100, and 500 francs.

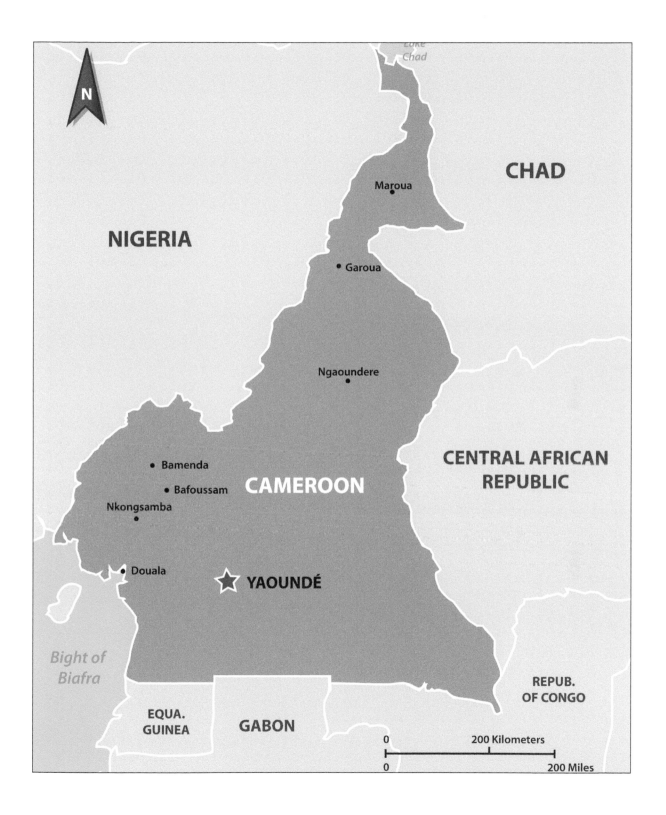

Principal Cities by Population (2015):

- Yaoundé (3,066,000)
- Douala (2,493,000)
- Kousséri (435,547)
- Bamenda (393,835)
- Garoua (436,899)
- Maroua (319,941)
- Bafoussam (290,768)
- Mokolo (275,239)
- Ngaoundéré (231,357)
- Edéa (203,149)

Land Area: 472,710 square kilometers (182,514 square miles)
Water Area: 2,730 square kilometers (1,054 square miles)
National Motto: "Paix, Travail, Patrie" (French, "Peace, Work, Fatherland")
National Anthem: "O Cameroun, Berceau de Nos Ancêtres" ("O Cameroon, Thou Cradle of Our Fathers")
Capital: Yaoundé
Time Zone: GMT +1
Flag Description: The flag of Cameroon features a tricolor design of three equal vertical bars of green (left), red (middle), and yellow (right). A five-pointed yellow star is centered within the red stripe. The colors represent Pan-Africanism, and are further stated to stand for unity (red), the sun and Cameroon's savanna landscapes (yellow), and the country's lush forests (green).

Population

Cameroon's population is made up of many different ethnic groups. The largest of these is the Bamiléké people, who live in the western part of the country. Other groups include the Fulani people, who live in the north, and the Douala (or Duala), Ewondo, and Fang people who inhabit the south and central regions. The Centre Region, occupying Cameroon's central plains, is the largest province (now region), with an estimated 2015 population of 2,672,533 million (followed closely by the Littoral, or Coastal, region, with a 2015 population of 2,202,340).

Urban areas, such as the capital city Yaoundé, contain a mix of ethnic groups, and ethnic tension and discrimination are common in Cameroon. Douala is the country's second largest city, with an unofficial population approaching that of Yaoundé. A large majority of Cameroonians are farmers who live outside of the major cities, in clay huts or rectangular brick houses; as of 2015, an estimated 54.4 percent of the population was urban. Most of the rural population is concentrated along Cameroon's forest, of which there are an estimated 19.8 million hectares (2015). Urban Cameroonians typically work in the service or manufacturing industries. Urban dwellings may either be modern structures or, in poorer areas, small shacks. In addition, there are many native people still living in tribal chiefdoms or kingdoms in remote areas of the country. As of 2015, the population growth rate was estimated at 3.6 percent.

Languages

Although French and English are the official languages, most Cameroonians speak at least one of 54 native African dialects as well. In the capital, over 20 indigenous languages are spoken, including pidgin (a combination of English, French, and local indigenous languages).

Native People & Ethnic Groups

People have lived in West Africa for more than 50,000 years. Cameroon's southeast rainforest is home to the Baka Pygmy tribes that are descended from the earliest inhabitants of the area. The Bantu people have been in Cameroon since 1000 BCE. Their long-term cultural influence is significant, as the Duala and the Fang people speak Bantu languages today.

In the ninth century, many Arab traders passed through Cameroon as they crossed the Sahara. These Arabs helped the spread of Islam, which remains a primary religion in modern Cameroon. These traders also took many native people captive, as part of the slave trade.

Today, the country's principal ethnicity is the Cameroon Highlanders, who make up an estimated 31 percent of the population. They include the Bamiléké people. In 2015, the country was home to an estimated 250 ethnicities. For the most part, Cameroon's demographic profile is characterized as being extremely complex.

Religions
Religion in Cameroon has been affected by colonialism, and the country is home to large Christian and Muslim populations. However, about 40 percent of Cameroonians practice a traditional African religion.

Climate
Cameroon's climate varies in different parts of the country. However, the entire country experiences generally warm or hot weather throughout the year. The northern savanna is the hottest and driest area, with an average temperature of 28° Celsius (82° Fahrenheit). Daytime temperatures in this area often reach 49° Celsius (120° Fahrenheit).

Temperatures are lower on the Adamawa Massif (in north-central Cameroon), averaging 24° Celsius (75° Fahrenheit). The coastal region experiences slightly higher temperatures of 27° Celsius (80° Fahrenheit), but receives the most rainfall of any region. Parts of the coastal region receive an average of 500 centimeters (200 inches) of rain annually. The average rainfall in other areas is about 254 centimeters (100 inches).

Yaoundé, the capital of Cameroon, has a tropical climate with a rainy season that lasts from July until October. The rest of the year is dry. Temperatures average between 19° and 27° Celsius (66° to 81° Fahrenheit), with high humidity. The city feels cooler at night, when the humidity dissipates. Yaoundé is sometimes cooled by rain as well and receives about 1,555 millimeters (61 inches) of precipitation per year. Most of the rain falls in the summer and early autumn.

ENVIRONMENT & GEOGRAPHY

Topography
There are four topographical regions in Cameroon. In the south and southeast, the land is mostly tropical rainforest. The central area, part of the Adamawa Massif (a plateau encompassing west-central Africa), is comprised of a high plateau separating the southern forests from the savanna

grasslands in the north. Finally, the western shore is mostly mountainous, and is the site of Mount Cameroon, the nation's highest point at 4,095 meters (13,435 feet). Mount Cameroon, like many of the mountains in the western region, is an active volcano. The volcano last erupted in May 2000.

There are several major rivers running through Cameroon, many of which contain natural waterfalls and hydroelectric dams. Some of the rivers, such as the Nyong and the Sanaga, flow west into the Bight of Biafra, the area of the Atlantic Ocean off Cameroon's shore. The Mbéré and the Logone flow north into Lake Chad, which lies above Cameroon's northern tip. Other major rivers include the Bénué and the Wouri. Lake Lagdo and Lake Mbakaou are the country's largest inland lakes.

Plants & Animals
Elephants, giraffes, antelopes, buffalo, lions, hippopotamuses, and rhinoceroses are all species native to Cameroon's forest plateau and savanna regions. Cameroon is also home to many endangered species. In recent years, conservation groups such as the World Wildlife Federation have been focused on preserving Cameroonian habitats.

Cameroon's rainforest also contains gorillas, chimpanzees, mandrills, monkeys, and many species of birds and reptiles. Rainforest birds include toucans, parrots and hornbills. Common reptiles are crocodiles, small lizards, and a variety of poisonous snakes. There are thousands of tropical flowers and vines in the rainforest, in addition to ebony, iroko, obeche, mahogany and rubber trees.

The coastal area is home to birds such as kingfishers, storks, flamingoes, and ibis, and a large variety of fish and amphibians. Coastal trees are mostly mangroves, which include species such as the rhizophora and avicennia.

CUSTOMS & COURTESIES

Greetings
Greetings vary in Cameroon, depending on the area. In Francophone Cameroon, close friends may greet one another by glancing cheeks

while embracing, then shaking hands, while Anglophone, or English language-speaking, Cameroonians generally greet with a handshake. However, Muslim men are unlikely to shake a woman's hand, as physical contact between genders in Muslim culture is discouraged. In addition, women rarely look another person in the eye, regardless of gender, and men show respect to those in a high social status or age by lowering their head. Cameroonians traditionally greet elders first as a sign of respect and do not rush the greeting process. Greetings are commonly said in either English or French, or a simplified mix of West African dialect and English, known as a pidgin language.

Gestures & Etiquette

When talking, Cameroonians are known to speak expressively, and talking over another is not considered rude. Because of the pervasive use of stories and myths throughout the culture, Cameroonians also commonly use many proverbs when talking on any number of subjects. Because Cameroon is essentially a conservative nation, religion and the practice of traditional customs are also important throughout the country, and are reflected in social etiquette. Thus, conservative dress is the norm, and the government even forbids the photographing of government buildings and personnel, as well as airports, bridges, and markets.

Eating/Meals

Those who can afford it eat three meals a day. Breakfast is usually light, and may consist of bread and fruit accompanied by tea or coffee in urban areas. In rural areas, smoked fish (along the coast), tea, and leftovers are common. Lunch is more popular in urban areas, and rural Cameroonians tend to eat more substantial dinners. One-course meals are typical, and commonly include soups and stews. Meat, such as beef, fish, or poultry, is consumed based on socioeconomics and region, and is often added to the stew or soup, along with vegetables. Rural Cameroonians eat bush meat, which includes crocodile, deer, snake, monkey, or other small

animals. Though Muslim Cameroonians occasionally eat beef, they are prohibited from eating pork.

Most Cameroonians, even in cities, eat at home. Traditionally, elders and male are served first when eating, followed by women and then children (who also may eat in separate rooms). Everyone is required to wash his or her hands, which is done in a communal bowl of water. When eating, it is common to use one's hands—the right, and not the left, since it is associated with the cleansing of the body—in rural areas and take from a communal bowl. Utensils are more commonly used in urban areas. Cameroonians may eat sitting on the floor or at a table, with the latter more common in urban areas.

Visiting

When visiting a Cameroonian's home, visitors are customarily expected to greet and shake hands with each household member, beginning with the eldest. A small gift, such as fruit, wine, or whiskey, might be expected, though a visitor to a Muslim household should refrain from bringing alcohol, as Muslims are forbidden to consume it. If the family has small children, it is also appropriate to present them with a small gift, such as sweets or pencils and paper for school. Traditionally, gifts are given with either both hands or only the right hand, and are usually opened upon receipt. When dining at a Cameroonian's home, guests are expected to show respect by dressing formally.

LIFESTYLE

Family

The family is of prime importance to Cameroonians, and the principal means through which they attain social standing and recognition within the wider community As such, extended families are the norm in the Cameroonian social system, and Cameroonian families and bloodlines can be large enough to encompass an entire village. The family's importance extends to the work environment, where family members hire one another, in part to have built-in trust with work colleagues. In addition, elders are traditionally cared for at home and by younger generations.

Though the marriage of one man to two or more women is common in Cameroon, Western educated families do not practice this tradition. Polygamy is more common in rural areas. Family members share responsibilities, such as maintenance and creation of wealth, though women do most of the childrearing. The entire family works together to sustain itself. With farming, women help raise food to feed the family, and men typically work to raise cash crops. Families in urban areas tend to help family members who migrate there from rural areas in search of economic opportunities.

Housing

Rural housing in Cameroon varies, and includes small, round wooden structures with thatched conical roofs made from palm trees, common in wooded areas, to homes made from baked mud, common in the grasslands. Such homes also have thatched roofs made from branches and grass. Homes are traditionally built in clusters in family compounds. In polygamist marriages, the different wives live separately in their own homes.

Urban homes are generally made from blocks made of concrete or a mix of concrete and ash. They tend to be square or rectangular shaped, and have roofs made of corrugated tin or wood. Apartment buildings or small, modern homes are more commonly built in cities.

Food

Cameroonian cuisine has distinct French, British, and Middle Eastern influences and varies according to the region. Seafood dishes are common in coastal areas, and include fried fish and fish stews; plantains are a staple in southern regions, and yams and cocoyams (also called taro) are featured in recipes in the western highlands. In the far northern areas of the country, rice, sorghum, and millet are staple ingredients. Throughout Cameroon, stewed vegetables of some kind are almost always included with meals. Regional foods are commonly shipped to other areas of the country, and many foods, such as spices and canned goods, are imported from other countries.

Many popular Cameroonian dishes are French-influenced, such as poulet, which is chicken flavored with spices, onion, garlic, and various peppers. It is fried in oil in a skillet and served with rice, roasted plantains, or millet, depending on the region. Because Cameroonian food is eaten with the fingers; many meals include pounded and formed starchy vegetables that can be dipped into sauces or stews. One of the most common dishes in Cameroon is achu, which is made by mashing cocoyams, and mounding it on a plate. A depression is made in the center of the mound, onto which is poured a sauce of palm oil and hot peppers. Cameroonians scoop the cocoyam on their finger and then dip the yam into the sauce. Fufu, made with pounded cocoyams, is formed into small dumplings, with a depression pushed into the small center, used to scoop up stew, soup, or vegetables. A thick vegetable stew called jammu-jammu is typically eaten with fufu. The national dish, ndolé, is a stewed preparation of a bitter leaf (similar to spinach) that includes oxtail, stock fish, peanuts, crayfish, onion, ginger, garlic, and salt and pepper.

Life's Milestones

Tradition plays a continuing role in marriage rites in Cameroonian culture. Though marriages are traditionally arranged, women and men occasionally meet without the assistance of their parents or families. Regardless, negotiations between the families can last for a period of months, as details about long-term obligations among the many family members require careful consideration. The actual wedding ceremony itself is simple in rural areas. In urban areas, Cameroonians often choose hold ceremonies that resemble those in European culture.

Death and the afterlife get special attention in Cameroonian culture, especially between the western Bamiléké and the eastern Maka. Bamiléké female relatives of the dead perform a wailing rite done to announce the death. All relatives of the recently deceased shave their heads

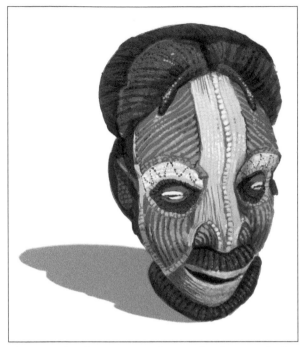

An example of a woven mask worn by dancers during a one-year anniversary of family member's death.

and dress in traditional blue and black cloth. The family might also display the deceased person's possessions to show the wealth that he or she passed to the heirs.

To mark the anniversary of the death, the family holds an official ceremony one year later. At this ceremony, the family digs up the deceased, removes the skull, and encases it in a shrine for viewing. The Baka of the eastern forested region mourn the dead with a ceremony in which a dancer wearing a raffia mask is believed to be inhabited by a forest spirit.

CULTURAL HISTORY

Art
Throughout history, the artistic practices of Cameroon's various ethnicities have served important social functions. For example, many Cameroonian ethnic groups have a long history of carving elaborate ceremonial masks, sculpting symbolic stools for chiefs, and making bronze sculpture. Special ceremonial masks, in particu-

lar, date back centuries. Traditionally, each mask is carved from one piece of wood to symbolize powerful animals or a chief, called a Fon. Masks might also be covered with brightly colored and patterned beads, adorned with raffia fringe (from raffia palm), intricately painted, or simply left plain.

The tradition of wearing masks, which has also existed for many centuries, serves important indigenous religious functions as well. They are worn during religious ceremonies for driving away evils spirits, curing disease, increasing fertility, and celebrating a harvest. Each mask is designed to serve one of these particular purposes. A chief makes the decisions involving masks, such as those what male wears the masks (masks are worn only by men) and the ritual for wearing them. Because the entire body is also covered in a special cloth and raffia costume to accompany the mask, the mask-wearer's identity is hidden from other villagers. Those chosen to wear masks dance or perform tribal dramas to symbolize the ritual. The Cameroonian ethnic groups who make the ritual masks are the Bamiléké, the Bamoun, and the Tikar, who are all part of the Semi-Bantu of the western grasslands.

Architecture
The distinct architecture of the Musgum (or Mousgoum) forms a prominent part of Cameroon's architectural heritage. The ethnic group, located in Cameroon's far north region, is known for its traditional conical huts, made from sun-dried mud. These tall, traditional mud houses feature a raised pattern, which can act as a type of scaffolding for repairs, and feature thicker walls at the base for stability. A circular opening at the domed dwelling's top allows air to circulate.

In general, Cameroon's architectural heritage has been influenced by the country's geographical and historical position of a crossroads of many civilizations and cultures, from the Bantu peoples to ancient kingdoms, such as the Sahel Kingdoms, to the colonial arm of Europe. Like most of West Africa, the country remains known for its vernacular architecture, as well as its traces of colonial architecture, which show a wide range in Cameroon, a country that has fallen under French, British, Dutch, and German control at various points. However, Cameroon's vernacular and colonial architectural heritage is in decline; urban areas have adopted uniformity in their architecture, and the transition to mud bricks has made the traditional huts of the Musgum obsolete.

Dance

More than 200 traditional dances have been recreated throughout Cameroon's history. Dances serve political, religious, and social situations, such as war, marriages, deaths, and the invoking of ancestors. Dance is also a culturally important part of Bikutsi music, which women perform as they sing about cultural and family issues. In indigenous religious dances, in order to communicate with the spirit world, dancers might dance until they are in a trance-like state. Additionally, western Semi-Bantu ethnic groups wear masks when they dance, giving the mask-wearer special power within the group. The Tipuri people dance in a circle carrying long sticks they hold upright.

Traditional dancers are typically restricted according to age, occupation, gender, and social status. Fons' wives and daughters are often not allowed to participate, and those who have higher social status do not usually dance with those who have lower social status. Though improvisation is used, dancers traditionally follow a choreographed sequence of moves that focus on moving certain regions of the body independently.

During the colonial era of the 19th and early 20th centuries, Cameroon's ethnic groups were mostly prevented and discouraged form performing traditional dances. Even after achieving independence in the early 1960s, a large number of traditional dances were no longer performed. However, many traditional dances have been revived and continue to hold social and cultural importance. Dance has also become an increasingly important method of social and political protest, and dancing in the street has been used as a way to air political views about political parties, including presidential candidates.

Music

Music in Cameroon was traditionally played on a number of instruments, all of which are still played in the early 21st century: the balafon, mvet, thumb piano, drums, and wooden flute. The balafon is similar to a wooden xylophone, but with between 15 and 19keys in the body of a hollow gourd. The Beti people of the Fang ethnic group were the pioneers of balafon music. To make this music, the musician uses a wooden hammer to strike the keys. A range of different balafons gives the instrument the capability to make unique sounds, such as that of a human voice.

The mvet is like a harp-zither, or a harp with two sides and special amplification. It is traditionally played when people of the Fang ethnic group tell their epic stories, which include mythology and real-world issues. Its strings were traditionally made out of strips from raffia palm branches but during the 20th-century, nylon replaced the natural fiber. The thumb piano is a carved wooden board on which varying lengths of wooden or metal keys are attached. The musician holds the board in his or her hands and plucks the keys with the thumbs. Women most often play the wooden flute, which they occasionally place in water beforehand to create a unique sound.

Musical traditions in Cameroon fall into the two essential kinds of music: makossa and bikutsi. Makossa (meaning "make me dance" in the Duala language) blends traditional Congo beats with jazz, swing, and soul. It became urban dance music in the city of Douala during the second half of the 20th century. Manu Dibango (1933–) helped introduce the music to the world with his best-selling album *Soul Makossa* (1972). Bikutsi (loosely translated as "beating the ground continuously") has intense rhythmic beats, which are accompanied by clapping and dancing. This native folk music gained widespread appeal in the capital of Yaoundé during the 1950s and 1960s, and developed from being traditionally based on war and fighting to include social issues as a prominent theme. Anne-Marie Nzié (1932–) was a major innovator of bikutsi, and popularized the music from the 1950s through the 1990s. She is known as the "golden voice of Cameroon" and the "queen mother of bikutsi." In the 1980s and 1990s, variations on makossa and bikutsi music took different musical forms in Cameroon and in Paris, France. Some forms combined both traditions, such as in the music of Henri Dikongué (1967–), who toured Europe and North America. Cameroonian-born Andy Allo (1989–) is a famous songwriter and rock star, now living in California.

Literature

The art of storytelling, which has its roots in tribal traditions, forms the basis of Cameroonian literature. This oral tradition has helped Cameroonians share their history throughout many generations, continuing their ethnic groups' social and cultural values. Primarily three types of tales, or fables, are most often told: tales about relationships between men and women, tales about the origin of things, and trickster tales. A trickster can be a human or an animal that uses wit to avoid danger. However, it wasn't until the 20th century that Cameroonians began to transcribe their oral history and stories and create new works of fiction.

Twentieth-century Cameroonian novels were written in either French or English, the two official languages. Not until after World War II did writers offer a critique of colonialism. Before that time, the best-known writers advocated the assimilation of Cameroonian culture into European culture. Ferdinand Oyono (1929–2010) criticized colonialism in *Une vie de boy* (Houseboy, 1966), a novel written in the form of a diary. Mongo Beti (1932–2001) criticized the newly independent government in Cameroon, causing his books to be banned in his home country and his exile to France. One of Cameroon's most famous writers was Francis Bebey (1929–2001). Bebey combined aspects of traditional and modern Cameroon culture, such as in *Le fils d'Agatha Moudio* (Agatha Moudio's Son, 1967). Calixthe Beyala (1961–) has written about women's struggles in traditional families, such as in *C'est le soleil qui m'a brûlée* (*It Is the Sun That Has Burnt Me*, 1987).

CULTURE

Arts & Entertainment

The contemporary arts in Cameroon use traditional themes and techniques to convey the country's history, and prominent themes include political independence and social issues. Film became a popular artistic medium shortly after independence in Cameroon. One of the first pioneers in Cameroon film was Thérèse Sita-Bella (1933–2006), who was also a pilot and the country's first female journalist. She was considered a feminist—and in that sense, a trailblazer in her traditional Beti tribe in southern Cameroon. Sita-Bella's film *Tam-Tam à Paris* (African Drums in Paris, 1963) documented the National Dance Company of Cameroon while on tour in Paris, where Sita-Bella studied. During the 1970s, Jean-Pierre Dikongué Pipa (1940–) wrote and directed films that focused on Cameroonian culture and society. His film *Muna Moto* (1975) concerned traditional Cameroonian culture and its many challenges in a changing world, including that of a post-colonial society. During the 21st century, Cameroonian cinema continues to develop and to truthfully express Cameroonian society. The film

Elaborately carved stools made for chiefs show the skill of Cameroon's woodcarvers.

Strange World (2008), by young filmmaker Balon Njilu, was made with what he called a collective work to bring together new talents to write and create a movie about a relationship between a man and his wives in Cameroonian society.

Woodcarving has been a significant traditional art in Cameroon for centuries. Traditional woodcarvings included scenes from religious ceremonies, family unity, and hunts. After colonial control, during which Christianity was imported into Cameroon, art became partly ornamental. In churches, biblical images were carved and painted into art objects and the actual building. Woodcarving remains important to 21st-century Cameroonian culture, especially in the western part of the country among the Bamiléké, the Bamoun, and the Tikar. It is often used to decorate functional items, such as house posts, stools, and doorframes. For example, fons (chiefs) use wooden stools carved with elaborate depictions of animal and human figures as seats of power, similar to a throne, and carved doorframes adorn the homes of important Bamiléké people. Themes of woodcarving are generally historical. For instance, wooden statues typically represent ancestral figures that are important in indigenous Cameroonian religions.

Dance in early 21st century Cameroon is either traditional, which includes traditional forms of Cameroonian music, such as makossa and bikutsi, or more urban, such as imported American hip-hop. Other imported forms of popular dance include the Nigerian ashiko and the abele. The ashiko is named after an African drum that is similar to the djembe, which has three primary tones. Nigerian highlife music, which originated in Ghana in the 19th century, is popular in dance clubs alongside popular dance music such as electronica.

Soccer is the most popular sport, as well as the most popular form of entertainment, in Cameroon by a wide margin. Cameroon's national professional team, les Lions Indomptables, has won several titles in the African Cup of Nations (1984, 1988, 2000, and 2002,) and is highly revered by African soccer fans. Other popular sports include boxing and volleyball.

Cultural Sites & Landmarks

The city of Limbe, on Cameroon's northwestern shore, is renowned for its climatic diversity. In fact, the city is represented by all of the African continent's major climate zones: mountains, coast, rainforest, and savanna. It is situated along the slopes of Mount Cameroon, an active volcano that painted the nearby black sand beaches. The region is also home to the Limbe Wildlife Center, which traces its origins as a horticultural site established in 1892. The center educates visitors about animal preservation and environmental conservation by showing how indigenous animals exist in the ecosystem. The wildlife center became a zoo in 1963, and the changing purposes of the gardens resemble larger cultural concerns and issues in Cameroon, such as the conservation of the environment.

The grasslands in Cameroon, called savanna, can be experienced in the northern region of the country. Waza National Park, in the Far North Region, became a biosphere reserve under the United Nations Educational, Scientific and Cultural Organization (UNESCO) in 1979. (A biosphere reserve promotes sustainable relationships among all the living systems contained in the area, including all that are on land, in the air, and in the water, including humans.) Along with native species such as lions, elephants, and giraffes, 379 species of birds are represented at the national park. Cameroon is also home to one World Heritage Site as recognized by UNESCO, the Dja Faunal Reserve. The reserve was recognized for its undisturbed rainforests and biodiversity, including a variety of primates. The largest protected Cameroon rainforest is in the Lake Lobeke Forest Reserve, which borders the Republic of Congo. Chimpanzees, monkeys, elephants, and buffalo, among other native animals, roam freely in this protected area. The reserve came under the protection of the World Wildlife Fund to protect certain animals from being overhunted. Local Cameroonians have depended on bush meat for generations, but dwindling numbers of animals have led to increased efforts to prevent the threat of extinction.

In addition to the many natural sites in Cameroon, remnants of previous ruling kingdoms and religious powers dot the landscape. The Foumban Royal Palace, built in 1917 by Bamoun king Ibrahim Njoya (1890–1923) was constructed in a style similar to a medieval chateau. The palace is a museum that showcases clothing from numerous royal families, musical instruments, carvings, and jewelry. In Yaoundé, the capital, a Benedictine monastery is now the Museum of Cameroonian Art. This museum, along with the National Museum and the Afhemi Museum, displays traditional Cameroonian arts and crafts. In December 2007, the National Museum of Yaoundé opened an exhibit that highlighted the efforts of 1,000 women from around the world who have contributed to developing peace, called "1000 Peace Women across the Globe."

Libraries & Museums

Yaoundé is home to several of the country's notable museums, including the Museum of Cameroon Art and le Musée National de Cameroon (Cameroon National Museum), both of which house works by Cameroonian artists, artifacts, and exhibits relating to the history of Cameroon. The Musée des Bénédictins is located within a Benedictine monastery. The Museum of Black Art and the Afhemi Museum are also popular attractions.

The National Library of Cameroon, established in 1966, and the National Archives are located in the capital. Other prominent libraries include the Library of the University of Buea, the Library of the Martin Luther King Memorial Foundation in Limbe, and the Library of the National Assembly of Cameroon in Yaoundé.

Holidays

Two national holidays are observed in Cameroon. Youth Day, which is a celebration of Cameroon's children, occurs on February 11. On this day, young Cameroonians march in a parade through the streets while wearing their school uniforms. National Day is observed on May 20, and is a celebration of the day in 1972 when Cameroon became an independent republic. Many Cameroonians also celebrate Christian or Muslim holidays as well.

Youth Culture

Sports are an important activity for Cameroonian youth, and include football (soccer), volleyball, boxing, and traditional sports such as canoeing and wrestling. Sports advocacy is an important part of national policy in Cameroon and youth sports are regulated by the sports ministry. In fact, Cameroon is one of only a handful of tropical nations to have participated in the Winter Olympics. The Cameroon national football team is also Africa's most successful national team, having qualified for the World Cup five times.

Cameroonian youth continue to face challenges in the early 21st century, most notably chronic unemployment, educational reform and inadequate career guidance, the spread of HIV/AIDS, and poverty (many youth are unable to afford schooling). In his address to the nation on February 10, 2009—the day prior to National Youth Day in Cameroon—President Paul Biya outlined the nation's commitment to empowering its youth. This included the implementation of a national action plan for youth employment, the opening of 16 private higher education institutions in 2008 (raising that number to 73), and the recruitment of over 5,000 teachers, also in 2008 (raising that number to over 25,000 nationwide).

SOCIETY

Transportation

Buses are the main mode of public transportation in Cameroon, and handle most transportation between cities. In urban areas, taxis are common, with bush taxis a common form of public transportation in rural areas. Traffic moves on the right-hand side of the road.

Transportation Infrastructure

Camrail, the country's rail network, operates three main lines and connects the southern and northern halves of Cameroon. Three road networks of the Trans-African Highway network also cross in Cameroon. Outside of these routes, the most developed roads have historically been along coastal regions. The national carrier, Cameroon Airlines, connects major cities domestically, as well as throughout West and Central Africa.

Media & Communications

The media industry in Cameroon is limited and tightly controlled by the state. Newspapers operate under certain government restrictions, including libel legislation, and self censorship is commonplace. The state, under the Cameroon Radio Television (CRTV), runs the national radio and television. There are also numerous private radio and television stations, and radio programming from the British Broadcasting Corporation (BBC) can be picked up. Overall, radio reaches nearly 80 percent of the Cameroon.

Telecommunications were largely liberalized at the turn of the 21st century. As of 2014, there were about 1.5 million Internet users in Cameroon, representing about 6.5 percent of the population. The inadequate land-based telephone system serves only 1.05 million people, but the rapid addition of cell phone users has increased great to about 17.3 million users in 2014.

SOCIAL DEVELOPMENT

Standard of Living

Cameroon ranked 152nd out of 187 countries on the 2013 United Nations Human Development Index, which measures quality of life and standard of living indicators.

Water Consumption

According to 2012 statistics released by the World Health Organization, approximately 74 percent of the Cameroonian population has access to improved drinking water, while an estimated 45 percent has access to improved sanitation, with the percentages of access much lower in rural areas. Further, it is estimated that nearly 20 percent of the rural population resides

30 minutes or more from a safe or clean supply of drinking water. Surface water pollution and waste mismanagement continue to be pressing issues in the country, particularly as the country experiences rapid urbanization.

Education

Cameroon has one of the highest rates of school attendance in Africa. Primary education is required of all children between six and 12 years of age. However, only about 28 percent of Cameroon's students continue their education beyond the primary level. Most families either consider secondary education to be unimportant, or they cannot afford to pay the tuition. Poverty, lack of professional qualifications among teachers, and poor quality of teaching remain hindrances in improving Cameroon's educational system.

Although only three percent of Cameroonian men and one percent of Cameroonian women attend college, there are several universities throughout the country. These include the University of Yaoundé, the University of Douala, and the University of Ngaoundéré. The average literacy rate among Cameroonian adults is 75 percent.

According to the 2013 Gender Inequality Index, which is published by the United Nations and measures gender equity in regard to economic, political, and educational opportunities, Cameroon ranked 152nd out of the 187 countries studied. In the specific area of educational attainment, Cameroon showed a large gap between men and women with secondary educational experience.

Women's Rights:

According to the Cameroonian constitution, which incorporated aspects of the UDHR and the African Charter of Human and People's Rights, women are guaranteed equal status before the law. In recent years, women have held high political offices in Cameroon—25 women have been appointed minister since 1970—and women continue to increase their representation in the national workforce. However, widespread unequal treatment of Cameroonian women and girls is commonplace and women have been persecuted by the state. Violence against women is also widespread, including domestically and at the hands of authorities. Women continue to be victim to arbitrary arrests and torture while in prison, and have been placed alongside men during their imprisonment.

According to the Committee on the Elimination of Discrimination against Women (CEDAW), monitoring the maltreatment, discrimination, and violence against women in Cameroon increased because efforts by the government to prevent the abuses were inadequate. As such, CEDAW has emphasized stronger punishment for these crimes. However, the Cameroonian government has pledged to increase its effort to reduce gender-based violence and discrimination, including that which occurs within the family. Yet, there is no specific law prohibiting domestic violence. Similarly, according to the World Health Organization (UNICEF), female genital mutilation (FGM) continues to affect about one percent of the female population and no specific legislation prohibits the traditional practice.

Women suffered the most discrimination in employment and in inheritance. Traditionally, only males can inherit property. When the husband dies, the widow typically is considered part of the deceased husband's property, and therefore his inheritance. Under the country's national system of laws, women can appeal such decisions through the court system. They can also seek help from the National Commission on Human Rights and Freedoms (CNDHL). Because of the frequent confusion between a traditional social structure, such as the lack of women's right to inherit, and constitutional rights, women are often uncertain which system to follow and often have no knowledge about available legal services.

Other cases of discrimination include polygamy (practice of multiple wives) and arranged marriages, both of which are permitted by law. Young girls are often forced into these marriage arrangements beginning at age 12. They are also forced to bear children at a young age, which poses a significant health risk for both mother and child. In addition, forced marriages and early pregnancy also force many young girls to drop out of school, adding to the already serious problem with illiteracy in Cameroon. In fact, of the estimated six million Cameroonians who are considered illiterate, roughly 63 percent are women.

Health Care

Cameroon's health care system relies heavily on foreign aid. The United States provides approximately $5 million (USD) annually to bolster Cameroon's education and health care programs. The health care system, like the school system, is regulated and organized by Christian churches.

Cameroon does not have a system to provide individual health care plans, and most citizens do not receive adequate medical attention. Life-threatening diseases such as malaria and HIV/AIDS are usually left untreated among most of the population. Life expectancy is relatively low, at 59 years for women and 57 years for men (2015 estimate).

GOVERNMENT

Structure

The Republic of Cameroon was formed in 1961, from the merger of British Cameroon and French Cameroon. The League of Nations had given control of Cameroon to Britain and France after World War I. Prior to that time, the region had been under German colonial control.

Today, Cameroon is a democratic republic with a president, prime minister, and a unicameral legislature. The president is elected to serve a seven-year term, and holds the most power in the central government. Presidential responsibilities include appointing the prime minister. The National Assembly is made up of 180 members. Twenty is the age of suffrage in Cameroon.

Political Parties

Several political parties exist, but the Cameroon People's Democratic Movement (CPDM) is the party with the most representation in the government. Other major parties include the Cameroon People's Party (CPP,) the Cameroonian Democratic Union (UDC,) and Movement of the Defense of the Republic (MDR.) In addition, as a multi-party system, minor parties abound in Cameroon.

Local Government

The nation is divided into 10 political provinces (called regions as of 2015), each headed by a governor. These administrative divisions are then subdivided into departments or divisions, and then arrondissements (sub-divisions) and districts. Local governance at the lower levels is handled by local government councils. The country is working to increase autonomy among local governments and to reduce central and provincial governmental influence or interference.

Judicial System

Cameroon's judiciary system is a mixture of the French civil law and English common law systems, and includes a Supreme Court, Court of Appeals (one based in each province, or region), and courts of first instance.

Taxation

Cameroon's tax rates are high, as the country has a top corporate tax rate of 38.5 percent and a top income rate of 35 percent. Other taxes levied include a property tax, value-added tax (VAT, similar to a consumption tax), and inheritance tax. The Cameroon tax system experienced significant reforms in 2008.

Armed Forces

The military of Cameroon consists of air, ground, and naval forces, and is considered a medium-sized force for the region. As of 2015, the military is estimated at about 14,000 active members. There is no conscription, and 18 years is the minimum age for voluntary military service. Cameroon celebrated the 50th anniversary of its armed forces in 2010.

Foreign Policy

Cameroon's foreign policy is generally perceived as one of noninterference. It joined the United Nations (UN) in 1960, the year of its independence, and its role in the UN has been one of supporting specific international peacekeeping efforts, environmental protections, and economic development in underdeveloped countries. The country has also supported UN peacekeeping efforts in Central Africa and has intentionally avoided criticizing human rights abuses in other countries. Regionally, Cameroon holds membership in the African Union (AU), the Islamic Development Bank (IDB), and the Economic and Monetary Community of Central Africa (CEMAC), among others.

Cameroon has maintained close ties with France, Britain, Canada, and the United States since its independence. Britain admitted Cameroon into the Commonwealth in 1995. France, Cameroon's former colonizer, is the country's primary means of defensive support. (China also supplies military assistance to Cameroon.) France and Cameroon also share economic and cultural agreements that have helped stabilize the country since independence. Cameroon has maintained a close bilateral relationship with Canada, as the two countries have a shared English and French heritage. However, in early 2009, the Canadian International Development Agency (CIDA) removed Cameroon as a developmental partner.

The U.S. has supported Cameroon's development through aid programs such as the bilateral U.S. Agency for International Development (USAID) and by providing Peace Corps workers to assist with education, health, community development, and agroforestry programs. The U.S. provides about $5 million (USD) in aid to Cameroon a year. Cameroon also signed an Economic Partnership agreement (EPA) with the European Union (EU) in January 2009, the first such trade agreement between the EU and a Central African nation.

The International Court of Justice (ICJ) resolved the border dispute with Nigeria during the 1980s and 1990s over the Bakassi Peninsula and its vast oil reserves. In 2002, the court ruled that the territory in the Lake Chad region is under the sovereignty of Cameroon. Under the guidance of the UN, Cameroon and Nigeria are peacefully resolving the transfer of territory, and several thousand Nigerians who had been living in the territory began moving back to Nigeria. Another area rich in oil reserves is near coastal Cameroon, where the country's territory borders Equatorial Guinea and Nigeria. Equatorial Guinea appealed to the ICJ for boundary protection to avoid a dispute with neighboring countries over the oil.

Human Rights Profile

International human rights law insists that states respect civil and political rights, and promote an individual's economic, social, and cultural rights. The United Nations Universal Declaration on Human Rights (UDHR) is recognized as the standard for international human rights. Its authors sought the counsel of the world's great thinkers, philosophers, and religious leaders, and were careful to create a document that reflected the core values shared by every world culture. (To read this document or view the articles relating to cultural human rights, visit http://www.udhr.org/UDHR/default.htm.)

Cameroon has a poor human rights record. Abuses and violations of the Cameroonian constitution's articles are widespread, including particular articles in the UDHR. Additionally, even though voters in the country are guaranteed the right to elect the president, widespread cases of voter fraud have been reported in past elections for President Paul Biya (1933–), who first assumed office in 1982. In 2008, Cameroon's parliament passed legislation amending term limits that essentially made President Biya's reelection in 2011 a formality. That same legislation also protected Biya from prosecution after his presidency.

The human rights organization, Amnesty International (AI), has documented numerous human rights abuses in Cameroon over the first decade of the 21st century. The government has reportedly prevented opposition movements from meeting in public or in private. In fact, in numerous cases, security forces have used violence, arrested opposition members arbitrarily, and unlawfully detained them without trial. The government has even persecuted human rights defenders in Cameroon by arresting and detaining them without trial as recently as 2008.

According to AI, the government has violently oppressed opposition and criticism, including a violent reprisal against demonstrators of a price hike during February 2008, and against a constitutional amendment to eradicate presidential term limits. Corruption is also a problem throughout the Cameroonian government, and the judiciary reportedly makes corrupt decisions under political influence. In 2004, a member of parliament and the ruling political party was reported to have killed the leader of an opposition movement. However, after protests against the killer's impunity, the government tried and convicted the accused killer and 11 accomplices, two of whom were acquitted and released.

The Cameroonian government repeatedly intimidates the press and harasses journalists, silencing any dissent. It has arrested and detained journalists, prevented the printing of newspapers, and closed television stations. The government has shut down radio stations, including one operated by the Roman Catholic Church. During opposition protests, security forces have been accused of abusing journalists and television reporters. The Cameroonian government is charged with systematically using torture—in some cases fatal—and failing to punish those who administer it. Prisons have been targeted by international monitoring agencies for their lack of medical care, adequate food, and sanitary facilities. Lastly, the government has committed numerous abuses including arbitrary arrests and detentions of people believed to have engaged in same-sex relationships; government officials show extreme prejudice against such relations and punish those accused harshly.

ECONOMY

Overview of the Economy

In the 1980s, Cameroon's natural resources and valuable cash crops made it the wealthiest nation in Africa. This led to technological advancements and the growth of the service sector. Eventually, the value of the crops declined, and Cameroon found itself in debt to foreign nations from which it had received loans. Despite efforts to rebuild the economy, the per capita gross domestic product (GDP) remains low, at $1,202.5 (USD) (2012 estimate).

Industry

Cameroon's small industrial sector is made up of manufacturing and processing activities. Manufactured goods include agricultural equipment and materials, oil equipment and materials, aluminum products, beer, cigarettes, shoes, soap, and soft drinks.

The service sector of Cameroon's industry includes transportation, trade, banking, and tourism. The service industry has been greatly affected by Cameroon's economic downturn, as the government cannot afford to repair damaged roads and railroads.

Yaoundé is Cameroon's manufacturing hub. The city's factories produce tobacco, bricks, lumber, soap, and vegetable oil. Primary exports are oil, timber, cocoa, coffee, and coffee. Imports include manufactured goods and fuel. Cameroon's major trading partners are France and other nations in the European Union, and China.

The other major industry in Yaoundé involves the processing and export of oil and natural gas. Cameroon exports its fossil fuels to many of its trading partners and uses hydroelectricity to meet its own power needs.

Labor

In 2014, Cameroon had an estimated labor force of 9.105 million. The agricultural sector employed over two thirds of the national work force in a 2001 estimate, while industry and the services sector accounted for 13 and 17 percent of the labor force, respectively. Unemployment is widespread. In a 2012 estimate, although the unemployment rate was only 3.8 percent, underemployment stood at 70 percent.

Energy/Power/Natural Resources

Oil and trees are the most valuable natural resources in Cameroon. Offshore drilling for oil has been a vital part of the economy for decades, but the country's petroleum deposits are nearly depleted. Pipelines from Chad have been built to help insure the future economic viability of Cameroon's oil industry.

Cameroon's trees have also been over-exploited. The southern rainforests in Cameroon contain over 300 species of trees with commercial value. Although these trees are essential to Cameroon's economy, the effects of logging have been devastating to the rainforest ecosystem, driving many of Cameroon's native animal species to endangered status. Efforts are being made to control the exploitation of the rainforests, which also provide rubber and palm oils for export. Other natural resources include natural gas, iron ore, bauxite, limestone, and hydroelectric power.

Fishing

Fishing is one of the major industries in Cameroon, reeling in over 140,000 tons of seafood annually. The top species that were exported by Cameroon fisheries include mackerel, shrimp and prawn, cod, and sardines. Artisanal fishing remains widespread, and relies on the smoking or drying of fish before distributed for local consumption. Over-fishing posits an environmental issue that may come to harm Cameroon's future fishing industry.

Forestry

As of 2015, Cameroon is home to 19.82 million hectares (48.99 million acres) of forested land. After an estimated 60 percent of Cameroon's forests had been logged in the 1980s, the country instituted tighter regulations in the following decade. However, logging, particularly illegal logging, and its resulting environmental degradation remain troubling concerns in Cameroon in the early 21st century. The forestry industry also represents approximately 25 percent of Cameroon's tax revenue, and the country remains the largest African exporter of timber products to the European Union. Timber is also harvested as fuel wood.

Mining/Metals

Significant mineral resources in Cameroon include bauxite, iron ore, nickel, and uranium.

However, the country lacks the infrastructure to exploit these resources. The petroleum sector remains the country's most significant mineral industry and resource. Cameroon also exports cement and sand.

Agriculture

In terms of labor, agriculture is Cameroon's largest economic sector. Over 50 percent of Cameroon's workforce is employed in farming, fishing, and forestry. Some of Cameroon's most valuable cash crops are cocoa, coffee, cotton, and sugar cane. Other important crops include beans, corn, yams, tea, cassava, millet, and groundnuts.

Animal Husbandry

Cameroon's primary livestock consist of cattle, sheep, and goats, with pigs and poultry raised to a lesser extent. Cattle are raised largely in the Adamawa Plateau region; in the Northwest Region, Fulani herders oversee more than 400,000 head of cattle.

Tourism

Cameroon's tourism industry is growing. There are a number of popular tourist attractions, both urban and rural. Beach resort towns such as Limbe and Kribi are often full of visitors, and major cities such as Yaoundé provide a wealth of restaurants, museums, and other modern tourist attractions.

One of the most popular tourist sites is Waza National Park, which features many native African animals, such as lions, giraffes, elephants, and zebras. At the Limbe Wildlife Centre, visitors can view many endangered species.

The Northwest Region is the center of Cameroon's rural tourist trade. It is comprised of many tribal villages, chiefdoms, and kingdoms. Ring Road, a 367–kilometer (228–mile) path that winds around Mount Oku, is a major tourist attraction in this area.

Kathryn Bundy, Richard Means, Amanda Wilding

DO YOU KNOW?

- In 1986, Lake Nyos released a large amount of toxic carbon dioxide, killing 1,700 people.
- Cameroon's name comes from Portuguese explorers who traveled up the Wouri River in 1472, and called it "Rio dos Camarões" (River of Prawns).
- The city of Ngaoundéré is named for its nearby mountain, which resembles a large belly button. The word Ngaoundéré means "navel."

Bibliography

Austen, Ralph. A. Jonathan Derrick, and Jonathan M. Derrick. "Middlemen of the Cameroon Rivers: The Duala and their Hinterland c. 1600– c. 1960." New York: *Cambridge University Press*, 1999.

Fowler, Ian and Verkijika Fanso, eds. "Encounter, Transformation, and Identity: Peoples of the Western Cameroon Borderlands, 1891–2000." New York: *Berghahn Books*, 2009.

Ignatowski, Clare A. "Journey of Song: Public Life and Morality in Cameroon." Bloomington, IN: *Indiana University Press*, 2006.

Mbaku Mukum, John. "Culture and Customs of Cameroon." Westport, CT: *Greenwood Press*, 2005.

Osseo-Asare, Fran. "Food Culture in Sub-Saharan Africa." Westport, CT: *Greenwood Press*, 2005.

Paden, John N. "Religion and Political Culture in Kano." New York: *ACLS Humanities E-Book*, 2008.

Regis, Helen and Helen A. Regis. "Fulbe Voices: Marriage, Islam, and Medicine in Northern Cameroon." Boulder, CO: Westview Press, 2002.

Tradition Njoh, Ambe J. "Culture and Development in Africa: Historical Lessons for Modern Development Planning." Surrey, UK: *Ashgate Publishing*, 2006.

Works Cited

"Background Note: Cameroon." *U.S. Department of State.* http://www.state.gov/r/pa/ei/bgn/26431.htm.

"Cameroon." https://www.cia.gov/library/publications/the-world-factbook/geos/cm.html. Central Intelligence Agency, *The World Factbook.*

"Cameroon: Language, Culture, Customs and Etiquette." http://www.kwintessential.co.uk/resources/global-etiquette/cameroon.html.

"Cameroon at the Crossroads." http://www.foreignaffairs.com/about-us/sponsors/cameroon-at-the-crossroads. *Foreign Affairs,* July/August 2008.

"Customs of Cameroon." *MSN Encarta.* http://encarta.msn.com/sidebar_631522180/customs_of_cameroon.html.

"Cameroon." http://www.geonames.org/advanced-search.html?q=&country=CM&featureClass=P&continentCode=. Geonames.

"Female Genital Mutilation/Cutting: A statistical overview and exploration of the dynamics of change." http://www.unicef.org/cbsc/files/UNICEF_FGM_report_July_2013_Hi_res.pdf/. UNICEF. (Accessed September 30, 2015).

"Human Development Reports: Cameroon." http://hdr.undp.org/en/countries/profiles/CMR. United Nations Human Development Programme. (Accessed September 30, 2015).

"Responses to the list of issues and questions with regard to the consideration of the combined second and third periodic reports: Cameroon." Pre-session working group, Forty-second session, 20 October–7 November 2008. *Committee on the Elimination of Discrimination against Women (CEDAW).* http://www.unhcr.org/refworld/publisher,CEDAW,STATEPARTIESREP,CMR,4948d5832,0.html.

"The Astonishing World of Musical Instruments." http://www.museevirtuel.ca/Exhibitions/Musique/html.html. Muséc Virtuel, Canada.

"UN Data: Cameroon." http://data.un.org/CountryProfile.aspx?crName=Cameroon. *The United Nations.* (Accessed September 30, 2015).

"West African Fisheries Profiles: Cameroon." http://www.imcsnet.org/imcs/docs/cameroon_fishery_profile_apr08.pdf. *US Aid for West Africa.* (Accessed September 30, 2015).

Ignatowski, Clare A. "Journey of Song: Public Life and Morality in Cameroon." Bloomington, Indiana: *Indiana University Press*, 2006.

Kummer, Patricia A. "Cameroon (Enchantment of the World Second Series)." New York, New York: *Children's Press*, 2004.

Mukum Mbaku, John. "Culture and Customs of Cameroon." Westport, Connecticut: *Greenwood Press*, 2005.

Osseo-Asare, Fran. "Food Culture in Sub-Saharan Africa." Westport, Connecticut: *Greenwood Press*, 2005.

Boats are an important aspect of life in the island nation of Cape Verde. iStock/corolanty.

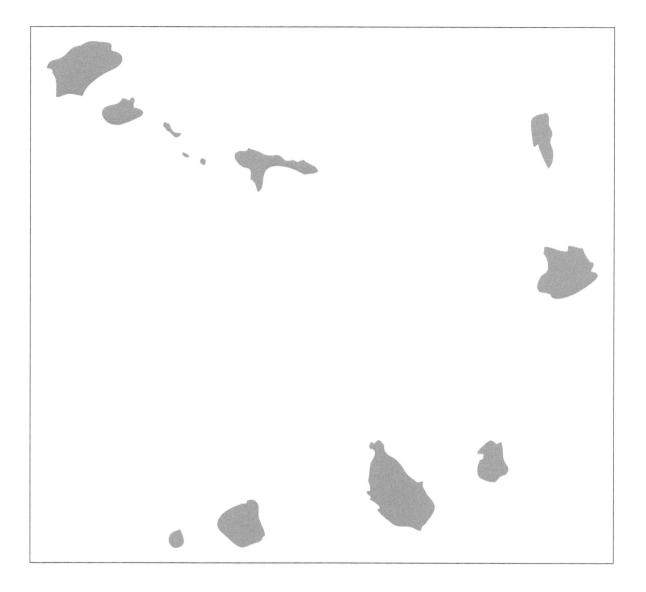

CAPE VERDE

Introduction

The Republic of Cape Verde, or Cabo Verde in Portuguese, is a small island state in the middle of the Atlantic Ocean, off the west coast of Africa. Santiago, or São Tiago, is the largest of the 10 volcanic islands and five islets that comprise the Cape Verde archipelago. The country was once a Portuguese slave-trading colony, but is now a stable democracy that maintains friendly, open relations with the rest of the world. Cape Verde has particularly maintained a cordial relationship with the United States since the early 18th century, when Cape Verdeans joined American whaling crews.

Cape Verde is at the crossroads of shipping lanes in the Atlantic and improvements made to its harbor infrastructure and the country's international airport have allowed Cape Verde to take advantage of its strategic position in recent decades. However, poor land and lack of water have hampered efforts to boost the economy of this archipelago of volcanic islands. As such, the expatriate population is larger than that of the islands themselves. Even with such large numbers of emigrants, Cape Verde is one of the most stable democracies in Africa.

The culture of Cape Verde is rich in music, literature, food, and crafts, with roots in the islands' slave trading past. The country has a long and multi-faceted musical tradition, and music accompanies almost every celebration, private or public. Traditional arts include basket and tapestry weaving, and coconut-shell crafts for decorative and utilitarian use.

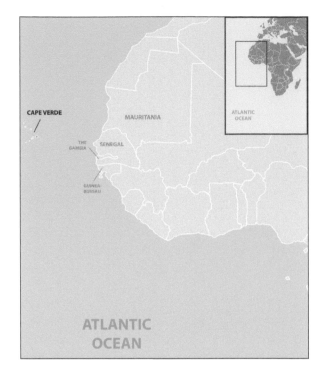

GENERAL INFORMATION

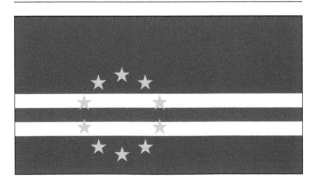

Official Language: Portuguese
Population: 545,993 (2015 estimate)
Currency: Cape Verdean escudo
Coins: Coins are available in denominations of 1, 5, 10, 20, 50, 100, and 200 escudos.
Land Area: 4,033 square kilometers (1,557 square miles)
National Motto: Unidade, Luta, Progresso (Portuguese "Unity, Work, Progress")
National Anthem: "Cântico de Liberdade" ("Song of Liberty")
Capital: Praia
Time Zone: GMT -1
Flag Description: The flag of Cape Verde is blue and features three horizontal bars in the flag's lower section: two white and one red. The white represents peace and the red represents the road to development. An off-center circle of 10 gold stars represents the country's 10 main islands.

Population

A little larger than the state of Rhode Island, Cape Verde has only two primary cities: the capital, Praia, on the island of Santiago, with approximately 148,000 inhabitants (though, unofficially, that number has been reported closer to 200,000),

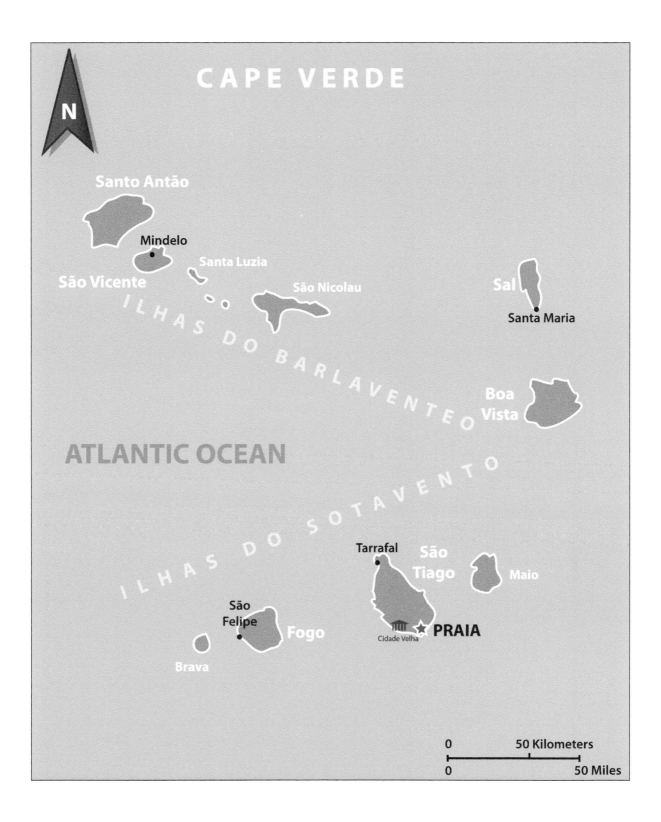

Principal Cities by Population (2014):

- Praia (147, 610)
- Mindelo (80,140)
- Santa Maria (32,210)
- Assomada (44,750)
- Pedra Badejo (26,440)
- Porto Novo (17,560)
- São Filipe (21,380)
- Tarrafal (18,370)
- Ribeira Grande (17,380)
- Calheta de São Miguel (14,870)

and Mindelo, on São Vicente, with a population of 80,140.

Approximately half of the population lives on the island of Santiago, followed by São Vicente (an estimated 80,140), Santo Antão (an estimated 41,190), and Fogo (an estimated 36,000). The remaining islands have population bases that range between 5,000 and 30,000.

The major ethnic groups are Creole (African and Portuguese mix- 71%), African (28%), and European (1%). Cape Verdeans commonly immigrate to the United States, Senegal, and Europe.

Languages
While the official language is Portuguese, many of the people speak Crioulo, a creole dialect based on old Portuguese that includes elements of African and other European languages.

Native People & Ethnic Groups
Cape Verde has no native peoples. The islands were uninhabited when the Portuguese arrived in 1456 and began importing people from West Africa to work as slaves on plantations. Cape Verde won its independence in 1975, after a bloody war of liberation. Today, the population is largely mixed, and Cape Verde has friendly relations with Portugal.

Religions
About 77 percent of Cape Verdeans are Roman Catholics, which is often combined with elements of indigenous beliefs. There are also small groups of Muslim and Baha'is. Although the constitution does not recognize any state religion, the Catholic Church does enjoy a privileged status. The church receives free television time, and several Catholic religious days are observed as national holidays.

Climate
The climate of Cape Verde is overwhelmingly dry. The archipelago receives little rainfall, and has only a small amount of fresh water. Severe droughts brought by the northeast trade winds are common and often result in food shortages. Droughts in Cape Verde sometimes last for years.

Average annual precipitation in Praia is 24 centimeters (9.5 inches). Most rain occurs from the end of July to early November. These rains are brought by the southwest monsoon season. The sun shines most of the year, although storms from the Sahara sometimes bring clouds in winter.

As it lies a little north of the equator, Cape Verde is warm, with little variation in temperature. The average temperature during February is 22° Celsius (72° Fahrenheit); the average September temperature is 27° Celsius (81° Fahrenheit).

ENVIRONMENT & GEOGRAPHY

Topography
The Cape Verde archipelago consists of 10 islands and five islets in the Atlantic Ocean, 500 kilometers (300 miles) off the west coast of Dakar, Senegal. The islands are arranged in two groups: the barlavento (or windward islands), and the sotavento (or leeward islands). The main windward islands are Santo Antão, São Vicente, Santa Luzia, São Nicolau, Sal, and Boa Vista. The major leeward islands include Maio, Santiago, Fogo, and Brava. Santa Luzia is the only large island that is uninhabited.

The highest point in Cape Verde, Pico de Cano (2,829 meters/9,281 feet), the only remaining active volcano in the archipelago, is on Fogo Island. There are no major rivers or lakes on the islands, and very little fresh water of any kind.

The islands, formed by volcanoes, are rugged and inhospitable to agriculture. They are comprised mainly of basalt and phonolite (volcanic rock). The islands nearest the mainland (Sal, Boa Vista, and Maio) are level and dry, and covered with sand dunes. Santiago, Fogo, Santo Antao, and São Nicolau, on the other hand, are mountainous, with sheer, rugged cliffs. Blowing sand has carved many rocks into unique formations.

Plants & Animals

Most of Cape Verde's native vegetation has been destroyed by improper land use. While some protected valleys still support lush growth, most surviving plants are those that have adapted to dry conditions, such as thorn bushes and aloe. As part of reforestation efforts, eucalyptus and acacia trees have been planted in areas where forests once stood.

Only a small number of wild animal species live on the islands. These include rodents, lizards, and wild goats.

CUSTOMS & COURTESIES

Greetings

Cape Verde's official language is Portuguese. Unique colloquial creoles, which are essentially Portuguese with influences from several West African languages, are commonly spoken on each of the nine inhabited islands. Greetings can be lengthy and may involve a brief discussion of health and family. The customary greeting is "Modi ki bu sta?" ("How are you?"). When conducting business with strangers, the Portuguese "Como estas?" ("How are you?") is typically used. There can be a great amount of physical contact in Cape Verdean conversations. Men may commonly hold hands, shake hands, and embrace, and women will often kiss on each cheek. Parents or elders are generally acknowledged with a kiss to one cheek.

Older people are respectfully addressed with an honorific title before their name, such as "Senhor" ("Mr.") or "Senhora" ("Mrs."). Parents and relatives are addressed by familial titles like "Pai" (creole for "Father") or "Papa" (Portuguese for "Father"), "Mae" (creole for "Mother") or "Mama" (Portuguese for "Mother").

Gestures & Etiquette

Cape Verdeans often stand close to each other while conversing and hand gestures and other forms of body language are often made to give signals or add emphasis to words and emotions. A wag of one's finger in front of another's face from left to right is not considered rude, but a common way to answer "no" to basic questions. Putting one's hands on top of one's head carries connotations of mourning. In addition, Cape Verdeans can be frank with their opinions and will often make uncensored remarks regarding another's appearance, style, or possessions.

The slow, tranquil pace of island life results in a general relaxed attitude toward time and punctuality. Meetings, appointments, or parties can start hours after the planned time, and it is customary for small talk about family or health to precede business discussions. Often, this small talk may take precedence over tangible transactions.

Eating/Meals

Breakfast usually consists of light fare, such as breads taken with milk or coffee. Lunch is traditionally the principal meal of the day. For wealthy Cape Verdeans, a late afternoon tea is served with cookies and cakes. However, a light snack such as a sandwich or cereal in the evening is more common.

Locally grown corn and rice are the staple foods in the Cape Verde diet. Corn is typically served with beans, pork, manioc (cassava), or sweet potatoes, while rice is often paired with locally caught fish and beans. Fruits such as mangoes, bananas, papayas, guavas, zimbrão, tambarindo, marmelos, azedinhas, tamaras, and coconuts may also be consumed. As in the West African tradition, these fruits may also be added to main dishes for richness and flavor.

Cape Verde towns will often host music and dance celebrations to honor Catholic saints—an estimated 77 percent of the population is Roman

Catholic—and food is an important aspect of these events. Cape Verdean women will spend days pounding corn, scaling fish, cleaning and cutting vegetables, and tenderizing meats in order to prepare for these special religious festivals.

Visiting

In rural areas of the island, the laid-back lifestyle allows ample time for frequent, informal visits to friends and relatives. For family affairs, cachupa, a slow-cooked stew (often considered the national dish) is often prepared and set out in a large pot for guests to snack on while they sit and chat. If cachupa is not available, Cape Verdean hosts will always offer something to drink along with some cookies, bread, or cake. In urban areas, many gather at the praça or town square in the early evening to meet with friends, share a bite to eat, and catch up on the day's events. These types of gatherings are often spontaneous, but can last until late into the night.

People in Cape Verde do things at a relaxed pace and are often late, sometimes by an hour or more. In particular, this is true for parties; a host will not be offended if guests do not arrive on time. A direct "no" to an invitation however implies that the invitation was not appreciated. When invited to an event, guests should always give a "yes" or "maybe," even if there are no intentions of following through.

LIFESTYLE

Family

Cape Verdeans tend to have large families, with several generations of relatives living together in the same house. Households are customarily patriarchal, though emigration and the practice of polygamy (multiple wives) have resulted in matriarchal households headed by single mothers. Women also work full time outside of the home and are also responsible for domestic tasks and child-rearing.

Communal childrearing and adoption is common among kin. Adolescents often work in the family's trade and, in addition to their studies, are expected to do a good deal of housework. Adult children, even those who are professionals, often live in their parents' house until they get married. The elderly are shown a great deal of obedience and respect and adult children often choose to take in elderly parents to care for them. Overall, the success of a family unit is considered more important than that of an individual. Accomplished Cape Verdeans feel it is their responsibility to help the less fortunate in their family and will often provide housing, salary paying jobs, loans, or assistance in emigration.

Housing

Modern architecture in Cape Verde is often integrated with colonial structures remaining from Portugal's possession of the island chain. Low- and middle-class country homes are typically stone structures with thatched or tiled roofs, while the wealthy generally live in colonial-style homes built from materials imported from Portugal and Africa.

Recently, there has been an exodus of residents from Cape Verde's inhabited islands, as people have moved into the capital of Praia seeking employment. Thousands of migrants build illegal houses each year that are constructed "junta mao" (creole for "hand to hand") and communally, often using dirt, plastic, and wood scraps. These homes generally have no access to legal electricity, proper roads, or sanitation and are threatened by erosion, disease, flooding, and crime.

Accordingly, the government has put into practice a national housing survey, land regulation reforms, and environmental protection laws in urban areas. New cinderblock structures, similar to American inner-city housing projects, have emerged to house the rapidly increasing population. The Ponta d'Agua project was the first urban community to develop as part of this initiative. The project aims not only to provide residents with legal housing, but also to help the communities obtain better water supply and social facilities.

Food

Cape Verde's cuisine has been influenced by the culinary traditions of its colonial past, as well as its dry, tropical environment. Enslaved Africans brought agricultural knowledge about tropical foods, while the Portuguese brought livestock, sugar, bananas, mangoes, papayas, and spices from Asia. Corn, a staple in the Cape Verdean diet, was first introduced to the islands by Portuguese colonists who were experimenting with foods native to the Americas.

The national dish, cachupa, is a slow-boiled stew of hominy or dried corn, beans, vegetables, spices, and marinated meat or fish (it varies regionally). Economic standing is often reflected in the quality of ingredients Cape Verdean families can put into their cachupa. Most people who live in rural areas maintain gardens to grow mandioca (cassava), beans, and greens; they also raise pigs for their cachupa. Cachupa prepared in wealthy families, or when made for a wedding celebration, is known as cachupa rica (or rich cachupa) and may contain imported Portuguese sausage, marinated meats, and vegetables such as greens, mandioca, potatoes, squash, and yams.

Cachupa guisada, or leftover cachupa, is often fried with onions until crispy on the bottom and served with a fried egg on top for breakfast. A steamed cornbread known as cuscus taken with honey and milk or coffee is another popular morning meal. Xerem, dried corn pounded to the fineness of rice, is a staple at many feasts.

Grog, or sugar cane liquor, is a popular Cape Verde drink, particularly among men, and is manufactured on the islands. Many women also use grog to cure anything from stomach ulcers to acne. Doce de leite (made of milk, sugar, and lemon) and doce de coco (made of coconut and sugar) are two popular desserts.

Life's Milestones

When a new baby arrives, Cape Verdean families host setes, or celebrations filled with dancing, eating, singing, and drinking. Traditionally, this gathering is held seven days after the mother gives birth. Relatives fuss over the newborn, and bless it with protection against evil spirits.

The selection of a spouse is made by individual choice, but parents and relatives wield a great deal of influence over the decision. Cohabitation (which generally extends to common-law marriage status) is common for most young couples. Church weddings followed by an evening reception are common only in wealthy families. In general, legal and church weddings have been uncommon in Cape Verde.

When a person dies, family members traditionally carry out a dramatized wailing ritual that lasts throughout the funeral and for seven days after. This tradition is a way to let the community know that someone has died. After the seventh day, the wailing will stop until the first anniversary of the death, and every year after. Traditionally, family members of the deceased dress in black for a full year after the funeral and are not permitted to dance or play music.

CULTURAL HISTORY

Art

Traditional arts form the core of Cape Verde's artistic heritage, and include basket and tapestry weaving, the use of natural resources such as coconut shells for decorative and utilitarian use, and, most importantly, ceramics. Cape Verdean pottery originates from western and central Africa and is one of the oldest types of folk art on the archipelago. Forms, ornamentation, and molding techniques used in Cape Verde ceramics date back thousands of years and are still practiced in African communities today. The potters, traditionally women, fire the pottery in an open pit of dried manure and branches for nearly nine hours This process not only hardens the piece, but provides the pottery with is customary reddish or bluish tint, depending on the clay's chemical composition.

Pottery making is traditionally a community event and usually done at night. Singing, feasting, and other celebratory activities may occur until the morning hours, when the ceramics have finished firing. Cape Verdean folk art utilizes local materials as well as themes of island life to depict the daily routines of its average citizens. The island of Boa Vista and Santiago are famous for their clay pottery. Textiles, stone and wood carving, and boat building are some of the other traditional folk arts practiced in Cape Verde.

Music & Dance

Traditional forms of African-European-influenced music include funáná, batuque, coladeira, and mornas. Funánás are played on an accordion and an iron bar used to tap out percussion beats. The dance that accompanies funáná music is an eroticized mix of Portuguese and African styles, with lower body movements typically African and upper body movements typically Portuguese. Funánás are customarily a couple's dance, with partners holding one another around the waist and with the hands while knee movements mark the rhythm.

Batuque music is performed by a circle of female musicians known as batucadeiras, who beat panos or sash clothes held between their legs like drums while singing. Batuque music is traditionally played at weddings, where humorous advice is traditionally sung to the bride and groom. Batuque music is also a feature at Cape Verde festivals and is accompanied by a unique form of solo dancing. A dancer waits in the middle of the batukadeiras's circle where drummers beat slow and steady rhythms on their panos. Once the beats have been established and internalized by the dancer, the rhythm accelerates and the dancer keeps time with pronounced hip circles and wriggles her buttocks.

The coladeira is said to be the most African of music in Cape Verde and uses satire, social criticism, jokes, and joyous themes to teach lessons or speak about life. This type of music is played on the violão (seven-string guitar) and cavaquinho (small guitar). It may include a violin, clarinet, or trumpet, and some form of percussion like a shaker, a güiro, a cowbell, or congas. Coladeira is a ballroom-style partnered dance. In coladeira, dancers hold arms while

hand-to-hand and press their bodies against one another ("cola" is the Portuguese word for glue). Body swings and side-to-side shoulder waves are used to mark the rhythm.

Morna, which emerged in the 19th century, is considered the national sound of Cape Verde. It blends European and African musical forms with lyrics of homesickness, longing, love, and sorrow. Traditional mornas are performed by a solo singer accompanied by string instruments and maracas. One of the most famous composers of morna, Eugenio Tavares (1867–1930), is honored with a statue in the town square of Villa Nova Sintra. Mornas are also danced to in a ballroom style of movement in pairs. Partners embrace while making rhythmic swinging motions with their bodies from side to side.

Literature

Cape Verde's rich literary history begins with the oral traditions of its slave-dependent colonial past. It specifically draws on the storytelling traditions of West Africa. These include colorful storytelling, riddles, proverbs, and mourning rituals, as well as spontaneous poems, songs, and dances which express the adversity of Cape Verdean life. This folkloric tradition was passed down from one generation to the next. Many traditional Cape Verdean parables feature animal characters who serve to teach lessons about character and etiquette. Nho Lobo, for example, is one such animal, usually portrayed as lazy, greedy, and frequently hungry. He always tries to swindle the other animals into doing his work or giving him food.

Written literature emerged in the second half of the 19th century with the creation of an academic seminary. The seminary, filled with Portuguese elite, published the first issue of its literary journal, *Almanach Luso-Africano,* in 1894. The first Cape Verdean writers to publish, known as classicists, imitated European writers. Writing in Portuguese, they were inspired by Portugal's scholars and academics rather than the day-to-day life of Cape Verde. Classicist Eugenio Tavares's (1867–1930) two volumes of love poetry were the first books of creative writing printed on the archipelago in 1916. Tavares, critical of the

Portuguese government, later began to use a creole as his chosen poetic language.

The claridade (clarity) movement of the 1930s marked a transition from writing about the European world and ideals to focusing on realism and Cape Verdean life, as well as the effects of colonialism. The movement encouraged artists to adopt a greater flexibility in their work and to reflect a realistic portrayal of island life. Jorge Barbosa (1902–1971) pioneered this movement with a collection of poems entitled *Arquipelago* in 1935. *Certeza,* a student-run literary journal, was influenced by *Claridade*—a periodical published from 1936 until 1960 whose topics on society, economics, and folklore came to define a distinct Cape Verdean art style—but took up issues dealing with social and political reform. Even though, the Portuguese government censored it after its second issue, this change in outlook led to the growth of the arts in Cape Verde nonetheless.

Writers such as Antonio Aurelio Goncalves (1901–1984) and Gabriel Mariano (1928–2002) depicted the underbelly of Cape Verdean society with stories of poverty, corruption, and other social ills. Perhaps the most famous work to emerge from Cape Verde is the novel *Chiquinho* (1947), written by Baltasar Lopes da Silva (1907–1989). Other very famous novels include *Chuva Braba* (Falling Rains, 1956) and *Os Flagelados do Vento Leste* (Victims of the East Wind, 1959) by Manuel Lopes (1907–2005). These three novels focus on their characters' affection for their homeland and their desire to find a suitable life abroad. Following the publication of these books, a movement to develop a standardized written form of creole was started. Although most contemporary literature is still written in Portuguese, many more writers today are writing in a modern, conversational style.

CULTURE

Arts & Entertainment

A predominant theme in almost all forms of contemporary Cape Verdean art is saudade. This term refers to the longing and homesickness usually felt as a result of emigration and separation from family. Themes of unrest and instability due to drought, famine, escape, or the impossibility of departure, also form the foundation for the small but growing body of contemporary literature, music, and visual arts.

Today, Cape Verdeans living on the islands or abroad still hold their nation close to heart, and this is reflected in the work of such artists as Cesária Évora (1941–2011). Known as the "barefoot diva," she sang mornas that evoke saudade with nostalgic images and enchanting lyrics of life and yearning for Cape Verde. After learning to sing in an orphanage choir and starting her singing career in bars and cafés, she brought Cape Verde's music to international attention. Some of her album titles that convey the sentiments she felt for her country include *Rogamar* (*Praise to the Sea*, 2006), *Mar Azul* (*Blue Sea,* 1991), *São Vicente di Longe* (*Distant Island of São Vicente*, 2001), and *Cabo Verde* (*Cape Verde*, 1997).

Cultural Sites & Landmarks

Discovered in 1462, Cidade Velha in Santiago is the oldest settlement in the Cape Verde chain. It was a chief port for trading slaves from West Africa to Brazil and the Caribbean. To protect the prosperous slave economy, forts were constructed to defend the Portuguese colony from French and British attacks. The biggest, Fortaleza Real de São Filipe, built in 1590, is over 120 meters (393 feet) in height and still surrounds the city today. Cidade Velha has the oldest colonial church and execution site in the colonial world, as well as Africa's oldest European-built street. It was inscribed as a World Heritage Site in 2009.

Praia, just a few miles from Cidade Velha, is the capital and largest city in Cape Verde. Colonial buildings and museums like the old city hall, the 19th-century Presidential Palace, the Igreja Nossa Senhora da Graca Church, the Culture Palace, and the Diogo Gomes Monument (the Portuguese navigator who discovered the island), surround central Albuquerque Square. This park, with its gardens and cobblestone walkways, is also enclosed by a fortified wall that once defended Santiago from European pirates and smugglers.

Near the center of the city of Tarrafal, on the island of Santiago, stand the remains of an old prison camp, Campo da Morte Lenta (Camp of Slow Death). Built in 1936 by Portuguese dictator António de Oliveira Salazar (1888–1970), it housed Portuguese antifascists, communists, and other opponents of Salazar's regime. It was used as a prison for political prisoners until it was closed in 1974, just before the Cape Verde islands won independence from Portugal. Pedra de Lume, on the island of Sal, is a small city famous for its salt flats and volcanic crater lake. During the 17ᵗʰ century, slave ships would make stops there to trade European textiles and merchandise for salt to bring to the Caribbean colonies. Salt is still excavated there today, but not at the rate it was in the city's heyday.

São Filipe, on the island of Fogo, is a European-influenced town with scenic squares, wide avenues, and pastel colored colonial homes. Views of Fogo's volcanic black sand beach, and the volcanic cone of Pico de Fogo, can be viewed from the town's boardwalk. Pico de Fogo is the highest point in the Cape Verde Island chain at 2,829 meters (6,562 feet) above sea level. Its last eruption occurred in 1995, and it is still active today. The summit crater stretches 500 meters (1,640 feet) in diameter and is over 180 meters (590 feet) deep. A round trip hike takes about 10 hours and includes views of the crater and the neighboring island of Santiago.

Libraries & Museums
The national library of Cape Verde, located in Praia, opened its doors in 1999. The Government Library was inaugurated in 2002. In 2005, the Cape Verdean Museum opened in East Providence, Rhode Island, in the United States. The museum, which was opened by a Cape Verdean native, pays tribute to the historical ties between Cape Verde and New England. In Assomada, a small museum, the Museu da Tabanka, plays a central role on the island of Santiago. It is dedicated to the cultural influence

of music, especially the tabanka, and the role of local folklore and traditional stories.

Holidays
Official holidays celebrated in Cape Verde include National Heroes Day (January 20), honoring freedom fighters of the independence movement; International Women's Day (March 8); Independence Day (July 5), commemorating independence from Portugal in 1975; Assumption Day (August 15); National Day (September 12); All Saints' Day (November 15); and Good Friday (March or April).

Youth Culture
Education is free and compulsory between the ages of seven and 14, with about 90 percent of students continuing on to high school. Students who opt to attend high school pay a fee based on their parents' income. Cape Verde has recently established institutes of higher education, but a university degree has historically had little bearing on employment in the islands.

Name brand labels associated with urban African American youth are preferred among fashionable Cape Verdean teens. It is common for young people from upper-class families to wear these types of designer fashions as a sign of their social status. However, poor Cape Verdeans often have relatives in the United States send them trendy clothing as well. Leisure time is spent socializing or in recreational pursuits such as basketball, baseball, or football (soccer)—the archipelago's most popular sport. For older youth, nightclubs and bars are the preferred places to socialize. Local music and dance styles popular among young Cape Verdeans include morna, coladeira, and funáná.

SOCIETY

Transportation
Private ownership of cars is uncommon in Cape Verde. The primary method of transport, particularly urban transport, is by shared mini-buses called aluguers. Aluguers can be flagged down at

the side of the road, and prices are agreed upon before departure. They depart only when they have filled all of their seats with passengers and have no set schedule. In the major cities, private taxis are also available to hire, and public buses run periodically. Traffic moves on the right-hand side of the road.

Transportation Infrastructure

Santiago is the oldest inhabited island in Cape Verde and thus benefits from a long-established infrastructure. Many roads throughout Cape Verde are the original dirt or cobblestone (approximately 418 of 1350 total kilometers are unpaved), but in and around Praia roads are typically paved. Praia also benefits from its port, the second largest in the country after Mindelo, located to the northwest on the windward island of São Vicente.

Cape Verde has three international airports: Amílcar Cabral International Airport on Sal Island, Praia International Airport on Santiago Island, and Rabil Airport on Boa Vista Island. International flights leave to and from Lisbon and Boston, and less frequently from other major European cities. Cape Verdeans typically choose to travel by air to Santiago, Sal, São Vicente, and the smaller islands; there are nine airports on the islands in total. Some travelers opt to take the inexpensive, though less comfortable and less reliable, ferry services.

Media & Communications

Much of the Cape Verdean media is state-run and broadcast or published in Portuguese, and to a lesser degree in Creole. Many independent and foreign outlets are also available. *Jornal Horizonte* and the independent *A Semana* are the weekly newspapers with the highest circulation. Though Cape Verde is considered a literate society, the high cost of newsprint and inter-island delivery costs make buying newspapers difficult for many people. Newspapers have thus begun using the Internet to regularly relay updated information throughout the country.

As of 2008, there are three television channels—one national and two others broadcasting from Portugal and Brazil. Local radio stations broadcast on an FM network; transmissions from Africa and France are picked up as well. Broadcast signals reach many parts of the island, but poor reception, especially in the mountains, is common. Radio and TV stations, like newspapers, also rely on the Internet for relaying updated information. As of 2014, there was an estimated 213,000 Internet users, representing nearly 40 percent of the population.

SOCIAL DEVELOPMENT

Standard of Living

Cape Verde ranked 123rd out of 195 countries on the 2013 United Nations Human Development Index, which measures quality of life and standard of living indicators.

Water Consumption

An estimated 92 percent of Cape Verdeans have access to clean, treated water. The availability of fresh water is limited by the lack of rainfall in the county. In July 2010, the European Union (EU) announced that it would provide $20 million (EUR) in funding for water supply and sanitation projects on Cape Verde, specifically on the islands of Santiago and São Vicente.

Education

Cape Verde requires six years of compulsory education, which begin at age six or seven. Secondary school begins at age 13, and consists of two cycles: three years of general education followed by two years of university preparation. As of 2011, education accounts for five percent of national expenditures.

The University of Cape Verde was established in 2006. Another university is the Jean Piaget University of Cape Verde, originally the island's only university. Many students attend college in the United States.

The adult literacy rate of Cape Verde was an estimated 87.6 percent in 2015. The youth literacy rate was an estimated 92.1 percent among males and 83.1 percent among females in 2007.

Women's Rights

Because of deep-rooted attitudes regarding a woman's societal role, Cape Verdean women are traditionally expected to bear between six and 10 children. Nonetheless, many receive little help from fathers to support these children. Macho attitudes, emigration, and rampant polygamy often leave women solely responsible for their children. In addition, women are expected to handle domestic tasks and participate in various sectors of the work force, including farming, construction, and commerce. However, they are radically underrepresented in white-collar professions and in the political system. Though women are generally respected for the massive workload they bear, in practice they often earn less than their male counterparts.

Domestic violence against women is widespread. The law encourages women to report spousal abuse, punishable by up the 13 years in prison, but cultural attitudes prevent them from doing so. Furthermore, punishment does not effectively prevent future abuse from occurring, and there are often delays in acting on domestic violence cases. Although it is illegal, prostitution and trafficking in women and girls is prevalent, especially in tourist areas, and the government generally does not impose any consequences for sex offenders. Sexual harassment is also widespread, but is not considered a crime. Offenders can face up to one year in prison, but law enforcement officials do not effectively enforce penalties against perpetrators.

The government has begun taking measures to create an infrastructure that support the progress of women in Cape Verde society. One such initiative is aimed at the residents of inner-city housing projects populated predominantly by poor women from the countryside with few material or educational resources who can no longer make a living in rural areas. Providing loans and support for women to create jobs for themselves has been a key strategy.

Women's organizations, such as the Women Jurists' Association, seek to establish a special family court to address domestic violence and abuse. The Women Jurists' Association provides free legal assistance to women suffering from discrimination, violence, and spousal abuse. Violence against women is kept at the forefront of the public eye through the media, government campaigns, and non-governmental organizations (NGOs) such as the Association in Support of Women's SelfPromotion in Development and the Cape Verdean Women's Organization.

Health Care

The average life expectancy in Cape Verde was estimated at 71 years in 2015 (69 for men, 74 for women). Healthy life expectancy (the approximate number of years a person can expect to live in good health) is 59 for men and 64 for women. Annual health care expenditure per capita is approximately $145 (USD). There are an estimated 17 doctors for every 100,000 people.

GOVERNMENT

Structure

Cape Verde's road to democracy has been rocky. During the 16th century, the colony was a center of the slave trade. It was also occasionally attacked by pirates. When the slave trade declined in the 18th century, so did the prosperity of the colony. Cape Verde was used as a ships' supply station for Portuguese sailors during the 19th century.

A growing spirit of nationalism led Portugal to change the status of Cape Verde from colony to overseas province in 1951. In the 1950s and 1960s, Cape Verdeans such as Amilcar Cabral joined with Guinea-Bissauans in a bloody struggle for independence. Cape Verde gained its independence on July 5, 1975.

The country was ruled under a one-party system until 1990. At that time, opposition groups formed the Movimento para a Democracia, or Movement for Democracy (MpD), and claimed the right to oppose the scheduled December 1990 presidential election. The one-party state ended on September 28, 1990. Elections with candidates from multiple parties were held for the first time in January 1991.

The president is the chief of state and is elected by popular vote to a five-year term. The prime minister, who is the head of government, is nominated by the National Assembly and appointed by the president. A Council of Ministers assists the prime minister in governing.

The Assembleia Nacional, or National Assembly, consists of 72 deputies elected to five-year terms. The judicial branch consists of the Supremo Tribunal de Justica, or Supreme Court, and various lower courts. The country is divided into 17 administrative districts.

Political Parties

Political parties include the Partido Africana da Independencia de Cabo Verde (African Party for the Independence of Cape Verde), the Democratic and Independent Cabo Verdean Union, Democratic Christian Party, the Movimento para a Democracia (Movement for Democracy), Partido da Convergencia Democratica (Party for Democratic Convergence), Partido da Renovacao Democratica (Democratic Renovation Party), Partido de Trabalho e Solidariedade (Party of Work and Solidarity), and Partido Socialista Democratico (Social Democratic Party).

Local Government

Cape Verde is subdivided into 22 municipalities and local governance occurs at the municipal level. Governance is in the form of an elected assembly or executive body, called the Câmara Municipal. Each island is also headed by a local authority.

Judicial System

A chief justice and at least five judges sit on Cape Verde's Supreme Court. Most are appointed by the Superior Judiciary Council, while one is appointed by the president and a second is appointed by the National Assembly. The country's constitution stipulates the right to a fair trial. A series of regional courts throughout the islands oversee minor legal items, and

legal counsel is provided to those who cannot acquire it.

Taxation

The government of Cape Verde collects a variety of taxes, including an income tax, corporate tax, and sales tax. Other taxes include a transfer tax, property taxes, a capital gains tax, and an inheritance tax. Although the government imposes a building tax, the prevalence of illegal housing has complicated the application and collection of this tax. In 2009, the government separated the income tax into an individual income tax and corporate income tax. Taxes and other revenue represent 24.2 percent of the GDP, according to 2014 estimates.

Armed Forces

The Armed Forces of Cape Verde (FAC) consist of two separate branches: an army (the National Guard) and coast guard (Guardia Costeira de Cabo Verde). The country has engaged in both land and sea operations, as well as air operations, in joint programs with countries such as the U.S., Spain, and Portugal to combat human and drug trafficking. In May 2010, the Counter-Narcotics and Maritime Security Interagency Fusion Center (CMIC) was completed in Cape Verde, with funding from the US Africa Command (or AFRICOM).

Foreign Policy

Cape Verde ranks as a middle-income developing country (MIC). It is known internationally for its nonpartisan foreign policy and its joint relations with diverse nations. Of particular focus for the island nation, which lacks natural resources, are the diversification of trade and foreign investment. The country has a longstanding history with Portugal and has developed closer economic and cultural ties to Brazil in recent years. Cape Verde holds membership in numerous international organizations including the African Development Bank (ADB) and the United Nations (UN), as well as associate status with the European Union (EU). In July 2008, Cape Verde became the 153rd member of the World Trade Organization (WTO) in order to improve its trade relations.

As a result of shared cultural heritage, economic dependency, and its proximity to Africa, Cape Verde is aiming for improved ties with the EU in the near future. Cape Verde and the EU signed the Cotonou Agreement in 2007 to strengthen and deepen relations. Some of the goals of this pact include improving trade associations, reforming immigration policy, developing higher education and information technology, and eradicating poverty. Cape Verde also maintains joint relations with Portuguese-speaking countries and is a founding member of the Lusophone organisation. Cape Verde seeks closer economic links with Brazil in order to serve as a transportation hub for trade with the EU. Cape Verde also is eligible for trade benefits under the African Growth and Opportunity Act (AGOA), which offers incentives for African countries to open their economies and markets. Since December 2011, Cape Verde has been a part of the GSP+ trade regime and in September 2014 the EU promised 55 million (EUR) to Cape Verde to help with economic growth, reduction in poverty and a continuation of the 2007 Cotonou Agreement.

Cape Verde's dry climate leaves only a small percentage of land usable for agriculture and the islands' produce does not meet the country's food needs. Foreign aid from the United States, Portugal, Holland, and other countries in Western Europe helps to supplement the country's insufficient food supply. Remittances from Cape Verdeans living abroad also make a considerable contribution to the islands' economy. The U.S. has provided emergency humanitarian aid and economic assistance to improve Cape Verde's public infrastructures in the past, and has given relief in the aftermath of natural disasters.

Human Rights Profile
International human rights law insists that states respect civil and political rights, and promote an individual's economic, social, and cultural rights. The United Nations Universal Declaration on Human Rights (UDHR) is recognized as

the standard for international human rights. Its authors sought the counsel of the world's great thinkers, philosophers, and religious leaders, and were careful to create a document that reflected the core values shared by every world culture. (To read this document or view the articles relating to cultural human rights, visit http://www.udhr.org/UDHR/default.htm.)

The Cape Verdean government generally respects the human rights of its citizens. However, violations that are commonly reported include flaws in the judicial process, poor prison conditions and police brutality, child abuse, and violence and discrimination against women.

Little crime exists in Cape Verde, though petty theft and robbery are becoming more of a problem. Suspects in police custody are granted rights including bail, contact with family members, and free legal representation. The law provides for a fair, public trial, and detainees are considered innocent unless proven guilty. Nevertheless, the judicial system is characterized as understaffed and disorganized and is often negligent concerning due process. In particular, lengthy pretrial detention has been a serious problem, with detainees often jailed without charge for more than a year. In addition, prison conditions are poor and overcrowded. Juveniles and pretrial detainees are often held together with adults and convicted prisoners, and there are frequent reports of police brutality. The government, however, does permit visits by international human rights monitors and allows media representatives to report on prison conditions.

The constitution provides for freedom of speech and press, and the government generally respects these rights. Freedom to practice a religion of choice is supported by the Cape Verdean government, though Catholicism is the preferred doctrine of the people. As of 2004, homosexuality, once illegal, was decriminalized under the condition that the age of sexual consent was set at 16 years of age. Child abuse and child labor continue to be serious issues that still need to be addressed. While the law prohibits trafficking in minors, Cape Verde has gained a reputation as an illegal shipping point for children and adults from West African countries to the Canary Islands and Europe. The Ministry of Justice and the Ministry of Internal Administration are implementing policies to combat these unlawful operations.

Workers have the right to form and join unions, and the right to strike within government limits. However, there are no established minimum wage rates, and often jobs do not provide a worker and his or her family a decent standard of living. The law provides for a 44-hour work week, prohibits excessive overtime, and requires just payment for overtime rendered. Women may experience discriminatory hiring practices and are often paid less than their male counterparts. Domestic violence against women is common, particularly in rural areas, and often goes unreported. The Ministry of Health and Social Affairs is working to uphold civil and human rights that are often withheld from both women and children.

Migration
In 2002, it was estimated that the population of the Cape Verdean diaspora outnumbers the population of the country's residents. A large number of Cape Verdeans continue to relocate to Portugal, mostly for employment reasons. The Migration Policy Institute has estimated that the number of emigrants leaving Cape Verde may decrease in coming decades as immigration laws in Europe and the United States become stricter.

ECONOMY

Overview of the Economy
The service sector is the largest part of Cape Verde's economy, accounting for 71.4 percent of the gross domestic product (GDP). Income sent home by Cape Verde's large expatriate community also affects the economy, accounting for roughly 20 percent of the nation's gross domestic product (GDP). The government actively encourages market-driven enterprises led by foreign and private investment ventures, such as property development, to strengthen and diversify the economy.

Industry
Major industries in Cape Verde include fishing and fish products, tourism, ship repair, and salt mining. Manufacturing activities include clothing, beverages, construction and building materials, furniture, and metal products. Exports of shoes, fish, clothes, and bananas accounts for 36.9 percent of the GDP annually.

Labor
The majority of Cape Verdeans are employed in the service industry and tourism remains a significant economic contributor on the islands. An estimated 72 percent of the country's GDP is comprised of commerce, transport, and public services dollars.

Energy/Power/Natural Resources
Among Cape Verde's few natural resources are salt, limestone, and fish and shellfish. The islands are also a source of pozzoluna, a volcanic ash that is used to make cement.

Current environmental issues include soil erosion (caused by overgrazing and the growing of crops on steep slopes), deforestation, desertification, and overfishing. This environmental damage has also threatened Cape Verde's bird and reptile species.

Fishing
Cape Verde has a small fishing industry that, combined with farming, represents approximately nine percent of the country's overall GDP. Regional fish include marlin and tuna, in addition to shellfish such as crab. Fish remains an essential element of Cape Verdean cuisine. A favorite local dish is a fish soup known as caldo de peixe.

Forestry
Although Cape Verde does not operate a significant forestry industry, it continues to face environmental problems related to the loss of its existing forests and forest cover. The country has seen widespread loss of its forests as Cape Verdeans search for more land for housing and agriculture. In addition, forests are used for firewood. Efforts to reforest the islands of Cape

Verde have been spearheaded by a group known as the Association of Friends of Nature (AAN).

Mining/Metals

Cape Verde does not have a significant mineral industry. Although the country produces some quantities of limestone, clay, gypsum, and salt, Cape Verde remains a net importer of minerals.

Agriculture

Only about 10 percent of Cape Verde's land is arable, and that is primarily on four of the main islands: Santiago, Santo Antao, Fogo, and Brava. Only 10 percent of the population is engaged in agriculture, although over 65 percent of the population lives in rural areas.

Important agricultural products include bananas, corn, beans, sugar cane, coffee, fruit, vegetables, and livestock. Fish and shellfish, particularly tuna and lobster, are plentiful in the waters surrounding the islands. Small amounts of the annual catch are exported. Because of the lack of fresh water, however, nearly all of Cape Verde's food must be imported.

Animal Husbandry

The large majority of Cape Verdeans practice traditional livestock management techniques.

Foreign-based development assistance organizations, such as the Peace Corps, have helped to introduce livestock vaccination procedures and sustainable land management practices. Species of livestock include goats, poultry, and cattle.

Tourism

Cape Verdeans, conscious of the benefits of a vigorous tourist trade, are working to increase tourism through the Centro Promocao Turistica, de Investimento Externo e das Exportacoes, the government office that promotes tourism and foreign investment.

Approximately 115,000 tourists visit Cape Verde each year. In Praia, tourism and other service-related industries account for a significant portion of the local economy (38.4% of total employment in 2013); tourism made up 20 percent of the country's GDP in 2014.

Popular tourist attractions include the scenic mountains of Santiago, Santo Antao, Fogo, and Brava, as well as the extensive beaches of Santiago, Sal, Boa Vista, and Maio. Cidade Velha was founded in 1462 as Ribeira Grande, the first permanent European city in the tropics.

Jennifer O'Donnell, Ellen Bailey, Meredith Reed O'Donnell

DO YOU KNOW?

- Praia became Cape Verde's capital in 1770 after pirates, including Sir Francis Drake, deemed the first major town, Cidade Velha, unsafe due to repeated attacks.

- In an attempt to earn money and escape harsh drought conditions, Cape Verdeans often took work on New England whaling ships, starting as early as the mid-1700s. New England is home to one of the largest Cape Verdean populations in the world. In fact, more Cape Verdeans reportedly live in the United States (mostly in New England) than in Cape Verde.

Bibliography

Batalha, Luis and Jorgen Carling, eds. *Transnational Archipelago: Perspectives on Cape Verdean Migration and Diaspora.* Amsterdam: Amsterdam University Press, 2008.

Carter, Katherine and Judy Aulette. *Cape Verdean Women and Globalization.* New York: Palgrave Macmillan, 2009.

Irwin, Aisling and Colum Wilson. *Cape Verde (Bradt Travel Guide).* Guilford, CT: Globe Pequot Press, 2014.

Lobban, Richard Andrew. *Historical Dictionary of the Republic of Cape Verde.* Lanham, MD: Scarecrow Press, 2007.

Rego, Marcia. *The Dialogic Nation of Cape Verde: Slavery, Language, Ideology.* Lanham, MD: Lexington Books, 2015.

University of Massachusetts Dartmouth Center for Portuguese Studies. *Cape Verde: Language, Literature, Music.* Dartmouth, MA: The Center, 2003.

Williams, Frederick G., ed. *Poets of Cape Verde.* Provo, UT: Brigham Young University Studies, 2010.

Works Cited

"Cape Verde 2007/2008." *Human Development Report.* http://hdrstats.undp.org/countries/country_fact_sheets/cty_fs_CPV.html.

"Cape Verde." *British Foreign and Commonwealth Office.* http://www.fco.gov.uk/en/about-the-fco/country-profiles/sub-saharan-africa/cape-verde?profile=intRelations&pg=4.

"Cape Verde." *Culture Crossing.* http://www.culturecrossing.net/basics_business_student.php?id=38.

"Cape Verde: Clandestine housing squeezes cities." *IRIN.* http://www.irinnews.org/report.aspx?ReportId=81340.

Lopes, Leao. "Cape Verdean Pottery." http://www.umassd.edu/SPECIALPrograms/caboverde/pottery.html.

"Cape Verde Country Specific information." *U.S. Department of State.* http://travel.state.gov/travel/cis_pa_tw/cis/cis_1083.html.

"Cape Verde." *U.S. State Department.* http://www.state.gov/r/pa/ei/bgn/2835.htm.

"Cape Verde Media Guide - February 2006." *Red Orbit.* http://www.redorbit.com/news/technology/376813/cape_verde_media_guide__february_2006/.

"Cape Verde." *Millennium Challenge Corporation.* http://www.mcc.gov/countries/capeverde/index.php.

"International Convention on the Elimination of all Forms of Racial Discrimination." *United Nations.* http://www.unhchr.ch/tbs/doc.nsf/(Symbol)/CERD.C.63.CO.3.En?Opendocument.

"Country Profile: Cape Verde." *BBC News.* http://news.bbc.co.uk/1/hi/world/africa/country_profiles/1021202.stm#media.

"Customs of Cape Verde." *Encarta.* http://encarta.msn.com/sidebar_631524667/customs_of_cape_verde.html.

"EU Relations with Cape Verde." *European Commission.* http://ec.europa.eu/development/geographical/regionscountries/countries/country_profile.cfm?cid=cv&lng=en&CFID=2577223&CFTOKEN=79470642&jsessionid=08061344d71373635a49.

"New Cape Verdean Talents." *African Colours.* http://capeverde.africancolours.net/content/13397.

"Travel & Tourism: Economic Impact 2014—Cape Verde." *World Travel & Tourism Council.* http://www.wttc.org/-/media/files/reports/economic%20impact%20research/country%20reports/cape_verde2014.pdf.

"World Fact Book Cape Verde." *Central Intelligence Agency.* https://www.cia.gov/library/publications/the-world-factbook/geos/cv.html.

Almeida, Ray. "A History of Ilha do Sal." http://www.umassd.edu/SPECIALPrograms/caboverde/salhist.html.

Brinkhoff, Thomas. "Jamaica." *City Population.* http://www.citypopulation.de/CapeVerde.html.

Eyre, Banning. "National Geographic, Morna." http://worldmusic.nationalgeographic.com/worldmusic/view/page.basic/genre/content.genre/morna_757.

Gérard, Albert. "The Literature of Cape Verde." *African Arts*, Vol. 1, No. 2. Winter, 1968.

Moacyr Rodrigues, Gabriel. "Traditional Festivities in Cape Verde." http://www.umassd.edu/specialPrograms/caboverde/cvfestas.html.

Raymond, Almeida. "Cachupa di Cabo Verde." *UMASS Amherst.* http://www.umassd.edu/SpecialPrograms/Caboverde/cachupa.html.

Robson, Paul. "Community Development in Cape Verde." *Review of African Political Economy*, Vol. 21, No. 59. March 1994.

Steede, Sabina. "Cape Verde and Cape Verdeans in the U.S." http://www2.bc.edu/~brisk/capeverde.htm.

A female mountain gorilla. iStock/JaysonPhotography.

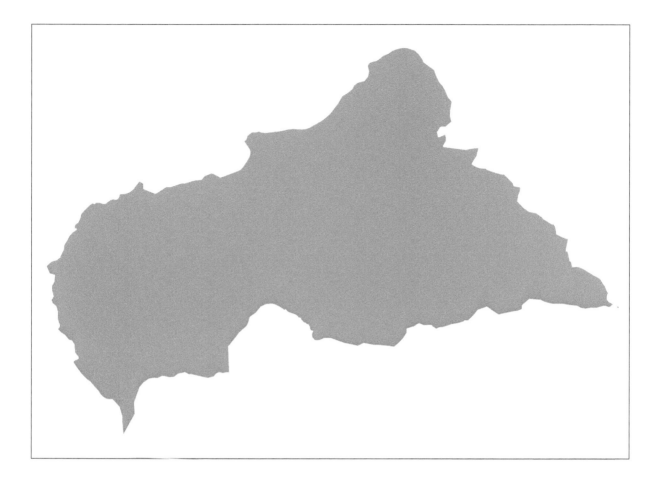

CENTRAL AFRICAN REPUBLIC

Introduction

The Central African Republic (CAR), formerly the French colony of Ubangi-Shari, is located in central Africa, just north of the equator. Its neighbors are Cameroon to the west, the Republic of the Congo and the Democratic Republic of the Congo to the south, Sudan and South Sudan to the east, and Chad to the north.

Since gaining independence in 1960, the landlocked country has suffered political instability and military dictatorship. For a brief period in the 1970s, it was known as the Central African Empire. A civilian government was established in the early 1990s, but fell to another military dictatorship, led by General Bozize, in 2003. In 2005, General Bozize was elected as president and he was reelected in 2011, but many believe the voting to have been fixed. Between 2011 and 2013 several rebel groups formed and were somewhat successful in taking parts of the country. A coalition government was formed by these groups but soon dissolved, and Bozize fled the country. Michel Djotodia, leader of a rebel group, established a National Transitional Council, which then elected Catherine Samba-Panza as interim president. Elections for a more permanent leader are scheduled to take place in 2015.

As in other central African nations, arts and entertainment in the Central African Republic reflect a wide mix of ethnic cultures. Traditional music plays a particularly important part in Central African culture, and modern genres such as soukous and Afrobeat, popular throughout the region, are prevalent in the nation as well. The country is also known for its beautiful rainforests and large wildlife populations.

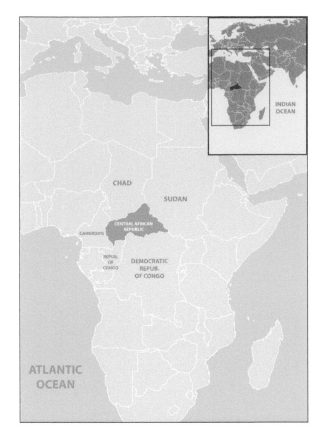

GENERAL INFORMATION

Official Language: French
Population: 5,391,539 (2015 estimate)
Currency: Communaute Financiere Africaine (CFA) franc
Coins: Coins are available in denominations of 1, 2, 5, 10, 25, 50, 100, and 500 francs
Land Area: 622,984 square kilometers (240,534 square miles)
National Motto: "Unité, Dignité, Travail" (French, "Unity, Dignity, Work")
National Anthem: "La Renaissance"
Capital: Bangui
Time Zone: GMT +1
Flag Description: The flag of the Central African Republic features four equal horizontal stripes (from top to bottom) of blue, white, green, and yellow, bisected with a centered red stripe. A gold star is emblazoned on the hoist (left) side of the blue stripe. The flag is a merging of the French tricolor (blue, white, and red) and Pan-African colors (red, green, and yellow). The red of the flag represents the blood of the people; the blue stands

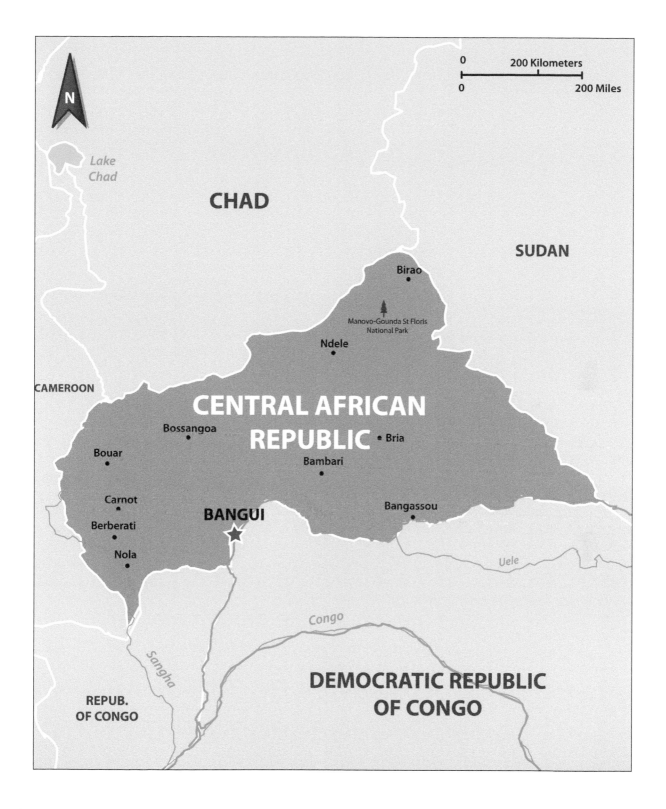

for freedom and the sky; the white represents peace; the green stands for hope; and the yellow symbolizes tolerance.

Population
The Central African Republic's population includes over 80 ethnic groups, none of which has a clear majority. The three largest groups are the Baya (33 percent of the population), Banda (27 percent), and Mandjia (13 percent). Other minority groups include the Sara (10 percent of the population), Mboum (seven percent), M'Baka (four percent), and Yakoma (four percent). Other ethnic groups consist of about two percent of the population, also including a small European population.

Over half of the population lives in rural areas and is engaged in subsistence agriculture. Chief agricultural centers are in the Bossangoa and Bambari areas. The capital, Bangui, is the major city, with an estimated population of 838,000. Bangui has a more diverse population than the nation as a whole, and supports a small population of foreign nationals and expatriates, most of whom are French or Congolese. Most inhabitants of Bangui are descended from one of several native ethnic groups, including the Baya and Banda, which together account for more than 50 percent of the population.

Languages
French is the official tongue and is used in all educational and administrative settings, but despite its official status, French is a minority language (although the major newspapers are in French). Most of the population speaks Sangho (related to Ngbandi), which serves as a "lingua franca," or common tongue; more than 90 percent of the

Bangui population uses Sangho as a primary language. The Sangho themselves are a small ethnic group living near the Oubangui River; they number around 350,000 in the Central African Republic, with approximately 54,000 more in Chad, Republic of the Congo, and the Democratic Republic of the Congo. Other languages spoken in the country include Arabic and Swahili. Tribal languages are also still in use regionally.

Native People & Ethnic Groups
Many ethnic groups have settled the Central African Republic since ancient times. The majority groups in the modern population, including the Baya (33 percent of the population), Banda (27 percent of the population), and Mandija (13 percent of the population), arrived from Sudan and Chad in the 18th and 19th centuries. Other ethnic groups include the Sara, Mboum, M'Baka, and Yakoma.

Slavery came to the area in the 1500s, as the region became a source for the European slave trade. The French began colonizing the area in the mid-1880s, establishing large plantations.

Religions
Roughly half of Central Africans are Christians (divided equally between Catholics and Protestants), while 35 percent practice traditional animism. The Catholic Church in the CAR is divided into nine dioceses, with an archdiocese based in Bangui. Christianity in Central Africa is a syncretic religion, in that many people have adopted animistic beliefs and practices in addition to Christian elements. There is also a sizeable Muslim minority, accounting for around 15 percent of the population.

Climate
The climate of the Central African Republic is largely equatorial, or tropical, in the south, while the northern part of the country is dry and sometimes desert-like. Winters are hot and dry, while summers are often hot, humid, and wet.

During the dry season, the average temperature is 30° Celsius (85° Fahrenheit); the average temperature during the rainy season is 25° Celsius (76° Fahrenheit). The rainy season lasts from May to September. Average rainfall ranges between 1,000 and 1,200 millimeters (40 and 50 inches), although the northeastern part of the country receives much less precipitation. Deforestation has intensified the effects of the hot harmattan winds that blow across the northern CAR.

ENVIRONMENT & GEOGRAPHY

Topography

The Central African Republic is largely a plateau, covered with savannah (grassland). Parts of the country are hilly, especially in the southwest and northeast. Much of the country is covered with forest, particularly tropical rainforest in the south. The northeastern part of the country is covered by desert.

The major rivers include the Oubangui (or Ubangi) River, which is a tributary of the Congo River and forms the country's southern border. In the north, the Chari River drains into Lake Chad. The Oubangui represents the country's lowest point, at 335 meters (1,099 feet) above sea level. The highest point is Mont Ngaoui, at 1,420 meters (4,659 feet) above sea level.

Bangui is situated in the western part of the Central African Republic, which is bordered by the Democratic Republic of the Congo, Sudan, South Sudan, Chad, Cameroon, and the Republic of the Congo. The capital is strategically located on the northern bank of the Oubangui River, which divides the Central African Republic from the DRC to the south, and its economy centers on its status as a river port. Most of the city lies in a floodplain created by the river and is surrounded by tropical grasslands and low hills that gradually blend into forest. The city is 396 meters (1,300 feet) above sea level.

Plants & Animals

Many wild species inhabit the CAR, notably forest elephants and several species of gorilla

The giant eland is a type of antelope found in the Central African Republic.

(lowland and mountain), as well as chimpanzees, baboons, and rhinoceroses. On the savannah live the African elephant, the giant eland (a type of antelope), and the roan antelope. Outside of the rainforest, most vegetation consists of grassland with some trees.

The forests in particular are rich in bird and insect species. Termites are common throughout the country. Hippopotamuses and crocodiles are typically found in the areas surrounding the country's major rivers, the Oubangui and the Chari.

Poaching is a major problem in the Central African Republic, and has severely diminished wildlife populations. There are several national parks which serve as refuges for wildlife. These include Dzanga-Sangha, Bamingui-Bongoran, and Manovo-Gounda St. Floris.

CUSTOMS & COURTESIES

Greetings

Greeting customarily takes the form of a handshake in formal situations. It is only acceptable to offer the right hand for a handshake, as the left hand is considered impure. If one individual is compelled to show deference due to social status or respect for elders, that person will shake right hands holding his right wrist in his left hand and bowing slightly. In addition, children are expected to avert their eyes when greeting those in authority and are customarily expected to curtsy or bow in cases of extreme deference. Small talk is also common, and failing to inquire about one's personal affairs may be perceived as rude.

French, the national language, is the appropriate language spoken in major cities and urban centers. As such, typical greetings include "Bonjour" ("Good day") and "Bonsoir" ("Good afternoon or evening"). Among Muslim populations "Salaam alaikum" ("Peace be unto you") is the customary greeting. French greetings may also be followed by a greeting in an indigenous language. The Sango example of this is "Bara ala" or "Bala mo" ("Greetings to you"). In rural areas, French is typically not used when greeting and individuals mostly speak indigenous languages.

Gestures & Etiquette

Central Africans are known for their physical expressiveness and gesturing. Some examples of these physical accents include raising one's eyebrows and inhaling rapidly when wishing to agree or answer yes to a question. In addition, friends of the same-sex may commonly hold hands. However, it is considered unacceptable for males and females to display affection in public. Between the young and the elderly, the proper protocol for interaction demands that younger generations avert their eyes, lower their voices, and cross their arms over their stomachs when speaking to elders.

In terms of dining etiquette, most Central Africans outside of urban centers use their hands for eating. For foods such as rice, this is accomplished by balling up the food and dipping it into sauce in small chunks. The right hand is exclusively used for eating and passing, as the left hand is associated with personal cleansing. In some tribal groups, it is customary for the

men to eat at the table or on the mat while the women and girls eat near the kitchen or cooking area, as they may be still preparing more food to bring out.

Eating/Meals

Central Africans generally eat their largest meal in the morning or at lunch. Breakfast is most commonly leftover dinner from the night before. Traditionally, food is usually cooked throughout the duration of the morning, and is then served for lunch. Dinner is generally the only time that families eat entirely together.

While Western conventions are increasing in urban areas, it is common is for an entire family to sit on a mat or at low tables when eating. Meals are traditionally communal and the family eats from shared dishes. It is customary for the woman who cooked the food to reduce the vegetables and meat into bite-sized pieces with her right hand and distribute them evenly to all family members. Because of this, women are usually the last to eat.

Visiting

Visiting the homes of family or neighbors is a common practice in the CAR. Visitors generally arrive unannounced, but commonly do so on a regular basis. When a visitor comes to one's home, the host is customarily required to offer a seat, particularly on a barambo (chair) or a straw mat. Guests are also frequently entertained outdoors, as many houses, especially in rural areas, are not conducive to indoor hosting. Generally, guests are invited to sit outside either on the porch of the main building or under the shade of a tree. Other facets of hospitality include the offering of a beverage or food. In Muslim homes, specifically those concentrated in urban areas, houses are more conducive to visits inside. Generally, the first room to the right or left of the entranceway is reserved for guests. This room is typically furnished (or contains mats) and may even have a television. Once an individual has visited another's home, he is expected to extend the same hospitality to his host.

LIFESTYLE

Family

For the vast majority of the nation's citizens, family life involves more traditional roles for males and females. Traditionally, men are the hunters, fishermen, and procurers of wild game for eating while women customarily grow and gather other staples for feeding their families. Women are also responsible for the household and child rearing. Once children reach an acceptable age, they are expected to accept more responsibility and are often involved in helping with younger siblings.

The Aka people who inhabit the southwestern-forested region of the CAR are known to practice some of the world's most unique parenting and family customs. For example, in the majority of Aka families, the woman hunts during the day while the man stays at home with the children. Infants are commonly left with the fathers, and women may even hunt up until their eighth month of pregnancy. Despite this role reversal, the Aka place great value on spending time with their offspring, the sex of the attending parent inconsequential.

Housing

Sixty percent of Central Africans live in rural areas, with most concentrated in the southern and western regions of the country. Traditional homes are characterized by their cylindrical shape and straw or bamboo, conical roofs. Generally, these homes are one-room buildings that may accommodate up to 15 people. Some families in the past were able to build several such buildings on one property to create a compound that includes additional housing for their children and cooking facilities. However, many villages have been burned down due to the internal conflict that ignited in the 1990s, leading to an increase in fragile, makeshift homes and leaving more than 300,000 citizens homeless. A lack of adequate infrastructure has also resulted in decreased access to safe water and sanitation, as well as other health concerns. In addition, the conflict of the past ten years has forced many to become refugees and further complicating these problems with infrastructure.

In urban areas, residents commonly reside in rectangular homes built from concrete. Housing styles in Bangui are some of the most diverse in the nation and include dilapidated French mansions, large, multi-room Muslim homes, and kodros, which are ethnic enclaves on the outskirts of the capital that have developed since World War II. Muslim homes generally have rooms centered on an outdoor courtyard, and include rooms in which the men can separately conduct their business. With the increased influx of rural migrants in the early 21st century, kodros have essentially become mini-villages transported from rural areas. Some even maintain their own regional governments.

Food

The Central African Republic diet mainly consists of some rather uniform staples. These include peanuts and groundnuts, crops such as plantains, cassava, and bananas, beef and goat, palm and peanut oil, and vegetables such as onion, garlic, okra, and other greens. More exotic dietary supplements include elephant and gazelle meat and steamed or fried termites. Each region of the country uses these ingredients similarly, and most common dishes include a base starch—generally rice, cassava, or yam—topped with sauce (also referred to as a soup or stew). Because rice generally does not grow well in the region, cassava and yam are more commonly grown. They are prepared by being pounded into a fine grain, fermented, and then steamed to form a thick starch.

The cuisine of the CAR is similar to that of neighboring Central African cultures, and sauces are typically palm oil-based or peanut oil-based. Common dishes include dongo-dongo, an okra stew served with beef or goat over steamed yam, and ngunja and ngunza, which are both variations of the same dish of cassava leaves in a tomato and garlic sauce. Muamba de galinha is a much less common dish consisting of chicken served in palm oil with okra. Chicken is considered a luxury and is generally reserved for special occasions. Common light fare or snacks include groundnuts, makala (fried dough), and kanda and mangbele (meat and cassava steamed in banana leaves). Banana leaves function as the primary tool for steaming.

Life's Milestones
Rites of passage in the Central African Republic are not only limited to the transition into adulthood, weddings, and funerals, but also include celebrations specific to migration, harvest, and hunting. Among the agrarian peoples in rural CAR, for example, seasonal celebrations involving elaborate dance, and singing marks the beginning of farming seasons. These observances are meant to foster strong crops and abundant harvests. The Aka people are well known for their seasonal celebrations aimed at influencing crop output or upon migration to another region.

Nearly every citizen commemorates the common milestones of birth, marriage, and death. Marriage, in particular, has maintained much of its traditional cultural mandates. The bride gift, for example, is required of the groom when he asks for a young woman's hand in marriage. He must be able to supply the bride's family with an acceptable amount of money or gifts. If he cannot, he is traditionally required to work for her family for many years until they deem the debt repaid. Once an agreement has been made, and couples have been arranged, the marriage is generally a family and village affair that can last for days. (It should be noted that a woman is not allowed to divorce her husband, but a husband may choose to divorce his wife.)

Birth is another milestone celebrated with singing and dancing, and traditionally includes the entire family and village. As for death, many Central Africans regard it in a spiritual or supernatural way, and often perceive the passing of another as bad luck or the cause of ill will. When a death occurs, families traditionally come together to mourn the dead (and possibly seek blame). Funerals generally include staying up all night and singing mournful songs to express grief.

CULTURAL HISTORY

Art
Human settlement in the region that constitutes the modern-day Central African Republic (CAR) dates back 8,000 years to societies that existed in the seventh millennium BCE. In this early and evolving age, artistic expression was represented by prehistoric rock art. Migrating groups of Adamawa-Ubangi- and Bantu-speaking peoples relocated to the area prior to the first century CE. These Bantu tribes carried out slash-and-burn farming and set up more permanent settlements, ultimately displacing many native pygmy groups. These people eventually formed states and had populations large enough to develop into large kingdoms. Art was collectively produced on a small scale, and generally consisted of wood sculpture, such as human figures, traditional instruments, and utilitarian objects, as well as woven textiles and baskets and pottery.

When the French began to colonize the region in the late 1800s, they disrupted many traditional art practices. As the country moved toward independence in the 20th century, local artists began to reflect on political and social conflicts. Jerome Ramedane (1936–1991), a self-taught painter, is one of the first artists to embody the reflection on the transition from colonial to self-rule. Originally a mural artist, he achieved wide-reaching fame both within the country and abroad by those who saw the honest emotion reflected in his simple style. Though only a part-time painter, his style and honesty about the cultural challenges facing his nation nonetheless met with universal understanding and influenced many other African artists.

Another influential artist is Cyr Perroni, who migrated from the Caribbean island of Martinique during the 1960s. Inspired by the independence movements and the development of African culture, Perroni settled in Bangui and founded an art studio that functioned as a haven for artists. Because of Perroni's efforts, artisan work flourished and underwent certain changes. For example, the elaborate carving styles of indigenous Central Africans were simplified to a more modernist and expressionist style. Today, most contemporary Central African arts remain similar to their traditional predecessors, with woodcarving the most popular medium. Unlike the artisan works in many former French colonies, art in the CAR has maintained a strong spiritual significance.

Architecture

The lifestyle of most Central Africans dictates their preferred architecture. The three main groups—nomadic hunters and gatherers, forest dwellers, and villagers—all rely on different materials and durability when designing their housing. The building style of the few remaining nomadic Central Africans is generally regarded as rudimentary, and incorporates natural materials such as large branches, leaves, tree bark, palm fronds, and a combination of straw and mud. They sink four large branches as corner posts and then weave leaves between branches or mix mud with straw to build the surrounding walls. Leaves are preferred by people living in the tropical regions because they allow for run-off of torrential rains.

In rural villages that feature more permanent settlements, mud bricks are the common building material and homes are typically constructed in a circular shape. French colonialism also had a rather significant impact on the arrangement of villages and urban architecture. Citing a complete lack of discernable organization and the inability to take an accurate census, the French imposed a village design whereby homes were to be built on either side of a single main road. Most established villages today bear this influence.

In cities such as the capital of Bangui, the influence of French architecture is evident in the whitewashed buildings and city layout, particularly the sectioned neighborhoods. In the 1960s, following increased investment in the newly independent nation, a series of high-rise buildings were constructed in Bangui. Today, many of these buildings suffer from staggering disrepair.

Drama

The film industry in CAR is still quite underdeveloped. This stems from a severe lack of funding and training—most Central African filmmakers have been trained in France—and from the destruction of much of the nation's infrastructure during the 2003 coup d'état. Early filmmakers included Joseph Akouissonne, who directed *Zo Kwe Zo* (*All People are People*, 1983)*,* and Léonie Yangba Zowe, who filmed a series of short, ethnographic films in the 1980s. Formally trained in France in the traditional French ethnographic style, Zowe used film to capture the dancing and ritual practices of various ethnic groups. Perhaps the most widely seen film associated with the CAR in the 21st century is *Le Silence de la Forêt* (*The Forest*, 2003) by Cameroonian director and writer Bassek Ba Kobhio (1957–). The film depicts a group of pygmies and village life in the forests of the CAR, and was screened at numerous prestigious film festivals.

Music

Music and dance were often the primary modes of artistic expression in the nation's early history. Of particular note are the music traditions of the African pygmy people, who still inhabit the same forested regions of the CAR. There are considered among the oldest modern humans in existence, and their culture, particularly their music, polyphonic in nature, has been the subject of continuous study. In 2003, the United Nations Educational, Scientific and Cultural Organization (UNESCO) named the oral traditions of the Aka Pygmies, specifically their polyphonic singing, as a Masterpiece of the Oral and Intangible Heritage of Humanity. They are most famous for their mostly a cappella performances rife with chanting and repetition.

Modern folk music of the Banda people is trumpet-based and uses ongos, or trumpet-like instruments made from the horns of antelopes, to add an element of jazz to the overall musicality. The smaller cultural enclave of the Nbaka peoples use the mbela, a simple instrument made from a tautly stretched string between two ends of a flexible tree branch, to create primitive, monotone sounds that have been prevalent in their music for centuries.

Literature

The national literature of the Central African Republic is rooted in the country's storytelling traditions. Initially, these traditions survived from generation to generation by being taught to younger members of a clan or village. Stories were performed dramatically, and still are in many places where literacy is low. With the arrival of Europeans, missionaries codified tribal languages in an effort to make the teaching of French much easier. This linguistic formalization allowed many Central Africans to begin writing stories in their native tongues.

As independence gained popularity and Central Africans learned writing and French in the French-run schools, national francophone authors such as Pierre Makombo Bamboté (1932–), the first writer from the CAR to be published, came to prominence. Faustin-Albert Ipéko-Etomane (1930–1980) translated and transcribed a series of traditional legends from his tribal language into French. As literature developed, important themes included cultural resistance, colonialism, independence, and the satirizing of the postcolonial government.

Other prominent writers include Pierre Sammy-Mackfoy (1935–2014), who explored the burden of modern Central Africans to reconcile traditional culture with modern trends. Étienne Goyémidé (1942–1997), a Central African writer who lived in France, wrote *Le Dernier Survivant de la caravane* (*The Last Survivor of the Caravan*, 1984), which is considered the first published novel to involve the theme of slavery in Africa. His most popular work, *Le Silence de la forêt* (*The Silence of the Forest*, 1984) follows the life of a modern Central African who abandons his sophisticated lifestyle to live among the pygmies. The book was adapted into a celebrated film in 2003.

CULTURE

Arts & Entertainment

In Bangui, the capital and primary city of the country, a blend of European and African culture defines the artistic and entertainment scene. The city's principal entertainment district, known as "Km5," lies 5 kilometers (3.1 miles) from the center of the city. This district offers a variety of clubs, restaurants, and other social venues. Daily markets and outdoor cafés also draw residents and visitors to the city's commercial districts. The capital is also home to the country's only university and other similar institutions of learning, and, typically, these educational and research institutions attract commercial business, such as cafés, bars, and other nightspots, adding to the city's recreational options.

Traditional music continues to maintain an important role in the culture of the Central African Republic. The Banda population has its own distinct folk music, which employs groups of trumpeters and other horn players. Instruments such as the sanza, a type of thumb piano, and the mbela, a stringed instrument played with the mouth, are also used in Central African music. Outside of these native music traditions, modern popular music mostly derives from neighboring central African countries such as the Republic of the Congo, or from West Africa and abroad, including jazz, rock and roll, soukous (or African rumba, a style of dance music), and other Latin-influenced styles.

Football (soccer) remains the most popular sport and recreational pastime. In 2009, the national football team captured the CEMAC Cup, a Central African football tournament. It was the team's first international championship. Other popular athletics include rugby and basketball, and youth basketball teams have competed on an international level. In the Olympics, athletes have represented the Central African Republic in the sports of taekwondo, judo, and boxing.

Cultural Sites & Landmarks

The cultural center of the Central African Republic is perhaps the capital of Bangui. The city was founded in 1880 by the French around a military post as they probed the region for mining and slaves. It was established alongside the goods-toting Ubangi (also spelled Oubangi) River, and wide avenues run out from several points on a central courtyard. The city center still bears the distinct mark of French colonialism in the whitewashed buildings. However, many of these buildings have fallen into disrepair, and the city is a run-down conglomerate of dingy colonial architecture, skeletal, concrete remains, and ad-hoc neighborhoods. The French quarter is more commonly referred to as the old town and is generally frequented by the upper class and dignitaries. Cultural sites include the central market, the Boganda Museum, which houses a vast collection of ancient cultural artifacts, and the nation's only university, the University of Bangui.

Outside of Bangui, the nation is known for its beautiful landscapes and diverse geography, ranging from savannah to forest. Its various tribal communities, particularly the sites of the Aka pygmies, have held cultural significance for centuries. The Central African Republic is also home to one World Heritage Site as recognized by UNESCO, the Manovo-Gounda St. Floris National Park. This wildlife sanctuary provides a natural habitat for black rhinos, elephants, cheetahs, leopards, wild dogs, red-fronted gazelle, and buffalo. Due to illegal poaching that persists in the region, the site is now categorized as a World Heritage Site in Danger. In addition, the Dzanga-Sangha National Park, in the southwestern corner of the CAR, is a vast expanse of forested region that provides a home to one of Central Africa's last elephant strongholds. The national park is also home to large families of gorilla and the Aka Pygmies.

Libraries & Museums

The Museé de Barthélemy Boganda (Boganda National Museum), established in 1964, is the national museum of the CAR, and was named after the nation's first prime minister. The ethnographic museum houses various collections of art and artifacts from the regions original tribal inhabitants, while also featuring a natural history collection with specimens of preserved local fauna.

Though created through legislation in the 1980s, the country still does not maintain a national library. In general, the public and school library systems throughout the country are underdeveloped or nonexistent. In 2010, however,

Libraries without Borders entered into an agreement to help build a library in CAR, with an endowment granted in 2012.

Holidays

The Central African Republic's national holiday is Republic Day (December 1), which commemorates the 1958 establishment of a self-governing republic within the "French Community." Independence Day, celebrated on August 13, commemorates full independence from France in 1960.

Several Christian holidays are also official, including Christmas and Easter Monday. Muslims have the right to take leave from work on their religious holidays, but these are not official.

Youth Culture

For the most part, Central African youth have relatively uniform expectations placed upon them by society. These include always showing respect for elders and helping around the house. It is rare to see a child act outside of these boundaries, with exceptions common only among orphaned children and child soldiers (or those kidnapped by northern rebel forces). During the 2003 coup d'état, the US Department of State estimated that nearly two-thirds of the nation's schools were destroyed. Since that time, NGOs and government initiatives have resulted in a concentrated rebuilding effort. In 2008, students were even returning to school in the most unstable northern region of the country. Despite this positive turn of events, many statistics still outline the severity of the lives of Central African youth.

In 2003, at the height of destruction, an estimated 60 percent of children did not attend school. As of 2008, that figure was closer to 49 percent, though an estimated 75 percent of children in conflict regions remained out of school. Overall literacy for males is just over 50 percent, and under 25 percent for females, as of 2015. In those same regions, many young boys have been stolen away by rebel forces. By 2007, over half of the most recently recruited child soldiers had been handed over to NGOs. These organizations are currently working to re-integrate these young men back into a society that may shun them for what they were forced to do. Additionally, as of 2015, the infant mortality rate was 90 in 1000 live births, with approximately 24 percent of children under 5 nationwide suffering from malnutrition.

SOCIETY

Transportation

The Central African Republic has one of the lowest car ownership rates in the world, at one car owned per 1,000 people. Walking is the most common mode of travel, particularly in rural areas, while minibuses are the most common mode of public transportation. These buses are typically constructed of old, imported car parts and have up to 24 seats. In addition to mini-buses, shared taxis are also common. Traffic moves on the right side of the road.

Transportation Infrastructure

The country's transportation infrastructure is characterized as underdeveloped and insufficient. In 2012, the World Bank granted $125 million to attempt to aid in overcoming this problem and build transportation infrastructure and increase regional trade. The road network in 2010 measured 20,278 kilometers (12,600 miles), a fifth of which are national roads, and a majority of which are unpaved. Vehicles are limited in their routes due to conflict and deteriorating or undeveloped infrastructure and natural elements; routes in the northern region are not well travelled or developed, and may be blocked by military or rebel forces.

There are no national railways and the Ubangi River and the nation's river system allows for travel and the transportation of goods. However, river port infrastructure requires overhaul. The Bangui M'Poko International Airport is located northwest of the capital. There are two airports with paved runways, along with 37 with unpaved.

Media & Communications

The Central African media is generally considered relatively free and fair. The constitution protects freedom of speech and the establishment of the High Council of Communications (HCC), an independent nine-member organization of journalists and other media experts, promotes the defense of such rights. Despite these protections, many journalists still claimed to have been the victims of government threats. The CAR has over thirty print newspapers, mainly limited to Bangui where the literacy rate is higher. Newspapers as *Le Citoyen*, *Le Confident*, and *Le Démocrate* are famous for their criticism of the government, but have little reach or influence outside Bangui.

Radio is the most popular medium and the privately owned Radio Ndeke Luka, backed by the United Nations, offers international programs. British Broadcasting Corporation (BBC) programming and Radio France Internationale are also available in the capital of Bangui. State-run radio stations typically refrain from broadcasting coverage of political opposition. Television broadcasting is monopolized by the government, as there are no private investors to begin an independent station.

The communications industry in CAR suffers from a lack of infrastructure. The vast majority of Central Africans are unable to afford mobile phones, and lack of satellite coverage renders them useless outside of major cities, but in the last few years there has been steady increase. Thus, according to UNICEF, about 23 out of every 100 people own and operate cell phones. As most people still have no running water or even electricity in their homes, landline telephones are also limited to only one for every 100 people. In addition, a 2010 estimate put the rate of Internet usage at 3 percent of the population, with the vast majority either foreigners or journalists in the capital.

SOCIAL DEVELOPMENT

Standard of Living

The Central African Republic ranked 185th out of 195 countries on the 2013 United Nations Human Development Index, which measures quality of life and standard of living indicators.

Water Consumption

According to UNICEF (United Nations International Children's Emergency Fund), the national average of access to improved drinking water is 67.1 percent nationally, breaking down into 92 percent in urban areas and 51 percent in rural areas. Access to improved sanitation is low, at a national average of 33.8 percent, with urban areas at 43.1 percent and rural areas at 27.8 percent. These numbers are low, but slowly improving from previous years' figures.

Education

The Central African Republic's education system is poor, but improving as well. It was reported in 2008 that less than one-third of eligible students complete primary school, but between 2008 and 2012 that number increased to 46 percent. In 2003, it was estimated that only about half of the population could read and write, but that too has increased. Literacy, however, continues much higher among men (672.3 percent) than among women (59.1 percent).

At the primary level, there are 92 students to each teacher. Teachers are ill-trained, with about half of the teaching population having only basic training.

Sangho is the main language of instruction in Central African schools. Relatively few people know French; as of 1996, the country's French-speaking population numbered only 9,000 speakers.

Education is secular, although religious schools are allowed; as of 2004, there were approximately a dozen Catholic schools in the capital. Little or no higher education existed during the colonial era; students traveled aboard, generally to France or Senegal, to attend universities.

The University of Bangui, established in 1969, is the only public university in the nation and attracts students from across the CAR and other parts of Africa. Bangui also has the National School of Arts, established in 1966, and a number of other French and African scientific and research institutions. Other institutions of higher learning include the National School of

Administration and Judiciary (ENAM), which trains civil servants.

Women's Rights

Central African women generally adhere to traditional roles in terms of family and daily life. These roles involve most domestic responsibilities, child rearing, and sometimes harvesting. While women are highly valued among their family and community as mothers and influential members of society, traditional customs and the law still limit their rights. For example, even though women are technically allowed to inherit property, this practice is rarely observed. Women in position to inherit land are commonly overlooked in favor of male family members. In addition, women are not legally allowed to be the head of a household under any circumstance. Under this law, widows, single women, and divorcees are not allowed to receive government funds, leading many women to marry or remarry for financial security. In extreme cases, they are forced to marry their deceased husband's brother or father in order to protect themselves and their children from poverty.

Polygamy, which is the practice of taking multiple wives, is legal in the CAR. According to the law, a man may have as many as four wives as long as he can provide for them equally. This practice is diminishing in urban areas as more women gain higher access to education and as both spouses enter the workforce. However, it continues in rural areas where multiple wives are a guaranteed way to provide more workers for farms and domestic tasks.

The constitution does not directly outlaw spousal abuse, but the crime can be filed under general assault. Nevertheless, cases are rarely reported as many women fear divorce or worse violence at home. The cultural acceptance of domestic abuse as a good punishment for an unsatisfactory wife also perpetuates the problem. Spousal rape is also not prohibited by law, and several non-governmental organizations (NGOs) have found cases to be rampant in rural CAR. Rape is against the law and is punishable by harsh physical labor. In general, women do report cases when they are encouraged to by their families. However, many families want to distance themselves from the shame of rape and avoid the chance that social stigma will affect their daughter's chances to marry. Sexual harassment and the trafficking of women, particularly for sexual exploitation, are also concerns, with the former alleged to be widespread.

While life can be harsh for many women in CAR, the current president is a woman, Catherine Samba-Panza, who was mayor before being elected to the presidency. There are opportunities available for women, but are largely out of reach for those without the social and economic resources that allow for extensive education and political and social mobility.

Health Care

Medical care is extremely poor in the Central African Republic, with high rates of HIV/AIDS and major infectious diseases such as hepatitis A and E, typhoid fever, dengue fever, meningococcal meningitis, and malaria. As of 2014, an estimated 135,400 people were infected and living with AIDS and there were 9,000 AIDS-related deaths. The bite of tsetse flies spreads African sleeping sickness (trypanosomiasis).

Because of these factors, the Central African Republic has a young population, with 40 percent of the male population under 14 and the median age of nineteen. Average life expectancy, as of 2012, in the CAR is approximately forty-nine and a half years. The infant mortality rate is high, at almost ninety-one deaths per 1,000 live births.

GOVERNMENT

Structure

The Central African Republic was the French colony of Ubangi-Shari from the late 19th century until after World War II. Established in 1894, Ubangi-Shari was merged in 1906 with the French colony of Chad. In 1910, France created French Equatorial Africa, a federation based at Brazzaville which included the territories of Ubangi-Shari, Chad, Gabon, and Middle Congo (the modern Republic of the

Congo). After World War II, the federation was part of the "French Community" of former colonies, an arrangement similar to the British Commonwealth of Nations.

In 1958, the member territories of French Equatorial Africa voted to become separate members of the French Community, and dissolved their federation. On August 13, 1960, Ubangi-Shari gained full independence as the Central African Republic. The CAR was unable to attain political stability, however, and suffered a string of dictatorships.

In the late 1970s, dictator Jean-Bédel Bokassa, who admired Napoleon Bonaparte, declared himself emperor of the Central African Empire and achieved international notoriety for his extravagance and extreme cruelty. He was deposed with the help of the French in 1979. During the 1980s and 1990s, the country alternated between civilian and military rule. In 2003, a military coup ended a decade of civilian government. Since 2011, the country has been continuing its transition back to democracy, but the international community remains concerned about the CAR's human rights record.

The president serves as chief of state. He or she is elected for a five-year term, and may serve two terms. The president appoints the vice president and a Council of Ministers. The prime minister, the head of government, is chosen by the political party that controls the legislature.

The unicameral legislature is known as the National Assembly (Assemblée nationale). There are 105 members, who are elected by popular vote and serve for five years.

The 1995 constitution was suspended following the 2003 military coup. A new constitution was approved on December 5, 2004, by a national referendum and updated in 2010. A new constitution was being readied for approval by the citizenry as of mid 2015.

Political Parties

The Central African Republic has several influential political parties. The National Convergence "Kwa Na Kwa," the Alliance for Democracy and Progress, Central African Democratic Rally, Civic Forum, Democratice Forum for Modernity, the Liberal Democratic Party, and Londo Association. In addition, the Movement for Democracy and Development, the Movement for the Liberation of the Central African People, the National Unity Party, The New Alliance for Progress, the Patriotic Front for Progress, the People's Union for the Republic, and the Social Democratic Party are some of the parties.

Local Government

The CAR is divided into 14 prefectures, with the capital Bangui as a self-governing commune. The prefectures are divided into many smaller units known as "subprefectures." Local administration is highly centralized, with the president appointing all prefects, subprefects, and communal authorities.

Judicial System

The nation's highest court is the Supreme Court (Cour Suprême). The Constitutional Court rules on constitutional law. Lower courts include the Court of Appeal, as well as criminal and lower courts. Traditional law plays an important part in CAR life, especially outside the capital. The CAR legal system is based on French law.

Taxation

The government of the Central African Republic levies income, corporate, value-added, social security, and property taxes. The income tax rate is high, levied at a top rate of 50 percent, while the corporate tax rate is relatively competitive, levied at a top rate of 30 percent. Taxes and other revenue make up 9.1 percent of the yearly GDP.

Armed Forces

The armed forces of the Central African Republic (Forces Armées Centrafricaines, or FACA) consist of five service branches: Ground Forces, Military Air Service, Gendarmerie (military police), Presidential Guard, and National Police. The armed forces accounted for less than one percent of the GDP in 2009. There is a two-year conscript service obligation.

Foreign Policy

The foreign policy of the Central African Republic focuses on regional stability and security, the handling of natural resources—namely gold, diamonds, timber, and uranium—and international support. The country is a participant in several African regional organizations, including the African Union (AU), the Economic Community of Central African States (CEEAC), the Bank of Central African States (BEAC), and the Community of Sahel-Saharan States (CEN-SAD). The country holds international membership in the World Bank and the UN, among other organizations, and generally votes with its regional block, the AU.

Since independence, the CAR has maintained close ties with France. While foreign aid from France has decreased over the past few decades, France remains the country's most important bilateral donor. The World Bank and International Monetary Fund (IMF) have also stepped in, simultaneously requiring economic reforms as the mandate for financial assistance. The country also receives assistance through the African Development Fund (ADF) and UN agencies. The CAR maintains good relations with the United States, though the U.S. has limited diplomatic representation in the country itself. The country remains one of the least developed nations in the world.

Human Rights Profile

International human rights law insists that states respect civil and political rights, and promote an individual's economic, social, and cultural rights. The United Nations (UN) Universal Declaration of Human Rights (UDHR) is recognized as the standard for international human rights. Its authors sought the counsel of the world's great thinkers, philosophers, and religious leaders, and were careful to create a document that reflects the core values shared by every world culture. (To read this document or view the articles relating to cultural human rights, visit http://www.udhr.org/UDHR/default.htm.)

Since achieving independence from France, the Central African Republic has experienced a brief but tumultuous history of self-rule, mainly characterized by military tyranny, most notably the regime of General Jean-Bédel Bokassa (1921–1996). Bokassa seized power from his cousin in January 1967, dissolving the 1959 constitution and breaking ties with China. Throughout his erratic reign (1966–1979), he ruled by decree, even declaring himself president for life. He transformed CAR into the Central African Empire (CAE) and later declared himself emperor. He even had a personal hand in the brutal murders of some of his suspected opponents. While the human rights situation has undoubtedly improved since he left office, there are still traces of Bokassa's oppressive reign.

The poor human rights record of the CAR largely stems from the continuous conflict between rebel forces in the northern region and the military. These rebel groups have a long-established presence due to lack of government control over the border with Chad. Since CAR's independence from France in 1960, the north has long acted as the regional headquarters of opposition groups. Today, the People's Army for the Restoration of Democracy (APRD) is believed to control most of the region, though its rebel tactics make it difficult to distinguish the APRD from regular citizens. As a result, the military is prone to attacking civilians in the search for militant rebels.

Human rights violations in the region include extrajudicial arrest and killing, rape, assault, torture, and the pillaging and arson of entire villages suspected of supporting rebels. While each of these offenses is illegal according to the constitution, the locals claim they are not protected by law or by military, leaving many to flee from their homes. More than 125,000 refugees from the north have dispersed throughout the south and into Chad to escape violence on both sides of the conflict. However, this movement is limited by military officials patrolling various inroads

into central and southern CAR. Migrants are often caught between forces with nowhere to go.

Harsh inconsistencies in the government's arrest and detention policies can best be observed in arrest of rebels, civilians, and military. Despite the violation of laws prohibiting torture, rape, murder, and unlawful detention, military personnel who committed these acts were granted immunity by the government. This contrasted starkly with the arrest of some 50 soldiers in 2007 accused of desertion when they were apprehended attempting to collect their overdue pay. This unbalanced approach to incarceration and punishment under the law applies to nearly all violent crimes as well.

The Central African Republic continues to be ravaged by this ongoing political and military crisis, although in the recent years, especially under the presidency of Catherine Samba-Panza, some of the violence has lessened. Other human rights issues that warrant addressing include poor prison conditions and corruption within the judicial system; censorship that stifles or limits criticism of the government (though to a lesser degree in recent years); the banning of certain religious groups; and child labor and the lack of adequate programs and funding for youth.

ECONOMY

Overview of the Economy

The Central African Republic is one of the world's poorest and least developed nations. Economic development has suffered from poor infrastructure, particularly the lack of energy and transportation networks. There are few paved roads and limited air travel. Rivers are the main means of travel, and hydroelectric power is the main energy source. Political corruption and instability are other obstacles to development.

Bangui is the economic center of the country because of its location along the Oubangui and near the Bangui M'Poko International Airport. Important exports include timber, cotton, sisal (a stiff fiber used in making rope), and coffee, as well as other plantation crops.

The country receives extensive international aid, including humanitarian assistance. In 2014, the per capita gross domestic product (GDP) was estimated at $600 (USD), $300 less than in 2009.

Industry

Agriculture represents over half of the Central African Republic's GDP. Industry accounts for roughly 12 percent of GDP, while services account for nearly 33 percent. Diamond mining and timbering are important industries, along with textile production. Major European markets including France, the Benelux nations, Germany, and Spain. Important African trading partners include Egypt and Côte d'Ivoire.

In Bangui, service and light manufacturing industries are large employers. Soap, processed food products, and textiles are the primary manufactured exports, and are often produced in factories in and around Bangui.

Labor

Though the unemployment rate in the nation was estimated at eight percent in 2001, the unemployment rate in Bangui was estimated at close to 23 percent, largely because political instability has prevented the economy from keeping pace with the growth of the city's population. The labor force in 2014 numbered 2.217 million people.

Energy/Power/Natural Resources

The CAR is rich in mineral and forest resources, though poor infrastructure development and political corruption have limited their economic impact. The country's main mineral resources are gold, diamonds, and uranium; of these, only diamonds have been exploited extensively. The country's rivers provide hydropower.

Fishing

As a landlocked nation, the Central African Republic has a small commercial fishing industry that is concentrated along its rivers. Commercial fish include tilapia, which are pond-raised. The fishing industry was largely destroyed by the civil war that occurred between 2004 and 2007,

and foreign aid has since helped to revitalize the river-based industry, including the purchasing of refrigeration, nets, and motors for fishing canoes.

Forestry

Though important economically, representing about 30 percent of exports and 10 percent of the country's GDP, the timber trade has led to extensive deforestation and environmental damage. In 2010, the government implemented a mapping and geo-spatial forest monitoring system to help manage the nation's forests.

Mining/Metals

In the early 21st century, the CAR was the world's fifth largest exporter of diamonds. Gold and uranium are also resources which can be exploited, but the industry is largely undeveloped, although increased interest in the CAR by mining companies has been reported.

Agriculture

Much of the population supports itself by subsistence agriculture, and much of the country is malnourished. Most farmers raise food crops, while a few in the western region raise cattle. Only three percent of the land is arable, with a fraction of that land planted with permanent crops (approximately 1 percent), and the quality of soil is poor.

Coffee and cotton are the most important crops grown for export. Central African farmers also grow food crops such as manioc (cassava), corn, rice, millet, and plantains. Tobacco, peanuts, and palm are also important to the agricultural economy.

Animal Husbandry

Raised livestock includes cattle, goats, pigs, sheep, and poultry, the majority of which is consumed domestically.

Tourism

Tourism is relatively low in the CAR, due to the country's ongoing political instability and violence. Tourists are often targeted by gangs as robbery victims. Among the main tourist attractions are the country's beautiful landscapes and nature preserves. The Central African rainforests are home to large populations of elephants and

gorillas, and are popular destinations for tourists and nature enthusiasts.

Kristen Pappas, Eric Badertscher, Micah Issitt

DO YOU KNOW?

- The name "Bangui" and the name of the Oubangui River are derived from the word "rapids" in the Bobangui language. The fast current near Bangui was an obstacle to early attempts at using the river for commerce, though shipping barges and fishing ships still use the river despite the danger.

- The French dialect spoken in Bangui, known as Central African French, differs from the standard form of the language used in France and other nations. Central African French features slightly different pronunciations and a number of unique additions to the basic vocabulary borrowed from other African dialects.

Bibliography

Hochschild, Adam. "King Leopold's Ghost: A Story of Greed, Terror, and Heroism in Colonial Africa." *Houghton Mifflin Harcourt*, September 1999.

Titley, Brian. "Dark Age: The Political Odyssey of Emperor Bokassa." *McGill-Queens University Press*, May 2002.

Carayannis, Tatiana and Louisa Lombard. *Making Sense of the Central African Republic.* London: *Zed Books*, 2015.

Kalck, Xavier-Samuel. "Historical Dictionary of the Central African Republic." *The Scarecrow Press*, December 2004.

Sarno, Louis. "Song from the Forest: My Life among the Pygmies." San Antonio, TX: *Trinity University Press*, 2015.

Schildkrout, Enid. "The Scramble for Art in Central Africa." *Cambridge University Press*, March 1998.

Woodfork, Jacqueline. "Culture and Customs of the Central African Republic." *Greenwood Press*, September 2006.

Works Cited

"Aka People." *Wikipedia Online*. http://en.wikipedia.org/wiki/Aka_(Pygmy_tribe)

"All titles from the Central African Republic." *Imdb*. http://www.imdb.com/List?tv=on&&countries=Central%20African%20Republic&&nav=/Sections/Countries/CentralAfricanRepublic/includetitles&&heading=8;All;Central%20African%20RepublicBarry Hewlett.

"Are the men of the Aka tribe the best fathers in the world?" *The Guardian Online*. http://www.guardian.co.uk/society/2005/jun/15/childrensservices.familyandrelationships.

"Central African Republic." *City Population Online*. http://www.citypopulation.de/Centralafrica.html

"Central African Republic." *Habitat for Humanity*. http://www.habitat.org/intl/ame/42.aspx

"Central African Republic profile—Leaders." *BBC News*. http://www.bbc.com/news/world-africa-13150042.

"Central African Republic: Country Reports on Human Rights Practices." Bureau of Democracy, Human Rights, and Labor: *U.S. Department of State*. http://www.state.gov/g/drl/rls/hrrpt/2006/78725.htm

"Central African Republic Human Rights." *Amnesty International*. http://www.amnestyusa.org/all-countries/central-african-republic/page.do?id=1011131

"Central African Republic Food & Dining." *Iexplore*. http://www.iexplore.com/dmap/Central+African+Republic/Dining

"Jean-Bédel Bokassa." *Wikipedia Online Encyclopedia*. http://en.wikipedia.org/wiki/Jean-Bédel_Bokassa

"Looking Back, Looking Forward." *Cambridge African Film Festival*. http://www.african.cam.ac.uk/cambridgeafricanfilmfestival2004/filmprogramme/filmprogramme2.html

"Manovo-Gounda St. Floris National Park." *UNESCO World Heritage Sites*. http://whc.unesco.org/en/list/475

"Monographs on African Artist." Jérôme Ramedane. 1936–1991. *Smithsonian Institute Online*. http://www.sil.si.edu/SILPublications/ModernAfricanArt/monographs_detail.cfm?artist=Ramedane,%20Jérôme,%201936-1991

"Music of the Central African Republic." *Wikipedia Online*. http://en.wikipedia.org/wiki/Music_of_the_Central_African_Republic

"Musical Bow, Mbela: Musical Instruments of Africa." *Cartage*. http://www.cartage.org.lb/en/themes/Arts/music/instruments/minstrumentafr/mbela/mbela.htm

"Traditional Pygmy Music of the Central African Republic." *Encarta Online*. http://encarta.msn.com/media_461564890_761574398_-1_1/Traditional_Pygmy_Music_of_the_Central_African_Republic.html

"Support for the Bakouma Library." *Libraries without Borders*. http://www.librarieswithoutborders.org/index.php/what-we-do/our-programs/abroad/sub-saharan-africa/central-african-republic/item/166-support-for-the-bakouma-library.

Chevigny, Blue. "Child Soldiers Demobalized in the Central African Republic." *UNICEF*. http://www.unicef.org/infobycountry/car_39740.html

Gikandi, Simon. *"Encyclopedia of African Literature." Google Book Search*. http://books.google.com/books?id=hFuWQmsM0HsC&pg=PA134&lpg=PA134&dq=Pierre+SammyMackfoy&source=bl&ots=0wez9Yoc7V&sig=02acgW8voyLssqG2BOxxA2h73pY&hl=en&ei=2KNSbXPHIiiNez3xacL&sa=X&oi=book_result&resnum=5&ct=result#PPA133,M1Thompson, Mike. "Deserted villages and abandoned lives." *BBC Online*. http://news.bbc.co.uk/today/hi/today/newsid_7779000/7779890.stm

Harrow, Kenneth W. "With Open Eyes." *Google Books Online*. http://books.google.com/books?id=IouwFbVrjPUC&pg=PA170&lpg=PA170&dq=leonie+yangba+zowe&source=bl&ots=YcSzFaSffb&sig=zvgYKw6zgu6CO0FSOmmTWiE0PM&hl=en&ei=ldONSaLNNaCYNZiWY0L&sa=X&oi=book_result&resnum=7&ct=result#PPA169,M1

Lovett,Richard A. "'Black' Diamonds May Come From Outer Space." *National Geographic News Online*. http://news.nationalgeographic.com/news/2007/01/070122-black-diamonds.html

Townsend, Dorn. "Campaign addresses three leading causes for child mortality in CAR." *UNICEF*. http://www.unicef.org/infobycountry/car_47033.html

Woodfork, Jacqueline Cassandra. "Culture and Customs of the Central African Republic." *Greenwood Publishing Group*, Google Books Online. http://books.google.com/books?id=7SEWjJ0_w2oC&pg=PA75&lpg=PA75&dq=architecture+in+bangui&source=web&ots=jpbJtB89EL&sig=eMqljXvvyuOH05a9Bc1Mdul-J7E&hl=en&sa=X&oi=book_result&resnum=2&ct=result#PPP1,M1

Homes in rural Chad are made from clay bricks and thatched with straw. iStock/retinal_experiments.

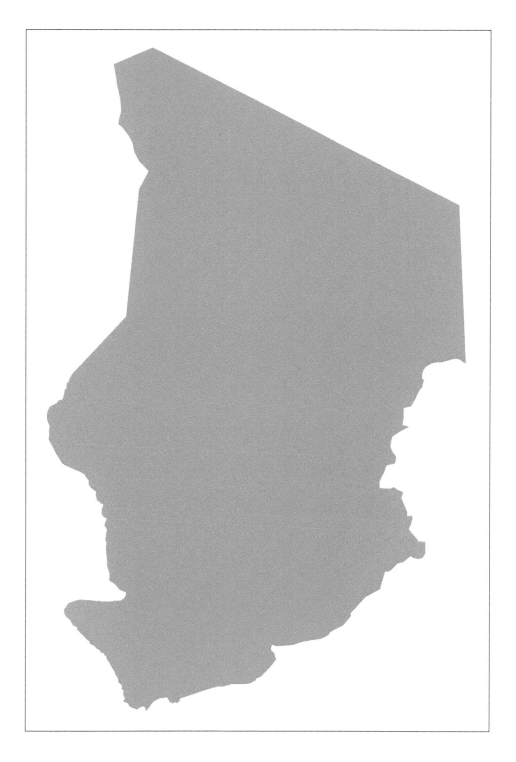

CHAD

Introduction

Chad is a landlocked nation in central Africa. It borders Sudan to the east, the Central African Republic to the south, Cameroon to the southwest, Niger and Nigeria to the west, and Libya to the north. Known for the uranium-rich Aouzou Strip, Chad was a colony of France from 1913 to 1960.

N'Djaména, the capital, which takes its name from the Arab word for "place of rest," was once considered an important staging ground for many humanitarian missions in the Central African region. However, recent warfare, both in Chad and in neighboring countries, has challenged Chad's stability, and the capital was the site of two rebel attacks, in 2006 and 2008, both named the Battle of N'Djaména. Furthermore, in 2015, Chad joined the fight against Boko Haram, a militant Islamist group operating in Africa, which led to a retaliatory attack by suicide bombers in the capital, killing 23 people.

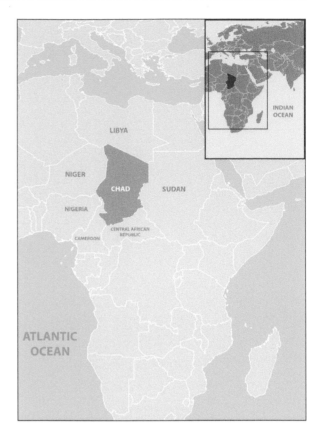

GENERAL INFORMATION

Official Language: French, Arabic
Population: 11,631,456 (2015)
Currency: Communaute Financiere Africaine franc/Central African CFA franc
Coins: Coins are available in denominations of 1, 2, 5, 10, 25, 50, 100, and 500 francs.
Land Area: 1,259,200 square kilometers (486,179 square miles)
Water Area: 24,800 square kilometers (9,575 square miles)

National Motto: "Unité, Travail, Progrès" (French, "Unity, Work, Progress")
National Anthem: "La Tchadienne" (The Chadian)
Capital: N'Djaména
Time Zone: GMT +1
Flag Description: Chad's flag features a vertical tricolor design of blue (left), yellow (center), and red (right) bands. The flag combines the colors of the French flag (Chad was part of French Equatorial Africa) and Pan-Africanism. More distinctly, blue symbolizes sky and water, and ostensibly hope; yellow represents the desert and the sun; while red represents not only the sacrificed blood of independence, but also ideals such as unity and progress.

Population

Chadians are divided into over 200 ethnic groups, among which 120 unique languages are spoken. The northernmost area of the country is dominated by the Toubou people, a clan-based group of nomadic herders who control the nation's government. Other groups in the

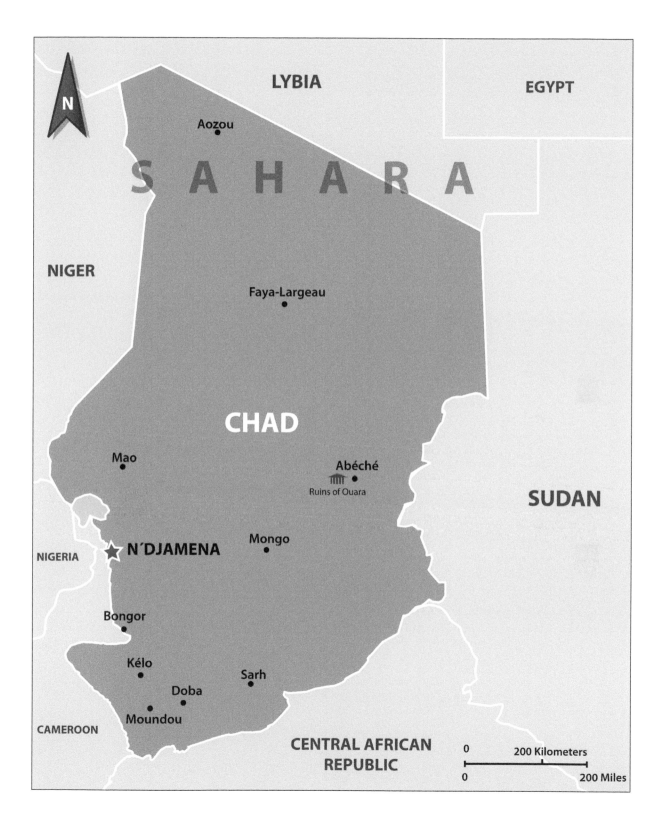

Principal Cities by Population (2010):

- N'Djaména (818,600)
- Moundou (141,200)
- Sarh (119,400)
- Abéché (77,400)
- Kelo (45,100)
- Pala (40,400)
- Koumra (38,400)
- Am Timan (31,400)
- Mongo (29,700)
- Bongor (29,400)

northern part of the country are the Gorane, Zaghawa, Kanembou, Ouaddaï, and Fulbe.

The Sahel region, in the central area of Chad, borders the Sahara Desert and is populated mostly by groups of Arab Muslims. More than 30 percent of Chadians are of Arab descent. Most of the Sahel region's Arab groups, which include the Maba people, are nomadic herders.

Black African ethnic groups dominate Chad's southern region. The Sara people are the largest indigenous group in the south, followed by the Massa, Moussei, and Moundang. Roughly one-third of all Chadians are Sara. There is also a very small minority French population living in Chad.

The capital and largest city in Chad is N'Djaména. Located in the southwest on the Nigerian border, N'Djaména is divided into a modernized wealthy community (the remnants of the French colonial period), and a poorer residential section with mud-brick dwellings. Due to extensive civil warfare in the 20th century, many parts of N'Djaména remain in ruin.

Other major cities in Chad are Abéché, the former capital of the ancient Ouaddaï Sultanate; Gaoui, which is built on the ruins of the capital of the Sao Kingdom of the first century BCE; the trading town of Mao; an agricultural settlement called Kélo; Moundou, center of the Sara people and the site of the Gala Beer Brewery; and Sarh, the country's cotton and sugarcane center.

Most of the population is rural. Eastern Chad, itself the site of insecurity and hostilities,

is home to more than 470,000 refugees, the majority from the Sudan and the Central African Republic, as well as some 111,000 internally displaced persons.

Languages

The predominant languages of Chad and its capital, N'Djaména, are French and Arabic, both of which are official languages of the country. Sara is also commonly spoken in the southern part of Chad. Regional African dialects are also common, and over 100 regional dialects are often spoken throughout Chad.

Native People & Ethnic Groups

Many rock paintings and engravings have been found in Chad. These paintings indicate that the area was inhabited as early as 5000 BCE. The Toubou, the Tuareg, and many other Chadian ethnic groups in the north are descended from the Berber people. Berbers came to Central Africa around 3000 BCE, and today primarily inhabit countries west of Chad. Arabs came to Chad near the beginning of the 12th century.

Although they are the majority among the black groups in the south, the Sara people have continually been abused by other groups in Chad. Arab traders from the north and European colonists enslaved and exploited the Sara for centuries. The Sara continue to face discrimination from non-black Chadians, despite the fact that the nation's first post-colonial president was Saran.

Ethnic disputes between the north and south are common. Civil war has broken out several times in Chad, mostly over issues of government representation. In an effort to combat rebellions in the Darfur region of Sudan, the Sudanese government and Janjawid militia groups have driven roughly 367,000 political refugees into eastern Chad. The Sudanese refugees are not included in Chad's population estimate.

Religions

Islam and Christianity are the nation's two most prominent religions. Roughly 53 percent of Chadians practice Islam and 20 percent practice

Christianity. For the most part, Islam is practiced in the northern regions, while Christianity is confined to the south. The remaining 27 percent of the population practices traditional African religions such as animism.

Climate

Like its topography, Chad's climate is divided into three zones. The Soudanian zone experiences an average temperature of 23° Celsius (73° Fahrenheit). The temperature in the Sahelian region often reaches 45° Celsius (113° Fahrenheit).

Chad receives an annual average of 50 centimeters (20 inches) of rain in the central region and 114 centimeters (45 inches) in the southern region. Rainfall is scarce in the northern zone, which contains part of the Sahara and the Tibesti Massif. Most of the country's rain comes during the wet season, which occurs between July and September.

The most prevalent natural hazard in Chad is the harmattan, which is a strong, often dangerous desert wind. Long droughts in the Sahelian region have caused extensive desertification and inhibit the growth of vegetation throughout the central region. Plagues of locusts and severely high temperatures are among other natural hazards.

ENVIRONMENT & GEOGRAPHY

Topography

Chad is divided into a mountainous northern region, the Sahel region in the center, and the Soudanian region in the south. The main topographical feature in Chad is the Tibesti Massif, a mountain range in the northeast. In this range is Emi Koussi, the country's highest peak at 3,415 meters (11,204 feet).

Chad contains several lakes, the largest of which is Lake Chad. Located in the southeast, it was once one of the largest freshwater lakes in the world. Lake Chad doubles in size during the wet season, and often shrinks significantly during dry spells. A Sahelian drought in 1984

caused the lake to disappear completely. Other major lakes include Lac Fitri in the south and Lac Yao in the north.

The Chari and the Logone are Chad's two main rivers. Both are located in the Soudanian zone in the south and flow into Lake Chad.

N'Djaména, the capital, is located on the western edge of Chad, which borders the nations of Sudan, Central African Republic, Cameroon, Niger, Nigeria, and Libya. Situated on the banks of the Chari River, directly across from the city of Kousséri in Cameroon, the capital is Chad's chief export center. Both the Chari and Logone rivers meet near N'Djaména and both are feeder systems for Lake Chad, one of the largest sources of freshwater in Africa.

Plants & Animals

Zakouma National Park is the only national park in Chad and contains much of the country's wildlife. However, many animals at Zakouma have been killed by poachers and warfare. With assistance from the European Union, the Chadian government has restocked the park with many of its indigenous species. Chad's native animals include elephants, giraffes, wildebeests, monkeys, lions, and antelopes.

Many varieties of trees are found in Chad's forests. The area surrounding Lake Chad is the most densely forested, and contains ebony, kapok, acacias, baobab, desert palms, date palms, and jujubes.

CUSTOMS & COURTESIES

Greetings

Because of the remarkable number of cultural groups and spoken languages in Chad, most Chadians are multilingual. The official languages are French and Arabic, but nearly all Chadians speak a local language as well. Chadian Arabic is perhaps the most popularly spoken language, and is infused with local dialects. Common greeting phrases include the more familiar "Lalê" ("Hello") and "Al-salâm alek" or "Al-salâm aleki," the latter used to greet women. A common greeting in the Sara languages, several of which are spoken in southern Chad, is "Lafia ngai" ("Hello").

Chadians will almost always shake hands when greeting and meeting people. A right-handed handshake is the most universal form of greeting. When meeting more than one person, or an entire group of people, it is customary to shake hands with each person. Between sexes and between women, greetings are usually verbal or are a simple nod of acknowledgment. When greeting an elder or someone of significantly higher social status, it is common for Chadians to bow or kneel while shaking hands. The precise form is generally dictated by the situation and the existing relationship between the individuals.

Greetings are generally followed by small talk. This includes polite inquiries about one's family, work, or crops. After a greeting or conversation, it is common for Muslim Chadians to place a hand on their chests, signaling that all is well.

Gestures & Etiquette

Due to the wide variety of religious and cultural backgrounds among Chadians, there is not one universal set of etiquette rules followed throughout the country. Common features, however, include respect for elders and conservative public behavior. For example, elders are customarily referred to by the honorific titles of "mother" and "father," regardless of actual familial relations. In addition, Muslims in northern Chad will often reference the family's eldest child.

Like many African and Middle Eastern cultures, customs regarding physical proximity and contact in Chad are often considerably different than they are in Western cultures. It is thus common for strangers, after having been introduced, to stand in close proximity to one other. It is also common for those of the same sex to hold hands in public, which is considered a display of friendship. Public displays of affection between men and women are not normal or generally accepted in Chad.

Common gestures include beckoning with the hand facing down and pulling the fingers toward the palm; agreeing by thrusting the chin forward and clicking the tongue; and catching someone's eye and rotating an open palm from a face down to face up position to mean, "What's up?" There are also many taboo gestures, including the use of the left hand in public to pass food or shake hands. This is because the left hand is associated with the cleansing of the body in Muslim culture, and is thus traditionally considered impure.

Eating/Meals

For Chadian families, mealtime is an important opportunity that traditionally brings the family together. A majority of the country is self-supporting by necessity and, as in many African cultures, cooking and meal preparation is customarily the responsibility of women. In most rural areas, meals are typically cooked over a three-rock fire on the ground or over an open charcoal fire.

Lunch is traditionally the main meal and is generally eaten at midday. A smaller meal is eaten near sundown. Morning meals have generally been rare. When breakfast is eaten, it is usually leftovers from the previous day's meals. Most meals are eaten while seated on the ground or floor and from a communal bowl, and men and women usually eat in separate areas. Traditionally, men and guests are served the best portions, children are served what remains, and women eat last, after the children have finished. As in many African and Arabic cultures, Chadians typically eat with their fingers, without utensils, and almost exclusively with their right hands.

Visiting

There is a great premium placed on hospitality in Chadian culture. Chadian hosts will invariably offer guests whatever is available; many times this might only be a glass of water or homemade millet beer. (Guest might also be offered water to wash their hands, face, and feet in the dry and dusty desert regions.) Though it is impolite to refuse what is offered, it is customary for a guest to make several token refusals before finally accepting. When visiting people or families socially or for business, it is polite and acceptable to give gifts. Small, practical, nonelectrical items are always best.

If a guest arrives at mealtime, he or she is typically invited to eat with the family. Mealtime is a particularly communal activity for many Chadians, and women will prepare enough food (if possible and practical) in case an unexpected visitor arrives. Guests should not begin eating until after the host has indicated that everyone should begin. When the guest stops eating, the meal is considered finished.

LIFESTYLE

Family

In Chad, different cultures often maintain unique traditions regarding the family, its structure, and its significance. Despite any differences that may exist, there are still many common features to most of these cultural groups, including deference for elders and the importance of the extended family. Traditionally, the family, rather than the individual, is viewed as the basic unit of social organization. This often takes the form of an extended family or a joint family of married brothers. As of 2015, it was estimated that each woman in Chad gave birth to an average of 4.55 children.

Chadian families are traditionally patrilineal, with the husband considered the absolute head of each household. Muslim law (known as Sharia) plays a key role in the lives and family structure in the northern regions of the country and among Muslim families throughout Chad. However, of declining significance among many of Chad's cultural groups, the traditional framework of clans continues to be important. Clan membership is particularly important to pastoralist groups such as the Tubu, Nar, and Tupuri.

Housing

A majority of Chad's population is rural, and resides in small villages comprised of homes made with natural elements. Houses are typically round with walls made of dried clay or adobe bricks mixed with straw. Roofs are cone-shaped

and made with straw, and built to be several inches thick. Many families adorn the tip of the roof with an object or symbol that represents the family and the clan to which they belong. A wealthy family might further embellish its home with a veneer of cement around the outer wall or replace the thatched roof with one of corrugated aluminum. In some regions of the country, homes are built with walls made of straw. Typically, this type of home is more temporary and built to be conveniently located near crops.

Houses are generally only one or two rooms and have few windows. They are primarily used for sleeping (away from the weather) and storage. Food is often cooked outdoors, but if a family has a kitchen, it usually occupies a separate building. In some regions, notably in and around the Sahel, homes are located within walled compounds.

Food

The semi-arid climate of much of Chad considerably limits the agricultural potential of the soil. Staple crops include cereal grain such as maize, sorghum, and millet, in addition to potatoes, rice, sesame, and beans. Because of the abundance of cultural groups, and the significant cultural divide between the people in the north and south, there is no single shared national food culture. The most common dish is boule, a porridge made with sorghum, millet, or corn that is shaped into bite-sized balls and then dipped into sauces. These various sauces typically contain meat, dried fish, okra, garlic, tomatoes, onions, and various spices. A variation of this dish that is often eaten in the morning is bouillie, which is a cold or warm dish made with millet and peanuts, and flavored with lemon and sugar.

Generally speaking, the southern diet contains a variety of tubers and spices, no fish, and very few dairy products. In the north, the typical diet and dietary restrictions resemble those of most other Muslim areas. Nomads throughout the country rely heavily on the dairy products of their livestock, including yogurt and milk. Special occasions in the south are cause to eat tan kul, which is a spiced sauce poured over fish or meat and beans. In the north, people often celebrate with nashif, which is meat cooked in a spicy tomato sauce.

Gala beer, brewed in Kélo; Moundou, is the nation's most popular alcoholic beverage. Beer is also brewed from millet. Soft drinks and a frozen fruit drink called jus are also widely drunk.

Life's Milestones

Most cultural groups in Chad honor and maintain their own traditions concerning major life milestones such as birth, puberty, marriage, and death. Rites and traditions important to initiation and healing rituals define many cultural and personal identities. Ceremonies central to Islam and Christianity have the most widespread influence and play significant roles in the religious lives of their adherents.

One local, secular ceremony of note among the Sara peoples is a traditional male initiation ceremony known as yondo. Every few years, village elders gather the young boys and conduct "meetings" at which the boys learn the traditions and customs of their village and culture. They also learn about the duties and responsibilities of men. At the end of the process, the boys are considered men and must live and eat separately from their female relatives. A similar version is also conducted for girls when they are taught about the traditional female duties of household maintenance, cooking, child rearing, and respect for male authority.

CULTURAL HISTORY

Art

Like many North African nations, Chad is home to a large collection of prehistoric rock art, most of which is located in the northeastern part of the country. Along with primitive stone tools, early jewelry such as beads and bracelets, and ceramics, these rock carvings represent the earliest forms of art in the region. In fact, the development of these early inhabitants is reflected in these pictographs, as the rock art progressed from simple depictions of wild animals and hunting scenes to show dancing and woman with baskets.

Humans, first depicted as stick figures, were later drawn holding more sophisticated weaponry, as well as with ornamental arrangements such as jewelry, hairstyles, and attire.

Despite the prevalence of fine art and traditional handicrafts from surrounding African countries, the traditional art and crafts of Chad have received comparatively little fanfare. Nonetheless, there are some 200 unique cultural groups within Chad, and many maintain a tradition of ornate decorations, including adorning their homes, clothing, and everyday artifacts created for their utilitarian value. Important handicrafts in modern Chad include basket weaving, pottery, woodcarving, and leatherwork. These art forms have produced regional and local artistic traditions and crafts that include woven mats, wood sculptures, jewelry, wool rugs, and carved gourds known as calabashes. In addition, women have historically developed embroidery skills while men have carved leather and soapstone statues.

Architecture

Traditional architecture in Chad is distinguished by the use of natural materials such as mud walls and thatched roofs. Houses are typically round with walls made of dried clay or adobe bricks mixed with straw. A wealthy family might further embellish its home with a veneer of cement around the outer wall. They might also replace the thatched roof with one of corrugated aluminum. In some regions of the country, homes are made with walls made of straw. Typically, this type of home is more temporary and built to be conveniently located near crops. Many government buildings and schools are also built with mud brick walls, but generally in a rectangular shape.

Drama

A form of artistic expression that is relatively new for the country is that of narrative film. Chad is not renowned for its films or filmmakers, but there have been several advances in recent years. Issa Serge Coelo (1967–) and Mahamat-Saleh Haroun (1961–) are two Chadian filmmakers, both living in France, who have become relatively well known. Coelo's best-known film, *Daresalam* (2000), is set in a fictional central African country, but recounts the ravages of Chad's civil war of the 1960s and 1970s. Critics have praised the film for accurately portraying the turbulent issues surrounding internal conflicts and civil war. Haroun's two most successful films, *Bye, Bye Africa* (1999) and *Abouna* (2002), are both stories about ordinary Chadians finding their way in society and the world. Both filmmakers won multiple international awards for their respective films. Owing to Haroun's success in the 2010 Cannes film festival, the Chadian government tasked Haroun with opening a film school in Chad with international standards in the upcoming years.

Music

In a general sense, the song and dance traditions of Chad have historically been linked to specific events, ceremonies, or occasions. Such forms of artistic expression usually occur during significant events in village life, including those that have religious and spiritual purposes. For many Chadians, music is also intimately connected with the natural world in which they live. In addition, each cultural group and region has their own unique varieties of music and dance, similar to traditional crafts.

Traditional music focuses on a number of wind, percussion, and stringed instruments. Common instruments associated with traditional music among Chad's cultures include the hu, kakaki, kinde harp, tam, kodio drum, balaphone, and zither. The hu is a stringed instrument amplified with "speakers" made of hollowed calabashes. The kakaki is one of many types of horn found throughout Chad; it is typically made out of tin. Similar horns and trumpets are made with other materials, including goat horns. These instruments are widely used in royal ceremonies such as coronations.

The kinde harp is a kind of bow harp and is typically associated with the ancient griot tradition of singing and oral storytelling. (Griots are West African wandering poets and praise singers, similar to a bard in European culture.) Many

types of drums, including the tam and kodio drum, are widely used in traditional Chadian music. They are probably most often associated with the southern Sara people, who also incorporate whistles and the balaphone (an instrument similar to the xylophone) into their music. Zithers (string instrument) are another common Chadian instrument, and are often associated with the Baguirmi people.

Literature

Chad, like many other African nations, has a rich oral tradition, including epics, folktales, and legends. As in many early cultures, these folktales and legends were proverbial and didactic in nature, and often featured animals as both protagonists and antagonists. These stories helped to impart values and moralistic lessons, as well as preserve history. Most of the cultural groups within Chad have maintained their storytelling traditions and continue to pass on their unique myths and narratives.

Some of the more notable Chadian literature to have developed in recent history has come from the expatriate community, particularly in France. This includes native Chadian writers such as playwright Baba Moustapha (1952–1982); playwright, poet, and novelist Koulsy Lamko (1959–); Nocky Djedanoum (1959–), director of the annual Fest'Africa festival in France and creator of a project to remember the genocide in Rwanda; and writer and politician Joseph Brahim Seid (1927–1980). Seid wrote two books which are today considered classics in Chad: *Au Tchad sous les étoiles* (*In Chad under the Stars*, 1962) and *Un enfant du Tchad* (*A Child of Chad*, 1967). The former was translated as *Told by Starlight in Chad* in 2007, and was hailed as presenting a new multicultural Chadian identity.

CULTURE

Arts & Entertainment

Completely landlocked within north-central Africa, Chad has been particularly susceptible to cultural trends and influences from surrounding cultures. Though there is a minor arts scene native to Chad, there is not a widespread arts culture that has significantly defined the country in modern times. Most art in Chad stems from practical and economic needs. For example, local handicrafts are generally utilitarian, and include woven mats and wool rugs, as well as jewelry and wood carvings. Chadian art also suffers from a substantial lack of patronage and government support, and only a few individual artists are able to maintain galleries in the capital of N'Djaména. Further exacerbating the situation is the fact that Musée National in N'Djaména (National Museum), already small in nature, has been subjected to looting and the loss of important artifacts during the country's recent history of conflict and instability.

Like many places in Africa, popular music in Chad is heavily influenced by the soukous music of the Democratic Republic of the Congo (DRC). Unique Chadian styles include sai which incorporates rhythms from the southern region of the country. Sai music was popularized by the group Tibesti. Other Chadian musical artists include International Challal, African Melody, Ahmed Pecos, and Clément Masdongar.

Chad's most popular sport, and one the nation's only professionally played sports, is soccer. Nambatingue Tokomon, a Chadian soccer player in France, is Chad's most famous athlete. Other popular sports include basketball, boxing, and wrestling.

Cultural Sites & Landmarks

With its desert climate and terrain—the Sahara Desert and Sahel region cover a vast majority of the country—and continuing instability, Chad's tourism sector remains relatively undeveloped. Nonetheless, the landlocked nation remains the fifth-largest country in Africa (and the twenty-first-largest country in the world) and has considerable natural and cultural sites. One of Chad's most important landmarks is Zakouma National Park, the nation's first national park. The park itself is surrounded by the Bahr Salamat Faunal Reserve and features forty-four species of mammals, including a sizeable elephant population.

Aside from the stark, desolate beauty of the Sahara, Chad is also home to several other notable natural sites, including the northern volcanic Tibesti Mountains, which extend into neighboring Libya and Niger. Within Chad is the summit of Emi Koussi, which, at 3,415 meters (11,204 feet), is the highest point in the Sahara. Chad's cultural sites include the hills of Tibesti, where prehistoric engravings of scenes depicting animals and hunters can be found.

Chad has also submitted a number of cultural sites and natural landmarks to the United Nations Educational, Scientific, and Cultural Organization (UNESCO) for consideration as World Heritage Sites. One notable site is the Ruins of Ouara. Ouara was the former capital of the Ouaddai Empire (1635–1912), which was abandoned in the 19th century. The ruins date back to the 17th century. Architectural remains include the sultan's palace, mosque, and city wall. Other submitted sites include the historic Lake Chad; the prehistoric engravings and paintings of Ennedi and Tibesti; the iron mines of Tele-Nugar, discovered in 1911; and the metallurgical site of Begon (or Begon II), dating back to between the ninth and 11th centuries CE.

The Grand Market in N'Djaména is a popular attraction and social center for the city, and where the majority of the region's agricultural products, textiles, and handicrafts can be purchased. With a large Muslim population, N'Djaména is home to the Great Mosque, built over a four-year period beginning in 1974. The building is a dominant part of Chad's skyline, and is located in the center of town. N'Djaména also has a large cathedral from its time as a French colony.

Libraries & Museums

The Place d'Independence, in N'Djaména, is the home to the Presidential Palace, government buildings, and foreign embassies. It also houses Chad's National Museum, which was founded in 1962. The museum is not large, with only five rooms containing artifacts from the pre-historic era to modern day, though it maintains an important collection of local traditions and culture, including indigenous art and paleontological discoveries such as fossilized tools.

The Sao-Kotoko Museum in Gaoui features artifacts salvaged from the ancient Sao Kingdom. In addition, traditional African crafts such as baskets, mats, dyed cloths, and masks are featured at N'Djaména's Centre Artisanal. The national library is also located in the capital.

Holidays

Chad's national holiday is Independence Day, which is celebrated on August 11. Other public holidays include Africa Freedom Day (May 25), Republic Day (November 28), and the Day of Liberty (December 1). Christian and Muslim holidays are also observed by Chadians throughout the year.

Youth Culture

Chad is a developing country with a noticeable lack of infrastructure outside of the capital of N'Djaména. Western-style entertainment options are few and virtually nonexistent outside of metropolitan areas, and Chad is one of the few remaining nations that have little, if any, contact with Western pop culture. In addition, young people generally have very little, if any, disposable income to spend on luxuries such as technology, designer clothing, or the latest personal accessories.

Outside of the capital and few other cities, most Chadians live without electricity, and children generally make their own toys out of scrap materials and spare parts. Most boys grow up playing football (soccer) and cultural and village-based ceremonies and events are the general form of entertainment in rural areas. Urban youth have more opportunities for leisure activities, including attending the cinema and socializing at bars and dance clubs. Attendance to primary school is mandatory, but very few children continue with further education. Children must learn responsibilities from an early age, as they are expected to help with daily chores around the home and in the fields. In fact, schools rarely assign homework as these afterschool responsibilities are an accepted part of children's lives.

Regardless of whether they live in the city or in the countryside, childhood is usually short in Chad. Youth have been heavily involved in the internal conflict that has plagued the country since the latter half of the 20th century. Urban violence among the youth culture of N'Djaména continues to be a huge concern, and youth are typically the perpetrators and victims of violence in the capital. It is believed that rapid urbanization in the capital, and the country abroad, is leading to an increase in street crime and gangs, especially as more youth are leaving rural areas for more opportunity. Youth are also being recruited into the Chadian army and rebel forces.

SOCIETY

Transportation

Around urban areas, particularly the capital of N'Djaména, shared taxis, minibuses, and clandos (motorcycle taxis) are the most common forms of transportation. Chad ranks low globally in terms of vehicles per capita and car ownership. Traffic moves on the right-hand side of the road.

N'Djaména International Airport is served by Air Tchad and Air France, as well as several other African airlines, including Cameroon Airlines, Ethiopian Airlines, Interair South Africa, and Sudan Airways. There are 59 airports in Chad, but only nine with paved runways.

Transportation Infrastructure

Chad is a sparsely populated country characterized by its desert climate and terrain. Much of the country is dominated by the Sahara and Sahel deserts, resulting in a population density that is only about 20 people per square mile. As a result, constructing and maintaining a viable transportation infrastructure has always been challenging. The country lacks a rail network and, as of 2011, had 206 km (128 miles) of paved highway of a total of 25,000 km (15,534 miles) of national and regional roads. In addition, Chad's rivers are only navigable during the rainy season, resulting in a lack of viable ports, harbors, or waterways.

Minibuses remain the primary mode of public transportation, while land cruisers and trucks are the primary—and most reliable—methods of long-distance travel. N'Djaména has Chad's only international airport.

Media & Communications

Radio is the most pervasive and important medium of mass communication in Chad. However, state control of public stations allows for few dissenting opinions. Several privately-owned stations broadcast in the country, and many of these are run by religious and non-profit organizations.

There is one nationally broadcast television station, Teletchad, which is state-controlled. Several newspapers are printed and distributed throughout Chad, and most of these are in French. The only daily newspaper is *Le Progres*. Other privately funded weekly newspapers include *N'Djaména Hebdo*, *L'Observateur*, *Le Temps*, and *Notre Temps*. Though the private newspapers tend to be the most critical of the government, they have relatively little impact due to their limited readership.

Mobile phones are quickly becoming popular among Chadians, with an estimated 46 users per 100 in 2014 (as opposed to only 23,000 installed and functioning land lines, which is less than 1 user per 100). In 2014, there were an estimated 273,900 Internet users, representing less than 2.5 percent of the total population.

SOCIAL DEVELOPMENT

Standard of Living

Chad ranked 184th out of 195 countries on the 2014 United Nations Human Development Index, which measures quality of life and standard of living indicators.

Water Consumption

It is estimated that only half of Chad's population has access to improved drinking water sources, including wells and piped water. In fact, Chad is one of six countries identified by the UN

as having less than 50 percent drinking water coverage (with sanitation coverage estimated at even lower). A 2010 United Nations report also estimates that nearly 85 percent of rural households might be sourcing their drinking water from areas used for defecation or waste disposal. Lake Chad, the continent's third-largest freshwater source, as well as a primary drinking water source in the region, is disappearing at an alarming rate, further exacerbating the issue of water consumption in the country. Flooding has also impacted access to drinking water in recent years.

Education

Primary education in Chad is compulsory for students up to age twelve. In the early 1980s, civil war caused the destruction of many of Chad's public schools. The education system remains inadequate. Overcrowding and a low number of trained teachers are the most significant problems. The average literacy rate among Chadians is 40 percent (48.5 percent for males and 31.9 percent for females).

Arab Muslims established Quranic secondary schools throughout Chad, which teach the Arabic language and the Islamic religion to students. The Ecole Mohamed Illech is among the nation's Quranic secondary schools. Chad's only university is the University of N'Djaména.

According to UNESCO, between 2005 and 2008, the primary/secondary gross enrollment ratio for women (per 100) was 37.6 and for men (per 100), was 58.5. Therefore, while educational attainment and literacy rates are generally lower in Chad, they are worse for women, who are underrepresented in primary, secondary, and tertiary education programs, where they represent only six percent of the total student population.

Women's Rights

The Chadian constitution provides equal rights for men and women and Chadian law directly prohibits domestic violence, rape, and prostitution. However, local culture continues to devalue the traditional roles and responsibilities of women, and all three continue to be serious problems in the country. Widespread discrimination and violence against women persists and, while rape is illegal, Chadian law does not provide for criminal penalties. Cases of domestic abuse continue rarely reported, and furthermore, rarely brought to trial.

The practice of female genital mutilation (FGM) is prohibited by law, but still widely practiced among many of Chad's cultural groups. Deeply rooted in tradition, it is estimated that the practice affects 45 percent of all Chadian women prior to puberty. It is primarily practiced in the eastern and southern regions of the country, particularly in those regions nearest to Sudan. A 1995 law theoretically made FGM a prosecutable offense, but no cases or charges have ever been made under the law. UNESCO reports that it is a steeply declining practice, however, with many, if not more, men speaking out against it.

Chad continues to be a patriarchal society where women traditionally assume domestic roles, including handling family responsibilities, household tasks, and child rearing. As such, women are unrepresented in politics, the military, and business, and Chad's pastoralist economy is almost exclusively under male influence. Educational opportunities for women are also limited, and many families arrange marriages for girls as young as eleven. Among some southern groups, the practice of polygamy (taking more than one wife) is common. Chadian law does not prohibit such practice and a husband may decide at any time that a marriage is polygamous.

Women are not significantly organized in public associations. However, there is a small and emerging group of female traders in N'Djaména and other cities. Generally speaking, women are not restricted in their ability to take part in the basics of society. They are free to move about in most spheres and actively engage in local economies. Among the northern Muslim groups, traditional Muslim customs such as the wearing of a veil in public are not prevalent, and there are no limits on the societal role of Chadian Muslim women.

Health Care

Health care and services in Chad are substandard. The largest and busiest hospital in the country is Hôpital Central in N'Djaména, but the facility is regarded as unsafe and unclean. Chadians are at high risk for contracting a number of infections and diseases, including meningitis, protozoal diarrhea, malaria, schistosomiasis, hepatitis A, typhoid fever, and HIV/AIDS.

Landmines left over from the civil war pose a serious threat to the safety of Chadians, particularly along the disputed Aouzou Strip. Life expectancy is estimated at 51 years for women and 48.5 years for men (2015 estimate).

GOVERNMENT

Structure

Chad experienced extensive civil warfare throughout the 20th century. Upon gaining independence from France in 1960, a Saran southerner named François Tomballage became the nation's first president. Tomballage oppressed Chadians by arresting political dissenters and banning any political parties from forming oppositions to his presidency; he was assassinated in 1975.

Escalating disputes between dissenters and supporters led to a full-scale civil war in 1979 between the Muslim north and the Christian south. In 1980, France and Libya intervened. Both sides agreed to remove their troops in an unofficial cease-fire in 1987. Libya broke the agreement and attacked. Chadian soldiers then forced Libya back over the border, and the country was relatively peaceful for the next few years.

In 1990, a Muslim warlord named Idriss Deby mobilized an army and assumed leadership of Chad, rigging elections to keep himself in office. A former minister of Deby's named Youssouf Togoimi formed the Movement for Democracy and Justice in Chad (MDJT) and launched a rebellion in 1998. However, Deby remained in power, tampering with election results to win the presidency again in 2001.

Chad is a democratic republic. The president, elected by popular vote to a five-year term, is the head of state and highest executive authority. The Council of State is the president's appointed cabinet. The council is overseen by the prime minister, who is the head of government.

A 155-member elected parliament, which is known as the National Assembly, comprises the legislative branch. The judicial branch consists of a Supreme Court, a Court of Appeals, Criminal Courts and Magistrate Courts.

The age of suffrage in Chad is 18. Although Chad is a democracy, its government continues to be characterized by oppression, corruption, and human rights violations.

Political Parties

Chad is considered a one-party dominant state. The ruling party, Patriotic Salvation Movement, has dominated Chadian politics since 1990. During the 2006 elections, the country's primary opposition parties boycotted the elections. Following the 2002 parliamentary elections, the Patriotic Salvation Movement controlled 113 seats, while the opposition parties Rally for Democracy and Progress and Federation Action for the Republic each won 10 seats. Two other opposition parties won five seats each, one party gained three seats, and nine parties each gained one seat.

Local Government

Local governance in Chad consists of 23 administrative divisions headed by an appointed governor.

Judicial System

Chad's legal system is based on modified French civil and criminal law. Courts include magistrate and criminal courts, court of appeal, and the country's Supreme Court. Generally, it is a mixed system of customary and civil law.

Taxation

Tax rates in Chad are high, with the highest personal income rate at 60 percent and the highest corporate tax rate at 40 percent. Other taxes levied in the country include a value-added tax

(VAT) and property tax. Taxes and other revenue make up 18.2 percent of the yearly GDP.

Armed Forces

The Chadian Armed Forces (Forces Armées Tchadiennes, or FAT) include a Ground Force, Air Force, and Gendarmerie. Conscription exists, and includes a three-year obligation (beginning at the age of twenty). Women are also required to complete a one-year term of compulsory military or civic service, beginning at age 21, but this is not fully utilized. The army has been engaged with Chadian rebel forces for much of the first decade of the 21st century; in 2010, after an offer of amnesty, many rebels laid down their arms. Ethnic conflict and hostilities continue to plague Eastern Chad.

Foreign Policy

As a landlocked nation, Chad has a significant interest in maintaining a peaceful and stable region. The government also advocates pan-Africanism and actively takes part in the Organization for African Unity (OAU), Central African Economic and Customs Union, the Lake Chad and Niger River Basin Commissions, and the Interstate Commission for the Fight against the Drought in the Sahel. Chad has generally good relations with four of its direct neighbors: Niger, Nigeria, Cameroon, and the Central African Republic (CAR). Chad has also accepted and provided shelter for approximately 280,000 refugees from the Darfur crisis in neighboring Sudan and 55,000 refugees from the CAR.

Chad's relations with Libya and Sudan have historically been strained and continue to suffer on several fronts. Those with Libya trace their roots back to the colonial era, and much of the resulting conflict since independence arose out of cross-border ethnic ties and territorial disputes. (Chad was a French colony and Libya was under Italian control.) After independence, many northern Chadians identified more with people in Libya than with the Chadian government based in the south of the country. Territorial disputes between the two countries continue to this day, though relations have improved greatly.

The conflict in the Darfur region of neighboring Sudan has essentially crossed the border and increased hostilities between Chad and Sudan. The two countries, though they signed a cease-fire agreement as recently as 2006, remain in a state of conflict.

Though officially nonaligned, Chad has close relations with its former colonial power, France, as well as other Western nations. A developing country, Chad remains strongly dependent on foreign aid from France, which supplies an estimated 30 percent of the national budget, as well as other members of the European Union (EU) and the United States. The assistance given to Chad is primarily used to finance the government and meet its routine expenses, to rebuild the economy and infrastructure following years of conflict, and to recover from drought and famine.

Relations with the U.S. are generally regarded as cordial, with the U.S. maintaining an embassy in the capital, N'Djaména, since Chad first achieved independence in 1960. Chad has also been a productive and cooperative partner to the U.S. in regional counter-terrorism operations.

Human Rights Profile

International human rights law insists that states respect civil and political rights, and promote an individual's economic, social, and cultural rights. The United Nations Universal Declaration on Human Rights (UDHR) is recognized as the standard for international human rights. Its authors sought the counsel of the world's great thinkers, philosophers, and religious leaders, and were careful to create a document that reflects the core values shared by every world culture. (To read this document or view the articles relating to cultural human rights, visit http://www.udhr.org/UDHR/default.htm.)

Chad continues to be the subject of criticism and concern from international human rights organizations due to the country's poor human rights record. A host of human rights abuses continue to occur, including widespread poverty; internal displacement of people; the incitement of ethnic and social tensions; corruption and a lack of government transparency; poor prison conditions and the unlawful treatment of detained suspects; relatively limited freedom of the press; and domestic violence against women. According to the US Department of State, human rights abuses have been on the increase and conditions in the country have been steadily worsening.

Civil war and armed rebellions have been recurring in Chad since independence was first achieved in 1960. In connection with the ongoing internal and external conflicts, armed banditry and reports of government-sanctioned killings are common. Security forces and the military are typically accused of using excessive force in their actions, often resulting in the death of civilians. Furthermore, the government has not prosecuted or punished any such apprehensive offenses conducted by or on behalf of the military.

Though Chad's constitution and laws forbid torture and the cruel and degrading treatment of suspects and prisoners, the government does not always respect these prohibitions in practice. In violation of Article 5 of the UDHR government-funded and sanctioned security forces have been known to torture, abuse, and rape individuals under their control. Again, no official punishment or actions have been brought against the forces that commit these acts.

Prisons in Chad are often cited for their disturbingly poor and life threatening conditions, generally due to overcrowding. In many instances, the overpopulation and lack of basic essentials unduly threatens the lives of prisoners and creates a serious health threat. Overcrowding is a perennial problem and, occasionally, juveniles younger than eighteen are housed in the same population as convicted adults. Though the government does not inhibit the work and monitoring of international non-governmental organizations (NGOs), there has been little improvement in conditions.

Article 19 of the UDHR outlines freedom of expression and the press. Chad's constitution and laws provide freedom of speech and of the press but, in practice, these rights are not always respected. Out of fear of reprisal, many journalists practice self-censorship and many have fled the country entirely. Journalists who attempt to cover the sensitive conflict with Sudan in the eastern part of the country do so at great peril and risk of being abducted by the government or rebel forces. There are no restrictions on Internet access though there have been reports of the government monitoring email communication.

Migration

The neighboring areas of Eastern Chad, Western Sudan, and the Central African Republic (south) have become a hotbed for forced migration and human rights concerns. Eastern and Southern Chad, specifically, host a large number of refugees—estimated at over 400,000 in seventeen camps—and internally displaced persons (often cited as numbering 110,000), and ethnic conflicts and armed rebel militia continue to plague a region already suffering food shortage, health epidemics, and general insecurity.

ECONOMY

Overview of the Economy

Chad is one of Africa's poorest nations. Its developing economy is highly dependent on foreign aid. Since 2000, the country has been expanding its oil pipelines; this effort is expected to boost the economy significantly. Nonetheless, with greater uncertainty and poor government control, the economic benefits of oil have not been able to create stability in the region or improve the country's infrastructure. Most of the population relies on subsistence farming. In 2014, the estimated per capita gross domestic product (GDP) was estimated at $2,600 (USD).

Although N'Djaména is considered the center of commerce for the entire country—and the only significant urban area in Chad—the economy of the capital, and the nation as a whole, has suffered due to instability. Drought, a lack of infrastructure, civil wars and unrest, as well as turmoil in neighboring countries, has also contributed to a slowing economy in N'Djaména.

Industry

Most of Chad's industrial activity is in the manufacturing sector. Manufactured products include cotton, textiles, beer, soap, cigarettes, and construction materials.

The country's leading exports are cotton, cattle, gum Arabic, and more recently, oil. Imported commodities include machinery and transportation equipment, industrial goods, petroleum products, food, and textiles. Chad's main trading partners are France, Cameroon, the United States, Portugal, Germany, Belgium, and China.

N'Djaména is the chief export center of Chad, and the primary industry of the city is meat processing. In addition, salt, dates, and grains are also primary exports. N'Djaména is also an ideal location as a regional market for agricultural goods because it is easily accessible for livestock and cotton farmers, as well as fishers in the outlying areas.

Labor

Chad's labor force was estimated at nearly five million in 2014. Subsistence agriculture, including fishing and farming, accounts for 80 percent of the labor force. Following a drought-plagued season, nearly one-fifth of the population will faced food shortages in 2010.

Energy/Power/Natural Resources

Chad's most important natural resource is the Aouzou Strip. This piece of land that forms the border between Chad and Libya contains large deposits of valuable uranium. Libya controlled and exploited the Aouzou Strip from 1977 to 1987, during which time the two nations used military force to fight for ownership of the region. Chad and Libya signed treaties in 1989 and 1994, and Chad has maintained ownership ever since.

Chad's southern Doba Basin contains a deposit of roughly one billion barrels of oil. Despite the efforts of national organizations such as the United Nations to restrict exploitation in the Doba Basin, Chad has been using the oil as an important economic resource. In addition to oil and uranium, other significant natural resources in Chad include natron, kaolin, fish, gold, limestone, sand, gravel, and salt.

Fishing

A landlocked nation, Chad's small fishing industry relies on inland freshwater fishing. A majority of fish is caught for domestic consumption. Lake Chad represents a main fisheries source in the country; according to the FAO, the lake's fisheries provide both employment and food to approximately 10 million people. However, the lake has shrunk considerably since the mid-20th century. The government instituted a ban on the export of fish caught in Lake Chad from 2009 to 2010 to aid local consumers.

Forestry

The use of wood as a heating source and for construction, desertification, and unsustainable herding practices have all contributed to the diminishment of forestry resources in Chad.

Mining/Metals

Oil remains the lynchpin of Chad's mining industry and is the single largest source of government revenue; in 2014, oil accounted for 60 percent of governmental export revenue. Other important mineral commodities include gold, salt, limestone, clay, and soda ash. Hostilities and instability continue to hamper the country's mining sector.

Agriculture

Nearly 80 percent of Chadians are subsistence farmers; most farming consists of livestock herding. Because of the focus on subsistence agriculture, Chad's agricultural sector is not as important to the economy as the industrial sector. Chad's major cash crops include cotton, gum arabic, cattle, sorghum, millet, peanuts, rice, potatoes, and manioc, much of which is consumed domestically. The most fertile land in the country is the south, and is dedicated largely to crops.

Animal Husbandry

The most common livestock are cattle, camel, sheep, goats, and, to a lesser extent, pigs. Cows, sheep, and goats predominate in the north, while the Saharan region can only accommodate camels and some goats.

Tourism

Outbreaks of guerrilla warfare in the Tibesti Massif have made the northern part of Chad unsafe for visitors. Chad's government has placed restrictions on the region, barring travelers from leaving specific areas of the country. Areas in the south and the west, including the Cameroonian border, are also closed to travelers. Furthermore, increases in terrorism and other forms of violence in the capital city have provoked the U.S. State Department to advise all travelers to leave Chad with haste and to have removed their own governmental personnel.

Visitors to Chad tend to remain in N'Djaména. The Musée National and Centre Artisanal are popular attractions. The wildlife at Zakouma National Park attracts visitors as well. Because Chad is politically unstable and there is a lack of security for foreigners, tourism is uncommon and revenues are negligible.

Jamie Greene, Richard Means, Ian Paul

DO YOU KNOW?

- The country of Chad is often referred to as the "Dead Heart of Africa" due to its landlocked status in the central region of the continent and the often-oppressive desert climate.
- N'Djaména was formerly known as Fort-Lamy.

Bibliography

Gordon, April A. and Donald L. Gordon. "Understanding Contemporary Africa." Boulder, CO: *Lynne Rienner Publishers*, 2012.

Seid, Joseph Brahim. "Told by Starlight in Chad." Trenton, NJ: *Africa World Press*, 2007.

Toingar, Esaie. "Idriss Deby and the Darfur Conflict." Jefferson, NC: McFarland & Co., 2013.

Works Cited

"2008 Human Rights Report: Chad." *U.S. State Department*. Bureau of Democracy, Human Rights, and Labor. http://www.state.gov/g/drl/rls/hrrpt/2008/af/118993.htm

"Chad." *Culture Crossing*. http://www.culturecrossing.net/basics_business_student.php?id=41

"Chad" *Encyclopedia Brittanica*. http://www.britannica.com/EBchecked/topic/104144/Chad

"Chad." *Freedom House*. http://www.freedomhouse.org/template.cfm?page=22&year=2007&country=7153

"Chad." *InfoPlease*. http://www.infoplease.com/ipa/A0107403.html

"U.S. Relations with Chad*." U.S. State Department*. Bureau of African Affairs. http://www.state.gov/r/pa/ei/bgn/37992.htm

"Welcome to Virtual Chad on the web!" http://www.tchad.org/enhome.html

Blair, David. "Boko Haram blamed as suicide bombers kill 23 in Chad." *The Telegraph*. Modified 15 June 2015. http://www.telegraph.co.uk/news/worldnews/africaandindianocean/chad/11675289/Suicide-attack-on-police-and-intelligence-offices-in-Chad-capital-says-minister.html

Collelo, Thomas, ed. 1988. "Chad: A Country Study." Washington, D.C.: *Library of Congress.*

Foster, Dean. 2002. "The Global Etiquette Guide to Africa and the Middle East." New York: *John Wiley & Sons, Inc.*

Kneib, Martha. 2006. "Cultures of the World: Chad." New York: *Marshall Cavendish Benchmark.*

Topping, Alexandra. "Mahamat Saleh Haroun Brings Chad to the World, and Vice Versa, through Film." *Guardian Africa Network*. The Guardian, 25 Feb. 2013. http://www.theguardian.com/world/2013/feb/25/mahamat-saleh-haroun-chad-film.

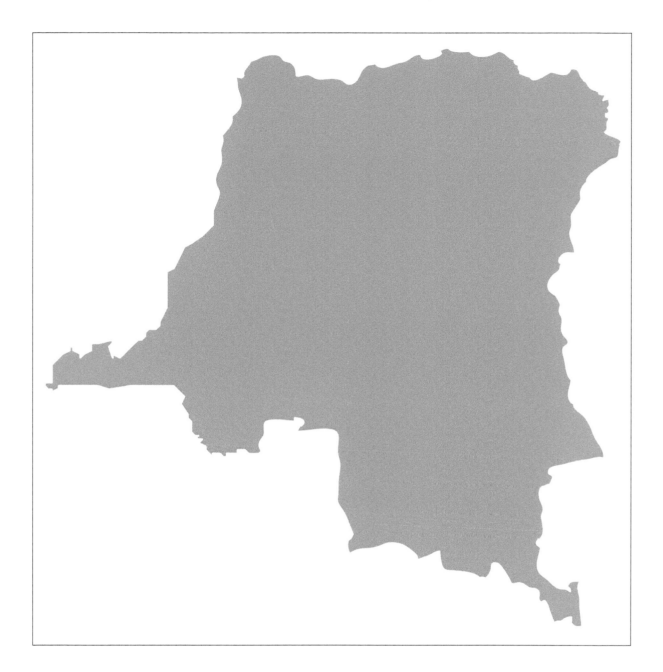

CONGO,
Democratic Republic of the

Introduction

The Democratic Republic of the Congo (DRC), located in Central Africa, is the third largest country on the African continent. The country's extensive natural resources have been sought after by competing powers for the last several centuries. First, a major center for the slave trade, it eventually came under the control of Belgium, which exploited the population for labor and profited from its natural resources. The colonial period lasted from the late 18th century until 1960, and left behind an impoverished nation faced with numerous development challenges.

Five years of civil conflict was followed by more than three decades of dictatorship. A devastating regional war broke out after dictatorial leader Mobutu Sese Seko was deposed in 1997. After a period of unrest under Laurent Kabila and his son Joseph Kabila, a transitional government was established in 2003, and elections took place in 2006. Further unrest, however, ensued starting in 2009, as various militias sought to gain power. Although Joseph Kabila was re-elected in 2011, the election results were disputed and some fighting continues today.

Music is one of the most well developed art forms in the DRC, and the one most well known outside of the country. Soukous, an urban dance music featuring guitar, drums, and vocals, boasts a wide following on the world music circuit, while Congolese jazz is also popular. Dancing and music played on traditional instruments remain important components of social occasions, and singing often accompanies work.

GENERAL INFORMATION

Official Language: French
Population: 79,375,136 (2015 estimate)
Currency: Congolese franc
Coins: The Congolese franc is subdivided into 100 centimes. However, circulating coins are considered nonexistent.
Land Area: 2,267,048 square miles (875,312 square miles)
Water Area: 77,810 square kilometers (30,043 square miles)
National Motto: "Justice, Paix, Travail" (French, "Justice, Peace, Work")
National Anthem: "Debout Congolais" ("Arise, Congolese")
Capital: Kinshasa
Time Zone: GMT +1
Flag Description: The flag of the DRC features an ascending diagonal design, with a stripe originating in the lower hoist (left) corner and extending to the upper fly corner (furthest from the flagpole). The stripe, red and bordered by thin

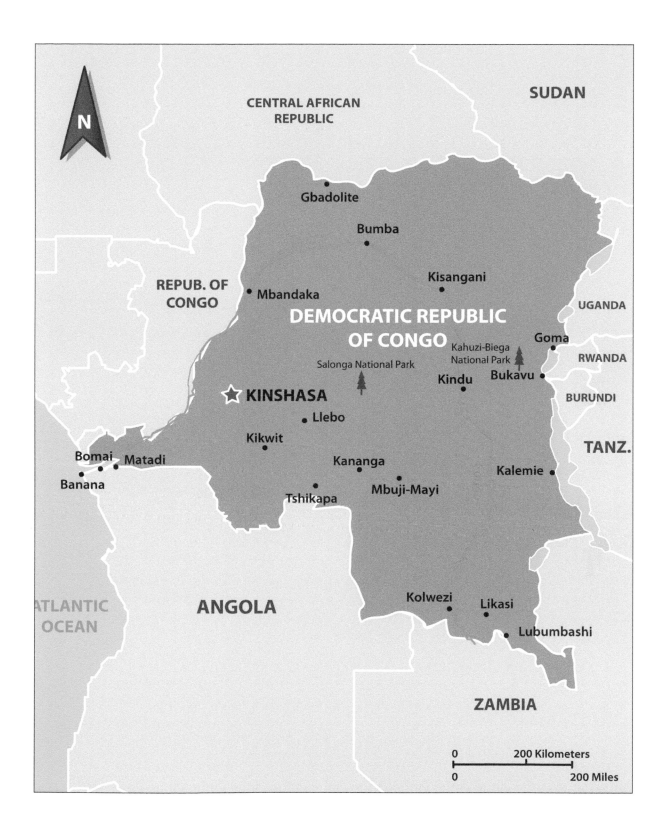

Principal Cities by Population (2012):

- Kinshasa (9,500,000)
- Lubumbashi (1,800,000)
- Mbuji-Mayi (1,700,000)
- Kananga (1,100,000)
- Bukavu (806,940)
- Tshikapa (587,548)
- Kisangani (535,977)
- Kolwezi (453,147)

golden-yellow stripes on each side, symbolizes the martyred blood of the nation's people. The upper left and lower right sections of the flag, divided diagonally by the red stripe, are both sky blue, representing hope. A five-pointed yellow star is situated in the upper left corner, representing unity.

Population

Though an estimated 250 ethnic groups make up the population, approximately 80 percent of the population speaks Bantu. The Luba, Kongo, and Mongo are the largest Bantu groups. Other groups live in the north and speak Nilo-Saharan languages include the Azande and the Mangbetu. Small groups of pygmies live in the rainforests, including the Mbuti and Efe tribes.

The highest concentration of people is along the Congo and other rivers. Approximately 70 percent of the population lives in small rural settlements. Kinshasa, the largest city, is situated on the Congo, where the river widens into the Malebo Pool. Much of the city's population explosion has been fueled by a tide of refugees fleeing fighting in other Congolese provinces as well as in neighboring countries such as the Republic of the Congo, Angola, and Rwanda. Most of these refugees inhabit shantytowns, where poor sanitation, malnutrition, overcrowding, and lack of any public health infrastructure have created a humanitarian crisis. Lubumbashi, Kolwezi, and Kisangani are other urban centers of note.

The DRC has a young, growing population but a low average life expectancy—55 years for

men and 58 years for women (2015 estimate). Families tend to be large, with each woman bearing an average of 4.66 children. An estimated half million Congolese refugees live outside their country, while several hundred thousand Africans from neighboring countries have found refuge in the DRC.

Languages

Over 200 languages and dialects have been identified in the DRC, the majority belonging to the Bantu family of languages. It is thus common for Congolese to be polyglot. The four most widely spoken African languages are Kikongo, Tshiluba, Swahili, and Lingala, a tonal Bantu language used for inter-tribal communication. French is the official language as well as the main language of business, government, literature, and higher education.

Native People & Ethnic Groups

What little evidence there is about the pre-history of the Congo region suggests that the ethnic groups represented in the DRC were present in the area by 2,000 years ago. The population became predominantly Bantu-speaking when these groups spread across the central and southern portion of the continent from the north. Their arrival for the most part displaced the indigenous pygmies, who currently survive as hunters and gatherers.

Religions

Christian missionaries left an important legacy in the DRC, which is reflected in the beliefs of the contemporary population. Half of the population is Roman Catholic, and 20 percent are Protestant. Muslims account for approximately 10 percent. The rest of the population either practices animism or syncretic religions, which combine Christianity and local animist traditions, such as Kimbanguism.

Climate

The DRC has a tropical climate dictated by its location on the equator. In the Congo River basin, it is hot and humid, with an average annual temperature of about 27° Celsius (80° Fahrenheit).

February is the hottest month. It is cooler in the uplands and in the eastern mountains, where annual temperatures average 19° Celsius (66° Fahrenheit). Though the highlands are cooler and receive less rainfall, the humidity is very high.

The central basin and the regions north and south of the equator experience different rainfall patterns. North of the equator, the rainy season lasts from April to October, and the dry season lasts from December to February. South of the equator, the rainy season lasts from November to March, and the dry season lasts from April to October. The eastern highlands average between 1,000 and 2,200 millimeters (between 39 and 87 inches) of rainfall annually. The Congo River basin, where the rainfall pattern is more even throughout the year, receives the most precipitation. Periodically, the southern uplands experience drought, while the Congo River can flood during the rainy seasons.

ENVIRONMENT & GEOGRAPHY

Topography

The DRC is bordered by Angola, Burundi, and the Central African Republic, the Republic of the Congo, Rwanda, Sudan, Tanzania, Uganda, and Zambia. It has 37 kilometers (23 miles) of coastline along the South Atlantic Ocean, where the Congo River drains.

The low-lying Congo River basin accounts for a third of the country's territory, measuring approximately 800,000 square kilometers (308,882 square miles). The basin is heavily forested and has areas of swamp and dry land. It is drained by the swift, wide Congo River, which flows for 4,374 kilometers (2,718 miles) and has many smaller tributaries feeding it; its upper portion is known as the Lualaba. The river is navigable for long distances and is an important source of hydroelectricity. It has its source on the Katanga Plateau, in the southeast of the country. Other important rivers include the Ubangi in the north and the Kasai in the south.

The country's most important lakes are also found in the Congo River Basin. Lake Tanganyika, the deepest lake in Africa, and Lake Kiyu both drain into the Congo River. These lakes, as well as the Mweru, Edward, and Albert Lakes, are part of the Great Rift Valley that runs along the eastern portion of the country. Lake Mai-Ndombe and Lake Tumba are located in the west.

North and south of the Congo River basin are regions of hills and plains that rise to an average elevation of 600 meters (1,969 feet). Rugged highlands dominate the east. The Ruwenzori Mountains contain the country's highest point, Marguerite Peak, which rises to 5,109 meters (16,762 feet) above sea level. The Virunga Mountains also rise in this region; the range is formed of both active and inactive volcanoes.

Kinshasa, the capital, is located on the southern bank of the Congo River, about 515 kilometers (320 miles) upstream from where that river empties into the Atlantic Ocean.

Plants & Animals

The ecosystems of the DRC are rich in plant and animal life. Dense forest covers three-quarters of its territory. The rainforests of the Congo River basin and the eastern highlands support various species of trees, including rubber trees, fruit trees, redwood, teak, ebony, cedar, and mahogany. Mangroves grow along the coast, while savannah interspersed with stands of trees dominates the drier regions of the far north, south, and east.

The extensive forests support a diverse range of animal species. Among the large mammals are gorillas, bonobos (endemic pygmy chimpanzees), chimpanzees, elephants, antelope, wild boar, and hippopotamuses. The savannah supports zebras, lions, leopards, giraffes, rhinoceroses, buffaloes, and hyenas. Bird and insect life are also abundant, and many species of fish thrive in the country's lakes and rivers.

Poaching and disturbance of natural habitats have taken a toll on the country's animal species. Approximately 10 percent of the total is considered threatened, several of them critically. Those listed as endangered include the African elephant, the bonobo, the chimpanzee, the gorilla, and the wild dog.

CUSTOMS & COURTESIES

Greetings

Greetings in the DRC vary according to region and community. This is a reflection of the country's diversity, which includes over 200 different ethnic groups and around 242 languages. People in urban areas commonly smile and shake hands while greeting one another. It is not customary for women to shake hands with men, although men may shake hands with other men. Men will sometimes greet each other by gently touching the other person's forehead while shaking hands. When greeting a man, instead of shaking hands, women generally clap their hands a few times and give a slight bow.

Since French is the official language of the DRC, it is common to hear "Bonjour" ("Hello") as a salutation. Lingala, a language spoken primarily in the northwest, is also used in urban settings. A person speaking to someone in Lingala would say "Mbote" ("Hello") and would ask "Sango nini?" ("What's new?") when inquiring about the other person's life. The Swahili greeting of "Jambo" ("Hello") is used more often in eastern and southeastern regions of the DRC.

Proper etiquette for greeting someone in the DRC involves not only saying "Hello," but also entails asking questions regarding the other person's personal life. Questions include how the person's family is faring, how his or her work is progressing, and how their religious and social lives are doing. A person is expected to inquire about general aspects of the other person's life before they can discuss other issues or conduct business matters. Failing to ask these questions may be considered impolite.

Gestures & Etiquette

In the Democratic Republic of the Congo, most locals make a point to dress in clean, fresh attire. Clothes are commonly colorful, and women wear long skirts or specifically pagnes (a tradi-tional wrap-around skirt) along with a matching blouse. Ties were banned by the government for decades, but have progressively been reintro-duced as a trendy accessory for men. Although casual apparel is socially accepted, it is generally understood that the people who dress well will receive more respect than the ones who are more informally dressed.

Congolese culture is overtly friendly. Camaraderie is expressed through touching a person, holding hands, or tapping the other person on the shoulder. Congolese are also generally frank in nature, and will approach most topics of conversation with candor. Constant eye contact is generally unwelcome and will make many Congolese uncomfortable. Continuous eye contact should especially be avoided when a person is speaking to a superior; this is considered impo-lite and can be misconstrued as a challenge to the person's rank.

Superiors should never be addressed by their first name. When asking a supervisor a question, it is expected that the person preface the question with, "Excuse me, sir." Furthermore, it is con-sidered proper etiquette to use formal language around superiors, even though colleagues are often addressed in an informal manner (similar to the way Congolese interact with their friends). Even among friends, it is considered inappropri-ate to create nicknames for others; people gener-ally prefer to be addressed by their actual names.

Eating/Meals

As with many things in the Democratic Republic of the Congo, eating customs vary according to community. In urban areas, it is typical for people to use silverware, whereas the indigenous people in rural areas will commonly eat with their hands. (However, they generally only use the fingers of their right hand.) Depending on ethnicity, meals are served either individually or in one commu-nal bowl. When people are sharing a communal bowl, it is customary for people to eat only from the section of the bowl that is in front of them. The elders at the meal, or the people who are of the highest rank, are allowed to portion out the meat to everyone. In some communities, men and women eat in separate areas. Meals are concluded with everyone washing their hands in bowls of warm, soapy water.

Nganda restaurants are a type of restaurant found in Kinshasa, the capital of the DRC. These restaurants serve food from specific ethnic groups from around the country. They are also aimed at serving specific clientele—some serve migrant workers and miners, while others serve high-ranking government officials.

Visiting

Socializing and maintaining a sense of community are important aspects of Congolese culture. Newcomers, acquaintances, and strangers should make formal arrangements with their hosts, even though impromptu visits by family members and friends are common. Guests that are not familiar with the family are expected to follow rules of proper etiquette, while close friends and family are given more autonomy to make themselves comfortable at the host's house.

Functions are usually held in outdoor courtyards. If a get-together is held inside a person's house, it is often an indication that the guests are significantly higher in social status than the host. Children are typically separated from the adults. When children attend a social gathering, they are usually sent to a different room, so that the adults are free to talk and socialize. Before they are dismissed, children are expected to greet each adult with a handshake, and sometimes a kiss on the cheek, depending on their relationship to the person.

It is at the discretion of the host that first-time visitors are seated. The other guests will remain seated during this process. When a host invites a guest to share a meal, it is considered polite for a guest initially to express ambivalence before accepting the invitation. It is also necessary for guests to try all of the food offered; an unwillingness to do so is interpreted as discourteous. First-time guests are not expected to give gifts, and doing so is considered improper behavior. Instead, visitors should wait until they have a closer relationship with the hosts before they bring a gift when they visit. Gifts are small and

are usually food items or something to decorate the host's house.

LIFESTYLE

Family

Traditionally, the concept of family in the DRC extends far beyond the nuclear family. It includes grandparents, cousins, aunts, uncles, nephews, nieces, and close friends of the family. The average family has five children, with the number of children in rural areas often nearing 10 per family. In a traditional household, women are expected to take care of any chores related to the house, including raising the children, preparing the food, and planting and harvesting food. The men that live in rural regions are typically responsible for hunting, while men that live in cities are responsible for financially supporting their family.

The DRC's familial support system has been thrown into disarray because of the country's civil war, poverty, and the high incidence of rape. Groups of street children, referred to as cheques, are a result of this disorganization. The number of these abandoned children is a fundamental problem in the country, especially since there are enough homeless children to have almost established a new social class.

Housing

Owing to the socioeconomic disparities within the DRC, there is not only a large difference between housing in urban and rural areas, there is also a disparity in the housing options within cities. The urban elite can afford to live in suburban houses or urban apartment buildings complete with all the modern amenities of a comfortable Western lifestyle. In contrast, the increasing numbers of urban poor live in shantytown settlements (communities consisting of poorly constructed shacks) that have sprawled out beyond the city limits. Most of these shacks are built out of corrugated iron or discarded materials.

A family's housing situation in most rural areas entails a series of round or rectangular mud huts that are enclosed in the same area.

The frame of each hut is formed from a number of sticks and the stems of palm tree leaves that are woven together by vines. This basic structure is then held together using a mixture of sand, water, and cement, with roofs that are fashioned out of grass. Each hut of the family is reserved for a specific activity; there is a hut for cooking, a hut for storage, and a hut for guests. Children are separated into different huts by gender.

Food

The cuisine of the Democratic Republic of the Congo, often referred to as Congolese cuisine, is similar to other Central African cuisines. Generally, cassava, a tropical starchy plant, is a staple food, particularly among the indigenous groups of the country. Like cassava, the other staples of the DRC diet reflect the natural resources of the land. These include groundnuts, beans, maize, rice, yams and potatoes, bananas, and fish. Other typically eaten fruits are mangoes, oranges, coconuts, and papayas.

The DRC has one national dish, referred to as moambe (which means "eight" in Lingala). As the name implies, it contains exactly eight ingredients: cassava leaves, chicken, fish, peanuts, palm nuts, bananas, rice, and hot pepper sauce. Another common dish is fufu. This is a sticky paste made from cassava flour and water. The resulting doughy substance is used as a basic starch dish, similar to rice, and is commonly prepared with a tomato-based or peanut-based sauce. Another standard dish that utilizes the cassava plant is shikwanga. This dish originates from the western area of the DRC. It is made from cassava root that is pounded into a paste and stored in banana leaves.

A typical meal in the DRC will include a series of sauces. Most sauces are cooked using traditional methods, even in urban settings. Traditional preparation of sauces usually involves a wood or charcoal fire, and sauces made from palm oil are particularly popular. Palm oil is found in the nuts of the African palm tree, which need to be crushed in order to produce the oil.

Life's Milestones

In Congolese culture, parents traditionally arrange the marriages of their children, although this practice is becoming less common, especially in urban areas. A societal custom related to the marriage ceremony is the establishment of the bride price, referred to as the dot. After the families of the bride and groom settle on the price of the dot, the groom must pay the amount to the bride's family before the wedding.

The morning after the wedding night, a ceremony is conducted to determine the bride's virginity. The ritual involves women from the groom and bride's families visiting the couple's bed. The women ask questions regarding the wedding night and look for blood, which is used as evidence of the bride's virginity. If the women are unable to confirm the bride's virginity, the husband is given the right to annul the marriage and ask that the bride's family return the dot.

CULTURAL HISTORY

Art

Numerous aspects of Congolese life are influenced by the Democratic Republic of the Congo's (DRC) colonial past. However, many elements of local art retain qualities that are completely native in technique and style. (Painting would not fully emerge as a prevalent visual art until the modern era, roughly during the early 20th century.) The early culture of the pre-colonial Kuba Kingdom (1625–1900), which makes up the modern-day nation of the DRC, was known for its embroidery and textile art, as well as ornately carved wooden masks and other objects. Other traditional arts that have retained their importance in contemporary DRC include ceramics, malachite, and copper art—the latter owing to a large copper industry in the southern Katanga region—as well as tattooing and sculpture, particularly carved masks and figures.

Since traditional African culture had no formal written language, methods for recording history were incorporated into art techniques such as tattooing. The practice of tattooing has been a general practice for the Bantu people, a large group comprised of people in central and southern Africa that are connected by similar linguistic roots. The art of cutting a design into a person's skin, leaving a permanent raised scar, served as an important means of chronicling history. Tattoos traditionally contain a person's ancestral information, their position in society, and membership in any secret organizations.

For two ethnic groups, the Bakuba and Baluba, the position of village sculptor is held in extremely high esteem. Customarily, in the province of Katanga, only members of the aristocracy were allowed to practice the craft of sculpting since it was considered one of the highest privileges. For the Baluba, a potential sculptor must survive apprenticeship training under a master and learn how to carve properly ivory and wood before they can become a true sculptor.

When a sculptor has completed his apprenticeship, he can begin to craft everything for the village, including magic amulets employed by witch doctors, and masks used for ritual dances. Some masks are fashioned after a human head. One mask traditionally used by the Bakuba is the bombo. A large, bulbous forehead, a large nose, and small eyes characterize the mask. Other masks are shaped after animals found in the surrounding jungle, such as a buffalo, leopards, elephants, and gnus (a large antelope native to Africa).

Architecture

The nation's colonial past often serves as the basis for the DRC's architectural heritage. Abandoned missions, prisons, forts, harbor infrastructure, and even factories are all vestiges of European colonization and Belgian Congo (1908–1960). As with many colonizers of the African continent, the Belgians attempted to replicate their own buildings and cities, and many architectural elements of the DRC's urban landscape retain distinct European influences, such as the grid structure and the use of green spaces and squares. Some of the best extant examples of colonial-built architecture are in the city Lubumbashi, founded by the Belgians in the early 19th century

in region of the country that grew prosperous due to its copper mining.

Music & Dance

Singing a cappella represented the earliest method of Congolese music. The Mbuti people, an indigenous hunter-gatherer tribe, are recognized for their unique vocal styles. It is a tradition that has been passed down from generation to generation within each family or with the aid of village elders. The method of singing involves many voices singing completely independent melodies at the same time. Percussion instruments, particularly upright drums, also figured prominently in early Congolese music. Other traditional instruments included the thumb piano, akin to a xylophone in some parts of the DRC, as well as the lute, harp, and zither (a stringed instrument).

Following colonization, Congolese music was influenced by Latin American and European styles. In imitating these new sounds, Congolese musicians began to incorporate new instruments such as the accordion, brass instruments, and, most importantly, the guitar. One musical genre of note is soukous, or African rumba, which has its origins in Caribbean, Afro-Cuban, and traditional or indigenous African rhythms. This style of dance music has resulted in various fusion styles and sub-genres throughout Africa and the DRC.

Dance is a fundamental aspect of traditional Congolese life, and can be divided into two categories: ritual dance and social dance. The former is rooted in the belief that the spirit world is intrinsically connected to everything that happens in daily life. Certain Congolese communities and ethnicities consider it necessary for the spirits to be acknowledged during important events, such as rites of passage, the birth of a child, the announcement of war, or the celebration of a successful harvest. These dances are considered highly specialized and sacred, and are exclusively performed by chosen trained individuals or villages.

Although many of the movements of social dance are derived from rituals, anyone is allowed to perform a social dance. These dances are typically not reserved for specific events and often improvised. Over the years, social dance has developed beyond the traditional moves of ritual dances thanks to the various ethnic groups in the DRC. Members of different groups regularly mingle at parties, festivals and nightclubs, and it is through these interactions that social dance has evolved.

Literature

The DRC first began to assert a national voice in its literature after the end of the 19th century. Early Congolese literature centered on rural life and the country's colonial past. Following World War II, Congolese literature began to flourish and reflect issues related to national and cultural identity. Other common themes included the clash between tradition and modernity and ethnic unity. Writers such as novelist Paul Lomami-Tshibamba (1914–), considered the "father of the Congolese novel," and poet Lisembe Elébé (1937–) have made significant contributions in establishing a Congolese literary voice while dealing with themes of alienation and African identity.

CULTURE

Arts & Entertainment

Art has also suffered from a lack of governmental support. Since the government has based its financial backing of the arts to projects that support its own political agenda, artisans must generally find other means of income. For this reason, many artists can be found working as agricultural laborers, while participation in underground commercial initiatives is also popular. For example, the DRC has a large number of street artists, and informal artisan communities have been set up in order to provide a makeshift support system for these artists.

After independence in 1960, many artists explored issues of Congolese identity, particularly in the context of colonialism. Many paintings in this post-independence period deal with

promoting an indigenous point of view rather than the colonial perspective that was formerly ingrained into the school and political system. Painters also began to delve into issues of inequality, poverty, and exploitation. One particularly important contemporary painter is Chéri Samba (1956–), whose work is housed in the Museum of Modern Art in New York and in Paris. His paintings are renowned for the commentary they offer on modern life in Africa.

Since the DRC represented the unification of many different ethnic groups sharing one piece of land, establishing a singular musical identity was difficult. Until the 1940s, each ethnicity was resolute in maintaining its own musical traditions. During World War II, the Cuban rumba beat revolutionized the Congolese music scene. Rumba is a unique blend of Latin and African music traditions. Musicians were also exposed to other types of international music, such as American swing, French cabaret, and Ghanaian highlife, a genre typified by the use of multiple guitars and jazzy horns.

Congolese musicians soon came together to adapt the sounds of the rumba to their own instruments and cultural traditions, and most performed in the Lingala language. The local music scene set itself apart in 1953 when Joseph "Grand Kalle" Kabasele (1930–1983), a man often considered to be the "father of modern Congolese music," headed African Jazz, the country's premier professional orchestra. African Jazz established itself as one of Africa's most famous and popular groups when it released "Independence Cha-Cha-Cha" in the 1960s. The song celebrated the DRC's independence, and ultimately developed into a political anthem for Africans. At this time, Kabasele was one of the DRC's first music celebrities, along with guitarist Francois Luambo Makiadi (1938–1989), commonly referred to as "Franco."

In 1969, the Congolese music scene was again electrified by a visit by James Brown, which launched a fascination with American rock and funk. This period of the late 1960s in Congolese music history is termed as the soukous era. The term soukous has developed into an all-encompassing name for African rumba. Traditional instruments, like the thumb piano and different drums, are often incorporated into soukous music to create a uniquely Congolese sound. Song themes vary from common topics of love and loss, to more controversial issues related to politics, gender, and abuse of power by the government.

Tabu Lei Rochereau (1940–2013) and Nico Kasanda (1939–1985) are regarded as the founders of modern soukous. They formed a group called African Fiesta in the late 1960s and began blending Congolese folk music with soul music. They also blended in classically Caribbean and Latin rhythms and instruments. A style of soukous with an extremely fast rhythm was developed, and became known as kwassa kwassa in the 1980s. Kwassa kwassa was originally named after a dance popularized by Pepe Kalle (1951–1998) in his music videos. The dance involves the dancer's hips rapidly moving back and forth while their hands move back and forth following the movement of the hips. Ndombolo is another style of soukous heard in dancehalls, whose name also originated from a style of dance.

The political unrest that the country has experienced since independence has contributed to the decline in the development of indigenous music, and by the early 1990s, many musicians had already left the country. Music has continued to serve as a strong medium for locals to express their opinions when they know it would be dangerous for them to discuss openly issues in public.

Football (soccer) is the most popular sport in the DRC. The national team has won the Africa Cup of Nations twice in its history. Other growing sports include rugby and basketball.

Cultural Sites & Landmarks

The DRC's location along the equator and the Congo River drainage basin has created a natural terrain comprised of numerous rainforests and swamps. This geography produces diverse habitats that lend themselves to a unique range of fauna and flora. The United National Educational, Scientific, and Cultural Organization (UNESCO) has recognized five national parks for inclusion on the World Heritage List. They include the Virunga National Park, the Kahuzi-Biéga National Park, the Salonga National Park, the Garamba National Park, and the Okapi Wildlife Reserve. Many of these parks are tourist destinations that offer access to some of the world's endangered animals and the rare landscapes they inhabit.

Virunga National Park is an example of exceptional biodiversity. It contains a range of different terrains, from icefields, savanna plains, and forests, to steppes and lava fields from two of Africa's most active volcanoes, Nyamuragira and Nyiragongo. These two volcanoes together make up two-fifths of all volcanic eruptions in the history of Africa, and consistently erupt every few years. Virunga is the world's second-oldest national park, and contains mountain gorillas, approximately 20,000 hippopotamuses, and Siberian birds that fly to the DRC for the winter.

The Kahuzi-Biéga National Park is situated in the eastern part of the country. Recognized in 1980 as a World Heritage Site, the park is particularly famous as a refuge for eastern lowland gorillas. The park was also the original site where renowned zoologist Dian Fossey (1932–1985) began her important and extensive study of gorillas before relocating to Rwanda. Due to the ongoing conflict in the country, the park was listed as a World Heritage Site in Danger in 1997.

The Salonga National Park is located at the very center of the Congo River basin and is only accessible by water. It remains Africa's largest tropical rainforest reserve and shelters various threatened species. Some of the endangered animals that live within the park's borders are the Congo peacock, the dwarf chimpanzee, the forest elephant, and the African slender-snouted crocodile. The protection of Garamba National Park is especially important since it serves as the home of the white rhinoceros. Garamba Park was the last place in the world where the Northern White rhinoceroses, now believed to be extinct in the wild, lived.

The Okapi Wildlife Reserve is close to the borders of Sudan and Uganda. It contains approximately one-sixth of the world's wild okapi population. The okapi is a forest mammal related to the giraffe, and characterized by its reddish-brown body, white cheeks, and the white stripes around its legs. Okapi Reserve also occupies the same land as two nomadic pygmy tribes, the Mbuti and Efe. Members of the tribe live a traditional hunter-gatherer lifestyle, primarily relying on the natural resources of the forest for food and shelter.

Kisangani, a major city in northern Congo, is also one of the country's significant cultural centers. Known as Stanleyville, the city was named after its founder, the famous explorer Henry Morton Stanley (1841–1904), and features colonial Belgian architecture. The capital of Kinshasa, considered the third largest city on the African continent, has its own cultural attractions. These include the Kinshasa Museum and the Kinshasa Fine Arts Academy, as well as the country's national stadium. The city was also founded by Stanley as a trading post in 1881.

Libraries & Museums

Kinshasa is the home of two notable museums. The first, located at Kinshasa University, highlights the ethnographic history of the local area. The second, the National Museum of Kinshasa, houses an extensive collection of Congolese art. Kinshasa's Academy of Fine Arts is a teaching institution that also features exhibits in ceramics, sculpture, painting, and metalwork. The National Library of the Democratic Republic of the Congo is also located in Kinshasa.

Holidays

The health care system in the DRC is very basic and cannot cope with the needs of the population. The government spends only a fraction of its resources on health care. There is a lack of facilities, supplies, and trained medical professionals, and many Congolese rely on traditional medicines and religious practices. Most facilities are located in urban centers.

Tropical illnesses such as malaria and sleeping sickness, in addition to poor sanitation and the recent war, all contribute to the dire state of public health. AIDS is also a major cause of death, and it has been estimated that over half a million Congolese are infected with the HIV virus. Malnutrition remains a widespread problem, especially among children.

Youth Culture

The youth living in the cities of the DRC are often affected by the phenomenon of "Americanization," whereby people become enamored by Western trends and mimic Western cultural behavior. This is particularly apparent in the fashion choices of young girls and women. Blue jeans and pants have become increasingly popular among the female population. Even though women prefer to maintain their cultural identity through certain items of dress, such as wearing pagnes (a wraparound skirt), the younger generation is partial to American styles. Girls living in urban areas often enjoy buying imported hairpieces instead of wearing the traditional braids preferred by the older generation.

Education continues to be the primary issue facing DRC youth. Outside of the primary level, education is neither free nor compulsory, and the student enrollment rate at the turn of the 21st century, at some estimates, was below 60 percent. The issue of child soldiers in the DRC also continues to remain prevalent, even after the government established a nationwide program to release and then reintegrate child soldiers back into society. As of 2006, it was estimated that 11,000 children were still unaccounted. Of particular concern are girl soldiers, who groups such as Amnesty International (AI) contend constitute the majority of child soldiers left to be found and disarmed.

SOCIETY

Transportation

The Democratic Republic of the Congo has a relatively small network of paved roads connecting its cities, and relies on rail service, air travel, and its waterway systems as necessary modes and avenues of transportation, as car ownership remains extremely limited. In fact, rivers offer a fundamental structure of highways and are the only means of traveling around two-thirds of the country. Barges regularly run between Kinshasa and Kisangani. However, like many other transportation options in the DRC, barges have no formal schedules and regularly break down. Buses operate within major cities, and the capital has an urban railway system. Traffic moves on the right-hand side of the road.

Transportation Infrastructure
The DRC's civil war has caused significant disturbances in the various transport networks, and the construction or reconstruction of adequate infrastructure is proving to be one of the most challenging endeavors on the entire continent. In the past, areas of the Congo River that could not be navigated by boat were connected via the railroad system. The political turmoil and civil unrest from the war has resulted in a defunct railway. Railway lines are dilapidated and the lack of governmental investment in infrastructure has further reduced the number of functioning rail lines between cities, where schedules are already irregular. It is estimated that the country has fewer than 3,000 kilometers (1,864 miles) of paved roads, and the unpaved roads that make up the majority of the road network are in poor condition.

The option of traveling around the country by air is considered risky due to the poor safety records of most DRC-based airlines and Congolese air traffic control. In July 2008, every DRC-certified airline was banned from flying in Europe. In 2010, South Africa's state-owned local and regional carrier announced plans to begin a domestic airline in the DRC.

Media & Communications
In the DRC, the radio serves as the primary resource for news. Several stations broadcast throughout the country, including the state-controlled Radio-Television Nationale Congolaise (RTNC) and Radio Okapi. The UN Mission in DR Congo, often referred to as Monuc, and Fondation Hirondelle, a Swiss-based non-profit organization, established Radio Okapi in

2002. The purpose of the radio station was to encourage communication between rival political groups. It is now one of the most popular radio stations in the nation, and includes pertinent news and information related to Monuc, in addition to music. Besides Radio Okapi and RTNC, there are over a hundred private radio stations, and listeners in Kinshasa have access to BBC radio programming as well as Radio France Internationale.

There are two daily newspapers in the DRC: the *Debout Congolais* and *La Reference*. The DRC's turbulent and violent political climate has created a volatile environment for the media. Reporters Without Borders, a non-governmental advocate group supporting freedom of the press, has reported cases of reporters being threatened, assaulted, and arrested for their work. Media workers, who are researching stories that expose corruption, are especially at risk. Still, the DRC does have media outlets, which speak for the views of opposition parties. Additionally, the media has been able to publish criticism of the government. Citizens of the DRC also have increasing access to the Internet, and it was estimated that less than one percent of the population were Internet users in the country as of March 2009.

SOCIAL DEVELOPMENT

Standard of Living
The DRC ranked 186th out of 187 countries on the 2014 United Nations Human Development Index, which measures quality of life and standard of living indicators.

Water Consumption
According to 2015 statistics from the World Health Organization, only 52 percent of the population of the DRC has access to an improved drinking water source, while only 28 percent had access to improved sanitation. The situation is proving to be particularly dire and challenging among the country's estimated 1.9 million internally displaced persons and refugees from neighboring countries who are fleeing armed conflict.

Education

The lack of funds, adequate facilities, materials, and qualified educators limits educational prospects in the DRC. In rural areas, the system is even less developed. The average literacy rate stands at 63 percent.

Catholic missionaries founded the educational system, and several Catholic private schools still operate in the country. The government subsidizes others. Six years of primary education are free and compulsory, though many eligible children do not attend. Many children must work in order to help support their family, and females are more underrepresented in schools than males. This trend is more common at the secondary level, which consists of four years with the option of attending technical school after the second year.

Kinshasa has two state universities, and the cities of Kisangani and Lubumbashi each have one. There are also colleges for teaching training.

Women's Rights

Alongside its human development index (HDI), the United Nations' Human Development Report establishes a gender-related development index (GDI) to gauge gender equality issues in areas such as health, education, and economic participation. In 2012, the Democratic Republic of the Congo's GDI was 681 and its HDI was 338. The presence of gender inequities in human development are represented in the disparity between GDI and HDI values. Of the 187 countries assigned GDI and HDI values that year, 185 countries had more favorable HDI/GDI ratios than the Democratic Republic of the Congo.

Women in the Democratic Republic of the Congo lack many of the personal liberties that their male counterparts exercise in social and political spheres. Even as non-governmental organizations (NGOs) work to create government-run schemes to enhance women's rights in the DRC, the social status of women remains low. Women who live in rural areas are especially pressured toward a life centered on domestic responsibilities and child-rearing. They are dissuaded from attending high school or higher levels of education, and are deterred from finding paid work. As a result, the social imbalance between both genders is maintained, since men are generally wealthier and have completed high school or pursued higher degrees. Women also remain underrepresented in government and high political positions, and though more women have entered the workforce since the late 20th century, they generally earn less than their male counterparts do.

The problem of rape and sexual violence in the DRC is so systemic and common that it is now reported to be the worst in the world. (Statistics, though difficult to calculate, estimate that as much as hundreds of thousands of women have been raped between 2006 and 2008.) The African Association for the Defense of Human Rights (ASADHO) released a report in 2006 detailing how women are raped in the context of the DRC's civil war, and how they are often kidnapped and forced into sexual slavery by soldiers. Furthermore, a report in July 2007 by the UN Special Rapporteur on Violence described how women are brutally raped as a wartime strategy of terrorism. This trend continued in the violence of recent years. Different army factions use rape as a weapon to destroy entire communities by publicly shaming and violating their women. The war has become so pervasive that civilians are increasingly committing rapes, in addition to military insurgents. After a woman is raped, it is common for her husband to abandon her and for her community to ostracize and blame her. Oftentimes, the community's rejection of the woman goes beyond social stigma and is based on fears that she has contracted HIV.

The situation for women remains particularly perilous as the country attempts to transition from the violent civil war whose effects are still felt by ethnic conflict. Women in Bukavu have established The Bukavu Women's Trauma Healing and Care Centre. This organization aims to help women recover from sexual violence through methods of self-empowerment. Similarly, the NGO Women for Women, helps women gain independence and reestablish their lives. They accomplish this by creating a support network, in addition to teaching survivors useful skills that will help them earn money in the future, such as how to read and write, how to cook, and how to make soap.

Impunity, or the virtual lack of a judicial system, has been listed as one of the main reasons that the rape problem has not been controlled. In 2008, the Congolese government did show signs of improving the judicial process by convicting and punishing more rapists than it had in the past. Bukavu, one of the DRC's largest cities, filed a record 103 rape cases in 2008. Rape prosecutions in some areas of the DRC, such as the town of Bunia, rose by as much as 600 percent over a five-year period. However, after renewed violence in 2012 rape prosecutions have fallen yet again.

Health Care

The health care system in the DRC is very basic and cannot cope with the needs of the population. The government spends only a fraction of its resources on health care. There is a lack of facilities, supplies, and trained medical professionals, and many Congolese rely on traditional medicines and religious practices. Most facilities are located in urban centers.

Tropical illnesses such as malaria and sleeping sickness, in addition to poor sanitation and the recent war, all contribute to the dire state of public health. AIDS is also a major cause of death, and over one million Congolese are currently infected with the HIV virus. Malnutrition remains a widespread problem, especially among children. Ten disasters alone in 2007 exacerbated the dire humanitarian situation, and fighting continues to impact any sustainable aid and health factors, such as basic care and access to safe and clean water.

GOVERNMENT

Structure

The DRC won its independence from Belgium in 1960, and five years later entered a 32-year period of dictatorship during which the Popular Movement for the Revolution was the sole legal political party. It was overthrown by rebel forces

in 1997, but a year later, fighting broke out between different rebel factions backed by neighboring countries, and the country descended into war. Widespread death and injury occurred, with three million Congolese killed and millions more displaced both inside the country and in neighboring countries. An end to the fighting was negotiated in 2002, and a transitional, multi-party government took power in 2003 under a new constitution.

The Constitution of the Third Republic came into effect in February of 2006. On June 30, 2006, the DRC held its first multi-party elections in over 40 years. However, the leader of the opposition party running against President Joseph Kabila did not participate. The election was conducted peacefully, but the results, which showed a victory for Kabila, were questioned by many.

The executive branch consists of a sixty-member cabinet, a president that serves as head of state, and a parliament-elected prime minister. The bicameral legislative branch consists of a Senate, the members of which are elected by provincial assemblies (and who serve five-year terms) and a 500-seat National Assembly (also serving five-year terms).

Political Parties

Free and fair elections have been the subject of much controversy in the DRC in the early 21st century, and many political parties have been founded in recent years (and nearly 280 are registered with the government.) With the disputed 2006 elections, and extending into the 2011 elections, the left-wing People's Party for Reconstruction and Democracy stood as the largest parliamentary party. The party is also the leading force of the Alliance of the Presidential Majority coalition or bloc, which consists of various other political parties. The largest opposition party is the Movement for the Liberation of the Congo.

Local Government

For administrative purposes, the DRC is divided into 10 provinces and one city (Kinshasa). Provincial governors were last elected in 2007.

The president is responsible for appointing the commissioner who oversees each administrative unit. In 2009, a new constitution decreed that local governance would be administratively divided among 26 provinces.

Judicial System

The judicial system is based on a mixture of Belgian and tribal law. The Constitutional Court is the highest court in the country; beneath it are county courts and appeal courts. The president is responsible for appointing judges.

Taxation

Tax rates in the Democratic Republic of the Congo are rather moderate, save for a high corporate tax rate of 40 percent. The highest income tax rate is 30 percent. Other taxes levied include a vehicle tax and sales tax.

Armed Forces

The armed forces of the Democratic Republic of the Congo are organized into an army, navy, and air force. The army was rebuilt following the Second Congo War in 2003. The United Nations Organization Stabilization Mission in the Democratic Republic of the Congo (MONUSCO)—formerly the United Nations Mission in the Democratic Republic of the Congo (MONUC)—continues to assist in peacekeeping and quelling ethnic conflict that has been rampant in the country. As of August 2010, 19,544 total uniformed personnel were stationed in the country as part of the mission. Many foreign fighters and rebel groups active in other surrounding nations have also found refuge in the DRC, and continue to pose challenges to the DRC military.

Foreign Policy

Due to the ongoing effects of the Second Congo War (1998–2003), the DRC's foreign relation policies are still heavily influenced by the neighboring and Western nations that intervened in the conflict. Besides the DRC, Uganda, Rwanda and Burundi (which all supported the rebel movement) and Namibia, Zimbabwe, Angola, and Chad (which all supported the new regime) were all engaged in armed conflict on DRC soil during the civil war. However, many of the countries that maintain a significant presence in the DRC's foreign relations agenda are competing for the DRC's natural resources. (In terms of natural resources, the DRC is one of the richest countries in the world, with valuable deposits of diamonds, gold, copper, uranium, oil, timber, and coltan, which is used in cell phones and computer chips.) This is of particular concern, since these same natural resources played a major role during the war. In July 2006, the DRC held its first democratic election for the presidency since it gained independence in 1960, though there was widespread suspicion that the candidates all worked for foreign government agencies.

Neighboring nations also have a significant number of refugees occupying DRC territory. In 2006, Angola was estimated to have around 106,772 refugees, while Rwanda had approximately 42,360. A considerable amount of refugees also come from Burundi, Uganda, Sudan, and the Republic of the Congo. (In addition, as of October 2010, the number of internally displaced persons in the DRC was listed at 1.9 million, with many in the North Kivu Province that borders Rwanda and Uganda, where fighting has spilled over.) The political struggle has had notable long-term effects on other countries that are formally allied with the Democratic Republic of the Congo. Between 1998 and 2000, Zimbabwe, one of those allied nations, sent troops into the DRC to assist DRC President Laurent-Désiré Kabila (1939–2001). The country's participation in the war resulted in the loss of hundreds of millions of dollars in the Zimbabwean economy.

Neighboring Rwanda has had a considerable effect on the DRC and its political history. Rising tensions between the Hutus and Tutsis, Rwanda's primary ethnic groups, led many Tutsis to flee into Uganda and the DRC (then known as Zaire) in the 1980s and 1990s. Following the Rwandan genocide of 1994, during which groups of Hutus proceeded to massacre Tutsis, the consequent civil war caused many Hutus to pour into Zaire as refugees. Mobutu attempted to begin his own campaign of ethnic cleansing against the Tutsi minority group in Zaire. This ultimately allowed Laurent Kabila to assume power in Zaire, as he became the rebel leader of the Tutsi minority, as well as anyone opposed to Mobutu's rule. The civil war has continued to divide the DRC and Rwanda. Rwanda has accused the DRC of supporting the Rwandan Hutu armed group, the Democratic Forces for the Liberation of Rwanda (FDLR), while the DRC has accused Rwanda of backing the National Congress for the Defense of the People (CNDP), a rebel group based in the eastern DRC.

When Kabila was assassinated in 2001, his son, Joseph Kabila (1971–), succeeded him. After assuming office, Joseph Kabila promoted an agenda of peace by visiting the heads of state in the US, France, Belgium, Britain, and the various Nordic countries. He additionally reopened a dialogue with the International Monetary Fund (IMF) and the World Bank to begin restructuring the country's failing economy. In 2002, the South African government negotiated the Pretoria Accord, an agreement to end the civil war in the DRC, which Kabila signed. Despite this agreement, and another peace accord signed in January 2008, fighting continued in North Kivu, a province in the eastern DRC, resulting ultimately in renewed violence in 2012, peace finally restored by UN forces the following year.

The International Committee in Support of the Transition (CIAT), which comprises the U.S., the European Union (EU), and South Africa, has considerable sway within the DRC. This is mainly attributed to the inability of the public to trust their own Congolese politicians, forcing many to turn to international governments for assistance. The CIAT demonstrated support for President Joseph Kabila before and during the 2006 election. Public wariness of the CIAT's investment in Kabila was reinforced when CIAT administrators rejected the proposal to reopen voter registration for a popular opposition leader, Etienne Tshisedeki (1932–), when Tshisekedi decided to reenter the election.

The United States, in particular, has been entrenched in Congolese politics, dating back to when the country was known as the Republic of Zaire (1971–1997). During that period, the US was the third largest donor of aid. It has also long been suspected that the U.S. Central Intelligence Agency (CIA) supported the presidency of Mobutu Sese Seko (1930–1997), the second president of the DRC, as a way to expand its influence in central Africa. Mobutu proved himself a staunch supporter of U.S. policies. For example, he condemned the Soviet invasion of Czechoslovakia in 1968, and regularly agreed with the U.S. position on Israel. The U.S. continues to support the peace process in the DRC, and emphasizes the importance of democratization to regional security in Central Africa.

Human Rights Profile

International human rights law insists that states respect civil and political rights, and promote an individual's economic, social, and cultural rights. The United Nations Universal Declaration on Human Rights (UDHR) is recognized as the standard for international human rights. Its authors sought the counsel of the world's great thinkers, philosophers, and religious leaders, and were careful to create a document that reflects the core values shared by every world culture. (To read this document or view the articles relating to cultural human rights, visit http://www.udhr.org/UDHR/default.htm.)

The Democratic Republic of the Congo's poor human rights record is a reflection of its recent violent history and ongoing internal conflict. The Second Congo War (also known as Africa's World War) and its aftermath have created a dangerous situation that has resulted in approximately 5.4 million deaths. Despite one of the largest UN peacekeeping missions in history—17,000 troops—attacks and violent behavior is a continuous problem. In particular, the systemic kidnapping of women and children in the eastern DRC is still a common occurrence. It is estimated that for every two children freed from both rebel and government military groups, another five children are abducted and forced into roles as child soldiers. Additionally, soldiers in the DRC army have been implicated in numerous human rights violations, including the killing and rape of civilians.

Five years removed from the civil war, ethnic violence is widespread and inadequate health services, and treatment has lead to outbreaks of malaria and other diseases. In some cases, basic care such as immunization is unavailable, furthering inflating the mortality rate of children under the age of five. Hunger continues to be a rampant problem and, along with disease, one of the leading causes of death in the postwar period. Overall, according to some 2008 reports, 45,000 people continue to die every month in the country.

The UDHR outlines the need for the government to adhere to a principle of equal rights for all citizens regardless of their race, religion, gender, or political affiliation. In 2003, the UN began investigating allegations of human rights abuses against the Pygmy populations, a minority group of hunter-gatherers. Accusations included reports that members of the Pygmy community were subject to mass killings, rapes, land evictions, and even cannibalism. Minority Rights Group International (MRG) testified that a large amount of evidence exists that substantiates these claims. The evidence links the Movement for the Liberation of Congo, a rebel group that is tied to the transitional government of the DRC, with the majority of the violence against Pygmies. Some reports even suggest that the Pygmies may be the target of cannibalism because of the conviction that they are "sub-human" and that their skin bestows magical attributes on whoever eats it.

Article 16 of the UDHR guarantees equal rights during marriage and at its dissolution. Although many families express the desire for their children to marry within the same ethnic group, it is becoming more common for people to choose spouses from a different ethnic group, particularly in urban areas. However, some traditions entailed in most marriage ceremonies in the DRC prevent Article 16 from being realized. Before a marriage, the families of the bride and the groom will agree upon a bride price, but if the marriage is annulled or a divorce occurs,

then the groom may request that the bride price be returned to him. Since women often do not have the financial freedom and ability to pay back their own bride price, they generally do not have the option to ask for a divorce, a right mostly reserved for men. In the instance of a husband's death, the DRC's Legal Code asserts that 30 percent of his estate must be allocated to his wife. However, this law is typically not enforced and widows regularly do not inherit anything from their husbands. Adultery is also considered an illegal act for women, but there is no law or social stigma attached to men who commit adultery. Similarly, polygamy is legal in the DRC, but polyandry (whereby women may have more than one husband) is illegal.

Other notable human rights abuses concern the right to freedom of expression and the right to assemble peacefully. Between the period of January and June 2006, in preparation for the DRC's democratic election, the UN censured the local police, the military, and the national information service for repeatedly preventing political demonstrations. The UN asserted that public demonstrations have been repressed through illegal means, such as random violent acts, arbitrary arrests, and illegitimate detainment.

ECONOMY

Overview of the Economy

Years of corruption, heavy debt, inflation, and war have stagnated the economy of the DRC. Statistics regarding the current state of affairs are often unavailable or hypothetical, but it has become one of the poorest countries in the world despite its wealth of natural resources.

The end of major hostilities and the transitional government's ostensible commitment to reform has resulted in slight improvements to the country's stability. In 2005, as part of a package of reforms designed to encourage foreign investor confidence, the government became a signatory to the Extractive Industries Transparency Initiative. The initiative supports improved accountability in resource-rich countries, through the verification and full publication of company payments and government revenues from oil, gas, and mining. Renewed mining activities modestly increased Kinshasa's export revenues and economic growth through 2015, and foreign aid and investment have to some degree returned.

In 2014, the gross domestic product (GDP) per capita was an estimated $700 USD. The underground economy is thought to be as large as the official economy.

Industry

The industrial sector accounts for only four percent of the GDP and employs only 13 percent of the labor force. Mining and mineral processing are the most important parts of the sector and have the potential to transform the economy, with diamonds, copper, and cobalt being the most important exports. Logging also has potential but is limited by the country's poor transportation system. Manufactured products include textiles, processed foods and beverages, and building materials.

Prior to the definitive collapse of the Congolese economy in the late 1990s, Kinshasa depended on its food and beverage processing, tanning, construction, and commercial ship repairing industries for revenue. Its manufacturing sector turned out textiles, shoes, tires, metalwork, paper, chemicals, mineral oils, and cement. Political turmoil, however, resulted in a breakdown of public order and civil institutions that in turn led to a wildly inflated currency and the disappearance of virtually all regular paying jobs. To survive, most residents rely on the informal sector, or black market economy.

Labor

The labor force was estimated at nearly 24 million in 2007. Both unemployment and underemployment remain significant problems. Much of the economic activity in the country occurs on the informal sector.

Political turmoil in Kinshasa resulted in the loss of virtually all regular paying jobs in the early 21st century. To survive, most residents of Kinshasa

make money in the city's black market economy. Many manage to make a living by peddling or bartering various wares, including bananas, drinking water, soccer balls, feather dusters, apples, brooms, sunglasses, popcorn, ice, air fresheners, toothpicks, wristwatches, and motor oil. The informal economy also relies heavily on the resale or trade of stolen or counterfeit merchandise, often in the form of construction materials such tools, bricks, lumber, pipes, used auto parts, and tires.

Energy/Power/Natural Resources

In terms of natural resources, the DRC is one of the richest countries in Africa. Among its mineral deposits are diamonds, gold, copper, silver, tin, manganese, tungsten, cobalt, coal, and uranium; offshore oil reserves are also present. The country's vast forests and plantations yield timber as well as rubber and palm oil, and its swift rivers have enormous potential for generating hydroelectricity. Its soil is also rich, especially where it has been mixed with volcanic ash.

Deforestation threatens the country's tropical forests and the animals that inhabit them where forests are cut for timber or cleared for agriculture. Soil erosion and water pollution are other problems faced by the country.

Fishing

Commercial fishing continues to be an unexploited area of the agricultural sector of the DRC. Kisangani and Mbandaka are the major fishing ports. The Congo River is also a primary fishery, and river communities rely on subsistence fishing.

Forestry

Despite the fact that two-thirds of the DRC—an estimated 122 million acres—is forested (equatorial), the timber industry is underdeveloped. In fact, an estimated six percent of the world's forests and 60 percent of the continent's forests are within DRC territory. Despite the opportunity for growth, illegal logging and unsustainable practices remain a concern.

Mining/Metals

The DCR is a nation endowed with tremendous mineral resources. It owns more than half of all the cobalt and 30 percent of all the diamonds in the world, in addition to enormous gold and copper deposits. However, the DRC has been unable to take advantage of these resources. Other important mineral commodities include aluminum, tungsten, crude steel, crushed stone, coal, and zinc.

Agriculture

Agriculture accounts for 58 percent of the GDP and employs the majority of the labor force. Farming is generally done on a small scale with basic agricultural implements, and many of the crops, such as corn, rice, cassava, bananas, and yams are locally consumed. Only three percent of the land is under cultivation because of the country's dense forests. Crops, which are raised for export, include coffee, rubber, and palm kernels, from which palm oil is derived.

The forests are sources of wild game, medicinal plants, and timber, and some people are still engaged in hunting and gathering. Freshwater fish are commonly caught for local consumption. However, foreign investment is necessary for the agricultural sector; including farming, fishing, and forestry, to reach its true potential or even facilitate growth.

Animal Husbandry

The most common domestic animals are sheep, goats, poultry, and pigs. In the southern and eastern parts of the capital, the raising of livestock, such as chickens, pigs, goats, and rabbits, is also common.

Tourism

The DRC has never been a major tourist destination despite its natural wonders and wildlife. Both civil unrest and a lack of infrastructure have prevented the industry's development. Should the country become safer and more developed, the Virunga, Garamba, and Salonga National Parks as well as other nature reserves will be the greatest attractions.

Danielle Chu, Michael Aliprandini, Beverly Ballaro

DO YOU KNOW?

- The Congo River is the fifth longest river in the world and the second longest on the African continent.

Bibliography

Berkeley, Bill. "The Graves are Not Yet Full: Race, Tribe, and Power in the Heart of Africa." New York: *Basic Books*, 2002.

Deibert, Michael. "The Democratic Republic of Congo: Between Hope and Despair." New York: *Zed Books*, 2013.

De Witte, Ludo. "The Assassination of Lumumba." New York: *Verso*, 2001.

Hochschild, Adam. "King Leopold's Ghost: A Story of Greed, Terror, and Heroism in Colonial Africa." New York: First Mariner Books, 1999.

Nzongola-Ntalaja, Georges. "The Congo: from Leopold to Kabila: A People's History." London: *Zed Books*, 2002.

Stewart, Gary. "Rumba on the River: A History of the Popular Music of the Two Congos." New York: *Verso*, 2000

Turner, Thomas. "The Congo Wars: Conflict, Myth, and Reality." London: *Zed Books*, 2007.

Van Reybrouck, David. "Congo: The Epic History of a People." New York: *Ecco*, 2014.

Works Cited

"Country Profile: Democratic Republic of Congo." November 2008. Accessed January 5, 2009. http://news.bbc.co.uk/1/hi/world/africa/country_profiles/1076399.stm

"Customs of Democratic Republic of the Congo," 2008. *MSN Encarta.* http://encarta.msn.com/sidcbar_631522281/Customs_of_Congo_(DRC).html

"Garamba National Park." *UNESCO.* http://whc.unesco.org/en/list/136

"List of Air Carriers of which all Operations are Subject to a Ban within the Community," The Member States of the European Community. http://ec.europa.eu/transport/air-ban/pdf/list_en.pdf

"Okapi Wildlife Reserve." *UNESCO.* http://whc.unesco.org/en/list/718

"Political and Economic Situation in Zaire," *U.S. Congress, Committee on Foreign Affairs, Subcommittee on Africa.* Fall 1981.

"The Lusaka Accords May Create More Instability." *Defense and Foreign Affairs Strategic Policy*, 27 (7): 3, 1999.

"Salonga National Park." *UNESCO.* http://whc.unesco.org/en/list/280

"UN denounces rise in rights violations ahead of DRC election." *Monuc*, UN Mission in DR Congo.

"Virunga National Park." *UNESCO.* http://whc.unesco.org/en/list/63

Bouvier, Paule and Pierre Englebert. "Congo's Implausible Democracy," *Foreign Policy*. July 2006.

Caputo, Robert. "Lifeline for a Nation: Zaire River." *National Geographic*, November 1991, 2–35.

Dynes, Michael. "Pygmies beg UN for aid to save them from Congo cannibals," *The Times*. May 23, 2003.

Gettleman, Jeffrey. "Rape Victims' Words Help Jolt Congo into Change," *New York Times Online*.

Haidcr ,Rizvi. "In Congo, Staggering Death Toll and a Move toward Peace." *OneWorld* U.S. January 26, 2008.

Jensen Arnett, Jeffrey. "International Encyclopedia of Adolescence: A Historical and Cultural Survey of Young People around the World." Boca Raton: *CRC Press*, 2007.

Kabwasa, Antoine Nsang-O'Khan. "African Cosmogony, Life's Philosophy and Development." *Lecture, University of Nairobi*, 17 February 1998.

Kisangani, Emizet. "The Massacre of Refugees in Congo." *Journal of Modern African Studies*, 38 (2): 162–174, 2000.

Koinange, Jeff. "Congo president on military rapes: 'Unforgivable.'" *CNN.com*, June 1, 2006.

McCrummen, Stephanie. "Prevalence of Rape in E. Congo Described as Worst in World," *The Washington Post*. September 9, 2008.

Schlein, Lisa. "UN: Recruitment of Child Soldiers in Congo on Rise," Voice of America News. January 2, 2009.

A Pygmy woman carrying goods to market. iStock/Guenter Guni.

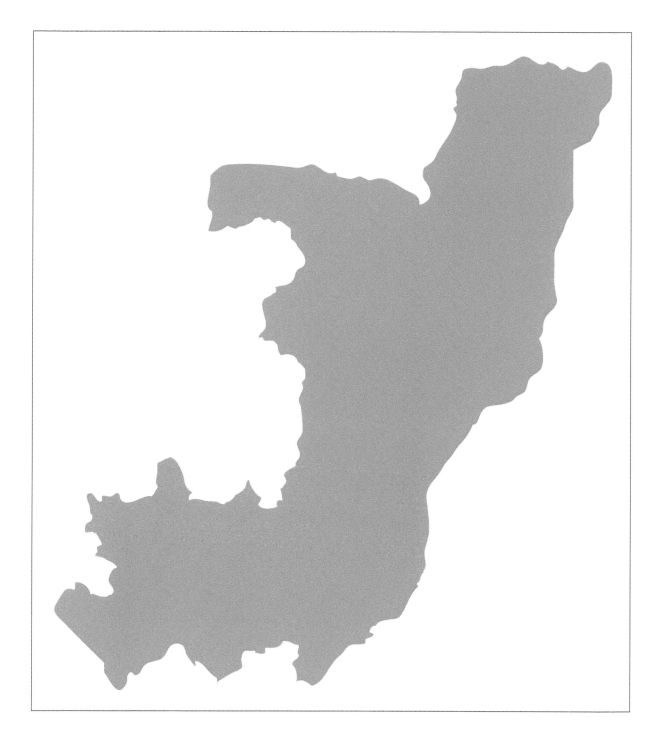

CONGO,
Republic of the

Introduction

The Republic of the Congo is located in the west of Central Africa, east of Gabon and west of the Democratic Republic of the Congo. Most of the nation is dense tropical rainforest with tributaries that drain into the Congo River. A portion of the country, between Angola and Gabon, borders the South Atlantic Ocean. The Congo Basin is home to the second largest tropical rainforest in the world, after the Amazon rainforest of Brazil. Although it is rich in oil reserves, the Republic of the Congo is among the world's least developed nations.

GENERAL INFORMATION

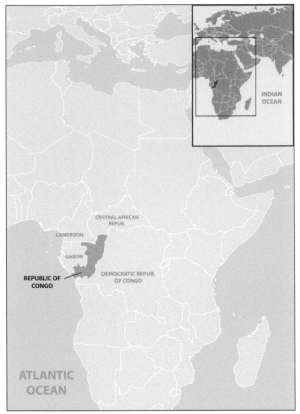

Official Language: French
Population: 4,755,097(2015 estimate)
Currency: Central African CFA franc
Coins: Coins are available in denominations of 1, 2, 5, 10, 25, 50, 100, and 500 francs.
Land Area: 341,500 square kilometers (132,041 square miles)
Water Area: 500 square kilometers (311 square miles)
National Motto: "Unité, Travail, Progrès" (French, "Unity, Work, Progress")
National Anthem: "La Congolaise" (The Concolese)
Capital: Brazzaville
Time Zone: GMT +1

Flag Description: The flag of the Republic of the Congo features a diagonal tricolor design. Divided diagonally from the lower hoist (left) side, it consists of a yellow stripe in the middle, and two equally sized triangles above (green) and below (red). The three colors represent the Pan-African colors.

Population

The southern part of the country is most densely populated, with nearly two-thirds of the Congolese population living in cities such as Brazzaville and Point-Noire; as of 2015, an estimated 65.4 percent of the population was urban. While the slow return of prosperity and stability is evident in the clean, modern streets of the capital's city center, surrounding sections have not fared as well. In recent years, Brazzaville has experienced a burst of unchecked growth as thousands of people displaced by civil conflict have come to inhabit shantytowns on the city's fringes.

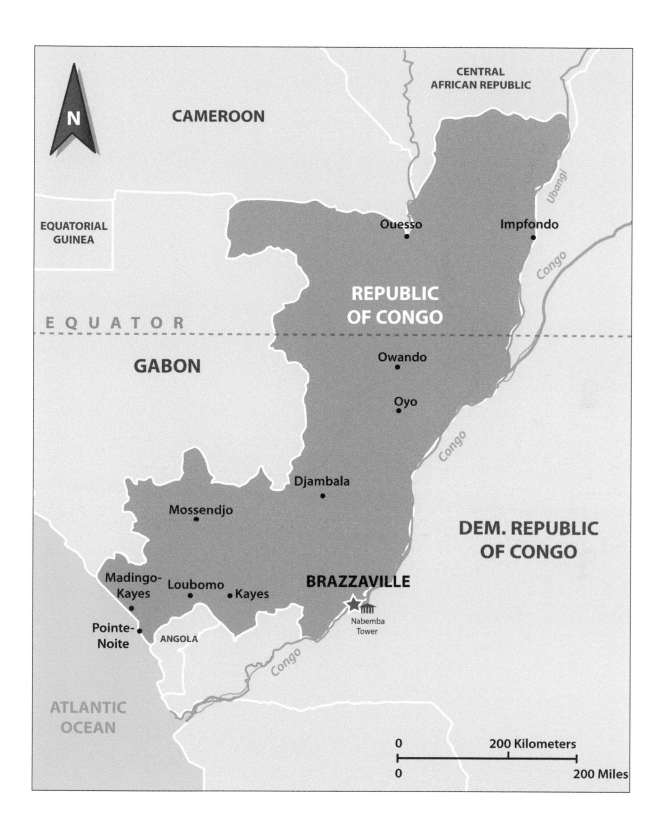

Principal Cities by Population (2007):

- Brazzaville (1,373,382)
- Pointe-Noire (715,334)
- Loubomo (83,798)
- Nkayi (71,620)
- Impfondo (33,911)
- Ouesso (28,179)

Overcrowding and a lack of municipal services such as potable water and the removal of trash and sewage have spawned significant public health and environmental hazards. In light of a United Nations Population Fund (UNFPA) report predicting the potential doubling of Brazzaville's population by 2021, the Congolese government is attempting to implement, with international assistance, new policies to alleviate the environmental, economic, and housing strains created by overcrowding.

As of 2015, the country had a population growth rate of two percent, a decrease from the 2010 rate of 2.8 percent.

Languages

While French is the official language, Lingala and Munukutuba are spoken as national or trade languages and are the lingua franca. There are also many native languages spoken, the most common being Kikongo. In all, there are approximately sixty-two languages spoken in Congo. Languages with over 10,000 speakers include Akwa, Bobangi, Bomwali, French, Kituba (a Kongo-based creole), Kunyi, Laari, Likuba, Likwala, Mbere, Mboko, Mbosi, Nbaka Ma"bo, Ngugwel, Njebi, Ombamba, Suundi, Teke-Ebbo, Teke-Ibali, Teke-Kukuyu, Teke-Nzikou, Teke-Tege, Teke-Tsaayi, Teke-Tyee, Tsaangi, Yay, and Yombe. All of these except for French fall within the Niger-Congo language classification, and all are considered living languages.

Native People & Ethnic Groups

The largest ethnic group is the Kongo people, who comprise 48 percent of the population. Smaller groups include the Sangah (20 percent of the total population), the M'Bochi (12 percent), and the Teke (17 percent). Europeans and other groups account for only three percent of the population.

The Bantu people have lived in Congo since the first century. Today, there are fifteen primary Bantu groups in the Republic of the Congo and seventy smaller groups. The largest include the Bacongo, Bateke, M'Bochi, Sangah, and Vili. A smaller population of less than 100,000 Pygmies resides in the rainforests.

In 2003, Pygmies living in the Lekoumou region in the south complained that due to the lack of documentation on their population, they were being paid less than their Bantu neighbors for identical work. Later that year, Pygmy groups produced a CD through the help of the United Nations Educational, Scientific, and Cultural Organization (UNESCO) in order to promote an awareness of indigenous Pygmy culture and the difficulties they currently endure, such as insufficient health care and education.

Religions

While, half of the Congolese had retained their traditional (animistic) beliefs, as of 2015 approximately 33.1 percent identify as Roman Catholic, approximately 42 percent as other Christian denominations, and 2 percent are Muslim.

Climate

Congo has a tropical climate, due to its location near the equator. The weather is hot and humid throughout the year, with temperatures between 27° and 32° Celsius (80° and 90° Fahrenheit). Most of the country receives a good deal of rain (as much as 70 inches/178 centimeters) throughout the year.

ENVIRONMENT & GEOGRAPHY

Topography

The Republic of the Congo is located in the west of Central Africa, east of Gabon and west of the Democratic Republic of the Congo. A portion of the country, between Angola and Gabon, borders the South Atlantic Ocean. Most of the nation is dense tropical rainforest with tributaries that drain into the Congo River.

The southwestern part of the country is a basin sloping south toward a coastal plain, drained by the Kouilou-Niari River. The Congo Basin is home to the second largest tropical rainforest in the world, after the Amazon rainforest of Brazil.

Central Congo is a plateau, and the northern part of the country descends again into a basin. The lowest point is at sea level along the Atlantic Coast, and the highest is at the tip of Mount Berongou, at an elevation of 903 meters (2,963 feet). The Congo and Ubangi are the country's major rivers, and are the primary routes for commercial water traffic.

Brazzaville is the country's capital. It is located in the southeastern section of the republic, on the northern bank of the Congo River. It is also directly opposite the port city of Kinshasa, which is the capital of the Democratic Republic of the Congo, formerly known as Zaire. Situated within viewing distance of each other, Brazzaville and Kinshasa represent the geographically closest pair of national capitals in the world.

Plants & Animals

Two valuable species of African mahogany, Entandrophramga cylindricum and Entandrophramga utile, account for nearly 70 percent of the timber harvested in Congo. The process by which the trees are harvested may permanently endanger the survival of both species.

In 2000, the Republic of the Congo expanded its Odzala National Park by four times its original size, to 3.2 million acres. This helps to ensure that Congo's large mammal population will be protected, including forest-dwelling elephants, water buffalo, gorillas, and lions. The part also provides a home for more than two-thirds of the more than 600 bird species found in the country.

At the Lossi Gorilla Sanctuary, located about 15 kilometers (nine miles) to the south and west of Odzala, researchers have noted that over 139 gorillas have disappeared since 2002, due to the Ebola virus. The virus seems to be spreading from the west and has infected humans who have been exposed to the ape carcasses. This has been a substantial setback to both the villagers and to environmentalists in the area.

Bush meat hunting is a severe problem in Congo. Bush meat markets are known to exist in Brazzaville and Pointe Noire, and elephant steak is often sold in high-end supermarkets. New roads constructed through the logging industry are making it easier for poachers to gain access to the animals.

In 1980, the Conkouati Reserve was formed at the border of Gabon and the Atlantic Ocean over an area of over 144,000 hectares (356,000 acres). The site is important due to its rich biodiversity, making it a critical zone to be conserved if the dense African forests are to last into the future. The portion of the reserve along the Atlantic is currently one of the most important sites for sea turtles to lay their eggs, and the Conkouati lagoon shelters a large population of manatees.

Some of the endangered species found in Congo include the broad-headed crocodile, chimpanzee, forest elephant, gorilla, leopard, and mandrill.

CUSTOMS & COURTESIES

Greetings

In formal situations in the Republic of the Congo, a handshake is the most common form of greeting. It is only acceptable to offer the right hand for a handshake, as the left hand is used for personal cleansing and is considered impure. Women often kiss each other on the cheek and embrace lightly.

Social status is an important aspect of interaction, and an individual is expected to show deference to others if applicable. This is accomplished by extending one's hand first or averting one's eyes while greeting. Honorific and formal titles are also customarily employed, and include "Ta," short for the Latin word "tata" ("father") or "Ma," short for the French word "maman" ("mother"). In rural areas, youth may occasionally bend one knee to greet an elder, though is this becoming rare among young males, and has been replaced by curtsies for young females.

Greetings are often offered in the indigenous language, particularly in rural areas. For example, "Mboté nayo" (loosely meaning "Hello, how are you?") derives from the original single strand of Bantu that came with migrating tribes hundreds of years earlier. However, in larger cities where ethnicities are more mixed, greetings are mainly conduced in French first, and appropriately include "Bonjour" ("Good day") and "Bonsoir" ("Good afternoon or evening"). Because of ethnic tension, many Congolese in cities will throw their names into a greeting to establish their tribal heritage. Once these formalities have been completed, the conversation will either continue in French or a common dialect of Bantu if it is shared.

Gestures & Etiquette

Gesturing is often an important facet of conversation in Congolese culture. For example, a question about someone's general well-being is commonly emphasized by putting out the right hand, palm up, and raising it. In addition, when greeting elders in some rural communities, curtsying is common among young girls, and men are traditionally expected to go down on one knee. Men may also raise their right hands to their foreheads when greeting each other in a sign of respect.

Eating/Meals

Congolese traditionally eat three meals daily. With the rising prices of food and the stagnation of wages in the early 21st century, many families have cut down on the number of meals eaten. Two larger meals are becoming increasingly common, but even this has been modified to just one large dinner with leftovers eaten the next day for breakfast.

Generally, breakfast may consist of a freshly stewed grain somewhat similar to porridge or leftover dinner from the night before. The majority of families living in rural areas know few recipes, so many of them eat the same dishes,

sometimes twice daily. Snacks and sandwiches can be purchased from street vendors, and include fried meats on skewers, fried bananas or plantains, peanuts or groundnuts, or fried dough. In the larger cities, men will commonly buy pastries and coffee on the way to work and eat sandwiches at lunchtime.

When eating, most families traditionally gather around a single dish that is placed on a mat on the floor. Shoes are customarily removed and the right hand is rinsed and dried with a rinsing bowl and towel. Meals are communal and the food is scooped with the right hand from the section immediately in front of an individual. (It is imperative to use only the right hand, as the left is designated for bathroom hygiene.)

Visiting

Visiting the homes of family or neighbors is a common practice in Congo. Generally, visitors are generally unannounced but rarely a surprise, as visiting is a regular occurrence. When a visitor comes to one's home, the host will generally offer them a seat either on a chair or on a straw mat on the ground. It is rare to host a guest indoors, as most homes are not conducive to this. Generally, guests are invited to sit outside either on the porch of the main building or under the shade of a tree. Beverages and food are also likely to be offered.

Two typical occasions for visiting include listening to the radio and watching soccer. Hospitality is reciprocal, and it may be expected that the wealthiest of the guests provide gifts and pay for their own transportation or that of their guests depending on who has to do the traveling.

LIFESTYLE

Family

The traditional Congolese family includes extended family members. This often includes a husband, his wife or wives (up to four), often four children per wife, grandparents, and siblings of the husband. In the south, where tribes are matrilineal, siblings of the wife and perhaps even distant cousins are commonly included. This is a result of both necessity and practicality. Most Congolese are subsistence farmers and require an extended household to care for the young and other domestic tasks while older children and parents work the fields. The necessity of an extended household also stems from civil unrest that has displaced tens of thousands of Congolese from their homes. In urban Congo, overcrowding is particularly prevalent, and large families often reside in one-floor apartments.

In the Republic of the Congo, all members of the family are expected to contribute. This may include farming, watching over younger siblings or the elderly, domestic tasks, or holding a job. In addition, a village or clan is often an extension of the family unit; in this case, it is customary for an entire community to involve itself in the affairs of an individual family. Villages are known to intervene in family disputes and even arbitrate minor crimes.

Housing

Most Congolese live in very cramped quarters, whether in rural villages or urban areas. This is mainly due to urban migration (over 65 percent of Congolese live in the major cities), refugees crowding into the homes of relatives, couples bearing numerous children (most families have four or more children—4.68 children per woman was the average in 2015), and lack of resources to build larger homes. Homes are generally called compounds in rural areas and include several one-room units built around an open courtyard or land. It is customary for husbands who have multiple wives to sleep alone or with their newest wife until she has conceived enough children. In urban Congo-Brazzaville, most families live in small apartments, often in dilapidated buildings. Most of these buildings were built before the civil war and have fallen into disrepair.

During the civil war of the late 1990s, tens of thousands of Congolese were displaced from their homes due to violence. This forced many people to live with their extended families, with many more seeking refuge in the inner forests. As a result, families were forced to build makeshift homes from natural or discarded materials. Many of these families remain in the bush and have since perfected their designs to accommodate for larger families. Multi-room homes are built from wood and large tropical fronds, and are primarily designed to keep out rain.

Food

A look at the traditional Congolese diet reveals a rich and healthy reliance on roots, greens, fruit, grains, and fresh meat. Most dishes in Congo involve a pounded starch such as millet, sorghum, maize, or manioc root. These starches are harvested and pounded by hand into tiny granules then stewed into a sticky porridge. All starches are accompanied by sauce, which can consist of combinations of beef or goat, fish, greens from the banana and cassava plants, peppers, eggplant, peanuts, and beans. Sauces usually contain onions and garlic, both cheap and flavorful staples of Congolese cuisine. In the forest regions, wild game is commonly eaten, and mainly includes gazelle meat. When snacking, most Congolese eat roasted and salted nuts, grilled meats, and fruit. Oranges, watermelon, and mangoes are also common.

In recent years, the diet of most Congolese has undergone a severe shift as the nation's large farms fell into disrepair and the government slowly grew more dependent on imports. Of the country's estimated 100 million hectares (247,105,381 acres) of farmable land, only. 2 percent is being farmed for permanent crops. Thus, with imports becoming so crucial to feed Congolese and the international economy dictating the price of food, it has raised the price to just out of reach of most Congolese. The number of daily meals has dropped from three to two, and getting closer to one. Staples rich in iron and protein are less and less available as white rice replaces cassava and other grains generally served as the main starch.

Life's Milestones

Like most cultures, the people of Congo celebrate birth, marriage, and death as life's major milestones. Different tribes have different traditions, but for the most part birth is a major achievement that is celebrated throughout entire communities. These celebrations generally last for days and may include musical performances, dancing, and feasts. These are all intended to protect the child and ensure a long life. Immediately after birth, the mother is given time to rest, which may last a few days or a couple of weeks. Often, female relatives will come from afar to help a new mother.

Marriage is not as frequently arranged as it used to be. When a man proposes, he traditionally offers the bride's family a "bride gift" to compensate for the loss of her domestic contribution at home. Depending on the status of each family, the gift ranges in size and content, and may include a monetary offering or a harvest of crops. If the couple chooses a monogamous marriage, they have the option to make that decision legal in a court of law. Having a civil service in which the groom promises to refuse polygamy has become the norm among educated couples recognizing the strain of multiple wives.

Death is not observed among most Congolese the way it is in some other African cultures. This is largely due to superstition that death is caused by evil spirits. While this belief is fading in urban areas, many rural Congolese remain superstitious. Some cultures even go so far as to blame someone in the community for cursing the deceased, ultimately bringing about his demise.

Other important life milestones include the coronation of a new king, something the Teke peoples still go through with each succession. These affairs often involve vast pomp and circumstance lasting for days.

CULTURAL HISTORY

Art

The earliest inhabitants of the densely forested regions of the Republic of the Congo (also known as Congo-Brazzaville or Congo) are believed to date back to 100,000–40,000 BCE. These individuals were forced to gather roots and other vegetation as the local environment made

hunting difficult. In the next tens of thousands of years, as humans grew in size and sophistication, these early inhabitants developed strong fishing abilities and expanded their diets to include freshwater fish from the Congo River. As is common with other prehistoric cultures, they also left traces of artistic expression in the form of rock art. Specifically situated in the Niari Valley, the rock art of Congo features drawings of lizards and geometric patterns.

With the influx of Bantu peoples, farming and metallurgy were brought to the region, and villages run by local chiefs became the norm. In the late first millennium, three distinct kingdoms emerged including the Loango Kingdom to the northeast of the Congo River basin, the Tio Kingdom of the northern plains, and the Bakongo or Kongo Kingdom of Congo River Basin. Sophisticated woodcarvings and sculpture, folk songs and dance, and indigenous traditions such as basketry and weaving were distinct to each kingdom. At the same time, the native Bantu language developed into two main strands that facilitated trading between the regions. In 1482, the Portuguese arrived, beginning a long relationship of trade and cultural exchange. This relationship was mutually beneficial at the outset. However, all three kingdoms had been destroyed or weakened by the time the French and British arrived in the late 17th century.

Despite the heavy European influence on culture in the country, Congolese people maintained many of their religious and artistic practices. Today, half of the population is Christian while nearly half still practice animism or other traditional beliefs. Elaborate dances, music, and crafts have also survived, but have become uniform through European influence.

Architecture

Architecture in Congo, like many other African nations, ranges from the most organic to imported colonial and modernist styles. In rural Congo, the vast majority of buildings are residences and small, one-story shops. Homes are generally one-room buildings positioned together in a single compound. They are often built in circular shapes from straw and mud and topped off with conical, thatched roofs. Other styles of rural architecture incorporate cement blocks to construct rectangular buildings. These generally have corrugated tin or cement roofs. A more primitive style of architecture is found in densely forested regions and consists of natural materials such as large branches and fronds. Inhabitation in such areas is largely from displacement during civil war or because of an ancestral link to the land.

In urban Congo, where the majority of the population is concentrated, the architecture is also varied. Both Pointe-Noire and Brazzaville, the two largest cities in Congo, have been strongly influenced by outside architectural styles, most notably the French, who implemented urban planning. Prior to French influence, villages were arranged in an egalitarian spread of family homes without centralized power. The French centralized settlements and introduced a style of architecture that mirrored French designs, including white-cement buildings, multiple-floored construction, and architectural elements such as windows and pillars. French colonial architecture is best exemplified in Brazzaville with the construction of St. Anne's Basilica in 1949. Considered the capital's most significant monument, it was designed by French architect Roger Erell (1907–1986). The angular cuts, triangular shapes, and green-tiled roofs of Brazzaville's distinct architectural style are also attributed to Erell.

Music & Dance

Traditional Congolese dance and music help commemorate life's milestones, and serve as means of communication. Many of the Congolese tribes, particularly those of the rainforest regions, are renowned for their traditional music and dance styles. These unique styles are used to communicate between tribal groups. Performers from different settlements often travel to neighboring tribes to share their musical and physical message. One of the most important musical instruments is the djembe drum, commonly known as the n'goma among the peoples of the rainforest region. A djembe drum is a large, goblet-shaped drum traditionally composed of carved wood and an animal hide stretched over the open top. The outside of the drum is generally carved with elaborate decorations.

The advent of European colonialism also brought the musical influence of the Latin American and Caribbean region. This influence was further strengthened by the introduction of the phonograph in the early 1900s, which the French used to play recordings of classical music, American jazz and the percussive rhythms of rumba. Originating in Cuba, rumba ultimately had the greatest impact on Congolese artists.

In the early 1900s, rural Congolese, many of which were skilled musicians, converged on both Kinshasa and Brazzaville, sister cities run by the Belgians and French, respectively, on either side of the Congo River. When they were not working for the colonial powers, they practiced their skills, spawning a burgeoning music and nightlife scene. This led to the development of soukous music (also known as African rumba), which combined European and Latin musical influences, This combination of native African sounds blended with rumba beats was widely popular in the 1930s and 1940s.

African popular music, or Afropop, which includes soukous, continues to be popular. Democratic Republic of the Congo (DRC) and American hip-hop influence most modern Congolese music.

Film

Although the Congolese cinema is still developing, the small nation has produced some strong artists. Notable Congolese directors include Léandre-Alain Baker (1960–), who has filmed both dramas and documentaries touching upon many issues facing West and Central Africa. His film *Ramata* (2007), a dramatic story of a wealthy and beautiful African woman married to a Senegalese official, was well received at international film festivals. The story highlights poverty and wealth among Africans while emphasizing fate and chance as having a strong power over the beliefs of Africans. Other films, nearly all documentaries, trace the various lives of Congolese. Another famous Congolese filmmaker is David Pierre Fila (1954–), whose documentaries trace the rich anthropological heritage of Congolese. He has lived and worked in Paris and organized screenings of African directors at the Center for African Studies.

Literature

Prior to written literature in Congo-Brazzaville, indigenous tribes maintained rich oral traditions through storytelling. Memorization of stories and proverbs has long been essential to the passing on of cultural and historical knowledge from one generation to the next. Proverbs are particularly common in early Congolese storytelling. Their moralistic content served different, albeit crucial, roles in the various tribal groups. Among the Teke people, for example, the memorization of proverbs is not only essential for historical preservation, but also a required tool for social engagement. At social gatherings, especially those for milestone or family events, an elder may recite the first proverb, and the group is expected to chant the proverb in response. The elder then designates the next person to dole out a proverb, and he or she will be chastised if they fail to fulfill the role.

When the French arrived, they built schools and taught French as the official language of the colony. With increased formal education and writing skills, Congolese began to express themselves on the page and in French. One of the first authors to gain international fame was Jean Malonga (1907–1985). His first published book, *Coeur d'Aryenne* (*Heart of Aryenne*, 1954), tells the story of an African boy and a European girl who fall in love despite the disapproval of their parents. For Malonga, the story illustrated the need for African and European coexistence in the postcolonial era. Congolese literature was also spurred on by the journal *Liaison* (1950–1960), which helped launch the writing careers of Malonga and other native authors.

CULTURE

Arts & Entertainment

Despite a tumultuous transition from colonial rule to self-governance, Congo established itself early on as a leader in contemporary African arts. French artist Pierre Lods recognized the need to establish an African style of painting. He believed firmly that the composition of rhythm and color harmony should be nurtured apart from the constraints of European formal training. His ideology contrasted with many African artists of the day who believed that Africa's true art history was one born of the blend of these two styles. In 1951, Lods founded the Poto Poto Art School, formally known as the Centre des Artes Africains, in Brazzaville.

As part of his style of teaching, Lods surrounded his artists with "props" or a milieu of artifacts and traditional art works, including masks, sculpture, and even readings of traditional proverbs and poems to inspire African artistry. As a result, the work to come out of Poto Poto generally shared common images associated stereotypically with African painting, such as an earth tone color scheme. In 1956, works from Poto Poto were chosen for an exhibition on African art at the Museum of Modern Art (MoMA) in New York City. With all of this international recognition, many others became interested in the teaching style of Lods, and he accepted a teaching position with the first art school of Dakar. This gave way to a second generation that is notably characterized by a stark transition from the Afrocentric teaching style of Lods to a more formal, European-style training. In 2002, in homage to the dismantled school, the Congolese Department of Arts and Culture promised a center based on the ideology of Poto Poto.

Most modern art in Congo-Brazzaville employs modern styles to portray traditional forms. This includes dance, visual arts, and even music. The world famous and award-winning dance company Li-Sangha (or Ballet Lisanga) Company operates in collaboration with the French Cultural Arts Center in Brazzaville to choreograph pieces reflective of this modern style with a traditional significance. Classically trained, the dancers tell the story of every day African life through their movements. The Congolese government also organizes the annual Pan-African Music Festival to bring together musicians from all over Africa to perform in a multi-day celebration of African music.

Cultural Sites & Landmarks

Congo's most significant landmark is perhaps the Odzala National Park located in the far northwestern region of the country. At roughly 13,600 square kilometers (5,250 square miles), Odzala is one of the least explored rainforest regions in the world. The park is home to a diverse range of flora and fauna, including the forest elephant and the western gorilla, two of the park's inhabitants that are more famous. In fact, it is believed that Congo-Brazzaville is home to over 80 percent of the world's entire population of gorillas, and the preservation of Odzala is crucial to their survival. Other wildlife living in the dense forested region include buffalo, leopards, monkeys, pygmy antelope, hippopotamus, hyena and the last remaining lions of Central Africa.

Another natural landmark is that of the Bateke Plateau, the historic home of the Teke tribes for hundreds of years. Unlike Odzala National Park, Bateke is an elevated stretch of land characterized by sand dunes, grassy plains, and light forest. The fauna is also different, but the most important contrast is the dense human population and its crucial role in the ecosystem. The Teke people, a hunting and gathering tribe, have long helped to maintain a balance of resources and consumption. However, with populations growing and the hunting and gathering lifestyle giving way to slash and burn farming, the Bateke Plateau is seeing its naturally maintained balance disrupted. Another famous natural landmark is the renowned Congo River, formerly known as the Zaire River. It is considered Africa's most powerful river and its rapids were first made famous by the explorer David Livingstone (1813–1873). Later, author Joseph

Conrad (1857–1924) named the violent river the "heart of darkness" in his famous novella of the same name.

Most Congolese live in Brazzaville and Pointe-Noire, the two largest cities. Originally, the Portuguese dubbed the main fishing village of the Bakongo kingdom, Pointe-Noir Ponta Negra in the early 1880s; Brazzaville derives its name from European explorer Pietro Paolo Savorgnan di Brazza (1852–1905). Pointe-Noire, located on the coast, is known for its golden beaches—it is a popular spot for surfing—and markets. Brazzaville, which has experienced moderate destruction due to recent conflicts, notably the Congo Civil War (1997–1999), is home to numerous landmarks and colonial architecture. Notable cultural sites include a controversial mausoleum erected to honor the colonizer Brazza; Nabemba Tower, the tallest structure in Central Africa at 106 meters tall (348 feet); St. Anne's Basilica is built in the beehive shape of traditional African homes; and the colonial Palais du Peuple (People's Palace), the seat of the presidency.

Libraries & Museums

The Republic of the Congo's national library, the People's National Library (Bibliothèque nationale populaire), is located in Brazzaville. There are 56 public libraries and 10 research libraries in the Republic. The National Museum of Congo (Musee National du Congo), founded in 1965, is also located in the capital of Brazzaville. As one of many African institutions to receive funding from the United States Ambassadors Fund for Cultural Preservation, the money allowed the museum to provide better protection and more storage space for its collection in 2010. The museum's collection consists of over 2,000 masks and various Congolese artifacts and crafts, such as musical instruments, pottery, and statuary.

Holidays

March 18 is celebrated as Marien Ngouabi Day, in honor of the man who served as military president from 1969 to 1977. An alleged suicide commando assassinated Ngouabi on March 18, 1977. Independence Day is celebrated on August 15.

Youth Culture

Youth culture in Congo is primarily one of subordination and deference. Family and village elders are given the utmost of respect from younger generations and Congolese youth are expected to demonstrate this through physical and verbal expression, such as averting their eyes and using honorific titles when speaking. Aside from showing respect to elders, the young Congolese generally spend their days going to school if their families can afford it, or helping around the house if they cannot.

The influence of American hip-hop and its related culture are popular among the Congolese youth, and can be particularly evident in regards to fashion. Generally, however, girls dress in long wraps, or skirts, with sleeveless shirts and cloth wraps on their heads. Young men tend to wear light pants and shirts. Young men are notably fond of football (soccer) and large groups are commonly seen playing in a range of places, including for organized neighborhood teams or in the street for those without the means to pay for membership. Street games may commonly substitute any material or garbage for a ball.

During the civil war that plagued the country, many children were either orphaned or kidnapped, and then forced to become child soldiers. The result of this has been the increase of street children in modern Congo. Many NGOs are working toward integrating these youth back into society, but their experiences with violence, rape, prostitution and trafficking makes it challenging.

SOCIETY

Transportation

Outside of walking, mini-buses and taxis are the most popular mode of transportation. Generally, mini-buses run routes along the most populous areas and are operated by independent drivers.

These buses, which are often vibrantly decorated, commonly run routes that can be determined by asking the driver. Road conditions in cities and throughout the country are mainly poor and affected by weather. For example, in the rainy season, most rural Congolese are isolated for months as the weather renders roads impassable. For this reason, most of the goods to be traded from Central Africa travel on barges along the Oubangui and Congo Rivers. Pirogues, for passengers and fishers, also make trips from town to town along the vast rivers. It may take as long as a few weeks to travel from the farthest inland regions to the coast, depending on the season and mode of transport. Traffic moves on the right-hand side of the road.

Transportation Infrastructure

The Central African sub-region, which includes Congo, is extremely poor and undeveloped in terms of transportation infrastructure; as of 2004, the length of paved roads in the region was estimated at 864 kilometers out of a total 17,289 km of roadways. As of 2009, Congo has approximately 2,000 kilometers (1,242 miles) of paved roads. Much of the transportation infrastructure in the Republic of the Congo was damaged during civil war. For example, rail transport was inoperable for six years following the outbreak of civil war in 1997. Rail service was also suspended in 2006 following fuel shortages and flooding. A deteriorating and underdeveloped transportation infrastructure has largely contributed to the Congo's widespread poverty and lack of economic investment.

Media & Communications

The constitution of the Republic of the Congo allows for the freedom of speech for all citizens in any medium, including journalists. Until recently, it was illegal for journalists to publish anything critical of the government. In 2001, President Denis Sassou-Nguesso (1943–) passed legislation to allow such criticisms. Despite this allowed freedom, the government reserves the right to punish individuals they deem guilty of inciting violence, racism or hatred of the government, an allowance used loosely by government officials to limit freedom of speech. This backdoor method for censorship is common in many African nations.

Most wide-reaching media groups are government-owned. Two of the largest radio stations, Radio Congo and Radio Brazzaville, are state-run and do not allow government criticism. The same policy exists for the government-owned television station TeleCongo, which reaches a large part of urban Congo. There is one private radio and television station apiece, each broadcasting occasional criticism of the government. They mainly run satellite-streamed news from international sources including the British Broadcasting Corporation (BBC), Radio France Internationale (RFI), and Voice of America (VOA). All of the newspapers in the Republic of the Congo are privately owned, but due to high levels of illiteracy, reach only one-third of the population. In 2014, there were an estimated 89,500 Internet users, representing less than 2 percent of the population.

SOCIAL DEVELOPMENT

Standard of Living
The Republic of Congo ranked 140th of 195 in the 2014 United Nations Human Development Index.

Water Consumption
Access to safe and cleaner water and basic sanitation continue to be significant issues in the African nation. The National Water Distribution Company (SNDE) is charged with water distribution, though the quality of that water is often seen as below standard and the cause of widespread diarrhea and child dysentery. As of 2014, the tap water was still not potable, but 76.5 percent of the total population had access to improved water sources.

Education
Since independence, the Congolese government has attempted to promote education beyond the elite ruling class, with marginal success. Education is free and compulsory for children between six and 16 years of age. Primary education lasts six years, and secondary education, which also consists of technical or trade schools, lasts for six or seven years (up to the 13th grade), and is divided into two cycles. Marien Ngouabi University is Congo's only state-funded institute of higher learning.

More than 79 percent of the adult population of Congo is literate—though some figures place that rate lower, at around 74 percent—with the literacy rate near 86 percent for men and 73 percent for women.

Women's Rights
The role of women in Congolese society remains relatively in line with centuries-old tradition, despite the efforts of numerous non-governmental organizations (NGOs) throughout the nation. Generally, the vast majority of women are responsible for raising their children, managing the home, and perhaps farming or selling crafts or food for additional income. In rural areas, it is common for women to maintain the family farm in addition to her daily responsibilities. Often, these same women will use the crops to make food to sell in a local village. Still, many more women living in urban Congo are required by their husbands to earn a living by cooking or craftwork that they then sell in city centers.

Because of this persistently uneducated role in society, women do not go very far in school, as this is seen as an unnecessary luxury. Furthermore, women are underrepresented politically and only nine out of 66 seats in the senate, and 10 out of 136 seats in the national assembly, were occupied by women in the 2012 election. In addition, the percentage of women in the official private sector is almost non-existent. NGOs are fighting this trend by advancing micro-lending practices in rural and urban areas to help women bolster their individual craft or food businesses. By funding part of their work, the NGOs allow women to diversify products and increase income.

Women hold very limited rights in terms of matrimony. For example, if a woman commits adultery she can be imprisoned or divorced by her husband. However, if a husband commits the same act, he suffers no punishment. The woman may divorce him, but at the risk of being forced to pay back the "bride price" he paid for her hand in marriage. If she is unable to pay back the bride price, she can never legally divorce him; this amount of money is nearly universally impossible for women to raise nationwide. Additionally, polygamy, or having multiple wives, is legal, while polyandry, or having multiple husbands, is illegal. Property rights give 30 percent of an estate to the widow upon her husband's death, but this is rarely observed.

Domestic violence and spousal rape was considered a national problem, though it was rarely prosecuted. This is largely due to the lack of official filings by abused women. There is no law against domestic abuse and cases must be filed under general assault. NGOs are working towards aiding women in abusive marriages, and in recent years, truth tribunals have been led in many Central African nations to give these women and their plight a voice. Some organizations have also designated the Republic of the Congo as a country of destination for human trafficking.

Health Care

Medical facilities are limited and medicines are in short supply, especially outside of the urban areas. Malaria is a persistent and sometime fatal disease. It is estimated that 80,700 Congolese are living with HIV (2014 estimate).

Infant mortality in the Republic of the Congo is high, at 57.92 deaths per 1,000 live births, though this figure has dropped significantly in the last decade. The average life expectancy for the Congolese is 58 years—57.5 years for men and almost 60 for women (2015 estimate).

GOVERNMENT

Structure

The Republic of the Congo, formerly the Middle Congo, was created on August 15, 1960, when it gained independence from France. A Marxist-styled government was formed soon after, which dissolved in 1990. A democratically elected government took power in 1992, but a civil war in 1997 marked a return to Marxism and an extended period of civil unrest, when many party leaders fled the country. A new constitution was adopted on January 20, 2002, which made the country a presidential republic and abolished the prime ministry in 2009. The new constitution also established a bicameral legislature (having two legislatures).

The Congolese government is comprised of an executive branch, with a president and his appointed Council of Ministers, and a legislative branch, consisting of a bicameral legislature with a Senate and National Assembly, as well as a judicial branch. There are 72 seats in the Senate and 139 in the National Assembly. Members of both houses are elected by popular vote to serve five-year terms. The president is elected by popular vote to a seven-year term. All adults over 18 years of age may vote.

Political Parties

There have been over 100 different political parties formed since the Marxist government collapsed in 1990, but not all of these are functioning. The most influential are the Action Movement for Renewal, the Congolese Labour Party, the Movement for Solidarity and Development, the Congolese Movement for Democracy and Integral Development (MCDDI). Also influential are the Pan-African Union for Social Development (UPADS), the Rally for Democracy and the Republic, the Rally for Democracy and Social Progress, the Rally of the Presidential Majority, the Union for Democracy and Republic, and the Union of Democratic Forces (UDF). Many smaller parties also exist.

Local Government

There are ten administrative regions in the nation: Bouenza, Cuvette, Cuvette-Ouest, Kouilou, Lékoumou, Likouala, Niari, Plateaux, Pool, and Sangha. The capital, Brazzaville, located on the Congo River in the southeastern part of the country, is considered a commune and not a part of any one region. Local governance consists of district, local, and regional councils.

Judicial System
A Supreme Court heads the judicial branch with a lower Court of Accounts and Budgetary Discipline. A Court of Appeal and a Constitutional Court were added with the 2002 constitution.

Taxation
The top personal income tax rate in Congo is 50 percent, while the top corporate tax rate is 38 percent. Other levied taxes include a tax on rental values and a value-added tax (VAT). Taxes and other revenue make up 46.1 percent of the yearly GDP.

Armed Forces
The Congolese Armed Forces consists of the Army (Armee de Terre), Navy, Congolese Air Force (Armee de l'Air Congolaise), Gendarmerie (national police force), and Special Presidential Security Guard (GSSP).

Foreign Policy
Congo-Brazzaville had achieved independence from France by 1960, marking the beginning of a period that would be defined by military ousters and takeovers. From 1971 to the early 1990s, as the world divided along democratic or socialist political ideologies, Congo-Brazzaville distanced itself from France to ally politically with the Soviet Union. With the fall of the Soviet Union in the late 20th century, the political view of Congo-Brazzaville shifted, and free market capitalism was favored by Pascal Lissouba (1931–). Despite these free economic tendencies, Lissouba dissolved the Congolese National Assembly, leading to violent eruptions by ethnic groups worried about diminishing political influence. The uprising was subdued with the help of international peacekeeping units, but would reemerge during the 1997 elections, when civil war broke out. This conflict continued for two years until the Angolan military intervened and Denis Sassou-Nguesso again became president (he had been president previously from 1979 until 1992).

Despite these consistent internal problems, Congo maintains its memberships in the African Union (AU), the United Nations (UN), the African Development Bank (ADB), the Non-Aligned Movement (NAM), and other regional and international organizations. The Republic of the Congo also was posted to the UN Security Council (UNSC) in 2006–2007 and President Sassou-Nguesso was elected to a one-year term as chair of the AU in 2006. As a developing nation, Congo receives substantial foreign aid through UN agencies, the U.S. Agency for International Development (USAID), and the European Union (EU) through the European Development Fund (EDF). Relations between the Republic of the Congo and the United States and other Western nations remain positive.

Human Rights Profile
International human rights law insists that states respect civil and political rights, and promote an individual's economic, social, and cultural rights. The United Nations Universal Declaration on Human Rights (UDHR) is recognized as the standard for international human rights. Its authors sought the counsel of the world's great thinkers, philosophers, and religious leaders, and were careful to create a document that reflects the core values shared by every world culture. (To read this document or view the articles relating to cultural human rights, visit http://www.udhr.org/UDHR/default.htm.)

Despite a rocky transition from colonialism to self-governance, the Republic of the Congo now claims a legitimate democracy. The 2002 elections were generally considered free and fair, despite the fact that the two major opponents were not allowed to run due to residency issues. The national government is now a multi-party system with a senate, the Congolese National Assembly, and multi-faceted judicial system. Despite this system being in place, the contrast between established and enforced laws was still a problem, and certain regions and ethnic groups claimed no representation in government. The Pool Region, for example, did not have its eight stipulated assembly seats filled in 2003, and there are still no Pygmy members in the national government.

Outside of the political sphere, there continues to be a number of human rights concerns. The national security forces continue to be suspected of abusing civilians, raping women, arbitrary arrest, looting, and soliciting bribes from the public. These actions are considered illegal under Sassou-Nguesso's constitutional reforms, but are alleged to persist unprosecuted. Violent attacks on civilians by both military officials trying to root out rebels and rebel forces trying to secure money and goods are also widespread. Furthermore, limitations on the freedom of movement were also enforced by government blockades despite the constitutional right of Congolese citizens to move about the country freely. In 2003, international human rights organizations cited the impunity of military forces in committing these crimes and accused the government of failing to act. The government responded by establishing committees to train soldiers about human rights.

The transparency of the use of oil and forestry revenue was once an issue of contention among Congolese who felt their government was embezzling funds. However, in a move to improve economic conditions and government transparency in Congo, President Sassou-Nguesso agreed to a deal with the International Monetary Fund (IMF) in which he would audit both the oil and forestry industries and maintain timely debt payments. The IMF, in turn, approved its participation in the Poverty Reduction Growth Facility (PRGF) aimed at improving many aspects of the nation's economy and infrastructure.

ECONOMY

Overview of the Economy

The economy is petroleum-based, supplemented by small-scale agriculture, handicrafts, and a historically overstaffed government bureaucracy. In 1994, pressure from international institutions such as the World Bank and the International Monetary Fund (IMF) forced the Congolese government to fire approximately 8,000 employees from its bloated payroll. By 1996, the nation had succeeded in restructuring its debt.

However, civil war broke out in June 1997, and the country has endured years of strife and civil unrest ever since. In 1998, oil prices fell and the transitional government was disrupted. The government and opposition adopted a new peace accord in 2003. Today, the nation enjoys a tenuous peace, and is renewing steps to stabilize its economy, pay down its debt, and reduce poverty. External debt in 2000 was estimated at $5 billion (USD). However, Congo became a net external creditor in 2011 and its external debt represented only 16 percent of the GDP ($3.956 billion) in 2014.

In 2014, the gross domestic product (GDP) was estimated at $28.04 billion (USD). The per-capita GDP was $6,600 (USD). Agriculture comprised 3.3 percent of the GDP, industry 74.4 percent, and services 22.3 percent.

Industry

Petroleum drives the Congolese economy, but may not be able to sustain it long-term. Other industries include brewing, cement, flour, lumber, palm oil, soap, sugar, and tobacco. Primary exports are cocoa, coffee, diamonds, lumber, petroleum, plywood, and sugar. Imports include construction materials and food. In 2014, exports totaled nearly $9 billion (USD). Imports totaled $4.389 billion (USD).

Labor

According to the 2011 World Factbook, Congo's workforce was estimated at 2.89 million. The unemployment rate is believed to be 53 percent.

Energy/Power/Natural Resources

The northern forests of the Republic of the Congo are some of the most pristine rainforests to be found anywhere in the world. Poachers are threatening many large mammal populations, and smaller animals are threatened by the reduction of the rainforest through logging.

As Congo's future reliance on petroleum may be problematic, logging is accelerating, and since the mid-1990s, over three million hectares (more than seven million acres) of forest have been allocated for logging. Other natural resources include copper, hydropower, lead, natural gas, phosphates, potash, uranium, and zinc.

Other environmental issues facing Congo include air pollution from vehicle emissions and water pollution due to the dumping of raw sewage. Much of the country's tap water is not potable.

Forestry

Prior to the discovery of oil, timber was the leading industry, but today it comprises less than seven percent of Congo's exports.

Mining/Metals

Crude petroleum and natural gas account for a large portion of Congo's mineral industry. As of 2011, the petroleum sector represented an estimated 290,000 bbl/day of Congo's exports, and over 60 percent of the country's GDP. Other significant mineral commodities include gold, iron-ore, and diamonds.

Agriculture

Primary crops grown in Congo include cassava, cocoa, coffee, corn, forest products, peanuts, rice, sugar, and vegetables. Most of these are grown by small farmers to feed their own families.

Much of the farming is done through slash-and-burn agriculture, also called swidden farming. While environmentalists complain of the smoke generated by this practice, it is a sustainable and highly efficient method of farming. Less than 25 percent of the population is employed through agriculture, and only two percent of the land is arable.

Tourism

Due to the volatility of the political situation and the lack of security, travel to the Republic of the Congo is not recommended. Brazzaville and the coastal town of Pointe Noir are relatively safe, but travel between the two towns should be done by air rather than by ground transportation, as robberies and extortion, even by police and security forces, are frequently reported. In general, the country's tourism infrastructure is not well-developed.

Kristen Pappas, Todd C. White, Beverly Ballaro

DO YOU KNOW?

- The Republic of the Congo is home to the largest concentration of lowland gorillas in the world.

- The Republic of the Congo was listed number ten on the list of the "30 Least Livable Countries" list published by the United Nations in 2004.

- Brazzaville sits in viewing distance of Kinshasa, capital of the Democratic Republic of Congo. The two cities represent the geographically closest pair of national capitals in the world.

- Pierre Savorgnan de Brazza, an Italian-born French explorer of the Congo River, founded Brazzaville in 1880.

- It is said that Brazzaville's longstanding rivalry with Kinshasa provided the motivation for the construction of the Nabemba Tower, which, as the tallest skyscraper in central Africa, was designed to signify Brazzaville's superiority over its neighbor.

Bibliography

Clarck, John F. *Failure of Democracy in the Republic of Congo*. Lynne Reinner Publishers Inc., January 2008.

Martin, Phyllis. *Leisure and Society in Colonial Brazzaville*. Cambridge University Press, August 2002.

Martin, Phyllis. *Catholic Women of Congo-Brazzaville: Mothers and Sisters in Troubled Times*. Indiana University Press, April 2009.

Mealer, Bryan. *All Things Must Fight to Live: Stories of War and Deliverance in Congo*. Bloomsbury, April 2008.

Rorison, Sean. *Congo—Democratic Republic. Republic (Bradt Travel Guide.)* Globe Pequot, 2012.

Stearns, Jason. *Dancing in the Glory of Monsters: The Collapse of the Congo and the Great War of Africa*. Public Affairs, 2012.

Works Cited

Jeanne, Jacob, Michael Ashkenazi. The World Cookbook for Students. *Greenwood Press*, January 2007. http://books.google.com/books?id=LohMBqO3nBYC&pg=PA221&lpg=PA221&dq=congo+brazzaville+cuisine&source=bl&ots=AhGqurw1bH&sig=aIKu-zXvgpJd2U0iHrbgObKLBTM&hl=en&ei=tvaWSdX5GpicNaD0mY4M&sa=X&oi=book_result&resnum=5&ct=result#PRA4-PA247,M1

"Congo." Encyclopædia Britannica. 2009. *Encyclopædia Britannica Online*. http://www.britannica.com/EBchecked/topic/132321/Congo-Brazzaville.

"Country Profile: Republic of the Congo." *BBC Online*. http://news.bbc.co.uk/2/hi/africa/country_profiles/1076794.stm

"Music of the Republic of the Congo." *Wikipedia*. http://en.wikipedia.org/wiki/Music_of_the_Republic_of_the_Congo

"Republic of the Congo." Bureau of African Affairs. *U.S. Department of State*. January 2009. http://www.state.gov/r/pa/ei/bgn/2825.htm

"Soukos." *Wikipedia*. http://en.wikipedia.org/wiki/Soukous

"Congo: Getting there and around." *Lonely Planet: Congo* http://www.lonelyplanet.com/congo

"Congo, Republic of: Country Reports on Human Rights Practices." *U.S. Department of State*. http://www.state.gov/g/drl/rls/hrrpt/2004/41598.htm

"Congo Brazzaville: Impunity perpetuates human rights abuses and instability." *Amnesty International Press Release*. http://www.amnesty.org.ru/library/Index/ENGAFR220022003?open&of=ENG-COG.

"Congo-Brazzaville: Government Moves to Curb Food Inflation 'Taking Time'." *RIN Humanitarian News and Analysis*, December 2008. http://allafrica.com/stories/200812030708.html

"U.S. Committee for Refugees World Refugee Survey 2003 - Congo-Brazzaville." *Refworld*. June 1, 2003. http://www.unhcr.org/refworld/country,,USCRI,,COG,456d621e2,3eddc49c8,0.html

"Congo–Brazzaville." *eDiplomat*. May 12, 2005. http://www.ediplomat.com/np/post_reports/pr_cg.htm

Coquery-Vidrovitch, Catherine, Beth Gillian Raps. African Women. *Westview Press, January 1997*. http://books.google.com/books?id=0ogzOgfliUC&pg=PA104&lpg=PA104&dq=modern+baTeke+family+africa&source=web&ots=eE0JHrcXC&sig=ho1wHkGBefpARKQP70j8Ax_ODNE&hl=en&ei=NSqaSemtLITcNOzisYkM&sa=X&oi=book_result&resnum=7&ct=result#PPP17,M1

"Central Africa: Congo-Brazzaville." *Modern African Art: Basic Reading List*. http://www.sil.si.edu/SILPublications/ModernAfricanArt/maadetail.cfm?subCategory=Congo%20(Brazzaville)

Harney, Elizabeth. In Senghor's Shadow. *Duke University Press*. http://books.google.com/books?id=GQkeAXWxtHwC&pg=PA65&lpg=PA65&dq=Pierre+Lods&source=bl&ots=UREcmngLsm&sig=ZpiI26ghf1d6H9UUdHwS1gljKy8&hl=en&ei=yYabSaT8NIT8NPeU2Y4F&sa=X&oi=book_result&resnum=5&ct=result#PPA65,M1

"Nicholas Ondongo: Artiste Contemporain du Congo." *Association pour la Défense Et l"Illustration des Arts d"Afrique et d"Océanie*. 9. http://www.adeiao.org/congo/nicolas-ondongo.html

"Li - Sangha Dance Company - CONGO BRAZAVILE." *Dance Meet Danse*. http://www.dmdfestival.org/dmd2007/li_sangha.html

"Poto Poto School." Simon, Njami, Lucy Durán. *Africa Remix: Contemporary Art of a Continent, Janaca Media*, 2007. http://books.google.com/books?id=rQbiP0M5tCUC&pg=PA247&lpg=PA247&dq=poto+poto+art+school&source=bl&ots=Qo91ULNKji&sig=LRObRDWwfpV6jfF_CktXZYyuGbA&hl=en&ei=mAmgSZfSKpDQnQcUwsn8DQ&sa=X&oi=book_result&resnum=5&ct=result

"Success Stories amongst Growing Numbers of Street Kids." *World Street Children News*, March 2007. http://streetkidnews.blogsome.com/category/1/africa/congo-brazzaville-streetkid-news/

"The man who would be Kongo's king." *BBC World News*, February 2003. http://news.bbc.co.uk/2/hi/africa/2752833.stm.

Reagan, Timothy G. Non-Western Educational Traditions, *Routledge* 2005. http://books.google.com/books?id=gFK9txcEYHYC&pg=PA66&lpg=PA66&dq=teke+traditions+africa&source=bl&ots=GMvcTZ_OXL&sig=3WRo3SRHM7AI6_Nk-czsXt9cloI&hl=en&ei=IS2gScPWNITUMcze3MQL&sa=X&oi=book_result&resnum=3&ct=result#PPA66,M1

"Biodiversity." *Wildlife Conservation Society – Congo*. http://www.wcs-congo.org/05wcscongoproj/06odzala/102biodiversity.html

"Pointe-Noir." *Wikipedia Online Encyclopedia*. http://en.wikipedia.org/wiki/Pointe-Noire

"The Congo River." *The Congo*. http://rainforests. mongabay.com/congo/congo_river.html

"Uncharted area of the Congo to be explored by Uni scientists." *University of Reading Press Releases*, September 2007. http://www.reading.ac.uk/about/ newsandevents/releases/PR8212.asp

Stewart, Gary. "Rumba on the River," *Verso* 2003. http://books.google.com/books?id=gKEHO1z 413EC&pg=PA119&lpg=PA119&dq=congo- brazzaville+dance&source=bl&ots=-uvjbdKFyg&sig =nnjTqmCbItDf3NntYHXKJgUpXUI&hl=en&ei=A- WhSe7bIZCKngfYwLX9DQ&sa=X&oi=book_result&r esnum=1&ct=result#PPP1,M1

"Congo (Rep.)." *City Population*. http://www. citypopulation.de/Congo.html

"David-Pierre Fila." *Centre d'*études africaines (Ceaf). http://lodel.ehess.fr/ceaf/document.php?id=461

"Leandre-Alain Baker." La maison des auteurs. http://www.lesfrancophonies.com/maison-des-auteurs/ baker-leandre

"News & Event Details." Sacramento World Music & Dance Festival, September 2008. http://www. sacramentoworldfestival.com/performers06.html

"Ramata." SudPlanete. http://www.sudplanete.net/index. php?menu=film&no=5752

"Where rich and poor collide." bd *The Architect's Website*, July 2005. http://www.bdonline.co.uk/story.asp?sectionc ode=431&storyCode=3053342

A cacao tree in Côte d'Ivoire. iSTock/Yves Grau.

CÔTE D'IVOIRE

Introduction

Côte d'Ivoire, formerly known as the Ivory Coast, is a nation in West Africa. It borders Ghana to the east, Mali and Burkina Faso to the north, Liberia and Guinea to the west, and the Atlantic Ocean to the south. Côte d'Ivoire, once known for its ivory trade, was a colony of France before gaining independence in 1960. Its people are known as Ivorians (or Ivoirians).

Traditional crafts remain one of the prominent art forms in Côte d'Ivoire, and include woodcarvings, dyed cloths, metalwork, and jewelry. Various ethnic groups create Ivorian art—the three most prevalent ethnic groups in the arts are the Baoulé, the Dan, and the Senufo—each of which has a distinct traditional style. In particular, Ivorian art often features aspects of storytelling or religious symbolism. Masks, usually carved from wood and decorated with shells and beads, are perhaps the most important works of art in Côte d'Ivoire, and are used in performances, rituals, and celebrations.

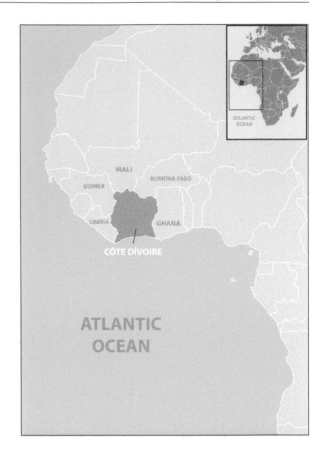

GENERAL INFORMATION

Official Language: French
Population: 23,295,302 (2015 estimate)
Currency: West African CFA franc
Coins: Coins are available in denominations of 1, 5, 10, 25, 50, 100, 200, 250, and 500 francs.
Land Area: 318,003 square kilometers (122,781 square miles)
Water Area: 4,460 square kilometers (1,722 square miles)

National Motto: "Union, Discipline, Travail" (French, "Unity, Discipline, Labor")
National Anthem: "L'Abidjanaise" (French, "Song of Abidjan")
Capital: Yamoussoukro (Abidjan is the de facto capital)
Time Zone: GMT +0
Flag Description: The flag of Côte d'Ivoire features a tricolor design of three equal vertical bands of orange (left), white (center), and green (right). The orange stripe stands for the land, particularly the northern savannah, and its fertility, white stands for peace, and green represents hope and the country's lush southern forests.

Population

Approximately 54 percent of Ivorians live in urban areas (2015 estimate). Abidjan is the largest city and cultural center of Côte d'Ivoire. Located on the southern coast, the city is divided into quarters by a lagoon. Yamoussoukro, located northwest of Abidjan, is the administrative

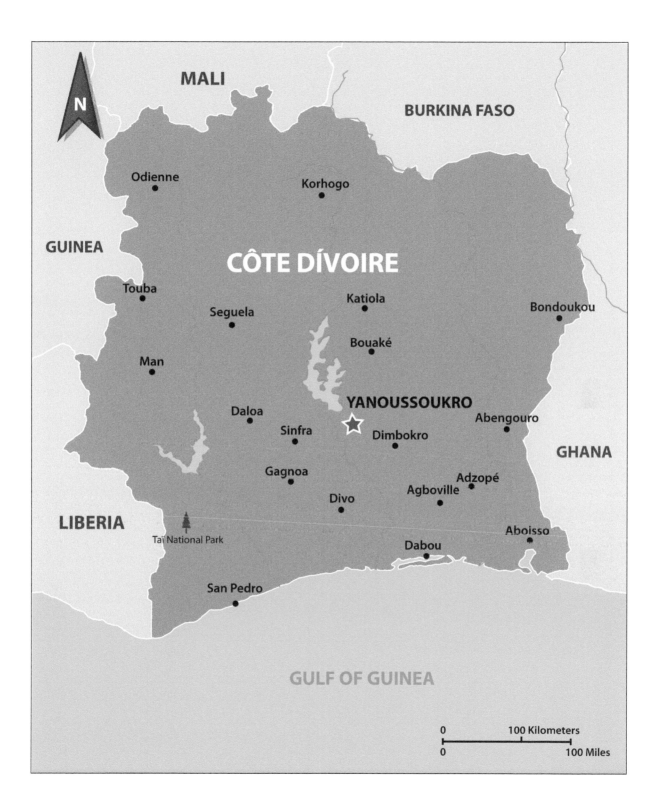

Principal Cities by Population (2012 estimate):

- Abidjan (4,400,000)
- Bouaké (649,841)
- Yamoussoukro (259.373)
- Daloa (261,789)
- Korhogo (225,547)
- Man (172,867)
- San Pédro (171,906)
- Gagnoa (153,935)
- Divo (147,379)

capital of Côte d'Ivoire. Bouaké, an inland city, is the site of much of the nation's commercial activity. Man, which is known as the "city of 18 mountains," is known for its art community and market.

A large percentage of Ivorians live in rural areas with their extended families or tribes. Mud huts with thatched roofs are the typical dwellings of these people, most of whom are farmers. Approximately three-quarters of the country's population are Ivorians (or Ivoirians), with the Akan ethnicity, largely residing in the east and center of the country, the largest ethnic group. Overall, the country is home to over 60 ethnic groups, including four other primary ethnicities: Lagoon (concentrated in the southeast); Krou (concentrated in the southwest); Southern Mande (concentrated in the west); and the Senufo (or Senoufo) and Lobi (concentrated in the north). Subgroups include the Baoulé peoples and the Malinke. The population growth rate was 1.91 percent in 2015.

Relationships between ethnic groups are strained. Foreign minorities, which make up nearly 33 percent of the country's population, are often the victims of discrimination. These include people from Mali, Burkina Faso, Guinea, Lebanon, France, and Syria.

Languages

Although Côte d'Ivoire's official language is French, the Dioula dialect is the most widely spoken language among Ivorians. Groups such as the Baoulé, Dan, Senoufo, and Agni speak unique dialects as well. The dialects of Côte d'Ivoire's ethnic groups belong to the Niger-Congo language family, and use changes in vocal tone and pitch to indicate meaning.

Native People & Ethnic Groups

Black Africans have inhabited West Africa for nearly 20,000 years. African tribal groups have been nomadic throughout history, and have therefore moved around the continent.

Most of the current population of Côte d'Ivoire is descended from groups that came to West Africa during the 18th and 19th centuries. Some groups, such as the Senoufo people, are descended from groups that arrived in the 15th century.

Because the country has no natural harbors, Côte d'Ivoire was not affected by the slave trade to the same extent as neighboring countries. The French arrived in the mid-19th century, and were primarily interested in exploiting the country's agricultural land, establishing coffee, banana, and cocoa plantations. Native farmers rebelled against French forced labor policies in the mid-20th century. The French language and the structure of the Ivorian government are the two most notable effects of the colonial period, which lasted from 1893 to 1960.

Today, Côte d'Ivoire's population consists of more than 60 ethnic groups. The largest is the Akan, who inhabit the central region of the country. The Akan people are divided into many tribal subgroups, the largest of which is the Baoulé. Like most of Côte d'Ivoire's tribal groups, the Baoulé live in chiefdoms, speak their own dialect, and are farmers. Roughly, 42 percent of Ivorians are of Akan ethnicity.

Other prominent ethnic groups in Côte d'Ivoire are the Voltaiques (also known as the Gur), who live in the northern areas of the country; the Kru, who inhabit the southwest region; and the Mandé, who live in the western region. Prominent subgroups are the Senoufo, the Bété, the Dan, the Agni, and the Dioula.

Religions

Roughly, 40 percent of Ivorians are Muslim and about 27 percent are Christian. Many Ivorians practice indigenous or traditional religions specific to their ethnic groups.

Climate

Average temperatures along the coast are slightly cooler than inland temperatures. Though both areas experience hot, humid weather throughout the year, the average coastal temperature is 26° Celsius (80° Fahrenheit), while the inland temperature often rises to 39° Celsius (103° Fahrenheit).

There are two wet seasons in the southern part of the country, which receives most of its rain from May to July and from October to November. In the north, most of the rain comes in the months between June and October. Côte d'Ivoire receives an average of 250 centimeters (100 inches) of rain annually. Coastal flooding is the country's main natural hazard.

Yamoussoukro, the capital, has a tropical climate; temperatures average around 27° Celsius (80° Fahrenheit). The city experiences three primary seasons. From November until March, the weather is warm and arid. It is typically hot and dry from March until May. Finally, from June to October, the temperature may reach 40° Celsius (104° Fahrenheit), but the heat is usually accompanied by humidity and rain.

ENVIRONMENT & GEOGRAPHY

Topography

Though it was once home to the largest rainforest in Africa, Côte d'Ivoire is now mostly grasslands and scrublands. The terrain along the coast is flat, but features rocky cliffs at some points. The northern areas of the country are dry savannahs. In the west are the Guinea Highlands, which rise to an elevation of 1,500 meters (5,000 feet). The highest point in Côte d'Ivoire is at the peak of Mont Nimba, which reaches 1,752 meters (5,748 feet) above sea level.

A large tropical rainforest previously existed behind the coastal area, but it has been mostly leveled due to deforestation. The country has several major rivers, the longest of which is the Bandama, which runs 800 kilometers (500 miles). Other important rivers are the Cavally, the Comoé, and the Sassandra.

Plants & Animals

Côte d'Ivoire's rainforest, which was once home to more than 200 species of trees, has been almost entirely destroyed by deforestation. Many of Côte d'Ivoire's indigenous plants and animals have also been lost as a result. The Taï National Park nature reserve is the only remaining unexploited forest in Côte d'Ivoire.

Baobab trees are common in the savannah region. Ferns, mosses, shrubs, and evergreens make up the majority of plant life. Trees native to the Ivorian rainforest include obeche, teak, and mahogany.

Animals native to Côte d'Ivoire include jackals, hyenas, panthers, antelope, hogs, elephants, chimpanzees, and reptiles such as lizards, snakes, and crocodiles. Manatees live offshore as well as in the country's rivers. Taï National Park is home to a number of pygmy hippopotamuses. Birds such as the guinea fowl and the blue-bellied roller bird are found in the savannah.

The African elephant is the national symbol of Côte d'Ivoire. However, the animal has been endangered by ivory hunters, and the government of Côte d'Ivoire has banned the trade of elephant tusks to protect the African elephant population.

CUSTOMS & COURTESIES

Greetings

Greetings are of the utmost importance in Ivorian society. Greetings must always be offered when meeting, and usually include "Bonjour" ("Hello"). It is important to maintain eye contact when greeting, but not for too long, which could be seen as a sign of disrespect. Hierarchy is also important, and Ivoirians are more formal than most North Americans. For example, in speaking French, Ivoirians use the formal "vous" form with strangers, people who are older, and those in positions of power.

Shaking hands is always the most appropriate greeting, but is less common in rural areas. After the handshake, it is customary for each person to make general inquiries into the health of the other's family members. People then ask each other for "les nouvelles" ("the news"). In rural areas, the exchange of information is usually more extensive than in the cities. Women in urban areas may greet with a bisou, or three light kisses on the cheeks. In both the city and rural areas, men who know each other well may greet by touching foreheads three times. This is more common, however, if two people have not seen one another for a long time. Lastly, touching the right forearm with the left hand when greeting an elder or superior is considered a mark of respect.

Gestures & Etiquette

Ivoirians are quite expressive and commonly use hand gestures when conversing. The extended right hand, twisting open, can mean, "How are you?' or "Where are you going?" Clapping hands together and opening them out means "Not much" or "Everything's the same." To express displeasure, people make a sort of sucking sound by inhaling through their teeth.

Touching is common among people of the same gender, and it is not unusual for men to hold hands with other men or women to hold hands with other women if they are friends. People maintain slightly less physical distance from each other than is common in North American culture. Depending on the ethnic group and religion, touching between men and women may be forbidden, or permissible only among friends and in the presence of others. Public displays of affection between couples are not common, although somewhat more common among young people. As with Muslim culture, the left hand is associated with the cleansing of the body, and is typically not used to touch another person.

Eating/Meals

Like many former French colonies, Côte d'Ivoire has retained many of the customs of its former colonial rulers. In the cities and bigger towns, breakfast may consist of coffee with condensed milk and a baguette, an omelet, or fried egg. People also follow the French custom of the long lunch break (although many people today do not nap after lunch). Dinner is usually a smaller meal. In the cities, people eat later in the evening, but in the rural areas, dinner starts when people come in from working in the fields.

Visiting

Ivoirians take hospitality quite seriously, and it is not necessary to call or make an appointment in advance before visiting. Feeding guests is important, and it is commonly expected that the host will ask the visitor to stay for a meal. The visitor is expected to accept the invitation.

When a visitor wants to leave, he or she is supposed to ask for permission to leave by saying "Je demande la route" (loosely, "I ask for the road" or "The road is calling."). Permission is given when the host says "Je te (or vous) donne la moitie" (which literally means, "I give you half," but implies "I will let you go now, but you must use the other half [of the road] to come back").

For honored guests and special occasions, a host will accompany a guest toward or out the door as they depart. This is seen as a mark of respect and affection. While gifts are generally not expected, it is customary for a visitor to offer some money, for example, to the children or the dependents of the household upon leaving after an extended stay.

LIFESTYLE

Family

The traditional family unit of all ethnic groups in Côte d'Ivoire includes extended family. While these extended family members such as aunts, uncles, and cousins may reside in different dwellings or villages, they are given much the same consideration as members of the nuclear family, with elders given particular respect. Some ethnic groups are matrilineal (descended through the mother's line) while others are patrilineal (descended through the father's line).

In recent years, many families in Côte d'Ivoire have been separated because of civil war and the increasing need to pursue work, both within and out of the country. As this trend continues in the 21st century, older generations are concerned about how it will affect traditions, which are an important part of the culture.

Housing

In the cities, many people live in mid or high-rise apartment buildings or smaller multi-family buildings. Abidjan and some of the other large cities have upper-class suburbs where there are European-style single-family homes. These are typically gated and often surrounded by security guards. Many cities also have shantytowns (informal settlements) in which houses are typically built using found materials such as corrugated metal or cardboard. In rural areas, people still live in traditional houses made of mud bricks and thatched or corrugated metal roofs. A more modern version of a simple rural home would be a cinderblock house.

Food

The staples of the Ivorian diet include foutou, fou, attieke, and kedjenou. Foutou is made from yams, cassava, or plantains that have been boiled and pounded into a paste and mixed with water. Similar to foutou, fou fou is a sticky, doughy paste made of boiled, mashed yams or plantains and oil, then formed into balls. Both dishes are usually served with rice and a spicy sauce made with peanuts, chilies, carrots, and onion called sauce arachide. Attieke is made from grated cassava (also called manioc). It is similar to couscous and is eaten with any main dish. Sauce gombo (an okra sauce), sauce graine (made from palm oil), and sauce clair (eggplant sauce) are other common accompaniments to any of the vegetable dishes. Kedjenou is typically made

with poultry or meat, tomatoes, and onions. It is cooked in a clay pot called a canari, which is shaken during cooking.

Because of Côte d'Ivoire's long coastline, fish is popular and traditionally served in stews or sauces, or braised. The Senegalese dish ceebu jen (fish cooked in a tomato sauce) is quite popular due to the influx of immigrants from Senegal. For a simple, inexpensive meal, Ivoirians often go to a maquis, an outdoor café, covered with a thatched roof or awning. A typical meal there might include braised chicken or fish along with some attieke, foutou, or fou fou.

In the north, where Muslims make up a large part of the population, alcohol is typically not consumed. In the south, it is common to have beer with a meal. Bandiji, an alcoholic drink made from juice extracted from palm or royal palm trees, is also popular. It is used in traditional ceremonies to help participants communicate with their ancestors.

Life's Milestones

Many of the milestones observed in Ivoirian culture are unique to certain ethnicities. For example, when a woman gives birth among the Akan, she then spends a few months with her child among the women of her family so she can recover and nurse. In Aboure culture, when someone dies, the family cannot say what happened to the deceased; at the actual burial, those in attendance act reserved, due to the belief that spirits prey upon the weak.

Among Muslim culture in the country, a body must be buried before sundown on the day of death. Ceremonies are held on the seventh and 40th days after death. In animist and Christian traditions, wakes can last for three days, and loud music is often played during the night.

CULTURAL HISTORY

Art

Most of the artistic heritage of the peoples of Côte d'Ivoire comes from sacred objects such as masks and wooden sculptures. Masks were used

Carved masks in Senofu may include non-human features.

to channel spirits during ceremonies and could only be made or worn by specific members of the community. The masks of each ethnic group are distinctive. Dan masks (worn only by men) are simple and realistic. Senufo masks are more elaborate and stylized, often with horns or other non-human features. Wooden sculptures were carved to represent spirits. Art was also used as a way to confer power. The Akan and Baoulé people carved wooden staffs and stools for the elders and kings. Different groups became known for different artistic specialties. The Senufo are known for their blacksmithing, while Lobi artwork is mostly wooden sculpture.

Architecture

Many of the people who live in modern-day Côte d'Ivoire are descended from the inhabitants of the medieval Asante Kingdom (includ-ing the Akan and Baoulé people) in what is now Ghana. Traditional Asante homes consisted of four separate clay construction single-room buildings attached with a low exterior wall to form an interior courtyard. Each building had a sloped, two-sided thatched roof with a steep pitch. Sacred buildings were decorated with bas-relief (or raised) designs. Malinke people, who came from what is now Mali, lived in round clay houses with conical thatched roofs. The Lobi, who came from what is now Burkina Faso, also built round houses, but the roofs were flat.

When the French arrived in the 19th century, they brought their architectural style. Many early French colonial government buildings still exist in present day Côte d'Ivoire. For example, just outside of Abidjan is the coastal resort town of Grand Bassam, which features some of the best-preserved examples of French colonial architecture in the country. It was the first French colonial capital in the late 19th century. Many of the buildings from that period still stand, including the Governor's Palace, which was built in 1893.

After independence in 1960, Côte d'Ivoire became one of the first African nations to feature modern cityscapes with skyscrapers and high-rises.

Music, Dance & Drama

Among the many peoples of Côte d'Ivoire, there is often no distinction between music, dance, storytelling, and drama—they are all performed simultaneously. Music and dance developed to accompany sacred celebrations and other important community events. Music was not limited to the sacred. Among some of the 60 ethnic groups in what is now Côte d'Ivoire, some groups had songs for working, "praise songs" to kings or chiefs, weather-related songs, and songs for celebrations such as weddings.

Drums have always been important in the music of all cultures in Côte d'Ivoire. The Malinke people brought the djembe to the area. The djembe is a drum with a wide top that tapers into a narrower base and is held between the legs while it is played. The "talking drums" used by

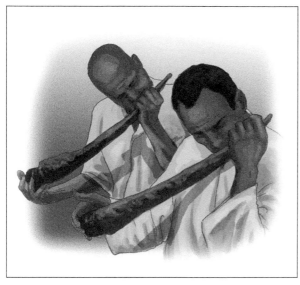

Gbofe horns are traditionally played by the men of the Tagbana tribe.

the Akan and other peoples have playable surfaces on each end and adjustable strings down the sides. The talking drums are used to pound out "words" that are recognized by all people in the community. Certain beats were used to get attention, then announcements would be made. The messages could be heard from distances and then repeated by nearby drummers who could spread them even further. It is said that each drummer could reach a radius of 40 kilometers (25 miles).

One of the traditional rituals of the Tagbana people is called gbofe. This ceremony involves long horns or trumpets which reproduce Tagbana language through long, cowhide-covered roots (also called gbofe). The gbofe horns were played by men accompanied by drums and female choirs that "interpreted" the words. This performance was used to convey different messages that are educational or express respect, praise, love, or mourning. Men who performed the gbofe had to follow an apprenticeship. In 2001, the gbofe and its associated performances were listed as one of the Masterpieces of the Oral and Intangible Heritage of Humanity by the United Nations Educational, Scientific, and Cultural Organization (UNESCO).

Masked dances are common among the peoples of the country. While behind the mask, the dancer was assumed not just to be a person in a mask, but actually be the spirit represented. In addition to masks, other ceremonial garb such as overcoats, headdresses and skirts were worn. Men and women typically danced separately. The masked stilt dancers of the Dan culture (all of whom were men) underwent three- to five-year apprenticeships to learn their skill, which includes doing flips while on stilts.

Literature

The ethnic groups of Côte d'Ivoire relied on oral traditions like storytelling to preserve history, transmit cultural and spiritual values, and for entertainment. There was informal storytelling between community elders, and formal storytelling. In groups such as the Mande, this was done by a griot who often traveled between villages. Griots were musical storytellers who sometimes wore costumes and were accompanied by musicians, and were thought of as a different social caste. Some were specifically "praise singers" who sang to glorify the king or chief, but others told comical stories. Female griots were called griottes.

Around the turn of the 20th century, the first Ivoirians attended formal schools where they learned to read and write in French. Ivoirian writer Bernard Dadié (1916–) wrote what is thought to be the first play written by an African and published his first collection of poems in 1950. Ahmadou Kourouma (1927–2003) gained international fame with his novel *The Suns of Independence* (1970), which was considered the first critical look at post-independence African governments by an African.

CULTURE

Arts & Entertainment

As Côte d'Ivoire experienced a long period of peace and prosperity, the arts thrived. People had money to spend on entertainment and the government made efforts to encourage and promote the arts. After the Ivoirian Civil War, the economy fell into decline and there was less money to invest in arts organizations. Many talented Ivoirians also chose to leave for countries with more stability. This led to many interesting developments in the arts, many of which eventually came back to Côte d'Ivoire.

Music is a very important part of life in Côte d'Ivoire. Ivoirians love to go to clubs and hear live music. In fact, many West African musicians record their music at Ivoirian studios. Abidjan is home to the International Festival of Black Music, International Jazz Festival of Abidjan, and other smaller music festivals.

Starting in the 1970s, reggae music from the Caribbean became popular in West Africa. Seydou Koné (1953–), who goes by the name of Alpha Blondy, is an Ivoirian reggae musician who rose to international fame. He sings in Diola, English, French, Arabic, and Hebrew, and his music is often political in nature. Brother Ayouba is another popular Ivoirian reggae singer who also performs in English, French, and Diola

In the 1980s and 1990s, a type of dance music called zouglou developed in Côte d'Ivoire and spread to other West African nations. Zouglou music is characterized by the humorous storytelling quality of the lyrics and uses a form of street language that blends French with local dialects. Zouglou emphasizes electronic instruments and blends European-style pop beats and hip-hop.

Because of the political unrest that unfolded at the turn of the 20th century, many Ivoirians moved to France, and coupé-décalé music developed among the Ivoirian diaspora. Very specific dance movements go along with the music, which is typically fast-paced, electronic pop music, and often doesn't include lyrics. From Paris, coupé-décalé spread back to Côte d'Ivoire and around Africa where it quickly became one of the most dominant trends in African music.

Going to the cinema is a popular Ivoirian pastime, and there are many outdoor movie theaters in Abidjan. Côte d'Ivoire has had a film industry since achieving independence, although today many of its filmmakers live in Paris. Many television sitcoms that are exported to other French-speaking African nations are produced in Côte d'Ivoire. Abidjan is also home to the International Festival of Short Film.

Since the time of independence, Ivoirian Theater has incorporated many Western styles of drama with local content and style, creating a new "postcolonial" form. Ivoirian playwrights such as Koffi Kwahulé (1956–) have gained international recognition for their work (most live in France). The International Festival of Theatres Without Borders has been held in Abidjan for a number of years, with the aim of exposing Ivoirians to different forms of theater and allowing the work of Ivoirian playwrights and actors to be recognized internationally. The festival draws performers and directors from Europe, Africa, and Asia. Côte D'Ivoire also has a national ballet company and many small traditional and contemporary dance troupes. Many Ivoirian dancers have gone on to become well-known teachers and choreographers in other parts of the world, most notably Alphonse Tiérou, who has written several books about African dance.

Competitive dance is traditional in many of the cultures of Côte d'Ivoire. Every November, the city of Man in the mountainous western region of the country hosts the Festival of Masks (Fêtes des Masques). This event brings people from regional villages together for masked dance competitions. Other smaller cities hold dance competition festivals as well. While Ivoirians do keep traditional dances alive, they are also always inventing new ones to go with musical fads or trends. The "bird flu dance" became popular after there was an outbreak of the flu in the country, and a dance craze called the bobaraba or "big bottom dance" became an international hit in 2008.

Soccer is the national sport of Côte d'Ivoire. Les Eléphants are the Ivorian national soccer team. Other popular sports include rugby, golf, basketball, and softball.

Cultural Sites & Landmarks

The capital of Yamoussoukro is home to numerous landmarks and cultural sites, including the tallest Christian church, the Basilica of Our Lady of Peace (Notre Dame de la Paix in French). Former Ivoirian President Félix Houphouët-Boigny conceived of the church as a way to bring attention to his hometown. Designed to resemble closely the Basilica of Saint Peter in Vatican City, the church is built of imported Italian marble and seats 7,000, with standing room for 11,000. Started in 1985, the project caused international controversy, particularly because less than 10 percent of the population is Catholic. In addition, the church cost an estimated $300 million (USD), which doubled the national debt of Côte d'Ivoire. In addition to the church, a palatial residence for the pope was also built.

Abidjan is the Côte d'Ivoire's largest city and former capital. Nicknamed the "Paris of the South," the city's wide boulevards were modeled after Paris and it features numerous cafés and restaurants. It is also one of the world's most populous French-speaking cites. Though it is no longer the capital, Abidjan remains the commercial center of Côte d'Ivoire, and the country's international businesses and foreign embassies are based here.

Tens of thousands of years ago, much of West Africa was covered in rainforest. Tai National Park, on Côte d'Ivoire's southwest coast and border with Liberia, is all that remains of that ecosystem. The park is particularly known for its rare large mammals, such as the pygmy hippo, elephants, and buffalos, and is home to leopards, civets, giant hogs, and over 250 species of birds. There are also 11 species of monkeys in the park, as well as a rare group of West African chimpanzees that were preserved by local populations because of their special place in the culture. Because of the park's flora and fauna, it was designated as a UNESCO World Heritage Site in 1982. Côte d'Ivoire is home to two other World Heritage Sites: Comoé National Park and Mount Nimba Strict Nature Reserve (shared with Guinea), both recognized for their rich biodiversity.

Libraries & Museums
In Abidjan, the Museum of Civilization details the ethnographic and sociological history of

Côte d'Ivoire. In Grand Bassam, just outside of Abidjan, is the National Museum of Costume, which features ceremonial masks and other clothing from many different ethnic groups, and serves as a center for local artisans to sell handcrafted items. Other museums include the state-run Musée des Armées, a military museum; the Cocody Municipal Museum of Contemporary Art, which exhibits paintings, textiles, photography, and sculpture; and the Adja Swa museum in the district of Yamoussoukro, which focuses on local culture.

The National Library of Côte d'Ivoire is located in Abidjan, but was shut down in the early 21st century due to lack of funding. As of 2010, the country was home to nearly ninety public libraries; the country reported only nine public libraries to the International Federation of Library Associations and Institutions in 2007, and most libraries are concentrated in the central northwestern area of the country.

Holidays
Côte d'Ivoire's national holiday is Independence Day, which is observed on August 7. The Fête du Dipri, held in April, is a festival in which women and children perform midnight rituals to remove evil spells from villages. In November, the Dan people celebrate the Fêtes des Masques. During this celebration, one of the best known in West Africa, people dance and wear masks honoring the spirits of the forest. The participants then vote for the best dancers in the community.

Other holidays observed amongst Ivorians are primarily religious, such as the Muslim month of Ramadan.

Youth Culture
Football (soccer) is the most popular activity for Ivoirian youth, both in terms of watching and playing. Even in the rural areas where there are no fields and a lack of proper equipment, the game still maintains its popularity. Games played by the national team and other African countries are broadcast on the radio.

Visiting is perhaps the main form of social activity among Ivoirian youth, and genders only mix in relatively large social groups. Many youth never finish their schooling, and are expected to work at home taking care of younger siblings. In urban areas, youth culture is similar to that in other countries, and dancing and live music are popular activities among teens.

SOCIETY

Transportation

In some cities, local bus service is available, and bus companies that offer long-distance routes between cities and to different countries. Bush taxis, a kind of informal taxi without a fixed route, are also a common mode of transportation in Côte d'Ivoire. Bush taxi service usually originates from a larger city and goes to rural areas. In the cities, it is also common for people to get around on bicycles or motorbikes. Traffic moves on the right-hand side of the road in Côte d'Ivoire.

Transportation Infrastructure

While there was once a good road system in Côte d'Ivoire, economic decline and civil war affected negatively the transportation infrastructure in the country. Due to this deterioration, traveling long distances by road has become more burdensome and time consuming. The rail system in Côte d'Ivoire is also not well developed. It connects between a few bigger cities within the country and has service to neighboring Burkina Faso. There are no passenger ferries in Côte d'Ivoire, but passengers can arrive from Europe on cargo liners. The international airport is Abidjan is served by regular passenger service and there are several other airports in the country with domestic service.

Media & Communications

Côte d'Ivoire is a multilingual country and less than half the population is literate. Access to television stations is rare in rural areas, so most Ivoirians (in the city or country) tend to get their news from the radio. Many radio stations are local, low-power stations, so their broadcasts have limited coverage. The government owns several radio stations, and the British Broadcasting Corporation (BBC) broadcasts in some of the larger cities and urban areas.

There are several daily and weekly French language newspapers in the country, one government-run, and one run by an opposition party; the rest are private. There is also a government news agency. The government also runs the main television station, but satellite TV is also available in the country.

Cell phone use is very popular in the country, as many people do not have landline service. As of 2014, there were an estimated 621,500 Internet users. There are Internet cafés in the bigger cities, and it is possible to get access at certain public institutions.

SOCIAL DEVELOPMENT

Standard of Living

Côte d'Ivoire ranked 171st out of 187 countries on the 2014 United Nations Human Development Index, which measures quality of life and standard of living indicators.

The standard of living in Côte d'Ivoire is low, mostly due to extreme poverty, high risk of disease, and recent outbreaks of violence against the government. In 2002, an attempt by rebels to overthrow the government caused civil war and economic collapse. Then, after a power struggle in 2010–2011, UN peacekeepers had to enter the country to restore peace. Nearly 500,000 Ivorians have fled their homes as a result.

Water Consumption

According to 2015 statistics from the World Health Organization, approximately 81 percent of Ivorians have access to an improved or safe source of drinking water, while an estimated 32 percent of the population has access to improved sanitation. Water and sanitation infrastructure have been negatively affected by conflict in the nation throughout the 21st century, and access to water and sanitation in rural areas is poor, with many people spending an inordinate amount of time traveling to a clean water supply or simply securing safe water. With help from UNICEF and the European Union, the country was able to implement water and sanitation programs between 2003 and 2009 that helped an estimated 8.5 million citizens.

Education

Education for Ivorians is free and compulsory at the primary level. Secondary school lasts for seven years, and is followed by university education. Many statistics regarding education in Côte d'Ivoire remain outdated, and the educational system experienced considerable disruption due to civil war in the early 21st century. It was estimated that in 2007, nearly one million children were not enrolled in or attending school, and that the literacy rate was hovering just over 50 percent.

There are several universities, the largest of which is the National University of Côte d'Ivoire in Abidjan (which was split into three universities—the University of Abidjan-Cocody (UAC), the University of Abobo-Adjamé, and the University of Bouaké). Other universities include the Catholic University of West Africa and the International University of Grand Bassam, as well as a polytechnic institute in Yamoussoukro, the National Polytechnical Institute Félix Houphouët-Boigny (INPHB). Many university students study abroad.

According to UNICEF (United Nations Children's Fund), nearly one of every two children between the ages of six and 11 does not attend school, with that gap larger for females and in rural areas. Even more, according to the UN, primary school enrollment dropped from 92 and 70 percent, respectively, for boys and girls in 2003 to just 81 and 64 percent in 2009. The expansion of poverty, mostly from the 2002 rebellion and ensuing civil wars, has been a primary factor of declining attendance rates, while a lack of investment in education—the government, for instance, cut down the length of teacher training, from three years to eight months—and infrastructure has led to a deterioration in the quality of education.

Education in Côte d'Ivoire was disrupted due to civil war and conflict in the early 21st century. During these periods of war and escalating violence, which saw the largely Muslim, rebel-held north pitted against the pro-government south, teachers were forced to flee and schools were closed. Following peace accords, the educational system slowly began to right itself as aid poured in and schools reopened, particularly in the rebel north (though the prolonged absence of an educational setting or school, sometimes for up to several years, considerably slowed the process). However, conflict stemming from a disputed election in November 2010 has placed the educational system of the country back in jeopardy as civil unrest began to mount and citizens began fleeing across the border.

Women's Rights

During the French colonial period, women gained some rights in the country through legislation that made the central government, not the local ethnic group, the authority on certain issues. Polygamy was outlawed, as was forced marriage. Women were also given the right to divorce more easily and couples were allowed to marry without the permission of their parents. Women earned the right to vote in 1953, just before the country became an autonomous republic.

Since independence in 1960, progress for women in the country has been mixed. Many more women have advanced degrees and have entered professions such as law, medicine, business, and higher education. Women are now employed in civil service, and many have risen to positions of power in the government. Legislation has been passed on pay equality, and in general, this rule is enforced. In the corporate world, however, most women are confined to lower level positions, in large part because of the perception that they are not career oriented.

Most women participating in business in Côte d'Ivoire are part of the informal sector, selling produce or handicrafts in markets, and are ineligible for benefits such as social security or pensions. It is difficult for women to get business loans, as these often require securities such as land ownership, which is still primarily held by men.

Inheritance laws in the country still discriminate against women as well. Côte d'Ivoire did sign the CEDAW (Convention on the Elimination of All Discrimination Against Women) in 1980, and has passed laws to ensure rights for Ivoirian women. However, these laws are not always enforced and many women are not aware of them. In rural areas, women still hold the traditional roles and are expected to take care of all the household duties and child rearing, as well doing the agricultural work. When a family cannot afford to send all of its children to school, the boys will be given preference over the girls.

Domestic violence is an issue for women in Côte d'Ivoire, as there is no legal definition. Many people, especially in rural areas, consider it a family matter, and women are very reluctant to report abuse to authorities. Police often do not take the issue seriously as a crime. Forced marriage and marriage of minors are still problems for women and young girls in rural areas despite national laws. Many women are not aware of their rights, and are reluctant to pursue legal action because of pressure from family and community members.

Female genital mutilation (FGM) is still common in many parts of the country, despite the fact that it is illegal. Women's groups in Côte d'Ivoire have undertaken public information campaigns to raise awareness about the physical and emotional damage of this practice.

Health Care

Health conditions in Côte d'Ivoire are desperate. Most Ivorians do not receive adequate medical attention, and the existing health care system is substandard. The civil war exacerbated an already dire situation, and medical infrastructure in rural parts of the country was practically non-existent during times of conflict. The war, in fact, destroyed much of the health infrastructure in the north of the country, particularly the Central Northwest region.

The HIV/AIDS epidemic is a major part of Côte d'Ivoire's public health crisis. Roughly, 460,100 Ivoirians are living with HIV/AIDS (2014 estimate). Bacterial diarrhea, hepatitis A, hepatitis B, dengue fever, typhoid fever, malaria, yellow fever, and schistosomiasis are common diseases and infections. Average life expectancy is 59 years for women and 57 years for men (2015 estimate). Eighteen is the age of suffrage.

GOVERNMENT

Structure

Côte d'Ivoire is a democratic republic with a multiparty system. The president is the chief executive, while the prime minister is the head of the government. The unicameral legislature consists of the 225-member National Assembly, and the highest judicial power is the Supreme Court. Côte d'Ivoire's constitution has been in effect since 2000.

The president, who is elected by popular vote, serves a term of five years and may be re-elected once. The prime minister and other ministers are appointed by the president.

The government of Côte d'Ivoire has been marked by corruption, as elections have been fixed, rightfully elected officials have been ousted, and human rights have been violated. There have been several attempts made by various groups to overthrow the government of Côte d'Ivoire. A coup d'état in 1999 was the first, followed by the larger, though unsuccessful, coup in 2002; in between, in 2000, Laurent Gbagbo became president after winning the October presidential elections.

Because of the failed 2002 coup, a large majority of the 750,000 displaced Ivorians moved into neighboring African countries. The nation erupted in civil war, with rebel forces in the north and loyalists in the south. In 2004, loyalist troops killed nine French peacekeepers during an airstrike. The United Nations responded by establishing an arms embargo on Côte d'Ivoire, and added 6,000 peacekeepers to the 4,000 French soldiers already stationed in Côte d'Ivoire. (The French also responded by destroying a majority of Ivorian military aircraft.) Gbagbo's five-year term was extended by a one-year period in 2005. In 2007, a peace accord was reached between the rebels and the Ivorian government, though presidential elections were consistently delayed until 2010.

Following the November 2010 presidential elections, Gbagbo was declared the loser against former Prime Minister Alassane Ouattara, but nonetheless clung to power, despite calls to stand down from the UN and the ECOWAS (Economic Community of West African States), along with backing from international bodies such as the European Union. (Gbagbo was also past the limit for reelection.) Violence followed the disputed election (the constitutional council threw out a substantial number of ballots from Ouattara strongholds in the north), and nearly 200 people were reported killed before the close of 2010 (while more than 10,000 Ivorians fled into North Liberia). Gbagbo, who began ousting foreign ambassadors, was mostly supported by the Christian south. Foreign military intervention was nominally hinted at in the media, lest the country fall back into civil war. ECOWAS also vowed to use military might to force out Gbagbo and, along with the African Union, suspended Côte d'Ivoire's membership. Gbagbo was finally forced out with the help of UN forces the following year, who have remained in the country ever since.

Political Parties

While Côte d'Ivoire is home to numerous political parties, the majority do not garner any national support. The Democratic Party of Côte d'Ivoire is one of the major political parties in the country, and the only legal party from 1960–1990. The party ultimately lost power after the 1999 coup, and entered into a coalition with several other parties, including the Rally of the Republicans, prior to the planned 2005 elections, eventually held in 2010. Another major party, the Ivorian People's Front, is the party of President Laurent Gbagbo, and won the majority of parliamentary seats—96 seats—following the December 2000 and January 2001 National Assembly elections. Overall, six parties were represented following

those elections, the most recently held legislative elections as of 2010.

Local Government

Côte d'Ivoire is subdivided into 19 regions and 81 departments. Each department and region maintains a central government representative and an elected government body. Communes, of which there are nearly 200, are overseen by an elected mayor. The Ivorian Civil War largely disrupted local governance in Côte d'Ivoire; for instance, many local government officials, called prefects, fled the north after war broke out.

Judicial System

Côte d'Ivoire's judiciary and legal system is based on a combination of customary law and French civil law. The system consists of a Supreme Court, the highest court, as well as an independent Constitutional Court. Below the Supreme Court are the Court of Appeals and other lower courts. The High Court of Justice maintains the responsibility of trying government officials. Traditional means of resolution remain in rural areas and at the village level, though formal systems are replacing these customary bodies of justice.

Taxation

The highest corporate tax rate in Côte d'Ivoire is 25 percent and the top income tax rate is 36 percent (2010). Other taxes levied include a value-added tax (VAT, similar to a consumption tax), at 18 percent, as well as a capital duty and stamp duty.

Armed Forces

The National Armed Forces of Côte d'Ivoire consist of a navy, army, and air force (though the naval forces are small in scope, and limited to patrol and gunboats, and the air force was decimated by the French in 2004). Conscription exists, and 18 is the minimum age for service. The United Nations Operation in Côte d'Ivoire, a UN mission aimed at maintaining peace following the Ivorian Civil War, maintains a peacekeeping force in the country.

Foreign Policy

Côte d'Ivoire gained independence from France in 1960, but France has remained its closest international ally in terms of diplomacy and trade. While other newly independent African nations tended to align themselves with the Soviet Union or China, Côte d'Ivoire was notably pro-Western in its foreign policy, and encouraged foreign investment in the country. As a result, the country experienced many years of stability and became what many considered a model for African democracies.

However, the country erupted into civil war in 2002. With many French citizens living in Côte d'Ivoire, France sent troops immediately to protect them. (The United States also sent a small number of troops to protect American citizens.) The United Nations imposed an arms embargo, froze assets of certain individual and organizations, and banned the import of diamonds from Côte d'Ivoire, but has also provided humanitarian assistance to the country. In 2003, a peace agreement negotiated by the French government gave rebel forces control of the north, and the government control of the south. UN peacekeepers and French troops then entered the country in 2004 to protect the agreements made in the peace process. However, when French soldiers were attacked that same year, France retaliated and completely destroyed the small Ivoirian air force. The two countries then undertook diplomacy to restore their relationship. UN forces, introduced in 2011, were largely French. Relations with the U.S. and the United Kingdom have generally been positive, although both nations have supported sanctions against Côte d'Ivoire in light of the civil war.

Within Africa, Côte d'Ivoire has close trade relationships with other French-speaking countries, such as the Democratic Republic of the Congo, Gabon, and Niger. Relationships with neighbors Mali, Guinea, and Burkina Faso (French-speaking) and Ghana have been less stable. Many Burkinabe (people from Burkina Faso) came to Côte d'Ivoire to work and became the target of violence due to the increase in anti-foreign sentiment during the war. Côte d'Ivoire's relationships with Guinea, Liberia, and Mali were less than friendly due to those countries' socialist policies, which contrasted with Côte d'Ivoire's capitalistic policies. Additionally, Côte d'Ivoire was one of the only countries that undertook direct diplomacy with South Africa in order to try to end apartheid rather than imposing sanctions on the country.

Côte d'Ivoire is a member of the UN (United Nations), African Union (AU), the Organization of African Unity (OAU), the World Health Organization (WHO), World Trade Organization (WTO), the International Monetary Fund (IMF), the World Bank, and other international organizations. In addition to the IMF and World Bank, Côte d'Ivoire has received direct financial assistance from France, Germany, and Canada.

Human Rights Profile

International human rights law insists that states respect civil and political rights, and promote an individual's economic, social, and cultural rights. The United Nations Universal Declaration on Human Rights (UDHR) is recognized as the standard for international human rights. Its authors sought the counsel of the world's great thinkers, philosophers, and religious leaders, and were careful to create a document that reflects the core values shared by every world culture. (To read this document or view the articles relating to cultural human rights, visit http://www.udhr.org/UDHR/default.htm.)

Since 2000, Côte d'Ivoire has experienced a great deal of political unrest. International observers report that many politically motivated human rights abuses have taken place, including torture, abduction, and execution. In political cases, there have been arbitrary arrests and denial of access to fair trials. The judicial system in Côte d'Ivoire is not independent from the ruling party, and therefore does not offer citizens free and fair legal process. Elections have been delayed due to the war, and people have not had the opportunity to vote to change the government.

While the many different ethnic groups of Côte d'Ivoire once lived together peacefully, the civil war promoted discrimination, hatred, and violence against minority groups. The government did not protect citizens from harassment, illegal searches of their homes, and extortion (the forced payment of bribes). In addition, the country's many immigrants (mostly from neighboring countries) were openly discriminated against by the government's policies.

Human trafficking, a problem in many countries in North and West Africa, is a problem in Côte d'Ivoire. Women and children in particular have been abducted for forced labor in different industries, and sometimes sent out of the country. People from other West and Central African countries are also brought to Côte d'Ivoire for forced labor. Ivoirian prisons extremely overcrowded and without proper sanitary conditions. In 2008, prisoners in one of the country's most overcrowded prisons rioted.

Freedom of the press in Côte d'Ivoire had been curtailed since the political unrest in the country started. Several foreign journalists were attacked or have disappeared, and the government has periodically suspended the broadcast of Radio France Internationale, an independent broadcaster. While there are independently owned and operated newspapers in the country, the government frequently brings charges against any that produce reports critical of its policies. There have been incidents of pro-government militia seizing operations from the broadcasters. The government has also used the state-run media to broadcast stories critical of the UN peacekeepers. In the rebel-controlled areas of the country, the rebels have taken over the state-run broadcasting sources.

Freedom of assembly and expression have also been limited since the country's civil war. The government has frequently denied permits to those wishing to hold outdoor demonstrations, and as of 2007, had banned such rallies. Academics at the country's universities have reported that there is an atmosphere of intimidation and faculty know that they can be transferred or lose their positions if they speak out. Since the war, the government has also imposed curfews, limiting citizens' freedom of movement. There are numerous roadblocks in the country, and opposition party members as well as foreigners

have reported that they have been forced to pay bribes in order to reach their destinations.

ECONOMY

Overview of the Economy

Côte d'Ivoire's economy has changed significantly in recent decades. A healthy timber trade spurred a boom during the 1960s and 1970s with France, but a long recession followed, leaving Côte d'Ivoire in debt and without exploitable timber resources. In 2014, the per capita gross domestic product (GDP) was estimated at $3,100 (USD). The country remains the largest producer and exporter of cocoa beans in the world, and is a primary global exporter of palm oil and coffee. Oil and gas production has also become important to the health of the Ivorian economy. The GDP was $33.96 billion in 2014.

Industry

Côte d'Ivoire's manufactures fertilizer, textiles, automobiles, building materials, and rubber. Other large industries include food processing, oil refining, and shipbuilding. The perfume industry serves as a major employer in Yamoussoukro and is a major contributor to the city's gross domestic product (GDP). Overall, Côte d'Ivoire's economy is focused on agriculture rather than industry. The existing industrial sector is a result of the government's attempts to diversify the nation's economy. The country has no natural harbors and few oil deposits.

Fuel and food are the country's two most significant imported commodities. Exports include cocoa, coffee, timber, petroleum, cotton, fruit, and fish. The majority of trade is conducted with France, Nigeria and Italy.

Labor

The bulk of Côte d'Ivoire's work force—an estimated 68 percent in 2007—is involved in agricultural production and exports. The unemployment rate was estimated at 40 to 50 percent in 2009. As of 2009, the country had an estimated labor force of 7.44 million.

Energy/Power/Natural Resources

Côte d'Ivoire is the world's leading exporter of cocoa beans that grow on cacao trees on the country's plantations. Other significant resources are coffee, petroleum, natural gas, and diamonds. In addition, minerals such as manganese, iron ore, cobalt, bauxite, copper, and gold are mined.

A hydroelectric plant on the Bandama River provides Côte d'Ivoire's primary energy resource. Timber was previously the country's leading natural resource, but has since been exhausted.

Fishing

In 2005, the fish production of Ivorian fisheries totaled 55,868 metric tons, and accounted for the direct employment of approximately 70,000. Exported commercial species include tuna (such as skipjack and yellowfin tuna), shrimp and prawn, octopus, and smoked fish such as herring. The tuna fleet, however, is foreign-owned, while domestic boats are mostly involved in the catch of smaller, pelagic fish (near to shore) such as sardines. Yamoussoukro's proximity to the Lac de Kossou makes it a hub for the fishing industry.

Forestry

Côte d'Ivoire has one of the highest rates of deforestation in West Africa as of 2008, at an annual rate of more than 660,000 hectares (1,630,895 acres). Deforestation and illegal logging remain concerns for a country boasting the highest level of biodiversity in its region; following the conclusion of the Ivorian Civil War, only approximately two percent of total land cover was primary forest in the country.

Mining/Metals

The mineral industry of Côte d'Ivoire produces industrial minerals and commodities such as cement, gravel, crushed stone, and clay, as well as gold and diamonds, natural gas and petroleum products, and types of ore. The country is also home to potential resources of nickel, iron ore, copper, bauxite, and cobalt. Beginning in 2002, the UN Security Council implemented a ban on diamond exports from the country.

Agriculture

What was once the largest forest resource in West Africa has been almost entirely depleted by deforestation. However, agriculture remains Côte d'Ivoire's most significant economic sector. Coffee and cocoa plantations were established during the period of French colonialism. Other than cocoa beans, important agricultural products include coffee, bananas, corn, rice, sugar, cotton, and rubber.

Côte d'Ivoire's economic struggles are related to the heavy focus on agriculture. Fluctuations in the prices of exported agricultural goods and agriculture's reliance on favorable weather make the economy vulnerable to recession. The rebel uprisings of 2002 have negatively affected Côte d'Ivoire's agricultural activity, as many cocoa workers have fled to neighboring countries.

Animal Husbandry

Approximately 90 percent or more of livestock production in the country is concentrated in the northern region. Cattle and poultry are two of the primary livestock raised in Côte d'Ivoire.

Tourism

Tourism in Côte d'Ivoire has been restricted by the country's civil war and closed borders. Generally, visitors are advised not to travel outside of Abidjan, as doing so is considered life-threatening. Furthermore, Abidjan is known for crimes against foreigners, and the police and soldiers in Abidjan do not deter crime. These problems make tourism insignificant to the nation's economy.

In years before the coups and civil war, Abidjan was nicknamed, "the Paris of West Africa." Tourism flourished due to Abidjan's cultural offerings, including museums, galleries, and architecture. For tourists who do visit, a popular destination is Yamoussoukro's Our Lady of Peace, the largest Christian church in Africa, and one of the largest in the world.

Joanne O'Sullivan, Richard Means, Amanda Wilding

DO YOU KNOW?

- Côte d'Ivoire was named by French sailors who traveled to the coast in the 14th century and established the ivory trade.

- For years, the country was called the Ivory Coast. To avoid confusion when translating this name, the government passed a law in 1985 stating that the country be called Côte d'Ivoire in every language.

Bibliography

Araoye, Ademola. *Côte d'Ivoire: The Conundrum of a Still Wretched of the Earth.* Trenton, NJ: *Africa World Press*, 2012.

Fischer, Eberhard, et al. "African Masters: Art form the Ivory Coast." Zurich: *Museum Rietberg*, 2014.

Hale, Thomas A. and Aissata Sidikou, eds. "Women's Songs from West Africa." Bloomington, IN: *Indiana University Press*, 2014.

McGovern, Mike. "Making War in Côte d'Ivoire." Chicago: *University of Chicago Press*, 2011.

Schwab, Peter. *Designing West Africa: Prelude to a 21st-Century Calamity.* New York: Palgrave Macmillan, 2004.

Works Cited

"Alpha Blondy." *The African Music Encyclopedia* http://www.africanmusic.org.

"African Heritage Classroom." *The Nationality Rooms Project, University of Pittsburgh,* http://www.pitt.edu.

"Côte d'Ivoire." *Ecowas.* http://www.ecowas.com.

"Côte d'Ivoire: Country Reports on Human Rights Practices, Bureau of Democracy, Human Rights, and Labor, Africa." *United States Department of State.* http://www.state.gov 2006.

"Côte d'Ivoire: Information Related to Intangible Cultural Heritage." *UNESCO.* http://www.unesco.org.

"Côte d'Ivoire: Business Travel." *U.S. Commercial Service West Africa.* http://www.buysua.gov.

"Côte d'Ivoire: Security Council Extends Diamond and Travel Sanctions." *UN News Service* 29 October 2008.

"Country Profile: Ivory Coast." *BBC.* http://news.bbc.co.uk

"Eco-Tourism: Ivory Coast." *Travel Africa.* Issue 20. http://www.travelafricamag.com

"EU Relations with Côte d'Ivoire." *The Official Web Site of the European Union,* 17 March 2008. http://ec.europa.eu.

"Female Ministers of the République de Côte d'Ivoire/Ivory Coast." *Guide to Women Leaders* http://www.guide2womenleaders.com

"Government Ban of RFI lifted after 3 Months." *Committee to Protect Journalists.* http://www.cpj.org. 6 May 2008.

"Ivory Coast Prison Protest Ends." *BBC News.* http://bbc.co.uk. 14 December 2008.

"Ivory Coast: Population." *Emporis.* http://ww.emporis.com

"Peace in Côte d'Ivoire, MASA 2007 for 5 Cities." *Francomix* http://www.francomix.com 6 March 2007.

"Tai National Park." *United Nations Environment Programme and World Conservation Monitoring Centre* http://www.unep-wcmc.org.

"The World Factbook: Côte d'Ivoire." *Central Intelligence Agency* http://www.cia.gov

Beaubien, Jason. "Ivory Coast Cathedral is the World's Largest Christian Church." *National Public Radio.* http://www.npr.org

Boudon, Laura. "Côte D'Ivoire." *Foreign Policy In Focus.* International Rescue Committee. http://www.irc-online.org

Cobb, Jr., Charles. "Côte d'Ivoire: U.S. Troops Ordered to West Africa." *All Africa News* 24 December 2002.

Ellis, David. "The President and the Basilica." *The Epoch Times* 24 January 2007.

Epstein, Daniel. "International Involvement in Côte d'Ivoire." *Global Politician* 26 June 2008.

Faul, Michelle. "News Travels Fast On Ivory Coast Drums." *Seattle Times.* 20 February 1994. http://seatteltimes.nwsource.com.

Gilman, Victoria. "Bird flu dance craze sweeps Ivory Coast." *National Geographic News.* 2 June 2006.

Griffis, Mike. "African Dan Masks of the Ivory Coast." *Buzzle* http://www.buzzle.com

Mitter, Siddhartha. The Hip Hop Generation: Ghana's Hip Life and Ivory Coast's Coupé-Decalé." *Afropop Worldwide.* http://www.afropop.org

Roy, Christopher. "The Lobi of Burkina Faso." *University of Iowa,* 2002.

Sopova, Jasmina. "Moving Africa with a Dance Rhythm." *UNESCO Courier.* http://www.unesco.org

Zijlma, Anouk. "Basilicas of Our Lady of Peace in Yamoussoukro." *African Travel* http://www.about.com.

A kalimba thumb piano. iStock.com/VIPDesignUSA.

EQUATORIAL GUINEA

Introduction

The Republic of Equatorial Guinea is a small West African nation located on the Gulf of Guinea near the Bight of Biafra. The country consists of the mainland territory known as Río Muni, as well as five coastal islands. The capital, Malabo, is located on Bioko, the largest island. Mainland neighbors include Gabon to the south and east, and Cameroon to the north. The island nation of São Tomé and Príncipe lies off Equatorial Guinea's southwestern coast.

Until 1968, the country was the Spanish colony of Spanish Guinea. Since independence, it has been governed by a perceived de facto dictatorship. Equatorial Guinea is rich in natural resources, particularly oil and natural gas. However, the revenue from these resources has not led to much improvement in living conditions for most Equatorial Guineans.

There are distinct differences between Equatoguinean culture found on the islands and that found on the mainland. The Spanish colonial influence is stronger in the islands, largely because the mainland was not under Spain's firm control until the 20th century. Indigenous cultures such as the Fang and Bubi in particular have maintained many of their traditional customs in the face of European colonialism.

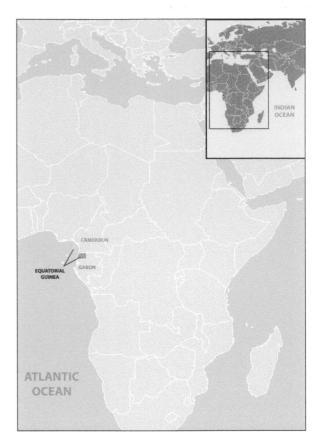

GENERAL INFORMATION

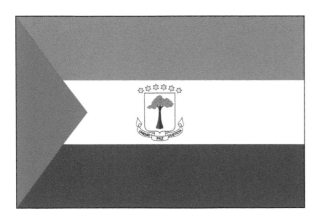

Official Language: Spanish and French
Population: 740,743 (2015 estimate)

Currency: Central African franc
Coins: Coins are available in denominations of 1, 2, 5, 10, 25, 50, 100, and 500 francs.
Land Area: 28,051 square kilometers (10,828 square miles)
National Motto: "Unidad, Paz, Justicia" ("Unity, Peace, Justice")
National Anthem: "Caminemos pisando la senda" ("Let Us Tread the Path")
Capital: Malabo
Time Zone: GMT +1
Flag Description: The flag of Equatorial Guinea features a blue isosceles triangle, the base of which is positioned on the hoist (left) side of flag. The flag also features three horizontal bands: green (top), white (middle), and red (bottom). In the center of the white band rests the country's coat of arms, which features six yellow stars, a gray shield, and a cotton tree, as well as the phrase "Unidad, Pax, Justicia," which translates to "Unity, Peace, Justice."

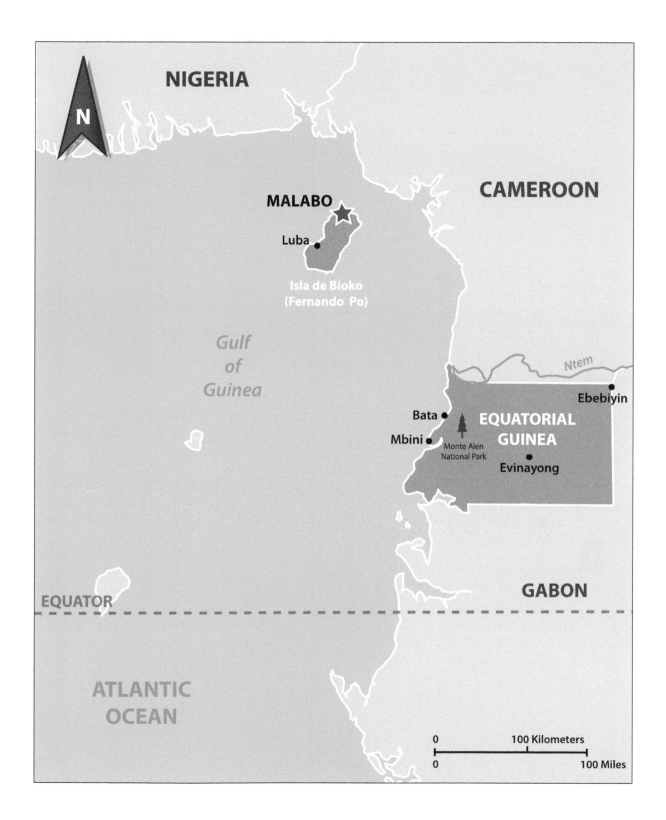

Principal Cities by Population (2012 estimate):

- Bata (250,770)
- Malabo (187,302)
- Ebebiyín (36,565)
- Aconibe (16,543)
- Añisoc (16,626

Population

The inhabitants of Equatorial Guinea (known as Equatorial Guineans or Equatoguineans) descend mostly from Bantu-speaking peoples. The Fang are the largest group on the mainland, while the islands represent a mix of peoples. The population of Bioko Island, formerly known as Fernando Po, is a mix of Bubi, Fang, and Nigerians, as well as "Fernandinos," many of whom are descended from freed slaves.

Around three-quarters of Equatorial Guineans live on the mainland. Bioko's population is growing rapidly, however, due to the oil boom that began in the mid-1990s. Tens of thousands of Equatoguineans live abroad, and form a distinct diaspora community; many have settled in Spain.

The capital, Malabo (formerly Santa Isabel), is located on the island of Bioko (formerly Fernando Po) and is the country's second-largest city. The population has doubled since the mid-1990s, when oil was discovered off the coast. The city has served as capital since 1969, replacing the mainland town of Bata. Malabo received its present name in 1973, as part of an effort to remove traces of European cultural influence.

The population of Equatorial Guinea is generally very young, with an estimated median age of 19 years. Just over 40 percent of the population is under 15 years of age, and four percent is older than 65 (2015).

Languages

Spanish and French are the official languages and are used in administrative and educational functions. 67.6 percent of the population is

fluent in Spanish. Spanish influence is greatest on Bioko, as the mainland was not fully colonized until the early 20th century. The main indigenous language is Fang, followed by Bubi and Ibo. A pidgin variety of English is also spoken, particularly by the Bubi. The population of the Annabón Province has a strong Portuguese element, and the people speak a creole form of Portuguese.

Native People & Ethnic Groups

The history of Equatorial Guinea's native peoples reflects the country's unique geography as a combination of mainland territory and coastal islands. The mainland, known as Río Muni, has been inhabited since ancient times, with the Pygmies as the original inhabitants. The population of Bioko, the largest island, is dominated by the Bubi, who began arriving in the 1600s.

The Portuguese began settling the islands in the mid-1470s, following explorer Fernão do Pó's 1472 discovery of Bioko (which was soon named after him). The Spanish took control of the islands, as well as the trade rights to the mainland in 1778, through a deal with Portugal. Spain did not receive territorial rights over Río Muni until 1990.

The British leased Fernando Po (now Bioko) from Spain from the late 1820s through the mid-1840s as a naval base to fight the slave trade. Many freed slaves chose to remain there, and became the ancestors of the Fernandino people; they are locally known as "Ferdinandos." After independence, many Fang migrated from the mainland to Bioko, and dominated the majority Bubi. During the 1970s, the reign of terror instituted by dictator Francisco Macías Nguema forced up to one-third of the population to flee. The Fang continue to dominate national politics.

The primary ethnic groups are the Fang and Bubi tribes. The Fang ethnic group comprises 85.7 percent of the population, which is further divided into over 60 subgroups. The Bubi are part of the Bantu tribal group and are native to Bioko Island; they make up 6.5 percent of the population. There is a small expatriate population in Malabo, primarily of Spanish descent, that comprises less than one percent of the population.

Religions
Most of the population (around 93 percent) is Christian. The vast majority belong to the Roman Catholic Church, with less than five percent belonging to the Reform Church of Equatorial Guinea.

Climate
As the name suggests, Equatorial Guinea is located on the equator and has a tropical climate. Conditions are hot and humid, especially on the mainland, and there are almost no seasonal changes. On average, the mainland receives about 2,000 millimeters (79 inches) of rain each year. Parts of Bioko receive as much of 10,000 millimeters (394 inches) of rain per year. The rainy season occurs between June and August, while the driest months are between December and February.

Average temperatures on the mainland range from 24° to 27° Celsius (75° to 80° Fahrenheit). The islands are also hot and humid, with temperatures regularly reaching the high 20°s or low 30°s Celsius (roughly 80° to 90° Fahrenheit).

ENVIRONMENT & GEOGRAPHY

Topography
Equatorial Guinea is located on the Gulf of Guinea near the Bight of Biafra, where the "bulge" of West Africa turns southward. The mainland section, Río Muni, is located between Cameroon and Gabon. The coastal region is covered with plains, though the interior is hilly. Three large rivers (the Congo, Niger, and Volta) drain into the Gulf. Much of the mainland is covered with rainforest.

The coastal islands of Equatorial Guinea are volcanic and widely separated; Bioko is about 40 kilometers (25 miles) from Cameroon, while Annobón is almost 600 kilometers (370 miles) southwest of Bioko. There are three smaller islands, just off the coast of Río Muni: Corisco, Elobey Grande (Big Elobey) and Elobey Chico (Small Elobey).

The country's highest point is at Pico Basile, an extinct volcano 3,008 meters (9,869 feet) above sea level.

Plants & Animals
Equatorial Guinea's wildlife is threatened with extinction due to human encroachment and poor resource management. The drill monkey, a kind of mandrill popular as "bushmeat," is threatened with extinction due to over-hunting. The goliath frog (Conraua goliath), an immense frog that is a foot long and weighs seven pounds, is threatened with the loss of its rainforest habitat due to pollution. Other species found on the mainland include the forest elephant and the lowland gorilla.

Most of the vegetation in Río Muni is tropical rainforest. The rugged mountain terrain of the islands is also forested.

The lowland gorilla is part of the wildlife found in Equatorial-Guinea.

CUSTOMS & COURTESIES

Greetings

Both French and Spanish are considered official languages in Equatorial Guinea, and several tribal languages are commonly spoken among the population. A majority of the population speaks or understands Spanish and it is the most common language spoken in the capital of Malabo and the surrounding region on Bioko Island. As such, greetings such as "Ola" ("Hello") and "Buenos dias" ("Good day"), for Spanish, and "Salut" ("Hello") and "Bonjour" ("Good day"), for French, are commonly used. Portuguese has also been gaining ground as an important language in the country. In 2007, President Teodoro Obiang Nguema Mbasogo (1942–) released a press statement to the effect that Portuguese would soon be named the country's third official language.

Many Equatoguineans, especially in the mainland, speak the ethnic Fang language, which is one of several tribal languages spoken in the country. Customary greeting phrases include "M'bolo" ("Hello"), while "M'bolani" is used when speaking to two or more people. The phrase "Yu num vah?" ("How are you?") is also commonly used as a greeting. Equatoguineans usually shake hands when greeting, extending the right hand. Friends, family, and acquaintances may kiss each other on the cheeks or embrace in greeting. However, men are expected to adopt a more reserved attitude regarding women, and should allow women to lead the pace of interaction.

Gestures & Etiquette

Equatoguineans typically stand close to one another when conversing and members of the same sex often touch while talking. Both men and women will hold hands when walking or embrace casually when talking. When meeting new people, Equatoguineans are more reserved, usually standing at arms length when conversing.

When calling to a person from a distance, Equatoguineans extend the entire hand with the palm facing downwards and curl the fingers towards the body. Extending the hand with the palm facing upward is considered impolite. Another common way to get someone's attention is to make a "hissing" sound.

Eating/Meals

Most Equatoguineans eat between two and three meals a day, roughly corresponding to breakfast, lunch, and dinner in the Western tradition. The morning meal is typically substantial, consisting of breads, grain, meat, and vegetables. In agricultural communities, individuals usually eat a large breakfast to maintain energy throughout the day.

The afternoon meal is typically light, consisting of fruits and grain or seafood and rice. The evening meal is generally reserved for family socialization and entertaining friends. A variety of dishes are served, including various types of seafood, roasted beef or goat, and numerous vegetable dishes. It is more common to serve dessert or sweets with the evening meal.

Most meals in Equatorial Guinea are served family style, with communal dishes placed in the center of the eating area. Individuals serve themselves from the dishes, using their right hand to retrieve food and eat, as the left hand is associated with personal cleansing, and considered unsanitary. In many Equatoguinean homes, individuals sit on the floor while eating, though some modern homes use a standard table and chairs. In rural areas, individuals often eat with their hands, though utensils are used at restaurants and often when entertaining guests.

Visiting

When visiting an Equatoguinean home, it is not expected to bring gifts for the hosts. As most Equatoguinean families are poor, providing food and drink for guests represents a significant expense for the family. It is therefore considered impolite to refuse any refreshment offered. Equatoguineans are known as a friendly people who will spare little expense to ensure the comfort of their guests. Reciprocity is important in native culture and, if invited to someone's home, the guest should extend a return invitation at the earliest convenience.

LIFESTYLE

Family

The basic unit of Equatoguinean society is the extended family, consisting of a married couple, their parents, grandparents, and other close relatives. Family life differs according to economic and ethnic group. The involvement of extended family members is essential among all the ethnic groups. Grandparents and older female relatives play an important role in child rearing and assist with domestic duties.

Among the Fang tribe, the largest and most influential ethnic group on Rio Muni, polygamy is common and families are patriarchal. Fang women are primarily responsible for domestic duties and child rearing and receive little in the way of compensation if divorced. According to tradition, women who divorce are required to return the dowry given by the male's family before the wedding. Marriages among the Fang are often arranged by the couple's parents and intended to enhance the family's stature by creating links between clans. The dowry is an important part of the marriage tradition, in which the family of the groom provides a gift of valuables, often cattle, to the bride's family to indicate the ability to provide for the family.

The Bubi ethnic group, which is the largest on Bioko Island, maintains a family tradition based on a matrilineal model. Women carry on the family name and are therefore granted higher stature within society. Married couples often live and work with the wife's family, and family stature within the community is often based on the social status of the clan's eldest female relatives.

Housing

Most Equatoguinean homes are simple, single-room dwellings, constructed from wood or thatched reeds. Families typically cluster their homes together and share a common outdoor garden for growing food and sometimes a shared irrigation system for water.

Few homes have indoor plumbing or electricity, except in Malabo and Bata. The traditional housing model on Rio Muni was the thatched hut, constructed from a wooden frame with palm leaves used for walls and roofing material. Alternatively, villagers sometimes used bamboo planks and earthen bricks in home construction.

Few homes have more than two rooms, and it is common for multiple members of a family to share a single room. In the cities, affordable apartments have become more common, though many apartments are small and consist of one or two rooms. In the capital and some of the other larger cities, there are remnants of Spanish colonial architecture. However, these are primarily used as official and administrative buildings. The nation's wealthiest families often live in former colonial homes, constructed from stone or earthen walls with tile roofing.

As temperatures can be uncomfortably high around the middle of the day, many Equatoguinean homes have many windows or open sections in the walls to allow airflow. Most homes also have angled roofing to protect from torrential rains during the wet season. Groups of houses are often built around a central well or near a river where villagers can obtain water and wash clothing and food.

Food

Equatoguinean cuisine is a blend of Spanish and African influences, and most Equatoguineans live on simple diets consisting of family-style meals. Fish is a common staple, especially on Bioko and in the coastal villages. Various types of animals are also raised for food, including chicken, native fowl, and zebu cattle. Paella, a common Spanish dish usually made with seafood, is also made in Equatorial Guinea, though the recipes have been altered with the use of African ingredients and spices. A common Equatoguinean version of paella uses guinea fowl, a native bird species, instead of seafood. In this native version, the fowl is cooked in a mixture of broth, onion, and spices, including hot peppers, turmeric, and oregano. Rice forms the base of the dish and is heated with the meat and stock until soft.

Fishing has always been a major part of Equatoguinean culture. Kingfish, tuna, or cod steaks are seasoned with salt and pepper and then baked with garlic, onion, and lime juice. The steaks may be served with rice and vegetables, including cassava, yams, potatoes, or carrots. Another common fish preparation is spicy fish stew, made with chunks of fish, usually redfish or snapper, mixed with potatoes, tomatoes, carrots, and spinach and flavored with salt, hot peppers, and lemon. Other spices include paprika, rosemary, and ground Ashanti pepper, a spice made from the ground seeds of a plant in the same family as black pepper. Another entrée served in Equatorial Guinea is kansiye, a stew made from chunks of red meat, usually beef or lamb, cooked with onion, clove, parsley, and tomatoes, and flavored with peanut sauce. The beef or lamb is usually served rare and with a side dish of white rice and vegetables.

Peanuts are common in Equatoguinean and West African cuisine. Equatoguineans make several varieties of peanut sauce, which is used with many types of food, including fish steaks, and as a garnish for vegetables and a dressing for salad. The basic peanut sauce includes peanut butter or mashed peanuts served with salt and pepper, beef or chicken broth, and tomato sauce or paste. Additional flavors added include thyme, hot peppers, lemon juice, and vinegar. Peanuts are also used in the preparation of other sauces, like avocado sauce, which mixes peanut paste with crushed avocados, lemon, garlic, onion, and peppers to create a creamy, flavorful sauce. Another variety uses steamed spinach, often cooked in fish broth, with peanut butter, garlic, and palm oil.

Life's Milestones

As a predominantly Catholic nation, most Equatoguineans follow the standard Catholic rites of passage, including baptism, communion, marriage, and funerary customs. Nearly 20 percent of Equatoguineans maintain some form of traditional, animistic religious beliefs, and may therefore follow different rites of passage.

A child's baptism and first communion are cause for celebration in the Catholic community. Families often throw a feast to which neighbors and members of the extended community are invited. While ceremonies are conducted in a church, according to Catholic tradition, the celebration that follows is usually held at a family home, complete with music, dancing, and food. It is common for guests to bring small gifts for the child and parents.

Marriage involves elements of Catholic and ancient African traditions. It is common for the male to present the bride's family with a dowry, often of cattle or other livestock, to signify the ability to care for the family. Marriages are typically arranged, though this practice is waning in modern Equatorial Guinea as more couples choose their own spouses outside of family custom. In the animist religious tradition, marriage also serves as the traditional marker of the transition to adulthood. Services are conducted by village elders and involve traditional song and dance ceremonies.

The funeral is one of the most important events in Equatoguinean life. In the traditional philosophy of both the Fang and Bubi, ancestors are revered and it is believed that they continue to play a role in guiding the lives of the living. Among Catholics and Christians in Equatorial Guinea, the belief in reverence for one's ancestors remains strong. Families hold solemn ceremonies to honor the death of a family member, followed by a gathering of family and friends for food and drink. Relatives and friends of the departed regularly visit the graves or tombs of deceased loved ones and leave gifts of food, flowers, and other items. Families may also keep the bones or ashes of their loved ones in a small tomb, which is usually an elaborately decorated box.

CULTURAL HISTORY

Art

The Fang people, the largest ethnicity in Equatorial Guinea, are known for their sculpture techniques, passed down through generations since the precolonial period. Fang sculptors create their works for both decorative and ceremonial functions. It is common for families to use a small bust or a

Fang artisans make carved wooden masks used in traditional ceremonies.

full figure sculpture to top the box containing the ashes or body of a dead relative. These funerary sculptures were intended to protect the deceased from evil and to guard the remains from harm. Fang sculptors often exaggerate features of their subjects, giving the figures large heads and eyes to communicate emotion.

Fang artisans also create a variety of wooden masks for ceremonial purposes that have become popular with tourists as souvenirs. Each type of mask is associated with an aspect of traditional ceremony used by one of the various Fang cults in the region. Many of the masks combine human and animal features, symbolizing the relationship between the tribe and the other animals living in the area. When wearing an animal-themed mask, the wearer is believed to have the ability to adopt characteristics of that animal. Antelope, leopard, lion, and elephant are some of the animals depicted in Fang masks.

Architecture

Spanish colonial architecture still exists in the country, such as the Malabo Cathedral, which

was completed in 1917. It is a popular destination for tourists and is designed according to a Gothic, Spanish architectural plan. The city of Bata also features many examples of Spanish colonial architecture; however, in the early 21st century, it has been noted that these structures tend to be poorly maintained.

Music & Dance

Music and dance are integral to the culture of Equatorial Guinea and carry much social and religious significance. The country's various tribes indigenous have strong oral traditions, and are known for their distinct folksongs and dances. Most traditional music is in the call-and-response style, accompanied by drums. The dances of the Bubi ethnic group, for instance, tend to feature wooden bells or drums and are often performed, at night, by both male and female dancers. One type of dance is the balele, which requires its dancers to shake, leap, and jump energetically. The national dance of the Fang tribe is known as the Ibanga.

Traditional musical instruments include the drum, harp, wooden trumpet, wooden xylophone, and the sanza, which is a small "thumb piano," typically made of bamboo.

Literature

Little is known about the literature of Equatorial Guinea before the end of the colonial period. There are several pieces of fiction and essays written during this time that have come to the attention of the international literary community. However, it was not until the postcolonial period that Equatoguinean literature began to develop unique cultural characteristics. The first Equatoguinean novel was *Cuando los Combes Luchaban* (1953) written by Leoncio Evita Enoy (1929–1996).

The most famous Equatoguinean writer is Donato Ndongo Bidyogo (1950–). A journalist and novelist, he has written several scholarly studies of Equatoguinean history and culture, including *History and Tragedy of Equatorial Guinea* (1977) and several well-respected short stories, such as "El Sueno" (1973). Ndongo

Bidyogo was one of the many Equatoguinean intellectuals who fled the country during the dictatorship of Francisco Nguema (1924–1979) in the mid-1970s. He spent more than 40 years living in Spain and traveled extensively in Europe and the United States, where he served as guest lecturer in Spanish language literature. Ndongo Bidyogo returned to Equatorial Guinea in 1979 and served as director of Equatorial Guinea's Hispano-Guinean Cultural Center from 1985 to 1992. He left the country again in 1994 after the government became hostile toward him when he reported on security forces arresting and detaining groups of intellectuals.

Another of the nation's famous writers, María Nsué Angüe (1945–), became the first Equatoguinean woman to have a book published with her 1985 novel *Ekomo*. Angüe spent most of her life living in Spain with her parents, who fled Equatorial Guinea during the Nguema dictatorship. She eventually returned to Equatorial Guinea where she served in a number of government offices, including becoming the first female to serve as minister of culture. Her novel *Ekomo* deals with the clash of gender and culture in Equatorial Guinea as the book's protagonist struggles with gender issues in society.

Another famous Equatoguinean writer, journalist, novelist, and poet Juan Tomás Ávila Laurel (1966–), began publishing poetry in the mid-1990s, becoming one of the most respected poets in the country. Avila Laurel has become well known in the international literary community for his eloquent prose, which communicates the struggles and issues faced in modern Equatoguinean life. Avila Laurel's 2008 novel, *Avión de Ricos*, *Ladrón de Cerdos*, tells the story of two Equatoguinean children struggling with poverty and homelessness.

CULTURE

Arts & Entertainment
While there are numerous craft traditions in Equatorial Guinea, arts funding is virtually non-existent and education is restricted to private

tutelage through established craft makers. Both the native Fang and Bubi tribes are known for their wood sculpture techniques and traditions. Many artisans take a small number of apprentices each year to maintain the island's native artistic techniques. Sculptors in modern Equatorial Guinea often fund their efforts by selling their art at the local market or to tourists.

Dance and music are also important elements of Equatoguinean culture, but have little integration into the administration. Basic music education is a part of the public curriculum, but students have few options for art or music education at higher levels. The maintenance of the country's musical traditions is largely through generational inheritance, with parents passing on musical theory and skills to the next generation.

As in many African countries, soccer is the most popular sport in Equatorial Guinea. The national team, part of the Confederation of African Football (CAF), competes internationally but has so far failed to qualify for the African Nations Cup.

Cultural Sites & Landmarks
Equatorial Guinea has a poorly developed tourism industry. Few travelers visit the country because of dangerous political conditions, high crime rates in the cities, and a lack of basic amenities. The potential exists to develop Equatorial Guinea's ecotourism industry because of the nation's wealth of natural resources, including several national parks, mountains, and coastal areas rich with diverse ecosystems of marine animals and plants.

The capital of Malabo, located on Bioko Island, is indicative of the struggling state of Equatorial Guinea. Despite being the largest city in the nation, its street network is underdeveloped and several unpaved roads lead into the capital. Nonetheless, the city is known for its colonial history, and the downtown area has several well-preserved examples of Spanish colonial architecture interspersed with modern buildings. The Malabo Cathedral is one of the oldest buildings in the city, built by Spanish colonists and designed in the Spanish Gothic style. The building is constructed from carved stone, with two towers rising above the intricately decorated face. The cathedral is located in the administrative district near the Presidential Palace and City Hall, both of which are designed in a colonial architectural style.

The Malabo Gardens are also in the administrative district, serving as a public park where visitors can relax near planted stands of tropical trees and bushes. The marketplace of Malabo is a popular spot for tourists and expatriates and forms a social hub for the community as a whole. Dozens of open stalls sell food, crafts, and other goods to crowds of customers often noisily bargaining for their purchases. The Malabo Port is largely commercial and is typically filled with commercial carriers serving the oil industry. The city of Malabo is located in the valley below Pico Basile, formerly Pico de Santa Isabel, and is a volcanic mountain that rises to over 3,000 meters (9,843 feet). Mountain climbers, nature enthusiasts, and hikers often visit the mountain, which has several cleared hiking trails leading from the forest floor into the tropical forests that cover the sides of the mountain.

Bata is the largest city of Rio Muni, or the Continental Region of Equatorial Guinea, and the center of the nation's oil industry. Once the capital of the nation, Bata still has a few colonial buildings, but has expanded with low-income housing stretching into the hills the surround the city. The downtown area has been in a state of rapid expansion due to an influx of revenue from the growing oil industry. On Rio Muni, Monte Alen National Park covers 1,200 square kilometers (463 square miles) of primary and secondary growth forest. There are hundreds of species inhabiting the park, including herds of wild elephant and families of gorilla. A number of private agencies provide permits and wildlife viewing tours through the park.

Libraries
The National Library of Equatorial Guinea is located in Malabo; it houses an estimated 12,000 volumes and in 2010, sponsored a literary contest to promote literacy and culture in the country.

Other literacy initiatives undertaken by the library include children's programs and mobile libraries.

Holidays
The country's national holiday is Independence Day (October 12), which celebrates independence from Spain. Other holidays include New Year's Day (January 1), the Presidents' Birthday (June 7), as well as religious holidays such as the Immaculate Conception, Corpus Cristi, and Good Friday.

Youth Culture
Extreme poverty limits the recreational and social lives of Equatoguinean children. Many begin working at an early age to aid their families, either by taking part in family businesses or working in the retail or agricultural sectors. Because many children are forced to begin working early, educational attainment is low. Few Equatoguineans pursue higher education, further limiting their employment and recreational options.

Sports are a common recreational option for Equatoguineans, and football (soccer) is the most popular sport in the nation. The national football team is a member of the Confederation of African Football (CAF), and many Equatoguineans follow their football team's progress throughout the year. Young children rarely have store-bought toys and instead create games using found or discarded objects. For teenagers, music forms a central component to their social and recreational lives. Traditional African music is still found in many parts of the country, but Equatoguinean teens often listen to reggae, hip-hop, and other music imported from the U.S. and other African nations.

SOCIETY

Transportation
There are limited options for public transportation in Equatorial Guinea, including a small, typically crowded bus service on Bioko that runs

on irregular schedules. There are private taxis operating around the main cities, and most offer transport to any location. For travel between Bata and Bioko Island, there are ships leaving the Bata harbor each day, some of which carry passenger traffic.

Traffic moves on the right-hand side of the road. There are only seven total airports in the entire country, six of which are paved runways.

Transportation Infrastructure

There are an estimated 2,880 kilometers (1,790 miles) of roads in Equatorial Guinea, most of which are unpaved and in poor condition. In most cases, automobile travel requires four-wheel-drive capability because of the uneven roads and potholes. A paved road to facilitate commercial shipments connects Bata and the city of Mbini. The main airport in Equatorial Guinea is Malabo International Airport on Bioko Island. On Rio Muni, Bata Airport, near the city of Bata, accepts short domestic flights from Malabo. The nation's other airports only provide flights within the country.

The port at Bata also serves as the country's chief commercial port, with agricultural and industrial goods shipped from the docks to nearby countries and to Bioko. The nation's other ports are located in the cities of Luba and Malabo.

Since 2003, the government has initiated a number of programs designed to enhance the infrastructure, particularly within the capital. Investments have included improvements to Malabo International Airport, located 9 kilometers (5.6 miles) from the city, which is the largest international hub in the region. Malabo has no public transportation system, but the government has indicated that progress is underway to initiate a system of bus lines.

Media & Communications

National law guarantees freedom of the press and expression, but the governmental places restrictions on all publishing and broadcast media. Criticism of general government policy is allowed. Criticizing the president, other members of the central government, or the security forces may be met with reprisal, fines, or detention. While government agents are able to exert significant control over print and radio, security forces lack the resources to supervise Internet broadcasts. Some reports indicate that restrictions on the press are beginning to change. In 2007 and 2008, reports indicated that government agents allowed some journalists to publish critical accounts of domestic policy issues. Despite minor improvements, Equatorial Guinea is recognized as one of the most censored nations in the world. The government also restricts the access and entrance of foreign media representatives and has been known to use threats of violence to control members of the media.

There are few independent media agencies active in the country and the government owns most of the television and print sources. *La Nation* and *La Opinion* are independently owned weekly publications providing news and entertainment coverage. *La Gaceta*, the nation's other independently owned publication, is published on a monthly basis. The state-owned *Ebano* primarily provides news and information about changes in official policy, and is used by the leading party to advertise for their administration. All publications are produced in Spanish and French with some limited English content.

Since 2001, the government-owned Television Nacional is the nation's sole television network, providing news and informative programming, as well as several select programs rebroadcast from foreign networks. The government also operates the state's largest radio network, Radio Nacional de Guinea Ecuatorial, which primarily provides news, but also allows some music programming.

According to evaluations by the United States Department of State, literacy rates remain low and there are few vendors selling books and magazines in the country. As of 2008, there were only two known bookstores in the country and three libraries, all operated by foreign groups or religious organizations. Some reports indicate that the number of vendors selling foreign newspapers and books is growing. In 2014, there were an estimated 115,100 Internet users, representing just over 15.9 percent of the population.

SOCIAL DEVELOPMENT

Standard of Living
Equatorial Guinea ranked 144th out of 187 countries on the 2013 United Nations Human Development Index, which measures quality of life and standard of living indicators.

As of 2015, the infant mortality rate was an estimated 69.17 deaths per 1,000 live births. Average life expectancy is 63.85 years; 62.7 years for men and 64.9 years for women (2009 estimate).

Water Consumption
In 2015, 72.5 percent of the urban population and 31.5 percent of the rural population had access to improved drinking water. An estimated 79.9 percent of the urban population and 71 percent of the rural population had access to improved sanitation systems that same year.

Education
Public education essentially began in Equatorial Guinean in the early 20th century. Before that, largely religious (usually Roman Catholic) groups provided education. During the 20th century, the colonial authorities established schools and promoted Spanish culture. Most education was at the elementary or primary level. There were very few opportunities for higher education in the country, though some students were able to travel to Spain for further education.

The educational system was severely damaged during the Nguema dictatorship, between 1968 and 1979. Conditions have improved only a little, despite revenues from the oil industry. Most of the population is literate, and education is free and compulsory for all native children. In 2007, roughly 90 percent of children between the ages of six and 12 attended primary school. As of 2015, according to the U.S. State Department, the adult literacy rate was estimated at 95.3 percent,

with slight disparity between genders (97.4 for men, and 93 for women).

In 1995, the National University of Equatorial Guinea was established in Malabo. It has several schools that specialize in the following areas: agriculture, fishing, medicine, business, engineering, social sciences, and education. Another college, Colegio Nacional Enrique Nvo Okenve, has two branches, one in Bata, and the other in Malabo. Many Equatoguineans still travel abroad, however, to receive advanced education.

Women's Rights
Domestic violence, though prohibited under national laws, remains a significant concern in Equatorial Guinea. NGO reports indicate that police are ineffective at addressing domestic issues. Women are reluctant to report abuse because of social stigma, fear of reprisal, and cultural permissiveness regarding the use of violence against women. Reports also indicate that police rarely investigate abuse cases and that most women believe that the police will do little to protect women from abusive spouses. In 2007, the government initiated a program, in cooperation with several NGOs, to educate women regarding their right to protection and legal remedies for abuse. Women's rights organizations have also criticized the government for failing to specify spousal rape in the penal code. While rape is illegal under national law, reports indicate that women are reluctant to report rape because of social stigmas and because rape victims may face discrimination within their communities.

Though women are guaranteed equal rights and equal opportunity to employment under the law, social norms and discrimination often confine women to domestic roles and certain industries. Women often worked in the educational, manufacturing, and agricultural industries. According to investigations by Amnesty International (AI) and other NGOs, women were not granted equal access to employment benefits, equal pay, or advancement opportunities. Though women are able to join the country's military service, within the Navy, they are only allowed administrative positions.

Health Care

Public health in Equatorial Guinea is extremely poor, the legacy of President Nguema's reign of terror in the 1970s. The health care system as it existed just before independence had been relatively extensive and well equipped, with around a dozen hospitals and Spanish-trained personnel. Major infectious diseases, such as malaria, were generally under control.

In the early 21st century, the risk of major infectious diseases is high; the most dangerous are malaria, bacterial diarrhea, hepatitis A, and typhoid fever. The incidence of HIV/AIDS is relatively low; as of 2014, only a little more than six percent of adults were infected.

In 2015, the infant mortality rate is high (69.17 deaths per 1000 live births), although conditions have improved in large part thanks to international aid agencies such as the United Nations International Children's Emergency Fund (UNICEF).

GOVERNMENT

Structure

The nation of Equatorial Guinea was established on October 12, 1968, out of the colony of Spanish Guinea. The colony had originally been two separate colonies: the coastal islands (governed from Fernando Po) and the mainland territory of Río Muni.

The first president of the new republic, Francisco Macías Nguema, was a former colonial administrator. He soon established a harsh dictatorship that destroyed the country's economic system and social infrastructure. Up to one-third of the population fled during his 11-year rule. He was deposed and executed in 1979 by his nephew, who became president.

Although less brutal than its predecessor, the new regime has received extensive criticism because of its poor record on human rights and lack of support for economic and social development. Multi-party democracy was established in the early 1990s, but foreign observers have alleged massive fraud in national elections. In

March 2004, the government foiled a coup attempt. The Fang ethnic group, from which the ruling dynasty comes, dominates national politics.

The president, who is popularly elected to a seven-year term, serves as head of state. The president appoints the prime minister, who serves as head of government, as well as the deputy prime ministers and the cabinet (Council of Ministers). In practice, all executive power is vested in the president. As of November 29, 2009, the president of Equatorial Guinea is Teodoro Obiang Nguema Mbasogo. He was re-elected with 95.8 percent vote; the next elections are to be held in 2016.

Equatorial Guinea has a single-house parliament, the House of People's Representatives (Camara de Representantes del Pueblo). The body has little power, however, and functions largely as a debating society. The 80 members serve five-year terms and are elected by popular vote.

The national constitution was approved by a referendum in November 1991 and amended in January 1995. International observers, however, argue that in practice the law is essentially in the hands of the executive branch, and have noted multiple cases of human rights abuses, including torture of prisoners.

Political Parties

Political parties in Equatorial Guinea include the Convergence Party for Social Democracy, led by Placido Mico Abogo; the Democratic Party for Equatorial Guinea, led by Teodoro Obiang Nguema Mbasogo; the Electoral Coalition; the Party for Progress of Equatorial Guinea, led by Severo Moto; and the Popular Action of Equatorial Guinea, led by Avelino Mocache.

Local Government

The country is divided into seven provinces: Annobon, Bioko Norte, Bioko Sur, Centro Sur, Litoral, Kie-Ntem, and Wele-Nzas. These provinces are further divided into 30 municipalities and around 1,000 village councils and associations. A governor is appointed by the president to oversee each province, while municipalities and village councils and associations are headed by elected mayors.

Judicial System

The highest court in Equatorial Guinea is the Supreme Court. The legal system is a mixture of Spanish and tribal law. In tribal areas, local elders handle legal issues. This system consists of nine judges and the chief justice.

Taxation

The top income and corporate tax rate in Equatorial Guinea is 35 percent (2010). Other taxes levied include an inheritance tax and a value-added tax (VAT). In 2014, taxes accounted for 33.8 percent of the country's GDP.

Armed Forces

Equatorial Guinea's armed forces include land, naval, and air branches. According to the U.S. State Department, the armed forces are 2,500 strong, and selective compulsory military service is two years.

Foreign Policy

Equatorial Guinea belongs to a number of international African organizations, including the Central African Economic and Monetary Union (CEMAC) and the Central African Franc Zone (CFA). The nation's petroleum supplies, after oil was discovered in 1991, have allowed the government to increase its status as an international trading partner. The US and China are two of the nation's most important trading partners, and the U.S. is the single biggest investor in Equatoguinean development programs. Through the U.S. Agency for International Development (USAID) program, the U.S. distributes funding to the Equatoguinean government, resulting in more than $40 million (USD) in development assistance.

Equatorial Guinea has a special relationship with Spain, the former colonial power, which includes select trade, diplomatic, and defense agreements. Despite strained relations due to opposition Equatoguinean governments operating in Spain, the country has maintained a functional relationship with Spanish leadership, and Spain remains one of the country's strongest supporters in terms of foreign aid and trade. Equatorial Guinea is also involved in a longstanding border dispute with the nations of Cameroon and Nigeria regarding ownership of coastal territory along the Gulf of Guinea. While the United Nations' International Court of Justice (ICJ) attempted to intervene and provide arbitration in 2002, the dispute between Cameroon and Equatorial Guinea resurfaced in 2006 and 2007.

International monitoring groups are concerned that Equatorial Guinea remains an active port for criminal industries, trafficking of children or kidnapping victims for sexual exploitation, and child labor. Lack of resources has prevented Equatorial Guinea from making significant progress towards addressing these issues. Kidnapping victims from Equatorial Guinea have been found in Benin, Cameroon, and China.

Human Rights Profile

International human rights law insists that states respect civil and political rights, and promote an individual's economic, social, and cultural rights. The United Nations (UN) Universal Declaration of Human Rights (UDHR) is recognized as the standard for international human rights. Its authors sought the counsel of the world's great thinkers, philosophers, and religious leaders, and were careful to create a document that reflects the core values shared by every world culture. (To read this document or view the articles relating to cultural human rights, visit http://www.udhr.org/UDHR/default.htm.)

Equatorial Guinea is controlled by a military regime that took power in 1979 and has been accused of using violent means to maintain political control. The administration of President Obiang represents the nation's native Fang ethnic group and tends to allow only representatives of the Fang to serve in the government. While there were efforts to improve human rights conditions in 2007 and 2008, monitoring agencies reported that violations were common. There were widespread reports that police and security forces regularly violated the human rights of criminal suspects, including engaging in unlawful killings and torture. Observers witnessed chambers within security offices with torture equipment, indicating that security forces commonly used torture as a method of obtaining confessions from suspected criminals.

The government of Equatorial Guinea has failed to ensure the safety and security of immigrants. Security forces conduct raids of immigrant neighborhoods, destroying property and using excessive violence on individuals suspected of illegal immigration. In addition, prison conditions, including both minimum-security detention centers and correctional facilities, do not meet international standards. Prisoners have inadequate access to medical care and basic sanitary facilities and are subject to violence from other prisoners and prison guards. Reports indicate that prison officials occasionally use torture to punish prisoners, and that the prison population included numerous political prisoners and foreign refugees, many of whom were arrested without due process.

Non-governmental organizations (NGOs) also object to the fact that juvenile and female offenders are not separated from the male prison population and that rape and child abuse occur. Similar reports indicate that individuals are sometimes held in temporary detention centers for periods exceeding several months, with no access to sanitary facilities. Though the government has allowed NGO organizations and UN committees to examine prisons and detention centers, authorities allow only partial, supervised access. NGO representatives believe that restricted prison areas may contain torture facilities and other examples of inhumane treatment.

Examinations of the Equatorial Guinea judicial system reveal numerous problems, including inefficient trial procedures, long detention periods without due process, and institutional corruption. In addition, numerous reports indicate that security forces regularly engage in arbitrary arrests without judicial consent and often hold detainees for long periods without formal

charges. While the government allows freedom of speech and the press to a limited extent, there are laws prohibiting criticism of the president or his family, either by the press or by private individuals. NGO reports indicate that government agents monitor the press and may monitor phone communication and the mail.

Other human rights abuses pertain to the freedom of religion and discrimination. The government allows only limited freedom of association and religion, as only government-sanctioned churches and organizations—mainly Christian—are allowed to congregate. The government does not provide adequate protection for persons with disabilities, and disabled persons suffer from discrimination in hiring and other forms of abuse. Similarly, widespread discrimination against homosexuals, HIV/AIDS sufferers, and ethnicities occurs with inadequate police intervention. As of 2014, 31,600 people in Equatorial Guinea were living with HIV/AIDS. NGO investigations also note that immigrants and members of ethnic minorities regularly face discrimination and abuse at the hands of security personnel. Lastly, the government does not adequately protect workers and maintains no statutes guaranteeing minimum acceptable working conditions. While there is a nationally mandated minimum wage, the government did not enforce wage laws and agricultural workers regularly earned less than the legal minimum.

ECONOMY

Overview of the Economy
Equatorial Guinea has gained immense wealth since the discovery of offshore petroleum in the mid-1990s, with the country becoming one of the largest oil suppliers in Africa. In 2014, the estimated gross domestic product (GDP) was estimated at $25.11 billion (USD). The per capita GDP for 2014 was estimated at $32,300 (USD).

Nonetheless, poverty remains widespread, despite the oil wealth, amid allegations of vast political corruption. Equatorial Guinea has lost much of its foreign aid partly because of corruption, but also due to its newfound natural resources.

Equatorial Guinea maintains strong economic links with other West African nations. It belongs to the Communaute Financiere Africaine (CFA, or Central African franc) franc currency zone, a monetary union mostly comprised of former French colonies. The currency's value is linked to that of the Euro.

Industry

In addition to oil, natural gas and timber are also important economic sectors. In 2014, agriculture contributes only 5.1 percent to GDP, but employs a significant percentage of the work force. Most industrial activity (85.7 percent to GDP) revolves around the oil industry, as well as cocoa beans, coffee, and timber.

Labor

The labor force comprises approximately 195,200 workers as of 2007. In 2009, the unemployment rate was 22.3 percent.

Energy/Power/Natural Resources

Equatorial Guinea has become one of the world's largest producers of petroleum, thanks to the discovery of large offshore deposits. The Zafiro field is the country's largest, holding most of the total proven reserves of 1.28 billion barrels. Natural gas is another important energy resource, and the country has an estimated 8.5 trillion cubic feet of proven resources, much of which is in the Alba field. In fact, natural gas reserves are so plentiful that the government is considering construction of a liquefied natural gas plant in the country in 2012.

Fishing

Fishing is a potentially significant, growing industry in Equatorial Guinea as the country has extensive fishing zones but poor infrastructure. In the early 21st century, the country is planning on improving and developing fishing industry infrastructure, including the construction of processing plants and modern fishing vessels.

Forestry

Timber has been an important resource for decades, but poor forestry practices as well as natural disasters have led to extensive deforestation.

Mining/Metals

Mineral resources include gold and diamonds, and industrial minerals such as bauxite, sand, gravel, and clay.

Agriculture

Most farming in Equatorial Guinea is at the subsistence level, focusing on food crops such as cassava, rice, and manioc. Less than five percent of the land is arable.

During the colonial era, the country was known for its production of export crops such as cocoa, coffee, and timber, but these declined sharply during the period of dictatorship. Cocoa was grown largely on Bioko, while the others were grown on the mainland.

Animal Husbandry

Cattle, sheep, and goat are the primary livestock breed in Equatorial Guinea. The livestock industry remains underdeveloped, and most agricultural activities occur at the subsistence level.

Tourism

Tourism in Equatorial Guinea is low and the European Union blacklists all of the country's airlines due to safety concerns. (Ten other African nations also have all of their registered airlines banned by the EU.) The country faces serious allegations of human rights abuse and poor health conditions. The majority of foreign visitors to the country are connected with the petroleum industry.

Micah Issitt, Eric Badertscher

DO YOU KNOW?

- The drill, a primate related to the baboon, is one of the world's most endangered primates. The largest current population lives on Bioko, though the animal is under pressure from hunting and loss of habitat.

- The Malabo pidgin dialect (also called Fernando Po Creole), spoken by the Island's Ferdinando population, contains elements of French, Spanish, English, and Portuguese, as well as African dialects from the Fang and Bubi tribes.

Bibliography

Falola, Toyin and Richard M. Lerner. "Teen Life in Africa." Westport, CT: *Greenwood Publishing Group*, 2004.

Lewis, Marvin A. "An Introduction to the Literature of Equatorial Guinea." Columbia, MO: *University of Missouri Press*, 2007.

Lininger-Goumaz, Max. "Small is Not Always Beautiful: The Story of Equatorial Guinea." London, UK: *Hurst Publishers*, 1989.

Osseo-Asare, Fran. "Food Culture in Sub-Saharan Africa." Westport, CT: *Greenwood Publishing*, 2005.

Peek, Philip M. and Kweshi Yankah. "African Folklore: An Encyclopedia." New York: *Taylor & Francis*, 2004.

Roberts, Adam. "The Wonga Coup: Guns, Thugs, and a Ruthless Determination to Create Mayhem in an Oil-rich Corner of Africa." New York: *Perseus Books Group*, 2007.

Scafidi, Oscar. "Equatorial Guinea (Bradt Travel Guide)." Guilford, CT: *Globe Pequot*, 2015.

Works Cited

"Background Note: Equatorial Guinea." *Bureau of African Affairs*. March 2009. http://www.state.gov/r/pa/ei/bgn/7221.htm

"Country Profile: Equatorial Guinea." *BBC News Online*. February 25, 2009. http://news.bbc.co.uk/2/hi/africa/country_profiles/1023151.stm

"Equatorial Guinea." *CIA World Factbook*. March 5, 2009. https://www.cia.gov/library/publications/the-world-factbook/geos/ek.html

"Equatorial Guinea: Country Reports on Human Rights Practices." Bureau of Democracy, Human Rights, and Labor. *U.S. Department of State Online*. March 11, 2008. http://www.state.gov/g/drl/rls/hrrpt/2007/100479.htm

"Equatorial Guinea Human Rights." *Amnesty International Online*. http://www.amnestyusa.org/all-countries/equatorial-guinea/page.do?id=1011149

"Equatorial Guinea: Language and Literature." Portals to the World. *Library of Congress Online*. http://www.loc.gov/rr/international/amed/eguinea/resources/eguinea-language.html

"Equatorial Guinea." Sub Saharan Africa. *Foreign Commonwealth Office*. http://www.fco.gov.uk/en/about-the-fco/country-profiles/sub-saharan-africa/equatorial-guinea/?view=Standard&version=2

"Equatorial Guinea Page." African Studies Center. *UPenn Online*. http://www.africa.upenn.edu/Country_Specific/Eq_Guinea.html

"Equatorial Guinea." *The Official Website for the Republic of Equatorial Guinea*. http://guinea-equatorial.com/

"Equatorial Guinea." *World Health Organization Profile*. http://www.who.int/countries/gnq/en/

"Equatorial Guinea." World News. *Guardian Online*. http://www.guardian.co.uk/world/equatorial-guinea

"Introducing Equatorial Guinea." Country Profiles. *Lonely Planet Press Online*. http://www.lonelyplanet.com/equatorial-guinea

"Languages of Equatorial Guinea." Country Index. *Ethnologue Online*. http://www.ethnologue.com/show_country.asp?name=Equatorial+Guinea

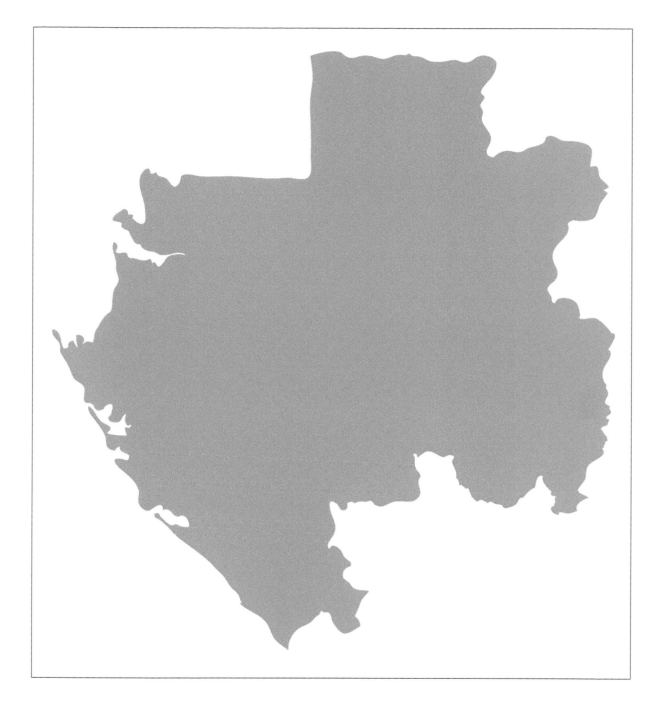

GABON

Introduction

The African nation of Gabon, or the Gabonese Republic, is located along the equator in West Africa. Gabon's success during the global rise in oil prices in the 1970s made the country unique among its West African neighbors. The standard of living and the expectations of Gabon's multiethnic population reflect this period of great wealth. Nonetheless, serious economic challenges continue to hinder Gabon's development. Gabon has worked with foreign aid organizations and governments to address its issues with widespread poverty and epidemic diseases. The country has also taken steps to improve its infrastructure.

Ruled for over four decades (1967–2009) by a single leader, Omar Bongo Ondimba, the country remained relatively stable. In the later years of Bongo's rule, however, weaknesses in the political system were exposed. Nevertheless, in 2009 Bongo's son, Ali Bongo Ondimba, was elected president, and the legacy of national stability has continued to the present.

Gabonese culture blends traditional African cultural elements with French elements, which remain as the legacy of France's colonial occupation of the country. Elements of traditional African culture include the country's open-air markets, which are often used as social centers; traditional crafts such as the wood-carved masks of the Fang, one of Gabon's largest ethnicities; and the country's oral traditions, which have influenced both Gabonese music and literature.

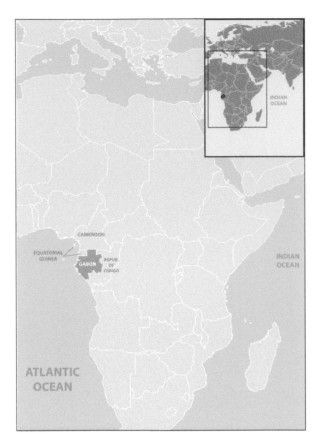

GENERAL INFORMATION

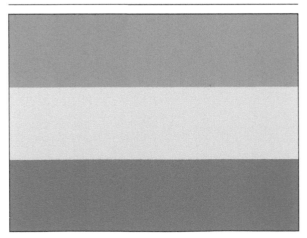

Official Language: French
Population: 1,705,336 (2015 estimate)
Currency: Communaute Financiere Africaine (CFA) franc
Coins: Coins are available in denominations of 1, 2, 5, 10, 25, 50, 100, and 500 francs.
Land Area: 257,667 square kilometers (99,485 square miles)
Water Area: 10,000 square kilometers (3,861 square miles)
National Motto: "Union, Travail, Justice" (French for "Union, Work, Justice")
National Anthem: "La Concorde"
Capital: Libreville
Time Zone: GMT +1
Flag Description: The flag of Gabon depicts three equal horizontal color bars: one green (top), one gold (middle), and one blue (bottom). The gold bar represents the equator, while the blue and green represent the sea and forest, respectively.

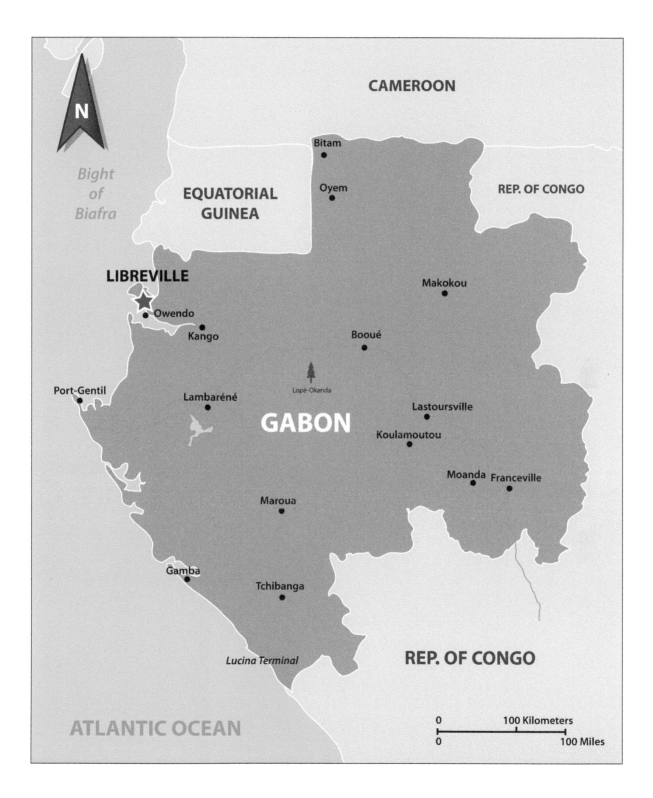

Principal Cities by Population (2014):

- Libreville (797,003)
- Port-Gentil (150,484)
- Franceville, or Masuku (59,231)
- Moando (41,564)
- Oyem (42,556)
- Mouila (30,974)

Population

Gabon has over 40 ethnic groups, most of which are offshoots of the Bantu ethno-linguistic family. Of these, the most prominent are the Fang, Bapounou, Nzebi, and the Obamba tribes. In addition, Gabon is home to people derived from other African and European settlers, including residents of French extraction and those who hold dual nationality.

It is estimated that over 80 percent of the Gabonese population lives in urban areas, with the capital, Libreville, also the country's largest city. In Libreville and other cities, European expatriates constitute a significant portion of the population and there are roughly10,700 French or dual French citizens living in Gabon.

Languages

French is the national language of Gabon and is spoken by over 90 percent of the population. Ethnic languages, such as Fang, Myene, and Eschira, are also common, especially in rural districts and villages. There are also significant pockets of Bapunu speakers in the south and Bandgabi speakers in and around the town of Franceville. French and English are commonly taught in the Gabonese school system.

Native People & Ethnic Groups

Gabon's coastal plains and lush interior were probably first settled by pygmies, ancestors of whom survive in small pockets in Gabon's most inaccessible areas. During the 11th century and after, however, neighboring Bantu tribes migrated into the region, displacing most of the pygmies.

At present, the descendants of the original tribes fall into ten large ethnic groups within Gabon, with the most dominant group being the Fang. Coming mostly from the north and east of present-day Gabon, the Fang have stamped traditional Gabonese life with their own language and culture. Other major ethnic groups, the Mbédé (including the Téké and Mbété) and the Eshira, come from the southeast and southwest, respectively. The Myéné settled most of Gabon's coastal plain areas.

Religions

The religious composition of Gabon was heavily influenced by the nation's European period. Between 55 and 75 percent of the population observes some form of Christianity. Animist religions are practiced in rural communities and occasionally in major cities. The practice of Islam has been growing in Gabon in recent years, but only accounts less than one percent of the population as a whole.

Climate

Gabon's location in West Africa along the equator gives the country its tropical climate. High temperatures range between 27° Celsius (81° Fahrenheit) and 31° Celsius (88° Fahrenheit) throughout the year.

The dry season lasts from May until September and is followed by another short dry season in December. Even during these seasons of reduced rainfall, the climate remains extremely hot and muggy. The frequent downpours during the rest of the year add up to rainfall amounts in excess of 250 centimeters (100 inches) in Libreville, and 380 centimeters (150 inches) further up the coast.

ENVIRONMENT & GEOGRAPHY

Topography

Bounded on three sides by Cameroon, Equatorial Guinea, and the Republic of the Congo, Gabon's lush, hilly interior gives way to a narrow coastal plain (30 to 200 kilometers or 18 to 125 miles wide) where the land meets the South Atlantic Ocean. Most of the country is actually part of the massive Ogowe River basin.

The Ogowe River, at over 160 kilometers (100 miles) long, cuts across the center of Gabon from the mountainous inland to the ocean. The mountain peaks in Gabon's interior rise to a height of up to 1,574 meters (5,165 feet) on the top of Mount Iboundiki. A rocky escarpment, almost 100 kilometers (60 miles) wide, separates the mountains from the coastal plain. Where riverbeds cut through the escarpment, deep channels have formed in the land.

In the northern slip of Gabon's coastline, estuaries, bays, and deltas spread out into the Atlantic. However, where the Ogwe meets the Atlantic to the south, mangrove swamps and lagoons make navigation difficult. In the southern and eastern portions of the country, grass savannahs provide habitats for rare and endangered species.

Libreville is located on the northern banks of the Gabon River, as the river expands into an estuary that leads to the Gulf of Guinea. The city is surrounded by year-round vegetation due to the numerous small streams branching from the Gabon River. Most of the urban area is arranged on a plateau rising to 15 meters (49 feet) above sea level. Portions of the city were built to have scenic views of the Gulf of Guinea, while other residential zones are arranged along the river.

Plants & Animals

Gabon's oil money and relatively low population have helped preserve the country's tropical rainforests. With only one percent of the original forestland sacrificed to agriculture, Gabon's rainforests still cover about three-quarters of the country's area. The rainforests, wetlands, and savannahs are home to incredible variety of plant and animal species.

Gabon has a collection of rare hardwood trees: ebony, purple heart, mahogany, and okume among them. Gabon has an equally impressive list of rare animals, including monkeys, baboons, lemurs, toucans, vipers, pythons, gorillas, hippopotamus, antelope, buffalo, crocodiles, and elephants to name only a few.

CUSTOMS & COURTESIES

Greetings

In Gabon, older people are likely to greet each other with several kisses on the cheeks or forehead. Younger people tend to use more Western-style manners, and will generally shake hands with each other. It is acceptable for women to kiss each other on the cheek. When men and women are interacting, they may kiss each other on the cheek or shake hands. Casual, friendly touching between the sexes is not frowned upon in Gabon. People are customarily addressed using honorific titles and last names, unless directed otherwise.

There are numerous ethnic groups in Gabon, and each has its own language. However, French is the dominant and accepted language. As such "Bonjour" ("Good day") is a common phrase of greeting. "Salut" ("Hello") is used in informal situations. In Fang, "Mbolo" ("Hello") is common. Greetings customarily involve inquiries into another's well-being and health.

Gestures & Etiquette

Gabon has been influenced by European manners and attitudes when it comes to gestures and etiquette. Additionally, it is a heavily Christian country, so behavior is not subject to many of the customs that are found in Muslim cultures. Therefore, most of the gestures that are considered appropriate in Western culture would likely be appropriate and understood in Gabon. For example, steady eye contact—and not a stare—is acceptable. It is not considered unusual for men to hold hands as they walk together, as this is seen as a sign of brotherhood. Pointing one's finger or whistling loudly to get attention are gestures that are considered rude. Showing the soles of one's feet or standing too close are small gestures that are frowned upon. Speaking to someone, especially an elder, with one's hands on their hips is considered disrespectful.

Eating/Meals

In Gabon, the main meal takes place during the middle of the day, and traditionally requires the shutting down of businesses for three hours starting at noon. The evening meal is generally light, often consisting of leftovers. In the case of a special holiday, the main meal may be served at night. In urban areas, the influence of the French is evident. In Libreville especially, restaurants of all kinds can be found.

Visiting

Gifts are not required when visiting in Gabon. If a gift is intended, flowers are an appropriate choice. The Gabonese do not insist that visitors remove their shoes before entering their homes, but it is polite for guests to take off their hats. People eat with either their left or right hand, but do not eat with both hands. Unlike in some cultures, it is all right to pass food or give gifts with the left hand. It is also important to at least try what food is offered, as not doing so might be considered disrespectful. In general, visiting is common, and often unexpected and unplanned in rural areas. Hospitality is generally expected to be reciprocated.

LIFESTYLE

Family

The Gabonese family, particularly in rural areas, is very traditional, and loyalty and familial obligations are important. The children live with their parents and the extended family lives nearby, and all very involved in each other's lives. Women are responsible for most chores, including cleaning, going to the market, working in the garden or the fields, and making food. When older children are at home, they help with the chores and farm work as well. Villages often function as an extended family.

In traditional communities, a woman may have to prove their fertility, and thus have children out of wedlock. If the marriage fails, these children live with the father. The Gabonese

typically marry within ethnicities, but not generally within villages. Families continue to wield significant influence in a child's spouse.

Housing

In cities, housing can vary from mansions to crowded apartment buildings. Cement is considered a sign of wealth, so government buildings and homes of the upper-class citizens are typically grand cement structures. Large cities such as Libreville often have rings of shanty towns (informal settlements) around them, where the workers who perform menial or domestic work within the city live.

In rural areas and villages, some houses might be built of wood, bark, or bricks. Roofs might be made of corrugated tin and brick houses may have a cement coating. The most important or wealthy citizens in the village might build their houses from cinder blocks. The simplest structures are huts that may use palm fronds for roofs. For example, the Babongo live in traditional, clustered huts called tudi that are made from forest material, such as saplings and leaves. The Mitsogo peoples traditionally live in huts made of mud.

Men and women traditionally have their own separate areas. Women have a separate kitchen hut where they keep pots, pans, and wood for fires, along with beds for resting. Men traditionally have an open space with low walls lined with benches and no roof. It is called a "corps de garde," or gathering of men, and used for socializing.

Food

Starches such as plantains, yams, or rice are typically part of any meal. Cassava, also called manioc or yucca, is a root that is used in a number of ways. It can be steamed, or pounded into flour, which is commonly cooked into porridge. Feuilles de manioc, or manioc leaves, are often added to stews and sauces. Batons de manioc is made by pounding the interior of a manioc root into a past, stuffing the leaves with the paste, and then steaming them. (The leaves are not eaten.)

It is important for people to choose the right kind of manioc—the leaves of the bitter kind (used in the batons de manioc) are poisonous and cannot be eaten. The leaves of the other kind, "sweet" manioc, can be eaten, although some scientists suspect that frequent consumption of these could still be harmful.

Meat and fish is common in urban areas. In rural areas, bushmeat is commonly eaten and includes antelopes, gazelles, wild boar, crocodiles, or snakes. Palm fruits, are known worldwide for the oil they produce. In Gabon, they are part of one of the most popular dishes, le poulet nyembwe, or chicken in nyembwe sauce. The sauce is made from crushed red palm fruits that are mixed with cayenne and chili peppers. The sap from the palm tree can be fermented and made into wine. Bananas and mangoes grow easily and are common dessert items or snacks. Sometimes bananas are breaded, fried, and served with sugar.

Life's Milestones

In Gabon, the celebration of life's milestones traditionally features the use of masks and dancing, and exact rituals vary with each ethnic group. For example, in Punu culture, stilted male dancers wear mukudj masks, which emphasize feminine traits, at funerals of elder males. Masks are also worn to offer protection during the passage from childhood to adulthood. Some groups have ceremonies that initiate boys and girls into adulthood. During these rituals, the girls and boys may spend a period of time in the forest with teachers, wise men, sorcerers, and medicine men. The acceptance into the bwiti religion also is marked with an elaborate ceremony involving music and dance.

Funerals are not seen as an end, but rather a transition to another phase of life for the deceased. The Babongo, one of the pygmy groups, believe that a dead spirit can haunt a village unless it is cleansed. The women wash the body and wrap it in cloth. The men then bury it in the forest. Afterward, the women use kaolin (soft white clay) to pain their faces white, and sing

Masks are an important part of the celebrations and rituals associated with life's milestones in Gabon.

and dance. The white symbolizes the purification of the spirit and the singing and dancing brings the dead person to rest. This lasts for three days. White is used in many ceremonies in Gabon to represent spirituality or purification.

CULTURAL HISTORY

Art

Undiscovered by Europeans until the 15th century, the peoples of Gabon were able to develop their own artistic traditions without outside influence. Even into the 19th century, when the country became a French protectorate, Western-style art did not have a significant effect on Gabonese art. Rather, the art of Gabon had an important effect on French art, as early modernist painters adapted the shapes and colors of art from the colonies into their own work.

The Fang, an ethnic group who moved into present-day Gabon in the 18th century, are known for their sculpture. The most famous pieces are parts of reliquaries, which are boxes or containers that held the bones (or other relics) of particularly important or wise ancestors that featured sculptures on top. The sculptures are known as "bieri," and are an important part of the Fang cult of the ancestor. The bieri, which were generally made of wood treated with oil, were used in ceremonies where they were consulted before important decisions or events.

The sculptures varied according to region. Some Fang groups used sculptures of just heads to top the relic container, although there is a school of thought that those heads may have been connected to a body sculpture. Others made the full figures. Depending on the group that carved them, the figure might be long and thin or short and squat. The heads are sometimes large in proportion to the body, or the neck elongated, and facial expressions are often exaggerated. There are two-dimensional bieri as well.

Most of the bieri that exist today are without their containers of relics. This is partially due to European collectors' lack of interest in the relics. However, among the Fang themselves, the sculptures were not the important part of the reliquary—a sculpture could be left behind and another made, but the relics were irreplaceable.

The Fang people used masks for important events. The Ngil, an all-male society that administered justice, wore masks during rituals where they sentenced wrongdoers. The masks were typically long, with a heart- or triangle-shaped face painted white. The eyes were typically narrow slits and the nose was long and thin. The So, another Fang society, wore masks that represented an antelope with long curling horns. This was worn during an initiation ceremony that was known to last for months at a time.

The Punu are known for the creation of mukudj masks. These masks are made to look like a beautiful woman's face, and typically include a carved representation of a hairstyle worn by Punu women. The eyes are closed, as if meditating, and the faces are painted white, a color associated with spiritualism and beauty. Small carved patterns decorate the faces. The patterns are based on the number nine, such as groups of nine squares, or nine domes. In Punu culture, nine is a powerful number. It is associated with healing, and gives the wearer the ability to perform the necessary rituals. The masks were traditionally worn by stilted male members during ceremonies for special events, such as funerals, initiations, or other occasions important to the village.

Drama

Theater in the European tradition began to appear in Gabon in the 20th century. Victor de Paul Nyonda (1918–1995), often called the "Father of Gabonese Theater," started out as a politician, but by the 1980s was concentrating on writing plays. His early plays dealt with the history and traditional culture of Gabon. Near the end of his life, he turned his eye toward criticism of contemporary Gabon. In 2000, Gabon established the Paul Nyonda Prize for young writers in honor of his contribution to Gabon's literary growth. Writers from other media also contributed to the theater—Laurent Owondo wrote the play *Les Impurs* (The Impure Ones) and Josephine Kama Bongo, before she reinvented herself as singer Patience Dabany, wrote the plays *Obali* and *Ayouma*.

Music & Dance

Music is an important part of the culture of Gabon. For example, music serves an important role in the initiation ceremony of the Bwiti religion, which incorporates ancestral worship, animism, and Christianity. The ceremony has been adopted by many of the peoples of Gabon, including the forest peoples and the Fang people. The initiation ceremony features a larger than normal dose of iboga, a hallucinogenic plant, that results in a deep trance. Musical accompaniment aids the initiate throughout the journey. The music uses repetition and a variety of contrasting rhythms.

Different instruments perform the traditional music that is part of the ceremony. The mouthbow is a bow with two strings where the player's lips are used to create varying tones. The bake is a percussion instrument played by several people at once, helping to create the mix of rhythms. Rattles, drums, and a sacred harp called the ngombi are also played. Since the people believe there are no voices in the land of the dead, there isn't any singing during the first part of the initiation. However, vocals are added toward the end when the initiate is returning to this world.

The pygmies, or forest peoples, are particularly known for their distinctive vocal technique called "jodel." The singer creates a yodeling type sound by quickly switching back and forth from their chest voice, or the part of the voice used for lower notes, to the head voice, the part that makes higher sounds. Pygmy music features complicated rhythms and repetition, but allow for improvisation on the part of the players. Their instruments include a variety of harps, drums, and the flute. The pygmies create songs that tell about their lives, and use them for events such as initiations into secret societies or elephant hunting.

Rituals and ceremonies in Gabon often feature dancing. In the Bwiti religion, the ngoze ceremony is a time when all members gather together to ingest the hallucinogenic iboga plants. The ritual generally lasts all night or longer for special occasions, and includes music and dancing. The dancing is taken very seriously—the local Bwiti leadership includes someone who is given the role of dance director. There is specific choreography for each type of dance. An often-seen dance involves a long line of people, with the leader executing a move that the rest than imitate until it reaches the end of the line. In another dance, performers use a lit torch.

Dances are used during important occasions such as funerals, and costumes and makeup feature prominently. In a funeral dance of the Bakoya people, a pygmy tribe, dancers' bodies are dotted with white makeup and they carry sprigs of leaves. These are meant to keep the dancers and mourners safe from evil spirits. The mukudj dancers of the Punu people are male but wear female masks.

The masks, with their beautiful serene features, are meant to be a contrast with the physically demanding, wild dance. The mukudj dancers perform on stilts that can be up to 3 meters (nine feet) tall, placing them high above their audiences. Dancers train from childhood in order to perform the difficult moves while balancing on the stilts. The complexity of the dance is such that the dancers are regarded as extraordinary people who are gifted with special, mysterious powers.

Literature

Gabon's oral tradition did not translate into written literature until recently. Due to France's long relationship with the country, French has been the language of choice for Gabonese writers since literary works began to first appear in the 20th century. A landmark event was the publication of *Contes Gabonais* (Gabonese Tales, 1967), a collection of folklore by André Raponda-Walker (1871–1968). In the 1970s, a number of Gabonese poets arose with the establishment of a supportive Ministry of Culture, including Georges Rawiri (1932–2006) and Quentin Ben Mongaryas (1948–). Gabonese novelists began to achieve recognition in the 1980s. The novels of Angèle Ntyugwetondo Rawiri's (1954–2010) deal with the lives of women and Laurent Owondo's (1948–) novel *Au bout du silence* (At the End of the Silence, 1985) made him one of Gabon's best-known literary figures.

CULTURE

Arts & Entertainment

No longer isolated, contemporary artists in Gabon often find themselves working to preserve their culture while also incorporating new forms. In the 20th century, one of the most influential figures on the Gabon musical scene is Pierre Akendengué (1943–). Trained in France, Akendengué combined elements of the French pop song with traditional music from Gabon. His work has covered everything from protest songs to new orchestrations of classical pieces inflected with Gabonese rhythms.

Patience Dabany (1944–) is one of Gabon's most famous contemporary singers. She was originally known to Gabonese as Josephine Bongo, the former wife of El Hadj Omar Bongo (1935–2009), who became president in 1967. She was the founder and lead singer of a group called Kounabeli (Superstars). She divorced her husband in 1986 and began recording under the name Patience Dabany. A drummer as well as a singer, she is known for music that mixes sounds from her Bateke culture with current music. Other popular musicians include Oliver N'Goma (1959–2010), a Gabonese singer whose music shows a reggae influence, and Didier Ontchanga, an African pop artist whose sound is reminiscent of the music from the Caribbean islands. A great deal of music, such as hip-hop and reggae, is imported from other areas.

Lack of funding has long inhibited the growth of filmmaking in Gabon. However, the establishment in the early 1990s of the Centre National du Cinéma Gabonais has begun to have a positive effect, with the number of Gabonese films increasing over the last two decades. One of the most successful filmmakers from Gabon is Imunga Ivanga (1967–). His 2000 film *Dôlè*, about poor young people in Libreville, won awards at several small film festivals and played at the famous Cannes Film Festival. Ivanga's 2006 film *L'Ombre de Liberty* dealt with a man's search for a cure for his dying son. Finding money and resources continues to be a battle for most Gabonese filmmakers.

Cultural Sites & Landmarks

Gabon is home to one World Heritage Site, as designated by the United Nations Educational, Scientific and Cultural Organization (UNESCO): the Ecosystem and Relict Cultural Landscape of Lopé-Okanda. The Lopé-Okanda National Park is notable both for the way it shows the natural history of Gabon and the evolution of civilization in the area. It includes a variety of environments, from dense, tropical rainforests, to wide open savannahs. A number of endangered species have made their homes there, and the River Oguooe, Gabon's most important river, winds

its way through the region. The Oguooe River valley was an important stop along the way for many migrating peoples in Africa, and evidence of settlements dating back 400,000 years can be found in the valley. Caves and other shelters, as well as ironworks, have been found in the area.

One of the most striking remnants of early civilization in the valley is the numerous examples of rock art. Dating back to the Iron Age, petroglyphs are inscriptions found on the surface of rocks. They often appear to have been chipped with metal tools, rather than carved into the surface of the rocks. About 1,800 petroglyphs have been found in the Lopé-Okanda area. The Kongo Boumba, a site located right on the river, contains 280 petroglyphs. Like most of the rock art in Gabon, the dominant design is concentric circles arranged in patterns. Some of the rocks at Kongo Boumba also include wavy lines weaving around the circles; others include lizards. One rock includes what appears to be a throwing knife, and another has a figure that appears to be a mammal. In September 2002, to build upon the country's natural beauty and heritage, a network of thirteen national parks was announced by the government.

Libreville, Gabon's capital, is home to numerous cultural site and landmarks, including the Ebando Association, found north of Libreville, which teaches visitors about the Bwiti religion. For a price, visitors can undergo the bwiti initiation, but it is an extremely complex ceremony. The Cathedral of St. Michael is another notable landmark. Its carved columns, each depicting a different scene from the Bible, were the work of a blind Gabonese artist. Another cultural site is the Schweitzer Hospital in Lambaréné, which is now a museum. The hospital was founded by Albert Schweitzer (1875–1965), a German doctor and musician who spent many years in Gabon in the early 20th century treating the people and studying infectious diseases. In the center of downtown Libreville is the Marché de Mont-Bouet, the city's largest open-air market, in which hundreds of vendors sell food and local crafts. The market is a popular destination for tourists and also serves as a meeting place for friends and family.

Libraries & Museums

The Musée des Arts et Traditions du Gabon, in Libreville, contains a broad collection of art and artifacts from Gabon's indigenous cultures as well as from the various periods of occupation. The museum features a large collection of the masks that are important to the different groups found in Gabon. The National Museum of Gabon is also located in Libreville and houses a collection of Gabonese artifacts and cultural relics. The Sainte-Exupéry French Cultural Centre is a small museum dedicated to collections of art and photography documenting the French involvement in Libreville and the rest of the nation.

The National Library of Gabon is housed in Libreville. The library's collection is divided among several buildings, containing over 25,000 books in total with a focus on Gabonese and African history.

Holidays

The Gabonese celebrate their independence for three days every August. In addition, practicing Christians celebrate the major Christian holidays, like Easter and Christmas. The country's few Muslim citizens celebrate Ramadan (a holy month of fasting between sunrise and sunset), Eid el-Fitr (the feast that ends Ramadan), and Tabaski, memorializing Abraham's sacrifice to the Old Testament God.

Youth Culture

Given Gabon's widespread poverty, leisure time and activities for youth are limited in most areas. Youth in the country's urban areas have more access to global pop culture. International television programs, films, and music are popular, particularly hip-hop and reggae music. Both rural and urban youth enjoy football (soccer), and will often construct a ball out of discarded materials if proper equipment is unavailable. More recently, basketball has also become popular among young Gabonese.

Education in Gabon follows the French system, with 13 grades and a concluding baccalaureate exam. However, it is very difficult for students to complete the entire program since many lack funding and supplies. In addition, in rural areas, youth commonly leave school during harvest seasons to help their families work in the fields. The travel required of some students is also often time-consuming, and some students spend an entire day traveling and completing their studies at home. Girls are traditionally expected to complete the majority of domestic chores, further limiting their school attendance and educational opportunities.

SOCIETY

Transportation

Within Libreville and other cities, cars and motorcycles are the primary sources of transportation. For travel outside of the city, people may ride in crowded taxis, minibuses, or trucks. However, road travel is difficult during the rainy season, which lasts from October to May. Traffic moves on the right-hand side of the road. Walking is the most common form of transportation for people in rural areas.

Transportation Infrastructure

The Trans-Gabon Railway System, which opened in the late 1970s, is considered the easiest and most inexpensive way to travel around Gabon. It connects Gabon to several of the nation's other larger cities. In 2014, there were roughly 649 kilometers (403 miles) of railway. As of 2009, there were roughly 9,170 kilometers (5698 miles) of road, of which only 1,097 kilometers (682 miles) were paved. Libreville International Airport is the country's busiest airport and provides business to nearby hotels and restaurants in Libreville. As of 2013, Gabon had a total of 44 airports (14 paved, 30 unpaved).

Media & Communications

The majority of broadcast media in Gabon is state-controlled. The government, operating under Radiodiffusion-Television Gabonaise, runs the two main TV and radio stations and the only daily newspaper, *L'Union*; other newspapers are private and published on a biweekly or bimonthly schedule. Paid satellite television service is also available, and Radio France Internationale (RFI) is available through an FM relay.

The constitution states that there is freedom of the press, but the reality is quite different. Reporters Without Borders (RWB) ranked Gabon 129 out of 175 nations in its 2009 Worldwide Press Freedom Index. The state-run media broadcasts the views and interests of the ruling party, and the state has suspended newspapers for government criticism. Self-censorship remains common, as does the harassment of both foreign and national journalists. In order to save printing costs, some private newspapers print in Cameroon, but the papers are then subject to inspection when they are brought across the border. There are no laws that allow for access to information for the public or journalists.

Cell phones are the most popular form of personal communication in Gabon. According to government statistics in 2014, there are 17,200 fixed telephone lines, 3.6 million cell phone users. The World Factbook shows that, in 2014, there were only 164,800 users.

SOCIAL DEVELOPMENT

Standard of Living
Gabon ranked 112th out of 187 countries on the 2013 United Nations Human Development Index, which measures quality of life and standard of living indicators.

Because of an AIDS crisis and the prevalence of malaria, sleeping sickness, and a tuberculosis epidemic, the death rate is at 13.12 people per 1,000. The infant mortality is 46.07 deaths for every 1,000 children born (2015 estimate). Life expectancy is low at 52.04 years—52.53 for women and only 51.56 years for men.

Water Consumption
According to 2009 statistics from the World Health Organization (WHO), an estimated 87 percent of the population has access to an improved source of drinking water, while an estimated 36 percent have access to improved sanitation. Both figures are above the regional average. Access to clean water remains a problem in Libreville, the largest city, however, and other statistics suggest that only 30 percent of the rural population has access to clean or improved water sources. Improper waste disposal and unsustainable environmental policies are major contributors to Gabon's water problem. In 2011, the total renewable water resources were 164 cubic kilometers.

Education
Primary education is free in Gabon, but secondary schools are not. A number of private institutions provide secondary and post-graduate education for Gabonese, at varying fees and quality. Thanks to the discovery of oil in Gabon, the Gabonese have become accustomed to a higher standard of living. The government has subsidized busing for students and travel to France for advanced degrees. Incomes among many of Gabon's upper and middle classes have been sufficient to pay for the rising costs of education.

International watch organizations claim that educational standards are dropping noticeably throughout the country, while educational costs continue to rise. In 2003, the passing rate for high school leaving exams dropped from approximately 60 percent to only 35 percent.

Student riots broke out in the capital in 2004 after the announcement of further government cutbacks to schools and busing programs. Many blamed the disappointing educational system on government favoritism and corruption, but few see any signs of improvement in the near future.

In 2015, Gabon's overall literacy rate was an estimated 83.2 percent (85.3 percent for men, 81 percent for women).

Women's Rights
The constitution of Gabon grants women equal rights and the country is a signatory of the Convention on the Elimination of All Forms of Discrimination against Women (CEDAW). However, in practice, social and cultural traditions prevent women from achieving full rights

and equal status. The written law discriminates against women in areas such as marriage, divorce, and child custody and the civil code states that women should obey their husbands. Polygamy continues to be an issue—the law reduced the number of wives a man can legally have from 30 to four. Women divorced from a polygamist lose much of their property. In addition, dowries, or payment to prospective husbands, have been outlawed, but the practice still continues. Similarly, the tradition that a widow is supposed to remarry a man in her husband's family still holds strong, although women technically have the right to refuse this.

There are laws against domestic violence, but it is widespread and the police have not shown a willingness to get involved. Rape is also illegal, but it is very difficult for women to bring legal action against their attackers. Additionally, women who have been raped have little access to medical help. Women who are employed as domestic workers are often subjected to violence and sexual abuse. They have little chance of receiving any aid, particularly since many are refugees or illegally trafficked into the country. There is also no law prohibiting sexual harassment.

Women are granted equal access to education; however, the overall literacy rate for women in Gabon is markedly lower than that of men. Women do own businesses in Gabon, and there have been women in governmental and judicial positions, but the numbers are low. In 2002, President Bongo stated that each election list should have at least three women candidates, but that has resulted in little progress. A 2007 UN report showed that women held only 12 of the 49 positions in the Gabonese government, and there were just 26 women out of the 211 members of parliament.

In 2012, a total of 36 women held position in both the lower (18) and upper (18) house of parliament.

Health Care
Gabon's health care system started off promisingly with Dr. Albert Schweitzer's Nobel Prize-winning efforts to provide medical care to Gabon's native population. The health clinic that he began in a chicken coop in 1912 eventually grew into a sophisticated medical center. Though the nation now has an established network of hospitals and clinics, corruption seems to have prevented Gabon's government from following up on Schweitzer's early efforts until recently.

Gabon is in the midst of a health crisis stemming from the spread of HIV/AIDS. Officials estimate that between six and eight percent of Gabon's sexually active population is infected with the virus, and that the numbers are closer to eight percent within the national capital of Libreville. Malaria, tuberculosis, and sleeping sickness (a virus spread by bites from tsetse flies) are also rampant in the country. In 2014, the estimated number of people living with AIDS in Gabon is 47,500.

In recent years, Gabon's Health Ministry has begun funding the International Center for Medical Research in Franceville (CIRMF), which is studying the spread and treatment of malaria and sexually transmitted diseases. The Ministry has also set aggressive targets for reducing malaria infection rates by the year 2020. International health organizations continue to be concerned about the country's progress in fighting these diseases, however. Organizations within the country, and even officials within the government, claim that corruption is still channeling necessary funds away from health care goals. The nation has no national health care system; patients are expected to pay for increasingly expensive medical care on their own.

The rapid increase in AIDS cases and virulence of tuberculosis in the country are likely to make Gabon's population even more vulnerable to viruses and secondary infections. As of 2014, there were roughly 47,500 citizens living with HIV/AIDS. The total death count from the disease for 2014 was 1,500. Large disparities in wealth make health care inaccessible to a large portion of the population, and malnutrition seems to be on the rise, suggesting even greater vulnerability to disease.

GOVERNMENT

Structure

In 1472, the Portuguese became the first of the European empires to arrive in the area that is now Gabon. By the 16th century, French, Dutch, and British merchants had made Gabon's coastal ports a regular stop for slave trading, ivory, and tropical timbers. Britain outlawed slavery in its colonies in 1843, and in 1849, a group of freed slaves immigrated to Libreville (literally, "Freetown") in what was then the Congo to establish a new settlement.

With the establishment of Libreville, missionaries from all over Europe traveled to Gabon. In 1904, however, Congo moved its capital from Libreville to Brazzaville, paving the way for the French to annex Gabon to their territories in Equatorial Africa in 1910.

Although slavery was no longer considered acceptable by the European powers, the French unofficially forced Gabon's African inhabitants to work for the French corporations that controlled the country's economy. The Gabonese responded with a series of revolts, and finally succeeded in wresting their independence from the French in 1960. However, the French had already depleted most of the country's accessible timber and mineral reserves. The establishment of processing plants for uranium and manganese, and the discovery of oil in the 1970s brought about an explosion in the Gabonese economy and continues to keep Gabon's government stable.

Gabon is a republic with a multiparty presidential regime. The current constitution was adopted on March 14, 1991. Gabon's president is elected by popular vote to seven-year terms. The president appoints the prime minister who, in consultation with the president, appoints a council of ministers. The legislature is bicameral. The Senate has 91 members, elected by members of municipal councils and departmental assemblies. The National Assembly has 120 members, who are elected by popular vote to serve five-year terms. The last assembly elections were held on December 8, 2012.

Political Parties

The dominant political party in Gabon is the Gabonese Democratic Party (PDG). Although other political parties are technically allowed to operate in the country, Gabon is essentially a one-party state. The PDG has remained in power in Gabon since it gained independence from France, winning consecutive parliamentary elections since Gabon established a multiparty system in 1990. The PDG has operating factions in both France and the United States. Although their influence is minimal, other political parties in Gabon include the African Development Movement, the Common Movement for Development, and the Circle of Reformist Liberals.

The most recent presidential elections were held on August 30, 2009. Ali Bongo Ondimba (the late president's son) won the race with 41.7 percent of the votes. The next such elections will be held in 2016.

Local Government

Gabon is divided into nine provinces: Estuaire, Haut-Ogooue, Moyen-Ogooue, Ngounie, Nyanga, Ogooue-Ivindo, Ogooue-Lolo, Ogooue-Maritime, and Woleu-Ntem. A governor is appointed to each province by the president. Provinces are sub-divided into 36 prefectures and eight sub-prefectures. Political authority in Gabon is highly centralized.

Judicial System

The Gabonese judicial system is divided into supreme courts, appeal courts, and lower courts. There are several different supreme courts in Gabon's, each over seeing a different area of law. Gabon's Judicial Supreme Court (Cour de Cassation) oversees criminal, social, commercial, and civil legal matters. The Administrative Supreme Court (Conseil d'Etat) oversees legal matters pertaining to the executive branch of Gabon's government and the Accounting Supreme Court (Counseil d'Etat) presides over government financial matters.

Gabon's Constitutional Court consists of nine judges. The president, president of the state, and the National Assembly each appoint three judges to the constitutional court. The Court of State Security oversees matters of treason and criminal proceedings of government officials.

Taxation

Taxes in Gabon are considered high in comparison to other African countries. The country's general tax code includes a personal income tax and capital gains tax. Corporations operating in Gabon pay a flat tax on profits. The International Monetary Fund (IMF) has been critical of Gabon's tax infrastructure for being corrupt. In 2014, taxes consist of 27.5 percent of Gabon's total GDP.

Armed Forces

Gabon maintains a small military divided into several branches, including an army, navy, and air force, as well as a national police force. There is no conscription and the voluntary age for service is twenty.

Foreign Policy

Gabon's foreign policy is based on nonalignment, international advocacy, and regional stability. Stability and peace in Central Africa is a key focus, and the country favors economic development and mediation when dealing with inter-African issues. Gabon has been involved in peacemaking and mediation efforts in nearby war-torn nations such as Chad, the Central African Republic (CAR), Cote d'Ivoire, Angola, the Republic of Congo, the Democratic Republic of the Congo (DRC), and Burundi. Gabon added military support to the Central African Economic and Monetary Community (CEMAC) mission to the CAR. Gabon's strong regional presence also includes membership in regional institutions such as the Organisation for the Harmonisation of Business Law in Africa (OHADA), the Economic Community of Central African States (ECCAS/CEEAC). and the African Intellectual Property Organisation (OAPI).

Outside of Africa, Gabon has been steadily increasing the number of nations with which

it has diplomatic relations. It is involved in numerous international organizations, including the United Nations (UN); the World Bank; the African Union (AU); the Organization of the Islamic Conference (OIC); the Nonaligned Movement (NAM); the International Monetary Fund (IMF); and the World Trade Organization (WTO). In 2004, Gabon assumed the presidency of the UN General Assembly (UNGA).

Gabon maintains strong relations with the United States. The two countries maintain an important trading relationship that includes the US importation of oil and Gabon's purchasing of military equipment. The US has also provided training for the Gabonese armed forces, and also provided grants directed toward human rights, cultural preservation, and support for democracy.

Although Gabon and France have historically been close since France's official occupation of the region in 1885, relations between the nations have deteriorated in recent years. France has criticized Gabon's one-party system and leveled corruption charges at President Bongo, who held the office since 1967 until his death in June 2009. (In February 2009, the French government froze President Bongo's French bank accounts after accusing him of accepting a bribe to release a French businessman jailed in Gabon.) Gabon has also stated a claim to three small islands in Corisco Bay, which is along the Gabonese-Equatorial Guinea maritime boundary. Both countries agreed to UN mediation in 2004.

Human Rights Profile

International human rights law insists that states respect civil and political rights, and also promote an individual's economic, social and cultural rights. The United Nations (UN) Universal Declaration of Human Rights is recognized as the standard for international human rights. Its authors sought the counsel of the world's great thinkers, philosophers, and religious leaders, and were careful to create a document that reflects the core values shared by every world culture. To read this document or view the articles relating to cultural human rights, visit http://www.udhr.org/UDHR/default.htm.

Gabon's constitution is in line with the UDHR, stating that it guarantees such basic human rights as freedom from discrimination, freedom of religion, freedom of the press, protection from illegal search and seizure, and equal access to education. However, according to a 2007 U.S. government report, Gabon's human rights record is poor. It includes restrictions on privacy and freedom of the press, rampant government corruption, child labor, and discrimination against women and people with HIV/AIDS. The Gabonese government has made improvements in certain areas, such as launching an aggressive campaign against human trafficking, the prosecution of those involved in child labor, and the abolition of the death penalty in 2007.

Gabon's constitution allows for the freedom of press and speech. However, the majority of the broadcast media is government-owned or affiliated, and self-censorship is widely practiced. In addition, all newspapers refrain from presidential criticism and both foreign and regional journalists have been detained on several occasions. Libel also can be considered a criminal offense and punishable by imprisonment. President Bongo has also threatened to revoke the passports of overseas citizens who criticize the government.

Arbitrary arrest and detention continues to be a human rights concern in Gabon. Security forces were responsible for numerous deaths and conducted warrantless searches. Prison conditions are also harsh and the abuse and torture of prisoners is widely reported. Exacerbating the situation is an alleged corrupt judicial system and an autocratic government that has been accused of conducting unfair elections. Widespread discrimination is also commonplace and directed at women, non-Africans, and those with HIV/AIDS. Amnesty International (AI) has also reported systemic discrimination against the Ba'aka, one of the indigenous pygmy groups that live in the forests of Gabon. Child trafficking and the ritualistic killing of children have also been reported.

ECONOMY

Overview of the Economy

The economy of Gabon is stronger than that of many African nations, but the country is still plagued by high levels of government debt, poverty, and a high unemployment rate. Oil production and refinement is the primary industry in Gabon and accounts for over 80 percent of the nation's exports and 40 percent of the gross domestic product (GDP). Including oil production, industrial manufacturing accounts for over 59 percent of the GDP and employs 15 percent of the total population. Oil production has been declining since the 1990s; this decline has contributed to the nation's financial difficulties. In 2014, Gabon's gross domestic product (GDP) was estimated at $36.35 billion (USD). The per capita GDP is approximately $22,900 (USD).

France is Gabon's most important trading partner, accounting for 20 percent of imported products. China is the largest export partner with 15.8 percent of the nation's exports. Other trading partners include Japan, Australia, the United States, and South Korea.

Industry

The oil industry accounts for about 61.7 percent of Gabon's income, primarily through petroleum extraction and refining. Though its dependence on other industries was alleviated by the discovery of oil reserves in the 1970s, the country still relies on the mining and export of manganese, gold mining, chemical production, ship repair, food and beverage export, textile manufacturing, cement production, and the timber industry. Libreville is the major hub for the Gabonese lumber industry and is also a globally important shipbuilding and ship repair facility. Libreville's ports ship lumber to Europe and to other African nations.

Labor

A lack of adequate employment has contributed to the sparse population of Gabon, except in cities like Libreville, where Gabonese can often find employment in the services and hospitality industries. The services industry employs 25 percent of the national population and over 50 percent of the population of Libreville.

Energy/Power/Natural Resources

French colonizers first mined Gabon for its precious metals and minerals. The country still has supplies of diamond, niobium, manganese, uranium, gold, timber, and iron ore, as well as hydropower. The country's most valuable resources by far, however, have been the oil and natural gas reserves that now seem to be reaching a state of depletion.

Fishing

Increased attention is being paid to Gabon's fishing industry as the reality of decreasing oil revenues becomes clearer. Industrialized fishing makes up approximately 4.5 percent of Gabon's GDP, though this figure does not include subsistence fishing. Large numbers of tilapia are fished each year from the waters off Gabon and the region is also home to tuna. Financial support from Japan has helped to improve Gabon's fishing infrastructure. In 2002, an estimated 9,000 tons of fish were harvested in Gabon, as well as 2,000 tons of shrimp.

Forestry

Forestry is Gabon's second largest export industry. There are over 400 species of trees in Gabon and over 80 percent of the country's territory is forested. Gabon is the world's largest supplier of the hardwood known as okume, which is used in the construction of plywood. In August 2010, the French timber firm GEB was purchased by China for $87 million, making it one of the dominant players in Gabon's forestry industry. Further development of Gabon's forestry industry has been hampered by its lack of sufficient transportation infrastructure. Development of the country's forestry industry continues. It is estimated that 25 percent of Gabon's forest resources remain untapped.

Mining/Metals

In addition to petroleum, Gabon is one of the world's leading producers of manganese, which is used to make steel and aluminum alloy. In addition, Gabon has limited resources of gold, diamond, uranium, and iron ore. Both Chinese and Canadian companies have worked with Gabon in the effort to further develop its mineral resources.

Agriculture

Agriculture is an important source of employment for the Gabonese, and approximately 60 percent of the population is involved in either subsistence or production agriculture. Despite its prevalence, agricultural exports only account for 6 percent of the GDP. Gabonese farms produce a variety of fruits and vegetables, as well as a number of plantation products, including rubber, cocoa, and sugar. Gabonese farms also produce coffee and palm oil. More than half of the country's labor force works in the agriculture sector. The labor force for agriculture in Gabon represents roughly half of the population.

Animal Husbandry

Gabonese raise numerous animals for domestic consumption, including cattle, hogs, sheep, goats, and chickens. The country's livestock industry has been negatively affected by the tsetse fly, which causes a deadly disease of the vertebrae in cattle. Experts have referred to the fly as the "poverty fly" because it kills off animals that could be used for food or used to harvest fields. Because of problems with the tsetse fly, Gabon relies on expensive imports of beef.

Tourism

Gabon's vast expanses of unspoiled tropical wilderness make it a natural draw for eco-tourists. Over 70 percent of Gabon remains undeveloped jungle habitat and the nation is becoming widely known, and visited, for its wildlife and other natural features. Tourist excursions from Libreville offer some of the best opportunities to observe gorillas in the wild. However, the country's infrastructure is underdeveloped and wildlife reserves and forested areas are difficult to access.

Kirsten Anderson, Amy Witherbee, Micah Issitt

DO YOU KNOW?

- The Trans-Gabon Railway is one of the most extensive rail projects ever undertaken in Africa. The railway project nearly left the country bankrupt when expenditures exceeded the budget. Plans for the railroad began in the 19th century, but the program was not approved and funded until the 1970s.

- Archeologists have found stone spearheads in Gabon that date back to 7000 BCE.

Bibliography

Bacquart, Jean-Baptiste. *The Tribal Arts of Africa*. New York: Thames and Hudson, 1998.

Frank, Katherine. *A Voyager Out: The Life of Mary Kingsley*. New York: Tauris Parke Paperbacks, 2005.

Gardinier, David and Douglas A. Yates. *Historical Dictionary of Gabon*. Lanham, Maryland: Scarecrow Press, Inc. 2006.

Hickendorff, Annelies. *Gabon (Bradt Travel Guide)*. Guilford, CT: Globe Pequot Press, 2014.

Ondo, Bonaventure Mve. *Wisdom and Initiation in Gabon: A Philosophical Analysis of Fang Tales, Myths, and Legends*. Lanham, MD: Lexington Books, 2013.

Works Cited

Gemma Pitcher, et al. "Lonely Planet Africa." Victoria: *Lonely Planet Publications*. 2007.

Philip M. Peek and Kwesi Yankah. "African Folklore: An Encyclopedia." Oxford: *Taylor & Francis*. 2004.

http://74.125.47.132/search?q=cache:tkn4U0rAPncJ:www. chr.up.ac.za/hr_docs/constitutions/docs/ GabonC%2520(english%2520summary)(rev),doc+gabon +constitution&hl=en&ct=clnk&cd=2&gl=us (Gabonese Constitution)

http://aflit.arts.uwa.edu.au/CountryGabonEN.html

http://globaledge.msu.edu/CountryInsights/history. asp?countryID=93&regionID=5

http://inadvertentgardener.wordpress.com/2006/11/page/2/

http://library.stanford.edu/depts/ssrg/africa/gabon.html

http://mbrugger.myweb.uga.edu/life2.html

http://news.bbc.co.uk/2/hi/africa/7912545.stm

http://spot.pcc.edu/~mdembrow/ivangainterview.htm

http://worldmusic.nationalgeographic.com/worldmusic/ view/page.basic/country/content.country/gabon_486

http://www.africaguide.com/culture/tribes/pygmies.htm

http://www.afrol.com/News/gab003_womens_rights.htm

http://www.amnestyusa.org/all-countries/gabon/page. do?id=1011274

http://www.amnestyusa.org/all-countries/gabon/page. do?id=1011274

http://www.bbc.co.uk/tribe/tribes/babongo/

http://www.bbc.co.uk/tribe/tribes/babongo/

http://www.bbc.co.uk/tribe/tribes/babongo/

http://www.bradshawfoundation.com/central-africa/gabon. php

http://www.chrysler.org/wom/wom0201.asp

http://www.forafricanart.com/Punu--Gabon_ep_28-1.html

http://www.gabonmagazine.com/images/G10-ENGLISH/ G10.palmoil.p18-23.pdf

http://www.gabonmagazine.com/images/G11-ENGLISH/ G11-pp22-25.pdf

http://www.genuineafrica.com/Art_Of_the_Fang.htm

http://www.hughes.com/HUGHES/Rooms/DisplayPages/ LayoutInitial?pageid=PAGE00000440&Container=com. webridge.entity.Entity[OID[ACE5D81A9C865B4D917F F96CAABD6273]]

http://www.ibogaine.org/samorini.html

http://www.ibogaine.org/samorini.html

http://www.infoplease.com/ce6/ent/A0856498.html

http://www.irinnews.org/country.aspx?CountryCode=GA& RegionCode=WA

http://www.irinnews.org/country.aspx?CountryCode=GA& RegionCode=WA

http://www.janes.com/extracts/extract/jwr/jwr_0216.html

http://www.legabon.org/livre/livredor_en.php

http://www.lonelyplanet.com/gabon/transport/getting- around

http://www.metmuseum.org/toah//ho/10/sfc/ho_2000.177. htm

http://www.metmuseum.org/toah//ho/10/sfc/ho_2000.177. htm

http://www.nationalgeographic.com/adventure/news/gabon- josh-ponte.html

http://www.nmafa.si.edu/exhibits/journey/guardian.html (reliquary)

http://www.novelguide.com/a/discover/jwec_03/ jwec_03_00178.html

http://www.nytimes.com/2007/10/05/arts/design/05afri. html

http://www.pygmies.info/baka/dances.html

http://www.pygmies.info/baka/music.html http://www. africaguide.com/culture/tribes/pygmies.htm

http://www.rebirth.co.za/fang/fang_mask_history.htm

http://www.rebirth.co.za/masks1.htm
http://www.state.gov/g/drl/rls/hrrpt/2007/100482.htm
http://www.state.gov/r/pa/ei/bgn/2826.htm
http://www.tageo.com/index-e-gb-cities-GA.htm
    (population)
http://www.tribalarts.com/feature/kwele/index5.html
http://www.uiowa.edu/~africart/toc/people/fang.html
http://www.voanews.com/english/archive/2007-10/2007-
    10-02-voa84.cfm

http://www.worldartandantiques.com/waagallery/v/fang/
http://www.worldtravelguide.net/country/95/
    communications/Africa/Gabon.html
http://www.worldtravelguide.net/country/95/top_things_to_
    see_and_do/Africa/Gabon.html
http://www.worldtraveltips.net/africa/view.
    cgi?country=Gabon
https://www.cia.gov/library/publications/the-world-
    factbook/print/gb.html

Wassu stone circles near burial sites in Gambia. iStock/trevkitt.

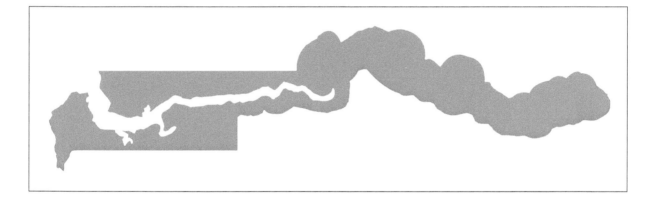

GAMBIA,
Republic of the

Introduction

The Republic of The Gambia is a West African nation whose territory is essentially an enclave of Senegal. Considered mainland Africa's smallest country, Gambia's long, slender territory stretches along the Gambia River from the North Atlantic Ocean on Africa's western coast. Once part of an expansive 14th-century Mali Empire, the region was divided up during colonial wars between the French and British during the 17th, 18th, and 19th centuries. The colonial divisions left The Gambia with a densely populated river valley, but few natural resources.

Banjul, the proclaimed gateway to West Africa, is the capital of Gambia. The British built it on an island at the mouth of the Gambia River. The lack of space in Banjul proper has spurred the rapid development of the suburban communities on the nearby shores of the river. As a result, Banjul is one of the few capitals in the developing world to have experienced a loss rather than an influx of population in the late 20th and early 21st centuries.

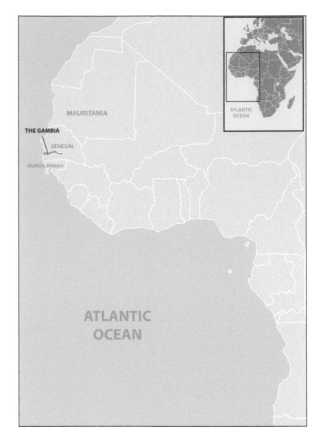

GENERAL INFORMATION

Official Language: English
Population: 1,967,709 (2015 estimate)
Currency: Gambian dalasi
Coins: The Gambian dalasi is divided into 100 bututs; coins are available in denominations of 1, 5, 10, 25, and 50 bututs, and 1 dalasi.

Land Area: 10,000 square kilometers (3,861 square miles)
Water Area: 1,295 square kilometers (500 square miles)
National Motto: "Progress, Peace, Prosperity"
National Anthem: "For The Gambia, Our Homeland"
Capital: Banjul
Time Zone: GMT +0
Flag Description: The flag of The Gambia (or Gambia) features a tricolor design consisting of horizontal bands of red (top), dark blue (middle), and green (bottom). The bands are separated by white fimbriations, or small stripes of color, with the middle blue band two-thirds the size of the other bands. The red represents the sun, the blue symbolizes the Gambia River, and the green represents the country's fertility and forests.

Population

About 99 percent of Gambians are of African descent. The most significant tribal affiliations

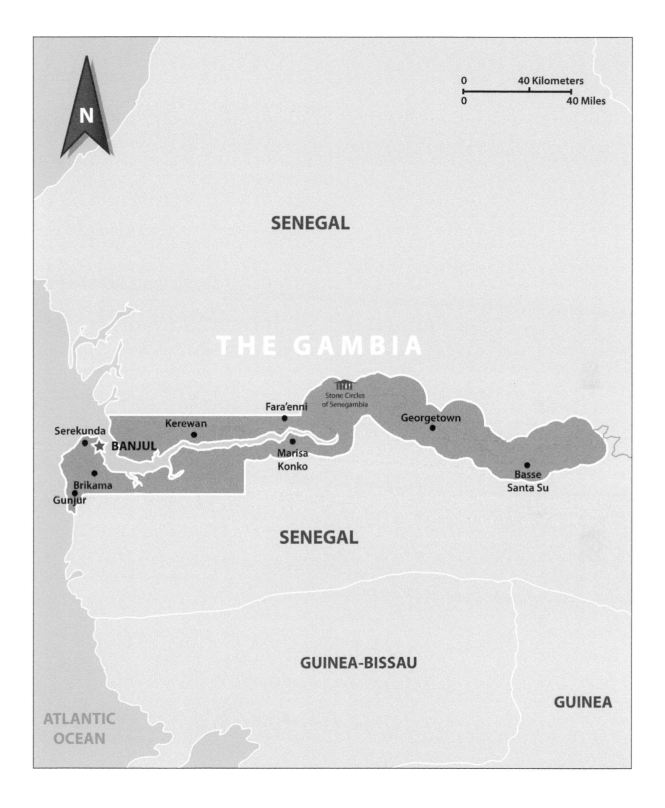

Principal Cities by Population (2012):

- Banjul (31,834)
- Serekunda (415,962)
- Brikama (101,119)
- Bakau (72,039)
- Lamin (39,112)
- Nama Kunku (31,834
- Brufut (31,692)

as of 2003 are the Mandinka (42 percent of the population), the Fula (18 percent), the Wolof (16 percent), the Jola (10 percent), and the Serahuli (nine percent).

Although roughly a quarter of the Gambian national population of 1.7 million people live in the greater Banjul area, the capital proper has experienced small declines in population in the late 20th and early 21st centuries. The migration of people from Banjul to the rapidly growing suburbs follows a period of explosive growth from the early 1960s through the 1980s, during which the capital's population more than doubled.

The initial waves of migrants to Banjul came to the capital in search of economic and educational opportunities as well as a more modern standard of living. The establishment of commuter infrastructures during the 1970s, however, permitted more citizens to work in the capital but live in the less congested communities in proximity to St. Mary's Island. Banjul is also home to significant communities of West African expatriates. Senegalese nationals comprise the largest of these groups, which also include people from the Republic of Guinea, Guinea Bissau, Mali, and Mauritania. Banjul also features a small Lebanese community. There is also a minority population of Britons in Gambia.

As of 2015, an estimated 59.6 percent of the population lived in urban areas. The growth rate was 2.16 percent in 2015.

Languages

English is Gambia's official language, a reflection of the nation's colonial past, and is used in government, commercial, and educational settings;

French is also taught in some area schools. Indigenous languages such as Mandinka, Wolof, Fula, Soninke, and Jola are also commonly spoken in Banjul. Most residents are, at minimum, bilingual.

Native People & Ethnic Groups

Most of the ancestors of The Gambia's largest ethnic groups, the Mandinka, Fula, Wolof, Jola, and Serahuli, probably migrated to the area beginning in the 14th century. Associated with Africa's Bantu speakers and influenced by Arab and Islamic traders, these varied peoples were present when the first European traders came to the area in 1456. The Portuguese who landed on St. James Island in the Gambia River estuary were followed by a larger contingent of Portuguese who expanded the existing slave trade in the area into a large-scale international affair.

As a result of European slave trading and other mercantile activities, the Gambia River Basin became a central point for trans-Atlantic trade and for the great African Diaspora. Today, more than 99 percent of Gambians are of African descent and practice traditional forms of religion, social customs, and economic practices that preserve a sense of regional and tribal identity.

Tribal groups are highly stratified, so that every member of a tribe is born into his or her social position and all of the constraints, customs, and freedoms that come with that tradition. Language differences, clothing, music, dance, cuisine, and customs maintain the differences between The Gambia's tribal groups. Ritualized greetings can establish position and tribal affiliation between two strangers, or reinforce social relations between family members or friends.

Religions

Most Gambians, about 90 percent, are adherents of Muslim. The remaining eight percent practice some form of Christianity, with two percent indigenous beliefs also exist alongside these more formal world religions.

Climate

The Gambia has a tropical climate, which varies slightly between the coastal areas to the west and the eastern inland area. Hot and humid conditions in the interior of the country can peak with temperatures of about 38° Celsius (100° Fahrenheit) during the warmest period between March and June.

Conditions are more moderate near the coast, with a dry period from mid-November to mid-May during which temperatures cool down. Between June and October, temperatures climb to 23° to 30° Celsius (73° to 88° Fahrenheit) and heavy rainfall is common. Average annual rainfall in the west is 1,295 centimeters (51 inches).

From January to March, the legendary harmattan wind blows across Western Africa from the Sahara Desert, creating dusty hazy conditions across the region.

Banjul has a subtropical climate in which warm, dry conditions prevail from December through February, and hot, humid weather dominates during the rainy season, which typically runs from July through September. During the rainy season, temperatures may run as high as 43° Celsius (110° Fahrenheit), but during the dry season, Banjul sometimes experiences overnight low temperatures of –7° Celsius (45° Fahrenheit).

ENVIRONMENT & GEOGRAPHY

Topography

Situated along the Gambia River, The Gambia's national territory is generally flat and at low elevations. In the east where The Gambia borders the North Atlantic, the country is about 45 kilometers (28 miles) wide and sits barely above sea level.

Inland, the country narrows, although elevations increase slightly as the land becomes a low plateau. The inland areas are occasionally dotted with small hills, which become rocky near the eastern border. The highest point of elevation is only 53 meters (174 feet) above sea level.

Banjul is located on St. Mary's Island in the estuary of the Gambia River, situated in a navigable stretch that extends some 300 kilometers (186 miles) from the West African interior to the Atlantic coastline. The Gambia River has for centuries served as key trade and transportation route in the region, a role it continues to play in the early 21st century, particularly when the high cost of fuel has made river transport a cost-effective alternative. The river narrows to a width of 5 kilometers (3 miles) at the location of the capital, which lies only 48 kilometers (26 miles) upstream from the ocean.

Plants & Animals

The Gambia's tropical climate and river basin have created mangrove swamps along the lower river and estuary, an ideal climate for wetlands vegetation. Dolphins, crocodiles, and the occasional hippopotamus are also found there. In this area, the 22,000-hectare (54,360-acre) Baobolong Wildlife Reserve has become a tourist destination for birdwatchers from around the globe.

Bamboo forests, tropical forests, and grasslands cover most of The Gambia's national territory. These areas host tropical woods like mahogany and rosewood and the country's growing wildlife preserves. Forest species include chimpanzees, vervet, patas, and red colobus monkeys as well as oribi and duikers (related to the antelope). The dry grasslands support waterbucks, elands, and warthogs.

CUSTOMS & COURTESIES

Greetings

In Gambia, people greet one another in English or one of Gambia's prominent tribal languages such as Mandinka or Wolof. (Other tribal languages include Fula, Jola, Sarahule, Serere, Krio, Marabout, Manjago, and Bambara.) English is the official language at work and school, but tribal languages are used at home and in casual social settings.

Most Gambians speak multiple languages. Common greetings include the Muslim saying "Asalamu alikum" ("Peace be unto you"), with the appropriate response being "Alaikum assalam" ("And unto you"). In addition, the phrases "Hera laata" and "Jamangen fanaan," in Mandinka and Wolof, respectively, are used for "Good morning, while "Fo waati koteng" and Ci jamma" are translated as "Goodbye."

Gambians greet one another in a hospitable and open manner. Handshakes are the most common physical greeting. As is Muslim custom, Gambians shake hands exclusively with their right hands, since the left hand is associated with personal cleansing, and thus considered impure. Alternatives to handshaking include offering an arm or raising clasped hands to chest level or above the head. Gambians acknowledge, exchange handshakes, and speak at least briefly with all the people with whom they come in contact during the day. Custom also dictates that Gambians stop what they are doing, even if it is important or complicated work, to greet people As a result of this custom, Gambians spend a lot of their day greeting one another. Lastly, greetings must come before any inquiry or conversation, and refusing to greet someone could cause offense.

In some areas of Gambia, traditional greeting custom involves repeating the names of all the family members that are known to one another. In this traditional practice, Gambians are symbolically greeting whole families (living and dead) and villages, rather than just one other person. This greeting also reveals the great respect Gambians have for their elders and ancestors. Young people greet elders first but avoid direct eye contact. Gambians are physically restrained in public.

Gestures & Etiquette

Gambia's British colonial past, tribal roots, and Muslim culture influence gestures and social etiquette. For example, because of Gambia's Muslim heritage, public displays of affection are rare and the right hand is exclusively used when physical contact is initiated with another. In addition, the etiquette and respect sometimes shown toward witch doctors and the supernatural is rooted in animism (the practice of investing natu-

ral objects with spiritual powers) and the tribal combination of Islamic and Christian beliefs. Gambians believe that witch doctors, diviners, and herbalists have power to protect against evil spirits, reverse curses, fix bad situations, and raise wealth and status.

In fact, taboos and superstitions about bad luck direct behavior and actions in Gambian society. For instance, Gambians may refrain from sitting in doorways, bathing in a lot of water, cutting babies' fingernails, sweeping the house at night, allowing children to eat fish, allowing pregnant women to eat eggs, or putting their hands on their heads except in mourning. In addition, Gambians believe that water jars should be left uncovered so that dead ancestors always have a water source. The act of pouring hot water on the ground may burn dead ancestors, while the act of pouring cold water in front of a house guarantees a good day.

Gestures are used in Gambia to convey a range of meanings, most commonly refusal, threat of physical punishment, the promise of doing something later rather than now, and friendly or peaceful greeting from a distance. Gambians communicate their refusal by flapping their arms like wings. Gambians convey a threat of physical punishment, often directed at a child, with a downward movement or flick of thumb and index finger. Gambians convey a promise of doing something later by moving index fingers in a circular motion. Gambians convey their friendly or peaceful greeting from a distance by clasping their hands together in front of their chests.

Despite common Gambian gestures and social etiquette rules, members of Gambia's tribal groups, such as the Mandinka, Wolof, Fula, and Jola, do have distinct versions and variations of traditions, gestures, social etiquette, and taboos.

Eating/Meals

In Gambia, the social aspects of dining are consistent across urban and rural areas. For example, family members traditionally share meals in all Gambian households or compounds, and families eat from a communal or shared food bowl. Gambians also wash their hands in a communal water bowl before all meals and only ever eat with their right hands. The communal food bowl is set upon in the middle of a large mat (called a basing). Family members remove their shoes as a sign of respect before sitting near the communal food bowl or on the eating mat. In some tribes and villages, men and women, including boys and girls, eat from different communal bowls. Visitors to the compound are always invited to join the meal. Bountiful meals, with extra portions for unexpected guests, are valued. The majority of Gambians eat their food with their right hand or a wooden spoon.

Traditionally, the head of the household will announce the beginning of a meal with the Arabic exclamation, "Bisimillah" ("In the name of God"). Hosts place the food in the center of the communal food bowl and watch over the meal to ensure that each person present gets a share of the food. Gambians do not talk during meals, though brief comments on the temperature or quality of the food are socially acceptable. Guests should offer thanks at the end of a meal. Hosts may end a meal by saying "Alhamdulilah" ("Thanks be to God").

Visiting

In Gambia, people frequently invite each other to their family homes, farms, or compounds for a social visit or meal. Visitors typically bring their hosts small gifts of rice or soap. Because Muslims refrain from alcohol, gifts of alcohol are rare. Visitors are expected to remove their shoes before they enter a home, which is seen as a demonstration of respect for the family that resides within the home. Some customs may be associated with the belief in the supernatural. For example, visits may be avoided on Saturdays due to a belief that the things done on Saturdays are likely to be repeated in the near future. Similarly, social visits are also generally avoided during late mornings and dusk, as these are the periods of time when spirits are believed to wander.

Gambians speak quietly when they enter a home. Visitors should not criticize a host's beliefs or home, but may comment on the behavior of the host's children. Negotiations and greetings

between friends and family tend to go on at great length, but traditionally occur without loud exclamations or big gestures. Gambians prefer to dress in bright and colorful clothing when out for social visits. Gambians of the same gender often hold hands as they walk about or socialize during leisurely walks or social visits.

LIFESTYLE

Family

Gambia's population is 90 percent Muslim and combines Muslim and tribal traditions. As such, the Muslim tradition of patrilineality (descent and inheritance through the man's family) and patrilocality (couples join the man's family) is commonplace. The typical Gambian family unit includes many generations living together, and most Gambian households include at least nine members. Polygamy is legal and common, and marriage between cousins and arranged marriage are encouraged practices. In fact, men can gain status by supporting a large household with multiple wives. Generally, families and households maintain a definitive hierarchy, starting with the head of the household, wife, children, son's children, daughter's children, and then moving to grandparents, aunts and uncles, and other extended family such as nieces and nephews.

Housing

Gambian houses, often called compounds, are built in response to the sub-tropical climate with its alternating dry and rainy seasons. Houses are well ventilated and may be single detached units or composed of several one-tier apartments. Local building materials include mud bricks and thatch, and concrete is used to ensure security. More affluent homes may have gates. Social status often dictates whether a household has electricity.

Gambians value their rural lifestyle and close family and village networks. Because of this close association between Gambian identity and rural life, the majority of Gambia's population lives in rural villages. Rural houses or huts are constructed of mud bricks, thatch, and corrugated metal, and are traditionally round and rectangle. Rural houses are usually built in family compounds, and two-room houses are common. Cooking and bathroom facilities are usually placed outside of the home.

Gambia's urban areas, including their planning and architectural styles, were influenced by British colonial rule. Urban housing is characterized by enduring British colonial aesthetics and design, as well as the growing problem of urban poverty. Colonial bungalows and squatter settlements fill urban areas, and wealthy Gambians may have guards to protect their homes. In recent years, young people have increasingly migrated to the capital of Banjul in search of work and opportunity.

Food

Gambia's cuisine is based on certain staples and ingredients, most notably rice, millet, peanuts, corn, cassava, okra, and palm kernels. In particular, Gambia's cuisine shares flavors and ingredients with neighboring Senegal. The national cuisine, with many recognizable Western foods, is also influenced by its identity as a former British colony. Commonly consumed meats come from cows, goats, and sheep. Peanut butter paste (called domoda) and palm oil (called chew deu terr) are used to prepare most main or savory dishes. Popular fruits in Gambia include mango, banana grapefruit, papaya, and orange.

Traditional Gambian dishes include fu-fu, afra, superkanja, benachin, chakery, and lakh. Fu-fu is a traditional yam dumpling prepared with a mixture of plantain, yam, potato, or cassava flour. It is commonly shaped by hand, boiled, or fried and eaten along with okra soup or stew. Afra is a popular stew made from slow-cooked lamb, onions, salt, chili powder, and water. Superkanja is okra stew and the main ingredients include beef, fish, palm oil, okra, onion, salt, and water. Superkanja is eaten with boiled rice or fu-fu. Benachin is a stew of spicy meat, rice, tomato sauce, and vegetables. It can be eaten by itself or over millet, couscous, or rice.

Chakery and lakh are popular sweet dishes. Chakery is couscous pudding made with warm couscous, evaporated milk, yogurt, and sour cream, fruit such as pineapple or mango, and nutmeg, vanilla, and sugar. Lakh is a sweet porridge made of baobab fruit, couscous, peanut butter, butter sugar, nutmeg, raisins, and vanilla.

Life's Milestones

Gambians achieve recognition, maturity, and social standing through milestones such as the naming ceremony, circumcision, and marriage. Friends and extended family, and sometimes even whole villages, participate in and witness these milestone ceremonies.

The Gambian naming ceremony, called ngente, is traditionally held eight days after a baby is born, and marks the baby's membership into the life of the family and the village. The morning ceremony occurs in the courtyard in front of the family's home, and families with available resources will typically arrange chairs and a tent. Family and guests wear their best clothing, and cake and bread are served. A spiritual leader, elder, or father of the baby cuts a piece of the baby's hair, pours water onto the baby, and whispers the baby's name. Only after this ritual will the baby's name be said aloud and announced to friends and extended family.

The circumcision ceremony, undertaken by both boys and girls, includes physical cutting of the genitals, a celebration, and education about sex, responsibilities, and traditions. The circumcision ceremony marks an adolescent's transition from childhood to adulthood. Female circumcision is becoming less common under international scrutiny and disapproval. The wedding ceremony marks a couple's union, as well as the alliances formed between the families and villages of the bride and groom.

CULTURAL HISTORY

Art

Gambia's artistic traditions are rooted in, and influenced by, rituals and ceremonies, economic need, and daily life. Art styles and traditions vary between the nation's eight different ethnic groups—the Mandinka, Fula, Jola, Wolof, Serer, Serahuli, Manjago, and Aku. They are also shaped by the availability of resources, such as clay, plant dyes, and fibers, as well as the nation's colonial past. These various crafts and traditions include mask making, woodcarving, textile dyeing, basket weaving, jewelry making, ceramics, and gourd art.

Gambia's wooden masks, carved from locally available wood, are used in tribal rituals, for entertainment, and in commerce. Ethnic tribes wear carved wooden masks in ceremonies such as coming of age celebrations and harvest festivals. Gambians believe that masks impart powers to those who wear them. A tribal chief, for example, may wear a mask to enhance his power to rule or decide tribal disputes. In addition to tribal use, Gambian masks are also made for the tourist trade. Other popular types of woodcarving include sculpture of human and animal figures and functional items such as spoons, bowls, and stools.

Gambia has a long tradition of basket weaving and textile art, including dyeing techniques such as batik and tie-dye. Gambian baskets, which are often made from dried palm leaves, are used by Gambians to carry and store items. Gambian women, particularly those from the Serahuli ethnic group, use local materials and dyes to produce images of abstract design and depictions of people and animals on fabrics. Dyed fabrics are made into traditional Gambian clothing styles, including kaftans (traditional men's clothing) and grandmubas (traditional women's clothing).

Pottery has been made in Gambia for over 6,000 years. Potters, who dig their clay from fields or riverbanks, shape their pottery by hand. Ceramics are most often produced by women, and functional items such as water containers and cooking pots are the most common uses for Gambian pottery.

Music & Dance

Griots (also called jeli or jalolu) are an integral part of Gambia's musical and oral traditions. Historically, griots were wandering musicians, or bards, who played drums and the kora (traditional stringed instrument) and who sung of praise and local history. The griot musical tradition, which preserves stories, customs, and traditions from one generation to the next, is rooted in the Mali Empire (1230–1600) in Africa. Today, griots continue to play traditional music in celebrations, such as rite of passage ceremonies, and at marketplaces. They tend to pass on the role or profession to their children. The griots' favored instrument, the kora, is found throughout West Africa, including the countries of Mali, Burkina Faso, Guinea, Sierra Leone, and Senegal. The kora is a complex instrument traditionally made from a calabash gourd, hardwood and fishing line. Skilled artisans make kora, which vary in size and sound.

Gambia's traditional music influences the sounds of Gambia's modern and popular music traditions. Gambia's popular music scene, which today includes hip-hop and blues, began in the 1960s. Political unrest in Gambia caused many Gambian musicians to move to foreign countries with greater stability and opportunity. Popular contemporary Gambian bands also play dance music and reggae.

In Gambia, traditional dances tend to be performed by either men or women, and rarely together. For instance, the taxuraan is a village dance exclusively performed by men. Women's dances are performed as a way of rejoicing for good news such as bountiful fishing trips or successful negotiation with a neighboring village. Gambia's traditional dance styles are also strongly associated with different ethnic groups. For example, the Jola, the Mandinka, and the Wolof, three of Gambia's main ethnic groups, have distinct dance styles. The Jola perform colorful and flamboyant dances. Masked dancers who twirl and balance on poles perform the Jola's most dramatic dance. The Mandinka perform dances with elaborate steps and footwork. People from the Wolof ethnic group tend to dance with their hips to the sounds and beats of contemporary music.

In Gambia, dancing and drumming are closely linked. The sound of djembe drumming, which is popular throughout West Africa, accompanies many traditional Gambian dances. The djembe drumbeat, made with two hands, is a strong and heavy percussion sound. The djembe drum is carved from a single piece of hardwood tree and covered with animal skin. Djembe drums can be played alone or together in a group depending on the event or purpose of the music.

Literature

Literary scholars date the beginning of Gambian literature to the 18th century. Gambian Poet Phillis Wheatley (1753–1784) is considered one of Gambia's first published writers. Wheatley was born in the Gambian region of Africa and taken to the United States as a slave when she was a young child. Wheatley, along with being among Gambia's first published writers, was one of the first African American poets published in the US.

Popular subjects for Gambian writers include the history of Gambia and contemporary life in Gambia. The book *I of Ebony*, by Nana Grey-Johnson (1951–), is a popular tale about 19th-century Gambia. *Magic Calabash*, also by Grey-Johnson, and *The Sun Will Soon Shine*, by Sally Singhateh (1977–) are popular stories about contemporary Gambia. Popular contemporary Gambian writers also include Lenrie Peters (1932–2009) and Ramatoulie Othman. However, few contemporary Gambian writers are known outside of Gambia and are limited by a lack of publishing opportunities within the country. Gambian writers with financial resources, such as Fodeh Baldeh (1948–), tend to self-publish and promote their own works.

Gambian writers are actively working to overcome their isolation and bring Gambian literature to an international audience. Recently, Gambian writers are increasingly sharing their work at international literary festivals. Gambia also hosted the SABLE International Literary Festival in 2007, which is sponsored by the London-based *Sable LitMag* literary publication. In addition, school programs in Gambia are increasingly working to promote literacy in the aim of producing self-sufficient Gambians as well as future Gambian writers.

CULTURE

Arts & Entertainment

The role of the arts in Gambia reflects the nation's 21st-century culture, traditions, collective experience, and social consciousness. In particular, the arts have been used widely as a vehicle for cultural survival and continuity after political coups and upheaval. Historically, during periods of slave capture and British colonial rule, the arts went underground to keep Gambia's tribal cultures alive. Griots, West African wandering bards or musicians, have preserved Gambia's oral tradition, history, and family or clan genealogies. Today, during a period of increased social and political control caused by failed political coups, wandering griots continue to preserve Gambia's history and stories, as well as influence the sound of Gambian music.

The arts have been influenced by Gambia's neighboring West African cultures (such as Guinea-Bissau, Senegal, and Guinea), prehistoric art (cave paintings and burial monuments), and Western art (British colonial aesthetics). Today, the tourist trade's demand for certain artistic items and colors influences Gambia's artistic production. Gambia's folk art traditions of basket weaving, textile dying, and mask carving are common throughout West Africa.

Gambians are proud of their arts and consider the arts to represent the best of Gambia's cultural skills, techniques, designs, and traditions. In particular, the performing arts, like music, dance, and drama, create cultural continuity over time, as well as a sense of a common or shared culture. Gambia has very little intertribal conflict. The tribes simultaneously preserve their own language, culture, and artistic traditions and contribute to the larger body of Gambian art. Gambia's arts community unites Gambia's multiple tribal and ethnic cultures, as well as provides temporary diversion from ongoing problems of poverty, health, and politics.

The arts promote a positive image of Gambian culture worldwide. For instance, the Gambian National Musical and Dance Troupe, which features traditional dance, songs, instruments, and culture of Gambia, perform at international festivals, universities, and cultural centers. The Gambian National Musical and Dance Troupe highlight traditional Gambian instruments, including the kora, the balafong, and the riti. The troupe performs dances from each of Gambia's distinct ethnic tribes. Two favorite dances include the cassa and the lenjengo. The cassa is a dance from the Jola tribe that involves fire, while the lenjengo is a traditional harvest celebration dance from the Mandinka tribe.

There is little government support for the arts in Gambia. As a result, Gambian writers often self-publish their own literary works and Gambian artists must be resourceful to support themselves and promote their art. Gambian musicians and artists also seek sponsorship, as well as performance and exhibition opportunities abroad. Within Gambia, local art galleries are increasingly highlighting the work of Gambia's visual artists.

Cultural Sites & Landmarks

The United Nations Educational, Scientific, and Cultural Organization (UNESCO) recognizes two sites in Gambia as requiring international recognition and preservation efforts. These sites include James Island and the Stone Circles of Senegambia. James Island and its related sites are a group of villages along the Gambia River that preserve aspects of early encounters between Africa and Europe during the 15th century, as well as pre-colonial and pre-slavery culture. In addition, James Island was an important location in the African slave trade and, as a result, holds an important place in African history.

The Stone Circles of Senegambia are four groupings of over 1,000 stone circles, pillars, and monuments, such as burial mounds, along the Gambia River. Archaeologists have uncovered iron weapons, pottery vessels, and gold and bronze ornaments in the burial mounds. The stone circles and pillars are made of local sandstone rocks that weigh between 75 to 100 tons. The four groupings, which date to as early as the third century BCE, are called Sine Ngayène, Wanar, Wassu, and Kerbatch. The building and organization required to erect over 1,000 stone circles,

pillars, and monuments reflects the prosperity and technological achievements of early inhabitants of the area. Gambians consider the site, which is part of a larger group of similar sites found throughout Africa and Europe, to be sacred.

Other important cultural sites and landmarks in Gambia include Fort Bullen built in 1827, and located at the mouth of the Gambia River. It was constructed to protect Britain's businesses and colonial officers, as well as fight the slave trade. The fort is a rectangular building with barracks and observation towers. Other attractions in the Banjul vicinity include the mangrove swamps surrounding the capital, which offer boat cruisers opportunities to view a wide variety of native birds and wildlife such as monkeys; the Katchikally Crocodile Pool, where visitors can observe crocodiles in their natural habitat; and the traditional village of Jufureh, home to an annual festival celebrating African heritage.

Libraries & Museums

Nestled amid Banjul's mixture of colonial-era architecture and modern office buildings is the Gambia National Museum, located on Independence Drive in the heart of the capital. The museum's exhibits document Banjul's history and culture, as well as Gambian achievements in the arts, politics, sports, and technology. Other important art, cultural, and history museums in Gambia include the Alliance Franco Gambienne, the Bansang Art Gallery, the Juffureh Museum, the Kaira Kunda Arts Promotion Center, and the Tanje Village Museum.

Gambian history is also reflected in the city gate of Banjul, called Arch 22. Built to commemorate the Second Republic of the Gambia that emerged in the aftermath of a bloodless coup in the summer of 1994, the arch sits astride four imposing columns. Its connecting platform is open to the public and affords a sweeping view of the capital and surrounding area. The top floor of the structure houses a textile museum.

Holidays

The Gambia's primary religious holidays are Muslim, and are set according to the Islamic lunar calendar. Eid Al Adha (the Feast of the Sacrifice) is celebrated in late January or early February. Mawlid an Nabi (the Prophet's birthday) is celebrated in late April or early May.

Ramadan ends the holy pilgrimage and begins a month-long holiday of fasting between dawn and dusk, private meditation and prayer, and communal time in the evenings. The end of Ramadan is marked with Eid al Fitr (usually in November), during which Muslims join in communal family celebrations, give money to the poor, and renew their faith.

The Gambia also officially recognizes the Christian holidays of Good Friday, Easter, Easter Monday, the Assumption of the Blessed Virgin, and Christmas.

State holidays include New Year's Day (January 1), Independence Day (February 18), and Labor Day (May 1).

Youth Culture

In Gambia, childhood and adolescence are brief. The average life expectancy is 54 years and women typically marry between the ages of 14 and 20. Men usually delay marriage until they can demonstrate their ability to support a family. Literacy and higher education attendance rates remain low in Gambia in the early 21st century. The government has standardized educational curriculum and most instruction occurs in English. However, the cost of schooling—school fees and uniforms are too expensive for many Gambian families—and the lack of academic preparation limit the educational opportunities of Gambian youth. Many poor Gambian families will educate a first-born son and keep other children at home to help with chores and agricultural labor.

Children and adolescents who do not attend school help their families with household labor. Girls accompany their mothers throughout the day and attend to domestic responsibilities while boys accompany their fathers to learn their trade. Older siblings are usually responsible for the care and safekeeping of their younger siblings. Gambian youth generally dress in a modest way as required by Muslim tradition, and female children and adolescents may spend hours each week braiding or plaiting their hair into traditional styles. Popular leisure activities include football (soccer), dancing, and listening to music. Western culture has made inroads in Gambian youth culture, and American and European films, as well as Western and African music videos, are popular.

SOCIETY

Transportation

Popular modes of transportation include by foot or bus and ferry service; few Gambians own their own cars. As of 2011, there were 3,740 km (2340 miles) of roadways of which 3,029 km (1882 miles) are paved. Taxis are also available, but passengers must tell the driver if they would like to pay for the taxi's exclusive use or allow multiple passengers. Traffic moves on the right-hand side of the road. As of 2013, there was only one airport in the country.

Transportation Infrastructure

Gambia, the smallest country in Western Africa, is small and narrow, and travel tends to be slow and unpredictable due to a lack of modern infrastructure or coordinated schedules. The vast majority of roadways in the country are unpaved. There is no rail network.

The Gambia River is large enough for small ocean vessels. Banjul, Gambia's capital, is the location of the country's port. Ships from many nations arrive in Banjul to bring goods and supplies to Gambia, and river ferries travel on the Gambia River and carry passengers between cities.

Media & Communications

While Gambia's constitution protects free speech, the Gambian government is known to punish political scrutiny and dissenting opinion by detaining journalists, closing publications, and prohibiting conferences and summits. Gambia's largest newspapers are *The Daily Observer*, which tends to be pro-government, *The Point, The Gambia Daily*, and *The Foroyaa*. However, as of 2015, Gambia's literacy rate was 55.5 percent, and the majority of Gambians continue to receive their information or news through media other than written sources. The Gambian government, through the Gambia Radio and Television Service, controls Gambia's only television station, and the station's signal reaches an estimated 60 percent of the country. A private satellite channel and Radio France Internationale (RFI) can also be accessed.

Gambia's communication system, including infrastructure and access, is considered adequate by international standards. In 2014, there were an estimated 274,000 Internet users, representing 14.2 percent of the population. Radio, television, and Internet access tends to be found primarily in urban areas.

SOCIAL DEVELOPMENT

Standard of Living

The Gambia ranked 172nd out of 187 countries on the 2013 United Nations Human Development Index, which measures quality of life and standard of living indicators.

The Gambian government continues to struggle to improve quality of life for its residents. Although HIV/AIDS prevalence is relatively low, at 1.82 percent, The Gambia's average life expectancy is only 62.27 years for men and 67 years for women (2015 estimate). Infant mortality is high at 63.9 deaths per 1,000 live births, and the birth rate stands at 30.8 per 1,000 citizens (2015 estimate).

The country's high mortality rates are due in part to the prevalence of contagious and environmentally-bound diseases. Bacterial and protozoal diarrhea, hepatitis A, typhoid fever, dengue fever, malaria, Crimean-Congo hemorrhagic fever, yellow fever, and in 2004, a deadly outbreak of meningococcal meningitis go uncontrolled as a result of poverty and a weak health care system.

Water Consumption

Gambia faces challenges related to water access. It is widely recommended that tap water be boiled for 20 minutes before it is consumed. Bottled water is widely available in the country. The Gambia River is the county's major water source. Water demands have increased greatly in the past decade as Gambia's urban population and economic activity have grown. The country's total renewable water resources stand at only eight cubic kilometers.

Education

The Gambia's educational system is notoriously weak. Education is only free through primary school (ages seven to 13), but families must pay for books, clothing, food, and transportation for students. In the wealthier, tourism-supported areas of the coast, charity has helped pay school fees and costs for students, but schools are badly under-funded in the poorer eastern part of the country.

Relatively few students proceed to secondary schools, training institutes, or universities. Instruction is given in English. In 2015, it is estimated that only about 55.5 percent of The Gambia's adult population is literate (63.9 percent of men, and 47.6 percent of women).

Women's Rights

Ethnic or tribal laws and sharia (Islamic law) combine to shape the role and treatment of women in Gambian society, culture, and political life. Sharia specifies women's treatment in areas of employment, marriage, divorce, and inheritance, while social customs perpetuate practices such as female genital mutilation (FGM), domestic abuse, and polygamy (the practice of taking multiple wives), which are harmful to women.

Gambian society expects that women and men will have different rights, roles, and responsibilities. Gambian women are not encouraged to seek out employment outside of the home or higher education and are expected to adhere to their husband's rules. Inheritance tends to favor male relatives, and arranged marriages and polygamy are common. These practices tend to weaken women's status as decision-makers or leaders in households or villages. Other practices, such as FGM and domestic abuse, have both severe physical and psychological consequences. Traditionally, FGM is a deeply entrenched practice, particularly in rural Gambia, which often causes dire physical complications for women. Domestic violence, including spousal rape, is considered a family matter rather than a legal matter, and law does not prohibit sexual harassment.

The role and treatment of women in Gambian society, culture, and political life is beginning to change because of international monitoring and grassroots involvement. Within Gambia, organizations are working to strengthen women's rights and opportunities. For example, the Gambia Committee for the Prevention of Harmful Traditional Practices (GAMCOTRAP) works to educate members of the Gambian Assembly about the negative consequences of FGM.

In 2009, the Gambian government, along with the University of Gambia, also undertook a national program to educate the population and raise awareness about the physical consequences of FGM. The Women in Service Development Organization & Management (WISDOM) and the Gambia Women's Finance Association (GWFA) help women build credit and savings. The Gambian Women's Bureau, empowered by the office of the vice president, operates, and oversees all government programs intended to improve women's health and development opportunities.

Women are allowed to take on leadership roles; however, in 2008, there were only five female ministers; and in 2012, only four women in parliament. As for women who owned land, this number accounted for about 5,700 women from 2001 to 2002.

Health Care
The Gambia's ground-level health care is provided through Village Health Services (VHS). Under this system, the government identifies outlying areas or villages with a population over 400 people that need a local health provider. Heath workers volunteer to see patients and to provide health education to the community, and the government funds the purchase of basic supplies

and equipment. Village workers serve under the supervision of VHS/Community Health trained nurses who visit villages on a regular basis.

The Gambia also has a Basic Health Service, which works in cooperation with the Village Health Services and supervises the activities of VHS/Community Health nurses. The Basic Health Services system includes major health centers, minor health centers, and dispensaries, although few distinctions now exist among these categories.

Health centers and dispensaries have at least one physician on staff and hold rotating clinics that, along with village services, provide the bulk of all health care in The Gambia. While local villagers may pay with food or farming services to allow their health workers to volunteer time, patients in the Basic Health Service centers pay a small fee based on the service provided.

Infant and childcare through age five is free after a child is registered with a service center. Divisional Health Teams are assigned to four regions of the country to supervise the Village and Basic Health Services for their areas.

Patients who need more specialized care are referred to one of The Gambia's three referral hospitals located in Banjul, Bansang, and Farafenni. A small number of private clinics and physician provide care for higher fees. These providers are not associated with the government system.

GOVERNMENT

Structure
The Gambia's government administration is divided into five districts (Central River, Lower River, North Bank, Upper River, and Western), with a separate administration for the capital of Banjul. The former colonial region received its independence from the British Empire in 1965 and briefly united with neighboring Senegal to form the federation of Senegambia in 1982.

Senegambia had fallen apart by 1989, and in 1991, The Gambia's government fell to a military coup. The reinstatement of a constitution and, at least in appearance, the return to multiparty elections in 1996 and 1997 has stabilized politics in the country, though corruption remains a problem.

A president and a unicameral National Assembly currently run the Gambian government. The president is elected by popular vote to a five-year term and appoints a vice president and cabinet. The legislature, or National Assembly, consists of 53 members, 48 of whom are elected by popular vote to five-year terms. The president appoints the remaining five members to five-year terms.

The most recent elections were held on November 24, 2011. The winner of the race was Yahya Jammeh (who was re-elected) with a 71.5 percent vote. The next election will be held in 2016.

Political Parties

The dominant political party in Gambia is the Alliance for Patriotic Reorientation and Construction. Although the government is technically a multi-party system, other parties do not have a legitimate chance of gaining political influence. These parties include the National Alliance for Democracy and Development (a conglomerate of smaller parties) and the Gambia Party for Democracy and Progress.

Local Government

Gambia's National Assembly passed a Local Government Act in 2002. The law organized government on a municipal level into seven districts, which are subdivided into wards. Wards then elect councils, which include members of regional tribal governments. Although the Local Government Act stipulated the federal government should provide administrative capital to municipal powers, issues related to the decentralization of government monies remain.

Judicial System

Gambia's judicial system is comprised of a Supreme Court, a Court of Appeal, a series of high courts, and eight magistrate courts. This court system consists of six judges and the chief

justice who are appointed by the president. In addition, Gambia has a Special Criminal Court. Some areas of the country have local courts that are administered by village authorities. Judicial corruption remains a significant issue in Gambia. This includes incidents of intimidation and imprisonment without representation.

Taxation

Gambia's system of taxation does not account for the country's widespread informal economy. Tax compliance remains an issue. New measures were announced by the government in late 2010, which aimed to increase the amount of revenue the government earned from taxes instead of continuing to rely on foreign loans. As of 2010, the highest corporate and income tax rates are 35 percent. In 2014, tax consisted of 19.3 percent of the country's GDP.

Armed Forces

The armed forces of The Gambia, officially the Gambian National Army, are composed of an infantry-based army, Gambia National Guard, and naval contingent. There is no conscription, and 18 is the minimum age for voluntary service. Recent estimates list the army as 1,900-strong. Less than one percent of the country's gross domestic product (GDP) is allocated for defensive or military expenditures.

The military serves as part of the Economic Community of West African States Monitoring Group, a West African regional force. In 2010, approximately 500 Gambian troops were deployed in a peacekeeping mission in Darfur, Sudan, joining United Nations and African Union troops. As of 2012, once enlisted, military members are required to serve a minimum of six months.

Foreign Policy

Gambia is a small country with limited international power and influence. Despite its size and resource limitations, Gambia works to maintain an active role in international affairs. Historically, Gambia has maintained strong foreign relations with the United Kingdom (UK) and is a strong participant in West African and Islamic affairs. The country is a member nation of the Economic Community of West African States (ECOWAS), and has participated in the effort to end civil war between Liberia and Sierra Leone, as well as disputes between Guinea-Bissau and Senegal. However, most Western nations suspended all non-humanitarian aid to Gambia from 1994 to 2002 in opposition to Gambia's election process. Relations with the West remained strained until Gambia's internationally monitored elections in 2001 and 2002. In 2005, Gambia received an estimated $58.15 million (USD) in economic aid.

Gambia's relations with the U.S. was strengthened by Gambia's free and fair democratic presidential and legislative elections in 2001 and 2002, but are increasingly strained by Gambia's human rights and free press violations. The U.S. offers Gambia aid to support and strengthen democratic government, human rights, education, HIV/AIDS prevention, and environmental preservation. The Peace Corps maintains an active presence in Gambia and Banjul International Airport (BIA) is one of four international sites selected as an emergency landing destination for US space shuttles.

International organizations have cited Gambia for not working to eliminate or decrease the problem of human trafficking. Gambia is considered a source and transit country for human trafficking, particularly for women and girls sent to Europe for the purpose of sexual exploitation or domestic servitude. Other areas of international dispute include refugees, arms smuggling, and cross-border raids. Gambia became a member of the United Nations Security Council (UNSC) for the first time in 1999. It has maintained membership in the UN since 1965.

Human Rights Profile

International human rights law insists that states respect civil and political rights, and promote an individual's economic, social, and cultural rights. The United Nations Universal Declaration on Human Rights (UDHR) is recognized as the standard for international human rights. Its authors sought the counsel of the world's great thinkers, philosophers, and religious leaders, and were careful to create a document that reflects the core values shared by every world culture. (To read this document or view the articles relating to cultural human rights, visit http://www.udhr.org/UDHR/default.htm.)

Article 2 of the UDHR, which states that everyone is entitled to legal rights and freedoms without distinction of race, color, sex, language, religion, political or other opinion, national or social origin, property, birth or other status, is mostly supported by the Gambian constitution. In particular, the Gambian constitution explicitly forbids discrimination based on race, religion, sex, disability, language, or social status. However, there are some notable distinctions in which Gambia does not adhere to international human rights law.

Gambia's current human rights policy is based on the need to control its citizens rather than encourage social, moral, economic, and cultural rights and freedoms. Tribal and Islamic laws regarding marriage and family tend to take precedence over constitutional law in Gambia. For instance, polygamy, arranged marriages, and intermarriage are accepted and common social practices in Gambia. In addition, the right to freedom of opinion and expression, protected by constitution law, is not honored by the Gambian government. The Gambian government has a record of intimidating, detaining, and censoring journalists.

Ultimately, Gambia's human rights profile, which was historically strong, began to worsen in 2007 because of a failed coup attempt against President Yahya Jammeh (1965–) and the Alliance for Patriotic Reorientation and Construction political party. In response to the coup attempt, the Gambian government has tightened control and lessened its commitment to human rights protections for its citizens. While the Gambian constitution and law offer explicit protection for most human rights, the current leadership has practiced unlawful arrests and detentions, restricted free press and speech, harassed journalists, allowed for continued human trafficking, and refused to recognize the problems of violence against women.

ECONOMY

Overview of the Economy
Since the late stages of its colonial history, The Gambia has relied heavily on the production of groundnuts (peanuts) and groundnut oil for export to world markets. The increase in groundnut prices after the country achieved independence in 1965 permitted the new government to begin development of health care, education, and other social programs. With the decline of the groundnut industry and political instability in the 1990s, much of this work was undone.

Banjul's strategic position and its well-sheltered, deep-water port have made the capital a hub for heavy commercial traffic along the river, as well as ocean-going vessels and cargo ships. Banjul's port, through which roughly 700,000 tons of cargo pass annually, plays a significant role in the both the local and regional economies. Peanuts and peanut products represent the most important source of revenue, while cotton, palm kernels, and beeswax are other key exports.

In February 2004, the Gambian government announced the discovery of oil reserves in its territorial waters off the coast. Officials hope that revenue from a new petroleum industry will replace the floundering agricultural base and allow for significant development in the struggling country. In 2014, The Gambia's per capita gross domestic product (GDP) was estimated at $1,600 (USD). Gambia's total GDP in 2014 was $825 million.

Industry
According to United States government figures, commerce, industry, and services combined account for less than 20 percent of The Gambia's labor force. Peanut processing, fishing, tourism, woodworking, metalworking, and clothing construction are among the most significant of The Gambia's industries, along with the assembly of agricultural machinery and the processing of beverages for sale.

Banjul's modest manufacturing sector includes peanut processing facilities and breweries. The production of woven fabrics, jewelry, and handicrafts also constitute important economic activities in the capital, as do commercial fishing operations based out of Banjul.

Labor
The work force was estimated at 777,100 in 2007. Unemployment and poverty rates are high, though the Gambian government has declined to issue any specific information on income or employment figures. As of the late 20th century, the bulk of the labor force—an estimated 75 percent—works in agriculture. Industry workers account for 19 percent, and services just six percent.

Energy/Power/Natural Resources
The Gambia has ample supplies of freshwater and saltwater fish. The country also has modest supplies of titanium, tin, zircon, and clay. Coastal beaches have yielded silica sand for export. In recent years, the government has been investigating petroleum reserves in the country's territorial waters in the Atlantic Ocean.

Fishing
Gambia has both a marine fishing industry and a freshwater fishing industry. The country is also trying to market itself as a sport-fishing destination. Although not a major contributor to the country's agricultural economy, the country does produce fish products for export and for domestic consumption. Artisanal (or non-commercial) fishers provide an estimated 90 percent of Gambia's domestic fish supply. Efforts to improve the country's fishing infrastructure, including storage and processing facility, are continuing.

Forestry
Forestry accounts for an estimated 0.5 percent of The Gambia's gross domestic product (GDP). Commercial logging provides wood fuel and timber; between 1968 and 1993, The Gambia experienced an 86 percent decrease in its forest area.

Mining/Metals
Gambia produces clay, zircon, and silica. However, mining is not a significant contributor

to the country's economy. Domestic petroleum needs are supplied solely by imports. Although Chinese companies have been working to investigate further Gambia's mineral sands, issues related to licensing have occurred.

Agriculture

The Gambia's economy is based on agriculture, relying heavily on the growth, harvesting, and production of rice, millet, sorghum, peanuts, corn, sesame, cassava, palm kernels. Palm kernels, cotton lint, and peanut products remain the country's most important exports. Most Gambian farmers operate at the subsistence level. Roughly, three-quarters of the country's population depends on subsistence farming for a living.

Animal Husbandry

Livestock species in Gambia include poultry, cattle, sheep, goats, and pigs. Although a large portion of livestock is reared for the informal economy and domestic consumption, livestock production represented an estimated five percent of the country's overall GDP in 2005. Gambia also has a small dairy farming industry. The country's livestock industry is administered by the Department of Livestock Services.

Tourism

Tourism has been a central feature of The Gambia's economy at least since independence. Tourism, in fact, accounts for more than 10 percent of the country's gross domestic product (GDP), and constitutes nearly a quarter of formal, private-sector employment. The country's tropical climate and location less than seven hours from Britain by air has helped The Gambia develop a strong tourist base; approximately 120,000 charter tourists arrive annually, primarily from Europe. In recent years, luxury resorts have appeared on Gambian beaches along the Atlantic coast. The government has set a goal of 500,000 tourist arrivals by 2012.

Eco-tourism is playing an increasingly large role in the national economy as the government works to expand wildlife preserve areas. River trips, safaris, village marketplaces, slavery-related historic sites, and the ruins of early empires draw tourists to The Gambia from Europe and North America. Tourism usually accounts for roughly a fifth of The Gambia's GDP. However, with the recent scare of Ebola, those figures have dropped.

Simone Flynn, Amy Witherbee, Beverly Ballaro

DO YOU KNOW?

- In its course from the Atlantic to the western boundaries of The Gambia, the Gambian River narrows from a width of 183 meters (600 feet) near the coast to a mere 6-meter (20-foot) channel near Barrow Kunda.

- The Gambia is home to more than 280 species of birds.

- At 15° longitude, The Gambia lies at a point equidistant from the equator and the Tropic of Cancer.

Bibliography

Briggs, Philip. "The Gambia (Bradt Travel Guide)." Guilford, CT: s, 2014.

Hughes, Arnold, ed. "The Gambia: Studies in Society and Politics." Birmingham, UK: *Birmingham University Press*, 2013.

Janson, Marloes. "Islam, Youth, and Modernity in the Gambia." New York: *Cambridge University Press*, 2014.

Raji, Wumi, ed. "Contemporary Literature of Africa: Tijan M. Sallah and Literary Works of the Gambia." Amherst, NY: *Cambria Press*, 2014.

Saine, Abdoulaye, et al., eds. "State and Society in the Gambia since Independence: 1965–2012." Trenton, NJ: *Africa World Press*, 2013.

Wright, Donald R. "The World in a Very Small Place in Africa: A History of Globalization in Niumi, the Gambia." New York: *Routledge*, 2010.

Works Cited

"A to Z of Gambia." *Gambia Guide*. http://www. accessgambia.com/information/a-z-gambia.html.

"Background Note: Gambia." *U.S. Department of State*. http://www.state.gov/r/pa/ei/bgn/5459.htm.

"Cities in Gambia." *Mongabay*. http://www.mongabay. com/igapo/2005_world_city_populations/Gambia.html.

"Culture and Traditions in Gambia and Africa." *WOW*. http://wow.gm/gambia/information.

"Culture of Gambia." *Countries and Their Cultures*. http:// www.everyculture.com/Cr-Ga/Gambia.html.

"Gambia." *CIA World Fact Book*. https://www.cia.gov/ library/publications/the-world-factbook/print/ga.html.

"Gambia." *UNESCO World Heritage List*. http://whc. unesco.org/en/statesparties/gm.

"Gambia." *U.S. Department of State Country Reports on Human Rights Practices*. http://www.state.gov/g/drl/rls/ hrrpt/2006/78736.htm.

"Gambia." *World Atlas* (n.d.). http://www.worldatlas.com/ webimage/countrys/africa/gm.htm.

"Gambian Literature and Writings." Gam Writers (n.d.). http://gamwriters.com/.

"Gambian Musicians." *Gambian Culture*. http://www. gambia.dk/cu.html.

"Greetings." *Gambia Guide*. http://www.accessgambia. com/information/gestures.html.

"Language and Culture." *The Gambia Experience*. http:// www.gambia.co.uk/Docs/About-The-Gambia/What-To-Expect/Language-And-Culture.aspx.

"The Gambia." *Encyclopedia of the Nations*. http://www. nationsencyclopedia.com/Africa/The-Gambia.html.

"Women's Organizations: Gambia." *The Global List of Women's Organizations*. http://www.distel.ca/womlist/ countries/gambia.html.

Goats are important livestock in Ghana. iStock/ruffraido.

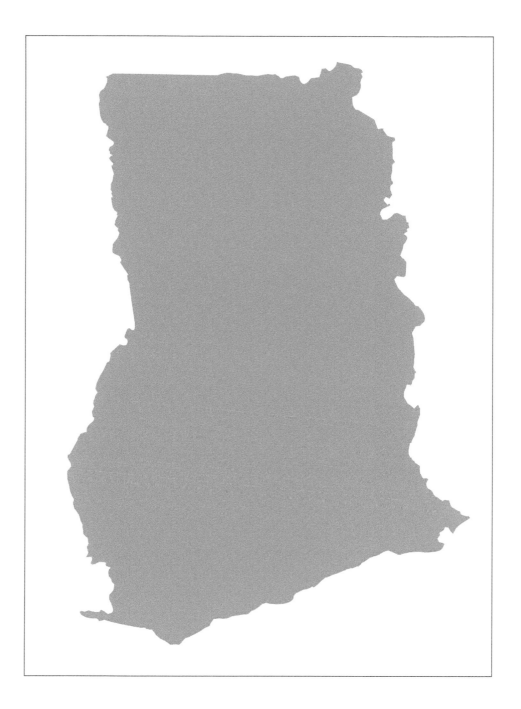

GHANA

Introduction

Ghana is a country in sub-Saharan Africa. A former British colony, Ghana declared its independence in 1957. It was the third country in Africa to become independent of colonial rule and the first country in Africa south of the Sahara to become free. Ghana is a major grower of cacao, the base ingredient in cocoa and chocolate. The country is also known for its traditional kente cloth, which is made by weavers throughout Ghana but a specialty of the city of Kumasi. The cloth's bright colors and tribal designs have symbolic meanings and are often worn by tribal chiefs.

GENERAL INFORMATION

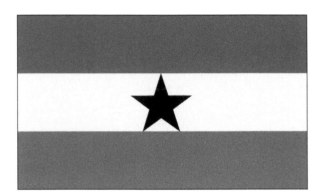

Official Language: English
Population: 26,327,649 (2015 estimate)
Currency: Cedi
Coins: 1 pesewa; 5 pesewa; 10 pesewa; 20 pesewa; 50 pesewa; 100 pesewa; 1 cedi
Land Area: 227,533 square kilometers (87,850 square miles)
Water Area: 11,000 square kilometers (4,247 square miles)
National Motto: "Freedom and Justice"
National Anthem: "God Bless Our Homeland Ghana"
Capital: Accra
Time Zone: GMT +0
Flag Description: The flag of Ghana features three horizontal bands (red, yellow, and green), with a black, five-pointed star in the center of the yellow band.

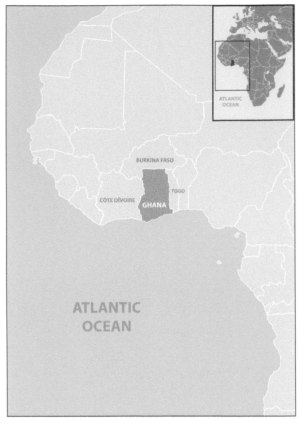

Population

Ghana has three main geographic areas: the urban coastal region, the central forest region, and the northern savannah. Each region has its own distinct population.

Approximately 70 percent of Ghana's population lives in the southern half of the country. About 54 percent of the population lives in the urban coastal region, which has historically had the most contact with European influences. The country's largest city is the capital, Accra, which is home to over two million people. All of the country's other urban areas are relatively small.

In 2009, Ghana experienced a 1.8 percent population growth rate. As of that same year, the median age was twenty years old, and the life expectancy for females was sixty-one years, and for men, sixty years. In 2007, roughly 21,000 deaths were attributed to HIV/AIDS. The death rate has since dropped in 2014 to 9,200 people. Currently, about 250,200 people are living with HIV/AIDS.

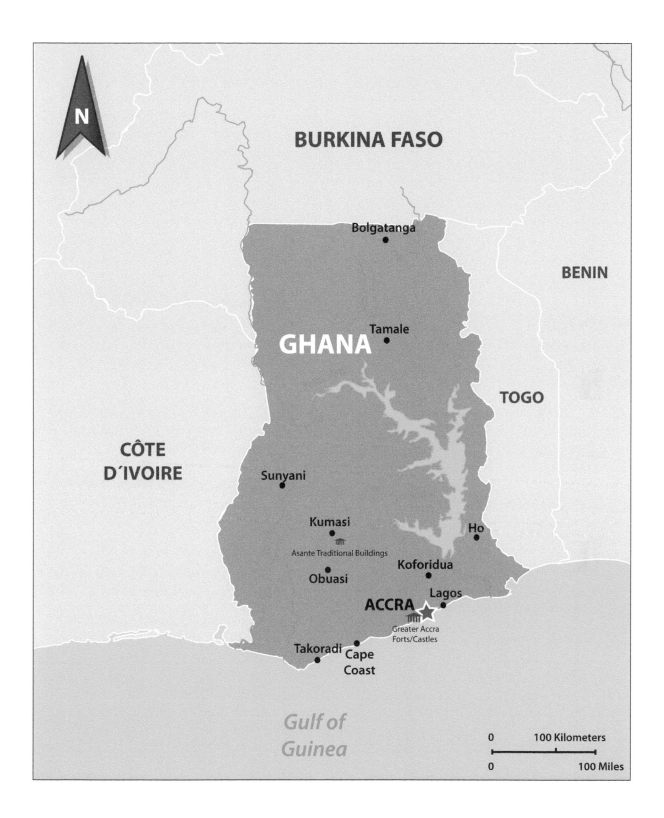

Principal Cities by Population (2012):

- Accra (2.3 million)
- Kumasi (2 million)
- Tamale (537,986)
- Teshie (160,939)
- Cape Coast (217,032)
- Obuasi (175,043)

Languages

Although English is the official language, many other languages are spoken, including Asante (16 percent), Ewe (14 percent), Fante (11.6 percent), Boron (4.9 percent), and Dagomba (4.4 percent).

Native People & Ethnic Groups

The Akan ethnic group makes up approximately 47.5 percent of Ghana's population and predominately resides in the southwest (coastal and forest) region of the country. When Europeans arrived on the coast of Ghana in the 15th century, they began a long-term interaction with the Akan, who, as a result, adopted some European cultural and linguistic aspects. In addition, people of Akan heritage often assume British surnames. The Akan ethnic group comprises many other subgroups, such as the Ashanti and the Akwamu.

The Ewe ethnic group, which makes up roughly 13.9 percent of the population, populates the southeastern area of the country. Other ethnic groups in the coastal region include the Ga-Dangme, which accounts for 7.4 percent of the total population. Traditionally, the coastal region had been split into various ethnic kingdoms, and its commerce was based in fishing. Other large cities include Cape Coast and Sekondi-Takoradi.

The ethnic groups that inhabit the agricultural forest region include the Akan, the Ewe, the Ashanti, the Akwapim, and the Akim. Much of the food Ghanaians eat comes from this region. Though there are fewer cities, the population density is greater around the region's cacao growing areas. The Ashanti held control of the middle forest region, especially the Kumasi area, from the 17th to the 19th century. They are still the dominant population, both culturally and politically.

The Dagomba and the Guang live in the northern savannah region. Most of the tribes are thought to have migrated to the area within the last 1,000 years. The Mamprussi and the Dagomba peoples are thought to be the first inhabitants of the area that is now Ghana. By the time Portuguese traders arrived in the 15th century, the tribes had migrated south through the savannah.

Aside from the larger ethnic groups, there are around 75 smaller subsets of tribes in Ghana. In addition to a small minority (less than two percent of the total population) of Europeans, there is a significant number of immigrants from other West African countries living in Ghana, including Liberians, Sierra Leoneans, and Togolese.

Religions

The 2010 census results state that 71.2 percent of the population of Ghana identify themselves as Christians, with denominations including Pentecostal, Protestant, and Roman Catholic. Roughly, 17.6 percent identify as Muslim, and approximately 5.2 percent practice traditional religions. Incorporation of traditional religious beliefs and practices into Christian and Muslim faiths is common. The majority of Ghana's Muslim population lives in the country's northern regions.

Climate

Ghana's climate is tropical, though temperatures vary from north to south, particularly during the rainy season. In the north, the rainy season lasts from March until September, while the rest of the country has two rainy seasons. The first runs from April until June, and the second runs from September to November. This translates into anywhere from 102 centimeters (40 inches) of rain in the north to 203 centimeters (80 inches) of rain in the south. This heavy rainfall is followed by a long dry season.

Another significant factor in Ghana's climate is the harmattan, a desert wind out of the northeast that follows the two rainy seasons. Evidence of the harmattan can be seen in the thin layer of red dust that covers furniture and cars throughout

Ghana's coast. Though the humidity is usually high, at or near 100 percent, it can dip as low as 12 percent during the harmattan season.

The hottest months in Ghana are February and March. Temperatures are usually between 26 and 29 degrees Celsius (78 and 84 degrees Fahrenheit). August tends to be the coolest month.

ENVIRONMENT & GEOGRAPHY

Topography
Ghana has three main geographic areas: the urban coastal region, the forest region, and the savannah to the north. Overall, the country is classified as lowland, though there is a series of hills at its eastern border with Togo. The country's highest point is Mount Afadjato, which 885 meters (2,903 feet) tall.

The forest region is the most agriculturally rich area of Ghana. This region is known for its production of cacao, which is the country's primary cash crop.

The savannah, in the northern part of Ghana, accounts for two-thirds of the country's area. It is the least-developed region of the country. Because of the lack of precipitation, little agriculture can be cultivated there.

The sandy beaches of the coastal region turn to coastal plains, dense with rivers and streams, further inland. The two main rivers in Ghana are the Black Volta and the White Volta. These join to form the Volta, which runs to the sea. Lake Volta, in the eastern part of the country, is one of the largest artificial lakes in the World.

Plants & Animals
Despite forest clearing activity in recent years, Ghana still has extensive forests. Some of the most notable trees found throughout the country are the giant silk cotton tree, the African mahogany, and the cedar. Evergreen forests are found in the southwest corner of Ghana.

The forests once covered approximately 77,700 square kilometers (30,000 square miles) of the country's area. Today, there are about 20,700 square kilometers (8,000 square miles) of forest left in Ghana.

Northern Ghana consists of grassland, while in the south, scrub and tall Guinea grass dominates the coastal savannah near Accra. Vegetation is interrupted by anthills that may reach up to 4 meters (14 feet) in height. Certain vegetation, such as the baobab plant, is often tough and resistant to drought or fire.

Ghana is home to many animals, including leopards, lions, antelope, hyenas, elephants, and several species of monkeys. There are also numerous reptiles, such as cobras, adders, mambas, and pythons. In addition, crocodiles are often found in the country's rivers. Birds include kingfishers, cuckoos, vultures, eagles, herons, and parrots.

CUSTOMS & COURTESIES

Greetings
In Ghana, greetings usually precede nearly every interaction. Greetings involve a smile, a wish for a good morning, afternoon or evening, or the respective Twi (a dialect of the Akan ethnic group) translation, and a loose handshake with the right hand. It is considered rude and strange to shake hands firmly as is common in the West. As a cultural rule, the left hand is never offered to another person. Following the handshake, it is customary to ask the other person about his family and work. If one is meeting a group, the same rules of conduct apply only one must apply them to each group member individually.

In many of the indigenous languages of Ghana, there are age-appropriate greetings that must be used. For example, the Twi phrase "Ya asone" is used for greeting someone of similar age and status, while "Ya aigya" and "Ya ehna" are used for older males and females, respectively.

If given the opportunity to speak with a tribal chief, Ghanaians approach him and bow, averting their eyes. Tourists will often be offered a handshake, but the average Ghanaian will have to settle for the bow. Tribal chiefs are usually not addressed directly, but through an intermediary.

Gestures & Etiquette

In general, Ghanaians share many of the same customs regarding gestures and etiquette as their West African neighbors. For example, public displays of affection between men and women are not common and generally considered unacceptable. However, it is very common to see two men or two women holding hands, as this is a sign of friendship.

Ghanaians will not offer their left hand in public arenas. As in other African countries, people tend to avoid using the left hand for social interaction, as this hand is used for bathroom hygiene and is generally considered unclean.

As many visitors notice, Ghanaians love to talk. In fact, they talk to each other so frequently and about so many other Ghanaians, that one might develop the notion that Ghanaians are gossips. However, it is simply a component of the culture to discuss nearly every matter openly. This is perhaps a reflection of the Ghanaian belief in the community as the ultimate family.

In Ghana, it is taboo to take photographs in some areas of the country. Taking photographs of government buildings and of the police or armed forces is frowned upon.

Eating/Meals

Ghanaians often eat together in large groups. Women do all of the cooking in most Ghanaian families and learn to cook through simple observation of their mothers and female elders throughout their young lives.

Ghanaians eat with their right hands, often after washing the hand in a dish of soapy water, then rinsing it in a dish of plain water and drying the hand on a communal towel. Eating of traditional dishes is usually done by balling the starch (cassava or fufu) and dipping it into the sauce, or by balling the starch with the sauce mixed in. Most Ghanaians eat three meals daily, with their supper being the largest meal. Meals are usually taken at home, except in the case of working members of the family and children attending school, who usually obtain food from "chop bars" and other food stands for breakfast and lunch.

Chop nearly literally translates as "to eat" in Twi. Every Ghanaian chop bar consists of a woman or women who prepare large quantities of soup or sauce in the morning and bring it to their establishment for serving at the lunch hour. Chop bar owners set up small shops or restaurants with indoor or outdoor seating. Often, dining areas are shaded with tents or umbrellas. The soup and sauces are kept covered until customers come for lunch hour, at which point the food is heated over a gas burner.

Visiting

Visiting family members and friends is a common practice among Ghanaians. Generally, guests stop by the homes of family and friends unannounced, but will declare their reason for visiting, if not simply to socialize, once formal greetings are out of the way. Sunday is the most common day for visiting another home, but visiting on Sunday is a more formal affair and often involves dressing in one's best clothes. Generally, Ghanaians will not visit during mealtimes, as it is considered somewhat impolite to impose on another family to provide meals. However, if a guest shows up unexpectedly during a meal, then the host will always offer food. A guest will normallh decline graciously or he will leave and come back later.

Ghanaians love to talk and discuss every aspect of local and international news and politics. As a result, visits often last many hours. As the visit is ends, Ghanaians often feel obligated to accompany their guests at least part of the way on their journey home. That may mean walking them to a main road, helping them find a cab, or walking with them half way home.

LIFESTYLE

Family

Lineage, in Ghanaian terms, refers to generations of a family traceable to the early ancestors, and can be matrilineal, traced through the women's ancestors, or patrilineal, traced through the men's ancestors. As part of a lineage, traditional Ghanaian cultural norms stipulate that family members enjoy rights to financial and proprietary benefits of the larger familial group, along with entitlement to a ceremonious burial. These rights are afforded to all in the lineage and take into consideration the family members who never marry or lose a spouse and would otherwise have no other guarantee of such protection. In return for these guarantees, each member of a lineage must uphold the moral standards of his family and be present in every commemoration of members' rites of passage. A family unit is a subunit of lineage.

Family structure in Ghana, like other African countries, is varied based on ethnic group. In the northern region, where many practice Islam, households are usually composed of brothers, their wives, and their children. Among the Ewe people, traditional culture holds that a husband and his wife or wives live in one household with their children. The Ga tradition requires husbands and wives to live separately. Historically, the Ga are patrilineal, husbands live with their fathers, and wives live with their mothers. When children are born, the sons and daughters are split in the same fashion. Generally, all Akan families are matrilineal, their nuclear family is managed just like the Ga, only husbands, and wives live with their respective mothers. Tribal traditions hold that mothers and daughters are obligated to feed their husbands three meals a day. Although ethnic identity is a source of pride in Ghana, most modern families in the country arrange relationships and family living situations in ways that parallel Western cultural traditions in America or the UK.

Today, economic development and an improved education system are changing the face of family in Ghana. With increased education, many young men and women are leaving rural areas for opportunities in larger cities. This flight of younger generations is leading to changes in rural life and traditional family relationships. This change is particularly evident among young men who find jobs in larger cities and acquire financial autonomy. They are then better able to attract a bride of their own choosing eliminating the family influence traditionally involved in

marriage. However, many young people choose to live and work in other countries or in Ghana's cities but remain active participants in family life by sending money and goods home to their relatives. They are therefore able to maintain a bond with their family.

Housing

Rural housing in Ghana often consists of a conglomeration of several individual rooms, either freestanding or separate, usually around a common courtyard. In some households, where men and women are forbidden from sharing a room, women's and men's rooms have separate courtyards. The women's courtyard often includes the kitchen, while the men's often includes the room reserved for visitors and social events. As more and more family members are born or as siblings and children get married, the compounds may be expanded to incorporate those new members.

In addition to this type of arrangement, Accra features numerous apartment complexes and more opportunity for families to live as smaller units, representing a Western influenced housing arrangement.

Food

Traditional Ghanaian food generally includes one main starch served with a soup, or a sauce. Generally, yam, cassava, cocoyam, plantain, and maize are pounded into a dough-like substance, which is then steamed or fried. The initial preparation of these starches is done by one or two women and a large mortar and pestle (pestles in Ghana can be as long as four feet and may weight several pounds). The larger the pestle, the finer the result. Women are admired for their ability to pound in a rhythmic fashion, lifting the pestle over their heads vertically and thrusting forcefully into the dish.

The most commonly eaten starches are fufu, made from pounded yam or a mix of cassava and cocoyam, and kenkey, or pounded maize. The preparation of kenke is nearly identical to preparation of maize by Native American cultures. Once the maize has been pounded, it is stuffed into the husk of a corncob and left to ferment.

Afterwards it is steamed, like a tamale. As these starches may take many hours to prepare, quickly steamed white rice is a popular substitute.

Commonly, on top of the starch, Ghanaians eat a sauce that may include any of the following: goat, beef, chicken, fish or dried fish, groundnut, peanut, spinach, palm leaves, and fresh hot peppers. Ghanaians believe that spicy food can cure most ailments. "Red red" is a popular dish that includes black-eyed peas and plantains stewed in palm oil. Jollof is another common dish of steamed rice, tomatoes, seafood or chicken and spicy peppers. It shares a close resemblance to "jambalaya," a dish popular in the southern United States. Along those lines, it is no coincidence that much of the food in the American South and the Caribbean share nearly identical recipes and ingredients with Ghanaian food. This is likely a result of slaves from West Africa having transported their culinary tradition to the Americas after being relocated to that region.

Life's Milestones

Ghanaians, like most people, commemorate birth, transition into adulthood, marriage, and death as the major milestones in life. When a new birth takes place in a family, for example, the entire family and close friends come together to hold a naming or "outdooring" ceremony. The ceremony can only take place once the infant has lived seven full days, the timeframe within which Ghanaians believe their children are most vulnerable. After that time, family members celebrate the event with food and gifts. Traditions vary, but the ceremony usually begins or ends with the father holding up the new baby, calling its name, and the entire family repeating it as an acknowledgement of his or her place on earth.

The Akan are also known for naming their children according to what day of the week they were born. For example, former President Kwame Nkrumah was so named because Kwame is the name given to all young men born on a Saturday.

Arranged marriages were common in Ghana for centuries, and still occur in some rural regions in the north. Families often arrange marriages for their children from a very young age in order to ensure that their children have a secure future. Marriage is viewed not only as a bond between two individuals but also of two families. In urban areas, arranged marriage is increasingly uncommon, as are large wedding gifts.

Ghanaians like to commemorate a person's death lavishly. Death is considered not an end but a transition from the physical to the spiritual world. Ghanaians celebrate this transition with large and extravagant funerals. The older the person, the bigger the celebration.

CULTURAL HISTORY

Art

Traditional Ghanaian art forms, like those of most African societies, were celebrated by Ghanaians not only as beautiful cultural expressions, but also as functional elements necessary to daily life. Each ethnic and tribal group, in accordance with ritual, ceremonial, religious, and political needs, developed a rich heritage of cloth weaving, sculpture, home decoration, jewelry design, and tool making. It was believed that the use of such items in daily life had the power to reaffirm the connection with ancestors, to lend power to the political strata and bridge the gap between life and death.

Patterns and symbols like these adorn the traditional woven kente cloth of Ghana to symbolize power and fertility.

Although there are many different ethnic groups within Ghana, certain elements of artistic expression are common to all groups. First of these is the use of textiles. In years past, the colorfully woven kente and adinkra cloths held a significant meaning based on the pattern and color of each individual design. Kente cloth, in particular, was used as a canvas for the most valuable symbolism of the Akan people including animals and vibrant patterns meant to symbolize power and fertility.

Traditionally, men exclusively wove both kente and adinkra cloths. It was the women's responsibility, however, to make and dye the thread the vibrant colors characteristic of finished cloths. These cloths continue to be produced in Ghana today. In the case of the kente cloth, the thread is spun on a narrow but tall loom measuring upwards of four feet from the base on the floor, where the weaver holds the thread in his toes. He controls the loom balanced against the weight of an attached boulder to create thin strips of woven material bearing the decided pattern. Once several of these strips have been woven, he then hand sews them together to create the larger pieces worn as clothes. Patterns are often composed of bright greens and golds offset in blocked patterns with black thread.

Adinkra cloth is woven much in the same fashion, but generally uses a thicker thread and a more subdued color scheme. Throughout history, Adinkra fabrics were an integral part of the Ashanti people's funerary ceremonies. Common colors in such rites of passage include earth tones ranging from granite and ebony to rust and deep reds. Textile goods of all kinds are popular with tourists visiting Ghana.

In addition to the historic importance of cloth weaving, sculpture is also a significant element of Ghanaian functional art. In particular, stool design is a rich tradition throughout Ghana. The basic structure of nearly all Akan stools is the same: a crescent-shaped seat supported by a single, thick column and a rectangular base. The specific detailed design of each stool is what has historically been used to distinguish its use. For example, images of leopards, elephants, lions or other majestic animals have traditionally been limited to royal stools. Traditional tribal beliefs held the stool as an extension of the owner and a validation of his or her place in this life. When the owner of a stool died, it was believed that his soul resides within the stool forever. The Golden Stool of the Ashanti is considered the most sacred of all stools, and is believed to have descended from the heavens at the time of the unification of the Ashanti Empire in the 19th century.

Hand-carved akuaba dolls depicting children or round-bellied, pregnant women were also traditionally valued as powerful tools of fertility among Akan women. It is believed that the first akuaba doll was given as a gift to a woman unable to bear children. Tribal legend holds that she cared for the wood doll as she would a child and eventually came to bear her own biological child.

Architecture

In Ghana, the contrast between rural and urban life may be seen in contrasting architectural influences. Rural areas are characterized by compounds, or several rooms or individual units built around a centralized courtyard. Other adjoining rooms include a kitchen, a bathroom and generally, a room reserved for socializing and social events. Depending on the size of families, many generations or many siblings may raise their families in the same compound.

Generally, homes are constructed of materials commonly used throughout West Africa: packed mud, dirt bricks, and loose cement blocks. Roofs are created from corrugated tin. Some villages in the northern regions still use the circular architecture with thatched roofs.

What distinguishes urban Ghana from rural, particularly in capital Accra, is the presence of both colonial and contemporary architecture. The architecture of present-day Accra is a snapshot of the different historical eras the coastal region of the country has experienced. From traditional living compounds, to large colonial forts, to modern office buildings and apartment complexes, Accra is a many-layered example of the various ways of life in Ghana.

Drama

Ghana's burgeoning film industry has undergone tremendous growth in the past several decades. This growth is due in large part due to the Ghana Film Industry Corporation. In the 1980s, a series of independent directors went out into greater Ghana to capture and tell various stories. As these films grew in popularity, directors became more sophisticated in their approach and technique. In 1996, Malaysian television production company Sistem Televisyen Malaysia Berhad of Kuala Lumpur purchased GFIC. Because of its roots as a television production company, it changed the focus of the company to primarily television dramas.

Themes in contemporary Ghanaian film often relate to societal grievances and especially the role of evil and supernatural forces underlying urbanization. In 2005, Oprah Winfrey produced a documentary film called *Emmanuelle's Gift* that traces a national bike ride made by a physically disabled young man. Throughout his journey, he confronts the issues facing the disabled in Ghana, where services and specialized facilities are not always available.

Music & Dance

As is the case with traditional Ghanaian visual arts, traditional dramatic arts have also served a functional and an aesthetic purpose throughout Ghana's history. In terms of music and dance, these two elements played integral roles in every rite of passage. Traditional songs were performed during birth, naming ceremonies, during transition into adulthood and certainly at weddings and funerals. Traditional dances featured movements aimed at ensuring safe passage through these life events. Song lyrics spoke of tribal ancestors their history. Other traditional songs offered lessons to children on how to behave and respect their elders. Traditionally, taking up the musical trade was an inherited vocation. Lifelong observation and experimentation was the customary method of training.

Traditional Ghanaian music incorporates numerous instruments, many of which are used in some form throughout West Africa, including the talking drum and the kora. Two distinctly Ghanaian instruments are the kpanlogo, a large deep drum played with the hands, and the gyil, an upper West African xylophone built from a large calabash gourd.

As trade with Middle Eastern and European markets increased in Ghana, so did the musical influence of these cultures. In particular, highlife was the first significant movement to develop from this interaction. Blending traditional Ghanaian styles with the foxtrot, waltz, calypso, and eventually Caribbean sounds led to an Afro-European blend that grew in popularity throughout the region. Highlife also contributed to a popular club and concert scene.

During the 1960s, the highlife genre lost some popularity as political revolution swept West Africa. By the 1980s, reggae and other music imports had taken the place of the highlife music style. In the 1990s, a Ghanaian musician living in London was becoming more and more influenced by hip-hop from Europe and the US. Inspired by what he called "African origins" in the music, Reggie Rockstone soon returned to Ghana to blend these sounds, and hip-life music was born. Rockstone is considered the "father" of hip-life because of his conscious choice to sing lyrics mainly in Twi. Hiplife remains widely popular in Ghana. In addition, R&B, hip-hop and dance music are also popular.

Literature

Ghana's literary history began as oral tradition rich in allegories. In the past, the stories of history, societal norms, and moral values were transmitted from one generation to the next by village or even family storytellers. Traditionally, the most highly regarded orators were the elders of a family. When performing such a story, the storyteller would incorporate the audience in the storytelling process. Stories typically involved animals displaying human attributes and suffering through human trials. Each story carried with it an intended message or lesson.

Another part of this oral tradition was the characteristic use of proverbs. The combined cultures within Ghana are said to have produced thousands of these clever adages that carefully or humorously cloak the intended message. Their intent was to transmit messages to others hidden in symbolism and almost riddle-like language. One traditional Ghanaian proverb holds that "The knot tied by a wise man cannot be undone by a fool."

Located on the coast in West Africa, Ghana has seen cultural influences from both the Middle East and North Africa. In addition, European influences are evident, due to the country's history as a British colony. As a result, in the north the influence of Islam in literature and writing is still prevalent, while most of the southern regions learned English from the British. English has since become the official national language and is the primary language taught in Ghanaian schools. However, traditional languages, particularly the Ashanti Twi language, still abound. Ayi Kwei Armah (1939–) is one of the most famous Ghanaian writers. A teacher and world traveler, he is famed for his depiction of cultural diversity in present-day Ghana.

CULTURE

Arts & Entertainment

Popular cultural events in Ghana include festivals held throughout the year based on historic tribal traditions. Many Ashanti people hold the Adae and Akwasidae festivals to honor their ancestors every forty-two days. The first day of the festival occurs on a Sunday, and the second part on the following Wednesday. These festivals are filled with bright costumes and dancing to djembe drum music. The participants drink palm wine to cleanse themselves, and the ceremony involves special golden stools that are reserved for the spirits of the people's ancestors.

In addition, Ghana is known for hiplife music, a local dance music played in its urban clubs that derives from the highlife music tradition of the 1960s. These clubs are also known as venues for Western hip-hop and R&B music.

Modern Ghanaian art reflects the conflict between modernity and tradition that faces most

Africans. Sculptor Vincent Kofi, in works such as *Mother and Child* and *Sankofa,* depicts familiar scenes that comment on the influence of colonialism and globalization. Contemporary painters such as Ato Delaquis, Wisdom Kutowor, and Godfried Donkor have been trained formally, and depict crowded urban markets, poverty, tribal scenes and other elements and challenges of daily Ghanaian life in their work. Donkor, in particular, is famous for turning images of historic black and African figures into abstract or socially significant scenes.

Performance arts share a strong link with traditional and colonial backgrounds. To establish a sense of national identity through the arts, President Kwame Nkrumah helped found the National Theatre Movement, which was charged with the task of developing Ghanaian theatre. Many playwrights and performers came to flourish because of this support. Among them was Afua Sutherland, playwright and eventual developer of Sutherland's Ghana Drama Studio in Accra. It was on this site in the early 1990s that dictator J.J. Rawlings declared that the Ghana National Theatre would be built.

The government of Ghana still struggles to support its contemporary arts sector, as limited financial resources are often allocated to the purveyors of traditional arts. These artists tend to sell more of their work to tourists. The future of many contemporary artists is uncertain, as their materials are often expensive and without government support, there is little opportunity for their work to be seen.

Cultural Sites & Landmarks

Some of the most widely known cultural landmarks in Ghana are the colonial forts that were built along the country's shoreline beginning in the 16th century. As the slave trade grew and became more and more lucrative, the forts increasingly shifted their function from storing goods to storing kidnapped Africans from all over West Africa. Half of the Africans transported from these forts never made it to their destinations alive, and those who survived were sold into a life of servitude in the Americas and the Caribbean.

Many of the forts still stand today, and serve as reminders of one of humankind's greatest tragedies. The Portuguese, for example, first built St. George's Castle at Elmina, in 1642 after they recognized the region's rich gold deposits. The castle, along with all of the others built along the coast, passed through the hands of many European powers over the course of the next few centuries. The castle still stands, and is the first European building in sub-Saharan West Africa.

Also on the coast is Ghana's capital, Accra, the most modern and congested city in the country. Diverse ethnic groups, shanty towns, wealthy suburbs, popular nightlife and national and international business thrive in this chaotic conglomeration of centuries-old fishing villages. The city also boasts national monuments honoring Ghana's first president, Kwame Nkrumah, and the civil rights activist W.E.B. DuBois. Vast markets, specializing in food, housewares, textiles and other goods are located throughout the city. The Makola Market is the largest such example in Accra, stretching through the winding and narrow streets of an entire neighborhood and selling everything from fresh fruit and vegetables to appliances and clothing.

The sites of historic and present-day Ashanti dwellings are also of great cultural significance. The Ashanti are famed not only for their unification of central Ghanaian tribes but also for their defiance of colonial rule. Kumasi is the capital of the Ashanti region and a center of trade for northern Ghana. The Ashanti built beautiful mud homes, palaces, and centers of worship with their characteristic grooved and swirling patterned walls. Most of those structures are gone today, but visitors to Kumasi can find examples of such design at the Prempeh II Cultural Center and the Manhyia Palace, built by the British for King Prempeh I upon his return from exile in 1925.

Libraries & Museums

The National Museum of Ghana, located in the capital of Accra, is the primary museum of the country, being the oldest and largest of the six state-administered museums in the West African nation. Artifacts on permanent exhibit include native Ghanaian instruments, traditional pottery and beads, and a collection of contemporary Ghanaian paintings. Other museums in Ghana include the Gramophone Records Museum, which celebrates highlife music; the Armed Forces Museum, a Ghanaian military museum; Kwame Nkrumah Mausoleum in Accra, a museum and mausoleum that houses the remains of Ghana's first president, Kwame Nkrumah; and the ethnographical and archeological Cape Coast Castle Museum, designated a World Heritage Site by UNESCO. The country is also home to numerous regional and university museums.

Libraries and archive institutions in Ghana include the Accra Central Library, the George Padmore Institute, a research library that acts as Ghana's national library, and the National Archives of Ghana, in Accra, as wells as regional and university libraries.

Holidays

Since the majority of the population is Christian, holidays such as Easter and Christmas are widely celebrated. Muslim holidays, such as Eid-al-Fitr and Eid-al-Adha, are also observed.

The main secular holiday in Ghana is Independence Day (March 6). Other holidays include Road Crossing Day (February 28), May Day (May 1), First Republic Day (July 1), and United Nations Day (October 24).

Youth Culture

Youth culture is seeing drastic change as Ghana continues its path toward economic development and increased outside influence. Like their Western counterparts, Ghanaian teens hang out with friends after school and on the weekends. Relationships between males and females are common and usually result in sexual activity, despite the disapproval of family. Fashion is thought to be fueling this increased activity, as girls are wearing more revealing clothing. It is now common for young women to wear skirts low enough on their hips to show their stomachs, a style known as, "I'm aware." The saying comes from the implication that someone dressing in this manner is aware of her own sexuality. Young men commonly dress in a style referred to as Otto-Pfister, derived from the German coach of the Ghanaian Black Stars. In this style, they wear loose-fitting and long pants that brush the ground.

Despite these changes, elders still hold much sway over youth in day-to-day interaction. This means youth traditionally address all elders as mother, father, grandmother, etc., and always avert their eyes during conversation.

Trokosi is a traditional practice in which families pledge one of their children to the local shrine in an attempt to atone for the offense of another family member. Generally, the family member to be given to the shrine is a young woman from the family. The practice is officially outlawed, but superstition and strong belief systems often trump the law.

SOCIETY

Transportation

There are numerous options for transportation in Ghana, including buses, tro-tros, taxis, boats, planes, and cars. As of 2013, there were 10 airports throughout Ghana. Most Ghanaians use tro-tros and buses when they need to travel longer distances. Tro-tro is the name for the numerous mini-buses and mini-vans found throughout the country. Taxi drivers and tro-tro drivers are exclusively male. Sometimes drivers hire an apprentice to work out of the back of the tro-tro and call out the route, attracting passengers and taking their fares. Tro-tros are decorated ornately with stickers and other adornments, reflecting the driver's personal tastes.

For longer trips, large buses or shared taxis are good options. Line taxis run specific routes, and shared taxis go the best route for all passengers. This helps to lower the cost and save time otherwise used in making stops on an entire bus route. Larger buses make long trips, sometimes over several days. Trips are often long because the driver is obligated to stop in many places, dropping off passengers and giving locals an opportunity to sell their goods at the bus windows.

People drive on the right side of the roadways in Ghana. Main road conditions are generally good; however, even within cities, some side streets may be in disrepair. Driving at night may be particularly hazardous, as there tends to be less-than-adequate street lighting, as well as pedestrians and bicyclists. Drivers should also consider that domesticated animals such as goats might be encountered on roadways. Another important consideration for drivers is the frequent checkpoints throughout the country, during which police may stop and search vehicles.

Transportation Infrastructure

Ghana has better roads than many of its West African neighbors. While paved roads are good, unpaved roads are generally very battered and rife with large potholes. As of 2009, Ghana's road network consisted of more than 109,515 kilometers (68049 miles) of road length. The government implemented a National Transport Policy in 2007, which includes the upgrading of infrastructure and the development of transportation services, particularly in urban areas. Many infrastructure improvements, such as revamping the railways and building a deep-sea port, are related to Ghana's 21st-century plans on becoming a major producer of gas and oil.

Media & Communications

The Ghanaian press developed out of interaction with colonial powers. The first people to hold media positions in Ghana were members of the elite ruling and European settlers. However, as the country swelled with talks of independence, newspapers and radio became catalysts for the spread of such ideas. Ironically, once Ghana had won its independence, its first president, Kwame Nkrumah (1909–1972), established national communications and outlawed the establishment of private forms of information dissemination. The national press and radio were also heavily censored to exclude any negative information about the president or his policies.

With the ousting of Nkrumah in the 1960s, Ghana saw freedom of the press restored. Today, Ghana is one of the best examples in all of Africa of a thriving and free communications infrastructure. There exists a plethora of both state-run and private publications. Radio and television shows bring information to nearly every corner of the nation. *The Daily Graphic* and *Ghanaian Times* are state-run, daily newspapers written entirely in English and covering Ghanaian, African and international news. Ghana Television, GTV, broadcasts nightly news in English and daily programming in English and Twi.

In addition to print and television, radio still maintains its status as a source of information for Ghanaians and an excellent example of Ghana's free and fair press. For example, call-in talk shows addressing development and the policies of current administrations are extremely popular.

Ghana was one of the first West African nations to have Internet access. As of 2014, there are nearly five million Internet users, representing 19.6 percent of the population. In 1992, Ghana launched the first cellular mobile network in sub-Saharan Africa. As of 2014, there are 30.4 million mobile phone users, and 260,000 fixed landlines.

SOCIAL DEVELOPMENT

Standard of Living

In 2013, Ghana's Human Development Index rank was 138th of 187 countries. Life expectancy at birth was 66.18 years in 2015.

Water Consumption

According to the Joint Monitoring Program for Water Supply and Sanitation (from UNICEF and WHO), 88 percent of Ghana's urban population and 64 percent of its rural population had access to water from sources such as dug wells, springs, and rainwater collections. However, only 37 percent of its urban and four percent of its rural populations had house connections to a water source. Sanitation is also an issue, with only 27 percent of the country's urban population and 11 percent of its rural having access to sanitation systems such as sewers, latrines, and septic systems.

In 2015, 92.6 percent of Ghana's urban population and 84 percent of the rural population had access to improved drinking water.

Schistosomiasis (also known as bilharzia), a disease caused by a parasitic worm found in water, affects over 100 million people on the African continent. In Ghana, populations living near Lake Volta, such as the inhabitants of the Aboam and Dominase villages, are particularly vulnerable to the disease.

Education

Education is free and compulsory in Ghana. Children begin attending nursery school around the ages of three and four and then take two years of kindergarten. Next, students complete primary school, junior secondary school, and senior secondary school, after which they may attend university. In school, students learn both English and at least one other ethnic language.

In 2005, the Ministry of Education eliminated school fees in attempt to increase access to education, as well as narrow the gender gap. By the next school year, kindergarten enrollment had increased by 67 percent, with the majority of the increase comprising female students.

In 2015, the literacy rate was 76.6 percent (82 percent for men and 71.4 percent for women). Relative to the rest of Africa, Ghana is one of the most educated countries. The current education system, in place since 1974, consists of three cycles, which lead to either a vocational program or university. There are seven public universities in Ghana, all supported by the government. They include the University of Ghana, located near Accra in Legon; the University of Science and Technology, in Kumasi; and the University of Cape Coast, which trains science teachers.

Women's Rights

Although Ghana's economy has grown, women and men do not share equally in the benefits. Traditional gender roles, for example, remain stagnant and strict, even in households in which women have full time jobs in addition to their responsibilities at home. This sense of duty to household affairs is ingrained in girls at a very young age, when labor is initially divided up among siblings. Most of the time, young girls are responsible for household chores while they are also attending school; as a result, many girls do not complete their education.

Women marry in their late teens or early 20s and generally have children immediately after marriage. Some women find work as teachers and nurses throughout Ghana. However, in the workplace, women still face significant discrimination from male coworkers.

Women are also regularly victims of spousal abuse and even rape. Although Ghanaian law prohibits violence against anyone, charges are rarely filed and arrests are much less frequent. Given the disparities in access to education, women in Ghana are generally less educated than their husbands are, and charges of abuse against a husband could require a woman to suffer through divorce that will render her homeless and without money to raise children. In the event of divorce, men do not battle for custody of their children, leaving women with the sole responsibility of raising them. Men may also be polygamous, especially in the northern part of the country.

Even though women have the right to hold political positions, after Ghana's elections in 2012, women held just 11 percent of the seats.

Health Care

Ghana is healthy relative to the rest of West Africa, but is considered unhealthy when compared with World standards. Health care is primarily provided through government hospitals and Christian missions. The government has been trying to boost public health by improving sanitation, nutrition, and the availability of drugs.

The country's health problems have centered on endemic, communicable diseases, such as pneumonia and malaria, as well as gastrointestinal diseases. Like the rest of Africa, Ghana has also been affected by HIV/AIDS. An estimated 1.47 percent of the adult population (about 387,016 people) suffers from AIDS (2014 estimate).

Other infectious diseases affecting Ghana include typhoid fever, yellow fever, and

schistosomiasis. The infant mortality rate, which has been improving along with the rest of the country's health, is approximately 37.4 deaths per 1,000 live births (2015 estimate).

GOVERNMENT

Structure
Ghana is a constitutional democracy. Its most recent constitution, reinstating multiparty politics, was adopted in 1992. In 1957, Ghana became the first sub-Saharan colony to gain its independence from Great Britain, though its initial statehood was defined by frequent coups.

Ghana has universal suffrage for citizens over the age of 18, and its legal system is based on English common law. Its executive branch is comprised of a chief of state and a head of government; both functions are fulfilled by the president (as in the United States government). The president nominates his Council of Ministers, which are then approved by Parliament. The president and the vice president are elected every four years by popular vote.

The legislative branch is comprised of a single-chamber, 230-seat parliament. The members of parliament are also elected to four-year terms by popular vote. The judicial branch is made up of a Supreme Court.

Political Parties
Political parties in Ghana include the New Patriotic Party (NPP), the National Democratic Congress Party, the Convention People's Party (CPC), and the Every Ghanaian Living Everywhere Party (EGLE), among others. (It should be noted that it is difficult to ascribe European and U.S. notions of liberalism and conservatism to the political parties of Ghana since the socioeconomic systems are so different.)

The National Democratic Congress Party was founded in 1992 and is considered a social democratic party. In 2012, the party's presidential candidate, John Dramani Mahama, won the election, earning just over 50.7 percent of the vote in a run-off election.

The Convention People's Party was formed in 1949 by Kwame Nkrumah, but was banned in 1966 after Nkrumah was lost power following a coup d'état by the National Liberation Council. The CPC reformed in 1996 because of the merging of the National Convention Party and the People's Convention Party. In the 2008 elections, the CPC won one parliamentary seat.

Local Government

In Ghana, executive power has been decentralized to the regional, district, and municipal levels, a process that began in 1988. There are 10 regions in Ghana, each headed by a presidentially appointed regional minister. Local governance is overseen by metropolitan, district, and municipal assemblies, with district assemblies having both legislative and executive powers. There are 138 district assemblies. Under municipal assemblies are zonal councils and unit committees, while urban/town/area councils fall under the district assemblies. The regional coordinating councils coordinate policy implementation among districts.

Judicial System

The higher court system in Ghana includes a Supreme Court, a Court of Appeal, a High Court, and 10 Regional Tribunals. The lower court system includes circuit courts, juvenile courts, and community and family tribunals.

Taxation

Ghana has a personal income tax and a value-added tax (VAT), and in the past has instituted a wealth tax that is not, as of 2010, being levied. The country also has a capital gains tax and gift tax, as well as a corporation/business tax. In 2014, taxes accounted for 23.2 percent of the country's GDP.

Armed Forces

The military of Ghana comprises an Army, Air Force, National Police Force, Navy, Palace Guard, and Civil Defense. To enlist, a candidate must be HIV/AIDS negative.

Foreign Policy

During the 1920s, Ghana showed some of the first stirrings of revolution, but local authorities quashed the sentiment. In 1957, however, Ghana became sub-Saharan Africa's first independent nation and Kwame Nkrumah was appointed as the first president. One of his first acts was to change the nation's name from the Gold Coast to Ghana. He then pushed strong legislation aimed at suppressing the various chiefs who were claiming rights to power of their own. He also limited the freedom of the press and embarked on steep borrowing from European nations to fund development projects.

Finally, in accordance with his determination to inspire the independence of all of Africa, he instituted the concept of Pan-Africanism. This was a policy by which Ghana sought to root out the influence of colonial powers by helping other nations develop free of outside political influence. He felt political ideology should be left out of this endeavor, and that other African nations should maintain their sovereignty.

With increasing poverty and civil unrest due to failed economic policies, Nkrumah was eventually ousted from power by the first of three coups that would follow before Jerry Rawlings assumed the presidency in 1982. When he came to power, he had drought, high national debt, and political corruption to tackle, among many other national concerns. A significant achievement in foreign policy during this time was Ghana's integral role in developing the Economic Organization of West African States (ECOWAS). This agreement among West African nations fueled trade in the region in the following decades. Rawlings held power until 2000, when the constitution mandated elections. The elections were considered free and fair by international observers and resulted in the election of opposition leader Dr. John Kufor.

Today, Ghana enjoys a reputation of stability in West Africa. In November 2008, citizens went to the polls for the second election since Rawlings willingly turned power over to Kufor in 2000. Though a runoff was necessary, the recount designated opposition leader John Atta Mills as the new president. Kufor congratulated the winner and the country thus passed through another democratic process with little conflict. Leaders all over the world acclaimed the transition.

Ghana's reputation as an example of successful West African democracy is also based on its assistance to its neighbors in times of crisis. Ghana has sent troops to join peacekeeping efforts in Sierra Leone and Liberia, as well as to Cambodia and Rwanda.

Human Rights Profile

International human rights law insists that states respect civil and political rights, and promote an individual's economic, social, and cultural rights. The United Nations Universal Declaration on Human Rights (UDHR) is recognized as the standard for international human rights. Its authors sought the counsel of the world's great thinkers, philosophers, and religious leaders, and were careful to create a document that reflects the core values shared by every world culture. (To read this document or view the articles relating to cultural human rights, visit http://www.udhr.org/UDHR/default.htm.)

Ghana is a constitutional democracy, which means it is a country of laws aimed at protecting the rights of its citizens equally. Nearly all of these laws were developed in accordance with the basic human rights outlined in the UDHR. Despite these protections, citizens and human rights advocacy groups see inconsistencies. In terms of criminal and prisoner protection, the law prohibits unlawful detention and inhumane treatment of criminals. However, human rights activists interviewing inmates found severe overcrowding of jails in Ghana. Some jails were operating at three times the intended capacity. This led to the spread of violence and disease, ultimately resulting in the deaths of inmates.

The freedom to demonstrate is also protected in the constitution but not practiced in reality. Many college demonstrations in past years have resulted in mass arrests and even police violence.

Workers' rights are also protected, as is the right to organize. The legal age at which young people are allowed to work is 15 for intensive labor, and thirteen for easier jobs. However, much younger children are forced into labor without pay in parts of rural Ghana.

These issues are thought by most Ghanaians to be the result of government corruption. According to the World Bank, while Ghana's government still has many problems regarding corruption, it has made significant progress since the 2004 elections. These improvements include legislation to improve the transparency of government. This legislation was introduced in 2002, however, and still has not been approved by the parliament. Ghana has also made headway with the introduction of the National Reconciliation Commission, established in 2001 to allocate reparations to families who suffered at the hands of the various military governments since 1957.

Ghana's constitution grants asylum to individuals qualifying as refugees in accordance with the 1951 United Nations Convention on Refugees. As a result, during the fifteen-year civil war in Liberia and neighboring Sierra Leone, Ghana allowed over 100,000 refugees to live in camps within Ghanaian borders. The Buduburam Camp is one of the most widely known, and has housed over 40,000 refugees since its inception. Despite providing asylum to so many refugees, some are unable to obtain work and do not receive proper protection from the police.

ECONOMY

Overview of the Economy

Ghana remains one of the world's poorest countries, and carries a lot of debt from international loans. As recently as the 1980s, the World Bank developed a program to resuscitate Ghana's economy, encouraging foreign companies to invest in public and private joint projects. In 1992, Ghana began to receive debt relief from the Heavily Indebted Poor Country program.

In 2014, the gross domestic product (GDP) of Ghana was an estimated $108.3 billion (USD).

Mainly agriculture and mineral mining drive the economy. Ghana's reputation as the "Gold Coast" has remained intact since the 15th century. Approximately 45 percent of the labor force works in agriculture, and 40.9 percent works in the service industry. Ghana is also looking to become a major commercial producer of gas and oil in the 21st century, and has been boosted by a $600 million loan by the IMF in 2009 to achieve this goal.

Industry

Relative to other West African countries, Ghana has a booming industry. In 2009, approximately 56 percent of the work force was employed in the agricultural industry. Beer, tobacco, aluminum, and cement are among the country's manufactured products. The timber industry supports several saw mills, and the Tema Oil Refinery Corporation operates a refinery in Ghana.

Labor

In 2013, the unemployment rate in Ghana was 5.2 percent. In 2014, the country's labor force was over 11.25 million.

Energy/Power/Natural Resources

Historically, Ghana's greatest natural resource is gold, which earned the country its nickname, the "Gold Coast," during the 15th century. The country also has deposits of oil and natural gas. Today, the country's most important natural resource is cacao.

Fishing

Fish for export includes tuna, tilapia, herring, mackerel, and barracuda. In 2009, the fishing industry accounted for 4.5 percent of Ghana's gross national product and employed approximately 10 percent of the population. That same year, the government announced plans to construct two fishing harbors and a dozen landing sites to encourage and promote the country's fishing industry.

Forestry

In January 2010, Ghana exported 26,421 cubic meters of wood products such as lumber, plywood, and billet. Ghana has a wide variety of tree species, including teak, eucalyptus, edinam, nyankom, wawa, and mahogany.

Mining/Metals

Gold, diamonds, iron, and silver are mined in Ghana.

Agriculture

More than half of Ghana's arable land is devoted to the cultivation of cacao, the primary ingredient in the production of chocolate. In 2009, Ghana produced approximately 14 percent of the world's cacao. Ghana also exports salt, which is collected from its lagoons and the Gulf of Guinea. Other products for export include coffee and sugar, as well as various fruits and vegetables.

Animal Husbandry

Livestock production includes goats, cattle, and chicken.

Tourism

Tourism is on the rise in Ghana, aided by the Ghana Tourist Board and Ghana Tourist Development Company. Most tourists come from nearby African countries, such as Nigeria and Cote d'Ivoire, but many tourists also visit from Great Britain, the United States, and Germany. Hotels are located in the more developed urban areas near the coast, such as Accra, or in larger central cities such as Kumasi.

Kristen Pappas, Barrett Hathcock

DO YOU KNOW?

- Lake Volta is one of the largest artificial lakes in the World.
- There are occasional earthquakes in Ghana, usually near Accra, the capital. A fault line runs along the eastern edge of the Akwapim-Togo mountain ranges.

Bibliography

Conrad, David C. *Empires of Medieval West Africa: Ghana, Mali, And Songhay (Great Empires of the Past)*. New York: Facts on File, 2005.

Cottrell, Anna. *Once upon a Time in Ghana: Traditional Ewe Stories Retold in English*. London: Troubador Publishing Ltd., 2007.

Gaines, Kevin K. *American Africans in Ghana: Black Expatriates and the Civil Rights Era (The John Hope Franklin Series in African American History and Culture)*. Chapel Hill, NC: University of North Carolina Press, 2007.

Hasty, Jennifer. *The Press and Political Culture in Ghana*. Bloomington, IN: Indiana University Press, 2005.

McCaskie, T.C. *Asante Identities: History and Modernity in an African Village, 1850–1950*. Bloomington, IN: Indiana University Press, 2001.

Miescher, Stephen F. *Making Men in Ghana*. Bloomington, IN: Indiana University Press, 2005.

Salm, Steven J, and Falola, Toyin. *Culture and Customs of Ghana (Culture and Customs of Africa)*. Westport, CT: Greenwood Press, 2002.

Stanliand, Martin. *The Lions of Dagbon: Political Change In Northern Ghana (African Studies)*. New York: Cambridge University Press, 2008.

Utley, Lynn. *Ghana—Culture Smart! The Essential Guide to Customs and Culture*. London: Kuperard, 2009.

Works Cited

"Achimota School Webpage. http://www.achimota.edu.gh/

"Akan Kente Cloths." Marshall University: Akan Cultural Symbols Project. http://www.marshall.edu/akanart/CLOTH_KENTE.HTML

"Ashanti Culture." Minnesota State e-Museum. http://www.mnsu.edu/emuseum/cultural/oldworld/africa/ashanti_culture.html

"Buduburam Camp," Metro TV News Video, Accra, Ghana. http://www.youtube.com/watch?v=uK-WuA1TkJM

"Contemporary Visual Art from Ghana," George Hughes. Review of Contemporary African Art: *Virtual Museum of Contemporary African Art*. http://www.vmcaa.nl/vm/magazine/002/artikel001/

"Customs of Ghana." Sidebar from Encarta. http://encarta.msn.com/sidebar_631522202/customs_of_ghana.html

"Anansi Stories." Kidipede: History and Science for Middle School Kids. http://www.historyforkids.org/learn/africa/literature/anansi.htm

"Country Profile: Ghana." BBC World News. http://news.bbc.co.uk/1/hi/world/africa/country_profiles/1023355.stm

"Elmina Castle." Wikipedia. http://en.wikipedia.org/wiki/Elmina_Castle

"Civilizations in West Africa: Ghana." Wisconsin State University: World Civilizations. http://www.wsu.edu:8080/~dee/CIVAFRCA/GHANA.HTM

"Foreign Relations: Guiding Principles and Objectives". U.S. Library of Congress Country Studies. http://countrystudies.us/ghana/107.htm

"Ghana: 1950 – 2050." World Urbanization Prospects: The 2007 Revision Population Database. http://esa.un.org/unup/p2k0data.asp

"Ghana." CIA World Factbook, December 2008. https://www.cia.gov/library/publications/the-world-factbook/geos/gh.html#Trans

"Ghana." International Encyclopedia of Adolescence http://books.google.com/books?id=lA606koL3EQC&pg=PA347&lpg=PA347&dq=youth+culture+ghana&source=bl&ots=6A0Fan9nA9&sig=vQqu6JJCsSJMfdRjSO4TH4mKA2E&hl=en&sa=X&oi=book_result&resnum=3&ct=result#PPA348,M1.

"Ghana." U.S. Department of State: Country Reports on Human Rights Practices 2007. http://www.state.gov/g/drl/rls/hrrpt/2007/100484.htm

"Ghana-Liberia: Liberian Refugees Still Wary of Returning Home." Humanitarian news and analysis: UN Office for the Coordination of Humanitarian Affairs. http://www.irinnews.org/report.aspx?reportid=57518

"Ghanaian Popular Cinema and Magic in and of Film." Brigit Meyer, 2002 African film Festival. http://www.africanfilmny.org/network/news/Fmeyer.html

"Kingdoms of Ghana." Boston University African Studies Center. http://www.bu.edu/africa/outreach/materials/handouts/k_o_ghana.html

"Kofi, Vincent Akwete, 1923–1974." Monograph on African Artists: *Smithsonian Institution Libraries*. http://www.sil.si.edu/SILPublications/ModernAfricanArt/monographs_detail.cfm?artist=Kofi,%20Vincent%20Akwete,%201923-1974

"Makola Market." Trip Advisor: Ghana. http://www. tripadvisor.com/Attraction_Review-g293797-d478881- Reviews-Makola_Market-Accra.html "Ghana Etiquette Tips." Vayama: International Travel Solved. http://www. vayama.com/ghana-etiquette

"The Empires of the Western Sudan: Ghana Empire". The Metropolitan Museum of Art, Heilbrunn Timeline of Art History. http://www.metmuseum.org/toah/hd/ghan/ hd_ghan.htm

"The Growth of a National Form of Theatre in Ghana," Steve Collins. Border Crossings. http://www. bordercrossings.org.uk/dilemma-ntgart.html

"Twi." Geocities.com http://www.geocities.com/asantedom/ webs/twi/indextwi.htm

Stanford University Africa South of the Sahara. http:// library.stanford.edu/depts/ssrg/africa/guide2.html

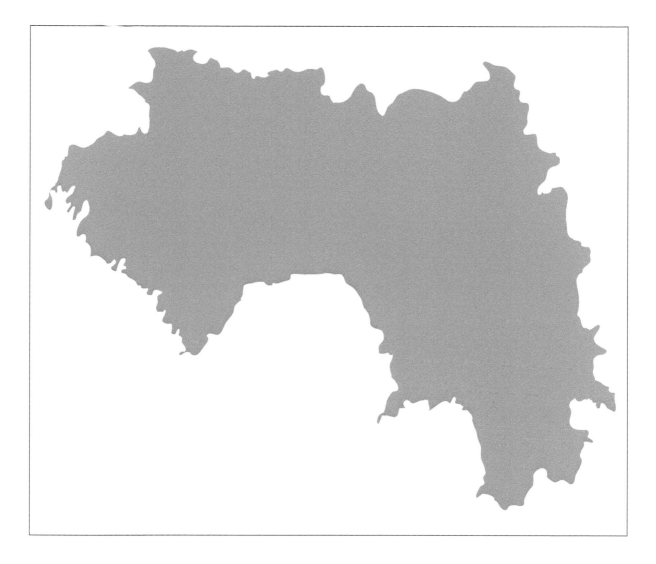

GUINEA

Introduction

The Republic of Guinea, formerly known as French Guinea, is located on the Atlantic coast of Africa and borders Guinea-Bissau, Senegal, Liberia, Côte d'Ivoire, Mali, and Sierra Leone. The name Guinea-Conakry is sometimes used to distinguish the country from its neighbor, Guinea-Bissau, and Equitorial Guinea. The nation contains portions of many of Africa's major rivers, including the Niger, Fatala, and the Rio Nuñez (Nunez River). Export along these rivers played a major role in encouraging immigration and settlement during the formation of the nation. Guinea is also referred to as Guinea-Conakry to distinguish itself from the Republic of Guinea-Bissau, another West African country that is northwest of Guinea.

In the decades since French officials abruptly withdrew from Guinea, the country has struggled to stimulate economic growth or achieve political compromise; until 2010, Guinea also operated under authoritarian rule since gaining its independence in 1958. However, in 2010, the first democratic elections were held for the office of president, while legislative elections were held in 2013, which determined the new National Assembly. As of January 2014, the first all-civilian presidential cabinet was also appointed. Still, corruption and violence are rampant in Guinea. Moreover, smuggling, banditry, and refugee movement plague Guinea's borders with Sierra Leone, Liberia, and Côte d'Ivoire, countries also struggling with their own civil unrest and development issues.

Different regions of Guinea are known for different sorts of crafts and artwork, and for its hand-dyed textiles, the country has developed an internationally renowned reputation that dates back centuries. Guinea's Fouta Djallon region is one of only a few in the world where natural indigo dyes from indigenous plants are still used to produce the vivid colors and patterns on hand-dyed textiles. Traditional music remains vibrant throughout the country, although African musicians have also been blending traditional rhythms, instruments, and themes with international musical styles.

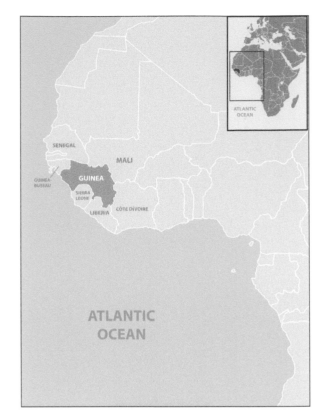

The country's newest challenge is the Ebola epidemic. As of 2015, the U.S. Centers for Disease Control (CDC) estimates that within Guinea, there are a possible 3,800 cases, with 3,340 of them lab-confirmed. Already 2,532 have died of the disease. The outbreak has hindered economic growth and caused widespread civil unrest and even violence against aid workers.

GENERAL INFORMATION

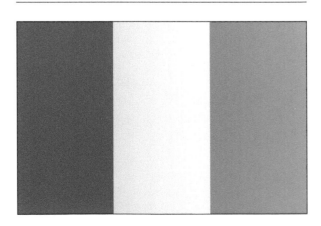

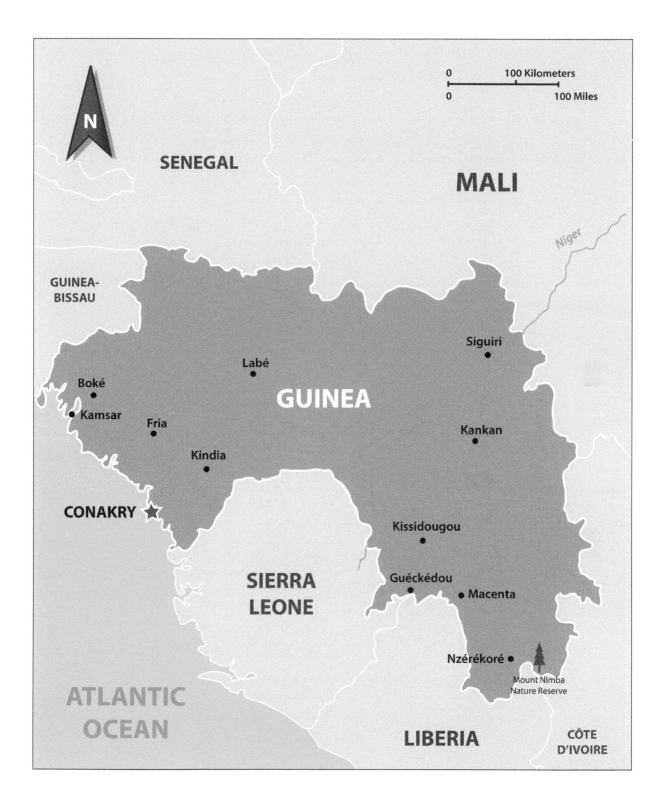

Principal Cities by Population (2014 estimates):

- Kankan (1,986,329)
- Conakry (1,667,864)
- Nzérékoré (1,663,582)
- Kindia (1,559,185)
- Labé (995,717)
- Mamou (732,117)
- Kissidougou (90,000)
- Port Kamsar (85,000)
- Guékédou (also, Guéckédougou) (63,000)
- Macenta (58,000)

Official Language: French
Population: 11,780,162 (2015 estimate)
Currency: Guinean franc (also, franc guinéen)
Coins: Coins are available in denominations of 1, 5, 10, 25, and 50 francs.
Land Area: 245,717 square kilometers (94,871 square miles)
Water Area: 140 square kilometers (54 square miles)
National Motto: "Travail, Justice, Solidarité" ("Work, Justice, Solidarity")
National Anthem: "Liberté" ("Liberty")
Capital: Conakry
Time Zone: GMT +0
Flag Description: The flag of Guinea features three vertical bands of color. Starting from the hoist side, they are red, yellow, and green. The red represents the people's sacrifice for work and liberty; yellow represents the sun, the country's national resources, and justice; and green represents both vegetation and unity. Red, yellow, and green are also the colors of the Pan-African movement and used commonly in national flags throughout Africa.

Population

Guinea's population is made up of a variety of African ethnic groups, including the Peuhl (also called Foula or Foulani), who make up about 40 percent of the population and live in the mountainous Fouta Djallon region. The Malinké (also called the Mandinka or Mandingo) are mostly

in the northern part of the country and account for about 30 percent of Guineans. The Soussou (or Susu) make up about 20 percent of the population, and live predominantly in the south around the capital. Smaller ethnic groups comprise approximately 10 percent of the remaining population.

Guinea also hosts a significant number of refugees who have fled civil violence in neighboring countries. While in the first decade of the 21st century, there were over 133,000 refugees from Liberia; 13,600 refugees from Sierra Leone; and 7,000 refugees from Côte d'Ivoire, the United National High Commissioner on Refugees (UNHCR) reports that, as of December 2014, the country has only 8,766 refugees and 281 asylum-seekers. Refugees leaving Guinea, according to the UNHCR, number 15,243, with 17,844 asylum-seekers. In 2014, Guinea's non-African population totaled 30,000 people, most of whom are from Lebanon, France, and other European countries.

There are approximately 1.7 million people living in Conakry. It is the second-most populous city in Guinea, after Kankan, which boasted nearly 2 million people in 2014. As of 2015, an estimated 37.2 percent of the population was urban. In 2015, Guinea had a population growth rate of 2.63 percent.

Languages

French is the official language in Guinea and is used in government, business, and education. In addition to French, native tribal languages such as Malinké, Fula, and Susu are commonly spoken. Kissi, Kpelle (also Guerzé), and Toma are spoken. There are more than 40 languages spoken within the country, and Arabic

Native People & Ethnic Groups

Guinea is located at a traditional crossroads where a large number of African tribes and empires, and later, European merchants, adventurers, and colonizers have all left their mark. Today, Guinea's largest ethnic tribes are the Peuhl (also the Foula or Foulani) at 40 percent, the Malinké (also called the Mandinka or

Mandingo) at 30 percent, the Soussou (or Susu) at 20 percent, the Kisi at 6.5 percent, the Kpelle 13 percent, and other smaller groups at approximately 11.6 percent.

Most of Guinea's native population survives on traditional methods of farming, herding, and artisanship. The Soussou and those who live in the lowlands grow rice, pineapples, palm kernels, and other fruits and vegetables that thrive in that fertile region. In the mountainous Fouta Djallon, the Fulani herd livestock in the cool, hilly prairies. In Upper Guinea, the Malinké farm hot, savanna grasslands and are famous for the skill of their artisans. Smaller tribes like the Kissi, Guerze, Toma, and Mano subsist with traditional hunting skills in the dense forests of southeastern Guinea. The majority of Guinea's population lives and works in Conakry and its environs.

Religions

Most of Guinea's population is Muslim, a legacy of the Holy Islamic War of the 18th century. Islamic holy days are recognized by the state and serve as a focus for community organization. About 85 percent of the population practices Islam, while eight percent practice some form of Christianity. Meanwhile, most Guineans maintain some customs or beliefs from traditional animist faiths, although the official number of those following indigenous beliefs is seven percent. Urban Conakry hosts a more diverse religious complement of Christian and animist groups, as well as those practicing other tribal-oriented beliefs.

Climate

Guinea's tropical climate varies slightly by region, but is essentially humid throughout. Most of the country experiences two rainy seasons: one between April and June, and the second lasting from September to November. The northern region, however, is subject to violent squalls in March and April. These dissipate into sporadic rain showers, which grow stronger toward the peak of this region's rainy season in September.

Annual rainfall in the country varies from 76 to 203 centimeters (30 to 80 inches) on average.

The capital of Conakry on the Atlantic coast may receive as much as 430 centimeters (14.1 feet) or rain per year, with significantly less falling in the Middle Guinea interior. The coastal regions often experience monsoons.

Temperatures throughout most of the country are highest in March and coolest in August. However, the overall temperature variations are slight, ranging from about 23° to 29° Celsius (73° to 84° Fahrenheit). From December until March, a dry desert wind (or harmattan) blows across the northeast of Guinea, creating hot days and cold nights in that region and filling the air with a fine, gray sand.

ENVIRONMENT & GEOGRAPHY

Topography

Guinea is bordered on the north by Guinea-Bissau and Senegal, on the northeast by Mali, on the east by Côte d'Ivoire, and on the south by Liberia and Sierra Leone. Only the western side of the country is protected by 320 kilometers (about 200 miles) of coastline along the North Atlantic. Its maritime claims amount to 12 nautical miles.

Guinea's coastal area, known as Lower Guinea, is an alluvial coastal plain, flat and wet, with large areas of fertile swampland. Middle Guinea, also known as the Fouta Djallon, is comprised of 77,700 square kilometers (30,000 square miles) of mountainous terrain and grasslands. This area, in the nation's interior, has an average altitude of 910 meters (about 3,000 feet).

In Upper Guinea, the interior mountains soften into a plain that sits at an average altitude of 305 meters (1,000 feet). Here, the land is covered in savanna grasses, with occasional rocky outcroppings. In spite of the gentler terrain, Upper Guinea boasts the country's highest point at Mont Nimba, which reaches an altitude of 1,752 meters (5,748 feet).

The republic's most inaccessible region, the highlands, is densely forested with tropical growth. Here, the Niger River and its tributary, the Milo, begin their journey across the interior to the Atlantic Ocean. The geology of the Guinea highlands is notable for the region's proliferation of granites, schist (metamorphic rock), and quartz.

The coastal region, which includes the capital, Conakry, is lined with swamps that blend into a sedimentary plain; mangrove forests are also common. Conakry is divided into two parts, generally known as Conakry 1 and Conakry 2, which are connected by an ocean bridge. The oldest portion, Conakry 1, is located on the largest of a small group of volcanic islands known as the Iles de Los. Conakry 2 is located on the Camayenne or Kaloum Peninsula. The Konkoure River, located north of the city, is used to generate hydroelectric power for Conakry.

Plants & Animals
Guinea's tropical rainforests, elevated grasslands, and alluvial coastal plains provide a rich array of habitats for plant and animal life. However, the region's extreme poverty has driven local populations deep into these natural habitats, often destroying species in the process. Guinea, therefore, has a long list of endangered species.

Some of Guinea's most notable species include large animals like the waterbuck, giraffe, hippopotamus, crocodiles, antelope, elephant, and African lions; and smaller creatures like the Liberian mongoose, fruit bats, several species of monkeys, and Johnston's genet. Guinea's Atlantic coastal waters are also home to several species of dolphin and African manatee. Guinée Écologie has begun working with BirdLife International and since 2008, has secured a protected 450,000 hectares (1,111,974 acres) area in the Fouta Djallon Highlands to ensure the survival the country's six species of vultures and other avian life.

CUSTOMS & COURTESIES

Greetings
Although there are many ethnic and regional languages spoken in Guinea, greetings and typical conversation is commonly conducted in French first, then Arabic. Thus, greetings generally begin

with "Bonjour" ("Good day") during the day and "Bonsoir" ("Good evening") at sunset. In Muslim areas, which now comprise nearly the entire nation, the French greeting is followed by the obligatory "Salaam alaikum" ("Peace be unto you"), with "Malaikum salaam" ("And also unto you") being the proper response.

Once this greeting has taken place, inquiries begin as to the health and well-being of one's family. These friendly questions are conducted nearly exclusively in tribal languages among Guineans, or in French among Guineans and foreigners. As is the custom throughout sub-Saharan Africa, if the introduction and inquiry is forgotten or ignored, a conversation is impossible. Generally, when introducing themselves, Guineans will use formal or honorific titles. This is often reserved for meeting strangers. More informal words, such as "frère" ("brother") and "seour" ("sister"), are used when Guineans greet family, friends, or close acquaintances.

When greeting, it is only appropriate to offer the right hand for a handshake, as the left hand is associated with the cleansing of the body and is considered impure. The only exception to this rule is when Guineans know they are saying farewell to a close friend for a long time. In this case, they will offer their left hand. The left-handed handshake is meant to convey the conviction that the two friends will see each other again in the future. Finally, while these greetings often shared between men and women, a conservative Muslim man will not shake the hand of a woman, but will instead place his right hand across his chest in a sign of deference.

Gestures & Etiquette
Compared to many other West African peoples, Guineans are on average more reserved and quiet in day-to-day interaction. Behavioral characteristics that demonstrate this include averting eye contact when speaking to someone in a position of authority and showing disapproval by wagging one's finger. Verbal disagreement is often considered aggressive and rude. This is not the rule, however, and more often good friends will be seen in public in animated discussion.

Personal space is limited throughout most of Guinea, and conversations are generally held in close quarters (as compared to an arm's length, which is often the appropriate or accepted distance in Western cultures). In fact, if one backs away from his conversational partner, the other may step in to fill the newly created void. Women and men are generally never seen touching in public, but friends of the same gender are commonly seen embracing or holding hands.

Eating/Meals

Most Guineans reside in rural areas and are considered subsistence farmers by trade. For such families, the largest meals are typically breakfast, eaten early in the morning, and then a larger dinner at dusk. During the day, when farmers are working, their wives may bring them meals or they may buy small items, like groundnuts and fried pastries. In urban areas, the largest meals are generally lunch and dinner. Lunch is usually eaten at home for those able to return during the lunch hour, or purchased from small stands and street vendors.

Customarily, meals eaten with family are communal, with the family members serving themselves from a large bowl. Eating is done strictly with the right hand and, in very rare cases, with a spoon. Traditionally, each person sits on the dining mat at his place around the bowl and eats from his corresponding section of the dish. In order to be able to eat from the communal dish, family members must first rinse their right hands, often in a dish provided for such a purpose.

Visiting

Guineans place a high value on social calls and visiting. Having a guest is an honor, and it is the host's duty to ensure the guest is treated appropriately. This involves offering a beverage and having a place to socialize. Guests must also uphold the social customs required when visiting someone's home. In most Guinean homes, or compounds, guests are first greeted at the entrance. After the greeting, guests are either brought to the one-room building dedicated to hosting guests, or they congregate in an area outside on the grounds of the compound. Most commonly, guests sit on a straw or plastic mat on the floor with their hosts. Shoes must always be removed before sitting on the mat.

Once a guest is seated, the women of the house will often offer a beverage. The guest will announce the reason for his visit, or if he did not show up unannounced, he will simply begin the conversation. The most common reasons for visits are to see family, something that may happen as frequently as once daily. It is not customary to bring gifts unless the visitors are from out of town. It is more polite to extend an invitation to one's hosts at the end of a visit in exchange for their hospitality.

LIFESTYLE

Family

Family structure throughout most of Guinea resembles that of other West African nations. Often, large extended families will live together on one compound. The Soussou of the southeastern regions maintain traditional male and female roles within their families. Most men are fishers or farmers, while the women stay at home and tend to domestic responsibilities and child rearing. Generally, the Soussou are known for marriage between family members, with second and even first cousins marrying. This is mainly an attempt to maintain a pure bloodline of Soussou. However, marriage between different ethnicities is becoming more common as younger generations migrate to urban areas.

Among all ethnic groups in Guinea, Islam is the dominant religion. As such, most husbands partake of their ordained right to engage in polygamy (having more than one wife). Islamic law states that a man may have up to four wives, so long as he can care for each of them and their children equally. In these families, it is the first wife's responsibility to maintain peace and harmony among all wives. In urban areas, where multiple wives are forced to live in close quarters with more limited funds, many women and men are opting for monogamous relationships.

An important characteristic of any Guinean family structure is the commonality of certain last names. For example, the Malinké people of the northern region share more than 25 common family names. Touré, the last name of the first Guinean president, is one example. When introducing themselves, Guineans will say their last names and the last names of all of their wives to notify the person to whom they speak of their tribal affiliation. Since most Guineans know the histories of these limited names, they may make premature judgments on the character of the individual before the conversation begins. Despite this strong tendency for family distinction, most Guineans will confer the title of brother, father, sister, or cousin, to a non-blood relative if they are a close friend.

Housing

Despite the clear cultural distinction between the three dominant ethnic groups in Guinea, the Peuhl, the Soussou, and the Malinké, most rural homes share a uniform style. More than 85 percent of Guineans are Muslims, and home construction is tied to traditional beliefs and the demands of religious customs. For example, as in most West African nations, the norm is to live with one's extended family, including grandparents, aunts, uncles, and cousins. In rural areas, when families amass several individual living units, their household is referred to as a compound, and several compounds grouped together make up rural villages. Urban housing is mainly a combination of rural styles, apartments, and larger, Western-style homes.

Rural households are broken up into individual one-room buildings with walls constructed from mud bricks or cement blocks and roofs made of corrugated tin or grass thatch. More often than not, women share one room with their children. Older children may begin sleeping with cousins, while the elderly and the head of the household generally have their own rooms.

Food

The cuisine of Guinea is similar to that found in other West African nations and is based on local foods, such as root vegetables, fruit, fish, groundnuts (peanuts), and rice. Most Guineans prefer their food bland and starchy, though Guinean cuisine is also known for its use of spices and hot chilies. Dishes are often four parts steamed rice and one part sauce, and most Guinean dishes include steamed African white rice. Depending on the region, there are three main Guinean sauces: in the north, a groundnut (peanut) sauce is served, while in central and southern Guinea, it is more common to have a sauce of palm oil and tomato paste or a sauce made from palm oil and manioc (cassava) leaves. Instead of rice, millet is also common in northern Guinea. Depending on the occasion or the wealth of the family, sauces may also include any combination of goat, beef, fish, the starchy cassava root, sweet potato, or squash.

Guinean snacks consist of grilled meats or fried dough, sweet or salty and served with hot pepper sauce. In the morning, families will often eat leftovers or simple, steamed rice. In the farming regions, stewed grains, like millet, are common for breakfast, while a café noir, a deeply black and espresso-like brew served very sweet, is often bought on the way to work.

Life's Milestones

Given the predominance of the Muslim faith, many milestones in Guinean culture are rooted in Islam. However, some rituals and practices remain unique to Guinea. In some families, newborns are kept on lockdown in the family home for the first seven days after their birth. The baby is then presented to the whole family for the naming ceremony. During this celebration, music and elaborate dances are performed to protect the child, and the baby is adorned with a silver bracelet or belly necklace to ward off bad spirits.

Most Guineans in rural areas are married by the age of 20 (for women) or 25 (for men). In Guinea, marriages are generally still arranged between two families after extensive research of respective reproductive and overall health history. If a direct arrangement is not carried out, the family still carries significant influence in the outcome of their children's matrimonial matches.

Once a match has been approved, the young man will sometimes present his bride's family with kola nuts as a symbol of his intentions to marry. If they break open the nuts, they symbolically consent to the match. The wedding traditionally involves a large celebration with both families, music performed by griots (traditional poet-singers), and dancing. In most rural areas, it is customary for the groom's family to present the bride's family with a gift of animals or food as a means of compensating for the loss of their daughter.

Funerals in Guinea are generally a celebration of life as opposed to a mournful event. The only time this is not true is when the death is unnatural or if the deceased is young.

CULTURAL HISTORY

Art

Prehistoric rock paintings in the Fouta Djallon highland region, extending through central Guinea, are a testament to the area's long history of human settlement, beginning with nomadic Africans. Traditional Guinean art is a product of vast migrations throughout the region starting in roughly 900 CE and ending at the turn of the 20th century. The continual influx of migrants from southwestern Sudan and the former Empire of Mali, as well as coastal and inland regions along the Atlantic Ocean, eventually displaced these original nomadic groups.

With that repopulation, art associated with original Guineans, such as traditional crafts like leatherwork and ceramics, was mostly incorporated into these new settlements. A prevalent art form during this early period included the decoration of functional items. Often, these designs were simple and geometric, such as a lined or boxed pattern woven or painted in a single, bold color, commonly red. (There is some question as to whether this practice originated among indigenous Guineans, or was carried by migratory peoples.)

These settlers from greater West Africa and southwestern Sudan developed their own dis-

tinct linguistic branches of the Mandé languages they originally spoke. Mandé languages include, among others, Mandinka, Soninke, Bambara, Dioula, Bozo, Mende, Susu, and Vai. The group that settled in the northern and central regions of the country came to be known as the Fulani people, who now speak Pulaar, a dialect of Fula. They are primarily Sunni Muslim and are the descendents of the original Baga people who moved into the region in as early as 900 CE. The Malinké, who speak Mandinka, is another group dominating the eastern regions of the country. Finally, the Soussou, or Susu, have settled mostly on the coast and speak primarily Soussou (also Susu). The arts of the region reflect this divergence of cultural development. The Ile-Ife peoples who predated some modern-day Yoruba are thought to have once dominated the entire Guinea coast region and brought with them the traditional woodcarving and bronze sculpting of their people.

Upon France's final consolidation of power over Guinea, many traditional art forms were preserved for their cultural value. However, in treating Guinean art solely as artifact and not an essential element of daily life, French demands on Guinean workmanship transformed traditional Guinean artists into slaves in bauxite mines. This severely repressed Guinea's creative capacity during colonial rule. Following independence, Guinea's first president, Ahmed Sékou Touré (1922–1984), abolished such primitive and animist art forms because he saw them as a direct threat to his authority.

Architecture

In most villages, homes are cylindrical with mud walls and thatched roofing. The mud walls are particularly useful for trapping cool air during the mid-day heat. These dwellings are commonly arranged in several clusters, or family compounds, around the village center. This style of arranging a village, based on few initial settlements that grow because of childbearing and additional migration, has always characterized Guinean village life. However, since the French during the colonial period, the layout and building style of some of Guinea's larger villages and towns has undergone significant change.

Larger settlements such as Kankan, Dalabal, Siguiri, and Conakry were fashioned according to popular European layouts after France colonized the region in 1890. These large towns typically feature straight-plotted grids with boulevards containing commercial and residential buildings, and a main street with political and administrative buildings. These buildings are juxtaposed against the traditional mud and brick structures built by Guineans since France's departure. Modern Guinean urban architecture was also influenced by Eastern Bloc architecture, most notably in Conakry. Apartment buildings were fashioned after the functional Soviet style, while the Palais du Peuple (Palace of the People) is a Chinese-built auditorium. Most wealthy foreigners and Guineans that live in Conakry reside in large, Western-style mansions.

Urban crowding in recent decades has also played a significant role in modern Guinean architecture. In Conakry, for example, home styles have undergone changes to make them more appealing to the ever-increasing urban overpopulation. Most homes within Conakry are built of cement, and are rectangular and either one or two stories high.

Drama

While Guinea's film industry remains small, it is broad in scope in terms of the cultural issues it portrays and examines. One of the more famous films to emerge in recent decades is *Dakan* (1997), a film about a homosexual relationship. Directed by Mohamed Camara (1959–), makes the assertion that homosexuality is innate and widespread across West Africa. In another film, *Allah Tantou* (*God's Will*, 1991), Guinean film director David Achkar (1960–1998) explores the events surrounding his father's execution at the hands of Touré's violent regime.

Music & Dance

Guinea's rich musical traditions closely resemble those of its West African neighbors. Sharing

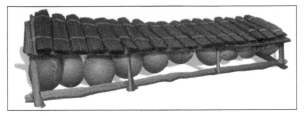

The bafalon, or Guinea xylophone, is an example of an instrument unique to Guinea.

use of the kora (a 21-stringed double-bridge-harp-lute), xylophones, handmade flutes, and traditional percussion instruments such as the hourglass-shaped talking drum, Guinea has created some of West Africa's most striking and beautiful music. Instruments unique to Guinea include the tambin, a flute made by the Fula people from hollowed dried vines, and the wooden-slatted bafalon, or Guinean xylophone. One particular bafalon, called Sosso-Bala, is considered the world's oldest such African xylophone and is kept in a town in Eastern Guinea. In 2001, the United Nations Educational, Scientific, and Cultural Organization (UNESCO) listed the age-old instrument as one of its Masterpieces of the Oral and Intangible Heritage of Humanity.

When Touré assumed the presidency in the late 1950s, he was the first and only African president to break all political ties with France. As part of his Africanist beliefs, he saw the importance of music and dance to developing a unified and independent Guinean culture. He allocated national funds for Guinean artists, resulting in some of the most creative blends of African and international music on the continent. Guinean music continues to stand out among other West African countries. Notable for its international big band sounds of the 1950s, the music relies heavily on Cuban horn and percussion sections. Nonetheless, just like its regional neighbors, Guinea's musical culture is dominated by a dedication to tradition, blended with the sounds and styles of colonial and modern influences.

In addition to the development of Guinean musical style, Les Ballets Africans is one of the most famous musical and performance groups to emerge from West Africa. First founded in Paris in the early 1950s by Guinean choreographer Fodéba Keïta (1921–1969), the dance company was invited to become Guinea's national performance troupe in 1958. By that time, the group had already toured nearly every major city of the Western world, sharing African music and dancing styles. Les Ballets maintains its status as National Ensemble and continues to share traditional Guinean music and dance worldwide.

Literature

Throughout much of its history, oral traditions have formed the basis of Guinea's literature. Early works were written using the Arabic alphabet, but literature written in French eventually emerged after World War II. As a result, many famous Guinean authors gained their acclaim outside of the country. This is particularly true of Camara Laye (1928–1980), perhaps the first famous author of Guinean decent. One of his most famous works, *L'Enfant noir* was published in French in 1953 and translated into English under the title *The Dark Child* in 1958. It won the Prix Charles Veillon writing prize. His other most famous novel, *Le Regard du roi* (*The Radiance of the King*, 1954) was, like *L'Enfant noir*, published during the author's schooling in France. Both books represent the earliest significant works of francophone African literature. These books trace the lives of Malinké individuals and their struggle for identity during the colonial period. After being exiled by Touré for his views on government, Laye completed several more works, some examining the role of Africans governing Africans.

Other famous authors include Tierno Monénembo (1947–) and Mohamed Alioum Fantouré (1938–). Monénembo is particularly renowned for capitalizing on Guinea's rich oral traditions in many of his works. Both writers are award-winning authors, with Monenembo winning the Prix Renaudot, a French literary

award, in 2008. In 1973, Fantouré won the Grand prix littéraire d'Afrique noire, awarded by the Association des Écrivains de Langue Française (Association of French Language Writers, or ADELF).

CULTURE

Arts & Entertainment

Following the end of colonial rule and the beginning of Guinea's independence from France, the nation's first president, Ahmed Sékou Touré, allied with Muslim factions of the north to do away with the idyllic sculpture of the Baga, or former Ile-Ife peoples, of northern Nigeria. These sculptures and Baga art in general often combined humans with animals. To the Muslims, these sculptures were a sacrilegious expression of a primitive culture and went against the principles of Islam, which forbids the depiction of human and animal forms. Outlawing Baga sculpture was also part of a larger conversion movement from animism to Islam. To Touré, allying with the Muslims at the onset of his presidency was the perfect means to attain a unified religious region, while simultaneously doing away with animist beliefs with which he had to compete for loyalty. This began a nearly 30-year era in which tribal artwork was suppressed in nearly all regions of the country.

While this suppression has since been lifted, the contemporary arts continue to suffer from a lack of funding in Guinea. Nevertheless, several painters have thrived, including Irina Condé, who has trained some of Guinea's most contemporary painters, including Ibrahima Barry, Seydouba Camara, Papus, Issa Bah, and Eugénie Condé. Camara, Papus, and Bah are all painters who work in oils and generally depict African scenes reminiscent of traditional Guinea. Other themes include the struggle for independence and development issues in present-day Guinea. Papus, in particular, has gained renowned for his combined impressionist and abstract style. Blending beautiful pastels, he portrays mainly tribal images of solitary Guineans who appear to be viewed through a rained-on window.

Ibrahima has relied on collage to add depth to his designs. Using fabrics, newspaper clippings, and other organic materials, he paints images of Guineans and craftily inserts the outside materials to enhance the dimension and meaning of his work. Condé is also a renowned sculptor who has attempted to reproduce the style of some of the sculpture work done away with during the Touré regime. In Guinea and other West African nations, communities of artists are taking garbage and creating three-dimensional collages of African scenes. The popularity of these street artists and the legitimacy of their work is a hotly debated topic.

Cultural Sites & Landmarks

Though it has recently become the site of intercommunal conflict and a refugee haven, the forest region of Guinea boasts a rich ecosystem and is considered one of the most important conservation areas in the world. A heavily forested region that extends into neighboring countries, such as Sierra Leone and Côte d'Ivoire, it is home to some of West Africa's most diverse wildlife, such as the endangered grey parrot and the goliath frog. Because of the abundant flora and fauna and the rapidly diminishing ranges of virgin rainforests, the Nimba Mountains and surrounding areas, collectively grouped as the Mount Nimba Strict Nature Reserve, are protected as a UNESCO World Heritage Site. However, the Guinean government under the rule of former president Lansana Conté (1934–2008) established iron mines in the mountains to extract the vast reserves of bauxite. Consequently, the Nimba Strict Nature Reserve has been categorized as a World Heritage Site in Danger since 1992.

North of the Forest Region of Guinea is Kankan, the country's second largest town, Kankan holds the unofficial title of capital of the Malinké peoples of West Africa. Originally, the town of Niani, located northeast of Kankan, was the capital and a major trading hub of the Mali Empire (1230s–1600s). The descendants of these original inhabitants comprise Guinea's present-day Malinké population, and they consider the entire central and northeastern region to be sacred land. During French colonization, Kankan also served as a major trade hub from the interior of the country to Conakry on the coast. The sister cities have long been connected by a train system that no longer runs.

The path to Conakry from Kankan runs directly through Fouta Djallon, also known at the Fouta Djallon Plateau. The region features lush and hilly land suitable for farming. Mainly inhabited by the Peuhl, or Fulani peoples, the land's fertility is the most sacred aspect of the region. It is thought to have supported some of the earliest villages in Guinea. Most of the subsistence farmers in the region work without the assistance of large machinery, such as tractors, and must rely on large herding animals. It is one of only a few areas in the world where natural indigo dyes from indigenous plants are still used to produce the vivid colors and patterns on hand-dyed textiles.

Conakry, Guinea's capital and largest city contains many of the country's important national landmarks. These include the main campus of the University of Guinea, the national sports stadium, and the Musée National that houses Guinea's largest collection of traditional masks and artifacts. Although deteriorating due to lack of maintenance—despite a significant monetary donation made in 2003 by the Kingdom of Saudi Arabia—the city Grande Mosquée is large enough for 2,500 female worshippers on the upper levels and 10,000 male worshippers on the lower levels, while some 12,500 people can be accommodated in the mosque's outdoor area. The much smaller Cathédrale Sainte-Marie reflects the minority Christian population. In addition, the Botanical Gardens in Conakry are famous for their extensive collections of tropical plants. First established by the French, the gardens also contain small collections of imported and international flora and provide a location for education and study of the native ecosystem.

Perhaps the most striking contemporary landmark is Camp Boiro, located in the heart of Conakry. During the 24-year reign of Guinea's first president, thousands of Guineans were tortured and either killed or left to die within the walls of this dilapidated military base and concentration camp.

Libraries & Museums

The Guinea National Museum (Musée National de Guinée), founded in 1960, is located in Conakry's central district, and features exhibits detailing the nation's history. Its collections include art and artifacts from the region's original tribal inhabitants. The National Museum, National Archive, and Conakry Library were all established after the nation gained its independence in 1958 and are of modern design. The Kissidougou Ethnology Museum, located in the southern city of Kissidougou, offers information explaining the region's prehistory and ethnological past; exhibits include masks, fetishes, and native art. Other museums in Guinea include the Musée Préfectoral de Boké, the Musée Préfectoral de Kissidougou, the Musée Préfectoral de Koundara, and the Musée Préfectoral de N'zerekore, each of which celebrate their region's tribal and ethnographic history. The Petit Musée du Fouta Djallon, operated by writer Koumanthio Diallo (1956–), places artifacts and documents in context.

Holidays

Most of Guinea's inhabitants celebrate Islamic holidays, although Christian Guineans mark Easter, Christmas, and All Saints Day. The most important holiday in Guinea is Tabaski (or Eid-al-Kabir), a feast to celebrate the Old Testament God's intercession to save Abraham's son from sacrifice. Also significant is Ramadan, the ninth month in the Muslim lunar calendar during which Muslims worldwide deepen their faith by fasting between sunrise and sunset. Ramadan ends with the feast of Eid-al-Fitr.

Muslims also celebrate Mouloud (Mohammed's birthday), always on 12th day of the Islamic month of Rabi' al-awwal, or the third month on the Islamic lunar calendar. Other public holidays include New Year's Day (January 1); Second Republic Anniversary (April 13), which celebrates the end of Sekou Touré's oppressive rule; Labor Day (May 1); Anniversary of the Women's Revolt (August 27), commemorating the uprising of Conakry market women against a presidential decree affecting their produce sales and livelihoods. Also included is Referendum Day (September 28), which memorializes a vote held on ejecting colonizers; Republic Day (October 2), which celebrates the country's independence from France in 1958; and the Day of the 1970 Invasion (November 22).

Youth Culture

Youth culture in Guinea is often dominated by societal demands to be domestically responsible. This means assuming significant portions of the physical labor, such as carrying water from a local freshwater source, as well as child-rearing and cooking. Following suit with adult responsibility, 17 is the legal age at which women may marry in Guinea. However, reports of parents selling daughters as young as 11 into marriage are common in rural regions. The youth of Guinea are also expected to show the utmost respect to elders. This includes never going against the wishes of elders, using appropriate titles in greeting, and averting one's eyes when interacting with any elder.

Many families send one or more of their sons to urban marabouts (Islamic religious teachers). These Muslim spiritual leaders adopt the young boys, who are then forced to reside in often-overcrowded one-room orphanages. Because the price for this shelter is high, boys are often sent out into the street to beg for money that the marabout then collects at night. These talibes (also talibé, or student, seeker), as the boys are known, are often subjected to severe abuse if they fail to bring in the required money. Child trafficking, specifically for mining blood diamonds, also remains a serious concern.

According to USAID, literacy rates and child mortality rates in Guinea are considered among the worst in the world. However, both rates have improved since the turn of the 21st century. In particular, access to primary education has improved steadily since 1999, though the nation-wide school system in Guinea is still considered inadequate, particularly as the population continues to grow.

SOCIETY

Transportation

As in most African countries, the preferred mode of transportation for most Guineans is walking. For longer commutes, bush taxis (share taxis) and minibuses are the common modes of public transportation, while bicyclists are common in rural areas. Bush taxis are the common vernacular for decades-old vehicles, mainly station wagons or light buses. Generally, bush taxis can be overcrowded and cover a route determined by the relative proximity of each person's destination. Minibuses are generally aging and hastily repaired vehicles that have more set routes. Larger buses are often referred to as "grand cars" and offer individual seating as opposed to the bench-seating common in minibuses. Traffic moves on the right-hand side of the road.

Transportation Infrastructure

Roads throughout Guinea vary in their conditions, but are typically paved between larger towns. There are currently 44,348 km (27,556 miles) of roads, although just 4,342 km (268 miles) are paved. There is also boat service on Guinea's larger rivers. (In fact, every major river in West Africa originates in Guinea, and the country is known as the "Water Tower of West Africa.") Approximately 1,300 km (808 miles) of these waterways are navigable by small, shallow-draft vessels.

The country's railways, which mostly ceased operating in the late 20th century, continue to be rebuilt and modernized, though mostly for commercial and industrial use. In 2014, the country had just 662 kilometers (411 miles) of narrow-gauge rail. As of 2013, Guinea had 16 airports, only four of which had paved runways.

Media & Communications

The media and communications industry in Guinea is thriving and diverse, but also restricted. When Guinea achieved independence in 1958, President Touré established a state-run press to portray government policy in a positive light. This served two functions: producing propaganda aimed at influencing the population's judgment of government policy and hiding the violent tactics used to subvert any opposition. Furthermore, the president made it illegal for other political parties to own newspapers and for journalists to publish anything critical of the government. Private radio and television stations were outlawed, and the government reserved the legal right to punish private-print journalists who criticized the government.

After Conté assumed power in 1984, he continued most of these media policies. However, with increased pressure from the international community, a law was established in 2006 to allow for public-owned radio stations. As radio is the most popular form of national media, (the majority of Guineans are illiterate), the government suspected that that wider access to anti-government slander caused national strikes in 2007. Citing a law that allows the government to punish journalists for inciting violence, Conté arrested, violently abused, and fined many journalists. Some were later exiled, jailed, or even killed for their reporting.

Little has changed, even under the new constitution, as evidenced by the ruling party's raid of Kankan-based radio station Batè FM's offices in 2013, during which all their broadcasting equipment was confiscated. The president's security forces are also accused of attacking an Escape TV camera operator two days before the radio station raid. In 2013, Reporters without Borders ranked Guinea 86th out of 179 countries on the press freedom index.

Today there are over 15 weekly, private print publications in Guinea, many of which print articles criticizing the government. There are also four private radio stations, but no private television stations. Thus, private programming is broadcasted on public stations. The government still reserves the legal right to censor any material run in its media that would cause a threat to the national party, and many journalists practice self-censorship out of fear of retribution, as evidenced by the examples above.

In addition, Guinea attained full Internet connectivity in 1997, but the telecommunications infrastructure remains underdeveloped. As of 2013, there were roughly 95,000 Internet subscribers in the country.

SOCIAL DEVELOPMENT

Standard of Living
Guinea ranked 179th out of 187 countries on the 2014 United Nations Human Development Index, which measures quality of life and standard of living indicators using 2012 data.

This ranking reflected in the country's disease and mortality rates. On average, more than 53 of every 1,000 babies born in the country die as infants (2015 estimate). As of 2015, average life expectancy was 62 years for women and 59 years for men. In addition, an estimated 118,000 people in Guinea are living with AIDS as of 2014. Nevertheless, the country's high birthrate brought the country's population growth rate to 2.63 percent in 2015. About 47 percent of Guinea's population lives below the poverty line.

Water Consumption
According to 2015 statistics from the World Health Organization (WHO), approximately 77 percent of the population had access to an improved source of drinking water, while only 20 percent of the population had access to improved sanitation. While the situation is slowly improving, it has been estimated that one-third (32.6 percent) of the rural population still does not have steady access to clean water, and some travel great distances to reach a potable water supply. Guinea, nonetheless, is rich in natural water,

with more than 20 waterways sourced above the capital itself and more rain than any other West African country. Water shortages were one of the main reasons behind a 2007 riot that witnessed protesters and police violently clashing, resulting in nearly 100 deaths. As of 2012, Guinea's Energy Ministry, with funding from the Islamic Development Bank, is currently working on a $15.7 million (USD) project to refurbish 15,000 extant water distribution points in 33 urban areas as well as create new boreholes that will allow for easier and more rapid water dispersal.

Education
Education is not compulsory in many parts of Guinea and only an estimated 30.4 percent of the population is literate (2015). While Guinea's educational system has been operating at the most basic level heading into the 21st century and educational efforts have been further crippled by the Ebola epidemic, 58.6 percent of children do finish primary school, according to UNICEF. In Conakry, education is more common and the literacy rate is higher due to the availability of basic educational services.

Guinea has two universities, the University of Conakry, formally known as Gamal Abdel Nasser University of Conakry, and the University of Kankan, or Julius Nyerere University of Kankan, named for the first president of Tanzania.

Women's Rights
Women in Guinea have suffered injustices similar to those endured by women in other West African nations. The role of women in Guinea is to share domestic and child-rearing responsibilities. Generally, females do not receive an education beyond primary levels, and are expected to marry by 20 years of age. In addition, most women in Guinea are one of several wives because polygamy is widely practiced and, despite Islamic law that requires a husband to provide for all his wives, their financial support typically diminishes as they age.

Domestic abuse is also a common practice among many husbands and a significant concern in Guinea. According to the constitution, domestic abuse is not specifically illegal, but may be filed as an assault case. Nevertheless, most women do not report abuse due to fear of retribution and social stigma. This is partially due to fear of divorce and destitution, but mainly due to the social acceptance of domestic abuse.

Rape is also against the law, although there were mass rapes of female opposition protestors reported during the September 2009 opposition crackdown by the Presidential Guard and hired mercenaries, many of whom are believed to have come from Liberia. After soldiers, known as "red berets" who represented the then-ruling junta government, fired at protestors in Conakry's main stadium, they began using their weapons, including knives and bayonets to tear clothing from women and subdue them. There are no official estimates of the number of rape victims, but survivors and observers reported to the BBC that women from every walk of life were subjected to this violence, even elderly women.

Outside of this incident, most cases of rape involve young girls under the age of 18. Prostitution and the trafficking of women and young girls are also widespread, though illegal, and few prosecutions are reported. As of 2014, Guinea was on the Tier 2 Watch List for human trafficking.

In terms of protection or property and custody rights, the law generally favors men. Women are not prohibited from owning property or having sole custody of their children. In most instances of divorce or death of the husband, property and the children were awarded to the highest-ranking male in the family. Widows thus, commonly end up marrying other male family members in order to survive.

Health Care

Guinea currently has one of the least effective systems of health care in the world. Up to 75 percent of Guineans have little or no access to health care, and the care that is available is generally poor, due to insufficient equipment, supplies, and staffing.

Since the 1980s, Guinea's government has been collaborating with foreign governments and non-governmental aid organizations to improve immunization rates, access to safe drinking water, emergency services, prenatal care, and disease prevention. While services have improved in some villages and towns, poverty and the prevalence of communicable diseases and air- and water-borne viruses are proving to be overwhelming obstacles to improving the quality of life in Guinea. The country continues to struggle with bacterial and protozoal diarrhea, hepatitis A, and typhoid fever, and even rabies, along with yellow fever, malaria, and dengue and lassa fevers. The water-borne parasite schistosomiasis, which enters through the skin and is often fatal in the long-term, is known as "snail fever" because freshwater snails carry it; it too presents challenges to the healthcare system. The recent Ebola epidemic has made the healthcare situation even more dire. As of September 2015, there are 3,800 cases and 2,532 confirmed deaths, according to the World Health Organization.

GOVERNMENT

Structure

Guinea accepted its independence from the French government in 1958. The area has had a long history of conquest. Part of the massive Mandé Empire in the 13th century, the Fulani herders swept into the area in the 15th century, just as European merchants arrived. During the centuries that followed, the slave trade established itself in the country. The Fouta Djallon fell under the control of the Fulani after the Holy Islamic War of 1725, which prompted the spread of Islam throughout the region. Guinea did not fall under French control until the coastal region was claimed as a protectorate in 1849. A century of resistance to French rule followed, including the heroic efforts of Guinea's national hero, Samori Touré, and frequent rebellions in Fouta Djallon.

In 1956, a poor Malinké man named Ahmed Sekou Touré (a descendent of Samori) formed a federation of African trade unions to throw off French rule. In 1958, French President Charles de Gaulle finally offered France's West African colonies a choice of complete independence or semi-autonomous status within a French-African community of states. Touré, on behalf of Guinea, was the only leader to choose total independence, and the French administration hit back by suddenly pulling out Guinea's government administration, records, and even phone lines. The country was plunged into overwhelming poverty, while the new leadership attempted to reorganize agriculture and industries under a communist state-run model.

Touré ruled Guinea as a brutally repressive military dictator until 1977, when the market women in Conakry revolted over a government effort to seize all agricultural produce for state-run markets. Touré backed down after the rioting spread to other towns and three governors were assassinated. Touré died in 1984 of heart failure. Since 1985, the government has worked with the IMF, the World Bank, and a long list of foreign nations and non-governmental organizations (NGOs) to improve conditions in Guinea.

Guinea emerged from decades of authoritarian rule and military governance in 2010, with the first democratic presidential elections, which saw Alpha Conde become president with 52.5 percent of the vote to Cellou Dalein Diallo's 47.5 percent. Upon election, the president, who serves as chief of state, holds a five-year term, as defined by the Loi Fundamentale (the constitution), which was completely redrafted in 2010 and passed on May 7, 2010. The Council of Ministers, the first to be all-civilian, are appointed by the president.

The head of government is the prime minister, who is appointed by the president and oversees the unicameral National Assembly, for which democractic elections were held in 2013. This legislative branch, called the Assemblé Nationale Populaire (People's National Assembly), has 114 members, 76 of whom are elected by a proportional representation vote and 38 are directly elected by majority vote. National Assembly members serve four-year terms.

Political Parties

Guinean politics was long dominated by the Party of Unity and Progress (PUP), led by Lansana Conté, and first elected to power in 2002. Although the 1990 constitution provided for the existence of more than one political party, the country was essentially a one-party state, and PUP won subsequent elections, although the results were widely claimed to have been rigged according to opposition parties. Upon Conté's death in late December 2008, the military seized power and PUP's rule came to an abrupt end that ultimately weakened the party. Following the adoption of a new constitution, approved in May 2010, democratic elections opened up the field to new political groups, and as of 2015, there are over 140 registered political parties. Among the most popular at present are: the National Party for Hope and Development (PEDN), the Rally for the Guinean People (RPG), Union of Democratic Forces of Guinea (UFDG), the Union for the Progress of Guinea (UPG), the Union for the Progress of Guinea (UPG), and the Union of Republican Forces (UFR). In the 2013 legislative elections, RPG won the majority, with 53 seats, while UFDG took 37 seats. UFR won 10 seats, and either independents or smaller political groups took 14.

Local Government

Guinea is divided into seven administrative regions—Boke, Faranah, Kankan, Kindia, Labe, Mamou, N'Zerekore—and one gouvenorat, Conarky, which is subdivided into five communes, Kaloum, Dixinn, Matam, Ratoma, and Matoto. The other seven regions are subdivided into 33 prefectures that are further divided into approximately 303 rural communes and 33 urban communes, aside from those that comprise Conakry. Although commune leaders are decided by elections, Guinea's government remains highly centralized even under the new constitution and the president selects officials and administrators at every level of government.

Judicial System

Because it was long controlled by a military government, Guinea's judicial is generally ineffective when compared to Western standards of law and justice. Moreover, even under the new constitution, it remains widely accepted that monetary corruption and political loyalty determines whether or not crimes are prosecuted. In addition, allegations of human rights violations against those who speak out against the government continue to occur.

Guinea's judicial system is headed by a Supreme Court (Cour Supreme), which is divided into various chambers, each with final authority over civil, penal, administrative, and constitutional cases. A court of appeals (Cour d'Appel) presides below the Supreme Court, under which the High Court of Justice (Cour d'Assises) and several courts of first instance (Tribunal de Premiere Instance) also operate. A court of special jurisdictions oversees, among other legal concerns, labor disputes, military tribunals, and justices of the peace. The effectiveness of Guinea's judicial system is hampered by corruption, lack of either educational services or training options for potential judges, the advancing age of existing judges, and the poor quality of existing judicial facilities and infrastructure.

While Guinea's judicial system struggles to reform, even under the new constitution, many prisoners remain incarcerated without charges and without trial dates.

Taxation

Guinea's formal economy is small, which results in a small tax base. An estimated 35 percent of government revenue in Guinea is obtained by taxes on the country's mining industry. The individual income tax rate, corporate tax rate, and capital gains are all 35 percent. In addition, both employees and corporations must contribute to social security at a rate of 17 percent and five percent, respectively. Other taxes collected include 20 percent on dividends, interest, remittances, and royalties, while a value-added tax (VAT) is levied at a rate of 18 percent. As of 2015, Guinea also added a petroleum tax.

The ability of Guinea's government to collect taxes is hampered by loose enforcement of tax regulations and poor infrastructure. The International Monetary Fund (IMF) has made efforts to upgrade and improve Guinea's tax system, but significant challenges remain.

Armed Forces

The National Armed Forces of Guinea are composed of several service branches, including an army; air force; navy, which includes marines; a Republican Guard; and a Presidential Guard. There is also a National Police Force, called the National Gendarmerie. Conscription exists for those between the ages of 18 and 25; as of 2012, there was an 18-month obligation for both compulsory and voluntary service. Both males and females are eligible to serve. In 2008, the military experienced some unrest over wages, which resulted in several deaths and looting by mutinous soldiers. Currently, Russia, Ukraine, France, and China are Guinea's biggest matériel suppliers.

Foreign Policy

Guinea's foreign policy is based on regional cooperation, national security, and an increasing presence on the international world stage. The country holds membership in numerous regional organizations, namely the African Union (AU), the African Development Bank (ADB), the Economic Community of West African States (ECOWAS), and the Organization of the Islamic Conference (OIC). Additionally, Guinea has maintained a secular foreign policy.

Guinea's foreign policy has been particularly shaped by the neighboring conflicts in Sierra Leone, Liberia, and Côte d'Ivoire. Guinea has been a refugee haven for those citizens fleeing from civil war and ethnic conflict in these West African nations. Since 1990, Guinea has offered asylum to an estimated 700,000 refugees. Guinea has also been involved in peacekeeping missions in these countries. Guinea's relations with Liberia were particularly contentious in the early 21st century, especially after Liberian-backed rebels killed over 1,000 Guineans. With the establishment of a new Liberian government in 2003, these relations have steadily improved. As of 2014, an estimated 6,580 refugees from Côte d'Ivoire are living in Guinea.

In recent years, Guinea's foreign relations with the West have improved, particularly as the country moves toward democratization. The country is a member of the UN, and the United States Mission in Guinea—which includes the Peace Corps and the U.S. Agency for International Development (USAID)—has provided military assistance and sustainable development, particularly concerning the promotion of health and education. However, Guinea's foreign policy priorities and relations remain somewhat unclear following a military coup in December 2008. In September 2009, the country signed an estimated $7 billion oil and mineral rights deal with China.

Human Rights Profile

International human rights law insists that states respect civil and political rights and promote an individual's economic, social, and cultural rights. The United Nations Universal Declaration on Human Rights (UDHR) is recognized as the standard for international human rights. Its authors sought the counsel of the world's great thinkers, philosophers, and religious leaders and were careful to create a document that reflects the core values shared by every world culture. (To read this document or view the articles relating to cultural human rights, visit http://www.ohchr.org/EN/UDHR/Pages/Introduction.aspx.)

From its inception as an independent nation, Guinea suffered from innumerable human rights violations at the hands of its government. Ahmed Sékou Touré, Guinea's first president, was infamous for his tight control of opposing political parties. In the first few years of his presidency, his favoritism toward his fellow Malinké people and murderous cruelty toward other ethnicities and political groups led to the deaths of hundreds of thousands of Guineans. Over one million more fled into surrounding nations as Touré's socialist policies rendered most land in Guinea property of the government. Farmers were removed from their land, while Guinea's crop and bauxite

output shrank by three quarters. Strict limits were also placed on freedom of speech.

In 1984, Touré died in office, which prompted a swift military takeover. Lansana Conté then became Guinea's second president, and in 1994, he returned Guinea to electoral rule when he ran for the presidency. However, Conté's 24-year presidency was also rife with human rights violations. Both the 1994 and 2003 elections were nearly swept by Conté, but considered corrupt by the international community. Most national parties stayed out of the elections assuming they would be harmed by government officials or unfairly beaten by corruption at the polls.

Since 2006, according to Amnesty International (AI) and the U.S. Department of State, Guinean citizens were still being subjected to unlawful and arbitrary detention, along with limits on their freedom of speech and assembly. In early 2007, mass demonstrations nationwide called for the resignation of Conté and the institution of a legitimate electoral government. According to Guinean law, however, any gathering of people is generally prohibited, and Conté declared his government under siege. Consequently, demonstrators were arrested, tortured, and, in many cases, even killed. It was estimated by Amnesty International that 135 citizens, some women and children, and most of them unarmed, perished.

Furthermore, Conté's government, which allowed international human rights groups to investigate the January human rights violations, refused to allow a national group to establish a museum at the site of mass killings by Touré's government. In 2008, Conté's death was followed by a military coup, and the announcement that national elections would be held in 2011. On September 28, 2009, the military junta was responsible for the deaths of at least 150 peaceful demonstrators, who had been protesting in a sports stadium against a plan by the junta's leader, Moussa Dadis Camara, to run in the presidential elections. In addition to the 150 deaths, when the Presidential Guard, known as "red berets," barricaded the exits and opened fire on protestors; 1,253 proterstors were injured and 30 were later arrested and detained. Women also reported having been raped by members of the Presidential Guard and plainclothes militia members, although no official count was recorded. However, the number of fatalities remains in dispute, as Human Rights Watch reported that bodies were retrieved from the massacre site and buried in mass graves.

Bribery, extortion, unlawful contracts, and misappropriation of public funds continue to be serious problems at every level of government, while the judiciary remains weak. However, the government of President Alpha Condé has made strides in curbing violence perpetrated by security forces and has even made efforts to pare down the previously vast security force, comprised of around 45,000 members. Still, political violence occurs, and since 2010, several hundred have died because of partisan violence, including incidents that occurred just before voting in 2013, when protestors alleged that incumbent Alpha Condé was attempting to rig the election.

Guinea is also considered a transit and source country for forced labor, including domestic servitude, as well as sex trafficking. The majority of victims are children. As of 2014, the country is on the Tier 2 Watch List, as the government does not comply with the necessary standards to hinder or end such activities and lacks laws that adequately address the issue. In 2013, of six open human trafficking cases, only one was prosecuted.

ECONOMY

Overview of the Economy
The Republic of Guinea is rich in natural resources, and has a productive agricultural sector. The mining industry contributes roughly 25 percent of the nation's exports, which amounted to $1.754 billion dollars in 2014. Despite Guinea's vast mineral wealth (it is the world's fifth-largest producer of bauxite), the country's economy remains underdeveloped, and unemployment and poverty are rampant. In 2014, the gross domestic product (GDP) was estimated at $14.97 billion (USD), with a per capita GDP of $1,300 (USD).

As of early 2015, Ebola has presented a significant challenge to Guinea's economy, as it has stalled several major projects, like offshore oil exploration and the Simandou iron ore project. Moreover, Ebola has compromised the country's labor force that currently stands at 5.045 million workers due to 3,200 confirmed cases and 2,100 deaths. Many workers fear contracting the disease and avoid labor in which they will be in close quarters with others.

There are more options for employment in Conakry, but unemployment and poverty remain major problems, and many of the city's residents live in poor conditions without access to significant or basic amenities, healthcare, and services. While there are no statistics kept on unemployment, the poverty rate remains at 46 percent of the population.

Due to a lack of investment, Conakry's infrastructure is also in dire need of repair. In 2006 and 2007, Conakry residents engaged in violent protests in an effort to bring attention to the needs of the city. One of the most pressing problems is a lack of adequate electricity. Much of the city's electricity is derived from hydroelectric plants; investment and refurbishment, however, is needed to update the system. In October 2011, the African Development Bank Group (AfDBG), allocated $818 million (USD) to fund58 infrastructure improvement projects among other studies and loans.

Industry
In 2014, Guinea's industrial production growth rate was estimated to be 4.4 percent, which suggests healthy expansion. The country's most prosperous industry is the mining and processing of bauxite, although other minerals, as well as gold, diamonds, and iron ore are also mined. Much of this work is run by international conglomerates, which often employ an expatriate staff for higher paid positions.

As the nation's principal shipping port, Conakry benefits from export revenues and peripheral businesses including refinement and processing of export commodities. The nation's chief exports are bauxite, gold, diamonds, iron, and refined metal, of which aluminum is the most important. Farms in rural areas produce coffee, rice, cocoa, palm kernels, sweet potatoes, and a variety of tropical fruits including pineapple, mangoes, cassava, and bananas.

Labor

As of 2014, Guinea's labor force numbered 5.045 million. The large majority of Guinea's labor force is employed in agriculture, including both the formal agricultural economy and subsistence farming. An estimated 76 percent of the labor force had agricultural occupations, while 24 percent were employed in the industry and services sectors.

Energy/Power/Natural Resources

Scientists estimate that Guinea has natural reserves totaling more than 29 billion metric tons of bauxite, just under one-quarter of the world's supply. According to the US State Department, the country has about four billion tons of high-grade iron ore, diamonds, gold, uranium, and salt deposits. Its major waterways and coastline also provide hydropower capabilities, and plentiful fish. The fertile soil and climate conditions are a lure to large-scale agricultural industries.

Fishing

Guinea's fishing industry provides more than 85,000 jobs. Generally, men work as fishers and women process the catch. Tuna provides the greatest tonnage and monetary returns. In the first decade of the 21st century, the African Development Bank has helped establish shrimp farms, while 14 prefectures now boast privately owned cold stage facilities specifically for the fishing industry.

Illegal, unregulated fishing is a significant problem in Guinea. According to Greenpeace, the country loses over an estimated $100 million (USD) each year to pirate fishing, which represents the largest annual economic loss from illegal fishing in all of Africa. Pirate fishing trawlers also damage artisanal fishing boats and negatively affect Guinea's marine environment. In general, Guinea lacks the infrastructure to enforce better marine regulations. Non-profit organizations, such as the Environmental Justice Foundation (EJF), continue to lobby the European Commission to assist with better enforcement of fishing laws in the waters of the coast of Guinea. In 2015, Greenpeace reported that since 2000, Chinese fishing vessels that are part of China's Distant Water Fishing (DFW) industry have been traveling into the territorial waters off Guinea, Guinea-Bissau, and Senegal and fishing illegally, while also underreporting their vessel's tonnage capacity. Weak enforcement has led to the continued arrival of rogue vessels in 2015 and placed significant strain on Guinea's domestic fishermen.

Forestry

Guinea is home to the largest remaining mangrove forests in West Africa, also home to some of the world's largest populations of chimpanzees. An estimated 26.5 percent of Guinea's territory is currently forested, down from 28 percent in the first decade of the 21st century. This is due in part to mismanagement by the Ministry of Agriculture and, to an even larger degree, overpopulation in forest regions, as violence has forced tribes inward in search of safety. In some areas, desertification is even becoming a serious concern. The Tropical Forestry Action Plan, adopted in 1993, is overseen by the country's Ministry of Agriculture. While the plan has helped to better manage Guinea's forest products and profits from wood processing, corruption within the Ministry of Agriculture still exists. USAID and the Jane Goodall Chimpanzee Conservation and Sensitization Program continue to work to sustain Guinea's natural resources and biodiversity.

Mining/Metals

As of 2014, Guinea is the world's fifth largest producer of both bauxite and diamonds, of which 70 to 80 percent are gem quality. According to some estimates, the country is home to 24 percent of the world's bauxite reserves, representing $222 billion (USD). The country's mining industry also produces gold, uranium, iron ore, and salt. Both Canadian and American mining companies are active in Guinea, the largest of which are Newmont

Mining Corp; Alcoa, Inc; and Anglo Aluminum Corp. In 2014, Guinea's industrial sector represented approximately 44.5 percent of overall GDP. The government revised the mining code in 2013, reducing taxes on royalties. In addition, as of 2015, international investors have begun to launch exploratory projects in Guinea, a prospect that will significantly advance Guinea's economy.

Agriculture

Most of the country's labor force, about 76 percent, is employed in agriculture, and much of that is at a subsistence level. Just over 58 percent of Guinea's land is arable, with 11.8 percent that is seasonally cultivated, 2.8 percent that is dedicated to permanent crops, and 43.5 percent that is permanent pasture for grazing. Approximately 949.2 square kilometers (366.4 square miles) is irrigated. Rice, pineapples, mangoes, cocoa, cassava, millet, coffee, palm kernels, bananas, sweet potatoes, potatoes, and timber harvests are significant throughout Guinea. An estimated 20.2 percent of Guinea's GDP is generated from agriculture.

Animal Husbandry

Livestock herding is predominant in Middle Guinea and cattle, sheep, and goats predominate. However, the country is not a significant exporter of livestock.

Tourism

Despite Guinea's natural beauty, the country is without a significant tourism industry due to its prevalent security concerns. Chronic food shortages and pervasive disease, as well as inadequate facilities and roadways, have prevented the growth of the tourist industry.

Conakry, the capital and largest city, is not considered a major tourist location and thus has few amenities to accommodate tourists. The beaches around Conakry are generally not suitable for swimming due to both pollution and dangerous geological features, such as large volcanic rocks. During the dry season, residents often travel to the Ilhe de Los where there are several beaches suitable for swimming and boating.

Conakry 1, located on Tombo Island, however, is a popular location for residents and visitors. (Conakry is divided into two parts, generally known as Conakry 1 and Conakry 2, which are connected by an ocean bridge; the oldest portion, Conakry 1, is located on the largest of a small group of volcanic islands known as the Iles de Los, while Conakry 2 is located on the Camayenne or Kaloum Peninsula.) Iles de Los offers beach resorts, swimming, and water sports, but few visit the island outside of the dry season from October to May. As the oldest part of the city, Conakry 1 also has a majority of the city's historic buildings and landmarks.

A significant attraction on the mainland is the Maison de Artisans in the Kouroula Quarter of Labé, where weavers, dyers, blacksmiths, and other artisans provide demonstrations and create works for sale.

Kristen Pappas, Amy Witherbee, Micah Issitt, Savannah Schroll Guz

DO YOU KNOW?

- Guinea is the fifth-most productive producer of bauxite in the world, after Australia, China, Brazil, and Indonesia. Bauxite, which is primarily used in the manufacture of aluminum, is found across Guinea and is processed there before being shipped around the world.

- The Republic of Guinea is the first African nation to establish a protected wilderness area specifically to safeguard vultures. The decision to establish the reserve came when conservationists realized that the nation's six species of native vultures were suffering significant population decline, due in part to the fact that the poisons used by livestock herders to control jackal, hyena, and lion populations were affect the scavenging birds when they ate the poisoned carcasses.

Bibliography

Caraway, Caren. African Designs of the Congo, Nigeria, the Cameroons and the Guinea Coast. *Stemmer House Publishers*, 1987. International Design Library Ser.

de Zurara, Gomes Eanes. The Chronicle of the Discovery and Conquest of Guinea. Cambridge, UK: *Cambridge University Press*, 2010. Cambridge Library Collection—Hakluyt First Ser.

Kastfelt, Niels. "The Role of Religion in African Wars." London: *C Hurst & Co Publishers Ltd.*, 2005.

Klein, Martin A. "Slavery and Colonial Rule in French West Africa." Cambridge, UK: *Cambridge University Press*, 1998. African Studies Ser.

Milne, June. "Kwame Nkrumah: The Conakry Years: His Life and Letters." London: *Panaf Books*, 1990.

Rémy, Mylene. "Guinea Today." Paris: *Jaguar Editions*, 1999.

Schmidt, Elizabeth. "Cold War and Decolonization in Guinea, 1946–1958." Athens, OH: *Ohio University Press*, 2007. Western African Studies Ser.

Works Cited

"Mobilizing the Masses: Gender, Ethnicity, and Class in the Nationalist Movement in Guinea, 1939–1958." Portsmouth, NH: *Heinemann*, 2005. Social History of Africa Ser.

"Africa: Guinea Coast." *Heilbrunn Timeline of Art History.* Metropolitan Museum of Art, 2015.

"Bauxite behemoths: the world's biggest bauxite producers." *Mining-technology.com.* Kable, 27 May 2014. Web. http://www.mining-technology.com/features/fcaturebauxite-behemoths-the-worlds-biggest-bauxite-producers-4274090/.

"Ebola in Guinea." Centers for Disease Control and Prevention. *CDC*, 2015. http://wwwnc.cdc.gov/travel/notices/warning/ebola-guinea.

"Ebola Situation Report—23 September 2015." Ebola Situation Reports. *WHO*, 2015. Web. http://apps.who.int/ebola/ebola-situation-reports.

"Guinea Economic Outlook." *African Development Bank Group.* AfDBC, 2015. Web. http://www.afdb.org/en/countries/west-africa/guinea/.

"Guinea." *2015 UNHCR subregional operations profile–West Africa. UN High Commissioner for Refugees*, 2015. http://www.unhcr.org/pages/49e484c66.html.

"Guinea." The World Factbook. *Central Intelligence Agency*, 15 Sept. 2015. Web. https://www.cia.gov/library/publications/the-world-factbook/geos/gv.html.

"Guinea: Guinea's Forest Region—Living on the edge." *IRIN: Humanitarian News and Analysis.* IRIN, 10 Jan. 2005. http://www.irinnews.org/IndepthMain.aspx?IndepthId=17&ReportId=62546.

"Guinea: September 28 Massacre Was Premeditated." *Human Rights Watch*, 27 Oct. 2009. https://www.hrw.org/news/2009/10/27/guinea-september-28-massacre-was-premeditated.

"Guinean Literature at a Glance." *Reading Women Writers and African Literatures.* The University of Western Australia, 25 Oct. 2008. http://aflit.arts.uwa.edu.au/CountryGuineaEN.html.

"Mount Nimba Strict Nature Reserve." *UNESCO World Heritage Centre.* United Nations/UNESCO, 2015. Web. http://whc.unesco.org/en/list/155.

"New evidence shows Chinese, West African governments must rein in rogue fishing fleet." *Greenpeace Africa*, 20 May 2015. http://www.greenpeace.org/africa/en/campaigns/Defending-Our-Oceans-Hub/Chinese-illegal-fishing-exposed/.

"Pirate Fishing." *Greenpeace International*, 2015. http://www.greenpeace.org/international/en/campaigns/oceans/which-fish-can-I-eat/pirate-fishing/.

"'Mass graves' found in Guinea." *BBC News.* BBC, 22 Oct. 2002. http://news.bbc.co.uk/2/hi/africa/2349639.stm.

"Universal Periodic Review: Guinea." *Human Rights Watch.* Human Rights Watch, 25 Jun. 2014. https://www.hrw.org/news/2014/06/25/universal-periodic-review-guinea.

Reporters Without Borders. "President's Supporters Ransack Provincial Radio Station." *Reporters Without Borders. Reporters sans Frontières*, 21 Aug. 2013. Web. http://en.rsf.org/guinea-president-s-supporters-ransack-21-08-2013,45081.html

"Serpent Headdress." Heilbrunn Timeline of Art History. *Metropolitan Museum of Art*, 2015. http://www.metmuseum.org/TOAH/ho/11/sfg/ho_1978.412.339.htm.

"Statistics." At a Glance: Guinea. *UNICEF*, 26 December 2013. http://www.unicef.org/infobycountry/guinea_statistics.html.

"Table 1: Human Development Index and its components." *Human Development Reports*, 2015. http://hdr.undp.org/en/content/table-1-human-development-index-and-its-components.

"Vulture reserve created in Republic of Guinea." *Wildlife Extra*, 2008. http://www.wildlifeextra.com/go/safaris/guinea-vultures.html#cr.

"Welcome to Les Ballets Africains." Les Ballets Africains: African Culture for the Modern World. *Department of Culture for the Republic of Guinea/Wordpress*, n.d. http://www.lesballetsafricains.com/.

Bah, Mahmoud. "Construire la Guinee apres Sekou Toure" (French Edition). Paris: *L'Harmattan*, 1990.

Caren Caraway. "African Designs of the Congo, Nigeria, the Cameroons and the Guinea Coast." *Stemmer House Publishers*, 1987. International Design Library Ser.

Elizabeth Schmidt. "Cold War and Decolonization in Guinea, 1946–1958." Athens, OH: *Ohio University Press*, 2007. Western African Studies Ser.

Gomes Eanes de Zurara. "The Chronicle of the Discovery and Conquest of Guinea." Cambridge, UK: *Cambridge University Press*, 2010. Cambridge Library Collection—Hakluyt First Ser.

June Milne. "Kwame Nkrumah: The Conakry Years: His Life and Letters." London: *Panaf Books*, 1990.

Martin A. Klein. "Slavery and Colonial Rule in French West Africa." Cambridge, UK: *Cambridge University Press*, 1998. African Studies Ser.

Mohamed Saliou Camara, Mohamed Saliou and Thomas O'Toole. "Historical Dictionary of Guinea." Lanham, MD: *Scarecrow Press, Inc.*, 2013. Historical Dictionaries of Africa Ser.

Moustapha Keita. "Guinea: Working to Provide Water and Electricity For All." *Interpress Service News Agency*. IPS-Inter Press Service, 1 Mar. 2012. Web. http://www.ipsnews.net/2012/03/guinea-working-to-provide-water-and-electricity-for-all/.

Mylene Rémy. "Guinea Today." Paris: *Jaguar Editions*, 1999.

Niels Kastfelt. "The Role of Religion in African Wars." London: *C Hurst & Co Publishers Ltd.*, 2005.

Ofeibea Quist-Arcton. "African view: Guinea's rape horror." *BBC News*, 6 Nov. 2009. Web. http://news.bbc.co.uk/2/hi/8342778.stm.

Sampson Jerry. "History and Culture of Guinea, Republic of Guinea." *Sonit Academy*, 2015.

Walter Rodney. "A History of the Upper Guinea Coast, 1545–1800." Ann Arbor, MI: *ACLS History E-Book Project*, 2006. http://www.metmuseum.org/TOAH/hi/hi_afgc.htm

GUINEA-BISSAU

Introduction

Formerly called Portuguese Guinea, Guinea-Bissau has long been associated with the trans-Atlantic slave trade and is part of the area in Africa once referred to as the Slave Coast. The Portuguese, who arrived around 1446, were central to the shipment of slaves to the New World, and an estimated two to three million West African men and women were exported from this region in exchange for tobacco, alcohol, textiles, and gold.

Since the country gained independence from Portugal in 1974—following a 13-year struggle between 10,000 PAIGC (African Party for the Independence of Guinea and Cape Verde) freedom fighters and 35,000 Portuguese-backed troops—it has been racked by coups, assassinations, and a devastating, yearlong civil war that erupted in June 1998. The most recent coup took place in April 2012, during which the constitution was temporarily suspended. Since the 2014 general elections, however, the country has worked to regain economic and political equilibrium. Still, nearly 70 percent of the population lives below the poverty line, and since 2007, the country has served as a transit point for cocaine moving from South America into Europe.

Guinea-Bissau is regarded as the birthplace of the kora, a stringed instrument thought to have been first assembled by the Mandinka people using a calabash gourd. Traditionally, the kora was played by griots, or storytellers. Today, however, it is used throughout Western Africa and in the global music scene.

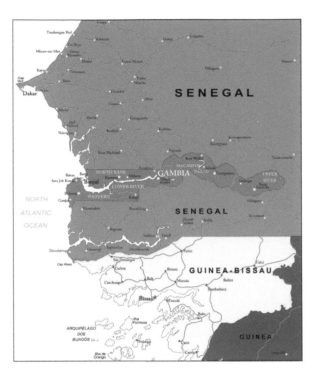

Official Language: Portuguese
Population: 1,726,170 (2015)
Currency: West African Communauté Financière Africaine (CFA [African Financial Community]) franc
Coins: Coins are available in denominations of 1, 5, 10, 25, 50, 100, 200, 250, 500 francs.
Land Area: 28,120 square km (10,875 square miles)
Water Area: 8,005 square km (3091 square miles)
National Motto: "Unidade, Luta, Progresso" (Portuguese "Unity, Struggle, Progress")
National Anthem: "Esta é a Nossa Pátria Bem Amada" ("This Is Our Beloved Homeland")
Capital: Bissau
Time Zone: UTC 0
Flag Description: The flag is comprised of three, equally wide bands of color. On the hoist (left-hand) side is a vertical red band, in which a five-pointed black star is centered. Projecting to the right are two horizontal bands: the top is golden yellow; the bottom is grass green. Green symbolizes hope, yellow signifies the sun, and red alludes to the bloody struggle for independence. The black star references African unity.

GENERAL INFORMATION

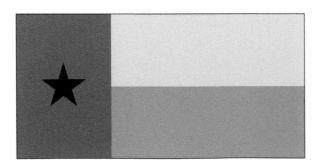

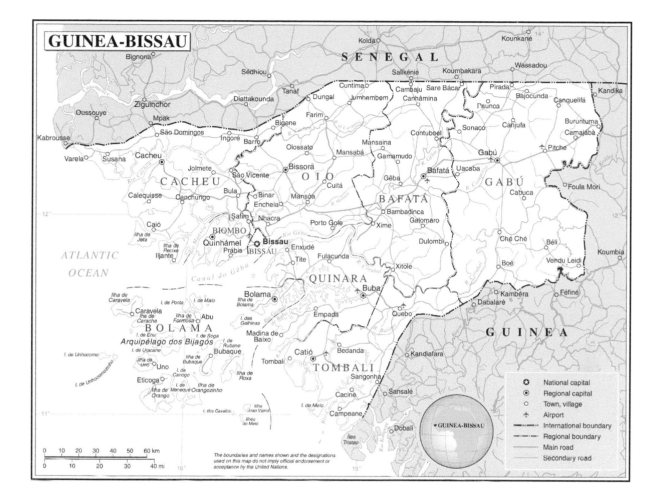

GUINEA-BISSAU

SENEGAL

Kolda
Kounkané
Bignona
Wassadou
Koumbakara
Sédhiou
Salikénié
Cuntimao
Cambaju
Oussouye
Ziguinchor
Tanaf
Dungal
Sare Bácar
Pirada
Bajocunda
Canquelifá
Kandika
Mpak
Diattakounda
Jumhembem
Canhâmina
Paunca
Farim
Contuboel
Sonaco
Canjufa
Buruntuma
Bigene
Kabrousse
São Domingos
Ingoré
Barro
Mansaina
Camajábá
Olossato
Mansabá
Gamamudo
Gabú
Pitche
Varela
Susana
Cacheu
Bissorá
Bafatá
Uacaba
Foula Mori
Jolmete
São Vicente
OIO
Gêba
GABÚ
CACHEU
Cuitá
Cabuca
Calequisse
Bula
Binar
Mansôa
BAFATÁ
Canchungo
Encheia
Bambadinca
Caió
Safim
Nhacra
Porto Gole
Galomaro
Ché Ché
Béli
Ilha de Jeta
BIOMBO
Xime
Dulombi
Koumbia
Ilha de Pecixe
Quinhámel
Prábis
BISSAU
Enxudé
Vendu Leidi
Iljante
Tite
Fulacunda
Boé
ATLANTIC
OCEAN
Canal do Gêba
Xitole
QUINARA
Buba
Kambéra
Féfiné
Bolama
Empada
Quebo
Dabalaré
Ilha de Caravela
I. de Ponta
I. de Maio
Ilha de Bolama
GUINEA
Caravela
Ilha de Caioche
Ilha de Formosa
Abu
I. das Galhinas
BOLAMA
I. de Enu
I. de Soga
Madina de Baixo
I. de Unhocomo
I. de Rubane
Arquipélago dos Bijagós
I. de Uracane
Bubaque
Kandiafara
Ilha de Bubaque
Tombali
Catió
Bedanda
I. de Uno
Uno
I. de Canogo
Eticoga
TOMBALI
Sangonha
I. de Meneque Orangozinho
Ilha de Roxa
Sansalé
I. de Unhocomozinho
Orango
Cacine
Ilha João Vieira
Dobali
Campeane
Ilhéu do Melo
I. de Melo
Ilhas Tristao

● National capital
◎ Regional capital
○ Town, village
✈ Airport
International boundary
Regional boundary
Main road
Secondary road

▼ GUINEA-BISSAU

0 10 20 30 40 50 60 km
0 10   20   30   40 mi

The boundaries and names shown and the designations used on this map do not imply official endorsement or acceptance by the United Nations.

Principal Cities by Population (2015):

- Bissau (492,000)
- Bafatá (22,521)
- Gabú (14,430)
- Bissorã (12,688)
- Bolama (10,769)
- Cacheu (10,490)

Population

Like many other African countries, Guinea-Bissau's population is very young, with nearly 40 percent under the age of 14 and 20 percent between 15 and 24 years of age. Life expectancy for men is comparatively short, on average just over 48 years. Women live approximately 52 years. Infant mortality is extremely high, with 89 deaths per 1,000 live births. However, with four children born to each woman in Guinea-Bissau, the population growth rate is still in the positive range, at nearly two percent as of 2015.

Languages

Although Portuguese is the country's official language, used in government, commerce, and education, it is spoken by just 27.1 percent of the population, while 5.1 percent and English speak French by 2.9 percent. The majority of people in Guinea-Bissau—approximately 90.4 percent—speak Kriolu, a pidgin form of Portuguese, or Portuguese-Creole.

Native People & Ethnic Groups

Native African groups make up 96 percent of Guinea-Bissau's population. These groups include the pastoral-nomadic Fula (28.5 percent); Balanta (22.5 percent), of which there are four subgroups; the Mandinka (14.7 percent), descendants of the Mali Empire; the agricultural Papel (9.1 percent), who live primarily around Bissau; the Manjaku (8.3 percent); the Biafada (3.5 percent), who are geographically dispersed into four groups. Also included are the Mancanha (3.1 percent), who occupy the central and northern coastal areas; the matriarchal Bijago (2.1 percent); the Felupe (1.7 percent), located in the country's northwest cor-

ner; Mansoanca (1.4 percent), and Balanta Mane (one percent). Those of European and Asian ancestry account for 1.8 percent of the population.

Religions

The principal religion in Guinea-Bissau is Islam, which 45.1 percent of the population practices. In fact, some of the largest ethnic groups in Guinea-Bissau, the Fula and Mandinka peoples, largely identify as Muslim. The Muslim majority is Malikite Sunni with a small minority of Shia and Ahmadiyya, a branch of Islam founded by Mirza Ghulam Ahmad (1835–1908). Christians comprise just over 22 percent of the population, while animists represent 14.9 percent, although some animists have merged their traditional beliefs with Christian teachings, possibly skewing these statistics. Christians and animists live in all parts of the country except the north, which is populated almost exclusively by Muslims. Exactly two percent identify with no faith.

Climate

The climate in Guinea-Bissau is hot, humid, and tropical, with a rainy season that extends from mid-May through the end of November. Temperatures are cooler between December and April, and the weather is comparatively dry. During the rainy season, temperatures generally range from 26° Celsius to 28° degrees Celsius (79° to 82° Fahrenheit), while in the dry season, when the dusty harmattan winds blow in from the Sahara, the temperature does not climb above 24° Celsius (75° Fahrenheit). December and January are the country's coldest months. While droughts have occurred in the latter half of the 20th century, in the 21st century, the country's annual rainfall has been consistently high, averaging in excess of 198 cm (78 inches).

ENVIRONMENT & GEOGRAPHY

Topography

Guinea-Bissau is bordered by Guinea, Senegal, and the North Atlantic. The country's mainland is primarily low coastal plain with mangrove-filled swamps and estuaries. Tidal waters regularly reach 62 miles inland. In the east, the landscape rises to become tropical forest interspersed with long swaths of tree-studded savanna and shrubby grasslands. In the southeast is the Fouta Djallon plateau, which rises 180 meters (600 feet) above sea level. The Boé Hills travel from this plateau to the Corubal River basin and Gabú Plain in the northeast. The east is home to the upper basin of the Gambia River system. While the country's lowest point is its twelve nautical miles of the Atlantic, its highest point is an unnamed 300-meter-high (984 feet) feature on the mainland's northeast corner.

Offshore, the Bissagos Archipelago (Arquipélago Dos Bijagós) is comprised of 88 islands, 18 of which are populated and 70 of which are small enough to be islets. These areas are filled with intertidal zones, in which salt-tolerant mangroves thrive, and covered by semi-dry forests, sandbanks, and coastal savannas flecked with shrubby vegetation. UNESCO named this archipelago a Biosphere Reserve in 1996.

Plants & Animals

Because of Guinea-Bissau's tidal estuaries and diverse landscape, the country is home to a wide range of flora and fauna. Flamingoes and pelicans are frequently spotted in the swamps along the coast, where crocodiles, endangered sea turtles, and water snakes are also common. Poaching has virtually extirpated native elephant populations. However, hyenas, leopards, monkeys, apes, and various species of gazelles, antelopes, and parrots inhabit the inland forests and savannas.

Guinea-Bissau is home to the edible African custard-apple; various species of orchid, like the *Aerangis biloba*; the saltwater-tolerant black mangrove; African mahogany trees; and the tamarind tree, which produces edible fruit pods. The tree-studded savannas and open grasslands are also home to the carnivorous annual *Utricularia firmula* and its equally carnivorous perennial cousins *Utricularia rigida*, *Utricularia* simulans (commonly known as fringed bladderwort), and *Utricularia tortilis*.

CUSTOMS & COURTESIES

Greetings

While Portuguese is the country's official language, and a large segment of the population speaks both French and English, Kriolu—a pidgin form of Portuguese—is Guinea-Bissau's *lingua franca*. It is particularly important for communication among ethnic groups speaking different tribal languages and is understood and spoken by over 90 percent of the population. A common pre-noon Kriolu greeting is "Bom dia" ("Good morning"). One might then follow with, "Kuma?" ("How are you?"), which may receive the reply, "N' sta bon" ("I am fine"). In the afternoon, Kriolu speakers greet others with the expression "Bo tardi" ("Good afternoon"), and after 5 p.m., the expression changes to "Bo noti" ("Good evening"). Handshakes are often exchanged on greeting, although they typically last longer than Westerners may be used to. Strangers may be addressed as "amigo" or "amiga" (friend).

Gestures & Etiquette

Because pointing with the finger is considered rude, when giving directions or referring to others, Bissau-Guineans often point with their tongues. In addition, it is not unusual to see people of the same gender holding hands or walking arm-in-arm; this is merely an expression of their friendship.

Women and men generally avoid direct eye contact with one another unless their relationship is romantic. Children, too, avoid eye contact with elders out of respect, and Muslim elders will often avoid looking directly at someone, opting instead to look sideways at their conversational partner. Indicating "yes" is indicated with a single click of the tongue, while "no" is indicated by waving the index finger from side to side and making two clicks with the tongue. Also important to note is that Bissau-Guineans prefer to stand in closer proximity when conversing than Westerners are used to, and often, they touch their conversational partner while speaking in order to indicate sincerity or underscore feelings.

Eating/Meals

Having three meals a day is common in Guinea-Bissau. However, the rainy season, which lasts from May to November, is also known as "the hungry season," and meals may be cut to as few as one per day. A period of significant food insecurity followed the coup in 2012, when civil unrest and strikes prevented some workers from getting enough food to feed their families. Many children suffered from malnutrition, and the World Food Programme stepped in to provide assistance through school-based food plans and investments in agricultural production.

Mealtimes vary, depending on location, and it is extremely rare for the average person to eat in a restaurant; very few people have the disposable income for such a luxury. Consequently, meals are enjoyed at home or shared during visits to relatives and friends homes. Breakfast in larger towns and cities is sometime between seven a.m. and nine a.m. and consists of either millet porridge or leftovers from the previous evening's meal. Lunch is between noon and three p.m. and is the largest meal of the day. Afterwards, time is always allotted for a short nap. Dinner is late by North American standards and occurs sometime between eight p.m. and 10 p.m. This evening meal is comparatively light, sometimes consisting of leftovers from the midday meal. Food is served on the floor in large bowls, and a family elder divides portions. While spoons are sometimes used in urban areas, most still eat with their hands. Only the right hand is employed in this activity, as the left hand is associated with personal hygiene and therefore perceived as inherently unclean.

Visiting

Visitors frequently arrive unannounced, and because the act of visiting is viewed as a thoughtful gesture, guests are always eagerly welcomed. A beverage is generally offered to visitors upon arrival, even if it is only water. If a meal is being eaten at the time of a visitors' arrival, a portion is shared with them. To refuse this gesture of hospitality is considered rude, and often, people will have at least a bite to please their hosts. Also important to note is that time is relatively fluid in Guinea-Bissau, and guests who are invited to visit at a particular time do not offend their hosts by arriving considerably later than originally scheduled. To demonstrate their appreciation, guests often bring a present for their hosts. Such gifts include kola nuts (a bitter-tasting nut containing high levels of caffeine that, when chewed, acts as a stimulant), cana (alcohol made from cane sugar), tobacco, bread, sugar, or fruit.

LIFESTYLE

Family

Family is central to the culture of Guinea-Bissau, and people sacrifice personal interests for its welfare. Families also tend to be large, with three generations within one household and, often, more than four children born to each woman. Women with as many as nine children are not uncommon. However, infant mortality rates are extremely high (89.21 deaths per 1,000 live births), and many women endure the loss of more than one child to malnutrition, diarrhea, and other largely preventable diseases. Another vital component to the extended family are elders, who help with childrearing, are held in high esteem, and often honored with dividing food portions at mealtimes.

Important to note is that many people do not have the money to pay for the marriage license the government requires to recognize a union as official. Instead, many couples whose unions are arranged by family members or urban couples who decide to set up a household together are considered married when they have their first child, although by the government's reckoning, these marriages are informal.

In families, there is a division of labor, with women responsible for childcare, cooking, and housekeeping as well as tending of any livestock, particularly pigs and chickens. In addition to subsistence farming and caring for any cattle, sheep, or goats the family has, Men provide financial support, food, and clothing for family members. In some cases, men even seek work outside Guinea-Bissau and send remittances home.

Housing

Just under half the population—that is, 49.3 percent—lives in urban areas, like Cacheu, Bissau, Bolama, or Gabu, where buildings are generally decaying remnants of the Portuguese colonial period. These are largely constructed of brightly colored, sometimes moldering, stucco or cinder blocks, with roofs of clay tile. In rural areas and on the Bijagós Islands, village-based homes are constructed of adobe, mudbrick, or quirinton, which are woven branches covered with either mud or bundles of straw. Roofs on these so-called "vernacular structures" are conical grass thatch, sometimes reinforced with a zinc foil that increases the roof's longevity. After dark, petrol lamps provide light. Whether urban or rural, most homes have neither electricity nor running water, and even fewer have any access to sewage systems or septic tanks.

Food

Military coups, corruption by both local authorities and border police, and overall inflation have led to significant food insecurity within Guinea-Bissau. Often, food imports are sometimes diverted from their intended destination or transporters are subjected to spontaneous tolls at police-manned checkpoints, making regular planned distribution difficult. For these reasons, many rely on subsistence farming to survive, although this is often complicated by droughts and civil unrest.

For those living along the coast of Guinea-Bissau, rice is a diet staple, while those living in the country's interior rely on millet. Fufu, a starchy side made from cassava flour, can be rolled into little balls and dipped in soups or stews. Soups and stews are most often made of some combination of sweet potatoes or yams, cassava root, manioc leaves, onions, tomatoes, and plantains. Legumes like black-eyed peas also find their way into soups and stews, while fish—either dried and flaked or fried in native palm oil—are similarly incorporated into the meal. Other meats, such as beef, are more costly and, therefore, reserved for special, often ceremonial occasions. However, venison, monkey, and beaver meat are not uncommon in native stews. Guinea-Bissau's most popular dish is *yassa*, chicken marinated with lemon, onion, and sometimes mustard. Having originated in Senegal and spread throughout West Africa, *yassa* is most often eaten to celebrate significant holidays, like national hero Amílcar Cabral's birthday on September 12 and Carnaval in February.

During colonial rule, the Portuguese encouraged the production of peanuts, called ground nuts in Africa. These feature prominently in recipes, as a flavoring agent or stand-alone element, as in peanut soup. Also important to the Bissau-Guinean cuisine are milk products, such as protein-rich whey. Spices and chilies are frequently used, as flavor enhancers, and an especially popular additive are the ground seeds of the *Aframomum melegueta*, also known as the Guinean pepper or "grains of paradise." It is actually a member of the ginger family and has a sharp, citrusy flavor.

Beer is extremely common in Guinea-Bissau and is a lucrative export. Cashew wine and palm wine are often enjoyed by non-Muslims, while rum is usually reserved for special occasions, like weddings, births, and circumcision ceremonies. The drink most frequently enjoyed is a sweet green tea called warga.

Life's Milestones

Regardless of ethnicity, births and marriages are generally celebrated with the sacrifice of cattle and, for non-Muslims, the drinking of palm wine, rum, or cana (sugar cane alcohol). For Muslims, burial occurs within 24 hours of death.

Rites of passage vary by ethnic group and tribe. The Balanta people, for example, have an initiation ritual for each phase of life, the most significant of which is Fanado, the male circumcision ceremony, during which men leave their families and remain for two months in what is known as "the sacred woods." After circumcision, they complete a series of endurance tests and have contact only with their maternal uncles and master guides. Some men do not survive the Fanado, but those who do, return to their villages wearing red hats symbolizing their newfound wisdom. By comparison, the Bijago people, who inhabit the Bissagos Islands, do not circumcise their youth. Instead, their rite of passage involves an initiation ceremony known as *Manratche*, during which young, post-adolescent men—part of the so-called *cabaro* age group—don *dugn'be* (ox) masks and perform a dance imitating a bull's aggressive nature.

CULTURAL HISTORY

Art

The art of Guinea-Bissau is closely associated with ritual and spirituality. The Bijago peoples' *dugn'be* (ox) masks, made of wood, leather, and cow horns, are created for use in the *Manratche* initiation ceremony, during which boys pass into manhood. A majority of the country's sculptural works are wooden figures known as *iran*, usually under two feet tall and intended as both memorial pieces and spiritual vessels. Animal sacrifices are sometimes made to the *iran* and a small portion of a successful crop is offered as a token of gratitude to the ancestor inhabiting the *iran*. Additionally, Animist priests (*oamcandjamos*) may consult the *iran* for advice. Many of these creative traditions continue not only in rural areas, where tribal culture persists, but also at the Centro Artistico Juvenil in Bissau, where young artisans create works like the *iran* for sale.

Drama

During the 1970s independence movement, the government developed a film industry to support the revolution, with an eye to creating social realist films. Although the industry was poorly funded and distribution channels were few, the effort influenced the work of filmmaker Flora Gomes (1949–). His 1988 movie *Mortu Nega* (*Those Whom Death Refuse*) was the first feature-length film ever shot in Guinea-Bissau, and it won the best film prize at the 1988 Pan-African Film and Television Festival (FESPACO). Since then, Gomes' work has continued to receive prestigious awards; his 1992 film *Os Olhos Azuis de Yonta* (*The Blue Eyes of Yonta*) won

the Un Certain Regard category at the Cannes Film Festival. In 2000, France named Gomes a *Chevalier des Arts et des Lettres*.

Music & Dance

The kingdom of Gabú, which broke from Mali in the 16th century and from which Guinea-Bissau developed, is considered the birthplace of the kora, a 21-stringed, lute-shaped harp believed to have been first assembled by the Mandinka using a calabash gourd. Kora are generally played by griots, West African storytellers, who often transmitted oral histories through song. However, musicians throughout Western Africa now use them. The independence movement and the assertion of unified cultural identity in the face of colonial suppression shaped a great deal of contemporary Bissau-Guinean music. The genre most associated with Guinea-Bissau is *gumbé*. With its fast tempo and driving percussion, *gumbé* has a sound similar to *zouk* music of the French Caribbean. The band Super Mama Djombo, founded during the 1960s when the members were still children, produces gumbé-style songs in the Kriolu language. The band's name pays homage to the spirit to which freedom fighters appealed during the country's independence war. Bissau-Guinean singers continue to use music as a form of protest against government corruption and oppression. José Carlos Schwarz's (1949–1977) song "Tustumunhus di aonti' ("Yesterday's Testimony") is one such example. Similarly, Justino Delgado, now living in Spain, was arrested and banned by the government after his songs disparaged the country's president.

Literature

Perhaps the country's most famous writer is national hero and freedom fighter Amílcar Lopes da Costa Cabral (1924–1973), whose many speeches and political tracts on national liberation have been reprinted in numerous volumes and spurred the Pan-African movement. Other important Bissau-Guinean literary figures include Paris-educated Manjaco poet António Baticã Ferreira (1939–), who earned a medical degree from the University of Lausanne, and who has been widely published in Europe. More recently, poet and short story writer Waldir Araújo (1971–) has come to prominence for work that confronts the everyday hardships of the poverty-stricken, post-independent nation in which he came of age.

Sports

Particularly popular in rural areas is *luta livre*, a Portuguese martial art that blends wrestling with a modified form of Judo. However, European football, or soccer, is the country's most beloved sport. Guinea-Bissau's football team, Federação de Futebol da Guiné-Bissau (FFGB)—nicknamed Djurtus—is a member of the Confederation of African Football (CAF) and is currently 147th in the FIFA world rankings. Djurtus has not yet qualified for participation in the World Cup.

CULTURE

Cultural Sites & Landmarks

In addition to the Bijagós Archipelago, a UNESCO International Biosphere Reserve since 1996, Guinea-Bissau has five other protected areas, four of which were established in 2000. Included in the protected areas are Cacheu River Mangroves Natural Park, 886 km (342 miles); Joao Vieira Poilao Islands Marine National Park, 495 km (191 miles); Lagoas Cufada Natural Park, a protected wetland of 890 km (344 miles); and Orango Islands National Park, which has two segments, one terrestrial (1582 km [611 miles]) and one marine-based (94,235 km [36,384 miles]). Established in 2007, Cantanhez Forest National Park is 1,057 km (408 miles).

In the capital city of Bissau, near the port, the spare Pidjiguiti Memorial commemorates the August 3, 1959 massacre of striking dockworkers, an event recognized with a national holiday. Also in Bissau is Fortaleza d'Amura, a colonial fortress that serves as a functioning army barracks and marks the boundary of the colonial quarter of Bissau. The tomb of national hero Amílcar Cabral is located inside, but entry is rare even for natives. Also in the Old City is the colonial-era presidential palace, which is currently in a state of decay, its roof having been bombed during the 1998–99 civil war.

Libraries & Museums

The National Institute of Studies and Research (*Instituto Nacional de Estudos e Pesquisa* (INEP), located in Bissau, suffered heavy damage during the 1998–99 civil war because it had been transformed into army barracks for Senegalese troops. In the process, a great deal of the Institute's library was severely damaged, with books, documents, and maps exposed to rain following several direct hits to the building's roof. With the help of international aid, restoration began in 2000, and today, INEP—of which the National Library is a part—has approximately 70,000 volumes and is working with the British Library and Portugal's Mario Soares Foundation to digitize works that are deteriorating as a result of their exposure during the civil war. Also in Bissau is the National Ethnographic Museum, which contains traditional sculpture, pottery, and examples of woven baskets, representing the country's various tribal cultures. It, too, has a library that boasts over 14,000 volumes.

Holidays

Both Christian and Muslim holidays are observed in Guinea-Bissau, including Christmas Day (December 25); Korité (August 31), which marks the end of Ramadan; and Tabaski (November 7), which celebrates the Feast of the Sacrifice, or Abraham's willingness to sacrifice his son as proof of his faith. Another significant historical holiday is Martyr's Day (August 3), which memorializes the striking dock workers killed during the Pidjiguiti massacre, an uprising against the Portuguese led by national hero Amílcar Cabral. Independence Day (September 24) celebrates the country's liberation from Portuguese rule, while the birthday of the late writer and freedom fighter Amílcar Cabral is commemorated annually on September 12.

Youth Culture

Guinea-Bissau's population is extremely young, with 60 percent under the age of 24. However, only slightly more than half of children under fourteen attend school. Because of the rampant poverty, child labor is a significant problem, with 226,316 children (57 percent of school-aged children) ages five to 14 engaged in some type of adult employment, such as cashew production, domestic service, mining, street vending, or sex worker. In addition, while Guinea-Bissau has ratified the UN CRC Optional Protocol on Armed Conflict and has begun to implement social programs to eliminate child labor in 2014, law enforcement is still weak and plagued by corruption.

Perhaps the greatest challenge to Guinea-Bissau's youth, however, is the country's new drug culture, which is facilitated by government corruption at all levels. Cocaine, packets of which washed up on the country's shores when a freighter ran aground at the turn of the 21st century, was, at first, something foreign. It has since saturated local cultures, creating a rising addiction problem among residents, the poorest of whom have turned to crack. In Bissau alone, it is estimated that between 20 and 30 percent of youth use crack, a figure that is expected to grow if the economy remains weak.

SOCIETY

Transportation

Outside the capital city, few roads are paved, making walking the most effective method of transport, particularly during the rainy season, when unpaved roads become impassible for wheeled vehicles. The U.S. Department of State actually advises against personnel driving outside the capital at night, citing numerous hazards, including bandits and carjackers; unreliable, even dangerous road conditions caused by potholes and landslips; and the peril of wild animals loose on the roadway. Within the capital city itself, small buses, called Toca-Tocas, transport people to various destinations, as do the more expensive taxis, which sometimes operate like a bus service, picking up as many passengers as there are available seats.

Traveling through the entirety of Guinea-Bissau is the paved Trans-West African Coastal Highway, which links 12 African nations from Nouakchott, Mauritania in the northwest to Lagos, Nigeria in the east. The segment of the highway that cuts through Guinea-Bissau, links Banjul, Gambia to Conakry, Guinea. Traffic moves on the right-hand side of the road in Guinea-Bissau.

Transportation Infrastructure

The country's transportation system is extremely underdeveloped, with poorly maintained bridges and roadways, many of which become impassible during periods of inclement weather. Some villages can only be reached by walking paths or boat. Of the country's 4,400 km (2,743 miles) of road, only 453 kilometers (281 miles) are paved, a majority of these are within and around the country's capital. Connections between other towns and villages are harder to navigate.

There is no railway system in Guinea-Bissau, although there was discussion of, and even an agreement with, Portugal in 1998 about creating a passenger and cargo line to Guinea. However, this project has never come to fruition.

There are approximately 30 airports within the country, three of which have paved runways. Osvaldo Vieira International Airport, located in the country's capital, Bissau, is one of the three airports with paved runways. ASKY Airlines, euroAtlantic, Royal Air Maroc, Senegal Airlines, and Transportes Aéreos de Cabo Verde (TACV) currently serve this airport, with flights to and from Lisbon, Portugal; Dakar, Senegal; Praia, Cape Verde; Lomé, Togo; and Casablanca, Morocco.

Because there is no rail service in Guinea-Bissau, imports, and exports enter and leave the country by boat, making ports vital to the Bissau-Guinean economy. The city of Bissau is home to the country's principal harbor, often referred to as Porto Pidjiguiti, which has a jetty and two piers. The country's three other smaller harbors include: Buba, in the south; Cacheu, in the northwest; and Farim, 217 km (135 miles) north of Cacheu.

Media & Communications

There is one state-owned radio station in Guinea-Bissau and several privately owned national broadcasters. A few community radio stations also intermittently transmit programming, but with a weaker signal. Overall, there is one AM station and four FM stations; the country offers no shortwave broadcasts.

In terms of television, the government has one station in operation, while a second cable and satellite channel, called Radio e Televisao de Portugal África (RTP África), offers Portuguese-language programming, like the primetime news show *Repórter África.*

Because literacy is low in Guinea-Bissau, there are very few newspapers produced in country. The exceptions are *Gazeta de Notìcias* and *Guiné-Bissau*, both offering coverage of national events in both print and digital editions. *Bissau Digital* is also a national news source, but offered only online and run by the Portuguese News Network.

Poverty has prevented the wider dispersion of telephone and internet. As of 2012, just 5,000 landlines and 1.1 million cell lines were registered, while only 2.9 percent of the population—that is 47,132 people—had any experience with the Internet.

SOCIAL DEVELOPMENT

Standard of Living

Guinea-Bissau ranks 177th out of 187 countries on the 2014 United Nations Human Development Index.

Water Consumption

Access to potable water has markedly improved in Guinea-Bissau, with nearly 99 percent of the urban population and 60.3 percent of rural populations enjoying access to improved water sources. Sanitation, however, remains underdeveloped. Only 33.5 percent of urban populations have improved sanitation facilities, and in rural areas, that number is even lower, just 20.8 percent. Approximately 226 square kilometers (87

square miles) of land is irrigated, while the country's total renewable water resources amount to 31 cubic kilometers (8,189 gallons).

Education

Primary school education is compulsory between the ages of seven and 14 in Guinea-Bissau. According to UNICEF, however, attendance during these grades is just 57 percent, and only 24 percent of those who attend primary school move on to secondary school, largely because the final two years must be completed in Bissau. Most who move to the secondary level only make it to grade nine. Largely, dropout rates are high because children are taught in Portuguese, which, for many, is a foreign language. There are marked gender disparities in the educational system, with perhaps the most obvious being literacy. While the illiteracy during the colonial period was nearly universal and equal among men and women, as of 2015, the adult literacy rate is just 59 percent, with nearly 72 percent of men and only 48.3 percent of women able to read. Protracted recovery from the 1998–99 civil war, a dearth of qualified teachers, particularly in rural areas, and economic pressures are all factors preventing many youth from advancing their education.

Women's Rights

Literacy is not the only area in which women in Guinea-Bissau arc left behind. While the country's constitution calls for equal treatment under the law and there are neither restrictions on women in public spaces nor prohibitions on their political participation, there are currently no quotas to safeguard their equal representation in the legislature. As of 2015, just 14 percent of the National Popular Assembly is female. However, while there is no organized women's movement in Guinea-Bissau, individual, women-led social organizations have begun to develop within the last few years.

Women are expanding their roles beyond the household, as an estimated 68 percent participate in the economy. New mothers, who work in government-regulated industry, are given 60 days paid maternity leave and labor discrimination is banned under the country's labor code. However, this is not true of the more informal agricultural sector, in which most women work.

Especially notable is that in June 2012, the National Popular Assembly passed a law making the practice of female genital mutilation illegal. Discussed for 16 years, the law was finally passed 64 to one. Still, UNICEF estimates that nearly 45 percent of women have undergone the practice, which leads to frequent renal and gynecological infections, chronic pain from nerve damage, and complications with both intercourse and childbirth.

Health Care

Thanks to foreign aid organizations, health care has improved since independence. However, many rural inhabitants have never seen a medical practitioner and are forced to rely on folk medicine when ill. In 2013, healthcare expenditures now account for 5.5 percent of the GDP, and there is one hospital bed per 1,000 people, a ratio higher than neighboring African nations. Yet, physicians are still remarkably few, with only 0.1 per 1,000 people. Nurses are also in demand, and the hospital in Bissau is frequently working without, or with very low supplies of, vital medicines, bandages, plasma, antibiotics, anesthetic, and basic equipment.

Largely preventable diseases cause the country's high infant mortality rate (89.21 deaths for every 1,000 live births) and low life expectancy—with the average age of death being 50.23 years. Bacterial and protozoal diarrhea, hepatitis A, typhoid, malaria, dengue fever, and yellow fever are rampant. The ultimately fatal parasite carried by freshwater snails, known as schistosomiasis or "snail fever," is also manageable with medicines, but few have access to them. Other widespread diseases in the country include cholera; filariasis, a parasite that can permeate the skin; rabies; and leprosy. As of 2014, 42,000 people—amounting to 3.7 percent of the population—are living with HIV or AIDS, and in 2014, 1,900 died from the disease. In the regions of Gabu and Tombali, the World Health Organization has set up centers to

deal with potential Ebola cases, and surveillance of borders with affected countries, like Senegal, Guinea, and Côte d'Ivoire has been implemented to help curb the spread of infection. As of October 2015, the country had no new cases of the disease.

GOVERNMENT

Guinea-Bissau has been in political upheaval since April 2012, when a military coup suspended its constitution and delayed scheduled elections. However, when the UN Security Council threatened sanctions against the country until the constitution was reinstated, order was restored, and elections were held in 2014. The first round of voting was conducted on April 13, 2014, with a run-off held on May 18, 2014, since no candidate had achieved a majority in the first round. In this second round of elections, Jose Mario Vaz of the African Party for the Independence of Guinea and Cape Verde (PAIGC) beat independent candidate Nuno Gomes Nabiam 61.9 percent to 38.1 percent.

The president is the chief of state, elected by majority vote to a five-year term. The prime minister is head of government and oversees the legislative branch. The president, who also appoints the prime minister, following conference with and the assent of party leaders and the National Assembly, appoint an advisory cabinet. The unicameral National People's Assembly (Assembleia Nacional Popular) has 102 seats. Members are directly elected to proportionally determined, multi-seat constituencies and serve four-year terms.

Political Parties

The democratic socialist African Party for the Independence of Guinea and Cape Verde (PAIGC) took 57 seats in the National People's Assembly. The center-left Party for Social Renewal took 41, while the Democratic Convergence Party took two seats. The New Democracy Party (PND) and the political alliance known as Union for Change each achieved one seat. The Republican Party for Independence and Development (PRID) lost three seats and now has no representation in the country's parliament. Overall, 15 parties competed for seats in the general elections of 2014.

Local Government

Guinea-Bissau is divided into nine administrative regions (regiões), including Bafata, Biombo, Bissau, Bolama/Bijagos, Cacheu, Gabu, Oio, Quinara, and Tombali. These regions are further divided into sectors (setores), including the city of Bissau, which is an autonomous sector. Committees govern villages (tabanca), while more urban towns and cities are overseen by councils.

Judicial System

Guinea-Bissau's legal system is heavily influenced by both Portuguese and French civil law codes. The country's highest court is the Suprema Tribunal Justica, or Supreme Court, which is presided over by nine judges and has civil, criminal, social, and administrative divisions. The Guinea-Bissau Supreme Court also has the capacity to rule on constitutional and last instance civil and administrative appeals. Other courts under the Suprema Tribunal Justica include, in descending order of instance, appeals courts, regional courts, and sectoral courts. Military courts operate independent of the civil, criminal, and administrative system.

Taxation

In Guinea-Bissau, corporate taxes are levied at a rate of 25 percent, with an additional corporate social security withholding of 14 percent. There is a 15 percent Value Added Tax (VAT), and social security contributions are withheld from employee wages at a rate of 8.3 percent. Tax on interest earned stands at 15 percent, and property taxes are also imposed, but rates and applicability are dependent upon location. In 2013, taxes contributed 16.1 percent to the country's GDP.

Armed Forces

The People's Revolutionary Armed Force (FARP) is comprised of the Army, Navy, and National Air Force, which is also known as the Forca Aerea Nacional. Guinea-Bissau's Presidential Guard is a paramilitary force that also operates under the purview of the military chief of staff. At present there is selective conscription for those 18 to 25 years old in the Army and Navy only; the Air Force engages personnel on a voluntary basis. As of 2015, there were an estimated 4,000 active military personnel. Both men and women may serve in the military, and those between 16 and 18 may serve with parental consent.

Foreign Policy

Guinea-Bissau follows a policy of non-alignment and seeks to remain on friendly terms with both its neighbors and other countries. As of 2015, Angola, Brazil, China, Cuba, France, Gambia, Germany, Guinea, Libya, Nigeria, Palestine, Portugal, Russia, Senegal, South Africa, and Spain all maintain embassies in the country's capital. Guinea-Bissau, in turn, maintains embassies in Algiers, Algeria; Brussels, Belgium; Brasilia, Brazil; Beijing, China; Havana, Cuba; Paris, France; Banjul, Gambia; Berlin, Germany; Conakry, Guinea; Tehran, Iran; Lisbon, Portugal; Moscow, Russia; Dakar, Senegal; and Madrid, Spain. In early 2010, Guinea-Bissau established bilateral relations with Botswana, although no embassies yet exist in either country.

The United States, which previously enjoyed strong bilateral relations with Guinea-Bissau, closed its embassies in the capital in 1998 following significant and sustained violence between rebel groups and the government.

Guinea-Bissau is currently a member of the United Nations (UN), the World Bank Group, the International Monetary Fund (IMF), the World Health Organization (WHO), the Food and Agriculture Organization (FAO), the African Development Bank, the Economic Community of West African States (ECOWAS). It is also a member of the West African Economic and Monetary Union (WAEMU), the African Union (AU), the Organization of Islamic Cooperation (OIC), and Permanent Interstate Committee for Drought Control in the Sahel (CILSS).

Human Rights Profile

International human rights law insists that states respect civil and political rights and promote an individual's economic, social, and cultural rights. The United Nations Universal Declaration on Human Rights (UDHR) is recognized as the standard for international human rights. Its authors sought the counsel of the world's great thinkers, philosophers, and religious leaders and were careful to create a document that reflects the core values shared by every world culture. (To read this document or view the articles relating to cultural human rights, visit http://www.ohchr.org/EN/UDHR/Pages/Introduction.aspx.)

Human trafficking, particularly of children, is a significant problem in Guinea-Bissau, and the U.S. State Department, indicating that it does not comply with minimum standards to combat trafficking and is making no effort to do so, currently rates the country as Tier 3. Most often, boys are forced into becoming street vendors or performing manual labor, while girls are similarly coerced into street vending, domestic service, and prostitution. Although the country developed a national action plan and enacted an anti-trafficking law, neither has been implemented and little has been done to stop the exploitation activities, identify victims, or prosecute offenders.

According to Amnesty International, Guinea-Bissau's armed forces have been responsible for the random arrest, detention, and torture of numerous civilians, who have either criticized or demonstrated against the government. There were also reports of two politicians having been badly beaten and the deportation of Portuguese journalist during the coup in 2012. Thus far, the government has done little to prosecute those who perpetrated these abuses, and in fact, government officials frequently sanction partisan and retributory violence.

Moreover, while the constitution permits freedom of assembly, both the current government and the post-coup, transitional governing body have not observed this right. The administration imposes license requirements on public meetings and demonstrations, and security forces have, in the past, cracked down on unlicensed, peaceful protests.

Migration

The UN Refugee Agency reports that some 8,684 refugees and 123 asylum-seekers were living in Guinea-Bissau as of December 2014. With elections scheduled for 2015 in Benin, Burkina Faso, Côte d'Ivoire, Ghana, Nigeria, and Togo, the UN High Commissioner for Refugees projects that additional émigrés may seek to escape volatile political circumstances by fleeing to Guinea-Bissau from these countries. As of early 2015, 1,307 Bissau-Guinean refugees and 1,784 Bissau-Guinean asylum-seekers were living outside the country's borders.

ECONOMY

Overview of the Economy

Subsistence farming is vital to Guinea-Bissau's economy and approximately 80 percent of the country's official export revenue comes from cashews, although a great deal of undocumented revenue is generated by the trafficking of illegal substances, most of which is destined for Europe. Fruits, vegetables, and other tubers provide minor cash crops for rural communities. The country has the potential to exploit reserves of bauxite, mineral sands, and phosphates, but this industry is in its infancy and has been interrupted by ongoing civil unrest. As of 2014, the country's GDP was $2.495 billion, while its per capita GDP was $1,400.

Industry

Guinea-Bissau's major industries involve agricultural processing, beer brewing, and the manufacture of soft drinks. Together they contribute just 7.5 percent to the country's GDP.

Labor

According to World Bank statistics, in 2013, Guinea-Bissau's labor force numbered 731,325. The percentage of women participating in the country's economy was just over 47 percent as of 2010. Exactly 82 percent of the labor force is employed in agricultural activities, while 18 percent are involved in the industry and services sector.

Energy/Power/Natural Resources

The country has significant, but still unexploited deposits of petroleum. As of 2013, the country consumed an estimated 3,020 barrels per day—all imported. Wood is still the principal source of fuel in many rural communities, which, along with illegal logging (see "Forestry") has led to deforestation concerns. Electricity is largely unavailable in rural areas and spotty in urban areas, and the government has drafted a long-range plan aimed at increasing its generating capacity, improving the distribution system, and curbing unmetered usage. Hydropower, which has not yet been implemented in Guinea-Bissau, is currently under development thanks to the multinational Sustainable Energy Fund for Africa (SEFA), which has invested $1 million (USD) to construct Salthino Hydroelectric Plant, the country's first.

Fishing

Fishing is a vital industry in Guinea-Bissau and for many along the coast and living in the archipelago, it is a way to feed their families. Therefore, most native fishing is artisanal. However, a fisheries partnership between the European Union and Guinea-Bissau started in June 2007 and is renewed every four years. Vessels from Spain, Portugal, Italy, France, and Greece fish legally in Guinea-Bissau's territorial waters. In return, Guinea-Bissau is given 9,200,000 Euros annually. There are separate per-tonnage and pole-and-line fees paid by each vessel owner. While the protocol was temporarily suspended in 2012, during the military coup, it was reestablished in October 2014. Overfishing is now a concern raised by environmental advocates.

Forestry

Just over 55 percent of the country is covered is forests, and timbering has become a booming industry. However, illegal logging remains a problem, particularly with native species like rosewood, for which China has great demand. Estimates indicate that between 2008 and 2014, harvesting of rosewood has increased from 80 to 15,000 cubic meters per year. Illegal logging has also grown because the demand for cashews has fallen, forcing local populations into the practice to order to survive. Government corruption, involving the bribery of high-level officials by Chinese import companies, keeps rosewood moving eastward, despite the efforts of environmental advocates and forestry officials.

Mining/Metals

Guinea-Bissau has rich deposits of phosphates, bauxite, clay, granite, limestone, and granite, along with largely unexplored reserves of diamonds, gold, heavy minerals (i.e., semi-precious gemstones, such as tourmaline or topaz), and petroleum. Foreign companies, like the Canadian firm GB Minerals Ltd have begun a 25-year plan to mine Guinea-Bissau's phosphate reserves near the northern town of Farim. Other firms involved in the mineral and mining industry include the South African-based companies AEL Mining Services and Earth Metallurgical Solutions, French-based ROC-Impact, and China-based Zhangqiu Ruinian Casting and Forging Co Ltd. Otherwise, this economic sector is largely underdeveloped and artisanal, with little effort made to investigate or exploit the country's petroleum assets.

Agriculture

Nearly 45 percent of Guinea-Bissau is devoted to agricultural land, with 6.9 percent devoted to permanent crops and nearly 30 percent devoted to pasture. In 2014, agriculture accounted for 45 percent of the GDP, and is the second largest income-generator for the country after the service industry, which accounts for 47.5 percent of the GDP. Subsistence agriculture is vital to the survival of many Bissau-Guinean families. In addition to the starchy cassava root and the edible manioc leaves that grow from it, other cultivated crops include rice, millet, corn, sorghum, sweet potatoes, yams, onions, and tomatoes. Principal agricultural exports are cashews, coconuts, palm nuts, and olives.

Animal Husbandry

Cattle have been kept throughout Guinea-Bissau for centuries as part of a subsistence pattern of living, and milk products have been an important component of the Bissau-Guinean diet. Truly large-scale herding has only been central to the Fula and Mandinka ethnic groups of the northern and eastern regions, however. There is even a division of labor in animal tending: men care for cattle, sheep, and goats, while women tend to hogs and poultry. In the first decade of the 21st century and continuing into the second, more than half a million cattle are being raised within the country.

Tourism

As of 2015, the U.S. State Department has issued a travel warning, advising tourists against visiting Guinea-Bissau due to ongoing civil unrest, particularly along the northwest border with Senegal, where the situation continues to be volatile. Important to note, too, is that throughout the country, unexploded landmines—a legacy of the Portuguese conflict—continue to pose serious risks for both residents and visitors, particularly those seeking to explore largely uncharted areas.

One of the country's greatest draws is the Bijagós Archipelago (Arquipélago dos Bijagós), a group of 88 islands in the Atlantic Ocean. There is a rich diversity of environments on these islands, from intertidal zones and palm forests to sand banks and coastal savannas, among many other ecosystems. In 1996, the UNESCO's Man and the Biosphere Programme named Bijagós an International Biosphere Reserve. The archipelago is home to marine turtles, hippos, and manatees.

Another site of interest is the River Zoo Farm, located 125 km (78 miles) from the country's capital. It is a 200-hectare (500-acre) preserve for thousands of birds, large mammals, and other native fauna, some of which are wild-captured and transported to the sanctuary for preservation purposes. While it is a wildlife breeding facility that works in conjunction with Guinea-Bissau Wildlife Department, bungalows are reserved for tourists.

Savannah Schroll Guz

DO YOU KNOW?

- The name of the Manjaku people, who make up 8.3 percent of Guinea-Bissau's population, actually translates to "I tell you."

- In 2005, when plastic packages of cocaine first washed up on Guinea-Bissau's shores from a damaged freighter, no one recognized what it was. Women mistook it for a flavoring agent and added it to sauces; one man mixed it with water and attempted to whitewash his house; others fed it to crops, believing it was fertilizer. Cocaine has since become a growing epidemic in the nation.

Bibliography

Chabal, Patrick. "Amílcar Cabral: Revolutionary Leadership and People's War." Trenton, NJ: *Africa World Press*, 2003.

Dhada, Mustafah. "Urgent Notice: Endangered by War, The National Institute of Studies and Research of Guinea-Bissau." *Journal of Contemporary African Studies* 17.1 (1999): 163–64.

Einarsdóttir, Jónína. "Tired of Weeping: Mother Love, Child Death, and Poverty in Guinea-Bissau." Madison: *U Wisconsin P*, 2004.

Figueira, Carla. "Languages at War: External Language Spread Policies in Lusophone Africa." Bern, Schweiz: *Peter Lang*, 2013. Duisburger Arbeiten zur Sprach- und Kulturwissenschaft Ser.

Gaynor, Lily and John Butterworth. "God's Needle: How Lily Gaynor Brought Hope and Healing to the Land of the Witchdoctors." Toronto, Ontario: Monarch Books, 2013.

Hawthorne, Walter. "Planting Rice and Harvesting Slaves: Transformations along the Guinea-Bissau Coast, 1400–1900." Portsmouth, NH: *Heinemann*, 2003. Social History of Africa Ser.

Manji, Firoze and Bill Fletcher, Jr., eds. "Claim No Easy Victories: The Legacy of Amílcar Cabral." Dakar, Senegal: *CODESRIA*, 2013.

Mendy, Peter Karibe and Richard A. Lobban, Jr. "The Historical Dictionary of Guinea-Bissau." 4th ed. Lanham, MD: *Scarecrow Press*, 2013.

Urdang, Stephanie. "Fighting Two Colonialisms: Women in Guinea-Bissau." New York: *Monthly Review Press*, 1979.

Vigh, Henrik. "Navigating Terrains of War: Youth and Soldiering in Guinea-Bissau." New York: *Berghahn Books*, 2006.

Works Cited

"2015 UNHCR subregional operations profile–West Africa." United Nations High Commissioner for Refugees. *UNHCR: The UN Refugee Agency*. United Nations High Commissioner for Refugees, 2015. http://www.unhcr.org/pages/49e484cd49.html.

"Africa: Guinea-Bissau." *The World Factbook. Central Intelligence Agency*, 2015. https://www.cia.gov/library/publications/the-world-factbook/geos/pu.html.

"At a Glance: Guinea-Bissau." *UNICEF*. UNICEF, 26 Dec. 2013. http://www.unicef.org/infobycountry/guineabissau_statistics.html.

"Ebola Situation Report – 30 September 2015." *World Health Organization*, 2015. http://apps.who.int/ebola/current-situation/ebola-situation-report-30-september-2015.

"Guinea-Bissau 2015 Crime and Safety Report." United States Department of State Bureau of Diplomatic Security. *Overseas Security Advisory Council/Bureau of Diplomatic Security*, 2015. https://www.osac.gov/pages/ContentReportDetails.aspx?cid=17636.

"Guinea-Bissau: Economic Overview" *The World Bank*. World Bank *Group*, 2015. http://www.worldbank.org/en/country/guineabissau/overview.

"Guinea-Bissau Human Rights." Amnesty International. *Amnesty International USA*, 2015. http://www.amnestyusa.org/our-work/countries/africa/guinea-bissau.

"Guinea-Bissau." 2014 Findings on the Worst Forms of Child Labor. *U.S. Dept. of Labor/Bureau of International Labor Affairs*, 2015. http://www.dol.gov/ilab/reports/child-labor/guinea-bissau.htm.

"Guinea-Bissau." Art & Life in Africa. *University of Iowa Museum of Art*, 2014. https://africa.uima.uiowa.edu/countries/show/11.

"Guinea-Bissau." Doing Business. *The World Bank Group*, 2015. http://www.doingbusiness.org/data/exploreeconomies/guinea-bissau/paying-taxes/.

"Guinea-Bissau." *EmbassyPages.com*. EmbassyPages.com, 2015. http://www.embassypages.com/guineabissau.

Guinea-Bissau." WPF.org. *World Food Programme*, 2015. https://www.wfp.org/countries/guinea-bissau.

Guinea-Bissau: Fisheries Partnership Agreement." European Comission Fisheries. *European Commission/Directorate-General for Maritime Affairs and Fisheries*, 18 May 2015. http://ec.europa.eu/fisheries/cfp/international/agreements/guinea_bissau/index_en.htm.

"Illegal Logging in Guinea-Bissau." BorgenProject.org. *The Borgen Project*, 31 Jul. 2014. http://borgenproject.org/illegal-logging-guinea-bissau/.

"INEP-About Us." *Instituto Nacional de Estudos e Pesquisa*. INEP, 2015. http://www.inep-bissau.org/Home/INEPAboutus/tabid/264/Default.aspx.

"New law prohibits practice of female genital mutilation in Guinea-Bissau." *UNICEF*. UNICEF, 24 Jul. 2012. http://www.unicef.org/health/guineabissau_59787.html.

"Phosphate Mining in West Africa: Farim Phosphate Project." *GB Minerals*. GB Minerals *Ltd.*, 2013. http://www.gbminerals.com/.

"River Zoo Farm: Wildlife Breeding Farm & Fauna Sanctuary." *River Zoo-farm*, 2004. http://www.riverzoofarm.com/.

"Supporting the Development of a Hydropower Plant in Guinea-Bissau." ECREEE: Towards Sustainable Energy. *ECOWAS Regional Centre for Renewable Energy and Energy Efficiency*, 2013. http://www.ecreee.org/news/supporting-development-hydropower-plant-guinea-bissau.

"Table 1: Human Development Index and its components." Human Development Reports. *UNDP*, 2015. http://hdr.undp.org/en/content/table-1-human-development-index-and-its-components.

"Tier Placements." *Trafficking in Persons Report 2014*. Office to Monitor and Combat Trafficking in Persons. U.S. Department of State, 2015. http://www.state.gov/j/tip/rls/tiprpt/2014/226649.htm.

Hatcher, Jessica. "Guinea-Bissau: How Cocaine Transformed a Tiny African Nation." *Time*. Time *Inc.*, 15 Oct. 2012. http://world.time.com/2012/10/15/guinea-bissau-how-cocaine-transformed-a-tiny-african-nation/.

Southern, Paul. "Waldir Araújo: Narratives of Guinea-Bissau's Troubled Identity." *The Culture Trip*. The Culture Trip *Ltd*, 2015. http://theculturetrip.com/africa/guinea-bissau/articles/waldir-ara-jo-narratives-of-guinea-bissau-s-troubled-identity/.

Yigitce, Erdinch. "Flora Gomes: Post-Colonial Cinema in Guinea-Bissau." *The Culture Trip*. The Culture Trip *Ltd.*, 2015. http://theculturetrip.com/africa/guinea-bissau/articles/flora-gomes-post-colonial-cinema-in-guinea-bissau/.

The hand-dyed textiles of Guinea. iStock/trevkitt.

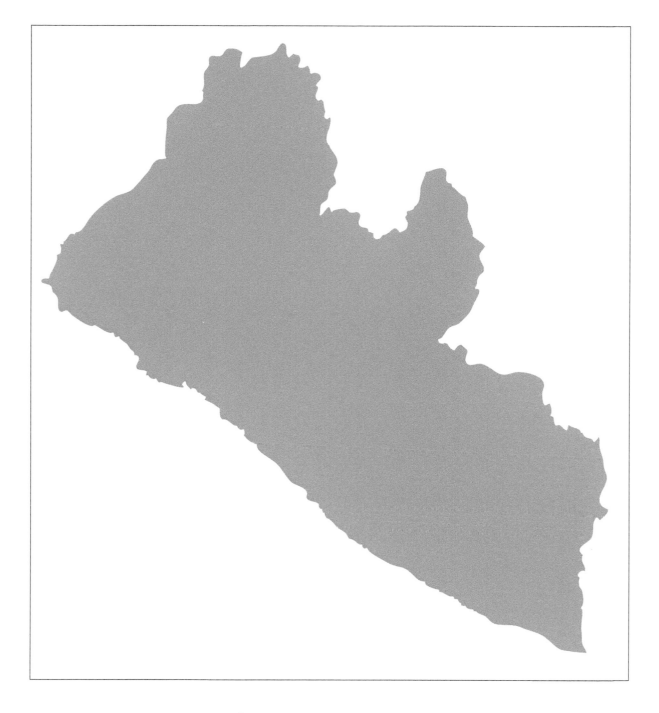

LIBERIA

Introduction

Located along Africa's North Atlantic coast between Sierra Leone, Guinea, and Côte d'Ivoire, the Republic of Liberia is Africa's oldest constitutionally defined government and is a country of rich resources whose people are still trying to recover from a brutal civil war. A military coup in 1980, followed by a second coup in 1989, brought about a civil war that lasted throughout most of the 1990s and into the 21st century. Although it is usually divided into two separate conflicts: the so-called "First Liberian Civil War," which lasted from 1989–1996, and the "Second Liberian Civil War," which extended from 1999 until 2003. The second conflict ended with an August 2003 peace agreement. However, Liberia's government is still striving to restore order throughout various parts of the country. In 2005, Ellen Johnson-Sirleaf (1938–) was elected Liberia's first female president and the first female president in Africa. A graduate of Harvard University's Kennedy School of Government and a former World Bank economist, Johnson-Sirleaf has led a focused effort to rebuild the country's shattered economy and infrastructure. In 2011, she won the Nobel Peace Prize for her nonviolent efforts in advancing women's rights.

Monrovia is the capital of Liberia and that nation's political, economic, and cultural center. Named in honor of the fifth president of the United States, James Monroe, Monrovia was originally founded in 1822—nearly four decades prior to the outbreak of the American Civil War—by freed slaves who wished to establish a new country on their ancestral home continent of Africa.

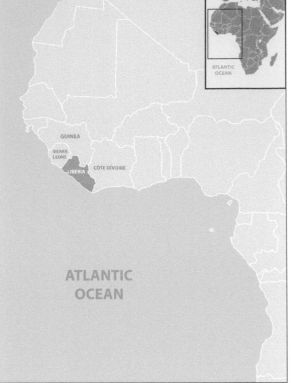

Official Language: English
Population: 4,195,666 (2015 estimate)
Currency: Liberian dollar
Coins: The Liberian dollar is subdivided into 100 cents; coins are available in denominations of 5, 10, 25, and 50 cents and 1 dollar.
Land Area: 96,320 square kilometers (37,189 square miles)
Water Area: 15,049 square kilometers (5,810 square miles)
National Motto: "The Love of Liberty Brought Us Here"
National Anthem: "All Hail, Liberia, Hail!"
Capital: Monrovia
Time Zone: GMT +0
Flag Description: The flag of Liberia is based upon the United States flag because the country's original settlers were freed American and Caribbean slaves sent to the country with the help of American Colonization Society. The flag consists of eleven alternating and equal stripes of red and white, with a red stripe adorning both the

GENERAL INFORMATION

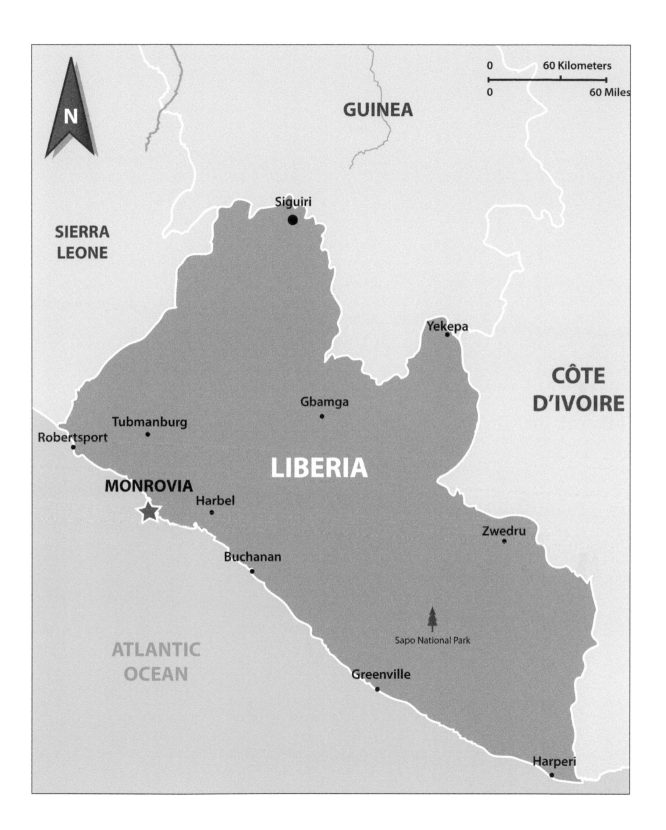

Principal Cities by Population (2013):

- Monrovia (1,264,000)
- Gbarnga (56,986)
- Buchanan (50,245)
- Ganta (42,077)
- Kakata (34,608)
- Zwedru (25,349)
- Harbel (25,309)
- Pleebo (also Plibo) (23,464)
- Voinjama (15,269)

top and bottom. In the upper hoist, or left, side of the flag, a five-pointed white star is centered within a small blue canton, or square. The blue square is represents the African mainland, while the alternating stripes of red (six) and white (five) signify the courage (red) and moral excellence (white) of the signatories of the 1847 Liberian Declaration of Independence. The white star symbolizes freedom.

Population

The vast majority of Liberia's people (95 percent) belong to one of the indigenous African tribes that lived in the region when American settlement began. Those tribes include the Kpelle (20.3 percent), Bassa (13.4 percent), Grebo (10 percent), Gio (eight percent), Mano (7.9 percent), Kru (six percent), Loma (also Lorma [5.1 percent]), Kissi (4.8 percent), and Gola (4.4 percent). Additionally, 17.6 percent of the population is comprised of other native ethnicities, including Gbandi, Krahn, Vai, Dei, Bella, Mandingo, and Mende. Finally, 2.5 percent consider themselves to be Americo-Liberians (descendants of freed slaves from the United States) or Congo People (descendants of West Indians freed from slave ships off the African coast).

Liberia's extended civil war wreaked havoc on the quality of life of the Liberian people. At of the end of 2004, over 200,000 Liberians were living as refugees in Guinea, Côte d'Ivoire, Sierra Leone, and Ghana. According to the UN, as of December 2014, that number dropped to 40,121.

Ironically, camps inside Liberia offer refuge to the victims of civil violence in neighboring Côte d'Ivoire and Sierra Leone. In late 2014, the number of refugees and asylum-seekers living inside Liberia totaled 15,932.

Approximately 49.7 percent of the population resides in urban areas (2015 estimate). As of 2015, the country had a population growth rate of 2.47 percent. Monrovia is the capital and largest city, and has an estimated population of more than 1.2 million. The capital is home to just over 30 percent of the Liberian population. The largest of these groups is the Kpelle, who speak a language belonging to the Mande language group, part of the Niger-Congo family. The second largest ethnic group is the Bassa, whose language belongs to the Kwa linguistic group. Monrovia also features significant communities made up of expatriates from African and European nations.

The so-called Americo-Liberians, or the descendants of the former American slaves who originally founded Liberia in particular, have historically dominated Liberia's coastal regions, and Monrovia. Although a small minority (they are outnumbered by the indigenous residents by a ratio of thirty to one), the educated elite—or "bookmen" as they are locally known—continue to wield much influence over Monrovia's political and economic landscape, although they are often viewed with suspicion by other natives.

Languages

Liberia's diversity is also reflected in its languages. Most of the indigenous tribes still converse, read, and write in their own languages. Others are bilingual and polylingual, though only 20 percent speak English, the country's official language. Another 20 regional languages are spoken and written within the country.

Native People & Ethnic Groups

A complex network of ethnic groups was already living in the area that is now Liberia when the first Americo-Liberians arrived less than 200 years ago. Most of Liberia's tribes migrated to the area from the Sudan in the 13th century, moving gradually from the hinterlands to the coast as populations grew.

The 16 ethnic groups that make up the majority of Liberia's indigenous population organize loosely into three language groups. The Mande tend to occupy most of northwest and central Liberia. This group includes the Kpelle (making up 20.3 percent of the entire population), the Ngbandi, Dan (Gio), Mano, Mende, Malinke, and the Vai, who are notable for having created their own distinct alphabet, though they are also literate in English and Arabic.

The Kwa-speaking peoples include the Basa (Monrovia's largest ethnic group), the Kru, Grebo, De, Belleh (Belle), and Krahn. The Kwa live primarily in the southern half of Liberia. The Kru and Grebo are some of the earliest African converts to Christianity.

The language group with the longest continuous presence in Liberia is the Mel. Located primarily in the north and coastal northwest, Mel speakers include the Gola and Kisi. As in other African countries, Liberia's national boundaries were superimposed on the area without regard to ethnic groupings. As a result, all of the indigenous tribes in Liberia have counterparts in neighboring countries, a factor which has affected civil wars in the region and the distribution of refugees.

Religions

Just over 85 percent of Liberians are practicing Christians, while 12.2 percent are Muslim. Less than one percent practices their religious faiths in keeping with local traditions, while 1.4 percent identify with no religion.

Climate

Liberia has a tropical climate. The average temperature is about 27° Celsius (81° Fahrenheit) year-round near the coast. In the mountains, the average is closer to 18° Celsius (64° Fahrenheit).

Liberia's rainy season lasts from May to October. Yearly rainfall in the country varies from 520 centimeters (205 inches) in some places on the coast to 178 centimeters (70 inches) on the central plateau. The harmattan winds blow dust from the Sahara across Liberia from December to March.

Monrovia features a warm, humid climate throughout the year. Temperatures generally hover between 27° Celsius (81° Fahrenheit) and 30° Celsius (86° Fahrenheit). The city also experiences a rainy season that lasts from May through October.

ENVIRONMENT & GEOGRAPHY

Topography

Liberia's gently rolling coastal lowlands extend for 579 kilometers (360 miles) along the Atlantic and 40 to 80 kilometers (25 to 50 miles) toward the interior. The coastal plain is fed with a multitude of rivers, streams, and lagoons that tend to flood during rainy seasons and storms. The country has 200 nautical miles of territorial sea, and is bordered by Guinea to the north, Sierra Leone to the northwest, and Cote d'Ivoire to the east.

At the edge of the coastal plain, the land rises dramatically to a string of 245-meter (800-foot) plateaus. On the plateaus, the Bong and Putu mountain ranges rise from wide grasslands and lush tropical rainforest. Liberia's highest point of elevation is the summit of Mount Wuteve, which soars to 1,440 meters (4,724 feet) near the border of Guinea and Sierra Leone.

Monrovia, the capital, is located in northwestern Liberia along the Atlantic coast at 6° 20′ north and 10° 46′ west. Built on a cluster of small islands and peninsulas, the city's lagoons are fed by the Mesurado River, which begins at the mouth of the Atlantic in Monrovia.

Plants & Animals

Poverty and the destruction of natural habitats have endangered a number of plant and animal species throughout Liberia. However, the grasslands, coastal wetlands, and rainforests still provide refuge for a vast array of wildlife.

Some of Liberia's rarest species include zebras, hippopotami, pygmy hippopotami, African elephants, chimpanzees, Diana monkeys, mona monkeys, dwarf crocodiles, fruit bats, and

Manatees are among the wildlife found in the coastal waters of Liberia.

Liberian mongooses. In the coastal waters, sperm whales, West African manatees, and spotted-neck otters are found.

CUSTOMS & COURTESIES

Greetings
When Liberians meet for the first time, such meetings commonly involve the question "What is your tribe?" This question dates back to when Liberia first became a republic in the mid-19th century, when a large number of indigenous tribes came under the rule of the newfound government. At that time, most groups had a vague understanding of each other and were suddenly forced into closer proximity under a single government.

Informal greetings often make use of a particular handshake, in which the right hands grasp, and the two middle fingers are pressed together and then pulled apart quickly to create a snapping sound. Various theories exist regarding the history of the handshake. One theory says that the unique greeting originated with African-American colonists in West Africa, who used it as a sign of solidarity. In addition, a regular handshake is common among adults. It is polite and expected that each person ask about the affairs of the other in greetings. If one fails to do so, he or she will often be reminded immediately.

Gestures & Etiquette
Generally, Liberians are considered friendly and upbeat, despite having experienced great adversity. More importantly, the sense of hope that rebuilding the country has infused into recent daily life is nearly universal. When speaking with each other, Liberians tend to staunchly avoid using "No" to respond to requests. In addition, an air of procrastination, or of putting things off, often defines the culture. Thus, as opposed to directly refusing a companion, it is more polite to say simply, "Maybe later" or "Tomorrow," or another such phrase. It can be construed as rude or impolite to do otherwise.

Eating/Meals
Liberians typically eat two meals each day, one in the morning and then either a big meal in the late afternoon or later in the evening. Rice is a staple of the Liberian diet and is eaten at least twice each day in most families. Generally, most Liberians eat with their fingers. However, some households may employ American customs and set the table with glassware and utensils. Snacking on street food takes place throughout the rest of the day.

After 14 years of conflict, malnutrition developed into a serious issue for many Liberians. This is due to food scarcity and the rising cost of fuel and basic foodstuffs. As of 2008, it was estimated that the number of urban children suffering from acute malnutrition surpassed figures that would define it as a nutritional crisis according to the World Health Organization (WHO). In 2014, the Ebola crisis further worsened food scarcity, as labor shortages caused food production to slow or even halt. In some areas, food scarcity has become such a serious problem; farmers are even eating the seeds intended for planting.

Visiting
In the years since Liberia has returned to relative political stability, most Liberians are rebuilding either their homes or working to get their

property back. Nonetheless, Liberians still pride themselves on being able to host guests for meals when they are able. Serving a meal is generally the focal point around which a gathering is organized. As is customary in most African cultures, a practical gift should be brought to the hosts. This most often includes a part of the meal to be served, such as rice or cassava.

LIFESTYLE

Family

As in most African nations, family structure in Liberia is rooted in the community at large and not simply the immediate family. Traditionally, households are composed of several generations and extended family, with all parties contributing in some way. Within the immediate family, women are customarily responsible for all domestic duties, including all child-rearing responsibilities, while men are responsible for earning and working, such as farming and selling crops in the rural areas. However, even before the violence erupted, family structure was suffering from increased teenage pregnancy (out of wedlock) and divorce rates.

Family life has been largely disrupted because of the political unrest and civil war. Because of the brutal practices of Charles Taylor's National Patriotic Front of Liberia (NPFL), in addition to the spread of HIV/AIDS, the number of "separated" children in Liberia has seen a drastic increase in the late 20th and early 21st centuries. Reuniting children with their families, now that the conflicts are largely over, is proving nearly impossible, as in many cases, parents have fled the country, been killed, or have died from fatal diseases. Most of unclaimed children end up categorized as orphans and never know the fate of their parents. This issue has been exacerbated by the February 2014 Ebola outbreak, which continued until September 2015. Also keeping many children homeless are the high numbers of former child soldiers. These former soldiers now choose to remain apart from their families, due

to shame or the inability to readjust to a life in which they do not have to care for themselves.

Housing

Traditional tribal homes in Liberia are generally cylindrical in shape with a conical roof, and are usually constructed of native materials such as mud, concrete, or palm fronds. As Liberia rebuilds after the conflict, more homes are being constructed from cinder blocks in a rectangular and with flat, corrugated tin roofs. Depending on the size of the family, the home may be divided inside with more tin sheets or, in some cases, with walls of mud. Additionally, most homes, particularly in rural areas, have no running water or electricity.

Much of Monrovia has been organized into what the locals refer to as slums or shantytowns (informal settlements). These are typically long chains of corrugated tin, one-room dwellings in which entire families live while they wait for new homes to be built. The majority of people residing in such settlements are those who have returned from refugee camps in nearby countries, only to find that their homes have been looted, destroyed, or taken over. Additionally, each slum is often considered its own township, and has schools, churches, mosques, and markets. However, most lack electricity, water, and proper sanitation.

Food

Generally, Liberian cuisine is similar to West African cuisine and has some distinct American influences. As in most West African countries, the diet in Liberia includes a foundation of rice or cassava, a starchy root that is cooked until it reaches a porridge-like consistency. Most dishes are served over steamed rice and often presented in a soupy consistency. For example, a common dish consists of rice topped with greens, palm oil, and meat or fish. Palm oil is used extensively, and other common ingredients include peppers, ginger, palm nuts, yams, mango, plantains (a starchy green banana), and beans. Sweet potato vines and cassava leaves (called manioc leaves) are the most common greens, and they are often fried in palm oil with onions, spices, and meat. Seafood is also common, particularly dried fish, as are chicken, beef, and bush meat (i.e., wild game, including amphibians, reptiles, and monkeys).

Dumboy (boiled and then pounded cassava root) and fufu (a derivative of cassava) are two staple dishes in Liberia, often eaten as sides. To prepare fufu, the starchy cassava root must first be ground and then allowed to ferment for several days. Once fermentation has occurred, the solid bits are removed, leaving only the liquid starch. This is boiled slowly until it takes on the texture of firm custard. This base, often rolled into balls, is then eaten with a side of soup. Dumboy, on the other hand, is much quicker to prepare. The cassava is boiled and then mashed in a large mortar and pestle. To keep it moist, water is poured around its edges until the soup is ready to take its place. In both instances, the preparation is meant to make the cassava a soft as possible. Another popular dish is goat soup, which is largely considered the national soup and thus served at important state functions.

Rice remains the most commonly eaten starch in Liberia. Most of Liberia's rice is imported. This imported rice is generally more popular, both because of Liberia's lack of farming infrastructure and because of rocks that often find their way into Liberian-grown rice during harvesting. Liberian cuisine is distinguished from that of other West African nations by its use of hot peppers. These are widely used because of the common belief that they prevent food from spoiling. Today, almost every vegetable stew is served spicy, but many Liberians add even more spice, such as cayenne.

Life's Milestones

Nearly 86 percent of the Liberian population identifies as Christian, while an estimated 12 percent are Muslim, with the remainder practicing various forms of animism, other traditional beliefs, or no religious faith at all. As such, many of the milestones honored and observed in Liberian culture are largely dictated by Christian and Muslim practices. Nonetheless, Liberia is home to a largely indigenous population, and the traditional rituals and practices of these varying ethnicities are still widespread.

Liberians commemorate birth, passage into adulthood, marriage, and death with various ceremonies. Most notably, Liberia is famous for its weddings and its celebrations commemorating the dead. Weddings are commonly large affairs that incorporate several important customs. For example, before the wedding, the groom's family prepares the calabash as a gift to the bride. The calabash, which is a large gourd, is dried and filled with a mat for the bride to sit on during the ceremony. The entire gourd and its contents are then wrapped in a cloth that the bride will wear over her head during the ceremony.

Decoration Day takes place in mid-March and is a day set aside to commemorate the dead. As the name suggests, Liberians are meant to visit and decorate the graves of their loved ones who have died. As nearly all of the graves are covered with white stone, this decoration generally involves whitewashing the grave and then decorating it with colorful paint, or even etching passages from the Bible into the stone. Liberians believe that by honoring the dead they will, in turn, inherit their wisdom from beyond the grave.

Another important rite is the initiation into Poro (also, Purrah) or Sande (also, Bundu) societies as a form of passage into adulthood. These gender-specific secret societies (Poro for males and Sande for females) exist throughout Liberia, but are most concentrated among the Lorma people of the west and other indigenous groups, particularly the Mande, in the northwest. Poro is the name given to the network of secret male societies. While the details vary from tribe to tribe, each of these clandestine groups is said to specialize in the strict training of Liberian boys.

Generally, training includes cultural norms and class systems, tribal life and history, and essential life skills. While the exact rituals and requirements are not widely discussed, the style of training is said to be on par with military training and can take up to four years. During this training, young men are forbidden from interacting with their mothers and typically do not see them until graduation. The corresponding female society is the Sande, and involves the same sort of training. However, this training focuses on instilling in females their proper role in Liberian society. As part of Sande, during which women are also taught appropriate sexual conduct, female circumcision (known as female genital mutilation [FGM]) is often performed as part of the initiation ritual.

CULTURAL HISTORY

Art

Liberia is perhaps most renowned as Africa's first republic, founded and built by freed American slaves in 1822, and it has strong ties to the United States. The nation features a complex culture infused by 16 different ethnic groups—the Kpelle in central and western Liberia is the largest ethnic group—that predate the arrival of the former slaves. In fact, the Americo-Liberians, as the descendants of the freed slaves that arrived in Liberia are called, comprise only an estimated 2.5 percent of the population as of 2015. As a result, nearly all of the historic art and culture in Liberia is rooted in the traditions of its indigenous people.

One example of Liberian artistic and cultural expression is the Dan mask, made by the Dan people and perhaps the most famous and widely used masks in Liberia. Nearly all Poros or Sandes—Liberia's secret societies—use these masks, which are believed to hold the highest spiritual strength, as part of the initiation ritual to ensure the safe transition of initiates into adulthood. During elaborate ceremonies, adult males don the masks and enter a trance-like state, during which they travel between the two worlds of the tribe and the spirit-inhabited forest. Generally, the masks depict faces of departed ancestors and are known for their slender, oval shape, large lips, narrow nose and eyes, and high cheekbones. Even though the masks allow for communication with spirit animals, they never represent such animals.

Following the repatriation of freed slaves in the 19th century, quilting became a popular and culturally important craft in Liberia. One famous quilter, Martha Ann Ricks (1816–1901), presented a quilt to Queen Victoria (1819–1901), then queen of the United Kingdom of Great Britain and Ireland. In fact, between 2007 and 2011, the "Liberia's Hope" Quilting Initiative was established at Union College in Schenectady, NY, to restore the cultural relevance of quilting and to empower women who had to abandon their craft and homeland due to civil war.

Architecture

Generally, architecture in Liberia blends traditional African styles with the architecture of the antebellum American South. Like most West African nations, the traditional Liberian housing style is a cylindrical, single-room structure, typically constructed of splintered wood and packed mud or concrete. The roofs are conical in shape and constructed from branches and palm fronds. The choice of leaves is essential in allowing rain to run off the sides and preventing water from leaking into homes. However, even before the political unrest of the late 20th century, Liberians were transitioning from the circular-shaped, mud-brick homes to a rectangular style with stucco or cinderblock walls and a corrugated tin roof. All new homes are constructed in this style.

In the wealthier neighborhoods of Monrovia, the architectural influences of the American South—introduced during the colonial period of the mid-19th century—are evident. Porches, columns, and a general tendency toward a neoclassical style are all common elements of these neighborhoods. However, the political violence uprooted most of the families in these neighborhoods, and witnessed the destruction of what many rebels saw as a symbol of their oppression. Additionally, the development of the vast majority of public buildings occurred in the period immediately following World War II, and feature European and American influences.

As Liberia has a relatively wet rainy season and is prone to flash floods, bridges are another crucial component of the national architecture. Many of the country's suspension bridges are constructed entirely out of existing natural materials, such as branches and rope.

Music

Use of the talking drum is common in Liberia, as it is in the rest of West Africa. Traditionally made from wood, animal hide, and hand-woven chords, this drum is typically a large hourglass shape that is topped with tightly stretched hide at both ends. Cords are attached to the outer rim of the hide and run from one end of the drum to the other. When playing the talking drum, Liberians hold the drum under their arm so that the cords are perpendicular to their chests. This allows them to hug the cords, which in turn either tightens or loosens the hide and changes the tone of the drum. The drum is said to be "talking" because it is thought to have a voice of its own that can change as pressure is applied to the cords.

Western music, including dance, hip-hop, and R&B from the United States and Europe, is also popular in Liberia.

Literature

Liberia's literary tradition is rooted in a rich history of storytelling. History and cultural norms were largely preserved through stories and allegories passed on orally from one generation to the next. In particular, the Dan people of Liberia, who subscribe to a complex tradition of animism, are known for their dramatic performances. These performances consist simply of storytellers who act out their stories. For the most part, these stories have been passed on through the Poros, or secret Liberian societies. This holds true today, since civil war destroyed much of Liberia's infrastructure, including schools.

Liberian literature largely developed in the 19th and 20th centuries, following the country's settlement by freed American slaves. This period saw the emergence of writers and literary figures such as Edward Wilmot Blyden (1832–1912), considered the father of Pan-Africanism—a philosophy and movement concerning the unity of native Africans. Other prominent Liberian literary figures include Roland T. Dempster (1910–1965), novelist Bai T. Moore (1916–1988), and

anthologist and author A. Doris Banks Henries (1913–1981). In modern times, more writers emerged to document, celebrate, and explore Liberia without fear of repercussions from the government. During the civil war, local writers in Monrovia began the Liberian Association of Writers (LAW). The goal of LAW was to draw in writers or those interested in expressing themselves through the written word. The organization continues to support many local writers.

CULTURE

Arts & Entertainment

Following the 14-year conflict that ravaged the nation, Liberia is in the process of rediscovering and restoring its national arts and culture. During the conflict, museums were destroyed, and arts and cultural institutions disappeared as artists fled the country. Furthermore, art supplies were nearly impossible to secure. However, this dire artistic scene has fueled a strong independent movement of artists, especially musicians.

In some ways, the development of modern Liberian music has mirrored the rise of hip-hop in inner cities in the United States. In fact, Liberians have fashioned their own style of hip-hop music, often referred to as "hipco," which fuses R&B and rap stylings with Liberian vernacular. This has become the primary vehicle for commenting on the state of Liberia today. This new style is also derived from highlife music, a music form developed in Ghana and Liberia in the early 20th century. Highlife blends sounds from American jazz and African and Latin guitar. Hipco blends these sounds with American-inspired hip-hop into a musical commentary on the country's political and social issues.

Cultural Sites & Landmarks

Monrovia, the nation's capital, is widely considered the most important site in Liberia. In particular, it is the epicenter of the nation's development as it emerges from fourteen years of civil war and strife. Monrovia was initially founded in 1822 by American colonists, and named in honor of U.S.

President James Monroe (1758–1831). The city's location—situated between the Atlantic Ocean to the west and the Mesurado River that flows east into the heart of the nation—made the city an ideal trading hub. Thus, Monrovia primarily functioned as a port of trade and center of commerce, but also as the heart of Liberia's government.

However, with the arrival of the First Liberian Civil War in 1989, Monrovia's location also made it the target of devastating destruction, vandalism, and squatters, and the city's infrastructure still bears these scars. In fact, the destruction was so total that it rendered Monrovia without electricity and running water for nearly 15 years. When the civil war finally ended, most of the city was left abandoned. Despite this destruction and abandonment—many refugees are now returning—some landmarks remain largely intact.

Liberia's National Museum, while damaged, still houses some of Liberia's most important artifacts, including tribal masks, jewelry, instruments, and various gifts to Liberian officials. However, much of Liberia's art was lost during the civil strife, and there are only roughly 100 artifacts left in the museum after looting. The famous Masonic Temple, founded over 150 years ago. is in Monrovia atop a hill overlooking the city. The temple was nearly destroyed by war, and what remained was used as a shelter and hospital for those fleeing conflict.

The Firestone Plantation, considered the largest rubber plantation in the world, is both a cultural site and national landmark. Like so many landmarks on the west coast of Africa, the Firestone Plantation carries with it an aura of the exploitation of African resources by Western nations. First founded in 1926, this one million-acre plot of land was rented from the Liberian government at $0.06 (USD) per acre, which equals a total rent of just $60,000 (USD) per year. At the time of its founding, and until the conclusion of World War II, the plantation employed over 20,000 Liberians. At the time, this accounted for 20 percent of the workforce. When Firestone was forced to cut back on production following the war, and then ceased operations altogether during the civil war, Liberia's economy suffered

greatly. The facility now offers tours, but has recently been charged with allegations of child labor and poor working conditions.

In 1964, the Kendeja National Cultural Center was established outside of Monrovia. The center was created to provide an educational and accurate depiction of tribal life and the customs of Liberia and featured representatives from 15 tribes living and working together. Programs that were highlighted at the center included wood carving, weaving, ceramics, bamboo crafts, and textiles. However, the center was looted during the 14 years of conflict and is now attempting to restore its cultural relevance.

Sapo National Park remains a true national treasure, and one of the only remaining virgin rainforests in the world. (A forest is dubbed "virgin" if it has never been subject to vast commercial logging.) Though Sapo has been subject to minor bouts of logging at the hands of guerilla soldiers, it remains largely unharmed. The national park is particularly renowned for its large collection of exotic flora and fauna.

Libraries & Museums
Monrovia's once bustling cultural scene was another casualty of the long civil conflict that engulfed Liberia until the late 1990s. The National Museum of Liberia (established in 1958 by an Act of the National Legislature), now housed in Monrovia's Supreme Court building, once held rich collections of ceremonial masks, musical instruments, and other artifacts from indigenous cultures, Several private galleries highlighted the work of contemporary Monrovian artists. Many of the National Museum's treasures fell into the hands of looters during the war years, but some have subsequently been recovered. Renovated in 1992 with international assistance, the National Museum of Liberia today features historical and ethnographical galleries containing items ranging from original maps and flags of Liberia to works of traditional local craftspeople.

Holidays
Liberia's public holidays include New Year's Day (January 1); Armed Forces Day (February 11);

Decoration Day (second Wednesday of March); the birthday of Liberia's first president, J. J. Roberts (March 15); Fast and Prayer Day (second Friday in April); Unification and Integration Day (May 14). Additional holidays include Independence Day (July 26); Flag Day (July 24); Thanksgiving Day (first Thursday of November); and President Tubman's Birthday, known as "Goodwill Day," which commemorates the birth of Liberia's longest-serving president (November 29).

Youth Culture

As of 2015, roughly 43 percent of the population is under the age of 15, while 18.3 percent is between 15 and 24 years. In the first decade of the 21st century, this was attributable to the flight of hundreds of thousands of adults during two decades of civil unrest. However, more than a decade later, the youth-heavy culture is due in part to Liberia's 2.47 percent population growth, high birthrate, and low life expectancy.

During Liberia's internal conflict, orphaned children were recruited to fight or sold into slavery, often to work in the harsh conditions of diamond mines in Sierra Leone. In fact, this conflict is perhaps most famed because of its widespread use of child soldiers and the brutality they often endured. Many children witnessed atrocities committed against their families or were even forced into committing atrocities themselves. In addition, these children and young people were often offered drugs and women as compensation for their work. As a result, post-conflict Liberia continues to have a significant drug problem among former child soldiers.

These former child-soldiers still struggle within a society that will not forget what they were forced to do by Charles Taylor. President Ellen Johnson Sirleaf made it one of her first priorities to help these men assimilate back into Liberian society through various governmental programs. In August 2005, she spearheaded the National Youth Conference, in which the Liberian National Youth Policy was drafted. The policy aims for improved education, healthcare, gender equality, HIV/AIDS prevention, and drug abuse prevention, among other key issues facing Liberian youth.

SOCIETY

Transportation

Public transportation exists in the form of bush taxis (light public transportation that usually consists of a mini-bus or wagon), which can be very expensive for the average Liberian. The most common mode of transportation remains walking. While there is no passenger train service, boats remain a popular mode of traveling from one coastal city to another. Again, safety is an issue, as these are generally fishing boats that are not built to navigate ocean waters. In addition, on roadways, speed limits are generally not established or otherwise enforced. Traffic moves on the right-hand side of the road in Liberia.

Transportation Infrastructure

Transportation in Liberia has been severely debilitated from past conflict and civil war. For example, the nation's three rail lines, used to transport iron ore from mines, were mostly shut down and destroyed during the wars. As of 2010, only one had been made operational again, but it does not serve passengers, only cargo. Moreover, there are no rail links between countries. The majority of Liberia's roads are unpaved and often are washed out during heavy rainfall, rendering them impassable. The only paved roads run between a few of the major cities, notably from Monrovia to nearby towns, but are commonly in poor condition and lack adequate markings or signage. There are seventy airports in Liberia, but only two have paved runways.

Media & Communications

Liberia's past internal conflicts led to both a physical and ideological destruction of the media. Even before the civil conflicts, however, Liberia suffered from leadership unwilling to give free rein to the press. In fact, former President William Tubman (1895–1971) was notorious for squashing reporters and newspapers who published anything remotely critical of his presidency.

When Charles Taylor seized power in 1997, media censorship reached a heightened level.

Public radio and television broadcasts were replaced with Taylor's Liberian Communication Network (LCN). This propaganda-ridden network aired only news that painted Taylor in a positive light. When Taylor resigned, he left behind no operating television stations and one public radio station that could not even reach the entire nation. Most of the former private stations were totally destroyed and looted during Taylor's regime.

Currently, the media in Liberia are rebuilding, and as of 2014, Freedom House considers the media under President Ellen Johnson Sirleaf to be "Partly Free" thanks, in large part, to her 2012 efforts to eliminate criminal defamation laws with the help of the Press Union of Liberia (PUL). There are now four private newspapers, two of which are dailies; four private television stations; and five radio stations, one of which is state-run. National broadcasting is now offered by UNMIL (the UN Mission to Liberia). As of 2015, the country is still struggling to repair its almost non-existent telecommunications system. As of 2013, just 4.6 percent of the population were Internet users.

SOCIAL DEVELOPMENT

Standard of Living

Liberia ranked 175th out of 187 countries on the 2014 United Nations Human Development Index, which measures quality of life and standard of living indicators using 2012 data.

Within Liberia, violence, disease, and the destruction of basic infrastructure including roads, airports, and hospitals have reduced average life expectancy to nearly 57 years for men and just over 60 years for women. The fertility rate is still high, at an average of 4.7 children for every woman of childbearing age, and this is reflected in a birth rate of 34 births for every 1,000 members of the population (2015 estimate). Liberia's infant mortality rate is one of the highest in the world, at nearly 68 deaths per 1,000 live births in 2015.

As of 2014 estimates, about 1.17 percent of the adult population is living with HIV/AIDS,

but other virulent diseases including Hepatitis A, typhoid, yellow fever, tuberculosis, dengue fever, and Lassa fever are also taking a toll on Liberia, as did the Ebola outbreak of 2015–15. The problem is made worse by the high rate of poverty and the lack of infrastructure. About 64 percent of Liberians live below the poverty line.

Water Consumption

According to 2015 statistics from the World Health Organization, approximately 75.6 percent of the Liberian population has access to an improved source of drinking water, while 16.9 percent has access to improved sanitation. Overall, however, data concerning water access and sanitation is generally unreliable, and the percentage of Liberians with access to clean water has been reported as low as 28 percent, with those with access to improved sanitation reported as low as 15 percent. Destruction of infrastructure from the county's civil war continues to hamper efforts to improve water and sanitation in the country. Poor sanitation continues to be a leading cause of death among Liberia's youth; a report by the World Health Organization in 2008 stated that 18 percent of deaths in the impoverished nation are a result of poor water and sanitation.

Education

In 2015, Liberia's literacy rate was an estimated 47.6 percent, with 62.4 percent of adult men and only 32.8 percent of Liberian women have basic literacy skills. Approximately half of Liberia's 1.8 million school-age children actually attend school, even though primary school from ages six to 16 is compulsory under Liberian law.

As in other areas of Liberia's social structure, the civil war has been to blame for the country's educational crisis. During the 14-year conflict, about 80 percent of the nation's 2,400 schools were destroyed or put out of service. Teacher training institutes were destroyed in two of the country's most populated regions, and about 800,000 children were forced to leave school when their parents fled, or when they were forced into military service.

While public schools are largely free, qualified teachers are few; books, materials, scientific equipment, labs, and libraries are often inadequate or unavailable, and absenteeism is frequently high. Even teachers sometimes fail to show up for the school day. Most parents who seek a quality education for their children send them to private schools, whose tuition ranges from $100 to $175 (USD) per year. Relief organizations and government officials have targeted school fees as a major obstacle to enrollment in a country where 52 percent of the population survives on less than $0.50 (USD) per day. Public school teachers earn only $40 (USD) per month. In May 2004, in response to continued problems within the educational system, the non-profit non-governmental organization Center for Transparency and Accountability in Liberia (CENTAL), which is registered with the Ministry of Planning and Economic Affairs, began operation in order to end corruption and nepotism in the education sector, so the system can improve. Education officials are also debating the possibility of using regional languages in some of the public schools where students are not fluent in English.

For those students who finish compulsory primary and junior level school, Liberia has implemented a standard examination from the West African Examination Council (WAEC). There is a junior high level for ninth and 10th graders and a senior high level for those graduating. Students who pass receive their West African Senior School Certificate. After passing an entrance examination, students may proceed to higher education at the University of Liberia in Monrovia; the African Methodist Episcopal University (AMEU), also in Monrovia; or Cuttington University in Suacoco (formerly Cuttington College, private and linked to the Episcopalian Church).

Women's Rights

Women make up just over half the Liberian population, and are represented by a woman president, Ellen Johnson Sirleaf, who was elected to the presidency in 2006. In fact, Johnson Sirleaf was elected with nearly 59 percent of the vote—and nearly the entire female vote—in Liberia's first free and fair election in decades. She became the first woman to hold such a high-ranking role in modern day Africa. Despite this historic achievement, Liberia still faces some of the worst human rights conditions for women. Part of Johnson Sirleaf's presidency is dedicated to fighting the culture of violence against women instilled by the Taylor regime.

Rape is a common occurrence in contemporary Liberia and the most frequently committed serious crime in the country, despite sentences of up to seven years in prison if convicted. During the war years, the UN estimates that 90 percent of all women, including young girls, were sexually abused, with some estimates as high as 94 percent. According to many Liberians, women often do not complain about or report sexual assault because they consider it a natural or accepted part of life. The comparatively small number of convictions as compared to cases deters women from bringing charges against an assailant.

During and following the political unrest in Liberia, sex also became a commodity. Many women, having already been desensitized by direct sexual abuse, found their survival dependent upon prostitution, which remains rampant today. Additionally, it is common practice for political officials, who can make life easier for families of these women, to solicit sex for favors and money. The practice is also often encouraged by a woman's family to lift some degree of financial burden.

In addition, cases of domestic abuse are widespread, but, similar to rape and other sexual crimes, are largely unreported due to social taboos. Female genital mutilation (FGM) also continues to be an issue in Liberia, particularly in rural areas, though it is believed that the rate of occurrence of this practice had dropped to an estimated low of 10 percent following the end of civil war. However, there are some experts who believe that percentage is increasing. Overall, sexual harassment in general is not prohibited by the law, and remains an issue.

Despite these hardships, women do share equal rights under the Liberian law. Women may own property, work in any profession, attend school, earn equal pay, own and run a business, and inherit property. However, many of the aforementioned are benefits almost exclusively enjoyed by Liberia's elite, while women in rural and poor areas continue to suffer the residual consequences of civil war.

An important figure in Women's Rights is Leymah Gbowee (1972–), who, along with President Ellen Johnson Sirleaf, was awarded the 2011 Nobel Peace Prize for her counseling of child soldiers and her nonviolent work to end the Second Liberian Civil War. Gbowee achieved this through threat of a curse on soldiers, sex strikes, a face-to-face meeting with Charles Taylor and his cabinet and, ultimately, leading a delegation of women to Ghana to negotiate peace between warring factions. In the process, Gbowee initiated a women's movement in Liberia, a legacy she continues.

Health Care

Since 2004, Liberia has been in the process of trying to rebuild a health care system after the civil war left roads, hospitals, clinics, and equipment destroyed. The war depleted the number of health care workers in the nation from 200 hundred doctors and 600 physician's assistants to 25 doctors and 125 paramedics. Health care services are run by international relief organizations, most under the guidance of the World Health Organization (WHO). Because of the severity of communicable diseases and disease stemming from malnutrition and poor sanitation, health care is now targeted almost exclusively at immunization, sanitation, and the provision of food. Violence has prevented relief organizations from getting to areas outside of Liberia's urban centers, such that three-quarters of Liberians have little or no access to health care.

The February 2014 Ebola outbreak further thinned these resources, although aid workers from the World Health Organization (WHO) arrived to fill the breach. Still, with the Ebola virus rampant until May 2015 and isolated outbreaks continuing until September 27, the WHO estimated that the country had 10,672 cases and

4,808 deaths. Of these numbers, 881 healthcare workers in Liberia, Guinea, and Sierra Leone were infected, with 513 of them dying. On September 3, 2015, Liberia was declared Ebola-free, but remains on heightened watch for new cases.

GOVERNMENT

Structure

Liberia is the oldest republic in Africa, dating to July 26, 1847, and one of the few areas never to be under the authority of a non-African government. However, the political history of the country has been far from peaceful.

In 1822, American leaders made their first efforts at settling the area with freed slaves. With the help of the American Colonization Society, thousands of freed slaves from the United States and from captured slave ships off the African coast settled in Liberia. The name "Liberia" is derived from Latin, meaning "Land of the Free."

Relations with the various African people already living in the region were hostile from the beginning. Skirmishes, attacks, and above all, linguistic differences kept barriers between immigrants from the United States, former West Indian slaves, and the different ethnic groups who had arrived in the region during the medieval era.

Throughout the remainder of the 19th century, Liberia struggled to maintain its borders against encroachment from the French in Côte d'Ivoire and the British in Sierra Leone, while always retaining its independence. By the 1930s, however, it became clear that Liberia's democratic government was not without problems. A League of Nations report showed that the government had taken advantage of ongoing slavery practices within some of the interior tribes—and of the huge disparities between Americo-Liberians and tribally affiliated Liberians—to obtain slave labor for government projects. The practice stopped soon afterward, but the elite position of the country's Americo-Liberian minority had been exposed.

A 1980 coup led by Liberian Army Master Sergeant and Kahn tribe member Samuel K. Doe (1951–1990) finally destroyed the Americo-Liberian power base. Unfortunately, Doe's regime proved to be brutally repressive toward all but his own tribal members, resulting in another coup in December 1989, this one led by Americo-Liberian descendant Charles Taylor. Taylor's government became famous for its own brutality, including attempts at genocide.

In 2003, with the country in a state of devastation, the Liberian government and two major rebel groups entered into peace negotiations. Charles Taylor (1948–) then resigned and was indicted by the United Nations for both war crimes and his participation in Sierra Leone's civil war. In April 2012, he was ultimately convicted of all 11 charges, including terror, rape, and murder, and was sentenced to 50 years in prison. The UN, with substantial support from the United States and ECOWAS (Economic Community of West African States), maintains peacekeeping troops in the country. In 2005, the first democratic elections were held, during which Ellen Johnson Sirleaf (1938–) was elected president. She achieved reelection in 2011.

Under the Liberian constitution, the president is both chief of state and head of government. The president is elected by popular vote to a six-year term, with a two-term limit. The cabinet is appointed by the president and confirmed by the Senate. The bicameral National Assembly consists of the upper Senate and the lower House of Representatives. Members of the Senate are all elected by popular vote to serve a maximum of two, nine-year terms. Elections are staggered over the nine-year period, so that 15 of the 30 total Senate seats are up for renewal every three years. Seats in the House of Representatives number 73, and members are elected by popular vote to six-year terms, with a two-term limit.

Political Parties

Liberia's multi-party system includes numerous political organizations. Coalition governments are formed through negations between various political parties. In the 2014 congressional

elections, 14 parties ran for seats in the Senate, including Congress for Democratic Change (two seats), the Liberty Party (two seats), the Unity Party (four seats), the National Patriotic Party (one seat), and the People's Unification Party (one seat). Also running for Senate seats were the Alternative National Congress (one seat), the Alliance for Peace and Democracy, the National Democratic Coalition (one seat), the Union for Liberian Democrats, Liberia Transformation Party, the Grassroots Democratic Party of Liberia, the Movement for Progressive Change, the Liberia National Union, and the Victory for Change Party.

Local Government

Liberia is divided into 15 counties, which include Bomi, Bong, Gbarpolu, Grand Bassa, Grand Cape Mount, Grand Gedeh, Grand Kru, Lofa, Margibi, Maryland, Montserrado, Nimba, River Cess, River Gee, and Sinoe. These counties are further divided into statutory districts, districts, and cities. Both elected officials and clan chiefs administer districts. Liberia's cities elect mayors that govern in conjunction with city councils.

Judicial System

Liberia's legal system is based on a blending of common and customary law and is heavily influenced by the Anglo-American tradition. The country's highest judicial authority is the Supreme Court, over which the presidentially appointed chief justice and four associate justices preside. Under the Supreme Court, which rules on constitutional matters, are circuit courts for cases involving criminal, civil, labor, and traffic issues. Below the circuit courts are magistrates and customary courts. The country's legal system continues to develop trained lawyers and experienced judges. Challenges related to judicial corruption remain.

Taxation

Corporate income tax is levied at a rate of 25 percent. There are also taxes imposed on rental properties, interest and dividends, goods and services, and fuel, along with scaled municipal taxes. An estimated 22 percent of government revenue comes from the collection of corporate and personal income taxes. Issues related to tax collection remain prevalent as a significant amount of trade occurs within the country's informal economy.

Armed Forces

The Armed Forces of Liberia (AFL), demobilized after years of civil war, is being rebuilt in the early 21st century (15,000-strong prior to the 13-year conflict, reportedly only six former military members were retained in rebuilding the new armed forces.) As of 2014, active personnel are estimated to number approximately 1,800 and comprise two infantry battalions; still, AFL efficacy is compromised by frequent desertions. Although mostly infantry-based, the armed forces recently added air force and naval branches. A small national coast guard patrols the country's maritime claims. The United States military has been a primary source for training for Liberia's armed forces, and the US government, through the Liberia Security Sector Reform program, has been a primary source of funding, although in fiscal year 2013–2014, Liberia allocated $12.9 million (USD) for military expenditures. The New National Defense Act of 2008 specifies that the Armed Forces of Liberia will participate in global peacekeeping missions as part of the Economic Community of West African States (ECOWAS) Standby Force and as a member of the African Union (AU).

Foreign Policy

Liberia was originally founded as a colony in 1822 by the American Colonization Society (ACS), which considered returning freed slaves to Africa as the ultimate freedom. In the 40 years after the land was purchased, over 6,000 former slaves left the U.S. to begin free lives in Liberia. These new settlers came to organize a government modeled after the U.S. Constitution and used it to subjugate the groups of indigenous Africans who lived there. In 1847, under the leadership of the first Americo-Liberian leader, the colonists declared their independence from

the U.S. and founded the Republic of Liberia, the first republic ever to exist in Africa. However, underlying this freedom was intense resentment of African natives in the region.

During the years leading up to World War II, Liberia opened its borders to the Firestone Tire and Rubber Company in a deal that allocated $5 million (USD) to the Liberian government in exchange for Firestone's use of 404,685 hectares (1 million acres) of rubber tree forest. However, Liberia's labor practices were exposed following the deal. In the 1930s, Liberia was rebuked by the League of Nations for its near slave-like treatment of indigenous workers in rubber manufacturing plants.

Liberia and the U.S. strengthened relations in the decades following World War II, and Liberia became one of the first countries to receive volunteers from the Peace Corps in the 1960s. However, after the death of President Tubman in 1971, Vice President William Tolbert assumed the presidency and expanded Liberia's foreign relations with nations of the Soviet bloc. During this era, Tolbert also helped to found the Economic Community of Western States (ECOWAS) in an effort to economically and politically link the nations of Western Africa.

The 1970s are commonly referred to by Liberians as the calm before the storm. In 1980, the continued marginalization of indigenous peoples inspired Liberia's first coup d'etat. This led to a decade and a half of political unrest and brutal violence during which Charles Taylor was elected to the presidency. In 1989, Taylor and the National Patriotic Front of Liberia (NPFL) invaded Liberia and embarked on the systemic killing of anyone suspected of dissent. Because of this devotion to brutal tactics, his election to the presidency in 1997 was almost unanimous. For six years, Taylor governed Liberia and engaged in rebel warfare in his own country and in Sierra Leone, where he profited from the diamond trade. As a result, relations with nearly every regional partner were strained.

In 2003, Taylor was indicted by the International Criminal Court of Justice to stand trial for crimes against humanity. Following

Taylor's resignation, ECOWAS stepped in with roughly 3,600 regional troops in conjunction with United Nations Mission in Liberia (UNMIL) to secure the country. As of 2009, over 15,000 such troops support Liberian security and development, one of the UN's largest such missions. Since that time, the forces have been working toward disarming former soldiers, revamping the police force and rebuilding infrastructure.

As a result, Liberia has seen political stability return and in 2005 saw the first election of a female president. The election of former United Nations Development Program (UNDP) economist Ellen Johnson Sirleaf led to less government corruption and improved relationships with the region and global institutions. Liberia has also been the recipient of substantial financial aid from foreign countries, with the U.S. contributing over $1 billion (USD) between 2004 and 2006. In 2012, Liberia received $73 million (USD) in international humanitarian assistance, with the EU its top donor, giving $19 million, and the U.S. the second largest benefactor, donating $14 million. Between 2003 and 2013, the U.S. donated $272 million to the country.

Human Rights Profile

International human rights law insists that states respect civil and political rights and promote an individual's economic, social, and cultural rights. The United Nations Universal Declaration on Human Rights (UDHR) is recognized as the standard for international human rights. Its authors sought the counsel of the world's great thinkers, philosophers, and religious leaders and were careful to create a document that reflects the core values shared by every world culture. (To read this document or view the articles relating to cultural human rights, visit http://www.ohchr.org/EN/UDHR/Pages/Introduction.aspx.)

Liberia and surrounding countries suffered terrible violence and cruelty under the leadership of Charles Taylor from 1989 until 2003. As head of the NPFL, Taylor proceeded to recruit a military force over 200,000 strong including over 6,000 child soldiers. These child soldiers were

often forced by their superiors to commit violent acts against their families as a means of baptizing them into the group.

Competition for diamonds led Taylor to support rebel groups within neighboring Sierra Leone with arms and manpower. The result of this support was a brutal civil war in Sierra Leone. Throughout Taylor's 14-year rule over Liberia, it is estimated that nearly 300,000 people died as a result and over one million more were displaced. Further, Taylor managed to secure some of the world's more expensive diamonds and stole more than $100 million (USD) from his government.

In 2003, the International Criminal Court at The Hague charged Taylor with crimes against humanity for his role in Sierra Leone's decade-long conflict. Still, Taylor refused to step down until he was pressured by the global community. In 2006, President Sirleaf requested his extradition from Nigeria, where he had gone into hiding, and the UN detained him in Sierra Leone, ultimately sending him to Penitentiary Institution Haaglanden in The Hague. In April 2012, he was found guilty of 11 charges, including terror, rape, and murder, and was sentenced to 50 years in prison. Taylor's son, Charles McArther Emmanuel (or Chuckie Taylor), who also came to Liberia during his father's rule, was extradited back to the U.S. following his father's arrest, and stood trial in Florida for conspiracy and torture. He is currently serving a 97-year sentence.

Today, Liberia still suffers from various problems with its penal system, including unfair detention of uncharged persons, occasional police brutality, and prison conditions that often lead to serious illness and death of inmates. Women, men, and children are often held in the same jail cells, resulting in various forms of abuse. When the UNMIL moved into Liberia in 2003, it was meant to replace the police who had served under Taylor. Most of the police force working for Taylor has since been removed and even detained for crimes against humanity, but police brutality at the hands of these individuals still exists in rural areas. The current administration contends that in order to rebuild the nation's military and police forces while maintaining the current peace, UNMIL must maintain its presence for several more years. As of 2015, the UN Security Council has extended the mission for one more year—until September 30, 2016—but has authorized a reduction in personnel, as Liberia is making progress on many development fronts.

Despite these persistent problems, human rights have improved drastically since Taylor resigned, the UNMIL stepped in, and President Ellen Johnson Sirleaf won the 2006 election. According to Johnson Sirleaf, the best means for improving human rights in Liberia will be to rebuild national security forces, rebuild roads and homes that were destroyed, and root out the fiscal corruption that plagued the Taylor government.

ECONOMY

Overview of the Economy

Since the civil war, Liberia has been dependent on foreign economic aid from the United States, China, Japan, and several Western European countries, like Germany. The country still manages to generate income by exporting rubber and timber. In 2014, the gross domestic product was estimated at $3.691 billion (USD) and a per capita GDP of $900. However, this is up significantly from 2008, when the GDP was $1.47 billion (USD) and the per capita GDP just $373.

Industry

Liberia's industries have included rubber processing, palm oil processing, timbering, and diamond and iron-ore mining. However, all industries were slowed or stopped during the civil war in the 1990s and early 2000s, and again during the Ebola outbreak of 2014–15. Still, between 2010 and 2013, industry grew significantly thanks to the return of businesses following the democratic elections of 2006. Monrovia, which had struggled to establish a modest manufacturing sector, began to stabilize, and the industrial growth rate climbed to a robust 50 percent by 2011. Factories

in and around the capital turned out construction materials such as cement, tiles, and bricks. Furniture, processed food, and beverage products were produced Monrovia factories. However, the rapid spread of Ebola in 2014 and isolated outbreaks in 2015 caused factories to close and businesses again to depart the country.

Labor

The labor force of Liberia was estimated at 1.554 million in 2014, while the unemployment rate was around 85 percent (based on 2003 estimates). As of the early 21st century, 70 percent of the labor force worked in agriculture; industry and the services sector accounted for roughly eight and 22 percent of the work force, respectively.

Energy/Power/Natural Resources

Liberia is rich in high-grade iron ore that was mined by foreign conglomerates between World War II and 1990, when violence put an end to the mining. With its tropical forests, Liberia also has a wealth of timber. Diamond, mineral, and gold reserves exist in unknown quantities. The country's major rivers and tributaries are also capable of providing hydropower. In January 2014, President Sirleaf initiated rehabilitation efforts at the Mount Coffee Hydropower Plant, located on the Saint Paul River, as an initial step in making Liberia more self-sufficient. The plant is slated for completion in 2016.

Fishing

In 2009, Liberia's Agriculture Ministry reported that the country was losing $12 million annually from illegal fishing by foreign entities, particularly China, in its territorial waters. Estimates in 2014 suggested that illegal vessels rob Liberia of as much as $100 million each year. While Liberia does operate a small fleet of industrial trawling boats and the country's fishing fleet includes a number of artisanal boats that harvest fish for domestic preparation and consumption, many fisherman complain that the foreign vessels' enormous capacities allow them to take everything of value in the surrounding area. Previously, artisanal fishing accounted for 60 percent of Liberia's domestic fish supply. However, with the illegal competition, this number has dropped significantly, although no official figures are currently available.

Forestry

In 2003, the United Nations restricted timber production in Liberia as a punishment to the regime of Charles Taylor, who reportedly used funds from the forestry industry to fund his oppressive regime. Following Taylor's arrest, the country's forestry industry has made steps to recover. In 2010, the UN lifted Liberia's wood products embargo and implemented regulations aimed at improving the health of its forestry industry while protecting rainforests as a natural resource. As of 2014, 44.6 percent of the land is still covered in forests.

Mining/Metals

Prior to civil war, mining was a major contributor to Liberia's economy. The country's mining industry continues to improve in its effort to return to pre-war production levels. Iron ore; diamonds; and, to a lesser extent, gold are the greatest income generators. In 2013, the mining sector contributed to 10.8 percent of the GDP.

Agriculture

Agricultural is still the foundation of Liberia's subsistence throughout most of the country and 28.1 percent of the country's land is devoted to agricultural use. Liberian plantations harvest rubber, coffee beans, cocoa, rice, cassava (tapioca, manoic), palm oil, sugarcane, and bananas. Liberia also harvests large amounts of timber.

The herding of sheep and goats is an essential part of rural life in the country. About 70 percent of Liberia's labor force works in agriculture.

Animal Husbandry

Liberia's livestock industry, like other sectors of the country's economy, continues to rebuild itself following the civil war. Although livestock production has never been a major part of Liberia's economy, the country does produce beef, pigs, sheep, goats, and poultry for domestic meat and dairy consumption.

Tourism

Monrovia's government planners are pinning their hopes for a brighter economic future on the development of the tourism industry. Monrovia shares many of the same assets—a hospitable climate, pristine beaches, and a rich and varied local cultural scene—with other African nations that have succeeded in turning tourism into an economic mainstay. The government also hopes that the rising popularity of surfing in the fishing village of Robertsport can help to enhance tourism statistics and, in turn, the country's economy. In addition, as the capital of the world's first republic settled by freed slaves, Monrovia also enjoys a unique historic heritage with the potential to attract visitors.

The creation of a significant tourism industry continues to be hampered, however, by the slow pace of efforts to rebuild the nation's infrastructure and transport network, while also restoring necessary institutions. Persistently high crime rates and widespread corruption among public officials also remain obstacles.

Kristen Pappas, Amy Witherbee, Beverly Ballaro, Savannah Schroll Guz

DO YOU KNOW?

- The American president for whom Monrovia is named, James Monroe (1758–1831)—who belonged to the American Colonization Society and who condemned the international slave trade as "abominable"—was a slave-owner.

Bibliography

"African Women and Peace Support Group." Liberian Women Peacemakers: Fighting for the Right to Be Seen, Heard, and Counted. Trenton, NJ: *Africa World Press*, 2004.

Ciment, James. "Another America: The Story of Liberia and the Former Slaves Who Ruled It." New York: *Hill & Wang*, 2014.

Ellis, Stephen. "The Mask of Anarchy Updated Edition: The Destruction of Liberia and the Religious Dimension of an African Civil War." New York: *NYU Press*, 2006.

Gbowee, Leymah and Carol Mithers. "Mighty Be Our Powers: How Sisterhood, Prayer, and Sex Changed a Nation at War." New York: *Beast Books*, 2013.

Hicks, Kyra E. "Martha Ann's Quilt for Queen Victoria. "Arlington, VA: Black Threads Press, 2012.

Hyman, Lester S. "United States Policy Towards Liberia, 1822 to 2003: Unintended Consequences." Cherry Hill, NJ: *Africana Homestead Legacy Publishers*, 2007.

Levitt, Jeremy I. "The Evolution of Deadly Conflict in Liberia: From 'Paternaltarianism' to State Collapse." Durham, NC: *Carolina Academic Press*, 2005.

McPherson, John Hanson Thomas. "History of Liberia." Reprint. Melbourne, AU: *Book Jungle*, 2008.

Mitchell, Michelle. "Righteous Propagation: African Americans and the Politics of Racial Destiny after Reconstruction." Chapel Hill: *UNC Press*, 2004.

Moran, Mary H. "Liberia: The Violence of Democracy." 2nd ed. Philadelphia: *University of Pennsylvania Press*, 2008. The Ethnography of Political Violence Ser.

Olukoju, Ayodeji. "Culture and Customs of Liberia." Westport, CT: *Greenwood Press*, 2006. Culture and Customs of Africa Ser.

Reef, Catherine. "This Our Dark Country: The American Settlers of Liberia." *Clarion Books*, 2002.

Sirleaf ,Ellen Johnson. "This Child Will Be Great: Memoir of a Remarkable Life by Africa's First Woman President." New York: *Harper Perennial*, 2010.

Waugh, Colin M. "Charles Taylor and Liberia: Ambition and Atrocity in Africa's Lone Star State." London: *Zed Books*, 2011.

Wulah, Teah. "The Forgotten Liberian: History of Indigenous Tribes." Bloomington, IN: AuthorHouse, 2005.

Works Cited

"2015 UNHCR country operations profile – Liberia." UNHCR. *The UN Refugee Agency*. UNHCR, 2015. http://www.unhcr.org/pages/49e484936.html.

"Biography." *Cheryl Dunye Website*. Cheryl Dunye, 2015. http://www.cheryldunye.com/about/.

"Dan Mask Art History." Rebirth African Art Gallery. *Rebirth*, 2000. http://www.rebirth.co.za/Dan_tribal_art_history_and_culture.htm.

"Dan Masks: Liberia and Ivory Coast Masks." *Rand African Art*. Rand African Art, 1 Jun. 2004. http://www.randafricanart.com/Dan_Gunyega_mask1.html.

"Ebola Situation Reports – 30 September 2015." Ebola Virus Disease Outbreak. *World Health Organization*HO, 30 Sept. 2015. http://apps.who.int/ebola/current-situation/ebola-situation-report-30-september-2015.

"Ellen Johnson Sirleaf–Facts." NobelPrize.org. *Nobel Media AB*, 2015. http://www.nobelprize.org/nobel_prizes/peace/laureates/2011/johnson_sirleaf-facts.html.

"I Will Not Send My Kids to Liberian Public School." Center for Transparency and Accountability in Liberia. *CENTRAL*, 2015. http://www.cental.org/index.php?option=com_content&view=article&id=115:-i-will-not-send-my-kids-to-liberian-public-school-&catid=37:edblog1&Itemid=79.

"In Pictures: Liberia's Museum." *BBC News*. BBC, 18 May 2005. http://news.bbc.co.uk/1/hi/in_pictures/4556849.stm.

"Iron Ladies of Liberia." Independent Lens. *Independent Television Service*, 2015. http://www.pbs.org/independentlens/ironladies/film.html.

"Liberia country profile – Overview." *BBC News*. BBC, 30 Jun. 2015. http://www.bbc.com/news/world-africa-13729504.

"Liberia Goes from War Zone to Surfing Mecca." *Time*. Time, Inc., 27 May 2014. http://time.com/119491/liberia-goes-from-warzone-to-surfing-mecca/.

"Liberia." Global Humanitarian Assistance. *Development Initiatives*, 2015. http://www.globalhumanitarianassistance.org/countryprofile/liberia.

"News & Announcements*." West African Examinations Council Corporate Website (Liberia). The West African Examinations Council, Liberia*, 2015. http://www.liberiawacc.org/news28.html.

"Overview of the Film *Liberia: America's Stepchild*." PBS Online. *WGBH Educational Foundation*, 2002. http://www.pbs.org/wgbh/globalconnections/liberia/film/overview.html.

Paying Taxes in Liberia." *Doing Business: Measuring Business Regulations. The World Bank Group*, 2013. http://www.doingbusiness.org/data/exploreeconomies/liberia/paying-taxes.

Sponsor a Child in Liberia." *SOS Children's Villages*. SOS Children's Villages UK, 2015. http://www.soschildrensvillages.org.uk/aids-africa/projects-by-country/aids-liberia-africa.htm.

"Table 1: Human Development Index and its components." Human Development Reports. UN Development Programme. *UNDP*, 2015. http://hdr.undp.org/en/content/table-1-human-development-index-and-its-components.

"With eye on security transition, Security Council extends UN mission in Liberia for another year." United Nations. *UN News Centre*. United Nations,

17 Sept. 2015. http://www.un.org/apps/news/story.
asp?NewsID=51905#.VhUpmmBdHVI.

"U.S. Relations with Liberia." *U.S. Department of State*.
U.S. State Department, 5 May 2015. http://www.state.
gov/r/pa/ei/bgn/6618.htm.

Curnow,K. "African Art." Allen Memorial Art Museum.
Oberlin College Conservatory, 2015. www.oberlin.edu/
amam/IvoryCoast.htm.

Frank, Cecil Franweah. "Tenth Anniversary of the
International Year of the Family: A Reflection on the
Status of the Family in Liberia." *The Perspective*. The
Perspective, 8 Mar. 2004. http://www.theperspective.
org/2004/mar/intlyearofthefamily.html.

Mathews, Elsa Sherin. "African Tales for American
Kids." *The Christian Science Monitor*. The Christian
Science Monitor, 17 Jun. 2008. http://www.csmonitor.
com/2008/0617/p18s01-hfks.html.

McFerron, Whitney. "Food Shortage as Farmers Eat
Seeds." *Bloomberg Business*. Bloomberg, LP, 20
Nov. 2014. http://www.bloomberg.com/news/
articles/2014-11-20/ebola-stokes-liberian-food-shortage-
as-farmers-eat-seeds.

Polgreen, Lydia. "A Master Plan Drawn in Blood."
New York Times. The New York Times *Company*,
2 Apr. 2006. www.nytimes.com/2006/04/02/
weekinreview/02polgreen.html.

Sankawulo, Sr., Wilton. "The Civil War and Liberian
Artists." *New Liberian*. NewLiberian.com, 11 Jan. 2008.
http://newliberian.com/?p=155.

Sengupta, Somini. "Liberia War Chokes the Life of
Monrovia." *New York Times*. The New York Times
Company, 30 Jun. 2003. http://www.nytimes.
com/2003/06/30/world/liberia-war-chokes-the-life-of-
monrovia.html.

Shaw, Elle. "Liberia Association of Writers (LAW)
Celebrates Redemption Road." *Liberia Stories*. Elle
Shaw/Blogger.com, 11 Oct. 2008. http://liberiastories.
blogspot.com/2008/10/liberia-association-of-writers.
html.

Smith, Zadie. "Letter from Liberia (Part Two)." *The
Observer*. Guardian News & Mmedia Limited, 28 Apr.
2007. www.guardian.co.uk/theobserver/2007/apr/29/
features.magazine87.

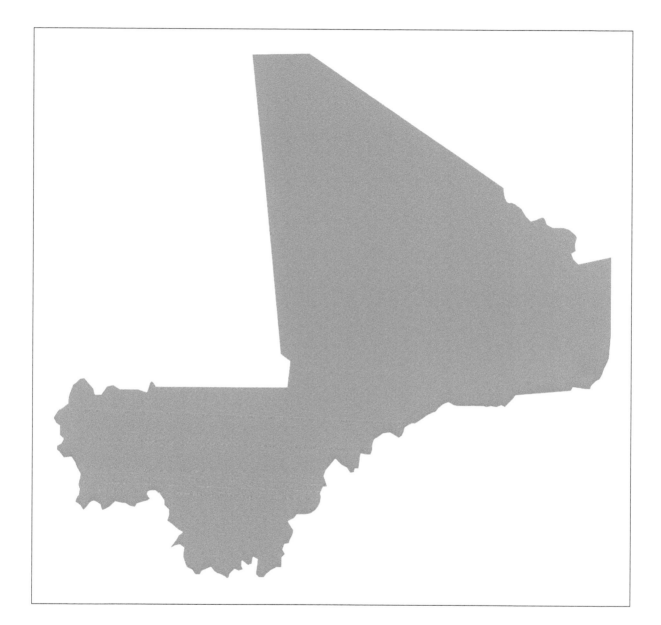

Mali

Introduction

The Republic of Mali, once known as French Sudan, is one of the largest countries in West Africa and among the twenty-five poorest nations in the world. The national capital is Bamako. The people of Mali are known as Malians. The country gained independence from France in 1960, but was ruled by dictatorship until a 1991 military coup paved the way for democratic rule. Following another military takeover in 2012 and the brief installation of a junta government, protracted civil unrest—along with occupation of the north by Islamist rebels, who declared the region independent and imposed strict Sharia law—further destabilized Mali's already frail economy, causing it to become further dependent on foreign aid. Both presidential and parliamentary elections in mid-2013 brought the resumption of relative harmony, although Al-Qaeda-sponsored groups continue to pose a threat to both the people and cultural sites of the north.

Indeed, throughout its history, Mali has experienced political corruption and unrest. Today, the country is trying to find a balance as it confronts a multitude of weighty issues: the internal displacement of its own people due to the northern conflict, the destruction of cultural symbols by Islamic extremists, and environmental problems, such as frequent droughts, descrtification, soil erosion, too little potable water, and flash flooding. Mali's government, back on track following the 2013 democratic elections, has instituted political, economic, and educational reforms in an effort to improve conditions in the country.

Globally, Mali is known for its music, including its drumming and guitar style. Native music in Mali has its roots in the musical traditions of the Mali Empire. Over the years, other musical traditions have been incorporated to produce a unique folk music style.

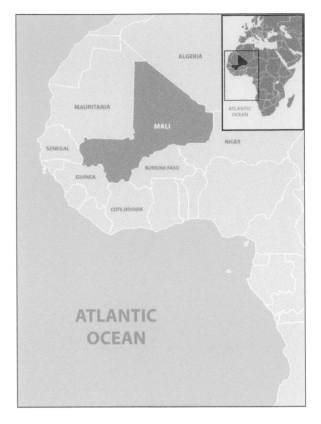

GENERAL INFORMATION

Official Language: French
Population: 16,955,536 (2015 estimate)
Currency: West African Communauté Financière Africaine (CFA [African Financial Community]) franc

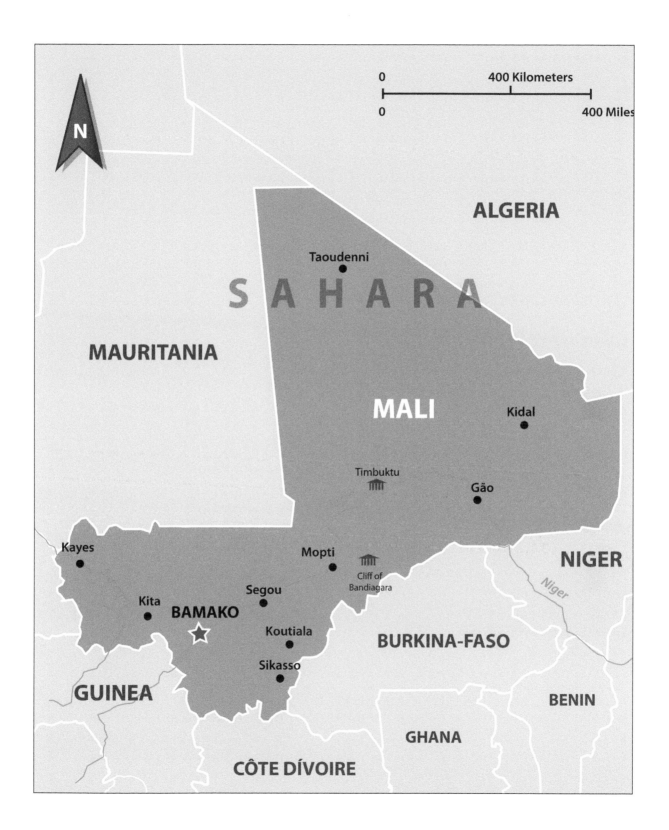

Principal Cities by Population (2014):

- Sikasso (2,643,179)
- Ségou (2,338,349)
- Mopti (2,036,209)
- Bamako (1,810,366)
- Koutiala (141,444)
- Kayes (126,319)
- Gao (86,353)
- Kati (84,500)

Coins: Coins are available in denominations of 1, 5, 10, 25, 50, 100, 200, 250, and 500 francs.
Land Area: 1,220,190 square kilometers (471,117 square miles)
Water Area: 20,002 square kilometers (7,722 square miles)
National Motto: "Un peuple, un but, une foi" ("One people, one goal, one faith")
National Anthem: "Pour L'Afrique et pour toi, Mali" ("For Africa and for You, Mali"); also known as simply "Le Mali"
Capital: Bamako
Time Zone: GMT +0
Flag Description: Mali's flag is a vertical tricolor of (beginning from the hoist side) green, gold, and red, which are the pan-African colors. The colors are in reverse order to those on the Guinean flag. In this case, the green stands for the fertile land, the gold for its wealth of minerals, while red symbolizes the blood of the people, shed while seeking liberty.

Population

Mali's capital, Bamako, has a population of approximately 1.8 million (according to 2014 estimates). Other large city population estimates include Ségou (population 2,338,349); Sikasso (population 2,643,179); Mopti (population 2,036,209); Gao (population 86,353); and Timbuktu, a UNESCO World Heritage Site (population 54,453). Approximately 10 percent of the population is nomadic.

More than 90 percent of Malians are descended from native African ethnic groups. The Mande (comprised of the Bambara, Malinke, and Soninke people) are the largest ethnic group, accounting for approximately 50 percent of the population.

Mali's capital, Bamako, holds the nation's largest and most diverse population, making it very different from the rest of the country's population. Here, the population is more diverse, containing larger numbers of immigrants, European expatriates, and members of other African ethnic groups. Bamako came to prominence through its strategic location as a shipping center, sending and receiving food, minerals, and slaves along the African interior toward the Atlantic Ocean. Named the capital of the French Sudan in the early 20th century, Bamako remained the capital of Mali after the nation's transition to independence in the 1960s. It has one of the fastest growing populations in Africa, and in 2008 and 2013, Bamako was ranked the sixth-fastest growing city in the world.

Languages

French is Mali's official language. It is used in administrative and educational settings. In addition to French, Mali has 13 other languages, which are spoken by various groups throughout the country. Bambara is spoken by 46.3 percent of the population, while Peul/foulfoulbe is spoken by 9.4 percent. Other languages include, in descending order of prevalence: Dogon (7.2 percent), Maraka/soninke (6.4 percent), Malinke (5.6 percent), Sonrhai/djerma (5.6 percent), Minianka (4.3 percent), Tamacheq (3.5 percent), Scnoufo (2.6 percent).

Native People & Ethnic Groups

Archaeological evidence shows that northern Mali has been inhabited for 50,000 years. Long ago, this area of the Sahara Desert was fertile grassland. Farming was introduced to the area around 5,000 BCE, and large communities had developed by 300 BCE.

Beginning in the first century, Mali was ruled by three successive kingdoms, each of which contributed to the country's modern day ethnic composition. The Ghana Empire, which ruled until the 11th century, was comprised of Soninke people. The Kingdom of Malinke followed, until it was displaced in the 15th century by the Songhai Empire. Each of these empires survived by trading gold, salt, and slaves.

After the decline of the Songhai, European ships began arriving in West African ports. France occupied the region in the late 1800s and established the territory of French Sudan in 1904. In 1958, the Sudanese Republic (comprised of Mali and Senegal) gained independence from France. The federation broke apart in 1960 and the Sudanese Republic became Mali.

There are several ethnic groups in Mali. The Mandé peoples (to which the Bambara, Malinké [Mandinka], Soninke ethnicities belong) are the largest group, accounting for 50 percent of the total population. Fula (or Peul), who are primarily herdsmen, account for another 17 percent. Minority groups include the Voltaic (12 percent), Songhai (six percent), and the Tuareg and Moor peoples (10 percent).

Religions

The majority of the population (94.8 percent) is Muslim. The city of Bamako has long served as a major center for Islam in Mali, and the city has numerous worship sites to serve the nation's Muslim population. While 2.4 percent practice Christianity, two percent are of the animist faith. Less than half a percent profess no religious affiliation.

Climate

Temperatures in Mali are typically very hot, with an average of 30° Celsius (86° Fahrenheit) during the day, although it has been known to climb as high as 40° Celsius (104° Fahrenheit) in the months of April, May, and June. The temperature drops significantly at night, however, falling as low as 18° to 20° Celsius (64° to 68° Fahrenheit).

The hottest months of the year are between April and July. The rainy season, characterized by thunderstorms and heavy downpours, lasts from June to October. The southern part of Mali receives the most rainfall, averaging around 1,397 millimeters (55 inches) annually, while the dryer north receives about 203 millimeters (8 inches). Timbuktu, in the center of the country, receives an average of 140 millimeters (5.5 inches) per year.

Droughts are rare in the capital city of Bamako because of the Niger River's volume, while other provinces, including Kidal, often experience droughts during the dry season. During the rainy season, flooding is a concern for neighborhoods located along the Niger or its tributary streams.

The hot, dusty, dry harmattan wind blows from the Sahara Desert, and spreads a fine dust over Mali's cities until June. The cooler alizé blows from November to January.

ENVIRONMENT & GEOGRAPHY

Topography

Mali is a landlocked country, bordered on the north by Algeria, on the east by Niger, on the south by Côte d'Ivoire and Burkina Faso, on the southwest by Guinea, and on the west by Senegal and Mauritania.

The country is mostly flat, and roughly 55.7 percent of its area is either semi-arid or desert. Mali may be divided into five distinct regions: the Sahara Desert in the north, flat farmland in the south, hilly forests in the west, the central savanna (the Sahel), and the Niger River Delta. The country's highest point is at the top of the Hombori Tondo mesa, 1,155 meters (3,789 feet) above sea level.

The Bafing River flows through Mali, and later joins the Semcfé to form the Senegal River. The Niger River flows 1,626 kilometers (1,010 miles) from southwestern Mali up to Timbuktu, then bends southeast toward the Atlantic. It is Africa's third-longest river (after the Nile and the Congo rivers), and Mali depends heavily on it for water and food.

The Niger River irrigates the soil around Mali's capital, Bamako, creating an oasis of lush, tropical vegetation that surrounds the city. The city was first established on the northern side of the river as a small village and shipping center. Modern Bamako expanded south of the river to accommodate an expanding population. While the Niger River is directly responsible for Bamako's growth and development, the river also complicates expansion as the floodplain and numerous small streams make construction impossible in some parts of the city.

Plants & Animals

Mali's plant life varies according to region. There is very little vegetation in the Sahara, but some trees such as mimosa, gum trees, and acacias survive there. In the more fertile Sahelian region, which receives about 600 millimeters (24 inches) of rain per year, date palms, acacia, and baobab trees flourish.

Drought has affected the country's animal population. Many animals are found in Mali's four protected national parks, the Wongo National Park, the Kouroufing National Park, the Boucle du Baoulé National Park, and the Parc National du Bafing. Heavy poaching has decimated a great number of the animals in these protected areas, including elephants, giraffes, buffaloes, and lions. Only chimps and other monkeys are visible in these areas as of 2015.

Wild animals found in Mali include several species of antelope, gazelle, hyenas, and desert fox. Typical African animals, such as cheetahs, lions, giraffes, and hippopotamuses, are found near the Niger River. Elephants also migrate through Mali, but are in constant danger from poachers.

Birds, including eagles, ostriches, bustards, and vultures, are abundant in Mali. Many species, including ibis, pelicans, ducks, herons, and kingfishers are found along the river.

CUSTOMS & COURTESIES

Greetings

Men and women alike use the handshake as their primary means of greeting, regardless of societal status. The right hand is typically used, and it is relatively common for a man to wait for a woman to extend her hand before offering his own. If an individual is entering a group for the first time, he will be introduced to everyone in descending age, and must shake hands with each person in that order. The only exceptions to this rule are the Moor and Tuareg peoples, both of Berber descent and usually Muslim; they do not believe that men and women should have any physical contact in public.

In verbal greetings, usually only the first name of each individual is given unless the speakers know each other well. In Malian culture, last names reveal caste and other socioeconomic factors about an individual, and are usually avoided. Thus, until each conversationalist feels comfortable, he or she will not release such sacred information. When leaving someone for a long period of time, it is customary to say farewell by shaking left hands only. This is a clear indicator that both people intend to see each other again.

Gestures & Etiquette

While Mali is a nation with a diverse cultural makeup, nearly 95 percent of the population practices Islam, regardless of tribal affiliation. As such, Islamic laws and traditions often figure prominently into Malian culture. For example, modesty, refraining from using the left land (it is traditionally used for cleansing, and thus considered impure) and avoiding conflict are all important characteristics defining social interaction in Mali. The latter is especially significant, considering the potential for tribal conflict. As a result, the Malians have also developed a system known as "cousinage," a French term used to describe the custom that forbids members of different tribes from fighting over ethnic differences. Instead, it is more common for different tribes to establish what is called in the Bambara language "sanankouya," which translates to "joking relationship."

When speaking to other people, Malians generally do not maintain eye contact for long periods of time, unless they are speaking to someone of the same status or age, or a long-time friend. If eye contact is maintained, it is typically considered impolite. For example, if a child makes extended eye contact with an elder, it is thought that the child is suggesting his own wisdom matches that of the older person. To Malians, this is both unlikely and rude.

In addition, when speaking or interacting with others, Malians generally adopt clear signals as to what they are feeling. Thus, emotion is conveyed accurately and without false pretenses.

This is especially true when being invited to events. In Malian culture, it is considered impolite, even offensive, to accept an invitation and then later turn it down. Instead, it is better to directly turn down an invitation if it makes one feel uncomfortable. When in public, it is also unacceptable to point at anything.

Eating/Meals

Meal time in Mali is largely considered a family affair. Traditionally, the entire family will sit together for meals, which are served in several bowls. The head of the household, typically the highest earning or most important male provider, decides who will be able to eat from each bowl. It can be any combination of people seated, but generally women and small children eat together from the same dishes. However, with the authority of women in the household increasing, this tradition is becoming less common among many Malians. Nonetheless, these guidelines are still prevalent in rural areas. Additionally, in the Islamic culture, the left hand is considered impure, so Malians typically use their right hand to eat or pass food at the table.

It is customary that individuals be served more than their fill and have leftovers. As such, it is considered appropriate to leave food in one's dish. Often, leftovers are stored for the next meal, most likely breakfast. If one does finish his entire bowl, the person will either be considered greedy by other family members, or will be given more food.

Visiting

Visiting the homes of other Malians is an important part of the country's social fabric. As is the case with most other African nations, it is customary to bring a gift for the family. This gift should consist of something practical for the family and most often includes a food item. It is always good to learn about the tastes of one's hosts before arriving. When everyone sits down and guests are served, generally the guest must make the gesture of offering food to the host. If not, the guest will be considered rude for eating in front of the host, while the host does nothing but watch.

While visiting a home, aside from eating, it is most likely that visitors will engage in dialogue with the entire family living there. Inquisitive conversations are not uncommon, and family members can be critical of other family members.

LIFESTYLE

Family

Family life is an integral part of Malian culture. Whether in rural or urban areas, Malians are typically surrounded by an extended family, consisting of several generations. Often, there are upwards of 25 people living in buildings positioned around the family courtyard. In addition, unlike many Western cultures, the act of conversing with parents and elders about appropriate behavior and life choices is a time honored tradition in Mali.

Because of the long-standing tradition of farming in Mali, most rural families have more children. These children are then raised to help work the farm and bring income into the home. Urban families are increasingly having fewer children, but the overall fertility rate in Mali remains very high in comparison with world statistics, with six children born to every woman, as of 2015.

Strictly arranged marriages are very uncommon in contemporary Mali society. However, young men and women are still influenced by their parents and extended families when selecting a spouse. Divorce, which is recently on the rise, is allowed for male or female spouses. This increase is thought to be the result of women having more independence in Mali. Once a couple divorces, each spouse will often return home to live with their respective families.

The concept of family is also extended to the caste system in Mali. Unlike castes of India, this one is not entirely socioeconomically based. The caste system in Mali, like that of other West African nations, is family-based, where occupations are often inherited alongside social status. The griot is the most elevated caste in Mali. If one is born to griot parents, then one is a griot by trade. This caste system is also matrimonially binding. While this system is practiced less in modern society, it is still influential.

Housing

Typically, three generations of a single family reside in one complex, which is generally built around a common courtyard. Depending on family size and wealth, these complexes vary in size and the number of housing units. It should be noted, though, that Mali has larger homes on average than many African nations. For example, a middle class family will generally have six or seven buildings constructed around a dirt courtyard, whereas lower class families will have perhaps one or two buildings. Generally, courtyards can be tiled and adorned with vegetation and pools, or simply dirt patches with lawn chairs, depending on a family's wealth.

In rural areas, the dwellings are often smaller in size and are more likely to be one-room homes with many generations under the same roof. In the Bambara and Bamana regions, homes are known as gwa, or households. Families within them are often large, with sometimes as many as 10 people living in the same residence. Though the actual homes in these regions may be smaller, land is generally larger due to the shared property of everyone living in that home. Subsistence farming is also conducted on the land adjacent to the dwellings, and everyone living there is responsible for farming duties and crop maintenance.

Food

The staples of the Malian diet are rice, millet and sorghum, as well as beans. Often, these ingredients are cooked as a type of porridge or plain stew, and typically served with a meat or fish, vegetables and sauce. Meats such as beef, lamb, and mutton are popular, as are poultry and fish, the latter served smoked or fresh. Commonly consumed vegetables and fruits include okra, tomatoes, yams, plantains, bananas, and mangoes. Many Arabic culinary traditions are also widely reflected in Malian cuisine, such as the use of certain spices. As with most countries,

Malian cuisine varies from region to region, largely due to the contrast of climates in the north and south, and the varying ethnic traditions of the Malian population.

Traditional dishes of the southern regions include tô, which consists of pounded millet and a beef sauce; poulet yassa, which is chicken with lemon and onion over rice; and riz arachide, beef with peanut sauce. In the northern desert regions, the Tuareg people eat a pounded grain cake that resembles a pancake with wild leaves as a garnish. Along the Niger River, Nile perch (freshwater fish), or capitaine as it is known among locals, is a common food. It is generally fried in palm oil or stewed and served over a grain.

Street food is becoming increasingly popular in urban Mali. These snacks generally include grilled beef or mutton skewers, corn, fried bananas or cassava, egg sandwiches or rice and sauce. To keep hunger away between meals, Malians often chew kola nuts, whose slightly bitter flesh contains high levels of caffeine and serves as a stimulant when chewed. Malian tea and millet beer are common drinks. In particular, a tea known as bissap, made from sugar, hibiscus leaves and water, is popular. This sweet and sour drink tastes and looks a lot like cranberry juice and is commonly served frozen in a small plastic bag.

Life's Milestones

Mali's diverse tribal makeup and strong Islamic influences largely dictate the recognition and celebration of life's milestones. The most commonly observed milestones by nearly every ethnic group in Mali include the passing of seasons, harvesting of crucial crops, birth, marriage, adulthood and death. Most of these milestones are celebrated in much the same way, with the tribesmen and women gathering together for elaborate ceremonies. These ceremonies may include dancing, masquerades, puppet shows and dramatic reenactments. Often, several tribesmen will dress as their ancestors and attempt to channel their wisdom from beyond the grave.

Kola nuts, which have a high level of caffeine, are central to Malian culture and often incorporated into ceremonies. They are even used as part of the betrothal process, when men seek approval to marry from potential in-laws. Kola nuts, which range in size, are not inexpensive, with the smallest examples costing as much as twenty-five francs. On the first meeting with the woman's family, the potential groom brings three kola nuts. If the meeting goes well, he returns with 10. And if approval is given, he brings his future in-laws a bucketful.

CULTURAL HISTORY

Art

The expression of art in Mali culture is rooted in the use of tools and materials found in nature. For example, one of the most famous forms of Malian art is the cloth tradition of bògòlanfini (mud cloth). This tradition originated among the Bambara people, an ethnicity largely concentrated in Mali. Generally, bògòlanfini involves the dyeing of a plain cloth with a specially fermented mud, a practice almost exclusively carried out by women. As part of the tradition, patterns are taught by mothers to their daughters, who are then expected to create their own variations. The mud used to paint the mud cloths is dyed a vibrant color using plant or tea extracts, and the finished cloths range in color and design.

Bògòlanfini are generally used in daily life and are prevalent in ceremonies and rites of passage, with the patterns reflecting the various uses. As such, the designs of a mud cloth may represent family ties, profession, or age. However, before the women paint with mud, local men must harvest and spin the natively grown cotton into thread. That thread is then woven into the cloth that will eventually act as a canvas. It is believed that this process originated before the first Malian Empire of the 13th century.

Bronze sculpture is another traditional Malian art form. Conventionally, the carvings begin as soft wax that is molded by hand near the warmth of an open fire, which keeps the wax pliable. This hardened wax sculpture, or "positive" is then covered with powdered earth that eventu-

ally hardens into a clay shell, or "negative." The artist finally melts the interior wax, a practice commonly known as the "lost-wax method," and fills the clay mold with molten bronze. When the bronze is cool, the clay is broken, revealing the unique sculpture; the work cannot be duplicated because the original cast has been destroyed during the sculpture's removal.

Mali is also famous for its wood and mask carving. Ebony, a very hard and dark wood, is the typical choice of wood carvers in West Africa. This is because it is native to the deserts of the Sahara and because ebony has a brilliant sheen on its black surface once polished. From wood carving grew the tradition of carving masks (Kpeliye'e). The carved masks of Malian tribes are renowned for both their beauty and their intimidating designs. Many prominent tribes have their own distinct style of mask, and in many cases, a single tribe uses several types of masks.

The Senufo people, for example, design masks specifically to be worn by a group of vigilantes. These vigilantes, whose identities are concealed by the masks, ward off criminal behavior among tribe members. In addition, the crocodile teeth and fire breathing mouths that are characteristic of these type of masks are also believed to scare off evil spirits. Other designs include animals and images from nature often associated with witchcraft and healing. Besides wood, other elements added to these masks include raffia fiber, animal horns, cotton cloth, feathers, and metal.

The Dogon people are famous for developing two distinct mask styles: the kanaga and sirige masks. The designs of the kanaga mask are similar to other ceremonial masks of Africa, except for the long poles jutting out of its top. These poles are then crossed by a perpendicular flat blade forming a T-shape. The tops of the masks are typically adorned with brightly colored fabrics. The sirige incorporates the geometric, angular traditional carving style of many African masks. However, one unique characteristic of the sirige is that they can be up to four meters (14 feet) long.

Architecture

Malian architecture is generally dependent on the region's climate and the lifestyles of its people. Because the northern region of the country is characterized by semi-desert and dry savanna conditions and the southern region is generally more tropical, there are different architectural styles for the distinct regions. In addition, many various ethnicities or tribes depend upon certain ways of life, such as herding, which shape their housing needs. These factors were largely influential in the development of three distinct architectural traditions in Mali: nomadic, earthen, and stone architecture.

In the case of the nomadic tribes such as the Turareg and Fulani, herders who move seasonally, architecture is largely based on their way of life. Because they move frequently, they use tent-like structures as housing. Typically, these structures consist of a wooden framework covered with materials such as fabric, hides, or mats. This style of housing is commonly found in the northern region, which is characterized by desert conditions.

Earthen architecture, though common in both rural and urban settings, is also usually found in the north. This style of architecture consists of adobe, or mud bricks. Since many buildings built in the northern region are constructed from the traditional mud brick, they almost never reach more than one story or must be tiered. This style of earthen architecture (known as Western Sudanese) is due to the mud brick's inability to support much weight. These homes often have flat roofs or terraces and thick walls that defend against the sand-laden desert winds.

An example of traditional earthen architecture in Mali is the Great Mosque of Djenné, considered the largest adobe building in the world and a UNESCO World Heritage Site. It was constructed by laying long wooden beams between various layers of brick to act as weight bearers for the otherwise weak bricks. In addition to having to account for the weight of building tall structures, buildings constructed of mud bricks must often be refinished frequently, as erosion due to strong desert wind often occurs. This is the case with Djenné's renowned mosque, a building that because of its stature and age must be restored every year to account for such erosions.

The homes and buildings of the southern region in Mali take on a more traditional African feel. More of these structures are built with stone, often mixed with clay or timber. Family homes are made from mud and wood with conical thatched roofing in the more rural areas. In addition, Muslim influence and the desire to deflect some of the intense heat have led many homes and public buildings to be designed with outdoor corridors and central courtyards lush with vegetation and standing pools. Most homes are also fitted with large wooden doors that families paint in whatever style they choose.

The Dogon people are a good example of how geography influences architecture in Mali. The Dogon originally settled in north central Mali because of the high cliffs in the area. They built their homes in the cliffs, using additional stone and mud to enhance the natural shelter created by caves. These lofty homes, accessible only by vertical rock formations or caves, serve as both a security measure and a means to avoid annual floodwaters.

Drama

Malian drama is an essential part of the nation's artistic heritage. In Malian terms, drama is referred to as "masquerading," which typically involves wearing an elaborate mask to perform a dramatic role. While the term was introduced by the French, this art form has been a part of Mali for centuries, and was practiced by the many ancient tribes that comprise Mali's diverse ethnic heritage. Masqueraders generally dress to play the role of a departed ancestor. Portraying these parts accurately is particularly revered. These performances usually offer a dramatic commentary on political and social issues, as well as the common aspects of Malian life such as agriculture, family and travel.

Cinema in Mali first emerged with the establishment of the Mali National Cinema Office in 1962. This company was in charge of the production and distribution of films in Mali, as well as the surrounding region, until 1993. During this period, Mali was largely considered the preeminent country for African film. However, after the company ceased operations, many theaters were forced to close.

Two of the most famous Malian filmmakers are Souleymane Cissé (b. 1940–), who is often considered the greatest African director of the 20th century, and Cheick Oumar Sissoko (b. 1945–), who would later become Mali's minister of culture in 2002. In fact, the film *Yeelen* (1987), directed by Cissé, was the first African film to win an award at the prestigious Cannes Film Festival. *Yeelen* is also considered the quintessential African film. In general, Malian cinema is known for its rich narratives and themes of tradition and modernity.

Music

Traditional music in Mali is rooted in the legacy of the griot. While French in origin, this term is used to describe an oral performer whose sole purpose is to compose songs and poetry about the history of Mali. The tradition dates back to the 14th century, when the first griot was given as a gift to the king of the Malian Empire. This man was considered an expert historian and advisor to the king. Eventually, the role of the griot, or performer, in Mali culture was integrated into the caste system. This meant that if one was born to griot parents, then they would also become a griot by trade. Today, the role is much less official, and people outside the caste, like Fatoumata Diawara (b. 1982–), have found success as griots.

Despite not having a regal responsibility in contemporary society, griots are still held in some degree of reverence in Mali, as they maintain the traditions and heritage of the Malian people. In fact, Malian singer Ali Farka Touré (1939–2006) was considered a griot among his countrymen. In 1994, he also became the first African to win a Grammy Award. Malian music has since experienced a growth in popularity in the international community. Malian artists such as Baba Sissoko (b. 1963–) and Habib Koité (b. 1958–) enjoy international acclaim.

The griot, or storyteller, holds the highest position in the Mali caste system.

Literature

As is the case with many African nations, literature in Mali can be traced back to oral storytelling traditions. However, these oral traditions in Mali were primarily expressed through song with the griots, whose lyrical poetry, once recorded, gave birth to a national literature. Perhaps the most famous tale of these ancient storytellers, still told in contemporary society, is that of the great King Sundiata (Sundiata Keita), often referred to as the "Lion King of Mali." The legend follows Sundiata as a handicapped and exiled young man who returns to Mali to unify the tribes and form the Empire of Mali in 1240 CE.

Another significant aspect of Mali's literary tradition began with Timbuktu's reign as the capital of Islamic scholarship during the 16th century. This was due, in large part, to Moorish refugees from Spain migrating into North Africa. Some of these refugees ended up in Timbuktu and began an intellectual tradition rooted in the founding of many mosques and other institutions of higher learning. It was at these institutions that documents containing anything from religious and philosophical writings to scientific findings were first published. Many Malians in the area learned about Islam, and contributed to these writings in Arabic. The documents are still housed in the museums of Timbuktu and are said to represent the "Renaissance of North Africa."

CULTURE

Arts & Entertainment

Mali is known worldwide for its music including its drumming and guitar style, both of which are a major part of the culture and are very much a part of the capital city's nightlife.

Folk music in Mali is based on the traditions of the Bambara, Soninke, and Malinke peoples, known collectively as the Mandé. Traditional musical instruments include the kora, 21-string lute-bridge-harp; ngoni (n'goni), an oblong lute; and several types of drums.

Musicians in Mali are known as jeliw (or griot) and come from a hereditary caste of musicians. Internationally famous blues musician Ali Farka Touré (1939–2006) was born in Mali. Other famous Malian musicians include Toumani Diabaté (1965–), a traditional kora player, and Afro-pop singer Salif Keita (1949–), who is not only an albino, but also a direct descendant of Sundiata Keita, founder of the Mali Empire. Such lineage makes Keita, known as the "Golden Voice of Africa," of the royal rather than the griot caste.

The Djenne region of Mali is famous for the sculptures of gold, terra cotta, and bronze produced there. Bambara artisans are skilled woodcarvers and mask makers. The best-known West African symbol is a Chiwara (Ci wara), a headpiece carved in the shape of an antelope and used in dances to signify a mythical being that was half human, half animal. Chiwara headdresses come in three styles: vertical (meaning vertically-oriented), horizontal (horizontally-oriented), and abstract. These works reflect the traditional animist faith.

The country's Muslim heritage is reflected in the architecture of mosques and other buildings. Islam prohibits the depiction of humans or other living creatures in art.

In Bamako, numerous markets scattered throughout the city serve as a center of social life. In addition to traditional Malian food, Bamako's restaurants serve a sampling of international cuisines, including French and Chinese.

Cultural Sites & Landmarks

Mali's ethnic diversity and eclectic landscapes provide a wealth of cultural landmarks. Most notably, Mali is home to four World Heritage Sites, as designated by the United Nations Educational, Scientific and Cultural Organization (UNESCO). They include the Cliff of Bandiagara, in north central Mali; the Old Towns of Djenné, an area inhabited since 250 BCE; the fabled city of Timbuktu, once the spiritual and intellectual center of Islam in the 15th and 16th centuries; and the Tomb of Askia, where the first emperor of the Songhai people, Askia Mohammad I (c. 1442–1538), is said to be entombed.

The Cliff of Bandiagara is also called Land of the Dogons, since the area is inhabited by the Dogon people. They live in homes constructed in caves high on the cliffs. The culture of the Dogon dates back over 700 years, when the tribe's founders fled persecution by Muslims. They fled to the cliff dwellings to seek safety in the camouflage and height of the jagged rock formations. Because of this remote location, their culture has been able to remain unchanged while all of Mali was changing around it.

The town of Djenné, in central Mali, was once an historic center of commerce and culture. It served as a base for trans-Saharan trade beginning in prehistoric times. In fact, it is the oldest known city in the sub-Saharan region. It is also famous for its traditional architecture, most notably the Great Mosque of Djenné, considered the most famous mosque in sub-Saharan Africa. Constructed with mud bricks, the mosque was built in the 13th century by Koi Konboro, one of the ancient kings of Djenné, and rebuilt in the early 20th century. Non-Muslims are forbidden from entering the building.

The legendary city of Tombouctou (Timbuktu) was established around 1100 CE by the nomadic Tuareg people. It began as a small village that the Tuareg used as a place to rest after long desert trips. As more and more people settled there, trying to benefit from the trans-Saharan trade route, the city rapidly grew. By the 15th and 16th centuries, after the Moors had been forced out of Spain and into North Africa, Timbuktu had developed into the center of Islamic scholarship. As a result, some of the most famous Islamic temples in Africa still stand in Timbuktu. One in particular, the Sankore Mosque—one of the largest mudbrick structures in Africa—was dubbed the "University of Timbuktu" and held somewhere between 40,000 and 70,000 manuscripts, some dating to the 12th century. Some of these manuscripts were recently smuggled out of Timbuktu in large trunks to the capital city of Bamako in order to protect them from Islamist rebels, who were destroying cultural symbols throughout the city. In fact, UNESCO estimated that the rebels who occupied Timbuktu in early 2013 destroyed 14 mausoleums, the El Farouk monument at the city's entrance, and more than 4,000 manuscripts from the Ahmed Baba Research Centre.

The Niger River also holds significant cultural importance as the main source of water for the majority of Malians. The river originates with an inland delta in the Fouta Djallon highlands of Guinea. It flows through Mali, Niger, and Benin before emptying into the Atlantic Ocean at the Gulf of Guinea on the coast of Nigeria. It supports fishing villages, rice and millet farms and is one of the major transportation routes to and from the Sahara. It has been used since the earliest Malian empires as an extension of the Saharan trade route. Among its most common cargoes are tourists boating from the south to Timbuktu.

In the capital, the Bamako Zoo and Bamako Botanical Gardens provide a valuable educational resource, with exhibits and information about Mali's native fauna and flora; both the zoo

and botanical gardens are located a short distance from the city center. The area near the Botanical Gardens, as the floodplain blends into the nearby mountains, is a popular spot for outdoor recreation known as Point G Hill. The area features a series of caves and ancient rock carvings, along with views of the Bamako plain.

The Bamako Grand Mosque is one of the most popular tourist destinations in the city and is used for religious ceremonies. The Grand Mosque is located near the core of activity in the northern part of the city and is connected by several bustling streets to the Grand Market, Bamako's largest and busiest outdoor market where visitors can purchase food, art, and other goods.

Libraries & Museums

The Bamako National Museum, located at the northern edge of the capital's urban district, features tools and art representing the region's earliest African tribes and inhabitants. The museum was first established under the French colonial government in the 1950s and it has become an archive for native African ethnographic materials since Mali's independence.

The Ethnological Museum in Timbuktu features the well of Bouctou (the legendary well from which the city gets its name) as well as a number of artifacts including clothing, musical instruments, and jewelry.

Holidays

Malians celebrate their independence from France on Independence Day (September 22). Other national holidays include Army Day (January 20), celebrating the country's armed forces; Labor Day (May 1); and African Unity Day (May 25). The martyrs of the 1991 Revolution are remembered on March 26.

Youth Culture

Generally, youth culture in Mali is characterized by family life and school. Public education is free for all youth between seven and 16 years old. However, students are responsible for their own uniforms and supplies, which can limit the ability of some families for whom this expenditure is not possible. It is estimated that only 67.2 percent of children are active students, with only 35.9 percent of them moving on to secondary school. (Most students leave school at age 12.)

Perhaps the most significant aspect of youth culture in Mali is the government-run committee of youth and sports programs. Through this committee, many of the nation's most popular pastimes are organized for youth participation on local and national levels. In addition, many of these recreational pastimes—which include sporting, theatrical, musical and dancing activities—culminate in a final national competition in Bamako during the nation's biennial Youth Week, which brings youth of all ages to compete in their individual events.

SOCIETY

Transportation

Two distinct geographical features—the Sahara, the world's largest hot desert, and the Niger River—have shaped mass transportation and travel in Mali. To cross the Saharan desert, traditional camel caravans are still commonly used. The Tuareg and the Moors, along with their ancestors, have been crossing the desert this way for centuries. Travelers have navigated the Niger River since the beginning of trans-Saharan trade. The route is still taken daily, but mostly by tourists, fishermen, and those involved in trade. Most travelers and fishermen use homemade motorized boats with woven mat awnings, called pinasses, and camp along the river at night.

Railways in Mali are in poor condition, as are many roads, which are largely unpaved. Buses, share taxis, and bush taxis move people from place to place in the south of Mali. In-country flights were offered by Air Mali beginning in 2005, although because of the conflict in the north, operations were suspended indefinitely in 2012. Car ownership in Mali is extremely low and traffic in the country drives on the right side of the road.

Transportation Infrastructure

Overall, the infrastructure in Mali is considered poor. In particular, railways are in poor condition, and breaks in the lines and closings due to rain are common. The Dakar-Bamako line, built in 1923, has seen such deterioration in services that its scheduled 35-hour trip often takes over three days. In addition, roads are generally not paved outside of urban areas. In southern Mali, where the majority of the population is concentrated, buses or share taxis, also called bush taxis (small passenger vehicles) are the most common modes of public transportation. Buses are often packed beyond capacity.

There is an international airport located just outside urban Bamako—Senou International Airport—which allows the city to benefit from business travel and tourism. Otherwise, of the country's 29 airports, only eight have paved runways. Trains and buses connect Bamako to other areas in Mali and other African nations. The Niger also supports local travel with boats carrying passengers into nearby cities.

Media & Communications

While low literacy rates and poor distribution channels remain challenging issues for Mali's media, there are still over 22 privately operated newspapers, both dailies and weeklies. Additionally, there are 125 radio stations, but just one national television station. Run by the Office de la Radiodiffusion Television du Mali (ORTM), the station offers numerous channels available by subscription. Radio is the most common form of communication, and most programming is in French. Newspapers are also published in French, including the national daily, L'Essor, as well as in Arabic and the various tribal languages prevalent in the country.

Internet use in Mali is low by world standards. As of 2013, 2.3 percent of the population had Internet access. This is largely due to a lack of infrastructure, widespread poverty, and lower literacy rates.

While Mali ranks low on the world scale of national infrastructure, it does rank very high in terms of the freedom of the press. For the most part, the media enjoys a favorable and fair environment. While the constitution still forbids harsh criticism of elected officials, these laws are rarely invoked, and daily headlines are often very critical of leaders when necessary. Nonetheless, quality and financial resources continue to be pressing issues for the media and communications industry in Mali.

SOCIAL DEVELOPMENT

Standard of Living
In 2014, Mali was ranked 176th out of the total 187 on the United Nations Human Development Index, which measures quality of life and standard of living indicators using 2012 data.

Water Consumption
According to UNICEF (United Nations International Children's Emergency Fund), 77 percent of the population has access to improved drinking water sources (96.5 percent in urban areas and 64.1 percent in rural areas). UNICEF also reports that 24.7 percent of the population has access to improved sanitation (37.5 percent in urban areas and 16.1 percent in rural areas). UNICEF has announced a 2010 program to improve water, soap, and latrine access to primary schools in Mali, accompanied by an education campaign to promote hygiene—specifically hand-washing. The program is targeted at promoting healthy hand-washing habits, but will have an extended impact that encourages girls (who lacked privacy because they did not have access to separate latrine facilities and, therefore, often dropped out of school) to stay in school.

Education
Primary school is free and compulsory in Mali for children between six and 15 years of age. However, there is a shortage of school buildings and materials, and many eligible students do not complete their education because their families cannot afford to buy supplies. The average adult has less than one year of formal schooling, and only 54.6 percent of girls were enrolled in primary schools in 2012. The average adult literacy rate is low, at 38.7 percent—with males at 48.2 percent and females at about 29.2 percent in 2015. The United Nations Educational, Scientific and Cultural Organization (UNESCO) and other international agencies are campaigning to improve education for all students in Mali. There is a national university in Bamako, with several campuses spread throughout the city.

Women's Rights
While gender equality in Mali is more prevalent than in many of its African neighbors, the suppression of women's rights is still pervasive throughout the nation.

Women in urban areas of Mali are better able to pursue professional positions because of their access to consistent childcare, either via servants or the extended family. Professions most widely available to women include teaching, law, civil service, and positions with local non-governmental organizations (NGOs). There are also an increasing number of women in the political arena. While most women are paid less than their male counterparts, women in politics receive more equitable pay. Despite this increase, the national female employment rate is still estimated at only 15 percent.

In more rural areas, where most of the population lives, the traditional role of women remains intact. Rural families generally stop the education of their daughters at a young age. It is considered more economical, and more in accordance with cultural and tribal demands, to educate young women in domestic tasks. Rural life is considerably more strenuous for women, as they are charged with both child-rearing and with nearly all of the physical labor around their homes. This generally means farming, cleaning, and preparing meals. In addition to these daily tasks, rural women must also travel several miles to get clean water.

Laws meant to protect women in Mali have rarely been used for their intended purposes. Such laws include prohibition of domestic abuse and laws against rape. More importantly, very few cases involving domestic abuse and rape are reported, with even fewer reaching the level of prosecution. Polygamy, in accordance with some Muslim and tribal beliefs, is also common.

Female genital mutilation (FGM) among girls from infancy to about six years of age still occurs throughout the country, with UNICEF estimating that 89 percent of girls have undergone the procedure, which can cause chronic pain, complications with intercourse and childbirth, and frequent renal and gynecological infections. While there is no law that explicitly forbids FGM, there is a law prohibiting certified practitioners from performing the procedure. The government has also tried to motivate practitioners to stop doing the procedure by training them in other services within the medical field.

By law, young women must be 18 to marry and men must be 21. Girls aged 15 or younger may also be married if their parents give permission. Despite the age limits, many parents still marry their daughters off as young as eleven, often to benefit financially. In addition, while women can request a divorce, they must pay $60 (USD) in order to do so, whereas men must simply make the request. Child custody and property rights are also nearly always on the side of the man, leaving a woman's children to be raised by the ex-husband's new wife or mother.

Women's rights have, most recently, been significantly curtailed in the northern regions by Islamist rebels, who have instituted a brutal form of Sharia law that imposes the veil on women, allows for their public flogging, and permits extrajudicial punishments, such as stoning, for inappropriate sexual activity.

Health Care
Health care in Mali is poor. The country has one of the highest infant mortality rates in the world, at 102.23 deaths for every 1,000 live births (2015 estimate). The rate of death among mothers is also high. The rate of HIV infection is lower in Mali than it is in most of Africa, with just 1.42 percent infected as of 2014; that translates to 133,400 people living with the disease. In 2014, there were 5,300 AIDS-related deaths.

Immunization rates are extremely low. Diseases such as diarrhea, hepatitis A, typhoid fever, malaria, schistosomiasis (an ultimately fatal and difficult-to-treat parasite carried by freshwater snails), and meningitis are prevalent. According to the World Health Organization, both rabies and polio have become a significant concern within the last five years. As of September 2015, an outbreak of polio was confirmed in Bamako.

As of January 18, 2015, the World Health Organization announced that the Ebola outbreak, which has had such a devastating impact on African populations, was no longer a threat in Mali.

Another, largely unrecognized problem is the health issues created by pesticides used in the cotton-growing industry. Many have suffered ill effects from working so often in the presence of the chemicals, which enter the body through the skin and respiratory system. Paracetamol tablets, a type of analgesic, are sold to combat the headaches that accompany pesticide toxicity. However, they are very expensive and can cost the equivalent of two kilos of cotton for one packet of eight pills. Overall, life expectancy is low in Mali, with just slightly more than 53 years for men and 57 years for women (2015 estimate).

GOVERNMENT

Structure
Mali suffered some political instability after gaining independence from France in 1960. The country's first president was overthrown in a 1968 military coup, and a multiparty political system was not introduced until 1991. Mali's present constitution was adopted on January 12, 1992; amended in 1999; and temporarily suspended following the military coup in April 2012. However, it was again in force in mid-2012 thanks, in part, to negotiations with the junta government conducted by Economic Community of West African States (ECOWAS). The country is still working to regain its equilibrium following the post-coup civil unrest and ongoing battles with Islamist rebels and Al-Qaeda-backed groups in the country's northern region.

Mali's executive branch consists of the president, who acts as the chief of state, and the prime minister, who is the head of the government. The president is popularly elected to a five-year term, with a two-term limit. The prime minister is appointed by the president.

The country's unicameral legislature is the Assemble Nationale (National Assembly). The 147 members are elected by majority vote to serve five-year terms. The country's legal system is based on French law, and the highest courts are the Cour Supreme (Supreme Court) and the Constitutional Court.

Political Parties

Presidential and parliamentary elections, as defined by the 1992 Constitution, were supposed to be held in 2012, but were delayed by the military coup. However, elections were resumed in late July 2013, and a run-off election for the presidency was held in August. Ibrahim Boubacar Keïta of Rally for Mali (RPM) bested Soumaïla Cissé of the Union for Republic and Democracy (URD) with 77.61 percent of the vote. In the parliamentary elections, RPM took 66 seats, while URD took 17 seats. Other important parties in Mali include the Alliance for Democracy in Mali, which took 16 seats in the 2013 elections; the Alternative Forces for Renewal and Emergence, which gained six seats; and the Convergence for the Development of Mali, which along with the African Solidarity for Democracy and Independence, each assumed five seats.

Local Government

Mali has been divided into eight regions and one district. The district includes Bamako, while the regions include Gao, Kayes, Kidal, Koulikoro, Mopti, Segou, Sikasso, and Tombouctou (Timbuktu). Each region is led by a governor and is subdivided into districts. Districts (or cercles) are subdivided into communes and then further divided into local villages or quarters. Districts are managed by prefects; elected mayors and municipal councils manage the affairs of their locality.

Judicial System

The Malian judicial system is based on the colonial French civil and customary law, with changes enacted in the recent past to tailor laws to Malian society. The Supreme Court (Cour Supreme) and Constitutional Court are the country's highest courts. The Ministry of Justice appoints the 19 judges serving within the four different Supreme Court chambers—three civil and one criminal—to five-year terms. Of the nine judges serving on the Constitutional Court, three are appointed by the president, three by the National Assembly, and three by Supreme Council of the Magistracy. Constitutional Court judges serve seven-year terms. County courts are local within towns and regions. The Appeals Court system hears appeals of County Court decisions. Mali also a High Court of Justice, which is reserved for only those cases involving high treason by the president or National Assembly ministers.

Taxation

The Malian government levies a personal income tax rate that ranges from three percent to 30 percent. There is also a corporate income tax of 30 percent, a value-added tax of 18 percent, and several other taxes, including a nine percent tax on interest and a 3.5 percent payroll tax.

Armed Forces

The Malian Armed Forces consist of the Army (Armee de Terre), Republic of Mali Air Force (Force Aerienne de la Republique du Mali, FARM), and the National Guard (Garde National du Mali). There is a two-year conscription obligation, beginning at 18 years of age. Both males and females are eligible to serve.

Foreign Policy

Mali's foreign policy is rooted in the trans-Saharan trade that dominated commerce and culture since ancient times. This trade route originated in Europe and the Middle East, and required passage through the Sahara, by way of Mali, to reach West Africa. It was this passageway that fueled much of the change and development in early Mali, and also allowed for a relatively high level of cultural tolerance in today's Mali, despite the rise in religious extremism and violence, which the country is now fighting.

Initially known as the Ghana Empire, the area of Mali reached all the way west to the Atlantic Ocean and east into modern-day Sudan. European colonization followed, largely under the French, who controlled the area and its rich resources—notably gold and cotton—under the name French Sudan. After gaining independence from France in 1960, Mali was associated with socialism, but eventually established a democracy. However, Mali's dependence on foreign monetary aid has left the country in a terrible financial state—in 2015, it was the 10th poorest country in the world. Malians attribute this dependence in large part to colonialism and corruption of current leaders.

Today, Mali shares strong bonds with the United States, which maintains an embassy in Bamako and considers Mali a significant regional ally in the US-led "war on terror." A member of the UN since 1960, Mali is also a member of various related committees, such as the International Monetary Fund (IMF) and The World Bank, two institutions on which Mali depends on for economic aid. Mali is also a member state of the Organization of African Unity (OAU), the Organization of the Islamic Conference (OIC) and the Non-Aligned Movement (NAM). It is also an associate member of the African Development Bank (ADB) and the European Community (EC), a pillar of the European Union (EU).

Regional integration has been difficult to establish and maintain due to various regional conflicts, particularly after the coup of 2012. Until this uprising and the temporary installation of the junta government, Mali had been a relatively stable nation since its previous military uprising in 1991 against the dictatorial regime of the militaristic General Moussa Traoré (b. 1936–). This uprising and the subsequent political calm was regarded favorably by the international community as a Malian dedication to maintaining a democratic government. This continues as the country regains stability following the rout

of Islamic extremist groups in the north in mid-2013. The people of Mali believe very strongly that their original forms of government, during the reign of their empires, were the first examples of democracy practiced in the country.

Mali's immediate neighbors, Ivory Coast and Niger, are prone to conflict. This is often seen by Malians as a disruption of their calm cousinage lifestyle. As such, the resolution of regional conflicts, particular in countries such as the Ivory Coast and Liberia, has become a major component of Mali's foreign policy. Currently, Mali holds membership in the African Union (AU), the Economic Community of West African States (ECOWAS), West African Economic Monetary Union (UEMOA), and Permanent Interstate Committee for Drought Control in the Sahel (CILSS), among other regional organizations aimed at greater interdependence of the region.

Human Rights Profile

International human rights law insists that states respect civil and political rights and also promote an individual's economic, social, and cultural rights. The United Nations Universal Declaration on Human Rights (UDHR) is recognized as the standard for international human rights. Its authors sought the counsel of the world's great thinkers, philosophers, and religious leaders and were careful to create a document that reflects the core values shared by every world culture. (To read this document or view the articles relating to cultural human rights, visit http://www.ohchr.org/EN/UDHR/Pages/Introduction.aspx.)

Before the 2012 military coup, Mali generally maintained a positive human rights record. This was due in large part to the country's successful constitutional democracy. Its constitution, written in the early 1960s, universally assured Mali citizens many of the same rights as other developed nations. However, certain freedoms are still limited or directly violated, a situation further complicated by Mali's status as one of the poorest nations in the world. However, in March 2012, the constitution was briefly suspended when the National Committee for the Restoration of Democracy and State

(CNRDR), a confederation of soldiers unhappy with President Amadou Toumani Touré, overran the presidential palace, the state television station, and the Bamako military barracks. Before Timbuktu was seized, CNRDR proposed a new constitution, and Timbuktu was seized. In April 2012, Mali's old constitution was reinstated, and CNRDR indicated the junta would step down, although they maintained widespread control of the country. Disturbingly, a mass grave of 21 soldiers, loyal to the former president and missing since the coup, was discovered in the town of Diago in December 2013.

The countrywide civil unrest stirred by the coup has largely calmed, thanks to French and Malian troops who have dispersed some of the problematic elements to the surrounding dessert. However, there are still significant outbursts of violence from both pro and anti-government forces, while general government corruption has created problems for citizens seeking healthcare, education, potable water, and many of the most basic resources. Moreover, the Al-Qaeda-linked groups—Ansar Dine and al-Qaeda in the Islamic Maghreb (AQIM), which overtook Timbuktu and the region along the border with Mauritania—instituted a brutal form of Sharia law that saw women flogged for failing to wear a veil and the extrajudicial penalization of suspected thieves by way of hand amputation. While Timbuktu was reclaimed, the Islamist rebels, and the human rights violations they impose, remain a threat.

Human rights violations committed directly by the Malian security forces include violence against civilians and rebels in government custody. According to Human Rights Watch, the Malian government has made little effort to prosecute those involved in civilian or rebel abuse. Prison conditions are generally considered poor and dangerous to the health of prisoners. In an attempt to remedy this situation, Mali consistently allows human rights officials to visit jails in an effort to improve conditions. Despite this effort, food is often scarce and overcrowding is prevalent, resulting in the poor health of the prison population. Often, the illnesses caused by

these conditions are fatal because prison medical facilities are limited or non-existent.

Mali also suffers from fairly widespread corruption among its political officials and a few major corporations. In the first decade of the 21st century, such occurrences included tax evasion in the telecommunications industry and a major financial embezzlement by the Office du Niger (ON), an irrigation system set up to ensure food security. While both scandals have resulted in major financial setbacks for Malian development, little has been done in the way of justice.

Another pervasive problem in Mali is the trafficking of children for labor. Despite the existence of serious punishment for this practice—a typical prison sentence carries a 20 years sentence—traffickers are relatively common. Complicating the situation is the fact that the constitution allows children to work beginning at the age of 12, though their hours must be limited. This has increased the trafficking of children into Mali, with forced child labor existing in all regions.

Additionally, as Mali developed from a caste system, people born into the lowest class of the caste are often considered slaves to the higher ranking classes. Practices related to the caste system still occur, with slavery one of the more serious problems still prevalent in Mali society. Despite slavery or compulsory labor being outlawed, the judicial system remains weak, and it has, therefore, proven difficult for Mali to uphold such laws. Many poverty-stricken citizens still find themselves in situations where higher ranking classes claim traditional ownership over them.

Migration

As of 2015, Mali's migration rate was −2.26 migrants per 1,000 people, indicating that over two people were leaving for every 1000 remaining within the country's borders. Migration, it is said, is part of Mali culture. Certainly, 10 percent of the country's population is nomadic, with movements occurring on a seasonal basis. In some areas, young people are told to wait to marry until they have left their community and come back. For most, however, the recent violence, rise of violent Islamist rebel groups, and poverty are the greatest motivators for migration. And according to the International Organization for Migration, in April 2013, there were approximately 301,027 internally displaced persons due to violence in the north, although this number dropped to 228,918 in mid-January 2013. The total number of border-crossing Malian refugees in May 2013 was 176,144.

ECONOMY

Overview of the Economy

Centuries ago, Mali was one of the richest empires in the world. Caravans passing through the country carried rich cargoes of gold and salt. Today, Mali is one of the poorest countries in the world, and usually does not meet UN development goals, placing the country in the lowest percentile on the global index. In 2014, the per capita gross domestic product (GDP) was estimated at $1,700 (USD).

Mali's economy relies on agriculture, with cotton and livestock being the chief exports aside from gold. Approximately 80 percent of the work force is engaged in farming, and the sector contributes to 38 percent of the total GDP. Cotton and gold are the country's greatest economic generators, garnering 80 percent of export revenue.

In contrast to the rest of the nation, the economy in the capital city is far more diverse. The service industries, including tourism, business travel, ecotourism, and recreational services, are a major source of employment for Bamako residents. The city's infrastructure was also improved following the city's 2002 hosting of the Africa Cup of Nations (CAN, or AFCON), a football (soccer) competition, and the influx of capital and tourism led to an explosion in the services sector, which continued to contribute 38.7 percent to the nation's GDP in 2014.

Mali continues to rely on foreign aid to combat fluctuations in the prices of its exports. The International Monetary Fund (IMF) and The

World Bank are also helping the country diversify its economy and attract foreign investment.

Industry

Mining, particularly the extraction of gold and phosphates, is the chief industry in Mali. Manufacturing is largely limited to the processing of agricultural products and food, although construction has become an emergent industry. Agriculture accounted for about 38 percent of the country's GDP in 2015. Almost all other products are imported.

In the capital, shipping remains one of Bamako's biggest industries and the second largest source of employment for residents. The city's ports along the Niger River ship a variety of agricultural and industrial products including corn, rice, millet, meat products, construction materials, stone, and several metal products harvested from nearby mining settlements.

In 2014, Mali's main export destinations were China (18.8 percent), India (14.4 percent), Indonesia (11.1 percent), Bangladesh (9.6 percent), Thailand (8.3 percent), and Australia (4.3 percent).

Labor

In 2004, between 25 and 30 percent of the nation's population was unemployed and income distribution was, and continues to be, a serious concern, with wide disparities between the nation's wealthiest and poorest citizens. As of 2012, however, the CIA reported that unemployment had dropped to 8.1 percent.

Energy/Power/Natural Resources

Despite having its own significant, albeit untapped, petroleum reserves in the north, Mali imports all its oil—approximately 4,698 bbl/day—and produces all of its own electricity, some 520 million kWh. In 2015, only about 25.6 percent of the population had access to electricity. Most electricity in rural areas is generated using kerosene or batteries. Efforts by various NGOs to help the country manage its forests (which are under threat by those needing wood fuel for cooking and heat), develop local economies, and introduce renewable energy options are helping to address the country's energy needs. Hydropower is a leading source of electricity, contributing nearly 52 percent of the country's total yield.

While gold is the country's most exploited natural resource, bauxite, copper, diamonds, gold, gypsum, iron ore, kaolin, limestone, lithium, manganese, phosphates, salt, silver, uranium, and zinc are also natural resources that have not yet been exploited to their full potential, although the country is making strides towards greater iron ore extraction.

Fishing

The Niger River is the nation's aquatic bread-basket. A significant commercial fishing industry is centered on the Niger River. During annual floods, which peak in August, the river over-flows its banks and many snatch perch, known as capitaine fish, struggling in receding waters. Fish leads meat as the country's leading protein, at annual consumption rates of 5.4 kilos (11.9 lbs.) per person to an average consumption of 4.7 kilos (10.3 lbs.) of meat. However, fishing is still a largely artisanal activity, dominated by two principal ethnic groups that live along the Niger: the Bozo people and the Somono people. Efforts supported by organizations such as USAID and The World Bank are promoting the development of aquaculture in three specific areas: pond culture, rice-fish culture, and fisheries planning.

Forestry

Mali's forests cover 10.2 percent of the nation's area. As wood is a major fuel source and subsistence farming is prevalent, Mali's forests are endangered and are in a state of rapid degradation. The FAO (Food and Agriculture Organization [UN]) is encouraging cross-sectoral policy coordination to address the threats to the nations remaining forests.

Mining/Metals

Mining, mostly for gold, is the chief industry in Mali. Other minerals are mined to a smaller extent. Further development of the mining indus-

try has been proposed as a means of expanding the nation's economy. In fact, the extraction of iron ore is under exploration within the country as of 2015.

Agriculture

More than 55 percent of the nation is arid or semi-desert, making farming difficult or impossible. In fact, just 5.6 percent of the land in Mali is arable; approximately 2,358 square kilometers (910 square miles) of farmland are irrigated.

Most agricultural production takes place on small farms, and 80 percent of the country's labor force is engaged in agricultural production. The country's small farms grow sorghum, millet, and maize. Cotton is also an important cash crop is cotton; 620,000 tons were produced in 2003–04, and Mali is the continent's second largest producer after Egypt. In 2010, 40 percent of the population relied on income from cotton crops to survive. Rice is grown along the Niger River, and wheat and groundnuts (peanuts) are grown in the eastern part of the country. In 2004, locusts decimated the country's grain crops, putting many Malians at risk for starvation.

Animal Husbandry

Livestock is an important part of the agricultural sector; cattle, sheep, and goats are all raised by Malian farmers for their meat. However, donkeys, camels, and horses are also bred and kept for their pack-carrying and draft-use potential. Chickens are also raised for their ability to supply meat and eggs. Recurrent droughts have a devastating effect on all of the country's herds.

Tourism

As of 2014, the U.S. Centers for Disease Control recommended against travel to Mali because of a November 2014 outbreak of Ebola. While the World Health Organization declared the outbreak over in January 2015 because the country had gone 42 days without a new case, the U.S. government has still recommended extreme caution.

Similarly, advisories against travel to northern Mali have also been issued by the Australian, Canadian, Irish, British, U.S., and New Zealand governments because Islamist rebels have captured significant amounts of northern territories, including historic Timbuktu, and declared the independence of the Azawad region. The rebel groups, who are allied with Al-Qaida have imposed strict Sharia law in these areas. Foreigners have been subject to kidnap and torture at the hands of rebels.

Tourism is a small but growing part of the Malian economy. The country's transportation system remains undeveloped. A rail line from Bamako to Senegal is the chief means of transportation in Mali. Most roads are unpaved.

Tourists come to Mali to view the wildlife in the country's national parks, see ancient cities such as Timbuktu, and witness the migration of elephants through the country. Other significant sites include Bandiagara Escarpment, which is a UNESCO World Heritage Site, and the city of Djenné, home to the mud-brick mosque, which is also a UNESCO World Heritage Site.

Karen Pappas, Roberta Baxter, Micah Issitt,
Savannah Schroll Guz

DO YOU KNOW?

- The Great Mosque of Djenné is the largest mud-brick building in the world, and is a UNESCO World Heritage Site.

- Timbuktu has three of the oldest mosques in Africa: Djinguereber (Djingareyber), Sankore, and Sidi Yahia; the country's oldest mosque, Djinguereber, was built in the 14th century.

- The word "Bamako," is taken from a Bambara term meaning "Crocodile's Back," and highlights the importance of the Niger River in the culture and history of the city. The name of the nation, "Mali" is also derived from a Bambara term meaning "Hippopotamus." Bambara terminology is common in Bamako and many of the streets and other features bear Bambara names.

Bibliography

Colleyn, Jean-Paul. "Bamana: Visions of Africa." Milan, Italy: *5 Continents*, 2008.

Collier, Paul. "The Bottom Billion: Why the Poorest Countries are Failing and What Can Be Done About It." Oxford, UK: *Oxford University Press*, 2008.

Drisdelle, Rheal. "Mali: A Prospect of Peace?" *Oxfam Publishing*, 1997. Oxfam Country Profile Ser.

Eyre, Banning. "In Griot Time." Philadelphia: *Temple University Press*, 2000.

Holloway, Kris. "Monique and the Mango Rains: Two Years with a Midwife in Mali." *Waveland Press*, 2006.

LaGamma, Alisa. "Genesis: Ideas of Origin in African Sculpture." 2nd ed. New York: *Metropolitan Museum of Art*, 2013.

Lucke, Lewis W. "Waiting for Rain: Life and Development in Mali, West Africa." Hanover, MA: *Christopher Publishing House*, 1998.

Mann, Gregory. "Native Sons: West African Veterans and France in the Twentieth Century." Durham, NC: *Duke University Press*, 2006. Politics, History, and Culture Ser.

Mann, Kenny. "Ghana Mali Songhay: The Western Sudan." Dillon, MT: *Dillon P*, 1996. African Kingdoms of the Past Ser.

Perinbam, Marie. "Family Identity And The State In The Bamako Kafu." Boulder, CO: *Westview Press*, 1998. African States & Societies in History Ser.

Sattin, Anthony. "The Gates of Africa: Death, Discovery, and the Search for Timbuktu." 3rd ed. London: *St. Martin's Press*, 2014.

Vanbeek, Walter E.A. "Dogon: Africa's People on the Cliffs." New York: *Harry N. Abrams*, 2001.

Works Cited

"Damage to Timbuktu's cultural heritage worse than first estimated reports UNESCO mission." *UNESCO Media Services*, 6 Jul. 2013. http://www.unesco.org/new/en/media-services/single-view/news/damage_to_timbuktus_cultural_heritage_worse_than_first_estimated_reports_unesco_mission/#.VgyxPmBdHmQ.

"Face Mask (Kpeliye'e)" The Collection Online. *The Metropolitan Museum of Art*, 2015. http://www.metmuseum.org/collection/the-collection-online/search/310950.

"Female Genital Mutilation/Cutting: A Statistical Overview and Exploration of the Dynamics of Change." New York: *UNICEF*, 2013.

"Global Food Security: First Report of Session, 2013–2014." Vol. 1 London: *House of Commons/The Stationery Office Ltd*, 2013.

"Government of Mali and WHO announce the end of the Ebola outbreak in Mali." *World Health Organization Regional Office for Africa*, 18 Jan. 2015. http://www.afro.who.int/en/media-centre/pressreleases/item/7293-government-of-mali-and-who-announce-the-end-of-the-ebola-outbreak-in-mali.html.

"Mali: Kola Nuts." Our Africa. *SOS Children's Villages*, n.d. http://www.our-africa.org/mali/kola.

"Mali." The World Factbook. *Central Intelligence Agency*, 2015. https://www.cia.gov/library/publications/the-world-factbook/geos/ml.html.

"Musée National du Mali: Art conservation, research and prevention." Sociolingo Africa. *Bram Posthumus*, 20 Apr. 2007. http://sociolingo.wordpress.com/2007/04/20/musee-national-du-mali-art-conservation-research-and-prevention/.

"Mali: From Timbuktu to Washington." *Center for Folklore and Cultural Heritage Website. Smithsonian Institution*, 2003. www.folklife.si.edu/resources/festival2003/mali.htm.

"Mali: Statistics." *UNICEF*, 27 Dec. 2013. http://www.unicef.org/infobycountry/mali_statistics.html.

"Polio outbreak confirmed in Mali." *World Health Organization Regional Office for Africa*, 7 Sept. 2015. http://www.afro.who.int/en/media-centre/pressreleases/item/7988-polio-outbreak-confirmed-in-mali.html.

"Table 1: Human Development Index and its components." *Human Development Reports*. UN Development Programme, 2015. http://hdr.undp.org/en/content/table-1-human-development-index-and-its-components.

"The Great Mosque of Djenné Official Website." *Ministry of Craft Industry & Tourism*, n.d. http://www.greatmosqueofdjenne.com/.

"U.S. Relations with Mali." Bureau of African Affairs. *U.S. Department of State*, 30 Apr. 2013. http://www.state.gov/r/pa/ei/bgn/2828.htmwww.state.gov/g/drl/rls/hrrpt/2006/78745.htm.

"World Report 2014: Mali." *Human Rights Watch*, 2015. https://www.hrw.org/world-report/2014/country-chapters/mali.

Cartier, Diana. "Mali Crisis: A Migration Perspective." Geneva, Switzerland: *International Organization for Migration*, 2013.

Day, Elizabeth. "The Desparate Plight of Africa's Cotton Farmers." *The Guardian*. Guardian News and Media Limited. 19 Apr. 2010.

Diarra, Adama. "Mass grave found in Mali near military base." *NBC News.com*, 4 Dec. 2015. http://www.nbcnews.com/news/other/mass-grave-found-mali-near-military-base-f2D11691386.

Gribble, James. "Family Planning in Ghana, Burkina Faso, and Mali." *Population Reference Bureau*, 2008. www.prb.org/Articles/2008/westafricafamilyplanning2.aspx.

Nurse, Earl and Teo Kermeliotis. "The Rise of Fatoumata Diawara, Mali's Pop Princess." CNN.com. *Cable News Network/Turner Broadcasting System, Inc.*, 14 Aug. 2013. http://www.cnn.com/2013/08/14/world/africa/the-rise-of-fatoumata-diawara-mali/.

Polgreen, Lydia. "Timbuktu Endured Terror under Harsh Shariah Law." The New York Times Company, 31 Jan. 2013. http://www.nytimes.com/2013/02/01/world/africa/timbuktu-endured-terror-under-harsh-shariah-law.html?_r=0.

Tran, Mark. "Inside Bamako: Africa's fastest-growing city—in pictures." The Guardian. *Guardian News and Media Limited*, 4 Oct. 2013. http://www.theguardian.com/global-development/gallery/2013/oct/04/inside-bamako-mali-in-pictures.

Smith, Alex Duval. "The country where you can choose your tax rate." *BBC News*, 17 Mar. 2015. http://www.bbc.com/news/magazine-31907670.

Iron ore is Mauitania's most important mineral resource. iStock/Adro_Hatxerre.

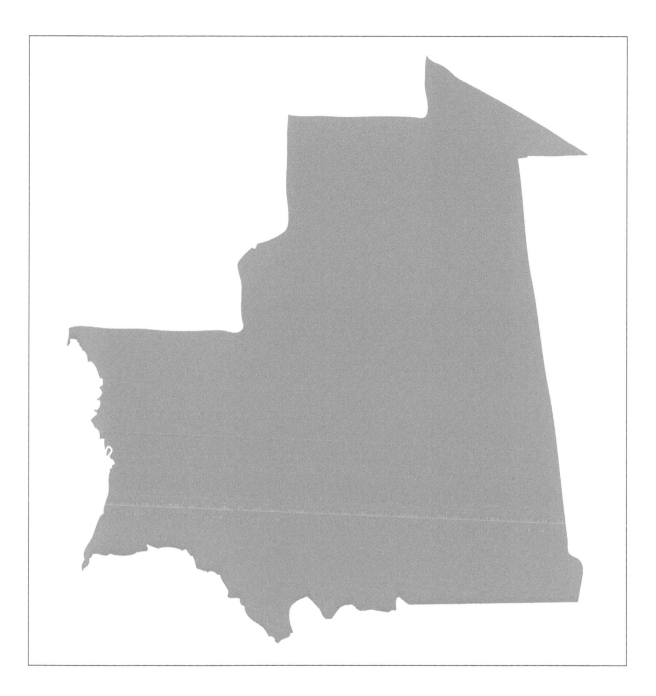

MAURITANIA

Introduction

Mauritania is officially known as the Islamic Republic of Mauritania (al-Jumhuriyah al-Islamiyah al-Muritaniyah in Arabic). The country is located in northwestern Africa, where much of the land is desert. Countries that share borders with Mauritania include Algeria to the northeast, Mali to the east and southeast, and Senegal to the southwest. The Western Sahara lies on the northwest, and the Atlantic Ocean on the west.

Mauritania gained independence from France in 1960. Its culture is influenced by the customs and history of a clan-based society, nomadic groups, and the desert geography. Islam and the Arabic language dominate; the language, religion, and law all stem from the country's Islamic traditions.

Although a number of Mauritanians continue to follow traditional nomadic lifestyles, following the water supply to herd animals like camels, goats, and sheep, many people are choosing to live in permanent settlements to pursue a higher quality of life.

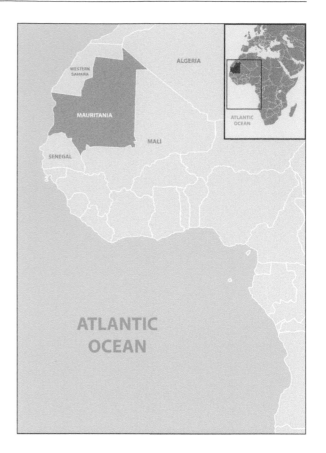

GENERAL INFORMATION

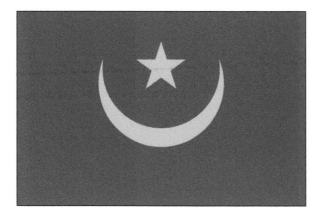

Official Language: Arabic
Population: 3,596,702 (2015 estimate)
Currency: Mauritanian ouguiya
Coins: The Mauritanian ouguiya is subdivided into five khoums; coins are available in denominations of 5, 10, and 20 ouguiya, with coin denominations of 1 khoum and 1 ouguiya rarely used.

Land Area: 1,030,070 square kilometers (397,712 square miles)
National Motto: "Honneur, Fraternité, Justice" ("Honor, Fraternity, Justice)
National Anthem: Simply listed as the "National Anthem of Mauritania." The anthem is based upon a centuries-old poem; the first line is "Be a helper for God, and censure what is forbidden."
Capital: Nouakchott
Time Zone: GMT + 0
Flag Description: The flag of Mauritania features a dark green field, or background, with a centered horizontal (upward-pointed) golden crescent below a five-pointed golden star (both symbols of Islam). The colors, gold and green, are Pan-African colors; green represents Islam while gold stands for the sands of the Sahara.

Population

The Mauritanians are a people primarily of Arab-Berber descent known as the Moors. The Moors make up around two-thirds of the country's

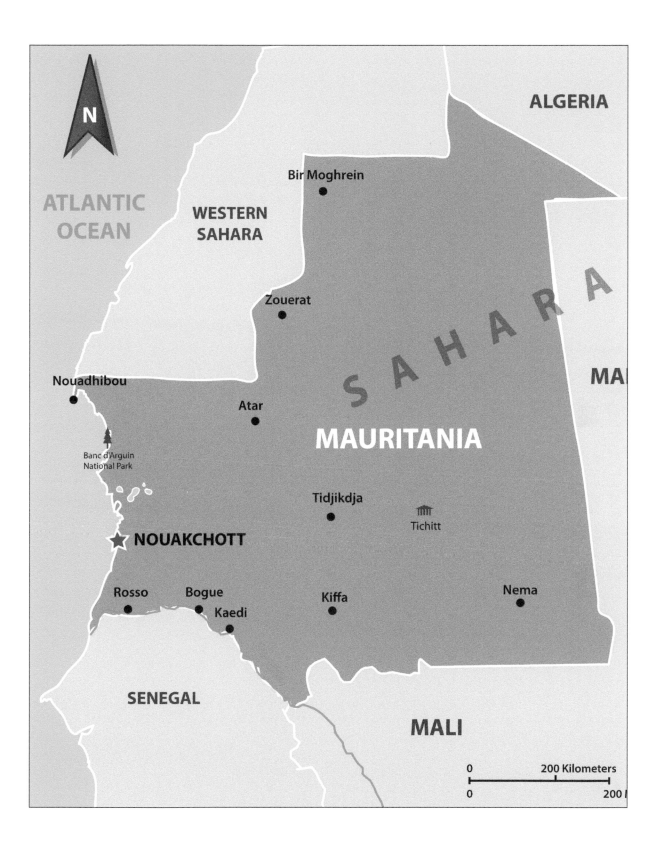

Principal Cities by Population (2012):

- Nouakchott (870,073)
- Kifah (91,336)
- Nouâdhibou (85,337)
- Rosso (80,936)
- Kayhaydi (59,942)
- Zuwarat (56,851)

population and can be divided into two distinct ethnic groups: the White Moors, who are called Beydane, and the Black Moors, or Haratine. White Moors are descended from Arab tribes that migrated to Mauritania beginning in the third century. Sudanese tribes are the ancestors of the Black Moors. Non-Moorish people living in Mauritania are known as kewrin.

Other ethnic groups are the Haalpulaar, Soninke, Fulani, Tukulor, and Wolof. These groups are related to those living in throughout sub-Saharan Africa, and many migrated to Mauritania after that country gained independence in 1960.

Slavery was officially abolished in Mauritania only recently, in 1981, and is still practiced in remote areas of the country. (Criminal laws were passed in 2007 to enforce the 1981 ban, including a two-year prison term for slavery apologists.) In 2002, the BBC news reported that there were an estimated 600,000 people living in slavery in Mauritania, a number that has been reiterated as the 21st century has progressed. Poverty and lack of education have contributed to the persistence of slavery in the country.

Population numbers for many areas in Mauritania are often difficult to calculate or substantiate, due to the traditional and nomadic ways of living of many of the country's residents. For example, as drought and other factors influence the migration of the rural population, many nomadic tribes will set up tents on the outskirts and center of the capital, Nouakchott, and move back and forth from the city as necessary. The increase in population has been a significant drain on Nouakchott's water resources. In 1958, French and Mauritanian engineers designed the city to

accommodate 15,000 new residents, a figure much smaller than current population numbers.

Approximately 59 percent of the population lives in urban areas (2015 estimate). As of 2015, the population growth rate was 2.23 percent.

Languages

Mauritania's official language is Arabic. Other languages spoken in the country include Hassaniya, which is a mixture of Arabic and Berber, and French, Pulaar, Wolof, and Soninke.

Native People & Ethnic Groups

Before Arabic and Berber tribes migrated to Mauritania in the third century, the region was part of the Ghana Empire. A black North African people known as the Bafour were the first inhabitants of modern Mauritania. The Bafour were the ancestors of the modern Soninke people, who live in the country.

With the arrival of the Arab and Berber invaders, the Bafour were forced to flee to the south, where Mauritania borders Senegal today. The invading tribes also enslaved the Bafour, beginning a tradition of ethnic social division in which Arabs enjoyed aristocratic status and black Africans were relegated to servant status.

Religions

Nearly the entire population of Mauritania is Sunni Muslim. Per the country's constitutional charter, Islam is the state religion.

Climate

The climate of Mauritania is arid, thanks to wind patterns such as the desert harmattan (dusty West African trade wind). It receives most of its precipitation during the rainy season, which takes place during the winter months. Most rainfall occurs in the south, while the north is the driest part of the country. In the south, the rainy season lasts from June to October, and averages around 635 millimeters (25 inches) of precipitation. The far north only sees around an inch or two of rain between September and November.

Mauritania is a hot country, the average temperature being 24° Celsius (75° Fahrenheit), with summer temperatures reaching between 38 and 46° Celsius (100 and 115° Fahrenheit). The temperature rarely falls below 20° Celsius (68° Fahrenheit).

ENVIRONMENT & GEOGRAPHY

Topography
Mauritania is primarily a flat country, with coastal plains that reach heights of up to 45 meters (150 feet). Most of the northern part of the country is desert, while a small portion of the south is fertile enough to support some agriculture.

In the country's interior, the plains reach altitudes of 182 to 228 meters (600 to 750 feet). These heights are part of a large plateau and system of ridges. The highest mountain in Mauritania is Mount Ijill, at 915 meters (3,002 feet) above sea level.

In the north, the Rigaibat region has many rocky hills and ridges. The Taoudeni Basin is located in the center of the country, and is surrounded by plateaus. Half of Mauritania is covered by sand dunes; wadis, or dry riverbeds, are common throughout the country, especially among the plateaus. Occasionally the wadis flood, but because the country receives very little rain, they are dry most of the time. The Senegal River runs through the southern part of the country.

The national capital, Nouakchott, is located in the western region of Mauritania on the Atlantic coast. Nouakchott is also located in the Sahara desert (the world's largest hot desert) and stands at the crossroads between the northern and southern parts of Mauritania.

Plants & Animals
Much of the southern part of Mauritania, which is not as arid as the north, is covered with savannah. There are also stands of baobab and palm trees. Southern vegetation includes shrubs such as acacia, euphorbia plants, and grasses like Indian sandbur (Cenchrus biflorus) and morkba (Panicum turgidum). The northern deserts are barren, and plants can only grow near wadis or in oases.

Large mammals native to Mauritania include antelope, lions, and elephants. Other common animals include warthogs, gazelles, crocodiles, panthers, lynx, and hyenas. The country is also home to the ostrich, the largest bird in the world.

CUSTOMS & COURTESIES

Greetings
Mauritanians greet one another with equal enthusiasm and sincerity, and greetings are one of the primary ways that Mauritanians show respect to one another. Mauritanians, both men and women, almost always shake hands in greetings and exchange multiple questions and answers regarding health, family, and general well-being. Similar to other Muslim cultures, the right hand is exclusively used when shaking hands; this is because the left hand is associated with the cleansing of the body, and thus considered impure. Some Mauritanians will touch their right hand to their chest or heart in greeting to convey that they hold the other person in their hearts.

Greetings could be exchanged in one of many different languages, depending on one's ethnicity and social class. The most commonly spoken languages in Mauritania include French and Hassaniya Arabic, the official language. Other commonly spoken languages include Fulani, Soninke, and Wolof. Common greetings in Hassaniya Arabic include "Is-selaamu aleykum" ("Peace be upon you"), "Ish haal is-sbaah" ("Good morning"), "Ish haal li-mgiil" ("Good afternoon"), "Eyaak il-khayr?" ("Are you in peace?"), "Ish haalak?" ("How are you?"), and "Ish haal usrtak?" ("How is the family?").

Gestures & Etiquette
Different ethnic groups in Mauritania have different social customs and etiquette. For example, the Moors are very socially conservative, while the Pulaar and Wolof are less so. Generally,

social etiquette in Mauritania dictates that people of the opposite sex do not stand close to one other or touch in public. Islamic law discourages men from having physical contact with all women, with the exception of their wives and close family. Women wearing head coverings also refrain from lifting their veils in public. People of the same sex who are involved in conversation with one another tend to stand very close and may hold hands as they talk. Friends and family do not value or preserve physical space. However, guests to a home will generally be given physical space as a sign of respect.

Gestures are often used to communicate respect. For example, young Mauritanians demonstrate respect for elders by taking the hand of an elder and placing the hand on their own head. A slight bend (like a bow or curtsy) during a greeting is also a common way of demonstrating respect to an elder. Mauritanian society also maintains numerous social taboos that reflect values and superstitions. For example, Mauritanians do not eat meals in front of their in-laws or call elders by name. In addition, staring at strangers is considered socially acceptable, while staring into the eyes of an elder, teacher, or employer is not.

Eating/Meals

In Mauritania, eating customs differ between urban and rural areas, ethnicities, and geographic areas. In urban areas, the colonial tradition of a French baguette at morning remains, while breakfast in rural areas is most likely rice or millet-based porridge. In addition, the southern half of Mauritania has experienced a severe food shortage, forcing the majority of the population to reduce food consumption to one meal a day. Inhabitants of northern Mauritania, on the other hand, have experienced better crop yields and have maintained their traditional eating customs.

Mauritanians traditionally eat meals from a communal tray or dish, such as a bowl or hollowed-out calabash gourd. Mauritanians generally eat with their own families and clans, and custom dictates that people refrain from eating in front of their in-laws. Fingers of the right hand, rather than utensils, are typically used to scoop food to the mouth (though utensils may be common in urban areas.) Meals are traditionally followed with a beverage such as hibiscus tea, mint tea, green tea, cold water, or sour milk. Most meals are served by young women or servants.

In recent years, Mauritanian culture has drawn international attention for the traditional practice of fattening women prior to marriage. Despite a severe food shortage in the early 21st century and several natural disasters, the practice of force-feeding women, referred to as "gavage," remains. Overall, Mauritanian men value plump and obese women, and if a Mauritanian man has such a wife, he is regarded as a man of resources and riches.

Visiting

Mauritanians generally socialize within their own families and clans. Popular times for visiting include the religious events of Ramadan (Islam's holy month of fasting) and Tabaski (the Feast of the Sacrifice). In addition, Mauritanians visit one another during non-secular events such as harvest celebrations and weddings. In areas with significant emigration, departing or returning family members will be acknowledged through family gatherings.

When visiting someone's home or mosque, custom dictates that any visitors remove their shoes. Visitors are traditionally offered food and drink. Male heads of household have specific responsibilities when hosting events. For example, married men are responsible for hosting the sacrificial feast during particular ceremonies and milestones, such as the end of Ramadan, marriages and funerals, or the return of pilgrims from Mecca. The male head of the household will traditionally sacrifice a lamb or sheep, and offer the grilled meat to guests within three days of slaughter. Guests are expected to partake of the feast. Additionally, when visiting a family member's home for a holiday celebration, visitors wear new clothes. Young girls and women might also paint their hands with henna dye to enhance their beauty.

LIFESTYLE

Family

Family and clans (a group of families sharing the same ancestors) are extremely important in Mauritania. The family unit traditionally consists of upwards of five or six children, and family compounds may house extended family or clan members. The eldest male usually leads the family and clan, and is responsible for making decisions about intermarriage between clans and property management. Family and clan members tend to share their land holdings and work them cooperatively. Polygamy is also culturally acceptable, and each multiple wife will reside with her own children separately.

Sharia (Muslim law) influences family dynamics and customs, including divorce and inheritance. Children generally do not leave the family house until marriage, and women live with their husband's kin. Under Sharia law, family elders are responsible for arranging marriages. Men must also pay their wife's family a bride price before the wedding to compensate the family for all that they have invested in the woman. In addition, marriage and divorce can occur against a woman's will, and children remain with their fathers if a divorce occurs. Men and women also receive different amounts of inheritance, and domestic roles and responsibilities are strictly divided by gender.

Housing

Mauritania's location and identity as a desert nation with ocean access has influenced the development of traditional building materials. Traditional Mauritanian homes are representative of Saharan or desert architecture, and houses in Mauritania were historically constructed of bricks made from sand, pebbles, cement, and crushed seashells. Flat roofs made from palm timber are common on traditional houses, and are suited to the hot and dry climate. In response to the hot weather, houses generally include an outdoor living space such as a courtyard or patio. Houses are built near to mosques whenever possible. Due to the sandy and unstable ground, houses tend be

single-story, compound-like structures built large enough to house extended family and visiting friends. In rural areas, permanent tent-like structures might also be common.

Due to urban migration, Mauritania is experiencing an urban housing shortage, particularly in the southern areas of the country. As a result, Mauritania's cities are filled with kébés (desert shantytowns) made of tents and shacks constructed of crude bricks and scrap wood and metal. People living in the shantytowns have little or no access to potable water. The government is working slowly to improve the urban and rural water supply, but have made little impact on the due to a lack of resources and the scale of the housing problem.

Food

Mauritanian cuisine is similar to other cuisines in the region and has been influenced by North African, Arabic, and French culinary traditions. The cuisine also varies by ethnicity and region. For example, the cuisine of Mauritanian Moors is similar to Moroccan cuisine, while cuisine in the south resembles Senegalese cuisine, and features more spices and vegetables. Traditional staples of the Mauritanian diet include meat, fish, millet, rice, and potatoes, and the main meal of the day in Mauritania is most often a stew. Traditional Mauritanian stews include camel chubbagin, lamb couscous, and chubbagin lélé et raabie.

Camel chubbagin is a stew prepared in one pot. It consists of cubed camel meat, rice, oil, eggplant, carrots, cabbage, sweet potato, onion, chili, garlic, tomato puree, hibiscus leaves, bouillon cubes, and salt and pepper. Lamb couscous (called couscous à l'agneau et aux légumes in French) combines readily available and much enjoyed meat and grain. The meat portion of the recipe needs cubed lamb meat, oil, chopped onion, turnips, carrots, cabbage, squash, and tomatoes. The couscous is cooked, usually in a steaming method, with dates, raisins, chickpeas, and butter. Chubbagin lélé et raabie is a traditional fish stew. The ingredients, including a whole fish, rice, oil, eggplant, cabbage, sweet potatoes, onion, parsley, chilies, tomato puree, garlic, hibiscus leaves, bouillon, salt, and pepper, are cooked together until soft. Roasted lamb is called mechoui, and is a popular meal throughout the country. Couscous, a mixture of semolina and vegetables, frequently accompanies stews and spicy fish.

Mauritanians often drink zrig, or camel's milk, and strong tea with mint. Drinking alcohol is forbidden by Islam.

Life's Milestones

Marriage is perhaps the most significant milestone for most Mauritanians. For women, a marriage means that she will leave her birth family and clan, and for men it signifies a new level of status and responsibility. Mauritanian society values families and every Mauritanian is expected to contribute to and strengthen society though marriage and childrearing. Arranged marriages are common, and men tend to be older and wealthier than women are when they marry. In addition, it is customary for the groom to pay a woman's family a bride price before the marriage can occur.

The traditional Mauritanian wedding ceremony involves two parts, including the aqd and the marwah. The aqd is the Islamic marriage contract that is signed at a mosque under the direction of a religious leader. The marwah

Traditional wedding garb in Mauritania.

is the reception or party during which the new bride is sent away to live with her husband's kin. Traditional wedding dress includes a black veil that covers the bride's face, and a white suit and a black turban for the groom.

CULTURAL HISTORY

Art

Historically, the arts in Mauritania include textiles, woodworking, leatherworking, metalworking, and pottery. Because early inhabitants were nomadic, early art was mostly utilitarian in nature. These works included leather pillows, cutlery, woven mats, and tents, and carved wooden boxes. Other art forms, such as silver jewelry, functioned as indications of wealth. As neighboring countries and migration influenced Mauritanian culture, local textile artists became known for their wall hangings and hand woven rugs, while Mauritanian metalworkers began creating gold jewelry. Another notable Mauritanian tradition is the art of henna (natural dye), which is applied to women's hands and forearms, often for ceremonial occasions such as weddings.

Mauritania's artistic traditions are also influenced by West African and Islamic art and aesthetics. West African influences on Mauritania's art are evident in the choice of materials and the focus on functionality, and included beaded jewelry and crafts, textile art, and elaborate woodcarvings. Islamic influence on Mauritania's art includes designs with arabesque (floral and geometric) patterns and a desire to impart beauty, as well as intricately detailed jewelry and silver handicrafts. According to the Islamic perspective, art pieces or objects are made to touch the emotions of the people who see or use the art. Islamic art also forbids the depiction of the human form.

Artists are also traditionally revered in Mauritanian culture because Mauritanians believe they pass down knowledge and skills to the next generation. These skilled artisans and craftspeople, known as mu'allmin, are part of the skilled caste. Castes refer to social classes rigidly separated by ethnicity, wealth, or profession.) Mauritania's caste system is hierarchical, with the religious and warrior caste at the top, the skilled caste in the middle, and the historian and musician caste toward the bottom.

Architecture

Mauritanian architecture is often dictated by the country's desert environment and the availability of building materials. For example, palm-timber flat roofs and outdoor living spaces accommodate the desert climate of the country, while housing typically consists of one-story structures due to the sandy, unstable ground; wattle-and-daub buildings have been traditionally predominate, while traditional building materials include bricks made from sand, pebbles, cement, and crushed seashells. Saharan architecture itself is defined by the use of flat roofs made from palms and mud-brick and red-stone houses and buildings, a style defined as "primitive" by early scholars. This style of architecture defines some of the region's trading centers that date back to medieval times. In the capital, Nouakchott, some buildings offer a reminder of the country's period of French colonialism, while Islamic architecture, particularly exemplified by mosques, predominates throughout the country.

Music

In Mauritania, musicians have traditionally been part of a lower caste referred to as the ighyuwn caste, which also includes poets and entertainers. (The lowest caste consisted of slaves.) Historically, musicians worked and performed at the request of upper caste members. Live musical performances remain common throughout Mauritania; however, few Mauritanian musicians have the means to record, market, or distribute their music. Mauritanian musicians are also predominantly men, as the nation's Islamic influence encourages women to remain modest and discourages female participation in the arts.

Folk music is popular in Mauritania, and is influenced by a blend of Arabic and African culture. Traditional Mauritanian music is particularly influenced by the West African tradition of the griot. Griots were wandering poet-praise singers and the keepers of their culture's words, music, and history. (The word "griot" is believed to derive from a transliterated Portuguese word meaning "servant," emphasizing the caste systems and the musician's traditional place in society.) Traditional Mauritanian folk instruments include the tidinit, a four-string Moorish lute played exclusively by male members of the ighyuwn caste; the ardin (or ardeen), a stringed harp-lute traditionally played by women; and the tbal, a large kettle drum.

Modern Mauritania is experiencing some growth in music festivals. The Nouakchott International Festival of Nomad Music (Festival international des Musiques Nomades), which began in 2004, is widely attended by Mauritanian and foreign musicians alike. The festival is organized by the Mauritanian Ministry of Culture, Youth, and Sports, along with the World Bank and French businesses. The festival provides opportunity to reach an international audience and promote the nation's musicians and its nomadic culture. In 2008, over 300 musicians from both Africa and Europe attended.

Dance & Drama

Mauritania's performance arts are rooted in the country's oral traditions, and poetic abilities and improvisation in storytelling are valued. Open-air performances by nomadic performers, dancers, and dramatists are popular, and dramatic readings, such of epics and poems, are still heard on the radio. Dramatic performances are also staged in a variety of languages, including Hassaniya (a Bedouin dialect), Fula, Soninke, Wolof, and French. Modern support for the performing arts has been scarce in Mauritania, but the bureau of educational and cultural affairs has established cultural programs. These include performing arts troupes and a national theater (inaugurated in 1988).

While Western-style theatrical art only emerged in Mauritania in the mid-20th century, Mauritania's contemporary dance styles are rooted in the country's nomadic heritage. As they evolved, they borrowed from Arabic and West

African dance traditions. In Mauritania, Islamic custom dictates that men should dance with men, and women should dance with women.

Literature

Mauritania has a rich oral history tradition. With the advent of Islam, poetry became an early dominant form of literature, born out of the culture's rich storytelling traditions and the ighyuwn caste (which includes entertainers and musicians). Mauritania is also known for its heritage of Arabic manuscripts. This tradition of scholarship is considered to be the richest in West Africa. Modern Mauritanian literature continues to be influenced by Islam, and largely focuses on Islamic affairs. Notable writers include Ahmad ibn al-Amin al-Shinqiti (1872–1913), considered the most famous Mauritanian writer; Ahmad Ben Abd al-Qader (1941–), who addressed social issues first through poetry, than fiction; and novelist Moussa Ould Ebnou (1956–), often referred to as one of the country's greatest novelists.

Because of the importance of Islam in the country, Mauritania has produced a number of religious scholars. Muhammad Yahya, formerly Muhammad al-Mukhtar, was a well-known religious writer who died in 1912.

CULTURE

Arts & Entertainment

In Mauritania, the arts reflect the country's 21st culture, traditions, collective experience, and social consciousness. The arts can be divided into two groups: function and entertainment. The functional arts include the important textiles, pottery, metal work, and wood and leather pieces made for everyday use. The entertainment or performing arts are a part of everyday life, and serve to unite Mauritania's many different ethnic groups.

Mauritanians do not generally own mass-produced objects. Instead, families rely on objects such as chairs, farm tools, and hand woven rugs made by skilled artists and craftspeople. The arts and crafts traditions, particularly textiles, wood-

working, leatherworking, metalworking, and pottery, contribute to the successful completion of daily chores and tasks. The pieces made by skilled artisans are made with Islamic principles and aesthetics in mind. Mauritanians believe that these works are strong examples of their country's unique and talented culture.

In Mauritania, the entertainment or performing arts are as important as the functional arts. The entertainment or performing arts unite different ethnic groups who might only be united through their faith and identity as Sunni Islam. Historically, the white and black Maur ethnic group has self-identified as Arab, while the black Arab ethnic groups has self-identified as African. Mauritania's performing arts are strongly influenced by Islamic content and principles, and ethnic tensions and clashes have been eased by the unifying power of shared Islamic-based entertainment. Storytellers perform religious stories, and performers of all ethnicities abide by Islamic traditions and standards, such as men and women refraining from dancing with one another.

The arts in Mauritania receive little government funding. As a result, the arts are largely community-based and independent in nature, and have been able to survive significant political change and turmoil. While political instability has not hurt the arts tradition, natural disasters, such as flood, draught, and locusts, are beginning to change the country's traditional nomadic culture and settlement patterns. Because of increasingly urban and sedentary lifestyles, some arts and cultural traditions, such as improvised storytelling and camel racing, are waning.

Music is an important form of cultural expression in Mauritania. Mauritanian folk singing is a combination of music and poetry. One famous griot, or folk singer, was Dimi Mint Abba (1958–2011), considered the country's most famous musician. Traditional music involves vocal performances accompanied by a lute-like instrument called the tidnit. Mauritanian singers perform in high-pitched tones and are occasionally accompanied by a harp known as an ardin, usually played by women. Drums and other percussion instruments are also featured in

Mauritanian music, such as the large tbal drum and the daghumma rattle.

Soccer, known as football, is the most popular sport in Mauritania. The country belongs to the Confederation of African Football, and its team is known as the Mourabitounes. However, the team rarely qualifies for the African Nations Cup or the World Cup tournaments.

Cultural Sites & Landmarks
The United Nations Educational, Scientific, and Cultural Organization (UNESCO) recognizes two sites in Mauritania as requiring international recognition and preservation efforts: Banc d'Arguin National Park and the Ancient Ksour of Ouadane, Chinguetti, Tichitt, and Oualata. (Ksour is plural for ksar, which is an ancient fortified settlement.) The Banc d'Arguin National Park is a protected area of islands, swamps, and sand dunes along the Atlantic coast. The park provides protection for species of migrating birds, sea turtles, fish, and dolphins. Scientists, preservationists, and artists alike consider the Banc d'Arguin National Park's blend of desert and marine environments to be of great natural and aesthetic importance.

The ancient ksour of Ouadane, Chinguetti, Tichitt, and Oualata are important centers of Islamic trade and religion. These ancient religious and trading centers generally include houses built around a mosque and other structures. The ancient ksour were the centers of Islamic life and culture, and date to the 11th and 12th centuries. The towns existed to meet the practical and spiritual needs of the many caravans of nomadic people that crossed the Sahara desert. Ouadane, Chinguetti, Tichitt, and Oualata are four ancient cities that preserve the culture and spirit of life along ancient trade routes.

Other important cultural sites and landmarks include the archaeological sites of Azougui, Tegdaoust, and Kumbi Saleh. Azougui was an ancient town in northwestern Mauritania. The town dates to the 11th century, though the site shows evidence of human settlement as early as the seventh century. Azougui's historical importance is traced to the town's function as a base for the Muslim Berbers as they conquered the Ghana Empire and Morocco. Tegdaoust is an important archaeological site in southern Mauritania that dates to the fifth century. Tegdaoust's historical importance is tied to the ancient city's identity as a medieval commercial center for Saharan trading routes. Throughout Tegdaoust's history, the Ghana Empire (790–1076 CE) and the Mali Empire (c. 1230–c. 1600s) ruled the city. Tegdaoust's development was influenced by the domestication of the camel and changes in the grassland and desert ecosystems.

The Kumbi Saleh is a significant archaeological site dating to the third century. Kumbi Saleh, located in southeastern Mauritania, is a settlement mound covering an area that was once an ancient city with mosques, residential suburbs, and a royal palace. (A settlement mound refers to a hill or mound of earth covering an area of land once inhabited or settled by humans.) Archeologists and historians have determined that Kumbi Saleh once served as the capital of the Ghana Empire. Kumbi Saleh's historical importance is linked to the ancient city's one-time identity as sub-Saharan Africa's largest urban area.

Libraries & Museums
The National Museum (or Musee National du Nouakchott) hosts a variety of ancient ceramic exhibits and presents a general history of the area, including detailed archeological and ethnographic histories of the country and region. Other museums include the Museum of Traditional Medicine of Mauritania and a manuscript museum located in the ancient town of Ouadane.

The National Library of Mauritania serves as the country's legal depository. It was established by decree in 1965. An Islamic library in the ancient trading center of Chinguetti, called the "library of the desert," contains manuscripts dating back centuries. (Renowned collections of ancient books and manuscripts are stored there by several families, in fact.)

Holidays
Islamic religious holidays such as Ramadan are widely observed in Mauritania. During the

month of Ramadan, eating and drinking are not permitted until after dark. In addition to Islamic holy days, Mauritanians celebrate their independence from France on November 28. They also commemorate the founding of the Organization of African Unity (OAU) on May 25, which is known as African Liberation Day.

Youth Culture

In Mauritania, youth culture is shaped by a combination of indigenous, Islamic, and black African culture. For the most part, youth fashion trends and social etiquette, such as behavior, are closely aligned with moderate Islamic traditions and expectations. Traditionally, young Mauritanians socialize almost exclusively within their families and clans until marriage. Younger children tend to make their own toys from discarded materials, and media influence and technology access remains limited for older youth.

Popular recreational sports include camel racing, horse racing, football (soccer), basketball, and wrestling. In recent years, Islamic fundamentalism and religious extremism are believed to have increased, particularly among Mauritania's young male population. This is attributed to the increasing violence in the region since the wars in Iraq and Afghanistan, as well as high unemployment rates and the traditionally nomadic country's 21st-century transition to an urban culture.

From the mid-1980s until the turn of the 21st century, Mauritania made significant improvements in its educational system. As of 1999, school enrollment in primary levels was an estimated 85 percent, up from 41 percent in 1985. Islamic education is a primary focus, and most children receive religious instruction. However, domestic duties, fees associated with schooling (such as books), and poor transportation services coupled with long distances continue to affect attendance, especially in Mauritania's more isolated regions. In addition, youth labor laws are not generally enforced and, as a result, many young people work outside of the home as day laborers or market helpers. Within the home, older youth tend to their siblings and may take increased responsibility in farm duties.

SOCIETY

Transportation

Due to the country's size and harsh climate, overland distances generally require a four-wheel drive vehicle. Passenger rail service operates between Nouâdhibou and Zouérat, and the Senegal River is passable by boat only in certain areas. Other modes of transportation include bush taxis and buses. (Vans or trucks might serve as group taxis.) Traffic moves on the right-hand side of the road. Bicycling, walking, and camel riding are also common modes of transportation. Nouakchott International Airport accommodates international air travel.

Transportation Infrastructure

There are four main roads in Mauritania, and they lead to and from Nouakchott; all other roads are generally unpaved. Only three highways link the capital to other major Mauritanian cities: Rosso in the south, Akjoujt in the northeast and Nema in the east. Of the country's approximately 11,066 kilometers (6,876 miles) of road, an estimated 26 percent is paved. Mauritania's main ports and terminals include Nouakchott and Nouâdhibou, which has services and infrastructure developed with assistance from the World Bank. The country's international airport is located in Nouakchott. There are 27 airports overall. Rail service is limited for passengers.

Media & Communications

Mauritania's media and communication systems are generally considered limited in scope and access. While the constitution provides protections for free speech and freedom of the press, the transitional government, which came to power after the 2008 military coup, controls the broadcast media (television and radio). Media censorship has since become a growing problem, and journalists have been banned for material that is deemed a threat to national security or that criticizes Islam. Private ownership is allowed in the print media, and includes *Akhbar Nouakchott*, which is an Arabic daily, and *Nouakchott Info*, a French-language daily; *Chaab*, printed in Arabic, and *Horizons*, printed in French, are the state-run dailies.

Mauritania's telecommunications infrastructure is limited and the national telecommunications company has a monopoly on landline telephone service. In 2014, Mauritania had an estimated 51,400 main telephone lines and 3.8 million mobile cellular lines. The same year there were an estimated 402,000 million Internet users, representing 11.4 percent of the population.

SOCIAL DEVELOPMENT

Standard of Living

Mauritania ranked 161st out of 187 countries on the 2014 United Nations Human Development Index, which measures quality of life and standard of living indicators.

Water Consumption

According to 2015 statistics from the World Health Organization, approximately 57 percent of all Mauritanians have access to improved drinking water (a number that has been reported as low as 20 percent in terms of access of clean or safe water), while an estimated 40 percent of the population has access to improved sanitation.

An arid country, it is estimated that external water supplies make up 97 percent of Mauritania's water access or supply.

Education

The population of Mauritania is not very well educated, and the country has faced problems such as poorly trained teachers, a shortage of funding, and a lack of school facilities. The adult literacy rate is around 52 percent.

Children must attend school between the ages of eight and 14, although only 89 percent of school-age children do so. The urban population is better educated and has more opportunities for learning than the rural population.

Along with traditional Islamic religious training, there are primary schools and secondary schools in Mauritania. The national library is located in the capital of Nouakchott. The city also has institutions for higher education, including the National College of Administration, the National College of Sciences, and the University of Nouakchott.

According to the United Nations, Mauritania ranked among the lowest Arab states (which include countries such as Libya, Algeria, Syria, Egypt, Saudi Arabia, and Sudan) in regard to female enrollment in higher education. Females represent less than 20 percent of secondary school enrollment (2003).

Women's Rights

The role of women in Mauritanian society and culture is very different from that of men. Secular law and Sharia (Muslim law) influence women's rights, particularly concerning marriage customs, inheritance rights, and legal options.

Women's bodies are subject to cultural beliefs and power relationships. For example, young girls, usually infants, undergo female genital mutilation (FGM) as an initiation, or birth ritual. In addition, girls are generally given more food to eat than boys are in an effort to fatten the girls and make them attractive marriage prospects. Young women are encouraged, sometimes even forced, to eat to the point of extreme obesity, so that they might better reflect a husband's wealth and prosperity. The practice of force-feeding young girls and women is called "gavage," which means, "to gorge" in French. Once particularly common among Mauritania's Moor Arab population, the practice has declined in recent years.

Women and men do not have equal rights under the law. For example, in situations where eyewitness testimony is required, the testimony of two women equals the testimony of one man. Women are more likely than men to be illiterate and unemployed. Women also inherit a smaller portion of an estate than male relatives do. A sister will usually inherit half or less than the amount of what her brother's inherits. Regarding marriage, polygamy is legal and common, and many marriages are arranged. Marriage and divorce do not generally require a woman's permission or consent. In fact, a woman's family may be force her to marry a man. Women may also be taken and made to work as slaves, and sexual exploitation of female slaves is common.

In cases of domestic problems, women in Mauritius have few legal options. While abuse and domestic are unlawful, police do not generally intervene in family matters or domestic disputes. Rape is also a growing problem; during periods of racial unrest or political turmoil, rape and violence against women are common tactics of intimidation and control. The transitional government, established after the 2008 military coup, does not generally enforce laws against rape and violence against women.

However, the transitional government is working with women's rights organizations to improve some areas of women's rights in Mauritania. While FGM is legal in Mauritania, the government and women's rights organizations are working to discourage the practice. Education campaigns about the problems caused by FGM are targeting hospitals, midwifes, and village doctors. For instance, organizations such as the High Islamic Council on Mauritania and the National Forum for Women's Rights teach the public that FGM is not a religious requirement, and that the practice has related health problems.

Health Care

The Mauritanian government provides free medical care for the poor, and services for the aged and disabled through the National Social Insurance Fund. The country's largest hospital is in the capital of Nouakchott, and a number of health clinics are located throughout the rest of the country; however, there are few up-to-date medical facilities. In addition to trained physicians and nurses, there are also many traditional medicine practitioners in the country. There are 10 physicians per 100,000 people.

Tuberculosis is one of the most troublesome health problems in Mauritania, and the malnutrition problem brought on by crop failures has seriously affected public health. There are an estimated 100,000 land mines located in Mauritania's desert, and these have caused deaths and injuries among the people living there.

GOVERNMENT

Structure

After independence, Mauritania was ruled by a president who was later overthrown in a bloodless coup in 1978. Between 1978 and 1992, a military council ruled the country. The military government was repressive and had a poor record on human rights issues, including the problem of slavery. Mauritania instituted a democratic election system in 1992 and elected a new president. Under the democratic system, multi-party elections are allowed.

Today, Mauritania is a republic that is divided into 13 administrative regions, known as wilaya. The executive branch of government consists of the president, who is the head of state. The bicameral national assembly forms the legislative branch; in the lower house, called the National Assembly, there are 81 members, while the upper house, or Senate, has 56 seats. The Supreme Court is the highest court in the land. Suffrage is universal for citizens age 18 and older.

Political Parties

Following the liberalization of Mauritania's politics in the early 21st century, the country transitioned from a one-party dominant state, though the country's commitment to transparency and democracy was questioned internationally, following a 2008 military coup. Parties have frequently adjusted their political views and stances, and alliances are often formed to gain political power. As of the 2006 parliamentary elections, in which Islamist parties were banned but Islamist candidates ran independently, a coalition that included the Rally of Democratic Forces garnered strong support, and their leader heads the opposition to the president following the 2007 presidential elections. In the 2007 Senate elections, a large majority of seats went to the collective Islamic independent candidates, often referred to as Al-Mithaq. Political parties in Mauritania include the Republican Party for Democracy and Renewal (PRDR), the Alliance for Justice and Democracy/Movement for Renewal, which represents the south's black minority population, and the Rally for Democracy and Unity. With the 2009 elections, the power structure was solidified and has remained relatively unchanged.

Local Government

Local governance in Mauritania is decentralized and divided among 13 regions, called wilayas. These regions are further broken down into departments (moughataa), districts, and communes, of which there are over 200. A governor (wali) oversees the 13 regions, while a prefect (hakem) oversees the departments and a district chief oversees districts.

Judicial System

Mauritania's legal system blends Sharia and French law. The president oversees the Supreme Council of the Judiciary. Courts of first instance are divided into moughataa, or district, courts and regional, or wilaya, courts. The latter are comprised of civil and commercial chambers. Other courts of first instance include labor courts, commercial courts (also with two separate chambers), and criminal courts. Higher court bodies include the Supreme Court, the Constitutional Court, and the High Court of Justice.

Taxation

Mauritania's corporate tax rates are relatively moderate—the highest rate is 25 percent—while the income tax rate is high, with the top rate at 40 percent. Other taxes levied include a value-added tax (VAT), similar to a consumption tax.

Armed Forces

The Military of Mauritania is mostly land-based, and consists of small contingents of air and naval forces, as well as a paramilitary force. The military participates in Operation Enduring Freedom–Trans Sahara, a United States-led operation that focuses on counterterrorism in sub-Saharan Africa and the surrounding region. Conscription in the country exists, and includes a two-year service obligation. Eighteen is the minimum age for military service.

Foreign Policy

Mauritania's foreign policy is shaped in large part by the country's economic need and national security. Mauritania tends to maintain a policy of neutrality, especially in regard to disputes between neighboring northern countries. Mauritania works together with neighboring countries, such as Senegal and Mali, on development projects and cooperates with neighboring countries on road improvement projects. However, one exception to Mauritania's neutral foreign relations stance concerns territory. Mauritania has ongoing international disputes with neighboring countries over ownership of areas of Western Sahara.

Mauritania was a French colony until 1960. Relations between Mauritania and France have remained positive since Mauritania's independence. Mauritania looks to France for political, military, social, and economic support. In fact, many of Mauritania's foreign relations decisions are tied to its economic situation. Mauritania amassed significant foreign debt because of drought, natural disasters, and questionable economic choices. In 2000, Mauritania received debt forgiveness as part of the Heavily Indebted Poor Countries (HPIC) initiative established by the International Monetary Fund (IMF) and the World Bank. In 2005, Mauritania received $190.4 million (USD) in economic aid. However, many international organizations have suspended ties and programs due to the 2008 military coup and resulting government leadership. For example, the International Monetary Fund and the World Bank have temporarily halted all economic programs in Mauritania. Mauritania was also suspended from the African Union (AU).

Mauritania is a member nation of the United Nations (UN), the International Labor Organization (ILO), the Economic Community of West African States (ECOWAS), the League of Arab States, the Non Aligned Movement (NAM), the Organisation of the Islamic Conference (OIC), and Islamic Development Bank (IDB), as well as numerous other regional and international bodies and institutions. Mauritania is also one of the EU's largest African partners, and is party to numerous environmental international agreements, including biodiversity, climate change, law of the sea, ozone layer protection, and marine pollution.

Human Rights Profile

International human rights law insists that states respect civil and political rights, and promote an individual's economic, social, and cultural rights. The United Nations Universal Declaration on Human Rights (UDHR) is recognized as the standard for international human rights. Its authors sought the counsel of the world's great thinkers, philosophers, and religious leaders, and were careful to create a document that reflects the core values shared by every world culture. (To read this document or view the articles relating to cultural human rights, visit http://www.udhr.org/UDHR/default.htm.)

Overall, Mauritania has a poor human rights record. Despite the social, moral, economic, and cultural rights guaranteed by Mauritania's constitution, Mauritania's citizens are ultimately limited by their nation's political instability, poverty, and underdeveloped infrastructure. Mauritania is also a centralized Islamic republic ruled by a military junta, and citizens are subject to strict religious control and are limited in their ability to influence the operations of their government. The political coup that occurred in Mauritania in 2008 has resulted in increasingly curtailed and limited constitutional rights.

Mauritanian law guarantees equality, but that ideal is seldom realized. In practice, Mauritanian law is guided by Islamic principles, and Islamic law influences how women and ethic minorities will be treated. Women in Mauritania experience discrimination and female genital mutilation (FGM), ethnic minorities experience discrimination and political disenfranchisement, and slave labor and exploitative child labor are common.

In addition, Article 18 of the UDHR, which supports the right to freedom of thought, conscience, and religion, is not supported by Mauritanian law. Mauritania's constitution declares that Islam shall be the religion of the people and of the state. Freedom of speech and of the press is also restricted, and the government oversees, and in some instances harasses, the broadcast media and journalists.

Non-governmental organizations (NGOs) and international monitoring agencies are also concerned about Mauritania's judiciary system, which is heavily influenced by executive branch or otherwise inefficient, and the prevalence of arbitrary arrests and detention. In addition, prison conditions are harsh and overcrowded. In a 2008 report from Amnesty International (AI), prisoners alleged that they were not allowed to leave their cells, often for years at a time, and some cells were inaccessible due to the number of inmates inhabiting them. AI also maintains that torture is the common interrogation method in prisons.

Despite Mauritania's overall poor human rights profile, the government is working slowly to improve some areas of human rights. For instance, in 2006, Mauritania's government held legislative and municipal elections and created a National Commission on Human Rights.

ECONOMY

Overview of the Economy

Mauritania is a relatively poor nation. Although it is a dry country, agriculture and fishing are its two most important industries. Iron ore is its richest resource. The capital of Nouakchott, an important deep-water harbor, is the major commercial center of the country. In fact, despite its small output, Nouakchott is the linchpin for the entire country's economy and the city was one of the main reasons that the United Nations (UN) named Mauritania as the best performing African economy in 2006.

In 2008, Mauritania's gross domestic product (GDP) was estimated at $5 billion (USD). The per capita GDP is approximately $4,300 (USD). The country's major trading partners are Italy, France, Africa, Spain, and Germany.

Industry

Because of the country's plentiful iron ore deposits, iron mining is one of the most important industries in Mauritania. Fishing is also an important source of income for many people. Industry accounts for 31 percent of the GDP. Growing industries include sugar refining, gypsum processing, flour milling, textile manufacturing, and fish processing.

Labor

The country's labor force was estimated at 1.292 million in 2014. The majority of the work force works in the agricultural sector, while industry accounts for only about one-tenth of the work force. The unemployment rate was 31 percent in 2012.

Energy/Power/Natural Resources

Mauritania's natural resources include fish, petroleum, gypsum, copper, phosphates, and salt. Its most important mineral resource is iron ore, which is a major export. Much of the country's iron ore is located around Mount Ijill.

While oil has been found in Mauritania, the oil industry has not yet been developed. There are hopes that the industry will grow and help to bolster the country's economy. Foreign companies are beginning to look for offshore petroleum and to invest in the industry.

Fishing

Mauritania's coastal waters are rich in resources and the country maintains an exclusive economic zone (EEZ) that provided for over $120 million in exports in the early 21st century, and 1.5 million tons are produced annually. Fishing, in fact, provides for over one-third of jobs for the country's modern sector. (Artisanal or traditional fishing exists, but fish consumption among the populace is low.) Commercial fish include pelagic fish and shrimp and lobster; overfishing and unlicensed fishing, however, remain concerns. Beginning in 2010, the government began the implementation of reforms to "Mauritanize" its fishing industry—the government sells fishing licenses to countries such as Russia and China, as well as the European Union—that includes processing at least half of the country's total catch domestically.

In 2010, Mauritania announced that the country was beginning the construction of a $120-million-dollar fisheries complex, funded by the Chinese. According to the government, the complex would include warehouse facilities, the construction of fishing vessels, and shipbuilding and maintenance facilities, as well as providing some 2,500 jobs. The country also received funding from Japan to support the development of small-scale fishing, and earlier in 2010, the European Union announced it would partially fund a $364-million, four-year plan to revitalize Mauritania's fishing industry. (It is estimated that approximately 200 European boats fish in Mauritanian waters.)

Mining/Metals

Mauritania ranks high globally in iron ore production, and was one of the top 10 exporters of the mineral. Other important commodities include copper, crude steel, gold, cement, crude oil, gypsum, and salt.

Agriculture

Agriculture accounts for more than 25 percent of Mauritania's GDP. However, growing crops and raising animals is only possible where there is adequate rainfall or irrigation. Droughts occur cyclically and can drastically affect crop production. The southern region affords the richest agricultural land, and has adequate water and forage for raising livestock. Dams and desalinization plants help to provide water for the population and for agricultural use.

The major crops of Mauritania are millet, sorghum, maize, wheat, dates, and rice. Date palm trees are also cultivated. Livestock and fisheries also contribute to the agricultural sector.

Animal Husbandry

Livestock herding and subsistence farming are the chief occupations of nomadic tribes, who raise sheep and goats for milk and meat. Livestock are an important source of income and food in the Hodh Basin, in the southeastern portion of the country. Camels, donkeys, and oxen provide transportation for nomads, who raise millet for food in the south. Pig farming is outlawed.

Tourism

Tourism is a developing economic sector in Mauritania. The country's infrastructure makes travel difficult; there are only 1,770 kilometers (1,100 miles) of paved roads, and the large stretches of sandy desert make travel problematic. Often, the desert dunes will shift and cover existing roads with deep sand. In addition to travel by automobile or camel, a local airline called Compagnie Mauritanienne des Transport Aeriens serves the country with a small fleet of airplanes.

While the Sahara creates harsh living conditions for the Mauritanians, there are hopes that more tourists will be attracted to the famous desert. The country also boasts ancient cave paintings and other artifacts. Most tourists who visit Mauritania come from France. In the early 21st century, terrorist attacks in the country linked to al-Qaeda negatively affected the country's tourism industry. In fact, during the 2007–08 tourist season, the number of tourist arrivals reportedly decreased by 60 percent. The tourism industry employs approximately 45,000 people.

Simone Isadora Flynn, Christina Healey, Ian Paul

DO YOU KNOW?

- Under French colonial rule, Mauritania was named for a province of ancient Rome.

- Prehistoric cave paintings found in Mauritania feature giraffes, which have long been extinct in the area.

- The Sahara Desert is the largest desert in the world, measuring around 1,600 kilometers (994 miles) wide and about 5,000 kilometers (3,100 miles) long.

- Many of Nouakchott's streets are named for important international historical figures such as Charles de Gaulle, the first president of France, John F. Kennedy, and former Egyptian President Abdel Nasser.

Bibliography

Foster, Noel. "Mauritania: The Struggle for Democracy." Boulder, CO: *FirstForumPress*, 2011.

McDougall, James and Judith Scheele. "Saharan Frontiers: Space and Mobility in Northwest Africa." Bloomington, IN: *Indiana University Press*, 2012.

Pazzanita, Anthony G. "Historical Dictionary of Mauritania." Lanham, MD: *Scarecrow Press*, 2008.

Robinson, David. "Paths of Accommodation: Muslim Societies and French Colonial Authorities in Senegal and Mauritania." Athens, OH: *Ohio University Press*, 2000.

Stewart, Charles, Sidi Ahmed Ould, and Ahmed Salim, eds. "The Arabic Literature of Africa, Vol. 2: Mauritania and Western Sahara." Leiden: *Brill Academic Publishers*, 2015.

Works Cited

"A Country Study: Mauritania." *Library of Congress Country Studies*. http://lcweb2.loc.gov/frd/cs/mrtoc.html.

"Background Notes: Mauritania." *U.S. Department of State*. http://www.state.gov/r/pa/ei/bgn/5467.htm.

"Culture of Mauritania." *Countries and Their Cultures*. http://www.everyculture.com/Ma-Ni/Mauritania.html.

"Greetings." *U.S. Embassy to Mauritania*. http://mauritania.usembassy.gov/uploads/images/HS0OuEgHmV2nIaRzlZnyOA/Greetings.pdf.

"Introduction to Hassaniya." *Peace Corps/Mauritania* (n.d.). http://multimedia.peacecorps.gov/multimedia/audio/languagelessons/mauritania/MR_Hassaniya_Language_Lessons.pdf.

"Mauritania." CIA World Fact Book. https://www.cia.gov/library/publications/the-world-factbook/print/mr.html.

"Mauritania." Encyclopedia of the Nations. http://www.nationsencyclopedia.com/Africa/Mauritania.html.

"Mauritania." World Food Program. http://www.wfp.org/countries/mauritania.

"Mauritania." UNESCO World Heritage List. http://whc.unesco.org/en/statesparties/mr.

"Mauritania." Women's Organizations. http://www.distel.ca/womlist/countries/mauritania.html.

"Mauritania." World Atlas (n.d.). http://www.worldatlas.com/webimage/countrys/africa/mr.htm.

"Mauritania." Culture Crossing (n.d.). http://www.culturecrossing.net/basics_business_student.php?id=131.

"Mauritania: Country Reports on Human Rights Practices." *U.S. Department of State,* (2007). http://www.state.gov/g/drl/rls/hrrpt/2006/78746.htm.

"Mauritania: Festival dedicated to the fast-disappearing nomadic way of life." *ITN Source* (Feb. 2009). http://www.itnsource.com/shotlist//RTV/2009/02/10/RTV240309/?utm_source=internal&utm_medium=video&utm_content=nomad.

"Mauritania and its Cuisine." *Celnet Recipes* (n.d.). http://www.celtnet.org.uk/recipes/mauritania.php.

"Mauritania Constitution." *International Constitutional Law* (2004). http://www.servat.unibe.ch/icl/mr00000_.html.

"Mauritania Page." *University of Pennsylvania African Studies Center.* http://www.africa.upenn.edu/Country_Specific/Mauritania.html.

"Newspapers in Mauritania." *International Media and Newspapers* (2009). http://www.4imn.com/mr/.

"Nouakchott International Nomad Music Festival kicks off." *Africa en ligne* (August 2008). http://www.afriquejet.com/news/africa-news/nouakchott-international-nomad-music-festival-kicks-off-200804091521.html.

"Population Estimates for Cities in Mauritania." Mongabay (2002). Retrieved 30 March 2009 http://www.mongabay.com/igapo/Mauritania.htm.

Brinkhoff, Thomas. "Mauritania: City Population." http://www.citypopulation.de/Mauritania.html.

Davies, Steven. "Fulfulde greetings." *Voices in the Desert.* http://www.voiceinthedesert.org.uk/weblog/archives/2004/07/fulfulde_greeti.html.

Foster, Dean. "The Global Etiquette Guide to Africa and the Middle East: Everything You Need to Know for Business and Travel Success." Hoboken, NJ: *John Wiley and Sons*, 2002.

Harter, Pascal. "Mauritania's 'wife-fattening' farm." *BBC News*, Jan. 2004. http://news.bbc.co.uk/2/hi/africa/3429903.stm.

Pestcoe, Shlomo. "From Ancient Egypt to West Africa: The Lute Connection." *Shlomo Music* (n.d.). http://www.shlomomusic.com/banjoancestors_egypt.htm.

Rubin, Don and Ghassan Maleh. "The world encyclopedia of contemporary theatre." London: *Taylor & Francis*, 1999.

Camels are a common means of transportation in Niger. iStock/trevkitt.

NIGER

Introduction

Niger (pronounced Ne-JAIR), is a country located in West Africa. Historically, it was an important hub of West African caravan trade routes, bringing together diverse peoples, cultures, and goods. The region was a French colony for nearly forty years, until it gained independence in 1960 as the Republic of Niger. Citizens of Niger are known as Nigeriens.

The country's northern region is partly covered by the Sahara Desert. Because most of the population survives by subsistence farming, the majority of Nigeriens live in the south, near the Niger River, where the land is more fertile and rainfall makes it hospitable to farming.

The main ethnic groups in the country are the Hausa and the Djerma-Songhai. Nomadic groups, including the Tuareg, also live in Niger. These groups have all made significant contributions to Niger's cultural life. At the same time, ethnic divisions, including divisions between the Tuareg of the north and other groups in the south, have led to ongoing conflicts.

GENERAL INFORMATION

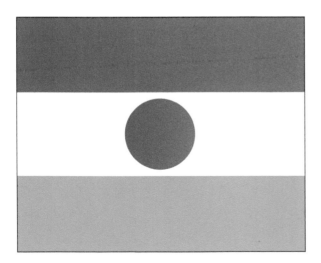

Official Language: French
Population: 18,045,729 (2015)
Currency: West African Communauté Financière Africaine (CFA) franc

Coins: Circulated coins are available in denominations of 1, 5, 10, 25, 50, 100, 200, 250, and 500 francs.
Land Area: 1,266,700 square kilometers (489,075 square miles)
Water Area: 300 square kilometers (115 square miles)
National Motto: French: "Fraternité, Travail, Progrés" ("Fraternity, Work, Progress")
National Anthem: "La Nigerienne"
Capital: Niamey
Time Zone: GMT +1
Flag Description: The flag of the Republic of Niger features a horizontal triband design consisting of an upper orange band, a middle white band, and a lower green band, equal in size. An orange disc, purportedly symbolizing the sun, is centered upon the central white stripe.

Population

Most of Niger's population consists of farmers settled in communities in the south; as of 2015, only an estimated 18 percent of the total popula-

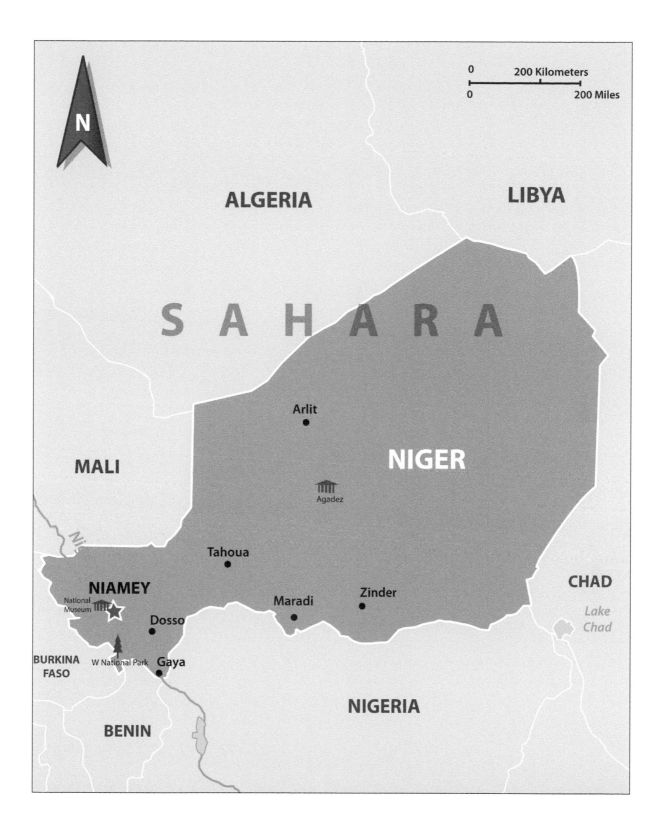

Principal Cities by Population (2012):

- Niamey (1,100,000)
- Zinder (253,766)
- Maradi (188,008)
- Arlit (128,807)
- Agedez (118647)
- Tahoua (110,046)
- Dasso (71,643)

tion was identified as urban. The largest ethnic group is the Hausa, who make up over half of the population. The second-largest group is the Djerma-Songhai people, who make up 22 percent of the population.

Today, around a quarter of the population is made up of a variety of tribal and ethnic groups. The nomadic peoples include the Fulani, Tuareg, and Kanuri; these groups primarily engage in livestock herding.

A small percentage of the population is made up of Arabs, as well as the Gourmantche and the Toubou people. While the Arabs and Toubou are nomadic peoples, the Gourmantche are settled farmers like the Hausa. Islam is the country's main religion, although a small percentage of the people practice traditional African religions or Christianity. As of 2015, the country had an estimated 3.25 population growth rate.

Languages

French is the official language, and many tribal languages are spoken throughout Niger. Hausa is the most important of the tribal languages, and is the most widely recognized and understood in the region. The second most widely used language is Songhai, which is also commonly spoken in Mali. Others include Djerma, Kanuri, and Tamachek. Arabic is also spoken in the country.

Native People & Ethnic Groups

Throughout history, a number of West African empires, kingdoms, and tribal groups have contested Niger's territory. The Hausa have historically been one of the strongest ethnic groups in the country, and today are the most numerous; as

of the 2001 census, they accounted for approximately 55 percent of the population. They primarily live in the southern regions of the country. The Songhai peoples are mostly found on the western borders and along the Niger River, along with the Zarma. Nomadic peoples such as the Tuareg and the Fulani can be found throughout Niger.

European explorers first arrived in Niger in the 19th century. Famous European explorers who visited the country include Mungo Park from Great Britain and Heinrich Barth from Germany. Niger eventually became a colony of France in 1922, after native resistance on the part of the Tuareg was suppressed.

Religions

Islam is the country's main religion, although a small percentage of the people practice traditional African religions or Christianity. In the capital of Niamey, most residents are Muslim, and are of Hausa and Djerma-Songhai ethnicity, while Fulanis, Tuaregs, and French ex-patriots are also present, to a lesser extent. Niamey is also home to small communities of Christians, Baha'is and animists.

Climate

Niger is a dry country that is mostly covered by desert. Contributing to the land's dryness is the dusty harmattan wind, which blows off the Sahara Desert.

Temperatures in Niger are extremely hot and only abate during the rainy season, which is typically very short and occurs around August. April and May are the hottest months, with temperatures reaching between 42° and 45° Celsius (108° and 113° Fahrenheit), depending on the region.

During the coldest months, generally between November and February, the temperature can reach freezing in the desert, but it usually averages around 32° Celsius (90° Fahrenheit). Niger also has generally high levels of humidity, particularly in October.

Rain in the northernmost part of the country is scarce and unpredictable. However, the rainy season typically varies throughout the country in both duration and volume of precipitation. The north can receive up to 160 millimeters (six inches) of rain during the course of the year, while around 600 millimeters (23 inches) fall in the south between June and September.

ENVIRONMENT & GEOGRAPHY

Topography

Niger is bordered by Burkina Faso and Mali on the west and by Libya and Chad on the northeast and east. Algeria lies to the northwest, and Nigeria and Benin form the country's southern border.

Niger's terrain consists mostly of desert and mountains, with some fertile savannahs in the south. The southern third of the country consists of sandstone plateaus with valleys and dallol, or fossilized valleys. There are many dry riverbeds and a rocky landscape, as well as sandstone highlands and a sandy plain. The Niger River, an important source of water in the country, is located in the south.

The national capital, Niamey, stands on the banks of the Niger River in southwestern Niger. There the country descends into the semi-arid Sahel zone south of the Sahara Desert.

Toward the north, the land becomes more arid and desert-like. The northern part of Niger contains the mountainous Aïr Massif, which runs across the middle of the country. There are a number of valleys that separate groups of mountains, and many high plateaus. The tallest mountain is Mount Gréboun, which measures 1,944 meters (6,379 feet) high.

The Nigerien Sahara is a sandy desert that surrounds the Aïr Massif. The desert to the west of the mountains is called the Talak region, while to the east it is called the Ténéré region. In the northern part of the Sahara, the sand dunes in the Tamesna region constantly drift due to wind conditions there.

Plants & Animals

As in other desert countries, the plant life in Niger primarily grows wherever there is water.

In the most barren parts of the country, plants such as date palms and maize can be found near oases. Less arid portions of the country are covered with grazing land, where grasses such as cram-cram (Cenchrus biflorus) grow, as well as the doum palm. Other plants commonly found in Niger include acacia trees, palmyra palms, and baobabs. The country's southern savannahs contain kapok and tamarind trees.

Most large animal species are rare in Niger, where big game hunting has been outlawed. There are small surviving populations of elephants, warthogs, lions, buffalo, and giraffes. These large species are primarily found in the Parc National du W ("W" National Park), where they are protected. Hippopotamuses and crocodiles live in the Niger River.

The Arabian camel or dromedary is able to survive in the desert because it can withstand the temperature and lack of water. Ostriches, the largest birds in the world, inhabit the grazing regions, along with herds of gazelles.

CUSTOMS & COURTESIES

Greetings

While handshaking is common in the cities, it is less common in rural areas. A man might also touch his upper chest with his right hand as a sign of respect rather than shake hands. Those who do shake hands do so lightly—more of a touch than a shake. Traditionally, men and women do not shake hands upon greeting. When meeting and greeting, Nigeriens tend to stand close to one another. This is partly because one is supposed to speak softly, and closer proximity allows one to do this while still being clearly heard.

A typical greeting in Hausa is "Ina kwana?" ("How did you sleep?"), to which the common answer would be "Lahiya lau" ("In health"). In the afternoon, one would ask "Ina kwana?" ("How did you pass the day?"). After an initial greeting, the conversation would typically progress to questions about a person's health and family. Nigeriens appreciate humor, and it is common to make a joke about the weather or one's own health. The Kanouri people greet by shaking their fist and saying "Wooshay, Wooshay" which means "Hello, Hello."

Gestures & Etiquette

In Niger, proper etiquette is important. The majority of the population is Muslim, and Islam exerts a strong influence over Nigerien culture. For example, Women are expected to dress modestly and cover their head, arms, and legs. In addition, public displays of emotion, including public affection, are not common outside of ritual settings such as weddings. Speaking loudly and public drunkenness are also frowned upon, and it is considered rude to maintain prolonged eye contact.

As in most Islamic countries, using the left hand is taboo. This is because the left hand is associated with personal cleansing, and considered impure. To beckon someone, the palm faces inward and the fingers downward. The traditional Western gesture (with palm out and fingers up) is considered a rude gesture. To signal agreement, Hausa people make a clicking sound deep at the back of the throat or suck in air through their mouths.

Eating/Meals

Due to poverty and famine, the Nigerien diet is limited. In rural areas, breakfast would typically consist of leftovers from the previous night's dinner. In urban areas, breakfast might be purchased at a food stall or small restaurant, and might consist of an egg with onions and spices served in a roll or baguette. Hura, which consists of finely pounded millet, water and milk (if available) is a common mid-morning drink. Because refrigeration is typically unavailable, the milk sours quickly, so the milk-flavored variety of hura has a tart taste.

Lunch at a food stall in the city might consist of a brochette (a skewer of grilled goat or chicken) and a side starch such as potatoes or rice with vegetable sauce. A common dinner in a rural area would be porridge made with of cooked, pounded millet with a sauce made from dried okra, a little peanut oil, water, and salt.

Since meat is expensive, it is typically saved for special occasions.

Traditionally, women eat with the women and the children of the family and men eat with men, a practice common in rural areas. A family sits on mats on the ground share food from a common pot or plate, using their hands. Tuareg people typically use spoons. Eating is more formalized in urban areas. Men and women typically do not eat together at restaurants. In fact, it is uncommon to see women eating out.

Visiting

Most Nigeriens are comfortable with and expect impromptu visits from family and friends. The population is generally sociable, and Nigeriens may often spend the better part of a day visiting with friends, family, and neighbors. With a majority Muslim population, it is common to exclaim "Salem aliekum" ("Peace be upon you") when approaching someone's door or courtyard. The traditional response would then be "Aliekum asalaam" ("Come in peace"). A visitor is expected to remove his or her shoes before entering the house. During mealtimes, guests are expected to eat as much as possible—the quantity of food consumed reflects the level of appreciation.

Gift-giving customs vary according to the length of the journey traveled. When a visitor has not traveled far for the visit, no gift is necessary. If a visitor arrives from a long distance, a gift such as soap or dates might be expected. Traditionally, wrapped gifts are not opened in front of the gift-giver.

Visitors are generally offered the food and water (or tea). Among the Tuareg people in the north, green or mint tea with sugar is offered to guests in a ritualized manner. The tea is made by the men and poured into three glasses that are stored in a special box when not in use. Men will serve men, but women must serve women. Each glass that is consumed is accompanied by a toast and has significance. For example, the first glass is for the host, the second for the guest, and the third for Allah. The tea is made and consumed in rounds, with each round made increasingly sweeter.

LIFESTYLE

Family

In rural areas, extended families traditionally live together, and could include distant relatives. Community members are also seen as a type of family, and it is common for neighbors to share child-rearing responsibilities. Elders have special status in the community and in the family, and taking care of them is seen as one of the most important duties of the family and community. Most marriages are arranged and the wife's family receives a "bride price" for their daughter, who then resides with her new husband's family. Many of Niger's ethnic groups have very stratified caste or class systems, and marrying outside of one's class is not acceptable. Polygamy is also common, and having more than one wife (up to a limit of four) is seen as a sign of success. In addition, people who achieve such relative wealth are expected to share their prosperity with family members. For example, if one relative has the means, he will often pay for the schooling of another relative's children.

Housing

Housing in Niger varies by region. In the southern part of the country, homes are typically made with mud-brick construction and thatched grass roofs. Large families generally reside in a compound of single-room structures grouped together. Polygamous families customarily maintain separate houses for each wife and her children, but share a common area for cooking. (The husband would also have his own structure.) Sleeping outside is common due to the arid climate, and most homes lack electricity or plumbing. In urban areas, people live in apartment buildings or detached homes, but often continue to sleep outside on the roof of patio because of the heat. In the northern, desert part of the country, nomadic people commonly live in tents made from goatskin stretched over poles.

Food

Nigerien food is based on the country's most common agricultural products, notably millet, sorghum, okra, yams, rice, beans, and groundnuts.

Millet is used to make two of the most common staples: tuwo, a pounded millet paste topped with tomato or okra sauce, and hura, a fermented milk beverage made with millet and hot pepper. It is also the basis for dégué, a millet ball served with yogurt. Rice is also used as a substitute for tuwo with the same kinds of sauces. Dumbou, a couscous and black-eyed pea dish, and fufu, a pounded yam dish accompanied by a meat or vegetable sauce, are also popular. The French influence is also still evident in Niger, particularly in urban areas. Baguettes are a common part of the diet, and French, Senegalese, Ghanaian, and Lebanese restaurants can be found in bigger cities.

Meat, mostly in the form of inexpensive brochettes (meat skewers typically made of goat, chicken, or guinea fowl), is common in cities, but not commonly consumed in rural areas, Kilishi, a dried beef jerky spiced with peanut sauce and cayenne is popular, as it lasts a long time and doesn't require refrigeration. Dates, mangos, and kola nuts are typical snacks, although they may be expensive to eat regularly. Starch dishes such as fried plantains and potatoes often accompany main dishes in restaurants and food stalls. Fried dough balls called beignets are also commonly found at markets and streets stalls. Many of the Peul and Tuareg people are goat herders, so goat milk and cheese are a large part of their diet. Because of the heat and lack of refrigeration, the cheese is eaten dry and has a chewy texture.

Life's Milestones

Approximately 90 percent of the Nigerien population is Muslim. Thus, many religious practices and life's milestones are observed in accordance with Islamic customs and law. In rural areas, traditional beliefs, such as Animism, may be practiced within a loose Islamic framework. In most of the ethnic groups in Niger, weddings are elaborate affairs to which everyone in the village is invited. They typically last three days, and consist of a feast for everyone as well as separate events for men and women.

There are some practices unique to Niger and its ethnicities. Among the Hausa people, a naming ceremony is held seven days after a baby is born. On the day of the ceremony, the house is cleaned and the father gives kola nuts to all of the guests. An animal is sacrificed, and the community religious leader gives blessings to the baby. The child's head is then shaved. Also in Hausa tradition, a wife mourns her husband for four months and 10 days. During this period, she should not adorn herself in any way and should generally stay in her home.

CULTURAL HISTORY

Art

Niger's ethnic groups are each known for their artistic contributions. The nomadic Tuareg specialize in silver jewelry, leatherwork, and beadwork. The Hausa are known for their textile arts (batiks) and pottery, which features engraved geometric surface designs. The Djerma/Songhai people developed a reputation for woodcarving, including sculptures and masks that are known for their abstract representations of human faces and figures.

Architecture

Niger was once at the center of African trading routes between the Songhaï Empire (c. 1340–1591), based in Mali and the Kanen-Bournu Empire, and in what is now Chad. The ruins of the Djado Plateau in northeast Niger typify the architecture of these early trade-route towns. The ruins include Sudanian-style clay buildings close together on high ground inside an exterior wall. In fact, the Djado Plateau was submitted to the United Nations Educational, Scientific, and Cultural Organization (UNESCO) as a tentative World Heritage Site. Its cultural landscape is a distinguishing feature, with abandoned forts and towns. Towns in other parts of the country featured the Sahelian architectural style common in the region: low, clay or mud-brick structures with flat roofs.

The spread of Islam influenced Niger's palatial and religious architecture. Ancient palaces featured conical towers, while mosques were often built with exposed wooden support struc-

tures and feature spiraling minarets. The old mosque at Agadez (a 19th-century replica of the original built in 1515) is thought to best exemplify medieval Nigerien architecture. Another grand example of Islamic architecture is the Grand Mosque of Niamey.

Niger is also known for the distinct architecture of the country's many ethnic groups. While the facades of most buildings were unadorned, the Hausa people often decorated the outside of their homes with geometric painting or bas-relief (raised designs on the surface of the building). The nomadic Tuareg who lived in the desert north made animal-hide tents that could be deconstructed and moved.

Drama & Film

Islam's predominance in Niger discourages public theatrical performance, but each ethnic group has a form of theater. Notable in Hausa tradition is the "dan kama" or "yan kama," who are performers similar to griots, who are storytellers, poets, and social commentators. Traditionally, they stage comedic shows that always center on food. Usually found performing in the market places, they juggle, perform parodies and gags, and try to "snatch" food from vendors who may be nearby. Another traditional performance is the gambara. It typically represents a kind of musical debate between two griots. Puppet performances have also been a mainstay of entertainment among the Djerma/Songhai people.

Niger established itself as a center of African film prior to independence, and several Nigerien directors have gained international acclaim since the 1960s. The poor Nigerien economy sent filmmakers to neighboring Nigeria in the 1980s, but film continues to be a popular medium in Niger.

Oumarou Ganda (1935–1981) is considered the greatest Nigerien filmmaker. His first film *Cabascabo*, debuted at the Cannes Film Festival in 1969. His film *Le Wazzou Polygame* (1970), about polygamy and forced marriage, won the Grand Prix in 1972 at the Panafrican Film and Television Festival of Ouagadougou (FESPACO), Africa's largest film festival. Moustapha Alassane (1942–2015) was the first

African filmmaker to use animation. *La morte da Gandji*, an animated satire about early postcolonial rulers, featured a toad king and his followers, and was considered groundbreaking for its time. Keita Rahmatou has been successful in Niger's documentary film industry.

Music

Most musical traditions in Niger evolved from the griot (or female version, the griotte), a kind of wandering West African bard (or praise singer) who told stories and preserved history. Griots in Niger date back to pre-Islamic times—before the eighth century—and were common among many of Niger's present-day ethnic groups. These include the Hausa, Peul (also known as Fulani), and the Djerma (also called Zarma or Songhai).

The influence of the Berbers, nomadic North Africans with whom the groups in Niger long traded, is felt in the rhythm and singing styles of Tuareg music. Traditional Tuareg instruments include the tendé, a goat-skin-covered drum that is suspended between ropes and held in place by a rock or boulder, and the imzad, a one-stringed violin that is played only by women. Choral singing, in which one woman "calls" and other women respond, is also traditional among the Tuareg. Peul music centers on vocals and percussive accompaniments made by clapping, clicking, and stomping. Traditional Djerma music generally features the molo, a stringed instrument similar to a lute, the tsiriki, a traditional flute, and the goge, a traditional fiddle. The Hausa also use a lute, called a kontigi, a fiddle called a goje, and a long trumpet called a kakakai, as well as talking drums and kettledrums.

Dance

Dance has always played an important function in the lives of Nigeriens. From harvest rituals to milestones of celebration or grief, dance has continuously accompanied commonplace and special moments in traditional Nigerien culture. Perhaps the best-known traditional dance in Niger is the Hausa bòòríí dance, a trance dance in which the dancers are said to become possessed of spirits. Similarly, the kora is an exor-

Men paint their faces as part of the traditional dance performed by male members of the Wodaabe group.

cism dance, which aims to rid an individual of an evil spirit. Both dances are community events that often last throughout the day. Another well-known traditional dance is the guéréwol dance, performed by male members of the Wodaabe group (a subgroup of the Fulani). Men paint their faces and wear elaborate feathered headgear and dance for seven days, with female judges determining which man is the best looking.

Literature

There was no written tradition among most of the people of Niger, although the Hausa people learned Arabic when they adopted Islam, and adapted Arabic script for use with their language. The Tuareg have a written alphabet called tifinagh, but they are best known for their spoken word poetry, which was often accompanied by music. As a result, most of Niger's stories, history, and legends were preserved through oral traditions, particularly by griots.

Niger's literary tradition developed after independence in 1960. Author Boubou Hama (1906–1982) is among the best-known Nigerien writers, noted for his autobiography *Kotia-nima*, which won the Grand Prix Littéraire d'Afrique Noir (Grand Prize of Black African Literature) in 1970. Mamani Abdoulaye (1932–1993) is another Nigerien author who gained recognition for his poetry, as well as his novel *Sarraounia*, about a Nigerien warrior queen who fought colonialism. Alfred Dogbe is known for his play, "Tiens bon, Bonkano," and for his short stories. Other famous playwrights from Niger include Idrissa Amadou, Idi Nouhou, and Rachid Ramane. Contemporary Nigerien writers have begun to write in local languages in addition to French.

CULTURE

Arts & Entertainment

Traditional music thrives in Niger, and griots (West African praise singers) are still influential. New forms of music such as hip-hop are also becoming increasingly popular, and many Nigerien hip-hop artists blend French and local languages such as Hausa or Zarma (spoken by the Djerma and Songhai peoples). There are frequent rap concerts in Niamey and other major cities, typically featuring local acts. In 2009, a group of 18 of Niger's best-known hip-hop artists took part in a national tour called the Hip-Hop Caravan, a music tour aimed at promoting peace and tolerance and fighting corruption. The Centre de Formation et de Promotion Musicale in Niamey is perhaps the center of music in Niger, and offers frequent workshops and classes by international musicians. "Tradi-moderne" music, which combines traditional music with modern instruments such as the saxophone or electronic instruments, is also popular.

Since independence, theater in Niger has built upon the French theatrical structures brought to the country, adapting to different ethnicities. Small, community-based student groups called samariyas have primarily led the Hausa theater movement. These groups perform plays that are often comical, somewhat improvised, and education-based. Samariyas tackle different commu-

nity themes, such as women's roles or education, and involve their audience in the plays. Since married Muslim women are not supposed attend public performances, the troupes often perform on radio and television. Dance dramas, which are referred to as ballets, have also become popular in Niger. Ballet troupe perform dances based on folktales or legends, mixing traditional and contemporary dancing styles.

Niger is also home to many artistic and cultural festivals. The Cure Salée (Festival of the Nomads), held in the north, is one of the most anticipated festivals, and celebrates the end of the rainy season. The famed guéréwol dance, in which men adorn themselves and dance for female judges, takes place during this festival. The festival also features camel and horseracing. The Festival de l'Air, held each December in the Air Mountains, features Tuareg songs, dance and artwork, as well as horse races and other competitions.

Niamey hosts the annual International Festival of African Fashion (FIMA), which brings designers, artists, and businesspeople from all over the continent to promote African textiles, crafts, and cosmetics. Developed by well-known Nigerien designer Alphadi (1957–), the festival has since come under protest by local Islamic groups. Lastly, the city of Dogondoutchi is home to an annual storytelling festival which brings in storytellers, dancers, traditional musicians, and from around Niger and from neighboring countries such as Burkina Faso, Benin, and Nigeria.

One of the most famous Nigerien athletes was Issake Dabore, who won a bronze medal in the light-welterweight boxing competition during the 1972 Olympic Games. Other popular sports are soccer (football) and traditional wrestling. Tourists in Niger may spend time fishing, horseback riding, or canoeing.

Cultural Sites & Landmarks

Niger is home to two UNESCO World Heritage Sites: W National Park and the Air and Ténéré Natural Reserves. Recognized for its unique ecosystem, W National Park contains the largest protected area of savanna in West Africa. Situated in a "w"-shaped bend in the Niger River, the park spans three countries: Niger, Benin, and Burkina Faso. The park is particularly known for its herd of West African giraffes, one of the last of its kind. Other large mammal populations include elephants, baboons, hippos, lions, leopards, and two types of wild cats, the serval, and caracal. The park is also known for its bird life, with nearly 400 species having been identified within its confines.

The Air and Ténéré Natural Reserves, collectively recognized as one World Heritage Site, is considered one of the largest protected areas in the world. Located in northern Niger, the World Heritage Site encompasses approximately 77,360 square kilometers (29,868 square miles), and includes a large variety of landscape features, as well as native plants and animals such as the ibex and mountain gazelle. The area itself has also become part of Niger's unique cultural landscape. The Ténéré Desert is part of the Sahara, but in the Air Mountains, there are several oases at which nomadic people have created permanent settlements. Also in the area are several important archeological sites, including a "dinosaur graveyard" and ancient petroglyphs (rock carvings) which depict wildlife that once existed in the region. An important rock carving found in 1987, thought to be 7,000 years old, features two eighteen-foot giraffes.

Just south of the Air Mountains is the city of Agadez, one of Niger's most popular tourist attractions until it was placed off-limits to travelers in 2007 because of the Tuareg conflict with the government. Agadez is an ancient city once a caravan stop for West African traders on their way to the Mediterranean. Later it was an outpost of the Songhaï Empire before it became a sultanate of the Tuareg, which it remains today. Notable buildings in Agadez include the Grand Mosque, a Sudanian-style structure originally built in 1515 then rebuilt in 1844. Also notable is the sultan's palace, home to the Sultan of Air, a traditional banco (mud brick) construction building. Agadez is also known for its annual desert horse race, camel market, and colorful central market.

Libraries & Museums

The Musée National du Niger (the National Museum of Niger) is one of West Africa's preeminent museums, and features exhibits about the natural and cultural history of Niger. The exhibits are set in outdoor pavilions built in the Hausa architectural style, an Islamic architectural style popular in the country. There is also a small zoo on the grounds and an artisan's market where craft-making techniques are demonstrated. Other museums include the Regional Museum of Dosso (Musée Régional de Dosso) and the Regional Museum of Zinder (Musée Régional de Zinder), a small museum focused on the Hausa culture.

Libraries in Niger are mostly limited to urban areas, while mobile library services, such as a fleet of vans, service rural and remote populations. Aside from inadequate staffing and funding, literacy and infrastructure regarding information and communication technologies continue to be major issues hindering library service in Niger. The National Archive of Niger is located in the capital of Niamey.

Holidays

One of the most famous Nigerien athletes was Issake Dabore, who won a bronze medal in the light-welterweight boxing competition during the 1972 Olympic Games. Other popular sports are soccer (football) and traditional wrestling. Tourists in Niger may spend time fishing, horseback riding, or canoeing.

Youth Culture

In rural areas, kids often use found objects or recycled materials to create their own toys or games. Football (soccer) is the most popular sport, followed by traditional wrestling. Wrestling is considered the national sport and has long been associated with harvest celebrations.

In urban areas, young people like to go to clubs to dance and hear music at night. American, French, and African popular music, such as hip-hop and Afropop, is popular. In rural areas, socialization typically occurs in the village, and might commonly consist of listening to the radio. One of the most popular pastimes for Nigerien kids is mancala, a game of strategy similar to checkers. It is traditionally played on a homemade board with dried camel dung pieces.

SOCIETY

Transportation

Common modes of public transportation in Niger include buses and bush taxis (share taxis), which are usually small vans that provide an informal service and have no fixed schedule or route. Bicycles and mopeds are also common in urban areas. In rural areas, more traditional modes of transportation such as donkey carts and horses and camels (used by nomadic peoples in the northern deserts) are common. There is no passenger rail service in Niger.

Paved "trunk" roads connect the major cities, while rural roads are primarily unpaved or not maintained; traffic moves on the right-hand side of the road.

Transportation Infrastructure

According to Euromonitor International, as of today, Niger's transportation structure is underdeveloped and in poor condition. There are six major airports in Niger, as well as many other smaller ones. The international airport in Niamey has service to neighboring African countries and Paris, France.

Media & Communications

Due to high illiteracy and undeveloped infrastructure, radio is the dominant medium in Niger. As of 2008, there were five privately run radio stations broadcasting in French and local languages, as well as one government-run station which broadcasts in French, Hausa, and local languages. Some of these stations broadcast international programs from the British Broadcasting Corporation (BBC) World Service, Voice of America (VOA), Radio France Internationale (RFI), and Deutsche Welle (a German international program). People in Niger can also pick up Africa 1, a pan-African station based in Gabon and Paris.

There are two large newspapers published in Niger: the government-run daily *Le Sahel* and the weekly *Le Republicain*, both published in French, as well as several private newspapers. There are also over forty smaller privately published newspapers, most published sporadically in French or Hausa. There are two private television stations in Niger, as well as one state-run station and one satellite station. Since there is no electricity in many of the rural areas, television is found mostly in larger towns or cities.

Niger suffers from an undeveloped communications infrastructure, with few telephone or electrical lines reaching rural areas. Cell phone use has increased dramatically in recent years, and there are several Internet cafés and long-distance call centers in Niamey. As of 2014, an estimated 1.6 percent of the population, or about 281,000 people, used the Internet frequently.

SOCIAL DEVELOPMENT

Standard of Living

One of the world's most impoverished nations, Niger ranked last out of 187 countries on the 2014 United Nations Human Development Index, which measures quality of life and standard of living indicators.

Water Consumption

According to UNICEF, an estimated three-quarters of Niger's rural population, which accounts for 62 percent of the total population, lack access to clean and safe drinking water, while only an estimated 10 percent of Nigeriens have access to proper or adequate sanitation.

Education

Niger has a very low level of success in education compared with other countries in West Africa. The literacy rate among adults is only 19 percent, and few children attend school regularly. The capital, Niamey, has one of the lowest literacy rates in the world, and it is not uncommon for businesses to use only pictures to advertise their services and goods. Although education is compulsory for six years in Niger, most people receive only a year or two of formal schooling. Typically, rural people receive less education than urban people do.

There is also a great disparity in education between men and women. In 2015, it was estimated that around 27 percent of men could read and write, while less than 12 percent of women were literate. Attitudes in the country that prevent women from being educated include fears that schools will corrupt girls, and concerns that education will not prepare women for traditional domestic roles as wives and mothers.

Primary and secondary schools are supported and operated by the Ministry of National Education, and are free to all. There are a few institutions for higher education, such as the teacher-training college, the Islamic University of Niger at Say, and Abdou Moumouni University.

Women's Rights

Niger signed the Convention on the Elimination of All Forms of Discrimination against Women (CEDAW) in 2005, committing to work toward legal equality for women. The government also established the Ministry for Women's Promotion and Children's Protection, tasked with improving the lives of Nigerien women. However, Nigerien women continue to face several hardships and rights abuses, including limited access to education and healthcare, limited constitutional rights, and domestic violence. In many rural areas, religious and traditional law and customs also continue to trump written law, to the point that discrimination is indoctrinated for most women.

Access to education continues to be a significant challenge for girls in Niger in the early 21st century. It is estimated that nearly 40 percent of children in the country are enrolled in primary school, and only a third of those students are female. Furthermore, many of those enrolled withdraw from school prior to or during the secondary level because of domestic responsibilities, and those that continue to attend do so sporadically. At the secondary school level, enrollment for girls decreases to 6 percent, with attendance still sporadic. Consequently, an esti-

mated 90 percent of women in Niger are illiterate in the early 21st century.

This lack of education severely limits women's economic opportunities. In rural areas, women typically work in the agricultural sector, making only subsistence wages. Moreover, while women constitute approximately half of the formal workforce, less than one quarter hold well-paid civil service and professional jobs. Women also continue to be unrepresented in the political arena, and have limited access to healthcare, especially in rural areas. Numerous women continue to die each year from childbirth complications, and Niger continues to have the highest infant and child mortality rates in the world.

Although the Nigerien constitution states that rights extend to all citizens regardless of gender, customary law prevails for much of the population. Depending on the ethnicity, customary law may dictate that women cannot own land or have limited inheritance rights. In some groups, women need their husbands' consent to apply for a loan and may not be permitted to travel without the escort of a male relative. Husbands also continue to assume the election votes of their wives, which has further isolated Nigerien women from political interest.

Although the legal age for marriage is 15, child marriage is still relatively common in Niger. Among some ethnic groups, girls as young as 10 or 12 are entered into arranged marriages. The law says that both parties must consent to the marriage, but in reality, girls of such a young age do not have the power to decline arrangements made by their parents. Polygamy (the practice of multiple wives) is also common in Niger. According to recent estimates, about one-third of all Nigerien women live in polygamous marriages.

Some ethnic groups in Niger still practice female genital mutilation (FMG), despite the practice being prohibited by law. The government has undertaken public education campaigns to increase awareness of the dangers of this traditional practice, and studies show that the practice has decreased somewhat in recent years. According to a 2008 government survey, the rate of FGM decreased from 5.8 percent to 2 percent during a recent eight-year span (1998–2006). In April 2009, the United Nations Children's Fund (UNICEF) also reported that ten villages in western Niger publicly denounced the practice.

Domestic violence is widespread and often socially accepted. According to one statistic taken from a 2006 survey conducted in the rural Zinder region of eastern Niger, 70 percent of women considered domestic violence such as rape and beatings normal. Although this type of abuse is against the law, domestic violence is rarely reported to the authorities and even more rarely prosecuted due to societal attitudes. The reluctance to report domestic violence also stems from family pressure on the victim and the overall lack of awareness of legal rights. If a victim does report the crime of abuse or spousal rape, it is typically to the leaders of the family or ethnic group, and the dispute is handled according to customary law. The government has recently started working with NGOs to conduct information campaigns that increase women's awareness of their rights.

Health Care

Niger has a weak health care system, and public health and welfare are threatened by poverty, hunger, and a lack of adequate treatment facilities. Administered by the Ministry of Public Health, Niger's health care system provides primary health care such as vaccination services.

The country is in need of trained health care professionals, and has been aided by non-governmental organizations such as Doctors without Borders. Common diseases in Niger include tuberculosis, smallpox, malaria, measles, and leprosy. Vaccination efforts have been effective against sleeping sickness and meningitis.

Niger has a high fertility rate and a very high rate of maternal mortality, or death due to childbirth or pregnancy complications. Many women also die from botched abortion procedures. Disease and health problems related to malnutrition are also a problem.

HIV/AIDS is a growing problem in Niger, with an estimated 40,500 people infected in

2013. Sexual health education efforts are limited. Work is being done to increase awareness, especially among young people, about the dangers of sexually transmitted disease.

GOVERNMENT

Structure

Niger is a republic with three separate branches of government. The executive branch consists of a president and a prime minister. There is a unicameral legislature known as the National Assembly that has 113 members. The country is divided into eight administrative regions. Suffrage in Niger is universal at 18 years of age.

Niger gained independence from France on August 3, 1960. In 1974, the country's first president was overthrown in a military coup. The military government remained in power until 1990, when democratic reforms were enacted and a multi-party political system was put in place. These reforms accompanied a period of political leadership known as the Third Republic, which was overthrown in 1996.

Among the challenges Niger has faced are political corruption, staging fair elections, and preserving civil rights. The government has imprisoned opposition leaders and journalists and stifled the free press. In addition to these problems, the Tuareg and Toubou tribes have launched revolts against the government since the early 1990s.

Political Parties

The National Movement for the Development of Society, the Democratic and Social Convention, and the Nigerien Party for Democracy and Socialism are among Niger's major political parties. There are numerous smaller parties as well. As of the 2011 parliamentary elections, nine parties were represented in parliament.

Following the ousting of President Mamadou Tandja in a military coup in February 2010, 17 Nigerien political parties formed an alliance in July of that same year to prepare for the next presidential election, scheduled for January 2011.

In the end, those elections did little to shift the political balance in the country.

Local Government

Local governance in Niger consists of eight regions, overseen by an appointed governor, which are subdivided into 36 districts, or departments, and then further subdivided into 266 urban and rural local councils, or communes.

Judicial System

The major courts of the judicial branch are the Constitutional Court, the Supreme Court, the Court of Appeals, and the High Court of Justice.

Taxation

Taxes in Niger range from moderate to high, with 30 percent being the top corporate tax rate and 45 percent being the top personal income tax rate. Other levied taxes include an insurance tax, capital gains tax, and a value-added tax (VAT).

Armed Forces

The armed forces of Niger consist of several service branches, including an army, air force, and the Republican Guard. Selective conscription exists, and military service consists of a two-year obligatory service term. As part of the ECOWAS (Economic Community of West African States), Niger has supplied the majority of troops to the organization's military missions. The Nigerian armed forces have been the subject of criticism from human rights organizations, particularly concerning their campaign against Tuareg rebels from 2007–2009.

Foreign Policy

Niger gained independence from France in 1960 and has maintained a close relationship with its former colonial ruler. France remains Niger's largest bi-lateral aid donor and trade partner, and provides military training and equipment. Significant multi-lateral aid also comes from the European Union (EU). In fact, over 40 percent of the government's revenue comes from international aid. In addition to international aid agencies such as the International Monetary Fund (IMF), the World Bank, and the United Nations (UN), Niger receives direct aid from the United States, Japan, Germany, China, Morocco, and Saudi Arabia, among other nations.

Niger has maintained cordial foreign relations both regionally and internationally. It was a charter member of the African Union (AU) and belongs to the UN, the IMF, the World Bank, the Economic Community of West African States (ECOWAS), the Non-aligned Movement (NAM), and the Organization of the Islamic Conference (OIC). Nigerien troops participated in the international coalition in the Gulf War, and the country sent troops to aid UN peacekeeping forces in neighboring Côte D'Ivoire when a civil war broke out in 2002. Niger participates in many international cultural, educational, and economic development programs, including the U.S. Fulbright Scholar program and the Peace Corps program, and hosted the 2005 Francophone Games, an international competitive sports event for athletes from French-speaking countries.

Niger has had a few territorial disputes with neighbors, including Benin, which claimed domain over several islands in the Niger River. The UN settled the issue peacefully in 2005 and the islands were ceded to Benin. Libya claims a large area of territory in northern Niger as its own, but neither country has aggressively pursued its claim. Niger is also involved in ongoing negotiations for water rights on Lake Chad, a lake that once bordered Cameroon, Chad, Niger, and Nigeria, but has shrunk dramatically over the past forty years due to climatic changes. While each country is attempting to resolve the dispute peacefully, conflicts have erupted locally.

Human Rights Profile

International human rights law insists that states respect civil and political rights, and promote an individual's economic, social, and cultural rights. The United Nations Universal Declaration on Human Rights (UDHR) is recognized as the standard for international human rights. Its authors sought the counsel of the world's great thinkers, philosophers, and religious leaders, and were careful to create a document that reflects the core values shared by every world culture. (To read this document or view the articles relating to cultural human rights, visit http://www.udhr.org/UDHR/default.htm.)

Niger is a signatory to the UDHR and has a national human rights commission called the National Commission on Human Rights and Fundamental Freedoms. Nonetheless, the country continues to struggle with human rights abuses and maintains an overall poor human rights record internationally. Human rights abuses include police brutality and arbitrary arrest; discrimination and violence against women; poor prison conditions; limited freedom of speech and the press; lack of government transparency; and human trafficking.

Niger's constitution prohibits police brutality, but human rights groups report that there are still instances of the police using force against anti-government demonstrators, including extra-judicial killings (state-sanctioned killing of political or social figures). There have also been reports of disappearances in conflicted northern Niger, with domestic security forces suspected of involvement. In addition, while Niger's constitution also prohibits arbitrary arrest and indefinite detention, both continued to be violated. The executive branch wields influence over the judiciary branch, and defendants with political ties are commonly afforded special treatment. Niger also has a separate legal system for customary law (the laws imposed by ethnicities on its members). In addition to the country's civil courts, there are customary courts which are presided over by lawyers, but which hear decisions made by the leaders of local ethnic groups. Women do not have equal status in customary courts.

Niger's prison conditions are considered extremely poor. Prisons are overcrowded and lack proper sanitation and access to nutrition, leading to the rampant spread of disease among inmates. Prison officials are also known for being corrupt, and there are instances reported wherein prisoners can pay for release. In fact, according to a World Bank report, corruption is a "severe problem" in Niger, within all levels of government. While international observers have

reported that national elections in Niger have been generally free and fair, there have been some irregularities. Freedom of assembly is generally protected, but the government has denied assembly permits to groups in some instances. Unions are legal, but few actually exist.

While the constitution guarantees freedom of the press, the practice of self-censor among journalists is commonplace. The government also uses intimidation tactics to stifle dissent. For example, one private radio station was suspended in 2008 for suspicion of libel, though journalists claim this was to quell criticism. Journalists are also frequently arrested for publishing reports that the government claims threaten national security or promote instability. When conflict broke out in the northern part of the country in 2007, journalists were prohibited from traveling to the region, and subject to arbitrary arrest if they did so. International media are permitted in Niger, but have also been restricted from covering the northern conflict, and two French journalists were arrested for entering the area.

Human rights groups report that trafficking in humans is a problem in Niger, and not specifically addressed under law. According to a 2005 survey from a non-governmental organization (NGO), nearly percent of households surveyed lost a family member to human trafficking. Niger is also considered a transit country for human trafficking in West Africa. Forms of slavery reportedly exist, particularly in the northern desert areas, where some ethnic groups have a traditional caste system that keeps members of the lowest caste essentially in unpaid servitude to higher castes. Lastly, while child labor is against the law, it is still practiced.

ECONOMY

Overview of the Economy

Niger is a very poor country. Most people survive through subsistence farming and raising livestock. However, underdeveloped agricultural methods, desertification, and drought have made farming difficult. The most important natural resource is uranium, which brings in over 70 percent of Niger's export income. The country has also begun developing mines in order to exploit its gold reserves, and may eventually become an important oil-producing nation.

The government has attempted to attract private investors to develop its industrial sectors. The International Monetary Fund (IMF) has provided Niger with debt relief, and the country has also received aid from the United Nations Development Program. During the early 21st century, the economy began to grow, in part due to successful agricultural production. In 2014, the gross domestic product (GDP) of Niger was $8 billion (USD). The per capita GDP was $1,000 (USD).

Industry

Industry brings in around 17 percent of the country's GDP. Major industries include textile and soap manufacturing, cement manufacturing, and the beverage industry. Uranium mining has been a major source of income for Niger, although the market for uranium is declining. With foreign investment, the country is starting to develop its gold mines and to begin petroleum exploration.

Labor

According to the CIA World Factbook, the labor force in Niger was an estimated 5.8 million in 2014. Approximately 90 percent of the labor force works in the agricultural sector.

Energy/Power/Natural Resources

Niger is rich in mineral resources such as gold, coal, iron ore, and tin. The country may have potentially valuable oil resources, although these have not yet been developed.

Mining/Metals

Niger has one of the richest deposits of uranium in the world, which has formed the backbone of its industrial economy. Niger has also begun to exploit its gold resources, and has large deposits of phosphates, limestone, and gypsum.

Agriculture

Although agriculture makes up 37 percent of Niger's GDP, its success is dependent on weather conditions. During times of drought, the country is unable to feed adequately its population; food must be imported or donated in order to prevent problems like malnutrition and starvation.

Only 15 percent of the country's land is suitable for farming, and soil depletion can be a problem. The most important subsistence crops in Niger are millet, sorghum, and cassava. The country exports cowpeas, onions, garlic, and peppers. Gum arabic and sesame seeds are exports of lesser importance.

Animal Husbandry

Livestock is a major source of food and livelihood for many Nigeriens, and is one of the country's most important exports. Livestock production centers primarily on herd animals like camels, sheep, goats, and cattle. The animals are valued for their meat and hides.

Tourism

Violence in Niger has hampered tourist travel. A Tuareg rebellion has sparked violence in the north. There have also been terrorist attacks in the region, which have prompted travel warnings. Still, tourism brings in approximately $250 million annually. The sector supports around 36,000 jobs, or 3.5 percent of the nation's workforce, and is expected to grow.

Tourist attractions in Niger include the Sahara Desert, camel racing, and traveling down the Niger River by dugout canoe or pirogue. Tourists may also travel through the desert by camel with tour guides. The large Parc National du W game reserve features lions, elephants, baboons, and cheetahs.

Joanne O'Sullivan, Christina Healey

DO YOU KNOW?

- "Niger" is a Tamashek word meaning "river among rivers."

- Each year during the Islamic holiday of Tabaski, Tuareg camel racers follow a course that winds through the city streets of Agadez.

- The Croix d'Agadez, a cross made by Nigerien silversmiths, is thought to protect its wearer from "the evil eye."

- The National Museum in Niamey is home to the Arbre du Ténéré, a renowned acacia tree that grew in the Sahara desert in northwestern Niger. Considered the most isolated tree in the world, it was destroyed in 1973 by a truck driver and replaced by a metal sculpture.

- The nomadic Tuareg refer to themselves as Kel Tamasheq or Kel Tamajaq, meaning "Speakers of Tamasheq," a Berber language.

Bibliography

Cushman, Amanda, ed. "Zarma Folktales of Niger." Florence, MA: *Quale Press*, 2010.

Fuglestad, Finn. "A History of Niger, 1850–1960." New York: *Cambridge University Press*, 2008.

Idrissa, Abdourahame. "Historical Dictionary of Niger." Lanham, MD: *Scarecrow Press*, 2012.

Walraven, Klaas van. "The Yearning for Relief: A History of the Sawaba Movement in Niger." Leiden: *Brill*, 2013.

Scott M. Youngstedt. "Surviving with Dignity: Hausa Communities of Niamey, Niger." Lanham, MD: *Lexington Books*, 2013.

Works Cited

"Caravans Across the Desert: The Tuareg Tea Ceremony." Africa: One Continent, Many Worlds, The Natural History Museum of Los Angeles County. http://www.nhm.org.

"Country Insights: Niger." *Center for Intercultural Learning,* 14 June 2006. http.//www.intercultures.ca

"Country Profile: Niger." *BBC.* http://news.bbc.co.uk

"Country Brief: Niger." The World Bank. http://web.worldbank.org

"La Maison du Tourism de Niger." http://www.maisontourisme-niger.com

"Le Republicain." *http://www www.republicain-niger.com*

"Niger: African Economic Outlook." *Organization for Economic Cooperation and Development.* http://www.oecd.org

"Niger: Background Notes." United States Department of State Undersecretary For Political Affairs. *Bureau of African Affairs,* January 2009. http://www.state.gov.

"Niger: Country Specific Information." United States State Department http://travel.state.gov

"Niger." Department for International Development, The British Government http://www.dfid.gov.uk

"Niger." *Division of Democracy, Human Rights and Labor, United States Department of State.* http://www.state.gov.

"Niger." Foreign and Commonwealth Office of the Government of the UK. *http://www.fco.uk.gov*

"Niger." *UNESCO.* http://www.unesco.org

"Niger's Dandy Gerewol Festival." *London Times,* 4 July 2004.

"The Web Site of the U.S. Embassy." *Niamey.* http://niamey.usembassy.gov

"The Web Site of the Embassy of Niger." *Canada.* http://niger.visahq.com.embassy.ca

"The World Factbook: Niger." *Central Intelligence Agency.* http://www.cia.gov.

"UN World Court Decides Niger, Benin Dispute." *UN News Centre,* 13 July 2005. http://www.un.org.

Banham, Martin, Errol Hill, and George Woodyard, eds. "The Cambridge Guide to African and Caribbean Theater." Cambridge: *Cambridge University Press,* 1994.

Bardeen, Sara. "Etran Finatawa and the Music of Niger." *National Public Radio,* 21 June 2006http://www.npr.org.

Coles, Catherine and Beverly Blow Mack. "Hausa Women in the Twentieth Century." Madison: *University of Wisconsin Press,* 1991

Gikandi, Simon, ed. "Encyclopedia of African Literature." London: *Routledge,* 2002

Johnson, Scott. "The Least Green Country on Earth." *Newsweek,* 14 July 2008. http://www.newsweek.com.

Osnes, Mary Beth and Sam Gill. *Acting: An International Encyclopedia.* Oxford: *ABC-Clio,* 2002.

Parris, Ronald. *Hausa* (Heritage Library of African Peoples, West Africa). New York: *Rosen,* 1996.

Rubin, Don and Ousmane Diakhaté. "World Encyclopedia of Contemporary Theatre: Africa, vol. 3." London: *Routledge,* 2000.

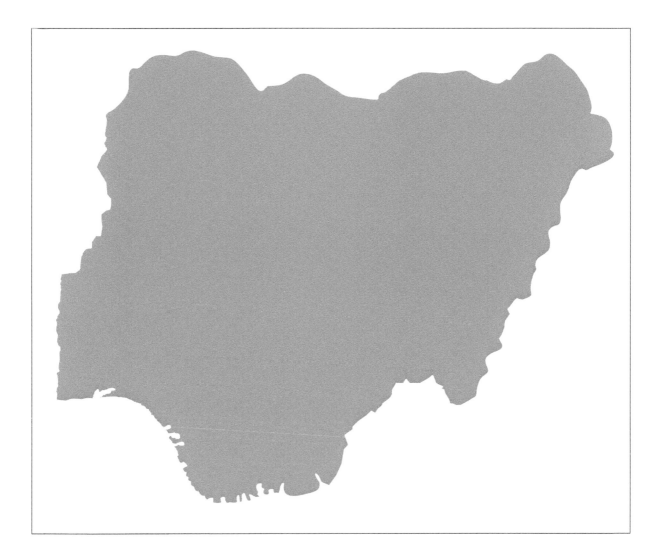

NIGERIA

Introduction

Nigeria's official name is the Federal Republic of Nigeria. It is situated in Western Africa, south of Niger, between Benin and Cameroon. It is the most populous country in Africa and includes more than 250 distinct ethnic tribal groups. The infant mortality rate in Nigeria is very high, with approximately 72 deaths for every 1000 births (2015 estimate). Average life expectancy is about 53 years—54 for men and 54 for women (2014). The country has experienced periods of relative stability interrupted by periods of conflict and violence.

Nigeria boasts a rich literary heritage. It is rooted in the oral traditions on which many Nigerians still rely, as well as historic influence from neighboring cultures. Nigeria's geographic position has led to cultural influence from both the Middle East and North Africa, as well as from Europe. Notable Nigerian author Chinua Achebe (1930–2013) received international acclaim for his beautiful prose and often challenging themes. Among African authors, he was the most widely read throughout the world. His famous novel, *Things Fall Apart* (1958), is one of the most widely read books in African literature.

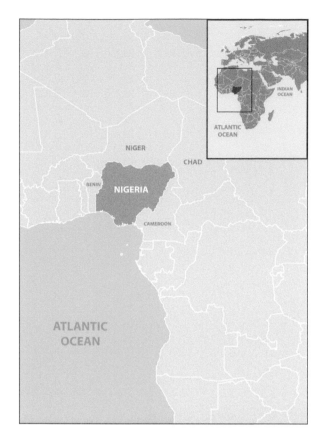

GENERAL INFORMATION

Official Language: English
Population: 181,562,056 (2015 estimate)
Currency: Naira

Coins: There are currently three coins in circulation, issued in February of 2007: the 50-kobo coin, and 1 and 2 naira.
Land Area: 910,768 square kilometers (351,649 square miles)
Water Area: 13,000 square kilometers (5,019 square miles)
National Motto: "Peace and Unity, Strength and Progress"
National Anthem: "Arise, O Compatriots, Nigeria's Call Obey"
Capital: Abuja
Time Zone: GMT +1
Flag Description: The flag of Nigeria is a tricolor design with three vertical and equal bands of green, white and then green. The two green stripes are said to represent the fertility of the land and agriculture, while white represents unity and peace. The flag was officially adopted in 1960.

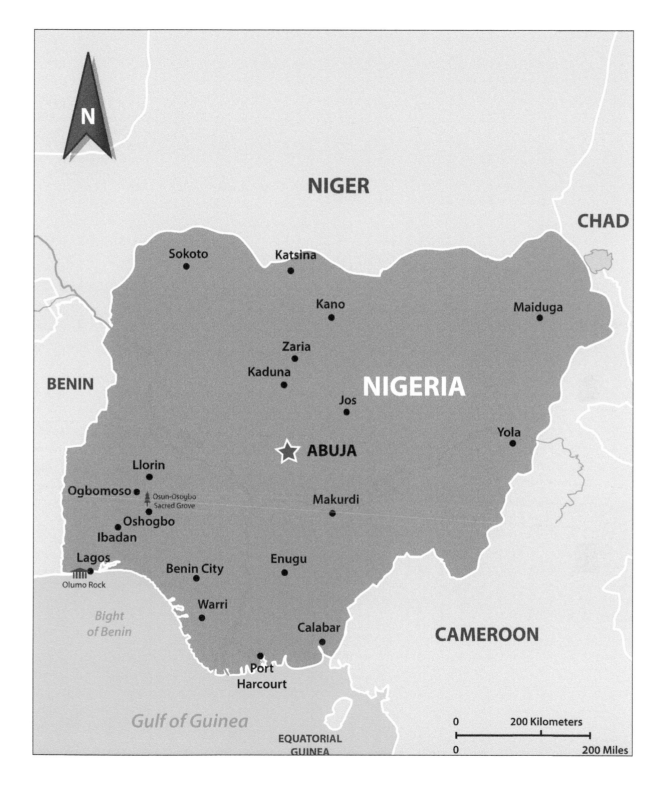

Principal Cities by Population (2012):

- Lagos (10,400,000)
- Ibadan (5,500,000)
- Benin (2,600,000)
- Kano (2,400,000)
- Port Harcourt (2,300,000)
- Kaduna (2,200,000)
- Aba (1,700,000)
- Abuja (1,600,000)
- Maiduguri (1,200,000)
- Ilorin (1,200,000)

Population

Nigeria is one of the world's most populated countries and has struggled for decades to provide an accurate account of its populace. In fact, a national controversy follows every official census, with the most recent occurring in 2006, the results of which remain controversial due to boycotts, protests, and allegations of inflated population numbers (and which resulted in 15 deaths). Before that, the last census was conducted in 1991. More than one-half of the latest census was also funded by foreign donors, most prominently the European Union.

According to the embattled 2006 census, half of Nigeria's population rests in the country's northern states, which are primarily Muslim. The most populous state is Kano, home to 9.4 million people; the state of Lagos is second with nine million, and is home to the city of Lagos, Nigeria's most populous city and, as of 2008, the fastest growing city in Africa. As of 2010, the state of Lagos may very well be the most populated state now in Nigeria due to the population growth in the city of Lagos. Overall, an estimated 30 percent of the population lives in urban areas.

The 2015 United Nations population estimate for Nigeria is 181,562,065. That same year, the country had an estimated growth rate of 2.45 percent. The country's HIV and AIDS epidemic continues to have a detrimental effect on the population; as of 2010, nearly 3.17 percent of the population is living with either AIDS or HIV, with approximately 174,300 people dying from

AIDS in 2014, up from an estimated 170,000 AIDS-related deaths in 2007, but down since 2009.

Languages

English is the official language of Nigeria. More than 250 distinct ethnic groups may be found in Nigeria, each distinguished by language. Recognized regional languages include Hausa, Igbo, and Yoruba.

Native People & Ethnic Groups

There are more than 250 distinct ethnic groups living in Nigeria, distinguished by language. The largest are the Hausa and Fulani (29 percent of the population), the Yoruba (21 percent), and the Igbo (or Ibo) at 18 percent.

The Yoruba and the Ibo, however, are not really one unified "tribe," but rather a collection of smaller units that share a common language. The 5 million Ibo are comprised of over 200 distinct groups, each with its own village system. The six million Yoruba are clustered into more than 50 distinct "kingdoms." Both Ibo and Yoruba are subsets of the language called Kwa, a subset within the Niger-Congo language family.

The Hausa are one of the rare African tribes that have a long written history, due to their having adopted an alphabet based on Arabic. They are divided between those who are Muslim and those who are pagan. Today, most Hausa are Muslim, as Islam has been a part of their culture since the middle of the 14th century. Their neighbors the Fulani are also primarily Muslim. Because they migrate with their cattle, they have been a strong force in the spread of Islam through West Africa.

Smaller ethnic groups include the Ijaw (10 percent), the Kanuri (four percent), and the Tiv (2.5 percent).

After World War I, the Tiv were isolated from the changes happening in the rest of Nigeria. The Dutch Reformed Church of South Africa established a mission in Tivland in 1911. American fundamentalist missionaries replaced the Dutch in the 1950s, as a result, many Tiv today identify as Christian, and only a few are devout Muslim.

The Tiv rioted in 1960 and 1964 on National (or Independence) Day, in order to assert their own independence and integrity as a people.

Religions

Despite Nigeria's ethnic diversity, only 10 percent of the population adheres to the region's indigenous religions. Half of the population now identifies as Muslim, and 40 percent is Christian.

Climate

Vast rolling plains and occasional gallery forests (formed along rivers) that receive between 100 and 115 centimeters (40 and 45 inches) of rainfall per year characterize the northern savanna. The southern savanna receives more rainfall and is therefore more densely forested.

In the southwestern part of the country, near Cameroon, rainfall totals approach 200 centimeters (80 inches) per year, and this increased level of moisture makes for denser forests and even swampland during the rainy season.

The rainy season throughout Nigeria begins and ends with dramatic thunderstorms. The rainy season begins in March in the south, and in May farther to the north. The dry season in the north lasts four months longer than in the south, making for dramatic climatic differences in Nigeria based on latitude. The climate is classified as arid in the north, tropical in the central region, and equatorial in the south.

ENVIRONMENT & GEOGRAPHY

Topography

Hausaland in northern Nigeria is a vast, rolling savanna, between 300 and 600 meters (1,000 and 2,000 feet) above sea level. Occasional outcroppings of rock and forests along rivers punctuate this landscape, which is bordered on the north by dry and hot semi-desert.

The Ibo live between the southern savannah and a low, flat region that becomes a 96-kilometer (60-mile) wide mangrove swamp during the wet season. This area collects an average of 195 centimeters (77 inches) of rain per year, most

of which falls between May and October. The Yoruba live on a vast, rocky plain in the western part of the country that yields to dense tropical forests to the south.

The Niger River from the west and Benue River from the east merge in the middle of the country and then flow southward to the ocean. The highest point in Nigeria is the crest of Mount Chappal Waddi, at 2,419 meters (7,935 feet), and the lowest point is at sea level along the South Atlantic coast.

Plants & Animals

Tropical hardwood trees found in the southern forests include iroko, mahogany, and obeche. Common animals include antelope, buffaloes, crocodiles, hyenas, hippopotamuses, leopards, lions, monkeys, and many different species of migrating birds.

One of the most dangerous animals in Nigeria is a tiny insect known as the tsetse fly. These carry a disease known as sleeping sickness, and spread animal African trypanosomiasis in cattle.

CUSTOMS & COURTESIES

Greetings

Nigeria, like its West African neighbors, has developed strict regulations that guide daily interactions. Nigerians typically greet each other formally. Thus, they use professional or honorific titles, or reference a person's social status. A greeting also customarily involves a smile. This initial introduction is then followed up with inquiries about family well-being and home life. If this social formality is overlooked, it is usually considered a sign of disrespect or rudeness. The young, in particular, must always remember to avert their eyes, bow, or curtsy, and use only last names and titles of respect when greeting elders. As a cultural rule, the left hand is never offered to another.

Because of Nigeria's vast cultural diversity, many tribes have developed their own takes on greetings. The Yoruba, for example, will often applaud a new visitor after he has given his introduction. The Nupe people are required to crouch to the ground, in the case of men, or to bow on one knee, in the case of women. When meeting up with old friends, the Nupe extend their arms fully and touch each other's fingertips.

Gestures & Etiquette

Nigerians have developed an intricate system of accepted gestures and etiquette over centuries of many cultural influences. In general, they share many of the same customs as their West African neighbors. For example, Nigerians never offer their left hand in public arenas. A common Muslim practice, this is because the left hand is associated with the cleansing of the body, and is considered impure. Thus, it is unacceptable to use the left hand for eating, accepting gifts, greeting, and gesturing.

Nigerians also prize face-to-face interaction. Nigerians typically stand close to someone when conversing, as it is seen as the best way with which to gauge the character of the person with whom they are interacting. Thus, most Nigerian businesspeople are reluctant to conduct business over the phone or computer. This also goes hand in hand with the Nigerian policy of being direct in speech and actions; to Nigerians, not being direct in one's actions is said to breed corruption.

Eating/Meals

Generally, the cultural divisions among urban and rural Nigerians can best be observed in two distinctive parts of life: eating and architecture. In terms of meals, most rural Nigerians eat porridge or another stewed starch in the morning. They may also east leftover dinner from the night before. During the day, rural Nigerians snack on nuts or fruit and then eat their largest meal in the early evening. They eat early enough to afford themselves ample time to digest before sleeping.

Urban Nigerians, however, have adopted more Western customs when eating. They typically eat three meals per day, with breakfast consisting generally of cereal or a sandwich. Lunch is usually eaten outside of the home, since most Nigerians in urban areas are in school or working. Often, these workers wait for their wives to

being them lunch or purchase a meal prepared by bukas, or small food stands. Women who run the bukas prepare traditional Nigerian dishes early in the morning and bring them to serve at lunchtime at stands equipped with picnic table seating. Dinner is the largest meal for urban Nigerians.

Many urban middle and upper-middle families eat in Western-style kitchens seated around a table with plated meals. However, the vast majority of Nigerians eat on mats sitting on the floor around a communal dish of food. Nigerians who eat in this fashion also typically refrain from using utensils; the food is eaten with the right hand only. Regardless of socioeconomic or geographical differences, it is customary to allow all elders and men to eat or be served first.

Visiting

Visiting in Nigeria is generally unplanned, so a family must always be prepared and expect that a guest will show up. Being prepared means always having enough food and drink on hand. When a guest arrives, it is customary that they remove their shoes and are shown to the room reserved for hosting. At this point, guests are traditionally offered a beverage by the women of the house. Once greetings are over the reason for the visit is announced. It is also customary to bring a small gift, including gifts for the children of the household.

More often than not, visitors come to visit their family members or to talk about a family issue or other pressing matters. Other reasons for visits include celebrations, rites of passage and holidays. However, one of the most common reasons for visiting another Nigerian home is to watch the national football (soccer) team play on television (football is the national sport). Nearly as sacred as religion, these games inspire intense devotion.

LIFESTYLE

Family

The role of family, just like many aspects of Nigerian culture, is undergoing considerable change. Traditional Nigerians identify with family on three levels: common lineage (ancestors), clan (living relatives) and community (or tribe). These are the three main facets of family life. Ties to the community date back to the first known West African societies, and has inspired such mantras as "the village raises the child," in which all community members are responsible for one another. The clan is comprised of many generations. Often, these generations live under the same roof (houses in rural areas are typically built to accommodate many people). Within most families, women are responsible for household duties and nearly exclusively responsible for child rearing.

Despite their traditional role, women command a great deal of respect in most Nigerian households. They often supplement family income with craftwork and cooking, traveling great distances to sell their goods. As women age, they are perceived as crucial advisors. This is because they have carried one of life's most important roles: motherhood. Despite this respect, women still struggle to fill roles outside of traditional ones. This is mainly due to the practice of girls being removed from school first if families are low on money. Furthermore, once women are married, which is typically young, they often leave school.

In the early 21st century, more youth are opting to leave village life, leading to the deterioration of the extended family cycle (young caring for the old). More Nigerian youth are also choosing their own spouses, a break from the tradition of arranged marriages, and choosing to live as a nuclear family unit (parents and their children). Despite this change, there is still a strong tie to village life, and many urban Nigerians send money and goods home to support their villages.

Housing

Nigerian housing reflects both cultural and socioeconomic diversity. Rural housing typically consists of groupings of single-room compounds, built to accommodate extended families. Depending on the region of the country, these compounds share distinct physical attributes. For example, most compounds in the northern region and those of the Yoruba in the southern region are single rectangular units joined in a larger rectangular around an open courtyard. In Nigeria's central regions, homes are cylindrical in shape and have conical roofs made of palms fronds or thatch. In both cases, the primary building material is mud or concrete.

Urban Nigeria has been subjected to much more international architectural influence. As a result, many family homes in large cities closely resemble those of Western countries. These homes are specifically designed for a nuclear family and are often two-story buildings with bedrooms upstairs and a kitchen, living room and bathroom downstairs. However, most urban Nigerians live in overcrowded dwellings or shantytowns (informal settlements) because of increasing city populations and a lack of adequate housing.

Food

Nigerian cuisine is similar to the cuisine of West Africa and involves the traditional combination of a prepared starch and a sauce, stew or soup. The most commonly consumed starches are rice, yam, cassava, and maize. Rice is generally steamed and served with very spicy dishes, while yam and cassava may be pounded and dried, then later boiled or steamed. When cassava is pounded and formed into dumplings, it is known as fufu. Sauces or soups are made daily from fresh ingredients including pumpkin and melon seeds, goat, beef and seafood, and vegetables and spices. Spices are considered essential, as many Nigerians believe spicy food promotes good health.

As with most countries, the cuisine varies by region. In the north, for example, Nigerians consume meats such as cattle and sheep. In the southern regions, seafood is commonly served. Additionally, Nigerians, like most West Africans, waste no part of the animal. Often, animal byproducts such as fish heads and internal organs are incorporated into meals. The most common snacks include dundu (yams fried in palm oil), kulikuli (baked nuts), grilled corn, chinchin (a wheat pastry), and suya (grilled meat skewers). It should be noted that the skewers are the only food traditionally deemed appropriate for men to cook.

Life's Milestones

Nigerians commemorate four main milestones: birth, transition into adulthood, marriage, and death. Each is traditionally seen as the step to another phase of existence, one that should be celebrated if reached at an appropriate age. The celebration of birth resembles most West African rituals and generally involves family gatherings at the home of one of the new grandparents. Family members must come to the gathering with one name in mind to suggest for the child. Generally, the parents decide the name, but everyone must suggest one as a confirmation of the life of the newborn.

The next celebration is the transition from childhood into adulthood. Nigerians mark this passage with a celebration that traditionally involves the entire village. However, these celebrations are often strictly gender-based. Young women are cleaned ceremoniously and paraded through the village, while young men are often required to perform physically demanding acts while the villagers watch.

As marriage is seen as the joining of two families, extensive family research is done on behalf of both sides leading up to the match. Disease, fertility of previous relatives, and wealth are all deciding factors when families choose mates for their children. Once the spouses have been selected, gifts of wealth are given to the bride's family. The fattening of the bride then commences so that she gains weight before the wedding, which, according to Nigerian society, also increases her beauty. Nigerian weddings often last a few days (eight days for Muslim ceremonies), and involve religious worship, feasts and gift giving.

Pregnancy in Nigeria is one of the most sacred rites of passage. Therefore, pregnant women are treated with great respect. However, discussing details of the pregnancy with the expectant mother is considered bad luck.

Nigerians celebrate death as a function of the person's life. For example, an individual who has lived through all other rites of passage is the most revered member of society. As a result, his or her funeral ceremony must be large to reflect a full life. (The deaths of children or victims of crime are often not commemorated much as they are considered unnatural.) After death, the body is cleaned ceremoniously and carefully to avoid contamination. Individuals are then buried with goods they loved in life to accompany them to the afterlife.

CULTURAL HISTORY

Art

The earliest Nigerian art form was sculpture, whether in wood, clay, stone or metal. The first examples of prolific, stylized sculpture in Africa occurred among an otherwise unknown African people living in northern Nigeria near the present-day village of Nok. It was there that fragments and larger sections of terracotta and clay sculptures were unearthed. Though there is little known about the Nok people, carbon dating has placed their culture in the Iron Age, which began in West Africa as early as 1200 BCE. Nok sculptures generally depict portrait heads, busts, and full body images of individuals. A unique aspect of these sculptures is that a majority seem to portray a different individual.

The subjects are both men and women, all sharing common traits of triangular, wide-set eyes and smooth, large foreheads. Women generally wear jewelry and skirts but no tops. Figures sometimes stand but are most often shown in a sitting position resting their chin on their knees. Occasionally the Nok sculptors created images of individuals displaying both animal and human features—such as an elephant man or a man with a tail. Some social scientists attribute this to disease and deformity, and believe that the Nok had a keen sense of its effects on the human body. That the sculptures still maintain their detailed designs even after aging is a testament to the refined skill of the artists.

Many social scientists have studied the similarities that exist between the sculpture of the Nok people and the modern woodcarvings of the Yoruba people of southern Nigeria. This is most likely due to the migration and assimilation of the Nok into the Benin Empire (1440–1897), a pre-colonial state. The use of wood by the Yoruba is attributed to the low cost and malleability of wood. The influence of Nok sculpture extends not only to the carvings of the Yoruba and terra cotta sculpture, but also to elaborate bronze and wood sculpture and to ivory carving within the Benin Empire. These intricately designed brass sculptures feature detailed and ornate etchings and generally portray individuals in similar positions to Nok figurines. These sculptures were created using the lost-wax casting method—in which brass is cast in a disposable wax mold—common in West Africa during the 15th and 16th centuries. Art during the Benin Empire also included masks and paintings, and was mostly ceremonial or commemorative in nature.

Architecture

Nigeria's rural architecture is relatively uniform, distinguished only by the shapes of buildings. In the northern and southern regions, most buildings are composed of mud bricks and are rectangular, and may have hardened mud or tin roofs. In the country's central region, cylindrical-shaped buildings are popular, and feature a conical roof formed from thatch. In urban Nigeria, the term "twin cities" has emerged as a term to describe most major centers of commerce. This is because these cities have distinctive historic and modern sections, the former characterized by high-rise structures and modern styles, and the latter consisting of traditional and colonial architecture.

Religious architecture, such as the styles found in mosques and churches, ranges from simple, one-room structures to elaborately decorated multi-room buildings and monuments. Generally, the most expensive materials were used in building religious structures in rural areas. It was thought that using such materials would help gain favor with God.

Music & Dance

Music plays an integral role in traditional Nigerian life. It is said that there are songs for every occasion, whether to celebrate hunting or a certain rite of passage. For example, agrarian workers developed a repertoire of chants and a cappella work songs to get them through the day. Royals, in particular, are each accorded their own unique musical sound that must never be played in honor of another.

Much of Nigeria's popular music since the 1920s developed because of a direct influence of foreign or neighboring cultures. The musical style of highlife is a prime example of this. Originally, a Ghanaian invention, this style of music—developed by E.T. Mensah (1919–1996)—fuses traditional Ghanaian sounds with calypso, waltz, and other European styles. Highlife was first brought to Nigeria when the Sugar Babies, a Ghanaian group, toured through West Africa. The music style grew exponentially in the 1940s after a performance by Mensah. By the 1950s, Nigerian bands were creating their own highlife sound.

Around this same time, another style of music was gaining popularity. Ju ju, unlike highlife, was developed solely by Nigerians, derived from a combination of European percussion instruments paired with traditional Yoruba drums. The lyrics were also firmly rooted in Yoruba tradition and moral code, often measuring the character of Nigeria's tumultuous political system by the acts of its ancestors. I.K Dairo (1930–1996) was the country's most prominent ju artist.

Other popular music styles that followed included Afrobeat, which combined dance music and the popular big band sound with traditional Nigerian rhythms and beats. Fela Kuti (1938–1997), who also fused messages of racial and political activism into his music, popularized this style of music. Christian music has also established a significant presence among Nigerians. Initially a peaceful style of reflective music when it was first brought by missionaries, modern Nigerian church music is now typically accompanied by hand clapping, loud singing and passionate dancing.

Literature

In terms of published and award-winning authors, gender equality, and translated works, Nigeria boasts a rich literary heritage. It is rooted in the oral traditions on which many Nigerians still rely, as well as historic influence from neighboring cultures. Nigeria's geographic position has led to cultural influence from both the Middle East and North Africa in the north, as well as from Europe along the southern coast. In the north, the influence of Islam in literature and writing is still prevalent. Many authors continue to write in Arabic and Ajami (a mix of indigenous Hausa and Arabic). Most of Nigeria's most popular authors write in English, however. Nigeria also boasts the highest number of formalized tribal languages that have standardized structures for writing and reading. An increasing number of authors are writing in these languages.

Notable Nigerian authors include Chinua Achebe (1930–2013) and Wole Soyinka (1934–), both of whom have risen to international acclaim for their beautiful prose and often challenging themes. Achebe, among African authors, is by far the most widely read throughout the world. His famous novel, *Things Fall Apart* (1958), is one of the most widely read books in African literature. Challenging the common sentiment of that period that considered traditional Nigerian culture unsophisticated, his Nigerian characters bring to light the complexity of maintaining tradition in the face of modernity. In 1986, Soyinka became the first African author to win the Nobel Prize in Literature.

CULTURE

Arts & Entertainment

Unlike many other African nations, Nigeria has made a rather quick leap to expressing itself through the contemporary arts. Though many artists still rely on traditional practices and styles to influence their work, exploring Nigerian identity through art has never solely relied on a resistance to formal training, but rather a desire to attain it.

This is largely due to Aina Onabulu (1882–1963), considered the "father of modern art" in Nigeria.

Despite the fact that he was not a skilled painter, Onabulu was the first Nigerian to travel abroad to learn formal European technique. Upon completing his training in London, he returned to Nigeria and became a teacher, inspiring Nigeria's next generation of painters. He simultaneously spurred the adoption of formal art training at many public and private schools. Following Onabulu's rise to fame was the painter and cartoonist Akinola Lasekan (1916–1974). Lasekan also chose to pursue formal training in London and used his skills to create political cartoons for local newspapers when he returned. His cartoons gained notoriety for their humorous take on British culture and colonial practices. He also figured prominently in Nigeria's independence movement.

Nigeria now boasts many public and private schools offering rigorous artistic training. Though sculpture was once the medium of choice, it has since been surpassed by painting. Contemporary artists in Nigeria demonstrate a mastery of both traditional methods and European styles such as abstract art, often combining the two to form groundbreaking pieces. Main themes of Nigerian artwork include tradition vs. modernity, Nigerian culture in a global context, social issues such as corruption and poverty, and religion, specifically Christianity, Islam, and animism.

Dubbed "Nollywood" by Nigerian film professionals, the film industry in Nigeria, which rakes in $250 million (USD) annually, is believed to be the third largest film industry in the world after the United States and India. The industry's growth is often attributed to the establishment of the Nigerian Film Corporation in 1979 (though some fault the corporation for power outages, lack of funding and restricted permits). As of 2006, the industry was producing anywhere from 400 to 800 films annually, with the average Nigerian film costing $15,000 (USD) to produce. This is in large part due to the straightforward nature of plots. Subject matter rarely strays from romance, action, and adventure, with comedy being the most popular genre. According to one

Nigerian filmmaker, films are generally treated as "home videos" rather than cinematic events, mostly to express both the personal subject matter and the Nigerian-based stories.

Cultural Sites & Landmarks

Nigeria has some of Africa's oldest and largest cultural sites. The northern town of Kano is one of the oldest cities in West Africa and still operates as a major metropolis. Established 1,400 years ago by Berbers and Nigerians trading along the trans-Saharan route, the city experienced great prosperity as the only link with southern Nigeria. Of note are the city's indigo pits dug into the ground, used as large tubs in which cloth is dyed indigo for the Tuareg peoples of the desert. Kano is also one of the few northern cities under the law of Sharia, or Muslim law.

Farther south are the Jos Plateau and the Osun-Osogbo Sacred Grove. Jos Plateau is considered one of the first regions in Nigeria to have been inhabited by a complex human society. Products of this society include the Nok terracotta sculptures and artifacts from the Benin Empire. The Osun-Osogbo Sacred Grove, in Yoruba territory, is a sacred forest that contains shrines and statues dedicated to Yoruba gods. The groves of the forests themselves are said to have been specifically allocated to worshipping the goddess Osun. Most statues today are in disrepair, but the grounds are said to hold spiritual power. The sacred forest was declared a World Heritage Site by the United Nations Educational, Scientific, and Cultural Organization (UNESCO).

Nigeria is home to one other World Heritage Site, the Sukur Cultural Landscape. The landscape contains extensive remains of the region's iron industry, including terraced fields, an ancient palace, and a village. Other cultural sites of importance include Sungbo's Erebo; a system of walls erected around 950 CE that is considered to be the largest manufacturer structure dating from Africa's pre-colonial period. Olumo Rock is an enormous granite chunk thought to contain magical powers in earlier times that contains many shrines and statues to Yoruba gods.

Libraries & Museums

The National Library Act of 1964 established Nigeria's national library, which is now located in Abuja. The national library has twenty-two state branches. To promote readership and to market the national library's modern facilities, the institution held "viewing" parties during the 2010 World Cup, a promotion that attracted a sizeable youth contingent. As with many African nations, the computerization of libraries, both at the public and university level, continues to be a challenge.

The national museum of Nigeria is the Nigerian National Museum, founded in 1957 and located in Lagos. The museum has a sizeable collection of Nigerian art and ethnographic and archeological collections, including artifacts from the Nok culture. A series of other national museums at the state level, operated by the National Commission for Museums and Monuments, are located throughout the country. Other cultural institutions include the National Gallery of Modern Art, in Lagos.

Participants in the Argungun fishing festival compete to wrestle fish from the river.

Holidays

Nigeria established its independence from the United Kingdom on October 1, 1960. Consequently, each October 1 is celebrated as National Day, or Independence Day.

In February and March, the Argungu International Fishing Festival is held near Sokotu, with thousands of anglers competing to wrestle the fish from the river. This tradition began in the 1930s and has grown to include other events such as canoe races and diving competitions.

Many communities celebrate harvest festivals, which in the south are centered on the harvesting of yams. Tribes in the southern delta region of Nigeria hold special festivals to celebrate regional water spirits, culminating in the appearance of the deity itself (actually a masked dancer).

Youth Culture

The youth culture in Nigeria is one of deeply ingrained respect for elders and family duty. According to most Nigerian adults, life can only continue when the young care for their elders. However, since the influx of Western culture and educational systems, the concept of caring for extended family is diminishing among Nigerian youth. This has resulted from increased education, even in rural areas, leading primarily young men to leave villages for jobs or university in the major cities. Once they have obtained work and an income of their own, they are capable of creating an adult life free of dependence on and influence from their families. Furthermore, as legal institutions become more involved in legal proceedings, families are rarely able to arbitrate on behalf of their children.

Children growing up in lower middle and lower classes generally have little means and rely on sports, invented games, and discarded neighborhood goods for recreation. A frequent creation is a metal wheel, fashioned from scrap metal, that children takes turns hitting so that it continuously rolls down the street. Children are often seen playing soccer with half-deflated balls or even cans or other kickable objects. Nigerian teens live similarly to those in Western nations

in that they spend most of their free time socializing. Gang activity is on the rise as the result of the illegal drug trade, and unemployment leaves many urban males without income.

SOCIETY

Transportation

Two popular modes of transportation in Nigeria are minibuses and okadas (motorcycle taxis). Minibuses are often older European buses, many of which feature fused parts and wooden planks serving as floorboards. These buses typically run local routes decided by the driver. In order to be sure of the route, passengers must ask where the bus is headed. The other option for inner-city travel is to hitch a ride on the back of a motorcycle or scooter. These motorcycle taxis are generally inexpensive but dangerous.

For longer distances, mini and larger buses make regular trips between most villages. Depending on the popularity of the destination, it may take anywhere from an hour to an entire day to find enough people to fill a bus. Rail travel, operated by the Nigerian Railway Corporation, is another option. Traffic moves on the right-hand side of the road.

Transportation Infrastructure

Heading into the 21st century, Nigeria's transportation infrastructure was assessed as inadequate and posed a challenge to the country's economic needs. In 2008, a series of bills—the Railway Bill, the National Inland Waterways Bill, the Ports and Harbour Reform Bill, and the National Roads Fund Bill, among others—were approved by the recently formed National Council on Privatisation (NCP) to help address the situation.

As of 2009, Nigeria's road network spanned about 190,000 kilometers (118,060 miles) and was responsible for between 90–95 percent of both freight and passenger traffic. Most of the roads in Nigeria are largely unpaved, with a large majority haven fallen into disrepair due to lack of maintenance. A three-year plan to address the deteriorating road infrastructure in Nigeria was announced in 2008. Nigeria's rail network is government owned and only accounts for a small percentage of freight and passenger traffic, though the government is committed to investing in the rail infrastructure from 2009–11.

Nigeria has about 21 airports, and the country's air cargo has increased exponentially between 2001 and 2007. The country's primary ports are located at Lagos, Onne, Calabar, Port Harcourt, Warri, and Sapele. The country maintains about 8,600 kilometers (5,343 miles) of inland waterways, most of which are underused.

Media & Communications

Nigeria introduced one of the first newspapers in West Africa in 1859. A Christian missionary publication, it focused on religious conversion as well as news reporting, and was published in the Yoruba dialect. During this time, European colonists also started a national radio program to propagate a positive European image while "culturalizing" the native population. It wasn't until the turn of the 20th century, and the advent of independence, that Nigerians began to control their own media.

After Nigeria achieved independence, however, freedom of press dwindled with successive military governments. These governments established state-run radio stations and newspapers, while private press suffered from strong political sentiment and bias. As of 2009, the largest broadcasting companies, the Federal Radio Corporation of Nigeria (FRCN) and the Nigerian Television Authority (NTA), were both run by the government. There are numerous daily newspapers, many of which are published in English.

Nigeria still boasts one of the largest news systems in Africa. However, while the law protects freedom of speech, harassment and violence still occurs. According to Reporters Sans Frontières (Reporters Without Borders, or RWB), an advocacy group monitoring the rights of the worldwide press world-wide, the harassment of Nigerian journalists who criticize the government has persisted in the form of imprisonment, torture and even murder.

In terms of communication, much of Nigeria's telecommunications infrastructure is inadequate, but improving. As of 2009, there were nearly 24 million Internet users, representing just over 15 percent of the total population. The country, in fact, has the largest number of Internet users on the African continent. Aside from work computers, cyber cafes remain the most popular Internet access point for Nigerians.

SOCIAL DEVELOPMENT

Standard of Living

In 2014, Nigeria ranked 152nd of 187 countries on the United Nations Human Development Index, which measures quality of life and standard of living indicators. Between 1990 and 2002, just over 70 percent of the population earned less than $1 (USD) per day, and 91 percent earned less than $2 (USD) per day. During this time, one-third of Nigeria's population lived below the national poverty line.

Water Consumption

With a network of rivers and streams and substantial groundwater resources, Nigeria boasts extensive water resources; however, much of the country's water supply has been characterized as "unreliable." A large portion of those resources—an estimated 70 percent at the turn of the 21st century—went to the agricultural sector. According to a recent 2015 report, just over 68 percent of the population has access to a piped water supply, while only 30 percent had access to adequate sanitation services. The Federal Ministry of Water Resources (FMWR) is the national body in charge of water management.

Education

Government expenditure on education in Nigeria is minimal, with less than one percent of the gross domestic product (GDP) being spent on education in 1990. Many Yoruba artisans and farmers are still illiterate or semi-literate, learning only enough to get by in their occupations. Wealthy Yoruba are highly educated and form a small but elite group, most of which reside in Ibadan.

In 2003, the illiteracy rate among those 15 years and older was 67 percent. This was hardly an improvement over 1990, when 49 percent were illiterate. For children under 15, approximately 74 percent were illiterate in 1990, increasing to 89 percent in 2002. As of 2015, more than half the population remains illiterate.

Women's Rights
The role of women in Nigeria remains for the most part within the confines of tradition. While some laws have been introduced to protect women, these are typically not consistently enforced and are gender-biased, particularly in areas where Sharia (traditional Muslim law) is prominent. A clear example is the punishment for adultery: if a man is found to be adulterous, his wife may choose to divorce him. However, when a woman is found to be adulterous, the husband is immediately granted a divorce and she may even be sentenced to death. Another example involves the unequal pay distribution to men and women performing the same job function.

In recent years, the situation for women has become even more dangerous with the rise of the Islamic extremist group Boko Haram. In 2014, the group, opposed to Western education especially for women, kidnapped 270 girls from a boarding school in the northeast of the country. Further kidnappings followed and, today, hundreds of girls and women are estimated to be held against their will.

Spousal abuse is also rampant among Nigerians, with 65 percent of women and 61 percent of men approving of it as an appropriate means of punishment. Nigerian law even allows a husband to hit or even beat his wife so long as his violence does not lead to any "grievous harm." However, despite even this minor protection, women rarely come forward for fear of divorce or other social stigmas. In addition, the trafficking of women, particularly for prostitution, occurs frequently.

Despite these realities, there are signs of progress. Nigerian women gained the right to vote and to run for political office in Nigeria in 1958. By 2001, nearly women held 23 percent of the government's ministerial positions. In 2004, women held more than six percent of the seats in the House of Representatives, and were nearly three percent of those in the Senate.

GOVERNMENT

Structure
The Federal Republic of Nigeria is comprised of 36 states and one territory. The 36 states that make up the republic include Abia, Adamawa, Akwa Ibom, Bauchi, Bayelsa, Benue, Borno, Cross River, Ebonyi, Edo, Ekiti, Enugu, Gombe, Imo, Jigawa, Kaduna, Kano, Katsina, Kebbi, Kogi, Kwara, Lagos, Nassarawa, Niger, Ogun, Ondo, Osun, Oyo, Sokoto, Taraba, Yobe, and Zamfara.

Nigeria's government is divided into three branches: executive, legislative, and judicial. The president is the head of the government and the chief of state, and is elected by popular vote and may not serve more than two four-year terms. The president's council of advisors is known as the Federal Executive Council.

The legislative branch is a bicameral National Assembly consisting of a Senate and a House of Representatives. There are 107 seats in the Senate and 346 in the House of Representatives, and all National Assembly members are elected by popular vote and serve four-year terms.

The president appoints Supreme Court justices in the judicial branch. The government, along with the Advisory Judicial Committee, appoints Federal Court of Appeals judges.

Political Parties
Major political parties in Nigeria include the All Nigeria People's Party (ANPP), the All Progressives Grand Alliance (APGA), the Alliance for Democracy (AD), the National Democratic Party (NDP), the People's Democratic Party

(PDP), the People's Redemption Party (PRP), the People's Salvation Party (PSP), and the United Nigeria People's Party (UNPP).

Since 2007, the PDP was the dominant party in both the House of Representatives and the Senate, with 223 and 76 seats, respectively, followed by the ANPP (96 and 27 seats, respectively) and the AD (34 and six seats, respectively). New elections have been postponed several times at the behest of the ruling party, citing the continuing threat of Boko Haram.

Local Government

Local governance in Nigeria consists of 36 states, each of which has enacted its own legislation, and the Abuja Federal Capital Territory, subdivided into six area councils. The 36 states are subdivided into 768 local government authorities. Local government's primary functions include education, regional roads and transport, trash collection, public health, and town planning, as well as facilities management (such as cemeteries) and sports and leisure.

Judicial System

The judiciary arm of government governs Nigeria's legal system, based on English common law. The Supreme Court is the highest court, followed by the Court of Appeal, and then the High Courts, which are trial courts with general jurisdiction. The lower-level courts include the Magistrates' and District Courts, under which are Area Courts and Customary Courts (which apply the laws of a specific ethnic group). There are also Sharia courts in Nigeria.

Taxation

Taxes are levied at a moderate rate in Nigeria. The corporate rate is 30 percent, while the highest income tax rate is 25 percent. Other taxes levied include a value-added tax (VAT), interest tax, and a capital gains tax.

Armed Forces

The Nigerian Armed Forces consists of an Army, Navy, and Air Force. To date, the Nigerian Army

has participated in 38 international peacekeeping operations.

Foreign Policy

Following independence, Nigeria's national politics have been plagued by turmoil and violence, most of which is rooted in tribal disputes and the distribution of vast oil revenues. According to many Nigerians, it was unnatural for a nation to be formed by combining the land of three regionalized ethnicities: the Hausa-Fulani, Igbo and Yoruba peoples (comprising northern, southeastern, and southwestern Nigeria, respectively). In fact, a series of coups and military governments has characterized 28 of the nearly fifty years of Nigerian rule. Nigeria has thus been associated with both tumultuous government and excessive corruption.

Nonetheless, because of its vast population and potential for economic growth, Nigeria is still perceived as a beacon of hope and potential leadership in the region, despite its tumultuous past and poor human rights record. Institutions such as the International Monetary Fund (IMF) and the World Bank have donated significant aid to fuel Nigeria's role as regional leader. (However, following Nigeria's failure to uphold loan agreements from a 2000 loan from the IMF, the organization dropped nearly all development programs and loans and developed stricter regulations for repayment.) Slowly, Nigerian politicians are showing more devotion to economic reform. This has included bettering the banking system, which is rife with corruption, and working to mediate ethnic disputes over the distribution of oil revenue.

As politics stabilize in the country, Nigeria is slowly emerging to fulfill its role as a peacekeeping and economic leader in the region. In particular, during the civil wars in both Liberia and Sierra Leone throughout the 1990s, Nigeria mediated much of the conflict through the Economic Community of West African States Monitoring Group (ECOMOG). This group of West African nations is charged with monitoring peace in the region. As of 2008,

Nigeria has nearly 6,000 Liberian refugees living inside its borders. Nigeria also holds membership in the Economic Community of West African States (ECOWAS), the Organization of Petroleum Exporting Countries (OPEC), and the Organization of African Unity (OAU). Internationally, Nigeria holds membership in the UN, the Non-Alignment Movement (NAM), and the Commonwealth of Nations, which is made up of former British colonies. It is also considered a regional leader in the fight against terrorism, as it continues to fight Islamic State–allied Boko Haram.

Human Rights Profile

International human rights law insists that states respect civil and political rights, and promote an individual's economic, social, and cultural rights. The United Nations Universal Declaration on Human Rights (UDHR) is recognized as the standard for international human rights. Its authors sought the counsel of the world's great thinkers, philosophers, and religious leaders, and were careful to create a document that reflects the core values shared by every world culture. (To read this document or view the articles relating to cultural human rights, visit http://www.udhr.org/UDHR/default.htm.)

The human rights situation in Nigeria is improving slowly but still in a precarious state. Amnesty International (AI) has characterized the human rights condition in Nigeria as a "crisis," and corruption and religious and ethnic violence remain rampant. However, compared to many neighboring nations, Nigeria is progressing.

The Nigerian government still maintains a firm hold on national press and radio, and the government owns nearly all radio stations. The Nigerian constitution protects every Nigerian's right to freedom of speech and assembly. However, demonstrations at universities have been broken up violently and with arrests. Furthermore, while no murders have been recorded in recent years, some journalists reported violent abuse from military and police. Many journalists practice self-censorship to avoid harsh punishment from the government.

Religious and ethnic freedoms are also protected in the national constitution. The constitution also declares it illegal for state and local governments to adopt official religion. Despite this, many citizens of northern Nigeria claim that states in the region have adopted Shari'a, or Islamic law, as a legal mandate, driven in large part by the well-armed and well-funded Boko Haram. Though these claims are disputed, the constitution does allow for states and local governments to use Shari'a in court. Those same laws state that non-Muslims should not be held to those standards. However, there have been claims that all court cases were tried under Shari'a even resulting in sentences of stoning to death for rape and adultery.

ECONOMY

Overview of the Economy

In 2014, the per capita gross domestic product (GDP) was estimated at $6,000 (USD), and the overall GDP was $573.7 billion (USD). Agriculture comprised about 20 percent of the GDP, while industry and services were about 25 and 53 percent respectively. Revenues in 2014 totaled $22.77 billion (USD) and expenditures were $34.62 billion (USD). Public debt was 11.7 percent of the GDP. Industrial production grew by just under five percent, but inflation was 8.1 percent.

Industry

Industrial jobs employ 10 percent of Nigeria's work force. Nigeria is an oil-rich nation, and oil production accounts for 20 percent of the GDP, 65 percent of annual budgetary revenues, and 95 percent of export earnings. Other industries include agriculture, animal hide production, mining, printing, steel production, and shipbuilding. Manufactured goods include cement, ceramics, chemicals and fertilizers, textiles and footwear.

Labor

According to the CIA World Factbook, Nigeria's labor force was an estimated 54.97 million in

2014. An estimated 70 percent of the labor force was employed in the agricultural sector, with 20 percent employed in the services sector and 10 percent in industry (though these figures date back to the turn of the 21st century). The unemployment rate was estimated at a whopping 23.4 percent in 2011.

Energy/Power/Natural Resources

Nigeria's most important natural resource is petroleum. Although prices have fluctuated since the 1990s, the country is one of the world's top oil producers, with large reserves both offshore and in the Niger Delta.

There are also large deposits of iron ore, tin, and columbite (used in steel manufacturing) throughout Nigeria. Other mined resources include coal, lead, limestone, and zinc.

Another important resource is arable land, most of which is found in the southern part of the country. Nigerian farmers cultivate more than one-third of this land.

Like many countries, Nigeria faces several environmental challenges, including oil pollution (in the air and water), soil degradation, and desertification.

Fishing

It is estimated that half of the demand for fish in Nigeria is met domestically. As with agriculture, the industry is mostly concentrated at the subsistence level, commercial fishing contributes very little to Nigeria's GDP, and fishing represents just 4 percent of the country's agricultural output. Offshore fishing continues to be dominated by foreign interests. Illegal fishing also remains a concern; in 2010, it was estimated that approximately 20,000 jobs were lost due to illegal fishing. Primary cultivated freshwater fish include tilapias, catfish, and carp.

Forestry

Overall, the forest reserves of Nigeria consist of swamp forests, tropical rainforests, and regrowth, or secondary, forests. The majority of Nigeria's protected forests are found in the country's southern half. The most common usage of Nigeria's forests is as domestic wood fuel for heating and cooking. Sawmills are the largest industrial sector involved in the forestry industry. Deforestation remains a concern, and sustainable forest management has become a government focus in the early 21st century.

Mining/Metals

The mining sector accounts for only about 1 percent of Nigeria's GDP. Nigeria mines coal and columbite, among other industrial minerals. To exploit the country's mineral reserves, which includes tin, uranium, lead, bitumen, zinc, and gold, foreign investment is needed. The country also has significant reserves of iron ore. In 2008, the Nigerian government set out a new policy to revitalize the mining sector, focusing on seven strategic minerals, including coal, gold, iron ore, lead, zinc, and bitumen.

Agriculture

Most of Nigeria's agriculture is subsistence-level, meaning that farmers grow food for their own consumption. More than half of the labor force is engaged in this occupation. Commercial farming remains limited. Important crops grown in Nigeria include cassava (manioc), cocoa, corn, cotton, millet, palm oil, peanuts, rice, rubber, sorghum, and yams. Guinea corn is grown in the northern Savanna regions, and cassava and kola nuts thrive in the rainier south. The Ibo are primarily yam farmers. They also grow cassava, and fruits such as oranges, mangoes, and bananas.

Nigeria once exported a substantial amount of agricultural products, but due to rapid population growth, the country must now import food. Timber and fish are natural resources that also contribute to Nigeria's agricultural economy.

Animal Husbandry

Many Nigerian farmers keep livestock, such as cattle, goats, sheep, chicken (raised mostly for subsistence rather than their eggs), and pigs. The majority of the cattle population—about 90 percent—is concentrated in the northern half of the country. Of the 40 percent that agriculture contributes to the GDP, livestock makes up about 10 percent.

Tourism

The Nigerian government launched its National Tourism Policy in 1990, to encourage tourism and encourage economic development. Nonetheless, the tourism sector remains largely underdeveloped. According to the World Travel and Tourism Council, the tourism sector contributes only five percent to the Nigerian GDP, and represents fewer than five percent of the country's total employment.

In addition to more than 800 kilometers (497 miles) of beaches, Nigeria also boasts eight national parks and many wildlife and game reserves, and other protected natural areas. The most popular of these is the Yankari Game Reserve, in Bauchi. The government hopes that these resources will attract eco-tourism to the country.

Kristen Pappas, Todd C. White

DO YOU KNOW?

- The Afikpo Ibo believe that bad luck is contagious, whereas good luck is attributed to fate.
- Cultural anthropologists report that the Yoruba people of Nigeria worship more than 400 deities.
- Portuguese traders were the first Europeans to encounter Nigerian tribes in the 15th century.

Bibliography

Achebe, Chinua. *The Trouble with Nigeria.* Fourth Dimension Publishing Co., 2000.

Achebe, Chinua. *Things Fall Apart.* W.W. Norton, 2008.

Adunbe, Omolade. *Oil, Wealth, and Insurgency in Nigeria.* Indiana University Press, 2015.

Akpan, Uwem. *Say You're One of Them.* Little, Brown and Company, 2008.

Bascom, William. *The Yoruba of Southwestern Nigeria.* Waveland Press, 1984.

Falola, Toyin. *Culture and Customs of Nigeria.* Greenwood Press, 2000.

Falola, Toyin and Heaton, Matthew. *A History of Nigeria.* Cambridge University Press, 2008.

Jordan Smith, Daniel. *A Culture of Corruption: Everyday Deception and Popular Discontent in Nigeria.* Princeton University Press, 2008.

Larkin, Brian. Signal and Noise: *Media, Infrastructure, and Urban Culture in Nigeria.* Duke University Press, 2008.

Ngozi Adichie, Chimamanda. *Half of a Yellow Sun.* Anchor, 2007.

Smith, Daniel Jordan. *A Culture of Corruption: Everyday Deception and Popular Discontent in Nigeria.* Princeton University Press, 2008.

Works Cited

"African Metal Working." *Pitt Rivers Museum Online.* http://www.prm.ox.ac.uk/pdf/metalworking_web.pdf

"Akinola Lasekan." *Nigeria Wiki.* http://nigerianwiki.com/wiki/Akinola_Lasekan

"Area boys." *Wikipedia*.org, http://en.wikipedia.org/wiki/Area_Boys

"Benin Empire." *Wikipedia Online Encyclopedia.* http://en.wikipedia.org/wiki/Benin_Empire

"Chinua Achebe: Things Fall Apart Study Guide." *Washington State University.* http://wsu.edu/~brians/anglophone/achebe.html

"Corporate Nigeria: The Business Trade and Investment Guide 2009." *Corporate Guides International Ltd.* http://www.corporate-nigeria.net/index.html

"Country Profile: Nigeria." *BBC Online.* http://news.bbc.co.uk/2/hi/africa/country_profiles/1064557.stm

"Inside Nigeria's Growing Film Industry: NPR's Interview with Jamie Meltzer and Nigerian film director Izu Ojukwu." *National Public Radio Online.* http://www.npr.org/templates/story/story.php?storyId=95695102

"Nigeria." *CIA World Factbook Online.* https://www.cia.gov/library/publications/the-world-factbook/geos/ni.html

"Nigeria: Country Reports on Human Rights Practices." *U.S. Department of State.* http://www.state.gov/g/drl/rls/hrrpt/2005/61586.htm

"Nigeria Human Rights." *Amnesty International.* http://www.amnestyusa.org/all-countries/nigeria/page.do?id=1011212

"Nigeria: Largest cities and towns and statistics of their population." *World Gazeteer Online.* http://world-gazetteer.com/wg.php?x=1230864178&men=gcis&lng=en&des=wg&geo=-1&srt=npan&col=abcdefghinoq&msz=1500&geo=-158

"Nok Information." *University of Iowa: Art & Life in Africa Website.* http://www.uiowa.edu/~africart/toc/people/Nok.html

"Nok Terracottas (500 B.C.–200 A.D.)." The Metropolitan Museum of Art: *Heilbrunn Timeline of Art History.* http://www.metmuseum.org/TOAH/HD/nok/hd_nok.htm

"Onabulu, Aina 1882–1963." *Smithsonian Institution Libraries: Monographs on African Artists.* http://www.sil.si.edu/SILPublications/ModernAfricanArt/monographs_detail.cfm?artist=Onabulu,%20Aina,%201882-1963

"Yoruba Art and Culture." *Hearst Museum Online.* http://hearstmuseum.berkeley.edu/outreach/pdfs/yoruba_teaching_kit.pdf

Peppercorns are an important agricultural export. iStock/mtcurado.

SÃO TOMÉ & PRÍNCIPE

Introduction

São Tomé and Príncipe, officially known as the Democratic Republic of São Tomé and Príncipe, is an island nation located off the Western coast of the African continent, specifically off the coast of Gabon and along the equator. It consists of two main islands, the larger São Tomé and the smaller Príncipe, as well as several very small rocky islands. A Portuguese-speaking nation, it was settled by Portugal in the 15th century, and achieved independence in 1975. The culture of São Tomé and Príncipe has been influenced by a blend of African and Portuguese heritage. Inhabitants of São Tomé and Príncipe are known as Santomeans (or Sao Tomeans).

GENERAL INFORMATION

Official Language: Portuguese
Population: 194,006 (2015 estimate)
Currency: Dobra
Coins: The São Tomé and Príncipe dobra is divided into 100 cêntimos. Coins are circulated in denominations of 50 cêntimos, and 1, 2, 5, 10 and 20 dobras. Larger denominations of 100, 250, 500, 1000 and 2000 dobras were introduced in 1997.
Land Area: 964 square kilometers (372 square miles)
National Motto: "Unidade, Disciplina, Trabalho" (Portuguese, "Unity, Discipline, Work")
National Anthem: "Independência Total" ("Total Independence")
Capital: São Tomé
Time Zone: GMT +0

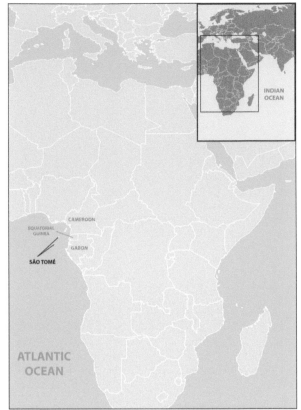

Flag Description: The flag of the Democratic Republic of São Tomé and Príncipe consists of a horizontal triband (green-yellow-green) design with a scarlet isosceles triangle based on the hoist (left) side. The central yellow band is one and a half times wider than the other two green bands. In the center stripe are two five-pointed black stars, which represent the two islands. Symbolically, the color red stands for the country's struggle for freedom and independence. The other colors—black, yellow, and green—are Pan-African colors.

Population

The country is made up of two islands. São Tomé holds the majority of the population and the nation's capital, while Príncipe, the smaller island, supports approximately 6,000 people. As of 2015, the country's urban population accounts for approximately 65 percent of the total population. Major changes in population took place in the 1970s, when 4,000 Portuguese left the islands

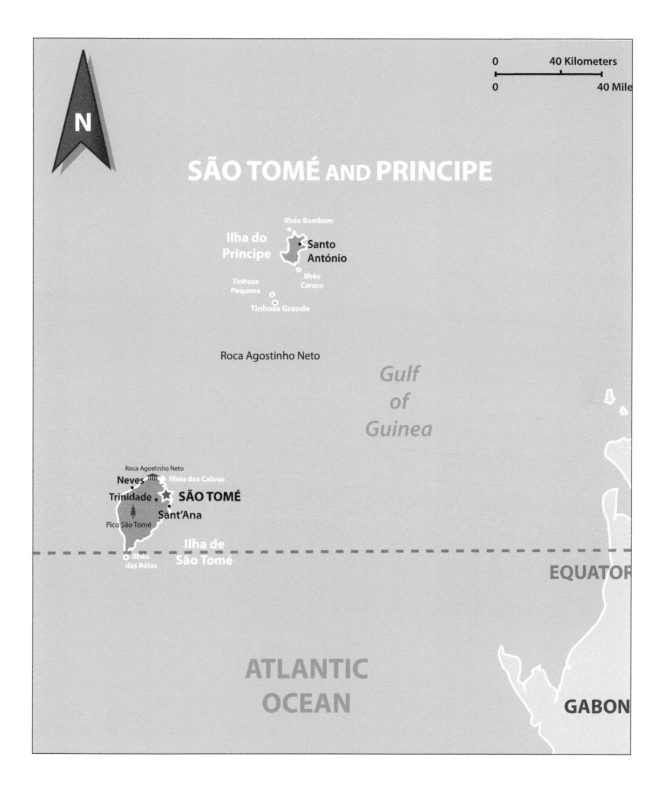

to return to Europe, and several hundred refugees from Angola arrived. Population-wise, São Tomé and Príncipe is the second smallest African country.

Languages

Although Portuguese is the official language, a number of other languages are spoken, including several Portuguese-based creoles. These include Forro, spoken primarily on São Tomé Island; Angolar (or Ngola), a language with Bantu influence spoken mainly in São Tomé's southernmost towns; and Principense (or Lung'iye), spoken by residents of Príncipe Island (and nearly extinct).

Native People & Ethnic Groups

The population of São Tomé and Príncipe is composed of six main ethnic groups. Mestiços (mixed blood) and forros (freed men) make up the majority of the population. The ancestors of the mestiços (also called filhos da terra, or sons of the land) were slaves from West Africa and European settlers. Forros are the descendants of freed slaves and are of African descent. A third ethnic group, the Angolares, descends from survivors of a slave shipwreck in 1540. These slaves from Angola settled in southern São Tomé and maintained a separate community until the 1800s, when they moved to other parts of the country. Many Angolares are fishers.

Other ethnicities include a small European minority, mostly from Portugal and of Portuguese descent, as well as modern immigrants, mostly from Cape Verde. There are also immigrant populations from Angola and Mozambique. Some of these immigrants work temporarily in São Tomé and are known as servicais (contract laborers). Their children are known as tongas.

These immigrants share a common culture and language with Santomeans and some have assimilated into Santomean society, especially Cape Verdeans.

Religions

The majority of Santomeans are Christian: 56 percent are Catholic and 9 percent belong to Evangelical, New Apostolic, and Adventist sects. A sizeable minority—about 20 percent—claims not to follow a religion, while an estimated 3 percent of the population adheres to non-Christian faiths such as Islam.

Climate

São Tomé and Príncipe is located near the equator and maintains a hot and humid climate year round. However, there are constant changes in the weather, since the country consists of two tropical islands, and it is common for it to be both sunny and hot, and later rainy and overcast in a single day. The rainy season takes place from October to May, when the average monthly rainfall reaches a maximum of 150 millimeters (5.9 inches). Meanwhile, the period from June to September has less rain and more sun, when average monthly rainfall decreases to a minimum of zero precipitation in July and August. The highest average temperature is 30° Celsius (86° Fahrenheit) in January and February, while the lowest average temperature is 21° Celsius (69.8° Fahrenheit) from July to September. The average annual temperature is 20° Celsius (68° Fahrenheit). Nevertheless, there are only four to six hours of sunshine a day.

ENVIRONMENT & GEOGRAPHY

Topography

São Tomé and Príncipe is the smallest country in Africa, and is located on two small volcanic islands (though the volcanoes are no longer active). The former volcano chain extends from Equatorial Guinea to Cameroon. The highest peak on the two islands is Pico de São Tomé (São Tomé Peak), which measures 2,024 meters (6,640 feet) tall. This mountain is located on São Tomé, which has higher altitudes than Príncipe. The lowest altitude is at sea level. Both islands have several large streams that run from the mountains to the ocean, which are used for irrigation. While permanent crops account for a little more than 50 percent of the land, only 9 percent of the remaining land is arable, due to poor land management and soil erosion. The two islands have a total of 209 kilometers (130 miles) of coastline.

Plants & Animals

About 90 percent of the country is covered by humid forests, including Atlantic rainforest called the Ôbo. It is in the forest where the majority of 800 plant species are found. Some of the flora is native to the islands, including several species of orchids and the giant begonia, a three meter (9.8 foot) tall flowering fern plant. To be exact, 95 species are native to São Tomé and 37species are native to Príncipe, with only sixteen native plant species in common. The Ôbo National Park, which consists of areas on both islands, was established to preserve the natural heritage of the country. The park comprises a third of the country's surface area.

The islands are also an important bird habitat and have 28 native or endemic species. This includes the rare São Tomé grosbeak and the lesser grey shrike. There are only a few native mammals, including the São Tomé shrew and two types of bats. A number of species are critically endangered due to small populations and hunting, including the dwarf olive ibis bird, the São Tomé grosbeak bird, and the São Tomé fiscal bird. The aforementioned species of shrew and bats are considered to be endangered due to habitat destruction and small populations. The islands are also important to five distinct species of sea turtles.

CUSTOMS & COURTESIES

Greetings & Etiquette

Common greeting expressions include "Seja lovadu" ("Hello"), "Bom dja ô" ("Good morning"), and "Que nomi bo e?" ("What's your name?"). Handshakes are the norm when greeting. Other typical social courtesies, such as removing one's shoes before entering a home, are also common. Because of the island country's strong and historic connection to Portugal, many Portuguese customs and courtesies are also commonplace. Generally, the Santomeans have a friendly and courteous air about them.

Visiting

Santomeans are a diverse people known for their friendliness and hospitality, which they extend to each other as well as to those visiting their country. The culture is known to be tourist-friendly, so those visiting the islands may be greeted warmly by the question "Tudo bem?" which means, "How are you?" or "Are you well?" One can respond, "Tudo bom," which means, "I'm well," or "leve-leve," which translates to "slowly, slowly."

Food

The cuisine of São Tomé and Príncipe largely consists of fresh seafood, tropical fruits (such as avocados, pineapples, and bananas) and root crops, and local livestock such as chicken. A majority of their culinary traditions are rooted in the island nation's Portuguese and West African influence, including the baking of breads and cakes, the use of spicy marinades and sauces as well as stewed dishes, and consumption of meat-stuffed rolls, usually filled with sausage or salami (from Portugal). The use of wine and tomato to flavor dishes is also common, deriving from the island's Portuguese heritage. Overall, meat dishes are not generally common, and fish is predominantly eaten.

Housing

Most domiciles on the islands are wooden structures that are raised on stilts. Those who live on plantations live in barrack-style structures and homes known as "sanzalas." Many large homes of former plantation owners can also be found on the islands.

An example of the style of housing typical on a plantation in São Tome.

CULTURAL HISTORY

Art

José Sobal de Almada Negreiros (1893–1970) was born in São Tomé and is one of the country's most renowned artists, though he spent most of his life in Europe. He was a poet and author as well as a painter, and worked with cubism and futurism, creating portraits and scenes of day-to-day life. He also made murals, designed scenery for theater productions, practiced printmaking, and created book illustrations. The contemporary art scene in São Tomé and Príncipe is relatively new, with a number of painters depicting rural scenes and everyday life on the islands. Other artists have explored more abstract-style paintings. Sculpture, using wood and stone, has also become a popular medium with artists. Beginning in 2000, the country has played host to the Bienal Internacional de Arte e Cultura (International Art & Cultural Biannual), an event held every other year celebrating local and international artists. The event includes exhibitions, theater performances, and art workshops.

Architecture

São Tomé and Príncipe's Portuguese influence is strongly reflected in its architecture, much of which dates back to the country's colonial period. Picturesque examples of the island nation's Portuguese heritage are largely located in the capital, and include the Presidential Palace, the 16th-century white-washed Santa Sé Cathedral—it is considered sub-Saharan Africa's oldest cathedral—and the São Sebastião fortress, an excellent example of Portuguese fortress architecture. Other examples of the Portuguese architecture include the various plantations and estates. A predominant style of the island nation's early architecture is the baroque style, a blend of the religious and secular that emphasized ornamentation, vivid or bright color, and contrast lighting.

Drama

The country has a long tradition of public theater. The tchiloli is a play that was brought to São Tomé in the 1500s by the Portuguese, introduced in Portugal by minstrels in the 11th century. The play integrates the Portuguese script with African music, dance, and pantomime. The play, which is performed during holidays throughout the year, is called *A tragédia do marquês de Mântua e do Imperador Carlos Magno* (The Tragedy of the Marquis of Mantua and the Emperor Charlemagne). The four-hour drama tells the story of a murder, which leads to King Charlemagne condemning his own son to death for the crime. The play is normally performed by an all-male troupe of approximately 30 people. Each actor plays his role for life and then passes the role on to his children. Performers have added local cultural twists and modern takes on the script, like integrating current affairs into the dialogue and using cell phones and watches as props. Príncipe also has its own drama tradition. The *Auto de Floripes* play is performed each year on August 10, the feast of Saint Lawrence. It is also a blend of Portuguese folklore and African culture, and centers on a battle between the Christians and the Moors in medieval Iberia.

Dance

A group of students from Sao Tome and Portugal founded Sao Tome FestFilm, an international film festival in 2014. The festival aims to promote interest in the history and culture of Sao Tome and Principe.

Dance

Santomean culture is best known for its music and dance, a blend of Portuguese and West African influences. Dances such as ússua and socopé are native to São Tomé, and mutual assistance groups come together to perform the dances using traditional costumes. Several drums and an accordion accompany Ússua, which resembles the waltz and was influenced by traditional Portuguese ballroom dancing. A conductor, called the mestre-sala, directs the dancers. The women wear long skirts, robes, and head wraps, while the men wear straw hats, black pants, and white jackets.

Socopé, which is less common, also comes from Portuguese dancing. It means "with only one foot" (só com um pé), and is an offshoot of ússua that emerged in São Tomé in the early 20th century. This dance is very patriotic, and dancers often carry the country's flag when performing it. The musicians use different types of drums and a bamboo flute, while the dancers are divided into various roles, including a leader and a group of singers. The women usually wear colorful skirts and scarves, and the men wear uniforms or informal suits. The danço congo is another dance tradition in São Tomé. Its main characters are from European theater, like the fool and the devil, but the performance uses African dance, song, and mime rather than words. The story describes the enslavement of a king from the Congo who is sent to São Tomé to toil on a plantation.

Angolan immigrants introduced the puita. This type of music, named after the main drum used, involves a variety of drums and percussion instruments. Traditionally, the dance was performed all night to honor a person's death, with lyrics written in the local creole language. It is popular throughout the islands, especially in the capital. The bulauê is a similar type of music popular among lower class Forros. Developed after the nation's independence, the songs are sung in Forro and are performed in cultural groups.

Literature

São Tomé has produced several notable writers. Alda do Espírito Santo (1926–2010) was one of the most acclaimed Portuguese-language African poets. She not only gained fame as a female writer but also as a government minister, serving as minister of education and culture as well as minister of information. Her most famous work is "É nosso o solo sagrada da terra" ("The sacred earth is ours"), written in 1978. Albertino Bragança (1944–) was also a politician and is famous for his novels, the most famous being *Rosa do Riboque.*

CULTURE

Cultural Sites & Landmarks

São Tomé and Príncipe is home to several important historical and ecological sites. São Tomé and Príncipe's history is inextricably linked to the sugar trade, and a number of historic plantations have been maintained. These include the Roça de Monteforte, Roça de Bombaim, and Roça de São João plantations, as well as Agostinho Neto, the largest in the country, and the Monte Café plantation, which used to be the largest coffee plantation on the islands. Here, visitors learn the history of São Tomé and about coffee production. Visitors can also explore the small historic towns of Santo Antonio, on Príncipe Island, and Porto Alegre, a fishing town on São Tomé. The Illhue das Rolas is a small island off the southern coast of São Tomé, through which the equator passes. The island has a monument marking the point where the equator crosses the land.

The majority of the country's points of interest are natural wonders. Hikers can climb Pico de São Tomé, over 2000 meters (6561 feet) above sea level, to see the views of the forest and the top of the extinct volcano. Jalé Beach, on the south edge of São Tomé, is home to a sustainable development and environmental protection project with the French Fund for World Environment (FFEM) and the protected areas network of Central Africa. Other natural points of interest include the Cascata São Nicolau, a waterfall in the mountains, and Boca de Inferno (Hell's Mouth), and a natural phenomenon where ocean waves shoot through a cave opening in the rocks.

Libraries & Museums

The National Museum (Museu Nacional), in operation since 1975, is housed in the São Sebastião Fort, built by the Portuguese in 1575. It contains colonial relics, old photographs, religious art, and information about slavery and plantation life. One of the museum's unique items is a box containing the skeletal remains of one of the country's cacao plantation owners. There is also a room dedicated to the island nation's marine turtle population.

SOCIETY

Transportation

There are two airports in the country. The main airport is located in São Tomé, and there is a ferry service between the two main islands. There are no railroads. Cars, taxis, and motorcycles are common modes of transportation. However, driving can be dangerous in rural areas since the roads are unlit at night and the unpaved roads can be difficult to navigate without four-wheel drive. Minibuses (large vans) and taxis are the only public transportation. Traffic moves on the right-hand side of the road.

Transportation Infrastructure

Overall, road infrastructure is limited and in poor condition; there is an estimated 320 kilometers (198 miles) of roadways, of which about 66 percent are paved. Creation of a deep-water port was begun in 2011. There are no railways in São Tomé and Príncipe.

Media & Communications

Though private companies are constitutionally allowed to run media outlets, the government runs the majority of the press, including newspapers, radio stations, and television stations.

There are four major newspapers: three are from the private sector and the fourth is run by the government. The most widely read are *Jornal de São Tomé*, *Tela Non*, and *Vitrina*. All of the television and radio stations are run by the government. There are only two domestic TV stations.

In 2014, there were 6,800 landline phones and 128,500 cell phone lines. As of June 2014, approximately 24 percent of the population were Internet users.

SOCIAL DEVELOPMENT

Standard of Living

The country ranked 142nd out of 187 countries listed on the United Nations Human Development Index (HDI), which ranks quality of life indicators. The country's infant mortality rate is 38 per 1,000 births. As of 2013, the country's projected life expectancy is approximately 66 to 66 for men and 56 for women.

Water Consumption

According to statistics from the World Health Organization, approximately 97 percent of the population has access to improved drinking water (2012), and 34 percent of the population has access to improved sanitation (2012).

Education

Education in São Tomé and Príncipe is free, universal, and compulsory up until the age of 14, or the sixth grade. As of the turn of the 21st century, the country had only ten secondary schools and one high school. According to the International Network for Higher Education in Africa (INHEA), there are two institutes of higher education in the country. Insufficient schools and financing, as well as a lack of trained or experienced teachers continue to hamper the educational system.

According to 2005 statistics, 88 percent of children attended primary school, a rate that decreased to approximately 59 percent for secondary education. The rate of school attendance is lower in urban areas—86 percent—than rural areas—90 percent. The rate of non-attendance is nearly 15 percent between six and 18 years of age.

As of 2014, the country had a literacy rate of approximately 70 percent. That number was higher among the youth population, specifically between the ages of 15 and 24.

Women's Rights

Women's rights are a prevalent issue on the island nation. Women have faced prejudice based on beliefs that a woman is responsible for taking care of children and the household, despite laws guaranteeing equal rights for both genders. Women have fewer opportunities to receive an education; in 2015, while 82 percent of males were literate, only 68 percent of women could read. There have also been reports of domestic violence and rape, though many women are afraid to report the incidents to the police. Sexual harassment is not illegal and has proved a problem for women in the workforce. After the October elections, women held 10 seats in National Assembly and one of 13 cabinet positions. Women held one seat on the five-member Supreme Court and six of the 12 judgeships on circuit courts.

Health Care

Access to health care services in São Tomé and Príncipe continues to be limited in the early 21st century, particularly among the rural population. The island of São Tomé houses the country's only hospital, and several clinics, mostly foreign-operated, is in operation as well. Of recent concern in the small island state is malaria control, prompting the establishment of community-based management programs as well as the free distribution of insecticide-treated nets (ITNs), which aimed to reduce the malaria-related mortality rate by 2009. The country ranked 133rd out of 190 countries on the World Health Organization's (WHO) ranking of the world's health systems.

GOVERNMENT

Structure

São Tomé and Príncipe is a republic with three branches of government: the executive, run by a president, a prime minister, and a council of ministers; the legislative, consisting of a single body, the National Assembly; and the judicial branch, run by the Supreme Court. Members of the National Assembly serve four-year terms, while the president serves a five-year term, though he can be re-elected. The president is elected directly by the citizens, who use secret ballots. All citizens eighteen years or older can vote. To be elected, the candidate has to receive a majority of the votes, or a runoff election is held. Once he is elected, the president selects a prime minister, who must be approved by the National Assembly's majority party. The prime minister chooses the members of the Council of Ministers. The judiciary used to be responsible to the National Assembly, but became independent in 1990.

Political Parties

The country achieved independence from Portugal in 1975, and the constitution was approved in 1990. Until the constitution's approval, the government was controlled by a single party, the Movement for the Liberation of São Tomé and Príncipe (MLSTP). The first democratic, multiparty elections were held in 1991. After that date, eight major parties have participated in government, including the MLSTP and new parties such as the Party of Democratic Convergence (PCD), the Christian Democratic Front-Socialist Union Party (FDC-PSU), and the Santomean Workers Party (PTS).

During the 2006 elections, the Force for Change Democratic Movement-Democratic Convergence Party (MDFM-PCD) coalition finished with the most seats, while the Movement for the Liberation of São Tomé and Príncipe/ Social Democratic Party (MLSTP/PSD) won twenty of fifty-five seats. The Independent Democratic Action (ADI) won eleven seats, while the New Way Movement party won only one seat. In 2008, the MDFM-PCD coalition agreed to a power-sharing arrangement with the Independent Democratic Action Party. Under the terms of the constitution, de Menezes (FORCE FOR CHANGE), like Trovoada (ADI) before him, was prohibited from seeking a third term as president, and several candidates stood in the 2011 presidential election to succeed him. The two front-runners from the first round of voting, held in July, were former president Pinto da Costa, running as an independent candidate, and the speaker of the National Assembly, Evaristo Carvalho, who was the ADI's candidate. When the two met again in the runoff election, held on August 7, 2011, Pinto da Costa garnered 52 percent of the vote to beat narrowly Carvalho. In 2012, three opposition parties combined in a no confidence vote to bring down the majority government of former Prime Minister Patrice TROVOADA. The new government of Prime Minister Gabriel Arcanjo Ferreira DA COSTA is entirely composed of opposition party members with limited experience in governance. (CIA FACTBOOK)

Local Government

The country is divided into two provinces, São Tomé and Príncipe, and in 1995, Príncipe won autonomy, and has been self-governed ever since. The two islands also are divided into seven municipalities: six in São Tomé and one in Príncipe. Each district is run by an independent council, run by locals elected every five years.

Judicial System

The judicial system of São Tomé and Príncipe is based largely on the Portuguese legal system and consists of a Supreme Court, with judges appointed by the National Assembly. The country does not have administrative or commercial courts.

Taxation

Taxation in São Tomé and Príncipe was reformed in 2009, when the personal income tax rate transitioned to a progressive rate between 10 and 20 percent—it had previously been a flat rate of 13 percent—and the corporate rate switched to a flat 25 percent rate (it was lowered from a 45 percent tax rate). Other levied taxes include a five percent sales tax, excise taxes, vehicle tax, and property tax.

Armed Forces

The Armed Forces consists of the Army, Coast Guard (Guarda Costeira de Sao Tome e Principe, GCSTP), and the Presidential Guard. It is considered the smallest armed forces in all of Africa.

Policy

São Tomé and Príncipe's foreign policy seeks to create political alliances, to improve its image abroad, to participate in international organizations, and to encourage economic support for the country. However, the policy tends to be one of non-alignment.

Historically, São Tomé's main diplomatic ties were exclusively with Portugal, but after independence, the government sought new partners abroad. In the 1980s, it allied itself with the Soviet Union and Cuba, but in the 1990s began to approach Western European countries and the US in search of financial support for economic development. São Tomé has a poor relationship with China, since it officially recognizes Taiwan as a country. When São Tomé decided to recognize Taiwan in 1997, China cut off diplomatic relations. More recently, however, China has become involved in the development of the deep-water port in São Tomé, along with other infrastructure projects.

The country has a friendly relationship with the U.S. São Tomé began sending an ambassador to the U.S. beginning in 1985, and the American ambassador to Gabon is also responsible for São Tomé. The U.S. installed a radio transmitter in São Tomé in 1992 to broadcast the Voice of America program, which is now heard across Africa. The U.S. also provides foreign assistance to the country, including a project through the government-run Millennium Challenge Corporation (MCC). In addition, the U.S. Navy began aiding São Tomé in 2005, providing military assistance and helping to build a boat ramp in 2007.

The government also sought diplomatic relationships with Portuguese-speaking African nations, due to a shared history and culture, and established closer relations with Cape Verde, Mozambique, and most of all, Angola. In 1978, the Angolese army helped protect the Santomean presidential palace after an attempted overthrow of the government. Also, in the 1990s, São Tomé established ties with geographic neighbors in western Africa, like Gabon and the Democratic Republic of Congo. São Tomé and Príncipe also increased its ties with Nigeria in the early 21st century due to their shared oil exploration agreement.

São Tomé is a member of nearly forty international and regional organizations, including the African Union (AU), which the country joined in 2000. The AU is an organization of fifty-four African countries, which seeks to forge economic and political cooperation to advance development and stability on the continent. The organization would like to eventually use a single currency in all of Africa, like the Euro, called the Afro. It also consists of a number of sub-organizations focused on specific issues, like the African Commission on Human and Peoples' Rights (ACHPR), the African Court of Justice, and the Pan-African Parliament. The country is also a member of the Non-Aligned Movement (NAM) and the Economic Community of Central African States (ECCAS).

Human Rights Profile

International human rights law insists that states respect civil and political rights, and also promote an individual's economic, social and cultural rights. The United Nations Universal Declaration on Human Rights (UDHR) is recognized as the standard for international human rights. Its authors sought the counsel of the world's great thinkers, philosophers, and religious leaders, and were careful to create a document that reflects the core values shared by every world culture. (To read this document or view the articles relating to cultural human rights, visit http://www.un.org/en/documents/udhr/.)

Though São Tomé and Príncipe has been cited for respecting human rights, there are a number of reported violations, including political corruption. In 2005, the attorney general held an investigation regarding the irregular process of awarding rights to oil blocks, but the inquiry did not yield any consequences for those accused of wrongdoing. In 2008, several high-level politicians were accused of embezzling millions of dollars in foreign aid, though the trial remained open in 2009. In addition, several judges are suspected of having accepted bribes, and the police force has been accused of corruption and impunity, with failed efforts to improve the investigative police unit. Despite laws meant to punish corruption, offenders did not face consequences, allowing for impunity.

The rights of prisoners and prison conditions also remain serious issues within the country. Prisoners often face long prison terms prior to trial, due to inadequate funding and a lack of lawyers and judges. In 2014, the prison population was 201, 11 percent was waiting to go to trial. Some prisoners wait for more than a year. Prison conditions are also very poor, with inadequate sanitation, food and medical care, as well as overcrowding (there is only one prison in the country). As a result, the prison population is mixed, with convicted prisoners being held with pretrial prisoners and minors.

ECONOMY

Overview of the Economy

The services sector is the largest contributor to the country's gross domestic product (GDP) at approximately 65 percent, followed by agriculture at nearly 19 percent and industry at 16 percent. Agriculture, however, remains the country's primary sector in its economy, accounting for an estimated 70 percent of the workforce.

In 2014, São Tomé and Príncipe's gross domestic product (GDP) was $624 million (USD), while the GDP per capita was $3,200 (USD). Services accounted for 65 percent of the GDP, whereas both agriculture and industry accounted for 14.6 percent of the GDP. In 2014, the GDP real growth rate was 4.5 percent, but the inflation rate was 7 percent the same year.

Industry

The country's main industries include logging, beer production, soap manufacturing, textile manufacturing, fishing, palm oil production, fish and shrimp processing, and construction. In 2014, the industrial growth rate was 4.2 percent.

São Tomé's major exports include copra, palm oil, cocoa, and coffee, though cocoa accounts for between 80 and 90 percent of all exports. In 2014, the country exported $12.6 million (USD) worth of products. In 2014, the Netherlands was São Tomé's major trading partner, followed by Belgium, Turkey, Spain, the United States, and Germany. The island imports a large number of products, including food, fuel, electrical equipment, consumer and manufactured products, and machinery. In 2014, the country spent $126.2 million (USD) on imports. In 2014, over 65 percent of imports came from Portugal, while the remainder came from Gabon and China. In the early 21st century, oil was discovered off the coast of the island. In 2001, São Tomé made an agreement with Nigeria to begin exploration in a 40–60 split, respectively. Chevron won the bid to begin exploration, which commenced in 2006. New oil discoveries in the Gulf of Guinea may attract increased attention to the small island nation.

The country has struggled with debt and the government has frequently sought help with international institutions. São Tomé received debt relief from the International Monetary Fund (IMF)'s Heavily Indebted Poor Countries (HIPC) Initiative in 2000, which reduced the national debt by $200 million (USD). The government signed another agreement in 2005 with the IMF for $4.3 million (USD). The estimated external national debt at the end of 2014 was $416.4 million (USD). In April 2011, the country completed a Threshold Country Program with The Millennium Challenge Corporation to help increase tax revenues, reform customs, and improve the business environment.

Labor

In 2014, the labor force was estimated at 70,200, ranking São Tomé and Príncipe 186th in the world in that category. Most of the population is involved in subsistence agriculture and fishing. The country lacks skilled workers and it is estimated that formal employment consists of fewer than 8,000 workers.

Energy/Power/Natural Resources

There are several natural resources used for local consumption as well as for export, including fish, cocoa, coffee, bananas, papayas, coconuts, copra (dried coconut kernels), palm kernels, pepper, cinnamon, and beans. In addition, hydropower and petroleum are two vital resources. Oil was discovered off the coast of the islands in the 1990s, and the government of São Tomé signed an agreement with Nigeria to divide exploration efforts, giving 40 percent of the share to São Tomé.

While cocoa is the major crop, the industry faced problems in the early 21st century due to climate problems, such as drought, and business issues, including the poor administration of crops.

The main threats to natural resources include erosion, soil depletion, and deforestation. The Ministry of Natural Resources and Environment of São Tomé collaborated with the British government's Darwin Initiative in 2007 to begin a sustainable development project to find a balance between agricultural and environmental preservation. (The British-based Darwin Initiative is a grant program that promotes conservation and sustainable resources in least developed nations.)

Fishing

Though overshadowed by the agricultural sector, fishing nonetheless is a vital part of the welfare of Santomeans. While offshore fisheries bring in important revenue, local fisheries provide an estimated 70 percent of the protein consumed by Santomeans. Fish found in the waters off São Tomé and Príncipe include grouper, blue marlin, sailfish, yellowfin tuna, wahoo, dorado (dolphin-fish), and red snapper. Foreign fleets, mostly

European, are permitted to fish in Santomean waters (though compensation is limited).

Agriculture

São Tomé has traditionally depended on agricultural exports and cash crops. Most of the land, formerly split into foreign-owned plantations and later owned by the government, is now run by private companies. Cocoa is the major agricultural product, which accounts for between 80 and 90 percent of the country's exports, although the industry began to face problems in the late 1990s due to poor management. Other agricultural products include fish, coconuts, palm kernels, pepper, coffee, cinnamon, poultry, bananas, beans, and copra. Despite this, the government must import food for domestic consumption.

Of the nation's 964 square kilometers (386 square miles), approximately half of the land—484 square kilometers (186 square miles)—is used for farming. Only a quarter of farmland is irrigated. In 2005, only 8 percent of unused land was suitable for farming due to land overuse and soil depletion. Agriculture accounted for less than 15 percent of the GDP in 2008. (agricultural land 50.7%; arable land 9.1%; permanent crops 40.6%; permanent pasture 1%; forest 28.1% (2011 estimate)

Tourism

São Tomé and Príncipe has a small but growing tourism industry. There was no formal tourism infrastructure until the 1990s, when German and Swiss businesspersons founded the first tourist accommodations. Since then, the government has collaborated with international organizations to increase infrastructure and services for tourists. The industry has added car rentals, tour guide companies, and boat and scuba cruises. The most famous hotels include the Miramar Hotel in São Tomé and the Bom Bom (translated as "goody-goody") Island Resort in Príncipe. Tourists can also stay at old plantation houses, since many have been converted to bed and breakfasts.

In 2000, the country received only 5,000 tourists, and in 2002, tourism expenditures accounted for approximately $1,000,000 (USD). In 2005, the country received 15,752 foreign visitors, of which approximately 10,000 were tourists. In 2014, the country was visited by 18,187 tourists, a 24.6% increase over the previous year. The majority of these tourists came from Portugal and France, as well as from Germany, Angola, and Cape Verde. At the beginning of 2014, CNN Travel chose São Tomé and Príncipe as one of 10 dream destinations worldwide.

The country's main tourism offerings are the large number of beaches and seaside hotels, as well as ecological excursions. Tourists can also visit the few historical sites, including São Sebastião Fort, the old plantations, and the small city of Santo Antonio. The islands' jungles make for excellent hiking trips and bird watching, while in the ocean, tourists can scuba dive and see the variety of marine species.

Rachel Glickhouse

DO YOU KNOW?

- The country is home to over 120 species of birds, some 28 of which are endemic to the island of São Tomé.

- The banknotes of the country's currency (the dobra) features what is believed to be a portrait of national hero Rei Amador, who led a slave revolt against the Portuguese in the late 16th century. A statue that was inaugurated in 2004 by the general secretary of the UN also commemorates Amador.

- The unofficial motto of the country is "leve-leve" ("slowly-slowly" or "light-light"), which expresses the relaxed pace of life on the islands.

Bibliography

Albertino, Francisco. *Exorcising Devils from the Throne: Sao Tome and Principe in the Chaos of Democratization.* New York: Algora Publishing, 2011.

Chabal, Patrick. *History of postcolonial Lusophone Africa.* Bloomington: Indiana University Press, 2002.

Ferraz, Luiz Ivens. *The Creole of Sao Tome.* Johannesburg: Witwatersrand University Press, 1979.

Garfield, Robert. *History of Sao Tome Island, 1470–1655 the key to Guinea.* San Francisco: Mellen Research University Press, 1992.

Hodges, Tony. *Sao Tome & Principe from plantation colony to microstate.* Boulder, Colorado: Westview Press, 1988.

Lloyd-Jones, Stewart, and Antonio Costa Pinto. *The Last Empire Thirty Years of Portuguese Decolonisation.* Bristol: Intellect, 2004.

Seibert, Gerhard. *Comrades, Clients and Cousins Colonialism, Socialism And Democratization in Sao Tome and Principe (African Social Studies Series) (African Social Studies Series).* New York: Brill Academic Press, 2006.

Williams, Frederick G., ed. *Poets of Sao Tome and Principe.* Provo, UT: BYU Studies, 2015.

Works Cited

"Activities." Sao Tome e Principe, Paradise on Earth. Illhue das Rolas. http://www.saotome.st/activities.php?intActivityID=2.

"African Union in a Nutshell." *Africa Union.* http://au.int/en/about/nutshell.

"Albertino Braganca - Memorias." Lusografias.http://lusografias.wordpress.com/2008/09/25/albertino-braganca-memorias/.

"Alda Espirito Santo." *Beto Gomes.* http://betogomes.sites.uol.com.br/AldaEspiritoSanto.htm.

"Average Conditions, Sao Tome e Principe." *BBC.* 2006. http://www.bbc.co.uk/weather/world/city_guides/results.shtml?tt=TT004850.

"Biodiversity, socioeconomics and agricultural development in Sao Tome and Principe." *Defra, UK Darwin Initiative.* 27 Mar. 2009 http://www.darwininitiative.org.uk/project/EIDPR080/.

"Boca de Inferno." Sao Tome e Principe, Paradise on Earth. 12 Mar. 2009 http://www.saotome.st/activities.php?intActivityID=7.

"A Brief History of Sao Tome & Principe." *About.* http://africanhistory.about.com/od/sotom/p/SaoTomeHist1.htm.

"Cascata Sao Nicolau." Sao Tome e Principe, Paradise on Earth. 19 Mar. 2009 http://www.saotome.st/activities.php?intActivityID=9.

"China and Sao Tome." 20 Nov. 2013. 08 Oct. 08 2015 http://www.chinausfocus.com/foreign-policy/china-and-sao-tome/

"CIA - The World Factbook -- Sao Tome and Principe." *Sao Tome & Principe.* 08 Oct. 2015. CIA. https://www.cia.gov/library/publications/the-world-factbook/geos/tp.html.

"Climate & when to go." *Lonely Planet Travel Guides and Travel Information.* http://www.lonelyplanet.com/sao-tome-and-principe/weather.

"Country profile: Sao Tome and Principe." *BBC NEWS.* 08 Oct. 2015 http://www.bbc.com/news/world-africa-14093493.

"Country Profile: Sao Tome and Principe." *Country Profiles.* British Foreign & Commonwealth Office. 28 Mar. 2009 http://www.fco.gov.uk/en/about-the-fco/country-profiles/sub-saharan-africa/sao-tome-principe?profile=history&pg=3.

"Culture of Sao Tome and Principe : The Navetur - Equatour Tourist Guide." *Navetur.* http://www.navetur-equatour.st/Culture.htm.

"Culture of Sao Tome and Principe." *Sao Tome & Principe, Tourism Portal.* http://www.turismo-stp.org/pages/en/cultura/tchiloli.htm.

"Deep water port project in Sao Tome and Principe attracts Angolan interest." 01 July 2013. 08 Oct. 2015 http://www.macauhub.com.mo/en/2013/07/01/deep-water-port-project-in-sao-tome-and-principe-attracts-angolan-interest/

"Ecology." *Navetur.* 03 Mar. 2009 http://www.navetur-equatour.st/Ecology.htm.

"Entrada de Estrangeiros." *Instituto Nacional de Estatistica, Sao Tome & Principe.* 15 Mar. 2009 http://www.ine.st/turismo/qresumo_entradas.htm.

"Excursion to the coffee plantation of Monte Cafe" *Navetur.* http://www.navetur-equatour.st/Monte_Cafe.htm.

"Forro language: Examples of Forro with Translations." *Wikipedia, the free encyclopedia.* 01 Jan. 2009. http://en.wikipedia.org/wiki/Forro_language.

"Fortificacao, Forte de Sao Sebastiao." *Fortalezas.* 13 June 2008.http://fortalezasmultimidia.com.br/fortalezas/index.php?ct=fortaleza&id_fortaleza=527.

"Getting Around, Sao Tome & Principe." *World Travel Guide.* http://www.worldtravelguide.net/country/241/internal_travel/Africa/S%E3o-Tom%E9-e-Pr%EDncipe.html.

"History of Sao Tome and Principe." *Navetur.* 05 Mar. 2009 http://www.navetur-equatour.st/History.htm.

"Introducing Sao Tome & Principe." *Lonely Planet.* http://www.lonelyplanet.com/sao-tome-and-principe.

"The IUCN Red List of Threatened species." *IUCN 2008 Red List.* 2008. http://www.iucnredlist.org/search.

"The jewel of Africa - a fairy-tale island state in the Gulf of Guinea." *Sao Tome und Principe.* 15 Mar. 2009 http://www.sao-tome.com/englisch/index.htm.

"The Non-Aligned Movement, Background Information." *Non Aligned Movement.* http://www.nam.gov.za/background/background.htm#1.1%20History.

"Orientacoes da politica externa, Objectivos e prioridades." *MNECC*. http://www.mnecc.gov.st/pexterna.htm.

Peek, Philip M., and Kwesi Yankah. *African Folklore: An encyclopedia*. New York: Routledge, 2004.

"Pico de Sao Tome." *Sao Tome e Principe, Paradise on Earth*. http://www.saotome.st/activities. php?intActivityID=8.

"Plantation houses." *Navetur*. http://www.navetur-equatour.st/Plantation_houses.htm.

"Quando tudo aconteceu." *Vidas Lusofonas*. http://www.vidaslusofonas.pt/almada_negreiros.htm.

"Republica Democratica de Sao Tome." *Arta Africa*. http://www.artafrica.info/html/paises/saotome.php.

"Sao Tome & Principe Newspapers." *ABYZ News Links*. http://www.abyznewslinks.com/saoto.htm.

"Sao Tome and Principe: People -- Britannica Online Encyclopedia." *Encyclopedia - Britannica Online Encyclopedia*. 08 Oct. 2015 http://www.britannica.com/place/Sao-Tome-and-Principe.

"Sao Tome and Principe." *National Anthems*. http://www.nationalanthems.info/st.htm.

"Sao Tome and Principe (01/09)." *Background Note: Sao Tome and Principe*. U.S. Department of State, Bureau of African Affairs. http://www.state.gov/r/pa/ei/bgn/5434.htm.

"Sao Tome and Principe." *United Nations Cyberschoolbus*. 08 Oct. 2015 http://www.un.org/cyberschoolbus/.

"Sao Tome and Principe." *U.S. Department of State*. http://www.state.gov/p/af/ci/tp/.

"Sao Tome and Principe Population 2015." http://worldpopulationreview.com/countries/sao-tome-and-principe-population/

"São Tomé and Príncipe receives over 18,000 tourists in 2014." Macauhub. 16 Apr. 2015. http://www.macauhub.com.mo/en/2015/04/16/sao-tome-and-principe-receives-over-18000-tourists-in-2014/

"São Tomé FestFilm." http://saotome-festfilm.com/index.php.

"Sao Tome opens new boat ramp with the help of Navy Sea Bees." *United States European Command*. 18 Sept. 2007. 08 Oct. 2015. http://www.eucom.mil/English/FullStory.asp?art=1425.

"Sao Tome, Principe and Annobon moist lowland forests." *World Wildlife*. 2001. http://www.worldwildlife.org/wildworld/profiles/terrestrial/at/at0127_full.html.

"Sao Tome & Principe Weather." *BBC*. http://www.bbc.co.uk/weather/world/country_guides/results.shtml?tt=TT004850.

"Sao Sebastiao Museum." *Sao Tome e Principe, Paradise on Earth*. http://www.saotome.st/activities.php?intActivityID=6.

"Sao Tome & Principe Culture and Geography." *PlacesOnLine*. http://www.placesonline.com/central_america/sao_tome_&_principe/culture_and_geography.asp.

"Sao Tome & Principe, historical data." *NationMaster*. http://www.nationmaster.com/time.php?stat=eco_tou_exp_int-economy-tourism-expenditures-international&country=tp-s-o-tom-pr-ncipe.

"Sao Tome e Principe nos Jogos OlÃmpicos de Pequim 2008." *Quadro de Medalhas*. 20 Mar. 2009 http://www.quadrodemedalhas.com/olimpiadas/jogos-olimpicos-pequim-2008/sao-tome-e-principe-jogos-olimpicos-pequim-2008.htm.

"Sao Tome & Principe." *Wikitravel*. http://wikitravel.org/en/Sao_Tome_and_Principe.

"Special wildlife months on Sao Tome & Principe." *Africa's Eden*. http://www.africas-eden.com/Wildlife-of-Sao-Tome-Principe.asp.

"There Is No Diplomatic Relations Between China and Sao Tome and Principe at Present." *Ministry of Foreign Affairs of the People's Republic of China*. 26 Aug. 2006. http://www.fmprc.gov.cn/eng/wjb/zzjg/fzs/gjlb/3069/t16567.htm.

"2015 Human Rights Report: Sao Tome & Principe." US Department of State. 08 Oct. 2015. http://www.state.gov/j/drl/rls/hrrpt/humanrightsreport/#wrapper

"U.S. Relations With Sao Tome and Principe." 29 Oct. 2014. http://www.state.gov/r/pa/ei/bgn/5434.htm.

"V Bienal de Sao Tome & Principe." *V Bienal de Sao Tome & Principe*. http://www.bienalstp.org/nprog.htm.

"Whale watching." *Sao Tome e Principe, Paradise on Earth*. http://www.saotome.st/activities.php?intActivityID=19.

"Where to Go in Sao Tome and Principe | iExplore." *Travel guides*. IExplore Adventure & World Travel. http://www.iexplore.com/dmap/Sao+Tome+and+Principe/Where+to+Go.

"World Prison Brief." http://www.prisonstudies.org/country/sao-tome-e-principe.

Baillie, Jonathan. "One month in the Forest of Principe."Gulf of Guinea Conservation Group of Guinea Islands' Biodiversity Network. http://www.ggcg.st/jon_principe.htm.

Banham, Martin. *A History of Theatre in Africa*. Cambridge: Cambridge University Press, 2004.

Gordon, Raymond G. "Languages of Sao Tome & Principe." *Ethnologue, Languages of the World*. 2005. Ethnologue. http://www.ethnologue.com/show_country.asp?name=ST.

Praia Jale. http://praiajale.free.fr/.

Seibert, Gerhard. *Comrades, Clients And Cousins: Colonialism, Socialism And Democratization in Sao Tome And Principe*. New York: Brill Academic, 2006.

A giant baobab tree. iStock/klublu.

SENEGAL

Introduction

The Republic of Senegal, commonly known as Senegal, is a small country that lies further west than any other nation on the African continent. One of the most developed and democratic nations of Africa, Senegal, and its modern capital, Dakar, are considered representative of the future of Africa.

Senegal is known for its poets, or griots. Often referred to as wandering musicians or storytellers, their talents range from musicians to oral historians, political commentators, comics, and poets. They maintain Senegal's oral history and culture through music and verse.

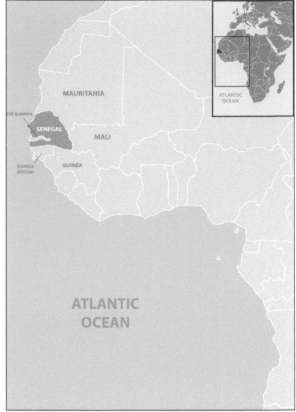

GENERAL INFORMATION

Official Language: French
Population: 13,975,834 (2015 estimate)
Currency: Communaute Financiere Africaine Franc (XOF)
Coins: Coins are issued in denominations of 1, 5, 10, 25, 50, 100, 200, and 500 CFA francs.
Land Area: 196,722 square kilometers (76,000 square miles)
National Motto: "Un peuple, un but, une foi" (French, "One people, one goal, one faith")
National Anthem: "Pincez Tous Vos Koras, Frappez les Balafons" (French, "Pluck Your Koras, Strike the Balafons")
Capital: Dakar
Time Zone: GMT +0

Flag Description: The flag of Senegal comprises three horizontal bands of green, yellow, and red. In the center of the yellow band is a five-pointed green star.

Population

In 2015, the population of Senegal was estimated to be almost 14 million, with 44 percent living in or near urban areas. The capital of Dakar is the largest, with a population of 3.52 million (2015 estimate). The city is divided into sections according to class, with wealthy people generally living in modern homes and the poor population living under substandard conditions. Outside of the cities, people live in areas according to family rather than economic status. Senegalese villages are arranged in family compounds consisting of large groups of huts. The huts in these rural areas are generally made from dried mud and clay, and have thatched or boarded roofs.

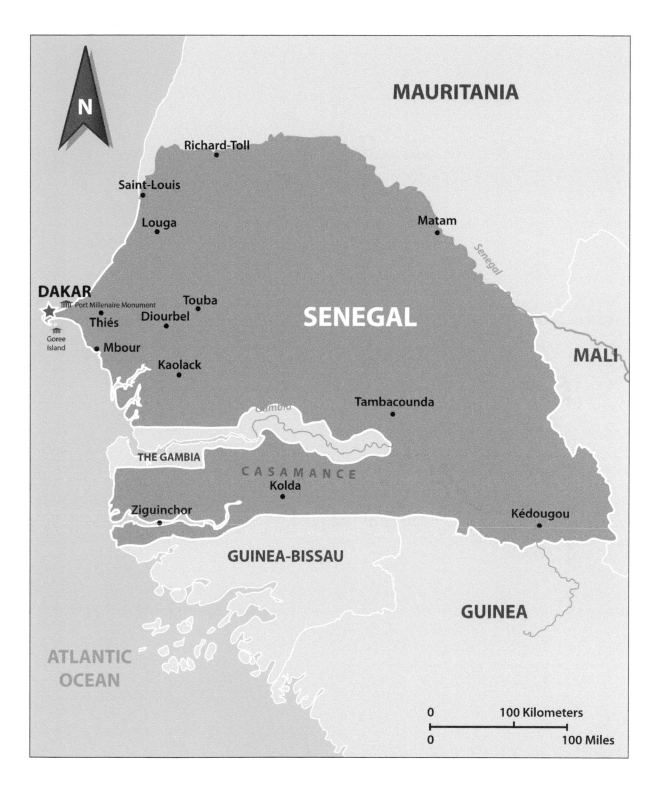

Principal Cities by Population (2013 census):

- Dakar (2,646,503)
- Touba Mosquee (753,315)
- Thies (317,763)
- Kaolack (233,708)
- Mbour (232,777)
- Rufisue (221,066)
- Saint-Louis (209,752)
- Ziguinchor (205,294)

Languages

Most Senegalese people speak Wolof, the language of the Wolof ethnic group, more frequently than they speak French. However, French remains the official language and the language of business, as it is more heavily used in urban centers such as Dakar.

Native People & Ethnic Groups

Many ethnic groups make up the population of Senegal. The majority ethnic groups are the Wolof, which make up 43 percent of the population, the Pular, which make up 29 percent, the Serer, which make up 15 percent, the Jola, which make up 4 percent, the Mandinka, which make up three percent, and the Soninkel, which make up one percent. These ethnic groups in modern Senegal have lived in Western Africa for thousands of years. About 10 percent of Senegal's inhabitants are European, Lebanese, or natives of other African countries.

Religions

Religion is very important to the people of Senegal. Senegalese society and politics are directly based on religious beliefs, thanks to the influence of Muslim leaders called marabouts. The vast majority of Senegalese are Muslim (94 percent as of 2014), and their devotion to Islam is evident throughout the culture.

Senegalese Muslims are divided into social factions called brotherhoods. The Mouride and the Tidjaniyya are the two brotherhoods with the most members. Brotherhoods are led by marabouts, or religious leaders. Among the non-Islamic population, Christianity is the most common religion, although several regional religions are also practiced.

Climate

Like many African nations, Senegal has no winter or summer season, only a dry season and a wet season. The wet season lasts for several months and produces about 50 centimeters (20 inches) of annual rainfall in the northern regions. In the Casamance, rainfall is substantially higher, with an average of 165 centimeters (65 inches) annually. Storms are infrequent, but usually come in the form of violent rain and tornados.

Generally speaking, western Africa has a hot, dry climate. Its terrain is classified as grassland, and much of the landscape is covered with patchy vegetation and sand. Average temperatures are quite high, ranging from 22° Celsius (71° Fahrenheit) on the coast to about 29° Celsius (84° Fahrenheit) inland.

ENVIRONMENT & GEOGRAPHY

Topography

The Republic of Senegal is a small country that occupies the westernmost area of the African continent. In addition, like the country, the capital Dakar sits on the westernmost tip of Senegal, on the Cap-Vert peninsula, at the edge of the Atlantic Ocean. Senegal is a generally flat country that is covered by sandy plains and low hills. Sand dunes characterize the coastal areas, including Dakar.

Gambia, a small, independent nation that occupies a strip of land running from the western shore and 200 kilometers (124 miles) up the Gambia River, is an important factor in Senegal's geography. Because of the location of the Gambia, Senegal is divided into a northern and a southern region. The region in the south is called the Casamance. The southern coast surrounding the Gambia has several inlets and bays, upon which several major cities are situated.

The coastal region, the Senegal River Valley, the Ferlo, the eastern region and the Casamance are geographic areas, but because of social struggles with the Gambia, the Casamance is a distinct political region as well.

Senegal's three major rivers, the Gambia, the Casamance, and the Senegal, all extend from the Atlantic Ocean into neighboring countries. Other topographical features include Lake Guiers in the north and the Fouta Djallon mountain range in the southeast.

Plants & Animals

With high levels of hunting and the increasing development of urban areas, the majority of Senegal's native animal species have become endangered or extinct. The Senegalese populations of wild lions, buffalo, zebras, and giraffes have been drastically depleted by hunting, but also because of diseases carried by the African tsetse fly.

Wild elephants, chimpanzees and crocodiles continue to inhabit Senegal, but in fewer numbers than in the past. The antelope, which lives primarily in the southern forests, is a more common example of Senegal's wildlife. There have been many efforts to preserve the region's remaining endangered species.

There is a great deal of rainfall in the Casamance, which allows for the growth of dense forests that are not typical in the drier northern areas. Rather, rubber trees, baobabs, oil palms, mahogany, and rosewood trees characterize the northern region. Many tropical fruits, such as mangoes, guavas, coconuts, oranges, and tamarinds, grow among the abundant elephant grass that covers this region.

CUSTOMS & COURTESIES

Greetings

Greetings signify more than good manners in Senegal. They are a way of establishing a common ground among people of all social, economic, religious, or ethnic backgrounds. In addition, Senegalese appreciate and expect an exchange of interest in one another's lives as signs of respect and community involvement. Denying a greeting can be perceived as a direct sign of disrespect or insult.

Long greetings of 15 minutes are not uncommon, and the exchange of niceties and courteous questions, however trivial, are important to social interaction in Senegal. Furthermore, a formal and sincere greeting is an important part of Senegalese courtesy and social interaction. Proper greetings typically consist of more than simply saying "Hello" or introducing a conversation. It is a respectful way to acknowledge another human being's value.

A meeting generally begins with a handshake – or forearm grasp if someone is busy eating or working – offering the right hand. Women, however, often forego the handshake and opt for a gesture of clasped hands raised as an acknowledgement. Men, too, offer this gesture in crowds or from distances. Salutations are often exchanged in French or another local language.

In addition, using a person's family name shows respect and engagement. Taking the time to invest this type of attention in someone's life before expressing needs or passing by is a way of connecting to others. In addition, close friends can be expected to use nicknames and forego the usual handshake for a hug and three kisses—left cheek, right cheek, left cheek.

Gestures & Etiquette

Diners typically take care to use only the right hand when eating in Senegal. Although this custom may no longer be applicable in many developing countries, the left hand is often considered unclean or rude. Thus, it is safer to favor the right hand so as not to appear insulting. Again, it is also important to note that Senegalese greet every new person they meet or encounter with a proper handshake and interest.

Respecting elders in the community is important, and measures should be taken to honor their status in the community. Avoiding direct eye contact, while considered impolite in other cultures, is an important way of honoring elders in Senegal. An appropriate professional title is typically used when greeting elders. The same can be said for most greetings, with the exception of familiar nicknames or among family.

Eating/Meals

In Senegal, eating is often considered an important way to engage with other people. It is not uncommon for women and men to be seated separately, but co-ed seating is also acceptable. Diners often wash up in special basins or by pouring clean water over their hands before beginning a meal. As in much of West Africa, meals are often shared in communal dishes. There is a formal honor system of gratefully accepting food offered while carefully considering the needs and portions remaining for others at the table. This concept, called "fayda," indicates a respect for fellow diners and a priority for sharing.

Visiting

In Senegal, the head of the family—typically the oldest man in the home—serves as an authority figure, responsible for the rules and guidelines for conduct in the home. Visitors should respect and honor the head of household and behave in compliance with the standards for that particular family. Because of the courtyard/patio design of many Senegalese homes, guests can expect to gather in the open area around which compounds are built, and to be greeted by extended family and neighbors. Again, the importance of proper greetings cannot be underestimated; visitors always make a point of extending greetings, handshakes and conversation to their hosts.

It is important to receive guests and visitors as though they are bringing the gift of their time. One may wish to return the generosity by paying visits to them and sharing their time and attention—for example, by bringing a small gift to their home. Sweets or fruit in decorative paper is a perfectly appropriate offering. In addition, Senegalese take care not to offer these gifts with the left hand.

LIFESTYLE

Family

In the Senegalese family structure, grandparents represent the head authorities. With men taking priority in each relationship, the grandfather is the primary decision-maker and commands respect throughout the household and community. The grandmother is second in the familial chain of command. Fathers and sons in nuclear families follow the lead and suggestions of the grandparents, and provide financial support. Women are often charged with domestic responsibilities and the provision of care and guidance for their children. In addition, it is the responsibility of the father to arrange marriages for their daughters. Cousins, siblings, nieces and nephews, step-siblings and godchildren may all live in familial communes, in which case they would refer to each other as "brother" and "sister," regardless of their technical relations.

The legal age for marriage is eighteen for men and sixteen for women. While both polygamy and divorce are legal, polygamy is only an option for men. However, both the wife and the husband are permitted to seek a divorce. Polygamous marriages allow for up to four wives for a husband, with provisions as to wives' legal rights within the union.

Housing

As in other Muslim countries, West African homes are often built as structures surrounding a courtyard used a family and communal gathering place. In rural villages, homes are typically basic, and built from straw and earth or brick. Often, rings of different crops that the inhabitants grow to support their community surround a home. Ethnic Jola villages, common in the Casamance region in southern Senegal, may have much larger populations, nearing 6,000.

In cities, brick homes with tin roofs are more common. Overcrowded homes are also common in large cities. Families may live in clustered homes forming compounds. Extended families often create an expansive familial community in this way. In the cities, nuclear families live in the same house, with husband and wife sharing a room. In more rural areas, however, it is not uncommon for couples to live separately in their own rooms, or even their own separate buildings.

Nearly one-fourth of Senegalese citizens live in the capital, Dakar. Homes there are very European in nature, with modern business buildings and Western-style apartment housing. Most of Senegal, however, is rural, consisting of small villages and familial communities.

Food

Senegal has a multicultural cuisine that is influenced by the country's French and Portuguese heritage, as well as its coastal location. The result is an exotic and unique flavor indicative of the region. Groundnuts—peanuts, specifically—are by far the most common food in Senegal, both in its cuisine and economic trade.

In addition to peanuts, seafood, and rice are the local mainstays of Senegalese cuisine. Chicken is also common. However, red meat, particularly lamb and beef, is also used; pork is not, as it is not an acceptable part of a Muslim diet. Colorful vegetables and tropical flair indicate the fusion of French and North African culinary influences. Couscous, a primarily North African grain dish similar to pasta, is also prevalent.

Fruit is common in drinks. The distinctly Senegalese baobab tree produces the monkey bread fruit, a unique pod whose seeds add sweet and tangy flavor to drinks as well as traditional soups. A yogurt drink called toufam is thinned with sugar water for a sweet and creamy treat. Palm wine and freshly brewed coffee are other common drinks. Mint tea is served at varying degrees of sweetness, allowing diners to progress from bitter to very sweet tastes throughout the course of a meal.

Life's Milestones

The naming of a child marks the first milestone in his or her life, as it introduces that child to the community. In Wolof culture, Senegalese children are not named until one week after they are born. They are then given a name that often incorporates words indicating details and circumstances of the child's birth. Muslim ritual is also an important part of marking the lives of Senegalese citizens. Young men undergo circumcision as a part of a religious ritual marking manhood. Although banned in 1999, female circumcision still occurs in rural regions of Senegal. Marriage is another important milestone and is often arranged by family and accompanied by traditional courtship.

CULTURAL HISTORY

Art

Senegal has a rich artistic heritage. The country's writers, musicians, filmmakers, and artisans are considered staples of classic African studies. Despite its legacy of French and Portuguese colonialism, Senegal has retained a strong sense of cultural identity independent of European influence.

Traditional arts and crafts are important to Senegalese culture. These historically significant art forms include jewelry making, basket weaving, and sand and "underglass" paintings. The latter are two popular and common Senegalese painting styles. Sand paintings emphasize local culture and identity by representing African scenes and images, using local sand as the medium. Artists typically paint with dyed sands from a variety of sources, including beaches, deserts, and volcanic remains. Underglass painting, also called "sous verre," involves a technique of literally painting on the reverse side of a piece of glass. Prior to 1960, these images often depicted Islamic themes. In contemporary Senegal, these paintings often cover a breadth of subject matter, including secular, or nonreligious, scenes.

Historically, Senegalese painters have emphasized religion in their work. One such movement is attributed to the Mouride brotherhood. This Muslim brotherhood is a Sufi branch born in the late 19th century, and well established in Senegal. (Sufism is a mystical tradition associated with Islam.) Art associated with Mouridism is often called Mouride art or Sufi art. It typically consists of visual representations of stories significant to their faith and culture. This includes giant murals and underglass paintings depicting images of peace and faith.

Architecture

Senegal's architecture was largely influenced by the French, who established a heavy colonial presence in the country beginning in the mid-19th century. This is particularly reflected in the country's capital, Dakar, where tree-lined streets with French façade are common. In French architecture, the façade is the exterior of a building, often the front, which is given particular architectural treatment or decoration. Other architectural styles are also common in Dakar. Traditional Islamic architecture is evident in the various mosques, and other styles of European architecture are revealed in the numerous cathedrals. Other parts of the capital, like the older medina, contrast sharply with their crowded streets, narrow paths and deteriorating buildings or dwellings.

In villages and less-developed urban areas, the architecture is often more rudimentary. Houses or buildings are often made from earth and straw, cement, or brick with tin roofing, as these materials are typically readily available. Homes often follow the Muslim tradition of gathering families and friends within house walls by building structures around an open courtyard or patio.

Drama

Senegalese cinema is known as one of the oldest in Africa. This is largely due to the influence of Senegalese director and writer Ousmane Sembene (1923–2007). As he began adapting his novels into films, Sembene embarked on a career in film that empowered social change and opened dialogue for political and social commentary. His films address issues of colonialism, development, and women's rights. His film *Moolaade* (2004) began a dialogue about female genital mutilation in modern times. Upon his death in 2007, he was praised as the "father of African film."

Music

West Africa is known for its poets, or griots. Often referred to as wandering musicians or "praise singers," these nomadic artists are trained in the oral tradition. They maintain an oral history through music and verse, and use their songs and poetry to preserve cultural integrity. They are also known for using music as a means for social criticism, humorous storytelling, and even gossip. Griots have been historically significant in Senegal, and continue to leave their artistic mark on Senegalese culture. In fact, the spoken word beat poetry known as Tallif, a 1,000-year-old tradition, has served as a backbone for the thriving hip-hop styles embraced by Senegalese youth. Griots are also known as "guewel" in Wolof, the most common tribal language in Senegal.

The signature percussion instrument of Senegal is the sabar. The term refers to both the type of drum and drumstick used and the style of music it creates. In addition, several types of drums and strings particular to the area create a signature Senegalese dance sound. They include the tama, tabala, kora, xalam, and djembe, all of which are important parts of mbalax music. Mbalax music is the national dance music of Senegal. It combines traditional sounds, such as the sabar, with Western styles such as jazz and rock and roll.

Literature

Frequently written in French, the country's official language, Senegalese literature often involves first-person accounts of overcoming oppression, grief, and strife. Novelist Ousmane Sembene, acclaimed author of *Les bouts de bois de Dieu* (*God's Bits of Wood*), wrote of mid-20th century colonial influences on the development of land and division of civil society. His works are considered fundamental examples of modern-day African fiction. His writing has been published in fifteen languages and has set a standard for African literature around the world.

A significant cultural and largely literary movement to influence Senegal was Negritude. The movement rejects and criticizes racism, and asserts African traditions and cultures by embracing them globally through the African diaspora. Largely developed in the 1930s in Paris, France, to oppose French colonialism, Negritude draws heavily from black art forms from around the world. It was particularly influenced by the Harlem Renaissance, a cultural movement in early-20th century America that explored and celebrated the historical experiences of African Americans. Former Senegalese President Leopold Senghor, who served as president during the 1960s, is credited as being one of the founders of the Negritude movement.

Senegal is also considered to be at the forefront of African feminism. In fact, the country has produced some of the most critically acclaimed women writers on the continent. In 1980, Mariama Ba (1929–1981), author of *Une Si Longue un Lettre* (*So Long a Letter*), became the first person to win the coveted Noma Prize for outstanding African literature. Her novel, written in the form of a letter to a friend, tells the story of a widow mourning the loss of her husband. Critics praised the book for capturing the impact of social and familial roles of women in the country. The book has left its mark on Senegalese culture by drawing attention to the issue of feminine identity. In addition, prominent poets include Birago Diop (1906–1989), one of the most influential griots, or poets, hailing from Senegal; Leopold Sedar Senghor (1906–2001), the former president; and Amadou Bamba Mbacke (1853–1927), a Senegalese spiritual leader who founded the Mouride brotherhood.

CULTURE

Arts & Entertainment

Art is encouraged and promoted as an important part of culture in Senegal. The Senegalese government often funds art projects and exhibitions. The government, because of their importance, sponsors theater and literature as vehicles for expression and social commentary. Such support reflects the fact that the Senegalese people consider art a fundamental part of their lives. History and significance, or meaning, are regarded as the two most important factors in traditional art and culture.

The tradition of griots, or storytellers, brings these together even in modern Senegalese society. Their talents range from musicians to oral historians, political commentators to comics, and poets. They belong to a caste, or social order, that generally only marries within its own social grouping. This is done in the hope of maintaining the integrity of the griot tradition as an art form.

Drawing from the griot tradition, Senegal supports a thriving movement of hip-hop artists and rappers. Outspoken on political themes, these artists strongly influence youth activism and social change within the country. In 2000, rap stars pushed a wave of young people to the polling booths, exercising their right to vote. Even the names of popular artists indicate the driving ethical forces behind their work. One significant group is called Positive Black Soul, while another rapper, Daara J, released an album called *Power of Unity*.

Clothing is also considered an art form in Senegal. While most men wear a long, lightweight garment called a boubou with baggy pants and a simple pair of flat, thin shoes, many women wear ornate, colorful boubous and handcrafted jewelry. Senegalese women are known for taking pride in the color and design of their clothing. Both men and women wear cloth waist wraps called pagnes.

Modern art forms such as film and pop music are also popular in Senegal, particularly in urban areas. Pop music is mainly dance music influenced by American and Caribbean beats. Senegalese pop musicians are known around the world for modernizing traditional African styles. Traditional Senegalese music is played on drums, such as the tahmal, and other percussion instruments, such as the balafon. Stringed music is often played on large gourd guitars called koras.

Sports such as wrestling (or lamb), cricket, and basketball are commonly played in Senegal. However, no sport is as popular in any Western African country as soccer. Many regions have professional teams that compete in the African Soccer Cup.

Cultural Sites & Landmarks

The capital Dakar hosts a number of cultural sites. One of the city's most striking natural landmarks is the corniche road, which is carved out of the limestone cliffs on the bank of Cape Manuel. It offers excellent views of Dakar's beaches and its famous harbor, as well as the surrounding islands. The highest point in Dakar is the Phare des Mamelles (Mamelles Lighthouse), located near the city's airport.

The Porte Millenaire monument, built in 2001, represents the city's past and future. The monument is made up of three nested rectangular arches, which symbolize doorways. Through these arches, viewers can view Goree Island, a symbol of Senegal's past, and the ocean, a symbol of the city's port and its bright future as a major maritime trading city in its own right. In addition, near the historic Gare Centrale train station is the Tirailleurs Senegalais monument, commemorating the Senegalese soldiers who were drafted to serve France in both world wars.

Goree Island is an important landmark in Senegal, because it played a significant role in the history of the Atlantic slave trade. In fact, the former European settlement served as a major slave-trading port governed first by the Portuguese, then the French. In addition to the multiple museums chronicling slave-trading activity in the area, the island is known for its volcanic rock landscapes.

The baobab tree is one of Senegal's most distinctive and important features.

Outside of Dakar, Saint-Louis is the most significant major city in Senegal. Once the capital of the country, Saint-Louis was named a United Nations Educational, Scientific, and Cultural Organization (UNESCO) World Heritage site in 2000.

National parks that highlight Senegal's wildlife include the Parc National du Niokola-Koba, a reserve for sub-Saharan wildlife. It is particularly known as the home of the green and hussar monkeys. There is also Parc National des Oiseaux du Djoudj, a bird sanctuary boasting an extraordinary array of African birds. Additionally, the baobab tree is a natural wonder and emblem of Senegal. The enormous trees grow and live for thousands of years, with trunk circumferences reaching 30 meters (98 feet).

Libraries & Museums

Senegal has many museums that feature collections of African art and foster the preservation of cultural heritage. The Dynamique Museum and the Tapestry Factory of Thies, both of Dakar, are two such examples. The Fundamental Institute of Black Africa museum (Dakar) houses collections of ancient African statues, musical instruments, and masks. Dakar is also home to the Soumbedioune, a distinctive marketplace known for its crafts and artisan displays.

The majority of libraries in Senegal are located in Dakar, such as the library of Sheikh Anta Diop University, which features half a million resources on social sciences and technology, as well as the country's national library, the Library of the Senegal Archives Directorate, which has a collection of over 1,700 periodicals and over 29,000 works. The Senegalese Research and Information Centre (CRDS) and the Gaston Berger University Library are both located in Saint-Louis.

Holidays

Senegal is a Muslim nation, and all major Islamic holidays are observed. Most Senegalese fast during daylight hours for the holy month of Ramadan, which ends with the celebration of Senegal's most important Muslim holiday, Korite. It is the custom for Senegalese to wear new, fine clothing when celebrating Korite with family.

Rites of passage and coming-of-age ceremonies are important to Senegalese society. Traditional dances such as the syniaka are incorporated into these gatherings to mark the transition into adulthood.

Youth Culture

Overall, youth culture in Senegal is similar to Western youth culture, though aspects are influenced by traditional Islamic culture. For example, drinking is not an important part of youth culture because the nation is predominantly Muslim. However, however, there is no legal drinking age. Dating is strictly controlled and more closely observed by the community in rural areas, largely due to West African traditions and customs. However, in urban areas, it is a much less formal custom and dating remains a common practice. Nonetheless, marriages are often arranged.

Senegalese youth are particularly engaged in social and political movements in Senegal, and are hugely influential considering 70 percent of the population is under 30 years old. For example, during the 1980s, young activists took to the streets in a form of non-violent protest known as "Set/Setal." Commenting on social disregard for community, employment, and respect, Senegalese youth took out their frustrations by cleaning the streets, beautifying cities, and incorporating art into everyday public life.

Music, particularly hip-hop and rap, is another art form critical to Senegalese youth culture. A politically influential art form, hip-hop music also talks about important issues shaping young people's lives. For example, artists like Baaba Maal and DJ Amadi address young people directly about sexual health and individual responsibility in preventing the spread of HIV/AIDS. By tackling otherwise taboo issues, popular music has helped draw attention to problems and concerns affecting the younger generations in Senegal.

SOCIETY

Transportation

Traffic moves on the right-hand side of the road in Senegal. Cell phone or mobile phone use while driving is prohibited, and helmets are mandatory for those operating motorcycles and scooters. Roadways tend to be poorly lit and poorly maintained, and drivers should be aware of pedestrians, bicyclists, motorcycles, livestock, and other animals on the roads.

Transportation Infrastructure

With several active seaports, a reliable rail system and extensive roadways, Senegal boasts a strong and generally effective transportation infrastructure, which sets it apart from many other African countries. Highly developed roads, including seven kilometers of expressways, are mostly dense in the heavily popular western region; however, small roads tend to be poorly maintained, and in the rainy season, some of the country's roads are impassable. There is an international airport located in Dakar and there are several domestic airports in other cities across the country.

A strong rail system connects major cities in Senegal and serves as both a means of industrial and agricultural transport and civilian travel within the country. Railroads are government-owned and stretch for 906 kilometers (562 miles) across the country. Transport lines and routes are dense in the more populated western region of the country, while less available throughout the inland. In addition, because of Senegal's location on the westernmost tip of Africa, various seaports serve both as important travel centers and are critical shipping centers for import-export business in the region.

Media & Communications

In 1996, Senegal achieved full Internet connectivity, allowing for increased technological business and personal communication. Phone lines are active and reliable throughout the more developed parts of the country. However, an energy crisis in 2006 and 2007 resulted in blackouts throughout the country, limiting access to non-print information media. In addition, almost one-quarter of the country's population has access to the Internet—3 million people, according to 2014 estimates.

Senegal has a well-respected and well-read output of print media. The most popular newspaper in the country is *Le Soleil*, followed by *Wal Fadjri L'Aurore*, *L'Observateur*, and *Sud Quotidien*, all published in French.

SOCIAL DEVELOPMENT

Standard of Living

In 2013, the country ranked 163rd out of 187 countries on the United Nations Human Development Index, which measures quality of life indicators. In 2015, the infant mortality rate was 51.54 deaths per 1,000 births.

Water Consumption

In 2007, it was estimated that 80 percent of the country's water consumption needs were met by underground aquifers. In 2015, more than three-quarters of the population had access to improved drinking water sources, and just over two-thirds had access to adequate sanitation. The country has a relatively high level of quality when it comes to water and sanitation services compared to other countries in sub-Saharan Africa.

Education

Senegal is a largely illiterate nation. The overall literacy rate (referring to persons over the age of fifteen who can read and write) is 57.7 percent (2015).Very few adults have developed reading and writing skills in French, English or Wolof. Despite a law requiring children to attend school for a minimum of six years, most do not. The lack of compliance with this law and the failure of officials to enforce it contribute to the poor education of the Senegalese.

Nearly half of the population attends elementary school, but very few continue their education at the secondary level. Higher education is not valued in Senegal as it is in some other African nations, and there are few universities. Major universities include the University of Dakar and Gaston Berger University. Most of the schools were established by the French, and are based on the Western system of education. In 2005, it was estimated that 15 percent of female students attended secondary school; the literacy rate is generally low, but more so for women, 46.6 percent of whom were literate in 2015 (compared with nearly 70 percent of men).

Most Senegalese children are raised in a family learning environment that includes the teaching of basic life skills. Children are often expected to learn the family trade and agriculture, and usually learn history and cultural traditions through folklore and music.

Women's Rights

Senegal falls below the international standards set for women's rights. While the nation retains an overall low level of civilian literacy, the female literacy rate is particularly low at only 46.6 percent. Because they are unskilled for work in many parts of the country, uneducated Senegalese, women often resort to prostitution as a means of employment, increasing their risk of HIV infection. Nonprofits such as World Education and the Association Contra La Lute de Sida (Association to Fight HIV/AIDS, or ARLS) are actively working in the country to educate and empower women to protect themselves. However, Senegalese women have full suffrage and are well represented in the voting process.

Once a source of significant controversy, female circumcision (or female genital mutilation) was banned in 1999. Though the practice still exists in rural communities, it is not viewed as an active human rights threat forced upon women as a rite of passage. The 1972 Family Laws established standards for women's sexual and familial rights, blending traditional Islamic laws with elements of Western legal systems. Notably missing from the list of rights granted and acknowledged is the recognition of marital rape. Economic problems facing women in Senegal tend to take priority over personal and health matters.

In March 2008, the Senegalese government signed a "virtual" petition spearheaded by the United Nations Development Fund for Women (UNIFEM), now called UN Women, voicing support for global advocacy against violence toward women.

Health Care

There is a severe lack of medical facilities and doctors in Senegal. Many Senegalese die from viral and bacterial infections contracted from food, water, and sexual activity. Parasitic worms and river blindness are two particularly devastating health problems that plague Western Africa. Senegal has a low life expectancy—59 years for men and 63 years for women (2015 estimate).

GOVERNMENT

Structure

France's colonial influence began in the 19th century and had a lasting effect in Senegal. It eliminated the power of Senegal's tribal chiefs and established a European system of governance that continues into the 21st century. Today, Senegal has a French-styled democratic system of government that includes a prime minister and a president, as well as a representative cabinet. The president has broad powers, and serves a seven-year term. Senegal's government includes a National Assembly of 150 members and several ministers appointed by the president and prime minister. Senegal's constitution was rewritten in 2001 and has been amended many times since then, most recently in 2009. Eighteen is the voting age in Senegal.

Political Parties

Although there is a unicameral legislature, there are several major political parties represented in the National Assembly, including a great number of active socialist groups and a democratic party. Abboulaye Wade, who was elected president in 2000 and reelected in the February 2007 presidential election, winning 56 percent of the vote, formed the Senegalese Democratic Party (PDS)

in 1974. His decision to run for a third presidential term sparked a large public backlash that led to his defeat in a March 2012 runoff election with Macky Sall, a former ally and prime minister. Sall ultimately won the 2012 runoff. Since taking office, he has launched an economic reform program aimed at boosting economic growth, and his administration has conducted corruption investigations against senior figures in Wade's government.

Local Government

Senegal comprises 14 regions that are each led by a governor, two deputy governors, and a regional assembly. The regions are divided into 34 departments and further subdivided into 320 rural councils.

Judicial System

The judicial system of Senegal comprises a Constitutional Council, Court of Final Appeals, Court of Cassation, and Council of State.

Taxation

The top income tax rate in Senegal is 50 percent and the country's top corporate tax rate is 25 percent. Other taxes levied include a vehicle tax, a value-added tax (VAT), real estate tax, stamp tax, and business license tax.

Armed Forces

The armed forces of Senegal comprise the Senegalese Navy, Army, and Air Force. In the early 21st century, Senegal dispatched soldiers for peacekeeping missions in African countries such as Sierra Leone and the Democratic Republic of Congo.

Foreign Policy

The French colonized Senegal in 1677. It remained a French territory until independence in 1960. During the colonial period, it was used as an important port for the slave trade with the West. In 1959, Senegal joined forces with the territory then known as the French Sudan to create the Mali Federation, an effort that was never brought to fruition and dissolved that very year.

However, that action sparked a movement that resulted in Senegal's independence. The country briefly merged with the Gambia, forming Senegambia Confederation in 1982. The countries broke apart seven years later and remain two separate territories.

In the late 20th century, President Abdou Diof worked to strengthen international relations and make his mark as an African leader in human rights advocacy. As such, Senegal maintains a strong cooperative relationship with France and is in good standing with other European countries and the U.S. It has been active in United Nations (UN) peace efforts, serving on the UN's Security Council in 1988–1989. In this capacity, Senegal provided aid and support to other African countries. Senegal has also actively intervened in crises in the Sudan, Cote d'Ivoire, and the Democratic Republic of Congo in efforts to gain peaceful conflict resolution. It also houses 13,699 refugees from Mauritania.

The international community has been supportive in aiding Senegalese programs for debt relief and economic reform. In addition, Senegal practices a conscription military service, enlisting soldiers for two-year terms. While generally free from conflict, the Senegalese military has supported a number of UN and Economic Community of West African States (ECOWAS) humanitarian and peacekeeping missions.

Civil strife has resulted in displacement issues that affect relations with neighboring countries, particularly in the southern Casamance region The people of Casamance, the southern strip of the country located just below the Gambia, are largely Christians and ethnic Diolas. They differ culturally from their mostly Muslim and Wolof neighbors to the north. Since 1982, activists and rebels have fought to break from Senegal and establish their own nation, leaving up to 24,000 still displaced people in 2014. Residents of the region have often sought refuge in the Gambia and Guinea-Bissau. These two countries have been supportive in receiving refugees and attempting to help resolve the conflict.

Human Rights Profile

International human rights law insists that states respect civil and political rights, and promote an individual's economic, social, and cultural rights. The United Nations Universal Declaration on Human Rights (UDHR) is recognized as the standard for international human rights. Its authors sought the counsel of the world's great thinkers, philosophers, and religious leaders, and were careful to create a document that reflects the core values shared by every world culture. (To read this document or view the articles relating to cultural human rights, visit http://www.un.org/en/documents/udhr/.)

With regard to Article 18 of the UN Declaration on Human Rights, women and men considered to be of age are allowed marriage rights. Inconsistencies in legal rights include an age difference allowing women to marry at a younger age than men, and men the right to polygamous marriages with up to four consenting wives. However, all decisions within these structures and the institution of marriage and divorce are to be consensual and given equal weight before the law. In 2004, the country abolished the death penalty, taking a bold step that advocates hope will influence other West African countries.

Regarding Articles 2 and 18—indicating freedom of thought, political and/or religious persuasion and equality regardless of race, ethnicity or gender—Senegal maintains a respectable record of pluralism, or the distribution of political power, and freedom. Still, both Senegalese and global free speech advocates criticize the government for controlling and censoring news media. Rappers and hip-hop artists, significant influences on youths' political views and social engagement in the late 20th and early 21st centuries, have been subject to taxation and harassment for refusing to support government figures and policies. In fact, such artists have come forward disclosing offers for tax breaks for favorable lyrics and tax increases for public criticism. Incidents such as the 2006 beating and threatening of a news reporter who voiced criticism of a well-known Muslim leader have further curbed freedom of speech in Senegal.

Additionally, there is a certain level of distrust among civilians who suspect that elections, such as those held in 2000 and 2007, have been rigged. Those critical of the Senegalese government maintain that it is more authoritarian than democratic. One example of government control is evident through the enforcement of "ordre publique" ("public order"), the government's effort to keep all demonstrations and public protests peaceful and with the interests of civilians in mind. Critics argue that government officials often ban or break up demonstrations that they consider threatening.

In 1982, Senegal signed the African Charter on Human and People's Rights. However, homosexuality is illegal in Senegal, punishable by jail time. Furthermore, there are no anti-discrimination laws, and activists often cite governmental tolerance of discrimination.

In addition, many activists are concerned that hostility toward homosexuality in Senegal contributes to the spread of the human immunodeficiency virus (HIV) and acquired immunodeficiency syndrome (AIDS). Senegal has a relatively low HIV/AIDS infection rate (0.53 percent of the population, or 44,000 people, were reported to have the virus in 2014) but is low on the United Nations Human Development Index (HDI), indicating a need for economic development, poverty reduction, and education and advocacy. Various non-governmental organizations (NGO) are active in the country battling these issues.

Healthcare in the country's urban centers is considered excellent in comparison to many other sub-Saharan African countries, and clinics, hospitals, and doctors are readily available for most of the country's citizens. When necessary, international aid programs such as the Red Cross and the World Health Organization (WHO) provide support.

ECONOMY

Overview of the Economy

The gross domestic product (GDP) of Senegal was $33.61 billion (USD) in 2014, with a per capita GDP of $2,300 (USD). Senegal is a distinctly poor nation. As a developing country, the importance of agriculture to the economy is great. Dakar's activity as a trading port is also crucial to the country's economic health, as most of Senegal's exported and imported goods come through the capital city. France has long been the primary trading partner of Senegal, and because of the brisk trade between the two countries, Senegal's industrial sector has survived. Nigeria, China, and the Netherlands are also trading partners with Senegal.

Food and beverages, and capital goods, in addition to coal and petroleum, are the country's chief imports. Most manufacturing jobs are related to agriculture, processing exported goods, and refining imported oil.

With an international airport and railroads, as well as radio, television, magazines and newspapers, Senegal's transportation and communication infrastructures are among the most

The capital Dakar is considered a major African port city owing to its location on the western edge of the African continent. Much of its industry is based around the port, including numerous import-export operations and fisheries.

Despite Senegal's relative poverty, Dakar's economy is among the strongest in Africa, attracting unemployed people from across the country to steady jobs in the ports and the military.

Industry

In 2014, the industry sector accounted for almost 24 percent of the country's GDP. Dakar's main industry is food processing; many of these products, including peanuts and peanut oil, gum arabic, and phosphoric salts, are exported. Dakar also has a petroleum refinery, and is considered a significant financial center in the region.

Labor

In 2014, the labor force of Senegal was 6.326 million. An estimated 77.5 percent of the labor force works in agriculture and 22.5 percent works in the industry and service sectors. The country's unemployment rate was 48 percent in 2007.

Energy/Power/Natural Resources

Western Africa has no natural coal or petroleum resources. For this reason, Senegal imports all of its major energy sources, and has a limited rate of industrial development. However, Senegal's land is rich in lime, which is the primary mineral export.

Fishing

The country's fishing industry is vital as it is a major domestic food source, accounting for 75 percent of the population's animal-protein consumption, and meets a growing international demand. In 2013, fishery exports brought in more than $250 million (USD). In 2009, it was estimated that the fishing industry provided 600,000 jobs in Senegal. The country's most plentiful and lucrative catch is tuna; other species caught include shrimp, prawn, octopus, and cuttlefish. Challenges to the fishing industry include a lack of infrastructure and diminishing annual catches from the late 20th to the early 21st century.

Forestry

Approximately 44 percent of Senegal is forested. In 2009, the forestry industry employed 12,700 people; that same year, it was estimated that the economic value of the country's wood production was $15 million (USD) and $3 million (USD) for non-timber forest products.

Mining/Metals

The minerals industry accounted for 20 percent of the country's GDP and made up roughly 20 percent of the country's exports in 2009. Commonly mined materials in Senegal include gold, iron ore, copper, and diamonds, as well as phosphates. Senegal's export of gold in 2013 was valued at $329 million (USD).

Agriculture

The majority of Senegalese people living in rural areas are farmers. Peanuts are farmed throughout Senegal and provide the overwhelming majority of agricultural revenue. In fact, peanuts are the largest economic resource in Senegal; in 2011, 13,806 tons of peanuts were exported.

Senegalese farmers are generally self-sufficient, and consume most of the rice, millet, cassava, and vegetables they grow. Although agriculture is essentially the primary economic sector, the land in Senegal is not ideal for farming. The ground is sandy and rocky, and the only significant rainfall occurs in the southern region.

Animal Husbandry

In the early 21st century, there were an estimated 3.2 million head of cattle in Senegal, as well as 9.3 million goats and sheep. Poultry (mainly in the form of chicken) numbered roughly 21 million, and there were approximately 330,000 pigs and over half a million horses. Areas in which the livestock industry is prominent include the poorer northern and southeast regions.

Tourism

Over the years, tourist traffic has fluctuated in Senegal. Dakar and other parts of the coastal region remain the most popular spots for visitors. Despite government-funded immersion programs for tourists interested in seeing the rural areas of Senegal, the political disputes in the Casamance have limited tourism to the coastal region.

Caroline Walker, Richard Means, Alex K. Rich

DO YOU KNOW?

- The Dakar Rally is an annual off-road automobile endurance race that has been held every year since 1977, when a racer became lost in the African desert. Although this has not been the case every year, the race traditionally either begins or ends in Dakar.

- Traditional Senegalese culture has many superstitions and mythologies. One popular myth is that the baobab tree was plucked out of the ground and replanted upside-down.

Bibliography

Buggenhagen, Beth A. *Muslim Families in Senegal.* Bloomington, IN: Indiana University Press, 2012.

Gadjigo, Samba and Faulkingham, Ralph. *Ousmane Sembene: Dialogues with Critics and Writers.* Amherst, MA: University of Massachusetts Press, 1993.

Harney, Elizabeth. *In Senghor's Shadow: Art, Politics, and the Avant-Garde in Senegal, 1960–1995.* Durham: NC: Duke University Press, 2004.

Jones, Hilary. *The Metis of Senegal.* Bloomington, IN: Indiana University Press, 2013.

Neveu Kringelbach, Helene. *Dance Circles: Movement, Morality, and Self-Fashioning in Urban Senegal.* New York: Berghahn Books, 2013.

Roberts, Allen F. and Roberts, Mary Nooter. *A Saint in the City: Sufi Arts of Urban Senegal.* Berkeley, CA: University of California Press, Fowler, 2003.

Sembene, Ousmane. *God's Bits of Wood.* London: Heinemann, 1996.

Tenaille, Frank. *Music is the Weapon of the Future: Fifty Years of African Popular Music.* Chicago, IL: Lawrence Hill Books, 2002.

Works Cited

"A Taste of Senegal." *Business Network: Food and Beverage Industry.* Online. Accessed July 13, 2008. http://findarticles.com/p/articles/mi_m3289/is_5_177/ai_n2545428

"African Underground Vol 1 – Hip Hop – Senegal." *Global Music Culture.* Online. http://www.flyglobalmusic.com/fly/archives/africamiddle_east_features/african_undergr.html

"Africa South of the Sahara: NATIONAL CINEMAS." *Film Reference.* Online. Accessed July 13, 2008. http://www.flimreference.com/encyclopedia/Academy-Awards-Crime-Films/Africa-South-of-the-Sahara-NATIONAL-CINEMAS.html

"Senegal." *CIA: The World Factbook.* Online. https://www.cia.gov/library/publications/the-world-factbook/geos/sg.html

"Senegal." *UN Data.* Online. http://data.un.org/CountryProfile.aspx?crName=senegal

"Senegal – Language, Culture, Customs and Etiquitte." Kwintessential Cross Cultural Solutions." Online. http://www.kwintessential.co.uk/resources/global-etiquette/senegal.html

"Senegal: Saving Women's Lives: Reducing Women's Vulnerability to HIV in Rural Senegal." World Education. Online. http://www.worlded.org/WEIInternet/features/senegal_saving_womens_lives.cfm

"Senegal with Lewis & Clark College." Online. http://www.lclark.edu/~senegal/.htm

"Senegalese President, Cabinet Ministers Sign UNIFEM's Say NO to Violence against Women Campaign." Online. http://www.unifem.org/news_events/story_detail.php?StoryID=660

"Sodomy Laws: Senegal." *Sodomy Laws.* Online. 2005. Online. http://www.sodomylaws.org/

"The Status of Human Rights Organizations in Sub-Saharan Africa: Senegal." *University of Minnesota Human Rights Library.* 1997. Online. http://www1.umn.edu/humanrts/africa/senegal.htm

"Women's Center in Rufisque, Senegal." *Open Architecture Network.* Online. March 12, 2007. Accessed July 1, 2008. http://www.openarchitecturenetwork.org/node/482

"World Cultures: Senegalese." *Every Culture.* Online. http://www.everyculture.com/wc/Rwanda-to-Syria/Senegalese.html

"In Senegal, a Movement to Reject Female Circumcision." Online. http://www.pbs.org/newshour/rundown/senegalese-movement-advocates-rejecting-female-circumcision/

African Cookbook: Senegal. Online. http://www.africa.upenn.edu/Cookbook/Senegal.html

BBC News Online. "Country Profile: Senegal." Online. http://www.bbc.com/news/world-africa-14093674

Senegal Embassy Homepage: Welcome to Senegal. "Senegalese Food and Drink." *Online.* Senegal Food and Dining." iExplore website. Online. http://www.iexplore.com/dmap/Senegal/Dining

Mclellan, Dennis. "Ousmane Sembene, 84; Senegalese hailed as 'the father of African film.'" Online. http://articles.latimes.com/2007/jun/14/local/me-sembene14

Teen Freedom website. "An International Survey: Senegal." Online. http://teenfreedom.wordpress.com/country-reports/senegal/

http://senegal.embassyhomepage.com/senegal_travel_information_senegalese_embassy_london_uk_cheap_flights_senegal_hotel_deals_senegal_holiday_travel_insurance.htm

City Population: Senegal website Online. Accessed http://www.citypopulation.de/Senegal.html

Quist-Artcton, "Senegal: Pop Stars and Youth Break Taboos to Spread AIDS Message." *Louga, Senegal.* Online. June 17, 2001. http://allafrica.com/stories/200106280576.html

UN Treaty No 16159. "France and Senegal: Agreement on cultural co-operation (with annexes)." March 29, 1974.

"Senegal." *Encyclopaedia Britannica*/Encyclopaedia Britannica Online. http://www.britannica.com/place/Senegal#toc55040

U.S. Department of State website. "Background Note: Senegal." Online. http://www.state.gov/r/pa/ei/bgn/2862.htm

Poling a canoe in the Turtle Islands of Sierra Leone. iStock/tropicalpixsingapore.

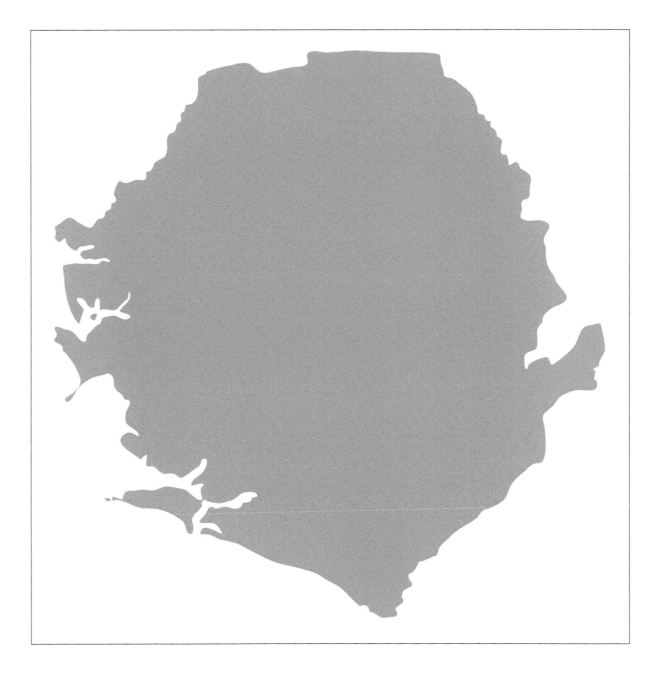

SIERRA LEONE

Introduction

Sierra Leone ("Lion Mountain" in Portuguese) is a small West African country. Officially known as the Republic of Sierra Leone, Guinea lies to the north and west, and Liberia to the southeast. The Atlantic Ocean lies to the south and west.

Sierra Leone is known for its mineral industries, particularly for its controversial diamond mines. However, its citizens rely mainly on subsistence and cash-crop agriculture, and the country has a very small urban population.

Sierra Leone is still recovering from a civil war that began in 1992 and continued until 2002, which damaged the economy and caused widespread poverty and starvation. In spite of modern problems like war, poverty, and illiteracy, Sierra Leone has a long tradition of intellectual and scientific accomplishment and was called the "Athens of West Africa" during the second half of the 19th century.

GENERAL INFORMATION

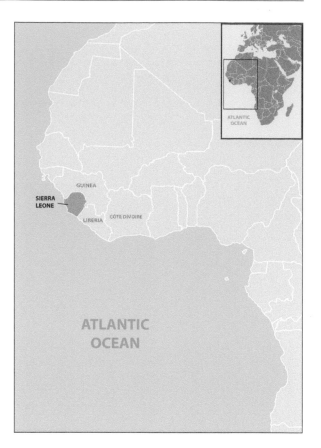

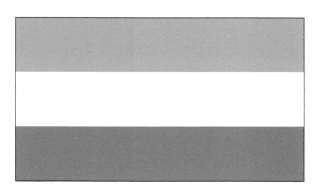

Official Language: English
Population: 6,100,000 (2013 estimate)
Currency: Leone
Coins: One hundred cents equal one leone. Coins are issued in denominations of 10, 50, 100, and 500 leone.
Land Area: 71,620 square kilometers (27,652 square miles)
Water Area: 120 square kilometers (46 square miles)

National Motto: "Unity - Freedom - Justice"
National Anthem: "High We Exalt Thee, Realm of the Free"
Capital: Freetown
Time Zone: GMT +0
Flag Description: Sierra Leone's flag is a horizontal tricolor of green (top), white (middle), and blue (bottom). The green symbolizes the mountains and natural resources, the blue represents the water, and the white represents justice.

Population

Sierra Leone has a diverse population, made up primarily of different indigenous African tribes. The largest tribal groups are the Temne (30 percent) and the Mende (30 percent). The Krio, or Creole descendants of freed slaves, make up around 10 percent of the population. Non-Africans, such as Lebanese, Indians, and Europeans, live in small communities in the country.

Principal Cities by Population (2012 estimate):

- Freetown (853,651)
- Bo (233,684)
- Kenema (182,106)
- Koidu (92,770)
- Makeni (109,125)
- Lunsar (24,450)
- Port Loko (23,195)

According to the government's statistics, about a third of the population resides in the Northern Province and a fifth of the population in the Western Area. The government attributes the rise in population growth in the west to displaced persons from the war as well as economic opportunities in the nation's capital. The density in the Bo, Kenema and Kailahun districts has much to do with the mining interests, associated industries, and agricultural development there and the availability of employment.

Languages

The major languages of the country are Krio, Mende, and Temne, which are spoken by the largest tribal groups. About 97 percent of the population understands Krio, which is considered the country's common language. English is also commonly spoken, and is used for administrative and business purposes. There are also a variety of other indigenous languages spoken in Sierra Leone.

Native People & Ethnic Groups

The native people of Sierra Leone include eighteen indigenous tribes. One of the largest, the Temne, lives in the northern part of the country. The Mende are the other major ethnic group, and are mostly found in the south. The Limba people, who also live in the north, are the third largest ethnic group in the country. Other indigenous tribes include the Koranko, Yalunka, Loko, Soso, Madingo, Fula, and Kissi.

The Portuguese were the first European explorers to reach the region in the 15th century. The British founded the colony of Sierra Leone, which was known as the "Province of Freedom," in 1787. The colony was a social experiment that would provide a home for freed slaves and poor black Europeans. After the abolition of the Atlantic slave trade in 1807, the capital of Freetown became a place where illegal slavers were tried by British courts. The black settlers began to prosper through trade.

The descendants of these black settlers are known today as the Krio. They have their own unique language and customs that have been influenced by African rituals, language, and folklore.

Religions

Islam is the major religion (71 percent of the population), especially in the north, although around 26 percent of the population is Christian. A small portion of the population follows African animist religious traditions.

Climate

Sierra Leone has a tropical rainforest climate, with a rainy season and a dry season. The rainy season lasts from April to November, with an average rainfall of 3,100 millimeters (122 inches). However, precipitation can range from 2,000 to 4,300 millimeters (78 to 169 inches) in some areas. The heaviest rainfall occurs in coastal areas.

The dry season lasts for the rest of the year, from November to April, and is characterized by dry winds or "harmattan," which originate in the Sahara Desert. The country also receives monsoon winds, which are cooler and blow in from the ocean. The hottest temperatures in Sierra Leone occur in March, and average around 33° Celsius (91° Fahrenheit). The coldest temperatures can reach 20° Celsius (68° Fahrenheit) in January. The northeastern part of the country tends to experience the most extreme temperatures.

ENVIRONMENT & GEOGRAPHY

Topography

Sierra Leone has four different physical and vegetative zones: coastal plains, interior plains, plateaus, and mountains. The coastal plain region is located in the west; it is a low-lying area made up of sand and clay soil that averages from 32 to 64 kilometers (20 to 40 miles) wide, and features mangrove swamps, rivers, estuaries, and lagoons. Some physical features of this region include beach ridges, alluvial plains, and coastal terraces. It is home to many of the country's waterfowl and fish species. The capital of Freetown is located on the Sierra Leone Peninsula on the central part of the western coast. The peninsula features forests and mountains, as well as coastal swamps.

The interior plains run from north to south and include "bolilands" or grassy savannas, rolling hills, and low plateaus. The altitude of the interior plains ranges from 40 to 200 meters (131 to 656 feet), and accounts for around 31,418 square kilometers (12,130 square miles) of the country's land area.

The plateau region is located in the eastern half of the country and is about half the size of the interior plains region, accounting for 7,691 square kilometers (2,969 square miles), or a little over 10 percent, of Sierra Leone's land area. The altitude of the plateau region reaches up to 700 meters (2,296 feet) above sea level. This area features rolling hills and plains.

The forested mountain regions of Sierra Leone reach altitudes of over 700 meters (2,296 feet). These mountains are often forested, and in the Loma Mountains in the northeast they can reach heights of over 1,828 meters (6,000 feet). Mount Loma Mansa, or Mount Bintimani, is the tallest peak in Sierra Leone, measuring 1,947 meters (6,391 feet). The 1,852-meter (6,079-foot) Sankanbiriwa Peak is another one of the country's tallest mountains; it is located in the Tingi Hills. Sierra Leone's major rivers include the Rokel, the Pampana, the Sewa, and the Moa.

Freetown sits 25.6 meters (84 feet) above sea level on a sloping landscape on the southern bank of the Sierra Leone River estuary. The western portion of the city is bordered by forested hills, some of which rise as high as 900 meters (2,700 feet). Freetown harbor, which marks the city's eastern border, is the third largest natural harbor in the world and is fed in part by the Rokel and Sierra Leone Rivers.

Plants & Animals

The rain forests and coastal and inland waters of Sierra Leone are known for their biological diversity. There are a large number of primates living in the country, including colobus monkeys, diana monkeys, and chimpanzees. Animals such as the pygmy hippopotamus, river otters, African elephants, leopards, fruit bats, lions, manatees, and zebras can also be found there.

There are numerous fish species native to Sierra Leone, including the mountain barbel, the Guinean killi, various species of lampeye and catfish, bull sharks, tetras, and gobies. Over 600 bird species have been recorded in the country, including plovers, swallows, parrots, starlings, hornbills, vultures, and bee-eaters.

Plant life is also diverse. Forests contain rare and valuable hardwood trees such as teak and African mahogany, although palm and cotton trees are more common. Areas of Sierra Leone that are covered with savanna feature plants and trees that are fire-resistant. Mangroves thrive in swampy areas, and sea grasses can be found along the coast. Coral reefs grow off the coast of the country.

CUSTOMS & COURTESIES

Greetings

English is the primary language in Sierra Leone, although the Krio dialect (descending from the Creole slaves who were emancipated in Sierra Leone) is also widely spoken, especially in Freetown, where the Krio people originated. Krio is derived from British English and the common phrases are easy to pick up.

When greeting, it is typical to shake hands. If one is shaking the hand of an elder or superior, it is polite to shake with the right hand and support one's forearm with the left hand. This implies that the superior's hand is weighty (thus acknowledging that they are of a higher status). In some tribal cultures, individuals shake hands and then touch their hand to their heart. When addressing others, honorific titles are customarily used as a courtesy. Also in keeping with the sense of community, peers are usually addressed affectionately as simply "brother" or "sister."

Greetings typically include any number of casual inquiries about one's health and family. For example, "Kusheh-o" ("Hello") is a ubiquitous greeting that can also be understood as "How are you?" The greeting "Padi, kusheh-o" ("Friend, how are you?") conveys the warm and casual nature of Sierra Leone. Other common greetings include "Aw di bohdi?" ("How are you?") or variations such as "Aw di fambul?" ("How's the family?").

Gestures & Etiquette

Sierra Leoneans are a nationalistic people who are collectively seasoned or acclimated to hardship, and are not timid in discussing it. They do not generally refrain from debating politics and current events, though some sensitivity remains from the brutal civil war that ravaged the country in the late 20th century. As for relations between men and women, there are no rigid codes of dress or conduct. However, men and women generally socialize separately in rural areas.

When eating, males are traditionally separated from the females. Rice, the staple food, is typically eaten with the hands (rolled as a ball and dipped in sauce) and elders are customarily served the choicest cuts of meat or food. Talking is traditionally not common during eating, as it shows disrespect for the food offered. Similar to Muslim culture, the right hand is exclusively used, as the left hand is used for the cleansing of the body, and is thus considered unclean.

Eating/Meals

Meals are eaten three times a day and almost always incorporate rice. Lunch is the largest meal of the day and usually consists of a communal bed of rice with sauce. Plasas is a common sauce consisting of potato or cassava leaves cooked in palm oil and tossed with beef or fish (seafood is plentiful in Freetown). Leftovers from lunch are generally set aside for breakfast, while dinner may be another rice dish or hearty stew. In the deep rural areas where meat and fresh produce are costly, many families eat simple meals of rice, potatoes, and cassava.

In the cities and towns, visitors can find a kukri (eating house) serving simple fare known as chop. There is also no shortage of inexpensive street snacks, with popular selections being fried chicken, roasted corn, fried plantains, mangoes, roasted peanuts, and skewers of grilled meat or fish. Poyo bars, which are popular hangouts for men, sell sweet fermented palm wine called poyo. Spicy ginger beer is also popular.

Food also plays a role in special occasions. Large platters of rice and sauce are served to guests, and portions are sometimes offered up to ancestors in honor of their memory.

Visiting

The culture of Sierra Leone is community-oriented and the act of visiting is central to the people's love of hospitality. Visits are frequent and typically unannounced. In fact, surprise visits are expected and invitations are rarely extended, as it is understood that spontaneous visits are welcome. Meeting times or events that are scheduled are done so with a very liberal sense of time. Guests may arrive hours after the announced time, and this is not considered a slight to the host.

Because visits are so frequent, they are generally very unceremonious. For example, men may gather outside to drink palm wine and women are likely to socialize in the kitchen. Despite the casual environment, guests are still considered a priority. Good hospitality is very personal to Sierra Leoneans and a host will often lavish the best of what they have on visitors. To reciprocate this hospitality, it is customary for a guest to present a gift to the host.

When dining, it is important for a guest to graciously accept whatever is offered, since it is generally understood that the family is likely offering the choicest items they have. Meals are typically served on a common platter, and usually on a bed of rice with hearty sauce poured in the middle. Food is customarily eaten with the hands, and portions are respectfully taken only from the part of the platter that is situated in front of each person. Often, a host will set aside certain meats and vegetables for the guest, especially in rural communities where meat or fresh vegetables are scarce. At the conclusion of the meal, water is traditionally passed around to wash hands. When leaving, hosts may escort their guests to the edge of their property.

LIFESTYLE

Family

The family unit is very sacred in Sierra Leonean culture, extending even to one's ancestors, who are sometimes offered ritual blessings and sacrifices. Many children are encouraged and as families expand, generations and extended families often reside under one roof. For example, when a son marries, his wife traditionally moves into his family's home. As they have children, additions are put on the home or another piece of property is purchased, creating a large compound. The mothers, aunts, sisters, and grandmothers all collaborate on domestic and child rearing responsibilities. Men provide the financial support and/or work the land.

There is a class system in Sierra Leone resulting in some distinction between residences, particularly in tribal areas. The chief's home can be readily identified as more elaborate and his compound often includes a separate home for his wives, as polygamy is sometimes practiced.

Housing

Civil war devastated Sierra Leone and the rebuilding process has been slow. Housing styles vary and depend on the availability of both financial and physical resources. In the urban areas, wood-framed houses have been replaced by modest and sturdy cinderblock structures. Although these are relatively inexpensive for urban dwellers, rural communities are limited

to natural resources. A typical rural home is a one- or two-room hut formed with mud bricks and topped with a thatched roof. Though these materials may be vulnerable to strong winds or sustained rains, they are also readily available and easily reconstructed. Electricity is not available in the rural areas and is inconsistent in the cities. Likewise, there is no reliable system of trash collection or disposal.

Food

Sierra Leone's cuisine is characterized by the use of locally grown staples like rice, fish, cassava, and peanuts seasoned with hot spices. Rice is the base of nearly every main dish and may be served with thick fish or meat stew ladled over the top and/or accompanied by an assortment of small vegetable dishes on the side. Groundnut stew is the most popular dish and has many varieties, depending upon which type of meat, poultry, or fish one wishes to incorporate. Groundnut stew with chicken is most often prepared at holiday celebrations. Other common ingredients include onions, peppers, yams, palm oil, and meats such as goat and pork. Fruits such as oranges, papayas, bananas, guavas, and mangoes are common, and typically eaten as snacks. Fried plantains are also a common snack. A classic dessert is ginger cake, shortbread-like cookies that are served with tea.

Life's Milestones

Marriages are not generally arranged but are strongly encouraged, and the community takes great interest in boys and girls of marrying age. Marriage is considered a foray into adulthood and, as the family unit is revered, perceived as a blessed opportunity to expand one's family tree. Most tribes have a certain initiation ceremony for young men and women of marrying age; these initiates are sometimes marked with white face paint so that they can be identified by the community.

Births and deaths are often observed with a traditional awujoh feast. This observance is designed to bring good fortune for new lives and a peaceful afterlife for those who have died.

Young people of marriageable age paint their faces white so they can be identified by the community in Sierra Leone.

CULTURAL HISTORY

Art

The history of Sierra Leone is a tumultuous one, marked by tribal conflict, subsequent European colonization, the struggle for independence and self-rule. The country has also experienced multiple generations of corruption and civil war. As a result, artistic endeavors have often taken a backseat to more pressing political concerns, and the arts were not actively patronized as they were in more stable African societies. Nonetheless, the arts, rooted in ancient tribal culture, managed to endure throughout the centuries. Rituals of folklore, dance and music, notably those of the Mende and Temne peoples—the two largest ethnicities in the country—laid the foundation for future generations. Although these art forms were introduced primarily as a mode of divine communication, or as a means of commerce, they have evolved into unique and lasting cultural expressions.

Ornamental masks carved out of bone, wood, and ivory are an integral part of tribal tradition. Used in political as well as spiritual ceremony, the masks generally showcase male forms, as men customarily wear the masks and perform the ceremonies. One exception is the Mende sowo mask, which has ties to the women's Sande society (an association that teaches females the responsibility of adulthood). The masks are carved with tall, delicate feminine features and decorated with raffia fronds that allude to female movement and dress. The aesthetics of the mask are intended to represent the female spirit. The mask is worn during initiation rituals and the final public ceremony, when the girls return to their village as marriageable women.

Carving was used domestically to channel a deity's favor. Soapstone figures known as nomoli depict crude representations of people (or sometimes human-animal hybrids) and were used as ritual offerings to bring about bountiful harvests. Their origin is vague, but they may date back as late as the eighth century. Ivory carving was especially popular in the 15th and 16th centuries when the Portuguese traders took notice of the "white gold" that was not available in their homeland. The soft texture of the ivory yields quite easily to carving. Shaped by local artisans into ornamental jewelry and other objects, the goods were so popular among European aristocrats that Sierra Leonean officials had to impose trade regulations.

Gara dyeing, also known as batik dyeing, dates back to the 19th century. The practice is named for the indigo dye that is extracted from the leaves of the gara plant (though other colors may be included, this is the most widely used). The leaves are pounded, formed into balls, and dried in the sun. A warm water bath is prepared and the gara balls are immersed to release the dye. Prewashed natural cotton fabric is then dipped repeatedly until the desired color or pattern is achieved.

Architecture

Architecture in Sierra Leone has cultural ties to two completely different pasts. On one hand are the traditional indigenous dwellings characterized by mud brick or wattle walls with thatched roofs. More modern versions of this simple structure may use concrete block and metal roofing materials. This is the architecture predominantly seen in villages and rural areas. As noted earlier, families tend to settle in compounds, which may consist of several of these structures.

The other architectural design tradition comes from resettled slaves, Krios, from the United Kingdom, North America, and the Caribbean. The structures built by this migration of settlers mirrors the plantation architecture seen in these countries, with one- or two-story wooden buildings or brightly painted plaster structures. In Freetown, Krio architecture dominates.

Drama

In keeping with its past, two traditions dominate Sierra Leone's dramatic history. Indigenous peoples have a strong oral or storytelling tradition that characterizes the dramatic traditions of tribal populations. Often, the storyteller has support from the audience in terms of refrains, clapping, and participation to further support the drama of the tale. Tribes also have their own rituals which have a dramatic element. For instance, the Temne, when hearing of the death of their leader, must act as if they know nothing of the death until it is announced by one of the chief's attendants. When the tribe is gathered, the attendant smashes a cooking pot, which prompts the community to publicly wail and grieve. Other tribes may have traditional dramas that they perform to celebrate milestones or natural cycles that include masks, costumes, dance and song.

The Krio culture in the 19th century often staged church-related dramas on Sunday mornings. At the same time, European (British) and American dramas were performed in urban areas to a Krio audience. Early 20th-century Sierra Leonean playwrights include Gladys Caeley-Hayford, who staged indigenous folk tales, and Professor N.J.G. Ballanta-Taylor, who penned African operas. They were followed in the 1950s by John Akar, who wrote of African life in his works such as *Valley Without Echo* (1957). Akar is also responsible for helping to establish the Sierra Leone National Dance Troupe in 1963.

Post-colonial plays dramatizing the lives of the urban and political elite include *Dear Parent and Ogre* (1965) and *The New Patriots* (1965) by R. Sarif Easmon. At this time, a Krio Theatre emerged, with works written in that language that were widely popular. Juliana John wrote both *Na Mami born Am* (1966) and *I Day I nor Du* (1966), which both enjoyed extended runs in Freetown. Other authors in this movement include Dele Charley and Yulisa Amadu Maddy, who would later be named minister of culture and then imprisoned for his criticism of the government.

Theater in Sierra Leone grew in the early 1980s, and Freetown's newly built city hall saw many performances. However, the government grew to dislike the criticism it was getting from the stage, particularly with works such as Kolosa John Kargbo's work *Poyo Tong Wahala* (1979), a socio-political critique. The government imposed censorship in its wake and the city hall was closed to dramatic productions in 1986. Following the government crackdown, theater troupes filled the void.

The civil strife between 1991 and 2002 hindered further development of the theater community, and in the 1990s, theater groups did much to educate the public about public health, safety, and political issues, Following the war, Western-style theater has begun to recover in Freetown, but not yet in rural areas.

Music

The music of Sierra Leone, like most African music, is characterized by infectious drumbeats and rhythms which naturally lend themselves to dance. Tribal dances are used for everything from prayer to celebration, and can last for hours. Dance music is very rhythmic, comprising either a group stomping and swaying in syncopated formations or one masked individual dancing within a circle of participants singing and chanting. This predominantly percussive style of music gave way to European influences with the arrival of the Portuguese. By introducing guitars, Sierra Leonean music took on a lighter, more nuanced sound known today as palm wine music (often compared to calypso).

SE Rogie, born Sooliman Rogers (c. 1940s–1994), is a renowned palm wine guitarist and singer who helped make the genre famous. His singular talent even earned him a performance for the Queen of England when Sierra Leone gained independence from Britain. Cultural musician Ebenezer Calendar (1912–1985) followed, and his song "Fire Fire" highlights a signature blend of palm music and gumbe drumbeats (borrowed from Jamaica), a sound often compared to samba. Palm wine and gumbe music further was revolutionized by Dr. Oloh, or Oloh Israel Olufemi Cole (1944–2007), who added his own special twist: empty Milo malt beverage cans filled with stones. This soulful percussive innovation earned him credit for the genre of milo jazz.

Literature

Sierra Leone's literary history is rooted in the storytelling traditions of tribal culture. This oral tradition was also a way to store history and tell morality tales of the various tribes, and served to both entertain and inform the community. The written word did not emerge until colonization and was mainly limited to journalism. However, as one of the world's most prominent trading sites, Sierra Leone provided its people with exposure to a variety of African, European, and West Indian cultures. These influences fueled a political spirit, particularly in the coastal region of the country. The freethinking Africanus Horton (1835–1883), a folklorist and Sierra Leone Creole writer, was an early advocate for independence, and one of the first Creoles to express a literary voice. A surgeon by trade, he worked for the British Army, but rallied for independence by publishing books that pushed for freedom from colonization.

CULTURE

Arts & Entertainment

Sierra Leone, affectionately referred to as "Sweet Salone" by locals, has the distinct misfortune of having experienced one of the most vicious civil wars in recent history. The Sierra Leone Civil War (1991–2002) lasted over a decade, and the country is still reeling from its devastating effects. One particular impact of the conflict was the lack of art patronage, as there was far too much instability to foster any art programs. However, grass roots initiatives have emerged, and the artistic expression of pre-war Sierra Leone, with its tribal offerings to the heavens and consumer trade with foreigners, has been reincarnated. Spiritual healing and economic progress are still very much at the root of local artistic endeavors. Sierra Leoneans are finding resourceful and creative ways to restore the spirit of their "Sweet Salone."

The art of gara dyeing is still practiced, and although it used to be reserved as decoration for the garb of chiefs, it is now popular everyday wear. The original techniques still apply with some new creative variations. For a more detailed result, hot wax is applied in intricate designs and cooled before the cotton is dipped. When the cotton is submerged in a cold water bath of dye, it is does not penetrate the wax, letting the design remain. These pieces are inexpensive to produce and, as it is primarily a women's craft, is a frequent choice for community associations looking to organize income-generating endeavors. Carving also remains a popular trade, though it is limited mostly to dark wood and bone. Local artisans use rudimentary tools sharpened by hand to shape masks, animals, and human forms of all shapes and sizes. Some woodwork is incorporated into ceremonial pieces, but most exquisite pieces are sold in the tourist trade.

As a catalyst of healing, war survivors are using the visual arts to deal with their grief. At one amputee camp in Freetown, victims have taken up painting to express their emotion. Local small businesses donate materials, mostly simple white paper and house paint. To help turn the therapy into an income generating effort, a division of the United Nations (UN) organizes gallery showings and the redemptive works have been selling out.

Literature is also on the rise in recent history—Syl Cheney-Coker (1945–) won the Commonwealth Writers' Prize (for African literature) for *The Last Harmattan of Alusine Dunbar* (1990). However, with an estimated 65 percent illiteracy rate, radio has become the most popular medium for entertainment.

An estimated 85 percent of the population reportedly listens to radio over watching television or reading the paper. The organization Search for Common Ground opened a production facility in Freetown called Talking Drum Studio which produces a variety of programming designed to help fellow citizens speak their minds about current affairs. One especially successful program is *The Golden Children*, a program for children that encourages dialogue about the state of the country and allows a forum to express their emotions.

Sierra Leone's music is influenced by African and European music. One popular type of music, known as palm wine or maringa music, is derived in part from calypso music. Other musical styles in Sierra Leone include bissaun gumbe music and milo-jazz.

Since the end of civil war, Sierra Leoneans, particularly the younger generations, have been inspired to speak their minds, using music as the voice of their politics. The music of the Baw Waw Society, whose mission is to use hip-hop as a vehicle for positive action, has been an anthem of change for young Sierra Leoneans who desire peace. It was not coincidence that the 2007 elections—the first since the war ended—and the withdrawal of the UN peacekeeping mission withdrew both corresponded with the release of the group's single "Ease di Tension" (Ease the Tension). It tells of needing a strong leader who will pull the country out of suffering. *Sweet Salone* is a documentary about the growing music scene in urban Freetown.

Another influential musical group is the Sierra Leone Refugee All Stars. Having fled to Guinea during the civil war, the members used music as a distraction to their fellow campmates. When the camp came under attack, the group stayed together and even acquired second-hand sound equipment and instruments from a Canadian refugee aid organization. With the help of various non-profit organizations that took an interest in the band, they organized a recording (some tracks were even field-recorded at the refugee camp). Their first album, *Living Like a Refugee*, was released in 2006. A mix of reggae and traditional drumbeats, the infectious rhythms combined with messages of hope earned them a performance on American television, most notably the *Oprah Winfrey Show.*

Cultural Sites & Landmarks

Historically, Sierra Leone is most notable for the role it played in the origin and termination of the slave trade, and the role it continues to play in the trade of conflict diamonds (also called blood diamonds). However, because of the region's rich tribal traditions and communities and the country's colonial history, Sierra Leone is home to a wealth of cultural and historical sites. Strategically located on the Atlantic coast of West Africa, Sierra Leone's varied climate also lends itself to an array of ecotourism activities. Its geographical patchwork includes coastlines, swampy rainforests, mountains, and dry savannahs. Sierra Leone's government is working fervently to develop these natural assets and lure foreign visitors.

The capital of Freetown boasts numerous cultural sites and landmarks. The Cotton Tree marks the place where transatlantic slaves were first bought and sold, as well as the site where the first free slaves gathered in 1787. When gathering to await resettlement by the British, the newly freed Krios passed under King's Yard Gate. York, a Krio village, has caves where the slaves stayed before being loaded and shipped. West of Tower Hill, the 19th-century wood-framed houses of the Krios still stand. Also located downtown are the Sierra Leone National Museum and the State House. Fourah Bay College, the oldest university college in West Africa, is located at the top of Mount Aureol and showcases dramatic views of Freetown. In addition, Bunce Island on the Sierra Leone River outside Freetown housed a British fort in 1663, and is home to the ruins of a European fort used for trading ivory and slaves. Freetown is also renowned for its beaches.

The famed landscape of Sierra Leone is accentuated by Mount Bintimani, the highest peak in the country at 1,945 meters (6,381 feet). The mountain is home to several parks and sanctuaries and a diverse array of wildlife. Sierra Leone is also home to several protected areas. The Loma Mountains Forest Reserve is a stretch of protected rainforests that house monkeys, elephants, hippos, crocodiles, baboons and buffalo. Outamba–Kilimi National Park, in northern Sierra Leone, is the nation's only national park. Devoid of roads, the park is a peaceful collection of virtually undisturbed hills, grasslands, rainforests, and rivers that can be explored by foot or canoe. South of the national park is the Tiwai Island Wildlife Sanctuary. An island on the Moa River, it holds Africa's highest concentration of primates in addition to other assorted wildlife.

Libraries & Museums

The Sierra Leone Museum is one of the country's few museums. It houses a replica of the Ruiter stone, a stone marked by Dutch sea captains that stands as the country's earliest evidence of European settlement. The Sierra Leone National Railway Museum holds a collection of railway locomotives and a coach built for Britain's Queen Elizabeth in 1961.

Sierra Leone has several heritage sites that are worthy of note, including Bunce Island, the British slave castle, and the Cotton Tree, an historical symbol of the nation's returning slave populations.

Holidays

Independence Day is celebrated in Sierra Leone on April 27. This holiday commemorates the granting of independence from Great Britain in 1961, and is marked with parades and other celebrations. One of the largest parades, the Lantern Parade, is held in Freetown. The country's Muslim and Christian populations also celebrate their respective religious holidays.

Youth Culture

The youth culture of Sierra Leone is typical of most youth cultures. Music is a defining

characteristic, socializing is a common activity, and sports, most notably football (soccer), is a popular activity and spectator event. Many youth are fans of the Leone Stars, the national football team. Although they have never made it to the World Cup, they have competed in the African Cup of Nations. Football is particularly popular among young boys, who can be found playing in the streets, while adolescent males and teenagers convene in coffee shops to watch football matches on TV or listen via the radio. Cricket and basketball are also popular sports. In the rural areas, girls enjoy crafting and generally stay close to home, whereas in the city both sexes typically mingle. Attending the cinema (mostly to see foreign films) and dancing at the disco are popular activities for older youth. Reggae music and Western Top 40 music are the most popular genres of music.

SOCIETY

Transportation

Sierra Leone's urban transportation system is modest. There is an international airport outside Freetown with flights running mainly to England or other West African countries. Private vehicle ownership is low, with only about three out of every 1,000 people owning a vehicle. Drivers travel on the right side of the road in Sierra Leone.

Private buses with no pre-determined routes, called poda poda, can be flagged like taxis, and are found in the cities and small towns. In the deep rural communities, roads are unpaved and the residents primarily walk between destinations.

Transportation Infrastructure

There is no active railway in Sierra Leone, although tracks remain from the defunct Sierra Leone Government Railway that folded in 1974. There are three ports, used mainly for cargo. There is also a paved highway system that is being absorbed into the Trans-West African Coastal Highway. This will be the only link between the infrastructure of Sierra Leone and its neighboring countries.

Media & Communications

English is the official language of Sierra Leone, although the different tribes have specific dialects that they use in informal contexts. Several of these languages are also broadcast on the government's local radio programs. Despite the 65 percent illiteracy rate, the Internet is hugely popular in Freetown and Internet cafés are plentiful; only 1.7 percent of the population is connected to the Internet as of 2013. According to the International Telecommunication Union in 2009, more than a million Sierra Leoneans own a cell phone.

Newspapers are less popular but nonetheless available. *Awoko* and *The Concord Times* are the two most prominent newspapers. As for television, the government-produced SLBS TV is scarcely watched for anything more than the occasional music video. Urban or rural, families swarm around their televisions to follow American serial dramas and Nigerian soap operas that air on the privately owned ABC Africa.

SOCIAL DEVELOPMENT

Standard of Living

The country ranked 183rd out of 187 on the 2014 United Nations Human Development Index (HDI), which measures quality of life indicators.

Water Consumption

Unsafe water conditions plague a significant portion of Sierra Leone's rural areas. The water and sanitation infrastructure suffered from the years of civil war. The Guma Valley Water Company regulates Freetown's vulnerable water supply. Currently 62 percent of the population has access to clean water.

A snail that carries bilharzia, a dangerous flatworm that causes the disease schistosomiasis, also inhabits many inland waterways, making drinking and swimming nearly impossible.

Education

Historically, Sierra Leone has had a sophisticated and influential educational system. The Fourah Bay College, an important African university, was founded in 1827. While it was under British colonial control, Sierra Leone had a highly educated and intellectual ruling class. The Krios became important participants in education and government.

The literacy rate in the country is around 48 percent, with men at almost 59 percent and women at 38 percent. Most children attend school, but those living in rural areas face many obstacles—students have to walk long distances to reach their schools, and balance schoolwork with domestic responsibilities that are important for their families' survival. Sierra Leone is working to modernize and rebuild its schools, and to train more teachers, but a shortage of resources is a serious impediment.

Women's Rights

The perceived status of women in Sierra Leone is rather contradictory. Within the country's culture, the family unit is revered and women are valued for the crucial role they play as child-bearers and child-rearers. Although men seemingly are the principle decision makers, with women deferring to them, this is often misinterpreted. Men are generally more educated and provide the household income and are the voice of the family outside of the home. However, within the home, the women are very much the center of the family nucleus and are essentially the driving force behind the development and nurturing of the family. Whereas Westernized nations may view this type of family as antiquated and oppressive, the women of Sierra Leone might traditionally view their role with satisfaction and empowerment.

Despite the insistence within Sierra Leone that women are highly valued, international human rights watch groups have shed light on some inarguable wrongs. Gender violence, for one, was particularly rampant during the recent civil war. It is estimated that over one third of the country's women and girls were abducted by rebels during the civil war and forced to endure sexual assault. Gender violence was used by the insurgents as a vehicle for intimidation and oppression, and the government has not taken steps to address the brutality. Whereas former child soldiers have been absorbed into orphanages and are granted resources for therapy and rehabilitation, victims of sexual violence have been left to provide for themselves. In addition, domestic violence, which is not specifically prohibited by law (nor is spousal rape), continues to be a major concern, as is rape, which is common. Sexual harassment is also considered to be common and human trafficking, particularly for sexual exploitation, remains a problem.

Another questionable practice is the Sande (known as Bondo in other regions of the country) society. Found in several West African cultures, Sande/Bondo is a rather powerful association of women that represents their social and political interests before the Poro, their male-counterpart organization. One of the primary objectives of the Sande/Bondo society is to guide young women in their transition from childhood to womanhood, schooling them in the ways of morality and personal conduct. One particularly concerning ritual for human rights groups is the ritual of initiation into womanhood. Adolescent girls are taken to a remote forest for weeks or months where they are trained in crafts and household duties, given surgical distinctions of their rite of passage such as female genital mutilation (FGM), and returned to their communities fully eligible for marriage. (This practice is not adhered to by the Christian Creole population in the Western Area.) While respecting the society as a cultural institution, human rights groups are adamant that the initiation deprives young girls of their freedom and the right to pursue their schooling.

Health Care

The health and welfare sectors in Sierra Leone are controlled by the central government. The country has a number of hospitals; the most modern and advanced medical clinics are located in the capital of Freetown and in the city of Bo. Public health and health care in Sierra Leone face many problems. Many people are too poor to buy medicine or to pay for medical services. The civil war destroyed much of the country's health infrastructure and equipment.

Infectious diseases such as malaria, dysentery, and other illnesses are a problem in the country, as are residual physical and mental health problems from the civil war. Common diseases include polio, diphtheria, tetanus, and measles; the government provides immunizations for these illnesses. Sierra Leone has one of the highest maternity mortality ratio, or rate of maternal death in childbirth, of any country in the world; its infant mortality rate is eighty deaths per 1,000 live births, putting it fourteenth in the world. The average life expectancy is 58 years—55 for men and 60 for women (2015 estimate).

In 2014 an Ebola virus epidemic began in Sierra Leone as part of a wider epidemic in West Africa. By the end of 2014, there were 13,500 cases reported of which nearly 4,000 died. In September of 2014 the country observed a nationwide three day quarantine called the Ouse to Ouse Tock. As of August 2015 teams fighting the disease say they may have seen the last of the cases.

GOVERNMENT

Structure

Today, Sierra Leone has positioned itself as a republic with a democratically elected president, but it is important to put the current structure in its historical context. Sierra Leone gained its independence from Great Britain on April 27, 1961, but the early government of the republic failed to represent all of the people adequately. It catered to the wealthier classes and to the powerful Mende ethnic group. As a result of tensions caused by political inequality, there was a military coup in March 1967. This coup began a period of political unrest that lasted until 1978, when the constitution was rewritten to ensure a one-party system of government.

The one-party system led to a number of problems, particularly during elections, which were marked by widespread corruption and murder in the 1980s. In 1991, after nearly three decades of political conflict, Sierra Leone returned to a multi-party system of government. However, a 1992 coup prevented the country from becoming a democracy. A civil war between the governing National Provisional Ruling Council and the Revolutionary United Front (RUF), a rebel group, followed. Thousands of people were killed and many were maimed, as the RUF often tortured its victims with amputation. The RUF also frequently kidnapped and drugged children, and used child soldiers in its ranks.

The 1999 Lome Peace Agreement was signed in order to placate the RUF leaders with political positions and to bring United Nations peacekeepers into the country, but it failed to achieve lasting peace. After a process of disarmament and ceasefire agreements in the late 1990s and early 2000s, the civil war was officially declared to be over in January 2002. There is still an ongoing process to reintegrate rebels into society, and former RUF members continue to be tried for war crimes. In March 2014 the UN Integrated Peacebuilding Office closed after 15 years of operation.

The president acts as head of government, and runs on the same ticket as the vice-president, who assumes office should the president resign or be unable to complete his five-year term. The president is popularly elected and appoints a cabinet which must be approved by the parliament. The unicameral parliament has 121 seats. One hundred nine seats are elected at the same time as the president, and the remaining seats are filled by the twelve paramount chiefs, one from each district.

Political Parties

Sierra Leone maintains a multi-party system. The two major parties in the country are the All People's Congress (APC), which represents those settled in the north of the country (essentially the Temne and Limba people), and the Sierra Leone People's Party (SLPP), which largely represents those from the southeast portion of the country (the Mende people). In the 2012 election, the APC prevailed by winning 59 seats and the SLPP took 43 seats. Another party, the People's Movement for Democratic Change (PMDC), received 3.23 per cent of the vote, but failed to take any seats; losing the 10 it won in 2007.

Local Government

Traditionally, chiefs and councils of elders head local governments throughout the country. Decentralization efforts have resulted in local elections in 2004 and 2008. The elections proved successful and in 2010, there are twelve district councils and five town councils outside of the Western Area. Within the Western Area, there is a Freetown city council and a rural council. Within local governments, elected councils are responsible for services and are working with chiefs on revenue collection. Chiefs and their councils are responsible for public safety (police) and local courts. As the nation sees further devolution, local governments may assume more local control of issues.

Judicial System

The Supreme Court is the highest court in the judicial branch of government. Other courts include local, traditional courts in rural areas, magistrate courts, a Court of Appeals and the High Court of Justice.

Taxation

Sierra Leone's government levies taxes on personal and corporate income, capital gains, sales, vehicles, interest, fuel, as well as social security taxes and local taxes and fees.

Armed Forces

The volunteer Republic of Sierra Leone Armed Forces consists of an army, which has an air and navy wing.

Foreign Policy

Sierra Leone has maintained strong diplomatic relationships with its African neighbors as well as the United States and the United Kingdom (UK). The government is a member of the African Union (AU), the African Development Bank

(AFDB), the Economic Community of West African States (ECOWAS), the Non-Aligned Movement (NAM), the Organization of the Islamic Conference (OIC), and the UN. Primary policy concerns are domestic: Sierra Leone has suffered decades of political instability, resulting in extreme poverty, and the repercussions have impacted all of Africa. The UN has been highly influential in supporting the country's nation building, with the understanding that the peaceful restoration of Sierra Leone will ultimately affect stability throughout Africa.

The large majority of Sierra Leone's population subsists on agriculture, and farming accounts for nearly half of the national income. The climate supports a range of produce, including palm oil, peanuts, carrots, eggplants, sweet potatoes, cassava, plantains, watermelon, mangos, and bananas. Farmed products are mainly for domestic consumption/ Although the agriculture industry is very active, the produce is not enough to sustain the population. Particularly as the country works to rebuild itself post-civil war, poverty is widespread and outside assistance (particularly the import of rice) is necessary to combat hunger.

Sierra Leone's economy depends largely on the trade of its natural resources. The country's primary trading partners are Belgium, the U.S., the UK, and Germany. In previous decades, as government corruption began to spread, the mining industry and the national economy slowed. By the 1990s, when civil war seized the country, diamond smuggling was rampant and the industry was reduced to corrupt transactions between rebel forces. Since 2002, when a resolution was finally negotiated by the UN, the health of the diamond trade has been targeted as a necessary building block of peace in Sierra Leone and, ultimately, all of Africa. Many nations, primarily the U.S. and Britain, have come forward to offer economic assistance and help restore the integrity of the industry.

So far, Sierra Leone's government has successfully maintained political stability. Though the country still relies heavily on international aid, the diamond trade is gaining strength and slowly bolstering the rest of the economy. As

the export of raw materials increases and money begins to flow within the country again, the government is exploring the growth of new industries like eco-tourism and the energy sector. Consequently, foreign investors, previously deterred by the persistent corruption and civil unrest, are recognizing the country's success and investing in the growth of its economy.

Human Rights Profile

International human rights law insists that states respect civil and political rights, and promote an individual's economic, social, and cultural rights. The United Nations Universal Declaration on Human Rights (UDHR) is recognized as the standard for international human rights. Its authors sought the counsel of the world's great thinkers, philosophers, and religious leaders, and were careful to create a document that reflects the core values shared by every world culture. (To read this document or view the articles relating to cultural human rights, visit http://www.udhr.org/UDHR/default.htm.)

The population of Sierra Leone has sustained an array of human rights violations in recent decades. Notable violations include the right to life, liberty, and security, freedom from slavery and servitude, freedom from torture, and the right to a healthy standard of living. One of the most immediate concerns has been conflict diamonds and the integrity of the diamond trade. Conflict diamonds are rough diamonds sold by rebel movements and their allies to finance the destabilization of legitimate governments. As one of the world's premier sources of raw diamonds, Sierra Leone's mines were a pawn for fraudulent politicians and rebel insurgents during the country's 10 years of civil unrest.

The corruption of the industry not only devastated the country's entire economy, causing deep poverty; it also funded the atrocities of war— namely, forcible deployment of child soldiers. Abducted from their homes, local children, some as young as five or six years old, were forced to serve in rebel armies under penalty of death. Generally, young boys were trained to wield guns and young girls were responsible for operations (cooking, cleaning) at the rebel camps. Today, thanks to the partnership of the local government and international relief organizations, these children are being rehabilitated so that they might assimilate into a civilized life and pursue their education. This ongoing success is due in large part to the regulation of the diamond industry.

In 2003, the UN sanctioned the launch of the Kimberley Process Certification Scheme in collaboration with African diamond-purchasing states. The Kimberley Process regulates the trade of rough diamonds and is designed to promote peace and prosperity among African nations. Participating governments agree to strict trade policies and uphold full transparency of their operations. Diamonds that pass through stringent controls are ultimately issued a Kimberly Process Certification, which guarantees compliance with the scheme, since participating countries may only trade certified diamonds. Whereas before the Kimberly Process conflict diamonds accounted for over 15 percent of global diamond production, they now comprise only a trace of 1 percent.

The stabilizing effect of these regulations has opened the door to further human rights reform in Sierra Leone. As the economy strengthens, the government is working to lessen its dependency on international relief and pull its population out of poverty. Progress is slow, but with the help of foreign investments, the country is working to implement small improvements, like consistent electricity and improved medical care, which will help restore the standard of living.

Migration
Sierra Leone's migration rate is –3.12 per 1,000 people, meaning that it is losing people to emigration, probably due to unemployment and severe economic conditions.

ECONOMY

Overview of the Economy
The mining and mineral industries continue to be the most important economic sector in Sierra Leone. Diamonds are the most valuable raw material found in the country, although they have been at the center of controversy over smuggling and corruption. "Conflict diamonds" are diamonds that are used in money-laundering operations to fund rebel groups and criminals, and to support war. They have been smuggled over Sierra Leone's borders. Political corruption also affects the diamond industry, and was particularly rampant during the civil war.

The war was devastating to Sierra Leone's economy. When it ended in 2002, international agencies and foreign countries provided aid, and the process of rebuilding the country's economy is ongoing. Sierra Leone currently belongs to the Economic Community of West African States and to the Mano River Union, a customs union. In 2013, the gross domestic product (GDP) was estimated at around $ 4.8 billion (USD), and the GDP per capita was $679 (USD).

Sierra Leone relies on aid donations from Great Britain, the United States, and Italy, among other countries. Nearly 70 percent of the population lives in poverty. Due to its weak economy, its health crises, and its history of violent civil unrest, Sierra Leone ranks among the least hospitable to human development.

Industry
The diamond industry remains the most important sector in Sierra Leone, and around $200-$300 million (USD) in diamonds is extracted there each year. The country has been struggling to maintain control of the industry in the face of smuggling and other illegal activities.

Sierra Leone's large deposits of rutile, or titanium dioxide, have made it an important trader of this mineral on the world market. Other industries that are important to Sierra Leone include forestry, the beverage and cigarette industries, construction materials, and tourism.

Labor
The labor force in Sierra Leone is at about 2.4 million people. About half of the population engages in subsistence agriculture.

Energy/Power/Natural Resources

The civil war that ended in 2002 knocked out most of Sierra Leone's power infrastructure. Residents in Freetown frequently experience blackouts and can spend more time without power than with it. Urban areas consume 90 percent of the nation's power. Generation of electricity is highly dependent on oil-powered generators, which makes electricity expensive to produce. In 2009, the Bumbuna Hydroelectricity Dam was commissioned, a first step in increasing access to electricity throughout the country.

Fishing

Sierra Leone boasts the largest fishing grounds for shrimp in West Africa. Other catch includes tuna, snapper, mackerel, lobster and crab. The country is highly dependent on artisanal fishing for local use, and overfishing by large industrial trawlers has become a threat to that way of life and to fish stocks.

Forestry

The country, because of a lack of government control during the civil war, has suffered from severe deforestation. As of 2005, about 38 percent of the country was forested and only 4.5 percent of the land is protected. The Gola Forest Reserve has been designated as a national park and in 2008 the government re-imposed an export ban on timber.

Mining/Metals

Diamonds are Sierra Leone's most economically important natural resource. The country is also rich in other minerals, including rutile (titanium dioxide) and bauxite. The country's mining operations were interrupted during the civil war,

when rebels took control of many of the mines. Gold, platinum, and chromite are also found in Sierra Leone.

Agriculture

Farming is important in the country, and over 30 percent of the land has agricultural potential. Subsistence agriculture is the most common form of agriculture in Sierra Leone, and is practiced by two-thirds of the population. Roughly, 25 percent of the land is cultivated, and agricultural exports account for 50 percent of the country's income. Some of the major products grown for export are coffee, rice, and peanuts. The country's tropical climate is suitable for growing bananas, cocoa, ginger, cassava, citrus fruits, and palm kernels. Sweet potatoes, plantains, and other vegetables are also grown.

Animal Husbandry

Cattle, sheep, goats, chickens, and pigs are raised for meat by Sierra Leonean farmers.

Tourism

Tourism is a growing sector in Sierra Leone. The civil war made the country very dangerous for visitors; however, Sierra Leone is attempting to modernize, to build more hotels and resorts, and to make itself more tourist-friendly.

About 72,000 extended jobs are attributed to Sierra Leone's tourism industry, which includes beachside resorts and eco-tourism operations. Bunce Island, a former British colonial prison for African slaves that was founded in 1670, is also a popular site among visitors.

Heidi Edsall, Christina Healey,
Meredith Reed O'Donnell

DO YOU KNOW?

- Sierra Leone (originally, Serra Lyoa: Lion Mountains) was named by Portuguese sea captain Pedro da Cintra in 1462. The landscape, noted da Cintra, reminded him of a lion at rest, while the crashing waves sounded like a lion's roar.

- Tiwai Island, the largest inland island in Sierra Leone, has the highest concentration and most diverse population of primates in the world.

- When Fourah Bay College was founded, it attracted students from all over West Africa and became known as the "Athens of Africa." In the 18th century, Freetown was also known as "Romarong," which means "the place of the wailers." It gained this name because of maritime disasters off the country's coast.

- The Portuguese Steps, located at Government Wharf, are more appropriately known as the Old Wharf Steps. Many captured and freed slaves climbed these steps when arriving in, or departing from, Freetown. The stones are thought to have been placed around 1818.

- The well-known 500-year-old Cotton Tree in downtown Freetown became a symbol of freedom for ex-slaves in the 18th and 19th centuries and an accommodating home for thousands of bats. This cotton tree is of the silk variety, and the fluff from its kapok fruit is used to stuff items such as pillows and life jackets.

- Freetown is home to the Sierra Leone chapter of PEN, an international writers' association. Local PEN member Michael Butscher edited "Book of Voices," an anthology published in 2006 that includes writings about the effects of war on Freetown and the people of Sierra Leone.

Bibliography

Abraham, Arthur. "Topics in Sierra Leone History: A Counter-Colonial Interpretation." Freetown, SL: *Leone Publishers*, 1976.

Beah, Ishmael. "A Long Way Gone: Memoirs of a Boy Soldier." New York, NY: *Farrar, Straus, and Giroux*, 2007.

Beah, Ishmael. "Radiance of tomorrow." New York, NY: *Sarah Chricton Books, Farrar, Straus, and Giroux*, 2014.

Butcher, Tim. "Chasing the devil." London, UK: *Chatto and Windus*, 2010.

Campbell, Greg. "Blood Diamonds: Tracing the deadly path of the world's most precious stones." Boulder, CO: *Westview Press*, 2002.

Ferme, Mariane Conchita. "The Underneath of Things: Violence, History and the Everyday in Sierra Leone." Berkeley, CA: *The University of California Press*, 2001.

Gberie, Lansana. "A dirty war in West Africa: the RUF and the destruction of Sierra Leone." Bloomington, IN: *University of Indiana Press*, 2005.

Stewart, Guy. "Black Man's Grave: Letters from Sierra Leone." Berkley Springs, WV: *Cold Run Books*, 2007.

Works Cited

"AfroPop." *Afropop Worldwide*. February 10, 2009 http://www.afropop.org.

"Africa: Sierra Leone." *CIA World Factbook* October 3, 2015. https://www.cia.gov/library/publications/the-world-factbook/geos/sl.html

"African Art." *Rand African Art*. February 5, 2009 http://www.randafricanart.com.

"Amnesty." *Amnesty International*. October 4, 2015. http://www.amnesty.org.

"BBC News." *The British Broadcast Corporation*, October 3, 2015. http://www.bbc.co.uk.

"Ebola in Sierra Leone: after 4000 deaths outbreak all but over." *Guardian*, October 3, 2015. https://www:thegaurdian.com/world/2015/aug/20/ebola-epidemic-in-sierra-leone-may-be-over-say-health-workers.

"Global Health Observatory (GHO): Sierra Leone." *World Health Organization*, October 3. http://www.who.int/gho/countries/sle/en/.

"Encarta." *MSN Encarta*. February 2, 2009 http://encarta. msn.com.

"Habitat for Humanity." *Habitat for Humanity*. March 4, 2015. http:/www.habitat.org.

"HRW." *Human Rights Watch*. March 3, 2015 http://www. hrw.org.

"KPCS." *Kimberly Process Certification Scheme*. February 2, 2009 http://www.kimberly process.com.

"Met Museum." *The Metropolitan Museum of Art* February 10, 2009 http://www.metmuseum.org.

"Open Democracy." *Open Democracy*. January 30, 2009 http://www.opendemocracy.net.

"PBS." *Public Broadcast System*. February 5, 2009 http:// www.pbs.org

"Peace-Links." *Peace Links* February 7, 2009 http://www. peace-links.org.

"PRB." *Population Reference Bureau*. January 28, 2009 http://www.prb.org.

"Search for Common Ground." *Search for Common Ground,* February 7, 2009 http://www.sfcg.org.

"SE Rogie." *Souliman Ernest Rogers* February 10, 2009 http://www.serogie.com.

"Sierra Leone." Nations of the world: a political, economic, and business handbook. 14th ed. Amenia, NY: *Grey House Publishing*. 2014.

"Sierra Leone." *Sierra Leone,* October 3, 2015. http://www. sierra- Leone.org.

"Sierra Leone." *United Nations Development Programme*, October 3 2015. http://www.sl.undp.org.

"Sierra Leone's Refugee All Stars." *Sierra Leone's Refugee All Stars*, February 7, 2009 http://www.sierra LeonesrefugeeallStars.org.

"UN." *United Nations*, October 4, 2015 http://www.un.org.

"UNICEF." *UNICEF*. October 4, 2015 http://www.unicef. org.

"UN Women News." *UN Women*, October 3, 2015 http:// www.unwomen.org/en.

"UNOG." *United Nations Office at Geneva*. January 30, 2009 http://www.unog.ch.

"U.S. Department of State." *U.S. Government*, October 4, 2015 http://www.state.gov.

"Welcome to Sierra Leone." *The Sierra Leone National Tourist Board*, February 12, 2009 http://welcometosierra Leone.org.

"World Music Central." *World Music Central* February 7, 2009 http://www.worldmusiccentral.org.

Atherton, John H. and Milan Kalous. "The Journal of African History, Volume 11." Cambridge, Great Britain: *Cambridge University Press*, 1970.

Bainbridge, James, Tim Bewer, Jean-Bernard Carillet, Paul Clammer, Mary Fitzpatrick, Michael Grosberg, Anthony Ham, Katharina Kane, Robert Landon, and Matt Phillips. "West Africa." Victoria, Australia: *Lonely Planet Publications*, 2006.

Broughton, Simon, Mark Ellingham, Oral Duane, Richard Trillo, and Vanessa Dowell. "World Music." London, Great Britain: *Rough Guides*, 2000.

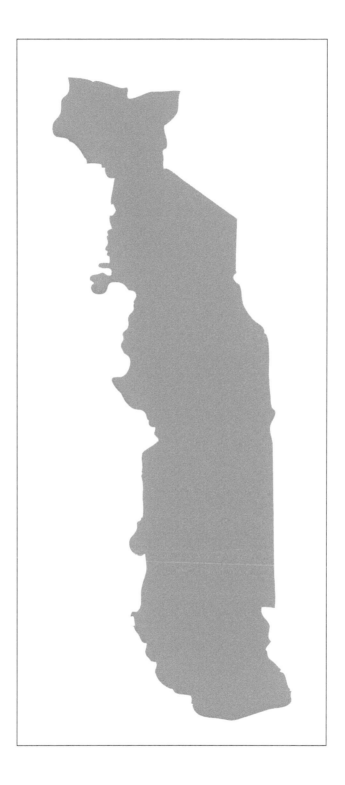

TOGO

Introduction

The Republic of Togo, or Togo, as it is generally known, is a thin strip of a country located on the southern coast of West Africa. It is slightly smaller than the American state of West Virginia. German and French colonial influences mingle with the cultural traditions of the nation's nearly 40 native ethnic groups.

GENERAL INFORMATION

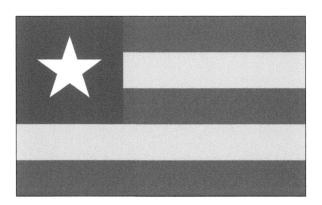

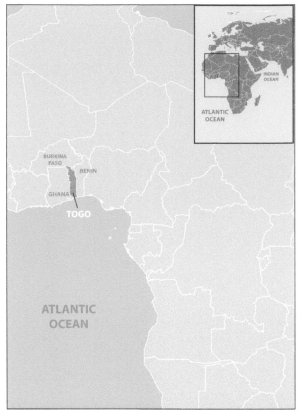

Official Language: French
Population: 6,820, 000 (2013 estimate)
Currency: Communaute Financiere Africaine (African Financial Community) franc (CFA XOF—for West African CFA franc)
Coins: Coins are issued in denominations of 500 and 200 CFA francs.
Land Area: 56,785 square kilometers (21,925 square miles)
Water Area: 2,400 square kilometers (926 square miles)
National Motto: Travail, Liberte, Patrie (French, "Work, Liberty, Homeland")
National Anthem: "Salut à toi, pays de nos aïeux" ("Hail to thee, land of our forefathers")
Capital: Lomé
Time Zone: GMT +0
Flag Description: Togo's flag has five equal and horizontal stripes of green and yellow (three green and two yellow) with a red square on the upper hoist side, emblazoned with a white five-pointed star. The stripes represent the five regions in Togo,

the red square stands for the people's loyalty to the country, and the white star stands for purity and peace. The yellow in the stripe recalls the country's mineral wealth and the faith of its people while green symbolizes fertility and agriculture.

Population

The vast majority of Togo's population (99 percent) is native African, with European and Syrian-Lebanese groups comprising only one percent. Since the 1960s, the population has increased substantially, growing from 1.4 million to nearly seven million; the 2014 population growth rate is 2.7 percent. A sizeable portion of the population lives in cities—39 percent in 2014.

The majority of the population has settled in the south, where Togo's largest city is Lomé, the capital, with a population of 1,820,000. Sokodé, with 115,692 people, is also in the south. Kpalime, with a population of 81,924, is the only major city in the northern part of the country.

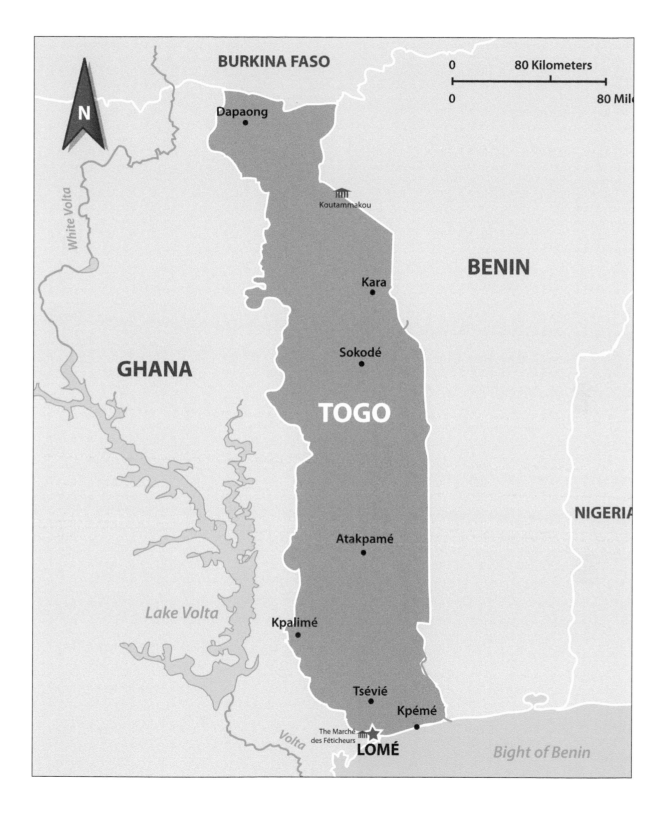

Principal Cities by Population (2012 estimate):

- Lomé (1,800,000)
- Sokodé (115,692)
- Kara (110,623)
- Atakpamé (85,408)
- Kpalimé (81,924)
- Dapaong (55,286)
- Tsévié (53,831)
- Notsé (38,973)

Languages

While French is the country's official language and the language of business, Ewé and Mina are spoken in the southern part of the country, and Kabyé and Dagomba in the north. In addition, English is taught in secondary schools, so many Togolese speak this language as well. Many also speak German.

Native People & Ethnic Groups

The people of Togo are comprised of approximately more than thirty ethnic groups. Major groups include the Ewé, Mina, Cotocoli (or Kotokoli), Moba, and Kabyé. The largest ethnic group is the Ewé, accounting for 21–25 percent of the population. They live in the south, where most of the country's population is concentrated. Many Ewé work as civil servants, merchants, and professionals.

The Kabyé, in contrast, constituting 12–15 percent of the population, live on the poor land in the northern Kara region and traditionally have served as soldiers and police officers. Young Kabyé often leave home for better opportunities in the south.

Religions

A majority of Togolese (51 percent) adhere to indigenous religions, including animism, polytheism, and voodoo. Approximately 29 percent of the population is Christian, and 20 percent is Muslim.

Climate

The climate is tropical, with the south experiencing high humidity and temperatures of 23–32 degrees Celsius (75–90 degrees Fahrenheit). The semiarid north has a greater temperature range, from 18–38 degrees Celsius (65–100 degrees Fahrenheit) and even higher.

The country experiences droughts periodically. The hot, dry harmattan wind (a West African wind that originates in the Sahara) blows across the north in the winter and reduces visibility.

ENVIRONMENT & GEOGRAPHY

Topography

Togo is a tiny, narrow country bounded on the west by Ghana, on the north by Burkina Faso, on the east by Benin, and on the south by the Bight of Benin (a bay in the Gulf of Guinea).

The country's north-south length is 579 kilometers (360 miles) At its broadest point, Togo is only 160 kilometers (200 miles) from west to east, with a mere 56 kilometers (34.8 miles) of coastline.

While the country is slightly smaller than West Virginia, the terrain varies widely from north to south. The sandstone Oti Plateau dominates the extreme north of the country, bounded by the Chaine du Togo, a range of hills stretching from the southwest to the northeast. This range is composed of the Togo and Atakora mountains.

South of the mountains lies the clay-soil Mono Tableland, and south of that is a region of fertile clay soil. Finally, a fringe of lagoons and creeks borders the southern coastal plain. The tableland is drained by the 400-kilometer (250-mile) Mono River, which rises near Benin at Sokodé. The lower part of the river forms the border between Togo and Benin.

The country's highest point is Mont Agou, at 986 meters (3,235 feet). Hydroelectric power is supplied by the Nangbeto Dam on the Mono River and by hydroelectric plants on Lake Volta in Ghana.

Plants & Animals

Togo faces a number of ecological and conservation concerns. There are few protected areas, and those have often been poorly managed. As a result, the animal population has declined. Deforestation has resulted from slash-and-burn agriculture and wood-burning for fuel.

In an effort to save its dwindling resources, the Togolese government has signed a number of agreements regarding biodiversity, climate change, desertification, endangered species, the ozone layer, ship pollution, tropical timber, and wetlands.

CUSTOMS & COURTESIES

Greetings
French is the official language of Togo. Along with French, public schools teach one of the languages of the country's two largest ethnic groups: Ewé in the south and Kabyé (Kabiyé) in the north. (Other spoken languages include Mina, also used in the south, as well as other local dialects.) English is also often taught in secondary schools and is the main language in neighboring Ghana. As a result, many Togolese, particularly along the Ghanaian border and in the south, speak at least basic or Pidgin English. Common expressions in Kabyé include "Un-la-waa lay" ("Good morning") and "Alafia way?" ("How are you?"). Common expressions in the Ewé language include "Nng di" ("Good morning") and "Nng-do" ("Good afternoon"). Handshakes are the common gesture of greeting, and members of the opposite sex customarily refrain from contact in public.

Gestures & Etiquette
Togolese often conduct their conversations in an animated manner, with loud voices and emphatic gestures. In traditional areas, they might also squat and touch their knees in greeting. Gender segregation remains a prominent part of Togolese culture, and many social gatherings are segregated by gender. Conservative dress is generally appropriate, especially in predominantly Muslim northern Togo, where women are expected to wear long sleeves and dresses. Respect for one's elders, particularly in villages, remains strong,

and it customary for youth to bow in their presence. Public affection is generally frowned upon.

Eating/Meals
Pâte, a starch-based thick porridge made from yams, corn, plantains, or other grains or vegetables, forms the basis for most midday and evening meals in Togo. The pâte is commonly served with a hot sauce and protein in the form of beans, beef, fish, or goat, and often contains much peanut paste or palm oil. While fruits and vegetables are widely available in Togo, they are not commonly eaten amongst the lower classes.

Most Togolese eat their meals at home. Other options include roadside stalls that sell omelets, peanuts, corn on the cob, cooked prawns, and brochettes (food grilled on skewers). In larger towns and cities, restaurants serve a variety of cuisines. In rural areas, where traditional hierarchical structures are maintained within most families, men typically eat before women, who then eat before children. The best food is usually saved for adults, especially the men.

LIFESTYLE

Family
The traditional Togolese family emphasizes kinship, and extended family structures remain strong and influential. Kinship provides a support network and extended family members are expected to participate in the various ceremonies marking life's milestones. Extended families also commonly live together, though the nuclear family unit has become increasingly common, especially in cities. The male continues to be the traditional head of the household; should a husband become deceased or absent, the wife's eldest brother takes charge.

There are three common types of marriages in Togo: Christian marriages, traditional marriages, and official marriages. While Togolese law requires that all marriages be sanctioned before a magistrate, the traditional marriage practices of each ethnic group persist and customary marriages, or marriages that are not legally sanctioned by the state, remain common. Polygamy, or the practice of multiple wives, has officially decreased, though it is suggested that unofficial polygamous relationships continue today. Although dowries (paid by the family of the bride to the family of the groom) are not common, many marriages involve a bride wealth (paid by the family of the groom to the family of the bride).

As socioeconomics begin to influence further Togolese society in the early 21st century, the conventional or traditional Togolese family structure is experiencing a breakdown. For example, more men are struggling to secure employment, thus delaying starting a family. In addition, more households are run by females. At the turn of the 21st century, a female headed an estimated 29 percent of urban families, and 22 percent of rural families. Economic difficulties have also made it more commonplace for a husband to remain with his parents, while a wife and children stays with her immediate family.

Housing

Traditional housing, which is constructed from mud (such as sun-dried bricks or plaster), straw, and wood, is still common in rural areas. Houses in villages are typically only three or two rooms, and may be arranged as a compound. Electricity and running water are not common in rural areas. Cement, bricks, and corrugated metals (such as iron or tin) are the common building materials in urban construction. Urban infrastructure rehabilitation has been a government priority in the early 21st century, particularly in the capital of Lomé.

Food

Togolese cuisine is often characterized as a traditional blend of African and European, particularly French, influences, with traditional starchy staples still commonly eaten. Grain crops such as millet and maize (corn) provide the primary dietary staple for Togo (as well as much of West Africa). Millet grows best in drier areas, is commonly grown in the north, while maize requires more water, and grows better in the southern regions. Other important crops include peanuts

Pounding yams to make fufu is traditionally women's work in Togo.

(also called groundnuts) and beans, as well as root vegetables such as yams and cassava, also known as manioc.

The main staple of Togolese cuisine is a thick starch-based porridge called pâte in French or akumé in Ewé. This dough-like substance can be made from grains such as maize or, in drier areas, sorghum, or millet. These grains are ground into flour and then mixed with water to make the porridge. Pâte can also be made from yams or plantains. Additionally, one particular pâte called kokonte is made from milled cassava. Pâte is typically served with a thick sauce made with meat or vegetables, similar to a stew. Common sauces might contain vegetables such as okra, spinach, or ademe, or meat such as smoked fish or crab. In addition to fish, chicken, goat, and beef, as well as cow skin or agouti ("grass-cutters"), a type of large bush rat, are also commonly eaten. Other bush meat, such as the guinea fowl, or pintade, may be widely eaten

In addition to pâte, a dish called fufu plays a prominent role in Togolese cuisine. Fufu, made from yams and similar to mashed potatoes, is prepared communally by a group of women. First, these women wash, peel, and chop up the yams before boiling them until soft. The cooked yams are then placed in a large pestle, or bowl, and pounded by two or three women at a time with large sticks. Eventually, the yams reach the consistency of bread dough and are then served, like pâte, with various sauces. Goat, palm nut, and peanut sauces are particularly popular with fufu. Other Togolese specialties include koliko (fried yams) and abobo (snails cooked on a skewer).

The legacy of Togo's German and French colonial administrations can also be seen in its food and drink. For example, the baguette, a long thin loaf of bread popular in France, is more common than round loaves in Togo. German-style beer is also popular. The most common Togolese-made alcoholic drink in the north is tchoukoutou, made from fermented millet. Palm wine is popular in the southern region, which also produces sodabe, an extremely potent clear liquor distilled from palm wine.

Life's Milestones

Ceremonies and celebrations mark many milestones in everyday Togolese life, which is frequently shaped by traditional superstitions and customs. Celebratory rites mark events such as birth, puberty, marriage, and death. Other rituals common to much of West Africa include the harvest celebration. In the central region of Togo, for example, people celebrate the millet harvest with singing and dancing.

As is common to many West African peoples, Togolese traditionally hold a special ceremony to celebrate the naming of a baby. This ceremony usually occurs when the baby is about one week old, and provides an opportunity for the baby's extended family, as well as friends and important village officials, to gather. Traditionally, each

guest whispers a wish into the baby's ear, perhaps for happiness or a long life.

Some rites vary by ethnic group. The funerary traditions of the Ewé, for instance, are heavily influenced by animist beliefs and the belief in the afterlife. They believe that after a person dies, the djoto (reincarnated soul) will return in the next child born in that family. The person's luvo (death soul), however, might remain trapped among the living and cause problems. Therefore, Ewé societies place great emphasis on the funeral ceremony. It includes several nights of drumming and dancing before rituals believed to free the luvo and encourage the djoto to return.

CULTURAL HISTORY

Art

Wooden sculpture is a prominent feature of Togolese art. Traditionally, sculptures and hunting trophies have been more common than masks. Contemporary woodcarvers from the Plateaux Region are famous for their "chains of marriage" sculptures. These sculptures portray two figures connected by rings that are carved from a single piece of wood. Other traditional crafts from Togo include textile dyeing (such as batik), leatherwork, ceramics, and weaving.

Contemporary Togolese visual artists have started to gain international recognition. The paintings of Sokey Edorh (1955–), for example, draw on Togo's desert regions for inspiration. Edorh demonstrates his interest in African history and civilization by incorporating symbols and writings that he has collected from various African tribes into his works. He also experiments with a variety of materials and frequently includes red clay from Africa in his compositions. Togolese artist Paul Ahyi (1930–2010) practiced zota, a type of pyro-engraving which involves decorating gourds with wood-burning techniques. A noted painter, writer, and ceramicist, his work was displayed throughout Lomé.

Architecture

Togo's architectural landscape is diverse and includes some of the most beautiful architecture on the African continent. The most notable is the house architecture of the Tamberma or Batammariba (which, as they refer to themselves, means "people who are the architects"), who live in Koutammakou in northeastern Togo. They are known for their fortress-style houses made of sun-dried mud (or clay), straw, and wood. These typically two-story houses resemble small castles and feature mud towers, attached granaries, and flat or thatched conical roofs. Traditionally, each fortified dwelling has a narrow entrance, with certain elements of the house, such as windows (eyes) or a grinding stone (teeth), mirroring the human form. In 2004, the United Nations Educational, Scientific, and Cultural Organization (UNESCO) recognized the cultural landscape of Koutammakou, or the Land of the Batammariba, as a World Heritage Site, and these towered houses have since come to symbolize Togo's cultural heritage.

Other rural and traditional architecture in Togo consists mainly of available or natural resources, such as wood or clay. Many rural homes are traditionally circular in shape with thatched roofs. Walls may be erected to protect these hut-style homes, and are used to mark land divisions as well. Many rural homes are clustered into villages. Togo's colonial legacy also contributed to its architectural heritage. A range of European-style architecture is evident in the country and includes English (neo-classical), German, and French architectural styles. Remnants of colonial architecture most notably remain in the capital of Lomé and in Aneho, the former German colonial capital, as well as along the coast.

Music

Traditionally, music in Togo has split along cultural or tribal lines, with the Kabyé in the north using the picancala (xylophone-like instrument with water flutes), the xokudu (a trumpet carved from the baobab tree), and other flutes and wind instruments. Congolese music has greatly influenced modern Togolese music. In the 1960s, Bella Bellow gained international recognition for her bluesy African style. She traveled to South America, the Caribbean, and Europe and came to influence many African artists, particularly women, including artists such as Angélique Kidjo.

In the south, folk music predominates, particularly with the Ewé. Anglers have songs that they sing while hauling in their nets—with heavy use of using percussion instruments. In fact, percussion and drums play an important part in music traditions throughout the country and the marking of life's milestones. According to Oxfam International, different areas of Togo have different drums and different rhythm affiliations.

King Mensah (1971–), known as the "golden voice of Togo," is a singer and songwriter, that relies heavily on percussion. His music blends the traditional with the punk, reggae, and other forms. Singing in Ewé and French, he has received international recognition.

Literature & Drama

The various peoples of Togo, as in many other African cultures, have a strong oral tradition. Until recently, few examples of literature written in Togo's vernacular languages existed. An Ewé-language theater tradition arose in the 20th century after European missionaries worked to standardize the language to promote Christianity among the Togolese people. This standardized language later gave rise to the works of playwrights such as Ferdinand Kwasi Fiawoo (1891–1969), author of *Toko Atolia* (The Fifth Landing Stage, 1937). He originally wrote the play in the Ewé language, and is considered that language's greatest writer. During Togo's French colonial period, which followed World War I, Ewé literary theater declined as French-language instruction was promoted in schools.

During the 20th century, church-based theater that was religious in nature, and which spread from Ghana, was popularized. Senouvo Zinsou (1946–) arguably became Togo's premier playwright during the 1970s and 80s, with plays such as *On joue la comédie* (We are Acting, 1975), *Le Club* (The Club, 1983), and *Yévi au pays des monstres* (Yévi in the Country of Monsters, 1987) that drew on previous theater traditions. He became the director of the Togolese National Theater Company in 1990. Togo's best-known contemporary writer is most likely Tété-Michel Kpomassie (1941–), author of *An African in Greenland* (1981). Kpomassie was born in Togo but later left Africa in a 10-year journey to the north of Greenland. His autobiography tells the tale of this journey. It won the Prix Littéraire Francophone International in 1981 and was translated from French into English in 1983.

CULTURE

Arts & Entertainment

Togo's music is as varied as its population, but certain styles of music are commonly heard in Togolese daily life and celebrations. Drumming is a prominent shared element across diverse musical styles and is often featured in any event, with the types of drums and other instruments varying by region. In the south, percussion instruments such as bells and gongs are most common. The central region features lithophones, which are percussion instruments made from stones. Here, songs might be sung in Fon (a Beninois language) or Yoruba rather than in Ewé or Kabyé. In the north, traditional music features the flute and the musical bow, which is played while holding an arrow. Throughout Togo, music is used to accompany dances that relate to life events, such as warfare, harvest, love, hunting, and fishing.

While traditional music and instruments remain common in Togo, some of these traditions have combined with musical styles and sounds from the rest of Africa, the West Indies, and South America to create new forms. Reggae and highlife, a Ghanaian genre of jazz music combining guitars and horns, are both popular, as is the fast-paced rumba called soukous. Soukous originated in the Congo region in the 1930s and 1940s, when African rhythms were combined with Caribbean and South American music.

Like its music, Togo's traditional crafts vary by region. Batik and wax-printed fabrics are made throughout Togo in a range of colors and designs. The batik fabrics made in Kloto are particularly famous and typically contain stylized depictions of everyday life in ancient times. The Ewé kente cloth, which has a muted color palette, is one of the country's best-known textiles. Ironwork, pottery, weaving, and hair braiding are common crafts throughout the country, but their forms and patterns change depending on what resources are available in a particular area. Similarly, wooden carvings of traditional masks or deities can be found throughout Togo, but differ according to local beliefs and customs. Decorative wood burning is particularly popular in the northwest region. Elaborate geometric patterns are burnt onto wooden vessels or calabashes (made from dried gourds), but might also appear on notable buildings and houses. Similar patterns are used in traditional body decoration, in which raised scars mark the skin.

Soccer and wrestling are the two main sports in Togo. To indulge their passion, the Togolese have formed several soccer leagues. In addition, a number of Togolese play on various European football (soccer) teams. Wrestling is so popular that there is a yearly national wrestling festival in Kara. The sport originated as a Kabyé test of manhood, but now wrestlers from all over the country compete in the festival every July. Wrestling is part of the fitness-training program for members of the armed forces. Many play basketball and handball, and, because of French influence, cycling is popular.

The many tribes of Togo have retained much of their original culture and rituals, and numerous folk festivals are celebrated throughout the country. For example, the Kabyé, an ancient tribe, hold the annual Evala wrestling competition for boys. At the Festival of Cutlasses in the third month of the Islamic calendar, men dance with swords. Moreover, about one month later, at the Dance of Fire, individuals prove their strength by dancing in a fire and swallowing coals.

Cultural Sites & Landmarks

Lomé, the capital of Togo, is home to a variety of cultural sites. The Marché des Féticheurs, or fetish market, contains ingredients for traditional fetishes, which are manmade objects attributed with supernatural powers. These might include horsehair, the skull of a donkey, or a parakeet's tail. The museum also sells fetishes and charms from all over Africa. Lomé is also known for its traditional and colonial architecture, including a cathedral built in the German gothic style and other colonial remnants.

Other Togolese cities of cultural importance include Togoville, which sits on the northern shore of Lake Togo, Aného, in southern Togo, and Kpalimé. Historically, Togoville was the center of Togolese vodun (voodoo) practices, and during the time of the slave trade, these vodun practitioners were taken as slaves to Haiti, where Haitian vodou has since flourished. Aného was Togo's colonial capital until 1920, and was once a prominent port in the slave trade between Africa and Brazil. Kpalimé is a town located on the edge of southern Togo's mountainous coffee- and cocoa-growing region. Its surrounding area is famous for its hiking and particularly for the butterfly walks in nearby Klouto.

Many of Togo's most important attractions and landmarks are its natural areas and ethnic landscapes, including the landscape of the Koutammakou, or the Land of the Batammariba, recognized as a World Heritage Site. The country is home to three national parks and nearly 90 forest reserves, and several of these natural sites, such as Fazao-Malfakassa National Park and Keran National Park, have been tentatively submitted to UNESCO for World Heritage status. However, conservation and park management have been a concern, and most of Togo's national parks have suffered from poaching and deforestation. Fazao-Malfakassa Park is in the process of restoring its wildlife and habitat in the early 21st century. The restoration, which began in 1995, has been moderately successful thus far, re-introducing elephants and many species of birds into the park.

Libraries & Museums

Togo's small two-room national museum, the Musée National (Togo National Museum), houses historical artifacts and documents, as well as traditional Togolese pottery, costumes, and woodcarvings. As of 2009, the museum averages 5,000 visitors per year. The International Museum of the Gulf of Guinea is also a major museum. Other museums include the National Geological and Mineral Museum and the Museum Agbedigo Gaston, an ethnographic museum founded in 1993. The regional museums in Sokodé and the savannah region display local artifacts. The National Library of Togo (Bibliotheque nationale du Togo) is also located in the capital of Lomé.

Holidays

Independence Day is April 27. Other holidays include Meditation Day (January 13), Day of Victory (January 24), and Day of the Martyrs (June 21).

Youth Culture

Football (soccer) is popular with Togo's youth, as well as with the general population. Togo's national football team, known as Les Eperviers (the Sparrow Hawks), maintains a huge following, and team qualified for its first World Cup in 2006. The team's victories are often celebrated with public parties in the streets and national holidays. The youth influence on Togo's music scene became evident in the late 1980s with the rise of Togolese hip-hop, and many hip-hop artists are now students. In 2003, the government established the Togo Hip-Hop Awards to celebrate this form and recognize hip-hop artists.

SOCIETY

Transportation

Common modes of transportation in Togo include minibuses, bush taxis (mostly unmetered), and taxi-motos (moped taxis), most of which are readily available in urban areas. Cars are driven on the right-hand side of the road in Togo.

Transportation Infrastructure

Togo's road infrastructure in the early 21st century is dilapidated, and the government has made improving road conditions a greater priority, especially in large cities such as Lomé. In June 2008, the Togolese government announced a pilot project with the World Bank—which, since 2002, had suspended aid disbursements to the African nation—to improve transportation infrastructure. The Trans-West African Coastal Highway crosses and connects Togo with Benin and Nigeria (in the east), as well as Ghana and Cote d'Ivoire (in the west). There is also a paved highway running north and south.

Togo has limited rail transportation. Togo's international airport is located just outside of Lomé, which, along with Kpemé, is one of the country's major ports.

Media & Communications

The premier media outlets in Togo are owned by the state, but private media outlets have increased since the 1990s. Nonetheless, while these private outlets have grown noticeably, the state-run outlets tend to have more stable finances and higher advertising revenue. The independent and privatized press frequently focuses on political topics, and most of the politicized material appears in print. The political commentary in private print media sometimes expresses explicit criticism of the government, while he official state-run media typically supports the government in its views and content.

Togo's constitution provides for freedom of the press and, according to an amendment of the 2002 media law, members of the press cannot be imprisoned for reporting or circulating information offensive to the government. Regardless, the government does not always respect media freedom, and journalists have been attacked for political reasons. The police have also raided newsstands and printing presses and closed certain radio stations. As a result, self-censorship is commonly practiced.

Radio is the most widespread and popular medium of mass communication in Togo, particularly in the more rural areas. By late 2006, over 80 radio stations were on the air. The state-run stations include the nationally broadcast Radio Togolaise, the northern region's Radio Kara, and the capital's Radio Lomé. Private stations include Omega FM, Kanal FM, Radio Legende, Nana FM, and Radio Zephyr; many of the privately owned radio stations are based in Lomé. Some of these private stations are in fact government-owned or otherwise associated with prominent political parties. The Catholic Church operates radio Maria Togo.

Togo's main daily newspaper is the government-owned *Togo-Presse*. Several privately run papers circulate weekly, including *Le Regard, Le Combat du Peuple, Nouveau Combat, Carrefour, Le Crocodile*, and *Motion d'Information*. The main television station in Togo is the government-owned Television Togolaise. The state also runs Telesports TV, which focuses on sports and cultural programs. Some private stations also have specific affiliations, such as the Christian-oriented TV Zion or the Islamic TV Djabal'nour.

Togo's telecommunications infrastructure has been characterized as fair, and the national telecommunications provider is Togo Telecom (Togotel). Togo did not fully establish a telecommunications regulatory agency until 2001. As of December 2014, there were 430,482 Internet users in Togo, representing less than six percent of the population.

SOCIAL DEVELOPMENT

Standard of Living

In 2014, Togo's Human Development Index rank, measuring longevity, education, literacy, and income, was 166th out of 187 countries. Most Togolese are extremely poor, living on less than the equivalent of $1.25 (USD) a day.

Water Consumption

According to UNICEF (United Nations Children's Fund), 62 percent of the total population has access to clean water (2014 estimate). This hides a large discrepancy, though, between urban and rural populations, where 86 percent of the urban population has access to clean water but only 40 percent of the rural population enjoys that benefit. Access to improved sanitation is poor, with the total population access at 12 percent (2014 estimate). Only 24 percent of the urban population has improved access to sanitation compared to three percent of the urban population.

In December 2009, those countries within the Volta River Basin, including Burkina Faso, Cote d'Ivoire, Benin, Ghana, Mali and Togo, reached an agreement to work together to develop water management policies to protect that water resource.

Education

Literacy in Togo is low. The literacy rate for older youth—those aged 15 and older—has risen to 53 percent (2003–2008 estimate); it was an estimated 44 percent in 1990. Only about 47 percent of adult women and 75 percent of adult men can read and write.

Education in Togo is based on the French system. In 2008, the government announced that primary education was free. This change opened doors for many families living in poverty who could not afford the annual fees for primary education. While the rate of school attendance is high in urban areas such as Lomé, attendance rates are estimated as low as 20 to 25 percent in some rural areas. In 2004, an estimated 85 percent of boys and 72 percent of girls were enrolled in primary school levels. Challenges facing the government, especially since the introduction of free primary school that resulted in a larger primary school population, include teacher shortages and basic student supplies such as desks, books, and utensils.

Students achieve their lycée degree before going on to university. There are five universities in Togo: the University of Lome, Kara University, which opened in January 2004 in borrowed buildings in the northern city of Kara, the Catholic University of West Africa, the National School of Administration and the African Crafts School of Architecture and Urbanism.

Women's Rights

Togo is a traditionally patriarchal society, and though women are considered equal under Togolese law, inherent gender discrimination persists. For example, a woman has no right to inherit wealth or property upon the death of her husband. In addition, women have no right to financial compensation or support if they are divorced or separated, and a husband is legally able to prevent his wife from seeking work or to take control of her earnings. Married women must also obtain their husband's permission to apply for a passport.

Women also face discrimination in employment, even though the labor code mandates equal pay for equal work. While this equality is practiced in most formal employment situations, many women receive lower pay than their male counterparts do. Gender inequality persists at the educational level as well, as fewer girls than boys are enrolled in primary school. Because traditional gender discrimination often carried over into the classroom, organizations like the United Nations Children's Fund (UNICEF) have been working to educate teachers to privilege equally girls and boys in educational environments.

Violence against women, particularly domestic violence, is common. While the law criminalizes rape, it does not specifically prohibit spousal rape. Because a social stigma is attached to rape, it is thought to be a vastly underreported problem. Domestic violence against women is also a widespread problem because it is not prohibited by law. In addition, because familial violence is traditionally considered a family matter, the police seldom intervene in cases of domestic abuse.

Female genital mutilation (FGM) also continues to be practiced among a small percentage of the population, despite its prohibition by a 1998 law. The most common form of FGM is excision, typically performed when girls are a few months old. Most cases of FGM occur in rural areas; however, the majority of Togo's larger ethnic groups do not practice FGM, and the government actively works to campaign and to offer educational seminars against the practice.

Health Care

Life expectancy in Togo is 59 years, and the infant mortality rate is almost 54 per 1,000 births (2014 estimate).

The major cause of these early childhood deaths is malaria, with measles and intestinal parasites following close behind. About 40 percent of the nation's health expenditure is for malaria. Many of the poorest, uneducated Togolese do not know that mosquitoes cause malaria. Only about 15 percent of children slept under mosquito nets until a recent United Nations Children's Fund (UNICEF) program began providing nets treated with repellent.

The $6 million UNICEF program has also treated children from nine months to five years old with pills for intestinal worms, polio vaccine and measles vaccine, and has provided health education to parents. In recent years, such programs have reduced deaths from measles by 94 percent.

GOVERNMENT

Structure

In the 11th and 14th centuries, the Ewé people moved into what is now Togo from the Niger River Valley. Portuguese traders and explorers came to the area in the 14th and 15th centuries. Because of its location in the middle of the Slave Coast, Togo became a center for the slave trade.

In the ensuing centuries, tribes in surrounding kingdoms threatened the area. When German representative Gustav Nachtigal arrived in the village of Togo (now Togoville) in 1884, he was able to obtain a treaty from Chief Mlapa III, giving Germany control. The country was then called German Togoland. After Germany's defeat in World War I, France and Great Britain took control of Togoland as a trusteeship. Western Togo, administered by the British, eventually became part of Ghana. Eastern Togo was known as French Togoland.

Togo became an independent republic in 1960. For several years after independence, politics in Togo were marked by assassinations, exiles, and coups, with each change of government accompanied by a new constitution. Stability came when Gnassingbe Eyadema was elected president in a national referendum. He remained in office for more than three decades, until his death on February 5, 2005. Upon his death, the Togolese Armed Forces installed his son (Faure Gnassingbé) as president, contradicting the constitution, which would have placed the president of the parliament in place pending elections. Facing internal conflict and international pressure, Gnassingbé resigned, called elections, and won the election with 60 percent of the vote in 2005; he won again in 2010, taking 60 percent of the vote.

The president, who is elected by popular vote, is the head of state. He appoints the prime minister, who is the head of government, and the Council of Ministers (Cabinet). The 81-seat National Assembly, elected by the party-list proportional representation system, is unicameral (it has a single house). Student protests against the one-party rule were answered with harsh government suppression, which resulted in riots in the early 1990s. As a result, a constitution allowing multiple parties was adopted in 1992.

Togo has universal adult suffrage and in 2007, the country adopted a proportional representation system. A proportional representation system allocates seats in the governing body (in this case, the National Assembly) by the number of votes attained by a political party, which has a prioritized list of party candidates. If the elections result in two seats for a party, the first two names on the prioritized list become members of the National Assembly. In the 2007 election, the new system resulted in a greater proportion of representation from the north of the country than had been seen before.

Political Parties

The parliamentary elections originally scheduled for 2012 were postponed due to civil unrest until 2013. In those elections the Union for the Republic (UNIR) won 62 seats, the Save Togo Collective (CST) won 19 seats, the Rainbow Alliance (a coalition including Action Committee for Renewal [CAR] and Democratic Convention of African Peoples [CDPA]) won six seats, and the Union of Forces for Change

(UFC) won three seats. Other parties of note in Togo include the Patriotic Pan-African Convergence (CPP), the Movement of the Believers of Peace and Equality (MOCEP), the Socialist Pact for Renewal (PSR), the National Alliance for Change (ANC), and the Rally for the Support for Development and Democracy (RSDD).

Local Government

There are 30 political prefectures in five administrative subdivisions. Each prefecture has an appointed prefect.

Judicial System

The Cour d'Apppel (Court of Appeals) and the Cour Supreme (Supreme Court) represent the judicial branch of the national government. In rural areas, the village chief or council of elders may try minor criminal and civil cases. The Togolese judicial system combines the Napoleonic Code with traditional law in criminal and civil trials—thus, defendants are not presumed innocent.

Taxation

Togo levies an income tax which can be as high as 45 percent of earnings. The corporate tax rate was 27 percent in 2015. Other tax revenues include a value-added tax (VAT), property taxes, and a vehicle tax.

Armed Forces

The military structure in Togo includes an army, navy, air force, and gendarmerie (national police force). The police operate under the direction of the Ministry of Security, which reports to the prime minister. The president, who also oversees the Ministry of Defense, on the other hand, directs the gendarmerie and military branches. Although officially the police and gendarmerie are responsible for law enforcement and the maintenance of order, he army is charged with maintaining external security and dominates domestic law enforcement. At age eighteen, individuals are eligible for selective compulsory or volunteer service.

Foreign Policy

Togo is generally proactive in its foreign policy and has a history of non-alignment. In recent years, the country's foreign policy has been characterized as generally pro-Western and market-oriented. Togo is particularly active in the West African region and holds membership in the African Union (AU), the Economic Community of West African States (ECOWAS), West African Economic and Monetary Union (UEMOA), and the Organisation of Islamic Conference (OIC). Togo has also maintained strong ties with former colonial powers France and Germany, though relations with Germany and the European Union (EU) have been strained due to political instability. Togo has been a member of the United Nations (UN) since 1960.

Togo is considered a heavily indebted poorer country, and much of its foreign relations and multilateral or bilateral agreements are based on developmental aid. However, due to political unrest and human rights abuses in the late 20th and early 21st century, aid to Togo was often suspended from the international community. In April 2009, the International Monetary Fund (IMF) disbursed $26.6 million (USD)—overall, totaling nearly $80 million—to Togo under a poverty reduction and economic growth initiative, and the World Bank has committed more than $765 million (USD) as of 2005.

Human Rights Profile

International human rights law insists that states respect civil and political rights, and promote an individual's economic, social, and cultural rights. The United Nations Universal Declaration on Human Rights (UDHR) is recognized as the standard for international human rights. Its authors sought the counsel of the world's great thinkers, philosophers, and religious leaders, and were careful to create a document that reflects the core values shared by every world culture. (To read this document or view the articles relating to cultural human rights, visit http://www.udhr.org/UDHR/default.htm.)

The 2005 election of President Fauré Gnassingbé (1966–), though seen as a step toward political reform, was marked by widespread voting irregularities and accusations of electoral fraud. Gnassingbé replaced his father, Gnassingbé Eyadema (1937–2005), who, with the support of his political party, the RPT, and the armed forces, maintained an authoritarian government for 38 years. Riots in Lomé following the election killed over 500 people. However, the October 2007 legislative elections for the national assembly were organized by the Independent National Electoral Commission (CENI) and widely declared free and fair. All major opposition parties were represented in the race.

Despite the country being largely re-welcomed into the international community following Eyadema's controversial regime, human rights abuses continue to be a concern in Togo. Togo's constitution prohibits torture, but the torture and mistreatment of detainees reportedly continues. Similarly, while the constitution and law do not permit arbitrary arrest and detention, both practices occur. The perpetrators of such abuses generally act with impunity, since the government does not prosecute publicly its officials for these acts. Prison conditions in Togo are also generally poor. Serious issues include severe overcrowding, widespread disease, poor sanitation, and nutrition, as well as pervasive drug abuse, sexual harassment of female prisoners, and insufficient medical facilities. Additionally, detainees awaiting trial are not housed separately from convicted prisoners.

The police force is largely ineffective, while corruption and impunity remain problematic since the government generally does not investigate or punish officials who commit violations. In 2005, the military was deployed to manage rioters following the presidential elections. It was estimated that 500 people died in those clashes. Following the 2010 election, clashes with security forces yielded some injuries, but nothing as serious as that seen in 2005.

Because the Togolese judicial system combines the Napoleonic Code with traditional law in criminal and civil trials, defendants are not presumed innocent. Detainees are sometimes not informed of the charges against them, and

may be held without charge for over the 48-hour legal limit. Furthermore, these detainees might be denied access to family members or attorneys for an extended period or altogether. In addition, detainees are sometimes held without the legally required pretrial investigation by a special judge to determine the bail, and whether or not there is sufficient evidence for a trial. A shortage of judges and an inefficient and corrupt judicial system means that some pretrial detainees might be held for several years, a longer period than they would have served if actually tried and convicted.

Law provides for all freedom of movement within Togo, foreign travel, emigration, and repatriation. However, in practice, the government restricts some of these rights, particularly domestic freedom of movement. Armed security personnel enforce checkpoints with arbitrary searches of vehicles and individuals. Often, these forces demand bribes in order to allow passage. Security forces sometimes institute additional unofficial checkpoints that also require bribes. The government does not use forced exile, which is constitutionally prohibited. However, some opposition figures and human rights workers live in self-exile because they fear arrest upon their return to Togo.

Certain social discriminations continue to persist in Togo. A 2005 law prohibits discrimination against persons with disabilities in education, employment, and access to health care. However, these prohibitions are not strongly enforced by the government, nor are all public and private facilities handicapped-accessible. Another 2005 law prohibits discrimination against persons infected with HIV/AIDS, but those infected are often socially marginalized. Homosexuality is illegal according to Togolese law, and discrimination based on sexual orientation occurs regularly. In addition, human trafficking, often that of children, remains a prominent issue for Togo. Children, particularly girls, are taken to Asia, the Middle East, or other West and Central African countries like Nigeria and Gabon to enter servitude that is frequently exploitative and akin to slavery. The Togolese government has also been accused of neglecting the enforcement of child labor laws.

In 2008, the government established Truth, Justice, and Reconciliation, a process intended to promote national unity and help to curb corruption and judicial impunity. In its first year, the organization more than doubled minimum wage and waived public primary school fees.

ECONOMY

Overview of the Economy
The nation suffered an economic collapse in the 1980s that forced many residents of the capital to leave. Violent protests and political violence in 1993 continued to reduce the population, as many Togolese fled to nearby Ghana, reducing the local workforce and causing a strain on the economy. The country's gross domestic product in 2014 was estimated at $4.518 billion (USD). The per capita gross domestic product (GDP) was estimated at $656 (USD) in 2014.

Though Togo has been the focus of economic international economic aid projects since the 1980s, notably from the International Monetary Fund (IMF) and World Bank, poverty is still common among the Togolese population. Thirty-two percent of residents live below the poverty line (2009 estimate).

Agriculture is the mainstay of the Togolese economy, employs 65 percent of the labor force, with coffee, cocoa, and cotton the major crops. The country is working towards privatization and political stability, issues that have hampered foreign investment and international aid.

Industry
The major industries in Togo include phosphate mining, agricultural products processing, cement production and the manufacture of handicrafts, textiles, and beverages. Industry accounts for five percent of the labor force.

Labor
Sixty-five percent of the labor force (3.222 million in 2013) is engaged in agriculture. Since the country depends primarily on subsistence and commercial agriculture, statistics on the employment rate are not available.

Energy/Power/Natural Resources
Marble, limestone and phosphates are found throughout the country. Water pollution is a hazard to the health of the people, and coastal pollution has hurt the fishing industry. Air pollution is increasing in cities, while desertification and erosion have reduced the amount of arable land.

Fishing
More than 23,000 metric tons of fish are landed yearly by the fishing industry in Togo.

Mining/Metals
The primary industry is phosphate mining. Togo is estimated to have 60 million metric tons of phosphate reserves, but phosphate production has dropped in recent years. Causes of the reduction include the drop in prices on the world market, foreign competition, and a decline in foreign investment. The industry's lack of the capital needed to make infrastructure improvements in the recovery of phosphate deposits has hampered growth. Substantial amounts of limestone and marble are also mined.

Agriculture
Only 44 percent of the land in Togo is arable. On farms with an average size of 1–3 hectares, the Togolese are able to grow sufficient crops and livestock for the country's domestic needs and some for export. Main crops include coffee, cocoa, cotton, yams, cassava (tapioca), corn, beans, groundnuts (peanuts), rice, millet, and sorghum.

Coffee, cocoa, cotton, and phosphates account for about 40 percent of the $438 million (USD) brought in by exports each year. In the last decade, cotton has replaced coffee and cocoa as the main cash crop.

Animal Husbandry
Sheep, goats, chickens, and cattle are typical livestock on Togolese farms. On the rocky northern plateau, livestock is especially important.

Tourism

Togo's formerly thriving tourist industry was badly damaged by the political disturbances of the 1990s. In an effort to rebuild the tourism industry, Togo has joined with Benin and Ghana to develop procedures to increase security for travelers and facilitate movement among the three countries.

Cultural tourism, ecotourism, and traditional tours are available for visitors to Togo. The ever-changing landscape and varieties of flora and fauna beg for ecotourism. The country's many lagoons and waterfalls such as Kuma Konda and Amegape, near Kpalime, and Yikpa/Evli, on the border with Ghana, are popular with tourists.

There are seven forest preserves, from the tiny Fosse aux Lions, of only 1.6 hectares (3.9 acres) in Tandjouaré Prefecture to the 195-hectare (481.8-acre) Fazao-Malfacassa in Sotouba-Bassar. The reserves and their surroundings provide beautiful vistas and wildlife. Lake Togo is the number one tourist site in the country, offering a variety of water sports and some fishing. In nearby Lomé, the fetish market is a popular place to buy voodoo souvenirs.

Alyssa Connell, Ellen Bailey, Micah Issitt

DO YOU KNOW?

- Some popular Togolese proverbs include "Don't butter the skillet before catching the fish," "The fox that arrives early gobbles up all the hens," and "Absence polishes passion, presence reinforces it."

Bibliography

"Background Note: Togo." *U.S. Department of State*. Jan. 2009. http://www.state.gov/r/pa/ei/bgn/5430.htm.

"Togo." *The Cambridge Guide to African and Caribbean Theatre*. Ed. Martin Banham, Errol Hill, and George Woodyard. Cambridge: Cambridge University Press, 1994. 117–119.

Blake, Susan Louise. "Letters from Togo." Iowa City, IA: *University of Iowa Press*, 1991.

Brownlie,Alison. *"West Africa: Food and Festivals."* Austin, TX: *Streck-Vaughn Company*, 1999.

Ham, Anthony, et al. "West Africa." 6th ed. Oakland, CA: *Lonely Planet Publications Pty Ltd*, 2006.

Kassindja, Fauziya. "Do they hear you when they cry [by] Fauziya Kassindja and Layli Miller Bashir." New York, NY: *Delacorte Press*, 1998.

Packer, George. "The village of waiting." New York, NY: *Farrar, Straus and Giroux*, 2001.

Winslow, Zachery. "Togo." New York: *Chelsea House*, 1988.

Works Cited

"Africa: Togo". *Internet world stats*. 4 October, 2015. http://internetworldstats.com/africa.htm#tg

"Afrol Gender Profiles: Togo." *Afrol.com*. 2 Apr. 2009. http://www.afrol.com/Categories/Women/profiles/togo_women.htm.

"Country Profile: Togo." *BBC News*. 18 Jun. 2008. 20 Mar. 2009. http://news.bbc.co.uk/2/hi/world/africa/country_profiles/1064470.stm.

"Highlife." *Wikipedia*. 12 Apr. 2009. 13 Apr. 2009. http://en.wikipedia.org/wiki/Highlife.

"Koutammakou, the Land of the Batammariba." *UNESCO World Heritage*. 23 Mar. 2009. 24 Mar. 2009. http://whc.unesco.org/en/list/1140.

"Sokey Edorh." *IFA Galleries*. 4 Apr. 2009. http://www.ifa.de/en/exhibitions/dt/rueckblick/2009/dakar/sokey-edorh/.

"Soukous." *Wikipedia*. 24 Mar. 2009. 12 Apr. 2009. http://en.wikipedia.org/wiki/Soukous.

"Tété-Michel Kpomassie." *The New York Review of Books*. 12 Apr. 2009. http://www.nybooks.com/nyrb/authors/7736.

"Togo." *Encyclopaedia Britannica*. 2009. Encyclopaedia Britannica Online. 4 Apr. 2009. http://proxy.library.upenn.edu:3225/eb/article-55363.

"Togo." *Nations of the world: a political, economic, and business handbook*. 14th ed. Amenia, NY: *Grey House Publishing*, 2014.

"Togo." *New World Encyclopedia*, 10 Apr. 2008. 5 Apr. 2009. http://www.newworldencyclopedia.org/entry/Togo.

"Togo." *UNESCO*, 4 October 2015. http://en.unesco.org/countries/togo.

"Togo." *Wikipedia*. 4 October 2015. http://en.wikipedia.org/wiki/Togo.

"Togo." *The World Bank* 4 October 2015. http://data.worldbank.org/country/togo.

"Togo 2013 Human Rights Report: Togo." *U.S. Department of State,* 4 October 2015 http://www.state.gov/documents/ organization/220381.pdf"Togo: Background." *UNICEF.org*. 4 October 2015. http://www.unicef.org/infobycountry/togo_1046.html.

"Togo – Facts and Figures." *CERF Around the World*, 2007. United Nations. 23 Mar. 2009. http://ochaonline.un.org/cerf/CERFinAction/Togo/tabid/1795/Default.aspx.

"Togolese Hip Hop." *Wikipedia*. 2 Jan. 2009. 13 Apr. 2009. http://en.wikipedia.org/wiki/Togolese_hip_hop.

"Togo political parties and leaders." *Index mundi*. 4 October, 2015. http://indexmundi.com/togo.

"Togolese parliamentary election, 2013. *Wikipedia*. 4 October 2015. http://en.wikipedia.org/wiki/togolese_parliamentary_election_2013.

"Virtual Journey of Togo." *Oxfam: Cool Planet*, 23 Mar. 2009. http://www.oxfam.org.uk/coolplanet/ontheline/explore/journey/togo/togoindex.htm.

"World Heritage List." *World Heritage Convention*. 4 October 2015. http://whc.unesco.org/en/list/

Appendix One:
World Governments

Commonwealth

Guiding Premise

A commonwealth is an organization or alliance of nations connected for the purposes of satisfying a common interest. The participating states may retain their own governments, some of which are often considerably different from one another. Although commonwealth members tend to retain their own sovereign government institutions, they collaborate with other members to create mutually agreeable policies that meet their collective interests. Some nations join commonwealths to enhance their visibility and political power on the international stage. Others join commonwealths for security or economic reasons. Commonwealth members frequently engage in trade agreements, security pacts, and other programs. Some commonwealths are regional, while others are global.

Typical Structure

A commonwealth's structure depends largely on the nature of the organization and the interests it serves. Some commonwealths are relatively informal in nature, with members meeting on a periodic basis and participating voluntarily. This informality does not undermine the effectiveness of the organization, however—members still enjoy a closer relationship than that which exists among unaffiliated states. Commonwealths typically have a president, secretary general, or, in the case of the Commonwealth of Nations (a commonwealth that developed out of the British Empire), a monarch acting as the leader of the organization. Members appoint delegates to serve at summits, committee meetings, and other commonwealth events and programs.

Other commonwealths are more formal in structure and procedures. They operate based on mission statements with very specific goals and member participation requirements. These organizations have legislative bodies that meet regularly. There are even joint security operations involving members. The African Union, for example, operates according to a constitution and collectively addresses issues facing the entire African continent, such as HIV/AIDS, regional security, environmental protection, and economic cooperation.

One of the best-known commonwealths in modern history was the Soviet Union. This collective of communist states was similar to other commonwealths, but the members of the Soviet Union, although they retained their own sovereign government institutions, largely deferred to the organization's central leadership in Moscow, which in turn deferred to the Communist Party leadership. After the collapse of the Soviet Union, a dozen former Soviet states, including Russia, reconnected as the Commonwealth of Independent States. This organization features a central council in Minsk, Belarus. This council consists of the heads of state and heads of government for each member nation, along with their cabinet ministers for defense and foreign affairs.

Commonwealth structures and agendas vary. Some focus on trade and economic development, as well as using their respective members' collective power to address human rights, global climate change, and other issues. Others are focused on regional stability and mutual defense, including prevention of nuclear weapons proliferation. The diversity of issues for which commonwealths are formed contributes to the frequency of member meetings as well as the actions carried out by the organization.

Role of the Citizen

Most commonwealths are voluntary in nature, which means that the member states must choose to join with the approval of their respective governments. A nation with a democratic government, therefore, would need the sanction of its popularly elected legislative and executive bodies in order to proceed. Thus, the role of the private citizen with regard to a commonwealth is indirect—the people may have the power to vote for or against a legislative or executive candidate based on his or her position concerning membership in a commonwealth.

Some members of commonwealths, however, do not feature a democratic government, or their respective governmental infrastructures are not yet in place. Rwanda, for instance, is a developing nation whose 2009 decision to join the Commonwealth of Nations likely came from the political leadership with very little input from its citizens, as Rwandans have very limited political freedom.

While citizens may not directly influence the actions of a commonwealth, they may work closely with its representatives. Many volunteer nonprofit organizations—having direct experience with, for example, HIV/AIDS, certain minority groups, or environmental issues—work in partnership with the various branches of a commonwealth's central council. In fact, such organizations are frequently called upon in this regard to implement the policies of a commonwealth, receiving financial and logistical support when working in impoverished and/or war-torn regions. Those working for such organizations may therefore prove invaluable to the effectiveness of a commonwealth's programs.

Michael Auerbach
Marblehead, Massachusetts

Examples

African Union
Commonwealth of Independent States
Commonwealth of Nations
Northern Mariana Islands (and the United States)
Puerto Rico (and the United States)

Bibliography

"About Commonwealth of Independent States." *Commonwealth of Independent States.* CIS, n.d. Web. 17 Jan. 2013.

"AU in a Nutshell." *African Union.* African Union Commission, n.d. Web. 17 Jan. 2013.

"The Commonwealth." *Commonwealth of Nations.* Nexus Strategic Partnerships Limited, 2013. Web. 17 Jan. 2013.

Communist

Guiding Premise

Communism is a political and economic system that seeks to eliminate private property and spread the benefits of labor equally throughout the populace. Communism is generally considered an outgrowth of socialism, a political and economic philosophy that advocates "socialized" or centralized ownership of the economy and the means of production.

Communism developed largely from the theories of Karl Marx (1818–83), who believed that a revolution led by the working class must occur before the state could achieve the even distribution of wealth and property and eliminate the class-based socioeconomic system of capitalist society. Marx believed that a truly equitable society required centralized control of credit, transportation, education, communication, agriculture, and industry, along with eliminating the rights of individuals to inherit or to own land.

Russia (formerly the Soviet Union) and China are the two largest countries to have been led by communist governments during the twentieth and twenty-first centuries. In both cases, the attempt to bring about a communist government came by way of violent revolutions in which members of the former government and ruling party were executed. Under Russian leader Vladimir Lenin (1870–1924) and Chinese leader Mao Zedong (1893–1976), strict dictatorships were instituted, curtailing individual rights in favor of state control. Lenin sought to expand communism into developing nations to counter the global spread of capitalism. Mao, in his form of communism, considered ongoing revolution within China a necessary aspect of communism. Both gave their names to their respective versions of communism, but neither Leninism nor Maoism managed to achieve the idealized utopia envisioned by Marx and other communist philosophers.

The primary difference between modern socialism and communism is that communist groups believe that a social revolution is necessary to create the idealized state without class structure, where socialists believe that the inequities of class structure can be addressed and eliminated through gradual change.

Typical Structure

Most modern communist governments define themselves as "socialist," though a national communist party exerts control over all branches of government. The designation of a "communist state" is primarily an external definition for a situation in which a communist party controls the government.

Among the examples of modern socialist states operating under the communist model are the People's Republic of China, the Republic of Cuba, and the Socialist Republic of Vietnam. However, each of these governments in fact operates through a mixed system of socialist and capitalist economic policies, allowing private ownership in some situations and sharply enforcing state control in others.

Typically, a communist state is led by the national communist party, a political group with voluntary membership and members in all sectors of the populace. While many individuals may join the communist party, the leadership of the party is generally selected by a smaller number of respected or venerated leaders from within the party. These leaders select a ruling committee that develops the political initiatives of the party, which are thereafter distributed throughout the government.

In China, the Communist Party elects both a chairperson, who serves as executive of the party, and a politburo, a standing committee that makes executive decisions on behalf of the party. In Cuba, the Communist Party selects individuals who sit for election to the National Assembly of People's Power, which then serves directly as the state's sole legislative body.

In the cases of China, Cuba, and Vietnam, the committees and leaders chosen by the communist party then participate directly in electing leaders to serve in the state judiciary. In addition, the central committees typically appoint individuals to serve as heads of the military and to lower-level, provincial, or municipal government positions. In China, the populace elects individuals to local, regional, and provincial councils that in turn elect representatives to sit on a legislative body known as the National People's Congress (NPC), though the NPC is generally considered a largely ceremonial institution without any substantial power to enact independent legislation.

In effect, most modern communist states are controlled by the leadership of the national communist party, though this leadership is achieved by direct and indirect control of lesser legislative, executive, and judicial bodies. In some cases, ceremonial and symbolic offices created under the communist party can evolve to take a larger role in state politics. In China, for instance, the NPC has come to play a more important role in developing legislation in the twenty-first century.

Role of the Citizen

In modern communist societies, citizens have little voice in selecting the leadership of the government. In many communist states, popular elections are held at local and national levels, but candidates are chosen by communist party leadership and citizens are not given the option to vote for representatives of opposing political parties.

In most cases, the state adopts policies that give the appearance of popular control over the government, while in actuality, governmental policies are influenced by a small number of leaders chosen from within the upper echelons of the party. Popularly elected leaders who oppose party policy are generally removed from office.

All existing communist states have been criticized for human rights violations in terms of curtailing the freedoms available to citizens and of enacting dictatorial and authoritarian policies. Cuba, Vietnam, and China, for instance, all have laws preventing citizens from opposing party policy or supporting a political movement that opposes the communist party. Communist governments have also been accused of using propaganda and misinformation to control the opinion of the populace regarding party leadership and therefore reducing the potential for popular resistance to communist policies.

Micah Issitt
Philadelphia, Pennsylvania

Examples
China
Cuba
Laos
North Korea
Vietnam

Bibliography
Caramani, Daniele. *Comparative Politics*. New York: Oxford UP, 2008. Print.
Priestland, David. *The Red Flag: A History of Communism.* New York: Grove, 2009. Print.
Service, Robert. *Comrades! A History of World Communism*. Cambridge: Harvard UP, 2007. Print.

Confederation/Confederacy

Guiding Premise

A confederation or confederacy is a loose alliance between political units, such as states or cantons, within a broader federal government. Confederations allow a central, federal government to create laws and regulations of broad national interest, but the sovereign units are granted the ultimate authority to carry out those laws and to create, implement, and enforce their own laws as well. Confederate governments are built on the notion that a single, central government should not have ultimate authority over sovereign states and populations. Some confederate governments were born due to the rise of European monarchies and empires that threatened to govern states from afar. Others were created out of respect for the diverse ideologies, cultures, and ideals of their respective regions. Confederations and confederacies may be hybrids, giving comparatively more power to a federal government while retaining respect for the sovereignty of their members. True confederate governments are rare in the twenty-first century.

Typical Structure

Confederate governments are typically characterized by the presence of both a central government and a set of regional, similarly organized, and sovereign (independent) governments. For example, a confederate government might have as its central government structure a system that features executive, legislative, and judicial branches. Each region that serves as members of the confederation would have in place a similar system, enabling the efficient flow of lawmaking and government services.

In some confederations, the executive branch of the central government is headed by a president or prime minister, who serves as the government's chief administrative officer, overseeing the military and other government operations. Meanwhile, at the regional level, another chief executive, such as a governor, is charged with the administration of that government's operations.

Legislative branches are also similarly designed. Confederations use parliaments or congresses that, in most cases, have two distinct chambers. One chamber consists of legislators who each represent an entire state, canton, or region. The other chamber consists of legislators representing certain populations of voters within that region. Legislatures at the regional level not only have the power to create and enforce their own laws, but also have the power to refuse to enact or enforce any laws handed down by the national government.

A confederation's judiciary is charged with ensuring that federal and regional laws are applied uniformly and within the limits of the confederation's constitutional framework. Central and regional governments both have such judicial institutions, with the latter addressing those legal matters administered in the state or canton and the former addressing legal issues of interest to the entire country.

Political parties also typically play a role in a confederate government. Political leadership is achieved by a party's majority status in either the executive or the legislative branches. Parties also play a role in forging a compromise on certain matters at both the regional and national levels. Some confederations take the diversity of political parties and their ideologies seriously enough to create coalition governments that can help avoid political stalemates.

Role of the Citizen

The political role of the citizen within a confederate political system depends largely on the constitution of the country. In some confederacies, for example, the people directly elect their legislative and executive leaders by popular vote. Some legislators are elected to open terms—they may technically be reelected, but this election is merely a formality, as they are allowed to stay in office until they decide to leave or they die—while others may be subject to term limits or other reelection rules. Popularly elected legislators and executives in turn draft, file, and pass new laws and regulations that ideally are favorable to the voters. Some confederate systems give popularly elected legislators the ability to elect a party leader to serve as prime minister or president.

Confederations are designed to empower the regional government and avoid the dominance of a distant national government. In this manner, citizens of a confederate government, in some cases, may enjoy the ability to put forth new legislative initiatives. Although the lawmaking process is expected to be administered by the legislators and executives, in such cases the people are allowed and even encouraged to connect and interact with their political representatives to ensure that the government remains open and accessible.

Michael Auerbach
Marblehead, Massachusetts

Examples
European Union
Switzerland
United States under the Articles of Confederation (1781–89)

Bibliography
"Government Type." *The World Factbook*. Central Intelligence Agency, n.d. Web. 17 Jan. 2013.
"Swiss Politics." *SwissWorld.org.* Federal Department of Foreign Affairs Presence Switzerland, n.d. Web. 17 Jan. 2013.

Constitutional Monarchy

Guiding Premise

A constitutional monarchy is a form of government in which the head of state is a monarch (a king or queen) with limited powers. The monarch has official duties, but those responsibilities are defined in the nation's constitution and not by the monarch. Meanwhile, the power to create and rescind laws is given to a legislative body. Constitutional monarchies retain the ceremony and traditions associated with nations that have long operated under a king or queen. However, the constitution prevents the monarch from becoming a tyrant. Additionally, the monarchy, which is typically a lifetime position, preserves a sense of stability and continuity in the government, as the legislative body undergoes periodic change associated with the election cycle.

Typical Structure

The structure of a constitutional monarchy varies from nation to nation. In some countries, the monarchy is predominantly ceremonial. In such cases, the monarch provides a largely symbolic role, reminding the people of their heritage and giving them comfort in times of difficulty. Such is the case in Japan, for example; the emperor of that country was stripped of any significant power after World War II but was allowed to continue his legacy in the interest of ensuring that the Japanese people would remain peaceful. Today, that nation still holds its monarchical family in the highest regard, but the government is controlled by the Diet (the legislature), with the prime minister serving in the executive role.

In other countries, the sovereign plays a more significant role. In the United Kingdom, the king or queen does have some power, including the powers to appoint the prime minister, to open or dissolve Parliament, to approve bills that have been passed by Parliament, and to declare war and make peace. However, the monarch largely defers to the government on these acts. In Bahrain, the king (or, until 2002, emir or hereditary ruler) was far more involved in government in the late twentieth and early twenty-first centuries than many other constitutional monarchs. In 1975, the emir of Bahrain dissolved the parliament, supposedly to run the government more effectively. His son would later implement a number of significant constitutional reforms that made the government more democratic in nature.

The key to the structure of this type of political system is the constitution. As is the case in the United States (a federal republic), a constitutional monarchy is carefully defined by the government's founding document. In Canada, for example, the king or queen of England is still recognized as the head of state, but that country's constitution gives the monarch no power other than ceremonial responsibilities. India, South Africa, and many other members of the Commonwealth of Nations (the English monarch's sphere of influence, spanning most of the former British colonies) have, since gaining their independence, created constitutions that grant no power to the English monarch; instead, they give all powers to their respective government institutions and, in some cases, recognize their own monarchs.

A defining feature of a constitutional monarchy is the fact that the monarch gives full respect to the limitations set forth by the constitution (and rarely seeks to alter such a document in his or her favor). Even in the United Kingdom itself—which does not have a written constitution, but rather a series of foundational documents—the king or queen does not step beyond the bounds set by customary rules. One interesting exception is in Bahrain, where Hamad bin Isa Al-Khalifa assumed the throne in 1999 and immediately implemented a series of reforms to the constitution in order to give greater definition to that country's democratic institutions, including resuming parliamentary elections in 2001. During the 2011 Arab Spring uprisings, Bahraini protesters called for further democratic reforms to be enacted, and tensions between the ruler and his opposition continue.

Role of the Citizen

In the past, monarchies ruled nations with absolute power; the only power the people had was the ability to unify and overthrow the ruling sovereign. Although the notion of an absolute monarchy has largely disappeared from the modern political landscape, many nations have retained their respective kings, queens, emperors, and other monarchs for the sake of ceremony and cultural heritage. In the modern constitutional monarchy, the people are empowered by their nation's foundational documents, which not only define the rights of the people but the limitations of their governments and sovereign as well. The people, through their legislators and through the democratic voting process, can modify their constitutions to expand or shrink the political involvement of the monarchy.

For example, the individual members of the Commonwealth of Nations, including Canada and Australia, have different constitutional parameters for the king or queen of England. In England, the monarch holds a number of powers, while in Canada, he or she is merely a ceremonial head of state (with all government power centered in the capital of Ottawa). In fact, in 1999, Australia held a referendum (a general vote) on whether to abolish its constitutional monarchy altogether and replace it with a presidential republic. In that case, the people voted to retain the monarchy, but the proposal was only narrowly defeated. These examples demonstrate the tremendous power the citizens of a constitutional monarchy may possess through the legislative process and the vote under the constitution.

Michael Auerbach
Marblehead, Massachusetts

Examples

Bahrain
Cambodia
Denmark
Japan
Lesotho
Malaysia
Morocco
Netherlands
Norway
Spain
Sweden
Thailand
United Kingdom

Bibliography

Bowman, John. "Constitutional Monarchies." *CBC News*. CBC, 4 Oct. 2002. Web. 17 Jan. 2013.
"The Role of the Monarchy." *Royal.gov.uk*. Royal Household, n.d. Web. 17 Jan. 2013.

Constitutional Republic

Guiding Premise

A constitutional republic is a governmental system in which citizens are involved in electing or appointing leaders who serve according to rules formulated in an official state constitution. In essence, the constitutional republic combines the political structure of a republic or republican governmental system with constitutional principles.

A republic is a government in which the head of state is empowered to hold office through law, not inheritance (as in a monarchy). A constitutional republic is a type of republic based on a constitution, a written body of fundamental precedents and principles from which the laws of the nation are developed.

Most constitutional republics in the modern world use a universal suffrage system, in which all citizens of the nation are empowered to vote for or against individuals who attempt to achieve public office. Universal suffrage is not required for a nation to qualify as a constitutional republic, and some nations may only allow certain categories of citizens to vote for elected leaders.

A constitutional republic differs from other forms of democratic systems in the roles assigned to both the leaders and the citizenry. In a pure democratic system, the government is formed by pure majority rule, and this system therefore ignores the opinions of any minority group. A republic, by contrast, is a form of government in which the government's role is limited by a written constitution aimed at promoting the welfare of all individuals, whether members of the majority or a minority.

Typical Structure

To qualify as a constitutional republic, a nation must choose a head of state (most often a president) through elections, according to constitutional law. In some nations, an elected president may serve alongside an appointed or elected individual who serves as leader of the legislature, such as a prime minister, often called the "head of government." When the president also serves as head of government, the republic is said to operate under a presidential system.

Typically, the executive branch consists of the head of state and the executive offices, which are responsible for enforcing the laws and overseeing relations with other nations. The legislative branch makes laws and has overlapping duties with the executive office in terms of economic and military developments. The judicial branch, consisting of the courts, interprets the law and the constitution and enforces adherence to the law.

In a constitutional republic, the constitution describes the powers allotted to each branch of government and the means by which the governmental bodies are to be established. The constitution also describes the ways in which governmental branches interact in creating, interpreting, and enforcing laws. For instance, in the United States, the executive and legislative branches both have roles in determining the budget for the nation, and neither body is free to make budgetary legislation without the approval of the other branch.

Role of the Citizen

In a constitutional republic, the citizens have the power to control the evolution of the nation through the choice of representatives who serve on the government. These representatives can, generally through complicated means, create or abolish laws and even change the constitution itself through reinterpretations of constitutional principles or direct amendments.

Citizens in a republic are empowered, but generally not required, to play a role in electing leaders. In the United States, both state governments and the federal government function according to a republican system, and citizens are therefore allowed to take part in the election of leaders to both local and national offices. In addition, constitutional systems generally allow individuals to join political interest groups to further common political goals.

In a constitutional democratic republic such as Guatemala and Honduras, the president, who serves as chief of state and head of government, is elected directly by popular vote. In the United States, a constitutional federal republic, the president is elected by the Electoral College, whose members are selected according to the popular vote within each district. The Electoral College is intended to provide more weight to smaller states, thereby balancing the disproportionate voting power of states with larger populations. In all constitutional republics, the citizens elect leaders either directly or indirectly through other representatives chosen by popular vote. Therefore, the power to control the government is granted to the citizens of the constitutional republic.

Micah Issitt
Philadelphia, Pennsylvania

Examples

Guatemala
Honduras
Iceland
Paraguay
Peru
United States
Uruguay

Bibliography

Baylis, John, Steve Smith, and Patricia Owens. *The Globalization of World Politics: An Introduction to International Relations*. New York: Oxford UP, 2010. Print.

Caramani, Daniele. *Comparative Politics*. New York: Oxford UP, 2008. Print.

Garner, Robert, Peter Ferdinand, and Stephanie Lawson. *Introduction to Politics*. 2nd ed. Oxford: Oxford UP, 2009. Print.

Hague, Rod, and Martin Harrop. *Comparative Government and Politics: An Introduction*. New York: Palgrave, 2007. Print.

Democracy

Guiding Premise

Democracy is a political system based on majority rule, in which all citizens are guaranteed participatory rights to influence the evolution of government. There are many different types of democracy, based on the degree to which citizens participate in the formation and operation of the government. In a direct democratic system, citizens vote directly on proposed changes to law and public policy. In a representative democracy, individuals vote to elect representatives who then serve to create and negotiate public policy.

The democratic system of government first developed in Ancient Greece and has existed in many forms throughout history. While democratic systems always involve some type of majority rule component, most modern democracies have systems in place designed to equalize representation for minority groups or to promote the development of governmental policies that prevent oppression of minorities by members of the majority.

In modern democracies, one of the central principles is the idea that citizens must be allowed to participate in free elections to select leaders who serve in the government. In addition, voters in democratic systems elect political leaders for a limited period of time, thus ensuring that the leadership of the political system can change along with the changing views of the populace. Political theorists have defined democracy as a system in which the people are sovereign and the political power flows upward from the people to their elected leaders.

Typical Structure

In a typical democracy, the government is usually divided into executive, legislative, and judicial branches. Citizens participate in electing individuals to serve in one or more of these branches, and elected leaders appoint additional leaders to serve in other political offices. The democratic system, therefore, involves a combination of elected and appointed leadership.

Democratic systems may follow a presidential model, as in the United States, where citizens elect a president to serve as both head of state and head of government. In a presidential model, citizens may also participate in elections to fill other governmental bodies, including the legislature and judicial branch. In a parliamentary democracy, citizens elect individuals to a parliament, whose members in turn form a committee to appoint a leader, often called the prime minister, who serves as head of government.

In most democratic systems, the executive and legislative branches cooperate in the formation of laws, while the judicial branch enforces and interprets the laws produced by the government. Most democratic systems have developed a system of checks and balances designed to prevent any single branch of government from exerting a dominant influence over the development of governmental policy. These checks and balances may be instituted in a variety of ways, including the ability to block governmental initiatives and the ability to appoint members to various governmental agencies.

Democratic governments generally operate on the principle of political parties, which are organizations formed to influence political development. Candidates for office have the option of joining a political party, which can provide funding and other campaign assistance. In some democratic systems—called dominant party or one-party dominant systems—there is effectively a single political party. Dominant party systems allow for competition in democratic elections, but existing power structures often prevent opposing parties from competing successfully. In multiparty democratic systems, there are two or more political parties with the ability to compete for office, and citizens are able to choose among political parties during elections. Some countries only allow political parties to be active at the national level, while other countries allow political parties to play a role in local and regional elections.

Role of the Citizen

The citizens in a democratic society are seen as the ultimate source of political authority. Members of the government, by contrast, are seen as servants of the people, and are selected and elected to serve the people's interests. Democratic systems developed to protect and enhance the freedom of the people; however, for the system to function properly, citizens must engage in a number of civic duties.

In democratic nations, voting is a right that comes with citizenship. Though some democracies—Australia, for example—require citizens to vote by law, compulsory participation in elections is not common in democratic societies. Citizens are nonetheless encouraged to fulfill their voting rights and to stay informed regarding political issues. In addition, individuals are responsible for contributing to the well-being of society as a whole, usually through a system of taxation whereby part of an individual's earnings is used to pay for governmental services.

In many cases, complex governmental and legal issues must be simplified to ease understanding among the citizenry. This goal is partially met by having citizens elect leaders who must then explain to their constituents how they are shaping legislation and other government initiatives to reflect constituents' wants and needs. In the United States, citizens may participate in the election of local leaders within individual cities or counties, and also in the election of leaders who serve in the national legislature and executive offices.

Citizens in democratic societies are also empowered with the right to join political interest groups and political parties in an effort to further a broader political agenda. However, democratic societies oppose making group membership a requirement and have laws forbidding forcing an individual to join any group. Freedom of choice, especially with regard to political affiliation and preference, is one of the cornerstones of all democratic systems.

Micah Issitt
Philadelphia, Pennsylvania

Examples

Denmark
Sweden
Spain
Japan
Australia
Costa Rica
Uruguay
United States

Bibliography

Barington, Lowell. *Comparative Politics*: *Structures and Choices*. Boston: Wadsworth, 2012. Print.

Caramani, Daniele. *Comparative Politics*. New York: Oxford UP, 2008. Print.

Przeworski, Adam. *Democracy and the Limits of Self Government*, New York: Cambridge UP, 2010. Print.

Dictatorship/Military Dictatorship

Guiding Premise

Dictatorships and military dictatorships are political systems in which absolute power is held by an individual or military organization. Dictatorships are led by a single individual, under whom all political control is consolidated. Military dictatorships are similar in purpose, but place the system under the control of a military organization comprised of a single senior officer, or small group of officers. Often, dictatorships and military dictatorships are imposed as the result of a coup d'état in which the regime in question directly removes the incumbent regime, or after a power vacuum creates chaos in the nation. In both situations, the consolidation of absolute power is designed to establish a state of strict law and order.

Typical Structure

Dictatorships and military dictatorships vary in structure and nature. Some come about through the overthrow of other regimes, while others are installed through the democratic process, and then become a dictatorship as democratic rights are withdrawn. Still others are installed following a complete breakdown of government, often with the promise of establishing order.

Many examples of dictatorships can be found in the twentieth century, including Nazi Germany, Joseph Stalin's Soviet Union, and China under Mao Tse-tung. A number of dictatorships existed in Africa, such as the regimes of Idi Amin in Uganda, Charles Taylor in Liberia, and Mu'ammar Gadhafi in Libya. Dictatorships such as these consolidated power in the hands of an individual leader. A dictator serves as the sole decision-maker in the government, frequently using the military, secret police, or other security agencies to enforce the leader's will. Dictators also have control over state institutions like legislatures. A legislature may have the ability to develop and pass laws, but if its actions run counter to the dictator's will, the latter can—and

frequently does—dissolve the body, replacing its members with those more loyal to the dictator's agenda.

Military dictatorships consolidate power not in the hands of a civilian but in an individual or small group of military officers—the latter of which are often called "juntas." Because military dictatorships are frequently installed following a period of civil war and/or a coup d'état, the primary focus of the dictatorship is to achieve strict order through the application of military force. Military dictatorships are often installed with the promise of an eventual return to civilian and/or democratic control once the nation has regained stability. In the case of North Korea, one-party communist rule turned into a communist military dictatorship as its leader, Kim Il-Sung, assumed control of the military and brought its leadership into the government.

In the late twentieth and early twenty-first centuries, dictatorships and military dictatorships are most commonly found in developing nations, where poverty rates are high and regional stability is tenuous at best. Many are former European colonies, where charismatic leaders who boast of their national heritage have stepped in to replace colonial governments. National resources are typically directed toward military and security organizations in an attempt to ensure security and internal stability, keeping the regime in power and containing rivals. Human rights records in such political systems are typically heavily criticized by the international community.

Role of the Citizen

Dictatorships and military dictatorships are frequently installed because of the absence of viable democratic governments. There is often a disconnect, therefore, between the people and their leaders in a dictatorship. Of course, many dictatorships are identified as such by external entities and not by their own people. For example, the government of Zimbabwe is technically identified as a parliamentary democracy, with Robert Mugabe—who has been the elected leader of the country since 1980—as its president. However, the international community has long complained that Mugabe "won" his positions through political corruption, including alleged ballot stuffing. In 2008, Mugabe lost his first reelection campaign, but demanded a recount. While the recount continued, his supporters attacked opposition voters, utilizing violence and intimidation until his opponent, Morgan Tsvangirai, withdrew his candidacy, and Mugabe was restored as president.

By definition, citizens do not have a role in changing the course of a dictatorship's agenda. The people are usually called upon to join the military in support of the regime, or cast their vote consistently in favor of the ruling regime. Freedom of speech, the press, and assembly are virtually nonexistent, as those who speak out against the ruling regime are commonly jailed, tortured, or killed.

Michael Auerbach
Marblehead, Massachusetts

Examples
Belarus (dictatorship)
Fiji (military dictatorship)
North Korea (military dictatorship)
Zimbabwe (dictatorship)

Bibliography
Clayton, Jonathan. "China Aims to Bring Peace through Deals with Dictators and Warlords." *Times* [London]. Times Newspapers, 31 Jan. 2007. Web. 6 Feb. 2013.
"Robert Mugabe—Biography." *Biography.com.* A+E Television Networks, 2013. Web. 6 Feb. 2013.

Ecclesiastical

Guiding Premise

An ecclesiastical government is one in which the laws of the state are guided by and derived from religious law. Ecclesiastical governments can take a variety of forms and can be based on many different types of religious traditions. In some traditions, a deity or group of deities are considered to take a direct role in the formation of government, while other traditions utilize religious laws or principles indirectly to craft laws used to manage the state.

In many cultures, religious laws and tenets play a major role in determining the formation of national laws. Historically, the moral and ethical principles derived from Judeo-Christian tradition inspired many laws in Europe and North America. Few modern governments operate according to an ecclesiastical system, but Vatican City, which is commonly classified as a city-state, utilizes a modernized version of the ecclesiastical government model. All states utilizing an ecclesiastical or semi-ecclesiastical system have adopted a single state religion that is officially recognized by the government.

In some predominantly Islamic nations, including the Sudan, Oman, Iran, and Nigeria, Islamic law, known as sharia, is the basis for most national laws, and government leaders often must obtain approval by the leaders of the religious community before being allowed to serve in office. Most modern ecclesiastical or semi-ecclesiastical governments have adopted a mixed theocratic republic system in which individuals approved by religious authorities are elected by citizens to hold public office.

Typical Structure

In an ecclesiastical government, the church or recognized religious authority is the source of all state law. In a theocracy, which is one of the most common types of ecclesiastical governments, a deity or group of deities occupies a symbolic position as head of state, while representatives are chosen to lead the government based on their approval by the prevailing religious authority. In other types of ecclesiastical governments, the chief of state may be the leading figure in the church, such as in Vatican City, where the Catholic Pope is also considered the chief of state.

There are no modern nations that operate on a purely ecclesiastical system, though some Islamic countries, like Iran, have adopted a semi-ecclesiastical form of republican government. In Iran, the popularly elected Assembly of Experts—comprised of Islamic scholars called mujtahids—appoints an individual to serve as supreme leader of the nation for life, and this individual has veto power over all other governmental offices. Iranian religious leaders also approve other individuals to run as candidates for positions in the state legislature. In many cases, the citizens will elect an individual to serve as head of government, though this individual must conform to religious laws.

In an ecclesiastical government, those eligible to serve in the state legislature are generally members of the church hierarchy or have been approved for office by church leaders. In Tibet, which functioned as an ecclesiastical government until the Chinese takeover of 1951, executive and legislative duties were consolidated under a few religious leaders, called lamas, and influential citizens who maintained the country under a theocratic system. Most modern nations separate governmental functions between distinct but interrelated executive, legislative, and judicial branches.

Many modern semi-ecclesiastical nations have adopted a set of state principles in the form of a constitution to guide the operation of government and the establishment of laws. In mixed constitutional/theocratic systems, the constitution may be used to legitimize religious authority by codifying a set of laws and procedures that have been developed from religious scripture.

In addition, the existence of a constitution facilitates the process of altering laws and governmental procedures as religious authorities reinterpret religious scriptures and texts.

Role of the Citizen

Citizens in modern ecclesiastical and semi-ecclesiastical governments play a role in formulating the government though national and local elections. In some cases, religious authorities may approve more than one candidate for a certain position and citizens are then able to exercise legitimate choice in the electoral process. In other cases, popular support for one or more candidates may influence religious authorities when it comes time to nominate or appoint an individual to office.

In ecclesiastical governments, the freedoms and rights afforded to citizens may depend on their religious affiliation. Christians living in a Christian ecclesiastical government, for instance, may be allowed to run for and hold government office, while representatives of other religions may be denied this right. In addition, ecclesiastical governments may not recognize religious rights and rituals of other traditions and may not offer protection for those practicing religions other than the official state religion.

Though religious authority dominates politics and legislative development, popular influence is still an important part of the ecclesiastical system. Popular support for or against certain laws may convince the government to alter official policies. In addition, the populace may join local and regional religious bodies that can significantly affect national political developments. As local and regional religious groups grow in numbers and influence, they may promote candidates to political office, thereby helping to influence the evolution of government.

Micah Issitt
Philadelphia, Pennsylvania

Examples

Afghanistan
Iran
Nigeria
Oman
Vatican City

Bibliography

Barrington, Lowell. *Comparative Politics*: *Structures and Choices*. Boston: Wadsworth, 2012. Print.
Hallaq, Wael B. *An Introduction to Islamic Law*. New York: Cambridge UP, 2009. Print.
Hirschl, Ran. *Constitutional Theocracy*. Cambridge, MA: Harvard UP, 2010. Print.

Failed State

Guiding Premise

A failed state is a political unit that at one point had a stable government that provided basic services and security to its citizens, but then entered a period marked by devastating conflict, extreme poverty, overwhelming political corruption, and/or unlivable environmental conditions. Often, a group takes hold of a failed state's government through military means, staving off rivals to fill in a power vacuum. The nominal leadership of a failed state frequently uses its power to combat rival factions, implement extreme religious law, or protect and advance illicit activities (such as drug production or piracy). Failed states frequently retain their external borders, but within those borders are regions that may be dominated by a particular faction, effectively carving the state into disparate subunits, with some areas even attaining relative stability and security—a kind of de facto independence.

Typical Structure

Failed states vary in appearance based on a number of factors. One such factor is the type of government that existed prior to the state's collapse. For example, a failed state might have originally existed as a parliamentary democracy, with an active legislature and executive system that developed a functioning legal code and administered to the needs of the people. However, that state may not have adequately addressed the needs of certain groups, fostering a violent backlash and hastening the country's destabilization. An ineffectual legislature might have been dissolved by the executive (a prime minister or president), and in the absence of leadership, the government as a whole ceased to operate effectively.

Another major factor is demographics. Many states are comprised of two or more distinct ethnic, social, or religious groups. When the ruling party fails to effectively govern and/or serve the interests of a certain segment of the population, it may be ousted or simply ignored by the marginalized faction within the state. If the government falls, it creates a power vacuum that rival groups compete to fill. If one faction gains power, it must remain in a constant state of vigilance against its rivals, focusing more on keeping enemies in check than on rebuilding crippled government infrastructure. Some also seek to create theocracies based on extreme interpretations of a particular religious doctrine. Frequently, these regimes are themselves ousted by rivals within a few years, leaving no lasting government and keeping the state in chaos.

Failed states are also characterized by extreme poverty and a lack of modern technology. Potable water, electricity, food, and medicine are scarce among average citizens. In some cases, these conditions are worsened by natural events. Haiti, for example, was a failed state for many years before the devastating 2010 earthquake that razed the capitol city of Port au Prince, deepening the country's poverty and instability. Afghanistan and Ethiopia—with their harsh, arid climates—are also examples of failed states whose physical environments and lack of resources exacerbated an already extreme state of impoverishment.

Most failed states' conditions are also worsened by the presence of foreigners. Because their governments are either unable or unwilling to repel terrorists, for example, failed states frequently become havens for international terrorism. Somalia, Afghanistan, and Iraq are all examples of states that failed, enabling terrorist organizations to set up camp within their borders. As such groups pose a threat to other nations, those nations often send troops and weapons into the failed states to engage the terrorists. In recent years, NATO, the United Nations, and the African Union have all entered failed states to both combat terrorists and help rebuild government.

Role of the Citizen

Citizens of a failed state have very little say in the direction of their country. In most cases, when a faction assumes control over the government, it installs strict controls that limit the rights of citizens, particularly such rights as freedom of speech, freedom of assembly, and freedom of religion. Some regimes allow for "democratic" elections, but a continued lack of infrastructure and widespread corruption often negates the legitimacy of these elections.

Citizens of failed states are often called upon by the ruling regime (or a regional faction) to serve in its militia, helping it combat other factions within the state. In fact, many militias within failed states are comprised of people who were forced to join (under penalty of death) at a young age. Those who do not join militias are often drawn into criminal activity such as piracy and the drug trade.

Some citizens are able to make a difference by joining interest groups. Many citizens are able to achieve a limited amount of success sharing information about women's rights, HIV/AIDS and other issues. In some situations, these groups are able to gain international assistance from organizations that were unable to work with the failed government.

Michael Auerbach
Marblehead, Massachusetts

Examples
Chad
Democratic Republic of the Congo
Somalia
Sudan
Zimbabwe

Bibliography
"Failed States: Fixing a Broken World." *Economist*, 29 Jan. 2009. Web. 6 Feb. 2012.
"Failed States." Global Policy Forum, 2013. Web. 6 Feb. 2012.
"Somalia Tops Failed States Index for Fifth Year." *CNN.com*. Turner Broadcasting System, 18 June 2012. Web. 6 Feb. 2012.
Thürer, Daniel. (1999). "The 'Failed State' and International Law." *International Review of the Red Cross*. International Committee of the Red Cross, 31 Dec. 1999. Web. 6 Feb. 2012.

Federal Republic

Guiding Premise

A federal republic is a political system that features a central government as well as a set of regional subunits such as states or provinces. Federal republics are designed to limit the power of the central government, paring its focus to only matters of national interest. Typically, a greater degree of power is granted to the regional governments, which retain the ability to create their own laws of local relevance. The degree to which the federal and regional governments each enjoy authority varies from nation to nation, based on the country's interpretation of this republican form of government. By distributing authority to these separate but connected government institutions, federal republics give the greatest power to the people themselves, who typically vote directly for both their regional and national political representation.

Typical Structure

A federal republic's structure varies from nation to nation. However, most federal republics feature two distinct governing entities. The first is a central, federal government, usually based in the nation's capital city. The federal government's task is to address issues of national importance. These issues include defense and foreign relations, but also encompass matters of domestic interest that must be addressed in uniform fashion, such as social assistance programs, infrastructure, and certain taxes.

A federal republic is comprised of executive, legislative, and judicial branches. The executive is typically a president or prime minister—the former selected by popular vote, the latter selected by members of the legislature—and is charged with the administration of the federal government's programs and regulations. The legislature—such as the US Congress, the Austrian Parliament, or the German Bundestag—is charged with developing laws and managing government spending. The judiciary is charged

with ensuring that federal and state laws are enforced and that they are consistent with the country's constitution.

The federal government is limited in terms of its ability to assert authority over the regions. Instead, federal republics grant a degree of sovereignty to the different states, provinces, or regions that comprise the entire nation. These regions have their own governments, similar in structure and procedure to those of the federal government. They too have executives, legislatures, and judiciaries whose foci are limited to the regional government's respective jurisdictions.

The federal and regional segments of a republic are not completely independent of one another, however. Although the systems are intended to distribute power evenly, federal and regional governments are closely linked. This connectivity ensures the efficient collection of taxes, the regional distribution of federal funds, and a rapid response to issues of national importance. A federal republic's greatest strength, therefore, is the series of connections it maintains between the federal, regional, and local governments it contains.

Role of the Citizen

A federal republic is distinguished by the limitations of power it places on the national government. The primary goal of such a design was to place the power of government in the hands of the people. One of the ways the citizens' power is demonstrated is by participating in the electoral process. In a federal republic, the people elect their legislators. In some republics, the legislators in turn elect a prime minister, while in others, the people directly elect a president. The electoral process is an important way for citizens to influence the course of their government, both at the regional and federal levels. They do so by placing people who truly represent their diverse interests in the federal government.

The citizen is also empowered by participating in government as opposed to being subjected to it. In addition to taking part in the electoral process, the people are free to join and become active in a political party. A political party serves as a proxy for its members, representing their viewpoint and interests on a local and national level. In federal republics like Germany, a wide range of political parties are active in the legislature, advancing the political agendas of those they represent.

Michael Auerbach
Marblehead, Massachusetts

Examples
Austria
Brazil
Germany

India
Mexico
Nigeria
United States

Bibliography
"The Federal Principle." *Republik Österreich Parlament.* Republik Österreich Parlament, 8 Oct. 2010. Web. 6 Feb. 2013.
"The Federal Republic of Germany." *Deutscher Bundestag.* German Bundestag, 2013. Web. 6 Feb. 2013.
Collin, Nicholas. "An Essay on the Means of Promoting Federal Sentiments in the United States." *Friends of the Constitution: Writings of the "Other" Federalists, 1787–1788.* Ed. Colleen A. Sheehan and Gary L. McDowell. Online Library of Liberty, 2013. Web. 6 Feb. 2013.

Federation

Guiding Premise

A federation is a nation formed from the unification of smaller political entities. Federations feature federal governments that oversee nation-wide issues. However, they also grant a degree of autonomy to the regional, state, or other local governments within the system. Federations are often formed because a collective of diverse regions find a common interest in unification. While the federal government is installed to address those needs, regions with their own distinct ethnic, socioeconomic, or political characteristics remain intact. This "separate but united" structure allows federations to avoid conflict and instability among their regions.

Typical Structure

The primary goal of a federation is to unify a country's political subunits within a national framework. The federal government, therefore, features institutions comprised of representatives from the states or regions. The representatives are typically elected by the residents of these regions, and some federal systems give the power to elect certain national leaders to these representatives. The regions themselves can vary considerably in size. The Russian Federation, for example, includes forty-six geographically large provinces as well as two more-concentrated cities as part of its eighty-three constituent federation members.

There are two institutions in which individuals from the constituent parts of a federation serve. The first institution is the legislature. Legislatures vary in appearance from nation to nation. For example, the US Congress is comprised of two chambers—the House of Representatives and the Senate—whose directly elected members act on behalf of their respective states. The German Parliament, on the other hand, consists of the directly elected Bundestag—which is tasked with electing the German federal chancellor, among other things—and the state-appointed Bundesrat, which works on behalf of the country's sixteen states.

The second institution is the executive. Here, the affairs of the nation are administered by a president or similar leader. Again, the structure and powers of a federal government's executive institutions varies from nation to nation according to their constitutional framework. Federal executive institutions are charged with management of state affairs, including oversight of the military, foreign relations, health care, and education. Similarly diverse is the power of the executive in relation to the legislative branch. Some prime ministers, for example, enjoy considerably greater power than the president. In fact, some presidents share power with other leaders, or councils thereof within the executive branch, serving as the diplomatic face of the nation but not playing a major role in lawmaking. In India, for example, the president is the chief executive of the federal government, but shares power with the prime minister and the Council of Ministers, headed by the prime minister.

In order to promote continuity between the federal government and the states, regions, or other political subunits in the federation, those subunits typically feature governments that largely mirror that of the central government. Some of these regional governments are modified according to their respective constitutions. For example, whereas the bicameral US Congress consists of the Senate and House of Representatives, Nebraska's state legislature only has one chamber. Such distinctive characteristics of state/regional governments reflect the geographic and cultural interests of the region in question. It also underscores the degree of autonomy given to such states under a federation government system.

Role of the Citizen

Federations vary in terms of both structure and distribution of power within government institutions. However, federal systems are typically democratic in nature, relying heavily on the participation of the electorate for installing representatives in those institutions. At the regional level, the people vote for their respective legislators and executives either directly or through political parties. The executive in turn appoints cabinet officials, while the legislators select a chamber leader. In US state governments, for example, such a leader might be a Senate president or speaker of the House of Representatives.

The people also play an important role in federal government. As residents of a given state or region, registered voters—again, through either a direct vote or through political parties—choose their legislators and national executives. In federations that utilize a parliamentary system, however, prime ministers are typically selected by the legislators and/or their political parties and not through a direct, national vote. Many constitutions limit the length of political leaders' respective terms of service and/or the number of times they may seek reelection, fostering an environment in which the democratic voting process is a frequent occurrence.

Michael Auerbach
Marblehead, Massachusetts

Examples

Australia
Germany
India
Mexico
Russia
United States

Bibliography

"Federal System of India." *Maps of India*. MapsOfIndia.com, 22 Sep. 2011. Web. 7 Feb. 2013.

"Political System." *Facts about Germany*. Frankfurter Societäts-Medien, 2011. Web. 7 Feb. 2013.

"Russia." *CIA World Factbook*. Central Intelligence Agency, 5 Feb. 2013. Web. 7 Feb. 2013.

Monarchy

Guiding Premise

A monarchy is a political system based on the sovereignty of a single individual who holds actual or symbolic authority over all governmental functions. The monarchy is one of the oldest forms of government in human history and was the most common type of government until the nineteenth century. In a monarchy, authority is inherited, usually through primogeniture, or inheritance by the eldest son.

In an absolute monarchy, the monarch holds authority over the government and functions as both head of state and head of government. In a constitutional monarchy, the role of the monarch is codified in the state constitution, and the powers afforded to the monarch are limited by constitutional law. Constitutional monarchies generally blend the inherited authority of the monarchy with popular control in the form of democratic elections. The monarch may continue to hold significant power over some aspects of government or may be relegated to a largely ceremonial or symbolic role.

In most ancient monarchies, the monarch was generally believed to have been chosen for his or her role by divine authority, and many monarchs in history have claimed to represent the will of a god or gods in their ascendancy to the position. In constitutional monarchies, the monarch may be seen as representing spiritual authority or may represent a link to the country's national heritage.

Typical Structure

In an absolute monarchy, a single monarch is empowered to head the government, including the formulation of all laws and leadership of the nation's armed forces. Oman is one example of a type of absolute monarchy called a sultanate, in which a family of leaders, called "sultans," inherits authority and leads the nation under an authoritarian system. Power in the Omani sultanate remains within the royal family. In the event of the sultan's death or incapacitation, the Royal Family Council selects a successor by consensus from within the family line. Beneath the sultan is a council of ministers, appointed by the sultan, to create and disseminate official government policy. The sultan's council serves alongside an elected body of leaders who enforce and represent Islamic law and work with the sultan's ministers to create national laws.

In Japan, which is a constitutional monarchy, the Japanese emperor serves as the chief of state and symbolic representative of Japan's culture and history. The emperor officiates national ceremonies, meets with world leaders for diplomatic purposes, and symbolically appoints leaders to certain governmental posts. Governmental authority in Japan rests with the Diet, a legislative body of elected officials who serve limited terms of office and are elected through popular vote. A prime minister is also chosen to lead the Diet, and the prime minister is considered the official head of government.

The Kingdom of Norway is another example of a constitutional monarchy wherein the monarch serves a role that has been codified in the state constitution. The king of Norway is designated as the country's chief of state, serving as head of the nation's executive branch. Unlike Japan, where the monarch's role is largely symbolic, the monarch of Norway has considerable authority under the constitution, including the ability to veto and approve all laws and the power to declare war. Norway utilizes a parliamentary system, with a prime minister, chosen from individuals elected to the state parliament, serving as head of government. Though the monarch has authority over the executive functions of government, the legislature and prime minister are permitted the ability to override monarchical decisions with sufficient support, thereby providing a system of control to prevent the monarch from exerting a dominant influence over the government.

Role of the Citizen

The role of the citizen in a monarchy varies depending on whether the government is a constitutional or absolute monarchy. In an absolute monarchy, citizens have only those rights given to them by the monarch, and the monarch has the power to extend and retract freedoms and rights at will. In ancient monarchies, citizens accepted the authoritarian role of the monarch, because it was widely believed that the monarch's powers were derived from divine authority. In addition, in many absolute monarchies, the monarch has the power to arrest, detain, and imprison individuals without due process, thereby providing a strong disincentive for citizens to oppose the monarchy.

In a constitutional monarchy, citizens are generally given greater freedom to participate in the development of governmental policies. In Japan, Belgium, and Spain, for instance, citizens elect governmental leaders, and the elected legislature largely controls the creation and enforcement of laws. In some countries, like the Kingdom of Norway, the monarch may exert significant authority, but this authority is balanced by that of the legislature, which represents the sovereignty of the citizens and is chosen to promote and protect the interests of the public.

The absolute monarchies of medieval Europe, Asia, and Africa held power for centuries, but many eventually collapsed due to popular uprisings as citizens demanded representation within the government. The development of constitutional monarchies may be seen as a balanced system in which the citizens retain significant control over the development of their government while the history and traditions of the nation are represented by the continuation of the monarch's lineage. In the United Kingdom, the governments of Great Britain and Northern Ireland are entirely controlled by elected individuals, but the continuation of the monarchy is seen by many as an important link to the nation's historic identity.

Micah Issitt
Philadelphia, Pennsylvania

Examples

Belgium
Bhutan
Japan
Norway
Oman
United Kingdom

Bibliography

Barrington, Lowell. *Comparative Politics: Structures and Choices.* Boston: Wadsworth, 2012. Print.

Dresch, Paul, and James Piscatori, eds. *Monarchies and Nations: Globalisation and Identity in the Arab States of the Gulf.* London: Tauris, 2005. Print.

Kesselman, Mark, et al. *European Politics in Transition.* New York: Houghton, 2009. Print.

Parliamentary Monarchy

Guiding Premise

A parliamentary monarchy is a political system in which leadership of the government is shared between a monarchy, such as a king or queen, and the members of a democratically elected legislative body. In such governments, the monarch's role as head of state is limited by the country's constitution or other founding document, preventing the monarch from assuming too much control over the nation. As head of state, the monarch may provide input during the lawmaking process and other operations of government. Furthermore, the monarch, whose role is generally lifelong, acts as a stabilizing element for the government, while the legislative body is subject to the periodic changes that occur with each election cycle.

Typical Structure

Parliamentary monarchies vary in structure and distribution of power from nation to nation, based on the parameters established by each respective country's constitution or other founding document. In general, however, parliamentary monarchies feature a king, queen, or other sovereign who acts as head of state. In that capacity, the monarch's responsibilities may be little more than ceremonial in nature, allowing him or her to offer input during the lawmaking process, to approve the installation of government officials, and to act as the country's international representative. However, these responsibilities may be subject to the approval of the country's legislative body. For example, the king of Spain approves laws and regulations that have already been passed by the legislative branch; formally appoints the prime minister; and approves other ministers appointed by the prime minister. Yet, the king's responsibilities in those capacities are subject to the approval of the Cortes Generales, Spain's parliament.

In general, parliamentary monarchies help a country preserve its cultural heritage through their respective royal families, but grant the majority of government management and lawmaking responsibilities to the country's legislative branch and its various administrative ministries, such as education and defense. In most parliamentary monarchies, the ministers of government are appointed by the legislative body and usually by the prime minister. Although government ministries have the authority to carry out the country's laws and programs, they are also subject to criticism and removal by the legislative body if they fail to perform to expectations.

The legislative body itself consists of members elected through a democratic, constitutionally defined process. Term length, term limit, and the manner by which legislators may be elected are usually outlined in the country's founding documents. For example, in the Dutch parliament, members of the House of Representatives are elected every four years through a direct vote, while the members of the Senate are elected by provincial government councils every four years. By contrast, three-quarters of the members of Thailand's House of Representatives are elected in single-seat constituencies (smaller districts), while the remaining members are elected in larger, proportional representation districts; all members of the House are elected for four-year terms. A bare majority of Thailand's senators are elected by direct vote, with the remainder appointed by other members of the government.

Role of the Citizen

While the kings and queens of parliamentary monarchies are the nominal heads of state, these political systems are designed to be democratic governments. As such, they rely heavily on the input and involvement of the citizens. Participating in legislative elections is one of the most direct ways in which the citizen is empowered. Because the governments of such systems are subject to legislative oversight, the people—through their respective votes for members of parliament—have influence over their government.

Political parties and organizations such as local and municipal councils also play an important role in parliamentary monarchies. Citizens' participation in those organizations can help shape parliamentary agendas and build links between government and the public. In Norway, for example, nearly 70 percent of citizens are involved in at least one such organization, and consequently Norway's Storting (parliament) has a number of committees that are tied to those organizations at the regional and local levels. Thus, through voting and active political involvement at the local level, the citizens of a parliamentary monarchy help direct the political course of their nation.

Michael Auerbach
Marblehead, Massachusetts

Examples
Netherlands
Norway
Spain
Sweden
Thailand
United Kingdom

Bibliography
"Form of Government." *Norway.org*. Norway–The Official Site in the United States, n.d. Web. 17 Jan. 2013.
"Issues: Parliament." *Governmentl.nl*. Government of the Netherlands, n.d. Web. 17 Jan. 2013.
"King, Prime Minister, and Council of Ministers." *Country Studies: Spain*. Lib. of Congress, 2012. Web. 17 Jan. 2013.
"Thailand." *International Foundation for Electoral Systems*. IFES, 2013. Web. 17 Jan. 2013.

Parliamentary Republic

Guiding Premise

A parliamentary republic is a system wherein both executive and legislative powers are centralized in the legislature. In such a system, voters elect their national representatives to the parliamentary body, which in turn appoints the executive. In such an environment, legislation is passed more quickly than in a presidential system, which requires a consensus between the executive and legislature. It also enables the legislature to remove the executive in the event the latter does not perform to the satisfaction of the people. Parliamentary republics can also prevent the consolidation of power in a single leader, as even a prime minister must defer some authority to fellow legislative leaders.

Typical Structure

Parliamentary republics vary in structure from nation to nation, according to the respective country's constitution or other governing document. In general, such a system entails the merger of the legislature and head of state such as a president or other executive. The state may retain the executive, however. However, the executive's role may be largely ceremonial, as is the case in Greece, where the president has very little political authority. This "outsider" status has in fact enabled the Greek president to act as a diplomatic intermediary among sparring parliamentary leaders.

While many countries with such a system operate with an executive—who may or may not be directly elected, and who typically has limited powers—the bulk of a parliamentary republic's political authority rests with the legislature. The national government is comprised of democratically elected legislators and their appointees. The length of these representatives' respective terms, as well as the manner by which the legislators are elected, depend on the frameworks established by each individual nation. Some parliamentary republics utilize a constitution for this purpose, while others use a set of common laws or other legal precepts. In South Africa, members of the parliament's two chambers, the National Assembly and the National Council of Provinces, are elected differently. The former's members are elected directly by the citizens in each province, while the latter's members are installed by the provincial legislatures.

Once elected to parliament, legislators are often charged with more than just lawmaking. In many cases, members of parliament oversee the administration of state affairs as well. Legislative bodies in parliamentary republics are responsible for nominating an executive—typically a prime minister—to manage the government's various administrative responsibilities. Should the executive not adequately perform its duties, parliament has the power to remove the executive from office. In Ireland, for example, the Dail Eireann (the House of Representatives) is charged with forming the country's executive branch by nominating the Taoiseach (prime minister) and approving the prime minister's cabinet selections.

Role of the Citizen

A parliamentary republic is a democratic political system that relies on the involvement of an active electorate. This civic engagement includes a direct or indirect vote for representatives to parliament. While the people do not vote for an executive as well, by way of their vote for parliament, the citizenry indirectly influences the selection of the chief executive and the policies he or she follows. In many countries, the people also indirectly influence the national government by their votes in provincial government. As noted earlier, some countries' parliaments include chambers whose members are appointed by provincial leaders.

Citizens may also influence the political system through involvement in political parties. Such organizations help shape the platforms of parliamentary majorities as well as selecting candidates for prime minister and other government positions. The significance of political parties varies from nation to nation, but such organizations require the input and involvement of citizens.

Michael Auerbach
Marblehead, Massachusetts

Examples
Austria
Greece

Iceland
Ireland
Poland
South Africa

Bibliography
"About the Oireachtas." *Oireachtas.ie*. Houses of the Oireachtas, n.d. Web. 7 Feb. 2013.
"Our Parliament." *Parliament.gov*. Parliament of the Republic of South Africa, n.d. Web. 7 Feb. 2013.
Tagaris, Karolina, and Ingrid Melander. "Greek President Makes Last Push to Avert Elections." *Reuters*. Thomson Reuters, 12 May 2012. Web. 7 Feb. 2013.

Presidential

Guiding Premise

A presidential system is a type of democratic government in which the populace elects a single leader—a president—to serve as both head of state and the head of government. The presidential system developed from the monarchic governments of medieval and early modern Europe, in which a royal monarch, holder of an inherited office, served as both head of state and government. In the presidential system, the president does not inherit the office, but is chosen by either direct or indirect popular vote.

Presidential systems differ from parliamentary systems in that the president is both the chief executive and head of state, whereas in a parliamentary system another individual, usually called the "prime minister," serves as head of government and leader of the legislature. The presidential system evolved out of an effort to create an executive office that balances the influence of the legislature and the judiciary. The United States is the most prominent example of a democratic presidential system.

Some governments have adopted a semi-presidential system, which blends elements of the presidential system with the parliamentary system, and generally features a president who serves only as head of state. In constitutional governments, like the United States, Mexico, and Honduras, the role of the president is described in the nation's constitution, which also provides for the president's powers in relation to the other branches of government.

Typical Structure

In most modern presidential governments, power to create and enforce laws and international agreements is divided among three branches: the executive, legislative, and judicial. The executive office consists of the president and a number of presidential advisers—often called the cabinet—who typically serve at the president's discretion and are not elected to office. The terms of office for the president are codified in the state constitution and, in most cases, the president may serve a limited number of terms before he or she becomes ineligible for reelection.

The president serves as head of state and is therefore charged with negotiating and administering international treaties and agreements. In addition, the president serves as head of government and is therefore charged with overseeing the function of the government as a whole. The president is also empowered, in most presidential governments, with the ability to deploy the nation's armed forces. In some governments, including the United States, the approval of the legislature is needed for the country to officially declare war.

The legislative branch of the government proposes new laws, in the form of bills, but must cooperate with the executive office to pass these bills into law. The legislature and the executive branch also cooperate in determining the government budget. Unlike prime ministers under the parliamentary system, the president is not considered a member of the legislature and therefore acts independently as the chief executive, though a variety of governmental functions require action from both branches of government. A unique feature of the presidential system is that the election of the president is separate from the election of the legislature.

In presidential systems, members of the legislature are often less likely to vote according to the goals of their political party and may support legislation that is not supported by their chosen political party. In parliamentary systems, like the government of Great Britain, legislators are more likely to vote according to party policy. Presidential systems are also often marked by a relatively small number of political parties, which often allows one party to achieve a majority in the legislature. If this majority coincides with the election of a president from the same party, that party's platform or agenda becomes dominant until the next election cycle.

The judicial branch in a presidential system serves to enforce the laws among the populace. In most modern presidential democracies, the president appoints judges to federal posts, though in some governments, the legislature appoints judges. In some cases, the president may need the approval of the legislature to make judicial appointments.

Role of the Citizen

In a democratic presidential system, citizens are empowered with the ability to vote for president and therefore have ultimate control over who serves as head of government and head of state. Some presidential governments elect individuals to the presidency based on the result of a popular vote, while other governments use an indirect system, in which citizens vote for a party or for individuals who then serve as their representatives in electing the president. The United States utilizes an indirect system called the Electoral College.

Citizens in presidential systems are also typically allowed, though not required, to join political parties in an effort to promote a political agenda. Some governmental systems that are modeled on the presidential system allow the president to exert a dominant influence over the legislature and other branches of the government. In some cases, this can lead to a presidential dictatorship, in which the president may curtail the political rights of citizens. In most presidential systems, however, the roles and powers of the legislative and executive branches are balanced to protect the rights of the people to influence their government.

In a presidential system, citizens are permitted to vote for a president representing one political party, while simultaneously voting for legislators from other political parties. In this way, the presidential system allows citizens to determine the degree to which any single political party is permitted to have influence on political development.

Micah Issitt
Philadelphia, Pennsylvania

Examples

Benin
Costa Rica
Dominican Republic
Guatemala
Honduras
Mexico
United States
Venezuela

Bibliography

Barington, Lowell. *Comparative Politics: Structures and Choices*. Boston: Wadsworth, 2012. Print.

Caramani, Daniele. *Comparative Politics*. New York: Oxford UP, 2008. Print.

Garner, Robert, Peter Ferdinand, and Stephanie Lawson. *Introduction to Politics*. 2nd ed. Oxford: Oxford UP, 2009. Print.

Republic

Guiding Premise

A republic is a type of government based on the idea of popular or public sovereignty. The word "republic" is derived from Latin terms meaning "matters" and "the public." In essence, a republic is a government in which leaders are chosen by the public rather than by inheritance or by force. The republic or republican governmental system emerged in response to absolute monarchy, in which hereditary leaders retained all the power. In contrast, the republican system is intended to create a government that is responsive to the people's will.

Most modern republics operate based on a democratic system in which citizens elect leaders by popular vote. The United States and Mexico are examples of countries that use a democratic republican system to appoint leaders to office. However, universal suffrage (voting for all) is not required for a government to qualify as a republic, and it is possible for a country to have a republican government in which only certain categories of citizens, such as the wealthy, are allowed to vote in elections.

In addition to popular vote, most modern republics are further classified as constitutional republics, because the laws and rules for appointing leaders have been codified in a set of principles and guidelines known as a "constitution." When combined with universal suffrage and constitutional law, the republican system is intended to form a government that is based on the will of the majority while protecting the rights of minority groups.

Typical Structure

Republican governments are typically led by an elected head of state, generally a president. In cases where the president also serves as the head of government, the government is called a "presidential republic." In some republics, the head of state serves alongside an appointed or elected head of government, usually a prime minister.

This mixed form of government blends elements of the republic system with the parliamentary system found in countries such as the United Kingdom or India.

The president is part of the executive branch of government, which represents the country internationally and heads efforts to make and amend international agreements and treaties. The laws of a nation are typically created by the legislative branch, which may also be composed of elected leaders. Typically, the legislative and executive branches must cooperate on key initiatives, such as determining the national budget.

In addition to legislative and executive functions, most republics have a judiciary charged with enforcing and interpreting laws. The judicial branch may be composed of elected leaders, but in many cases, judicial officers are appointed by the president and/or the legislature. In the United States (a federal republic), the president, who leads the executive branch, appoints members to the federal judiciary, but these choices must be approved by the legislature before they take effect.

The duties and powers allotted to each branch of the republican government are interconnected with those of the other branches in a system of checks and balances. For instance, in Mexico (a federal republic), the legislature is empowered to create new tax guidelines for the public, but before legislative tax bills become law, they must first achieve majority support within the two branches of the Mexican legislature and receive the approval of the president. By creating a system of separate but balanced powers, the republican system seeks to prevent any one branch from exerting a dominant influence over the government.

Role of the Citizen

The role of the citizen in a republic depends largely on the type of republican system that the country has adopted. In democratic republics, popular elections and constitutional law give the public significant influence over governmental development and establish the people as the primary source of political power. Citizens in democratic republics are empowered to join political groups and to influence the development of laws and policies through the election of public leaders.

In many republican nations, a powerful political party or other political group can dominate the government, preventing competition from opposing political groups and curtailing the public's role in selecting and approving leaders. For instance, in the late twentieth century, a dominant political party maintained control of the Gambian presidency and legislature for more than thirty years, thereby significantly limiting the role of the citizenry in influencing the development of government policy.

In general, the republican system was intended to reverse the power structure typical of the monarchy system, in which inherited leaders possess all of the political power. In the republican system, leaders are chosen to represent the people's interests with terms of office created in such a way that new leaders must be chosen at regular intervals, thereby preventing a single

leader or political entity from dominating the populace. In practice, popular power in a republic depends on preventing a political monopoly from becoming powerful enough to alter the laws of the country to suit the needs of a certain group rather than the whole.

Micah Issitt
Philadelphia, Pennsylvania

Examples
Algeria
Argentina
Armenia
France
Gambia
Mexico
San Marino
South Sudan
Tanzania
United States

Bibliography
Caramani, Daniele. *Comparative Politics*. New York: Oxford UP, 2008. Print.
Przeworski, Adam. *Democracy and the Limits of Self-Government*. New York: Cambridge UP, 2010. Print.

Socialist

Guiding Premise

Socialism is a political and economic system that seeks to elevate the common good of the citizenry by allowing the government to own all property and means of production. In the most basic model, citizens cooperatively elect members to government, and the government then acts on behalf of the people to manage the state's property, industry, production, and services.

In a socialist system, communal or government ownership of property and industry is intended to eliminate the formation of economic classes and to ensure an even distribution of wealth. Most modern socialists also believe that basic services, including medical and legal care, should be provided at the same level to all citizens and not depend on the individual citizen's ability to pay for better services. The origins of socialism can be traced to theorists such as Thomas More (1478–1535), who believed that private wealth and ownership led to the formation of a wealthy elite class that protected its own wealth while oppressing members of lower classes.

There are many different forms of socialist philosophy, some of which focus on economic systems, while others extend socialist ideas to other aspects of society. Communism may be considered a form of socialism, based on the idea that a working-class revolution is needed to initiate the ideal socialist society.

Typical Structure

Socialism exists in many forms around the world, and many governments use a socialist model for the distribution of key services, most often medical and legal aid. A socialist state is a government whose constitution explicitly gives the government powers to facilitate the creation of a socialist society.

The idealized model of the socialist state is one in which the populace elects leaders to head the government, and the government then oversees the distribution of wealth and goods among the populace, enforces the laws, and provides for the well-being of citizens. Many modern socialist governments follow a communist model, in which a national communist political party has ultimate control over governmental legislation and appointments.

There are many different models of socialist states, integrating elements of democratic or parliamentary systems. In these cases, democratic elections may be held to elect the head of state and the body of legislators. The primary difference between a socialist democracy and a capitalist democracy can be found in the state's role in the ownership of key industries. Most modern noncommunist socialist states provide state regulation and control over key industries but allow some free-market competition as well.

In a socialist system, government officials appoint leaders to oversee various industries and to regulate prices based on public welfare. For instance, if the government retains sole ownership over agricultural production, the government must appoint individuals to manage and oversee that industry, organize agricultural labor, and oversee the distribution of food products among the populace. Some countries, such as Sweden, have adopted a mixed model in which socialist industry management is blended with free-market competition.

Role of the Citizen

All citizens in a socialist system are considered workers, and thus all exist in the same economic class. While some citizens may receive higher pay than others—those who work in supervisory roles, for instance—limited ownership of private property and standardized access to services places all individuals on a level field with regard to basic welfare and economic prosperity.

The degree to which personal liberties are curtailed within a socialist system depends upon the type of socialist philosophy adopted and the degree to which corruption and authoritarianism play a role in government. In most modern communist governments, for instance, individuals are often prohibited from engaging in any activity seen as contrary to the overall goals of the state or to the policies of the dominant political party. While regulations of this kind are common in communist societies, social control over citizens is not necessary for a government to follow a socialist model.

Under democratic socialism, individuals are also expected to play a role in the formation of their government by electing leaders to serve in key positions. In Sri Lanka, for instance, citizens elect members to serve in the parliament and a president to serve as head of the executive branch. In Portugal, citizens vote in multiparty elections to elect a president who serves as head of state, and the president appoints a prime minister to serve as head of government. In both Portugal and Sri Lanka, the government is constitutionally bound to promote a socialist society, though both governments allow private ownership and control of certain industries.

Citizens in a socialist society are also expected to provide for one another by contributing to labor and by forfeiting some ownership rights to provide for the greater good. In the Kingdom of Sweden, a mixed parliamentary system, all citizens pay a higher tax rate to contribute to funds that provide for national health care, child care, education, and worker support systems. Citizens who have no children and require only minimal health care benefits pay the same tax rate as those who have greater need for the nation's socialized benefits.

Micah Issitt
Philadelphia, Pennsylvania

Examples
China
Cuba
Portugal
Sri Lanka
Venezuela
Zambia

Bibliography
Caramani, Daniele. *Comparative Politics*. New York: Oxford UP, 2008. Print.
Heilbroner, Robert. "Socialism." *Library of Economics and Liberty*. Liberty Fund, 2008. Web. 17 Jan. 2013.
Howard, Michael Wayne. *Socialism*. Amherst, NY: Humanity, 2001. Print.

Sultanate/Emirate

Guiding Premise

A sultanate or emirate form of government is a political system in which a hereditary ruler— a monarch, chieftain, or military leader—acts as the head of state. Emirates and sultanates are most commonly found in Islamic nations in the Middle East, although others are found in Southeast Asia as well. Sultans and emirs frequently assume titles such as president or prime minister in addition to their royal designations, meshing the traditional ideal of a monarch with the administrative capacities of a constitutional political system.

Typical Structure

A sultanate or emirate combines the administrative duties of the executive with the powers of a monarch. The emir or sultan acts as the head of government, appointing all cabinet ministers and officials. In Brunei, a sultanate, the government was established according to the constitution (set up after the country declared autonomy from Britain in 1959). The sultan did assemble a legislative council in order to facilitate the lawmaking process, but this council has consistently remained subject to the authority of the sultan and not to a democratic process. In 2004, there was some movement toward the election of at least some of the members of this council. In the meantime, the sultan maintains a ministerial system by appointment and also serves as the nation's chief religious leader.

In some cases, an emirate or sultanate appears similar to a federal system. In the United Arab Emirates (UAE), for example, the nation consists of not one but seven emirates. This system came into being after the seven small regions achieved independence from Great Britain. Each emirate developed its own government system under the leadership of an emir. However, in 1971, the individual emirates agreed to join as a federation, drafting a constitution that identified the areas of common interest to the entire group of emirates. Like Brunei, the UAE's initial government structure focused on the authority of the emirs and the various councils and ministries formed at the UAE's capital of Abu Dhabi. However, beginning in the early twenty-first century, the UAE's legislative body, the Federal National Council, has been elected by electoral colleges from the seven emirates, thus further engaging various local areas and reflecting their interests.

Sultanates and emirates are at times part of a larger nation, with the sultans or emirs answering to the authority of another government. This is the case in Malaysia, where the country is governed by a constitutional monarchy. However, most of Malaysia's western political units are governed by sultans, who act as regional governors and, in many cases, religious leaders, but remain subject to the king's authority in Malaysia's capital of Kuala Lumpur.

Role of the Citizen

Sultanates and emirates are traditionally non-democratic governments. Like those of other monarchs, the seats of emirs and sultans are hereditary. Any votes for these leaders to serve as prime minister or other head of government are cast by ministers selected by the emirs and sultans. Political parties may exist in these countries as well, but these parties are strictly managed by the sultan or emir; opposition parties are virtually nonexistent in such systems, and some emirates have no political parties at all.

As shown in the UAE and Malaysia, however, there are signs that the traditional sultanate or emirate is increasingly willing to engage their respective citizens. For example, the UAE, between 2006 and 2013, launched a series of reforms designed to strengthen the role of local governments and relations with the people they serve. Malaysia may allow sultans to continue their regional controls, but at the same time, the country continues to evolve its federal system, facilitating multiparty democratic elections for its national legislature.

Michael Auerbach
Marblehead, Massachusetts

Examples
Brunei
Kuwait
Malaysia
Qatar
United Arab Emirates

Bibliography
"Brunei." *The World Factbook*. Central Intelligence Agency, 2 Jan. 2013. Web. 17 Jan. 2013.
"Malaysia." *The World Factbook*. Central Intelligence Agency, 7 Jan. 2013. Web. 17 Jan. 2013.
"Political System." *UAE Interact*. UAE National Media Council, n.d. Web. 17 Jan. 2013.
Prime Minister's Office, Brunei Darussalam. Prime Minister's Office, Brunei Darussalam, 2013. Web. 17 Jan. 2013.

Theocratic Republic

Guiding Premise

A theocratic republic is a type of government blending popular and religious influence to determine the laws and governmental principles. A republic is a governmental system based on the concept of popular rule and takes its name from the Latin words for "public matter." The defining characteristic of a republic is that civic leaders hold elected, rather than inherited, offices. A theocracy is a governmental system in which a supreme deity is considered the ultimate authority guiding civil matters.

No modern nations can be classified as pure theocratic republics, but some nations, such as Iran, maintain a political system largely dominated by religious law. The Buddhist nation of Tibet operated under a theocratic system until it was taken over by Communist China in the early 1950s.

In general, a theocratic republic forms in a nation or other governmental system dominated by a single religious group. The laws of the government are formed in reference to a set of religious laws, either taken directly from sacred texts or formulated by religious scholars and authority figures. Most theocratic governments depend on a body of religious scholars who interpret religious scripture, advise all branches of government, and oversee the electoral process.

Typical Structure

In a typical republic, the government is divided into executive, legislative, and judicial branches, and citizens vote to elect leaders to one or more of the branches of government. In most modern republics, voters elect a head of state, usually a president, to lead the executive branch. In many republics, voters also elect individuals to serve as legislators. Members of the judiciary may be elected by voters or may be appointed to office by other elected leaders. In nontheocratic republics, the citizens are considered the ultimate source of authority in the government.

In a theocratic republic, however, one or more deities are considered to represent the ultimate governmental authority. In some cases, the government may designate a deity as the ultimate head of state. Typically, any individual serving as the functional head of state is believed to have been chosen by that deity, and candidates for the position must be approved by the prevailing religious authority.

In some cases, the religious authority supports popular elections to fill certain governmental posts. In Iran, for instance, citizens vote to elect members to the national parliament and a single individual to serve as president. The Iranian government is ultimately led by a supreme leader, who is appointed to office by the Assembly of Experts, the leaders of the country's Islamic community. Though the populace chooses the president and leaders to serve in the legislature, the supreme leader of Iran can overrule decisions made in any other branch of the government.

In a theocratic republic, the power to propose new laws may be given to the legislature, which works on legislation in conjunction with the executive branch. However, all laws must conform to religious law, and any legislation produced within the government is likely to be abolished if it is deemed by the religious authorities to violate religious principles. In addition, religious leaders typically decide which candidates are qualified to run for specific offices, thereby ensuring that the citizens will not elect individuals who are likely to oppose religious doctrine.

In addition, many modern nations that operate on a partially theocratic system may adopt a set of governmental principles in the form of a constitution, blended with religious law. This mixed constitutional theocratic system has been adopted by an increasing number of Islamic nations, including Iraq, Afghanistan, Mauritania, and some parts of Nigeria.

Role of the Citizen

Citizens in a theocratic republic are expected to play a role in forming the government through elections, but they are constrained in their choices by the prevailing religious authority. Citizens are also guaranteed certain freedoms, typically codified in a constitution, that have been formulated with reference to religious law. All citizens must adhere to religious laws, regardless of their personal religious beliefs or membership within any existing religious group.

In many Middle Eastern and African nations that operate on the basis of an Islamic theocracy, citizens elect leaders from groups of candidates chosen by the prevailing religious authority. While the choices presented to the citizens are more limited than in a democratic, multiparty republic, the citizens nevertheless play a role in determining the evolution of the government through their voting choices.

The freedoms and rights afforded to citizens in a theocratic republic may depend, in part, on the individual's religious affiliation. For instance, Muslims living in Islamic theocracies may be permitted to hold political office or to aspire to other influential political positions, while members of minority religious groups may find their rights and freedoms limited. Religious minorities living in Islamic republics may not be permitted to run for certain offices, such as president, and must follow laws that adhere to Islamic principles but may violate their own religious principles. Depending on the country and the adherents' religion, the practice of their faith may itself be considered criminal.

Micah Issitt
Philadelphia, Pennsylvania

Examples

Afghanistan
Iran
Iraq
Pakistan
Mauritania
Nigeria

Bibliography

Cooper, William W., and Piyu Yue. *Challenges of the Muslim World: Present, Future and Past.* Boston: Elsevier, 2008. Print.
Hirschl, Ran. *Constitutional Theocracy.* Cambridge: Harvard UP, 2010. Print.

Totalitarian

Guiding Premise

A totalitarian government is one in which a single political party maintains absolute control over the state and is responsible for creating all legislation without popular referendum. In general, totalitarianism is considered a type of authoritarian government where the laws and principles used to govern the country are based on the authority of the leading political group or dictator. Citizens under totalitarian regimes have limited freedoms and are subject to social controls dictated by the state.

The concept of totalitarianism evolved in fascist Italy in the 1920s, and was first used to describe the Italian government under dictator Benito Mussolini. The term became popular among critics of the authoritarian governments of Fascist Italy and Nazi Germany in the 1930s. Supporters of the totalitarian philosophy believed that a strong central government, with absolute control over all aspects of society, could achieve progress by avoiding political debate and power struggles between interest groups.

In theory, totalitarian regimes—like that of Nazi Germany and modern North Korea—can more effectively mobilize resources and direct a nation toward a set of overarching goals. Adolf Hitler was able to achieve vast increases in military power during a short period of time by controlling all procedural steps involved in promoting military development. In practice, however, pure totalitarianism has never been achieved, as citizens and political groups generally find ways to subvert complete government control.

Totalitarianism differs from authoritarianism in that a totalitarian government is based on the idea that the highest leader takes total control in order to create a flourishing society for the benefit of the people. By contrast, authoritarian regimes are based on the authority of a single, charismatic individual who develops policies designed to maintain personal power, rather than promote public interest.

Typical Structure

In a fully realized totalitarian system, a single leader or group of leaders controls all governmental functions, appointing individuals to serve in various posts to facilitate the development of legislation and oversee the enforcement of laws. In Nazi Germany, for instance, Adolf Hitler created a small group of executives to oversee the operation of the government. Governmental authority was then further disseminated through a complex network of departments, called ministries, with leaders appointed directly by Hitler.

Some totalitarian nations may adopt a state constitution in an effort to create the appearance of democratic popular control. In North Korea, the country officially operates under a multiparty democratic system, with citizens guaranteed the right to elect leaders to both the executive and legislative branches of government. In practice, the Workers' Party of North Korea is the only viable political party, as it actively controls competing parties and suppresses any attempt to mount political opposition. Under Supreme Leader Kim Il-sung, the Workers' Party amended the constitution to allow Kim to serve as the sole executive leader for life, without the possibility of being removed from office by any governmental action.

In some cases, totalitarian regimes may favor a presidential system, with the dictator serving officially as president, while other totalitarian governments may adopt a parliamentary system, with a prime minister as head of government. Though a single dictator generally heads the nation with widespread powers over a variety of governmental functions, a cabinet or group of high-ranking ministers may also play a prominent role in disseminating power throughout the various branches of government.

Role of the Citizen

Citizens in totalitarian regimes are often subject to strict social controls exerted by the leading political party. In many cases, totalitarian governments restrict the freedom of the press, expression, and speech in an effort to limit opposition to the government. In addition, totalitarian governments may use the threat of police or military action to prevent protest movements against the leading party. Totalitarian governments maintain absolute control over the courts and any security agency, and the legal/judicial system therefore exists only as an extension of the leading political party.

Totalitarian governments like North Korea also attempt to restrict citizens' access to information considered subversive. For instance, North Korean citizens are not allowed to freely utilize the Internet or any other informational source, but are instead only allowed access to government-approved websites and publications. In many cases, the attempt to control access to information creates a black market for publications and other forms of information banned by government policy.

In some cases, government propaganda and restricted access to information creates a situation in which citizens actively support the ruling regime. Citizens may honestly believe that the social and political restrictions imposed by the ruling party are necessary for the advancement of society. In other cases, citizens may accept governmental control to avoid reprisal from the military and police forces. Most totalitarian regimes have established severe penalties, including imprisonment, corporal punishment, and death, for criticizing the government or refusing to adhere to government policy.

Micah Issitt
Philadelphia, Pennsylvania

Examples

Fascist Italy (1922–1943)
Nazi Germany (1933–1945)
North Korea
Stalinist Russia (1924–1953)

Bibliography

Barrington, Lowell. *Comparative Politics: Structures and Choices*. Boston: Wadsworth, 2012. Print.
Gleason, Abbot. *Totalitarianism: The Inner History of the Cold War*. New York: Oxford UP, 1995. Print.
McEachern, Patrick. *Inside the Red Box: North Korea's Post-Totalitarian Regime*. New York: Columbia UP, 2010. Print.

Treaty System

Guiding Premise

A treaty system is a framework within which participating governments agree to collect and share scientific information gathered in a certain geographic region, or otherwise establish mutually agreeable standards for the use of that region. The participants establish rules and parameters by which researchers may establish research facilities and travel throughout the region, ensuring that there are no conflicts, that the environment is protected, and that the region is not used for illicit purposes. This system is particularly useful when the region in question is undeveloped and unpopulated, but could serve a number of strategic and scientific purposes.

Typical Structure

A treaty system of government is an agreement between certain governments that share a common interest in the use of a certain region to which no state or country has yet laid internationally recognized claim. Participating parties negotiate treaty systems that, upon agreement, form a framework by which the system will operate. Should the involved parties be United Nations member states, the treaty is then submitted to the UN Secretariat for registration and publication.

The agreement's founding ideals generally characterize the framework of a treaty. For example, the most prominent treaty system in operation today is the Antarctic Treaty System, which currently includes fifty nations whose scientists are studying Antarctica. This system, which entered into force in 1961, focuses on several topics, including environmental protection, tourism, scientific operations, and the peaceful use of that region. Within these topics, the treaty system enables participants to meet, cooperate, and share data on a wide range of subjects. Such cooperative activities include regional meetings, seminars, and large-scale conferences.

A treaty system is not a political institution in the same manner as state governments. Rather, it is an agreement administered by delegates from the involved entities. Scientists seeking to perform their research in Antarctica, for example, must apply through the scientific and/or government institutions of their respective nations. In the case of the United States, scientists may apply for grants from the National Science Foundation. These institutions then examine the study in question for its relevance to the treaty's ideals.

Central to the treaty system is the organization's governing body. In the case of the Antarctic Treaty, that body is the Antarctic Treaty Secretariat, which is based in Buenos Aires, Argentina. The Secretariat oversees all activities taking place under the treaty, welcomes new members, and addresses any conflicts or issues between participants. It also reviews any activities to ensure that they are in line with the parameters of the treaty. A treaty system is not a sovereign organization, however. Each participating government retains autonomy, facilitating its own scientific expeditions, sending delegates to the treaty system's main governing body, and reviewing the treaty to ensure that it coincides with its national interests.

Role of the Citizen

Although treaty systems are not sovereign government institutions, private citizens can and frequently do play an important role in their function and success. For example, the Antarctic Treaty System frequently conducts large-scale planning conferences, to which each participating government sends delegates. These teams are comprised of qualified scientists who are nominated and supported by their peers during the government's review process. In the United States, for example, the State Department oversees American participation in the Antarctic

Treaty System's events and programs, including delegate appointments.

Another area in which citizens are involved in a treaty system is in the ratification process. Every nation's government—usually through its legislative branch—must formally approve any treaty before the country can honor the agreement. This ratification is necessary for new treaties as well as treaties that must be reapproved every few years. Citizens, through their elected officials, may voice their support or disapproval of a new or updated treaty.

While participating governments administer treaty systems and their secretariats, those who conduct research or otherwise take part in activities in the region in question are not usually government employees. In Antarctica, for example, university professors, engineers, and other private professionals—supported by a combination of private and government funding—operate research stations.

Michael Auerbach
Marblehead, Massachusetts

Example
Antarctic Treaty System

Bibliography

"Antarctic." *Ocean and Polar Affairs.* US Department of State, 22 Mar. 2007. Web. 8 Feb. 2013.

"About Us." *Antarctic Treaty System.* Secretariat of the Antarctic Treaty, n.d. Web. 8 Feb. 2013.

"United Nations Treaty Series." *United Nations Treaty Collection.* United Nations, 2013. Web. 8 Feb. 2013.

"Educational Opportunities and Resources." *United States Antarctic Program.* National Science Foundation, 2013. Web. 8 Feb. 2013.

Appendix Two:
World Religions

African Religious Traditions

General Description

The religious traditions of Africa can be studied both religiously and ethnographically. Animism, or the belief that everything has a soul, is practiced in most tribal societies, including the Dogon (people of the cliffs), an ethnic group living primarily in Mali's central plateau region and in Burkina Faso. Many traditional faiths have extensive mythologies, rites, and histories, such as the Yoruba religion practiced by the Yoruba, an ethnic group of West Africa. In South Africa, the traditional religion of the Zulu people is based on a creator god, ancestor worship, and the existence of sorcerers and witches. Lastly, the Ethiopian or Abyssinian Church (formally the Ethiopian Orthodox Union Church) is a branch of Christianity unique to the east African nations of Ethiopia and Eritrea.

Number of Adherents Worldwide

Some 63 million Africans adhere to traditional religions such as animism. One of the largest groups practicing animism is the Dogon, who number about six hundred thousand. However, it is impossible to know how many practice traditional religion. In fact, many people practice animism alongside other religions, particularly Islam. Other religions have spread their adherence and influence through the African diaspora. In Africa, the Yoruba number between thirty-five and forty million and are located primarily in Benin, Togo and southwest Nigeria. The Zulu, the largest ethnic group in South Africa, total over eleven million. Like Islam, Christianity has affected the number of people who still hold traditional beliefs, making accurate predictions virtually impossible. The Ethiopian or Abyssinian Church has over thirty-nine million adherents in Ethiopia alone.

Basic Tenets

Animism holds that many spiritual beings have the power to help or hurt humans. The traditional faith is thus more concerned with appropriate rituals rather than worship of a deity, and focuses on day-to-day practicalities such as food, water supplies, and disease. Ancestors, particularly those most recently dead, are invoked for their aid. Those who practice animism believe in life after death; some adherents may attempt to contact the spirits of the dead. Animists acknowledge the existence of tribal gods. (However, African people traditionally do not make images of God, who is thought of as Spirit.)

The Dogon divide into two caste-like groups: the inneomo (pure) and innepuru (impure). The hogon leads the inneomo, who may not sacrifice animals and whose leaders are forbidden to hunt. The inneomo also cannot prepare or bury the dead. While the innepuru can do all of the above tasks, they cannot take part in the rituals for agricultural fertility. Selected young males called the olubaru lead the innepuru. The status of "pure" or "impure" is inherited. The Dogon have many gods. The chief god is called Amma, a creator god who is responsible for creating other gods and the earth.

The Dogon have a three-part concept of death. First the soul is sent to the realm of the dead to join the ancestors. Rites are then performed to remove any ritual polluting. Finally, when several members of the village have died, a rite known as dama occurs. In the ritual, a sacrifice is made to the Great Mask (which depicts a large wooden serpent and which is never actually worn) and dancers perform on the housetops where someone has died to scare off any lingering souls. Often, figures of Nommo (a worshipped ancestral spirit) are put near funeral pottery on the family shrine.

The Yoruba believe in predestination. Before birth, the ori (soul) kneels before Olorun, the wisest and most powerful deity, and selects a destiny. Rituals may assist the person in achieving his or her destiny, but it cannot be altered. The Yoruba, therefore, acknowledge a need for ritual and sacrifice, properly done according to the oracles.

Among the Yoruba, the shaman is known as the babalawo. He or she is able to communicate with ancestors, spirits and deities. Training for this work, which may include responsibility as a doctor, often requires three years. The shaman is consulted before major life decisions. During these consultations, the shaman dictates the right rituals and sacrifices, and to which gods they are to be offered for maximum benefit. In addition, the Yoruba poetry covers right conduct. Good character is at the heart of Yoruba ethics.

The Yoruba are polytheistic. The major god is Olorun, the sky god, considered all-powerful and holy, and a father to 401 children, also gods. He gave the task of creating human beings to the deity Obatala (though Olorun breathed life into them). Olorun also determines the destiny of each person. Onlie, the Great Mother Goddess, is in some ways the opposite of Olorun. Olorun is the one who judges a soul following death. For example, if the soul is accounted worthy, it will be reincarnated, while the unworthy go to the place of punishment. Ogun, the god of hunters, iron, and war, is another important god. He is also the patron of blacksmiths. The Yoruba have some 1,700 gods, collectively known as the Orisa.

The Yoruba believe in an afterlife. There are two heavens: one is a hot, dry place with potsherds, reserved for those who have done evil, while the other is a pleasant heaven for persons who have led a good life. There the ori (soul) may choose to "turn to be a child" on the earth once more.

In the Zulu tradition, the king was responsible for rainmaking and magic for the benefit of the nation. Rainmakers were also known as "shepherds of heaven." They performed rites during times of famine, drought or war, as well as during planting season, invoking royal ancestors for aid. Storms were considered a manifestation of God.

The Zulu are also polytheistic. They refer to a wise creator god who lives in heaven. This Supreme Being has complete control of everything in the universe, and is known as Unkulunkulu, the Great Oldest One. The Queen of heaven is a virgin who taught women useful arts; light surrounds her, and her glory is seen in rain, mist, and rainbows.

The Ethiopian Church incorporates not only Orthodox Christian beliefs, but also aspects of Judaism. The adherents distinguish between clean and unclean meats, practice circumcision, and observe the seventh-day Sabbath. The Ethiopian (or Abyssinian) Church is monotheistic and believes in the Christian God.

Sacred Text

Traditional religions such as animism generally have no written sacred texts. Instead, creation stories and other tales are passed down orally. The Yoruba do have some sacred poetry, in 256 chapters, known as odus. The text covers both right action in worship and ethical conduct. The Ethiopian Church has scriptures written in the ancient Ge'ez language, which is no longer used, except in church liturgy.

Major Figures

A spiritual leader, or hogon, oversees each district among the Dogon. There is a supreme hogon for the entire country. Among the Yoruba, the king, or oba, rules each town. He is also considered sacred and is responsible for performing rituals. Isaiah Shembe is a prophet or messiah among the Zulu. He founded the Nazareth Baptist Church (also called the amaNazaretha Church or Shembe Church), an independent Zulu Christian denomination. His son, Johannes Shembe, took the title Shembe II. In the Ethiopian Church, now fully independent, the head of the church is the Patriarch. Saint Frumentius, the first bishop of Axum in northern Ethiopia, is credited with beginning the Christian tradition during the fourth century. King Lalibela, noted for authorizing construction of monolithic churches carved underground, was a major figure in the twelfth century.

Major Holy Sites

Every spot in nature is sacred in animistic thinking. There is no division between sacred and profane—all of life is sacred, and Earth is Mother. Sky and mountains are often regarded as sacred space.

For the Yoruba of West Africa, Osogbo in Nigeria is a forest shrine. The main goddess is Oshun, goddess of the river. Until she arrived, the work done by male gods was not succeeding. People seeking to be protected from illness and women wishing to become pregnant seek Osun's help. Ilé-Ifè, an ancient Yoruba city in Nigeria, is another important site, and considered the spiritual hub of the Yoruba. According to the Yoruba creation myth, Olorun, god of the sky, set down Odudua, the founder of the Yoruba, in Ilé-Ifè. Shrines within the city include one to Ogun. The shrine is made of stones and wooden stumps.

Mount Nhlangakazi (Holy Mountain) is considered sacred to the Zulu Nazareth Baptist Church (amaNazaretha). There Isaiah Shembe built a High Place to serve as his headquarters. It is a twice-yearly site of pilgrimage for amaNazarites.

Sacred sites of the Ethiopian Church include the Church of St. Mary of Zion in Axum, considered the most sacred Ethiopian shrine. According to legend, the church stands adjacent to a guarded chapel which purportedly houses the Ark of the Covenant, a powerful biblical relic. The Ethiopian Church also considers sacred the eleven monolithic (rock-hewn) churches, still places of pilgrimage and devotion, that were recognized as a collective World Heritage Site by the United Nations Educational, Scientific and Cultural Organization.

Major Rites & Celebrations

Most African religions involve some sacrifice to appease or please the gods. Among the Yoruba, for example, dogs, which are helpful in both hunting and war, are sacrificed to Ogun. In many tribes, including the Yoruba, rites of passage for youth exist. The typical pattern is three-fold: removal from the tribe, instruction, and return to the tribe ready to assume adult responsibilities. In this initiation, the person may be marked bodily through scarification or circumcision. The Yoruba also have a yearly festival re-enacting

the story of Obatala and Oduduwa (generally perceived as the ancestor of the Yorubas). A second festival, which resembles a passion play, re-enacts the conflict between the grandsons of these two legendary figures. A third festival celebrates the heroine Moremi, who led the Yoruba to victory over the enemy Igbo, an ethnicity from southeastern Nigeria, and who ultimately reconciled the two tribes.

Yoruba death rites include a masked dancer who comes to the family following a death, assuring them of the ancestor's ongoing care for the family. If the person was important in the village, a mask will be carved and named for them. In yearly festivals, the deceased individual will then appear with other ancestors.

Masks are also used in a Dogon funeral ritual, the dama ceremony, which is led by the Awa, a secret society comprised of all adult Dogon males of the innepuru group. During ceremonial times, the hogon relinquishes control and the Awa control the community. At the end of the mourning period the dama ceremony begins when the Awa leave the village and return with both the front and back of their heads masked. Through rituals and dances, they lead the spirit of the deceased to the next world. Control of the village reverts to the hogon at that point. The Wagem rites govern contact with the ancestors. Following the dama ceremony, the eldest male descendant, called the ginna bana, adds a vessel to the family shrine in the name of the deceased. The spirit of the ancestor is persuaded to return to the descendents through magic and sacrificial offerings, creating a link from the living to the first ancestors.

Ethiopian Christians observe and mark most typical Christian rites, though some occur on different dates because of the difference in the Ethiopian and Western calendars. For example, Christmas in Ethiopia is celebrated on January 7.

ORIGINS

History & Geography

The Dogon live along the Bandiagara Cliffs, a rocky and mountainous region. (The Cliffs of Bandiagara, also called the Bandiagara Escarpment, were recognized as a UNESCO World Heritage Site due to the cultural landscape, including the ancient traditions of the Dogon and their architecture.) This area is south of the Sahara in a region called the Sahel, another region prone to drought (though not a desert). The population of the villages in the region is typically a thousand people or less. The cliffs of the Bandiagara have kept the Dogon separate from other people.

Myths of origin regarding the Dogon differ. One suggestion is that the Dogon came from Egypt, and then lived in Libya before entering the the region of what is now Burkina Faso, Mauritania, or Guinea. Near the close of the fifteenth century, they arrived in Mali.

Among the Yoruba, multiple myths regarding their origin exist. One traces their beginnings to Uruk in Mesopotamia or to Babylon, the site of present-day Iraq. Another story has the Yoruba in West Africa by 10,000 BCE.

After the death of the Zulu messiah Isaiah Shembe in 1935, his son Johannes became the leader of the Nazareth Baptist Church. He lacked the charisma of his father, but did hold the church together. His brother, Amos, became regent in 1976 when Johannes died. Johannes's son Londa split the church in 1979 when Amos refused to give up power. Tangled in South African politics, Londa was killed in 1989.

The Ethiopian Orthodox Church is the nation's official church. A legend states that Menelik, supposed to have been the son of the Queen of Sheba and King Solomon, founded the royal line. When Jesuits arrived in the seventeenth century, they failed to change the church, and the nation closed to missionary efforts for several hundred years. By retaining independence theologically and not being conquered politically, Ethiopia is sometimes considered a model for the new religious movements in Africa.

Founder or Major Prophet

The origins of most African traditional religions or faiths are accounted for through the actions of deities in creation stories rather than a particular founder. One exception, however, is Isaiah Shembe, who founded the Nazareth Baptist Church, also known as the Shembe Church or amaNazarite Church, in 1910 after receiving a number of revelations during a thunderstorm. Shembe was an itinerant Zulu preacher and healer. Through his influence and leadership, amaNazarites follow more Old Testament regulations than most Christians, including celebrating the Sabbath on Saturday rather than Sunday. They also refer to God as Jehovah, the Hebrew name for God. Shembe was regarded as the new Jesus Christ for his people, adapting Christianity to Zulu practice. He adopted the title Nkosi, which means king or chief.

The Ethiopian Orthodox church was founded, according to legend, by preaching from one of two New Testament figures—the disciple Matthew or the unnamed eunuch mentioned in Acts 8. According to historical evidence, the church began when Frumentius arrived at the royal court. Athanasius of Alexandria later consecrated Frumentius as patriarch of the church, linking it to the Christian church in Egypt.

Creation Stories

The Dogon believe that Amma, the sky god, was also the creator of the universe. Amma created two sets of twins, male and female. One of the males rebelled. To restore order, Amma sacrificed the other male, Nommo, strangling and scattering him to the four directions, then restoring him to life after five days. Nommo then became ruler of the universe and the children of his spirits became the Dogon. Thus the world continually moves between chaos and order, and the task of the Dogon is to keep the world in balance through rituals. In a five-year cycle, the aspects of this creation myth are re-enacted at altars throughout the Dogon land.

According to the Yoruba, after one botched attempt at creating the world, Olorun sent his son Obatala to create earth upon the waters. Obatala tossed some soil on the water and released a five-toed hen to spread it out. Next, Olorun told Obatala to make people from clay. Obatala grew bored with the work and drank too much wine. Thereafter, the people he made were misshapen or defective (handicapped). In anger, Olorun relieved him of the job and gave it to Odudua to complete. It was Odudua who made the Yoruba and founded a kingdom at Ilé-Ifè.

The word *Zulu* means "heaven or sky." The Zulu people believe they originated in heaven. They also believe in phansi, the place where spirits live and which is below the earth's surface.

Holy Places

Osun-Osogbo is a forest shrine in Nigeria dedicated to the Yoruba river goddess, Osun. It may be the last such sacred grove remaining among the Yoruba. Shrines, art, sculpture, and sanctuaries are part of the grove, which became a UNESCO World Heritage site in 2005.

Ilé-Ifè, regarded as the equivalent of Eden, is thought to be the site where the first Yoruba was placed. It was probably named for Ifa, the god associated with divination. The palace (Afin) of the spiritual head of the Yoruba, the oni, is located there. The oni has the responsibility to care for the staff of Oranmiyan, a Benin king. The staff, which is eighteen feet tall, is made of granite and shaped like an elephant's tusk.

Axum, the seat of the Ethiopian Christian Church, is a sacred site. The eleven rock-hewn churches of King Lalibela, especially that of Saint George, are a pilgrimage site. According to tradition, angels helped to carve the churches. More than 50,000 pilgrims come to the town of Lalibela at Christmas. After the Muslims captured Jerusalem in 1187, King Lalibela proclaimed his city the "New Jerusalem" because Christians could no longer go on pilgrimage to the Holy Land.

AFRICAN RELIGIONS IN DEPTH

Sacred Symbols

Because all of life is infused with religious meaning, any object or location may be considered or become sacred in traditional African religions. Masks, in particular, have special meaning and may be worn during ceremonies. The mask often represents a god, whose power is passed to the one wearing the mask.

Sacred Practices & Gestures

The Yoruba practice divination in a form that is originally Arabic. There are sixteen basic figures—combined, they deliver a prophecy that the diviner is not to interpret. Instead, he or she recites verses from a classic source. Images may be made to prevent or cure illness. For example, the Yoruba have a smallpox spirit god that can be prayed to for healing. Daily prayer, both morning and evening, is part of life for most Yoruba.

In the amaNazarite Church, which Zulu Isaiah Shembe founded, singing is a key part of the faith. Shembe himself was a gifted composer of hymns. This sacred music was combined with dancing, during which the Zulu wear their traditional dress.

Rites, Celebrations & Services

The Dogon have three major cults. The Awa are associated with dances, featuring ornately carved masks, at funerals and on the anniversaries of deaths. The cult of the Earth god, Lebe, concerns itself with the agricultural cycles and fertility of the land; the hogon of the village guards the soil's purity and presides at ceremonies related to farming. The third cult, the Binu, is involved with communication with spirits, ancestor worship, and sacrifices. Binu shrines are in many locations. The Binu priest makes sacrifices of porridge made from millet and blood at planting time and also when the help of an ancestor is needed. Each clan within the Dogon community has a totem animal spirit—an ancestor spirit wishing to communicate with descendents may do so by taking the form of the animal.

The Dogon also have a celebration every fifty years at the appearing of the star Sirius B between two mountains. (Sirius is often the brightest star in the nighttime sky.) Young males leaving for three months prior to the sigui, as it is called, for a time of seclusion and speaking in private language. This celebration is rooted in the Dogon belief that amphibious creatures, the Nommo, visited their land about three thousand years ago.

The Yoruba offer Esu, the trickster god, palm wine and animal sacrifices. Because he is a trickster, he is considered a cheater, and being on his good side is important. The priests in Yoruba traditional religion are responsible for installing tribal chiefs and kings.

Among the Zulu, families determine the lobola, or bride price. They believe that a groom will respect his wife more if he must pay for her. Further gifts are then exchanged, and the bride's family traditionally gives the groom a goat or sheep to signify their acceptance of him. The groom's family provides meat for the wedding feast, slaughtering a cow on the morning of the wedding. The families assemble in a circle and the men, in costume, dance. The bride gives presents, usually mats or blankets, to members of her new family, who dance or sing their thanks. The final gift, to the groom, is a blanket, which is tossed over his head. Friends of the bride playfully beat him, demonstrating how they will respond if he mistreats his new wife. After the two families eat together, the couple is considered one.

In the traditional Zulu religion, ancestors three generations back are regarded as not yet settled in the afterlife. To help them settle, offerings of goats or other animals are made and rituals to help them settle into the community of ancestors are performed.

Christmas is a major celebration in Ethiopian Christianity. Priests rattle an instrument derived from biblical times, called the sistra, and chant to begin the mass. The festivities include drumming and a dance known as King David's dance.

Judy A. Johnson, MTS

Bibliography

A, Oladosu Olusegun. "Ethics and Judgement: A Panacea for Human Transformation in Yoruba Multireligious Society." *Asia Journal of Theology* 26.1 (2012): 88–104. Print.

Barnes, Trevor. *The Kingfisher Book of Religions*. New York: Kingfisher, 1999. Print.

Dawson, Allan Charles, ed. *Shrines in Africa: history, politics, and society*. Calgary: U of Calgary P, 2009. Print.

Doumbia, Adama, and Naomi Doumbia. *The Way of the Elders: West African Spirituality*. St. Paul: Llewellyn, 2004. Print.

Douny, Laurence. "The Role of Earth Shrines in the Socio-Symbolic Construction of the Dogon Territory: Towards a Philosophy of Containment." *Anthropology & Medicine* 18.2 (2011): 167–79. Print.

Friedenthal, Lora, and Dorothy Kavanaugh. *Religions of Africa*. Philadelphia: Mason Crest, 2007. Print.

Hayes, Stephen. "Orthodox Ecclesiology in Africa: A Study of the 'Ethiopian' Churches of South Africa." *International Journal for the Study of the Christian Church* 8.4 (2008): 337–54. Print.

Lugira, Aloysius M. *African Religion*. New York: Facts on File, 2004. Print.

Mbiti, John S. *African Religions and Philosophy*. 2nd ed. Oxford: Heinemann, 1991. Print.

Monteiro-Ferreira, Ana Maria. "Reevaluating Zulu Religion." *Journal of Black Studies* 35.3 (2005): 347–63. Print.

Peel, J. D. Y. "Yoruba Religion as a Global Phenomenon." *Journal of African History* 5.1 (2010): 107–8. Print.

Ray, Benjamin C. *African Religions*. 2nd ed. Upper Saddle River: Prentice, 2000. Print.

Thomas, Douglas E. *African Traditional Religion in the Modern World*. Jefferson: McFarland, 2005. Print.

Bahá'í Faith

General Description
The Bahá'í faith is the youngest of the world's religions. It began in the mid-nineteenth century, offering scholars the opportunity to observe a religion in the making. While some of the acts of religious founders such as Buddha or Jesus cannot be substantiated, the modern founders of Bahá'í were more contemporary figures.

Number of Adherents Worldwide
An estimated 5 to 7 million people follow the Bahá'í faith. Although strong in Middle Eastern nations such as Iran, where the faith originated, Bahá'í has reached people in many countries, particularly the United States and Canada.

Basic Tenets
The Bahá'í faith has three major doctrines. The first doctrine is that there is one transcendent God, and all religions worship that God, regardless of the name given to the deity. Adherents believe that religious figures such as Jesus Christ, the Buddha, and the Prophet Muhammad were different revelations of God unique to their time and place. The second doctrine is that there is only one religion, though each world faith is valid and was founded by a ""manifestation of God" who is part of a divine plan for educating humanity. The third doctrine is a belief in the unity of all humankind. In light of this underlying unity, those of the Bahá'í faith work for social justice. They believe that seeking consensus among various groups diffuses typical power struggles and to this end, they employ a method called consultation, which is a nonadversarial decision-making process.

The Bahá'í believe that the human soul is immortal, and that after death the soul moves nearer or farther away from God. The idea of an afterlife comprised of a literal "heaven" or "hell" is not part of the faith.

Sacred Text
The Most Holy Book, or the Tablets, written by Baha'u'llah, form the basis of Bahá'í teachings. Though not considered binding, scriptures from other faiths are regarded as "Divine Revelation."

Major Figures
The Bab (The Gate of God) Siyyad 'Ali Mohammad (1819–50), founder of the Bábí movement that broke from Islam, spoke of a coming new messenger of God. Mirza Hoseyn 'Ali Nuri (1817–92), who realized that he was that prophet, was given the title Baha'u'llah (Glory of God). From a member of Persia's landed gentry, he was part of the ruling class, and is considered the founder of the Bahá'í faith. His son, 'Abdu'l-Bahá (Servant of the Glory of God), who lived from 1844 until 1921, became the leader of the group after his father's death in 1892. The oldest son of his eldest daughter, Shogi Effendi Rabbani (1899–1957), oversaw a rapid expansion, visiting Egypt, America, and nations in Europe. Tahirih (the Pure One) was a woman poet who challenged stereotypes by appearing unveiled at meetings.

Major Holy Sites
The Bahá'í World Center is located near Haifa, Israel. The burial shrine of the Bab, a pilgrimage site, is there. The Shrine of Baha'u'llah near Acre, Israel, is another pilgrimage site. The American headquarters are in Wilmette, Illinois. Carmel in Israel is regarded as the world center of the faith.

Major Rites & Celebrations
Each year, the Bahá'í celebrate Ridvan Festival, a twelve-day feast from sunset on April 20 to sunset on May 2. The festival marks Baha'u'llah's declaration of prophethood, as prophesized by the Bab, at a Baghdad garden. (Ridvan means Paradise.) The holy days within that feast are the first (Baha'u'llah's garden arrival), ninth (the arrival

of his family), and twelfth (his departure from Ridvan Garden)—on these days, the Bahá'í do not work. During this feast, people attend social events and meet for devotions. Baha'u'llah referred to it as the King of Festivals and Most Great Festival. The Bahá'í celebrate several other events, including World Religion Day and Race Unity Day, both founded by Bahá'í, as well as days connected with significant events in the life of the founder. Elections to the Spiritual Assemblies, and the national and local administrations; international elections are held every five years.

ORIGINS

History & Geography

Siyyad 'Ali Muhammad was born into a merchant family of Shiraz in 1819. Both his parents were descendents of the Prophet Muhammad, Islam's central figure. Like the Prophet, the man who became the Bab lost his father at an early age and was raised by an uncle. A devout child, he entered his uncle's business by age fifteen. After visiting Muslim holy cities, he returned to Shiraz, where he married a distant relative named Khadijih.

While on pilgrimage in 1844 to the black stone of Ka'bah, a sacred site in Islam, the Bab stood with his hand on that holy object and declared that he was the prophet for whom they had been waiting. The Sunni did not give credence to these claims. The Bab went to Persia, where the Shia sect was the majority. However, because Muhammad had been regarded as the "Seal of the Prophets," and the one who spoke the final revelation, Shia clergy viewed his claims as threatening, As such, nothing further would be revealed until the Day of Judgment. The authority of the clergy was in danger from this new movement.

The Bab was placed under house arrest, and then confined to a fortress on the Russian frontier. That move to a more remote area only increased the number of converts, as did a subsequent move to another Kurdish fortress. He

was eventually taken to Tabriz in Iran and tried before the Muslim clergy in 1848. Condemned, he was caned on the soles of his feet and treated by a British doctor who was impressed by him.

Despite his treatment and the persecution of his followers—many of the Bab's eighteen disciples, termed the "Letters of the Living," were persistently tortured and executed—the Bab refused to articulate a doctrine of jihad. The Babis could defend themselves, but were forbidden to use holy war as a means of religious conquest. In three major confrontations sparked by the Shia clergy, Babis were defeated. The Bab was sentenced as a heretic and shot by a firing squad in 1850. Lacking leadership and grief-stricken, in 1852 two young Babis fired on the shah in 1852, unleashing greater persecutions and cruelty against those of the Bahá'í faith.

A follower of the Bab, Mirza Hoseyn 'Ali Nuri, announced in 1863 that he was the one who was to come (the twelfth imam of Islam), the "Glory of God," or Baha'u'llah. Considered the founder of the Bahá'í Faith, he was a tireless writer who anointed his son, 'Abdu'l-Bahá, as the next leader. Despite deprivations and imprisonments, Baha'u'llah lived to be seventy-five years old, relinquishing control of the organization to 'Abdu'l-Bahá before the time of his death.

'Abdu'l-Bahá, whom his father had called "the Master," expanded the faith to the nations of Europe and North America. In 1893, at the Parliament of Religions at the Chicago World's Fair, the faith was first mentioned in the United States. Within a few years, communities of faith were established in Chicago and Wisconsin. In 1911, 'Abdu'l-Bahá began a twenty-eight month tour of Europe and North America to promote the Bahá'í faith. Administratively, he established the spiritual assemblies that were the forerunner of the Houses of Justice that his father had envisioned.

During World War I, 'Abdu'l-Bahá engaged in humanitarian work among the Palestinians in the Holy Land, where he lived. In recognition of his efforts, he was granted knighthood by the British government. Thousands of people, including many political and religious dignitaries, attended his funeral in 1921.

'Abdu'l-Bahá conferred the role of Guardian, or sole interpreter of Bahá'í teaching, to his eldest grandson, Shoghi Effendi Rabbani. To him, all questions regarding the faith were to be addressed. Shoghi Effendi Rabbani was a descendent of Baha'u'llah through both parents. He headed the Bahá'í faith from 1921 to 1963, achieving four major projects: he oversaw the physical development of the World Centre and expanded the administrative order; he carried out the plan his father had set in motion; and he provided for the translating and interpreting of Bahá'í teachings, as the writings of both the Bab and those of Baha'u'llah and 'Abdu'l-Bahá have been translated and published in more than eight hundred languages.

Beginning in 1937, Shoghi Effendi Rabbani began a series of specific plans with goals tied to deadlines. In 1953, during the second seven-year plan, the house of worship in Wilmette, Illinois, was completed and dedicated.

Although the beliefs originated in Shi'ite Islam, the Bahá'í Faith has been declared a new religion without connections to Islam. To followers of Islam, it is a heretical sect. During the reign of the Ayatollah Khomeini, a time when Iran was especially noted as intolerant of diverse views, the Bahá'í faced widespread persecution.

Founder or Major Prophet

Mirza Husayn Ali Nuri, known as Baha'u'llah, was born into privilege in 1817 in what was then Persia, now present-day Iran. At twenty-two, he declined a government post offered at his father's death. Although a member of a politically prestigious family, he did not follow the career path of several generations of his ancestors. Instead, he managed the family estates and devoted himself to charities, earning the title "Father of the Poor."

At twenty-seven, he followed the Babis's movement within Shia Islam, corresponding with the Bab and traveling to further the faith. He also provided financial support. In 1848, he organized and helped to direct a conference that explained the Bab's teaching. At the conference, he gave

symbolic names to the eighty-one followers who had attended, based on the spiritual qualities he had observed.

Although he managed to escape death during the persecutions before and after the Bab's death, a fact largely attributed to his upbringing, Baha'u'llah was imprisoned several times. During a four-month stay in an underground dungeon in Tehran, he realized from a dream that he was the one of whom the Bab had prophesied. After being released, he was banished from Persia and had his property confiscated by the shah. He went to Baghdad, refusing the offer of refuge that had come from Russia. Over the following three years a small band of followers joined him, including members of his family. When his younger brother attempted to take over the leadership of the Babis, Baha'u'llah spent two years in a self-imposed exile in the Kurdistan wilderness. In 1856, with the community near anarchy as a result of his brother's failure of leadership, Baha'u'llah returned to the community and restored its position over the next seven years.

Concerned by the growing popularity of the new faith, the shah demanded that the Babis move further away from Persia. They went to Constantinople where, in 1863, Baha'u'llah revealed to the whole group that he was "He Whom God Will Make Manifest." From there the Bahá'í were sent to Adrianople in Turkey, and at last, in 1868, to the town of Acre in the Holy Land. Baha'u'llah was imprisoned in Acre and survived severe prison conditions. In 1877, he moved from prison to a country estate, then to a mansion. He died in 1892 after a fever.

Philosophical Basis

The thinking of Shia Muslims contributed to the development of Bahá'í. The writings incorporate language and concepts from the Qur'an (Islam's holy book). Like Muslims, the Bahá'í believe that God is one. God sends messengers, the Manifestations of God, to instruct people and benefit society. These have included Jesus Christ, the Buddha, the Prophet Muhammad, Krishna, and the Bab. Bahá'í also goes further than Islam in accepting all religions—not just Judaism, Christianity, and Islam—as being part of a divinely inspired plan.

Shia Muslims believe that Muhammad's descendents should lead the faithful community. The leaders, known as imams, were considered infallible. The Sunni Muslims believed that following the way (sunna) of Muhammad was sufficient qualification for leadership. Sunni dynasties regarded the imams as a threat and executed them, starting with two of Muhammad's grandsons, who became Shia martyrs.

In Persia, a state with a long tradition of divinely appointed rulers, the Shia sect was strong. When the Safavids, a Shia dynasty, came to power in the sixteenth century, the custom of the imamate was victorious. One tradition states that in 873, the last appointed imam, who was still a child, went into hiding to avoid being killed. For the following sixty-nine years, this twelfth imam communicated through his deputies to the faithful. Each of the deputies was called bab, or gate, because they led to the "Hidden Imam." Four babs existed through 941, and the last one died without naming the next bab. The Hidden Imam is thought to emerge at the end of time to bring in a worldwide reign of justice. From this tradition came the expectation of a Mahdi (Guided One) to lead the people.

During the early nineteenth century, many followers of both the Christian and Islamic faiths expected their respective messiahs to return. Shia teachers believed that the return of the Mahdi imam was near. In 1843, one teacher, Siyyid Kázim, noted that the Hidden Imam had disappeared one thousand lunar years earlier. He urged the faithful to look for the Mahdi imam.

The following year in Shiraz, Siyyad 'Ali Mohammad announced that he was the Mahdi. (Siyyad is a term meaning descended from Muhammad.) He referred to himself as the Bab, though he expanded the term's meaning. Eighteen men, impressed with his ability to expound the Qur'an, believed him. They became the Letters of the Living, and were sent throughout Persia (present-day Iran) to announce the dawning of the Day of God.

In 1853, Mirza Husayn Ali Nuri experienced a revelation that he was "He Whom God Shall Make Manifest," the one of whom the Bab prophesied. Accepted as such, he began writing the words that became the Bahá'í scriptures. Much of what is known of the early days of the faith comes from a Cambridge academic, Edward Granville Browne, who first visited Baha'u'llah in the 1890. Browne wrote of his meeting, introducing this faith to the West.

The emphasis of the Bahá'í faith is on personal development and the breaking down of barriers between people. Service to humanity is important and encouraged. Marriage, with a belief in the equality of both men and women, is also encouraged. Consent of both sets of parents is required prior to marrying.

Holy Places

The shrine of the Bab near Haifa and that of Baha'u'llah near Acre, in Israel, are the two most revered sites for those of the Bahá'í faith. In 2008, the United Nations Educational, Scientific, and Cultural Organization (UNESCO) recognized both as World Heritage Sites. They are the first such sites from a modern religious tradition to be added to the list of sites. Both sites are appreciated for the formal gardens surrounding them that blend design elements from different cultures. For the Bahá'í, Baha'u'llah's shrine is the focus of prayer, comparable to the significance given to the Ka'bah in Mecca for Muslims or to the Western Wall for Jews.

As of 2013, there are seven Bahá'í temples in the world; an eighth temple is under construction in Chile. All temples are built with a center dome and nine sides, symbolizing both diversity and world unity. The North American temple is located in Wilmette, Illinois. There, daily prayer services take place as well as a Sunday service.

THE BAHÁ'Í FAITH IN DEPTH

Governance

Elected members of lay councils at international, national, and local levels administer the work of the faith. The Universal House of Justice in Haifa, Israel, is the location of the international nine-member body. Elections for all of these lay councils are by secret ballot, and do not include nominating, candidates, or campaigns. Those twenty-one and older are permitted to vote. The councils make decisions according to a process of collective decision-making called consultation. They strive to serve as a model for governing a united global society.

Personal Conduct

In addition to private prayer and acts of social justice, those of the Bahá'í faith are encouraged to have a profession, craft, or trade. They are also asked to shun and refrain from slander and partisan politics. Homosexuality and sexual activity outside marriage are forbidden, as is gambling.

The Bahá'í faith does not have professional clergy, nor does it engage in missionary work. However, Bahá'í may share their faith with others and may move to another country as a "pioneer." Pioneers are unlike traditional missionaries, and are expected to support themselves through a career and as a member of the community.

Avenues of Service

Those of the Bahá'í Faith place a high value on service to humanity, considering it an act of worship. This can be done through caring for one's own family or through one's choice of vocation. Within the local community, people may teach classes for children, mentor youth groups, host devotional programs, or teach adult study circles. Many are engaged in economic or social development programs as well. Although not mandated, a year or two of service is often undertaken following high school or during college.

United Nations Involvement

Beginning in 1947, just one year after the United Nations (UN) first met, the Bahá'í Faith was represented at that body. In 1948, the Bahá'í International Community was accredited by the UN as an international nongovernmental organization (NGO). In 1970, the faith received special consultative status with the UN Economic

and Social Council (ECOSOC). Following World War I, a Bahá'í office opened in Geneva, Switzerland, where the League of Nations was headquartered. Thus the Bahá'í Faith has a long tradition of supporting global institutions.

Money Matters

The International Bahá'í Fund exists to develop and support the growth of the faith, and the Universal House of Justice oversees the distribution of the money. Contributions are also used to maintain the Bahá'í World Center. No money is accepted from non-Bahá'í sources. National and local funds, administered by National or Local Spiritual Assemblies, are used in supporting service projects, publishing endeavors, schools, and Bahá'í centers. For the Bahá'í, the size of the donation is less important than regular contributions and the spirit of sacrifice behind them.

Food Restrictions

Bahá'í between fifteen and seventy years of age **fast** nineteen days a year, abstaining from food and drink from sunrise to sunset. Fasting occurs the first day of each month of the Bahá'í calendar, which divides the year into nineteen months of nineteen days each. The Bahá'í faithful do not drink alcohol or use narcotics, because these will deaden the mind with repeated use.

Rites, Celebrations & Services

Daily prayer and meditation is recommended in the Bahá'í faith. During services there are mediations and prayers, along with the reading of Bahá'í scriptures and other world faith traditions. There is no set ritual, no offerings, and no sermons. Unaccompanied by musical instruments, choirs also sing. Light refreshments may be served afterwards.

Bahá'í place great stress on marriage, the only state in which sex is permitted. Referred to as "a fortress for well-being and salvation," a monogamous, heterosexual marriage is the ideal. To express the oneness of humanity, interracial marriages are encouraged. After obtaining the consent of their parents, the couple takes the following vow: "We will all, verily, abide by the will of God." The remainder of the service may be individually crafted and may also include dance, music, feasting, and ceremony. Should a couple choose to end a marriage, they must first complete a year of living apart while trying to reconcile differences. Divorce is discouraged, but permitted after that initial year.

Judy A. Johnson, MTS

Bibliography

Albertson, Lorelei. *All about Bahá'í Faith*. University Pub., 2012. E-book.

Bowers, Kenneth E. *God Speaks Again: an Introduction to the Bahá'í Faith*. Wilmette: Bahá'í, 2004. Print.

Buck, Christopher. "The Interracial 'Bahá'í Movement' and the Black Intelligentsia: The Case of W. E. B. Du Bois." *Journal of Religious History* 36.4 (2012): 542–62. Print.

Cederquist, Druzelle. *The Story of Baha'u'llah*. Wilmette: Bahá'í, 2005. Print.

Echevarria, L. *Life Stories of Bahá'í Women in Canada: Constructing Religious Identity in the Twentieth Century*. Lang, 2011. E-book.

Garlington, William. *The Bahá'í Faith in America*. Lanham: Rowman, 2008. Print.

Hartz, Paula R. *Bahá'í Faith*. New York: Facts on File, 2006. Print.

Hatcher, William S. and J. Douglas Martin. *The Bahá'í Faith: The Emerging Global Religion*. Wilmette: Bahá'í, 2002. Print.

Karlberg, Michael. "Constructive Resilience: The Bahá'í Response to Oppression." *Peace & Change* 35.2 (2010): 222–57. Print.

Lee, Anthony A. *The Bahá'í Faith in Africa: Establishing a New Religious Movement, 1952–1962*. Brill NV, E-book.

Momen, Moojan. "Bahá'í Religious History." *Journal of Religious History* 36.4 (2012): 463–70. Print.

Momen, Moojan. *The Bahá'í Faith: A Beginner's Guide*. Oxford: Oneworld, 2007. Print.

Smith, Peter. *The Bahá'í Faith*. Cambridge: Cambridge UP, 2008. Print.

Wilkinson, Philip. *Religions*. New York: DK, 2008. Print.

Buddhism

General Description

Buddhism has three main branches: Theravada (Way of the Elders), also referred to as Hinayana (Lesser Vehicle); Mahayana (Greater Vehicle); and Vajrayana (Diamond Vehicle), also referred to as Tantric Buddhism. Vajrayana is sometimes thought of as an extension of Mahayana Buddhism. These can be further divided into many sects and schools, many of which are geographically based. In Buddhism, these different divisions or schools are regarded as alternative paths to enlightenment (Wilkinson 2008).

Number of Adherents Worldwide

An estimated 474 million people around the world are Buddhists. Of the major sects, Theravada Buddhism is the oldest, developed in the sixth century BCE. Its adherents include those of the Theravada Forest Tradition. From Mahayana Buddhism, which developed in the third to second centuries BCE, came several offshoots based on location. In what is now China, Pure Land Buddhism and Tibetan Buddhism developed in the seventh century. In Japan, Zen Buddhism developed in the twelfth century, Nichiren Buddhism developed a century later, and Soka Gakkai was founded in 1937. In California during the 1970s, the Serene Reflection Meditation began as a subset of Sōtō Zen. In Buddhism, these different divisions or schools are regarded as alternative paths to enlightenment.

Basic Tenets

Buddhists hold to the Three Universal Truths: impermanence, the lack of self, and suffering. These truths encompass the ideas that everything is impermanent and changing and that life is not satisfying because of its impermanence and the temporary nature of all things, including contentment. Buddhism also teaches the Four Noble Truths: All life is suffering (Dukkha). Desire and attachment cause suffering (Samudaya). Ceasing to desire or crave conceptual attachment

ends suffering and leads to release (Nirodha). This release comes through following the Noble Eightfold Path—right understanding (or view), right intention, right speech, right conduct, right occupation, right effort, right mindfulness, and right concentration (Magga).

Although Buddhists do not believe in an afterlife as such, the soul undergoes a cycle of death and rebirth. Following the Noble Eightfold Path leads to the accumulation of good karma, allowing one to be reborn at a higher level. Karma is the Buddhist belief in cause-effect relationships; actions taken in one life have consequences in the next. Ultimately, many refer to the cessation or elimination of suffering as the primary goal of Buddhism.

Buddhists do not believe in gods. Salvation is to be found in following the teachings of Buddha, which are called the Dharma (law or truth). Buddhism does have saint-like bodhisattvas (enlightened beings) who reject ultimate enlightenment (Nirvana) for themselves to aid others.

Sacred Text

Buddhism has nothing comparable to the Qur'an (Islam's holy book) or the Bible. For Theravada Buddhists, an important text is the Pāli Canon, the collection of Buddha's teachings. Mahayana Buddhists recorded their version of these as sutras, many of them in verse. The Lotus Sutra is among the most important. The Buddhist scriptures are written in two languages of ancient India, Pali and Sanskrit, depending on the tradition in which they were developed. Some of these words, such as karma, have been transliterated into English and gained common usage.

Major Figures

Siddhartha Gautama (ca. 563 to 483 BCE) is the founder of Buddhism and regarded as the Buddha or Supreme Buddha. He is the most highly regarded historical figure in Buddhism.

He had two principle disciples: Sariputta and Mahamoggallana (or Maudgalyayana). In contemporary Buddhism, the fourteenth Dalai Lama, Tenzin Gyatso, is a significant person. Both he and Aung San Suu Kyi, a Buddhist of Myanmar who was held as a political prisoner for her stand against the oppressive regime of that nation, have been awarded the Nobel Peace Prize.

Major Holy Sites

Buddhist holy sites are located in several places in Asia. All of those directly related to the life of Siddhartha Gautama are located in the northern part of India near Nepal. Lumbini Grove is noted as the birthplace of the Buddha. He received enlightenment at Bodh Gaya and first began to teach in Sarnath. Kusinara is the city where he died.

In other Asian nations, some holy sites were once dedicated to other religions. Angkor Wat in Cambodia, for example, was constructed for the Hindu god Vishnu in the twelfth century CE. It became a Buddhist temple three hundred years later. It was once the largest religious monument in the world and still attracts visitors. In Java's central highlands sits Borobudur, the world's largest Buddhist shrine. The name means "Temple of Countless Buddhas." Its five terraces represent what must be overcome to reach enlightenment: worldly desires, evil intent, malicious joy, laziness, and doubt. It was built in the eighth and ninth centuries CE, only to fall into neglect at about the turn of the millennium; it was rediscovered in 1815. The complex has three miles of carvings illustrating the life and teachings of the Buddha. In Sri Lanka, the Temple of the Tooth, which houses what is believed to be one of the Buddha's teeth, is a popular pilgrimage site.

Some of the holy sites incorporate gifts of nature. China has four sacred Buddhist mountains, symbolizing the four corners of the universe. These mountains—Wŭtái Shān, Éméi Shān, Jiŭhuá Shān, and Pŭtuó Shān—are believed to be the homes of bodhisattvas. In central India outside Fardapur, there are twenty-nine caves carved into the granite, most of them with frescoes based on the Buddha's life. Ajanta, as the site is known, was created between 200 BCE and the fifth century CE. Five of the caves house temples.

The Buddha's birthday, his day of death, and the day of his enlightenment are all celebrated, either as one day or several. Different traditions and countries have their own additional celebrations, including Sri Lanka's Festival of the Tooth. Buddhists have a lunar calendar, and four days of each month are regarded as holy days.

ORIGINS

History & Geography

Buddhism began in what is now southern Nepal and northern India with the enlightenment of the Buddha. Following his death, members of the sangha, or community, spread the teachings across northern India. The First Buddhist Council took place in 486 BCE at Rajagaha. This council settled the Buddhist canon, the Tipitaka. In 386 BCE, a little more than a century after the Buddha died, a second Buddhist Council was held at Vesali. It was at this meeting that the two major schools of Buddhist thought—Theravada and Mahayana—began to differ.

Emperor Asoka, who ruled most of the Indian subcontinent from around 268 to 232 BCE, converted to Buddhism. He sent missionaries across India and into central parts of Asia. He also set up pillars with Buddhist messages in his own efforts to establish "true dharma" in the kingdom, although he did not create a state church. His desire for his subjects to live contently in this life led to promoting trade, maintaining canals and reservoirs, and the founding a system of medical care for both humans and animals. Asoka's son Mahinda went to southern Indian and to Sri Lanka with the message of Buddhism.

Asoka's empire fell shortly after his death. Under the following dynasties, evidence suggests Buddhists in India experienced persecution. The religion continued to grow, however, and during the first centuries CE, monasteries and monuments were constructed with support from local rulers. Some additional support came from women within the royal courts. Monastic centers also grew in number. By the fourth century CE, Buddhism had become one of the chief religious traditions in India.

During the Gupta dynasty, which lasted from about 320 to 600 CE, Buddhists and Hindus began enriching each other's traditions. Some Hindus felt that the Buddha was an incarnation of Vishnu, a Hindu god. Some Buddhists showed respect for Hindu deities.

Also during this era, Mahavihara, the concept of the "Great Monastery," came to be. These institutions served as universities for the study and development of Buddhist thinking. Some of them also included cultural and scientific study in the curriculum.

Traders and missionaries took the ideas of Buddhism to China. By the first century CE, Buddhism was established in that country. The religion died out or was absorbed into Hinduism in India. By the seventh century, a visiting Chinese monk found that Huns had invaded India from Central Asia and destroyed many Buddhist monasteries. The religion revived and flourished in the northeast part of India for several centuries.

Muslim invaders reached India in the twelfth and thirteenth centuries. They sacked the monasteries, some of which had grown very wealthy. Some even paid workers to care for both the land they owned and the monks, while some had indentured slaves. Because Buddhism had become monastic rather than a religion of the laity, there was no groundswell for renewal following the Muslim invasion.

Prominent in eastern and Southeast Asia, Buddhism is the national religion in some countries. For example, in Thailand, everyone learns about Buddhism in school. Buddhism did not begin to reach Western culture until the nineteenth century, when the Lotus Sutra was translated into German. The first Buddhist temple in the United States was built in 1853 in San Francisco's Chinatown.

Chinese Communists took control of Tibet in 1950. Nine years later, the fourteenth Dalai Lama left for India, fearing persecution. The Dalai Lama is considered a living teacher (lama) who is to instruct others. (The term *dalai* means "great as the ocean.") In 1989, he received the Nobel Peace Prize.

Buddhism experienced a revival in India during the twentieth century. Although some of this new beginning was due in part to Tibetan immigrants seeking safety, a mass conversion in 1956 was the major factor. The year was chosen to honor the 2,500th anniversary of the Buddha's death year. Buddhism was chosen as an alternative to the strict caste structure of Hinduism, and hundreds of thousands of people of the Dalit caste, once known as untouchables, converted in a ceremony held in Nagpur.

Founder or Major Prophet
Siddhartha Gautama, who became known as the "Enlightened One," or Buddha, was a prince in what is now southern Nepal, but was then northern India during the sixth century BCE. The name Siddhartha means "he who achieves his aim." He was a member of the Sakya tribe of Nepal, belonging to the warrior caste. Many legends have grown around his birth and early childhood. One states that he was born in a grove in the woods, emerging from his mother's side able to walk and completely clean.

During Siddhartha's childhood, a Brahmin, or wise man, prophesied that he would grow to be a prince or a religious teacher who would help others overcome suffering. Because the life of a sage involved itinerant begging, the king did not want this life for his child. He kept Siddhartha in the palace and provided him with all the luxuries of his position, including a wife, Yashodhara. They had a son, Rahula.

Escaping from the palace at about the age of thirty, Gautama first encountered suffering in the form of an old man with a walking stick. The following day, he saw a man who was ill. On the third day, he witnessed a funeral procession. Finally he met a monk, who had nothing, but who radiated happiness. He determined to leave his privileged life, an act called the Great Renunciation. Because hair was a sign of vanity in his time, he shaved his head. He looked for enlightenment via an ascetic life of little food or sleep. He followed this path for six years, nearly starving to death. Eventually, he determined on a Middle Way, a path neither luxurious as he had known in the palace, nor ascetic as he had attempted.

After three days and nights of meditating under a tree at Bodh Gaya, Siddhartha achieved his goal of enlightenment, or Nirvana. He escaped fear of suffering and death.

The Buddha began his preaching career, which spanned some forty years, following his enlightenment. He gave his first sermon in northeast India at Sarnath in a deer park. The first five followers became the first community, or sangha. Buddha died around age eighty, in 483 BCE after he had eaten poisoned food. After warning his followers not to eat the food, he meditated until he died.

Buddhists believe in many enlightened ones. Siddhartha is in one tradition regarded as the fourth buddha, while other traditions hold him to have been the seventh or twenty-fifth buddha.

His disciples, who took the ideas throughout India, repeated his teachings. When the later Buddhists determined to write down the teachings of the Buddha, they met to discuss the ideas and agreed that a second meeting should occur in a century. At the third council, which was held at Pataliputta, divisions occurred. The two major divisions—Theravada and Mahayana—differ over the texts to be used and the interpretation of the teachings. Theravada can be translated as "the Teachings of the Elders," while Mahayana means "Great Vehicle."

Theravada Buddhists believe that only monks can achieve enlightenment through the teachings of another buddha, or enlightened being. Thus they try to spend some part of their lives in a monastery. Buddhists in the Mahayana tradition, on the other hand, feel that all people can achieve enlightenment, without being in a monastery. Mahayanans also regard some as bodhisattvas, people who have achieved the enlightened state but renounce Nirvana to help others achieve it.

Philosophical Basis

During Siddhartha's lifetime, Hinduism was the predominant religion in India. Many people, especially in northern India, were dissatisfied with the rituals and sacrifices of that religion. In addition, as many small kingdoms expanded and the unity of the tribes began to break down, many people were in religious turmoil and doubt. A number of sects within Hinduism developed.

The Hindu belief in the cycle of death and rebirth led some people to despair because they could not escape from suffering in their lives. Siddhartha was trying to resolve the suffering he saw in the world, but many of his ideas came from the Brahmin sect of Hinduism, although he reinterpreted them. Reincarnation, dharma, and reverence for cows are three of the ideas that carried over into Buddhism.

In northeast India at Bodh Gaya, he rested under a bodhi tree, sometimes called a bo tree. He meditated there until he achieved Nirvana, or complete enlightenment, derived from the freedom of fear that attached to suffering and death. As a result of his being enlightened, he was known as Buddha, a Sanskrit word meaning "awakened one." Wanting to help others, he began teaching his Four Noble Truths, along with the Noble Eightfold Path that would lead people to freedom from desire and suffering. He encouraged his followers to take Triple Refuge in the Three Precious Jewels: the Buddha, the teachings, and the sangha, or monastic community. Although at first Buddha was uncertain about including women in a sangha, his mother-in-law begged for the privilege.

Greed, hatred, and ignorance were three traits that Buddha felt people needed to conquer. All three create craving, the root of suffering. Greed and ignorance lead to a desire for things that are not needed, while hatred leads to a craving to destroy the hated object or person.

To the Four Noble Truths and Eightfold Path, early devotees of Buddhism added the Five Moral Precepts. These are to avoid taking drugs and alcohol, engaging in sexual misconduct, harming others, stealing, and lying.

The precepts of the Buddha were not written down for centuries. The first text did not appear for more than 350 years after the precepts were first spoken. One collection from Sri Lanka written in Pāli during the first century BCE is known as Three Baskets, or Tipitaka. The three baskets include Buddha's teaching (the Basket of Discourse), commentary on the sayings (the Basket of Special Doctrine), and the rules for monks to follow (the Basket of Discipline). The name Three Baskets refers to the fact that the sayings were first written on leaves from a palm tree that were then collected in baskets.

Holy Places

Buddhists make pilgrimages to places that relate to important events in Siddhartha's life. While Lumbini Grove, the place of Siddhartha's birth, is a prominent pilgrimage site, the primary site for pilgrimage is Bodh Gaya, the location where Buddha received enlightenment. Other pilgrimage sites include Sarnath, the deer park located in what is now Varanasi (Benares) where the Buddha first began to teach, and Kusinara, the city where he died. All of these are in the northern part of India near Nepal.

Other sites in Asia that honor various bodhisattvas have also become pilgrimage destinations. Mountains are often chosen; there are four in China, each with monasteries and temples built on them. In Japan, the Shikoku pilgrimage covers more than 700 miles and involves visits to eighty-eight temples along the route.

BUDDHISM IN DEPTH

Sacred Symbols

Many stylized statue poses of the Buddha exist, each with a different significance. One, in which the Buddha has both hands raised, palms facing outward, commemorates the calming of an elephant about to attack the Buddha. If only the right hand is raised, the hand symbolizes friendship and being unafraid. The teaching gesture is that of a hand with the thumb and first finger touching.

In Tibetan Buddhism, the teachings of Buddha regarding the cycle of rebirth are symbolized in the six-spoke wheel of life. One may be reborn into any of the six realms of life: hell, hungry spirits, warlike demons called Asuras, animals, humans, or gods. Another version of the wheel has eight spokes rather than six, to represent the Noble Eightfold Path. Still another wheel has twelve spokes, signifying both the Four Noble Truths and the Noble Eightfold Path.

Tibetan Buddhists have prayer beads similar to a rosary, with 108 beads representing the number of desires to be overcome prior to reaching enlightenment. The worshipper repeats the Triple Refuge—Buddha, dharma, and sangha—or a mantra.

The prayer wheel is another device that Tibetan Buddhists use. Inside the wheel is a roll of paper on which the sacred mantra—Hail to the jewel in the lotus—is written many times. The lotus is a symbol of growing spiritually; it grows in muddied waters, but with the stems and flowers, it reaches toward the sun. By turning the wheel and spinning the mantra, the practitioner spreads blessings. Bells may be rung to wake the hearer out of ignorance.

In Tantric Buddhism, the mandala, or circle, serves as a map of the entire cosmos. Mandalas may be made of colored grains of sand, carved or painted. They are used to help in meditation and are thought to have a spiritual energy.

Buddhism recognizes Eight Auspicious Symbols, including the banner, conch shell, fish, knot, lotus, treasure vase, umbrella, and wheel. Each has a particular significance. A conch shell, for example, is often blown to call worshippers to meetings. Because its sound travels far, it signifies the voice of Buddha traveling throughout the world. Fish are fertility symbols because they have thousands of offspring. In Buddhist imagery, they are often in facing pairs and fashioned of gold. The lotus represents spiritual growth, rooted in muddy water but flowering toward the sun. The umbrella symbolizes protection, because servants once used them to protect royalty from both sun and rain.

Sacred Practices & Gestures

Two major practices characterize Buddhism: gift-giving and showing respect to images and relics of the Buddha. The first is the transaction between laity and monks in which laypersons present sacrificial offerings to the monks, who in return share their higher state of spiritual being with the laity. Although Buddhist monks are permitted to own very little, they each have a begging bowl, which is often filled with rice.

Buddhists venerate statues of the Buddha, bodhisattvas, and saints; they also show respect to his relics, housed in stupas. When in the presence of a statue of the Buddha, worshippers have a series of movements they repeat three times, thus dedicating their movements to the Triple Refuge. It begins with a dedicated body: placing hands together with the palms cupped slightly and fingers touching, the devotee raises the hands to the forehead. The second step symbolizes right speech by lowering the hands to just below the mouth. In the third movement, the hands are lowered to the front of the chest, indicating that heart—and by extension, mind—are also dedicated to the Triple Refuge. The final movement is prostration. The devotee first gets on all fours, then lowers either the entire body to the floor or lowers the head, so that there are five points of contact with the floor.

Statues of the Buddha give a clue to the gestures held important to his followers. The gesture of turning the hand towards the ground indicates that one is observing Earth. Devotees assume a lotus position, with legs crossed, when in meditation.

Allowing the left hand to rest in the lap and the right hand to point down to Earth is a gesture used in meditation. Another common gesture is to touch thumb and fingertips together while the palms of both hands face up, thus forming a flat triangular shape. The triangle signifies the Three Jewels of Buddhism.

Food Restrictions

Buddhism does not require one to be a vegetarian. Many followers do not eat meat, however, because to do so involves killing other creatures. Both monks and laypersons may choose not to eat after noontime during the holy days of each month.

Rites, Celebrations, & Services

Ancient Buddhism recognized four holy days each month, known as *uposatha*. These days included the full moon and new moon days of each lunar month, as well as the eighth day after each of these moons appeared. Both monks and members of the laity have special religious duties during these four days. A special service takes place in which flowers are offered to images of the Buddha, precepts are repeated, and a sermon is preached. On these four days, an additional three precepts may be undertaken along with the five regularly observed. The three extra duties are to refrain from sleeping on a luxurious bed, eating any food after noon, and adorning the body or going to entertainments.

In Theravada nations, three major life events of the Buddha—birth, enlightenment, and entering nirvana—are celebrated on Vesak, or Buddha Day. In temples, statues of Buddha as a child are ceremonially cleaned. Worshippers may offer incense and flowers. To symbolize the Buddha's enlightenment, lights may be illuminated in trees and temples. Because it is a day of special kindness, some people in Thailand refrain from farm work that could harm living creatures. They may also seek special merit by freeing captive animals.

Other Buddhist nations that follow Mahayana Buddhism commemorate these events on three different days. In Japan, Hana Matsuri is the celebration of Buddha's birth. On that day, people create paper flower gardens to recall the gardens of Lumbini, Siddhartha's birthplace. Worshippers also pour perfumed tea over statues of Buddha; this is because, according to tradition, the gods provided scented water for Siddhartha's first bath.

Poson is celebrated in Sri Lanka to honor the coming of Buddhism during the reign of Emperor Asoka. Other holy persons are also celebrated in the countries where they had the greatest influence. In Tibet, for instance, the arrival of

Padmasambhava, who brought Buddhism to that nation, is observed.

Buddhists also integrate their own special celebrations into regular harvest festivals and New Year activities. These festivities may include a performance of an event in the life of any buddha or bodhisattva. For example, troupes of actors in Tibet specialize in enacting Buddhist legends. The festival of the Sacred Tooth is held in Kandy, Sri Lanka. According to one legend, a tooth of Buddha has been recovered, and it is paraded through the streets on this day. The tooth has been placed in a miniature stupa, or sealed mound, which is carried on an elephant's back.

Protection rituals have been common in Buddhism from earliest days. They may be public rituals meant to avoid a collective danger, such as those held in Sri Lanka and other Southeast Asia nations. Or they may be designed for private use. The role of these rituals is greater in Mahayana tradition, especially in Tibet. Mantras are chanted for this reason.

Customs surrounding death and burial differ between traditions and nations. A common factor, however, is the belief that the thoughts of a person at death are significant. This period may be extended for three days following death, due to a belief in consciousness for that amount of time after death. To prepare the mind of the dying, another person may read sacred texts aloud.

Judy A. Johnson, MTS

Bibliography

Armstrong, Karen. *Buddha*. New York: Penguin, 2001. Print.

Barnes, Trevor. *The Kingfisher Book of Religions*. New York: Kingfisher, 1999. Print.

Chodron, Thubten. *Buddhism for Beginners*. Ithaca: Snow Lion, 2001. Print.

Eckel, Malcolm David. *Buddhism*. Oxford: Oxford UP, 2002. Print.

Epstein, Ron. "Application of Buddhist Teachings in Modern Life." *Religion East & West* Oct. 2012: 52–61. Print.

Harding, John S. *Studying Buddhism in Practice*. Routledge, 2012. E-book. Studying Religions in Practice.

Harvey, Peter. *An Introduction to Buddhism: Teachings, History and Practices*. 2nd ed. Cambridge UP, 2013. E-book.

Heirman, Ann. "Buddhist Nuns: Between Past and Present." *International Review for the History of Religions* 58.5/6 (2011): 603–31. Print.

Langley, Myrtle. *Religion*. New York: Knopf, 1996. Print.

Low, Kim Cheng Patrick. "Three Treasures of Buddhism & Leadership Insights." *Culture & Religion Review Journal* 2012.3 (2012): 66–72. Print.

Low, Patrick Kim Cheng. "Leading Change, the Buddhist Perspective." *Culture & Religion Review Journal* 2012.1 (2012): 127–45. Print.

McMahan, David L. *Buddhism in the Modern World*. Routledge, 2012. E-book.

Meredith, Susan. *The Usborne Book of World Religions*. London: Usborne, 1995. Print.

Morgan, Diane. *Essential Buddhism: A Comprehensive Guide to Belief and Practice*. Praeger, 2010. E-book.

Wilkinson, Philip. *Buddhism*. New York: DK, 2003. Print.

Wilkinson, Philip. *Religions*. New York: DK, 2008. Print.

Christianity

General Description

Christianity is one of the world's major religions. It is based on the life and teachings of Jesus of Nazareth, called the Christ, or anointed one. It is believed that there are over thirty thousand denominations or sects of Christianity worldwide. Generally, most of these sects fall under the denominational families of Catholicism, Protestant, and Orthodox. (Anglican and Oriental Orthodox are sometimes added as separate branches.) Most denominations have developed since the seventeenth-century Protestant Reformation.

Number of Adherents Worldwide

Over 2.3 billion people around the world claim allegiance to Christianity in one of its many forms. The three major divisions are Roman Catholicism, Eastern Orthodox, and Protestant. Within each group are multiple denominations. Roman Catholics number more than 1.1 billion followers, while the Eastern Orthodox Church has between 260 and 278 million adherents. An estimated 800 million adherents follow one of the various Protestant denominations, including Anglican, Baptist, Lutheran, Presbyterian, and Methodist. Approximately 1 percent of Christians, or 28 million adherents, do not belong to one of the three major divisions

There are a number of other groups, such as the Amish, with an estimated 249,000 members, and the Quakers, numbering approximately 377,000. Both of these churches—along with Mennonites, who number 1.7 million—are in the peace tradition (their members are conscientious objectors). Pentecostals have 600 million adherents worldwide. Other groups that are not always considered Christian by more conservative groups include Jehovah's Witnesses (7.6 million) and Mormons (13 million) (Wilkinson, p. 104-121).

Basic Tenets

The summaries of the Christian faith are found in the Apostles Creed and Nicene Creed.

In addition, some churches have developed their own confessions of faith, such as Lutheranism's Augsburg Confession. Christianity is a monotheistic tradition, although most Christians believe in the Trinity, defined as one God in three separate but equal persons—Father, Son, and Holy Spirit. More modern, gender-neutral versions of the Trinitarian formula may refer to Creator, Redeemer, and Sanctifier. Many believe in the doctrine of original sin, which means that the disobedience of Adam and Eve in the Garden of Eden has been passed down through all people; because of this sin, humankind is in need of redemption. Jesus Christ was born, lived a sinless life, and then was crucified and resurrected as a substitute for humankind. Those who accept this sacrifice for sin will receive eternal life in a place of bliss after death. Many Christians believe that a Second Coming of Jesus will inaugurate a millennial kingdom and a final judgment (in which people will be judged according to their deeds and their eternal souls consigned to heaven or hell), as well as a resurrected physical body.

Sacred Text

The Bible is the sacred text of Christianity, which places more stress on the New Testament. The canon of the twenty-six books of the New Testament was finally determined in the latter half of the fourth century CE.

Major Figures

Christianity is based on the life and teachings of Jesus of Nazareth. His mother, Mary, is especially revered in Roman Catholicism and the Eastern Orthodox tradition, where she is known as Theotokos (God-bearer). Jesus spread his teachings through the twelve apostles, or disciples, who he himself chose and named. Paul (Saint Paul or Paul the Apostle), who became the first missionary to the Gentiles—and whose writings comprise a bulk of the New Testament—is a key figure for the theological treatises embedded in his letters to early churches. His conversion occurred after Jesus' crucifixion. All of these figures are biblically represented.

Under the Emperor Constantine, Christianity went from a persecuted religion to the state religion. Constantine also convened the Council of Nicea in 325 CE, which expressed the formula defining Jesus as fully God and fully human. Saint Augustine (354–430) was a key thinker of the early church who became the Bishop of Hippo in North Africa. He outlined the principles of just war and expressed the ideas of original sin. He also suggested what later became the Catholic doctrine of purgatory.

In the sixth century, Saint Benedict inscribed a rule for monks that became a basis for monastic life. Martin Luther, the monk who stood against the excesses of the Roman Catholic Church, ignited the seventeenth-century Protestant Reformation. He proclaimed that salvation came by grace alone, not through works. In the twentieth century, Pope John XXIII convened the Vatican II Council, or Second Vatican Council, which made sweeping changes to the liturgy and daily practice for Roman Catholics.

Major Holy Sites

The key events in the life of Jesus Christ occurred in the region of Palestine. Bethlehem is honored as the site of Jesus's birth; Jerusalem is especially revered as the site of Jesus's crucifixion. The capital of the empire, Rome, also became the center of Christianity until the Emperor Constantine shifted the focus to Constantinople. Rome today is the seat of the Vatican, an independent city-state that houses the government of the Roman Catholic Church. Canterbury, the site of the martyrdom of Saint Thomas Becket and seat of the archbishop of the Anglican Communion, is a pilgrimage site for Anglicans. There are also many pilgrimage sites, such as Compostela and Lourdes, for other branches of Christianity. In Ethiopia, Lalibela is the site of eleven churches carved from stone during the twelfth century. The site serves as a profound testimony to the vibrancy of the Christian faith in Africa.

Major Rites & Celebrations

The first rite of the church is baptism, a water-related ritual that is traditionally administered to infants or adults alike through some variant of sprinkling or immersion. Marriage is another rite of the church. Confession is a major part of life for Roman Catholics, although the idea is also present in other branches of Christianity.

The celebration of the Eucharist, or Holy Communion, is a key part of weekly worship for the liturgical churches such as those in the Roman Catholic or Anglican traditions. Nearly all Christians worship weekly on Sunday; services include readings of scripture, a sermon, singing of hymns, and may include Eucharist. Christians honor the birth of Jesus at Christmas and his death and resurrection at Easter. Easter is often considered the most significant liturgical feast, particularly in Orthodox branches.

Many Christians follow a calendar of liturgical seasons. Of these seasons, perhaps the best known is Lent, which is immediately preceded by Shrove Tuesday, also known as Mardi Gras. Lent is traditionally a time of fasting and self-examination in preparation for the Easter feast. Historically, Christians gave up rich foods. The day before Lent was a time for pancakes—to use up the butter and eggs—from which the term Mardi Gras (Fat Tuesday) derives. Lent begins with Ash Wednesday, when Christians are marked with the sign of the cross on their foreheads using ashes, a reminder that they are dust and will return to dust.

ORIGINS

History & Geography

Christianity was shaped in the desert and mountainous landscapes of Palestine, known as the Holy Land. Jesus was driven into the wilderness following his baptism, where he remained for forty days of fasting and temptation. The Gospels record that he often went to the mountains for solitude and prayer. The geography of the deserts and mountains also shaped early Christian spirituality, as men and women went into solitude to pray, eventually founding small communities of the so-called desert fathers and mothers.

Christianity at first was regarded as a sect within Judaism, though it differentiated itself early in the first century CE by breaking with the code of laws that defined Judaism, including the need for circumcision and ritual purity. Early Christianity then grew through the missionary work of the apostles, particularly Paul the Apostle, who traveled throughout the Mediterranean world and beyond the Roman Empire to preach the gospel (good news) of Jesus. (This is often called the Apostolic Age.)

Persecution under various Roman emperors only served to strengthen the emerging religion. In the early fourth century, the Emperor Constantine (ca. 272-337) made Christianity the official religion of the Roman Empire. He also convened the Council of Nicea in 325 CE to quell the religious controversies threatening the Pax Romana (Roman Peace), a time of stability and peace throughout the empire in the first and second centuries.

In 1054 the Great Schism, which involved differences over theology and practice, split the church into Eastern Orthodox and Roman Catholic branches. As Islam grew stronger, the Roman Catholic nations of Europe entered a period of Crusades—there were six Crusades in approximately 175 years, from 1095-1271—that attempted to take the Holy Land out of Muslim control.

A number of theologians became unhappy with the excesses of the Roman church and papal authority during the fifteenth and sixteenth centuries. The Protestant Reformation, originally an attempt to purify the church, was led by several men, most notably Martin Luther (1483-1546), whose ninety-five theses against the Catholic Church sparked the Reformation movement. Other leaders of the Protestant Reformation include John Knox (ca. 1510-1572), attributed as the founder of the Presbyterian denomination, John Calvin (1509-1564), a principle early developer of Calvinism, and Ulrich Zwingli (1484-1531), who initially spurred the Reformation in Switzerland. This period of

turmoil resulted in the founding of a number of church denominations: Lutherans, Presbyterians, and Anglicans. These groups were later joined by the Methodists and the Religious Society of Friends (Quakers).

During the sixteenth and seventeenth centuries, the Roman Catholic Church attempted to stem this wave of protest and schism with the Counter-Reformation. Concurrently, the Inquisition, an effort to root out heresy and control the rebellion, took place. There were various inquisitions, including the Spanish Inquisition, which was led by Ferdinand II of Aragon and Isabella I of Castile in mid-fifteenth century and sought to "guard" the orthodoxy of Catholicism in Spain. There was also the Portuguese Inquisition, which began in 1536 in Portugal under King John III, and the Roman Inquisition, which took place in the late fifteenth century in Rome under the Holy See.

During the modern age, some groups became concerned with the perceived conflicts between history (revealed through recent archaeological findings) and the sciences (as described by Charles Darwin and Sigmund Freud) and the literal interpretation of some biblical texts. Fundamentalist Christianity began at an 1895 meeting in Niagara Falls, New York, with an attempt to define the basics (fundamentals) of Christianity. These were given as the inerrant nature of the Bible, the divine nature of Jesus, his literal virgin birth, his substitutionary death and literal physical resurrection, and his soon return. Liberal Christians, on the other hand, focused more on what became known as the Social Gospel, an attempt to relieve human misery.

Controversies in the twenty-first century throughout Christendom focused on issues such as abortion, homosexuality, the ordination of women and gays, and the authority of the scriptures. An additional feature is the growth of Christianity in the Southern Hemisphere. In Africa, for example, the number of Christians grew from 10 million in 1900 to over 506 million a century later. Initially the result of empire-building and colonialism, the conversions in these nations have resulted in a unique blend of native religions and Christianity. Latin America has won renown for its liberation theology, which was first articulated in 1968 as God's call for justice and God's preference for the poor, demonstrated in the ministry and teachings of Jesus Christ. Africa, Asia, and South America are regions that are considered more morally and theologically conservative. Some suggest that by 2050, non-Latino white persons will comprise only 20 percent of Christians.

Founder or Major Prophet

Jesus of Nazareth was born into a peasant family. The date of his birth, determined by accounts in the Gospels of Matthew and Luke, could be as early as 4 or 5 BCE or as late as 6 CE. Mary, his mother, was regarded as a virgin; thus, Jesus' birth was a miracle, engendered by the Holy Spirit. His earthly father, Joseph, was a carpenter.

At about age thirty, Jesus began an itinerant ministry of preaching and healing following his baptism in the Jordan River by his cousin, John the Baptist. He selected twelve followers, known as apostles (sent-ones), and a larger circle of disciples (followers). Within a short time, Jesus' ministry and popularity attracted the negative attention of both the Jewish and Roman rulers. He offended the Jewish leaders with his emphasis on personal relationship with God rather than obedience to rules, as well as his claim to be coequal with God the Father.

For a period of one to three years (Gospel accounts vary in the chronology), Jesus taught and worked miracles, as recorded in the first four books of the New Testament, the Gospels of Matthew, Mark, Luke, and John. On what has become known as Palm Sunday, he rode triumphantly into Jerusalem on the back of a donkey while crowds threw palm branches at his feet. Knowing that his end was near, at a final meal with his disciples, known now to Christians as the Last Supper, Jesus gave final instructions to his followers.

He was subsequently captured, having been betrayed by Judas Iscariot, one of his own twelve apostles. A trial before the Jewish legislative body, the Sanhedrin, led to his being condemned for blasphemy. However, under Roman law, the Jews did not have the power to put anyone to death. A later trial under the Roman governor, Pontius Pilate, resulted in Jesus being crucified, although Pilate tried to prevent this action, declaring Jesus innocent.

According to Christian doctrine, following the crucifixion, Jesus rose from the dead three days later. He appeared before many over a span of forty days and instructed the remaining eleven apostles to continue spreading his teachings. He then ascended into heaven. Ultimately, his followers believed that he was the Messiah, the savior who was to come to the Jewish people and deliver them. Rather than offering political salvation, however, Jesus offered spiritual liberty.

Philosophical Basis

Jesus was a Jew who observed the rituals and festivals of his religion. The Gospels reveal that he attended synagogue worship and went to Jerusalem for celebrations such as Passover. His teachings both grew out of and challenged the religion of his birth.

The Jews of Jesus' time, ruled by the Roman Empire, hoped for a return to political power. This power would be concentrated in a Messiah, whose coming had been prophesied centuries before. There were frequent insurrections in Judea, led in Jesus' time by a group called the Zealots. Indeed, it is believed that one of the twelve apostles was part of this movement. Jesus, with his message of a kingdom of heaven, was viewed as perhaps the one who would usher in a return to political ascendancy.

When challenged to name the greatest commandment, Jesus answered that it was to love God with all the heart, soul, mind, and strength. He added that the second was to love one's neighbor as one's self, saying that these two commands summarized all the laws that the Jewish religion outlined.

Jewish society was concerned with ritual purity and with following the law. Jesus repeatedly flouted those laws by eating with prostitutes and tax collectors, by touching those deemed unclean, such as lepers, and by including

Gentiles in his mission. Women were part of his ministry, with some of them providing for him and his disciples from their own purses, others offering him a home and a meal, and still others among those listening to him teach.

Jesus's most famous sermon is called the Sermon on the Mount. In it, he offers blessings on those on the outskirts of power, such as the poor, the meek, and those who hunger and thirst for righteousness. While not abolishing the law that the Jews followed, he pointed out its inadequacies and the folly of parading one's faith publicly. Embedded in the sermon is what has become known as the Lord's Prayer, the repetition of which is often part of regular Sunday worship. Much of Jesus' teaching was offered in the form of parables, or short stories involving vignettes of everyday life: a woman adding yeast to dough or a farmer planting seeds. Many of these parables were attempts to explain the kingdom of heaven, a quality of life that was both present and to come.

Holy Places

The Christian church has many pilgrimage sites, some of them dating back to the Middle Ages. Saint James is thought to have been buried in Compostela, Spain, which was a destination for those who could not make the trip to the Holy Land. Lourdes, France, is one of the spots associated with healing miracles. Celtic Christians revere places such as the small Scottish isle of Iona, an early Christian mission. Assisi, Italy, is a destination for those who are attracted to Saint Francis (1181-1226), founder of the Franciscans. The Chartres Cathedral in France is another pilgrimage destination from the medieval period.

Jerusalem, Rome, and Canterbury are considered holy for their associations with the early church and Catholicism, as well as with Anglicanism. Within the Old City of Jerusalem is the Church of the Holy Sepulchre, an important pilgrimage site believed to house the burial place of Jesus. Another important pilgrimage site is the Church of the Nativity in Bethlehem. It is built on a cave believed to be the birthplace of Jesus, and is one of the oldest operating churches in existence.

CHRISTIANITY IN DEPTH

Sacred Symbols

The central symbol of Christianity is the cross, of which there are many variant designs. Some of them, such as Celtic crosses, are related to regions of the world. Others, such as the Crusader's cross, honor historic events. The dove is the symbol for the Holy Spirit, which descended in that shape on the gathered disciples at Pentecost after Jesus's ascension.

Various symbols represent Jesus. Candles allude to his reference to himself as the Light of the World, while the lamb stands for his being the perfect sacrifice, the Lamb of God. The fish symbol that is associated with Christianity has a number of meanings, both historic and symbolic. A fish shape stands for the Greek letters beginning the words Jesus Christ, Son of God, Savior; these letters form the word *ichthus*, the Greek word for "fish." Fish also featured prominently in the scriptures, and the early apostles were known as "fishers of man." The crucifixion symbol is also a popular Catholic Christian symbol.

All of these symbols may be expressed in stained glass. Used in medieval times, stained glass often depicted stories from the Bible as an aid to those who were illiterate.

Sacred Practices & Gestures

Roman Catholics honor seven sacraments, defined as outward signs of inward grace. These include the Eucharist, baptism, confirmation, marriage, ordination of priests, anointing the sick or dying with oil, and penance. The Eastern Orthodox Church refers to these seven as mysteries rather than sacraments.

Priests in the Roman Catholic Church must remain unmarried. In the Eastern Orthodox, Anglican, and Protestant denominations, they may marry. Both Roman Catholic and Eastern Orthodox refuse to ordain women to the priesthood.

The Orthodox Church practices a rite known as chrismation, anointing a child with oil following its baptism. The "oil of gladness," as it is known, is placed on the infant's head, eyes, ears, and mouth. This is similar to the practice of confirmation in some other denominations. Many Christian denominations practice anointing the sick or dying with oil, as well as using the oil to seal those who have been baptized.

Many Christians, especially Roman Catholics, use a rosary, or prayer beads, when praying. Orthodox believers may have icons, such as small paintings of God, saints or biblical events, as part of their worship. There may be a font of water that has been blessed as one enters some churches, which the worshippers use to make the sign of the cross, touching fingers to their forehead, heart, right chest, and left chest. Some Christians make the sign of the cross on the forehead, mouth, and heart to signify their desire for God to be in their minds, on their lips, and in their hearts.

Christians may genuflect, or kneel, as they enter or leave a pew in church. In some churches, particularly the Catholic and Orthodox, incense is burned during the service as a sweet smell to God.

In some traditions, praying to or for the dead is encouraged. The rationale for this is known as the communion of saints—the recognition that those who are gone are still a part of the community of faith.

Catholic, Orthodox, and some branches of other churches have monastic orders for both men and women. Monks and nuns may live in a cloister or be engaged in work in the wider world. They generally commit to a rule of life and to the work of prayer. Even those Christians who are not part of religious orders sometimes go on retreats, seeking quiet and perhaps some spiritual guidance from those associated with the monastery or convent.

Food Restrictions

Historically, Christians fasted during Lent as preparation for the Easter celebration. Prior to the Second Vatican Council in 1962, Roman Catholics did not eat meat on Fridays. Conservative Christians in the Evangelical tradition tend to eliminate the use of alcohol, tobacco, and drugs.

Rites, Celebrations & Services

For churches in the liturgical tradition, the weekly celebration of the Eucharist is paramount. While many churches celebrate this ritual feast with wine and a wafer, many Protestant churches prefer to use grape juice and crackers or bread.

Church services vary widely. Quakers sit silently waiting for a word from God, while in many African American churches, hymns are sung for perhaps an hour before the lengthy sermon is delivered. Some churches have a prescribed order of worship that varies little from week to week. Most services, however, include prayer, a sermon, and singing, with or without musical accompaniment.

A church's architecture often gives clues as to the type of worship one will experience. A church with the pulpit in the center at the front generally is a Protestant church with an emphasis on the Word of God being preached. If the center of the front area is an altar, the worship's focus will be on the Eucharist.

Christmas and Easter are the two major Christian celebrations. In liturgical churches, Christmas is preceded by Advent, a time of preparation and quiet to ready the heart for the coming of Christ. Christmas has twelve days, from the birth date of December 25 to the Epiphany on January 6. Epiphany (to show) is the celebration of the arrival of the Magi (wise men) from the East who came to worship the young Jesus after having seen his star. Their arrival is believed to have been foretold by the Old Testament prophet Isaiah, who said "And the Gentiles shall come to thy light, and kings to the brightness of thy rising" (Isaiah 60:3). Epiphany is the revealing of the Messiah to the Gentiles.

In the early church, Easter was preceded by a solemn period of fasting and examination, especially for candidates for baptism and penitent sinners wishing to be reconciled. In Western churches, Lent begins with Ash Wednesday, which is six and half weeks prior to Easter. By excluding Sundays from the fast, Lent thus gives a forty-day fast, imitating that of Jesus in the wilderness. Historically forbidden foods during the fast included eggs, butter, meat, and fish. In the Eastern Church, dairy products, oil, and wine are also forbidden.

The week before Easter is known as Holy Week. It may include extra services such as Maundy Thursday, a time to remember Jesus's new commandment (*maundy* is etymologically related to *mandate*) to love one another. In some Catholic areas, the crucifixion is reenacted in a Passion play (depicting the passion—trial, suffering, and death—of Christ). Some churches will have an Easter vigil the Saturday night before or a sunrise service on Easter morning.

Judy A. Johnson, MTS

Bibliography

Bakker, Janel Kragt. "The Sister Church Phenomenon: A Case Study of the Restructuring of American Christianity against the Backdrop of Globalization." *International Bulletin of Missionary Research* 36.3 (2012): 129–34. Print.

Bandak, Andreas and Jonas Adelin Jørgensen. "Foregrounds and Backgrounds—Ventures in the Anthropology of Christianity." *Ethos: Journal of Anthropology* 77.4 (2012): 447–58. Print.

Barnes, Trevor. *The Kingfisher Book of Religions*. New York: Kingfisher, 1999. Print.

Chandler, Daniel Ross. "Christianity in Cross-Cultural Perspective: A Review of Recent Literature." *Asia Journal of Theology* 26.2 (2012): 44–57. Print.

Daughrity, Dyron B. "Christianity Is Moving from North to South—So What about the East?" *International Bulletin of Missionary Research* 35.1 (2011): 18–22. Print.

Kaatz, Kevin. *Voices of Early Christianity: Documents from the Origins of Christianity*. Santa Barbara: Greenwood, 2013. E-book.

Langley, Myrtle. *Religion*. New York: Alfred A. Knopf, 1996.

Lewis, Clive Staples. *Mere Christianity*. New York: Harper, 2001. Print.

McGrath, Alistair. *Christianity: An Introduction*. Hoboken, New Jersey: Wiley, 2006. Print.

Meredith, Susan. *The Usborne Book of World Religions*. London: Usborne, 1995. Print.

Ripley, Jennifer S. "Integration of Psychology and Christianity: 2022." *Journal of Psychology & Theology* 40.2 (2012): 150–54. Print.

Stefon, Matt. *Christianity: History, Belief, and Practice*. New York: Britannica Educational, 2012. E-book.

Wilkinson, Philip. *Christianity*. New York: DK, 2003. Print.

Wilkinson, Philip. *Religions*. New York: DK, 2008. Print.

Zoba, Wendy Murray. *The Beliefnet Guide to Evangelical Christianity*. New York: Three Leaves, 2005. Print.

East Asian Religions

General Description

East Asian religious and philosophical traditions include, among others, Confucianism, Taoism, and Shintoism. Confucianism is a philosophy introduced by the Chinese philosopher Confucius (Kongzi; 551–479 BCE) in the sixth century BCE, during the Zhou dynasty. Taoism, which centers on Tao, or "the way," is a religious and philosophical tradition that originated in China about two thousand years ago. Shinto, "the way of the spirits," is a Japanese tradition of devotion to spirits and rituals.

Number of Adherents Worldwide

Between 5 and 6 million people, the majority of them in China, practice Confucianism, once the state religion of China. About 20 million people identify as Taoists. Most of the Taoist practitioners are in China as well. In Japan, approximately 107 million people practice Shintoism, though many practitioners also practice Buddhism. Sects of Shinto include Tenrikyo (heavenly truth), founded in 1838, with nearly 2 million devotees. Shukyo Mahikari (divine light) is another, smaller sect founded in the 1960s. Like other sects, it is a blend of different religious traditions (Wilkinson 332–34).

Basic Tenets

Confucianism is a philosophy of life and does concerns itself not with theology but with life conduct. Chief among the aspects of life that must be tended are five key relationships, with particular focus on honoring ancestors and showing filial piety. Confucianism does not take a stand on the existence of God, though the founder, Confucius, referred to "heaven." Except for this reference, Confucianism does not address the question of life after death.

Taoists believe that Tao (the way or the flow) is in everything. Taoism teaches that qi, or life energy, needs to be balanced between yin and yang, which are the female and male principles

of life, respectively. With its doctrine of the evil of violence, Taoism borders on pacifism, and it also preaches simplicity and naturalness. Taoists believe in five elements—wood, earth, air, fire and water—that need to be in harmony. The five elements lie at the heart of Chinese medicine, particularly acupuncture. In Taoism, it is believed that the soul returns to a state of nonbeing after death.

Shinto emphasizes nature and harmony, with a focus on lived experience rather than doctrine. Shinto, which means "the way of the gods," is a polytheistic religion; Amaterasu, the sun goddess, is the chief god. At one point in Japan's history, the emperor was believed to be a descendant of Amaterasu and therefore divine. In Tenrikyo Shinto, God is manifested most often as Oyakami, meaning "God the parent."

Shinto teaches that some souls can become kami, a spirit, following death. Each traditional home has a god-shelf, which honors family members believed to have become kami. An older family member tends to the god-shelf, placing a bit of food and some sake (rice wine) on the shelf. To do their work, kami must be nourished. The Tenrikyo sect includes concepts from Pure Land Buddhism, such as an afterlife and the idea of salvation.

Sacred Texts

Five classic texts are sacred to the Confucians. These include the I Ching, or Book of Changes; the Book of Odes; the Book of History; the Book of Rites; and the Annals of Spring and Autumn. The Analects, a collection of Confucius's sayings, is another revered classic. The Tao Te Ching (The Way of Power) is the most sacred book of the Taoists. Those who practice Shinto hold sacred two works: the Kojiki (Record of Ancient Matters) and the Nihon-gi (Chronicles of Japan). Both texts, which contain legends and creation myths, were written during the eighth century.

Major Figures

Confucius, who lived during the sixth century, was the first great philosopher of China. Mengzi (Meng-tzu; 371–289 BCE), known in the West as Mencius, developed Confucius's teachings about the higher power guiding human life. Another ancient Chinese philosopher, Laozi(or Lao-tzu), is the founder of Taoism. He is believed to have been a contemporary of Confucius's in the central region of China. Modern scholars are not certain he ever existed, though one account includes the story of Confucius visiting Laozi. Chuang Tzu wrote of Laozi and his ideas during the fourth and third centuries BCE. Shinto's major figures include Ō no Yasumaro (d. 723), the compiler of the Kokiji who acted under the orders of Empress Gemmei and consulted a bard known to have an infallible memory; the scholar Motoori Norinaga (1730–1800), whose work led to a revived interest in ancient Shinto texts; and Nakayama Miki (1798–1887), the farmer's wife who founded Tenrikyo.

Major Holy Sites

Most Confucian sacred places are located within private homes, where an ancestral shrine and an altar to gods and spirits are maintained. In China's Shandong Province is Qufu, the site of Confucius's family mansion, temple, and cemetery. The temple was built in 478 BCE, only a year after Confucius's death, and has been maintained and enlarged. In addition to its status as a holy site, the United Nations Educational, Scientific, and Cultural Organization (UNESCO) has placed it on their World Heritage List.

Taoists regard mountains as a way to communicate with Earth's primeval powers and with those who are immortal. Five of the nine sacred mountains in China are associated with Taoism: Hengshan in both the north and the south, Songshan in the south, Taishan in the east, and Huashan in the west. The holiest of the five is Taishan, which symbolizes stability, prevents natural disasters, and ensures fertility.

Shintoism has a high regard for natural beauty. As such, Shinto shrines are everywhere, particularly in mountains or near waterfalls.

Mountains in particular are regarded as homes of the gods. Mount Fuji is the holiest Shinto mountain, and climbing it to reach the shrine on its peak is an act of worship. More than forty thousand shrines are dedicated to Inari, the rice god.

Shinto was formalized during the Yamato period (the name for ancient Japan), and because the emperor of the imperial dynasty was from the Yamato area and was considered divine, the whole region is revered. At Ise, located near the coast in Mie Prefecture, southeast of Nara, the shrine has been rebuilt every twenty years for at least fourteen centuries. This rebuilding ensures that Toyouke-Ōmikami (the harvest goddess) and Amaterasu (the sun goddess) are renewed in vigor, which in turn invigorates both the rice crop and the imperial line. Those who have died in war are revered as kami in Japan. In Tokyo, a shrine called Yasukuni is dedicated to them. However, there is controversy surrounding the place because of its association with Japan's extreme nationalism prior to World War II.

Sacred Texts

Five classic texts are sacred to the Confucians. These include the I Ching, or Book of Changes; the Book of Odes; the Book of History; the Book of Rites; and the Annals of Spring and Autumn. The Analects, a collection of Confucius's sayings, is another revered classic. The Tao te Ching (The Way of Power) is the most sacred book of the Taoists. Those who practice Shinto hold sacred two works: the Kojiki (Record of Ancient Matters) and the Nihon-gi (Chronicles of Japan). Both texts, which contain legends and creation myths, were written during the eighth century.

Major Figures

Confucius, who lived during the sixth century, was the first great philosopher of China. Mengzi (Meng-tzu; 371–289 BCE), known in the West as Mencius, developed Confucius's teachings about the higher power guiding human life. Another ancient Chinese philosopher, Laozi,(or Lao-tzu) is the founder of Taoism. He is believed to have been a contemporary of Confucius in the central region of China. Modern scholars are not certain he ever existed, though one account includes the story of Confucius visiting Laozi. Chuang Tzu wrote of Laozi and his ideas during the fourth and third centuries BCE. Shinto's major figures include Ō no Yasumaro, the compiler of the Kokiji who acted under the orders of Empress Gemmei and consulted a bard known to have an infallible memory; the scholar Motoori Norinaga (1730–1800), whose work led to a revived interest in ancient Shinto texts; and Nakayama Miki (1798–1887), the farmer's wife who founded Tenrikyo.

Major Holy Sites

Most Confucian sacred places are located within private homes, where an ancestral shrine and an altar to gods and spirits are maintained. In China's Shandong Province is Qufu, the site of Confucius's family mansion, temple and cemetery. The temple was built in 478 BCE, only a year after Confucius's death, and has been maintained and enlarged. In addition to being a holy site, the United Nations Educational, Scientific, and Cultural Organization (UNESCO) has placed it on their World Heritage List.

Taoists consider mountains as a way to communicate with Earth's primeval powers and with those who are immortal. Five of the nine sacred mountains in China are associated with Taoism. They are Hengshan in both the north and south, Songshan in the south, Taishan in the east, and Huashan in the west. The holiest of the five is Taishan, which symbolizes stability, prevents natural disasters, and ensures fertility.

Shintoism has a high regard for natural beauty. As such, Shinto shrines are everywhere, particularly in mountains or near waterfalls. Mountains in particular are regarded as homes of the gods. Mount Fuji is the holiest Shinto mountain, and climbing it to reach the shrine on its peak is an act of worship. More than forty thousand shrines are dedicated to Inari, the rice god.

Shinto was formalized during the Yamato period (the name for ancient Japan), and because the emperor of the imperial dynasty is from the Yamato area, and was considered divine, the whole region is revered. At Ise, located near the coast in the Mie prefecture southeast of Nara, the shrine has been rebuilt every twenty years for at least fourteen centuries. This rebuilding ensures that Toyouke-Ōmikami (the harvest goddess) and Amaterasu (the sun goddess) are renewed in vigor, which in turn invigorates both the rice crop and the imperial line. Those who have died in war are revered as kami in Japan. In Tokyo, a shrine called Yasukuni is dedicated to them. However, there is controversy surrounding the place because of its association with Japan's extreme nationalism prior to World War II.

Major Rites & Celebrations

Confucian celebrations have to do with honoring people rather than gods. At Confucian temples, the philosopher's birthday is celebrated each September. In Taiwan, this day is called "Teacher's Day." Sacrifices, music and dance are part of the event.

Taoism has a jiao (offering) festival near the winter solstice. It celebrates the renewal of the yang force at this turning of the year. During the festival priests, who have been ritually purified, wear lavish clothing. The festival includes music and dancing, along with large effigies of the gods which are designed to frighten away the evil spirits. Yang's renewal is also the focus of New Year celebrations, which is a time for settling debts and cleaning house. Decorations in the yang warm colors of gold, orange and red abound.

Many of the Shinto festivals overlap with Buddhist ones. There are many local festivals and rituals, and each community has an annual festival at the shrine dedicated to the kami of the region. Japanese New Year, which is celebrated for three days, is a major feast. Since the sixteenth century, the Gion Festival has taken place in Kyoto, Japan. Decorated floats are part of the celebration of the shrine.

ORIGINS

History & Geography

During the Zhou dynasty (1050–256 BCE) in China, the idea of heaven as a force that controlled events came to the fore. Zhou rulers believed that they ruled as a result of the "Mandate of Heaven," viewing themselves as morally superior to those of the previous dynasty, the Shang dynasty (1600-1046 BCE). They linked virtue and power as the root of the state.

By the sixth century the Zhou rulers had lost much of their authority. Many schools of thought developed to restore harmony, and were collectively known as the "Hundred Schools." Confucius set forth his ideas within this historical context. He traveled China for thirteen years, urging rulers to put his ideas into practice and failing to achieve his goals. He returned home to teach for the rest of his life and his ideas were not adopted until the Han dynasty (206 BCE–220 CE). During the Han period, a university for the nation was established, as well as the bureaucratic civil service that continued until the twentieth century. When the Chinese Empire fell in 1911, the Confucian way became less important.

Confucianism had influenced not only early Chinese culture, but also the cultures of Japan, Korea, and Vietnam. The latter two nations also adopted the bureaucratic system. In Japan, Confucianism reached its height during the Tokugawa age (1600–1868 CE). Confucian scholars continue to interpret the philosophy for the modern period. Some regard the ideas of Confucius as key to the recent economic booms in the so-called "tiger" economies of East Asia (Hong Kong, Singapore, South Korea, Taiwan, and Thailand). Confucianism continues to be a major influence on East Asian nations and culture.

Taoism's power (te) manifests itself as a philosophy, a way of life, and a religion. Philosophically, Taoism is a sort of self-help regimen, concerned with expending power efficiently by avoiding conflicts and friction, rather than fighting against the flow of life. In China, it is known as School Taoism. As a way of life, Taoism is concerned with increasing the amount of qi available through what is eaten and through meditation, yoga, and tai chi (an ancient Chinese martial art form). Acupuncture and the use of medicinal herbs are outgrowths of this way of life. Church Taoism, influenced by Buddhism and Tao Chiao (religious Taoism), developed during the second century. This church looked for ways to use power for societal and individual benefit.

By the time of the Han dynasty (206–220 CE), Laozi had been elevated to the status of divine. Taoism found favor at court during the Tang dynasty (618–917 CE), during which the state underwrote temples. By adapting and encouraging people to study the writings of all three major faiths in China, Taoism remained relevant into the early twentieth century. During the 1960s and 1970s, Taoist books were burned and their temples were destroyed in the name of the Cultural Revolution (the Great Proletarian Cultural Revolution). Taoism remains popular and vital in Taiwan.

Shinto is an ancient religion, and some of its characteristics appeared during the Yayoi culture (ca. 300 BCE–300 CE). The focus was on local geographic features and the ancestry of local clan leaders. At first, women were permitted to be priests, but that equality was lost due to the influence of Confucian paternalism. The religion declined, but was revived in 1871 following the Meiji Restoration of the emperor. Shoguns (warlords) had ruled Japan for more than 250 years, and Shinto was the state religion until 1945. It was associated with the emperor cult and contributed to Japan's militarism. After the nation's defeat in World War II, the 1947 constitution forbade government involvement in any religion. In contemporary Shinto, women are permitted to become priests and girls, in some places, are allowed to carry the portable shrines during festivals.

Founder or Major Prophet

Confucius, or Kongzi ("Master Kong"), was a teacher whose early life may have included service in the government. He began traveling throughout the country around age fifty, attempting and failing to interest rulers in his ideas for creating a harmonious state. He returned to his home state after thirteen years, teaching a group of disciples who spread his ideas posthumously.

According to legend, Taoism's founder, Laozi, lived during the sixth century. Laozi may be translated as "Grand Old Master," and may be simply a term of endearment. He maintained the archives and lived simply in a western state of China. Weary of people who were uninterested in natural goodness and perhaps wanting greater solitude in his advanced years, he determined to leave China, heading for Tibet on a water buffalo. At the border, a gatekeeper wanted to persuade him to stay, but could not do so. He asked Laozi to leave behind his teachings. For three days Laozi transcribed his teachings, producing the five-thousand-word Tao Te Ching. He then rode off and was never heard of again. Unlike most founders of religions, he neither preached nor promoted his beliefs. Still, he was held with such regard that some emperors claimed descent from him.

No one is certain of the origin of Shinto, which did not have a founder or major prophet. Shinto—derived from two Chinese words, *shen* (spirit) and *dao* (way)—has been influenced by other religions, notably Confucianism and Buddhism.

Philosophical Basis

Confucianism sought to bring harmony to the state and society as a whole. This harmony was to be rooted in the Five Constant Relationships: between parents and children; husbands and wives; older and younger siblings; older and younger friends; and rulers and subjects. Each of these societal relationships existed to demonstrate mutual respect, service, honor, and love, resulting in a healthy society. The fact that three of the five relationships exist within the family highlights the importance of honoring family. Ritual maintains the li, or rightness, of everything, and is a way to guarantee that a person performed the correct action in any situation in life.

Taoism teaches that two basic components—yin and yang—are in all things, including health, the state, and relationships. Yin is the feminine principle, associated with soft, cold, dark, and moist things. Yang is the masculine principle,

and is associated with hard, warm, light, and dry things. By keeping these two aspects of life balanced, harmony will be achieved. Another concept is that of wu-wei, action that is in harmony with nature, while qi is the life force in all beings. The Tao is always in harmony with the universe. Conflict is to be avoided, and soldiers are to go as if attending a funeral, solemnly and with compassion. Taoism also teaches the virtues of humility and selflessness.

Shinto is rooted in reverence for ancestors and for the spirits known as kami, which may be good or evil. By correctly worshipping the kami, Shintoists believe that they are assisting in purifying the world and aiding in its functioning.

Holy Places

Confucianism does not always distinguish between sacred and profane space. So much of nature is considered a holy place, as is each home's private shrine. In addition, some Confucian temples have decayed while others have been restored. Temples do not have statues or images. Instead, the names of Confucius and his noted followers are written on tablets. Like the emperor's palace, temples have the most important halls placed on the north-south axis of the building. Temples are also internally symmetrical, as might be expected of a system that honors order. In Beijing, the Temple of Heaven, just south of the emperor's palace, was one of the holiest places in imperial China.

Taoism's holy places are often in nature, particularly mountains. The holiest of the five sacred mountains in China is Taishan, located in the east. Taoism also reveres grottoes, which are caves thought to be illuminated by the light of heaven.

In the Shinto religion, nature is often the focus of holy sites. Mount Fuji is the most sacred mountain. Near Kyoto the largest shrine of Inari, the rice god, is located. The Grand Shrines at Ise are dedicated to two divinities, and for more than one thousand years, pilgrims have come to it. The Inner Shrine (Naiku) is dedicated to Amaterasu, the sun goddess, and is Shinto's most holy location. The Outer Shrine (Geku) is dedicated to

Toyouke, the goddess of the harvest. Every twenty years, Ise is torn down and rebuilt, thus renewing the gods. Shinto shrines all have torii, the sacred gateway. The most famous of these is built in the sea near the island of Miyajima. Those going to the shrine on this island go by boat through the torii.

EAST ASIAN RELIGIONS IN DEPTH

Sacred Symbols
Water is regarded as the source of life in Confucianism. The water symbol has thus become an unofficial symbol of Confucianism, represented by the Japanese ideogram or character for water, the Mizu, which somewhat resembles a stick figure with an extra leg. Other sacred symbols include the ancestor tablets in shrines of private homes, which are symbolic of the presence of the ancestor to whom offerings are made in hopes of aid.

While not a sacred symbol as the term is generally used, the black and white symbol of yin and yang is a common Taoist emblem. Peaches are also of a symbolic nature in Taoism, and often appear in Asian art. They are based on the four peaches that grew every three thousand years and which the mother of the fairies gave to the Han emperor Wu Ti (140–87 BCE). They are often symbolic of the Immortals.

The Shinto stylized sun, which appears on the Japanese flag, is associated with Amaterasu, the sun goddess. The torii, the gateway forming an entrance to sacred space, is another symbol associated with Shinto.

Sacred Practices & Gestures
Confucian rulers traditionally offered sacrifices honoring Confucius at the spring and autumnal equinoxes. Most of the Confucian practices take place at home shrines honoring the ancestors.

Taoists believe that one can reach Tao (the way) through physical movements, chanting, or meditation. Because mountains, caves, and springs are often regarded as sacred sites, pilgrimages are important to Taoists. At a Taoist

funeral, a paper fairy crane is part of the procession. After the funeral, the crane, which symbolizes a heavenly messenger, is burned. The soul of the deceased person is then thought to ride to heaven on the back of the crane.

Many Shinto shrines exist throughout Japan. Most of them have a sacred arch, known as a torii. At the shrine's entrance, worshippers rinse their mouths and wash their hands to be purified before entering the prayer hall. Before praying, a worshipper will clap twice and ring a bell to let the kami know they are there. Only priests may enter the inner hall, which is where the kami live. During a festival, however, the image of the kami is placed in a portable shrine and carried in a procession through town, so that all may receive a blessing.

Rites, Celebrations & Services
Early Confucianism had no priests, and bureaucrats performed any rituals that were necessary. When the Chinese Empire fell in 1911, imperial ceremonies ended as well. Rituals have become less important in modern times. In contemporary times the most important rite is marriage, the beginning of a new family for creating harmony. There is a correct protocol for each aspect of marriage, from the proposal and engagement to exchanging vows. During the ceremony, the groom takes the bride to his family's ancestor tablets to "introduce" her to them and receive a blessing. The couple bows to the ancestors during the ceremony.

After a death occurs, mourners wear coarse material and bring gifts of incense and money to help defray the costs. Added to the coffin holding are food offerings and significant possessions. A willow branch symbolizing the deceased's soul is carried with the coffin to the place of burial. After the burial, family members take the willow branch to their home altar and perform a ritual to add the deceased to the souls at the family's shrine.

Confucians and Taoists celebrate many of the same Chinese festivals, some of which originated before either Confucianism or Taoism began and reflect aspects of both traditions. While some festivals are not necessarily Taoist, they may be led by Taoist priests. During the Lantern Festival, which occurs on the first full moon of the New Year, offerings are made to the gods. Many of the festivals are tied to calendar events. Qingming (Clear and Bright) celebrates the coming of spring and is a time to remember the dead. During this time, families often go to the family gravesite for a picnic. The Double Fifth is the midsummer festival that occurs on the fifth day of the fifth month, and coincides with the peak of yang power. To protect themselves from too much of the male force, people don garments of the five colors—black, blue, red, white, and yellow—and with the five "poisons"—centipede, lizard, scorpion, snake, and toad—in the pattern of their clothes and on amulets. The gates of hell open at the Feast of the Hungry Ghosts. Priests have ceremonies that encourage the escaped evil spirits to repent or return to hell.

Marriage is an important rite in China, and thus in Taoism as well. Astrologers look at horoscopes to ensure that the bride and groom are well matched and to find the best day for the ceremony. The groom's family is always placed at the east (yang) and the bride's family to the west (yin) to bring harmony. When a person dies, the mourners again sit in the correct locations, while the head of the deceased points south. White is the color of mourning and of yin. At the home of the deceased, white cloths cover the family altar. Mourners may ease the soul's journey with symbolic artifacts or money. They may also go after the funeral to underground chambers beneath the temples to offer a sacrifice on behalf of the dead.

In the Shinto religion, rites exist for many life events. For example, pregnant women ask at a shrine for their children to be born safely, and the mother or grandmother brings a child who is thirty-two or thirty-three-days-old to a shrine for the first visit and blessing. A special festival also exists for children aged three, five or seven, who go to the shrine for purifying. In addition, a bride and groom are purified before the wedding, usually conducted by Shinto priests. Shinto priests may also offer blessings for a new car or building. The New Year and the Spring Festival are among the most important festivals, and shrine virgins, known as miko girls, may dance to celebrate life's renewal. Other festivals include the Feast of the Puppets, Boys' Day, the Water Kami Festival, the Star Feast, the Festival of the Dead, and the autumnal equinox.

Judy A. Johnson, MTS

Bibliography

Barnes, Trevor. *The Kingfisher Book of Religions*. New York: Kingfisher, 1999. Print.

Bell, Daniel A. "Reconciling Socialism and Confucianism? Reviving Tradition in China." *Dissent* 57.1 (2010): 91–99. Print.

Chang, Chung-yuan. *Creativity and Taoism: A Study of Chinese Philosophy, Art and Poetry*. London: Kingsley, 2011. E-book.

Coogan, Michael D., ed. *Eastern Religions*. New York: Oxford UP, 2005. Print.

Eliade, Mircea, and Ioan P. Couliano. *The Eliade Guide to World Religions*. New York: Harper, 1991. Print.

Lao Tzu. *Tao Te Ching*. Trans. Stephen Mitchell. New York: Harper, 1999. Print.

Li, Yingzhang. *Lao-tzu's Treatise on the Response of the Tao*. Trans. Eva Wong. New Haven: Yale UP, 2011. Print.

Littlejohn, Ronnie. *Confucianism: An Introduction*. New York: Tauris, 2011. E-book.

Littleton, C. Scott. *Shinto*. Oxford: Oxford UP, 2002. Print.

Mcvay, Kera. *All about Shinto*. Delhi: University, 2012. Ebook.

Merton, Thomas. *The Way of Chuang Tzu*. New York: New Directions, 1965. Print.

Oldstone-Moore, Jennifer. *Confucianism*. Oxford: Oxford UP, 2002. Print.

Poceski, Mario. *Chinese Religions: The EBook*. Providence, UT: Journal of Buddhist Ethics Online Books, 2009. E-book.

Van Norden, Bryan W. *Introduction to Classical Chinese Philosophy*. Indianapolis: Hackett, 2011. Print.

Wilkinson, Philip. *Religions*. New York: DK, 2008. Print.

Hinduism

General Description

Hinduism; modern Hinduism is comprised of the devotional sects of Vaishnavism, Shaivism, and Shaktism (though Smartism is sometimes listed as the fourth division). Hinduism is often used as umbrella term, since many point to Hinduism as a family of different religions.

Number of Adherents Worldwide

Between 13.8 and 15 percent of the world's population, or about one billion people, are adherents of Hinduism, making it the world's third largest religion after Christianity and Islam. The predominant sect is the Vaishnavite sect (Wilkinson, p. 333).

Basic Tenets

Hinduism is a way of life rather than a body of beliefs. Hindus believe in karma, the cosmic law of cause and effect that determines one's state in the next life. Additional beliefs include dharma, one's religious duty.

Hinduism has no true belief in an afterlife. Rather, it teaches a belief in reincarnation, known as samsara, and in moksha, the end of the cycle of rebirths. Different sects have different paths to moksha.

Hinduism is considered a polytheist religion. However, it is also accurate to say that Hinduism professes a belief in one God or Supreme Truth that is beyond comprehension (an absolute reality, called Brahman) and which manifests itself in many forms and names. These include Brahma, the creator; Vishnu, the protector; and Shiva, the re-creator or destroyer. Many sects are defined by their belief in multiple gods, but also by their worship of one ultimate manifestation. For example, Shaivism and Vaishnavism are based upon the recognition of Shiva and Vishnu, respectively, as the manifestation. In comparison, Shaktism recognizes the Divine Mother (Shakti) as the Supreme Being, while followers of Smartism worship a particular deity of their own choosing.

Major Deities

The Hindu trinity (Trimurti) is comprised of Brahma, the impersonal and absolute creator; Vishnu, the great preserver; and Shiva, the destroyer and re-creator. The goddesses corresponding to each god are Sarasvati, Lakshimi, and Parvati. Thousands of other gods (devas) and goddesses (devis) are worshipped, including Ganesha, Surya, and Kali. Each is believed to represent another aspect of the Supreme Being.

Sacred Texts

Hindus revere ancient texts such as the four Vedas, the 108 Upanishads, and others. No single text has the binding authority of the Qur'an (Islam's holy book) or Bible. Hindu literature is also defined by Sruti (revealed truth), which is heard, and Smriti (realized truth), which is remembered. The former is canonical, while the latter can be changing. For example, the Vedas and the Upanishads constitute Sruti texts, while epics, history, and law books constitute the latter. The Bhagavad Gita (The Song of God) is also considered a sacred scripture of Hinduism, and consists of a philosophical dialogue.

Major Figures

Major figures include: Shankara (788–820 CE), who defined the unity of the soul (atman) and absolute reality (Brahman); Ramanuja (1077–1157 CE), who emphasized bhakti, or love of God; Madhva (1199–1278 CE), scholar and writer, a proponent of dualism; Ramprahsad Sen (1718–1775 CE), composer of Hindu songs of devotion, poet, and mystic who influenced goddess worship in the; Raja Rammohun Roy (1772–1833 CE), abolished the custom of suttee, in which widows were burned on the funeral pyres of their dead husbands, and decried polygamy, rigid caste systems, and dowries; Rabindranath Tagore (1861–1941 CE), first Asian to win the Nobel Prize in Literature; Dr. Babasaheb R. Ambedkar (1891–1956 CE), writer of India's constitution and leader of a mass conversion to Buddhism; Mohandas K. Gandhi (1869–1948 CE), the "great soul" who left a legacy of effective use of nonviolence.

Major Holy Sites

The major holy sites of Hinduism are located within India. They include the Ganges River, in whose waters pilgrims come to bathe away their sins, as well as thousands of tirthas (places of pilgrimage), many of which are associated with particular deities. For example, the Char Dham pilgrimage centers, of which there are four—Badrinath (north), Puri (east), Dwarka (west) and Rameshwaram (south)—are considered the holy abodes or sacred temples of Vishnu. There are also seven ancient holy cities in India, including Ayodhya, believed to be the birthplace of Rama; Varanasi (Benares), known as the City of Light; Dwarka; Ujjian; Kanchipuram; Mathura; and Hardwar.

Major Rites & Celebrations

Diwali, the Festival of Lights, is a five-day festival that is considered a national holiday in India. Holi, the Festival of Colors, is the spring festival. Krishna Janmashtmi is Krishna's birthday. Shivaratri is Shiva's main festival. Navaratri, also known as the Durga festival or Dasserah, celebrates one of the stories of the gods and the victory of good over evil. Ganesh Chaturthi is the elephant-headed god Ganesha's birthday. Rathayatra, celebrated at Puri, India, is a festival for Jagannath, another word for Vishnu.

ORIGINS

History & Geography

Hinduism, which many people consider to be the oldest world religion, is unique in that it has no recorded origin or founder. Generally, it developed in the Indus Valley civilization several thousand years before the Common Era. The faith blends the Vedic traditions of the Indus Valley civilization and the invading nomadic tribes of the Aryans (prehistoric Indo-Europeans). Most of what is known of the Indus Valley

civilization comes from archaeological excavations at Mohenjo-Daro (Mound of the Dead) and Harappa. (Because Harappa was a chief city of the period, the Indus Valley civilization is also referred to as the Harappan civilization.) The Vedas, a collection of ancient hymns, provides information about the Aryan culture.

The ancient Persian word *hind* means Indian, and for centuries, to be Indian was to be Hindu. Even now, about 80 percent of India's people consider themselves Hindu. The root word alludes to flowing, as a river flows. It is also etymologically related to the Indus River. At first, the term Hindu was used as an ethnic or cultural term, and travelers from Persia and Greece in the sixteenth century referred to those in the Indus Valley by that name. British writers coined the term *Hinduism* during the early part of the nineteenth century to describe the culture of India. The Hindus themselves often use the term Sanatana Dharma, meaning eternal law.

The Rigveda, a collection of hymns to various gods and goddesses written around 1500 BCE, is the first literary source for understanding Hinduism's history. The Vedas were chanted aloud for centuries before being written down around 1400 CE. The Rigveda is one of four major collections of Vedas, or wisdom: Rigveda, Yajurveda, Samaveda, and Atharvaveda. Together these four are called Samhitas.

Additionally, Hinduism relies on three other Vedic works: the Aranyakas, the Brahamans, and the Upanishads. The Upanishads is a philosophical work, possibly written down between 800 and 450 BCE, that attempts to answer life's big questions. Written in the form of a dialogue between a teacher (guru) and student (chela), the text's name means "to sit near," which describes the relationship between the two. Along with the Samhitas, these four are called Sruti (heard), a reference to their nature as revealed truth. The words in these texts cannot be altered.

Remaining works are called Smriti, meaning "remembered," to indicate that they were composed by human writers. The longer of the Smriti epics is the Mahabharata, the Great Story of the Bharatas. Written between 300 and 100 BCE, the epic is a classic tale of two rival, related families, including teaching as well as story. It is considered the longest single poem in existence, with about 200,000 lines. (A film made of it lasts for twelve hours.)

The Bhagavad Gita, or Song of the Lord, is the sixth section of the Mahabharata, but is often read as a stand-alone narrative of battle and acceptance of one's dharma. The Ramayana is the second, shorter epic of the Mahabharata, with about fifty thousand lines. Rama was the seventh incarnation, or avatar, of Vishnu. The narrative relates the abduction of his wife, Sita, and her rescue, accomplished with the help of the monkey god, Hanuman. Some have regarded the Mahabharata as an encyclopedia, and the Bhagavad Gita as the Bible within it.

Although many of the practices in the Vedas have been modified or discontinued, sections of it are memorized and repeated. Some of the hymns are recited at traditional ceremonies for the dead and at weddings.

Hinduism has affected American life and culture for many years. For example, the nineteenth-century transcendental writers Margaret Fuller and Ralph Waldo Emerson were both influenced by Hindu and Buddhist literature, while musician George Harrison, a member of the Beatles, adopted Hinduism and explored his new faith through his music, both with and without the Beatles. In 1965, the International Society for Krishna Consciousness (ISKCON), or the Hare Krishna movement, came to the Western world. In addition, many people have been drawn to yoga, which is associated with Hinduism's meditative practices.

Founder or Major Prophet

Hinduism has no founder or major prophet. It is a religion that has developed over many centuries and from many sources, many of which are unknown in their origins.

Philosophical Basis

Hinduism recognizes multiple ways to achieve salvation and escape the endless cycle of rebirth. The way of devotion is the most popular. Through worship of a single deity, the worshipper hopes to attain union with the divine. A second path is the way of knowledge, involving the use of meditation and reason. The third way is via action, or correctly performing religious observances in hope of receiving a blessing from the gods by accomplishing these duties.

Hinduism is considered the world's oldest religion, but Hindus maintain that it is also a way of living, not just a religion. There is great diversity as well as great tolerance in Hinduism. While Hinduism does not have a set of dogmatic formulations, it does blend the elements of devotion, doctrine, practice, society, and story as separate strands in a braid.

During the second century BCE, a sage named Patanjali outlined four life stages, and the fulfilled responsibilities inherent in each one placed one in harmony with dharma, or right conduct. Although these life stages are no longer observed strictly, their ideas still carry weight. Traditionally, these codes applied to men, and only to those in the Brahman caste; members of the warrior and merchant classes could follow them, but were not obligated. The Shudra and Dalit castes, along with women, were not part of the system. Historically, women were thought of as protected by fathers in their childhood, by husbands in their youth and adulthood, and by sons in old age. Only recently have women in India been educated beyond the skills of domestic responsibility and child rearing.

The earliest life stage is the student stage, or brahmacharya, a word that means "to conduct oneself in accord with Brahman." From ages twelve to twenty-four, young men were expected to undertake learning with a guru, or guide. During these twelve years of studying the Veda they were also expected to remain celibate.

The second stage, grihastha, is that of householder. A Hindu man married the bride that his parents had chosen, sired children, and created a livelihood on which the other three stages depended.

Vanaprastha is the third stage, involving retirement to solitude. Historically, this involved leaving the house and entering a forest dwelling.

A man's wife had the option to go with him or to remain. This stage also involved giving counsel to others and further study.

At the final stage of life, sannyasis, the Hindu renounces material goods, including a home of any sort. He may live in a forest or join an ashram, or community. He renounces even making a fire, and lives on fruit and roots that can be foraged. Many contemporary Hindus do not move to this stage, but remain at vanaprastha.

Yoga is another Hindu practice, more than three millennia old, which Patanjali codified. The four forms of yoga corresponded to the Hindu avenues of salvation. Hatha yoga is the posture yoga seeking union with god through action. Jnana yoga is the path to god through knowledge. Bhakti yoga is the way of love to god. Karma yoga is the method of finding god through work. By uniting the self, the practitioner unites with God. Yoga is related etymologically to the English word *yoke*—it attempts to yoke the individual with Brahman. All forms of yoga include meditation and the acceptance of other moral disciplines, such as self-discipline, truthfulness, nonviolence, and contentment.

Aryan society was stratified, and at the top of the social scale were the priests. This system was the basis for the caste system that had long dominated Hinduism. Caste, which was determined by birth, affected a person's occupation, diet, neighborhood, and marriage partner. Vedic hymns allude to four varnas, or occupations: Brahmins (priests), Kshatriyas (warriors), Vaishyas (merchants and common people), and Shudras (servants). A fifth class, the Untouchables, later known as Dalit (oppressed), referred to those who were regarded as a polluting force because they handled waste and dead bodies. The belief was that society would function properly if each group carried out its duties. These varnas later became wrongly blended with castes, or jatis, which were smaller groups also concerned with a person's place in society.

The practice of Hinduism concerns itself with ritual purity; even household chores can be done in a ritualistic way. Some traditions demand ritual purity before one can worship. Brahmin priests, for example, may not accept water or food from non-Brahmins. Refusal to do so is not viewed as classism, but an attempt to please the gods in maintaining ritual purity.

Mohandas Gandhi was one of those who refused to use the term *Untouchable*, using the term *harijan* (children of God), instead. Dr. Babasaheb R. Ambedkar, who wrote India's constitution, was a member of this class. Ambedkar and many of his supporters became Buddhists in an attempt to dispel the power of caste. In 1947, following India's independence from Britain, the caste system was officially banned, though it has continued to influence Indian society.

Ahimsa, or dynamic harmlessness, is another deeply rooted principle of Hinduism. It involves six pillars: refraining from eating all animal products; revering all of life; having integrity in thoughts, words, and deeds; exercising self-control; serving creation, nature, and humanity; and advancing truth and understanding.

Holy Places

In Hinduism, all water is considered holy, symbolizing the flow of life. For a Hindu, the Ganges River is perhaps the most holy of all bodies of water. It was named for the goddess of purification, Ganga. The waters of the Ganges are said to flow through Shiva's hair and have the ability to cleanse sin. Devout Hindus make pilgrimages to bathe in the Ganges. They may also visit fords in the rivers to symbolize the journey from one life to another.

Pilgrimages are also made to sites associated with the life of a god. For example, Lord Rama was said to have been born in Ayodhya, one of the seven holy cities in India. Other holy sites are Dwarka, Ujjian, Kanchipuram, Mathura, Hardwar, and Varanasi, the City of Light.

After leaving his mountain home, Lord Shiva was thought to have lived in Varanasi, or Benares, considered the holiest city. Before the sixth century, it became a center of education for Hindus. It has four miles of palaces and temples along the river. One of the many pilgrimage circuits covers thirty-five miles, lasts for five days, and includes prayer at 108 different shrines. Because of the river's sacred nature, Hindus come to bathe from its many stone steps, called ghats, and to drink the water. It is also the place where Hindus desire to be at their death or to have their ashes scattered. Because Varanasi is regarded as a place of crossing between earth and heaven, dying there is thought to free one from the cycle of rebirth.

The thirty-four Ellora Caves at Maharashtra, India, are known for their sculptures. Built between 600 and 1000 CE, they were cut into a tufa rock hillside on a curve shaped like a horseshoe, so that the caves go deeply into the rock face. Although the one-mile site includes temples for Buddhist, Jain, and Hindu faiths, the major figure of the caves is Shiva, and the largest temple is dedicated to Shiva.

Lastly, Hindu temples, or mandirs, are regarded as the gods' earthly homes. The buildings themselves are therefore holy, and Hindus remove their shoes before entering.

HINDUISM IN DEPTH

Sacred Symbols

The wheel of life represents samsara, the cycle of life, death and rebirth. Karma is what keeps the wheel spinning. Another circle is the hoop of flames in which Shiva, also known as the Lord of the Dance, or Natraja, is shown dancing creation into being. The flames signify the universe's energy and Shiva's power of both destruction and creation. Shiva balances on his right foot, which rests on a defeated demon that stands for ignorance.

The lotus is the symbol of creation, fertility, and purity. This flower is associated with Vishnu because as he slept, a lotus flower bloomed from his navel. From this lotus Brahma came forth to create the world. Yoga practitioners commonly assume the lotus position for meditation.

Murtis are the statues of gods that are found in both temples and private homes. They are often washed with milk and water, anointed with oil, dressed, and offered gifts of food or flowers. Incense may also be burned to make the air around the murti sweet and pure.

One of Krishna's symbols is the conch shell, a symbol of a demon he defeated. A conch shell is blown at temples to announce the beginning of the worship service. It is a visual reminder for followers of Krishna to overcome ignorance and evil in their lives.

For many years, the Hindus used the swastika as a holy symbol. (*Swastika* is a Sanskrit word for good fortune and well-being.) The four arms meet at a central point, demonstrating that the universe comes from one source. Each arm of the symbol represents a path to God and is bent to show that all paths are difficult. It is used at a time of new beginnings, such as at a wedding, where it is traditionally painted on a coconut using a red paste called kum kum. The symbol appears as a vertical gash across the horizontal layers on the southern face of Mount Kailas, one of the Himalayas's highest peaks, thought to have been the home of Shiva. The mountain is also near the source of the Ganges and the Indus Rivers. The use of the swastika as a symbol for Nazi Germany is abhorrent to Hindus.

Some Hindus use a mala, or rosary, of 108 wooden beads when they pray. As they worship, they repeat the names of God.

Sacred Practices & Gestures

Many homes have private altars or shrines to favorite gods. Statues or pictures of these deities are offered incense, flowers and food, as well as prayers. This daily devotion, known as puja, is generally the responsibility of women, many of whom are devoted to goddesses such as Kali or Sita. A rich family may devote an entire room of their house to the shrine.

Om, or Aum, a sacred syllable recorded first in the Upanishads, is made up of three Sanskrit letters. Writing the letter involves a symbol resembling the Arabic number three. Thus, it is a visual reminder of the Trimurti, the three major Hindu gods. The word is repeated at the beginning of all mantras or prayers.

Each day the Gayatri, which is perhaps the world's oldest recorded prayer, is chanted during the fire ritual. The prayer expresses gratitude to the sun for its shining and invokes blessings of prosperity on all. The ritual, typically done at large consecrated fire pits, may be done using burning candles instead.

Holy Hindu men are known as sadhus. They lead ascetic lives, wandering, begging, and living in caves in the mountains. Regarded as having greater spiritual power and wisdom, they are often consulted for advice.

Food Restrictions

Many Hindus are vegetarians because they embrace ahimsa (reverence for and protection of all life) and oppose killing. In fact, Hindus comprise about 70 percent of the world's vegetarians. They are generally lacto-vegetarians, meaning that they include dairy products in their diets. However, Hindus residing in the cold climate of Nepal and Tibet consume meat to increase their caloric intake.

Whether a culture practices vegetarianism or not, cows are thought to be sacred because Krishna acted as a cowherd as a young god. Thus cows are never eaten. Pigs are also forbidden, as are red foods, such as tomatoes or red lentils. In addition, garlic and onions are also not permitted. Alcohol is strictly forbidden.

Purity rituals before eating include cleaning the area where the food is to be eaten and reciting mantras or praying while sprinkling water around the food. Other rituals include Annaprasana, which celebrates a child's eating of solid food—traditionally rice—for the first time. In addition, at funerals departed souls are offered food, which Hindus believe will strengthen the soul for the journey to the ancestors' world.

Serving food to those in need also generates good karma. Food is offered during religious ceremonies and may later be shared with visiting devotees of the god.

To show their devotion to Shiva, many Hindus fast on Mondays. There is also a regular fast, known as agiaras, which occurs on the eleventh day of each two-week period. On that day, only one meal is eaten. During the month of Shravan, which many consider a holy month, people may eat only one meal, generally following sunset.

Rites, Celebrations & Services

Many Hindu celebrations are connected to the annual cycle of nature and can last for many days. In addition, celebrations that honor the gods are common. Shiva, one of the three major gods, is honored at Shivaratri in February or March. In August or September, Lord Krishna is honored at Krishnajanmashtmi. Prayer and fasting are part of this holiday.

During the spring equinox and just prior to the Hindu New Year, Holi is celebrated. It is a time to resolve disputes and forgive or pay debts. During this festival, people often have bonfires and throw objects that represent past impurity or disease into the fire.

Another festival occurs in July or August, marking the beginning of the agricultural year in northern India. Raksha Bandhan (the bond of protection) is a festival which celebrates sibling relationships. During the festivities, Hindus bind a bauble with silk thread to the wrists of family members and friends.

To reenact Rama's defeat of the demon Ravana, as narrated in the Ramayana, people make and burn effigies. This festival is called Navaratri in western India, also known as the Durgapuja in Bengal, and Dasserah in northern India. It occurs in September or October each year as a festival celebrating the victory of good over evil. September is also time to celebrate the elephant-headed god Ganesha's birthday at the festival of Ganesh Chaturthi.

Diwali, a five-day festival honoring Lakshmi (the goddess of good fortune and wealth), occurs in October or November. This Festival of Lights is the time when people light oil lamps and set off fireworks to help Rama find his way home after exile. Homes are cleaned in hopes that Lakshmi will come in the night to bless it. People may use colored rice flour to make patterns on their doorstep. Competitions for designs of these patterns, which are meant to welcome God to the house, frequently take place.

Jagannath, or Vishnu, is celebrated during the festival Rathayatra. A large image of Jagannath rides in a chariot pulled through the city of Puri.

The temple for Hindus is the home of the god. Only Brahmin priests may supervise worship there. The inner sanctuary of the building is called the garbhagriha, or womb-house; there the god resides. Worshippers must be ritually pure before the worship starts. The priest recites the mantras and reads sacred texts. Small lamps are lit, and everyone shares specially prepared and blessed food after the service ends.

Judy A. Johnson, MTS

Bibliography

Barnes, Trevor. *The Kingfisher Book of Religions.* New York: Kingfisher, 1999. Print.

Harley, Gail M. *Hindu and Sikh Faiths in America.* New York: Facts on File, 2003. Print.

Iyengar, B. K. S. and Noelle Perez-Christiaens. *Sparks of Divinity: The Teachings of B. K. S. Iyengar from 1959 to 1975.* Berkeley: Rodmell, 2012. E-book.

"The Joys of Hinduism." *Hinduism Today* Oct./Dec. 2006: 40–53. Print.

Langley, Myrtle. *Religion.* New York: Knopf, 1996. Print.

Meredith, Susan. *The Usborne Book of World Religions.* London: Usborne, 1995. Print.

Rajan, Rajewswari. "The Politics of Hindu 'Tolerance.'" *Boundary 2* 38.3 (2011): 67–86. Print.

Raman, Varadaraja V. "Hinduism and Science: Some Reflections." *Journal of Religion & Science* 47.3 (2012): 549–74. Print.

Renard, John. *Responses to 101 Questions on Hinduism.* Mahwah: Paulist, 1999. Print.

Siddhartha. "Open-Source Hinduism." *Religion & the Arts* 12.1–3 (2008): 34–41. Print.

Shouler, Kenneth and Susai Anthony. *The Everything Hinduism Book.* Avon: Adams, 2009. Print.

Soherwordi, Syed Hussain Shaheed. "'Hinduism'—A Western Construction or an Influence?" *South Asian Studies* 26.1 (2011): 203–14. Print.

Theodor, Ithamar. *Exploring the Bhagavad Gita: Philosophy, Structure, and Meaning.* Farnham and Burlington: Ashgate, 2010. E-book.

Whaling, Frank. *Understanding Hinduism.* Edinburgh: Dunedin, 2010. E-book.

Wilkinson, Philip. *Religions.* New York: DK, 2008. Print.

Islam

General Description

The word *Islam* derives from a word meaning "submission," particularly submission to the will of Allah. Muslims, those who practice Islam, fall into two major groups, Sunni and Shia (or Shi'i,) based on political rather than theological differences. Sunni Muslims follow the four Rightly Guided Caliphs, or Rashidun and believe that caliphs should be elected. Shia Muslims believe that the Prophet's nearest male relative, Ali ibn Abi Talib, should have ruled following Muhammad's death, and venerate the imams (prayer leaders) who are directly descended from Ali and the Prophet's daughter Fatima.

Number of Adherents Worldwide

Approximately 1.6 billion people, or 23 percent of the world's population, are Muslims. Of that total, between 87 and 90 percent of all Muslims are Sunni Muslims and between 10 and 13 percent of all Muslims are Shia. Followers of the Sufi sect, noted for its experiential, ecstatic focus, may be either Sunni or Shia.

Basic Tenets

Islam is a monotheistic faith; Muslims worship only one God, Allah. They also believe in an afterlife and that people are consigned to heaven or hell following the last judgment.

The Islamic faith rests on Five Pillars. The first pillar, Shahadah is the declaration of faith in the original Arabic, translated as: "I bear witness that there is no god but God and Muhammad is his Messenger." The second pillar, Salah, are prayers adherents say while facing Mecca five times daily at regular hours and also at the main service held each Friday at a mosque. Zakat, "the giving of a tax," is the third pillar and entails giving an income-based percentage of one's wealth to help the poor without attracting notice. The fourth pillar is fasting, or Sawm, during Ramadan, the ninth month of the Islamic calendar. Certain groups of people are excused from the fast, however. The final pillar is the Hajj, the pilgrimage to Mecca required of every able-bodied Muslim at least once in his or her lifetime.

Sacred Text

The Qur'an (Koran), meaning "recitation," is the holy book of Islam.

Major Figures

Muhammad, regarded as the Prophet to the Arabs—as Moses was to the Jews—is considered the exemplar of what it means to be a Muslim. His successors—Abu Bakr, Umar, Uthman, and Ali—were known as the four Rightly Guided Caliphs.

Major Holy Sites

Islam recognizes three major holy sites: Mecca, home of the Prophet; Medina, the city to which Muslims relocated when forced from Mecca due to persecution; and the Dome of the Rock in Jerusalem, believed to be the oldest Islamic building in existence. Muslims believe that in 621 CE Muhammad ascended to heaven (called the Night Journey) from a sacred stone upon which the Dome was constructed. Once in heaven, God instructed Muhammad concerning the need to pray at regular times daily...

There are also several mosques which are considered primary holy sites. These include the al-Aqsa Mosque in the Old City of Jerusalem, believed by many to be the third holiest site in Islam. The mosque, along with the Dome of the Rock, is located on Judaism's holiest site, the Temple Mount, where the Temple of Jerusalem is believed to have stood. Muslims also revere the Mosque of the Prophet (Al-Masjid al-Nabawi) in Medina, considered the resting place of the Prophet Muhammad and the second largest mosque in the world; and the Mosque of the Haram (Masjid al-Haram or the Sacred or Grand Mosque) in Mecca, thought to be the largest mosque in the world and site of the Ka'bah, "the sacred house," also known as "the Noble Cube," Islam's holiest structure.

Major Rites & Celebrations

Two major celebrations mark the Islamic calendar. 'Id al-Adha, the feast of sacrifice—including animal sacrifice—held communally at the close of the Hajj (annual pilgrimage), commemorates the account of God providing a ram instead of the son Abraham had been asked to sacrifice. The second festival, 'Id al-Fitr, denotes the end of Ramadan and is a time of feasting and gift giving.

ORIGINS

History & Geography

In 610 CE, a forty-year-old businessman from Mecca named Muhammad ibn Abdullah, from the powerful Arab tribe Quraysh, went to Mount Hira to meditate, as he regularly did for the month of Ramadan. During that month, an entire group of men, the hanif, retreated to caves. The pagan worship practiced in the region, as well as the cruelty and lack of care for the poor, distressed Muhammad. As the tribe to which he belonged had become wealthy through trade, it had begun disregarding traditions prescribed by the nomadic code.

The archangel Jibra'il (Gabriel) appeared in Muhammad's cave and commanded him to read the words of God contained in the scroll that the angel showed him. Like most people of his time, Muhammad was illiterate, but repeated the words Jibra'il said. Some followers of Islam believe that this cave at Jebel Nur, in what is now Saudi Arabia, is where Adam, the first human Allah created, lived.

A frightened Muhammad told only his wife, Khadija, about his experience. For two years, Muhammad received further revelations, sharing them only with family and close friends. Like other prophets, he was reluctant about his calling, fearing that he was—or would be accused of being—possessed by evil spirits or insane. At one point, he tried to commit suicide, but was stopped by the voice of Jibra'il affirming his status as God's messenger.

Muhammad recalled the words spoken to him, which were eventually written down. The Qur'an is noted for being a book of beautiful language, and Muhammad's message reached many. The Prophet thus broke the old pattern of allegiance to tribe and forged a new community based on shared practice.

Muhammad considered himself one who was to warn the others of a coming judgment. His call for social justice and denunciation of the wealthy disturbed the powerful Arab tribe members in Mecca. These men stood to lose the status and income derived from the annual festival to the Ka'bah. The Prophet and his followers were persecuted and were the subject of boycotts and death threats. In 622 CE, Muslim families began a migration (hijrah) to Yathrib, later known as Medina. Two years earlier, the city had sent envoys seeking Muhammad's leadership for their own troubled society. The hijrah marks the beginning of the Islamic calendar.

The persecutions eventually led to outright tribal warfare, linking Islam with political prowess through the victories of the faithful. The Muslims moved from being an oppressed minority to being a political force. In 630 CE, Muhammad and ten thousand of his followers marched to Mecca, taking the city without bloodshed. He destroyed the pagan idols that were housed and worshipped at the Ka'bah, instead associating the hajj with the story of Abraham sending his concubine Hagar and their son Ishmael (Ismail in Arabic) out into the wilderness. With this victory, Muhammad ended centuries of intertribal warfare.

Muhammad died in 632, without designating a successor. Some of the Muslims believed that his nearest male relative should rule, following the custom of the tribes. Ali ibn Abi Talib, although a pious Muslim, was still young. Therefore, Abu Bakr, the Prophet's father-in-law, took the title khalifah, or caliph, which means successor or deputy. Within two years Abu Bakr had stabilized Islam. He was followed by three additional men whom Muhammad had known. Collectively, the four are known as the Four Rightly Guided Caliphs, or the Rashidun. Their rule extended from 632 until 661. Each of the final three met a violent death.

Umar, the second caliph, increased the number of raids on adjacent lands during his ten-year rule, which began in 634. This not only increased wealth, but also gave Umar the authority he needed, since Arabs objected to the idea of a monarchy. Umar was known as the commander of the faithful. Under his leadership, the Islamic community marched into present-day Iraq, Syria, and Egypt and achieved victory over the Persians in 637.

Muslims elected Uthman ibn Affan as the third caliph after Umar was stabbed by a Persian prisoner of war. He extended Muslim conquests into North Africa as well as into Iran, Afghanistan, and parts of India. A group of soldiers mutinied in 656, assassinating Uthman.

Ali, Muhammad's son-in-law, was elected caliph of a greatly enlarged empire. Conflict developed between Ali and the ruler in Damascus whom Uthman had appointed governor of Syria. The fact that the governor came from a rival tribe led to further tensions. Increasingly, Damascus rather than Medina was viewed as the key Muslim locale. Ali was murdered in 661 during the internal struggles.

Within a century after Muhammad's death, Muslims had created an empire that stretched from Spain across Asia to India and facilitated the spread of Islam. The conquerors followed a policy of relative, though not perfect, tolerance toward adherents of other religions. Christians and Jews received special status as fellow "People of the Book," though they were still required to pay a special poll tax in exchange for military protection. Pagans, however, were required to convert to Islam or face death. Later, Hindus, Zoroastrians, and other peoples were also permitted to pay the tax rather than submit to conversion. Following the twelfth century, Sufi mystics made further converts in Central Asia, India, sub-Saharan Africa, and Turkey. Muslim traders also were responsible for the growth of Islam, particularly in China, Indonesia, and Malaya.

The Muslim empire continued to grow until it weakened in the fourteenth century, when it was replaced as a major world power by European states. The age of Muslim domination ended with the 1683 failure of the Ottoman Empire to capture Vienna, Austria.

Although lacking in political power until recent years, a majority of nations in Indonesia, the Middle East, and East and North Africa are predominately Islamic. The rise of Islamic fundamentalists who interpret the Qur'an literally and seek victory through acts of terrorism began in the late twentieth century. Such extremists do not represent the majority of the Muslim community, however.

Like Judaism and Christianity, Islam has been influenced by its development in a desert climate. Arabia, a region three times the size of France, is a land of steppe and desert whose unwelcoming climate kept it from being mapped with any precision until the 1950s. Because Yemen received monsoon rains, it could sustain agriculture and became a center for civilization as early as the second millennium BCE. In the seventh century CE, nomads roamed the area, guarding precious wells and oases. Raiding caravans and other tribes were common ways to obtain necessities.

Mecca was a pagan center of worship, but it was located not far from a Christian kingdom, Ethiopia, across the Red Sea. Further north, followers of both Judaism and Christianity had influenced members of Arab tribes. Jewish tribes inhabited Yathrib, the city later known as Medina. Neither Judaism nor Christianity was especially kind to those they considered pagans. According to an Arabian tradition, in 570 the Ethiopians attacked Yemen and attempted an attack on Mecca. Mecca was caught between two enemy empires—Christian Byzantine and Zoroastrian Persia—that fought a lengthy war during Muhammad's lifetime.

The contemporary clashes between Jews and Muslims are in part a result of the dispersion of Muslims who had lived in Palestine for centuries. More Jews began moving into the area under the British Mandate; in 1948, the state of Israel was proclaimed. Historically, Jews had been respected as a People of the Book.

Founder or Major Prophet

Muslims hold Allah to be the founder of their religion and Abraham to have been the first Muslim. Muhammad is God's prophet to the Arabs. The instructions that God gave Muhammad through the archangel Jibra'il and through direct revelation are the basis for the Islamic religion. These revelations were given over a period of twenty-one years. Because Muhammad and most of the Muslims were illiterate, the teachings were read publicly in chapters, or suras.

Muhammad did not believe he was founding a new religion. Rather, he was considered God's final Prophet, as Moses and Jesus had been prophets. His task was to call people to repent and to return to the straight path of God's law, called Sharia. God finally was sending a direct revelation to the Arab peoples, who had sometimes been taunted by the other civilizations as being left out of God's plan.

Muhammad, who had been orphaned by age six, was raised by an uncle. He became a successful businessman of an important tribe and married Khadija, for whom he worked. His integrity was such that he was known as al-Amin, the trusted one. He and Khadija had six children; four daughters survived. After Khadija's death, Muhammad married several women, as was the custom for a great chief. Several of the marriages were political in nature.

Muhammad is regarded as the living Qur'an. He is sometimes referred to as the perfect man, one who is an example of how a Muslim should live. He was ahead of his time in his attitudes toward women, listening to their counsel and granting them rights not enjoyed by women in other societies, including the right to inherit property and to divorce. (It should be noted that the Qur'an does not require the seclusion or veiling of all women.)

Islam has no religious leaders, especially those comparable to other religions. Each mosque has an imam to preach and preside over prayer at the Friday services. Although granted a moral authority, the imam is not a religious leader with a role comparable to that of rabbis or priests.

Philosophical Basis

Prior to Muhammad's receiving the Qur'an, the polytheistic tribes believed in Allah, "the god." Allah was far away and not part of worship rituals, although he had created the world and sustained it. He had three daughters who were goddesses.

Islam began pragmatically—the old tribal ways were not working—as a call for social justice, rooted in Muhammad's dissatisfaction with the increasing emphasis on accumulating wealth and an accompanying neglect of those in need. The struggle (jihad) to live according to God's desire for humans was to take place within the community, or the ummah. This effort was more important than dogmatic statements or beliefs about God. When the community prospered, this was a sign of God's blessing.

In addition, the revelation of the Qur'an gave Arab nations an official religion. The Persians around them had Zoroastrianism, the Romans and Byzantines had Christianity, and the Jews of the Diaspora had Judaism. With the establishment of Islam, Arabs finally could believe that they were part of God's plan for the world.

Four principles direct Islam's practice and doctrine. These include the Qur'an; the traditions, or sunnah; consensus, or ijma'; and individual thought, or ijtihad. The term sunnah, "well-trodden path," had been used by Arabs before Islam to refer to their tribal law.

A fifth important source for Islam is the Hadith, or report, a collection of the Prophet's words and actions, intended to serve as an example. Sunni Muslims refer to six collections made in the ninth century, while Shia Muslims have a separate Hadith of four collections.

Holy Places

Mecca was located just west of the Incense Road, a major trade route from southern Arabia to Palestine and Syria. Mecca was the Prophet's home and the site where he received his revelations. It is also the city where Islam's holiest structure, the Ka'bah, "the sacred house," was located. The Ka'bah was regarded as having been built by Abraham and his son Ishmael. This forty-three-foot gray stone cube was a center for pagan idols in the time of Muhammad. In 628 the Prophet removed 360 pagan idols—one for each day of the Arabic lunar year—from inside the Ka'bah.

When the followers of Muhammad experienced persecution for their beliefs, they fled to the city of Medina, formerly called Yathrib. When his uncle Abu Talib died, Muhammad lost the protection from persecution that his uncle had provided. He left for Ta'if in the mountains, but it was also a center for pagan cults, and he was driven out. After a group of men from Yathrib promised him protection, Muhammad sent seventy of his followers to the city, built around an oasis about 215 miles north. This migration, called the hijra, occurred in 622, the first year of the Muslim calendar. From this point on, Islam became an organized religion rather than a persecuted and minority cult. The Prophet was buried in Medina in 632, and his mosque in that city is deeply revered.

Islam's third holiest site is the Dome of the Rock in Jerusalem. Muslims believe that the Prophet Muhammad ascended to heaven in 621 from the rock located at the center of this mosque. During this so-called night journey, Allah gave him instructions about prayer. In the shrine at the Dome of the Rock is a strand of hair that Muslims believe was Muhammad's.

Shia Muslims also revere the place in present-day Iraq where Ali's son, Husayn, was martyred. They regard the burial place of Imam Ali ar-Rida in Meshed, Iran, as a site of pilgrimage as well.

ISLAM IN DEPTH

Sacred Symbols

Muslims revere the Black Stone, a possible meteorite that is considered a link to heaven. It is set inside the Ka'bah shrine's eastern corner. The Ka'bah is kept covered by the kiswa, a black velvet cloth decorated with embroidered calligraphy in gold. At the hajj, Muslims walk around it counterclockwise seven times as they recite prayers to Allah.

Muslim nations have long used the crescent moon and a star on their flags. The crescent moon, which the Ottomans first adopted as a symbol during the fifteenth century, is often placed on the dome of a mosque, pointing toward Mecca. For Muhammad, the waxing and waning of the moon signified the unchanging and eternal purpose of God. Upon seeing a new moon, the Prophet confessed his faith in God. Muslims rely on a lunar calendar and the Qur'an states that God created the stars to guide people to their destinations.

Islam forbids the making of graven images of animals or people, although not all Islamic cultures follow this rule strictly. The decorative arts of Islam have placed great emphasis on architecture and calligraphy to beautify mosques and other buildings. In addition, calligraphy, floral motifs, and geometric forms decorate some editions of the Qur'an's pages, much as Christian monks once decorated hand-copied scrolls of the Bible. These elaborate designs can also be seen on some prayer rugs, and are characteristic of Islamic art in general.

Sacred Practices & Gestures

When Muslims pray, they must do so facing Mecca, a decision Muhammad made in January 624 CE. Prior to that time, Jerusalem—a holy city for both Jews and Christians—had been the geographic focus. Prayer involves a series of movements that embody submission to Allah.

Muslims sometimes use a strand of prayer beads, known as subhah, to pray the names of God. The beads can be made of bone, precious stones, or wood. Strings may have twenty-five, thirty-three or 100 beads.

Food Restrictions

Those who are physically able to do so fast from both food and drink during the daylight hours of the month Ramadan. Although fasting is not required of the sick, the aged, menstruating or pregnant women, or children, some children attempt to fast, imitating their parents' devotion. Those who cannot fast are encouraged to do so the following Ramadan. This fast is intended to concentrate the mind on Allah. Muslims recite from the Qur'an during the month.

All meat must be prepared in a particular way so that it is halal, or permitted. While slaughtering the animal, the person must mention the name of Allah. Blood, considered unclean, must be allowed to drain. Because pigs were fed garbage, their meat was considered unclean. Thus Muslims eat no pork, even though in modern times, pigs are often raised on grain.

In three different revelations, Muslims are also forbidden to consume fermented beverages. Losing self-control because of drunkenness violates the Islamic desire for self-mastery.

Rites, Celebrations, and Services

The **mosque** is the spiritual center of the Muslim community. From the minaret (a tower outside the mosque), the call to worship occurs five times daily—at dawn, just past noon, at midafternoon, at sunset, and in the evening. In earliest times, a muezzin, the official responsible for this duty, gave the cry. In many modern countries, the call now comes over a speaker system. Also located outside are fountains to provide the necessary water for ritual washing before prayer. Muslims wash their face, hands, forearms, and feet, as well as remove their shoes before beginning their prayers. In the absence of water, ritual cleansing may occur using sand or a stone.

Praying involves a series of movements known as rak'ah. From a standing position, the worshipper recites the opening sura of the Qur'an, as well as a second sura. After bowing to demonstrate respect, the person again stands, then prostrates himself or herself to signal humility. Next, the person assumes a sitting posture in silent prayer before again prostrating. The last movement is a greeting of "Peace be with you and the mercy of Allah." The worshipper looks both left and right before saying these words, which are intended for all persons, present and not.

Although Muslims stop to pray during each day when the call is given, Friday is the time for communal prayer and worship at the mosque. The prayer hall is the largest space within the mosque. At one end is a niche known as the mihrab, indicating the direction of Mecca, toward which Muslims face when they pray. At first, Muhammad instructed his followers to pray facing Jerusalem, as the Jewish people did. This early orientation was also a way to renounce the pagan associations of Mecca. Some mosques serve as community centers, with additional rooms for study.

The hajj, an important annual celebration, was a custom before the founding of Islam. Pagan worship centered in Mecca at the Ka'bah, where devotees circled the cube and kissed the Black Stone that was embedded in it. All warfare was forbidden during the hajj, as was argument, speaking crossly, or killing even an insect.

Muslims celebrate the lives of saints and their death anniversaries, a time when the saints are thought to reach the height of their spiritual life. Mawlid an-Nabi refers to "the birth of the Prophet." Although it is cultural and not rooted in the Qur'an, in some Muslim countries this is a public holiday on which people recite the Burdah, a poem that praises Muhammad. Muslims also celebrate the night that the Prophet ascended to heaven, Lailat ul-Miraj. The Night of Power is held to be the night on which Allah decides the destiny of people individually and the world at large.

Like Jews, Muslims practice circumcision, a ceremony known as khitan. Unlike Jews, however, Muslims do not remove the foreskin when the male is a baby. This is often done when a boy is about seven, and must be done before the boy reaches the age of twelve.

Healthy adult Muslims fast between sunrise and sunset during the month of Ramadan. This commemorates the first of Muhammad's revelations. In some Muslim countries, cannons are fired before the beginning of the month, as well as at the beginning and end of each day of the month. Some Muslims read a portion of the Qur'an each day during the month.

Judy A. Johnson, MTS

Bibliography

Al-Saud, Laith, Scott W. Hibbard, and Aminah Beverly. *An Introduction to Islam in the 21st Century*. Wiley, 2013. E-book.

Armstrong, Lyall. "The Rise of Islam: Traditional and Revisionist Theories." *Theological Review* 33.2 (2012): 87–106. Print.

Armstrong, Karen. *Islam: A Short History*. New York: Mod. Lib., 2000. Print.

Aslan, Reza. *No god but God: The Origins, Evolution, and Future of Islam*. New York: Random, 2005. Print.

Badawi, Emran El-. "'For All Times and Places': A Humanistic Reception of the Qur'an." *English Language Notes* 50.2 (2012): 99–112. Print.

Barnes, Trevor. *The Kingfisher Book of Religions*. New York: Kingfisher, 1999. Print.

Ben Jelloun, Tahar. *Islam Explained*. Trans. Franklin Philip. New York: New, 2002. Print.

Esposito, John L. *Islam: the Straight Path*. New York: Oxford UP, 1988. Print.

Glady, Pearl. *Criticism of Islam*.Library, 2012. E-book.

Holland, Tom. "Where Mystery Meets History." *History Today* 62.5 (2012): 19–24. Print.

Langley, Myrtle. *Religion*. New York: Knopf, 1996. Print.

Lunde, Paul. *Islam: Faith, Culture, History*. London: DK, 2002. Print.

Nasr, Seyyed Hossein. *Islam: Religion, History, and Civilization*. New York: Harper, 2002. Print.

Pasha, Mustapha Kamal. "Islam and the Postsecular." *Review of International Studies* 38.5 (2012): 1041–56. Print.

Sayers, Destini and Simone Peebles. *Essence of Islam and Sufism*. College, 2012. E-book.

Schirmacher, Christine. "They Are Not All Martyrs: Islam on the Topics of Dying, Death, and Salvation in the Afterlife." *Evangelical Review of Theology* 36.3 (2012): 250–65. Print.

Wilkinson, Philip. *Islam*. New York: DK, 2002. Print.

Wilkinson, Philip. *Religions*. New York: DK, 2008. Print.

Jainism

General Description

Jainism is one of the major religions of India. The name of the religion itself is believed to be based on the Sanskrit word *ji*, which means "to conquer or triumph," or *jina*, which means "victor or conqueror." The earliest name of the group was Nirgrantha, meaning bondless, but it applied to monks and nuns only. There are two sects: the Svetambaras (the white clad), which are the more numerous and wear white clothing, and the Digambaras (the sky clad), the most stringent group; their holy men or monks do not wear clothing at all.

Number of Adherents Worldwide

Jainism has about five million adherents, most of them in India (in some estimates, the religion represents approximately 1 percent of India's population). Because the religion is demanding in nature, few beyond the Indian subcontinent have embraced it. Jainism has spread to Africa, the United States, and nations in the Commonwealth (nations once under British rule) by virtue of Indian migration to these countries.

Basic Tenets

The principle of nonviolence (ahimsa) is a defining feature of Jainism. This results in a pacifist religion that influenced Mohandas Gandhi's ideas on nonviolent resistance. Jains believe that because all living creatures have souls, harming any of those creatures is wrong. They therefore follow a strict vegetarian diet, and often wear masks so as to not inhale living organisms. The most important aspect of Jainism is perhaps the five abstinences: ahimsa, satya (truthfulness), asteya (refrain from stealing), brahmacarya (chaste living), and aparigraha (refrain from greed).

A religion without priests, Jainism emphasizes the importance of the adherents' actions. Like Buddhists and Hindus, Jainists believe in karma and reincarnation. Unlike the Buddhist and Hindu idea of karma, Jainists regard karma as tiny particles that cling to the soul as mud clings to shoes, gradually weighing down the soul. Good deeds wash away these particles. Jainists also believe in moksha, the possibility of being freed from the cycle of death and rebirth. Like many Indian religions, Jainism does not believe in an afterlife, but in a cycle of death and rebirth. Once freed from this cycle, the soul will remain in infinite bliss.

While Jains do not necessarily believe in and worship God or gods, they believe in divine beings. Those who have achieved moksha are often regarded by Jains in the same manner in which other religions regard deities. These include the twenty-four Tirthankaras (ford makers) or jinas (victors), those who have escaped the cycle of death and rebirth, and the Siddhas, the liberated souls without physical form. The idea of a judging, ruling, or creator God is not present in Jainism.

Jainists believe that happiness is not found in material possessions and seek to have few of them. They also stress the importance of environmentalism. Jainists follow the Three Jewels: Right Belief, Right Knowledge, and Right Conduct. To be completely achieved, these three must be practiced together. Jainists also agree to six daily obligations (avashyaka), which include confession, praising the twenty-four Tirthankaras (the spiritual leaders), and calm meditation.

Sacred Text

The words of Mahavira were passed down orally, but lost over a few centuries. During a famine in the mid-fourth century BCE, many monks died. The texts were finally written down, although the Jain sects do not agree as to whether they are Mahavira's actual words. There are forty-five sacred texts (Agamas), which make up the Agam Sutras, Jainism's canonical literature. They were probably written down no earlier than 300 BCE. Two of the primary texts are the Akaranga

Sutra, which outlines the rule of conduct for Jain monks, and the Kalpa Sutra, which contains biographies of the last two Tirthankara. The Digambaras, who believe that the Agamas were lost around 350 BCE, have two main texts and four compendia written between 100 and 800 CE by various scholars.

Major Figures

Jainism has no single founder. However, Mahavira (Great Hero) is one of the Tirthankaras or jinas (pathfinders). He is considered the most recent spiritual teacher in a line of twenty-four. Modern-day Jainism derives from Mahavira, and his words are the foundation of Jain scriptures. He was a contemporary of Siddhartha Gautama, who was revered as the Buddha. Both Mahavira and Rishabha (or Adinatha), the first of the twenty-four Tirthankaras, are attributed as the founder of Jainism, though each Tirthankara maintains founding attributes.

Major Holy Sites

The Jain temple at Ranakpur is located in the village of Rajasthan. Carved from amber stone with marble interiors, the temple was constructed in the fifteenth century CE. It is dedicated to the first Tirthankara. The temple has twenty-nine large halls and each of the temple's 1,444 columns has a unique design with carvings.

Sravanabegola in Karnataka state is the site of Gomateshwara, Lord Bahubali's fifty-seven-foot statue. It was constructed in 981 CE from a single chunk of gneiss. Bahubali is considered the son of the first Tirthankara. The Digambara sect believes him to have been the first human to be free from the world.

Other pilgrimage sites include the Palitana temples in Gujarat and the Dilwara temples in Rajasthan. Sometimes regarded as the most sacred of the many Jain temples, the Palitana temples include 863 marble-engraved temples. The Jain temples at Dilwara were constructed of marble during the eleventh and thirteenth centuries CE. These five temples are often considered the most beautiful Jain temples in existence.

Major Rites & Celebrations

Every twelve years, the festival of Mahamastakabhisheka (anointing of the head) occurs at a statue of one of Jain's holy men, Bahubali, the second son of the first Tirthankara. The statue is anointed with milk, curd, and ghee, a clarified butter. Nearly a million people attend this rite. Jainists also observe Diwali, the Hindu festival of lights, as it symbolizes Mahavira's enlightenment.

The solemn festival of Paryusana marks the end of the Jain year for the Svetambaras (also spelled Shvetambaras). During this eight-day festival, all Jains are asked to live as an ascetic (monk or nun) would for one day. Das Laxana, a ten-day festival similar to that of Paryusana, immediately follows for the Digambara sect. During these special religious holidays, worshippers are involved in praying, meditating, fasting, forgiveness, and acts of penance. These holy days are celebrated during August and September, which is monsoon season in India. During the monsoons, monks prefer to remain in one place so as to avoid killing the smallest insects that appear during the rainy season. The Kalpa Sutra, one of the Jain scriptures, is read in the morning during Paryusana.

The feast of Kartaki Purnima follows the four months of the rainy season. It is held in the first month (Kartik) according to one calendar, and marked by a pilgrimage to the Palitana temples. Doing so with a pure heart is said to remove all sins of both the present and past life. Those who do so are thought to receive the final salvation in the third or fifth birth.

ORIGINS

History & Geography

In the eastern basin of the Ganges River during the seventh century BCE, a teacher named Parshvanatha (or Parshva) gathered a community founded on abandoning earthly concerns. He is considered to be the twenty-third Tirthankara (ford-maker), the one who makes a path for salvation. During the following century, Vardhamana, called Mahavira (Great Hero), who was considered the twenty-fourth and final spiritual teacher of the age, formulated most Jain doctrine and practice. By the time of Mahavira's death, Jains numbered around 36,000 nuns and 14,000 monks.

A division occurred within Jainism during the fourth century CE. The most extreme ascetics, the Digambaras (the sky-clad), argued that even clothing showed too great an attachment to the world, and that laundering them in the river risked harming creatures. This argument applied only to men, as the Digambaras denied that a soul could be freed from a woman's body. The other group, the Svetambaras (the white-clad), believed that purity resided in the mind.

In 453 or 456 CE, a council of the Svetambara sect at Saurashtra in western India codified the canon still used. The split between the Digambaras, who did not take part in the meeting, and Svetambaras thus became permanent. Despite the split, Jainism's greatest flowering occurred during the early medieval age. After that time, Hindu sects devoted to the Hindu gods of Vishnu and Shiva flourished under the Gupta Empire (often referred to as India's golden age), slowing the spread of Jainism. Followers migrated to western and central India and the community became stronger.

The Digambaras were involved in politics through several medieval dynasties, and some Jain monks served as spiritual advisers. Royalty and high-ranking officials contributed to the building and maintenance of temples. Both branches of Jainism contributed a substantial literature. In the late medieval age, Jain monks ceased to live as ascetic wanders. They chose instead to don orange robes and to live at temples and other holy places.

The Muslims invaded India in the twelfth century. The Jains lost power and fractured over the next centuries into subgroups, some of which repudiated the worship of images. The poet and Digambara layman Banarsidas (1586-1643) played a significant role in a reform movement during the early 1600s. These reforms focused on the mystical side of Jainism, such as spiritual exploration of the inner self (meditation),

and denounced the formalized temple ritual. The movement, known as the Adhyatma movement, resulted in the Digambara Terapanth, a small Digambara sect.

The Jainists were well positioned in society following the departure of the British from India. Having long been associated with the artisan and merchant classes, they found new opportunities. As traditional Indian studies grew, spurred by Western interest, proponents of Jainism began to found publications and places of study (In fact, Jain libraries are believed to be the oldest in India.) The first Jain temple outside India was consecrated in Britain during the 1960s after Jains had gone there in the wake of political turmoil.

The Jains follow their typical profession as merchants. They publish English-language periodicals to spread their ideas on vegetarianism, environmentalism, and nonviolence (ahimsa). The ideas of ahimsa were formative for Mohandas Gandhi, born a Hindu. Gandhi used nonviolence as a wedge against the British Empire in India. Eventually, the British granted independence to India in 1947.

Virchand Gandhi (1864–1901) is believed to be the first Jain to arrive in America when he came over in 1893. He attended the first Parliament of World Religions, held in Chicago. Today North America has more than ninety Jain temples and centers. Jains in the West often follow professions such as banking and business to avoid destroying animal or plant life.

Founder or Major Prophet

Mahavira was born in India's Ganges Basin region. By tradition, he was born around 599 BCE, although some scholars think he may have lived a century later. His story bears a resemblance to that of the Buddha, with whom he was believed to have been a contemporary. His family was also of the Kshatriya (warrior) caste, and his father was a ruler of his clan. One tradition states that Mahavira's mother was of the Brahman (priestly) caste, although another places her in the Kshatriya.

Because he was not the eldest son, Mahavira was not in line for leadership of the clan.

He married a woman of his own caste and they had a daughter. Mahavira chose the life of a monk, with one garment. Later, he gave up wearing even that. He became a wandering ascetic around age thirty, with some legends stating that he tore out his hair before leaving home. He sought shelter in burial grounds and cremation sites, as well as at the base of trees. During the rainy season, however, he lived in towns and villages.

He followed a path of preaching and self-denial, after which he was enlightened (kevala). He spent the next thirty years teaching. Eleven disciples, all of whom were of the Brahman caste, gathered around him. At the end of his life, Mahavira committed Santhara, or ritual suicide through fasting.

Philosophical Basis

Like Buddhists and the Brahmin priests, the Jains believe in human incarnations of God, known as avatars. These avatars appear at the end of a time of decline to reinstate proper thinking and acting. Such a person was Mahavira. At the time of Mahavira's birth, India was experiencing great societal upheaval. Members of the warrior caste opposed the priestly caste, which exercised authority based on its supposed greater moral purity. Many people also opposed the slaughter of animals for the Vedic sacrifices.

Jainists share some beliefs with both Hinduism and Buddhism. The Hindu hero Rama, for example, is co-opted as a nonviolent Jain, while the deity Krishna is considered a cousin of Arishtanemi, the twenty-second Tirthankara. Like Buddhism, Jainism uses a wheel with twelve spokes; however, Jainism uses the wheel to explain time. The first half of the circle is the ascending stage, in which human happiness, prosperity, and life span increase. The latter half of the circle is the descending stage, involving a decrease of life span, prosperity, and happiness. The wheel of time is always in motion.

For Jainists, the universe is without beginning or ending, and contains layers of both heaven and hell. These layers include space beyond, which is without time, matter, or soul. The cosmos is depicted in art as a large human. The cloud layers surrounding the upper world are called universe space. Above them is the base, Nigoda, where lowest life forms live. The netherworld contains seven hells, each with a different stage of punishment and misery. The middle world contains the earth and remainder of the universe—mankind is located near the waist. There are thirty heavens in the upper world, where heavenly beings reside. In the supreme abode at the apex of the universe, liberated souls (siddha) live.

Jainism teaches that there are six universal entities. Only consciousness or soul is a living substance, while the remaining five are non-living. They include matter, medium of rest, medium of motion, time, and space. Jainism also does not believe in a God who can create, destroy, or protect. Worshipping goddesses and gods to achieve personal gain or material benefit is deemed useless.

Mahavira outlined five basic principles (often referred to as abstinences) for Jainist life, based on the teachings of the previous Tirthankara. They are detachment (aparigraha); the conduct of soul, primarily in sexual morality (brahmacharya); abstinence from stealing (asteya); abstinence from lying (satya); and nonviolence in every realm of the person (ahimsa).

Like other Indian religions, Jainism perceives life as four stages. The life of a student is brahmacharya-ashrama; the stage of family life is gruhasth-ashrama; in vanaprasth-ashrama, the Jainist concentrates on both family and aiding others through social services; and the final stage is sanyast-ashrama, a time of renouncing the world and becoming a monk.

Like many religions, Jainism has a bias toward males and toward the rigorous life of monks and nuns. A layperson cannot work off bad karma, but merely keeps new bad karma from accruing. By following a path of asceticism, however, monks and nuns can destroy karma. Even members of the laity follow eight rules of behavior and take twelve vows. Physical austerity is a key concept in Jainism, as a saint's highest ideal is to starve to death.

Holy Places

There are four major Jain pilgrimage sites: the Dilwara temples near Rajasthan; the Palitana temples; the Ranakpur temple; and Shravan Begola, the site of the statue of Lord Bahubali. In addition, Jains may make pilgrimages to the caves of Khandagiri and Udayagiri, which were cells for Jain monks carved from rock. The spaces carved are too short for a man to stand upright. They were essentially designed for prayer and meditation. Udayagiri has eighteen caves and Khandagiri has fifteen. The caves are decorated with elaborate carvings.

JAINISM IN DEPTH

Sacred Symbols

The open palm (Jain Hand) with a centered wheel, sometimes with the word *ahimsa* written on it, is a prominent Jain symbol. Seen as an icon of peace, the open palm symbol can be interpreted as a call to stop violence, and also means "assurance." It appears on the walls of Jain temples and in their publications. Jainism also employs a simple swastika symbol, considered to be the holiest symbol. It represents the four forms of worldly existence, and three dots above the swastika represent the Three Jewels. The Jain emblem, adopted in 1975, features both the Jain Hand (the open palm symbol with an inset wheel) and a swastika. This year was regarded as the 2,500th anniversary of Mahavira being enlightened.

Sacred Practices & Gestures

Jains may worship daily in their homes at private shrines. The Five Supreme Beings stand for stages in the path to enlightenment. Rising before daybreak, worshippers invoke these five. In addition, devout Jainists set aside forty-eight minutes daily to meditate.

To demonstrate faithfulness to the five vows that Jains undertake, there are four virtuous qualities that must be cultivated. They are compassion (karuna), respect and joy (pramoda), love and friendship (maitri), and indifference toward and noninvolvement with those who are arrogant (madhyastha). Mahavira stressed that Jains must be friends to all living beings. Compassion goes beyond mere feeling; it involves offering both material and spiritual aid. Pramoda carries with it the idea of rejoicing enthusiastically over the virtues of others. There are contemplations associated with these virtues, and daily practice is suggested to attain mastery.

Some Jainists, both men and women, wear a dot on the forehead. This practice comes from Hinduism. During festivals, Jains may pray, chant, fast, or keep silent. These actions are seen as removing bad karma from the soul and moving the person toward ultimate happiness.

Food Restrictions

Jainists practice a strict vegetarian way of life (called Jain vegetarianism) to avoid harming any creature. They refuse to eat root vegetables, because by uprooting them, the entire plant dies. They prefer to wait for fruit to drop from trees rather than taking it from the branches. Starving to death, when ready, is seen as an ideal.

Rites, Celebrations & Services

Some festivals are held annually and their observances are based on a lunar calendar. Mahavir Jayanti is an example, as it celebrates Mahavira's birthday.

Jains may worship, bathe, and make offerings to images of the Tirthankaras in their home or in a temple. Svetambaras Jains also clothe and decorate the images. Because the Tirthankaras have been liberated, they cannot respond as a deity granting favors might. Although Jainism rejects belief in gods in favor of worshipping Tirthankaras, in actual practice, some Jainists pray to Hindu gods.

When Svetambara monks are initiated, they are given three pieces of clothing, including a small piece of white cloth to place over the mouth. The cloth, called a mukhavastrika, is designed to prevent the monk from accidentally eating insects.

Monks take great vows (mahavratas) at initiation. These include abstaining from lying, stealing, sexual activity, injury to any living thing, and personal possessions. Monks own a broom to sweep in front of where they are going to walk so that no small creatures are injured, along with an alms bowl and a robe. The Digambara monks practice a more stringent lifestyle, eating one meal a day, for which they beg.

Nuns in the Svetambaras are three times more common than are monks, even though they receive less honor, and are required to defer to the monks. In Digambara Jainism, the nuns wear robes and accept that they must be reborn as men before progressing upward.

The observance of Santhara, which is religious fasting until death, is a voluntary fasting undertaken with full knowledge. The ritual is also known as Sallekhana, and is not perceived as suicide by Jains, particularly as the prolonged nature of the ritual provides ample time for reflection. It is believed that at least one hundred people die every year from observing Santhara.

Judy A. Johnson, MTS

Bibliography

Aristarkhova, Irina. "Thou Shall Not Harm All Living Beings: Feminism, Jainism, and Animals." *Hypatia* 27.3 (2012): 636–50. Print.

Aukland, Knut. "Understanding Possession in Jainism: A Study of Oracular Possession in Nakoda." *Modern Asian Studies* 47.1 (2013): 103–34. Print.

Barnes, Trevor. *The Kingfisher Book of Religions*. New York: Kingfisher, 1999. Print.

Langley, Myrtle. *Religion*. New York: Knopf, 1996. Print.

Long, Jeffery. *Jainism: An Introduction*. London: I. B. Tauris, 2009. Print.

Long, Jeffrey. "Jainism: Key Themes." *Religion Compass* 5.9 (2011): 501–10. Print.

Rankin, Aidan. *The Jain Path*. Berkeley: O Books, 2006. Print.

Shah, Bharat S. *An Introduction to Jainism*. Great Neck: Setubandh, 2002. Print.

Titze, Kurt. *Jainism: A Pictorial Guide to the Religion of Non-Violence*. Delhi: Motilal Banarsidass, 2001. Print.

Tobias, Michael. *Life Force: the World of Jainism*. Berkeley:Asian Humanities, 1991. E-book, print.

Wiley, Kristi L. *The A to Z of Jainism*. Lanham: Scarecrow, 2009. Print.

Wiley, Kristi L. *Historical Dictionary of Jainism*. Lanham: Scarecrow, 2004. Print.

Wilkinson, Philip. *Religions*. New York: DK, 2008. Print.

Judaism

General Description

In modern Judaism, the main denominations (referred to as movements) are Orthodox Judaism (including Haredi and Hasidic Judaism); Conservative Judaism; Reform (Liberal) Judaism; Reconstructionist Judaism; and to a lesser extent, Humanistic Judaism. In addition, the Jewry of Ethiopia and Yemen are known for having distinct or alternative traditions. Classical Judaism is often organized by two branches: Ashkenazic (Northern Europe) and Sephardic Jews (Spain, Portugal, and North Africa).

Number of Adherents Worldwide

Judaism has an estimated 15 million adherents worldwide, with roughly 41 percent living in Israel and about 41 percent living in the United States. Ashkenazi Jews represent roughly 75 percent, while Sephardic Jews represent roughly 25 percent, with the remaining 5 percent split among alternative communities. Within the United States, a 2000-01 survey stated that 10 percent of American Jews identified as Orthodox (with that number increasing), 35 percent as Reform, 26 percent as Conservative, leaving the remainder with an alternative or no affiliation. [Source: Wilkinson, 2008]

Orthodox Judaism, which was founded around the thirteenth century BCE, has 3 million followers. Members of Reform Judaism, with roots in nineteenth-century Germany, wanted to live peacefully with non-Jews. Therefore, they left the laws that prevented this vision of peace and downplayed the idea of a Jewish state. Reform Judaism, also known as Progressive or Liberal Judaism, allows women rabbis and does not require its adherents to keep kosher. About 1.1 million Jews are Reform; they live primarily in the United States. When nonkosher food was served at the first graduation ceremony for Hebrew Union College, some felt that the Reform movement had gone too far. Thus the Conservative movement began in 1887. A group of rabbis founded the Jewish Theological Seminary in New York City, wanting to emphasize biblical authority above moral choice, as the Reform tradition stressed. Currently about 900,000 Jews practice this type of Judaism, which is theologically midway between Orthodox and Reform. The Hasidim, an ultra-conservative group, began in present-day Ukraine around 1740. There are 4.5 million Hasidic Jews.

Basic Tenets

Though there is no formal creed (statement of faith or belief), Jews value all life, social justice, education, generous giving, and the importance of living based on the principles and values espoused in the Torah (Jewish holy book). They believe in one all-powerful and creator God, Jehovah or Yaweh, a word derived from the Hebrew letters "YHWH," the unpronounceable name of God. The word is held to be sacred; copyists were required to bathe both before and after writing the word. Jews also believe in a coming Messiah who will initiate a Kingdom of Righteousness. They follow a complex law, composed of 613 commandments or mitzvot. Jews believe that they are God's Chosen People with a unique covenant relationship. They have a responsibility to practice hospitality and to improve the world.

The belief in the afterlife is a part of the Jewish faith. Similar to Christianity, this spiritual world is granted to those who abide by the Jewish faith and live a good life. Righteous Jews are rewarded in the afterlife by being able to discuss the Torah with Moses, who first received the law from God. Furthermore, certain Orthodox sects believe that wicked souls are destroyed or tormented after death.

Sacred Text

The complete Hebrew Bible is called the Tanakh. It includes the prophetic texts, called the Navi'im, the poetic writings, the Ketubim, and the Torah, meaning teaching, law, or guidance. Torah may refer to the entire body of Jewish law or to the first five books of the Hebrew Bible, known as the Pentateuch (it is the Old Testament in the Christian Bible). Also esteemed is the Talmud, made up of the Mishnah, a written collection of oral traditions, and Gemara, a commentary on the Mishnah. The Talmud covers many different subjects, such as law, stories and legends, medicine, and rituals.

Major Figures

The patriarchs are held to be the fathers of the faith. Abraham, the first patriarch, was called to leave his home in the Fertile Crescent for a land God would give him, and promised descendents as numerous as the stars. His son Isaac was followed by Jacob, whom God renamed Israel, and whose twelve sons became the heads of the twelve tribes of Israel. Moses was the man who, along with his brother Aaron, the founder of a priestly line, and their sister Miriam led the chosen people out of slavery in Egypt, where they had gone to escape famine. The Hebrew Bible also details the careers of a group of men and women known as judges, who were really tribal rulers, as well as of the prophets, who called the people to holy lives. Chief among the prophets was Elijah, who confronted wicked kings and performed many miracles. Several kings were key to the biblical narrative, among them David, who killed the giant Goliath, and Solomon, known for his wisdom and for the construction of a beautiful temple.

Major Holy Sites

Most of Judaism's holy sites are within Israel, the Holy Land, including Jerusalem, which was the capital of the United Kingdom of Israel under kings David and Solomon; David captured it from a Canaanite tribe around 1000 BCE. Within the Old City of Jerusalem is the Temple Mount (where the Temple of Jerusalem was built), often considered the religion's holiest site, the Foundation Stone (from which Judaism claims the world was created), and the Western (or Wailing) Wall. Other sites include Mount Sinai

in Egypt, the mountain upon which God gave Moses his laws.

Major Rites & Celebrations

The Jewish calendar recognizes several important holidays. Rosh Hashanah, literally "first of the year," is known as the Jewish New Year and inaugurates a season of self-examination and repentance that culminates in Yom Kippur, the Day of Atonement. Each spring, Passover commemorates the deliverance of the Hebrew people from Egypt. Shavuot celebrates the giving of the Torah to Moses, while Sukkot is the harvest festival. Festivals celebrating deliverance from enemies include Purim and Hanukkah. Young adolescents become members of the community at a bar or bat mitzvah, held near the twelfth or thirteenth birthday. The Sabbath, a cessation from work from Friday at sundown until Saturday when the first star appears, gives each week a rhythm.

ORIGINS

History & Geography

Called by God perhaps four thousand years ago, Abraham left from Ur of the Chaldees, or the Fertile Crescent in Mesopotamia in present-day Iraq, to go the eastern Mediterranean, the land of Canaan. Several generations later, the tribe went to Egypt to escape famine. They were later enslaved by a pharaoh, sometimes believed to have been Ramses II (ca. 1279–1213 BCE), who was noted for his many building projects. The Israelites returned to Canaan under Moses several hundred years after their arrival in Egypt. He was given the law, the Ten Commandments, plus the rest of the laws governing all aspects of life, on Mount Sinai about the thirteenth century BCE. This marked the beginning of a special covenant relationship between the new nation, known as Israel, and God.

Following a period of rule by judges, kings governed the nation. Major kings included David, son-in-law to the first king, Saul, and David's son, Solomon. The kingdom split at the beginning of the reign of Solomon's son

Rehoboam, who began ruling about 930 BCE. Rehoboam retained the ten northern tribes, while the two southern tribes followed a military commander rather than the Davidic line.

Rehoboam's kingdom was known as Israel, after the name Jehovah gave to Jacob. Judah was the name of the southern kingdom—one of Jacob's sons was named Judah. Prophets to both nations warned of coming judgment unless the people repented of mistreating the poor and other sins, such as idolatry. Unheeding, Israel was taken into captivity by the Assyrians in 722 BCE. and the Israelites assimilated into the nations around them.

The Babylonians captured Judah in 586 BCE. After Babylon had been captured in turn by Persians, the Jewish people were allowed to return to the land in 538 BCE. There they began reconstructing the temple and the walls of the city. In the second century BCE, Judas Maccabeus led a rebellion against the heavy taxes and oppression of the Greek conquerors, after they had levied high taxes and appointed priests who were not Jewish. Judas Maccabeus founded a new ruling dynasty, the Hasmoneans, which existed briefly before the region came under the control of Rome.

The Jewish people revolted against Roman rule in 70 CE, leading to the destruction of the second temple. The final destruction of Jerusalem occurred in 135 under the Roman Emperor Hadrian. He changed the city's name to Aelia Capitolina and the name of the country to Palaestina. With the cultic center of their religion gone, the religious leaders developed new methods of worship that centered in religious academies and in synagogues.

After Christianity became the official state religion of the Roman Empire in the early fourth century, Jews experienced persecution. They became known for their scholarship, trade, and banking over the next centuries, with periods of brutal persecution in Europe. Christians held Jews responsible for the death of Jesus, based on a passage in the New Testament. The Blood Libel, begun in England in 1144, falsely accused Jews of killing a Christian child to bake unleavened bread for Passover. This rumor persisted for centuries, and was repeated by Martin Luther during the Protestant Reformation. England expelled all Jews in 1290; they were not readmitted until 1656 under Oliver Cromwell, and not given citizenship until 1829. Jews were also held responsible for other catastrophes—namely poisoning wells and rivers to cause the Black Death in 1348—and were often made to wear special clothing, such as pointed hats, or badges with the Star of David or stone tablets on them.

The relationship between Muslims and Jews was more harmonious. During the Muslim Arab dominance, there was a "golden age" in Spain due to the contributions of Jews and Muslims, known as Moors in Spain. This ideal and harmonious period ended in 1492, when both Moors and Jews were expelled from Spain or forced to convert to Christianity.

Jews in Russia suffered as well. An estimated two million Jews fled the country to escape the pogroms (a Russian word meaning devastation) between 1881 and 1917. The twentieth-century Holocaust, in which an estimated six million Jews perished at the hands of Nazi Germany, was but the culmination of these centuries of persecution. The Nazis also destroyed more than six hundred synagogues.

The Holocaust gave impetus to the creation of the independent state of Israel. The Zionist movement, which called for the founding or reestablishment of a Jewish homeland, was started by Austrian Jew Theodor Herzl in the late nineteenth century, and succeeded in 1948. The British government, which had ruled the region under a mandate, left the area, and Israel was thus established. This ended the Diaspora, or dispersion, of the Jewish people that had begun nearly two millennia before when the Romans forced the Jews to leave their homeland.

Arab neighbors, some of whom had been removed forcibly from the land to create the nation of Israel, were displeased with the new political reality. Several wars have been fought, including the War of Independence in 1948, the Six-Day War in 1967, and the Yom Kippur War in 1973. In addition, tension between Israel and its neighboring Arab states is almost constant.

When the Jewish people were dispersed from Israel, two traditions began. The Ashkenazi Jews settled in Germany and central Europe. They spoke a mixture of the Hebrew dialect and German called Yiddish. Sephardic Jews lived in the Mediterranean countries, including Spain; their language, Ladino, mixed Hebrew and old Spanish.

Founder or Major Prophet

Judaism refers to three major patriarchs: Abraham, his son Isaac, and Isaac's son Jacob. Abraham is considered the first Jew and worshipper in Judaism, as the religion began through his covenant with God. As the forefather of the religion, he is often associated as the founder, though the founder technically is God, or Yahweh (YHWH). Additionally, the twelve sons of Jacob, who was also named Israel, became the founders of the twelve tribes of Israel.

Moses is regarded as a major prophet and as the Lawgiver. God revealed to Moses the complete law during the forty days that the Jewish leader spent on Mount Sinai during the wilderness journey from Egypt to Canaan. Thus, many attribute Moses as the founder of Judaism as a religion.

Philosophical Basis

Judaism began with Abraham's dissatisfaction with the polytheistic worship of his culture. Hearing the command of God to go to a land that would be shown to him, Abraham and his household obeyed. Abraham practiced circumcision and hospitality, cornerstones of the Jewish faith to this day. He and his descendents practiced a nomadic life, much like that of contemporary Bedouins. They migrated from one oasis or well to another, seeking pasture and water for the sheep and goats they herded.

The further development of Judaism came under the leadership of Moses. A Jewish child adopted by Pharaoh's daughter, he was raised and educated in the palace. As a man, he identified with the Jewish people, killing one of the Egyptians who was oppressing a Jew. He subsequently fled for his life, becoming a shepherd in the wilderness, where he remained for forty years. Called by God from a bush that burned but was not destroyed, he was commissioned to lead the people out of slavery in Egypt back to the Promised Land. That forty-year pilgrimage in the wilderness and desert of Arabia shaped the new nation.

Holy Places

The city of Jerusalem was first known as Salem. When King David overcame the Jebusites who lived there, the city, already some two thousand years old, became the capital of Israel. It is built on Mount Zion, which is still considered a sacred place. David's son Solomon built the First Temple in Jerusalem, centering the nation's spiritual as well as political life in the city. The Babylonians captured the city in 597 BCE and destroyed the Temple. For the next sixty years, the Jews remained in exile, until Cyrus the Persian conqueror of Babylon allowed them to return. They rebuilt the temple, but it was desecrated by Antiochus IV of Syria in 167 BCE. In 18 BCE, during a period of Roman occupation, Herod the Great began rebuilding and expanding the Temple. The Romans under the general Titus destroyed the Temple in 70 CE, just seven years after its completion.

The city eventually came under the rule of Persia, the Muslim Empire, and the Crusaders before coming under control of Britain. In 1948 an independent state of Israel was created. The following year, Jerusalem was divided between Israel, which made the western part the national capital, and Jordan, which ruled the eastern part of the city. The Western or Wailing Wall, a retaining wall built during Herod's time, is all that remains of the Second Temple. Devout Jews still come to the Wailing Wall to pray, sometimes placing their petitions on paper and folding the paper into the Wall's crevices. The Wall is known as a place where prayers are answered and a reminder of the perseverance of the Jewish people and faith. According to tradition, the Temple will be rebuilt when Messiah comes to inaugurate God's Kingdom.

The Temple Mount, located just outside Jerusalem on a natural acropolis, includes the Dome of the Rock. This shrine houses a rock held sacred by both Judaism and Islam. Jewish tradition states that it is the spot from which the world was created and the spot on which Abraham was asked to sacrifice his son Isaac. Muslims believe that from this rock Muhammad ascended for his night journey to heaven. Much of Jerusalem, including this holy site, has been and continues to be fought over by people of three faiths: Judaism, Islam, and Christianity.

Moses received the law from God on Mount Sinai. It is still regarded as a holy place.

JUDAISM IN DEPTH

Sacred Symbols

Observant Jewish men pray three times daily at home or in a synagogue, a center of worship, from the word meaning "meeting place." They wear a tallis, or a prayer shawl with tassles, during their morning prayer and on Yom Kippur, the Day of Atonement. They may also cover their heads as a sign of respect during prayer, wearing a skullcap known as a kippah or yarmulka. They find their prayers and blessings in a siddur, which literally means "order," because the prayers appear in the order in which they are recited for services. Jewish daily life also includes blessings for many things, including food.

Tefillin or phylacteries are the small black boxes made of leather from kosher animals that Jewish men wear on their foreheads and their left upper arms during prayer. They contain passages from the Torah. Placing the tefillin on the head reminds them to think about the Torah, while placing the box on the arm puts the Torah close to the heart.

The Law of Moses commands the people to remember the words of the law and to teach them to the children. A mezuzah helps to fulfill that command. A small box with some of the words of the law written on a scroll inside, a mezuzah is hung on the doorframes of every door in the house. Most often, the words of the Shema,

the Jewish recitation of faith, are written on the scroll. The Shema is repeated daily. "Hear, O Israel: the Lord your God, the Lord is one. . . . Love the Lord your God with all your heart, and with all your soul, and with all your might."

Jews adopted the Star of David, composed of two intersecting triangles, during the eighteenth century. There are several interpretations of the design. One is that it is the shape of King David's shield. Another idea is that it stands for daleth, the first letter of David's name. A third interpretation is that the six points refer to the days of the work week, and the inner, larger space represented the day of rest, the Sabbath, or Shabot. The Star of David appears on the flag of Israel. The flag itself is white, symbolizing peace and purity, and blue, symbolizing heaven and reminding all of God's activity.

The menorah is a seven-branch candlestick representing the light of the Torah. For Hanukkah, however, an eight-branched menorah is used. The extra candle is the servant candle, and is the one from which all others are lit.

Because the Torah is the crowning glory of life for Jewish people, a crown is sometimes used on coverings for the Torah. The scrolls of Torah are stored in a container, called an ark, which generally is covered with an ornate cloth called a mantle. The ark and mantle are often elaborately decorated with symbols, such as the lion of Judah. Because the Torah scroll, made of parchment from a kosher animal, is sacred and its pages are not to be touched, readers use a pointed stick called a yad. Even today, Torahs are written by hand in specially prepared ink and using a quill from a kosher bird. Scribes are trained for seven years.

A shofar is a ram's horn, blown as a call to repentance on Rosh Hashanah, the Jewish New Year. This holiday is the beginning of a ten-day preparation for the Day of Atonement, which is the most holy day in the Jewish calendar and a time of both fasting and repentance.

Sacred Practices & Gestures

Sacred practices can apply daily, weekly, annually, or over a lifetime's events. Reciting the Shema, the monotheistic creed taken from the

Torah, is a daily event. Keeping the Sabbath occurs weekly. Each year the festivals described above take place. Circumcision and bar or bat mitzvah are once-in-a-lifetime events. Each time someone dies, the mourners recite the Kaddish for seven days following death, and grieve for a year.

Food Restrictions

Kosher foods are those that can be eaten based on Jewish law. Animals that chew the cud and have cloven hooves, such as cows and lamb, and domestic poultry are considered kosher. Shellfish, pork, and birds of prey are forbidden. Keeping kosher also includes the method of preparing and storing the food. This includes animals which are slaughtered in a way to bring the least amount of pain and from which all blood is drained. In addition, dairy and meat products are to be kept separate, requiring separate refrigerators in the homes of the Orthodox.

Rites, Celebrations & Services

Sabbath is the weekly celebration honoring one of the Ten Commandments, which commands the people to honor the Sabbath by doing no work that day. The practice is rooted in the Genesis account that God rested on the seventh day after creating the world in six days. Because the Jewish day begins at sundown, the Sabbath lasts from Friday night to Saturday night. Special candles are lit and special food—included the braided egg bread called challah—for the evening meal is served. This day is filled with feasting, visiting, and worship.

Boys are circumcised at eight days of age. This rite, B'rit Milah, meaning "seal of the covenant," was first given to Abraham as a sign of the covenant. A trained circumciser, or mohel, may be a doctor or rabbi. The boy's name is officially announced at the ceremony. A girl's name is given at a special baby-naming ceremony or in the synagogue on the first Sabbath after she is born.

A boy becomes a "son of the commandment," or bar mitzvah, at age thirteen. At a special ceremony, the young man reads a portion of

Torah that he has prepared ahead of time. Most boys also give a speech at the service. Girls become bat mitzvah at age twelve. This ceremony developed in the twentieth century. Not all Orthodox communities will allow this rite. Girls may also read from the Torah and give a sermon in the synagogue, just as boys do.

When a Jewish person dies, mourners begin shiva, a seven-day mourning period. People usually gather at the home of the deceased, where mirrors are covered. In the home, the Kaddish, a collection of prayers that praise God and celebrate life, is recited. Traditionally, family members mourn for a full year, avoiding parties and festive occasions.

The Jewish calendar offers a series of feasts and festivals, beginning with Rosh Hashanah, the Jewish New Year. At this time, Jews recall the creation. They may also eat apples that have been dipped into honey and offer each other wishes for a sweet New Year. The next ten days are a time of reflection on the past year, preparing for Yom Kippur.

This Day of Atonement once included animal sacrifice at the Temple. Now it includes an all-day service at the synagogue and a twenty-five-hour fast. A ram's horn, called a shofar, is blown as a call to awaken to lead a holier life. The shofar reminds Jewish people of the ram that Abraham sacrificed in the place of his son, Isaac.

Passover, or Pesach, is the spring remembrance of God's deliverance of the people from slavery in Egypt. In the night that the Jewish people left Egypt, they were commanded to sacrifice a lamb for each household and sprinkle the blood on the lintels and doorposts. A destroying angel from God would "pass over" the homes with blood sprinkled. During the first two nights of Passover, a special meal is served known as a Seder, meaning order. The foods symbolize different aspects of the story of deliverance, which is told during the meal by the head of the family.

Shavuot has its origins as a harvest festival. This celebration of Moses receiving the Torah on Mount Sinai occurs fifty days after the second day of Passover. To welcome the first fruits of the season, the synagogue may be decorated with fruit and flowers. Traditionally, the Ten Commandments are read aloud in the synagogue.

Purim, which occurs in February or March, celebrates the deliverance of the Jews during their captivity in Persia in the fifth century BCE. The events of that experience are recorded in the Book of Esther in the Hebrew Bible (Tanakh). The book is read aloud during Purim.

Sukkot, the feast celebrating the end of the harvest, occurs in September or October. Jews recall God's provision for them in the wilderness when they left Egypt to return to Canaan. Traditionally, huts are made and decorated with flowers and fruits. The conclusion of Sukkot is marked by a synagogue service known as Simchat Torah, or Rejoicing in the Law. People sing and dance as the Torah scrolls are carried and passed from person to person.

Hanukkah, known as the Festival of Lights, takes place over eight days in December. It celebrates the rededicating of the Temple under the leader Judas Maccabeus, who led the people in recapturing the structure from Syria in 164 BCE. According to the story, the Jews had only enough oil in the Temple lamp to last one day, but the oil miraculously lasted for eight days, after which Judas Maccabeus re-dedicated the Temple. On each day of Hanukkah, one of the eight candles is lit until all are burning. The gift-giving custom associated with Hanukkah is relatively new, and may derive from traditional small gifts of candy or money. The practice may also have been encouraged among those integrated with communities that exchange gifts during the Christmas season.

Judy A. Johnson, MTS

Bibliography

Barnes, Trevor. *The Kingfisher Book of Religions*. New York: Kingfisher, 1999. Print.

"A Buffet to Suit All Tastes." *Economist* 28 Jul. 2012: Spec. section 4–6. Print.

Charing, Douglas. *Judaism*. London: DK, 2003. Print.

Coenen Snyder, Saskia. *Building a Public Judaism: Synagogues and Jewish Identity in Nineteenth-Century Europe*. Cambridge: Harvard UP, 2013. E-book.

Diamant, Anita. *Living a Jewish Life*. New York: Collins, 1996. Print.

Exler, Lisa and Rabbi Jill Jacobs. "A Judaism That Matters." *Journal of Jewish Communal Service* 87.1/2 (2012): 66–76. Print.

Gelernter, David Hillel. *Judaism: A Way of Being*. New Haven: Yale UP, 2009. E-book.

Kessler, Edward. *What Do Jews Believe?* New York: Walker, 2007. Print.

Krieger, Aliza Y. "The Role of Judaism in Family Relationships." *Journal of Multicultural Counseling & Development* 38.3 (2010): 154–65. Print.

Langley, Myrtle. *Religion*. New York: Knopf, 1996. Print.

Madsen, Catherine. "A Heart of Flesh: Beyond 'Creative Liturgy.'" *Cross Currents* 62.1 (2012): 11–20. Print.

Meredith, Susan. *The Usborne Book of World Religions*. London: Usborne, 1995. Print.

Schoen, Robert. *What I Wish My Christian Friends Knew About Judaism*. Chicago: Loyola, 2004. Print.

Stefnon, Matt. *Judaism: History, Belief, and Practice*. New York: Britannica Educational, 2012. E-book.

Wertheimer, Jack. "The Perplexities of Conservative Judaism." *Commentary* Sept. 2007: 38–44. Print.

Wilkinson, Philip. *Religions*. New York: DK, 2008. Print.

Sikhism

General Description

The youngest of the world religions, Sikhism has existed for only about five hundred years. Sikhism derives from the Sanskrit word *sishyas*, which means "disciple"; in the Punjabi language, it also means "disciple."

Number of Adherents Worldwide

An estimated 24.5 million people follow the Sikh religion. Most of the devotees live in Asia, particularly in the Punjab region of India (Wilkinson, p. 335).

Basic Tenets

Sikhism is a monotheistic religion. The deity is God, known as Nam, or Name. Other synonyms include the Divine, Ultimate, Ultimate Reality, Infinity, the Formless, Truth, and other attributes of God.

Sikhs adhere to three basic principles. These are hard work (kirt kao), worshipping the Divine Name (nam japo), and sharing what one has (vand cauko). Meditating on the Divine Name is seen as a method of moving toward a life totally devoted to God. In addition, Sikhs believe in karma, or moral cause and effect. They value hospitality to all, regardless of religion, and oppose caste distinctions. Sikhs delineate a series of five stages that move upward to gurmukh, total devotion to God. This service is called Seva. Sahaj, or tranquility, is practiced as a means of being united with God as well as of generating external good will. Sikhs are not in favor of external routines of religion; they may stop in their temple whenever it is convenient during the day.

Sikhism does not include a belief in the afterlife. Instead, the soul is believed to be reincarnated in successive lives and deaths, a belief borrowed from Hinduism. The goal is then to break this karmic cycle, and to merge the human spirit with that of God.

Sacred Text

The Guru Granth Sahib (also referred to as the Aad Guru Granth Sahib, or AGGS), composed of Adi Granth, meaning First Book, is the holy scripture of Sikhism. It is a collection of religious poetry that is meant to be sung. Called shabads, they were composed by the first five gurus, the ninth guru, and thirty-six additional holy men of northern India. Sikhs always show honor to the Guru Granth Sahib by carrying it above the head when in a procession.

A second major text is the Dasam Granth, or Tenth Book, created by followers of Guru Gobind Singh, the tenth guru. Much of it is devoted to retelling the Hindu stories of Krishna and Rama. Those who are allowed to read and care for the Granth Sahib are known as granthi. Granthi may also look after the gurdwara, or temple. In the gurdwara, the book rests on a throne with a wooden base and cushions covered in cloths placed in a prescribed order. If the book is not in use, it is covered with a cloth known as a rumala. When the book is read, a fan called a chauri is fanned over it as a sign of respect, just as followers of the gurus fanned them with chauris. At Amritsar, a city in northwestern India that houses the Golden Temple, the Guru Granth Sahib is carried on a palanquin (a covered, carried bed). If it is carried in the city, a kettle drum is struck and people welcome it by tossing rose petals.

Major Figures

Guru Nanak (1469–1539) is the founder of Sikhism. He was followed by nine other teachers, and collectively they are known as the Ten Gurus. Each of them was chosen by his predecessor and was thought to share the same spirit of that previous guru. Guru Arjan (1581–1606), the fifth guru, oversaw completion of the Golden Temple in Amritsar, India. Guru Gobind Singh (1675–1708) was the tenth and last human guru. He decreed that the True Guru henceforth would be the Granth Sahib, the scripture of the Sikhs. He also founded the Khalsa, originally a military order of male Sikhs willing to die for the faith; the term is now used to refer to all baptized Sikhs.

Major Holy Sites

Amritsar, India, is the holy city of Sikhism. Construction of the city began under Guru Ram Das (1574–1581), the fourth guru, during the 1570s. One legend says that the Muslim ruler, Emperor Akbar, gave the land to the third guru, Guru Amar Das (1552–74). Whether or not that is true, Amar Das did establish the location of Amritsar. He chose a site near a pool believed to hold healing water.

When construction of the Golden Temple began, only a small town existed. One legend says that a Muslim saint from Lahore, India, named Mian Mir laid the foundation stone of the first temple. It has been demolished and rebuilt three times. Although pilgrimage is not required of Sikhs, many come to see the shrines and the Golden Temple. They call it Harmandir Sahib, God's Temple, or Darbar Sahib, the Lord's Court. When the temple was completed during the tenure of the fifth guru, Arjan, he placed the first copy of the Guru Granth Sahib inside.

Every Sikh temple has a free kitchen attached to it, called a langar. After services, all people, regardless of caste or standing within the community, sit on the floor in a straight line and eat a simple vegetarian meal together. As a pilgrimage site, the langar serves 30,000–40,000 people daily, with more coming on Sundays and festival days. About forty volunteers work in the kitchen each day.

Major Rites & Celebrations

In addition to the community feasts at temple langars, Sikhs honor four rites of passage in a person's life: naming, marriage, initiation in Khalsa (pure) through the Amrit ceremony, and death.

There are eight major celebrations and several other minor ones in Sikhism. Half of them commemorate events in the lives of the ten gurus.

The others are Baisakhi, the new year festival; Diwali, the festival of light, which Hindus also celebrate; Hola Mahalla, which Gobind Singh created as an alternative to the Hindu festival of Holi, and which involves military parades; and the installing of the Guru Granth Sahib.

ORIGINS

History & Geography

The founder of Sikhism, Nanak, was born in 1469 CE in the Punjab region of northeast India, where both Hinduism and Islam were practiced. Both of these religions wanted control of the region. Nanak wanted the fighting between followers of these two traditions to end and looked for solutions to the violence.

Nanak blended elements of both religions and also combined the traditional apparel of both faiths to construct his clothing style. The Guru Granth Sahib further explains the division between Sikhs and the Islamic and Muslim faiths:

Nanak would become the first guru of the Sikh religion, known as Guru Nanak Dev. A Muslim musician named Bhai Mardana, considered the first follower, accompanied Nanak in his travels around India and Asia. Guru Nanak often sang, and singing remains an important part of worship for Sikhs. Before his death, Nanak renamed one of his disciples Angad, a word meaning "a part of his own self." He became Guru Angad Dev, the second guru, thus beginning the tradition of designating a successor and passing on the light to that person.

Guru Baba Ram Das, the fourth guru, who lived in the sixteenth century, began constructing Amritsar's Golden Temple. The structure was completed by his successor, Guru Arjan Dev, who also collected poems and songs written by the first four gurus and added his own. He included the work of Kabir and other Hindu and Muslim holy men as well. This became the Adi Granth, which he placed in the Golden Temple.

Guru Arjan was martyred in 1606 by Jehangir, the Muslim emperor. His son Hargobind became the sixth guru and introduced several important practices and changes. He wore two swords, representing both spiritual and worldly authority. Near the Golden Temple he had a building known as Akal Takht, or Throne of the Almighty, erected. In it was a court of justice as well as a group of administrators. Even today, orders and decisions enter the community from Akal Takht. Guru Hargobind was the last of the gurus with a direct link to Amritsar. Because of conflict with the Muslim rulers, he and all subsequent gurus moved from the city.

The tenth guru, Gobind Singh, created the Khalsa, the Community of the Pure, in 1699. The members of the Khalsa were to be known by five distinctive elements, all beginning with the letter *k*. These include kes, the refusal to cut the hair or trim the beard; kangha, the comb used to keep the long hair neatly combed in contrast to the Hindu ascetics who had matted hair; kaccha, shorts that would allow soldiers quick movement; kara, a thin steel bracelet worn to symbolize restraint; and kirpan, a short sword not to be used except in self-defense. Among other duties, members of this elite group were to defend the faith. Until the middle of the nineteenth century, when the British created an empire in India, the Khalsa remained largely undefeated.

In 1708, Guru Gobind Singh announced that he would be the final human guru. All subsequent leadership would come from the Guru Granth Sahib, now considered a living guru, the holy text Arjan had begun compiling more than a century earlier.

Muslim persecution under the Mughals led to the defeat of the Sikhs in 1716. The remaining Sikhs headed for the hills, re-emerging after decline of Mughal power. They were united under Ranjit Singh's kingdom from 1820 to 1839. They then came under the control of the British.

The British annexed the Punjab region, making it part of their Indian empire in 1849, and recruited Sikhs to serve in the army. The Sikhs remained loyal to the British during the Indian Mutiny of 1857–1858. As a result, they were given many privileges and land grants, and with

peace and prosperity, the first Singh Sabha was founded in 1873. This was an educational and religious reform movement.

During the early twentieth century, Sikhism was shaped in its more modern form. A group known as the Tat Khalsa, which was more progressive, became the dominant way of understanding the faith.

In 1897, a group of Sikh musicians within the British Army was invited to attend the Diamond Jubilee of Queen Victoria in England. They also traveled to Canada and were attracted by the nation's prairies, which were perfect for farming. The first group of Sikhs came to Canada soon after. By 1904, more than two hundred Sikhs had settled in British Columbia. Some of them later headed south to Washington, Oregon, and California in the United States. The first Sikh gurdwara in the United States was constructed in Stockton, California, in 1912. Sikhs became farmers, worked in lumber mills, and helped to construct the Western Pacific railroad. Yuba City, California, has one of the world's largest Sikh temples, built in 1968.

Sikh troops fought for Britain in World War I, achieving distinction. Following the war, in 1919, however, the British denied the Sikhs the right to gather for their New Year festival. When the Sikhs disobeyed, the British troops fired without warning on 10,000 Sikhs, 400 of whom were killed. This became known as the first Amritsar Massacre.

The British government in 1925 did give the Sikhs the right to help manage their own shrines. A fragile peace ensued between the British and the Sikhs, who again fought for the British Empire during World War II.

After the war ended, the Sikh hope for an independent state was dashed by the partition of India and Pakistan in 1947. Pakistan was in the Punjab region; thus, 2.5 million Sikhs lived in a Muslim country where they were not welcome. Many of them became part of the mass internal migration that followed Indian independence.

In 1966, a state with a Sikh majority came into existence after Punjab boundaries were redrawn. Strife continued throughout second half of twentieth century, however, as a result of continuing demands for Punjab autonomy. A second massacre at Amritsar occurred in 1984, resulting in the death of 450 Sikhs (though some estimates of the death toll are higher). Indian troops, under orders from Indian Prime Minister Indira Gandhi, fired on militant leaders of Sikhs, who had gone to the Golden Temple for refuge. This attack was considered a desecration of a sacred place, and the prime minister was later assassinated by her Sikh bodyguards in response. Restoration of the Akal Takht, the administrative headquarters, took fifteen years. The Sikh library was also burned, consuming ancient manuscripts.

In 1999, Sikhs celebrated the three-hundredth anniversary of the founding of Khalsa. There has been relative peace in India since that event. In the United States, however, Sikhs became the object of slander and physical attack following the acts of terrorism on September 11, 2001, as some Americans could not differentiate between Arab head coverings and Sikh turbans.

Founder or Major Prophet

Guru Nanak Dev was born into a Hindu family on April 15, 1469. His family belonged to the merchant caste, Khatri. His father worked as an accountant for a Muslim, who was also a local landlord. Nanak was educated in both the Hindu and Islamic traditions. According to legends, his teachers soon realized they had nothing further to teach him. After a direct revelation from Ultimate Reality that he received as a young man, Nanak proclaimed that there was neither Muslim nor Hindu. God had told Nanak "Rejoice in my Name," which became a central doctrine of Sikhism.

Nanak began to preach, leaving his wife and two sons behind. According to tradition, he traveled not only throughout India, but also eventually to Iraq, Saudi Arabia, and Mecca. This tradition and others were collected in a volume known as Janamsakhis. A Muslim servant of the family, Mardana, who also played a three-stringed musical instrument called the rebec, accompanied him, as did a Hindu poet, Bala Sandhu, who had been a friend from childhood

(though the extent of his importance or existence is often considered controversial).

Nanak traveled as an itinerant preacher for a quarter century and then founded a village, Kartarpur, on the bank of Punjab's Ravi River. Before his death he chose his successor, beginning a tradition that was followed until the tenth and final human guru.

Philosophical Basis

When Guru Nanak Dev, the first guru, began preaching in 1499 at about age thirty, he incorporated aspects of both Hinduism and Islam. From Hinduism, he took the ideas of karma and reincarnation. From Islam, he borrowed the Ultimate as the name of God. Some scholars see the influence of the religious reformer and poet Kabir, who lived from 1440 until 1518. Kabir merged the Bhakti (devotional) side of Hinduism with the Islamic Sufis, who were mystics.

Within the Hindu tradition in northern India was a branch called the Sants. The Sants believed that God was both with form and without form, unable to be represented concretely. Most of the Sants were illiterate and poor, but created poems that spoke of the divine being experienced in all things. This idea also rooted itself in Sikhism.

Guru Nanak Dev, who was raised as a Hindu, rejected the caste system in favor of equality of all persons. He also upheld the value of women, rejecting the burning of widows and female infanticide. When eating a communal meal, first begun as a protest against caste, everyone sits in a straight line and shares karah prasad (a pudding), which is provided by those of all castes. However, Sikhs are expected to marry within their caste. In some cases, especially in the United Kingdom, gurdwaras (places of worship) for a particular caste exist.

Holy Places

Amritsar, especially the Golden Temple, which was built in the sixteenth century under the supervision of the fifth guru, Guru Arjan, is the most sacred city.

Ram Das, the fourth guru, first began constructing a pool on the site in 1577. He called it

Amritsar, the pool of nectar. This sacred reflecting pool is a pilgrimage destination. Steps on the southern side of the pool allow visitors to gather water in bottles, to drink it, to bathe in it, or to sprinkle it on themselves.

SIKHISM IN DEPTH

Sacred Symbols

The khanda is the major symbol of Sikhism. It features a two-edged sword, representing justice and freedom, in the center. It is surrounded by a circle, a symbol of both balance and of the unity of God and humankind. A pair of curved swords (kirpans) surrounds the circle. One sword stands for religious concerns, the other for secular concerns. The khanda appears on Sikh flags, which are flown over every temple.

Members of the Khalsa have five symbols. They do not cut their hair, and men do not trim their beards. This symbol, kes, is to indicate a harmony with the ways of nature. To keep the long hair neat, a comb called a kangha is used. The third symbol is the kara, a bracelet usually made of steel to represent continuity and strength. When the Khalsa was first formed, soldiers wore loose-fitting shorts called kaccha. They were worn to symbolize moral restraint and purity. The final symbol is a short sword known as a kirpan, to be used only in self-defense. When bathing in sacred waters, the kirpan is tucked into the turban, which is worn to cover the long hair. The turban, which may be one of many colors, is wound from nearly five yards of cloth.

Sacred Practices & Gestures

Sikhs use Sat Sri Akal (truth is timeless) as a greeting, putting hands together and bowing toward the other person. To show respect, Sikhs keep their heads covered with a turban or veil. Before entering a temple, they remove their shoes. Some Sikhs may choose to wear a bindhi, the dot on the forehead usually associated with Hinduism.

When Guru Gobind Singh initiated the first men into the Khalsa, he put water in a steel bowl and added sugar, stirring the mixture with his sword and reciting verses from the Guru Granth as he did so. He thus created amrit (immortal), a holy water also used in baptism, or the Amrit ceremony. The water represents mental clarity, while sugar stands for sweetness. The sword invokes military courage, and the chanting of verses brings a poetic spirituality.

The Sikh ideal of bringing Ultimate Reality into every aspect of the day is expressed in prayers throughout the day. Daily morning prayer (Bani) consists of five different verses, most of them the work of one of the ten gurus; there are also two sets of evening prayers. Throughout the day, Sikhs repeat the Mul Mantra, "Ikk Oan Kar" (There is one Being). This is the first line of a brief creedal statement about Ultimate Reality.

Food Restrictions

Sikhs are not to eat halal meat, which is the Muslim equivalent of kosher. Both tobacco and alcohol are forbidden. Many Sikhs are vegetarians, although this is not commanded. Members of the Khalsa are not permitted to eat meat slaughtered according to Islamic or Hindu methods, because they believe these means cause pain to the animal.

Rites, Celebrations, & Services

The Sikhs observe four rite of passage rituals, with each emphasizing their distinction from the Hindu traditions. After a new mother is able to get up and bathe, the new baby is given a birth and naming ceremony in the gurdwara. The child is given a name based on the first letter of hymn from the Guru Granth Sahib at random. All males are additionally given the name Singh (lion); all females also receive the name Kaur (princess).

The marriage ceremony (anand karaj) is the second rite of passage. Rather than circle a sacred fire as the Hindus do, the Sikh couple walks four times around a copy of the Guru Granth Sahib, accompanied by singing. The bride often wears red, a traditional color for the Punjabi.

The amrit initiation into the Khalsa is considered the most important rite. It need not take place in a temple, but does require that five

Sikhs who are already Khalsa members conduct the ceremony. Amrit initiation may occur any time after a child is old enough to read the Guru Granth and understand the tenets of the faith. Some people, however, wait until their own children are grown before accepting this rite.

The funeral rite is the fourth and final rite of passage. A section of the Guru Granth is read. The body, dressed in the Five "K's," is cremated soon after death.

Initiation into the Khalsa is now open to both men and women. The earliest gurus opposed the Hindu custom of sati, which required a widow to be burned on her husband's funeral pyre. They were also against the Islamic custom of purdah, which required women to be veiled and covered in public. Women who are menstruating are not excluded from worship, as they are in some religions. Women as well as men can be leaders of the congregation and are permitted to read from the Guru Granth and recite sacred hymns.

The Sikh houses of worship are known as gurdwaras and include a langar, the communal dining area. People remove their shoes and cover their heads before entering. They touch their foreheads to the floor in front of the scripture to show respect. The service itself is in three parts. The first segment is Kirtan, singing hymns (kirtans) accompanied by musical instruments, which can last for several hours. It is followed by a set prayer called the Ardas, which has three parts. The first and final sections cannot be altered. In the first, the virtues of the gurus are extolled. In the last, the divine name is honored. In the center of the Ardas is a list of the Khalsa's troubles and victories, which a prayer leader recites in segments and to which the congregation responds with Vahiguru, considered a word for God. At the end of the service, members eat karah prasad, sacred food made of raw sugar, clarified butter, and coarse wheat flour. They then adjourn for a communal meal, Langar, the third section of worship.

Sikhism does not have a set day for worship similar to the Jewish Sabbath or Christian Sunday worship. However, the first day of the month on the Indian lunar calendar, sangrand, and the darkest night of the month, masia, are considered special days. Sangrand is a time for praying for the entire month. Masia is often considered an auspicious time for bathing in the holy pool at the temple.

Four of the major festivals that Sikhs observe surround important events in the lives of the gurus. These are known as gurpurabs, or anniversaries. Guru Nanak's birthday, Guru Gobind Singh's birthday, and the martyrdoms of the Gurus Arjan and Tegh Bahadur comprise the four main gurpurabs. Sikhs congregate in the gurudwaras to hear readings of the Guru Granth and lectures by Sikh scholars.

Baisakhi is the Indian New Year, the final day before the harvest begins. On this day in 1699, Guru Gobind Singh formed the first Khalsa, adding even more importance to the day for Sikhs. Each year, a new Sikh flag is placed at all temples.

Diwali, based on a word meaning string of lights, is a Hindu festival. For Sikhs, it is a time to remember the return of the sixth guru, Hargobind, to Amritsar after the emperor had imprisoned him. It is celebrated for three days at the Golden Temple. Sikhs paint and whitewash their houses and decorate them with candles and earthenware lamps.

Hola Mohalla, meaning attack and place of attack, is the Sikh spring festival, which corresponds to the Hindu festival Holi. It is also a three-day celebration and a time for training Sikhs as soldiers. Originally, it involved military exercises and mock battles, as well as competitions in archery, horsemanship, and wrestling. In contemporary times, the festival includes athletic contests, discussion, and singing.

Judy A. Johnson, MTS

Bibliography

Barnes, Trevor. *The Kingfisher Book of Religions*. New York: Kingfisher, 1999. Print.

Dhanjal, Beryl. *Amritsar*. New York: Dillon, 1993. Print.

Dhavan, Purnima. *When Sparrows Became Hawks: The Making of the Sikh Warrior Tradition, 1699–1799*. Oxford: Oxford UP, 2011. Print.

Eraly, Abraham, et. al. *India*. New York: DK, 2008. Print.

Harley, Gail M. *Hindu and Sikh Faiths in America*. New York: Facts on File, 2003. Print.

Jakobsh, Doris R. *Sikhism and Women: History, Texts, and Experience*. Oxford, New York: Oxford UP, 2010. Print.

Jhutti-Johal, Jagbir. *Sikhism Today*. London, New York: Continuum, 2011. Print.

Langley, Myrtle. *Religion*. New York: Knopf, 1996. Print.

Mann, Gurinder Singh. *Sikhism*. Upper Saddle River: Prentice, 2004. Print.

Meredith, Susan. *The Usborne Book of World Religions*. London: Usborne, 1995. Print.

Sidhu, Dawinder S. and Neha Singh Gohil. *Civil Rights in Wartime: The Post-9/11 Sikh Experience*. Ashgate, 2009. E-book.

Singh, Nikky-Guninder Kaur. *Sikhism*. New York: Facts on File, 1993. Print.

Singh, Nikky-Guninder Kaur. *Sikhism: An Introduction*. Tauris, 2011. E-book.

Singh, Surinder. *Introduction to Sikhism and Great Sikhs of the World*. Gurgaon: Shubhi, 2012. Print.

Wilkinson, Philip. *Religions*. New York: DK, 2008. Print.

Index